APPLIED ETHICS

Fifth Edition

APPLIED ETHICS
A MULTICULTURAL APPROACH

edited by

Larry May
Vanderbilt University

Kai Wong
Washington University

Jill Delston
Washington University

Prentice Hall
Boston   Columbus   Indianapolis   New York   San Francisco   Upper Saddle River
Amsterdam   Cape Town   Dubai   London   Madrid   Milan   Munich   Paris   Montreal   Toronto
Delhi   Mexico City   São Paulo   Sydney   Hong Kong   Seoul   Singapore   Taipei   Tokyo

Editorial Director: Craig Campanella
Editor in Chief: Dickson Musslewhite
Publisher: Nancy Roberts
Editorial Assistant: Nart Varoqua
Director of Marketing: Brandy Dawson
Senior Marketing Manager: Laura Lee Manley
Marketing Assistant: Patrick Walsh
Managing Editor: Maureen Richardson
Project Manager/Production: Shelly Kupperman
Senior Operations Supervisor: Nick Sklitsis
Operations Specialist: Amanda Smith
Manager, Cover Visual Research & Permissions: Jayne Conte
Cover Designer: Bruce Kenselaar
Cover Art: Fotolia/gemalter Hintergrund © Sunnydays
Full-Service Project Management/Composition: Saraswathi Muralidhar, PreMediaGlobal
Printer/Binder: Courier Companies, Inc.
Cover Printer: Courier Companies, Inc.
Text Font: 10 pt. Times New Roman

Credits and acknowledgments borrowed from other sources and reproduced, with permission, in this textbook appear within text.

Many of the designations by manufacturers and seller to distinguish their products are claimed as trademarks. Where those designations appear in this book, and the publisher was aware of a trademark claim, the designations have been printed in initial caps or all caps.

Library of Congress Cataloging-in-Publication Data

Applied ethics : a multicultural approach / edited by Larry May, Kai Wong, Jill Delston.—5th ed.
    p. cm.
  Includes bibliographical references.
  ISBN-13: 978-0-205-70808-6
  ISBN-10: 0-205-70808-0
 1. Applied ethics.   2. Multiculturalism—Moral and ethical aspects.   I. May, Larry.   II. Wong, Kai.   III. Delston, Jill.
  BJ1031.A66 2010
  170—dc22

                                                    2010009675

10 9 8 7 6 5 4 3 2 1

Prentice Hall
is an imprint of

PEARSON

www.pearsonhighered.com

ISBN 10:   0-205-70808-0
ISBN 13: 978-0-205-70808-6

CONTENTS

PREFACE

This book has filled an existing gap in the literature used in applied ethics courses. The major anthologies in applied ethics contain essays written almost exclusively by American social and moral philosophers. These anthologies leave the student with the impression that there are no viewpoints other than those expressed by Americans, and that ethical and social philosophy has little to do with perspectives of other nations and cultures. More and more courses that include the perspectives of diverse cultures are being added to the curriculum. There is no applied ethics volume comparable to ours—indeed philosophy has been very slow to respond to the call for multiculturalism in our curricula.

Our volume addresses various topics in applied ethics from Western and non-Western perspectives. As a result, the typical instructor will have an easier time approaching the material than if the material were segregated, or if the issues were not already well known in the West. Nonetheless, since our book devotes significant attention to the moral perspectives of many different cultures and ethnicities, students will come away from our text having a deeper appreciation for other cultures. We believe that the increasing emphasis on multiculturalism and internationalism across disciplines has set the stage for a very positive reception for a book like ours.

Let us briefly address some of the terminology in the book. We have chosen to use the term "American Indian" rather than "Native American" because of the increasing use of the former instead of the latter in such titles as "American Indian Studies" and because many American Indian people believe that the term "Native American" does not adequately capture their identity since many non-Indians may also claim to be Native Americans. We have used the term "African American" when referring to Blacks living in America and have retained the term "Blacks" when the designated group was not restricted to Americans.

Many people provided us with valuable suggestions and assistance throughout the years that we worked on this project. We would like to thank Margaret Battin, Karen Warren, Iris Young, Mary Mahowald, Marilyn Friedman, Denward Wilson, and Gloria Cuádraz for valuable suggestions about the book's format and selections. We are especially grateful to Dana Klar from Washington University's Center for American Indian Studies for help with some of the multicultural material. In addition, Kenneth Sharratt, Marilyn Broughton, and Debi Katz have helped in the more technical phases of the book's production. The following reviewers provided helpful suggestions and useful insights for the editions: Gene Torisky; Charles H. Rossell, Montana State University, Great Falls; John P. Clark, Loyola University, New Orleans; Don Collins Reed, Wittenberg University; Carol Quinn, University of North Carolina, Charlotte; Chris McCord, Kirkwood Community

College; Corlette Bell, University of North Florida; Elliott Wreh-Wilson, Edinboro University of Pennsylvania; and Jan C. Gordon, Surry Community College; and many others who used the first edition and gave valuable help on the second edition and as did our students. We would also like to thank Benedict Chan for valuable suggestions on the human rights section. And finally, we would like to thank Ross Miller and the rest of the Prentice Hall staff for their invaluable help and support.

APPLIED ETHICS

INTRODUCTION

Our first resource is human compassion, gained through the clear use of our minds, which will allow us to make the best use of the human family. And another of our best resources emerges when we think clearly about the peoples who have alternative answers to the questions that are not being answered by our society. For the first time . . . it is possible . . . to make the world our library.
—JOHN MOHAWK[1]

This anthology presents a new approach to the study of applied ethics. Its premise is that the issues in applied ethics are addressed too often from narrow North American perspectives, with little attention paid to viewpoints from other cultures. The sixty-seven essays collected here attempt to present a wide view of the standard issues in contemporary applied ethics such as abortion, euthanasia, world hunger, discrimination, war, and the environment. To these standard issues we have added discussions of gender roles, violence, human rights, and cloning. We have attempted to find the best recent literature—indeed, over half the essays in our book have been written in the last ten years. In addition, more than half the essays either take a non-Western perspective or address themselves to the international context of an applied ethics issue, and many of the essays are written by people who are indigenous to the cultures about which they are writing.

Each section of our anthology begins with a well-known essay on a major issue such as hunger, war, or abortion. This is followed by a very recent essay, usually responding to the "classical" essay. In addition, each section includes several essays that approach the topic from Third World perspectives, and many sections have pieces that relate the topic of the section to relevant international issues. It is our intention to broaden the range of perspectives, in addition to making the issues come alive in ways they often do not when a more limited range of perspectives is considered.

THE CASE FOR A MULTICULTURAL APPROACH TO ETHICS

Lawrence Blum offers the following definition of *multiculturalism*:

> Multiculturalism involves an understanding, appreciation, and valuing of one's own culture, and an informed respect and curiosity about the ethnic cultures of others. It involves a valuing of other cultures, not in the sense of approving of all aspects of those cultures, but of attempting to see how a given culture can express value to its own members.[2]

In this view—a view we largely share—a multicultural approach to ethics, or any subject, does not require that we be uncritical of the practices and beliefs of other cultures. Indeed, just as a consideration of the many distinctly North American perspectives on abortion does not require that we agree with all of these views, so a consideration of the many diverse cultural perspectives on applied ethics issues does not require that we agree with all of these views either.

Our approach to multiculturalism begins with a sincere belief in the words written one hundred years ago by John Stuart Mill:

> Only through diversity of opinion is there, in the existing state of human intellect, a chance of fair play to all sides of the truth.[3]

The key component in the case for multiculturalism is diversity of opinion. To give just one example: In the contemporary American debate on abortion, virtually no one defends late-term abortions. But we have included an essay by several Chinese physicians who defend this practice in countries such as theirs, countries that are struggling to curb a population explosion. We have included this essay not because we necessarily agree with it, but because we think that it is important that this opinion be heard and reflected upon to see whether there is any part of the truth that is revealed by such a consideration.

Another important part of the case for multicultural approaches to ethics, and to other subjects, is to combat the ethnocentrism and racism that often result from ignorance of other peoples and cultures. There is little doubt that our ignorance of people who are different from us has, historically, contributed to much hatred and violence. By remaining uninformed about people of other cultures, we miss the opportunity to see how much alike they are to us and avoid having to try to understand the basis for our differences.

Yet another argument in favor of a multicultural approach to ethics, or to any other subject, has to do with the importance of understanding those who are our competitors and those who we hope will eventually be our partners in the development of the global village. In the past, the restricted vision of traditional approaches in the West worked to a limited extent only because the world was cut into many self-contained units. In a fragmented world, one group could survive simply by closing its doors and regarding everyone else as the enemy. With increasing global interdependence, this narrow approach is becoming counterproductive. John Mohawk makes the case well when he says:

> We are living in a world in which difference is just a simple fact of life, but our collective thinking has yet to truly come to grips with this reality. This *has* to change. A workable world mentality means that we are going to have to make peace with those who are different from us.[4]

The reach of many issues today—environmental degradation, racial and sexual oppression, the AIDS epidemic—is global. Intellectual disciplines such as applied ethics cannot afford to be myopic, since the survival of the West will surely depend in the near future on its ability to understand the much more populous areas of the Third World, as well as disparate cultures that exist side by side with, and sometimes within, Western cultures.

Finally, there is a strong moral case for discussions of cultures different from one's own. Such discussions foster respect for others. Respect is generally recognized as a moral value by most cultures. And the most important component of respect is an appreciation for another person as different from oneself. An appreciation for different cultures will make us better able to appreciate differences among individuals, especially between ourselves and those who, in many minor and some major ways, are different from us. If it is true that understanding breeds respect, then a consideration of a diverse set of cultural perspectives, such as those contained in this anthology, will advance the moral goal of increasing respect among peoples and individuals in the world.

Let us end this introduction with a comment about method. While we have tried to provide a representative sample of Western and non-Western perspectives on applied ethics, we have not provided a sample of differences in method that exist in non-Western philosophical writing about ethics. Rather we have tried to find pieces that all have an argument that can be analyzed in terms of Western philosophical methods. In this sense, the essays all speak to one another, in terms of arguments and counterarguments, even though this method may not be common in the cultures in question. Nonetheless, even though most of our essays are Western in form, we feel that they are not so "westernized" as to misrepresent their cultural perspectives.

It is our hope that this anthology will spawn future works in applied ethics by those who take non-Western perspectives. In constructing our book we found a large literature—larger than most Western-trained philosophers would expect to find. It is hoped that our success will cause other Western philosophers to explore Third World perspectives on applied ethics in greater depth. We would be grateful to hear from anyone who is working in this area or who knows of good essays that we have not included here. We have provided a brief bibliography at the end of each part to point the reader toward some of the essays that we were not able to include in this book.

We have included two essays as part of our Introduction. In the first essay, Lawrence Blum provides an excellent discussion of what values are important to be taught to students in a pluralistic society. These values are opposition to racism, respect for other cultures, a sense of interracial community, and treating persons as individuals. Blum thus helps us see how a discussion of different cultures, and an appreciation of those cultures, is worthwhile, especially in a very heterogeneous society such as the United States. Most important, such a consideration will counter the "misleading tradition in our thinking about community" where people think they can feel a sense of community only with people who are the same as themselves. Blum's essay stresses the need to appreciate people's differences for what they are, as instances of our shared humanity. We must be open to an appreciation of these differences so as to have a stronger community.

In the second essay, Martha Nussbaum presents us with a good test case of how to deal with clashes of culture over a moral issue. Some would contend that it is wrong to criticize another culture since moral values are relative to cultures, and people outside the culture are in no position to appreciate or condemn a culture's practices. In this context, Nussbaum discusses the problem of female genital mutilation (FGM), a practice common in parts of Africa and Asia, but strongly condemned in the United States and Western Europe. The practice involves cutting, or removing, the clitoris and other parts of the female genitalia. FGM is a ritualized "purification" of girls and women prior to marriage. Nussbaum defends those who have condemned this practice against charges that such condemnation manifests a kind of cultural imperialism and insensitivity, as well as those who

say that condemnation of FGM involves a double standard since similar practices are not condemned in the United States or Western Europe. Nussbaum carefully distinguishes FGM from Western practices aimed at increasing the sexual appeal of women. There are two main differences. First, women consent to beautifying procedures in the West, but women are not asked to consent to FGM in Africa. Second, FGM leaves women permanently unable to experience certain sexual sensations and often permanently experiencing continued serious pain, whereas the beautifying procedures do not have these injurious characteristics. Nussbaum concludes that we can still be sympathetic to cultural difference and yet strongly condemn practices such as FGM.

NOTES

1. John Mohawk, "Epilogue: Looking for Columbus." *The State of Native America*, edited by M. Annette Jaimes (Boston: South End Press, 1992), p. 443.
2. Lawrence Blum, "Antiracism, Multiculturalism, and Interracial Community: Three Educational Values for a Multicultural Society," a monograph published by the University of Massachusetts, Boston, 1991.
3. John Stuart Mill, *On Liberty* [1859] (Indianapolis: Hackett Publishing, 1978), p. 46.
4. John Mohawk, "Epilogue," p. 442.

Antiracism, Multiculturalism, and Interracial Community: Three Educational Values for a Multicultural Society

Lawrence A. Blum

Lawrence A. Blum is a distinguished professor of liberal arts and education in addition to being professor of philosophy at University of Massachusetts at Amherst. He is the author of many articles in ethics and of *Friendship, Altruism, and Morality* (1980), *A Truer Liberty: Simone Weil and Marxism* (1989), *Moral Perception and Particularity* (1994), and "I'm Not a Racist, But . . .": The Moral Quandary of Race (2002). He is also actively involved in programs promoting inter-cultural understanding, both at the higher and secondary levels of education.

Blum maintains that central to education for a multicultural society are four distinct but interrelated values—antiracism, multiculturalism, interracial community, and respect for persons as individuals—of which the first three are the focus of this article. The value of antiracism education is to counter those attitudes of superiority that seek to perpetuate unjustified advantages of one group over another's. The value of multiculturalism involves the appreciation of values different from those of one's culture, and the value of sense of a community is to foster solidarity among various groups in spite of their ethnic and cultural differences.

I want to argue that there are a plurality of values that one would want taught in schools and families. None of these can be reduced to the others, nor can any take the place of the others. Without claiming comprehensiveness for my list, I want to suggest that there are at least four values, or families of values, essential to a program of value education for a multiracial society. . . .

Lawrence Blum, "Antiracism, Multiculturalism, and Interracial Community: Three Education Values for a Multicultural Society," a monograph published by the University of Mass., Boston, 1991, edited version. Reprinted by permission.

The first value is *antiracism* or *opposition* to racism:

Racism is the denial of the fundamental moral equality of all human beings. It involves the expression of attitudes of superior worth or merit justifying or underpinning the domination or unjust advantage of some groups over others. Antiracism as a value involves striving to be without racist attitudes oneself as well as being prepared to work against both racist attitudes in others and racial injustice in society more generally.

The second value is *multiculturalism*:

Multiculturalism involves an understanding, appreciation and valuing of one's own culture, and an informed respect and curiosity about the ethnic culture of others. It involves a valuing of other cultures, not in the sense of approving of all aspects of those cultures, but of attempting to see how a given culture can express value to its own members.

The third value is a sense of *community*, and in particular an *interracial community*:

> This involves a sense, not necessarily explicit or articulated, that one possesses human bonds with persons of other races and ethnicities. The bonds may, and ideally should, be so broad as to encompass all of humanity; but they may also be limited to the bonds formed in friendships, schools, workplaces, and the like.

The fourth value is *treating persons as individuals*:

> This involves recognizing the individuality of each person—specifically, that while an individual person is a member of an ethnic or racial group, and while that aspect may be an important part of who she is, she is more than that ethnic or racial identity. It is the lived appreciation of this individuality, not simply paying lip service to it, that constitutes the value I will call treating persons as individuals. . . .

Again, I claim that these four are distinct though related values, and that all of them are essential to multicultural value education. Failure to appreciate their distinctness poses the danger that one of them will be neglected in a value education program. At the same time there are natural convergences and complementarities among the four values taken in any combination; there are ways of teaching each value that support the promotion of each one of the other values. On the other hand, I will claim there can also be tensions, both practical and theoretical, between various of the values; that is, some ways of teaching one of the values may work against the conveying of one of the others. Since the values can be either convergent or in tension, it will be crucial to search for ways of teaching them that minimize the tension and support the convergences.

I have designated *antiracism* as the first value for this value education. In contrast to the three others, this one is stated negatively—in opposition to something rather than as a positive goal to be striven for. Why do I not refer to this value positively as

"racial equality" or "racial justice"? One reason is that the oppositional definition brings out that a central aspect of the value of antiracism involves countering an evil and not just promoting a good. An important component of what children need to be taught is how to notice, to confront, to oppose, and to work toward the elimination of manifestations of racism. Particular moral abilities and traits of character, involving certain forms of empowerment, are required for activities of *opposition* that are not required merely for the promotion of a good goal. Of course, antiracism does presuppose the positive value of racial justice; hence, the positive element is implicitly contained in the value of antiracism.

To understand the value of antiracism we must first understand *racism*. The term racism, while a highly charged and condemnatory one, has no generally agreed upon meaning. On the one hand all can agree that using a racial slur, telling a Chicano student that one does not like Chicanos and wishes they were not in one's school, or carving "KKK" on . . . [an] African American student's door, are racist acts. At the same time the conservative writer Dinesh D'Souza has given voice to a suspicion, shared I am sure by others, that the term "racism" is in danger of losing its meaning and moral force through a too broad usage.

I agree that there has sometimes been a tendency to inflate the meaning of the word racism so it becomes virtually a catchall term for any behavior concerning race or race relations that its user strongly condemns. This development ill serves those like myself who wish racism to be taken more seriously than it presently is. Like the boy who cried "wolf," the inflation of the concept of racism to encompass phenomena with questionable connection to its core meaning desensitizes people to the danger, horror, and wrongfulness of true racism.

Here is my definition of racism, which I present without further defense: Racism refers both to an institutional or social structure of racial domination or injustice—as when we speak of a racist institution—and also to individual actions, beliefs, and attitudes, whether consciously held or not, which express, support, or justify the superiority of one racial group to another. Thus, on both the individual and institutional levels, racism involves denying or violating the equal dignity and worth of all human beings independent of race; and, on both levels, racism is bound up with dominance and hierarchy.

There are three components of (the value of) *antiracism* as I see it.

One is the belief in the equal worth of all persons regardless of race, not just as an intellectual matter, but rooted more deeply in one's attitudes and emotions; this is to have what one might call a *nonracist* moral consciousness. But it is not enough to learn to be nonracist as an individual; students must also be taught to *understand* the particularity of racism as a psychological and historical phenomenon. This is partly because one aspect of antiracism is learning to perceive racism and to recognize when it is occurring. Just being nonracist cannot guarantee this. For one may sincerely subscribe to the right principles of racial justice and yet not see particular instances of racism right under one's nose, in either institutional or individual forms; for example, not recognizing unintended patterns of exclusion of people of color, or not recognizing a racial stereotype.

There are three components to this second feature of antiracism (understanding racism). The first is the *psychological* dynamic of racism, such as scapegoating and stereotyping, rigidity and fear of difference, rationalization of privilege and power, projecting of unwanted wishes onto others, and other psychological processes contributing to racist attitudes. The second is the *historical* dynamic of racism in its particular forms: slavery, colonialism, segregation, Nazism, the mistreatment of native Americans, and the like. Involved also must be learning about movements *against* racism, such as abolitionism, civil rights movements, and the black power movement; and learning about institutional racism as well. The third component is the role of *individuals* in sustaining or resisting racist institutions, patterns, and systems—how individuals can change racist structures; how they may contribute to or help to perpetuate racist patterns even if they themselves are not actually racist.

Studying the historical dynamics of racism necessarily involves teaching the victimization of some groups by others. While some conservative critics of multicultural education ridicule and derogate focusing on a group's history as victims of racism, it would nevertheless be intellectually irresponsible not to do so. One can hardly understand the historical experience of African Americans without slavery, of Jews without the Holocaust, of Asian-Americans without the historic barriers to citizenship and to family life and without the World War II internment camps.

Nevertheless, from the point of view of historical accuracy as well as that of value education, it is vital not to *confine* the presentation of a group to its status as victim. One needs to see subordinate groups as agents in their own history—not just as suffering victimization but as responding to it, sometimes by active resistance both cultural and political, sometimes by passive resistance, sometimes by accommodation. The study of social history is invaluable here in providing the framework for seeing that victims made their own history in the face of their victimization, and for giving concrete embodiment to the philosophical truth that human beings retain the capacity for agency even when oppressed and dominated by others.

The third component of antiracist education (in addition to nonracism and understanding racism) is *opposition to racism*; for nonracism implies only that one does all one can to avoid racism in *one's own* actions and attitudes. This is insufficient, for students need also to develop a sense of responsibility concerning manifestations of racism in other persons and in the society more generally. For example, since students will almost inevitably witness racist acts, to confine their own responsibility simply to ensuring that they individually do not participate in such actions themselves is to give students a mixed message about how seriously they are being asked to take racism.

• • •

The second educational value, *multiculturalism*, encompasses the following three subvalues: (a) affirming one's own cultural identity; learning about and valuing one's own cultural heritage; (b) respecting and desiring to understand and learn about (and from) cultures other than one's own; (c) valuing and taking delight in cultural diversity itself; that is, regarding the existence of distinct cultural groups within one's own society as a positive good to be treasured and nurtured. The kind of respect involved in the second condition (respecting others) is meant to be an informed (and not uncritical) respect grounded in an understanding of another culture. It involves an attempt to see the culture from the point of view of its members and in particular to see how members of that culture value the expression of their own culture. It involves an active interest in and ability in some way to enter into and to enjoy the cultural expressions of other groups.

Such an understanding of another culture in no way requires an affirmation of every feature of that culture as positively good, as some critics of multiculturalism fear (or at least charge). It does not preclude criticism, on the basis either of norms of that culture itself which particular practices in that culture might violate, or of standards external to that culture. Of course when it is legitimate to use a standard external to a culture (e.g., a particular standard of equality between men and women drawn from the Western liberal tradition) is a complex issue. And multiculturalism always warns both against using a legitimate criticism of some feature of a culture as moral leverage to condemn the culture as a whole—declaring it not worthy of serious curricular attention, or disqualifying it as a source of moral insight to those outside that culture, for example—as well as alerting us to the difficult-to-avoid failure to scrutinize the basis of that criticism for its own cultural bias. Nevertheless, multiculturalism need not and should not identify itself with the view that members of one culture never have the moral standing to make an informed criticism of the practices of another culture.

The outward directedness of the second feature of multiculturalism (respecting other cultures) is an important complement to the inward focus of the first feature (learning about and valuing one's own culture). This dual orientation meets the criticism sometimes made of multiculturalism that it creates divisions between students. For the second feature prescribes a reaching out beyond one's own group and thus explicitly counters the balkanizing effect of the first dimension of multiculturalism alone. Nevertheless, that first feature—learning about and valuing one's own culture—is an integral part of multiculturalism, not merely something to be tolerated, treated as a response to political pressure, or justified simply on the grounds of boosting self-esteem. An individual's cultural identity is a deeply significant element of herself, and understanding of her own culture should be a vital part of the task of education. An understanding of one's own culture as contributing to the society of which one is a part is a significant part of that first element of multiculturalism.

The third component of multiculturalism is the valuing of diversity itself. Not only do we want our young people to respect specific other cultures, but also to value a school, a city, a society in which diverse cultural groups exist. While this diversity may certainly present problems for young people, one wants them to see the diversity primarily as something to value, prefer, and cherish.

Three dimensions of culture seem to be deserving of curricular and other forms of educational attention in schools. The first is the *ancestor culture* of the ethnic group, nation, or civilization of origin. For Chinese-Americans this would involve understanding Chinese culture, including ancient Chinese cultures, philosophies, religions, and the like. For Irish-Americans it would be Irish history and culture. For Mexican-Americans it would include attention to some of the diverse cultures of Mexico—the Aztec, the Mayan, as well as the Spanish, and then the hybrid Spanish/indigenous culture which forms modern Mexican culture.

While all ethnic cultures have an ancestor culture, not all current groups bear the same relationship to that ancestor culture. For example, African Americans' connection to their ancestor culture is importantly different from that of immigrant groups like Italians, Eastern European Jews, and Irish. Although scholars disagree about the actual extent of influence of various African cultures on current African American cultural forms, it was a general feature of American slavery systematically to attempt to deprive African slaves of their African culture. By contrast voluntary immigrant groups brought with them an intact culture, which they renegotiated in the new conditions of the United States. In fact the label "African American" can be seen as an attempt to forge a stronger analogy between the experience of black Americans and that of other immigrant groups than do other expressions, such as "black" or even "Afro-American." The former conceptualization emphasizes that American blacks are not simply a product of America but do indeed possess an ancestor culture, no matter how brutally that culture was attacked. Note, however, that there is an important difference between this use of "African American" and that applied, for example, to second-generation Ethiopian-Americans. The latter is a truer parallel to white ethnic "hyphenate Americans."

Other differences among groups, such as the current ethnic group's distance in time from its original emigration, variations, and pressures to assimilate once in the United States and the effects of racism affect the significance of the ancestor culture for a current ethnic group. Nevertheless ancestor culture plays some role for every group.

A second dimension of culture to be encompassed by multicultural education is the *historical experience* of the ethnic group within the United States. Generally it will attend to the historical experiences, ways of life, triumphs and setbacks, art and literature, contributions, and achievements of ethnic groups in the United States. The latter point is uncontroversial; all proponents of multicultural education agree in the need to correct the omission in traditional curricula and textbooks of many ethnic groups' experiences and contributions to our national life. But distinguishing this dimension from the ancestor culture and giving attention to both of them is crucial. For the culture of the Chinese-American is *not* the same as the culture of traditional or modern China; it is a culture with its own integrity: neither the purer form of ancestor culture nor that of middle America. It can be called "intercultural," influenced by more than one culture (as indeed the ancestor culture itself may have been), yet forming a culture in its own right.

A third dimension of culture is the *current ethnic culture* of the group in question. This is the dimension most directly embodied in the student member of that culture. This current ethnic culture—family ethnic rituals, foods, customs regarding family roles and interactions, values, musical and other cultural preferences, philosophies of life, and the like—bears complex relationships to the ancestor culture as well as to the group's historical ethnic experience in the United States. It changes over time and is affected in myriad ways by the outer society. As with ancestor culture and historical ethnic experience, the student's current ethnic culture must be given respect. What such respect consists of is a complex matter, as the following examples indicate.

In one case, respect can involve allowing Arab girls to wear traditional headgear in school if they so desire. In another, it can mean seeing a child's remark in class as containing insight stemming from her cultural perspective that might otherwise be missed or seem off the mark. Another form of respect for culture involves, for example, recognizing that a Vietnamese child's failure to look a teacher in the eye is not a sign of evasiveness or lack of interest, but a way of expressing a deference to teachers and authority, culturally regarded as appropriate. Thus, respect for ethnic cultures sometimes involves a direct valorizing of a part of that culture; at other times neither valorizing nor disvaluing, but allowing for its expression because it is important to the student. In another context, it can involve reshaping one's own sense of what is educationally essential, to take into account another culture's difference. Finally, it can sometimes involve seeing a cultural manifestation as a genuine obstacle to learning, but respecting the cultural setting in which it is embedded and the student's own attachment to that cultural feature and finding ways to work with or around that obstacle to accomplish an educational goal.

In summary, ancestor culture, ethnic historical experience in the United States, and current ethnic culture are three dimensions of ethnic culture requiring attention in a multicultural education. They are all dimensions that children need to be taught and taught to respect—both in their own and others' cultures.

The context of multicultural education presupposes a larger society consisting of various cultures. Thus, teaching an attitude of appreciation toward a particular one of these cultures in the three dimensions just mentioned will have both a particular and general aspect. We will want students to appreciate cultures in their own right, but also in their relationship to the larger society. This simple point can help us to avoid two familiar and contrasting pitfalls of multicultural education that can be illustrated with the example of Martin Luther King Jr.

One pitfall would be exemplified by a teacher who portrayed King as an important leader of the black community, but who failed to emphasize that he should be seen as a great *American* leader more generally—as a true hero for all Americans, indeed for all humanity, and not *only* for or of African Americans. The teacher fails to show the non-African-American students that they too have a connection with King simply as Americans.

Yet an exactly opposite pitfall is to teach appreciation of the contribution of members of particular cultures *only* insofar as those contributions can be seen in universal terms or in terms of benefiting the entire society. This pitfall would be exemplified by seeing Dr. King only in terms of his contribution to humanity or to American society more generally, but *not* acknowledging him as a product and leader specifically of the African American community. Multicultural education needs to enable non-African-American students (whether white or not) to be able to appreciate a leader of the African American community in that role itself, and not *only* by showing that the leader in question made a contribution to everyone in the society. Thus, multicultural education needs to emphasize both the general or full society dimension of each culture's contributions and heroes and also the particular or culture-specific dimension.

Many people associate multiculturalism with the idea of moral *relativism* or cultural relativism and specifically with the view that because no one from one culture is in a position to judge another culture, no one is in a position to say which culture should be given priority in the allocation of respect, curricular inclusion, and the like. Therefore, according to this way of thinking, every culture has a claim to equal inclusion and respect, because no one is in a position to say which ones are *more* worthy of respect. While the philosophic relativism on which this version of multiculturalism rests needs to be taken seriously—it has a long and distinguished philosophic history—there is an alternative, quite different and nonrelativistic, philosophic foundation for multiculturalism as well. This view—which might be called *pluralistic*—agrees that cultures manifest different values, but affirms that the values of a given culture can be, or can come to be, appreciated (as well as assessed) by someone from a different culture. Thus, while cultures are different, they are at least partly accessible to one another.

According to this pluralist, nonrelativist line of thought, multicultural education should involve exposing students to, and helping them to appreciate the range of, values embodied in different cultures. Both whites and Cambodian immigrant students can come to appreciate Toni Morrison's novels of black life in America. African American students can come to understand and appreciate Confucian philosophy. This pluralist view should not minimize the work often necessary to see beyond the parochial assumptions and perspectives of one's own culture in order to appreciate the values of another culture. Indeed, one of the undoubted contributions of the multicultural movement has been to reveal those obstacles as well as the dominant culture's resistance to acknowledging them. Nevertheless, the fact that such an effort can be even partially successful provides a goal of multicultural education that is barely conceivable within the pure relativist position.

• • •

The third value for an educational program that I want to discuss is the *sense of community*—specifically a sense of community that embraces racial and cultural differences. While the idea of a multiracial integrated community has historically been linked with the struggle against racism, I think there is reason for focusing on it as a value distinct from antiracism. The sense of community that I mean involves a sense of bond with other persons, a sense of shared identification with the community in question (be it a class, a school, or a workplace), a sense of loyalty to and involvement with this community. I will make the further assumption that the experience of interracial community in such institutions is an important contributor to being able fully to experience members of other races and cultures as fellow citizens and fellow human beings throughout one's life.

It is true that the achievement of or the experience of interracial community is likely to contribute to a firm commitment to nonracist and antiracist values. Nevertheless, there is an important difference between the two families of values. A sense of community is defeated not only by racist attitudes, in which members of one group feel themselves superior to members of another group, but simply by experiencing members of other races and cultural groups as *other*, as distant from oneself, as people with whom one does not feel comfortable, and has little in common. . . . What defeats a sense of community is to see members of a group primarily as *they*, as a kind of undifferentiated group counterposed to a *we*, defined by the group one identifies with oneself. One becomes blind to the individuality of members of the *they* group. One experiences this group as deeply different from oneself, even if one cannot always account for or explain that sense of difference. This anticommunal consciousness can exist in the absence of actual racist attitudes toward the other group, although the former is a natural stepping-stone toward the latter. I think many students in schools, of all races and cultures, never do achieve the experience of interracial community, never learn to feel comfortable with members of other racial and ethnic groups, even though these students do not really have racist attitudes in the strict sense. Rather, the sense of group difference simply overwhelms any experiencing of commonality and sharing that is necessary for developing a sense of community.

Fortunately, we need not choose between the values of interracial community and antiracism; rather, we should search for ways of teaching antiracist values that minimize the potential for harming or preventing interracial community. I will briefly mention two general guidelines in this regard. One is constantly to emphasize the internal variety within a group being studied; not to say "whites" and "blacks" all the time as if these were monolithic groups. For example, in discussing slavery, make clear that not all blacks were slaves during the period of slavery, that there were many free blacks. Similarly, most whites did *not* own slaves, and a few whites even actively aligned themselves with the cause of abolition, aiding free blacks who organized the underground railroads and the like. Exhibiting such internal variety within "white," "black," and other groups helps to prevent the formation of rigid or undifferentiated images of racial groups that lend themselves readily to a *we/they* consciousness that undermines community.

A second guideline is to try to give students the experience (in imagination at least) of being both discriminated against, excluded, or demeaned, and also being the discriminator, the excluder, the advantaged one. . . .

Encouraging students to attempt as much as possible to experience the vantage points of advantaged and disadvantaged, included and excluded, and the like, provides an important buffer to a "we/they" consciousness in the racial domain. This buffering is accomplished not so much by encouraging, as the first guideline does, the appreciation of internal diversity in a given group, as by bridging the gulf between the experience of the dominant and that of the subordinate. This is achieved by showing children that there is at least *some* dimension of life on which they occupy the dominant, and on others the subordinate, position (even if these dimensions are not of equal significance).

Some broad guidelines are the following: (a) Invite children's participation in cultures studied, so as to make "other" cultures as accessible as possible to nonmembers. For example, have children in the class interview one another, posing questions about each others' cultures that the questioners feel will help them to comprehend the culture in question. Establish an "intercultural dialogue" among students. This approach will use a recognition of genuine cultural differences to bring children together rather than keep them apart. (b) Recognize cultures' internal variety (even contradictory strands within a given culture), their change over time, and (where appropriate) their interaction with other cultures—rather than presenting cultures as frozen in time, monolithic, and totally self-contained. (c) Recognize cultural universals and commonalities. It is not contrary to the spirit of multiculturalism—to the acknowledgment of authentic cultural differences—to see that distinct cultures may share certain broad features. For example, every culture responds to certain universal features of human life, such as birth, death, the rearing of children, a search for meaning in life. Both (b) and (c) prevent an inaccurate and community-impairing "theyness" in the presentation of other cultures.

Finally, our conception of interracial community must itself allow for the recognition of difference. A powerful, but misleading, tradition in our thinking about community is that people only feel a sense of community when they think of themselves as "the same" as the other members of the community. But, as Robert Bellah and his colleagues argue in *Habits of the Heart*, the kind of community needed in the United States is *pluralistic* community, one which involves a sense of bond and connection stemming from shared activity, condition, task, location, and the like—and grounded ultimately in an experience of shared humanity—yet recognizing and valuing cultural differences (and other kinds of differences as well).[1]

NOTE

1. Robert Bellah, et al., *Habits of the Heart: Individualism and Commitment in American Life* (Berkeley: University of California Press, 1985).

Judging Other Cultures: The Case of Genital Mutilation

Martha Nussbaum

Martha Nussbaum is professor of law and ethics at the University of Chicago. She is the author of *The Fragility of Goodness* (1986), *Love's Knowledge* (1990), *The Therapy of Desire* (1994), *Poetic Justice* (1996), *Cultivating Humanity* (1997), and *Sex and Social Justice* (1999).

Nussbaum presents an argument against the practice of female genital mutilation, a common practice in Africa and other parts of the world. In arguing against this practice, Nussbaum confronts the challenge of cultural relativism. She concludes that we can be sensitive to other cultures and yet condemn certain cultural practices.

In June 1997, the Board of Immigration Appeals of the United States Immigration and Naturalization Service (INS) granted political asylum to a nineteen-year-old woman from Togo who had fled her home to escape the practice of genital mutilation.[1] Fauziya Kassindja is the daughter of Muhammed Kassindja, a successful owner of a small trucking business in Kpalimé. Her father opposed the ritual practice: He remembered his sister's screams during the rite and her suffering from a tetanus infection she developed afterwards. Hajia, his wife, recalled the death of her older sister from an infection associated with the rite; this tragedy led Hajia's family to exempt her from cutting, and she, too, opposed the practice for her children. During his lifetime, Muhammed, being wealthy, was able to defy the tribal customs of the Tchamba-Kunsuntu, to which he belonged. Both illiterate themselves, the Kassindjas sent Fauziya to a boarding school in Ghana, so that she could learn English and help her father in his business. Meanwhile, her four older sisters married men of their own choice, genitals intact.

Fauziya's family was thus an anomaly in the region. Rakia Idrissou, the local genital exciser, told a reporter that girls usually have the procedure between the ages of four and seven. If weak, they are held down by four women; if stronger, they require five women, one to sit on their chests and one for each arm and leg. They must be kept still, she said, because if they jerk suddenly the razor blade used for the surgery can cut too deep.

When Fauziya was fifteen, however, her father died. Her mother was summarily turned out of the house by hostile relatives, and an aunt took control of the household, ending Fauziya's education. "We don't want girls to go to school too much," this aunt told a reporter from the *New York Times*. The family patriarch then arranged for Fauziya to become the fourth wife of an electrician; her prospective husband insisted that she have the genital operation first. To avoid the marriage and the mutilation that would have preceded it, Fauziya decided to leave home; her mother gave her $3,000 of the $3,500 inheritance that was her only sustenance. On her wedding day, Fauziya left

Martha Nussbaum, "Judging Other Cultures: the Case of Genital Mutilation" from *Sex and Social Justice*, pp. intro 15–24, 1999. Reprinted by permission of Oxford University Press.

12

her aunt's house, flagged down a taxi, and, with nothing but the clothes on her back, asked the driver to take her across the border into Ghana, some twenty miles away. Once in Ghana, she got on a flight to Germany; with help from people who befriended her there, she got a flight to the United States.

On landing in Newark she confessed that her documents were false and asked for political asylum. After weeks of detention in an unsanitary and oppressive immigration prison, she got legal assistance again with the help of her mother, who contacted a nephew who was working as a janitor in the Washington area. Scraping together $500, the nephew hired a law student at American University, Ms. Miller Bashir, to handle Fauziya's case. At first, Bashir was unsuccessful and a Philadelphia immigration judge denied Fauziya's request for asylum. Through the determined efforts of activists, journalists, and law faculty at American University, she successfully appealed the denial. The appellate ruling stated that the practice of genital mutilation constitutes persecution and concluded: "It remains particularly true that women have little legal recourse and may face threats to their freedom, threats or acts of physical violence, or social ostracization for refusing to undergo this harmful traditional practice, or attempting to protect their female children."

In recent years, the practice of female genital mutilation has been increasingly in the news, generating a complex debate about cultural norms and the worth of sexual functioning. This chapter attempts to describe and to sort out some aspects of this controversy. First, however, a word about nomenclature. Although discussions sometimes use the terms "female circumcision" and "clitoridectomy," "female genital mutilation" (FGM) is the standard generic term for all these procedures in the medical literature. "Clitoridectomy" standardly designates a subcategory, described shortly. The term "female circumcision" has been rejected by international medical practitioners because it suggests the fallacious analogy to male circumcision, which is generally believed to have either no effect or a positive effect on physical health and sexual functioning.[2] Anatomically, the degree of

cutting in the female operations described here is far more extensive. (The male equivalent of the clitoridectomy would be the amputation of most of the penis. The male equivalent of infibulation would be "removal of the entire penis, its roots of soft tissue, and part of the scrotal skin."[3]) This discussion is confined to cases that involve substantial removal of tissue and/or functional impairment; I make no comment on purely symbolic procedures that involve no removal of tissue, and these are not included under the rubric "female genital mutilation" by international agencies that study the prevalence of the procedure.[4]

Three types of genital cutting are commonly practiced: (1) In *clitoridectomy*, a part or the whole of the clitoris is amputated and the bleeding is stopped by pressure or a stitch. (2) In *excision*, both the clitoris and the inner lips are amputated. Bleeding is usually stopped by stitching, but the vagina is not covered. (3) In *infibulation*, the clitoris is removed, some or all of the labia minora are cut off, and incisions are made in the labia majora to create raw surface. These surfaces are either stitched together or held in contact until they heal as a hood of skin that covers the urethra and most of the vagina.[5] Approximately 85% of women who undergo FGM have type 1 or type 2; infibulation, which accounts for only 15% of the total, nonetheless accounts for 80 to 90% of all operations in certain countries, for example, the Sudan, Somalia, and Djibouti.

The practice of female genital mutilation remains extremely common in Africa, although it is illegal, and widely resisted, in most of the countries where it occurs.[6] The World Health Organization estimates that overall, in today's world between 85 and 115 million women have had such operations. In terms of percentages, for example, 93% of women in Mali have undergone genital cutting, 98% in Somalia, 89% of women in the Sudan, 43% in the Central African Republic, 43% in the Ivory Coast, and 12% in Togo.[7] Smaller numbers of operations are now reported from countries such as Australia, Belgium, France, the United Kingdom, and the United States.

Female genital mutilation is linked to extensive and in some cases lifelong health problems.

These include infection, hemorrhage, and abscess at the time of the operation; later difficulties in urination and menstruation; stones in the urethra and bladder due to repeated infections; excessive growth of scar tissue at the site, which may become disfiguring; pain during intercourse; infertility (with devastating implications for a woman's other life chances); obstructed labor and damaging rips and tears during childbirth.[8] Complications from infibulation are more severe than those from clitoridectomy and incision; nonetheless, the false perception that clitoridectomy is "safe" frequently leads to the ignoring of complications.

Both in the implicated nations and outside, feminists have organized to demand the abolition of this practice, citing its health risks, its impact on sexual functioning, and the violations of dignity and choice associated with its compulsory and nonconsensual nature. These opponents have been joined by many authorities in their respective nations, both religious and secular. In Egypt, for example, both the Health Minister, Ismail Sallem, and the new head of Al Azhar, the nation's leading Islamic institution, support a ban on the practice. The World Health Organization has advised health professionals not to participate in the practice since 1982 and repeated its strong opposition in 1994; the practice has also been condemned by the U.N. Commission on Human Rights, UNICEF, the World Medication Organization, Minority Rights Group International, and Amnesty International.[9]

At the same time, however, other writers have begun to protest that the criticism of genital mutilation is inappropriate and "ethnocentric," a demonizing of another culture with our own.[10] They have also charged that the focus on this problem involves a Western glamorization of sexual pleasure that is inappropriate, especially when we judge other cultures with different moral norms. To encounter such positions we do not need to turn to scholarly debates. We find them in our undergraduate students who are inclined to be ethical relativists on such matters, at least initially, hesitant to make any negative judgment of a culture other than their own. Because it seems important for anyone interested in political change in this area to understand these views in their popular and nonacademic

form, I shall illustrate them from student writings I have encountered, both in my own teaching and in my research for a book on liberal education, adding some points from the academic debate.[11]

Many students, like some participants in the academic debate, are general cultural relativists, holding that it is always inappropriate to criticize the practices of another culture, and that cultures can appropriately be judged only by their own internal norms. That general position would indeed imply that it is wrong for Westerners to criticize female genital mutilation, but not for any reasons interestingly specific to genital mutilation itself. For that reason, and because I have already considered that family of views in chapter 1 discussing the views of relativists in anthropology and development policy, I shall focus here on four criticisms that, while influenced by relativism, stop short of the general relativist thesis:

(1) It is morally wrong to criticize the practices of another culture unless one is prepared to be similarly critical of comparable practices when they occur in one's own culture. (Thus, a typical student reaction is to criticize the "ethnocentrism" of a stance that holds that one's own culture is the benchmark for "the principles and practices that are appropriate for all people.")[12]

(2) It is morally wrong to criticize the practices of another culture unless one's own culture has eradicated all evils of a comparable kind.[13] (Thus, a typical undergraduate paper comments that criticism of genital mutilation is unacceptable "when one considers the domestic problems we are faced with in our own cultures.")

(3) Female genital mutilation is morally on a par with practices of dieting and body shaping in American culture. (I observed quite a few courses in which this comparison played a central role, and the comparison has often been suggested by my own students. In a similar vein, philosopher Yael Tamir writes that, "Western conceptions of female beauty encourage women to undergo a wide range of painful, medically unnecessary, and potentially damaging processes."[14])

(4) Female genital mutilation involves the loss of a capacity that may not be especially central to the lives in question, and one to which

Westerners attach disproportionate significance. Thus "references to clitoridectomy commonly reveal a patronizing attitude toward women, suggesting that they are primarily sexual beings."[15]

These are significant charges, which should be confronted. Feminist argument should not be condescending to women in developing countries who have their own views of what is good. Such condescension is all the more damaging when it comes from women who are reluctant to criticize the flaws in their own culture, for then it is reminiscent of the worst smugness of "white man's burden" colonialism. Our students are surely right to think that withholding one's own judgment until one has listened carefully to the experiences of members of the culture in question is a crucial part of intelligent deliberation. On the other hand, the prevalence of a practice, and the fact that even today many women endorse and perpetuate it, should not be taken as the final word, given that there are also many women in African cultures who struggle against it, and given that those who do perpetuate it may do so in background conditions of intimidation and economic and political inequality. How, then, should we respond to these very common charges?

The first thesis is true, and it is useful to be reminded of it. Americans have all too often criticized other cultures without examining their own cultural shortcomings. It is less clear, however, that lack of self-criticism is a grave problem for Americans on such issues. We find no shortage of criticism of the ideal female body image, or of practices of dieting intended to produce it. Indeed, American feminists would appear to have devoted considerably more attention to these American problems than to genital mutilation, to judge from the success of books such as Naomi Wolf's *The Beauty Myth* and Susan Bordo's *Unbearable Weight*. Indeed, a review of the recent feminist literature suggests the problem may lie in exactly the opposite direction, in an excessive focusing on our own failings. We indulge in moral narcissism when we flagellate ourselves for our own errors while neglecting to attend to the needs of those who ask our help from a distance.

The second thesis is surely false. It is wrong to insist on cleaning up one's own house before

responding to urgent calls from outside. Should we have said "Hands off Apartheid," on the grounds that racism persists in the United States? Or, during the Second World War, "Hands off the rescue of the Jews," on the grounds that in the 1930s and 1940s every nation that contained Jews was implicated in anti-Semitic practices? It is and should be difficult to decide how to allocate one's moral effort between local and distant abuses. To work against both is urgently important, and individuals will legitimately make different decisions about their priorities. But the fact that a needy human being happens to live in Togo rather than Idaho does not make her less my fellow, less deserving of my moral commitment. And to fail to recognize the plight of a fellow human being because we are busy moving our own culture to greater moral heights seems the very height of moral obtuseness and parochialism.

We could add that FGM is not as such the practice of a single culture or group of cultures. As recently as in the 1940s, related operations were performed by U.S. and British doctors to treat female "problems" such as masturbation and lesbianism.[16] Nor is there any cultural or religious group in which the practice is universal. As Nahid Toubia puts it, "FGM is an issue that concerns women and men who believe in equality, dignity and fairness to all human beings, regardless of gender, race, religion or ethnic identity. . . . It represents a human tragedy and must not be used to set Africans against non-Africans, one religious group against another, or even women against men."[17]

If the third thesis were true, it might support a decision to give priority to the local in our political action (though not necessarily speech and writing): If two abuses are morally the same and we have better local information about one and are better placed politically to do something about it, that one seems to be a sensible choice to focus on in our actions here and now. But is the third thesis true? Surely not. Let us enumerate the differences.

1. Female genital mutilation is carried out by force, whereas dieting in response to culturally constructed images of beauty is a matter of choice, however seductive the persuasion. Few mothers restrict their

children's dietary intake to unhealthy levels in order to make them slim; indeed most mothers of anorexic girls are horrified and deeply grieved by their daughters' condition. By contrast, during FGM small girls, frequently as young as four or five, are held down by force, often, as in Togo, by a group of adult women, and have no chance to select an alternative. The choices involved in dieting are often not fully autonomous: They may be the product of misinformation and strong social forces that put pressure on women to make choices, sometimes dangerous ones, that they would not make otherwise. We should criticize these pressures and the absence of full autonomy created by them. And yet the distinction between social pressure and physical force should also remain salient, both morally and legally. (Similarly, the line between seduction and rape is difficult to draw; frequently it turns on the elusive distinction between a threat and an offer, and on equally difficult questions about what threatened harms remove consent.) Nonetheless, we should make the distinction as best we can, and recognize that there remain relevant differences between genital mutilation and dieting, as usually practiced in America.

2. Female genital mutilation is irreversible, whereas dieting is, famously, far from irreversible.

3. Female genital mutilation is usually performed in conditions that in and of themselves are dangerous and unsanitary, conditions to which no child should be exposed; dieting is not.

4. Female genital mutilation is linked to extensive and in some cases lifelong health problems, even death. (In Kassindja's region, deaths are rationalized by the folk wisdom that profuse bleeding is a sign that a girl is not a virgin.) Dieting is linked to problems of this gravity only in the extreme cases of anorexia and bulimia, which, even then, are reversible.

5. Female genital mutilation is usually performed on children far too young to consent even were consent solicited; dieting involves, above all, adolescents and young adults.[18] Even when children are older, consent is not solicited. Typical is the statement of an Ivory Coast father of a twelve-year-old girl about to be cut. "She has no choice," he stated. "I decide. Her viewpoint is not important." His wife, who personally opposes the practice, concurs. "It is up to my husband," she states. "The man makes the decisions about the children."[19]

6. In the United States, as many women as men complete primary education, and more women than men complete secondary education; adult literacy is 99% for both females and males. In Togo, adult female literacy is 32.9% (52% that of men); in the Sudan, 30.6% (56% that of men); in the Ivory Coast, 26.1% (56%); in Burkina Faso, 8% (29%). Illiteracy is an impediment to independence; other

impediments are supplied by economic dependency and lack of employment opportunities. These facts suggest limits to the notions of consent and choice, even as applied to the mothers or relatives who perform the operation, who may not be aware of the extent of resistance to the practice in their own and relevantly similar societies. To these limits we may add those imposed by political powerlessness, malnutrition, and intimidation. The wife of the patriarch in Fauziya Kassindja's clan told a reporter that she is opposed to the practice and would have run away like Fauziya had she been able—but nonetheless, she will allow the operation for her infant daughter. "I have to do what my husband says," she concludes. "It is not for women to give an order. I feel what happened to my body. I remember my suffering. But I cannot prevent it for my daughter."

7. Female genital mutilation means the irreversible loss of the capability for a type of sexual functioning that many women value highly, usually at an age when they are far too young to know what value it has or does not have in their own life. In the rare case in which a woman can make the comparison, she usually reports profound regret. Mariam Razak, a neighbor of the Kassindjas, was fifteen when she was cut, with five adult women holding her down. She had had sex with the man who is now her husband prior to that time and found it satisfying. Now, they both say, things are difficult. Mariam compares the loss to having a terminal illness that lasts a lifetime. "Now," her husband says, "something was lost in that place. . . . I try to make her feel pleasure, but it doesn't work very well."[20]

8. Female genital mutilation is unambiguously linked to customs of a male domination. Even its official rationales, in terms of purity and propriety, point to aspects of sex hierarchy. Typical is the statement of Egyptian farmer Said Ibrahim, upset about the government ban. "Am I supposed to stand around while my daughter chases men?" To which Mohammed Ali, age seventeen, added, "Banning it would make women wild like those in America." Sex relations constructed by the practice are relations in which intercourse becomes a vehicle for one-sided male pleasure rather than for mutuality of pleasure.[21]

By contrast, the ideal female body image purveyed in the American media has multiple and complex resonances, including those of male domination, but also including those of physical fitness, independence, and boyish nonmaternity.

These differences help explain why there is no serious campaign to make ads for diet programs, or the pictures of emaciated women in *Vogue*, illegal, whereas FGM is illegal in most of the countries in which it occurs.[22] (In the Sudan, the practice is punishable by up to two years' imprisonment.) Such laws are not well enforced, but their existence is evidence of a widespread movement against the practice in the countries implicated. Women in local regions where the practice is traditional give evidence of acquiescing, insofar as they do, out of intimidation and lack of options; women in adjacent regions where the practice is not traditional typically deplore it, citing health risks, loss of pleasure, and unnecessary suffering.[23]

These differences also explain why Fauziya Kassindja was able to win political asylum. We shall not see similar arguments for political asylum for American women who have been pressured by the culture to be thin—however much it remains appropriate to criticize the norms of female beauty displayed in *Vogue* (as some advertisers have begun to do), the practices of some mothers, and the many covert pressures that combine to produce eating disorders in our society. Similarly, whereas the prospect of footbinding of the traditional Chinese type (in which the bones of the feet were repeatedly broken and the flesh of the foot became rotten[24]) would, in my view, give grounds for political asylum; the presence of advertisements for high-heeled shoes surely would not, however many problems may be associated with the fashion. Even the publication of articles urging women to undergo FGM should be seen as altogether different from forcing a woman to undergo the procedure.

How, then, is FGM traditionally justified, when it is? In social terms, it is highly likely that FGM emerged as the functional equivalent to the seclusion of women. African women, unlike their counterparts in India, Pakistan, and elsewhere, are major agricultural producers. There is no barrier to women's work outside the home, and indeed the entire organization of agriculture in Africa traditionally rests on the centrality of female labor.[25] In India, women's purity is traditionally guaranteed by seclusion; in Africa, this guarantee was absent, and another form of control emerged. But this functional history clearly does not justify the practice. What arguments are currently available?

It is now generally agreed that there is no religious requirement to perform FGM. The prophet Mohammed's most cited statement about the practice (from a reply to a question during a speech) makes the process nonessential, and the force of his statement seems to have been to discourage extensive cutting in favor of a more symbolic type of operation.[26] The one reference to the operation in the *hadith* classifies it as a *makrama*, or nonessential practice. FGM is not practiced at all in many Islamic countries, including Pakistan, Algeria, Tunisia, Saudi Arabia, Iran, and Iraq. Defenses appealing to morality (FGM keeps women from extramarital sex) have resonance because they connect with the practice's likely original rationale, but they presuppose an unacceptable picture of women as whorish and childish. However sincerely such arguments are addressed, they should not be accepted by people with an interest in women's dignity. Defenses in terms of physical beauty are trickier, because we know how much cultures differ in what they regard as beautiful, but even perceptions of beauty (also at issue in Chinese footbinding) should yield before evidence of impairment of health and sexual functioning. Arguments claiming that without the practice women will not be acceptable to men may state something true in local circumstances (as was also the case with footbinding) and may therefore provide a rationale for individual families to defer to custom as the best of a bad business (although this is less true now than formerly, given the widespread resistance to the practice in most areas where it occurs). Such arguments, however, clearly cannot justify the practice in moral or legal terms; similarly, arguments advising slaves to behave themselves if they do not want to be beaten may give good advice but cannot justify the institution of slavery.

The strongest argument in favor of the practice is an argument that appeals to cultural continuity. Jomo Kenyatta and others have stressed the constitutive role played by such initiation rites in the formation of a community and the disintegrative effect of interference.[27] For this reason, Kenyatta opposed criminalization of the surgery and recommended a more gradual process of education and persuasion.

Although one must have some sympathy with these concerns, it is still important to remember that a community is not a mysterious organic unity but a plurality of people standing in different relations of power to one another. It is not obvious that the type of cohesion that is effected by subordination and functional impairment is something we ought to perpetuate. Moreover, sixty years after Kenyatta's ambivalent defense, we see widespread evidence of resistance from within each culture, and there is reason to think that the practice is kept alive above all by the excisers themselves, paramedical workers who enjoy both high income and high prestige in the community from their occupation. These women frequently have the status of priestesses and have great influence over social perceptions.[28] Countries that move against the practice should certainly make provision for the economic security of these women, but this does not mean taking them as unbiased interpreters of cultural tradition. To the extent that an initiation ritual is still held to be a valuable source of cultural solidarity, such rituals can surely be practiced (as they already are in some places) using a merely symbolic operation that does not remove any tissue.

Let me now turn to the fourth thesis. A secondary theme in recent feminist debates about FGM is skepticism about the human value of sexual functioning. Philosopher Yael Tamir, for example, argues that hedonistic American feminists have ascribed too much value to pleasure. She suggests that it is men, above all, whose interests are being served by this, because female sexual enjoyment in our society is "seen as a measure of the sexual power and achievements of men," and because men find women who do not enjoy sex more intimidating than those who do.

I am prepared to agree with Tamir to this extent: The attention given FGM seems to me somewhat disproportionate among the many gross abuses the world practices against women: unequal nutrition and health care, lack of the right to assemble and to walk in public, lack of equality under the law, lack of equal access to education, sex-selective infanticide and feticide, domestic violence, marital rape, rape in police custody, and many more. Unlike Tamir, I believe that the primary reason for this

focus is not a fascination with sex, but the relative tractability of FGM as a practical problem, given the fact that it is already widely resisted and indeed illegal, and given that it is not supported by any religion. How much harder to grapple with women's legal inequality before Islamic courts, their pervasive hunger, their illiteracy, their subjection to battery and violence? But surely Tamir is right that we should not focus on this one abuse while relaxing our determination to make structural changes that will bring women closer to full equality worldwide. And she may also be right to suggest that the fascination with FGM contains at least an element of the sensational or even the prurient.

Tamir, however, does not simply criticize the disproportionate focus on FGM: She offers a more general denigration of the importance of sexual pleasure as an element in human flourishing. This part of her argument is flawed by the failure to make a crucial distinction: that between a function and the capacity to choose that function. Criticizing her opponents for their alleged belief that the capacity for sexual pleasure is a central human good, she writes:

> Nuns take an oath of celibacy, but we do not usually condemn the church for preventing its clergy from enjoying an active sex life. Moreover, most of us do not think that Mother Teresa is leading a worse life than Chichulina, though the latter claims to have experienced an extensive number of orgasms. It is true that nuns are offered spiritual life in exchange for earthly goods, but in the societies where clitoridectomy is performed, the fulfilling life of motherhood and child bearing are offered in exchange. Some may rightly claim that one can function as a wife and a mother while still experiencing sexual pleasures. Others believe that full devotion to God does not require an oath of celibacy. Yet these views are, after all, a matter of convention.[29]

There are a number of oddities in this argument. (It is hard, for example, to know what to make of the assertion that the possibility of combining sexual pleasure with motherhood is a mere "matter of convention.") More centrally, however, Tamir mischaracterizes the debate. No feminist opponent of FGM is saying or implying that celibacy is bad, that nuns all have a starved life, that orgasms are the be-all and end-all of existence. I know of no opponent who would not agree with Tamir's statement that women "are not merely sexual agents, that their ability to lead rich and rewarding lives does not depend solely on the nature of their sex life." But there is a great difference between fasting and starving; just so, there is also a great difference between a vow of celibacy and FGM. Celibacy involves the choice not to exercise a capability to which nuns, insofar as they are orthodox Roman Catholics, ascribe considerable human value.[30] Its active exercise is thought good for all but a few of those humans, and even for them it is the choice not to use a capacity one has (as in the case of fasting) that is deemed morally valuable. (A Catholic should hold that a survivor of FGM cannot achieve the Christian good of celibacy.) FGM, by contrast, involves forgoing altogether the very possibility of sexual functioning—and, as I said, well before one is of an age to make such a choice.[31] We all know that people who are blind or unable to walk can lead rich and meaningful lives; nonetheless we would all deplore practices that deliberately disabled people in those respects, nor would we think that critics of those practices are giving walking or seeing undue importance in human life.

Can even the mothers of these girls make an informed choice as to the value of female sexual pleasure? They have been immersed in traditional beliefs about women's impurity; lacking literacy and education, as a large proportion do, they have difficulty seeking out alternative paradigms. As the immigration report points out, their situation is made more difficult by fear and powerlessness. Equally important, their own experience of sexual life cannot have contained orgasmic pleasure if they themselves encountered FGM as girls; even if they did not, they are highly likely to have experienced marriage and sexual life as a series of insults to their dignity, given the ubiquity of domestic violence and marital rape. Should they believe that FGM is a bad thing for their daughters—as a remarkable proportion of the women interviewed in the recent stories clearly do—they have no power to make their choices effective and many incentives to conceal the views they hold. Such facts do not show that women who have had a

more fortunate experience of marriage and sexuality are making a mistake when they hold that the capacity for sexual pleasure should be preserved for those who may choose to exercise it. There is certainly something wrong with any social situation in which women are viewed only or primarily as sex objects; but criticizing such perceptions has nothing to do with defending FGM.

Nor does Tamir give us any reason to suppose that the importance of women's sexual pleasure is a mythic construct of the male ego. Many women have reported enjoying sex a good deal, and there is no reason to think them all victims of false consciousness. It is probably true that some men find women who do not enjoy sex more intimidating than those who do, but it would be more than a little perverse to deny oneself pleasure simply in order to intimidate men. Moreover, in the situation we are contemplating in the case of FGM, the operative male fear is surely that of women's sexual agency, which is a sign that the woman is not simply a possession and might even experience pleasure with someone other than her owner. It would be highly implausible to suggest that African women can gain power and intimidate men by undergoing FGM. The attack on FGM is part and parcel of a more general attempt by women to gain control of their sexual capacities; it is thus a relative of attacks on rape, marital rape, sexual harassment, and domestic violence. It is precisely this challenge to traditional male control that many men find threatening.

In the concluding section of her discussion of FGM, Yael Tamir imagines a country called Libidia, where women with unnaturally enlarged clitorises find they cannot do anything else but have sex and therefore seek to remove the clitoris in order to have better lives. In this way she suggests that sexual pleasure undermines other valuable human functions—one might plausibly deem its removal a helpful thing, rather like a trip to the dentist to get rid of a diseased tooth. She here expresses a Platonic idea about the relationship between continence and intellectual creativity that may be true for some individuals at some times but is surely not a universal datum of human experience. Plato did indeed hold in the *Phaedo* that mental life would be much better if the bodily appetites could be put to one side insofar as possible—even though he did not maintain this position with absolute consistency, nor did he suggest genital mutilation as a remedy.[32] Aristotle, on the other hand, held that someone who was insensible to the full range of the bodily pleasures would be "far from being a human being." We do not need to decide which thinker is right—or indeed for which people each of them is right—to decide sensibly that FGM is not like an appendectomy—that it involves the removal of a capability for whose value history and experience have had a great deal to say. Individuals may then choose whether and how to exercise it, just as we also choose whether and how to use our athletic and musical capacities.

Internal criticism is slowly changing the situation in the nations in which FGM has traditionally been practiced. The eighteen-year-old son of the patriarch of the Kassindja family told reporters that he wanted to marry a woman who had not been cut, because teachers in his high school had influenced his thinking. The patriarch himself now favors making the practice optional, to discourage more runaways who give the family a bad name. The very fact that the age of cutting in Togo has been moving steadily down (from twelve to four), in order (the exciser says) to discourage runaways, gives evidence of mounting resistance to the practice. But many of the women and men in the relevant nations who are struggling against this practice are impoverished or unequal under the law or illiterate or powerless or in fear—and often all of these. There is no doubt that they wish outside aid. There is also no doubt that they encounter local opposition—as is always the case when one moves to change a deeply entrenched custom connected with the structures of power. (As I have suggested, some of the people involved have strong personal economic and status interests in the status quo.) Suzanne Aho, director of Togo's office for the Protection and Promotion of the Family, explains that she tries to counsel men about women's rights of choice, but she encounters the dead weight of custom. Of the Kassindja patriarch she says: "'You cannot force her,' I told him. He understood, but he said it is a tradition."

These upholders of tradition are eager, often, to brand their internal opponents as Westernizers, colonialists, and any other bad thing that may carry public sentiment. Even so, Fauziya's father was accused of "trying to act like a white man." But this way of deflecting internal criticism should not intimidate outsiders who have reasoned the matter out, at the same time listening to the narratives of women who have been involved in the reality of FGM. The charge of "colonialism" presumably means that the norms of an oppressor group are being unthinkingly assimilated, usually to carry favor with that group. That is not at all what is happening in the case of FGM. In the United Nations, in Human Rights Watch, in many organizations throughout the world, and in countless local villages the issue has been debated. Even the not very progressive Immigration and Naturalization Service (INS) has been swayed by the data it collected. The vigor of internal resistance should give confidence to those outside who work to oppose the practice. Frequently external pressure can assist a relatively powerless internal group that is struggling to achieve change.

In short, international and national officials who have been culpably slow to recognize gender-specific abuses as human rights violations are beginning to get the idea that women's rights are human rights, and that freedom from FGM is among them. Without abandoning a broader concern for the whole list of abuses women suffer at the hands of unjust customs and individuals, we should continue to keep FGM on the list of unacceptable practices that violate women's human rights, and we should be ashamed of ourselves if we do not use whatever privilege and power has come our way to make it disappear forever.

NOTES

1. See Celia W. Dugger, "U.S. Gives Asylum to Woman Who Fled Genital Mutilation," *New York Times*, June 20, 1996; and "A Refugee's Body Is Intact but Her Family Is Torn," *New York Times*, September 11, 1996. For related stories, see Neil MacFarquhar, "Mutilation of Egyptian Girls: Despite Ban, It Goes On," *New York Times*, August 8, 1996, A3; Celia W. Dugger, "African Ritual Pain: Genital Cutting," *New York Times*, October 5, 1996; Celia W. Dugger, "New Law Bans Genital Cutting in United States," *New York Times*, October 12, 1996, A1.

2. Moreover, the male operation, in both Judaism and Islam, is linked with membership in the dominant male community rather than with subordination.

3. Nahid Toubia, *Female Genital Mutilation: A Call for Global Action* (hereafter *FGM*) (New York: UNICEF, 1995), 5. Toubia was the first woman surgeon in the Sudan. She is an advisor to the World Health Organization, vice chair of the Women's Rights Project of Human Rights Watch, and director of the Global Action against FGM Project at the Columbia University School of Public Health. Other medical discussions include Toubia, "Female Circumcision as a Public Health Issue," *England Journal of Medicine*, 331 (1994), 712 ff. Amy O. Tsui, Judith N. Wasserheit, and John G. Haaga, eds., *Reproductive Health in Developing Countries: Expanding Dimensions, Building Solutions* (Washington, DC: National Academy Press, 1997), 32–3 with bibliography; N. El-Saadawi, "Circumcision of Girls," and R. H. Dualeh and M. Fara-Warsame, "Female Circumcision in Somalia," in *Traditional Practices Affecting the Health of Women and Children*, ed. T. Baasher, R. H. Bannerman, H. Rushwan, and I. Sharif (Alexandria, Egypt: the World Health Organization, 1982); C. P. Howson et al., eds., *In Her Lifetime, Female Morbidity and Mortality in Sub-Saharan Africa* (Washington, DC: National Academy Press, 1996); World Health Organization, "WHO Leads Action Against Female Genital Mutilation," *World Health Forum*, 15 (1994), 416 ff; L. Heise, "Gender-based Violence and Women's Reproductive Health," *International Journal of Gynecology and Obstetrics*, 46 (1994), 221–9.

4. See *FGM*, 10, stating that ritualistic circumcisions never involve only the removal of the skin around the glans, without damage to the sensitive part of the organ—although such "male style female circumcisions" have been documented in modern surgical settings. In this sense, one lengthy recent contribution to the debate appears to bypass the main issue. Leslye Obiora, "Bridges and Barricades: Rethinking Polemics and Intransigence in the Campaign Against Female Circumcision," *Case Western Reserve Law Review*, 47 (1997), 275–378, begins by attacking the campaign against the operation as an example of Western paternalism and condescension, but in the end it emerges that what she herself would accept may be limited to a merely symbolic pricking. She recommends "clinicalizing" the practice, that is, permitting it but requiring it to be done in a hospital or clinic setting; she strongly implies that in such a setting no tissue would be removed, and a symbolic pricking would be the only thing that would occur. However, her own normative position remains extremely unclear because she does not ask what is in fact occurring in clinical settings in Djibouti, which has adopted the medicalization solution, and where there is no reason at all to suppose that a mere pricking is being preferred to traditional forms of the practice. See Isabelle Gunning, "Commentary," *Case Western Law Review*, 47 (1992), 445–460, which emphasizes that the Djibouti campaign has focused on a shift from infibulation to any lesser surgery; given this emphasis, a considerable amount of tissue is still removed under the medicalized form of the procedure; nor does Obiora state that her own approval of medicalization would be contingent upon the operation's being merely symbolic.

5. See *FGM*, 10–11, with anatomical drawings.

6. Twenty-four countries have legislation or ministerial regulations against FGM per se; several others cover FGM under laws relating to child abuse; it is also illegal under the Convention on the Rights of the Child (CRC) and the Convention to Eliminate All Forms of Discrimination Against Women (CEDAW), which most of the countries in question have ratified. See *FGM*, 44.

7. See *FGM*, 25, reporting WHO data. Another valuable source of data is the *Country Reports on Human Rights Practices for 1996*, report submitted, to the Committee on Foreign Relations, U.S. Senate and Committee on International Relations, U.S. House of Representatives by the Department of State (Washington, DC: U.S. Government Printing Office, 1997). The data, arranged by individual countries, are similar to the WHO data. See also *Human Rights are Women's Right* (London: Amnesty International, 1995), 131–4.

8. See *FGM*; and also N. Toubiam, "Female Genital Mutilation," in *Women's Rights, Human Rights* (hereafter WRHR), ed. J. Peters and A. Wolper (New York: Routledge, 1994), 224–37, bibliography.

9. See Amnesty International, 132–4.

10. An African defense that has influenced many Western commentators is that of Jomo Kenyatta, *Facing Mount Kenya* (London: Secker and Warburg, 1938), 130–62. For a related anthropological account, see J. S. La Fontaine, *Initiation* (Manchester: Manchester University Press, 1985), 109–12, 166–80. Obiora gives an overview of other anthropological perspectives; unfortunately, however, she fails to acknowledge the extent of African women's resistance to FGM. See Gunning's commentary, with references, and also comments by African activist Seble Dawit, cited in "Preface," *Case Western Law Review* 47 (1997), 28. A recent U.N. report shows that the request to use the term "female genital mutilation" rather than "female circumcision" to describe the practice came from African women, not from outsiders. See *Report of the United Nations Seminar on Traditional Practices Affecting the Health Of Women and Children*, Subcommission on Prevention of Discrimination and Protection of Minorities, Commission on Human Rights, 43d Sess. 32, U.N. Doc. E/CN.4/Sub.2./1991/48 (1991). At times, Obiora appears to recognize that "culture" includes contestation and resistance; at other times seems to treat all resistance and protest as evidence of an alien "Western" ideology. Other African critiques of FGM can be found in Asma A'Haleem, "Claiming Our Bodies and Our Rights: Exploring Female Circumcision as an Act of Violence," *Freedom from Violence*, ed. Margaret Schuler (OEF International: 1992), available from United Nations/UNIFEM; Raqiya H. D. Abdalla, *Sisters in Affliction: Circumcision and Infibulation of Women in Africa* (London: Zed Books, 1982); Olayinka Koso-Thomas, *The Circumcision of Women: A Strategy for Eradication* (London: Zed Books, 1992); Efua Dorkenoo, *Cutting the Rose: Female Genital Mutilation—The Practice and Its Prevention* (Minority Rights Publication, 1994); Marie B. Assad, "Female Circumcision in Egypt: Social Implications, Current Research, and Prospects for Change," *Studies in Family Planning* 11, (1980). For a general treatment of human rights issues in Islamic perspective, see Abdullahi

An-Na'im, *Toward an Islamic Reformation: Civil Liberties, Human Rights, and International Law* (Syracuse, NY: Syracuse University Press, 1990).

11. For further discussion of student writing in a course on practices of control and shaping of the female body at St. Lawrence University, see *Cultivating Humanity: A Classical Defense of Reform in Higher Education* (Cambridge, MA: Harvard University Press, 1997), chap. 6. One example of an academic article that could easily be read as advancing such claims is Tamir, "Hands off Clitoridectomy," *The Boston Review*, 21(3/4) (1996), 21–2. See also Tamir's response to critics in the following issue, where she clarifies her position, suggesting that she did not intend to endorse any of the four claims in the form in which I have stated them here.

12. Quotations from student writing are from the St. Lawrence course.

13. For analysis of a (typical) student essay that advanced this thesis, see *Cultivating Humanity*, chap. 4.

14. Tamir, 21. Compare Obiora, 318–20.

15. Tamir, 21.

16. *FGM*, 21.

17. Ibid., 7.

18. See Toubia, in WRHR, 233.

19. "African Ritual Pain."

20. Toubia has encountered rare cases in which women who have undergone clitoridectomy and even intermediate infibulation convince her that they have experienced orgasm. She attributes this to unusual psychological resourcefulness, together with the capacities of secondary sources of sexual stimulation.

21. For valuable reflections on this point I am indebted to Grant Cornwell's "Suffering and Sexuality," a description of his experience in Kenya, as a part of a faculty group from St. Lawrence University.

22. Toubia suggests the more pertinent analogy to artificial breast implants, which do involve serious health risks but do not impair functioning in a similar way.

23. For accounts of such views in a Kenyan village, I am indebted to manuscripts by Eve Stoddard, Grant Cornwell, and the members of the St. Lawrence University Culture Encounters Group.

24. For an especially vivid description of this practice, see Jung Chang, *Wild Swans: Three Daughters of China* (London and New York: HarperCollins, 1992). See also Andrea Dworkin, *Woman Hating* (New York: Dutton, 1974), 95–116, with citations to scholarly studies and memoirs.

25. On the two styles of agricultural organization, the classic work is Esther Boserup, *Women's Role in Economic Development*, 2nd ed. (Aldershot, England: Gower Publishing, 1986). (Original work published 1971).

26. See Toubia in WRHR, 236; cf. *FGM*, 31. Mohammed told his listeners to "circumcise" but not to "mutilate," for not destroying the clitoris would be better for the man and would make the woman's face glow—a directive that many interpret as calling for "a male-type circumcision where the prepuce is removed, making the clitoris even more sensitive to touch." Toubia, in WRHR, 236. See also Marie Aimée Hélie-Lucas, "Women Living Under Muslim Laws," in *Ours By Right: Women's Rights as Human Rights*, ed. Joanna Kerr (London: Zed Books, 1993), 53. Obiora attacks this argument against the religion-based defense, saying, "The originating claim for the position holds only for persons favorably disposed to denigrating indigenous African religion as a farce" (350). But the bare fact that the practice predates the arrival of Islam and Christianity into Africa does not show that it is religious rather than cultural, and Obiora offers no argument that would help us to distinguish these two spheres. Furthermore, the legal question must be whether today the practice is defended as part of a religious system of belief, not whether at one time it had such a connection. In any case, as Obiora notes, even in the United States, with its very liberal understanding of religious freedom, the protection of the well-being and health of children has typically been understood to override the parent's interest in initiating the child into a religious practice. See *Prince v. Massachusetts*, 321 U.S. 158 (1944).

27. Kenyatta, *Facing Mount Kenya*.

28. *FGM*, 29.

29. Tamir, 21.

30. Of course, in the past many women were forced to become nuns by their families; in this situation (which may still exist today in some countries), Christian celibacy is more directly comparable to FGM.

31. Thus it is not surprising that Christians have been among the leading opponents of the practice. See *FGM*, 32, stressing the role of Christian leaders in raising the issue in the British parliament. Toubia notes, however, that the Coptic church has been silent about FGM, and the Ethiopian Orthodox Church actively supports it.

32. See, however, Catullus poem 65, where a devotee of an Asian cult castrates himself in the service of the goddess—and is promptly referred to by the female pronoun!

Part I

THEORETICAL PERSPECTIVES

WHAT DOES ETHICS CONCERN?

According to many Western and non-Western perspectives, ethics generally is understood to address the question: How ought we to lead our lives? Ethics, as a branch of philosophy, raises a number of questions that can be addressed conceptually or theoretically, namely:

- Is ethical knowledge possible?
- What are the sources of such knowledge?
- What are the theoretical strategies for resolving conflicts among these sources?
- Which are the most important values and how are they related to each other?

Applied ethics pursues these various conceptual or theoretical questions within the framework of particular contemporary issues.

In Western thought, it is common to distinguish between two large subgroups of questions in ethics. *Personal ethics* deals with the questions

- What determines the rightness or wrongness of particular actions?
- What determines how social responsibility will divide into the individual shares of responsibility for the members of a community?

Then there are large-scale, collective issues in ethics, which we will call *social ethics*, such as

- What determines the rightness or wrongness of various social policies?
- What are communities collectively responsible for?

There is a long-standing controversy in Western thought about the relationship between personal and social ethics. Some thinkers have believed that ethics mainly concerns what one's individual conscience tells one to do, and that

one should not be concerned about what the society at large could do. Others, such as the utilitarians, have thought that ethics primarily concerns deciding what is best for the society at large, with each person's own happiness counting for no more than any other person's happiness. Some non-Western approaches deny that there is a significant difference between these two approaches.

Neither of these approaches, personal or social, excludes the other. Indeed, environmental ethics is a clear case of a blend between the two: It involves a set of issues that ultimately require collective action, yet it also involves issues that individuals in North America, for instance, face every day in the way they decide about such personal matters as whether to use a recycling bin. All issues in ethics have a personal dimension in that they have an effect on individual lives and call for some kind of judgment on the individual's part. In addition, most ethical issues have a social dimension in that, for their resolution, they require some sort of group action by the community at large. In this text, we will stress social ethics first, in order to push ourselves to think about the effects of our actions on distant parts of the world, thereby extending the horizon of our ethical gaze.

WHERE DO WE BEGIN?

In any study of ethics, the first and most difficult question we face concerns the subject matter itself: What do we study in an ethics course? What data, if any, are we concerned with? There are three types of "data" most commonly mentioned in ethics:

- Intuitions
- Rules and codes
- Social roles

Some philosophers would also include *reason* as a major source of ethical knowledge. But it seems to us that reason alone cannot tell us very much in ethics, unless it has something to operate on. Although rationality is terribly important in ethics, since it sets the ground rules for discussion and deliberation, an appeal to reason alone is unlikely to lead very far in ethics.

The most commonly cited "data," especially in Western approaches to ethics, are people's *intuitions*. Intuitions concern what people actually think, especially after they have engaged in reflection about what is right and wrong. Most discussions of ethics begin with what people think is wrong about such issues as starvation or murder. Of course, there is significant disagreement about such things, and so an appeal to intuitions alone will not resolve many ethical questions. What one can hope for, indeed what our book aims at, is an increasingly reflective approach toward one's intuitions, informed by an understanding of the intuitions and reasoning of a wide spectrum of the population. As we will see, there is an emerging consensus concerning issues raised in certain ethical questions. On some other issues, we are far away from anything remotely resembling a consensus.

Rules and *codes* are another important starting point in ethics. Most communities have explicit or implicit sets of moral rules and taboos, and many societies have codes of conduct that are enforced against their members in much the same way that civil laws are enforced. These rules and codes often reflect the considered judgments of many people over many generations. In this sense, rules and codes often represent an intergenerational consensus about what is right or wrong. But rules and codes can conflict with an individual person's intuitions when applied to a particular case. In such cases of conflict it is not clear that the rules or codes should be given priority over one's intuitions. One such example is Huck Finn's dilemma: He was drawn toward his friend, Jim, and was inclined not to turn him in as a runaway slave; but Huck was also strongly motivated by the rules of his society, which dictated that slaves were property, and when they escaped they were in effect stealing from their masters. It is extremely important that we not treat any code or set of rules (or intuition) as unchallengeable, for like the slavery rules, even the consensus of a community may be ethically flawed.

Social roles are another interesting starting point for ethics discussions. Taking on, or having been thrust into, a particular role, such as "father" or "mother," "teacher" or "friend," "employer" or "employee," is often thought to involve a change in one's moral status. Social roles create obligations or expand our responsibilities. Understanding what the status of these roles is may be an important first step toward understanding what is right or wrong to do in a given situation. But like rules and codes, social roles may conflict with intuitions, and worse yet, the different roles each person assumes may offer conflicting guidance about what is right or wrong in particular cases. So again, we should not, indeed we cannot, regard social roles as unimpeachable sources of ethics. Rather, we need to consider intuitions, rules, codes, and social roles as each providing input into a process of ethical deliberation. What is crucial in such a process is the ability to resolve conflicts that exist among these sources of ethical knowledge.

HOW ARE MORAL JUDGMENTS MADE?

In Western thought there are three standard ways of making moral judgments, especially in cases in which there are conflicts among our sources of ethical knowledge:

- Consequentialism—of which utilitarianism is the most prominent variation.
- Deontological theory—of which Kantianism and rights theory are the most prominent variations.
- Virtue theory—of which Aristotelianism and Thomistic theory are the most prominent variations.

Each of these theoretical perspectives has achieved prominence, and for each perspective there are significant groups of defenders among contemporary moral philosophers.

Consequentialism is the view that judgments about whether an action is morally right should be made based on an assessment of the probable effects, or consequences, of alternative acts that are open to the person in question. Consequentialists contend that an act is morally right insofar as it maximizes the best results for everyone. But there is considerable disagreement about how to assess what the best consequence is. Is pleasure or happiness the main basis for deciding what is best? Or is there some other criterion, such as goodness, that should be the basis for deciding what is best for everyone? Another question that arises is this: Should greater emphasis be placed on short-term or long-term effects? And also, should we take account of the effects the application of a particular rule would have on the society at large?

Some consequentialists, such as classical utilitarians, believe that a person can measure the quantity of happiness likely to be produced by an act and the quantity of happiness likely to be produced by all alternative acts, and then by comparing these quantities, decide which act is morally best. Duties and rights are reconceived as merely rules of thumb for guiding us toward what is best for everyone. Our first reading, an excerpt from John Stuart Mill's book *Utilitarianism*, ends by arguing that rights are merely highly likely to advance the greatest happiness for the greatest number. Rights, in this view, have no intrinsic value.

Other consequentialists, such as rule utilitarians, take a more subtle view of moral duties and rights. Rather than weighing the likely consequences of alternative acts, these consequentialists weigh the likely consequences of alternative rules. If a rule, such as "honesty is the best policy," has been proven to be productive of very good consequences, and no other more useful rule is applicable, then the right thing to do is to conform to the rule of honesty. Both duties and rights are understood as forms of rule. On this view it would be right to act according to a weighty rule, such as the honesty rule, even though it appears that better consequences could be had in this one case by acting dishonestly. Duties and rights have weight here, but the weight is still a function of their ability to produce the best consequences in the society as a whole.

Deontological theory is the view that we should perform those acts that conform to duties and rights, quite independently of the consequences. In general, deontological views characterize morally right acts as those that display the most intrinsic value. The value of an act is determined by examining the act in light of moral principles. Here are two common deontological principles:

- Always treat a person as an end, never as a means only.
- Treat people the way you would want to be treated.

Deontological theorists are generally concerned about what a person intends to do, rather than about the actual results of what that person does. Some deontological theorists believe that the principles used to assess acts must be universal in scope, and others believe that it is sufficient that the principles reflect a consensus in a particular society.

Ronald Dworkin, one of the best-known contemporary defenders of a deontological approach to rights, argues that rights should be treated as trump cards. Whenever they are applicable, they should not be overridden by considerations of social well-being. If a government is willing to disregard a person's fundamental rights for some useful social purpose, that government fails to respect the dignity of the person and thereby undermines the idea of equality and justice within its domain. For example, when a government denies fundamental rights of free speech to one of its citizens, Dworkin argues, that government insults the citizen, and the government thereby undermines respect for law. Deontological theory is attractive because of its firm stand against the denial of rights to any citizen. Many of the essays in our book embrace such a perspective, especially the United Nations Declaration and the essay by Onora O'Neill.

Virtue theory is the view that judgments about what is morally right should be made in terms of promoting good character or other natural ends. The key to making good judgments is to have developed good habits to which one can merely refer now that one is uncertain about what to do. Morality is very much a matter of context as well as habit; the virtuous person is supposed to have developed a fine sense of appropriateness that is sensitive to differences in context. In this respect, virtue theory shares much in common with various non-Western perspectives, such as Buddhism. Unlike consequentialism and deontological theory, virtue theory focuses on the person's character rather than the person's behavior.

One way of understanding the virtuous life is in terms of conforming to what is "natural." In deciding what to do, one should pursue the path that is most in keeping with what is most natural in a given context. In this sense, virtue theory and *natural law theory* share much in common. Natural law theory is the view that morality is grounded in something larger than our human circumstances, namely in a natural (in many cases God-given) order. Natural law theory is most prominently espoused by Catholic theorists and by other theorists who support a strong connection between religion and ethics. Natural law has been understood, at least since Thomas Aquinas, as God's eternal law applied to natural entities, most especially to humans. In its more recent manifestations, there has been much controversy in natural law theory as to what precisely is the relationship between God's law and human laws.

Each of these theories may give a different answer to the question of how to resolve a particular conflict between sources of ethical knowledge. There is no consensus about which of these theories is best. Our view is that each of these theories contains a grain of truth, and that some combination of these theoretical perspectives may turn out to be the best overall theory. Until such a combination is devised, it is worthwhile to consider each perspective seriously whenever one is faced with a conflict of sources of ethical knowledge. This may seem unsatisfactory to those who were hoping that ethics would always provide a single solution to any ethical question. In our view, ethics is not a science that provides such solutions; rather, the study of ethics enriches one's deliberations but leaves the conclusion of those deliberations often unresolved.

WHAT ARE SOME OF THE CHIEF VALUES?

In most Western discussions of ethics, from a philosophical perspective, various values are subjected to the most intense conceptual scrutiny. Each of these values can be understood from the standpoint of personal or social ethics. Among the chief values are:

- Autonomy
- Justice
- Responsibility
- Care

Autonomy is often thought to be a paradigmatic value in personal ethics. Being autonomous means being true to our own principles and acting in a way that we have chosen or that we endorse. Autonomy is closely connected to self-respect, for the person who is true to his or her own principles generally esteems himself or herself. Autonomy also has a social ethics dimension. For autonomy to be maintained and maximized in a population, it is crucial that social institutions be designed to minimize interference with the life choices of individuals. Highly intrusive institutions will make it much more difficult for individuals to attain autonomy. In the field of medicine, the more fully patients are informed about treatment options, the more likely they are to make autonomous decisions.

Justice is also sometimes characterized as a value of personal ethics. In this view, justice is best understood as giving to each person his or her due, based on what that individual has a legitimate right to. When rights are understood as a contract between two equal parties, they undergird a personal ethics conception of justice. But justice is also concerned with the fair distribution of goods and services within a society. The fairness of distributions is not solely determined by contractual rights. This is especially true, as we will see in several of our essays, when we approach distributive justice from a global perspective. It may be true that no one is owed our help to be saved from starvation, but it seems to many philosophers that it would be unjust to spend one's resources on luxuries while others die highly painful deaths from starvation because they have no resources with which to purchase food.

Responsibility, like justice, has a personal and social orientation. Responsibility can be understood as accountability for the consequences that one has explicitly and directly caused. According to this understanding, one can limit one's responsibility simply by not doing very much that has effects in the world. But if we think of the consequences of what people have failed to do, as well as what they have explicitly done, then responsibility can be seen as a social category that is related to our membership in various communities. This latter sense of responsibility implies that in order to avoid acting irresponsibly, people will have to worry about their contribution, or lack of contribution, to group action as well as about their own individual personal actions. For example, racist violence on one's campus may not seem to be a particular student's responsibility if that student did not engage in the violence. But if the student could have helped in preventing the violence, but chose not to, there is a sense in which the student may share responsibility for that violence.

Care has recently been discussed as a decidedly different value from justice. Justice, even in its social, distributive form, calls for us to be impartial in assigning to people what is considered their due. But care calls for partiality, especially toward those who cannot protect themselves and to those with whom we are in special relationships. Our own children may not be owed any more than children in distant parts of the world; indeed our own children are probably owed less, given their already privileged position. But there is a value in preferring one's own child and striving to aid him or her. In our section on gender roles, we will encounter a recent dispute on whether and to what extent justice and care are different.

This concludes a brief overview of some of the main currents in contemporary Western philosophical approaches to ethics. In the next section, we will explain how an emphasis on multiculturalism will further enrich our deliberations about both personal and social ethics.

A BRIEF ACCOUNT OF SOME NON-WESTERN PERSPECTIVES

The main non-Western perspectives represented in this anthology are these:

- African
- Confucian
- Buddhist
- Indian Hindu
- Islamic
- American Indian

We have also included a significant number of both Western and non-Western feminist pieces. As will become clear, there is considerable overlap among many of these non-Western perspectives. It is for this reason that it is sometimes appropriate to talk of a Third World perspective, even though each of these non-Western perspectives is unique. In the remainder of this introduction, we will give a very brief overview of these perspectives.

The question of whether there is a single, distinct African perspective is hotly debated. What most of our authors mean by an African perspective is one that is centered on several traditional key ideas. Ifeanyi Menkiti provides a good summary of some of these ideas. Africans deny that the concept of a person

> can be defined by focusing on this or that physical or psychological characteristic of the lone individual. Rather, man is defined by reference to the environing community . . . the reality of the community takes precedence over the reality of individual life histories, whatever these may be . . . persons become persons only after a process of incorporation. Without incorporation into this or that community, individuals are considered to be mere danglers, to whom the description "person" does not fully apply.[1]

In addition, as we will see, the experiences of poverty and hunger, so prevalent in many parts of Africa, have meant that Africans put much more emphasis on economic considerations than on political rights, such as the right to free speech. Furthermore, the well-being of the community is paramount, and the well-being of the individual is inextricably linked to that of the community. Claude Ake's essay on African conceptions of human rights (in Part II) is a good place to begin to understand the ethical perspective that is connected to the view of personhood central to traditional African thought.

The traditional Confucian ethical perspective, to some degree resembling the African perspective, also emphasizes the importance of the community to the individual. In order for one to realize one's identity and sense of value, one has to fulfill a set of obligations defined by one's roles in a nexus of relationships. And by living in harmony with others through the proper execution of these obligations, the individual nurtures and develops his or her human nature, which is held to be fundamentally good. The failure to live up to these duties and to find one's roles would reduce a person to insignificance and render him or her unable to lead a virtuous life. Nonetheless, it is important to add that for the truly virtuous individual, occasions may arise when he or she has to stand up for what is right in spite of opposition from the community at large.

Like Confucian ethics, the Buddhist outlook places no less weight on the interrelatedness of the individual with other people and nature. However, the way in which the Buddhist regards self, others, and nature could not differ more from a Confucian. Whereas a Confucian locates his or her sense of value and significance in a virtuous life within a fabric of relationships, the Buddhist assumes an attitude of nonattachment toward persons and things in the world, however valuable they are. By "nonattachment," the Buddhist does *not* mean that one should totally drop out of commitments and relationships, but rather one should not be encumbered by or ensnared in anything in the world, whether it is something as vicious as greed or hatred or even as good as justice or friendship. For it is precisely this "clinging" and "grasping" attitude that accounts for suffering in this world. Once one realizes that one's own existence, one's relationships, and the world are products of contingency and transitoriness, one is willing to let go of the things one holds dear when the time comes. Only with this orientation of nonattachment can one live with an openness that is free to show

patience and compassion to humanity and all of creation that struggle and suffer in the same way. (For more on the Buddhist perspective, see Inada and the editors' notes that accompany it.)

Indian Hindu perspectives on ethics share many features in common with Buddhist perspectives, but there are also important differences. I. C. Sharma has provided a good summary of some of the key Indian ethical ideas. Indian philosophies all start with the idea of a person who is suffering, and "who is to be rescued from endless torture, misery, disease, destruction, old age, even death."[2] For most Indian philosophers, the path to take in ending suffering is as important as the ending of suffering itself. Mohandas Gandhi epitomizes one of the great differences between Hindu and Buddhist ethical perspectives. Gandhi stressed an active intervention into the world to make it better, whereas Buddhists often prefer a more patient and passive approach. Gandhi's nonviolence and pacifism are inspired by a drive toward mitigating as much suffering as one can in the present.

Traditional Islamic perspectives on ethics are deeply intertwined with religious conceptions. Like some Hindu perspectives, Islamic ethics is highly activist and interventionist. Most interesting for our purposes, Islamic ethics are highly partialist. The Koran specifies that there will be strict rules for the ethical conduct of men and quite different, some would say even stricter, rules for women. In addition, non-Muslims are to be treated quite differently from Muslims. This ethical perspective shares some features in common with those Western philosophers in the virtue ethics tradition who have argued for different sets of norms for how one behaves toward one's family members and toward those who are outside of one's family. But the Islamic perspective is especially difficult to reconcile with any claims of universal human rights, or of women's equal rights, as we will see in the essays about Islam in the sections on human rights and on gender roles.

American Indian perspectives, although often quite different from tribe to tribe, are deeply infused with a respect for the group, as is true for African perspectives. Added to this is a respect for the integrity and inherent importance of the natural world. . . . This is a very central belief which seems consistent across many Native American cultures—that the Earth is a living, conscious being that must be treated with respect and loving care.[3]

American Indians are also deeply affected by the extreme forms of suffering and discrimination their people have been forced to withstand while living in a dominant white society. Their insights are particularly important, as we will see, both in discussions of environmental ethics and in those on racial and gender discrimination.

Finally, let us say just a few words about feminism, a perspective that falls in between Western and non-Western philosophies. Many recent feminist writings have stressed the importance of relationships and interdependence rather than autonomy and individual rights. In this respect, some feminist perspectives share many views in common with African and American Indian perspectives.[4] Most feminists have offered often cogent critiques of Western ethical views, especially concerning the nature and importance of justice, the commitment to universal principles, the rigidity of gender roles, as well as the status of pregnant women and the distribution of health care. Essays addressing these subjects can be found throughout our anthology.

Our first reading is one of the best-known discussions of consequentialist ethics in general. John Stuart Mill, a defender of utilitarianism, presents one of the most plausible interpretations of utilitarianism, that is, the theory of ethics that equates moral rightness with the maximization of pleasure and the minimization of pain. Mill explains the importance of distinguishing between pleasures qualitatively. He argues that the test for deciding which of two pleasures is the best is simply which is preferred by those who have experienced both. Mill's general defense of the principle of utility proceeds from the idea that only when people prefer or desire something do we have any basis for regarding that thing as good. He then proceeds to show that happiness is the only thing that is desired for its own sake. Virtue and rights are valued in terms of their promotion of happiness or utility. At the end, Mill recognizes that justice is a term for various moral requirements that protect rights, and that while justice is merely a form of social utility, it is an especially important and weighty kind of utility.

Our second reading presents a simplified account of a dominant deontological approach rivaling Mill's consequentialism—the ethics of Kant. In this selection, Onora O'Neill explicates the Formula of the End in Itself, one of the key formulations of Kant's fundamental moral principle, the Categorical Imperative. According to this formulation, moral rightness consists of treating oneself and others always as an end and not merely as a means. To treat a person as an end, in O'Neill's analysis, is in essence to allow the person, at least in principle, a choice between accepting and rejecting one's proposed course of action, which Kant calls a *maxim*. Absent such a choice, whether due to coercion or deception, the other person is treated merely as a means, and one's intended act cannot be morally acceptable. O'Neill proceeds to point out that unlike Mill's utilitarianism, which sees an individual's value as capable of compromise or sacrifice for the happiness of all, Kant's deontology rules out this possibility.

Our third reading presents John Rawls's contract theory. Rawls considers his theory to be a Kantian theory although it differs from Kant in several ways. According to Rawls, questions of distributive justice, which are at the heart of most public policy disputes, are best addressed as questions of what principles would be acceptable as fair to all free and equal people. Rawls proposes that this way of characterizing justice eliminates the kind of bias that comes when people realize that because of their positions in society they will benefit differentially by policy decisions. For policies to be fair, the principles that they are based on must not be biased. But this does not mean that principles of justice must be strictly egalitarian, in that everyone is treated exactly the same. Rather, rational people will choose principles of justice that will work out to the greatest benefit of them all, regardless of what social and economic positions they occupy. Ultimately this will result in principles of justice being seen as fair insofar as they result in making even the least advantaged better off than he or she was before.

Our fourth reading presents an account of virtue ethics. Rosalind Hursthouse presents virtue theory as both an agent-centered and an act-centered ethic, thereby distinguishing virtue theory from both consequentialism and deontological (Kantian) theory. But she also tries to present virtue theory as a theoretical perspective on ethics from which decisions about the right thing to do can be generated. Hursthouse presents us with a version of virtue theory that holds first that a "virtuous agent is one who has, and exercises, certain character traits, namely the virtues"; and second, a virtue is a character trait that conforms to certain rules, namely that "act charitably, honestly, and kindly . . . and so on." On this account, virtue ethics gives the same type of guidance that utilitarianism and Kantian theory do, but it provides a context that makes more sense of the moral rules that people follow by connecting the prohibition not to act dishonestly with the reason that doing so would "be dishonest, and dishonesty is a vice."

Our fifth reading presents a non-Western approach to ethics, from the Hindu tradition. Debabrata Sen Sharma discusses one of the oldest non-Western perspectives on ethics. One of the central tenets of Hindu ethics is that no person should be subject to misery or unhappiness. Unlike utilitarianism, this principle is not based on a respect for individual self-determination, but on the oneness of all aspects of the universe. All things, animate and inanimate, are to be in harmony. For humans, such harmony is blocked when they are subject to disease, starvation, or unhappiness. The general outlook here is that of "Universal Being," where what matters is not what country or what faith a person belongs to, but only that one is a member of humanity and ultimately of the world. When faced with a moral question, Hindu theorists urge that we appeal to our consciences, the voice of humanity within us.

We end this part with a selection from Carol Gilligan. Gilligan is the best-known person doing empirical work on gender and morality. In this early piece of hers, we find a discussion of two children, one male and one female, who interpret a moral dilemma in very different ways, illustrating what Gilligan thinks are different moral voices that correlate with different genders. Amy is concerned about maintaining relationships, while Jake is concerned with rules and fairness. Jake sees people standing alone whereas Amy sees them as always situated in relationships of interdependence. From these different conceptions of self emerge very different orientations toward morality, an appreciation of which helps us understand differences between what has been considered appropriate ways for men and women to treat each other.

—LARRY MAY

NOTES

1. Ifeanyi Menkiti, "Person and Community in African Traditional Thought," in *African Philosophy*, 3rd ed. edited by Richard Wright (Lanham, MD: University Press of America, 1984), pp. 171–72.
2. I. C. Sharma, *Ethical Philosophies of India* (New York: Harper & Row, 1965), p. 55.
3. Annie Booth and Harvey Jacobs, "Ties that Bind: Native American Beliefs as a Foundation for Environmental Consciousness," *Environmental Ethics*, vol. 12 (Spring 1990), pp. 30, 32.
4. See Sandra Harding's fascinating essay, "The Curious Coincidence of Feminine and African Moralities," in Eva Kittay and Diana Meyers, eds., *Women and Moral Theory* (Totowa, NJ: Rowman and Littlefield, 1987).

Utilitarianism

John Stuart Mill

John Stuart Mill was one of the leading intellectuals of the nineteenth century. He was a member of Parliament as well as a popular philosopher. He is the author of *A System of Logic* (1843), *On Liberty* (1859), *Utilitarianism* (1861), *Considerations on Representative Government* (1861), *The Subjection of Women* (1869), and *Principles of Political Economy* (1871).

Mill's defense of the principle of utility is the most influential modern account of a consequentialist moral theory. In this excerpt from his book *Utilitarianism*, Mill clearly sets out the principle of the greatest happiness for the greatest number and defends it against several of the most obvious objections. He then offers a limited defense of the principle. He ends by explaining the intimate relationship between utility and rights.

WHAT UTILITARIANISM IS

The creed which accepts as the foundation of morals "utility" or the "greatest happiness principle" holds that actions are right in proportion as they tend to promote happiness; wrong as they tend to produce the reverse of happiness. By happiness is intended pleasure and the absence of pain; by unhappiness, pain and the privation of pleasure. To give a clear view of the moral standard set up by the theory, much more requires to be said; in particular, what things it includes in the ideas of pain and pleasure, and to what extent this is left an open question. But these supplementary explanations do not affect the theory of life on which this theory of morality is grounded—namely, that pleasure and freedom from pain are the only things desirable as ends; and that all desirable things (which are as numerous in the utilitarian as in any other scheme) are desirable either for pleasure inherent in themselves or as means to the promotion of pleasure and the prevention of pain.

Now such a theory of life excites in many minds, and among them in some of the most estimable in feeling and purpose, inveterate dislike. To suppose that life has (as they express it) no higher end than pleasure—no better and nobler object of desire and pursuit—they designate as utterly mean and groveling, as a doctrine worthy only of swine, to whom the followers of Epicurus were, at a very early period, contemptuously likened; and modern holders of the doctrine are occasionally made the subject of equally polite comparisons by its German, French, and English assailants.

When thus attacked, the Epicureans have always answered that it is not they, but their accusers, who represent human nature in a degrading light, since the accusation supposes human beings to be capable of no pleasures except those of which swine are capable. If this supposition were true, the charge could not be gainsaid, but would then be no longer an imputation; for if the sources of pleasure were precisely the same to human beings and to swine, the rule of life which is good enough for the one would be good enough for the other. The comparison of the Epicurean life to that of beasts is felt as degrading, precisely because a beast's pleasures do not satisfy a human being's conceptions of happiness. Human beings have faculties more elevated than the animal appetites and, when once made conscious of them, do not regard anything as happiness which does not include their gratification. I do not indeed, consider the Epicureans to have been by any means faultless in drawing out their scheme of consequences from the utilitarian principle. To do this in any sufficient manner, many Stoic, as well as Christian, elements require to be included. But there is no known Epicurean theory of life which does not assign to the pleasures of the intellect, of the feelings and imagination, and of the moral sentiments a much higher value as pleasures than to those of mere sensation. It must be admitted, however, that utilitarian writers in general have placed the superiority of mental over bodily pleasures chiefly in the greater permanency, safety, uncostliness, etc., of the former—that is, in their circumstantial advantages rather than in their intrinsic nature. And on all these points utilitarians have fully proved their case; but they might have taken the other and, as it may be called, higher ground with entire consistency. It is quite compatible with the principle of utility to recognize the fact that some kinds of pleasure are more desirable and more valuable than others. It would be absurd that, while in estimating all other things quality is considered as well as quantity, the estimation of pleasure should be supposed to depend on quantity alone.

If I am asked what I mean by difference of quality in pleasures, or what makes one pleasure more valuable than another, merely as a pleasure, except its being greater in amount, there is but one possible answer. Of two pleasures, if there be one to which all or almost all who have experience of both give a decided preference, irrespective of any feeling of moral obligation to prefer it, that is the more desirable pleasure. If one of the two is, by those who are competently acquainted with both, placed so far above the other that they prefer it, even though knowing it to be attended with a

greater amount of discontent, and would not resign it for any quantity of the other pleasure which their nature is capable of, we are justified in ascribing to the preferred enjoyment a superiority in quality so far outweighing quantity as to render it, in comparison, of small account.

Now it is an unquestionable fact that those who are equally acquainted with and equally capable of appreciating and enjoying both do give a most marked preference to the manner of existence which employs their higher faculties. Few human creatures would consent to be changed into any of the lower animals for a promise of the fullest allowance of a beast's pleasures; no intelligent human being would consent to be a fool, no instructed person would be an ignoramus, no person of feeling and conscience would be selfish and base, even though they should be persuaded that the fool, the dunce, or the rascal is better satisfied with his lot than they are with theirs. They would not resign what they possess more than he for the most complete satisfaction of all the desires which they have in common with him. If they ever fancy they would, it is only in cases of unhappiness so extreme that to escape from it they would exchange their lot for almost any other, however undesirable in their own eyes. A being of higher faculties requires more to make him happy, is capable probably of more acute suffering, and certainly accessible to it at more points, than one of an inferior type; but in spite of these liabilities, he can never really wish to sink into what he feels to be a lower grade of existence. We may give what explanation we please of this unwillingness; we may attribute it to pride, a name which is given indiscriminately to some of the most and to some of the least estimable feelings of which mankind are capable; we may refer it to the love of liberty and personal independence, an appeal to which was with the Stoics one of the most effective means for the inculcation of it; to the love of power or to the love of excitement, both of which do really enter into and contribute to it; but its most appropriate appellation is a sense of dignity, which all human beings possess in one form or other, and in some, though by no means in exact, proportion to their higher faculties, and which is so essential a part of the happiness of those in whom it is strong that nothing which conflicts with it could be otherwise than momentarily an object of desire to them. Whoever supposes that this preference takes place at a sacrifice of happiness—that the superior being, in anything like equal circumstances, is not happier than the inferior—confounds the two very different ideas of happiness and content. It is indisputable that the being whose capacities of enjoyment are low has the greatest chance of having them fully satisfied; and a highly endowed being will always feel that any happiness which he can look for, as the world is constituted, is imperfect. But he can learn to bear its imperfections, if they are at all bearable; and they will not make him envy the being who is indeed unconscious of the imperfections, but only because he feels not at all the good which those imperfections qualify. It is better to be a human being dissatisfied than a pig satisfied; better to be Socrates dissatisfied than a fool satisfied. And if the fool, or the pig, are of a different opinion, it is because they only know their own side of the question. The other party to the comparison knows both sides.

It may be objected that many who are capable of the higher pleasures occasionally, under the influence of temptation, postpone them to the lower. But this is quite compatible with a full appreciation of the intrinsic superiority of the higher. Men often, from infirmity of character, make their election for the nearer good, though they know it to be the less valuable; and this no less when the choice is between two bodily pleasures than when it is between bodily and mental. They pursue sensual indulgences to the injury of health, though perfectly aware that health is the greater good. It may be further objected that many who begin with youthful enthusiasm for everything noble, as they advance in years, sink into indolence and selfishness. But I do not believe that those who undergo this very common change voluntarily choose the lower description of pleasures in preference to the higher. I believe that, before they devote themselves exclusively to the one, they have already become incapable of the other. Capacity for the nobler feelings is in most natures a very tender plant, easily killed, not only by hostile influences, but by mere want of

sustenance; and in the majority of young persons it speedily dies away if the occupations to which their position in life has devoted them, and the society into which it has thrown them, are not favorable to keeping that higher capacity in exercise. Men lose their high aspirations as they lose their intellectual tastes, because they have not time or opportunity for indulging them; and they addict themselves to inferior pleasures, not because they deliberately prefer them, but because they are either the only ones to which they have access or the only ones which they are any longer capable of enjoying. It may be questioned whether anyone who has remained equally susceptible to both classes of pleasures ever knowingly and calmly preferred the lower, though many, in all ages, have broken down in an ineffectual attempt to combine both.

From this verdict of the only competent judges, I apprehend there can be no appeal. On a question which is the best worth having of two pleasures, or which of two modes of existence is the most grateful to the feelings, apart from its moral attributes and from its consequences, the judgment of these who are qualified by knowledge of both, or, if they differ, that of the majority among them, must be admitted as final. And there needs be the less hesitation to accept this judgment respecting the quality of pleasures, since there is no other tribunal to be referred to even on the question of quantity. What means are there of determining which is the acutest of two pains, or the intensest of two pleasurable sensations, except the general suffrage of those who are familiar with both? Neither pains nor pleasures are homogeneous, and pain is always heterogeneous with pleasure. What is there to decide whether a particular pleasure is worth purchasing at the cost of a particular pain, except the feelings and judgment of the experienced? When, therefore, those feelings and judgment declare the pleasures derived from the higher faculties to be preferable *in kind*, apart from the question of intensity, to those of which the animal nature, disjoined from the higher faculties, is susceptible, they are entitled on this subject to the same regard.

I have dwelt on this point as being part of a perfectly just conception of utility or happiness considered as the directive rule of human conduct. But it is by no means an indispensable condition to the acceptance of the utilitarian standard; for that standard is not the agent's own greatest happiness, but the greatest amount of happiness altogether; and if it may possibly be doubted whether a noble character is always the happier for its nobleness, there can be no doubt that it makes other people happier, and that the world in general is immensely a gainer by it. Utilitarianism, therefore, could only attain its end by the general cultivation of nobleness of character, even if each individual were only benefited by the nobleness of others, and his own, so far as happiness is concerned, were a sheer deduction from the benefit. But the bare enunciation of such an absurdity as this last renders refutation superfluous.

According to the greatest happiness principle, as above explained, the ultimate end, with reference to and for the sake of which all other things are desirable—whether we are considering our own good or that of other people—is an existence exempt as far as possible from pain, and as rich as possible in enjoyments, both in point of quantity and quality; the test of quality and the rule for measuring it against quantity being the preference felt by those who, in their opportunities of experience, to which must be added their habits of self-consciousness and self-observation, are best furnished with the means of comparison. This, being according to the utilitarian opinion the end of human action, is necessarily also the standard of morality, which may accordingly be defined "the rules and precepts for human conduct," by the observance of which an existence such as has been described might be, to the greatest extent possible, secured to all mankind; and not to them only, but, so far as the nature of things admits, to the whole sentient creation. . . .

OF WHAT SORT OF PROOF THE PRINCIPLE OF UTILITY IS SUSCEPTIBLE

It has already been remarked that questions of ultimate ends do not admit of proof, in the ordinary acceptation of the term. To be incapable of proof by reasoning is common to all first principles, to the first premises of our knowledge, as well as to those of our conduct. But the former, being matters of fact, may be the subject of a direct appeal to the faculties which judge of fact—namely, our senses and our internal consciousness. Can an appeal be made to the same faculties on questions of practical ends? Or by what other faculty is cognizance taken of them?

Questions about ends are, in other words, questions of what things are desirable. The utilitarian doctrine is that happiness is desirable, and the only thing desirable, as an end; all other things being only desirable as means to that end. What ought to be required of this doctrine, what conditions is it requisite that the doctrine should fulfill—to make good its claim to be believed?

The only proof capable of being given that an object is visible is that people actually see it. The only proof that a sound is audible is that people hear it; and so of the other sources of our experience. In like manner, I apprehend, the sole evidence it is possible to produce that anything is desirable is that people do actually desire it. If the end which the utilitarian doctrine proposes to itself were not, in theory and in practice, acknowledged to be an end, nothing could ever convince any person that it was so. No reason can be given why the general happiness is desirable, except that each person, so far as he believes it to be attainable, desires his own happiness. This, however, being a fact, we have not only all the proof which the case admits of, but all which it is possible to require, that happiness is a good, that each person's happiness is a good to that person, and the general happiness, therefore, a good to the aggregate of all persons. Happiness has made out its title as *one* of the ends of conduct and, consequently, one of the criteria of morality.

But it has not, by this alone, proved itself to be the sole criterion. To do that, it would seem, by the same rule, necessary to show, not only that people desire happiness, but that they never desire anything else. Now it is palpable that they do desire things which, in common language, are decidedly distinguished from happiness. They desire, for example, virtue and the absence of vice no less really than pleasure and the absence of pain. The desire of virtue is not as universal, but it is as authentic a fact as the desire of happiness. And hence the opponents of the utilitarian standard deem that they have a right to infer that there are other ends of human action besides happiness, and that happiness is not the standard of approbation and disapprobation.

But does the utilitarian doctrine deny that people desire virtue, or maintain that virtue is not a thing to be desired? The very reverse. It maintains not only that virtue is to be desired, but that it is to be desired disinterestedly, for itself. Whatever may be the opinion of utilitarian moralists as to the original conditions by which virtue is made virtue, however they may believe (as they do) that actions and dispositions are only virtuous because they promote another end than virtue, yet this being granted, and it having been decided, from considerations of this description, what *is* virtuous, they not only place virtue at the very head of the things which are good as means to the ultimate end, but they also recognize as a psychological fact the possibility of its being, to the individual, a good in itself, without looking to any end beyond it; and hold that the mind is not in a right state, not in a state conformable to utility, not in the state most conducive to the general happiness, unless it does love virtue in this manner—as a thing desirable in itself, even although, in the individual instance, it should not produce those other desirable consequences which it tends to produce, and on account of which it is held to be virtue. This opinion is not, in the smallest degree, a departure from the happiness principle. The ingredients of happiness are very various, and each of them is desirable in itself, and not merely when considered as swelling an aggregate. The principle of utility does not mean that any given pleasure, as music, for instance, or any given exemption from pain, as for example health, is to be looked upon as means to a collective something termed happiness, and to be desired on that account. They are desired and desirable in and for themselves; besides being means, they are a part of the end. Virtue, according to the utilitarian doctrine, is not naturally and originally a part of the end, but it is

capable of becoming so; and in those who live it disinterestedly it has become so, and is desired and cherished, not as a means to happiness, but as a part of their happiness.

To illustrate this further, we may remember that virtue is not the only thing originally a means, and which if it were not a means to anything else would be and remain indifferent, but which by association with what it is a means to comes to be desired for itself, and that too with the utmost intensity. What, for example, shall we say of the love of money? There is nothing originally more desirable about money than about any heap of glittering pebbles. Its worth is solely that of the things which it will buy; the desires for other things than itself, which it is a means of gratifying. Yet the love of money is not only one of the strongest moving forces of human life, but money is, in many cases, desired in and for itself; the desire to possess it is often stronger than the desire to use it, and goes on increasing when all the desires which point to ends beyond it, to be compassed by it, are falling off. It may, then, be said truly that money is desired not for the sake of an end, but as part of the end. From being a means to happiness, it has come to be itself a principal ingredient of the individual's conception of happiness. The same may be said of the majority of the great objects of human life: power, for example, or fame, except that to each of these there is a certain amount of immediate pleasure annexed, which has at least the semblance of being naturally inherent in them—a thing which cannot be said of money. Still, however, the strongest natural attraction, both of power and of fame, is the immense aid they give to the attainment of our other wishes; and it is the strong association thus generated between them and all our objects of desire which gives to the direct desire of them the intensity it often assumes, so as in some characters to surpass in strength all other desires. In these cases the means have become a part of the end, and a more important part of it than any of the things which they are means to. What was once desired as an instrument for the attainment of happiness has come to be desired for its own sake. In being desired for its own sake it is, however, desired as *part* of happiness. The person is made, or thinks he would be made, happy by its mere possession; and is made unhappy by failure to obtain it. The desire of it is not a different thing from the desire of happiness any more than the love of music or the desire of health. They are included in happiness. They are some of the elements of which the desire of happiness is made up. Happiness is not an abstract idea but a concrete whole; and these are some of its parts. And the utilitarian standard sanctions and approves their being so. Life would be a poor thing, very ill provided with sources of happiness, if there were not this provision of nature by which things originally indifferent, but conducive to, or otherwise associated with, the satisfaction of our primitive desires, become in themselves sources of pleasure more valuable than the primitive pleasures, both in permanency, in the space of human existence that they are capable of covering, and even in intensity.

Virtue, according to the utilitarian conception, is a good of this description. There was no original desire of it, or motive to it, save its conduciveness to pleasure, and especially to protection from pain. But through the association thus formed it may be felt a good in itself, and desired as such with as great intensity as any other good; and with this difference between it and the love of money, of power, or of fame—that all of these may, and often do, render the individual noxious to the other members of the society to which he belongs, whereas there is nothing which makes him so much a blessing to them as the cultivation of the disinterested love of virtue. And consequently, the utilitarian standard, while it tolerates and approves those other acquired desires, up to the point beyond which they would be more injurious to the general happiness than promotive of it, enjoins and requires the cultivation of the love of virtue up to the greatest strength possible, as being above all things important to the general happiness.

It results from the preceding considerations that there is in reality nothing desired except happiness. Whatever is desired otherwise than as a means to some end beyond itself, and ultimately to happiness, is desired as itself a part of happiness, and is not desired for itself until it has become so. . . .

ON THE CONNECTION BETWEEN JUSTICE AND UTILITY

In all ages of speculation one of the strongest obstacles to the reception of the doctrine that utility or happiness is the criterion of right and wrong has been drawn from the idea of justice. The powerful sentiment and apparently clear perception which that word recalls with a rapidity and certainty resembling an instinct have seemed to the majority of thinkers to point to an inherent quality in things; to show that the just must have an existence in nature as something absolute, generically distinct from every variety of the expedient and, in idea, opposed to it, though (as is commonly acknowledged) never, in the long run, disjoined from it in fact. . . .

The idea of justice supposes two things—a rule of conduct and a sentiment which sanctions the rule. The first must be supposed common to all mankind and intended for their good. The other (the sentiment) is a desire that punishment may be suffered by those who infringe the rule. There is involved, in addition, the conception of some definite person who suffers by the infringement, whose rights (to use the expression appropriated to the case) are violated by it. And the sentiment of justice appears to me to be the animal desire to repel or retaliate a hurt or damage to oneself or to those with whom one sympathizes, widened so as to include all persons, by the human capacity of enlarged sympathy and the human conception of intelligent self-interest. From the latter elements the feeling derives its morality; from the former, its peculiar impressiveness and energy of self-assertion.

I have, throughout, treated the idea of a *right* residing in the injured person and violated by the injury, not as a separate element in the composition of the idea and sentiment, but as one of the forms in which the other two elements clothe themselves. These elements are a hurt to some assignable person or persons, on the one hand, and a demand for punishment, on the other. An examination of our own minds, I think, will show that these two things include all that we mean when we speak of violation of a right. When we call anything a person's right, we mean that he has a valid claim on society to protect him in the possession of it, either by the force of law or by that of education and opinion. If he has what we consider a sufficient claim, on whatever account, to have something guaranteed to him by society, we say that he has a right to it. If we desire to prove that anything does not belong to him by right, we think this done as soon as it is admitted that society ought not to take measure for securing it to him, but should leave him to chance or to his own exertions. Thus a person is said to have a right to what he can earn in fair professional competition, because society ought not to allow any other person to hinder him from endeavoring to earn in that manner as much as he can. But he has not a right to three hundred a year, though he may happen to be earning it; because society is not called on to provide that he shall earn that sum. On the contrary, if he owns ten thousand pounds three-percent stock, he *has* a right to three hundred a year because society has come under an obligation to provide him with an income of that amount.

To have a right, then, is, I conceive, to have something which society ought to defend me in the possession of. If the objector goes on to ask why it ought, I can give him no other reason than general utility. If that expression does not seem to convey a sufficient feeling of the strength of the obligation, nor to account for the peculiar energy of the feeling, it is because there goes to the composition of the sentiment, not a rational only but also an animal element—the thirst for retaliation; and this thirst derives its intensity, as well as its moral justification, from the extraordinarily important and impressive kind of utility which is concerned. The interest involved is that of security, to everyone's feelings the most vital of all interests. All other earthly benefits are needed by one person, not needed by another; and many of them can, if necessary, be cheerfully forgone or replaced by something else; but security no human being can possibly do without; on it we depend for all our immunity from evil and for the whole value of all and every good, beyond the passing moment, since nothing but the gratification of the instant could be of any worth to us if we could be deprived of everything the next instant by whoever

was momentarily stronger than ourselves. Now this most indispensable of all necessaries, after physical nutriment, cannot be had unless the machinery for providing it is kept unintermittedly in active play. Our notion, therefore, of the claim we have on our fellow creatures to join in making safe for us the very groundwork of our existence gathers feelings around it so much more intense than those concerned in any of the more common cases of utility that the difference in degree (as is often the case in psychology) becomes a real difference in kind. The claim assumes that character of absoluteness, that apparent infinity and incommensurability with all other considerations which constitute the distinction between the feeling of right and wrong and that of ordinary expediency and inexpediency. The feelings concerned are so powerful, and we count so positively on finding a responsive feeling in others (all being alike interested) that *ought* and *should* grow into *must*, and recognized indispensability becomes a moral necessity, analogous to physical, and often not inferior to it in binding force.

If the preceding analysis, or something resembling it, be not the correct account of the notion of justice—if justice be totally independent of utility, and be a standard *per se*, which the mind can recognize by simple introspection of itself—it is hard to understand why that internal oracle is so ambiguous, and why so many things appear either just or unjust, according to the light in which they are regarded. . . .

It appears from what has been said that justice is a name for certain moral requirements which, regarded collectively, stand higher in the scale of social utility, and are therefore of more paramount obligation, than any others, though particular cases may occur in which some other social duty is so important as to overrule any one of the general maxims of justice. Thus, to save a life, it may not only be allowable, but a duty, to steal or take by force the necessary food or medicine, or to kidnap and compel to officiate the only qualified medical practitioner. In such cases, as we do not call anything justice which is not a virtue, we usually say, not that justice must give way to some other moral principle, but that what is just in ordinary cases is, by reason of that other principle, not just in the particular case. By this useful accommodation of language, the character of indefeasibility attributed to justice is kept up, and we are saved from the necessity of maintaining that there can be laudable injustice.

The considerations which have not been adduced resolve, I conceive, the only real difficulty in the utilitarian theory of morals. It has always been evident that all cases of justice are also cases of expediency; the difference is in the peculiar sentiment which attaches to the former, as contradistinguished from the latter. If this characteristic sentiment has been sufficiently accounted for; if there is no necessity to assume for it any peculiarity of origin; if it is simply the natural feeling of resentment, moralized by being made coextensive with the demands of social good; and if this feeling not only does but ought to exist in all the classes of cases to which the idea of justice corresponds—that idea no longer presents itself as a stumbling block to the utilitarian ethics. Justice remains the appropriate name for certain social utilities which are vastly more important, and therefore more absolute and imperative, than any others are as a class (though not more so than others may be in particular cases); and which, therefore, ought to be, as well as naturally are, guarded by a sentiment, not only different in degree, but also in kind; distinguished from the milder feeling which attaches to the mere idea of promoting human pleasure or convenience at once by the more definite nature of its commands and by the sterner character of its sanctions.

A Simplified Account of Kant's Ethics

Onora O'Neill

Onora O'Neill is now principal of Newnham College, Cambridge University. She has taught philosophy at the University of Essex and Barnard College. She has published articles on ethics and is also the author of *Acting on Principle* (1975), *Faces of Hunger* (1986), and *Constructions of Reason* (1989).

Kant's ethics represent the prevailing approach to deontological moral theory. In this selection, O'Neill elucidates and provides an interpretation of one of the formulations of the Categorical Imperative, The Formula of the End in Itself, in terms of the notion of consent. She also highlights the differences between utilitarianism and Kantian ethics on the value of human life.

Kant's moral theory has acquired the reputation of being forbiddingly difficult to understand and, once understood, excessively demanding in its requirements. I don't believe that this reputation has been wholly earned, and I am going to try to undermine it. . . . I shall try to reduce some of the difficulties. . . . Finally, I shall compare Kantian and utilitarian approaches and assess their strengths and weaknesses.

The main method by which I propose to avoid some of the difficulties of Kant's moral theory is by explaining only one part of the theory. This does not seem to me to be an irresponsible approach in this case. One of the things that makes Kant's moral theory hard to understand is that he gives a number of different versions of the principle that he calls the Supreme Principle of Morality, and these different versions don't look at all like one another. They also don't look at all like the utilitarians' Greatest Happiness Principle. But the Kantian principle is supposed to play a similar role in arguments about what to do.

Onora O'Neill, "A simplified account of Kant's ethics" from *Matters of Life and Death*, edited by Tom Regan, 1986. © 1986 The McGraw-Hill Companies. Reprinted by permission.

Kant calls his Supreme Principle the *Categorical Imperative*; its various versions also have sonorous names. One is called the Formula of Universal Law; another is the Formula of the Kingdom of Ends. The one on which I shall concentrate is known as the *Formula of the End in Itself*. To understand why Kant thinks that these picturesquely named principles are equivalent to one another takes quite a lot of close and detailed analysis of Kant's philosophy. I shall avoid this and concentrate on showing the implications of this version of the Categorical Imperative.

THE FORMULA OF THE END IN ITSELF

Kant states the Formula of the End in Itself as follows:

> Act in such a way that you always treat humanity, whether in your own person or in the person of any other, never simply as a means but always at the same time as an end.

To understand this we need to know what it is to treat a person as a means or as an end. According to Kant, each of our acts reflects one or more *maxims*. The maxim of the act is the principle on which one sees oneself as acting. A maxim expresses a person's policy, or if he or she has no settled policy, the principle underlying the particular intention or decision on which he or she acts. Thus, a person who decides "This year I'll give 10 percent of my income to famine relief" has as a maxim the principle of tithing his or her income for famine relief. In practice, the difference between intentions and maxims is of little importance, for given any intention, we can formulate the corresponding maxim by deleting references to particular times, places, and persons. In what follows, I shall take the terms "maxim" and "intention" as equivalent.

Whenever we act intentionally, we have at least one maxim and can, if we reflect, state what it is. (There is of course room for self-deception here—"I'm only keeping the wolf from the door" we may claim as we wolf down enough to keep ourselves overweight, or, more to the point, enough to feed someone else who hasn't enough food.)

When we want to work out whether an act we propose to do is right or wrong, according to Kant, we should look at our maxims and not at how much misery or happiness the act is likely to produce, and whether it does better at increasing happiness than other available acts. We just have to check that the act we have in mind will not use anyone as a mere means, and, if possible, that it will treat other persons as ends in themselves.

USING PERSONS AS MERE MEANS

To use someone as a *mere means* is to involve them in a scheme of action *to which they could not in principle consent*. Kant does not say that there is anything wrong about using someone as a means. Evidently we have to do so in any cooperative scheme of action. If I cash a check I use the teller as a means, without whom I could not lay my hands on the cash; the teller in turn uses me as a means to earn his or her living. But in this case, each party consents to her or his part in the transaction. Kant would say that though they use one another as means, they do not use one another as *mere* means. Each person assumes that the other

has maxims of his or her own and is not just a thing or a prop to be manipulated.

But there are other situations where one person uses another in a way to which the other could not in principle consent. For example, one person may make a promise to another with every intention of breaking it. If the promise is accepted, then the person to whom it was given must be ignorant of what the promisor's intention (maxim) really is. If one knew that the promisor did not intend to do what he or she was promising, one would, after all, not accept or rely on the promise. It would be as though there had been no promise made. Successful false promising depends on deceiving the person to whom the promise is made about what one's real maxim is. And since the person who is deceived doesn't know that real maxim, he or she can't in principle consent to his or her part in the proposed scheme of action. The person who is deceived is as it were, a prop or a tool—a mere means—in the false promisor's scheme. A person who promises falsely treats the acceptor of the promise as a prop or a thing and not as a person. In Kant's view, it is this that makes false promising wrong.

One standard way of using others as mere means is by deceiving them. By getting someone involved in a business scheme or a criminal activity on false pretenses, or by giving a misleading account of what one is about, or by making a false promise or a fraudulent contract, one involves another in something to which he or she in principle cannot consent, since the scheme requires that he or she doesn't know what is going on. Another standard way of using others as mere means is by coercing them. If a rich or powerful person threatens a debtor with bankruptcy unless he or she joins in some scheme, then the creditor's intention is to coerce; and the debtor, if coerced, cannot consent to his or her part in the creditor's scheme. To make the example more specific: If a money-lender in an Indian village threatens not to renew a vital loan unless he is given the debtor's land, then he uses the debtor as a mere means. He coerces the debtor, who cannot truly consent to this "offer he can't refuse." (Of course, the outward form of such transactions may look like ordinary commercial dealings, but we know very well that some offers and demands couched in that form are coercive.)

In Kant's view, acts that are done on maxims that require deception or coercion of others and so cannot have the consent of those others (for consent precludes both deception and coercion), are wrong. When we act on such maxims, we treat others as mere means, as things rather than as ends in themselves. If we act on such maxims, our acts are not only wrong but unjust: such acts wrong the particular others who are deceived or coerced.

TREATING PERSONS AS ENDS IN THEMSELVES

Duties of justice are, in Kant's view (as in many others'), the most important of our duties. When we fail in these duties, we have used some other or others as mere means. But there are also cases where, though we do not use others as mere means, still we fail to use them as ends in themselves in the fullest possible way. To treat someone as an end in him or herself requires in the first place that one not use him or her as mere means, that one respect each as a rational person with his or her own maxims. But beyond that, one may also seek to foster others' plans and maxims by sharing some of their ends. To act beneficently is to seek others' happiness, therefore to intend to achieve some of the things that those others aim at with their maxims. If I want to make others happy, I will adopt maxims that not merely do not manipulate them but that foster some of their plans and activities. Beneficent acts try to achieve what others want. However, we cannot seek everything that others want; their wants are too numerous and diverse, and, of course, sometimes incompatible. It follows that beneficence has to be selective.

There is then quite a sharp distinction between the requirements of justice and of beneficence in Kantian ethics. Justice requires that we act on *no* maxims that use others as mere means. Beneficence requires that we act on *some* maxims that foster others' ends, though it is a matter for judgment and discretion which of their ends we foster. Some maxims no doubt ought not to be

fostered because it would be unjust to do so. Kantians are not committed to working interminably through a list of happiness-producing and misery-reducing acts; but there are some acts whose obligatoriness utilitarians may need to debate as they try to compare total outcomes of different choices, to which Kantians are stringently bound. Kantians will claim that they have done nothing wrong if none of their acts is unjust, and that their duty is complete if in addition their life plans have in the circumstances been reasonably beneficent.

In making sure that they meet all the demands of justice, Kantians do not try to compare all available acts and see which has the best effects. They consider only the proposals for action that occur to them and check that these proposals use no other as mere means. If they do not, the act is permissible; if omitting the act would use another as mere means, the act is obligatory. Kant's theory has less scope than utilitarianism. Kantians do not claim to discover whether acts whose maxims they don't know fully are just. They may be reluctant to judge others' acts or policies that cannot be regarded as the maxim of any person or institution. They cannot rank acts in order of merit. Yet, the theory offers more precision than utilitarianism when data are scarce. One can usually tell whether one's act would use others as mere means, even when its impact on human happiness is thoroughly obscure.

THE LIMITS OF KANTIAN ETHICS: INTENTIONS AND RESULTS

Kantian ethics differs from utilitarian ethics both in its scope and in the precision with which it guides action. Every action, whether of a person or of an agency, can be assessed by utilitarian methods, provided only that information is available about all the consequences of the act. The theory has unlimited scope, but owing to lack of data, often lacks precision. Kantian ethics has a more restricted scope. Since it assesses actions by looking at the maxims of agents, it can only assess intentional acts. This means that it is most at home in assessing individuals' acts; but it can be extended to assess acts of agencies that (like corporations and governments and student unions) have decision-making procedures. It can do nothing to assess patterns of action that reflect no intention or policy, hence it cannot assess the acts of groups lacking decision-making procedures, such as the student movement, the women's movement, or the consumer movement.

It may seem a great limitation of Kantian ethics that it concentrates on intentions to the neglect of results. It might seem that all conscientious Kantians have to do is to make sure that they never intend to use others as mere means, and that they sometimes intend to foster others' ends. And, as we all know, good intentions sometimes lead to bad results and correspondingly, bad intentions sometimes do no harm, or even produce good. If Hardin is right, the good intentions of those who feed the starving lead to dreadful results in the long run. If some traditional arguments in favor of capitalism are right, the greed and selfishness of the profit motive have produced unparalleled prosperity for many.

But such discrepancies between intentions and results are the exception and not the rule. For we cannot just *claim* that our intentions are good and do what we will. Our intentions reflect what we expect the immediate results of our action to be. Nobody credits the "intentions" of a couple who practice neither celibacy nor contraception but still insist "we never meant to have (more) children." Conception is likely (and known to be likely) in such cases. Where people's expressed intentions ignore the normal and predictable results of what they do, we infer that (if they are not amazingly ignorant) their words do not express their true intentions. The Formula of the End in Itself applies to the intentions on which one acts—not to some prettified version that one may avow. Provided this intention—the agent's real intention—uses no other as mere means, he or she does nothing unjust. If some of his or her intentions foster others' ends, then he or she is sometimes beneficent. It is therefore possible for people to test their proposals by Kantian

arguments even when they lack the comprehensive causal knowledge that utilitarianism requires. Conscientious Kantians can work out whether they will be doing wrong by some act even though it blurs the implications of the theory. If we peer through the blur, we see that the utilitarian view is that lives may indeed be sacrificed for the sake of a greater good, even when the persons are not willing. There is nothing wrong with using another as a mere means provided that the end for which the person is so used is a happier result than could have been achieved any other way, taking into account the misery the means have caused. In utilitarian thought persons are not ends in themselves. Their special moral status derives from their being means to the production of happiness. Human life has therefore a high, though derivative value, and one life may be taken for the sake of greater happiness in other lives, or for the ending of misery in that life. Nor is there any deep difference between ending a life for the sake of others' happiness by not helping (e.g., by triaging) and doing so by harming. Because the distinction between justice and beneficence is not sharply made within utilitarianism, it is not possible to say that triaging is a matter of not benefiting, while other interventions are a matter of injustice.

Utilitarian moral theory has then a rather paradoxical view of the value of human life. Living, conscious humans are (along with other sentient beings) necessary for the existence of everything utilitarians value. But it is not their being alive but the state of their consciousness that is of value. Hence, the best results may require certain lives to be lost—by whatever means—for the sake of the total happiness and absence of misery that can be produced.

KANT AND RESPECT FOR PERSONS

Kantians reach different conclusions about human life. Human life is valuable because humans (and conceivable other beings, e.g., angels or apes) are the bearers of rational life. Humans are able to choose and to plan. This capacity and its exercise are of such value that they ought not to be sacrificed for anything of lesser value. Therefore, no one rational or autonomous creature should be treated as mere means for the enjoyment or even the happiness of another. We may in Kant's view justifiably—even nobly— risk or sacrifice our lives for others. For in doing so we follow our own maxim and nobody uses us as mere means. But no others may use either our lives or our bodies for a scheme that they have either coerced or deceived us into joining. For in doing so they would fail to treat us as rational beings; they would use us as mere means and not as ends in ourselves.

It is conceivable that a society of Kantians, all of whom took pains to use no other as mere means, would end up with less happiness or with fewer persons alive than would some societies of complying utilitarians. For since the Kantians would be strictly bound only to justice, they might without wrongdoing be quite selective in their beneficence and fail to maximize either survival rates or happiness, or even to achieve as much of either as a strenuous group of utilitarians, who know that their foresight is limited and that they may cause some harm or fail to cause some benefit. But they will not cause harms that they can foresee without this being reflected in their intentions.

UTILITARIANISM AND RESPECT FOR LIFE

From the differing implications that Kantian and utilitarian moral theories have for our actions toward those who do or may suffer famine, we can discover two sharply contrasting views of the value of human life. Utilitarians value happiness and the absence or reduction of misery. As a utilitarian one ought (if conscientious) to devote one's life to achieving the best possible balance of happiness over misery. If one's life plan remains in doubt, this will be because the means to this end are often unclear. But whenever the causal

tendency of acts is clear, utilitarians will be able to discern the acts they should successively do in order to improve the world's balance of happiness over unhappiness.

This task is not one for the fainthearted. First, it is dauntingly long, indeed interminable. Second, it may at times require the sacrifice of happiness, and even of lives, for the sake of a greater happiness. Such sacrifice may be morally required not only when the person whose happiness or even whose life is at stake volunteers to make the sacrifice. It may be necessary to sacrifice some lives for the sake of others. As our control over the means of ending and presenting human life has increased, analogous dilemmas have arisen in many areas for utilitarians. Should life be preserved at the cost of pain when modern medicine makes this possible? Should life be preserved without hope of consciousness? Should triage policies, because they may maximize the number of survivors, be used to determine who should be left to starve? Should population growth be fostered wherever it will increase the total of human happiness—or on some views so long as average happiness is not reduced? All these questions can be fitted into utilitarian frameworks and answered *if* we have the relevant information. And sometimes the answer will be that human happiness demands the sacrifice of lives, including the sacrifice of unwilling lives. Further, for most utilitarians, it makes no difference if the unwilling sacrifices involve acts of injustice to those whose lives are to be lost. It might, for example, prove necessary for maximal happiness that some persons have their allotted rations, or their hard-earned income, diverted for others' benefit. Or it might turn out that some generations must sacrifice comforts or liberties and even lives to rear "the fabric of felicity" for their successors. Utilitarians do not deny these possibilities, though the imprecision of our knowledge of consequences often somehow makes the right calculations. On the other hand, nobody will have been made an instrument of others' survival or happiness in the society of complying Kantians.

A Theory of Justice

John Rawls

John Rawls taught philosophy at Princeton, Cornell, MIT, and Harvard universities. He is perhaps the most important political philosopher of the twentieth century. His books include *A Theory of Justice* (1971), *Political Liberalism* (1993), and *The Law of Peoples* (1999).

In this excerpt from his book, *A Theory of Justice*, Rawls argues that justice is best understood as a certain kind of fairness, where people agree to principles in an initial situation that free and equal people would see as reasonable. But from within this position, the principle of utility would not be considered fair. Instead, Rawls proposes that people would accept as fair a set of principles that would work out to the benefit of the least well-off person.

My aim is to present a conception of justice which generalizes and carries to a higher level of abstraction the familiar theory of the social contract as found, say, in Locke, Rousseau, and Kant. In order to do this we are not to think of the original contract as one to enter a particular society or to set up a particular form of government. Rather, the guiding idea is that the principles of justice for the basic structure of society are the object of the original agreement They are the principles that free and rational persons concerned to further their own interests would accept in an initial position of equality as defining the fundamental terms of their association. These principles are to regulate all further agreements; they specify the kinds of social cooperation that can be entered into and the forms of government that can be established. This way of regarding the principles of justice I shall call justice as fairness.

Thus we are to imagine that those who engage in social cooperation choose together, in one joint act, the principles which are to assign basic rights and duties and to determine the division of social benefits. Men are to decide in advance how they are to regulate their claims against one another and what is to be the foundation charter of their society. Just as each person must decide by rational reflection what constitutes his good, that is, the system of ends which it is rational for him to pursue, so a group of persons must decide once and for all what is to count among them as just and unjust The choice which rational men would make in this hypothetical situation of equal liberty, assuming for the present that this choice problem has a solution, determines the principles of justice.

In justice as fairness the original position of equality corresponds to the state of nature in the traditional theory of the social contract. This original position is not, of course, thought of as an actual historical state of affairs, much less a primitive condition of culture. It is understood as a purely hypothetical situation characterized so as to lead a certain conception of justice. Among the essential features of this situation is that no one knows his place in society, his class position or social status, nor does anyone know his fortune in the distribution of natural assets and abilities, his intelligence, strength, and the like. I shall even assume that the parties do not know their conceptions of the good or their special psychological propensities. The principles of justice are chosen behind a veil of ignorance. This ensures that no one is advantaged or disadvantaged in the choice of principles by the outcome of natural chance or the contingency of social circumstances. Since all are similarly situated and no one is able to design principles to favor his particular condition, the principles of justice are the result of a fair agreement or bargain. For given the circumstances of the original position, the symmetry of everyone's relations to each other, this initial situation is fair between individuals as moral persons, that is, as rational beings with their own ends and capable, I shall assume, of a sense of justice. The original position is, one might say, the appropriate initial status quo, and thus the fundamental agreements reached in it are fair. This explains the propriety of the name "justice as fairness": it conveys the idea that the principles of justice are agreed to in an initial situation that is fair. The name does not mean that the concepts of justice and fairness are the same, any more than the phrase "poetry as metaphor" means that the concepts of "poetry and metaphor" are the same.

Justice as fairness begins, as I have said, with one of the most general of all choices which persons might make together, namely, with the choice of the first principles of a conception of justice which is to regulate all subsequent criticism and reform of institutions. Then, having chosen a conception of justice, we can suppose that they are to choose a constitution and a legislature to enact laws, and so on, all in accordance with the principles of justice initially agreed upon. Our social situation is just if it is such that by this sequence of hypothetical agreements we would have contracted into the general system of rules which defines it. Moreover, assuming that the original position does determine a set of principles (that is, that a particular conception of justice would be chosen), it will then be true that whenever social institutions satisfy these principles those engaged in them can say to one another that they are cooperating on terms to which they would agree if they were free and equal persons whose relations with respect to one another were fair. They could all view their arrangements as meeting the stipulations which they would acknowledge in an initial situation that embodies widely accepted and reasonable constraints on the choice of principles. The general recognition of this fad would provide the basis for a public acceptance of the corresponding principles of justice. No society can, of course, be a scheme of cooperation which men enter voluntarily in a literal sense; each person finds himself placed at birth in some particular position in some particular society, and the nature of this position materially affects his life prospects. Yet a society satisfying the principles of justice as fairness comes as close as a society can to being a voluntary scheme, for it meets the principles which free and equal persons would assent to under circumstances that are fair. In this sense its members are autonomous and the obligations they recognize self-imposed.

One feature of justice as fairness is to think of the parties in the initial situation as rational and mutually disinterested. This does not mean that the parties are egoists, that is, individuals with only certain kinds of interests, say in wealth, prestige, and domination. But they are conceived as not taking an interest in one another's interests. They are to presume that even their spiritual aims may be opposed, in the way that the aims of those of different religions may be opposed. Moreover, the concept of rationality must be interpreted as far as possible in the narrow sense, standard in economic theory, of taking the most effective means to given ends. I shall modify this concept to some extent, as explained later, but one most try to avoid introducing into it any controversial ethical elements. The initial situation must be characterized by stipulations that are widely accepted.

In working out the conception of justice as fairness one main task clearly is to determine which principles of justice would be chosen in the original position. To do this we must describe this situation in some detail and formulate with care the problem of choice which it presents. These matters I shall take up in the immediately succeeding chapters. It may be observed, however, that once the principles of justice are thought of as arising from an original agreement in a situation of equality, it is an open question whether the principle of utility would be acknowledged. Offhand it hardly seems likely that persons who view themselves as equals, entitled to press their claims upon one another, would agree to a principle which may require lesser life prospects for some simply for the sake of a greater sum of advantages enjoyed by others. Since each desires to protect his interests, his capacity to advance hit conception of the good, no one has a reason to acquiesce in an enduring loss for himself in order to bring about a greater net balance of satisfaction. In the absence of strong and lasting benevolent impulses, a rational man would not accept a basic structure merely because it maximized the algebraic sum of advantages irrespective of its permanent effects on his own basic rights and interests. Thus it seems that the principle of utility it incompatible with the conception of social cooperation among equals for mutual advantage. It appears to be inconsistent with the idea of reciprocity implicit in the notion of a well-ordered society. Or, at any rate, so I shall argue.

I shall maintain instead that the persons in the initial situation would choose two rather different principles; the first requires equality in the assignment of basic rights and duties, while the second holds that social and economic inequalities, for example inequalities of wealth and authority, are just only if they result in compensating benefits for everyone, and in particular for the least advantaged members of society. These principles rule out justifying institutions on the grounds that the hardships of some are offset by a greater good in the aggregate. It may be expedient but it is not just that some should have less in order that others may prosper. But there is no injustice in the greater benefits earned by a few provided that the situation of persons not so fortunate is thereby improved. The intuitive idea is that since everyone's well-being depends upon a scheme of cooperation without which no one could have a satisfactory life, the division of advantages should be such at to draw forth the willing cooperation of everyone taking part in it, including those less well situated. . . . The two principles mentioned seem to be a fair agreement on the basis of which those better endowed, or more fortunate in their social position, neither of which we can be said to deserve, could expect the willing cooperation of others when some workable scheme is a necessary condition of the welfare of all. Once we

decide to look for a conception of justice that nullifies the accidents of natural endowment and the contingencies of social circumstance as counters in quest for political and economic advantage, we are led to these principles. They express the result of leaving aside those aspects of the social work that seem arbitrary from a moral point of view.

The problem of the choice of principles, however, is extremely difficult. I do not expect the answer I shall suggest to be convincing to everyone. It is, therefore, worth noting from the outset that justice as fairness, like other contract views, consists of two parts: (1) an interpretation of the initial situation and of the problem of choice posed there, and (2) a set of principles which, it is argued, would be agreed to. One may accept the first part of the theory (or some variant thereof), but not the other, and conversely. The concept of the initial contractual situation may seem reasonable although the particular principles proposed are rejected. . . .

Justice as fairness is an example of what I have called a contract theory. Now there may be an objection to the term "contract" and related expressions, but I think it will serve reasonably well. Many words have misleading connotations which at first are likely to confuse. The terms "utility" and "utilitarianism" are surely no exception. They too have unfortunate suggestions which hostile critics have been willing to exploit; yet they are clear enough for those prepared to study utilitarian doctrine. The same should be true of the term "contract" applied to moral theories. As I have mentioned, to understand it one has to keep in mind that it implies a certain level of abstraction. In particular, the content of the relevant agreement is not to enter a given society or to adopt a given form of government, but to accept certain moral principles. Moreover, the undertakings referred to are purely hypothetical: a contract view holds that certain principles would be accepted in a well-defined initial situation.

The merit of the contract terminology is that it conveys the idea that principles of justice may be conceived as principles that would be chosen by rational persons, and that in this way conceptions of justice may be explained and justified. The theory of justice is a part, perhaps the most significant part, of the theory of rational choice. Furthermore, principles of justice deal with conflicting claims upon the advantages won by social cooperation; they apply to the relations among several persons or groups. The word "contract" suggests this plurality as well as the condition that the appropriate division of advantages must be in accordance with principles acceptable to all parties. The condition of publicity for principles of justice is also connoted by the contract phraseology. Thus, if these principles are the outcome of an agreement, citizens have a knowledge of the principles that others follow. It is characteristic of contract theories to stress the public nature of political principles. Finally there is the long tradition of the contract doctrine. Expressing the tie with this line of thought helps to define ideas and accords with natural piety. There are then several advantages in the use of the term "contract." With due precautions taken, it should not be misleading. . . .

11. TWO PRINCIPLES OF JUSTICE

I shall now state in a provisional form the two principles of justice that I believe would be chosen in the original position. In this section I wish to make only the most general comments, and therefore the first formulation of these principles is tentative. As we go on I shall run through several formulations and approximate step by step the final statement to be given much later. I believe that doing this allows the exposition to proceed in a natural way.

The first statement of the two principles reads as follows.

> First: each person is to have an equal right to the most extensive scheme of equal basic liberties compatible with a similar scheme of liberties for others.
> Second: social and economic inequalities are to be arranged so that they are both(a) reasonably expected to be to everyone's advantage, and(b) attached to positions and offices open to all.

There are two ambiguous phrases in the second principle, namely "everyone's advantage" and "open to all." . . .

These principles primarily apply, as I have said, to the basic structure of society and govern the assignment of rights and duties and regulate the distribution of social and economic advantages. Their formulation pre-supposes that, for the purposes of a theory of justice, the social structure may be viewed as having two more or less distinct parts, the first principle applying to the one, the second principle to the other. Thus we distinguish between the aspects of the social system that define and secure the equal basic liberties and the aspects that specify and establish social and economic inequalities. Now it is essential to observe that the basic liberties are given by a list of such liberties. Important among these are political liberty (the right to vote and to hold public office) and freedom of speech and assembly; liberty of conscience and freedom of thought; freedom of the person, which includes freedom from psychological oppression and physical assault and dismemberment (integrity of the person); the right to hold personal property and freedom from arbitrary arrest and seizure as defined by the concept of the rule of law. These liberties are to be equal by the first principle.

The second principle applies, in the first approximation, to the distribution of income and wealth and to the design of organizations that make use of differences in authority and responsibility. While the distribution of wealth and income need not be equal, it must be to everyone's advantage, and at the same time, positions of authority and responsibility must be accessible to all. One applies the second principle by holding positions open, and then, subject to this constraint, arranges social and economic inequalities so that everyone benefits.

These principles are to be arranged in a serial order with the first principle prior to the second. This ordering means that infringements of the basic equal liberties protected by the first principle cannot be justified, or compensated for, by greater social and economic advantages. These liberties have a central range of application within which they can be limited and compromised only when they conflict with other basic liberties. Since they may be limited when they clash with one another, none of these liberties is absolute; but however they are adjusted to form one system, this system is to be the same for all. It is difficult, and perhaps impossible, to give a complete specification of these liberties independently from the particular circumstances—social, economic, and technological—of a given society. The hypothesis is that the general form of such a list could be devised with sufficient exactness to sustain this conception of justice. Of course, liberties not on the list, for example, the right to own certain kinds of property (e.g., means of production) and freedom of contract as understood by the doctrine of laissez-faire are not basic; and so they are not protected by the priority of the first principle. Finally, in regard to the second principle, the distribution of wealth and income, and positions of authority and responsibility, are to be consistent with both the basic liberties and equality of opportunity.

The two principles are rather specific in their content, and their acceptance rests on certain assumptions that I must eventually try to explain and justify. For the present, it should be observed that these principles are a special case of a more general conception of justice that can be expressed follows.

> All social values—liberty and opportunity, income and wealth, and the social bases of self-respect—are to be distributed equally unless an unequal distribution of any, or all, of these values is to everyone's advantage.

Injustice, then, is simply inequalities that are not to the benefit of all. Of course, this conception is extremely vague and requires interpretation.

As a first step, suppose that the basic structure of society distributes certain primary goods, that is, things that every rational man is presumed to want. These goods normally have a use whatever a person's rational plan of life. For simplicity, assume that the chief primary goods at the disposition of society are rights, liberties, and opportunities, and income and wealth. (Later on in Part III the primary good of self-respect has a central place.) These are the social primary goods. Other primary goods such as health and vigor, intelligence and imagination, are natural goods; although their possession is influenced by the basic structure, they are not so directly under its control. Imagine, then, a hypothetical initial arrangement in which all the social primary goods are equally distributed: everyone has similar rights and duties, and income and wealth are evenly shared. This state of affairs provides a benchmark for judging improvements. If certain inequalities of wealth and differences in authority would make everyone better off than in this hypothetical starting situation, then they accord with the general conception.

Now it is possible, at least theoretically, that by giving up some of their fundamental liberties men are sufficiently compensated by the resulting social and economic gains. The general conception of justice imposes no restrictions on what sort of inequalities are permissible; it only requires that everyone's position be improved. We need not suppose anything so drastic as consenting to a condition of slavery. Imagine instead that people seem willing to forego certain political rights when the economic returns are significant. It is this kind of exchange which the two principles rule out; being arranged in serial order they do not permit exchanges between basic liberties and economic and social gains except under extenuating circumstances. . . .

24. THE VEIL OF IGNORANCE

The idea of the original position is to set up a fair procedure to that any principles agreed to will be just. The aim it to use the notion of pure procedural justice as a basis of theory. Somehow we must nullify the effects of specific contingencies which put men at odds and tempt than to exploit social and natural circumstances to their own advantage. Now in order to do this I assume that the parties are situated behind a veil of ignorance. They do not know how the various alternatives will affect their own particular case and they are obliged to evaluate principles solely on the basis of general considerations.

It is assumed, then, that the parties do not know certain kinds of particular facts. First of all, no one knows his place in society, his class position or social status; nor does he know his fortune in the distribution of natural assets and abilities, his intelligence and strength, and the like. Nor, again, does anyone know his conception of the good, the particulars of his rational plan of life, or even the special features of his psychology such as his aversion to risk or liability optimism or pessimism. More than this, I assume that the parties do not know the particular circumstances of their own society. That is, they do not know its economic or political situation, or the level of civilization and culture it has been able to achieve. The persons in the original position have no information as to which generation they belong. These broader restrictions on knowledge are appropriate in part because questions of social justice arise between generations as well as within them, for example, the question of the appropriate rate of capital saving and of the conservation of natural resources and the environment of nature. There is also, theoretically anyway, the question of a reasonable genetic policy. In these cases too, in order to carry through the idea of the original position, the parties must not know the contingencies that set them in opposition. They must choose principles the consequences of which they are prepared to live with whatever generation they turn out to belong to.

As far as possible, then, the only particular facts which the parties know is that their society is subject to the circumstances of justice and whatever this implies. It is taken for granted, however, that they know the general facts about human society. They understand political affairs and the principles of economic theory; they know the basis of social organization and the laws of human psychology. Indeed, the parties are presumed to know whatever general facts affect the choice of the principles of justice. There are no limitations on general information, that is, on general laws and theories, since conceptions of justice must be adjusted to the characteristics of the systems of social cooperation which they are to regulate, and there is no reason to rule out these facts. It is, for example, a consideration against a conception of justice that, in view of the laws of moral psychology, men would not acquire a desire to act upon it even when the institutions of their society satisfied it. For in this case there would be difficulty in securing the stability of social cooperation. An important feature of a conception of justice is that it should generate its own support. Its principles should be such that when they are embodied in the basic structure of society men tend to acquire the corresponding sense of justice and develop a desire to act in

accordance with its principles. In this case a conception of justice is stable. This kind of general information is admissible in the original position. . . .

Thus there follows the very important consequence that the parties have no basis for bargaining in the usual sense. No one knows his situation in society nor his natural assets, and therefore no one is in a position to tailor principles to his advantage. We might imagine that one of the contractees threatens to hold out unless the others agree to principles favorable to him. But how does he know which principles are especially in his interests? The same holds for the formation of coalitions: if a group were to decide to band together to the disadvantage of the others, they would not know how to favor themselves in the choice of principles. Even if they could get everyone to agree to their proposal, they would have no assurance that it was to their advantage, since they cannot identify themselves either by name or description. . . .

The restrictions on particular information in the original position are, then, of fundamental importance. Without them we would not be able to work out any definite theory of justice at all. We would have to be content with a vague formula stating that justice is what would be agreed to without being able to say much, if anything, about the substance of the agreement itself. The formal constraints of the concept of right, those applying to principles directly, are not sufficient for our purpose. The veil of ignorance makes possible a unanimous choice of a particular conception of justice. Without these limitations on knowledge the bargaining problem of the original position would be hopelessly complicated. Even if theoretically a solution were to exist, we would not, at present anyway, be able to determine it. . . .

Now the reasons for the veil of ignorance go beyond mere simplicity. We want to define the original position so that we get the desired solution. If a knowledge of particulars is allowed, then the outcome is biased by arbitrary contingencies. As already observed, to each according to his threat advantage is not a principle of justice. If the original position is to yield agreements that are just, the parties must be fairly situated and treated equally as moral persons. The arbitrariness of the world must be corrected for by adjusting the circumstances of the initial contractual situation. Moreover, if in choosing principles we required unanimity even when there is full information, only a few rather obvious cases could be decided. A conception of justice based on unanimity in these circumstances would indeed be weak and trivial. But once knowledge is excluded, the requirement of unanimity is not out of place and the fact that it can be satisfied is of great importance. It enables us to say of the preferred conception of justice that it represents a genuine reconciliation of interests. . . .

DEMOCRATIC EQUALITY AND THE DIFFERENCE PRINCIPLE

To illustrate the difference principle, consider the distribution of income among social classes. Let us suppose that the various income groups correlate with representative individuals by reference to whose expectations we can judge the distribution. Now those starting out as members of the entrepreneurial class in property-owning democracy, say, have a better prospect than those who begin in the class of unskilled laborers. It seems likely that this will be true even when the social injustices which now exist are removed. What, then, can possibly justify this kind of initial inequality in life prospects? According to the difference principle, it is justifiable only if the difference in expectation is to the advantage of the representative man who is worse off, in this case the representative unskilled worker. The inequality in expectation is permissible only if lowering it would make the working class even more worse off. Supposedly, given the rider in the second principle concerning open positions, and the principle of liberty generally, the greater expectations allowed to entrepreneurs encourages them to do things which raises the long-term prospects of laboring class. Their better prospects act as incentives so that the economic process is more efficient, innovation proceeds at a faster pace, and so on. Eventually the resulting material benefits spread throughout the system and to the least advantaged. I shall not consider how far these things are true. The point is that something of

this kind must be argued if these inequalities are to be just by the difference principle.

THE TENDENCY TO EQUALITY

We see then that the difference principle represents, in effect, an agreement to regard the distribution of natural talents as a common asset and to share in the benefits of this distribution whatever it turns out to be. Those who have been favored by nature, whoever they are, may gain from their good fortune only on terms that improve the situation of those who have lost out. The naturally advantaged are not to gain merely because they are more gifted, but only to cover the costs of training and education and for using their endowments in ways that help the less fortunate as well. No one deserves his greater natural capacity nor merits a more favorable starting place in society. But it does not follow that one should eliminate these distinctions. There is another way to deal with them. The basic structure can be arranged so that these contingencies work for the good of the least fortunate. Thus we are led to the difference principle if we wish to set up the social system so that no one gains or loses from his arbitrary place in the distribution of natural assets or his initial position in society without giving or receiving compensating advantages in return.

In view of these remarks we may reject the contention that the injustice of institutions is always imperfect because the distribution of natural talents and the contingencies of social circumstance are unjust, and this injustice must inevitably carry over to human arrangements. Occasionally this reflection is offered as an excuse for ignoring injustice, as if the refusal to acquiesce in injustice is on a par with being unable to accept death. The natural distribution is neither just nor unjust; nor is it unjust that men are born into society at some particular position. These are simply natural facts. What is just and unjust is the way that institutions deal with these facts. Aristocratic and caste societies are unjust because they make these contingencies the ascriptive basis for belonging to more or less enclosed and privileged social classes. The basic structure of these societies incorporates the arbitrariness found in nature. But there is no necessity for men to resign themselves to these contingencies. The social system is not an unchangeable order beyond human control but a pattern of human action. In justice as fairness men agree to share one another's fate. In designing institutions they undertake to avail themselves of the accidents of nature and social circumstance only when doing so is for the common benefit. The two principles are a fair way of meeting the arbitrariness of fortune; and while no doubt imperfect in other ways, the institutions which satisfy these principles are just.

A further point is that the difference principle expresses a conception of reciprocity. It is a principle of mutual benefit. We have seen that, a least when chain connection holds, each representative man can accept the basic structure as designed to advance his interests. The social order can be justified to everyone, and in particular to those who are least favored; and in this sense it is egalitarian. But it seems necessary to consider in an intuitive way how the condition of mutual benefit is satisfied. Consider any two representative men A and B, and let B be the one who is less favored. Actually, since we are most interested in the comparison with the least favored man, let us assume that B is this individual. Now B can accept A's being better off since A's advantages have been gained in ways that improve B's prospects. If A were not allowed his better position, B would be even worse off than he is. The difficulty is to show that A has no grounds for complaint. Perhaps he is required to have less than he might since his having more would result in some loss to B. Now what can be said to the more favored man? To begin with, it is clear that the well-being of each depends on a scheme of social cooperation without which no one could have a satisfactory life. Secondly, we can ask for the willing cooperation of everyone only if the terms of the scheme are reasonable. The difference principle, then, seems to be fair basis on which those better endowed, or more fortunate in their social circumstances, could expect others to collaborate with them when some workable arrangement is a necessary condition of the good of all.

There is a natural inclination to object that those better situated deserve their greater advantages whether or not they are to the benefit of others. At this point it is necessary to be clear about the notion of desert. It is perfectly true that given a just system of cooperation as a scheme of public rules and the expectations set up by it, those who, with the prospect of improving their condition, have done what the system announces that it will reward are entitled to their advantages. In this sense the more fortunate have a claim to their better situation; their claims are legitimate expectations established by social institutions, and the community is obligated to meet them. But this sense of desert presupposes the existence of the cooperative scheme; it is irrelevant to the question whether in the first place the scheme is to be designed in accordance with the difference principle or some other criterion.

Perhaps some will think that the person with greater natural endowments deserves those assets and the superior character that made their development possible. Because he is more worthy in this sense, he deserves the greater advantages that he could achieve with them. This view, however, is surely incorrect. It seems to be one of the fixed points of our considered judgments that no one deserves his place in the distribution of native endowments, any more than one deserves one's initial starting place in society. The assertion that a man deserves the superior character that enables him to make the effort to cultivate his abilities is equally problematic; for his character depends in large part upon fortunate family and social circumstances for which he can claim no credit. The notion of desert seems not to apply to these cases. Thus the more advantaged representative man cannot say that he deserves and therefore has a right to a scheme of cooperation in which he is permitted to acquire benefits in ways that do not contribute to the welfare of others. There is no basis for his making this claim. From the standpoint of common sense, then, the difference principle appears to be acceptable both to the more advantaged and to the less advantaged individual. Of course, none of this is strictly speaking an argument for the principle, since in a contract theory arguments are made from the point of the original position. But these intuitive considerations help to clarify the nature of the principle and the sense in which it is egalitarian.

On Virtue Ethics

Rosalind Hursthouse

Rosalind Hursthouse is professor of philosophy at University of Auckland in New Zealand. She is the author of *On Virtue Ethics* (1999).

Hursthouse attempts to provide a clear and concise formulation of virtue ethics that will allow us to compare it to its chief rivals, utilitarianism and Kantian ethics. She is especially interested in rebutting the claim that virtue ethics, with its emphasis on character formation, cannot give us guidance about what we ought to do in particular situations.

Virtue ethics has been characterized in a number of ways. It is described (1) as an ethics which is "agent-centred" rather than "act-centred"; (2) as concerned with Being rather than Doing; (3) as addressing itself to the question, "What sort of person should I be?" rather than to the question, "What sorts of action should I do?"; (4) as taking certain areteic concepts (*good, excellence, virtue*) as basic rather than deontic ones (*right, duty, obligation*); (5) as rejecting the idea that ethics is codifiable in rules or principles that can provide specific action guidance.

I give this list because these descriptions of virtue ethics are so commonly encountered, not because I think they are good ones. On the contrary, I think that all of them, in their crude brevity, are seriously misleading. Of course, there is some truth in each of them, which is why they are so common, and I shall return to them as we proceed, to note what truth, with what qualifications, they may be seen as containing. Readers familiar with the recent literature I mentioned in the Introduction, which has blurred the lines of demarcation between the three approaches in normative ethics, will no doubt have discarded or qualified them long since. But here, at the outset, it seems best to begin at a simple level, with the descriptions most readers will recognize, and work our way through to some of the complications and subtleties that are not so well known.

RIGHT ACTION

The descriptions, especially when encountered for the first time, can easily be read as all making roughly the same point, and one way in which they are all misleading is that they encourage the thought that virtue ethics cannot be a genuine rival to utilitarianism and deontology. The thought goes like this:

> If virtue ethics is "agent-centred rather than act-centred," concerned with "What sort of person should I be?" rather than "What sorts of action should I do?" (with "Being rather than Doing"), if it concentrates on the *good* or *virtuous* agent rather than on *right* action and on what anyone, virtuous or not, has an *obligation* to do; how can it be a genuine rival to utilitarianism and deontology? Surely ethical theories are supposed to tell us about right action, i.e. about what sorts of act we should do. Utilitarianism and deontology certainly do that; if virtue ethics does not, it cannot be a genuine rival to them.

Now the descriptions do not actually say that virtue ethics does not concern itself at all with right action, or what we should do; it is in so far as

Rosalind Hursthouse, Excerpt from On Virtue Ethics, pp. 51–57, 1999. Reprinted by permission of Oxford University Press.

it is easy to take them that way that they are misleading. For virtue ethics can provide action guidance. The way it does this can most helpfully be shown by comparing it with the guidance given by some versions of utilitarianism and deontology, all laid out in a similar way.

Suppose an act utilitarian began her account of right action as follows:

P.1. An action is right iff it promotes the best consequences.

This premise provides a specification of right action, forging the familiar act-utilitarian link between the concepts of right action and *best consequences*, but gives no one guidance about how to act until one knows what to count as the best consequences. So these must be specified in a second premise, for example:

P.2. The best consequences are those in which happiness is maximized—which forges the familiar utilitarian link between the concepts of *best consequences* and *happiness*.

Many simple versions of deontology can be laid out in a way that displays the same basic structure. They begin with a premise providing a specification of right action:

P.1. An action is right iff it is in accordance with a correct moral rule or principle.

Like the first premise of act utilitarianism, this one gives no guidance about how to act until, in this case, one knows what to count as a correct moral rule (or principle). So this must be specified in a second premise, which begins

P.2. A correct moral rule (principle) is one that . . .

and this may be completed in a variety of ways, for example,

(1) . . . is on the following list—(and then a list follows, perhaps completed with an "etc."), or
(2) . . . is laid down for us by God, or
(3) . . . is universalizable/acategorical imperative, or
(4) . . . would be the object of choice of all rational beings,

and so on.

Although this way of laying out fairly familiar versions of utilitarianism and deontology is hardly

controversial, it shows that there is something wrong with an over-used description of them, namely the slogan, "Utilitarianism begins with" (or "takes as its fundamental concept," etc.) "the Good, whereas deontology begins with the Right."[1] If the concept a normative ethics "begins with" is the one it uses to specify right action, then utilitarianism might indeed be said to begin with the Good (taking this to be the same concept as that of the best), but we should surely hasten to add, "but only in relation to consequences or states of affairs, not, for instance, in relation to *good* agents, or living *well*." And even then, we shall not be able to go on to say that most versions of deontology "begin with" the Right, for they use the concept of moral rule or principle to specify right action. The only versions which, in this sense, "begin with" the Right would have to be versions of what Frankena calls "extreme act-deontology,"[2] which (I suppose) specify a right action as one which just *is* right.

And if the slogan is supposed to single out, rather vaguely, the concept which is "most important," then the concepts of *consequences* or *happiness* seem as deserving of mention as the concept of the Good for utilitarianism, and what counts as most important for deontologists (if any one concept does) would surely vary from case to case. For some it would be God, for others universalizability, for others the Categorical Imperative, for others rational acceptance, and so on. (Should we say that for Kant it is the good will, or the Categorical Imperative, or both?)

It is possible that too slavish a reliance on this slogan contributes to the belief that virtue ethics cannot provide its own specification of right action. For many who rely on it go on to say, "Utilitarianism derives the concept of the Right from that of the Good, and deontology derives the Good from the Right; but how can virtue ethics possibly derive the Good and the Right from the concept of the Virtuous Agent, which it begins with?" Now indeed, with no answer forthcoming to the questions, "Good *what*? Right *what*?," I have no idea. But if the question is "How can virtue ethics give an account of right action in such a way as to provide action guidance?," the answer is easy. Here is its first premise:

P.1. An action is right iff it is what a virtuous agent would characteristically (i.e. acting in character) do in the circumstances.

This specification rarely, if ever, silences those who maintain that virtue ethics cannot tell us what we should do. On the contrary, it tends to provoke irritable laughter and scorn. "That's no use," the objectors say. "It gives us no guidance whatsoever. Who are the virtuous agents?"

But if the failure of the first premise of an account of right action, the premise which forges a link between the concept of right action and a concept distinctive of a particular normative ethics, may provoke scorn because it provides no practical guidance, why not direct similar scorn at the first premises of act utilitarianism and deontology in the form in which I have given them? Of each of them I remarked, apparently in passing, but really with a view to this point, that they gave us no guidance. Act utilitarianism must specify what are to count as the best consequences, and deontology what is to count as a correct moral rule, producing a second premise, before any guidance is given. And, similarly, virtue ethics must specify who is to count as a virtuous agent. So far, the three are all in the same position.

Of course, if the virtuous agent can be specified only as an agent disposed to act in accordance with correct moral rules, as is sometimes assumed, then virtue ethics collapses back into deontology and is no rival to it. So let us add a subsidiary premise to this skeletal outline, intended to show that virtue ethics aims to provide a non-deontological specification of the virtuous agent *via* a specification of the virtues, which will be given in its second premise.

P.1a. A virtuous agent is one who has, and exercises, certain character traits, namely, the virtues.
P.2.   A virtue is a character trait that . . .

This second premise of virtue ethics, like the second premise of some versions of deontology, might be completed simply by enumeration—"is on the following list"—and then a list is given, perhaps completed with "etc." Or we might interpret the Hume of the second *Enquiry* as espousing virtue ethics. According to Hume, we might say, a virtue

is a character trait (of human beings) that is useful or agreeable to its possessor or to others (inclusive "or" both times). Or we might give the standard neo-Aristotelian completion, which claims that a virtue is a character trait a human being needs for *eudaimonia*, to flourish or live well.

Here, then, we have a specification of right action, whose structure closely resembles those of act utilitarianism and many simple forms of deontology. Comparing the three, we see that we could say, "Virtue ethics (in its account of right action) is agent-centred rather than consequences- or rules-centred. It is agent-centred in that it introduces the concept of the virtuous *agent* in the first premise of its account of right action, where utilitarianism and deontology introduce the concepts of *consequences* and *moral rule* respectively." That's true; it does. But note that it is not thereby "agent-centred *rather than* act-centred." It has an answer to "How shall I decide what to do?"

So there is the first misunderstanding cleared away. Virtue ethics does have something to say about right action. But this is only a first step in dealing with the misunderstanding, for many people find what it has to say unsatisfactory. The reasons for their dissatisfaction are so varied that they will occupy us for several chapters; in this one, I shall concentrate on some that are naturally expressed in the complaint that virtue ethics does not and cannot tell us what to do; the complaint that it does not and cannot provide moral guidance.

"Virtue ethics does not provide us with moral guidance"—how can it fail to, when it has provided a specification of right action? Sometimes people suspect that it has provided only a circular specification, not a specification that we could use to guide us. "It has told us that the right action is what a virtuous agent would do. But that's a truism. Of course the virtuous agent "does what is right"; if she didn't, she wouldn't be virtuous; we are just going round in circles."

Now it is true that the first premise of virtue ethics' account of right action has the air of being a truism. For although act utilitarians will want to deny the deontologists' first premise ("No! We should break the rule if the consequences of doing so would be better than those of keeping it"), and deontologists will deny the utilitarian one ("No! We must stick to the rules regardless of the consequences"), it is quite likely that both of them would accept what virtue ethics says: "An action is right iff it is what a virtuous agent would do." But, if they did, they would each be assuming that they had settled what right action was already, using their first and second premises, and were then using the truism to specify what, for them, counted as a virtuous agent: "A virtuous agent is one who does what is right (in my sense of "right")."[3]

What I need to emphasize is that the apparent truism, "An action is right iff it is what a virtuous agent would characteristically do in the circumstances," is not figuring as a truism in virtue ethics' account of right action. It is figuring as the first premise of that account, a premise that, like the first premises of the other two accounts, awaits filling out in the second premise. Perhaps I could make this clearer by restating the first premise, and its supplement, in a way that made the necessity for filling them out glaringly obvious, thus:

P.1.   An action is right iff it is what an X agent would characteristically do in the circumstances, and
P.1.a. An X agent is one who has and exercises certain character traits, namely the Xs.

And put that way, P.1 does not look at all like a truism.

Unfortunately, it now looks uninformative, once again, apparently, contrasting unfavourably with the first premises of act utilitarianism and deontology: "We all have some idea about what best consequences might be and of what correct moral rules or principles are, but what on earth is an X agent?" But now I must repeat the point made earlier. The other first premises, taken strictly, are equally uninformative. We overlook this point because the utilitarian specifications of best consequences are so familiar, and all the deontologists we know cite familiar moral rules. But, for all that is said in the first premise of either, strange things might emerge in the second.

Someone might specify the "best consequences" as those in which the number of Roman Catholics was maximized (and the number of non-Catholics minimized). It would be a very odd view

to hold; no proper Catholic could hold it, but some madman brought up in the Catholic faith might. Or someone might specify the "best consequences" as those in which certain moral rules were adhered to. "We all have some idea of what best consequences might be," not because this is *given* in the first premise of the act utilitarian account, but because we are all familiar with the idea that, by and large, if an action has, as a consequence, that many people are made happy, or much suffering is relieved, this counts as a good consequence.

Similarly, when we read the deontologist's first premise, we suppose that "we all have some idea of what correct moral rules or principles are." We expect (something like) "Do not kill" and "Keep promises." We do not expect "Purify the Aryan race," "Keep women in their proper place, subordinate to men," "Kill the infidel." But we know only too well that these not only might be specified, but have been specified, as correct moral rules. As far as the first premise of the deontological account of right action goes, we do not, in fact, have any idea, given by that premise, of what correct moral rules or principles are; we bring our own ideas to it.

So, understood as a first premise comparable to those of act utilitarianism and deontology, "An action is right iff it is what a virtuous agent would, characteristically, do in the circumstances," far from being a truism, is, *like* the first premises of the others, uninformative. All three start to be informative only when the second premise is added.

MORAL RULES

A common objection goes as follows:

> Deontology gives a set of clear prescriptions which are readily applicable. But virtue ethics yields only the prescription, "Do what the virtuous agent—the one who is just, honest, charitable, etc.—would do in these circumstances." And this gives me no guidance unless I am (and know I am) a virtuous agent myself—in which case I am hardly in need of it. If I am less than fully virtuous, I shall have no idea what a virtuous agent would do, and hence cannot apply the only prescription virtue ethics has given me. True, act utilitarianism also yields only a

single prescription ("Do what maximizes happiness"), but there are no parallel difficulties in applying that; it too is readily applicable. So there is the way in which virtue ethics' account of right action fails to be action guiding where deontology and utilitarianism succeed.

In response, it is worth pointing out that, if I know that I am far from perfect, and am quite unclear what a virtuous agent would do in the circumstances in which I find myself, the obvious thing to do is to go and ask one, should this be possible. This is far from being a trivial point, for it gives a straightforward explanation of an important aspect of our moral life, namely the fact that we do not always act as "autonomous," utterly self-determining agents, but quite often seek moral guidance from people we think are morally better than ourselves. When I am looking for an excuse to do something I have a horrid suspicion is wrong, I ask my moral inferiors (or peers if I am bad enough), "Wouldn't you do such-and-such if you were in my shoes?" But when I am anxious to do what is right, and do not see my way clear, I go to people I respect and admire: people who I think are kinder, more honest, more just, wiser, than I am myself, and ask them what they would do in my circumstances. How, or indeed whether, utilitarianism and deontology can explain this fact, I do not know, but, as I said, the explanation within the terms of virtue ethics is straightforward. If you want to do what is right, and doing what is right is doing what the virtuous agent would do in the circumstances, then you should find out what she would do if you do not already know.

Moreover, seeking advice from virtuous people is not the only thing an imperfect agent trying to apply the "single prescription" of virtue ethics can do. For it is simply false that, in general, "if I am less than fully virtuous, then I shall have no idea what a virtuous agent would do," as the objection claims. Recall that we are assuming that the virtues have been enumerated as, say, honesty, charity, fidelity, etc. So, *ex hypothesi*, a virtuous agent is one who is honest, charitable, true to her word, etc., So what she characteristically does is what is honest, charitable, true to her word, etc., and not what would be dishonest, uncharitable, untrue to her word. So, given such an enumeration of the virtues, I may well have a perfectly good idea of what the virtuous person would do in my circumstances, despite my own imperfection. Would she lie in her teeth to acquire an unmerited advantage? No, for that would be both dishonest and unjust. Would she help the wounded stranger by the roadside even though he had no right to her help, or pass by on the other side? The former, for that is charitable, and the latter callous. Might she keep a death-bed promise even though living people would benefit from its being broken? Yes, for she is true to her word. And so on.[4]

This second response to the objection that virtue ethics' account of right action fails to be action guiding amounts to a denial of the oft-repeated claim that "virtue ethics does not come up with any rules," (which is another version of the thought that it is concerned with Being rather than Doing), and needs to be supplemented with rules. We can now see that it comes up with a large number of rules. Not only does each virtue generate a prescription—do what is honest, charitable, generous—but each vice a prohibition—do not do what is dishonest, uncharitable, mean.[5]

Once this point about virtue ethics is grasped (and it is remarkable how often it is overlooked), can there remain any reason for thinking that virtue ethics cannot tell us what we should do? Yes, there is one. The reason given is, roughly, that rules such as "Do what is honest, do not do what is uncharitable," are, like the rule "Do what the virtuous agent would do," still the wrong sort of rule, still somehow doomed to fail to provide the action guidance supplied by the rules (or rule) of deontology and act utilitarianism.

But how so? It is true that these rules of virtue ethics (henceforth "v-rules") are couched in terms, or concepts, that are certainly "evaluative" in *some* sense, or senses, of that difficult word. Is it this which dooms them to failure? Surely not, unless many forms of utilitarianism and deontology fail for this reason too.

There are, indeed, some forms of utilitarianism which aim to be entirely "value-free" or empirical, such as those which define happiness in terms of the satisfaction of actual desires or preferences, regardless of their content, or as a mental state whose presence is definitively established by introspection. Such forms run into well-known problems, and have always seemed to me the least plausible, but I accept that anyone who embraces them may consistently complain that v-rules give inferior action guidance in virtue of containing "evaluative" terms. But a utilitarian who wishes to employ any distinction between the higher and lower pleasures, or pronounce on what rational preferences would be, or rely on some list of goods (such as autonomy, friendship, or knowledge of important matters) in defining happiness, must grant that even her single rule is implicitly "evaluative." (This is why, briefly, I think that utilitarianism is not generally immune to the threat of moral relativism or scepticism, as I mentioned above.)

What about deontology? If we concentrate on the single example of lying, defining lying to be "asserting what you believe to be untrue, with the intention of deceiving your hearer(s)," then we might, for a moment, preserve the illusion that a deontologist's rules do not contain "evaluative" terms. But as soon as we remember that few deontologists will want to forego principles of nonmaleficence and (or) beneficence, the illusion vanishes. For these principles, and their corresponding rules (do no evil or harm to others, help others, promote their well-being), rely on terms or concepts which are at least as "evaluative" as those employed in the v-rules.

We see revealed here a further inadequacy in the slogan "Utilitarianism begins with Good, deontology with the Right" when this is taken as committing deontology to making the concept of the Good (and, presumably, the Bad or Evil) somehow derivative from the concept of the Right (and Wrong). A "utilitarian" who relied on the concept of right, or virtuous, action in specifying his concept of happiness would find it hard to shrug off the scare quotes, but no one expects a deontologist to be able to state each of her rules without ever employing a concept of *good* which is not simply the concept of *right action for its own sake*, or without any mention of *evil* or *harm*.

We might also note that few deontologists will rest content with the simple, quasi-biological

"Do not kill," but more refined versions of that rule, such as "Do not murder," or "Do not kill the innocent," once again employ "evaluative" terms, and "Do not kill unjustly" is itself a particular instantiation of a v-rule.

Supposing this point were granted, a deontologist might still claim that the v-rules are markedly inferior to deontological rules as far as providing guidance for children is concerned. Granted, adult deontologists must think hard about what really constitutes harming someone, or promoting their well-being, or respecting their autonomy, or murder, but surely the simple rules we learnt at our mother's knee are indispensable. How could virtue ethics plausibly seek to dispense with these and expect toddlers to grasp "act charitably, honestly, and kindly, don't act unjustly," and so on? Rightly are these concepts described as "thick"! Far too thick for a child to grasp.

Strictly speaking, this objection is rather different from the *general* objection that v-rules fail to provide action guidance, but it arises naturally in the context of the general one and I am more than happy to address it. For it pinpoints a condition of adequacy that any normative ethics must meet, namely that such an ethics must not only come up with action guidance for a clever rational adult, but also generate some account of moral education, of how one generation teaches the next what they should do. But an ethics inspired by Aristotle is unlikely to have forgotten the question of moral education, and the objection fails to hit home. Firstly, the implicit empirical claim that toddlers are taught only the deontologist's rules, not the "think" concepts, is surely false. Sentences such as "Don't do that, it hurts the cat, you mustn't be cruel," "Be kind to your brother, he's only little," "Don't be so mean, so greedy," are commonly addressed to toddlers. For some reason, we do not seem to teach "just" and "unjust" early on, but we certainly teach "fair" and "unfair."

Secondly, why should a proponent of virtue ethics deny the significance of such mother's-knee rules as "Don't lie," "Keep promises," "Help others"? Although it is a mistake (I have claimed) to define a virtuous agent simply as one disposed to act in accordance with deontologist's moral rules, it is a very understandable mistake, given the obvious connection between, for example, the exercise of the virtue of honesty and refraining from lying. Virtue ethicists want to emphasize the fact that, if children are to be taught to be honest, they must be taught to love and prize the truth, and that *merely* teaching them not to lie will not achieve this end. But they need not deny that, to achieve this end, teaching them not to lie is useful, or even indispensable.

So we can see that virtue ethics not only comes up with rules (the v-rules, couched in terms derived from the virtues and vices) but, further, does not exclude the more familiar deontologists' rules. The theoretical distinction between the two is that the familiar rules, and their applications in particular cases, are given entirely different backings. According to deontology, I must not tell this lie because, applying the (correct) rule "Do not lie" to this case, I find that lying is prohibited. According to virtue ethics, I must not tell this lie because it would be dishonest to do so, and dishonesty is a vice.[6]

NOTES

1. For a particularly illuminating critique of Rawls's distinction, see G. Watson, "On the Primacy of Character" (1990). See also Hudson, "What Is Morality All About?," (1990) and Herman, *The Practice of Moral Judgment*, ch. 10, who both challenge the slogan in relation to Kant's deontology.
2. W. Frankena, *Ethics* (1973).
3. Cf. Watson's opening paragraphs in "On the Primacy of Character."
4. Cf. Anscombe: "It would be a great improvement if, instead of "morally wrong," one always named a genus such as "untruthful," "unchaste," "unjust" . . . the answer would sometimes be clear at once." "Modern Moral Philosophy" (1958, repr. 1981), 33.
5. Making this point in earlier articles, I expressed the generated rules adverbially—act honestly, charitably, generously; do not act dishonestly, etc. But the adverbs connote not only doing what the virtuous agent would do, but also doing it "in the way" she would do it, which includes "for the same sort(s) of reason(s)," and it has seemed to me better here to separate out the issue of the virtuous agent's reasons for a later chapter.
6. This clear distinction (between deontology and virtue ethics) is just one of the many things that has been blurred by the recent happy convergence of Kantians and virtue ethicists.

Hindu Values

Debabrata Sen Sharma

Debabrata Sen Sharma teaches Hinduism at the University of Calcutta, India. He is the author of many books and articles on various aspects of Hinduism.

Debabrata Sen Sharma focuses on the values that are most prominent in Hinduism: happiness and well-being. He relates these values to the search for the ultimate unfolding of our true nature.

INTRODUCTION

Hinduism, as is well known, is one of the oldest religions in the world. It has a vast literature and great following even today. It is the most ancient religion in Asia dating back several millennia before Christ. Ancient Hindu scriptures refer to *Sanatana-Dharma*, the religious tradition which has come down to us from time immemorial. It is believed to be eternal in this part of the globe, and lasting as long as man lives on this earth. The word "Hindu" does not appear anywhere in our religious texts. It was coined by the Arabs in the medieval period to classify people of this country belonging to this particular faith.

The socioreligious writers in the past were not merely social thinkers and theoreticians; a large majority of them were seers who had obtained a direct vision of the Supreme Truth. They had developed an intuitive vision which enabled them to look at man as the Universal Being, not belonging to a particular country or conditioned by a particular time. Their perspective was so all-encompassing that nothing was left out which concerned man's existence on the earth. They never talked about man as belonging to one particular faith, but man as entire humanity. Our ancient thinkers looked upon man as the finest specimen of creation on the earth who possesses an innate capacity to elevate himself to the highest level of perfection. They focused their attention on him, considering his problems, seeking to alleviate his suffering.

THE *SANATANA-DHARMA*

Early writers spoke in terms of the universal man (*manava*) and his socioreligious beliefs as the universal religion (*manava dharma*). Rabindranath Tagore explained it as the "religion of man." These writers discussed about the ultimate values, the goal in life which all humanity cherished, irrespective of time or place. Their motto was "regard the entire world as one family."[1] Every devout Hindu still utters the following prayer at the close of every religious ceremony, "let all people be happy, let all be free from disease, let us see the well-being prevailing everywhere, let no person be subject to misery or unhappiness."[2]

This universal outlook was the consequence of the perception that there is one spiritual principle underlying creation: The cosmos or universe, which encompasses not only all humanity, but all animate and inanimate things, is bound by a thread of one Unified Spiritual Principle, as it were. "All

Debabrata Sen Sharma, "Terrorism and Morality" in *Asian Values: Encounter with Diversity* by J. Cauquelin et al., 2000. Routledge.

exists in One, and One exists in all"—this is the supreme understanding of Hinduism's ancient seers, on which their philosophy is based.

Some of the distinguishing characteristics of Hinduism or the *Sanatana-Dharma* are its open-mindedness and its infinite capacity for assimilation from similar religious traditions. These unique qualities in the Hindu religious tradition have provided it with inner strength which has enabled the *Sanatana-Dharma* not only to survive the attacks of other religions, but also to gain strength. Hindu seers welcomed moral and social ideas from outside as they proclaimed "Let thoughts enter into us from all sides." The attitude of confrontation and conflict is not found in Hinduism's religious tradition: it is the "religion of man." For instance, the ideals of non-violence (*ahimsa*), austerity (*tapas*), complete non-attachment (*vairagya*), stress on following the middle path (*madhyama pratipada*) in spiritual discipline and the Eightfold Path (*astanga marga*) figure prominently in Jainism and Buddhism respectively, and have been accepted with some modification and given prominent place by Hinduism's religious thinkers and have enriched Hindu thinking. The Buddha was included as one of many incarnations of God.

One might ask why Sankaracarya and Ramanuja, the protagonists of Vedic religion in a later period were so vehement in their challenge to Jain and Buddhist teachers, refuting their religious thoughts and beliefs, while their teachings had been tolerated and assimilated before. The main reason for this attack was that the Buddhists and Jains did not accept the authority of the Vedas, the holy scriptures of the *Sanatana-Dharma*, and were branded as atheists or nonbelievers, worthy of condemnation by the Vedic schools. Hindu philosophers did not reject the ethical or moral and spiritual code of conduct prescribed by the Buddhists and Jains. The criticism of the Buddhists and Jains by Sankaracarya and others was based on philosophical grounds. In fact, Sankaracarya himself borrowed many philosophical ideas from the Buddhists, especially the *Madhyamika* and *Yogacara* schools and was labelled by later philosophers as pseudoBuddhist. The main cause for the disappearance of Buddhism from India was not criticism by the orthodox Hindu teachers, but lack of royal patronage which declined after the death of Emperor Asoka.

Hindu thinkers always spoke of the purpose of human life, the ultimate destiny, the revelation of man's divine nature, which every individual would eventually reach in his life.

THE NOTION OF VALUE

The notion of value is a Western concept which attempts to shed light on what is valuable or precious to man, or important for the qualitative improvement of his life. It is a subjective notion as it attempts to define what is excellent in life and conducive to his happiness. The Hindus are practical in outlook, they do not believe mere speculation, they define values as principles of life, seeking man's improvement in ethical, spiritual, and social terms so that he may enjoy happiness in this world and attain perfection in the end.

Threefold Values

The threefold values are the moral or ethical values, the spiritual values, and the social values. These systems are not mutually exclusive; they overlap and form one unified set of values. Most of the ancient Indian texts on Hindu law and the epics, the *Puranas* and others such as Kautilyas *Arthasastra*,[3] refer to values which aim at achieving all-round improvement in the quality of life, making men happy and well contented. The two ideals in life are discussed in the texts: first is the ideal of the upliftment of man in the worldly sense, the enjoyment of material comforts and happiness; second, the ideal of the attainment of the Supreme Goal in life, the unfolding of man's true spiritual nature.

Moral Values

The moral or ethical values advocated by the Hindu, Buddhist, or Jain thinkers serve a dual purpose: the purification of the mind, culminating in the revelation of the self. Moral values emphasize excellence in social behaviour, and the removal of all causes for conflict between one individual and another. The individual striving for excellence should abstain from violence in any form, and should refrain from causing injury to anyone through deed, word, or thought. This is called noninjury (*ahimsa*). It has been asserted that the individual adopting *ahimsa* becomes completely fearless and invincible. Every individual should always stick to the truth and follow the path of righteousness. He should never deviate from the path of Truth, for Truth always triumphs (*satyam eva jayate*). Mahatma Gandhi tried to apply the ideal of truth to the politicians. Linked with this is the virtue of honesty which one should observe in one's behaviour. Hypocrisy has no place in the behaviour of a person whose goal is self-purification. No one should take by force that which does not belong to him; he should not steal. Men should observe sexual restraint and man should not allow himself to be seized by passion and lust as these desires not only disturb the tranquility of mind but also pervert his social behaviour. The exercise of self-control advocated by our religious thinkers does not imply repression and inhibition so much talked about today by Western psychologists, for these have been condemned by Lord Krishna in the *Bhagavad Gita*. The *Gita* says that "even a mind that knows the right path can be dragged from his path when the senses are so unruly. But he who controls the senses and recollects his mind and fixes it on the God, I [Lord Krishna] call him the illumined."[4] Direction rather than repression is the method prescribed by our holy men for achieving self-control.

A person striving to gain excellence should not amass more wealth than is essential for the maintenance of his life. Man has a natural propensity for amassing material wealth for his personal enjoyment. Little does he know that the thirst for enjoyment, for the gratification of his senses, cannot be satiated. He should purify his mind by observing cleanliness, both external and internal. One should cultivate a sense of nonattachment towards worldly goods in order to achieve contentment of mind; the mind then becomes free from tension. One of the methods for conserving energy

is to observe silence. Anger, arrogance, and vanity are considered vices which inhibit the achievement of purification. The *Bhagavad Gita* refers to these vices as demonic tendencies that deprave men (XIV, 1–4). Anger is considered to be the worst of all vices as it is said to delude man, and he loses the power of discrimination between good and bad, useful and harmful. Hindu scriptures stress self-examination in order to develop the ability to seek perfection. Moral or ethical values, when put into practice, not only improve the personal life and behaviour of the individual, but they also contribute to a better society.

Spiritual Values

The spiritual values advocated by the practitioners of Yoga and by Indian teachers are similar to moral values. Purification of the mind is an essential prerequisite for spiritual studies. The values which a spiritual aspirant should practise include the withdrawal of the senses from the sense objects by practising austerity as enjoined in our scriptures. He should develop a renunciatory attitude in life. The *Isavasy-opanisad* prescribes enjoyment through the practice of renunciation.[5] Renunciation is the beginning, the middle, and the end of spiritual life. The *Bhagavad Gita* regards renunciation as inseparable from the yoga of action, the yoga of knowledge, and the yoga of devotion. However, it does not imply adopting a monastic way of life, for it can be practised by all, the monk as well as the householder who pursues the spiritual path. Other-worldliness does not mean shunning the duties and obligations of family life. The *Bhagavad Gita* teaches that the duties of life can be undertaken with a heart free from attachment and thoughts of worldly gain. It insists on the performance of one's secular duties (*svadharma*) in the spirit of yoga in the initial stage, but later, when following the spiritual path, all *dharmas* or worldly duties can be abandoned and refuge can be taken in the Supreme Being. Complete detachment and self-surrender are the best ways for realizing the divine consciousness, thereby attaining eternal life and infinite peace. The ultimate goal of a spiritual aspirant, in the

Indian view, is to be released from the cycles of birth and death, by realizing the true nature of the self according to some schools of spiritual thought, or by realizing one's divine nature according to others. Some Hindu religious schools teach that the discovery of the presence of the Divine in themselves by spiritual aspirants is the highest ideal. The religious texts of these schools declare that every individual being is potentially divine, but he is not aware of this because he is enveloped in a thick veil of ignorance. The spark of divinity lying latent in him must be kindled by the knowledge of his real nature. The Vedic seer therefore prays to the Supreme Being—"lead me from the untruth to the truth, from darkness to the light, from death to immortality."[6] The cherished goal of man is to make the whole world divine, according to some of our spiritual masters. Hindu seers do not hope to see individual but collective excellence, in order that the kingdom of heaven may be built on this earth.

The most refined ideal, the virtue of love, arises from the realization that one spirit permeates all creation. The sage Yajnavalkya told Gargi, his wife, "One does not love his son because he is his offspring, but because he sees his own reflection in his children. His wife is not dear to him because she is wedded to him. He loves his wife because he sees his own image in her." The presence of the universal self in the individual arouses the spontaneous feeling of love and this is the most ennobling and sanctifying experience that men can ever have. Our scriptures advise us to feel the presence of God, the Divine Being everywhere, in every plant and creature; they advise us to see God in each other. This God is not a deity different from our inner self: Until and unless we experience the presence of the universal self in all creation, we shall not break through the barrier of individuality which we have ourselves created.

Social Values

Social values cannot be divorced from the moral and spiritual values which the individual has been encouraged to pursue by Hindu religious teachers. Social values are seen as integral to moral and spiritual values: The main aim of social values is to improve society as a whole and thus benefit the individual. This universal outlook is undoubtedly the unique characteristic of the Hindu religious tradition which is not seen elsewhere. Hindu teachers always stressed the need for enlarging our perspective, giving up narrowness and selfishness, and developing the feeling of brotherhood among all human beings. When Swami Vivekananda addressed learned scholars and representatives of different faiths in the Parliament of Religions at Chicago more than a hundred years ago using the words "O brothers and sisters of America," it created a sensation. No one before him had addressed the gathering in that way; no one had experienced the oneness of people living together in society. The young Swami had realized the presence of the universal being, his inner self in the gathering of people, and these spontaneous words endeared him to all.

Our teachers advised us to cultivate a feeling of respect for elders and show hospitality to guests. The seer in one of the *Upanisads* gives this advice to his students, who on completing their study in the house of the teacher are about to leave: "Regard your mother as goddess and treat her accordingly. Look upon your father as God and treat him accordingly. Consider the guest as a god and show him due respect." This exemplifies a noble ideal. One should always honour the teacher, as he is responsible for the student's enlightenment. We should respect others, we should never speak disparagingly about anyone.

Hindu law enjoins man to keep a sizeable part of his income to be given to the poor and needy (*dana*). Charity brings people nearer to each other; it creates fellow feeling. The Hindu ancient texts advise giving charity in secret; in that way the donor cannot demonstrate his superiority, which is considered to be sinful.

The values of *maitri* (friendliness) and *karuna* (mercy) are essential in an enlightened being, and their importance has been emphasized by both Hindus and Buddhists.

The Hindu teachers were aware that it is not possible to prescribe a set of absolute values or a standard code of conduct applicable to all men on the earth. They postulated that we should follow whichever virtue leads to the attainment of the Supreme Goal in life, i.e. achievement of liberation or revelation of our real nature. We should avoid following the path of vice and refrain from sinful actions as they obstruct our realization of the Supreme Goal. Hindu teachers advise that we should observe the conduct of people who were better trained morally and better placed in society: "Perform only those actions which might be regarded as faultless by the society. When you are faced with a dilemma and are unable to decide what is good and what is not, look towards the conduct of those Brahmins [learned and wise people] who are free from blemish, follow their path."[7] It is interesting to note that the Greek scholar Aristotle also expressed the view that the opinion of a trained character should count as the principle of moral authority when one feels bewildered and is not able to choose the way of moral action on account of ignorance.

The importance of the voice of our conscience was recognized by our ancient teachers. When we are faced with a crisis, it is conscience which puts us on the right road. We should not still the voice of conscience by arrogance and vanity, but should hear it in our inner being if our minds are pure. Tolerance of other views is another virtue which can remove the cause of conflict and discord, making our lives peaceful and happy. The advice given by Jain teachers is worthy of emulation; they said that every object of knowledge is multidimensional and we can grasp only one dimension at a time. Our knowledge is always partial and one-sided, but is not totally false; it is incomplete. We should always beware of our limitations and refrain from attacking the perception of others.

THE ROLE OF *KARMA* IN MAINTAINING MORAL BALANCE

According to the doctrine of *Karma*, accepted by all ancient faiths in India with the sole exception of the hedonist materialists, every action we perform leaves residual impressions on our minds which accumulate without our being aware of

them. After a time, these impressions, called "seeds" of action, produce certain tendencies which motivate all our future actions. All our actions come under two categories: meritorious deeds and sinful deeds, producing in turn agreeable results and painful results. There is a well-known biblical proverb "for whatsoever a man soweth, that shall he reap."[8] Such is the law of nature. The *Bhagavad Gita* prescribes the yoga of *Karma* which enables us to escape from the bondage created by our actions. Our faith in the doctrine of *Kharma* and the fear of suffering caused by sinful deeds have served as a deterrent in the past; it has helped society in maintaining its moral balance, forcing people to follow the path of virtue.

THE EFFECT OF CASTE ON HINDU SOCIETY

Modern social scientists and anthropologists blame the old Hindu laws for creating an artificial hierarchy in an otherwise homogenous society by introducing the caste system. There is no doubt that the caste system as it is prevalent now, is a curse responsible for many ills. It has created divisions and raised artificial barriers between people professing one faith and one spiritual philosophy. One tragic consequence of the caste system is that it has negated the basic tenet of Hindu philosophy—namely, the oneness of the Spirit pervading all creation.

The much maligned caste system in modern Hindu society is only a degenerated form of another kind of classification made by the Vedic seers, which was based on men's different capacities and inclinations. It was called *Varna-Vyavastha* (literally, the classification based on the "colour" of the individual). The earliest reference to this unique kind of division of Hindu society is found in one of the hymns in the *Rgveda*, where all human society is conceptualized as the body of the Universal Being, called *Purusa* (the primordial man), and the different classes of humans as his different limbs. It was said that the *Brahmans*, the most talented section of the society from his mouth, the *Ksatriyas*, people of the warrior class from his hands, the *Vaisyas*, experts in business and agriculture from his belly, and *Sudras* or people with no talent emerged from his feet.[9] The hierarchy reflected in this metaphorical description shows that the Vedic seers did not divide society on an arbitrary basis. They noticed that men do not possess the same talent, or capacity for work, because this is against the law of nature. Variety and differentiation is inherent in the act of creation. The Vedic seers had noticed this inequality inherent in men, and devised this classification as a way of maintaining social balance. It was a sound and scientific principle for a division of labour in which the capacity and the inclination of the individual members were taken into account.

This kind of hierarchy lasted until the age of the epics, as may be evident from a statement made by Lord Krishna in the *Bhagavad Gita*, where he declares "I [the Supreme Being] created this fourfold *Varna*-division on the basis of talent, qualities, and inclination of individual beings for the efficient functioning of Society."[10] There are many cases recorded in the Vedic texts of persons born in the family of inferior castes having elevated themselves to a higher caste by dint of endeavour, cultivating and developing the superior qualities generally seen in people of a higher class (*Varnas*). This situation continued till the end of the Vedic age and the beginning of the age of the epics.

When the Hindu law makers saw that people made intertribal marriages, throwing all past practice to the winds, the ancient hierarchical stratification was replaced by a rigid mode of class division based on the birth of the individual, in the family. The original flexible division of society based on the different talents and capacities of the individual, degenerated in the course of time and was forced into a fixed order. This happened just before the appearance of Manu, the father of modern Hindu law. It appears that the need for maintaining the purity of different classes (or the operation of the law of eugenics) became the prime concern for the Hindu lawmakers in the post-Vedic period, with the disastrous consequences with which we are all so familiar. Despite the attempt by the Hindu social reformers like Guru Nanak, Swami Dayanand, and Raja Ram Mohan Roy to do away with the caste system, this stigma of Hindu social structure persists today. Political leaders have recently wrought havoc by exploiting the caste-based division of Hindu society purely for their personal gain. The situation on this front is grave indeed.

THE PRESENT SITUATION

There is always a gap between theory and practice, and this applies equally to the pursuit of values by Hindus in modern times. It is unfortunate that the country which once preached sublime spiritual ideals and exalted values should face crisis and confusion today in moral and spiritual fields. The educated youth of India today has, in the name of modernity and progress, not only abandoned the path shown by our forefathers, they have also turned blind eye to our rich and glorious past. The glamour of the modern Western way of living has blinded their vision to such an extent that they now ape Western materialistic utilitarian pursuits. The only idea that catches their imagination today is the value of material comforts of life at all costs. The pursuit of a materialistic goal is nothing new or alien in India. The hedonist schools like Carvaka and Ajivaka in the Buddhist and post-Buddhist periods preached a materialistic philosophy of life, but they were vehemently criticized by all other schools of Indian philosophical thought. Now the old spiritual ideals have been replaced by new materialistic goals, old values have been abandoned for a new set of materialistic values. Young people have little faith in the Hindu doctrine of *Karma*.

One example of the changes in modern Hindu society is the joint family system. It was the norm in the past for one family of parents and grandparents, brothers and their families to live together. The grandchildren learnt moral values and good conduct from their grandfathers and grandmothers through stories. Men and women learnt the value of tolerance and adjustment by living together in the joint family. This joint family system has been replaced by single family units in the towns for economic reasons, depriving children of the wisdom of their grandparents. Materialistic consumerism has brought with it a form of spiritual decline as fewer and fewer people continue to follow the old ideals and cherish the age-old values of life that are perennial as well as universal.

NOTES

1. Vasudhaiva Kutumbakam.
2. *Sarve sukhinah santu sarve santu niramaya / sarvatra bhadrani pasya ma kascid duhkhabhag bhavet.*
3. Vedic texts on *Dharmasastra* are the *Grhyasutras*, the *Kalpasutras*, etc. Later texts on Hindu law, that are popular, are the *Manusmrti*, the *Yajnavalkya smrti*, the *Parasara smrti*. The epics are the *Ramayana* and the *Mahabharata*. The *Purana* texts are eighteen in number, and the *Arthasastra* of Kautilya is a well-known ancient work on Indian policy.
4. *Bhagavad Gita* Chap. II, verse 60 s.
5. Op. cit.: *Tena tyaktena bhunjitha.* v. 1.
6. *Asato ma sad gamaya, tamaso ma jyotir gamaya, mrtyor mamrtam gamaya/Upanisad.*
7. Taittiriya Upanisad, Siksavalli.
8. Galatians 6:7.
9. Op. cit., X, 90, 12.
10. Op. cit., IV, 13.

Images of Relationship

Carol Gilligan

Carol Gilligan is a developmental psychologist and professor of education at Harvard University. She is the author of *In a Different Voice* (1982), *Remapping the Moral Domain* (1988), and many articles.

Gilligan focuses on different responses by males and females to the Heinz dilemma. Heinz is faced with either breaking into a drug store and stealing a drug his sick wife needs to live, or watching his wife die. Boys tend to see the problem as a self-contained problem in "moral logic" involving a reconciliation of conflict factors. Girls tend to see the problem as one of relationships. These different approaches correlate with different, gendered approaches to morality.

In 1914, with his essay "On Narcissism,"[1] Freud swallows his distaste at the thought of "abandoning observation for barren theoretical controversy" and extends his map of the psychological domain. Tracing the development of the capacity to love, which he equates with maturity and psychic health, he locates its origins in the contrast between love for the mother and love for the self. But in thus dividing the world of love into narcissism and "object" relationships, he finds that while men's development becomes clearer, women's becomes increasingly opaque. The problem arises because the contrast between mother and self yields two different images of relationships. Relying on the imagery of men's lives in charting the course of human growth, Freud is unable to trace in women the development of relationships, morality, or a clear sense of self. This difficulty in fitting the logic of his theory to women's experience leads him in the end to set women apart, marking their relationships, like their sexual life, as "a "dark continent" for psychology" (1926, p. 212).

Thus the problem of interpretation that shadows the understanding of women's development arises from the differences observed in their experience of relationships. To Freud, though living surrounded by women and otherwise seeing so much and so well, women's relationships seemed increasingly mysterious, difficult to discern, and hard to describe. While this mystery indicates how theory can blind observation, it also suggests that development in women is masked by a particular conception of human relationships. Since the imagery of relationships shapes the narrative of human development, the inclusion of women, by changing that imagery, implies a change in the entire account.

The shift in imagery that creates the problem in interpreting women's development is elucidated by the moral judgments of two eleven-year-old children, a boy and a girl, who see, in the same dilemma, two very different moral problems. While current theory brightly illuminates the line and the logic of the boy's thought, it casts scant light on that of the girl. The choice of a girl whose moral judgments elude existing categories of developmental assessment is meant to highlight the issue of interpretation rather than to exemplify sex differences per se. Adding a new line of interpretation, based on the imagery of the girl's thought, makes it possible not only to see development where previously development was not discerned, but also to consider differences in the understanding of relationships without scaling these differences from better to worse.

The two children were in the same sixth-grade class at school and were participants in the rights and responsibilities study, designed to explore different conceptions of morality and self. The sample selected for this study was chosen to focus the variables of gender and age while maximizing developmental potential by holding constant, at a high level, the factors of intelligence, education, and social class that have been associated with moral development, at least as measured by existing scales. The two children in question, Amy and Jake, were both bright and articulate and, at least in their eleven-year-old aspirations, resisted easy categories of sex-role stereotyping, since Amy aspired to become a scientist while Jake preferred English to math. Yet their moral judgments seem initially to confirm familiar notions about differences between the sexes, suggesting that the edge girls have on moral development during the early school years gives way at puberty with the ascendance of formal logical thought in boys.

The dilemma that these eleven-year-olds were asked to resolve was one in the series devised by Kohlberg to measure moral development in adolescence by presenting a conflict between moral norms and exploring the logic of its resolution. In this particular dilemma, a man named Heinz considers whether or not to steal a drug which he cannot afford to buy in order to save the life of his wife. In the standard format of Kohlberg's interviewing procedure, the description of the dilemma itself—Heinz's predicament, the wife's disease, the druggist's refusal to lower his price—is followed by the question, "Should Heinz steal the drug?" The reasons for and against stealing are then explored through a series of questions that vary and extend the parameters of the dilemma in a way designed to reveal the underlying structure of moral thought.

Jake, at eleven, is clear from the outset that Heinz should steal the drug. Constructing the dilemma, as Kohlberg did, as a conflict between the values of property and life, he discerns the logical priority of life and uses that logic to justify his choice:

> For one thing, a human life is worth more than money, and if the druggist only makes $1,000, he is still going to live, but if Heinz doesn't steal the drug, his wife is going to die. (*Why is life worth more than money?*) Because the druggist can get a thousand dollars later from rich people with cancer, but Heinz can't get his wife again. (*Why not?*) Because people are all different and so you couldn't get Heinz's wife again.

Asked whether Heinz should steal the drug if he does not love his wife, Jake replies that he should, saying that not only is there "a difference between hating and killing," but also, if Heinz were caught, "the judge would probably think it was the right thing to do." Asked about the fact that, in stealing, Heinz would be breaking the law, he says that "the laws have mistakes, and you can't go writing up a law for everything that you can imagine."

Thus, while taking the law into account and recognizing its function in maintaining social order (the judge, Jake says, "should give Heinz the lightest possible sentence"), he also sees the law as man-made and therefore subject to error and change. Yet his judgment that Heinz should steal the drug, like his view of the law as having mistakes, rests on the assumption of agreement, a societal consensus around moral values that allows one to know and expect others to recognize what is "the right thing to do."

Fascinated by the power of logic, this eleven-year-old boy locates truth in math, which, he says, is "the only thing that is totally logical." Considering the moral dilemma to be "sort of like a math problem with humans," he sets it up as an equation and proceeds to work out the solution. Since his solution is rationally derived, he assumes that anyone following reason would arrive at the same conclusion and thus that a judge would also consider stealing to be the right thing for Heinz to do. Yet he is also aware of the limits of logic. Asked whether there is a right answer to moral problems, Jake replies that "there can only be right and wrong in judgment," since the parameters of action are variable and complex. Illustrating how actions undertaken with the best of intentions can eventuate in the most disastrous of consequences, he says, "like if you give an old lady your seat on the trolley, if you are in a trolley crash and that seat goes through the window, it might be that reason that the old lady dies."

Theories of developmental psychology illuminate well the position of this child, standing at the juncture of childhood and adolescence, at what Piaget describes as the pinnacle of childhood intelligence, and beginning through thought to discover a wider universe of possibility. The moment of preadolescence is caught by the conjunction of formal operational thought with a description of self still anchored in the factual parameters of his childhood world—his age, his town, his father's occupation, the substance of his likes, dislikes, and beliefs. Yet as his self-description radiates the self-confidence of a child who has arrived, in Erikson's terms, at a favorable balance of industry over inferiority—competent, sure of himself, and knowing well the rules of the game—so his emergent capacity for formal thought, his ability to think about thinking and to reason things out in a logical way, frees him from dependence on authority and allows him to find solutions to problems by himself.

This emergent autonomy follows the trajectory that Kohlberg's six stages of moral development trace, a three-level progression from an egocentric understanding of fairness based on individual need (stages one and two), to a conception of fairness anchored in the shared conventions of societal agreement (stages three and four), and finally to a principled understanding of fairness that rests on the free-standing logic of equality and reciprocity (stages five and six). While this boy's judgments at eleven are scored as conventional on Kohlberg's scale, a mixture of stages three and four, his ability to bring deductive logic to bear on the solution of moral dilemmas, to differentiate morality from law, and to see how laws can be considered to have mistakes, points toward the principled conception of justice that Kohlberg equates with moral maturity.

In contrast, Amy's response to the dilemma conveys a very different impression, an image of development stunted by a failure of logic, an inability to think for herself. Asked if Heinz should steal the drug, she replies in a way that seems evasive and unsure:

> Well, I don't think so. I think there might be other ways besides stealing it, like if he could borrow the money or make a loan or something, but he really shouldn't steal the drug—but his wife shouldn't die either.

Asked why he should not steal the drug, she considers neither property nor law but rather the effect that theft could have on the relationship between Heinz and his wife:

> If he stole the drug, he might save his wife then, but if he did, he might have to go to jail, and then his wife might get sicker again, and he couldn't get more of the drug, and it might not be good. So, they should really just talk it out and find some other way to make the money.

Seeing in the dilemma not a math problem with humans but a narrative of relationships that extends over time, Amy envisions the wife's continuing need for her husband and the husband's continuing concern for his wife and seeks to respond to the druggist's need in a way that would sustain rather than sever connection. Just as she ties the wife's survival to the preservation of relationships, so she considers the value of the wife's life in a context of relationships, saying that it would be wrong to let her die because, "if she died, it hurts a lot of people and it hurts her." Since Amy's moral judgment is grounded in the belief that, "if somebody has something that would keep somebody alive, then it's not right not to give it to them," she considers the problem in the dilemma to arise not from the druggist's assertion of rights but from his failure of response.

As the interviewer proceeds with the series of questions that follow from Kohlberg's construction of the dilemma, Amy's answers remain essentially unchanged, the various probes serving neither to elucidate nor to modify her initial response. Whether or not Heinz loves his wife, he still shouldn't steal or let her die; if it were a stranger dying instead, Amy says that "if the stranger didn't have anybody near or anyone she knew," then Heinz should try to save her life, but he should not steal the drug. But as the interviewer conveys through the repetition of questions that the answers she gave were not heard or not right, Amy's confidence begins to diminish, and her replies become more constrained and unsure. Asked again why Heinz should not steal the drug, she simply repeats, "Because it's not right." Asked again to explain why, she states again that theft would not be a good solution, adding lamely, "if he took it, he might not know how to give it to his wife, and so his wife might still die." Failing to see the dilemma as a self-contained problem in moral logic, she does not discern the internal structure of its resolution; as she constructs the problem differently herself, Kohlberg's conception completely evades her.

Instead, seeing a world comprised of relationships rather than of people standing alone, a world that coheres through human connection rather than through systems of rules, she finds the puzzle in the dilemma to lie in the failure of the druggist to respond to the wife. Saying that "it is not right for someone to die when their life could be saved," she assumes that if the druggist were to see the consequences of his refusal to lower his price, he would realize that "he should just give it to the wife and then have the husband pay back the money later." Thus she considers the solution to the dilemma to lie in making the wife's condition more salient to the druggist or, that failing, in appealing to others who are in a position to help.

Just as Jake is confident the judge would agree that stealing is the right thing for Heinz to do, so Amy is confident that, "if Heinz and the druggist had talked it out long enough, they could reach something besides stealing." As he considers the law to "have mistakes," so she sees this drama as a mistake, believing that the world should just share things more and then people wouldn't have to steal. Both children thus recognize the need for agreement but see it as mediated in different ways—he impersonally through systems of logic and law, she personally through communication in relationship. Just as he relies on the conventions of logic to deduce the solution to this dilemma, assuming these conventions to be shared, so she relies on a process of communication, assuming connection and believing that her voice will be heard. Yet while his assumptions about agreement are confirmed by the convergence in logic between his answers and the questions posed, her assumptions are belied by the failure of communication, the interviewer's inability to understand her response.

Although the frustration of the interview with Amy is apparent in the repetition of questions and its ultimate circularity, the problem of interpretation is focused by the assessment of her response. When considered in the light of Kohlberg's definition of the stages and sequence of moral development, her moral judgments appear to be a full stage lower in maturity than those of the boy. Scored as a mixture of stages two and three, her responses seem to reveal a feeling of powerlessness in the world, an inability to think systematically about the concepts of morality or law, a reluctance to challenge authority or to examine the logic of received moral truths, a failure even to conceive of acting directly to save a life or to consider that such action, if taken, could possibly have an effect. As her reliance on relationships seems to reveal a continuing dependence and vulnerability, so her belief in communication as the mode through which to resolve moral dilemmas appears naive and cognitively immature.

Yet Amy's description of herself conveys a markedly different impression. Once again, the hallmarks of the preadolescent child depict a child secure in her sense of herself, confident in the substance of her beliefs, and sure of her ability to do something of value in the world. Describing herself at eleven as "growing and changing," she says that she "sees some things differently now, just because I know myself really well now, and I know a lot more about the world." Yet the world she knows is a different world from that refracted by Kohlberg's construction of Heinz's dilemma. Her world is a world of relationships and psychological truths where an awareness of the connection between people gives rise to a recognition of responsibility for one another, a perception of the need for response. Seen in this light, her understanding of morality as arising from the recognition of relationship, her belief in communication as the mode of conflict resolution, and her conviction that the solution to the dilemma will follow from its compelling representation seem far from naive or cognitively immature. Instead, Amy's judgments contain the insights central to an ethic of care, just as Jake's judgments reflect the logic of the justice approach. Her incipient awareness of the "method of truth," the central tenet of nonviolent conflict resolution, and her belief in the restorative activity of care, lead her to see the actors in the dilemma arrayed not as opponents in a contest of rights but as members of a network of relationships on whose continuation they all depend. Consequently, her solution to the dilemma lies in activating the network by communication, securing the inclusion of the wife by strengthening rather than severing connections.

But the different logic of Amy's response calls attention to the interpretation of the interview itself. Conceived as an interrogation, it appears instead as a dialogue, which takes on moral dimensions of its own, pertaining to the interviewer's uses of power and to the manifestations of respect. With this shift in the conception of the interview, it immediately becomes clear that the interviewer's problem in understanding Amy's response stems from the fact that Amy is answering a different question from the one the interviewer thought had been posed. Amy is considering not *whether* Heinz should act in this situation ("*should* Heinz steal the drug?") but rather *how* Heinz should act in response to his awareness of his wife's need ("Should Heinz *steal* the drug?"). The interviewer takes the mode of action for granted, presuming it to be a matter of fact; Amy assumes the necessity for action and considers what form it should take. In the interviewer's failure to imagine a response not dreamt of in Kohlberg's moral philosophy lies the failure to hear Amy's question and to see the logic in her response, to discern that what appears, from one perspective, to be an evasion of the dilemma signifies in other terms a recognition of the problem and a search for a more adequate solution.

Thus in Heinz's dilemma these two children see two very different moral problems—Jake a conflict between life and property that can be resolved by logical deduction, Amy a fracture of human relationship that must be mended with its own thread. Asking different questions that arise from different conceptions of the moral domain, the children arrive at answers that fundamentally diverge, and the arrangement of these answers as successive stages on a scale of increasing moral maturity calibrated by the logic of the boy's response misses the different truth revealed in the judgment of the girl. To the question, "What does he see that she does not?" Kohlberg's theory provides a ready response, manifest in the scoring of Jake's judgments a full stage higher than Amy's in moral maturity; to the question, "What does she see that he does not?" Kohlberg's theory has nothing to say. Since most of her responses fall through the sieve of Kohlberg's scoring system, her responses appear from his perspective to lie outside the moral domain.

Yet just as Jake reveals a sophisticated understanding of the logic of justification, so Amy is equally sophisticated in her understanding of the nature of choice. Recognizing that "if both the roads went in totally separate ways, if you pick one, you'll never know what would happen if you went the other way," she explains that "that's the chance you have to take, and like I said, it's just really a guess." To illustrate her point "in a simple way," she describes her choice to spend the summer at camp:

> I will never know what would have happened if I had stayed here, and if something goes wrong at camp, I'll never know if I stayed here if it would have been better. There's really no way around it because there's no way you can do both at once, so you've got to decide, but you'll never know.

In this way, these two eleven-year-old children, both highly intelligent and perceptive about life, though in different ways, display different modes of moral understanding, different ways of thinking about conflict and choice. In resolving Heinz's dilemma, Jake relies on theft to avoid confrontation and turns to the law to mediate the dispute. Transposing a hierarchy of power into a hierarchy of values, he defuses a potentially explosive conflict between people by casting it as an impersonal conflict of claims. In this way, he abstracts the moral problem from the interpersonal situation, finding in the logic of fairness an objective way to decide who will win the dispute. But this hierarchical ordering, with its imagery of winning and losing and the potential for violence which it contains, gives way in Amy's construction of the dilemma to a network of connection, a web of relationships that is sustained by a process of communication. With this shift, the moral problem changes from one of unfair domination, the imposition of property over life, to one of unnecessary exclusion, the failure of the druggist to respond to the wife.

This shift in the formulation of the moral problem and the concomitant change in the imagery of relationships appears in the responses of two eight-year-old children, Jeffrey and Karen, asked to describe a situation in which they were not sure what was the right thing to do:

Jeffrey When I really want to go to my friends and my mother is cleaning the cellar, I think about my friends, and then I think about my mother, and then I think about the right thing to do. (*But how do you know it's the right thing to do?*) Because some things go before other things.

Karen I have a lot of friends, and I can't always play with all of them, so everybody's going to have to take a turn, because they're all my friends. But like if someone's all alone, I'll play with them. (*What kinds of things do you think about when you are trying to make that decision?*) Um, someone all alone, loneliness.

While Jeffrey sets up a hierarchical ordering to resolve a conflict between desire and duty, Karen describes a network of relationships that includes all of her friends. Both children deal with the issues of exclusion and priority created by choice, but while Jeffrey thinks about what goes first, Karen focuses on who is left out.

The contrasting images of hierarchy and network in children's thinking about moral conflict and choice illuminate two views of morality which are complementary rather than sequential or opposed. But this construction of differences goes against the bias of developmental theory toward ordering differences in a hierarchical mode. The correspondence between the order of developmental theory and the structure of the boys' thought contrasts with the disparity between existing theory and the structure manifest in the thought of the girls. Yet in neither comparison does one child's judgment appear as a precursor of the other's position. Thus, questions arise concerning the relation between these perspectives: What is the significance of this difference, and how do these two modes of thinking connect? These questions are elucidated by considering the relationship between the eleven-year-old children's understanding of morality and their descriptions of themselves:

(*How would you describe yourself to yourself?*)

Jake Perfect. That's my conceited side. What do you want—any way that I choose to describe myself?

Amy You mean my character? (*What do you think?*) Well, I don't know. I'd describe myself as, well, what do you mean?

(*If you had to describe the person you are in a way that you yourself would know it was you, what would you say?*)

Jake I'd start off with eleven years old. Jake [last name]. I'd have to add that I live in [town], because that is a big part of me, and also that my father is a doctor, because I think that does change me a little bit, and that I don't believe in crime, except for when your name is Heinz; think school is boring, because I think that kind of changes your character a little bit. I don't sort of know how to describe myself, because I don't know how to read my personality. (*If you had to describe the way you actually would describe yourself what would you say?*) I like corny jokes. I don't really like to get down to work, but I can do all the stuff in school. Every single problem that I have seen in school I have been able to do, except for ones that take knowledge, and after I do the reading, I have been able to do them, but sometimes I don't want to waste my time on easy homework. And also I'm crazy about sports. I think, unlike a lot of people, that the world still has hope . . . Most people that I know I like, and I have the good life, pretty much as good as any I have seen, and I am tall for my age.

Amy Well, I'd say that I was someone who likes school and studying, and that's what I want to do with my life. I want to be some kind of a scientist or something, and I want to do things, and I want to help people. And I think that's what kind of person I am, or what kind of person I try to be. And that's probably how I'd describe myself. And I want to do something to help other people. (*Why is that?*) Well, because I think that this world has a lot of problems, and I think that everybody should try to help somebody else in some way, and the way I'm choosing is through science.

In the voice of the eleven-year-old boy, a familiar form of self-definition appears, resonating to the inscription of the young Stephen Daedalus in his geography book: "himself, his name and where he was," and echoing the descriptions that appear in *Our Town*, laying out across the coordinates of time and space a hierarchical order in which to define one's place. Describing himself as distinct by locating his particular position in the world, Jake sets himself apart from that world by his abilities, his beliefs, and his height. Although Amy also enumerates her likes, her wants, and her beliefs, she locates herself in relation to the world, describing herself through actions that bring her into connection with others, elaborating ties through her ability to provide help. To Jake's ideal of perfection, against which he measures the worth of himself, Amy counterposes an ideal of care, against which she measures the worth of her activity. While she places herself in relation to the world and chooses to help others through science, he places the world in relation to himself as it defines his character, his position, and the quality of his life.

The contrast between a self defined through separation and a self delineated through connection, between a self measured against an abstract ideal of perfection and a self assessed through particular activities of care, becomes clearer and the implications of this contrast extend by considering the different

ways these children resolve a conflict between responsibility to others and responsibility to self. The question about responsibility followed a dilemma posed by a woman's conflict between her commitments to work and to family relationships. While the details of this conflict color the text of Amy's response, Jake abstracts the problem of responsibility from the context in which it appears, replacing the themes of intimate relationship with his own imagery of explosive connection:

(*When responsibility to oneself and responsibility to others conflict, how should one choose?*)

Jake You go about one-fourth to the others and three-fourths to yourself.

Amy Well, it really depends on the situation. If you have a responsibility with somebody else, then you should keep it to a certain extent, but to the extent that it is really going to hurt you or stop you from doing something that you really, really want, then I think maybe you should put yourself first. But if it is your responsibility to somebody really close to you, you've just got to decide in that situation which is more important, yourself or that person, and like I said, it really depends on what kind of person you are and how you feel about the other person or persons involved.

(*Why?*)

Jake Because the most important thing in your decision should be yourself, don't let yourself be guided totally by other people, but you have to take them into consideration. So, if what you want to do is blow yourself up with an atom bomb, you should maybe blow yourself up with a hand grenade because you are thinking about your neighbors who would die also.

Amy Well, like some people put themselves and things for themselves before they put other people, and some people really care about other people. Like, I don't think your job is as important as somebody that you really love, like your husband or your parents or a very close friend. Somebody that you really care for—or if it's just your responsibility to your job or somebody that you barely know, then maybe you go first—but if it's somebody that you really love and love as much or even more than you love yourself, you've got to decide what you really love more, that person, or that thing, or yourself. (*And how do you do that?*) Well, you've got to think about it, and you've got to think about both sides, and you've got to think which would be better for everybody or better for yourself, which is more important, and which will make everybody happier. Like if the other people can get somebody else to do it, whatever it is, or don't really need you specifically, maybe it's better to do what you want, because the other people will be just fine with somebody else so they'll still be happy, and then you'll be happy too because you'll do what you want.

(*What does responsibility mean?*)

Jake It means pretty much thinking of others when I do something, and like if I want to throw a rock, not throwing it at a window, because I thought of the people who would have to pay for that window, not doing it just for yourself, because you have to live with other people and live with your community, and if you do something that hurts them all, a lot of people will end up suffering, and that is sort of the wrong thing to do.

Amy That other people are counting on you to do something, and you can't just decide, "Well, I'd rather do this or that." (*Are there other kinds of responsibility?*) Well, to yourself. If something looks really fun but you might hurt yourself doing it because you don't really know how to do it and your friends say, "Well, come on, you can do it, don't worry," if you're really scared to do it, it's your responsibility to yourself that if you think you might hurt yourself, you shouldn't do it, because you have to take care of yourself and that's your responsibility to yourself.

Again Jake constructs the dilemma as a mathematical equation, deriving a formula that guides the solution: one-fourth to others, three-fourths to yourself. Beginning with his responsibility to himself, a responsibility that he takes for granted, he then considers the extent to which he is responsible to others as well. Proceeding from a premise of separation but recognizing that "you have to live with other people," he seeks rules to limit interference and thus to minimize hurt. Responsibility in his construction pertains to a limitation of action, a restraint of aggression, guided by the recognition that his actions can have effects on others, just as theirs can interfere with him. Thus rules, by limiting interference, make life in community safe, protecting autonomy through reciprocity, extending the same consideration to others and self.

To the question about conflicting responsibilities, Amy again responds contextually rather than categorically, saying "it depends" and indicating how choice would be affected by variations in character and circumstance. Proceeding from a premise of connection, that "if you have a responsibility *with* somebody else, you should keep it," she then considers the extent to which she has a responsibility to herself. Exploring the parameters of separation, she imagines situations where, by doing what you want, you would avoid hurting yourself or where, in doing so, you would not thereby diminish the happiness of others. To her, responsibility signifies response, an extension rather than a limitation of action. Thus it connotes an act of care rather than the restraint of aggression. Again seeking the solution that would be most inclusive of everyone's needs, she strives to resolve the dilemma in a way that "will make everybody happier." Since Jake is concerned with limiting interference, while Amy focuses on the need for response, for him the limiting condition is, "Don't let yourself be guided totally by others," but for her it arises when "other people are counting on you," in which case "you can't just decide, "Well, I'd rather do this or that." " The interplay between these responses is clear in that she, assuming connection, begins to explore the parameters of separation, while he, assuming separation, begins to explore the parameters of connection. But the primacy of separation or connection leads to different images of self and of relationships.

Most striking among these differences is the imagery of violence in the boy's response, depicting a world of dangerous confrontation and explosive connection, where she sees a world of care and protection, a life lived with others whom "you may love as much or even more than you love yourself." Since the conception of morality reflects the understanding of social relationships, this difference in the imagery of relationships gives rise to a change in the moral injunction itself. To Jake, responsibility means *not doing* what he wants because he is thinking of others; to Amy, it means *doing* what others are counting on her to do regardless of what she herself wants. Both children are concerned with avoiding hurt but construe the problem in different ways—he seeing hurt to arise from the expression of aggression, she from a failure of response.

NOTE

1. Sigmund Freud, "On Narcissism: An Introduction," 1914, in Vol. XIV of *The Standard Edition of the Complete Psychological Writings of Sigmund Freud*, trans. and ed. James Strachey, London: The Hogarth Press, 1961.

STUDY QUESTIONS: ETHICAL PERSPECTIVES

1. Outline Mill's discussion of the concept of justice. How is justice related to the principle of utility? What are some of the objections that might be brought against Mill's position?
2. What is a maxim, according to Onora O'Neill's understanding of Kant? In what sense does treating someone merely as a means reveal a failure to respect his or her maxim? In what sense does treating persons as an ends involve consideration of his or her maxim?
3. Explain why Rawls thinks that the principle of utility would not be chosen from behind the veil of ignorance. Why does Rawls think that economic inequalities would only be chosen if they worked out for the benefit of the least well off? How would Mill respond to Rawls's argument? Which position do you find most plausible?
4. Hursthouse argues that virtue theory can give us guidance about what to do. Construct an example of such guidance from virtue theory's perspective, and then compare how utilitarianism would address the example.
5. Hinduism, according to Sharma, puts great emphasis on self-control. What does self-control mean and why think that it is morally valuable?
6. According to Gilligan what is the difference between care reasoning and justice reasoning? Provide two different arguments, one from the care perspective and one from the justice perspective, in favor of Heinz stealing the drug from the pharmacist. Which argument do you find most plausible? Why?

Part II

HUMAN RIGHTS

Human rights are rights that people have simply in virtue of fact they are human. These rights provide us with standards of acceptable behavior for treating one another independently of considerations of race, color, sex, language, religion, birth, or national origin. In that respect, human rights are thought to be universal. This universality is corroborated by the fact that the United Nations Universal Declaration of Human Rights was ratified with no dissenting votes. And an ever-increasing number of nations is taking this human rights document seriously. Despite the claim of universality of human rights, there remains an ongoing debate about the nature, extent, justification, and enumeration of human rights. We cover this topic at the beginning of our anthology because it is central to all of the subsequent discussions— environmental rights; the right to be fed; the rights of those fighting in, or the right not to have to fight in, wars; the rights of sexual and racial equality; the right to health care; the right to free choice; as well as the right to life and the right to die.

In general, rights are considered to be extremely important moral considerations. Rights form the basis upon which individuals can make claims against other individuals or against whole societies or governments. If Jane has a right of free speech, then she has a strong basis for complaint if someone tries to prevent her from speaking, regardless of whether anyone wants to hear what she says. Indeed, according to the deontological tradition, the existence of a right provides an individual with a nearly unchallengeable basis for exercising that right, even when the vast majority of fellow citizens would be better off if the individual were not allowed to exercise her right.

Hardly anyone, at least in Western societies, denies that there are human rights, but there is a long-standing debate about what the basis of these rights is and which human rights are the most fundamental. Some argue that civil and political rights are more basic, while others believe that social and economic rights are even more rudimentary. Civil and political rights include the rights to vote, speak, assemble, and participate equally in political affairs. Social and economic rights have to do with the livelihood and survival of a person in terms of food, shelter, clothing, and opportunities for education. Many socialists, feminists, and members of certain non-Western societies have challenged the Western-oriented dominance of civil and political rights over social and economic rights.

In some non-Western societies, as we will see, questions are raised about whether there are human rights that are universal in scope, or whether they vary according to gender or race. Another challenge often brought against conceptions of human rights is that they are too focused on the individual rather than on the group. Ancient and medieval discussions of ethics in the West, especially discussions of natural rights, did not have this emphasis. The universalistic and individualistic dimensions of a Western conception of rights, as some critics claim, are the products of the modern age. In a sense, some of the non-Western approaches we will examine resemble ancient and medieval Western conceptions much more than they do modern ones, and there are parallels between premodern and non-Western approaches that it would be interesting to explore.

To set the stage for our discussion, we begin with what many believe to be the authoritative statement of human rights—the United Nations Universal Declaration of Human Rights. Passed by the General Assembly in 1948, this document was created in the aftermath of World War II in an effort to prevent future massive violations of persons' rights. It enumerates the variety of civil, political, legal, economic, and welfare rights that each individual, independently of sex, race, religion, social status, and national origin, is entitled to enjoy. Notice that while these human rights may not be effective until a government implements them through legislation or a society integrates them into their practice, they are nonetheless normative standards that any government or legal system is expected to respect and on the basis of which their practices can be criticized. It is also important to bear in mind that these rights constitute only minimum standards for "decent social and governmental practice."[1] They are not meant to be directives for comprehensive solutions of moral problems.

The idea of human rights as commonly embraced in the West is, however, not without its critics. Charlotte Bunch challenges the priority assigned to civil and political rights over socioeconomic rights in the Western conception of human rights in light of women's situation. She observes that since the oppression and the violence directed against women across the globe are carried out by men who hold positions of power over them, protecting women's civil or political rights will not necessarily end such practices as sexual slavery, nor will it diminish the extent to which men are able to exercise arbitrary power over their social and economic status. Notice that Bunch does not claim that human rights are unimportant. She only intends to bring out the fact that unless the actual problems faced by women are treated of equal concern as the problems faced by men, human rights discussions will not have much to offer women.

In contrast with Bunch, Abdullahi Ahmed An-Na'im discusses a society in which the very legitimacy of human rights is called into question by the practices of the religious leadership. An-Na'im points out that some societies, such as those in the Islamic world, do not clearly endorse the view that all people should be accorded the same fundamental protections. Islamic society is partialist, in the sense that non-Muslims are treated quite differently from Muslims. The idea of equal respect, which is held to be the hallmark of human rights theory, is lacking in practice, although arguably it is something that can be justified by reference to some main Islamic texts. In those societies that do not accept the principle of equal respect, talk of human rights will not have much meaning, he concludes.

Speaking from an African context, Claude Ake argues that individual civil and political liberties are of little benefit to communities of people suffering from hunger, poverty, and disease. In his view, the best society is the one that leads to the greatest amount of economic development and liberation for the members of society. Thus, economic considerations should outweigh civil or political considerations. Furthermore, to better account for the African context, which views a person's interests as inextricably bound up with those of the community as a whole, the idea of human rights should be expanded from the rights of the individuals to include communities as rights-bearers, namely, collective human rights.

On the other hand, Daniel Bell points out that it is often counterproductive to impose human rights as understood in the Western liberal tradition on the East Asian context. To gain support from peoples of East Asia for human rights, one would need to show that there are cultural values in East Asia that could form the basis for their own understanding of human rights. And in fact, as Bell contends, there is such a basis. Moreover, one would have to allow for an expanded understanding of human rights that is sensitive to the East Asian context. For instance, the value of filial piety may call for a right of elderly parents to demand financial support from their grown children.

In contrast with the dominant discourse on human rights, which regards individuals as discrete persons making adversarial claims against each other, the Buddhist conception of human rights emphasizes the interconnectedness of nature and people. Central to the Buddhist perspective, Kenneth Inada explains, are the notions of mutuality, holism, and emptiness. Whereas mutuality and holism focus on the reciprocity and the openendedness of our relationships and experience, emptiness takes into account the contingency, fortuity, and fragility in the constitution of one's self and the world. On the basis of this understanding, a human right conception, according to the Buddhist, has to incorporate a sense of compassion not only for human beings but other sentient and even non-sentient beings as well.

We have covered various approaches to human rights from diverse cultural, philosophical, and religious perspectives. The question remains whether it is possible to arrive at a crosscultural consensus on human rights with different groups and communities having different background reasons for why humans rights are to be justified. Charles Taylor argues for such a possibility. He identifies four kinds of conflict between the Western language of human rights and other major contemporary cultures. The first kind of conflict could be resolved by legal innovation, according to Taylor, whereas the other three kinds of conflict can be resolved through reconsideration and recreations within the philosophical or cultural traditions at issue.

We end this section with a discussion of human rights and democracy. If one looks at Article 21 of The Universal Declaration of Human Rights, it is not difficult to see that democratic participation is recognized as a human right, even though the Universal Declaration does not explicitly use the term "democracy." Nevertheless, to claim that right to democratic participation is a human right raises questions concerning the relationship of human rights and democracy. Why is democratic form of participation, but not other forms of political government or participation, a human right? Is democracy the best form of political society to uphold human rights? Is democracy a universal value? Amartya Sen addresses some of these questions in his piece, "Democracy as a Universal Value." He argues that democracy is universally valuable, not only because it serves the instrumental purpose of reducing errors in policies by allowing people to express diverse viewpoints but also because political participation is itself an important human good. Democratic participation also shapes or reshapes people's understanding of their values and needs. Besides, Sen writes, we should not focus so much on whether a country is "deemed fit *for* democracy" as on whether it should become "fit *through* democracy."

—KAI WONG

NOTE

1. James Nickel, *Making Sense of Human Rights* (Berkeley: University of California Press, 1987), p. 4.

United Nations Universal Declaration of Human Rights

The Universal Declaration of Human Rights was approved unanimously by the General Assembly of the United Nations on December 10, 1948, by forty-eight nations with eight abstentions (including six members in the Soviet bloc at the time, South Africa, and Saudi Arabia) to be the common universal standard of human rights for all nations and peoples. The Declaration enumerates all rights and freedoms that each individual is to enjoy irrespective of "race, color, sex, language, religion, political or other opinion, national or social origin, property, birth, or other status."

The General Assembly

proclaims This Universal Declaration of Human Rights as a common standard of achievement for all peoples and all nations, to the end that every individual and every organ of society, keeping this Declaration constantly in mind, shall strive by teaching and education to promote respect for these rights and freedoms and by progressive measures, national and international, to secure their universal and effective recognition and observance, both among the peoples of Member States themselves and among the peoples of territories under their jurisdiction.

ARTICLE 1

All human beings are born free and equal in dignity and rights. They are endowed with reason and conscience and should act towards one another in a spirit of brotherhood.

ARTICLE 2

Everyone is entitled to all the rights and freedoms set forth in this Declaration, without distinction of any kind, such as race, colour, sex, language, religion, political or other opinion, national or social origin, property, birth, or other status.

Furthermore, no distinction shall be made on the basis of the political, jurisdictional, or international status of the country or territory to which a person belongs, whether it be independent, trust, non-self-governing, or under any other limitation of sovereignty.

ARTICLE 3

Everyone has the right to life, liberty, and security of person.

ARTICLE 4

No one shall be held in slavery or servitude; slavery and the slave trade shall be prohibited in all their forms.

ARTICLE 5

No one shall be subjected to torture or to cruel, inhuman, or degrading treatment or punishment.

ARTICLE 6

Everyone has the right to recognition everywhere as a person before the law.

Reprinted with the permission of United Nations Publications.

ARTICLE 7

All are equal before the law and are entitled without any discrimination to equal protection of the law. All are entitled to equal protection against any discrimination in violation of this Declaration and against any incitement to such discrimination.

ARTICLE 8

Everyone has the right to an effective remedy by the competent national tribunals for acts violating the fundamental rights granted him by the constitution or by law.

ARTICLE 9

No one shall be subjected to arbitrary arrest, detention, or exile.

ARTICLE 10

Everyone is entitled in full equality to a fair and public hearing by an independent and impartial tribunal, in the determination of his rights and obligations and of any criminal charge against him.

ARTICLE 11

1. Everyone charged with a penal offence has the right to be presumed innocent until proved guilty according to law in a public trial at which he has had all the guarantees necessary for his defence.

2. No one shall be held guilty of any penal offence on account of any act or omission which did not constitute a penal offence, under national or international law, at the time when it was committed. Nor shall a heavier penalty be imposed than the one that was applicable at the time the penal offence was committed.

ARTICLE 12

No one shall be subjected to arbitrary interference with his privacy, family, home, or correspondence, nor to attacks upon his honour and reputation. Everyone has the right to the protection of the law against such interference or attacks.

ARTICLE 13

1. Everyone has the right to freedom of movement and residence within the borders of each state.

2. Everyone has the right to leave any country, including his own, and to return to his country.

ARTICLE 14

1. Everyone has the right to seek and to enjoy in other countries asylum from persecution.

2. This right may not be invoked in the case of prosecutions genuinely arising from non-political crimes or from acts contrary to the purposes and principles of the United Nations.

ARTICLE 15

1. Everyone has the right to a nationality.

2. No one shall be arbitrarily deprived of his nationality nor denied the right to change his nationality.

ARTICLE 16

1. Men and women of full age, without any limitation due to race, nationality, or religion, have the right to marry and to found a family. They are entitled to equal rights as to marriage, during marriage, and at its dissolution.

2. Marriage shall be entered into only with the free and full consent of the intending spouses.

3. The family is the natural and fundamental group unit of society and is entitled to protection by society and the State.

ARTICLE 17

1. Everyone has the right to own property alone as well as in association with others.

2. No one shall be arbitrarily deprived of his property.

ARTICLE 18

Everyone has the right to freedom of thought, conscience, and religion; this right includes freedom to change his religion or belief and freedom, either alone or in community with others and in public or private, to manifest his religion or belief in teaching, practice, worship, and observance.

ARTICLE 19

Everyone has the right to freedom of opinion and expression; this right includes freedom to hold opinions without interference and to seek, receive, and impart information and ideas through any media and regardless of frontiers.

ARTICLE 20

1. Everyone has the right to freedom of peaceful assembly and association.

2. No one may be compelled to belong to an association.

ARTICLE 21

1. Everyone has the right to take part in the government of his country, directly or through freely chosen representatives.

2. Everyone has the right of equal access to public service in his country.

3. The will of the people shall be the basis of the authority of government; this will shall be expressed in periodic and genuine elections which shall be by universal and equal suffrage and shall be held by secret vote or by equivalent free voting procedures.

ARTICLE 22

Everyone, as a member of society, has the right to social security and is entitled to realization, through national effort and international co-operation and in accordance with the organization and resources of each State, of the economic, social, and cultural rights indispensable for his dignity and the free development of his personality.

ARTICLE 23

1. Everyone has the right to work, to free choice of employment, to just and favourable conditions of work, and to protection against unemployment.

2. Everyone, without any discrimination, has the right to equal pay for equal work.

3. Everyone who works has the right to just and favourable remuneration ensuring for himself and his family an existence worthy of human dignity, and supplemented, if necessary, by other means of social protection.

4. Everyone has the right to form and to join trade unions for the protection of his interests.

ARTICLE 24

Everyone has the right to rest and leisure, including reasonable limitation of working hours and periodic holidays with pay.

ARTICLE 25

1. Everyone has the right to a standard of living adequate for the health and well-being of himself and of his family, including food, clothing, housing and medical care and necessary social services, and the right to security in the event of unemployment, sickness, disability, widowhood, old age, or other lack of livelihood in circumstances beyond his control.

2. Motherhood and childhood are entitled to special care and assistance. All children, whether born in or out of wedlock, shall enjoy the same social protection.

ARTICLE 26

1. Everyone has the right to education. Education shall be free, at least in the elementary and fundamental stages. Elementary education shall be compulsory. Technical and professional education shall be made generally available and higher education shall be equally accessible to all on the basis of merit.

2. Education shall be directed to the full development of the human personality and to the strengthening of respect for human rights and fundamental freedoms. It shall promote understanding, tolerance and friendship among all nations, racial or religious groups, and shall further the activities of the United Nations for the maintenance of peace.

3. Parents have a prior right to choose the kind of education that shall be given to their children.

ARTICLE 27

1. Everyone has the right freely to participate in the cultural life of the community, to enjoy the arts, and to share in scientific advancement and its benefits.

2. Everyone has the right to the protection of the moral and material interests resulting from any scientific, literary, or artistic production of which he is the author.

ARTICLE 28

Everyone is entitled to a social and international order in which the rights and freedoms set forth in this Declaration can be fully realized.

ARTICLE 29

1. Everyone has duties to the community in which alone the free and full development of his personality is possible.

2. In the exercise of his rights and freedoms, everyone shall be subject only to such limitations as are determined by law solely for the purpose of securing due recognition and respect for the rights and freedoms of others and of meeting the just requirements of morality, public order, and the general welfare in a democratic society.

3. These rights and freedoms may in no case be exercised contrary to the purposes and principles of the United Nations.

ARTICLE 30

Nothing in this Declaration may be interpreted as implying for any State, group or person any right to engage in any activity or to perform any act aimed at the destruction of any of the rights and freedoms set forth herein.

Women's Rights as Human Rights: Toward a Re-Vision of Human Rights

Charlotte Bunch

Charlotte Bunch is the director of the Center for Global Issues and Women's Leadership at Rutgers University. She is the author of *Passionate Politics: Feminist Theory in Action* (1987). She is the editor of seven books, including *Class and Feminism* (1974) and *Learning Our Way: Essays in Feminist Education* (1983).

Bunch criticizes the Western conception of human rights for leaving women's rights largely out of the picture. Many women's rights are socioeconomic—that is, centered on food, shelter, and work. In addition, political oppression and systematic forms of violence against women are not taken as seriously as rights to free speech and press—rights that are only marginally important to many women, especially those in the Third World. Bunch concludes with some practical guidelines for transforming Western conceptions of human rights to ensure that women's rights are also counted as human rights.

Significant numbers of the world's population are routinely subject to torture, starvation, terrorism, humiliation, mutilation and even murder simply because they are female. Crimes such as these against any group other than women would be recognized as a civil and political emergency as well as a gross violation of the victims' humanity. Yet, despite a clear record of deaths and demonstrable abuse, women's rights are not commonly classified as human rights. This is problematic both theoretically and practically, because it has grave consequences for the way society views and treats the fundamental issues of women's lives. This paper questions why women's rights and human rights are viewed as distinct, looks at the policy implications of this schism, and discusses different approaches to changing it.

Women's human rights are violated in a variety of ways. Of course, women sometimes suffer abuses such as political repression that are similar to abuses suffered by men. In these situations, female victims are often invisible, because the dominant image of the political actor in our world is male. However, many violations of women's human rights are distinctly connected to being female—that is, women are discriminated against and abused on the basis of gender. Women also experience sexual abuse in situations where their other human rights are being violated, as political prisoners or members of persecuted ethnic groups, for example. In this paper, I address those abuses in which gender is a primary or related factor because gender-related abuse has been most neglected and offers the greatest challenge to the field of human rights today.

The concept of human rights is one of the few moral visions ascribed to internationally. Although its scope is not universally agreed upon, it strikes deep chords of response among many. Promotion of human rights is a widely accepted goal and thus provides a useful framework for seeking redress of gender abuse. Further, it is one of the few concepts that speaks to the need for transnational activism and concern about the lives of people globally. The Universal Declaration of Human Rights,[1] adopted in 1948, symbolizes this world vision and defines human rights broadly. While not much is said about women, Article 2 entitles all to "the rights and freedoms set forth in this Declaration, without distinction of any kind, such as race, colour, sex, language, religion, political or other opinion, national or social origin, property, birth, or other status." Eleanor Roosevelt and the Latin American women who fought for the inclusion of sex in the Declaration and for its passage clearly intended that it would address the problem of women's subordination.[2]

Since 1948 the world community has continuously debated varying interpretations of human rights in response to global developments. Little of this discussion, however, has addressed questions of gender, and only recently have significant challenges been made to a vision of human rights which excludes much of women's experiences. The concept of human rights, like all vibrant visions, is not static or the property of any one group; rather, its meaning expands as people reconceive of their needs and hopes in relation to it. In this spirit, feminists redefine human rights abuses to include the degradation and violation of women. The specific experiences of women must be added to traditional approaches to human rights in order to make women more visible and to transform the concept and practice of human rights in our culture so that it takes better account of women's lives.

In the next part of this article, I will explore both the importance and the difficulty of connecting women's rights to human rights, and then I will outline four basic approaches that have been used in the effort to make this connection.

BEYOND RHETORIC: POLITICAL IMPLICATIONS

Few governments exhibit more than token commitment to women's equality as a basic human right in domestic or foreign policy. No government determines its policies toward other countries on the basis of their treatment of women, even when some aid and trade decisions are said to be based on a country's human rights record. Among nongovernmental organizations, women are rarely a priority, and Human Rights Day programs on 10 December seldom include discussion of issues like violence against women or reproductive rights. When it is suggested that governments and human rights organizations should respond to women's rights as concerns that deserve such attention, a number of excuses are offered for why this cannot be done. The responses tend to follow one or more of these lines: (1) sex discrimination is too trivial, or not as important, or will come after larger issues of survival that require more serious attention; (2) abuse of women, while regrettable, is a cultural, private, or individual issue and not a political matter requiring state action; (3) while appropriate for other action, women's rights are not human rights per se; or (4) when the abuse of women is recognized, it is considered inevitable or so pervasive that any consideration of it is futile or will overwhelm other human rights questions. It is important to challenge these responses.

The narrow definition of human rights, recognized by many in the West as solely a matter of state violation of civil and political liberties, impedes consideration of women's rights. In the United States, the concept has been further limited by some who have used it as a weapon in the cold war almost exclusively to challenge human rights abuses perpetrated in communist countries. Even then, many abuses that affected women, such as forced pregnancy in Romania, were ignored.

Some important aspects of women's rights do fit into a civil liberties framework, but much of the abuse against women is part of a larger socioeconomic web that entraps women, making them vulnerable to abuses which cannot be delineated as exclusively political or solely caused by states. The inclusion of "second generation" or socioeconomic human rights to food, shelter, and work—which are clearly delineated as part of the Universal Declaration of Human Rights—is vital to addressing women's concerns fully. Further, the assumption that states are not responsible for most violations of women's rights ignores the fact that such abuses, although committed perhaps by private citizens, are often condoned or even sanctioned by states. I will return to the question of state responsibility after responding to other instances of resistance to women's rights as human rights.

The most insidious myth about women's rights is that they are trivial or secondary to the concerns of life and death. Nothing could be farther from the truth: sexism kills. There is increasing documentation of the many ways in which being female is life-threatening. The following are a few examples:

- Before birth: Amniocentesis is used for sex selection leading to the abortion of more female fetuses at rates as high as 99 percent in Bombay, India; in China and India, the two most populous nations, more males than females are born even though natural birth ratios would produce more females.[3]
- During childhood: The World Health Organization reports that in many countries, girls are fed less, breast fed for shorter periods of time, taken to doctors less frequently, and die or are physically and mentally maimed by malnutrition at higher rates than boys.[4]
- In adulthood: the denial of women's rights to control their bodies in reproduction threatens women's lives, especially where this is combined with poverty and poor health services. In Latin America, complications from illegal abortions are the leading cause of death for women between the ages of fifteen and thirty-nine.[5]

Sex discrimination kills women daily. When combined with race, class, and other forms of oppression, it constitutes a deadly denial of women's right to life and liberty on a large scale throughout the world. The most pervasive violation of females is violence against women in all its manifestations, from wife battery, incest, and rape, to dowry deaths,[6] genital mutilation,[7] and female sexual slavery. These abuses occur in every country and are found in the home and in the workplace, on streets, on campuses, and in prisons and refugee camps. They cross class, race, age, and national lines; and at the same time, the forms this violence takes often reinforce other oppressions such as racism, "able-bodyism," and imperialism. Case in point: in order to feed their families, poor women in brothels around U.S. military bases in places

like the Philippines bear the burden of sexual, racial, and national imperialism in repeated and often brutal violation of their bodies.

Even a short review of random statistics reveals that the extent of violence against women globally is staggering:

- In the United States, battery is the leading cause of injury to adult women, and a rape is committed every six minutes.[8]
- In Peru, 70 percent of all crimes reported to police involve women who are beaten by their partners; and in Lima (a city of seven million people), 168,970 rapes were reported in 1987 alone.[9]
- In India, eight out of ten wives are victims of violence, either domestic battery, dowry-related abuse, or, among the least fortunate, murder.[10]
- In France, 95 percent of the victims of violence are women; 51 percent at the hands of a spouse or lover. Similar statistics from places as diverse as Bangladesh, Canada, Kenya, and Thailand demonstrate that more than 50 percent of female homicides were committed by family members.[11]

Where recorded, domestic battery figures range from 40 percent to 80 percent of women beaten, usually repeatedly, indicating that the home is the most dangerous place for women and frequently the site of cruelty and torture. As the Carol Stuart murder in Boston demonstrated, sexist and racist attitudes in the United States often cover up the real threat to women; a woman is murdered in Massachusetts by a husband or lover every 22 days.[12]

Such numbers do not reflect the full extent of the problem of violence against women, much of which remains hidden. Yet rather than receiving recognition as a major world conflict, this violence is accepted as normal or even dismissed as an individual or cultural matter. Georgina Ashworth notes that:

> The greatest restriction of liberty, dignity and movement and at the same time, direct violation of the person is the threat and realization of violence. . . . However, violence against the female sex, on a scale which far exceeds the list of Amnesty International victims, is tolerated publicly; indeed some acts of violation are not crimes in law, others are legitimized in custom or court opinion, and most are blamed on the victims themselves.[13]

Violence against women is a touchstone that illustrates the limited concept of human rights and highlights the political nature of the abuse of women. As Lori Heise states: "This is not random violence. . . . [T]he risk factor is being female."[14] Victims are chosen because of their gender. The message is domination: stay in your place or be afraid. Contrary to the argument that such violence is only personal or cultural, it is profoundly political. It results from the structural relationships of power, domination, and privilege between men and women in society. Violence against women is central to maintaining those political relations at home, at work, and in all public spheres.

Failure to see the oppression of women as political also results in the exclusion of sex discrimination and violence against women from the human rights agenda. Female subordination runs so deep that it is still viewed as inevitable or natural, rather than seen as a politically constructed reality maintained by patriarchal interests, ideology, and institutions. But I do not believe that male violation of women is inevitable or natural. Such a belief requires a narrow and pessimistic view of men. If violence and domination are understood as a politically constructed reality, it is possible to imagine deconstructing that system and building more just interactions between the sexes.

The physical territory of this political struggle over what constitutes women's human rights is women's bodies. The importance of control over women can be seen in the intensity of resistance to laws and social changes that put control of women's bodies in women's hands: reproductive rights, freedom of sexuality whether heterosexual or lesbian, laws that criminalize rape in marriage, etc. Denial of reproductive rights and homophobia are also political means of maintaining control over women and perpetuating sex roles and thus have human rights implications. The physical abuse of women is a reminder of this territorial domination and is sometimes accompanied by other forms of human rights abuse such as slavery (forced prostitution), sexual terrorism (rape), imprisonment (confinement to the home), and torture (systematic battery). Some cases are extreme, such as the women in Thailand who died in a brothel fire because they were chained to their beds. Most situations are more ordinary like denying women decent educations or jobs which leaves them prey to abusive marriages, exploitative work, and prostitution.

This raises once again the question of the state's responsibility for protecting women's human rights. Feminists have shown how the distinction between private and public abuse is a dichotomy often used to justify female subordination in the home. Governments regulate many matters in the family and individual spheres. For example, human rights activists pressure states to prevent slavery or racial discrimination and segregation even when these are conducted by nongovernmental forces in private or proclaimed as cultural traditions as they have been in both the southern United States and in South Africa. The real questions are: (1) who decides what are legitimate human rights; and (2) when should the state become involved and for what purposes. Riane Eisler argues that:

> the issue is what types of private acts are and are not protected by the right to privacy and/or the principle of family autonomy. Even more specifically, the issue is whether violations of human rights within the family such as genital mutilation, wife beating, and other forms of violence designed to maintain patriarchal control should be within the purview of human rights theory and action. . . . [T]he underlying problem for human rights theory, as for most other fields of theory, is that the yardstick that has been developed for defining and measuring human rights has been based on the male as the norm.[15]

The human rights community must move beyond its male-defined norms in order to respond to the brutal and systematic violation of women globally. This does not mean that every human rights group must alter the focus of its work. However, it does require examining patriarchal biases and acknowledging the rights of women as human rights. Governments must seek to end the politically and culturally constructed war on women rather than continue to perpetuate it. Every state has the responsibility to intervene in the abuse of women's rights within its borders and to end its collusion with the forces that perpetrate such violations in other countries.

TOWARD ACTION: PRACTICAL APPROACHES

The classification of human rights is more than just a semantics problem because it has practical policy consequences. Human rights are still considered to be more important than women's rights. The distinction perpetuates the idea that the rights of women are of a lesser order than the "rights of man," and, as Eisler describes it, "serves to justify practices that do not accord women full and equal status."[16] In the United Nations, the Human Rights Commission has more power to hear and investigate cases than the Commission on the Status of Women, more staff and budget, and better mechanisms for implementing its findings. Thus, it makes a difference in what can be done if a case is deemed a violation of women's rights and not of human rights.[17]

The determination of refugee status illustrates how the definition of human rights affects people's lives. The Dutch Refugee Association, in its pioneering efforts to convince other nations to recognize sexual persecution and violence against women as justifications for granting refugee status, found that some European governments would take sexual persecution into account as an aspect of other forms of political repression, but none would make it the grounds for refugee status per se.[18] The implications of such a distinction are clear when examining a situation like that of the Bangladeshi women who, having been raped during the Pakistan–Bangladesh war, subsequently faced death at the hands of male relatives to preserve "family honor." Western powers professed outrage but did not offer asylum to these victims of human rights abuse.

I have observed four basic approaches to linking women's rights to human rights. These approaches are presented separately here in order to identify each more clearly. In practice, these approaches often overlap, and while each raises questions about the others, I see them as complementary. These approaches can be applied to many issues, but I will illustrate them primarily in terms of how they address violence against women in order to show the implications of their differences on a concrete issue.

1. *Women's Rights as Political and Civil Rights.* Taking women's specific needs into consideration as part of the already recognized "first generation," political and civil liberties is the first approach. This involves both raising the visibility of women who suffer general human rights violations as well as calling attention to particular abuses women encounter because they are female. Thus, issues of violence against women are raised when they connect to other forms of violation such as the sexual torture of women political prisoners in South America.[19] Groups like the Women's Task Force of Amnesty International have taken this approach in pushing for Amnesty to launch a campaign on behalf of women political prisoners which would address the sexual abuse and rape of women in custody, their lack of maternal care in detention, and the resulting human rights abuse of their children.

Documenting the problems of women refugees and developing responsive policies are other illustrations of this approach. Women and children make up more than 80 percent of those in refugee camps, yet few refugee policies are specifically shaped to meet the needs of these vulnerable populations who face considerable sexual abuse. For example, in one camp where men were allocated the community's rations, some gave food to women and their children in exchange for sex. Revealing this abuse led to new policies that allocated food directly to the women.[20]

The political and civil rights approach is a useful starting point for many human rights groups; by considering women's experiences, these groups can expand their efforts in areas where they are already working. This approach also raises contradictions that reveal the limits of a narrow civil liberties view. One contradiction is to define rape as a human rights abuse only when it occurs in state custody but not on the streets or in the home. Another is to say that a violation of the right to free speech occurs when someone is jailed for defending gay rights, but not when someone is jailed or even tortured and killed for homosexuality. Thus, while this approach of adding women and stirring them into existing first generation human rights categories is useful, it is not enough by itself.

2. Women's Rights as Socioeconomic Rights. The second approach includes the particular plight of women with regard to "second generation" human rights such as the rights to food, shelter, health care, and employment. This is an approach favored by those who see the dominant Western human rights tradition and international law as too individualistic and identify women's oppression as primarily economic.

This tendency has its origins among socialists and labor activists who have long argued that political human rights are meaningless to many without economic rights as well. It focuses on the primacy of the need to end women's economic subordination as the key to other issues including women's vulnerability to violence. This particular focus has led to work on issues like women's right to organize as workers and opposition to violence in the workplace, especially in situations like the free-trade zones which have targeted women as cheap, nonorganized labor. Another focus of this approach has been highlighting the feminization of poverty or what might better be called the increasing impoverishment of females. Poverty has not become strictly female, but females now comprise a higher percentage of the poor.

Looking at women's rights in the context of socioeconomic development is another example of this approach. Third World peoples have called for an understanding of socioeconomic development as a human rights issue. Within this demand, some have sought to integrate women's rights into development and have examined women's specific needs in relation to areas like land ownership or access to credit. Among those working on women in development, there is growing interest in violence against women as both a health and development issue. If violence is seen as having negative consequences for social productivity, it may get more attention. This type of narrow economic measure, however, should not determine whether such violence is seen as a human rights concern. Violence as a development issue is linked to the need to understand development not just as an economic issue but also as a question of empowerment and human growth.

One of the limitations of this second approach has been its tendency to reduce women's needs to the economic sphere which implies that women's rights will follow automatically with Third World development, which may involve socialism. This has not proven to be the case. Many working from this approach are no longer trying to add women into either the Western capitalist or socialist development models, but rather seek a transformative development process that links women's political, economic, and cultural empowerment.

3. Women's Rights and the Law. The creation of new legal mechanisms to counter sex discrimination characterizes the third approach to women's rights as human rights. These efforts seek to make existing legal and political institutions work for women and to expand the state's responsibility for the violation of women's human rights. National and local laws which address sex discrimination and violence against women are examples of this approach. These measures allow women to fight for their rights within the legal system. The primary international illustration is the Convention on the Elimination of All Forms of Discrimination Against Women.[21]

The Convention has been described as "essentially an international bill of rights for women and a framework for women's participation in the development process . . . [which] spells out internationally accepted principles and standards for achieving equality between women and men."[22] Adopted by the UN General Assembly in 1979, the Convention has been ratified or acceded to by 104 countries as of January 1990. In theory, these countries are obligated to pursue policies in accordance with it and to report on their compliance to the Committee on the Elimination of Discrimination Against Women (CEDAW).

While the Convention addresses many issues of sex discrimination, one of its shortcomings is failure to directly address the question of violence against women. CEDAW passed a resolution at its eighth session in Vienna in 1989 expressing concern that this issue be on its agenda and instructing states to include in their periodic reports information about statistics, legislation, and support services in this area.[23] The Commonwealth Secretariat in its manual on the reporting process for the Convention also interprets the issue of violence against women as "clearly fundamental to the spirit of the Convention," especially in Article 5 which calls for the modification of social and cultural patterns, sex roles, and stereotyping that are based on the idea of the inferiority or the superiority of either sex.[24]

The Convention outlines a clear human rights agenda for women which, if accepted by governments, would mark an enormous step forward. It also carries the limitations of all such international documents in that there is little power to demand its implementation. Within the United Nations, it is not generally regarded as a convention with teeth, as illustrated by the difficulty that CEDAW has had in getting countries to report on compliance with its provisions. Further, it is still treated by governments and most nongovernmental organizations as a document dealing with women's (read "secondary") rights, not human rights. Nevertheless, it is a useful statement of principles endorsed by the United Nations around which women can organize to achieve legal and political change in their regions.

4. *Feminist Transformation of Human Rights.* Transforming the human rights concept from a feminist perspective, so that it will take greater account of women's lives, is the fourth approach. This approach relates women's rights and human rights, looking first at the violations of women's lives and then asking how the human rights concept can change to be more responsive to women. For example, the GABRIELA women's coalition in the Philippines simply stated that "Women's Rights are Human Rights" in launching a campaign last year. As Ninotchka Rosca explained, coalition members saw that "human rights are not reducible to a question of legal and due process. . . . In the case of women, human rights are affected by the entire society's traditional perception of what is proper or not proper for women."[25] Similarly, a panel at the 1990 International Women's Rights Action Watch conference asserted that "Violence Against Women is a Human Rights Issue." While work in the three

previous approaches is often done from a feminist perspective, this last view is the most distinctly feminist with its woman-centered stance and its refusal to wait for permission from some authority to determine what is or is not a human rights issue.

This transformative approach can be taken toward any issue, but those working from this approach have tended to focus most on abuses that arise specifically out of gender, such as reproductive rights, female sexual slavery, violence against women, and "family crimes" like forced marriage, compulsory heterosexuality, and female mutilation. These are also the issues most often dismissed as not really human rights questions. This is therefore the most hotly contested area and requires that barriers be broken down between public and private, state and nongovernmental responsibilities.

Those working to transform the human rights vision from this perspective can draw on the work of others who have expanded the understanding of human rights previously. For example, two decades ago there was no concept of "disappearances" as a human rights abuse. However, the women of the Plaza de Mayo in Argentina did not wait for an official declaration but stood up to demand state accountability for these crimes. In so doing, they helped to create a context for expanding the concept of responsibility for deaths at the hands of paramilitary or right-wing death squads which, even if not carried out by the state, were allowed by it to happen. Another example is the developing concept that civil rights violations include "hate crimes," violence that is racially motivated or directed against homosexuals, Jews, or other minority groups. Many accept that states have an obligation to work to prevent such rights abuses, and getting violence against women seen as a hate crime is being pursued by some.

The practical applications of transforming the human rights concept from feminist perspectives need to be explored further. The danger in pursuing only this approach is the tendency to become isolated from and competitive with other human rights groups because they have been so reluctant to address gender violence and discrimination. Yet most women experience abuse on the grounds of sex, race, class, nation, age, sexual preference, and politics as interrelated, and little benefit comes from separating them as competing claims. The human rights community need not abandon other issues but should incorporate gender perspectives into them and see how these expand the terms of their work. By recognizing issues like violence against women as human rights concerns, human rights scholars and activists do not have to take these up as their primary tasks. However, they do have to stop gate-keeping and guarding their prerogative to determine what is considered a "legitimate" human rights issue.

As mentioned before, these four approaches are overlapping and many strategies for change involve elements of more than one. All of these approaches contain aspects of what is necessary to achieve women's rights. At a time when dualist ways of thinking and views of competing economic systems are in question, the creative task is to look for ways to connect these approaches and to see how we can go beyond exclusive views of what people need in their lives. In the words of an early feminist group, we need bread and roses, too. Women want food and liberty and the possibility of living lives of dignity free from domination and violence. In this struggle, the recognition of women's rights as human rights can play an important role.

NOTES

1. Universal Declaration of Human Rights, *adopted* 10 December 1948, G.A. Res. 217A(III), U.N. Doc. A/810 (1948).
2. Blanche Wiesen Cook, "Eleanor Roosevelt and Human Rights: The Battle for Peace and Planetary Decency," Edward P. Crapol, ed. *Women and American Foreign Policy: Lobbyists, Critics, and Insiders* (New York: Greenwood Press, 1987), 98–118; Georgina Ashworth. "Of Violence and Violation: Women and Human Rights," *Change Thinkbook II* (London, 1986).
3. Vibhuti Patel. *In Search of Our Bodies: A Feminist Look at Women, Health, and Reproduction in India* (Shakti, Bombay, 1987); Lori Heise, "International Dimensions of Violence Against Women," *Response*, vol. 12, no. 1 (1989): 3.
4. Sundari Ravindran, *Health Implications of Sex Discrimination in Childhood* (Geneva: World Health Organization, 1986). These problems and proposed social programs to counter them in India are discussed in detail in "Gender Violence: Gender Discrimination Between Boy

and Girl in Parental Family," paper published by CHETNA (Child Health Education Training and Nutrition Awareness), Ahmedabad, 1989.
5. Debbie Taylor, ed., *Women: A World Report, A New Internationalist Book* (Oxford: Oxford University Press, 1985), 10. See Joni Seager and Ann Olson, eds., *Women in the World: An International Atlas* (London: Pluto Press, 1986) for more statistics on the effects of sex discrimination.
6. Frequently a husband will disguise the death of a bride as suicide or an accident in order to collect the marriage settlement paid him by the bride's parents. Although dowry is now illegal in many countries, official records for 1987 showed 1,786 dowry deaths in India alone. See Heise, note 3 above, 5.
7. For an in-depth examination of the practice of female circumcision see Alison T. Slack, "Female Circumcision: A Critical Appraisal," *Human Rights Quarterly* 10 (1988): 439.
8. C. Everett Koop, M.D. "Violence Against Women: A Global Problem," presentation by the Surgeon General of the U.S., Public Health Service, Washington D.C., 1989.
9. Ana Maria Portugal, "Cronica de Una Violacion Provocada?" *Fempress* especial "Contraviolencia," Santiago, 1988; Seager and Olson, note 5 above, 37.
10. Ashworth, note 2 above, 9.
11. "Violence Against Women in the Family," Centre for Social Development and Humanitarian Affairs, United Nations Office at Vienna, 1989.
12. Bella English, "Stereotypes Led Us Astray," *The Boston Globe*, 5 Jan. 1990, 17, col. 3. See also the statistics in *Women's International Network News*, 1989; United Nations Office, note 11 above; Ashworth, note 2 above; Heise, note 3 above; and *Fempress*, note 9 above.
13. Ashworth, note 2 above, 8.
14. Heise, note 3 above, 3.
15. Riane Eisler, "Human Rights: Toward an Integrated Theory for Action," *Human Rights Quarterly* 9 (1987): 297. See also Alida Brill, *Nobody's Business: The Paradoxes of Privacy* (New York: Addison-Wesley, 1990).
16. Eisler, note 15 above, 291.
17. Sandra Coliver, "United Nations Machineries on Women's Rights. How Might They Better Help Women Whose Rights Are Being Violated?" in Ellen L. Lutz, Hurst Hannum, and Kathryn J. Burke, eds., *New Directions in Human Rights* (Philadelphia: Univ. of Penn. Press, 1989).
18. Marijke Meyer, "Oppression of Women and Refugee Status," unpublished report to NGO Forum, Nairobi, Kenya, 1985 and "Sexual Violence Against Women Refugees" Ministry of Social Affairs and Labour, The Netherlands, June 1984.
19. Ximena Bunster describes this in Chile and Argentina in "The Torture of Women Political Prisoners: A Case Study in Female Sexual Slavery," in Kathleen Barry, Charlotte Bunch, and Shirley Castley, eds., *International Feminism: Networking Against Female Sexual Slavery* (New York: IWTC, 1984).
20. Report given by Margaret Groarke at Women's Panel, Amnesty International New York Regional Meeting, 24 Feb. 1990.
21. Convention on the Elimination of All Forms of Discrimination Against Women, G.A. Res. 34/180, (1980).

22. International Women's Rights Action Watch. "The Convention on the Elimination of All Forms of Discrimination Against Women" (Minneapolis: Humphrey Institute of Public Affairs, 1988), 1.

23. CEDAW Newsletter, 3rd Issue (13 Apr. 1989), 2 (summary of U.N. Report on the Eighth Session, U.N.Doc. A/44/38, 14 April 1989).

24. Commonwealth Secretariat, "The Convention on the Elimination of All Forms of Discrimination Against Women: The Reporting Process—A Manual for Commonwealth Jurisdictions," London, 1989.

25. Speech given by Ninotchka Rosca at Amnesty International New York Regional Conference, 24 Feb. 1990, 2.

Islam, Islamic Law, and the Dilemma of Cultural Legitimacy for Universal Human Rights[1]

Abdullahi Ahmed An-Na'im

Abdullahi Ahmed An-Na'im is a professor of law at Emory University. He is the author of *Islam and the Secular State: Negotiating the Future of Shari'a* (2008) and *Toward an Islamic Reformation: Civil Liberties, Human Rights and International Law* (1990). His edited or coedited works include *Human Rights under African Constitutions* (2003) and *Human Rights in Cross Cultural Perspectives* (1992).

Islamic societies generally do not place a high value on the protection of what we deem as human rights. An-Na'im argues that human rights need to be perceived as culturally legitimate in order for them to be given more than lip service. Since countries are largely left unsupervised in terms of the protection of the human rights of their own citizens, the leaders must be persuaded that the human rights of all their citizens are deserving of equal respect. But in Islamic cultures, a deep division exists between those who are Muslim and those who are not, as well as between men and women. As long as these divisions exist, appeals to universal human rights will continue to clash with deeply held cultural and religious views.

Although Islam is often discussed in the contexts of North Africa and the Middle East, the majority of Muslims live outside this region. The clear majority of the Muslims of the world live in the Indian subcontinent.[2] The Muslim population of Indonesia alone is equal to the combined Muslim population of Egypt and Iran, the largest countries of the so-called Muslim heartland of North Africa and the Middle East. In terms of percentage to the total population, Muslims constitute 97% of the total population of Pakistan, 82.9% of that of Bangladesh and 80% of that of Indonesia. While Muslims constitute

Edited Excerpt from Abdullahi Ahmed An-Na'im, "Islam, Islamic Law and the Dilemma of Cultural Legitimacy for Universal Human Rights," in Asian Perspectives on Human Rights, Claude E. Welch and Virginia Leary, editors. 1990. Reprinted by permission of the author.

slightly less than half the population of Malaysia, Islam is perceived as an important element of Malay ethnicity which receives special protection under the constitution.[3] As we shall see, Pakistan has been struggling with the meaning and implications of its purported Islamic identity since independence. Bangladesh also appears to be heading in the same direction. It is therefore important to consider the Islamic dimension of human rights policy and practice in South and Southeast Asia.

It is important to note that Islamic norms may be more influential at an informal, almost subconscious psychological level than they are at the official legal or policy level. One should not, therefore, underestimate the Islamic factor simply because the particular state is not constituted as an Islamic state, or because its legal system does not purport to comply with historical Islamic law, commonly known as Shari'a.[4] Conversely, one should not overestimate the Islamic factor simply because the state and the legal system are publicly identified as such. This is particularly important from a human rights point of view where underlying social and political attitudes and values may defeat or frustrate the declared policy and formal legal principles.

This chapter is concerned with both the sociological as well as the legal and official impact of Islam on human rights. The chapter begins by explaining the paradox of declared commitment to human rights, on the one hand, and the low level of compliance with these standards in daily practice, on the other. It is my submission that this paradox can be understood in light of the competing claims of the universalism and relativism of human rights standards. It is my thesis that certain standards of human rights are frequently violated because they are not perceived to be culturally legitimate in the context of the particular country. To the extent that political regimes and other dominant social forces can explicitly or implicitly challenge the validity of certain human rights norms as alien or at least not specifically sanctioned by the primary values of the dominant indigenous culture, they can avoid the negative consequences of their violation.

Such analysis would seem to suggest the need for establishing cultural legitimacy for human rights standards in the context of the particular society. However, this enterprise raises another problem. If indigenous cultural values are to be asserted as a basis of human rights standards, we are likely to encounter "undesirable" aspects of the indigenous culture. In other words, while it may be useful to establish cultural legitimacy for human rights standards, certain elements of the indigenous culture may be antithetical to the human rights of some segments of the population. This chapter will illustrate the dilemma of cultural legitimacy for human rights in the Islamic tradition.

THE HUMAN RIGHTS PARADOX

1988 marked the fortieth anniversary of the Universal Declaration of Human Rights, which was adopted by the General Assembly of the United Nations on the 10th of December 1948.[5] Several UN and regional human rights conventions have since been ratified as binding international treaties by scores of countries from all parts of the world.[6] At the domestic level, many human rights receive strong endorsement in the constitutional and legal system of most countries of the world. Moreover, human rights issues are continuously covered by the news media as a supposedly important consideration in national and international politics.

Despite these formal commitments to human rights, and apparently strong concern with their violation, there is a mounting crisis in practical compliance with human rights standards throughout the world. Gross and consistent violations of human rights in many countries are recorded daily. Activist groups and non-governmental organizations continue to charge almost every government in the world of involvement or complicity in violating one or more human rights in its national and/or international policies.[7]

This glaring disparity between apparent commitment in theory and poor compliance in practice is what may be called the paradox of human rights. On the one hand, the idea of human rights is so powerful that no government in the world today can afford to reject it openly.[8] On the other hand, the most basic and fundamental human rights are being consistently violated in all parts of the world. It is therefore necessary to understand and resolve this paradox if human rights are to be respected and implemented in practice. As correctly stated by Jenks: "The potentially tragic implication of this paradox is the ever-present danger that the denial of human rights may, as in the past, express, permit, and promote a worship of the State no less fatal to peace than to freedom; by failure to make a reality of the Universal Declaration of Human Rights and United Nations Covenants of Human Rights we may leave mankind at the mercy of new absolutism which will engulf the world."[9]

One obvious explanation of the dichotomy between the theory and practice of human rights is the cynical manipulation of a noble and enlightened concept by many governments and politicians in all countries of the world. It may therefore be said that this is merely the current manifestation of an ancient phenomenon in human affairs. However, without disputing the historical validity of this analysis, one can point to the other side of the coin as the concrete manifestation of another ancient phenomenon in human affairs, namely the capacity of people to assert and realize their rights and claims in the face of adversity and cynicism. From this perspective, what is therefore significant is not the cynical abuse of the human rights idea, but the fact that oppressive governments and ambitious politicians find expressing their support of human rights useful, if not necessary, for gaining popular support at home and legitimacy abroad. This tribute paid by vice to virtue is very significant and relevant to future efforts at bridging the gap between the theory and practice of human rights.

In order to hold governments to their declared commitment to human rights, it is essential to establish the principle that human rights violations are not matters within the exclusive domestic jurisdiction of any state in the world.[10] Under traditional international law, national sovereignty was taken to include the right of each state to treat its own subjects in whatever manner it deemed fit. Consequently, it was perceived to be unwarranted interference in the internal affairs of a sovereign state for other states to object to or protest any action or policy of that state towards its own subjects. The Charter of the United Nations apparently endorsed these notions. Article 2.7 expressly stated that the Charter does not "authorize the United Nations to intervene in matters which are essentially within the domestic jurisdiction of any state or shall require the Members to submit such matters to settlement under the present Charter." Other authoritative statements of international law continue to emphasize the traditional definition of national sovereignty. For example, these notions feature prominently in the 1970 UN Declaration on Principles of International Law Concerning Friendly Relations and Cooperation among States in Accordance with the Charter of the United Nations.[11]

However, Article 2.7 of the UN Charter stipulates that the principle of non-interference in matters essentially within the domestic jurisdiction of any state shall not apply to UN action with respect to threats to the peace, breaches of the peace, and acts of aggression. It could be argued that serious and consistent violations of at least some fundamental human rights constitute a threat to international peace and security, and are therefore within this exception to the "essentially domestic jurisdiction" clause of the UN Charter. In other words, since serious and consistent violations of certain human rights constitute a threat to international peace and security, the UN can act against the offending state because the matter is beyond the "essentially domestic jurisdiction" of the state. It may also be possible to construe some of the language of the above-cited 1970 UN Declaration on Friendly Relations as permitting international action in promoting and protecting at least some fundamental human rights.

Despite its problems, national sovereignty appears to be necessary for the exercise of the right of peoples to self-determination. In any case, it is too strongly entrenched to hope for its total repudiation in the foreseeable future. Nevertheless, it is imperative to overcome national sovereignty objections to international action for the protection and promotion of human rights without violating the legitimate scope of such sovereignty. "The renunciation of intervention [in the internal affairs of states] does not constitute a policy of nonintervention; it involves the development of some form of *collective intervention*."[12]

In order to support this position, it is necessary to repudiate any plausible argument which claims that action in support of human rights violates the national sovereignty of the country. It has been argued, for example, that the established international standards are not consistent with the cultural traditions or philosophical and ideological perspectives of the given country.[13] It is not enough to say that this argument may be used as a pretext for violating human rights because such manipulation would not be viable if there is no validity to the argument itself. In other words, this argument is useful as a pretext precisely because it has some validity which makes the excuse plausible. It is therefore incumbent upon human rights advocates to address the element of truth in this argument in order to prevent its cynical abuse in the future.

THE LEGITIMACY DILEMMA

If we take the UN Charter and the Universal Declaration of Human Rights as the starting point of the modern movement for the promotion and protection of human rights, we will find it true that the majority of the peoples of Africa and Asia had little opportunity for direct contribution to the formulation of these basic documents. Since the majority of the peoples of these two continents were still suffering from the denial of their collective human right to self-determination because of colonial rule and foreign domination at the time, they were unable to participate in the drafting and adoption processes.[14] It is true that some of the representatives of the older, mainly Western, nations were sensitive to the cultural traditions of the unrepresented peoples,[15] but that could have hardly been a sufficient substitute for direct representation.

Many more African and Asian countries subsequently achieved formal independence and were able to participate in the formulation of international human rights instruments. By ratifying the UN Charter and subscribing to the specialized international instruments which incorporated and elaborated upon the Universal Declaration of Human Rights, the emerging countries of Africa and Asia were deemed bound by those earlier documents in addition to the subsequent instruments in which they participated from the start. Thus, the vast majority of the countries of Africa and Asia can be seen as parties to the process by which international human rights standards are determined and formulated. Nevertheless, this official and formal participation does not seem to have achieved the desired result of legitimizing international human rights standards in the cultural traditions of these peoples. This failure is clearly illustrated, in my view, by the lack of sufficient popular awareness of and support for these standards among the majority of the population of the countries of

Africa and Asia. Given this lack of awareness and support for the international standards, it is not surprising that governments and other actors are able to evade the negative consequences of their massive and gross violations of human rights throughout Africa and Asia.

It is my submission that formal participation in the formulation and implementation processes by the elites of African and Asian countries will never achieve practical respect and protection for human rights in those regions unless that participation reflects the genuine consensus of the population of those countries. I would further suggest that the peoples of these regions have not had the chance to develop such consensus by reexamining their own cultural traditions in terms of universal and international human rights. It seems that the elites of these countries have come to the international fora where human rights standards were determined and formulated without a clear mandate from their own peoples.

As an advocate of international human rights, I am not suggesting that the international community should scrap the present documents and start afresh. This would be an impracticable and dangerous course of action because we may never recover what would be lost through the repudiation of the present instruments and structures. What I am suggesting is that we should supplement the existing standards and continue to develop them through the genuine participation of the widest possible range of cultural traditions. In furtherance of this approach, it is incumbent on the advocates of human rights to work for legitimizing universal standards of human rights within their own traditions.

However, this approach presents us with the other horn of the dilemma. Almost every existing cultural tradition (including philosophical or ideological positions) in the world has some problems with respect to the full range of fundamental human rights. Generally speaking, for example, whereas the liberal tradition(s) of the West have difficulties in accepting economic, social, and cultural rights and in conceiving of collective rights such as a right to development, the Marxist tradition has similar difficulties with respect to civil and political rights.[16] More specifically, prevailing notions of freedom of speech under the Constitution of the United States, for instance, may protect forms of speech and expression which advocate racial hatred in violation of the international standards set by the Covenant for the Elimination of All Forms of Racial Discrimination of 1965.

The main difficulty in working to establish universal standards across cultural boundaries is the fact that each tradition has its own internal frame of reference and derives the validity of its precepts and norms from its own sources. When a cultural tradition relates to other traditions and perspectives, it is likely to do so in a negative and perhaps even hostile and antagonistic way. In order to claim the loyalty and conformity of its own members, a tradition would normally assert its own superiority over, and tend to dehumanize the adherents of, other traditions. This tendency would clearly undermine efforts to accord members of other traditions equality in status and rights, even if they happen to live within the political boundaries of the same country.[17]

Nevertheless, I believe that all the major cultural traditions adhere to the common normative principle that one should treat other people as he or she wishes to be treated by them. This golden rule, which may be called the principle of reciprocity, is shared by all the major traditions of the world. Moreover, the moral and logical force of this simple proposition can easily be appreciated by all human beings of whatever cultural tradition or philosophical persuasion. If construed in an enlightened manner so that the "other" includes all other human beings, this principle is capable of sustaining universal standards of human rights.

In accordance with this fundamental principle of reciprocity, I would take universal human rights to be those rights which I claim for myself, and must therefore concede to others. The practical implications of this fundamental principle would have to be negotiated through the political process to develop consensus around specific policies and concrete action on what the majority or other dominant segment of the population would accept for itself and would therefore have to concede to minorities and individuals. Although theoretical

safeguards and structures may be devised to ensure the constitutional and human rights of all individuals and groups, the ultimate safeguard is the goodwill and sense of enlightened political expediency of the majority or other dominant segment of the population. Unless the majority or dominant segment of the population is persuaded to respect and promote the human rights of minorities and individuals, the whole society will drift into the politics of confrontation and subjugation rather than that of reconciliation and justice.

THE LEGITIMACY DILEMMA IN THE MUSLIM CONTEXT

When I consider Shari'a as the historical formulation of my own Islamic tradition I am immediately confronted with certain inadequacies in its conception of human rights as judged by the above-stated principle of reciprocity and its supporting arguments. In particular, I am confronted by Shari'a's discrimination against Muslim women and non-Muslims and its restrictions on freedom of religion and belief. Unfortunately, most contemporary Muslim writings on the subject tend to provide a misleadingly glowing view of Shari'a on human rights without any reference to the above-cited problematic aspects of Shari'a.[18] Moreover, some of those Muslim authors who are willing to candidly state the various features of conflict and tension between Shari'a and current standards of human rights tend to take an intransigent position in favor of Shari'a without considering the prospects of its reconciliation with current standards of human rights.[19]

It is true that Shari'a had introduced significant improvements in the status and rights of women as compared to its historical contemporaries between the seventh and nineteenth centuries A.D.[20] Under Shari'a, Muslim women enjoy full and independent legal personality to own and dispose of property and conclude other contracts in their own right. They are also guaranteed specific shares in inheritance and other rights in family law. However, Shari'a did not achieve complete legal equality between Muslim men and women.

Whereas a man is entitled to marry up to four wives and divorce any of them at will, a woman is restricted to one husband and can only seek judicial divorce on very limited and strict grounds. Women receive only half a share of a man in inheritance, and less monetary compensation for criminal bodily harm (*diya*). Women are generally incompetent to testify in serious criminal cases. Where their testimony is accepted in civil cases, it takes two women to make a single witness.[21] Other examples of inequality can be cited. In fact, the general rule of Shari'a is that men are the guardians of women, and as such have the license to discipline them to the extent of beating them "lightly" if they fear them to become unruly.[22] Consequently, Shari'a holds that Muslim women may not hold any office involving exercising authority over Muslim men.

Similarly, Shari'a granted non-Muslim believers, mainly Christians and Jews who submit to Muslim sovereignty, the status of *dhimma*, whereby they are secured in person and property and permitted to practice their religion and regulate their private affairs in accordance with their own law and custom in exchange for payment of a special tax, known as *jiziya*.[23] Those classified by Shari'a as unbelievers are not allowed to live within an Islamic state except with a special permit of safe conduct, known as *aman*, which defines their status and rights.[24] If the residence of a *musta'min*, an unbeliever allowed to stay within an Islamic state under *aman*, extends beyond one year, some Shari'a jurists would allow him to assume the status of *dhimma*. However, neither *dhimma* nor *aman* would qualify a non-Muslim to full citizenship of an Islamic state or guarantee such a person complete equality with Muslim citizens.[25] For example, Shari'a specifically requires that non-Muslims may never exercise authority over Muslims.[26] Consequently, non-Muslims are denied any public office which would involve exercising such authority.

The third example of serious human rights problems with Shari'a, indicated above, is freedom of religion and belief. It is true that *dhimma* and possibly *aman* would guarantee a non-Muslim a measure of freedom of religion in that he would be free to practice his officially sanctioned religion. However, such freedom of religious practice is inhibited by the limitations imposed on non-Muslims in public life, including payment of *jiziya*, which is intended by Shari'a to be a humiliating tax.[27]

Another serious limitation of freedom of religion and belief is the Shari'a law of apostasy, *ridda*, whereby a Muslim would be subject to the death penalty if he should repudiate his faith in Islam, whether or not in favor of another religion.[28] Some modern Muslim writers have argued that apostasy should not be punishable by death.[29] However, this progressive view has not yet been accepted by the majority of Muslims. Moreover, even if the death penalty is abolished, other serious consequences will remain, such as the possibility of other punishment, confiscation of the property of the apostate and the nullification of his or her marriage to a Muslim spouse.[30] In contrast, non-Muslims, including Christians and Jews, are encouraged to embrace Islam. Whereas Muslims are supported by the state and community in their efforts to proselytize in order to convert non-Muslims to Islam, non-Muslims are positively prohibited from undertaking such activities.

All of the above features of discrimination against Muslim women and non-Muslims and restrictions on freedom of religion and belief are part of Shari'a to the present day. Those aspects of discrimination against Muslim women which fall within the scope of family law and inheritance are currently enforced throughout the Muslim world because Shari'a constitutes the personal law of Muslims even in those countries where it is not the formal legal system of the land.[31] Discrimination against non-Muslims and the Shari'a law of apostasy are enforced in those countries where Shari'a is the formal legal system. For example, Article 13 of the Constitution of the Islamic Republic of Iran expressly classifies Iranians in terms of their religious or sectarian beliefs. By the terms of this Article, Baha'is are not a recognized religious minority, and as such are not entitled even to the status of second-class citizens under the principle of *dhimma* explained above. Moreover, as recently as January 1985, a 76-year-old man was executed for apostasy in the Sudan.[32]

What is more significant for our present purposes, however, is the fact that all of these and other aspects of Shari'a are extremely influential in shaping Muslim attitudes and policies even where Shari'a is not the formal legal system. In other words, so long as these aspects of Shari'a are held by Muslim legislators, policy makers, and executive officials to be part of their cultural tradition, we can only expect serious negative consequences for human rights in predominantly Muslim countries, regardless of whether or not Shari'a is the basis of the formal constitutional and legal system of the land. . . .

CONCLUSION: REVISED AGENDA FOR THE HUMAN RIGHTS MOVEMENT

Thus, if we are to bridge the gap between the theory and practice of human rights in the contemporary world, we must all be ready to shed or modify those preconceptions which seem to obstruct or frustrate the efficacy of international cooperation in the field of human rights. This would require a modification of the concept of national sovereignty in order to enhance the principle of international accountability for violating human rights. The international community must firmly establish, as a matter of international law and, as well, of practice, that violations of universal human rights are not matters of "essentially domestic jurisdiction." The legal framework for such action can easily be established under the UN Charter and existing international and regional human rights instruments. What may be lacking is the political will among states to relinquish their traditional national pride in favor of the international rule of law.

Another concept that needs to be modified is the cultural conception of the term "right." In the Western liberal tradition, rights are primarily entitlements or claims which the individual person has against the state. This conception has led many Western governments and human rights advocates to deny human rights status to claims which they deem to be too vague or not amenable to enforcement against the state, such as economic rights and collective rights to development. Non-Western cultural traditions, in contrast, not only conceive of such claims as human rights, they insist that they must be granted that status. Some of the human rights treaties and literature already reflect a broader conception of rights than originally envisaged by liberal theory. However, there is little evidence to show that this is more than a token concession by liberal governments. The developed countries of the world should not expect other peoples of the world, including the Muslim peoples, to examine and reevaluate their cultural and philosophical traditions in the interest of more genuine respect for and greater compliance with international standards of human rights *unless* they (the developed countries) are willing to examine and re-evaluate their own cultural traditions.

It is my submission that these and other related considerations must now be injected into human rights discourse at official, scholarly and popular levels of debate and action. It is not difficult, for example, to develop the appropriate formulations and implementation mechanisms and procedures for collective claims or entitlement as human rights which do not necessarily correspond to the established Western notion of "right." For this course of action to be useful, however, the existing human rights standards and mechanisms for their enforcement must be opened up for new ideas and influences. The process of definition, formulation, and implementation of universal human rights must be genuinely universal and not merely Western in orientation and techniques.

In conclusion, the dilemma of cultural legitimacy must be resolved if the glaring disparity between the theory and practice of human rights is to be narrowed. To achieve this end, human rights advocates need to undertake a massive educational effort, drawing on all the religious and other normative resources of each community in support of universal human rights. They must build from the immediately local, through the national and regional levels, towards greater international cooperation in the promotion and protection of human rights. Greater emphasis must be placed on the role of grass-roots non-governmental organizations and the role of indigenous mechanisms for enhancing the cultural legitimacy of human rights.

NOTES

1. A first draft of this chapter was prepared under a grant from the Woodrow Wilson International Center for Scholars, Washington, D.C. The statements and views expressed herein are those of the author and are not necessarily those of the Wilson Center. I have prepared the final draft of this chapter while holding the position of Ariel F. Sallows Professor of Human Rights at the College of Law, University of Saskatchewan, Canada in 1989–90.

2. For statistics on Muslim peoples and their percentages of the total population of all the countries of the world, see Richard V. Weeks, ed., *Muslim Peoples, A World Ethnographic Survey*, second ed. (Westport, CT: Greenwood Press, 1984), pp. 882–911.

3. F. A. Trindade and H. P. Lee, editors, *The Constitution of Malaysia: Further Perspectives and Developments* (Singapore: Oxford University Press, 1986), pp. 5–12. See further the review of this book by Abdullahi A. An-Na'im in *Columbia Journal of Transnational Law* 26 (1988), pp. 1101–1107.

4. It is misleading to think of Shari'a as merely law in the strict modern sense of the term. Shari'a is the Islamic view of the whole duty of humankind, and includes moral and pastoral theology and ethics, high spiritual aspirations and detailed ritualistic and formal observance, as well as legal rules in the formal sense. See S. G. Vesey-Fitzgerald, "The Nature and Sources of the Shari'a," in M. Khadduri and H. J. Liebesny, eds., *Law in the Middle East* (Washington: The Middle East Institute, 1955), pp. 85ff.; and Majid Khadduri, "Nature and Sources of Islamic Law," *George Washington Law Review* 22 (1953), pp. 6–10.

5. For the full text of the Universal Declaration of Human Rights see Ian Brownlie, ed., *Basic Documents on Human Rights*, second ed. (Oxford: Clarendon Press, 1981), pp. 21–27.

6. These include the International Convention on the Elimination of All Forms of Racial Discrimination of 1963; the International Covenant on Economic, Social and Cultural Rights, and the International Covenant on Civil and Political Rights, both of 1966; and the Convention on the Elimination of All Forms of Discrimination Against Women of 1979. For the texts of these instruments, see *ibid*. pp. 150–63, pp. 118–27 and pp. 94–107, respectively. There are three regional conventions currently in force for Europe, the Americas and Africa. See *ibid*. pp. 242–57 and pp. 391–416 for the European and American Conventions respectively. The African Charter is included as Appendix I in Claude E. Welch, Jr. and Ronald I. Meltzer, eds., *Human Rights and Development in Africa* (Albany: State University of New York Press, 1984), pp. 317–29.

7. See, for example, the Annual Reports of Amnesty International, and the periodic reports of Human Rights Internet and the Minority Rights Group. Of special interest to the subject of this paper, see Lawyers Committee for Human Rights, *Zia's Law: Human Rights under Military Rule in Pakistan* (New York/Washington: The Lawyers Committee for Human Rights, 1985). The Lawyers Committee has also published two other reports on human rights in Pakistan: *Violations of Human Rights in Pakistan*, June 1981; and *Justice in Pakistan*, July 1983.

8. Louis Henkin, Introduction, in Louis Henkin, ed., *The International Bill of Rights: The Covenant on Civil and Political Rights* (New York: Columbia University Press, 1981), p. 1.

9. C. Wilfred Jenks, *The World Beyond the Charter in Historical Perspective* (London: George Allen and Unwin, Ltd., 1969), pp. 130–31.

10. Henkin, *The International Bill of Rights*, pp. 3–8. See generally, Richard Falk, *Human Rights and State Sovereignty* (New York: Holmes & Meier, 1982).

11. G.A. Res. 2625 (XXXV 1970). For the full text of this Declaration see Louis Henkin, Richard C. Pugh, Oscar Schachter and Hans Smit, eds., *Basic Documents Supplement to International Law: Cases and Materials*, second ed. (St. Paul, MN: West Publishing Co., 1987), pp. 75–83.

12. Richard Falk, *Legal Order in a Violent World* (Princeton: Princeton University Press, 1968), p. 339. Emphasis added.

13. This argument was recently advanced by official spokesmen of the Islamic Republic of Iran. See Edward Mortimer, "Islam and Human Rights," *Index on Censorship* (1983), p. 5.

14. Only eleven African and Asian countries were founding Members of the UN, with seven more joining over the next ten years. Jenks, *The World Beyond the Chattel in Historical Perspective*, p. 92.

15. See, for example, "Human Rights, Comments and Interpretations," a symposium edited by UNESCO, London, 1949, reprinted in *Human Rights Teaching*, IV (1985), pp. 4–31.

16. These conceptual difficulties and cultural differences were the underlying cause of the development of two separate covenants, one for civil and political rights and the other for economic, social and cultural rights, rather than a single bill of human rights as originally envisaged. Henkin, *The International Bill of Rights*, pp. 5–6.

17. See, generally, Patrick Thornberry, "Is There a Phoenix in the Ashes? International Law and Minority Rights." *Texas International Law Journal* 15 (1980), p. 421.

18. See, for example, Ali Abedl Wahid Wafi, "Human Rights in Islam," *Islamic Quarterly* 11 (1967), p. 64; and Isma'il al-Faruqi, "Islam and Human Rights," *Islamic Quarterly* 27 (1983), p. 12. One of the better and more constructive works by contemporary Muslim authors is Riffat Hassan's "On Human Rights and the Qur'anic Perspectives," *Journal of Ecumenical Studies* 19 (1982), p. 51.

19. See, for example, Tabandeh, *A Muslim Commentary on the Universal Declaration of Human Rights* (London: F. T. Goulding and Co., 1970).

20. On the relative improvements in the status of women introduced by Shari'a, see Ameer Ali, *The Spirit of Islam* (London: Christophers, 1922), pp. 222–57; and Fazlur Rahman, "Status of Women in The Qur'an," in G. Nashat, ed., *Women and Revolution in Iran* (Boulder, CO: Westview Press, 1983), p. 37.

21. For sources and discussion of these aspects of Shari'a, see Abdullahi Ahmed An-Na'im, "The Rights of Women and International Law in the Muslim Context," *Whittier Law Review* (1987), pp. 493–97.

22. Verse 4:34 of the Qur'an. The Qur'an is cited here by number of chapter followed by number of verse in that chapter.

23. Verse 9:29 of the Qur'an. See *The Encyclopedia of Islam, New Edition*, vol. II, p. 227; and Majid Khadduri, *War and Peace in the Law of Islam* (Baltimore: The Johns Hopkins University Press, 1955), p. 177 and pp. 195–99.

24. Khadduri, *War and Peace in the Law of Islam*, pp. 163–69; Muhammad Hamidullah, *The Muslim Conduct of State*, 5th edition (Lahore: Sh. M. Ashraf, 1966), pp. 201–02.

25. Majid Khadduri, "Human Rights in Islam," *The Annals of the American Academy of Political and Social Science* 243 (1946), p. 79. Cf. Majid Khadduri, *The Islamic Concept of Justice* (Baltimore and London: The Johns Hopkins University Press, 1984), p. 233.

26. This is held to be so because verses of the Qur'an, such as 3:28, 4:144, 8:72 and 73, etc. prohibit Muslims from taking non-Muslims as *awliya*, guardians and supporters.

27. This connotation is reflected in the language of verse 9:29 of the Qur'an which requires that *dhimmis* pay *jiziya* in humiliation and submission.

28. Khadduri, *War and Peace in the Law of Islam*, p. 150; Rudoph Peters and Gert J. De Vries, "Apostasy in Islam," *Die Welt des Islams* XVII (1976–77), p. 1.

29. See, for example, A. Rahman, *Punishment of Apostasy in Islam* (Lahore: Institute of Islamic Culture, 1972).

30. On these other consequences of apostasy see Abdullahi Ahmed An-Na'im, "The Islamic Law of Apostasy and its Modern Applicability: A Case from the Sudan," *Religion* 16 (1986), p. 212.

31. Coulson, *A History of Islamic Law*, p. 161; Herbert Liebesny, *The Law of the Near and Middle East* (Albany: State of New York Press, 1975), p. 56.

32. For a full explanation and discussion of this case see An-Na'im, "The Islamic Law of Apostasy and Its Modern Applicability: A Case from the Sudan."

The African Context of Human Rights

Claude Ake

Claude Ake was professor of political science at the University of Port Harcourt in Nigeria. He was the author of *A Theory of Political Integration* (1967), *Revolutionary Pressures in Africa* (1978), and *A Political Economy of Africa* (1981).

Ake points out that Western liberal notions of human rights are not very interesting or meaningful for African societies. He contends that if a person is starving to death, the right to free speech does not do him or her much good. Ake also argues that a strong emphasis on rights will block various development policies. He believes that socialism rather than procedural liberalism provides the best grounding for a conception of human rights that will effectively address the current problems of poverty and fascism in African countries. In this context, collective rights, especially for those of disadvantaged groups, will be of greater concern than individual rights.

Nobody can accuse Africa of taking human rights seriously. In a world which sees concern for human rights as a mark of civilized sensitivity, this indifference has given Africa a bad name. It is not unlikely that many consider it symptomatic of the rawness of life which has always been associated with Africa. I am in no position to say with any confidence why Africa has not taken much interest in human rights, but I see good reasons why she should not have done so.

Before going into these reasons let us be clear what we are talking about. The idea of human rights is quite simple. It is that human beings have certain rights simply by virtue of being human. These rights are a necessary condition for the good life. Because of their singular importance, individuals are entitled to, indeed, required to claim them and society is enjoined to allow them. Otherwise, the quality of life is seriously compromised.

The idea of human rights, or legal rights in general, presupposes a society which is atomized and individualistic, a society of endemic conflict. It presupposes a society of people conscious of their separateness and their particular interests and anxious to realize them. The legal right is a claim which the individual may make against other members of society, and simultaneously an obligation on the part of society to uphold this claim.

The values implicit in all this are clearly alien to those of our traditional societies. We put less emphasis on the individual and more on the collectivity, we do not allow that the individual has any claims which may override that of the society. We assume harmony, not divergence of interests, competition and conflict; we are more inclined to think of our obligations to other members of our society rather than our claims against them.

The Western notion of human rights stresses rights which are not very interesting in the context of African realities. There is much concern with the right to peaceful assembly, free speech and thought, fair trial, etc. The appeal of these rights is sociologically specific. They appeal to people with

Excerpt from Claude Ake, "The African Context of Human Rights," Africa Today, Vol. 34, No. 142, pp. 5–13, 1987. Reprinted by permission of Indiana University Press.

a full stomach who can now afford to pursue the more esoteric aspects of self-fulfillment. The vast majority of our people are not in this position. They are facing the struggle for existence in its brutal immediacy. Theirs is a totally consuming struggle. They have little or no time for reflection and hardly any use for free speech. They have little interest in choice for there is no choice in ignorance. There is no freedom for hungry people, or those eternally oppressed by disease. It is no wonder that the idea of human rights has tended to sound hollow in the African context.

The Western notion of human rights lacks concreteness. It ascribes abstract rights to abstract beings. There is not enough concern for the historical conditions in which human rights can actually be realized. As it turns out, only a few people are in a position to exercise the rights which society allows. The few who have the resources to exercise these rights do not need a bill of rights. Their power secures them. The many who do not have the resources to exercise their rights are not helped any by the existence of these rights. Their powerlessness dooms them.

The idea of human rights really came into its own as a tool for opposing democracy. The French Revolution had brought home forcefully to everyone the paradox of democracy, namely that its two central values, liberty and equality, come into conflict at critical points. There is no democracy where there is no liberty for self-expression or choice. At the same time there is no democracy where there is no equality, for inequality reduces human relations to subordination and domination. The French Revolution and Jean Jacques Rousseau revealed rather dramatically the paradoxical relation between these two central values of democracy by leaning heavily towards equality. They gave Europe a taste of what it would be like to take the idea of equality and the correlative idea of popular sovereignty seriously.

Bourgeois Europe was horrified. The idea of a popular sovereign insisting on equality and having unlimited power over every aspect of social life was unacceptable. For such power was a threat to the institution of private property as well as the conditions of accumulation. So they began to emphasize liberty rather than the collectivity. This emphasis was also a way of rejecting democracy in its pure form as popular sovereignty. That was the point of stressing the individual and his rights and holding that certain rights are inalienable. That was the point of holding that the individual could successfully sustain certain claims and certain immunities against the wishes of the sovereign or even the rest of society. It is ironic that all this is conveniently forgotten today and liberal democrats can pass as the veritable defenders of democracy.

CHANGING STATUS OF HUMAN RIGHTS IN AFRICA

Africa is at last beginning to take interest in human rights. For one thing, the Western conception of human rights has evolved in ways which have made it more relevant to the African experience, although its relevance still remains ambiguous. Because human rights is such an important part of the political ideology of the West, it was bound to register in Africa eventually. Human rights record is beginning to feature in Western decisions of how to relate to the countries and leaders of Africa. Western decisions on this score have been made with such cynical inconsistency that one wonders whether human rights record really matters to them at all. However, our leaders ever so eager to please are obliged to assume that it matters and to adjust their behavior accordingly. Also, the authoritarian capitalism of Africa is under some pressure to be more liberal and thereby create political conditions more conducive to capitalist efficiency.

If these are the reasons why Africa is beginning to take more interest in human rights, they are by no means the reason why she ought to do so. The way I see it is that we ought to be interested in human rights because it will help us to combat social forces which threaten to send us back to barbarism. Because it will aid our struggle for the social transformation which we need to survive and to flourish. To appreciate this, let us look at the historical conditions of contemporary Africa.

I hope we can all agree that for now, the most salient aspect of these conditions is the crisis. It has been with us for so long we might well talk of the permanent crisis. No one seems to know for sure what its character is but we know its devastating effects only too well. We Africans have never had it so bad. The tragic consequences of our development strategies have finally come home to us. Always oppressed by poverty and deprivation, our lives become harsher still with each passing day as real incomes continue to decline. We watch helplessly while millions of our people are threatened by famine and look pitifully to the rest of the world to feed us. Our social and political institutions are disintegrating under pressure from our flagging morale, our dwindling resources and the intense struggle to control them. What is the problem? I am not sure. But I am convinced that we are not dealing simply or even primarily with an economic phenomenon. There is a political dimension to it which is so critical, it may well be the most decisive factor.

This is the problem of democracy or the problem of political repression. A long time ago our leaders opted for political repression. Having abandoned democracy for repression, our leaders are delinked from our people. Operating in a vacuum, they proclaim their incarnation of the popular will, hear echoes of their own voices, and reassured, pursue with zeal, policies which have nothing to do with the aspirations of our people and which cannot, therefore, mobilize them. As their alienation from the people increases, they rely more and more on force and become even more alienated.

CONSEQUENCES OF THE PROBLEM OF DEMOCRACY

The consequences of this are disastrous. In the first place, it means that there is no development. Political repression ensures that the ordinary people of Africa who are the object of development remain silent, so that in the end nobody really speaks for development and it never comes alive in practice. Development cannot be achieved by proxy. A people develops itself or not at all. And it can develop itself only through its commitment and its energy. That is where democracy comes in. Self-reliance is not possible unless the society is thoroughly democratic, unless the people are the

end and not just the means of development. Development occurs, in so far as it amounts to the pursuit of objectives set by the people themselves in their own interest and pursued by means of their own resources.

Another consequence of repression is the brutalization of our people. Look around you. The willful brutalization of people occurring among us is appalling. Human life is taken lightly, especially if it is that of the underprivileged. All manner of inhuman treatment is meted out for minor offenses and sometimes for no offenses at all. Ordinary people are terrorized daily by wanton display of state power and its instruments of violence. Our prison conditions are guaranteed to traumatize. The only consensus we can mobilize is passive conformity arising from fear and resignation. As we continue to stagnate, this gets worse.

Yet another disaster threatens us. I am referring to fascism. In all probability this is something which nobody wants. But we might get it anyway because circumstances are moving steadily in that direction. All the ingredients of fascism are present now in most parts of Africa: a political class which has failed even by its own standards, and which is now acutely conscious of its humiliation and baffled by a world it cannot control; a people who have little if any hope or sense of self-worth yearning for redeemers; a milieu of anomie; a conservative leadership pitted against a rising popular radicalism and poised to take cover in defensive radicalism. That is what it takes and it is there in plenty. If Africa succumbs it will be terrible—fascism has always been in all its historical manifestations.

It seems to me that for many African countries the specter of fascism is the most urgent and the most serious danger today. Unless we contain it effectively and within a very short time, then we are in a great deal of trouble.

If this analysis is correct, then our present agenda must be the task of preventing the rise of fascism. To have a chance of succeeding, this task requires a broad coalition of radicals, populists, liberals, and even humane conservatives; that is, a coalition of all those who value democracy not in the procedural liberal sense, but in the concrete socialist sense. This is where the idea of human rights comes in. It is easily the best ideological framework for such a coalition.

AN AFRICAN CONCEPTION OF HUMAN RIGHTS

We have now seen the relevance of human rights in the African context. But on a level of generality which does not tell us very much and so does not really settle the question of the applicability of the Western concept of human rights. I do not see how we can mobilize the African masses or the intelligentsia against fascism or whatever by accepting uncritically the Western notion of human rights. We have to domesticate it, recreate it in the light of African conditions. Let me indicate very briefly how these conditions redefine the idea of human rights.

First, we have to understand that the idea of legal rights presupposes social atomization and individualism, and a conflict model of society for which legal rights are the necessary mediation. However, in most of Africa, the extent of social atomization is very limited mainly because of the limited penetration of capitalism and commodity relations. Many people are still locked into natural economies and have a sense of belonging to an organic whole, be it a family, a clan, a lineage or an ethnic group. The phenomenon of the legal subject, the largely autonomous individual conceived as a bundle of rights which are asserted against all comers has not really developed much especially outside the urban areas.

These are the conditions which explain the forms of consciousness which we insist on misunderstanding. For instance, ethnic consciousness and ethnic identity. It is the necessary consciousness associated with nonatomized social structures and mechanical solidarity. Ethnic consciousness will be with us as long as these structural features remain, no matter how we condemn it or try to engineer it out of existence.

All this means that abstract legal rights attributed to individuals will not make much sense for most of our people; neither will they be relevant to their consciousness and living conditions. It is necessary to extend the idea of human rights to include collective human rights for corporate social groups such as the family, the lineage, the ethnic group. Our people still think largely in terms of collective rights and express their commitment to it constantly in their behavior. This disposition underlies the zeal for community development and the enormous sacrifices which poor people readily make for it. It underlies the so-called tribalist voting pattern of our people, the willingness of the poor villager to believe that the minister from his village somehow represents his share of the national cake, our traditional land tenure systems, the high incidence of cooperative labor and relations of production in the rural areas. These forms of consciousness remain very important features of our lives. If the idea of human rights is to make any sense at all in the African context, it has to incorporate them in a concept of communal human rights.

For reasons which need not detain us here, some of the rights important in the West are of no interest and no value to most Africans. For instance, freedom of speech and freedom of the press do not mean much for a largely illiterate rural community completely absorbed in the daily rigors of the struggle for survival.

African conditions shift the emphasis to a different kind of rights: rights which can mean something for poor people fighting to survive and burdened by ignorance, poverty and disease; rights which can mean something for women who are cruelly used; rights which can mean something for the youth whose future we render more improbable every day. If a bill of rights is to make any sense, it must include, among others, a right to work and to a living wage, a right to shelter, to health, to education. That is the least we can strive for if we are ever going to have a society which realizes basic human needs.

Finally, in the African context, human rights have to be much more than the political correlate of commodity fetishism which is what they are in the Western tradition. In that tradition the rights are not only abstract, they are also ascribed to abstract persons. The rights are ascribed to the human being from whom all specific determinations have been abstracted: The rights have no content, just as individuals who enjoy them have no determination, and so do not really exist.

All these problems which usually lurk beneath the surface, appear in clear relief when we confront them with empirical reality. Granted, I have the freedom of speech. But where is this freedom, this right? I cannot read, I cannot write. I am too busy trying to survive. I have no time to reflect. I am so poor, I am constantly at the mercy of others. So where is this right and what is it really? Granted, I have the right to seek public office. That is all very well. But how do I realize this right? I am a full-time public servant who cannot find the time or the necessary resources to put up the organization required to win office. If I take leave from my work, I cannot hold out for more than one month without a salary. I have no money to travel about and meet the voters, even to pay the registration fees for my candidature. If I am not in a position to realize this right, then what is the point of saying that I have it? Do I really have it?

In Africa liberal rights make less sense even as ideological representations. If rights are to be meaningful in the context of a people struggling to stay afloat under very adverse economic and political conditions, they have to be concrete. Concrete in the sense that their practical import is visible and relevant to the conditions of existence of the people to whom they apply. And most importantly, concrete in the sense that they can be realized by their beneficiaries.

To be sure, there are rights which are realizable and there are people in Africa who effectively realize their rights. However, the people who are in a position to realize their rights are very few. They are able to realize their rights by virtue of their wealth and power. The litmus test for rights is those who need protection. Unfortunately, these are precisely the people who are in no position to enjoy rights. Clearly, that will not do in African conditions. People are not going to struggle for formalities and esoteric ideas which will not change their lives.

Therefore, a real need arises; namely, to put more emphasis on the realization of human rights.

How is this to be? Not in the way we usually approach such matters: by giving more unrealizable rights to the powerless and by begging the powerful to make concessions to them in the name of enlightened self-interest, justice and humanity. That approach will fail us always. Rights, especially those that have any real significance for our lives are usually taken, not given—with the cooperation of those in power if possible, but without it if necessary. That is the way it was for other peoples and that is the way it is going to be in Africa.

The realization of rights is best guaranteed by the power of those who enjoy the rights. Following this, what is needed is the empowerment by whatever means, of the common people. This is not a matter of legislation, although legislation could help a little. It is rather a matter of redistributing economic and political power across the board. That means that it is, in the final analysis, a matter of political mobilization and struggle, and it will be a protracted and bitter struggle because those who are favored by the existing distribution of power will resist heartily.

CONCLUSION: HUMAN RIGHTS AND SOCIAL TRANSFORMATION

It is at this point that the ideal of human rights is fully articulated for it is now that we see its critical dialectical moment. Initially part of the ideological prop of liberal capitalism, the idea of human rights was a conservative force. It was meant to safeguard the interests of the men of property especially against the threatening egalitarianism of popular sovereignty. It was not of course presented as a tool of special interests but a universal value good for humanity. That went down well, and it has been able to serve those who propagated it behind this mystification.

But ideas have their own dynamics which cannot easily be controlled by the people who brought them into being. In the case of human rights, its dynamics soon trapped it in a contradiction somewhat to the dismay of its protagonists. Fashioned as a tool against democracy, the idea became an important source of legitimation for those seeking the expansion of democracy. But in Europe, this contradiction never fully matured. An agile and accommodating political class and unprecedented affluence saw to that.

In Africa, prevailing objective conditions will press matters much further, particularly the question of empowerment. In all probability, the empowerment of people will become the primary issue. Once this happens, the social contradictions will be immensely sharpened and the idea of human rights will become an asset of great value to radical social transformation. I cannot help thinking that Africa is where the critical issues in human rights will be fought out and where the idea will finally be consummated or betrayed.

Asian Justifications for Human Rights

Daniel A. Bell

Daniel A. Bell has degrees from McGill University and Oxford University. He is now a professor of philosophy at Tsinghua University in Beijing. He is the author of *East Meets West* (2000) and *Communitarian and Its Critics* (1993). He has recently published *Beyond Liberal Democracy: Political Thinking for an East Asian Context* (2006), from which this selection is drawn.

  Bell argues that human rights could be justified from an East Asian cultural context, not simply from the Western liberal tradition. Moreover, while there is international agreement on a core set of human rights standards, there may be cultural variations in the conceptions of some human goods, which may have to call for a more expanded understanding of rights that include the right of elderly parents to demand care or support from grown children.

ASIAN JUSTIFICATIONS FOR HUMAN RIGHTS

Human Rights: Is Liberalism the Only Moral Foundation?

According to the prominent human rights theorist Jack Donnelly, "the idea that all human beings, simply because they are human, have certain inalienable political rights" was essentially foreign to traditional Asian political thought as well as to premodern Western political thought.[1] The theory of human rights was first fully developed in John Locke's *Second Treatise on Government.* These ideas spread broadly in response to the dual threats to human dignity posed by modern centralized states and socially disruptive free markets in seventeenth-century Europe.

The claim that the concept of human rights is foreign to East Asian political traditions may be out of date: China, for example, has been the site of a rich discourse on rights for the last century or so, every [sic] since the term "rights" began to be translated into the Chinese term *quanli.*[2] Moreover, several East Asian intellectuals argued that values similar to aspects of Western conceptions of human rights can also be found in some "premodern" non-Western traditions. For example, the distinguished Islamic scholar Nurcholish Madjid notes that "Islam too recognizes the right to found a family, the right to privacy, the right to freedom of movement and residence, the right to use one's own language, the right to practice one's own culture and the right to freedom of religion."[3] The University of Hong Kong political philosopher Joseph Chan argues that values similar to aspects of Western conceptions of human rights can also be found in the Confucian tradition.[4] The notion of *ren* (variously translated as benevolence, humanity, or love), for example, expresses the value of impartial concern to relieve human suffering, In Mencius's famous example of a child on the verge of falling into a well, a person with *ren*

Excerpt from Daniel Bell, Beyond Liberal Democracy: Political Thinking for an East Asian Context, 2006. Reprinted by permission of Princeton University Press.

would be moved by compassion to save the child, not because he or she had personal acquaintance with the child's parents, nor because he or she wanted to win the praise of fellow villagers or friends, but simply because of his or her concern for the suffering of a human person. Such concern shows that Confucianism allows for duties or rights that belong to human persons *simpliciter,* independent of their roles.[5]

In addition, the functional equivalents of some human rights *practices* can be found in Asian traditions. For example, the idea of curbing the ruler's exercise of arbitrary state power figured prominently in Confucian political regimes.[6] Jongryn Mo argues that the Censorate provided an effective institutional restraint on the ruler's power in Choson dynasty Korea. The Censorate consisted of three organs that were explicitly designed to prevent abuse in the exercise of political and administrative agents. The censors were not only judicial and auditing agents but also voices of dissent and opposition, playing roles similar to that of opposition parties in modern democracies.[7]

There were also functional equivalents of some social and economic rights. Classical Confucians strongly emphasized that the first obligation of government is to feed the people, and this norm was often put into practice in imperial China. In the Song dynasty (960–1279 C.E.), the central government established a granary in each district for the storing of rice that came from the public land, as rent. Each of the four classes of people was given rice and sometimes clothes. In the Qing dynasty (1644–1911), there were strict legal sanctions to punish officials who failed to secure the "right to food": "According to the Law Code of the Tsing [Qing] Dynasty, if the officials do not support the four classes, the very sick person and the infirm and superannuated who need public support, they shall be punished by sixty blows of the long stick."[8]

In short, the Western liberal tradition may not be the only moral foundation for realizing the values and practices associated with human rights regimes. But why does this matter, practically speaking?

Increasing Commitment to Human Rights in East Asia: Strategic Considerations

While it may be possible to defend the argument that human rights ideas and practices resonate to some extent with Asian cultural traditions, are there any particular reasons for proponents of human rights to adopt culturally sensitive strategies for the promotion of rights, either instead of, or as a complement to, other strategies? If the ultimate aim of human rights diplomacy is to persuade others of the value of human rights, it is more likely that the struggle to promote human rights can be won if it is fought in ways that build on, rather than challenge, local cultural traditions.[9] To deny the possibility that human rights norms and practices are compatible with Asian traditions translates into dependence on a foreign standard for promoting human rights. This approach has a number of drawbacks.

First, the argument that Western liberalism is the only moral foundation for human rights unwittingly plays into the hands of nasty forces in East Asia who seek to stigmatize human rights voices as "agents of foreign devils" and defamers of indigenous traditions. Similarly, the argument that the development of human rights is contingent on the development of capitalism strengthens the position of antimodernists who oppose human rights, while the argument that human rights is contingent on anthropocentric arguments strengthens advocates of a theocentric view who oppose human rights.[10] Worse, arguments that present a stark choice between religion and human rights (as opposed to an approach that promises to reconcile religious insights with human rights ideas) may lead politically moderate religious persons into developing feelings hostile to human rights positions.[11]

Second, it is a widespread belief within the United States—currently the dominant voice/actor on the world diplomatic stage—that exporting U.S. political practices and institutions is necessary for the promotion of human rights abroad. As Stephen Young, former assistant dean at the Harvard Law School, puts it,

> Many Americans seem to believe that the constitutional pattern of governance in the United States

today—as formalized in the Declaration of Independence, the Constitution, and the Bill of Rights—is a necessary prerequisite for protecting human rights. Thus, they evaluate the performance of other countries in the field of human rights by comparing their conduct with the standards of American politics?[12]

It may well have been feasible to act on this belief in the post–World War II era, when the United States was powerful enough to insist upon human rights norms. The U.S. capacity to dictate appropriate forms of government to Japan in the immediate post–World War II period is a classic example. Today, however, the relative economic and military strength of East Asia means that the United States must now rely primarily on moral authority to promote human rights in Asia. However, several factors undermine U.S. moral authority in this respect.

Widely publicized social problems in the United States no longer make it the attractive political model that it may once have been. For example, Tokyo University's Onuma Yasuaki is an active proponent of human rights in Japan, but he is also a harsh critic of the attempt to export the U.S.-style rights regime, which emphasizes civil and political liberties over social and economic rights.[13] Onuma argues that this regime—with its excessive legalism and individualism—contributes to various social diseases, such as high rates of drug use, collapsing families, rampant crime, growing economic inequality, and alienation from the political process.[14]

It is obvious that recent foreign policy developments, particularly since the Iraq War, have undermined U.S. moral credibility in Asia and, elsewhere.[15] The tendency to subordinate human rights concerns when they conflict with security and commercial considerations contributes to cynicism regarding the true motivation of U.S. policymakers, not just among government officials, but also among ordinary citizens.[16] The refusal to make amends for past misdeeds such as the Vietnam War further undermines U.S. moral authority in Asia,[17] just as Japan's refusal to accept full responsibility for its war of aggression weakens its own moral authority in Asia. For the

foreseeable future, the attempt to export "American ideals" is likely to fall on deaf ears, if not be counterproductive, in the East Asian region.

Third, appeal to the Universal Declaration of Human Rights (UDHR) as a standard for promoting human rights in East Asia is not without drawbacks. Although the UDHR has served as an effective tool in some human rights struggles in East Asia (for example, by human rights campaigners in the Philippines during Marcos' rule),[18] in many parts of East Asia the UDHR and other U.N. documents are not nearly as relevant.

Since the UDHR was formulated without significant input from East Asia, it is not always clear to East Asians why the UDHR should constitute "our" human rights norms (the Bangkok Declaration was significant because it was the first organized expression of Asian opposition to the UDHR).[19] Although the UDHR is normatively binding, most East Asian states endorsed it for pragmatic, political reasons and not because of a deeply held commitment to the human rights norms it contains. The UDHR thus does not have the normative force and political relevance of a constitution that emerges from genuine dialogue between interested parties keen on finding a long-term solution to a shared political dilemma.[20] The lack of a proper enforcement mechanism for the International Bill of Human Rights, as the UDHR and subsequent documents are called, further reduces the practical viability of this standard.

Another fundamental weakness of the U.N. documents is that they are pitched at too high a level of abstraction (perhaps necessarily so in view of the need to reach agreement among many states) to be of use for many actual social and political problems.[21] For example, does the "right to life" (article 3 of the UDHR) mean that capital punishment should be abolished? It is much easier to secure agreement at the level of high principle than to secure agreement over the application of those principles to particular cases. Moreover, U.N. documents do not provide much guidance when rights conflict or need to be violated preemptively to prevent further violations of rights.

In short, U.S. and "international" justifications for human rights do not seem particularly promising from a tactical point of view, and to be effective human rights activists may need to pay more attention to local justifications for human rights in Asia. There are also positive reasons in favor of drawing on the resources of indigenous cultural traditions to persuade East Asians of the value of human rights.

First, awareness of "values in Asia" allows the human rights activist to draw on the most compelling *justifications* for human rights practices. Many rights battles will be fought within societies according to local norms and justifications. Consider the example of the Sisters in Islam, an autonomous, nongovernmental organization of Muslim women in Malaysia.[22] This group challenges the way that Islam has been (mis)used by powerful forces to justify patriarchal practices, often contravening Islam's central ideas and animating principles. It tries to advocate women's rights in terms that are locally persuasive, meaning that it draws upon Islamic principles for inspiration.[23] For example, the Sisters in Islam submitted a memorandum to the prime minister of Malaysia urging the Federal Parliament not to endorse the *hudud* law passed by the Kelantan state legislature. The *hudud* punishments included such troubling features as the inadmissibility of women as eyewitnesses. Sisters in Islam argued against the endorsement of these punishments by rejecting the crude equation of *hudud* with *Shari'a* and *Shari'a* with Islam that helped to justify the Kelantan enactments. Apparently this campaign was effective, because the Federal Parliament states that it will not pass the Kelantan *hudud* code. The Sisters in Islam also engage in long-term human rights work, such as distributing pamphlets on Quranic conceptions of rights and duties of men and women in the family that provide the basis for a more egalitarian view of gender relations than the regressive ideas typically (and misleadingly) offered in the name of Islam itself. The assumption is that building human rights on traditional cultural resources—on the customs and values that people use to make sense of their lives—is more likely to lead to long-term commitment to human rights ideas and practices. Conversely, the group seems to recognize that defending rights by

appealing to "universal human rights" (not to mention Western feminist ideas) is likely to be ineffective, if not counterproductive.[24]

It can be argued that predominantly Islamic societies present a special case, where people's outlooks and "habits of the heart" are profoundly informed by religious values. In this context, it seems obvious that defenders of human rights are more likely to be effective if they work within the dominant tradition. But cultural traditions may also be relevant for human rights activists and democratic reformers elsewhere. For example, Wang Juntao—a long-time democratic activist who spent nearly five years in jail after the 1989 Beijing massacre—argues that many of the key figures in Chinese democracy movements drew inspiration from Confucian values. From the late nineteenth century to the present, nearly all the important figures in the history of democracy movements in mainland China, Taiwan, and Hong Kong tried to revive Confucianism in order to support democratization. Wang Juntao supports this aspiration, partly on the grounds that democracy may be easier to implement in the Chinese context if it can be shown that it need not conflict with traditional political culture: "If Confucianism is consistent with democracy, the traditional culture may be used as a means of promoting democratization in East Asia. At the very least, the political transition will be smoother and easier, with lower costs, since there will be less cultural resistance."[25] Of course, there is an element of speculation here since the "effectiveness" of Confucian—based arguments for democracy remains to be proven in mainland China, but such arguments, at minimum, can be deployed to counter official attempts to use "Confucianism" to justify constraints on democratic rule.

Second, local traditions may shed light on the *groups* most likely to bring about desirable social and political change. For example, Han Sangjin of Seoul National University suggests that students from universities in Korea, centers of "cultural authority," could draw on the Confucian tradition of respect for intellectual elites and hence play a crucial role in establishing a society-wide commitment on the need for improving the human rights situation in Korea.[26] It may be that intellectual elites are granted uncommon (by Western standards) amounts of respect in societies shaped by Confucian traditions, with the implication that human rights activists need to target this group in particular, as opposed to investing their hopes in a mythical liberalizing middle class that often supports human rights reforms only insofar as they maintain a political order conducive to the accumulation of wealth.[27]

Third, regardless of the substance or the moral justification for one's arguments, awareness of local traditions may shed light on the appropriate attitude to be employed by human rights activists. For example, Onuma Yasuaki reminds us that "[i]n Japanese culture, modesty is highly valued. Even if one believes in certain values, proselytizing for them is regarded as arrogant, uncivilized, and counterproductive. Instead, one should find ways to induce others to appreciate these values in a quiet and modest manner."[28] This has implications for cross-cultural critics of human rights violations: instead of the high-decibel "naming and shaming" approach[29] that is often seen in East Asia as high-minded and self-righteous, even by dissident intellectuals, criticism of human rights violations in East Asia is often more effective if it is presented in a more subtle and indirect way.

Fourth, local traditions may also make one more sensitive to the possibility of alternative, nonlegalistic mechanisms for the protection of the vital human interests normally secured by a rights regime in a Western context.[30] As Onuma (himself a professor of international law) notes, "legalistic thinking has been rather foreign to many Japanese . . . to resort to juridical measures and to enforce one's rights is not appreciated. Rather, one is expected to reach the same goal by resorting to less forceful measures such as patient negotiations, mediation, and other conciliatory measures.[31] In such a context, human rights activists can suggest nonjuridical mechanisms for the protection of vital human interests, emphasizing that legal means are to be employed only as a last resort.[32]

It would seem, then, that strategic considerations of practical relevance speak strongly in favor of local justifications for the values and practices that, in the Western world, are normally realized through a human rights regime. Perhaps, however, the deepest and most controversial question remains to be addressed: Can one identify aspects of East Asian cultural traditions relevant not just in the strategic sense of how best to persuade East Asians of the value of a human rights regime, but also in the sense that they may provide a moral foundation for political practices and institutions different from the human rights regimes typically favored in Western countries? It is to this topic that we now turn.

Values in Asia versus Western Liberalism: Justifiable Moral Differences?

A human rights regime is supposed to protect our basic humanity—the fundamental human goods (or needs or interests) that underpin any "reasonable" conception of human flourishing. But which human goods are fundamental? There is little public dispute over rights against murder, torture, slavery, and genocide (though, needless to say, many governments continue to engage in nasty deeds off the record). As Singaporean government official Bilahari Kausikan puts it, "It makes a great deal of difference if the West insists on humane standards of behavior by vigorously protesting genocide, murder, torture, or slavery. Here there is a clear consensus on a core of international law that does not admit of any derogation on any grounds.[33] However, beyond this agreed upon core, it may well be possible to identify "civilizational" faultlines with respect to differing conceptions of vital human interests.

To repeat, both Western and Asian cultural traditions are complex and change a great deal in response to various internal and external pressures. Nonetheless, it is possible that most politically relevant actors, both officials and intellectuals, in East Asian societies typically endorse a somewhat different set of fundamental human goods than their counterparts in Western societies now and for the foreseeable future. Different societies may typically have different ideas regarding which human goods must be protected regardless of competing considerations, and which human goods can be legitimately subject to trade-offs with other goods as part of everyday politics. If there is some truth in these propositions, it is essential for purposes of improving mutual understanding and minimizing cross-cultural conflict to take them into account. It may mean that some Western conceptions of human rights are actually culturally specific conceptions of fundamental human goods, not readily accepted elsewhere, too encompassing in some cases and too narrow in others.

Limiting the Set of Human Rights for an East Asian Context

For example, it is not only defenders of "Asian" autocratic rule who question the "American" idea that individuals have a vital interest in speaking freely, so long as they do not physically harm others, along with the political implication that the government has a "sacred" obligation to respect this interest. Consider the case of Dr. Sulak Sivaraksa, a leading prodemocracy activist in Thailand and a nominee for the Nobel Peace Prize. In 1991 the Thai ruler, General Suchinda, pressed charges against Sulak for *lèse-majesté*—derogatory remarks directed at the royal family—and for defaming the general in a speech given at Thammasat University in Thailand. Fearing for his life, Sulak fled the country, but he returned in 1992 to face charges after the Suchinda government had fallen. In court, Sulak did not deny that he had attacked the "dictator" Suchinda, but he did deny the charge of *lèse-majesté,* referring to the many services he had performed for the loyal family. Sulak explains:

> I did not . . . stake my ground on an absolute right to free speech. My defense against the charge of *lése-majesté* was my innocence of the charge; my defense was my loyalty to the King and the Royal Family and, even where I discussed the use of the charge of *lèse-majesté* in current Siamese political practice, it was to highlight abuse and to point to the ways in which abuse might undermine the monarchy, rather than to defend any theoretical right to commit this action. I am not affirming, nor would I affirm, a right to commit *lèse-majesté*. This aspect of the case is particularly concerned with my being Siamese and belonging to the Siamese cultural tradition.[34]

In other words, Sulak aimed to persuade fellow citizens that the dominant political system should be replaced with an alternative, relatively democratic political structure, but he made it explicit that this did not mean advocating the removal of the existing constraint on direct criticism of the Thai king. Perhaps Sulak, like many Thais, would feel deeply offended, if not personally harmed, by an attack on the king. In such a case—where a constraint on the freedom of speech seems to be endorsed by both defenders and critics of the prevailing political system—there should be a strong presumption[35] in favor of respecting this deviation from American-style free speech.[36]

Other examples put forward by East Asian intellectuals regarding the possibility of narrowing the definition of vital human interests more than would typically be the case in liberal Western countries—hence narrowing the list of rights that belong to the core of the human rights zone—include the following:

1. In Singapore, there is a law that empowers the police and immigration officers to "'test the urine for drugs of any person who behaves in a suspicious manner. If the result is positive, rehabilitation treatment is compulsory.'"[37] Joseph Chan comments that "[t]his act would be seen by Western liberals as an unjustifiable invasion of privacy. But for some Asians this restriction may be seen as a legitimate trade-off for the value of public safety and health."[38]

2. In democratic South Korea, each household is required to attend monthly neighborhood meetings to receive government directives and discuss local affairs,[39] What may be viewed as a minor inconvenience in Korea would almost certainly outrage most U.S. citizens, and it is likely that the U.S. Supreme Court would strike down a governmental policy that forced citizens to associate for political purposes of this sort as a violation of the First Amendment. Once again there seems to be more willingness in East Asia among the general population to serve the common good by limiting individual freedom, perhaps as a residue of the Confucian cultural tradition.

3. Islamic legal scholar and human rights activist Abdullahi A. An-Na'im offers the following example from Islamic criminal law. According to Islamic law, which is based on the Quran and which Muslims believe to be the literal and final word of God, and on the Sunna, or traditions of the

Prophet Muhammad, theft is punishable by the amputation of the right hand and homicide by exact retribution or payment of monetary compensation. An-Na'im notes that

> Islamic law requires the state to fulfill its obligation to secure social and economic justice and to ensure decent standards of living for all its citizens before it can enforce these punishments. The law also provides for very narrow definitions of these offenses, makes an extensive range of defenses against the charge available to the accused person, and requires strict standards of proof. Moreover, Islamic law demands total fairness and equality in law enforcement. In my view, the prerequisite conditions for the enforcement of these punishments are extremely difficult to satisfy in practice and ate certainly unlikely to materialize in any Muslim country in the foreseeable future.[40]

Notwithstanding the practical impediments to the legitimate implementation of corporeal punishment under Islamic law, An-Na'im argues that Islamic criminal law is endorsed in principle by the vast majority of Muslims today,[41] whereas most Western liberals and human rights activists would almost certainly regard it as a violation of the human right not to he subjected to cruel, inhuman, or degrading treatment or punishment.

Expanding the Set of Human Rights for an East Asian Context

The East Asian challenge, however, is not simply an argument for shortening the set or rights typically endorsed by members of Western liberal societies. In some areas, there may be a case for *widening* the scope of fundamental human goods to be protected by a rights regime, In Japanese society, for example, well-developed empathetic ability is regarded as one of the necessary conditions for the pursuit of the good life. Such ability is normally acquired via warm, intimate human relationships in early stages of life, leading Teruhisa Se and Rie Karatsu to argue that "a new right could be included in the category of human rights: a right to be brought up in an intimate community."[42]

Consider also the value of filial piety, what Confucians consider to be "the essential way of learning to be human."[43] East Asian societies influenced by Confucianism strongly emphasize the idea that adult children have a duty to care for elderly parents,[44] a duty to be forsaken only in the most exceptional circumstances.[45] Thus, whereas it is widely seen as morally acceptable in the West to commit elderly parents to nursing homes,[46] from an East Asian perspective this often amounts to condemning one's parents to a lonely and psychologically painful death and thus should be considered as a violation of a fundamental human good. In political practice, the value of filial piety means that it is incumbent on East Asian governments to provide the social and economic conditions that facilitate the realization of the duty to care for elderly parents.[47] This can take the form of laws that make it mandatory for children to provide financial support for elderly parents, as in mainland China,[48] Taiwan,[49] Japan, and Singapore, and/or reliance on more indirect methods such as tax breaks and housing benefits that simply make at-home care for the elderly easier, as in Korea, Hong Kong, and Singapore.[50] In some cases, the right to be cared for by adult children is secured in the constitution itself, along with other "constitutional essentials."[51]

In sum, East Asian conceptions of vital human interests may well justify deviations from the human rights standards typically endorsed by liberal theorists, Western governments, and international human rights documents formulated without substantial input from East Asia. The position that different societies can draw different lines between the core of the human rights regime and less important value is not particularly controversial in East Asia.[52] However, many otherwise progressive liberal voices in the West still seem compelled by a tradition of universalist moral reasoning that proposes one final solution to the question of the ideal polity yet paradoxically draws only on the moral aspirations and political practices found in Western societies.

One obvious implication of these reflections is to allow for the possibility of justifiable deviations from Western-style human rights regimes in East Asia. If otherwise critical East Asian voices endorse their government's "autocratic" measures,

Western human rights activists need to think twice before intervention. Let me put it differently. Given the extent of human suffering in today's world, with so many obvious and uncontroversial violations of the minimal conditions of human well-being, it is difficult to understand why Western human rights groups would want to spend (scarce) time and money critiquing human rights "violations" that would not be viewed as such by East Asians with no particular axe to grind.

NOTES

1. Donnelly, "Human Rights and Asian Values," [in The East Asian Challenge for Human Rights, edited by Joanne R. Bauer and Daniel A. Bell (New York: Cambridge University Press, 1999)] 62.
2. See Stephen C. Angle, *Human Rights and Chinese Thought: A Cross-Cultural Inquiry* (New York: Cambridge University Press, 2002), and Marina Svensson, *Debating Human Rights in China: A Conceptual and Political History* (Lanham, MD: Rowman and Littlefield, 2002). Angle and Svensson have coedited and translated *The Chinese Human Rights Reader* (Armonk, NY: M. E. Sharpe. 2002), which includes many of the key Chinese-language documents and essays on human rights.
3. Nurcholish Madjid, "Islam, Modernization and Human Rights: A Preliminary Examination of the Indonesian Case," paper presented at the Hakone workshop (on file with author) (quoting Chandra Muzaffar), 7. Since the downfall of Suharto, Nurcholish Madjid has played an important role in aiding the transition to democratic rule, and his views have been respected partly, if not mainly, because he appeals to Islamic foundations and is personally respected for his religious piety.
4. In the same vein, Stephen Angle argues that the Chinese rights discourse owes much to neo-Confucian theories about legitimate desires that date back to the sixteenth century. Angle's main argument is not that there is an exact convergence between Western and Chinese views on human rights, but rather that the Chinese background has shaped a distinctively Chinese discourse about rights, I have critically evaluated this argument in my review of Angle's book, "Human Rights and Social Criticism in Contemporary Chinese, Political Theory," *Political Theory,* vol. 32, no. 3 (June 2004), pp. 397–400.
5. See Chan, "A Confucian Perspective on Human Rights," 218.
6. It is rather surprising that Alasdair MacIntyre, known for his supposed hostility to Western-style rights discourse, has argued that modern states necessarily must draw on that discourse in a way that precludes Confucianism: "my view does involve a denial that any modern State, Asian or Western, could embody the values of a Mencius or a Xunzi. The political dimensions of a Confucianism that took either or both of them as its

teachers would be those of the local community, not of the state." MacIntyre, "Questions for Confucians: Reflections on the Essays in Comparative Study of Self, Autonomy, and Community," in *Confucian Ethic: A Comparative Study of Self, Autonomy, and Community,* ed. Kwong-loi Shun and David B. Wong (New York: Cambridge University Press, 2004), 217. But if some aspects of Confucian-inspired practices and institutions can serve as the functional equivalent of Western-style practices and institutions that secure civil and political rights, then why take such a hard line against "political Confucianism?" MacIntyre underestimates the potential of Confucian-inspired political institutions, just as he overestimates the potential of Confucian ethics to structure ethical life at the level of local community. Few contemporary adherents of Confucianism regard Confucianism as a "well-defined concept of (he kind of community within which relationships could be defined by the relevant norms, and the four virtues would provide the standards for practice" (ibid., 215); rather, Confucianism is viewed as part of the good life, particularly relevant for structuring relationships with elderly parents, but most Confucians freely draw upon other ethical resources such as Christianity and Buddhism for structuring ethical lives.
7. Jongryn Mo, "The Challenge of Accountability: Implications of the Censorate," in *Confucianism for the Modern World,* ed. Daniel A. Bell and Hahm Chaibong (New York: Cambridge University Press, 2003).
8. Chen, Huan-Chang, *The Economic Principles of Confucius and His School, vol. 2* (New York: Columbia University Press, 1911), p. 599. Quoted in Joseph Chan, "Giving Priority to the Worst-Off: A Confucian Perspective on Social Welfare," in *Confucianism for the Modern World,* ed. Daniel A. Bell and Hahm Chaibong (New York: Cambridge University Press, 2003), pp. 241–42.
9. The conception of tradition refers to an ongoing argument about the good of the community whose identity it seeks to define. The cultural traditions of interest to human rights activists, in other words, should be living in the sense that fundamental values still have the capacity to motivate action in the contemporary era. For similar accounts of tradition, see Robert Bellah et al., *Habits of the Heart* (Berkeley: University of California Press, 1985), pp. 27–28, 335–36; and Alasdair MacIntyre, *Whose Justice? Which Rationality?* (London: Duckworth, 1988).
10. John L. Esposito points out that "[t]oo often analysis and policymaking have been shaped by a liberal secularism that fails to recognize it too represents a world view, not the paradigm for modern society, and can easily degenerate into a 'secularist fundamentalism' that treats alternative views as irrational, extremist, and deviant." Esposito, "Political Islam: Beyond the Green Menace," *Current History,* vol. 93, no. 579 (January 1994), 24. The problem with "secular fundamentalism" is not just that it fails to respect nonliberal cultural traditions, but that it plays into the hands of "religious fundamentalists" who also seek to reject wholesale values and practices associated with the Western liberal tradition.
11. This is not to deny that aspects of religious traditions are inconsistent with contemporary human rights values and practices, but only to suggest that aspects of religious

traditions may be supportive of human rights and to offer the possibility that contemporary members of religious traditions may be able to formulate persuasive interpretations while excising "contingent" aspects inimical to human rights concerns. See the discussion of Islamic feminism below.

12. Stephen B. Young, "Human Rights Questions in Southeast Asian Culture: Problems for American Response," in *The Politics of Human Rights,* ed. Paula Newberg (New York: New York University Press, 1980), 187. Young then proceeds to criticize this standpoint: "Although the Anglo-American political and legal tradition has been a forceful expositor of human rights causes, it is not the only basis upon which to build a political system that respects individual dignity." Nonetheless, he falls into his own universalist trap when he fails to distinguish between democracy and human rights, apparently assuming that Western-style electoral mechanisms are necessary and sufficient to secure basic human rights (see ibid., 187–88, 209). It is important to keep in mind that nondemocratic governments sometimes do fairly well at securing human rights (e.g., contemporary Hong Kong or the Republic of Venice for most of the previous millennium), whereas democratic governments can sometimes have atrocious human rights records at home (e.g., Sri Lanka and El Salvador under Duarte) and abroad (e.g., the United States in Vietnam and Iraq).

13. The U.S.-style priority of civil and political rights refers to the official policies of the U.S. government (its invocations of "human rights and democracy" lend to refer to civil and political rights), the works of trading American political philosophers (e.g., John Rawls's *A Theory of justice),* and U.S.-based human rights groups (e.g., Human Rights First, formerly known as the Lawyers Committee for Human Rights). It is worth noting, however, that the U.S. branch of Amnesty International is explicitly critical of the official U.S. devaluation of economic rights (see the following chapter).

14. Onuma Yasuaki, "Toward an Intercivilizational Approach to Human Rights," in *The East Asian Challenge for Human Rights,* ed. Joanne R. Bauer and Daniel A. Bell, eds. (New York: Cambridge University Press. 1999), 107.

15. The lack of moral authority in the rest of world was explicitly recognized by the U.S. State Department when it postponed the annual release of its (2004) Country Reports on Human Rights Practices following the public release of photos depicting the torture ("abuse," as the U.S. government called it) of Iraqi prisoners at Abu Ghraib prison.

16. On the case of China, see Randall Peerenboom, "Assessing Human Rights in China; Why the Double Standard?," *Cornell International Law Journal,* vol. 38, no. 1 (February 2004), 73, n. 7.

17. The Bush administration, needless to say, is not likely to apologize for the Vietnam War. More surprisingly, perhaps, the Clinton administration added insult to injury by pressuring the Vietnamese government to repay $145 million in debts incurred by the U.S.-backed government of the former South Vietnam, effectively putting "Hanoi in the position of retroactively footing part of the bill for a war against itself." Clay Chandler, "Ghosts of War Haunt Rubin's Vietnam Trip," *International Herald Tribune,* 11 April 1997.

18. One can explain this phenomenon in part by the fact that the Marcos regime depended to a great extent on U.S. economic and military support. Because of this, Marcos was extremely conscious of his public image before the world. This, in turn, led him to employ legalistic justifications for his policies. As Maria Serena Diokno puts it, "what better way than to apply international instruments he had publicly proclaimed as the guiding principles of his rule?" Letter from Maria Serena Diokno to Daniel Bell (20 November 1995) (on file with author).

19. Sumner B. Twiss notes that the Chinese delegate to the drafting process of the UDHR argued for the inclusion of the Confucian idea of *ren* in article 1, which was eventually reflected in the idea that human beings are endowed not just with "reason," but also with "conscience." Twiss, "A Constructive Framework for Discussing Confucianism and Human Rights," in *Confucianism and Human Rights,* ed. Wm. Theodore de Bary and Tu Weiming (New York: Columbia University Press, 1998), 41. If that is the only concrete manifestation of an East Asian contribution to the UDHR, however, it won't quell the critics who view it as a "Westcentric" document.

20. One might also ask why the government's voice should count as the normatively binding final interpretation of human rights issues in East Asia. Ironically, the same critics who point out that East Asian governments illegitimately present their own interpretations of human rights (often self-interested arguments for the denial of rights) as though it represents a society-wide consensus are saying, in effect, that international human standards upheld in the UDHR should be upheld because their governments endorsed this document.

21. Similar problems arise with principles laid out in state constitutions: on the (mistaken) tendency to think that constitutionalizing property rights is sufficient to secure those rights, see Greg Alexander, "Property in Global Constitution-Making: Avoiding the Formalist Trap" (ms. on file with the author).

22. See Norani Othman, "Grounding Human Rights Arguments in Non-Western Culture: *Shari'a* and the Citizenship Rights of Women in a Modern Islamic State," in *The East Asian Challenge for Human Rights,* ed. Joanne R. Bauer and Daniel A. Bell (New York: Cambridge University Press, 1999). chap. 7.

23. Similar arguments have been put forward by Islamic feminists in Morocco: see Wendy Kristianasen, "Debits entre femmes en terres d'islam," *Le Monde Diplomatique,* Avril 2004, 20. In Kenya, the argument that female genital cutting is inconsistent with the teachings of the Quran (Koran) has been relatively effective at changing the minds of (former) practitioners of genital cutting. Mark Lacey, "Genital Cutting Shows Signs of Losing Favor in Africa," *The New York Times,* 8 June 2004, A3.

24. Note, however, that the strategy adopted by Sisters of Islam is not without controversy. At the Bangkok workshop, a representative of the group was severely criticized by a devout Muslim from Malaysia, who questioned the Islamic credentials of the group, including the fact that some members could not read the Quran in Arabic. Such criticisms suggest that local justifications are most effective if deployed by "true believers" of the tradition: in the case of Islam, if a nonbeliever draws on

Islam to push forward values similar to human rights in an Islamic context, the strategic use of the religion is not likely to be viewed as sincere and may be rejected as another form of cultural imperialism. Needless to say, I do not mean to imply that the members of Sisters of Islam are not true believers: in fact, their successes in the Malaysian political area suggests that they are taken seriously by other Muslims. In this case, it appears to be a dispute between competing interpretations of Islam, nor between believers and nonbelievers.

25. Wang Juntao, "Confucian Democrats in Chinese History," in *Confucianism for the Modern World*, ed. Daniel A. Bell and Hahm Chaibong (New York: Cambridge University Press, 2003), 69.

26. Han Sangjin, "Political Liberalization, Stability, and Human Rights" (paper presented at the Hakone workshop, on file with author), 21.

27. See David Brown and David Martin Jones, "Democratization and the Myth of the Liberalizing Middle Classes," in Daniel A. Bell et al., *Towards Illiberal Democracy in Pacific Asia* (London and New York: Macmillan/St. Antony's College and St. Martin's Press, 1995), 78–106.

28. Onuma Yasuaki, "In Quest of Intercivilizational Human Rights: 'Universal vs. Relative' Human Rights Viewed from an Asian Perspective," Centre for Asian Pacific Affairs, The Asia Foundation, Occasional Paper no. 2, 1996, 4.

29. See the discussion in the following chapter of the "naming and shaming" approach defended by Human Rights Watch.

30. If human rights practices and institutions refer by definition only to the legal protection of individual rights, then, needless to say, nonlegalistic mechanisms for the protection of those same individual rights cannot be termed "human rights practices." However, if the end result is the same—that is, the protection and promotion of vital human interests, which is presumably the whole point of a human rights regime—it is unclear why one should place too much emphasis on this terminological issue.

31. Onuma, "In Quest of Intercivilizational Rights," 4. See also Albert H. Y. Chen, "Mediation, Litigation, and Justice: Confucian Reflections in a Modern Liberal Society," in *Confucianism for the Modern World*, ed. Daniel A. Bell and Hahm Chaibong (New York: Cambridge University Press, 2003) chap. 11. Several areas of conflict, such as traffic and industrial accidents, that would be dominated by private litigation in the United States are settled by administrative procedures in China. William C. Jones points to the imperial roots of such practices and suggests that administrative agencies can also protect and promote freedom in China's future. William C. Jones, "Chinese Law and Liberty," in *Realms of Freedom in Modern China*, ed. William C. Kirby (Stanford: Stanford University Press, 2004), 55–56.

32. For the view that legalistic human rights language is generally counterproductive (i.e., not just in the East Asian context) given what it is trying to achieve, see Charles Blattberg, "Two Concepts of Cosmopolitanism" (ms. on file with author).

33. Bilahari Kausikan, "Asia's Different Standard," *Foreign Policy*, vol. 92 (1993), 39, The consensus, soon breaks down once it comes to the application of general prohibitions to particular cases, as illustrated by disputes over the whether the abuse of Iraqi prisoners constitutes "torture." There may even be disputes over the application of "torture" in everyday, familial settings: an American student of Indian descent told me that her parents forced her to eat spicy food as a child even after she was crying from the pain, telling her that God would punish her if she didn't eat it (if the point of this child-rearing practice was to promote the love of spicy food, it was effective in this case).

34. Sulak Sivaraksa, "Buddhism and Human Rights," paper presented at the Bangkok workshop on Cultural Sources of Human Rights in East Asia, Match 1996 (on file with author).

35. I do not mean to deny that this presumption can be overridden. For example, the foreign human rights advocate would not have an obligation to refrain from critique of the Thai king if the king were to call for an unjustified war against a neighboring state, even if all Thais support this call. But such an eventuality is very unlikely (at least under the current king, who is widely admired and recognized to be a benevolent ruler), hence the strong presumption in favor of deferring to the "Thai" constraint on free speech.

36. At the Bangkok workshop (March 1996), Charles Taylor pointed out that relatively uncontroversial laws against hate speech also exist in Canada. It could be argued, however, that the Thai case is more of a deviation from American-style free speech because the core of this ideal is the right to criticize political leaders, which is precisely the right being called into question here.

37. Joseph Chan, "The Asian Challenge to Universal Human Rights: A Philosophical Appraisal," in *Human Rights and International Relations in the Asia Pacific*, ed. James T. H. Tang (London: Pinter, 1995), 25, 36 (quoting Won Kan Seng, "The Real World of Human Rights," address at the Second World Conference on Human Rights, Vienna, 1993).

38. Ibid.

39. Kim Dae Jung, "Is Culture Destiny?" *Foreign Affairs*, November/December 1994, 190.

40. Abdullahi A. An-Na'im, "Toward a Cross-Cultural Approach to Defining International Standards of Human Rights: The Meaning of Cruel, Inhuman, or Degrading Treatment or Punishment," in *Human Rights in Cross-Cultural Perspectives: A Quest for Consensus* (Philadelphia: University of Pennsylvania Press, 1992), 34.

41. Ibid.

42. Teruhisa Se and Rie Karatsu, "A Conception of Human Rights Based on Japanese Culture: Promoting Cross-cultural Debates," *Journal of Human Rights*, vol. 3, no. 3 (September 2004), 283. He and Rie point to the possibility that such new fights can improve the human rights scheme prevailing in Western cultures (ibid., 284–85), though my view is that well-developed empathetic ability is not nearly so central to the Western liberalism and is not likely to be adopted as the foundation for new rights in the West.

43. Tu Wei-ming, *Confucianism in an Historical Perspective*, Institute of East Asian Philosophies, Occasional Paper and Monograph Series no. 13, 1989, 15.

44. Interestingly, this moral outlook still seems to inform the practices of Asian immigrants to other societies.

According to the *New York Times* (11 July 2001), fewer than one in five whites in the United States help care for or provide financial support for their parents, in-laws, or other relatives, compared with 28 percent of African Americans, 34 percent of Hispanic American, and 42 percent of Asian Americans. Those who provide the most care also feel the most guilt that they are not doing enough. Almost three-quarters of Asian Americans say they should do more for their parents, compared with two-thirds of Hispanics, slightly more than half of African Americans, and fewer than half of whites.

45. The obligations of filial piety do not end with the death of one's parents: equally, if not more important, are the mourning period and the subsequent rituals designed to show ongoing respect for one's parents. In Korea, for example, the large majority of families endorse the practice of ancestor worship. Geir Helgesen, *Democracy and Authority in Korea: The Cultural Dimension in Korean Politics* (Richmond, England: Curzon, 1988), 128. Arnold Schwarzenegger expressed a contrasting approach in the film *Pumping Iron,* where he seemed proud of the fact that he chose to train for a body-building competition rather than return home for his father's funeral.

46. This is not to deny that Westerners sometimes agonize over the decision to commit a parent to an old-age home. It is only to say that, generally speaking, East Asians are more likely to provide personal care for older parents (see also chapter 10).

47. In the case of elderly parents without family members, Mencius argues that the obligation falls to the state: see the discussion in Chan, "Giving Priority to the Worst-Off," 238–42.

48. In China's basic courts, appeals by parents for support from their children constitute 5–10 percent of the cases. Upham comments that "Confucian values notwithstanding, the refusal of young Chinese to obey their legal obligation to support their parents is a significant social problem" (Upham, "Who Will Find the Defendant?")(ms. on file with the author). But the fact that young Chinese have such a legal obligation shows the continuing relevance of the value of filial piety (the point is to punish the minority of young Chinese who do not pay the "costs" of this value).

49. It is interesting to note that laws meant to secure the traditional value of filial piety are not subject to political debate in Taiwan, one of the few areas of consensus in an otherwise highly polarized society where the government seems intent on casting aside manifestations of traditional "Chinese" values and practices (see chapter 6).

50. The Singapore state, for example, promotes the ideal of "three generations under one roof" by means of policies that give priorities of allocation for publicly subsidized accommodation or additional housing subsidies for newly married couples who live within a certain distance of their old neighborhood where their parents continue to live. Antonio I., Rappa and Sor-hoon Tan, "Political Implications of Confucian Familism," *Asian Philosophy*, vol. 13, nos. 2/3 (July 2003), 90.

51. The right to be cared for by adult children may not be expressed in rights language—for example, the 1992 Mongolian Constitution specifies the duty to care for elderly parents. But if adult children can be punished for neglecting their parents, the difference is terminological rather than substantive.

52. I leave aside the question of cultural differences that may affect different ways of determining the core of human rights *within* societies. For example, newly arrived Hmong immigrants to the United States believe that ritual killings of animals is necessary to heal sick family members, but once the practice became known to residents of Merced, California, the city passed an ordinance banning the slaughter of livestock and poultry within city limits. See Anne Fadiman, *The Spirit Catches You and You Fall Down*: *A Hmong Child, Her American Doctors, and the Collision of Two Cultures* (New York: Farrar, Straus, and Giroux, 1997), 107–8. Were the Hmong to frame their grievances in terms of the language of human rights, they would have a good case to argue that their basic rights are being violated.

A Buddhist Response to the Nature of Human Rights

Kenneth K. Inada

Kenneth K. Inada is a professor emeritus of philosophy at the State University of New York at Buffalo. He is the author of *Guide to Buddhist Philosophy* (1985) and *Buddhism and American Thinkers* (1984).

Inada contends that a Buddhist perspective places much more importance on the fluidity of human relationships than does a Western perspective. This means that a Buddhist conception of human rights will be softer, more accommodating, and more flexible than a Western conception of human rights; it will be more compassionate, more forgiving, and less inclined to set up strong oppositions between parties. In contrast to the Western perspective, a Buddhist conception of human rights is less interested in legal formalities and more interested in the nurturance of feelings that will promote humanistic existence.

It is incorrect to assume that the concept of human rights is readily identifiable in all societies of the world. The concept may perhaps be clear and distinct in legal quarters, but in actual practice suffers greatly from lack of clarity and gray areas due to impositions by different cultures. This is especially true in Asia, where the two great civilizations of India and China have spawned such outstanding systems as Hinduism, Buddhism, Jainism, Yoga, Confucianism, Taoism, and Chinese Buddhism. These systems, together with other indigenous folk beliefs, attest to the cultural diversity at play that characterizes Asia proper. In focusing on the concept of human rights, however, we shall concentrate on Buddhism to bring out the common grounds of discourse.

Alone among the great systems of Asia, Buddhism has successfully crossed geographical

Excerpt from Kenneth K. Inada, "A Buddhist Response to the Nature of Human Rights," from Asian Perspectives on Human Rights, edited by Claude E. Walsh and Virginia Leary, 1990. Reprinted by permisson of the author.

and ideological borders and spread in time throughout the whole length and breadth of known Asia. Its doctrines are so universal and profound that they captured the imagination of all the peoples they touched and thereby established a subtle bond with all. What then is this bond? It must be something common to all systems of thought which opens up and allows spiritual discourse among them.

In examining the metaphysical ground of all systems, one finds that there is a basic feeling for a larger reality in one's own experience, a kind of reaching out for a greater cosmic dimension of being, as it were. It is a deep sense for the total nature of things. All this may seem so simple and hardly merits elaborating, but it is a genuine feeling common among Asians in their quest for ultimate knowledge based on the proper relationship of one's self in the world. It is an affirmation of a reality that includes but at once goes beyond the confines of sense faculties.

A good illustration of this metaphysical grounding is seen in the Brahmanic world of Hinduism. In it, the occluded nature of the self (*atman*) constantly works to cleanse itself of defilements by yogic discipline in the hope of ultimately identifying with the larger reality which is Brahman. In the process, the grounding in the larger reality is always kept intact, regardless of whether the self is impure or not. In other words, in the quest for the purity of things, a larger framework of experience is involved from the beginning such that the ordinary self (*atman*) transforms into the larger Self (*Atman*) and finally merges into the ultimate ontological Brahman.

A similar metaphysical grounding is found in Chinese thought. Confucianism, for example, with its great doctrine of humanity (*jen*), involves the ever-widening and ever-deepening human relationship that issues forth in the famous statement, "All men are brothers." In this sense, humanity is not a mere abstract concept but one that extends concretely throughout the whole of sentient existence. Confucius once said that when he searched for *jen*, it is always close at hand.[1] It means that humanity is not something external to a person but that it is constitutive of the person's experience, regardless of whether there is consciousness of it or not. It means, moreover, that in the relational nature of society, individual existence is always more than that which one assumes it to be. In this vein, all experiences must fit into the larger cosmological scheme normally spoken of in terms of heaven, earth, and mankind. This triadic relationship is ever-present and ever-in-force, despite one's ignorance, negligence, or outright intention to deny it. The concept that permeates and enlivens the triadic relationship is the *Tao*. The *Tao* is a seemingly catchall term, perhaps best translated as the natural way of life and the world. In its naturalness, it manifests all of existence; indeed, it is here, there, and everywhere since it remains aloof from human contrivance and manipulation. In a paradoxical sense, it depicts action based on nonaction (*wu-wei*), the deepest state of being achievable. The following story illustrates this point.

A cook named Ting is alleged to have used the same carving knife for some 19 years without sharpening it at all. When asked how that is possible, he simply replied:

> What I care about is the way (*Tao*), which goes beyond skill. When I first began cutting up oxen, all

I could see was the ox itself. After three years I no longer saw the whole ox. And now—now I go at it by spirit and don't look with my eyes. Perception and understanding have come to a stop and spirit moves where it wants. I go along with the natural makeup, strike in the big hollows, guide the knife through the big openings, and follow things as they are. So I never touch the smallest ligament or tendon, much less a main joint. . . . I've had this knife of mine for nineteen years and I've cut up thousands of oxen with it, and yet the blade is as good as though it had just come from the grindstone.[2*]

Such then is the master craftsman at work, a master in harmonious triadic relationship based on the capture of the spirit of *Tao* where the function is not limited to a person and his or her use of a tool. And it is clear that such a spirit of *Tao* in craftsmanship is germane to all disciplined experiences we are capable of achieving in our daily activities.

Buddhism, too, has always directed our attention to the larger reality of existence. The original enlightenment of the historical Buddha told of a pure unencumbered experience which opened up all experiential doors in such a way that they touched everything sentient as well as insentient. A Zen story graphically illustrates this point.

Once a master and a disciple were walking through a dense forest. Suddenly, they heard the clean chopping strokes of the woodcutter's axe. The disciple was elated and remarked, "What beautiful sounds in the quiet of the forest!" To which the master immediately responded, "You have got it all upside down. The sounds only make obvious the deep silence of the forest!" The response by the Zen master sets in bold relief the Buddhist perception of reality. Although existential reality refers to the perception of the world as a singular unified whole, we ordinarily perceive it in fragmented ways because of our heavy reliance on the perceptual apparatus and its consequent understanding. That is to say, we perceive by a divisive and selective method which, however, glosses over much of reality and indeed misses its holistic nature. Certainly, the hewing sounds of the woodcutter's axe are clearly audible and delightful to the ears, but they are so at the expense of the basic silence of the forest (i.e., total reality). Or, the forest in its silence constitutes the necessary background, indeed the basic source, from which all sounds (and all activities for that matter) originate. Put another way, sounds arising from the silence of the forest should in no way deprive nor intrude upon the very source of their own being. Only human beings make such intrusions by their crude discriminate habits of perception and, consequently, suffer a truncated form of existence, unknowingly for the most part.

Now that we have seen Asian lives in general grounded in a holistic cosmological framework, we would have to raise the following question: How does this framework appear in the presence of human rights? Or, contrarily, how do human rights function within this framework?

Admittedly, the concept of human rights is relatively new to Asians. From the very beginning, it did not sit well with their basic cosmological outlook. Indeed, the existence of such an outlook has prevented in profound ways a ready acceptance of foreign elements and has created tension and struggle between tradition and modernity. Yet, the key concept in the tension is that of human relationship. This is especially true in Buddhism, where the emphasis is not so much on the performative acts and individual rights as it is on the matter of manifestation of human nature itself. The Buddhist always takes human nature as the basic context in which all ancillary concepts, such as human rights, are understood and take on any value. Moreover, the context itself is in harmony with the extended experiential nature of things. And thus, where the Westerner is much more at home in treating legal matters detached from human nature as such and quite confident in forging ahead to establish human rights with a distinct emphasis on certain "rights," the Buddhist is much more reserved but open and seeks to understand the implications of human behavior, based on the fundamental nature of human beings, before turning his or her attention to the so-called "rights" of individuals.

An apparent sharp rift seems to exist between the Western and Buddhist views, but this is not really so. Actually, it is a matter of perspectives and calls for a more comprehensive understanding of what takes place in ordinary human relationships. For the basic premise is still one that is focused on human beings intimately living together in the selfsame world. A difference in perspectives does not mean noncommunication or a simple rejection of another's view, as there is still much more substance in the nature of conciliation, accommodation, and absorption than what is initially thought of. Here we propose two contrasting but interlocking and complementary terms, namely, "hard relationship" and "soft relationship."

The Western view on human rights is generally based on a hard relationship. Persons are treated as separate and independent entities or even bodies, each having its own assumed identity or self-identity. It is a sheer "elemental" way of perceiving things due mainly to the strong influence by science and its methodology. As scientific methodology thrives on the dissective and analytic incursion into reality as such, this in turn has resulted in our perceiving and understanding things in terms of disparate realities. Although it makes way for easy understanding, the question still remains: Do we really understand what these realities are in their own respective fullness of existence? Apparently not. And to make matters worse, the methodology unfortunately has been uncritically extended over to the human realm, into human nature and human relations. Witness its ready acceptance by the various descriptive and behavioral sciences, such as sociology, psychology, and anthropology. On this matter, Cartesian dualism of mind and body has undoubtedly influenced our ordinary ways of thinking in such a manner that in our casual perception of things, we habitually subscribe to the clearcut subject–object dichotomy. This dualistic perspective has naturally filtered down into human relationships and has eventually crystallized into what we refer to as the nature of a hard relationship. Thus, a hard relationship is a mechanistic treatment of human beings where the emphasis is on beings as such, regardless of their inner nature and function in the fullest sense; it is an atomistic analysis of beings where the premium is placed on what is relatable and manipulable without regard for their true potentials for becoming. In a way it is externalization in the extreme, since the emphasis is heavily weighted on seizing the external character of beings themselves. Very little attention, if any, is given to the total ambience, inclusive of inner contents and values, in which the beings are at full play. In this regard, it can be said that postmodern thought is now attempting to correct this seemingly lopsided dichotomous view created by our inattention to the total experiential nature of things. We believe this is a great step in the right direction. Meanwhile, we trudge along with a heavy burden on our backs, though unaware of it for the most part, by associating with people on the basis of hard relationships.

To amplify on the nature of hard relationships, let us turn to a few modern examples. First, Thomas Hobbes, in his great work, *Leviathan*,[3] showed remarkable grasp of human psychology when he asserted that people are constantly at war with each other. Left in this "state of nature," people will never be able to live in peace and security. The only way out of this conundrum is for all to establish a reciprocal relationship of mutual trust that would work, i.e., to strike up a covenant by selfish beings that guarantees mutual benefits and gains, one in which each relinquishes certain rights in order to gain or realize a personal as well as an overall state of peace and security. This was undoubtedly a brilliant scheme. But the scheme is weak in that it treats human beings by and large mechanically, albeit psychologically too, as entities in a give-and-take affair, and thus perpetuates the condition of hard relationships.

Another example can be offered by way of the British utilitarian movement which later was consummated in American pragmatism. Jeremy Bentham's hedonic calculus[4] (e.g., intensity of pleasure or pain, duration of pleasure or pain, certainty or uncertainty of pleasure or pain, purity or impurity of pleasure or pain, etc.) is a classic example of quantification of human experience. Although this is a most expedient or utilitarian way to treat and legislate behavior, we must remind ourselves that we are by no means mere quantifiable entities. John Stuart Mill introduced the element of quality in order to curb and tone down the excesses of the quantification process,[5] but, in the final analysis, human nature and relationships are still set in hard relations. American pragmatism fares no better since actions by and large take place in a pluralistic world of realities and are framed within the scientific mode and, therefore, it is unable to relinquish the nature of hard relationships.

In contemporary times, the great work of John Rawls, *A Theory of Justice*,[6] has given us yet another twist in pragmatic and social contract theories. His basic concept of justice as fairness is an example of the reciprocal principle in action, i.e., in terms of realizing mutual advantage and benefit for the strongest to the weakest or the most favored to the least favored in a society. Each person exercises basic liberty with offices for its implementation always open and access available. It is moreover a highly intellectual or rational theory. It thus works extremely well on the theoretical level but, in actual situations, it is not as practical and applicable as it seems since it still retains hard relationships on mutual bases. Such being the case, feelings and consciousness relative to injustice and inequality are not so readily sported and corrected. That is to say, lacunae exist as a result of hard relationships and they keep on appearing until they are detected and finally remedied, but then the corrective process is painfully slow. Thus the theory's strongest point is its perpetually self-corrective nature which is so vital to the democratic process. Despite its shortcomings, however, Rawls' theory of justice is a singular contribution to contemporary legal and ethical thought.

By contrast, the Buddhist view of human rights is based on the assumption that human beings are primarily oriented in soft relationships; this relationship governs the understanding of the nature of human rights. Problems arise, on the other hand, when a hard relationship becomes the basis for treating human nature because it cannot delve deeply into that nature itself and functions purely on the peripheral aspects of things. It is another way of saying that a hard relationship causes rigid and stifling empirical conditions to arise and to which we become invariably attached.

A soft relationship has many facets. It is the Buddhist way to disclose a new dimension to human nature and behavior. It actually amounts to a novel perception or vision of reality. Though contrasted with a hard relationship, it is not in contention with it. If anything, it has an inclusive nature that "softens," if you will, all contacts and allows for the blending of any element that comes along, even incorporating the entities of hard relationships. This is not to say, however, that soft and hard relationships are equal or ultimately identical. For although the former could easily accommodate and absorb the latter, the reverse is not the case. Still, it must be noted that both belong to the same realm of experiential reality and in consequence ought to be conversive with each other. The nonconversive aspect arises on the part of the "hard" side and is attributable to the locked-in character of empirical elements which are considered to be hard stubborn facts worth perpetuating. But at some point, there must be a break in the lock, as it were, and this is made possible by knowledge of and intimacy with the "soft" side of human endeavors. For the "soft" side has a passive nature characterized by openness, extensiveness, depth, flexibility, absorptiveness, freshness, and creativity simply because it remains unencumbered by "hardened" empirical conditions.

What has been discussed so far can be seen in modern Thailand where tradition and change are in dynamic tension. Due to the onslaught of elements of modernity, Buddhism is being questioned and challenged. Buddhist Thailand, however, has taken up the challenge in the person of a leading monk named Buddhadasa who has led the country to keep a steady course on traditional values.[7]

> The heart of Buddhadasa's teaching is that the Dhamma (Sanskrit, Dharma) or the truth of Buddhism is a universal truth. Dhamma is equated by Buddhadasa to the true nature of things. It is everything and everywhere. The most appropriate term to denote the nature of Dhamma is *sunnata* (Sanskrit, *sunyata*) or the void. The ordinary man considers the void to mean nothing when, in reality, it means everything—everything, that is, without reference to the self.

We will return to the discussion of the nature of the void or *sunata* later, but suffice it to say here that what constitutes the heart of Buddhist truth of existence is based on soft relationships where all forms and symbols are accommodated and allows for their universal usage.

Robert N. Bellah has defined religion as a set of normative symbols institutionalized in a society or internalized in a personality.[8] It is a rather good definition but does not go far enough when it comes to describing Buddhism, or Asian religions in general for that matter. To speak of symbols being institutionalized or internalized without the proper existential or ontological context seems to be a bit artificial and has strains of meanings oriented toward hard relationships. Bellah, being a social scientist, probably could not go beyond the strains of a hard relationship, for, otherwise, he would have ended in a nondescriptive realm. The only way out is to give more substance to the nature of religious doctrines themselves, as is the case in Buddhism. The Buddhist Dharma is one such doctrine which, if symbolized, must take on a wider and deeper meaning that strikes at the very heart of existence of the individual. In this respect, Donald Swearer is on the right track when he says:

> the adaptation of symbols of Theravada Buddhism presupposes an underlying ontological structure. The symbol system of Buddhism, then, is not to be seen only in relationship to its wider empirical context, but also in relationship to its ontological structure. This structure is denoted by such terms as Dhamma or absolute Truth, emptiness and nonattachment. These terms are denotative of what Dhiravamsa calls "dynamic being." They are symbolic, but in a universalistic rather than a particularistic sense.[9]

Swearer's reference to an underlying ontological structure is in complete harmony with our use of the term soft relationship. And only when this ontological structure or soft relationship is brought into the dynamic tension between tradition and modernity can we give full accounting to the nature of human experience and the attendant creativity and change within a society.

Let us return to a fuller treatment of soft relationships. In human experience, they manifest themselves in terms of the intangible human traits that we live by, such as patience, humility, tolerance, deference, nonaction, humaneness, concern, pity, sympathy, altruism, sincerity, honesty, faith, responsibility, trust, respectfulness, reverence, love, and compassion. Though potentially and pervasively present in any human relationship, they remain for the most part as silent but vibrant components in all experiences. Without them, human intercourse would be sapped of the human element and reduced to perfunctory activities. Indeed, this fact seems to constitute much of the order of the day where our passions are mainly directed to physical and materialistic matters.

The actualization and sustenance of these intangible human traits are basic to the Buddhist quest for an understanding of human nature and, by extension, the so-called rights of human beings. In order to derive a closer look at the nature of soft relationships, we shall focus on three characteristics, namely, mutuality, holism, and emptiness or void.

MUTUALITY

Our understanding of mutuality is generally limited to its abstract or theoretical nature. For example, it is defined in terms of a two-way action between two parties and where the action is invariably described with reference to elements of hard relationships. Except secondarily or deviously, nothing positive is mentioned about the substance of mutuality, such as the feelings of humility, trust, and tolerance that transpire between the parties concerned. Although these feelings are present, unfortunately, they hardly ever surface in the relationship and almost always are overwhelmed by the physical aspect of things.

What is to be done? One must simply break away from the merely conceptual or theoretical understanding and fully engage oneself in the discipline that will bring the feelings of both parties to become vital components in the relationship. That is, both parties must equally sense the presence and value of these feelings and thus give substance and teeth to their actions.

Pursuing the notion of mutuality further, the Buddhist understands human experience as a totally open phenomenon, that persons should always be wide open in the living process. The phrase, "an open ontology," is used to describe the unclouded state of existence. An illustration of this is the newborn child. The child is completely an open

organism at birth. The senses are wide open and will absorb practically anything without prejudice. At this stage, also, the child will begin to imitate because its absorptive power is at the highest level. This open textured nature should continue on and on. In other words, if we are free and open, there should be no persistence in attaching ourselves to hard elements within the underlying context of a dynamic world of experience. The unfortunate thing, however, is that the open texture of our existence begins to blemish and fade away in time, being obstructed and overwhelmed by self-imposed fragmentation, narrowness and restriction, which gradually develop into a closed nature of existence. In this way, the hard relationship rules. But the nature of an open ontology leads us onto the next characteristic.

HOLISM

Holism of course refers to the whole, the total nature of individual existence and thus describes the unrestrictive nature of one's experience. Yet, the dualistic relationship we maintain by our crude habits of perception remains a stumbling block. This stunted form of perception is not conducive to holistic understanding and instead fosters nothing but fractured types of ontological knowledge taking. Unconscious for the most part, an individual narrows his or her vision by indulging in dualism of all kinds, both mental and physical, and in so doing isolates the objects of perception from the total process to which they belong. In consequence, the singular unified reality of each perceptual moment is fragmented and, what is more, fragmentation once settled breeds further fragmentation.

The Buddhist will appeal to the fact that one's experience must always be open to the total ambience of any momentary situation. But here we must be exposed to a unique, if not paradoxical, insight of the Buddhist. It is that the nature of totality is not a clearly defined phenomenon. In a cryptic sense, however, it means that the totality of experience has no borders to speak of. It is an open border totality, which is the very nature of the earlier mentioned "open ontology." It is a noncircumscribable totality, like a circle sensed, which does not have a rounded line, a seamless circle, if you will. A strange phenomenon, indeed, but that is how the Buddhist sees the nature of individual existence as such. For the mystery of existence that haunts us is really the nature of one's own fullest momentary existence. Nothing else compares in profundity to this nature, so the Buddhist believes.

Now, the open framework in which experience takes place reveals that there is depth and substance in experience. But so long as one is caught up with the peripheral elements, so-called, of hard relationships one will be ensnared by them and will generate limitations on one's understanding accordingly. On the other hand, if openness is acknowledged as a fact of existence, then the way out of one's limitations will present itself. All sufferings (*duhkha*), from the Buddhist standpoint, are cases of limited ontological vision (*avidya*, ignorance) hindered by the attachment to all sorts of elements that obsess a person.

Holism is conversant with openness since an open experience means that all elements are fully and extensively involved. In many respects, holistic existence exhibits the fact that mutuality thrives only in unhindered openness. But there is still another vital characteristic to round out or complete momentary experience. For this we turn to the last characteristic.

EMPTINESS**

Emptiness in Sanskrit is *sunyata*.[10] Strictly speaking, the Sanskrit term, depicting zero or nothing, had been around prior to Buddhism, but it took the historical Buddha's supreme enlightenment (*nirvana*) to reveal an incomparable qualitative nature inherent to experience. Thus emptiness is not sheer voidness or nothingness in the nihilistic sense.

We ordinarily find it difficult to comprehend emptiness, much less to live a life grounded in it. Why? Again, we return to the nature of our crude habits of perception, which is laden with unwarranted forms. That is, our whole perpetual process is caught up in attachment to certain forms or elements which foster and turn into so-called empirical and cognitive biases. All of this is taking place in such minute and unknowing ways that we hardly, if ever, take notice of it until a crisis situation arises, such as the presence of certain obviously damaging prejudice or discrimination. Then and only then do we seriously wonder and search for the forms or elements that initially gave rise to those prejudicial or discriminatory forces.

Emptiness has two aspects. The first aspect alerts our perceptions to be always open and fluid, and to desist from attaching to any form or element. In this respect, emptiness technically functions as a force of "epistemic nullity,"[11] in the sense that it nullifies any reference to a form or element as preexisting perception or even postexisting for that matter. Second and more importantly, emptiness points at a positive content of our experience. It underscores the possibility of total experience in any given moment because there is now nothing attached to or persisted in. This latter point brings us right back to the other characteristics of holism and mutuality. Now, we must note that emptiness is that dimension of experience which makes it possible for the function of mutuality and holism in each experience, since there is absolutely nothing that binds, hinders, or wants in our experience. Everything is as it is (*tathata*), under the aegis of emptiness; emptiness enables one to spread out one's experience at will in all directions, so to speak, in terms of "vertical" and "horizontal" dimensions of being. As it is the key principle of enlightened existence, it makes everything both possible and impossible. Possible in the sense that all experiences function within the total empty nature, just as all writings are possible on a clean slate or, back to the Zen story, where the sounds are possible in the silence (emptiness) of the forest. At the same time, impossible in the sense that all attachments to forms and elements are categorically denied in the ultimate fullness of experience. In this way, emptiness completes our experience of reality and at the same time, provides the grounds for the function of all human traits to become manifest in soft relationships.

It can now be seen that all three characteristics involve each other in the selfsame momentary existence. Granted this, it should not be too difficult to accept the fact that the leading moral concept in Buddhism is compassion (*karuna*). Compassion literally means "passion for all" in an ontologically extensive sense. It covers the realm of all sentient beings, inclusive of nonsentients, for the doors of perception to total reality are always open. From the Buddhist viewpoint, then, all human beings are open entities with open feelings expressive of the highest form of humanity. This is well expressed in the famous concept of *bodhisattva* (enlightened being) in Mahayana Buddhism, who has deepest concern for all beings and sympathetically delays his entrance to nirvana as long as there is suffering (ignorant existence) among sentient creatures. It depicts the coterminous nature of all creatures and may be taken as a philosophic myth in that it underscores the ideality of existence which promotes the greatest unified form of humankind based on compassion. This ideal form of existence, needless to say, is the aim and goal of all Buddhists.

As human beings we need to keep the channels of existential dialogue open at all times. When an act of violence is in progress, for example, we need to constantly nourish the silent and passive nature of nonviolence inherent in all human relations. Though nonviolence cannot counter violence on the latter's terms, still, its nourished presence serves as a reminder of the brighter side of existence and may even open the violator's mind to common or normal human traits such as tolerance, kindness, and noninjury (*ahimsa*). Paradoxically and most unfortunately, acts of violence only emphasize the fact that peace and tranquility are the normal course of human existence.

It can now be seen that the Buddhist view on human rights is dedicated to the understanding of persons in a parameter-free ambience, so to speak, where feelings that are extremely soft and tender, but nevertheless present and translated into human traits or virtues that we uphold, make up the very fiber of human relations. These relations, though their contents are largely intangible, precede any legal rights or justification accorded to human beings. In brief, human rights for the Buddhist are not only matters for legal deliberation and understanding, but they must be complemented by and based on something deeper and written in the very feelings of all sentients. The unique coexistent nature of rights and feelings constitutes the saving truth of humanistic existence.

NOTES

1. *Lun Yu* (The Analects of Confucius): VII, 29.
2. *The Complete Works of Chuang Tzu*, translated by Burton Watson (New York: Columbia University Press, 1960), pp. 50–51.
3. Thomas Hobbes, *Leviathan* (New York: Hafner, 1926).
4. Jeremy Bentham, *An Introduction to the Principles of Morals and Legislation* (New York: Hafner, 1948).
5. John Stuart Mill observed, "It is better to be a human being dissatisfied than a pig satisfied; better to be a Socrates dissatisfied than a fool satisfied." *Utilitarianism*, cited in Louis P. Pojman, *Philosophy: The Quest for Truth* (Belmont, CA: Wadsworth, 1989), p. 357.
6. John Rawls, *A Theory of Justice* (Cambridge: Harvard University Press, 1971). Rawls also has a chapter on civil disobedience but it too is treated under the same concept of justice as fairness and suffers accordingly from the elements of hard relationships.
7. Donald K. Swearer, "Thai Buddhism: Two Responses to Modernity," in Bardwell L. Smith, ed., *Contributions to Asian Studies*, Volume 4: *Tradition and Change in Theravada Buddhism* (Leiden: EJ. Brill, 1973), p. 80. "Without reference to the self" means to uphold the Buddhist doctrine of nonself (Sanskrit, *anatman*) which underlies all momentary existence and avoids any dependence on a dichotomous self-oriented subject–object relationship. For an updated and comprehensive view of Buddhadasa's reformist's philosophy, see Donald K. Swearer, ed., *Me and Mine: Selected Essays on Bhikkhu Buddhadasa* (Albany: State University of New York Press, 1989).
8. Robert N. Bellah, "Epilogue" in Bellah, ed., *Religion and Progress in Modern Asia* (New York: Free Press, 1965), p. 173.
9. Swearer, "Thai Buddhism," p. 92.
10. Etymologically *sunyata* (in Pali, *sunnata*) means the state of being swollen, as in pregnancy, or the state of fullness of being. Thus, from the outset the term depicted the pure, open and full-textured nature of experiential reality.
11. Kenneth Inada, "Nagarjuna and Beyond," *Journal of Buddhist Philosophy* 2 (1984), pp. 65–76, for development of this concept.

EDITOR'S NOTES

*On the Ting Story (p. 108)

As exaggerated as the story may sound, Ting's manual dexterity provides a vivid illustration of the centrality of the idea of embodiment in Taoism and in Eastern philosophy in general. Perhaps a different example may help toward understanding what Ting means by "the ox ceasing to be an ox" and "the spirit moves where it wants." Take for instance a person gone blind as a result of an injury to her eyes. She has to learn to go about her daily affairs with a walking stick. At the beginning of this new phase of her life, she is constantly aware of *the* stick—the pressure and the various sensations impinging on her hand as her stick comes into contact with the ground and different objects. But after habituating herself to the use of the stick, her attention is now transferred to the farther end of the stick, and she no longer needs to make self-conscious determinations of the distance between the two ends of the stick. In other words, the stick now *becomes* a part of her bodily extension—an extended hand: what was once only a tool, a thing, is now incorporated into her self.

The moral of Ting's story is that what stands out as an alien object can be made "natural" through this embodied integration into one's own self by a process of skillful habituation. Once the makeup of the ox, the tendons, the ligaments, the difficult joints, become as familiar to the cook as his own body, the animal will cease to appear to be a thing that stands opposed to the cook and to have to be consciously mastered. With this embodied knowledge, the cook knows which parts of the animal's body most easily yield to his knife, and thus he can guide his knife as effortlessly as "the spirit moves where it wants." As dramatic as it sounds, after he submits thousands of oxen to the blade, it still remains as though "it had just come from the grindstone."

**On Emptiness (p. 114)

The idea of "emptiness" deserves a more detailed clarification here because of a very common but mistaken association that the term generates. There is a tendency among Western philosophers to construe this Buddhist idea of emptiness as nihilism, thanks to one of the most influential Western philosophers of the last century, Friedrich Nietzsche. (See, for example, his *Will to Power*.) But this characterization cannot be further from the truth. For one thing, Buddhism has always been a secular philosophy. There is no concept of a transcendent God, who is the ultimate source of all values. One's existence and place in the universe are contingent and in constant flux all along. The absence of God does not plunge one into a kind of despair that totally negates the ground of one's existence, because one's self-identification and sense of significance begin and end with the universe. More importantly, for the Buddhist, even when faced with extreme disappointment and misfortune, one should not "wallow" in meaninglessness and despair, because even meaninglessness and despair *are*, as paradoxical as it may sound, ultimately "empty." One should not hang onto good things such as friendship and justice any more than one should unpleasant feelings of meaninglessness and despair, because all of these will vanish in the ephemeral order of things after all, ignorance of which fact causes a person unnecessary suffering.

Conditions of an Unforced Consensus on Human Rights

Charles Taylor

Charles Taylor is one of the most influential political philosophers living today. He is the author of many books including *A Secular Age* (2007), *Multiculturalism: Examining the Politics of Recognition* (1994), *The Ethics of Authenticity* (1991), and *Sources of the Self* (1989). He is a professor of philosophy at McGill University.

Charles Taylor holds that it is possible for diverse cultural and religious communities to arrive at an unforced consensus on international norms of human rights even as they differ in their justifications for such norms. To resolve the conflicts between the current Western notions of human rights and those of other contemporary cultures, Taylor suggests that the connection between a legal culture of rights enforcement and its philosophical underpinning be loosened. Through the use of different examples, he shows how justifications acceptable to diverse groups can be found within their own philosophical and spiritual traditions and in the form of internal legal innovations.

INTRODUCTION

What would it mean to come to a genuine, unforced international consensus on human rights? I suppose it would be something like what Rawls describes in his *Political Liberalism* as an "overlapping consensus."[1] That is, different groups, countries, religious communities, and civilizations, although holding incompatible fundamental views on theology, metaphysics, human nature, and so on, would come to an agreement on certain norms that ought to govern human behavior. Each would have its own way of justifying this from out of its profound background conception. We would agree on the norms while disagreeing on why they were the right norms, and we would be content to live in this consensus, undisturbed by the differences of profound underlying belief.

The idea was already expressed in 1949 by Jacques Maritain: "I am quite certain that my way of justifying belief in the rights of man and the ideal of liberty, equality, fraternity is the only way with a firm foundation in truth. This does not prevent me from being in agreement on these practical convictions with people who are certain that their way of justifying them, entirely different from mine or opposed to mine, . . . , is equally the only way founded upon truth."[2]

Is this kind of consensus possible? Perhaps because of my optimistic nature, I believe that it is. But we have to confess at the outset that it is not entirely clear around what the consensus would form, and we are only beginning to discern the obstacles we would have to overcome on the way there. I want to talk a little about both these issues here.

First, what would the consensus be on? One might have thought this was obvious: on human rights. That's what our original question was about, but there is an immediate obstacle that has often been pointed out. Rights talk is something that has roots in Western culture. Certain features of this talk have roots in Western history, and there only. This is not to say that something very like the underlying norms expressed in schedules of rights don't turn up elsewhere, but they are not expressed in this language. We can't assume without further examination that a future unforced world consensus could be formulated to the satisfaction of everyone in the language of rights. Maybe yes, maybe no. Or maybe partially yes, partially no, as we come to distinguish among the things that have been associated in the Western package.

This is not to say that we already have some adequate term for whatever universals we think we may discern between difficult cultures. Jack Donnelly speaks of "human dignity" as a universal value.[3] Onuma Yasuaki criticizes this term, pointing out that "dignity" has itself been a favorite term in the Western philosophical stream that has elaborated human rights. He prefers to speak of the "pursuit of spiritual and material well-being" as the universal.[4] Where "dignity" might be too precise and culture-bound a term, "well-being" might be too vague and general. Perhaps we are incapable at this stage of formulating the universal values in play here. Perhaps we shall always be incapable of this. This wouldn't matter, because what we need to formulate for an overlapping consensus are certain norms of conduct. There does seem to be some basis for hoping that we can achieve at least some agreement on these norms. One can presumably find in all cultures condemnations of genocide, murder, torture, and slavery, as well as of, say, "disappearances" and the shooting of innocent demonstrators.[5] The deep underlying values supporting these common conclusions will, in the nature of the case, belong to the alternative, mutually incompatible justifications.

I have been distinguishing between norms of conduct and their underlying justification. The Western rights tradition in fact exists at both of these levels. On one plane, it is a legal tradition, legitimating certain kinds of legal actions and empowering certain kinds of people to make them. We could, and people sometimes do, consider this legal culture as the proper candidate for universalization, arguing that its adoption can be justified in more than one way. Then a legal culture entrenching rights would define the norms around which world consensus would supposedly crystallize.

Some people already have trouble with this, such as Lee Kwan Yew and those in East Asia who sympathize with him. They see something dangerously individualistic, fragmenting, dissolvent of community in this Western legal culture. (Of course, they have particularly in mind—or in their sights—the United States.[6]) In their criticism of Western procedures, they also seem to be attacking the underlying philosophy, which allegedly gives primacy to the individual, whereas supposedly a "Confucian" outlook would have a larger place for the community and the complex web of human relations in which each person stands.

The Western rights tradition also contains certain views on human nature, society, and the human good and carries some elements of an underlying justification. It might help the discussion to distinguish these two levels, at least analytically, so that we can develop a more fine-grained picture of what our options are. Perhaps in fact, the legal culture could "travel" better, if it could be separated from some of its underlying justifications. Or perhaps the reverse is true, that the underlying picture of human life might look less frightening if it could find expression in a different legal culture. Or maybe neither of these simple solutions will work (this is my hunch), but modifications need to be made to both; however, distinguishing the levels still helps, because the modifications are different on each level.

In any case, a good place to start the discussion would be to give a rapid portrait of the language of rights that has developed in the West and of the surrounding notions of human agency and the good. We could then proceed to identify certain centers of disagreement across cultures, and we might then see what if anything could be done to bridge these differences.

THE LANGUAGE OF RIGHTS

Many societies have held that it is good to ensure certain immunities or liberties to their members—or sometimes even to outsiders (think of the stringent laws of hospitality that hold in many traditional cultures). Everywhere it is wrong to take human life, at least under certain circumstances and for certain categories of persons. Wrong is the opposite of right, so this is relevant to our discussion.

A quite different sense of the word is invoked when we start to use the definite or indefinite articles, or to put it in the plural, and speak of "a right" or "rights," or when we start to attribute these to persons, and speak of "your rights" or "my rights." This is to introduce what has been called "subjective rights." Instead of saying that it is wrong to kill me, we begin to say that I have a right to life. The two formulations are not equivalent in all respects, because in the latter case the immunity or liberty is considered as it were the property of someone. It is no longer just an element of the law that stands over and between all of us equally. That I have a right to life says more than that you shouldn't kill me. It gives me some control over this immunity. A right is something that in principle I can waive.[7] It is also something which I have a role in enforcing.

Some element of subjective right exists in all legal systems. The peculiarity of the West is that, first, the concept played a bigger role in European medieval societies than elsewhere in history, and, second, it was the basis of the rewriting of Natural Law theory that marked the seventeenth century. The older notion that human society stands under a Law of Nature, whose origin is the Creator, and that is thus beyond human will, became transposed. The fundamental law was reconceived as consisting of natural rights, attributed to individuals prior to society. At the origin of society stands a Contract, which takes people out of a State of Nature, and puts them under political authority, as a result of an act of consent on their part.

Subjective rights are not only crucial to the Western tradition; even more significant is the fact that they were projected onto Nature and formed the basis of a philosophical view of humans and their society, one that greatly privileges individuals' freedom and their right to consent to the arrangements under which they live. This view has become an important strand in Western democratic theory of the last three centuries.

The notion of (subjective) rights both serves to define certain legal powers and also provides the master image for a philosophy of human nature, of individuals and their societies. It operates both as legal norm and as underlying justification. Moreover, these two levels are not unconnected. The force of the underlying philosophy has brought about a steady promotion of the legal norm in our politicolegal systems so that it now occupies pride of place in a number of contemporary polities. Charters of rights are now entrenched in the constitutions of a number of countries, and also of the European Union. These are the bases of judicial review, whereby the ordinary legislation of different levels of government can be invalidated on the grounds of conflict with these fundamental rights.

The modern Western discourse of rights involves, on one hand, a set of legal forms by which immunities and liberties are inscribed as rights, with certain consequences for the possibility of waiver and for the ways in which they can be secured—whether these immunities and liberties are among those from time to time granted by duly constituted authority or among those that are entrenched in fundamental law. On the other hand, it involves a philosophy of the person and of society, attributing great importance to the individual and making significant matters turn on his or her power of consent. In both these regards, it contrasts with many other cultures, including the premodern West, not because some of the same protections and immunities were not present, but because they had a quite different basis.[8]

When people protest against the Western rights model, they seem to have this whole package in their sights. We can therefore see how resistance to the Western discourse of rights might occur on more than one level. Some governments might resist the enforcement of even widely accepted norms because they have an agenda that involves their violation (for example, the contemporary

Peoples Republic of China). Others, however, are certainly ready, even eager, to espouse some universal norms, but they are made uneasy by the underlying philosophy of the human person in society. This seems to give pride of place to autonomous individuals, determined to demand their rights, even (indeed especially) in the face of widespread social consensus. How does this fit with the Confucian emphasis on close personal relationships, not only as highly valued in themselves but also as a model for the wider society? Can people who imbibe the full Western human rights ethos, which reaches its highest expression in the lone courageous individual fighting against all the forces of social conformity for her rights, ever be good members of a "Confucian" society? How does this ethic of demanding what is due to us fit with the Theravada Buddhist search for selflessness, for self-giving and *dana* (generosity)?[9]

Taking the rights package as a whole is not necessarily wrong, because the philosophy is plainly part of what has motivated the great promotion enjoyed by this legal form. But the kinds of misgivings expressed in the previous paragraph, which cannot be easily dismissed, show the potential advantages of distinguishing the elements and loosening the connection between a legal culture of rights enforcement and the philosophical conceptions of human life that originally nourished it.

It might help to structure our thinking if we made a tripartite distinction. What are we looking for, in the end, is a world consensus on certain norms of conduct enforceable on governments. To be accepted in any given society, these would in each case have to repose on some widely acknowledged philosophical justification, and to be enforced, they would have to find expression in legal mechanisms. One way of putting our central question might be this: What variations can we imagine in philosophical justifications or in legal forms that would still be compatible with a meaningful universal consensus on what really matters to us, the enforceable norms?

Following this line of thinking, it might help to understand better just what exactly we might want to converge on in the world society of the future, as well as to measure our chances of getting there, if we imagine variations separately on the two levels. What I propose to do is look at a number of instances in which there seem to be obvious conflicts between the present language of human rights and one or more major contemporary cultures. The goal will be to try to imagine ways in which the conflict might be resolved and the essential norms involved in the human rights claim preserved, and this through some modification either of legal forms or of philosophy.

ALTERNATIVE LEGAL FORMS

I would like to look at four kinds of conflict. The first could be resolved by legal innovation, and I will briefly discuss this possibility, but it can best be tackled on the philosophical level. The other three involve the basic justification of human rights claims. In developing these, I will have to spell out much further the justificatory basis for Western thinking and practice about rights than I have in my rather sparse remarks about Natural Rights theory. I shall return to this later.

Let us take the kind of objection that I mentioned at the outset, that someone like Lee Kwan Yew might raise about Western rights practice and its alleged unsuitability for other societies, in particular East Asian ones. The basic notion is that this practice, obviously nourished by the underlying philosophy I described in the previous section, supposes that individuals are the possessors of rights and encourages them to act, to go out and aggressively seek to make good their rights. But this has a number of bad consequences. First of all, it focuses people on their rights, on what they can claim from society and others, rather than on their responsibilities, what they owe to the whole community or to its members. It encourages people to be self-regarding and leads to an atrophied sense of belonging. This in turn leads to a higher degree of social conflict, more and more many-sided, tending ultimately to a war of all against all. Social solidarity weakens, and the threat of violence increases.

This scenario seems rather overdrawn to some. However, it seems to have elements of truth to others, including to people within Western societies, which perhaps might make us doubt that we are on to a difference *between* civilizations here. In fact, there is a long tradition in the West warning against pure rights talk outside a context in which the political community has a strong positive value. This "communitarian" theorizing has taken on a new urgency today because of the experience of conflict and alienation and the fraying of solidarity in many Western democracies, notably but not only the United States. Does this mean that Lee Kwan Yew's formula might offer a solution to present-day America?

The absurdity of this suggestion brings us back to the genuine differences of culture that exist today. But if we follow through on the logical of the "communitarian" critique in the West we can perhaps find a framework in which to consider these differences.

One of the key points in the critique of a too-exclusive focus on rights is that this neglects the crucial importance of political trust. Dictatorships, as Tocqueville pointed out, try to destroy trust between citizens,[10] but free societies vitally depend on it. The price of freedom is a strong common commitment to the political formula that binds us, because without the commitment the formula would have to be aggressively enforced and this threatens freedom. What will very quickly dissolve the commitment for each and every one of us is the sense that others no longer share it or are willing to act on it. The common allegiance is nourished on trust.

This goes for a political regime centered on the retrieval of rights as much as for any other. The condition of our being able to go out and seek to enforce our own rights is that the system within which this is carried out retains the respect and allegiance of everybody. Once rights retrieval begins to eat into this, once it begins to create a sense of embattled grievance pitting group against group, undermining the sense of common allegiance and solidarity, the whole system of freewheeling rights enforcement is in danger.

The issue is not "individualism" as such. There are many forms of this, and some have grown up together with modern, democratic forms of political society. The danger is in any form of

either individualism or group identity that undercuts or undermines the trust that we share a common allegiance as citizens of this polity.

I don't want to pursue here the conditions of political trust in Western democracies, at least not for its own sake,[11] but I want to use this requirement as a heuristic tool, in search of a point of consensus on human rights. One way of considering a claim, similar to that of Lee Kwan Yew's, that the Western rights focus does not fit a certain cultural tradition would be to ask how certain fundamental liberties and immunities could be guaranteed in the society in question, consistent with the maintenance of political trust. This means, of course, that one will not consider satisfactory any solution that does not preserve these liberties and immunities while accepting whatever modifications in legal form one needs to generate a sense of common acceptance of the guaranteeing process in the society concerned.

In the concrete case of Lee Kwan Yew's Singapore, this would mean that his claim in its present form is hardly receivable. There is too much evidence of the stifling of dissent and of the cramping (to say the least) of the democratic political process in Singapore. However, this kind of claim should lead us to reflect further on how immunities of the kinds we seek in human rights declarations can best be preserved in "Confucian" societies.

Turning back to Western societies, we note that judges and the judicial process enjoy in general a great deal of prestige and respect.[12] In some countries, this respect is based on a long tradition in which some notion of fundamental law played an important part, and hence in which its guardians had a special place. Is there a way of connecting rights retrieval in other societies to offices and institutions that enjoy the highest moral prestige there?

Adverting to another tradition, we note that in Thailand at certain crucial junctures the immense moral prestige of the monarchy has been used to confer legitimacy on moves to end military violence and repression and return to constitutional rule. This was the case following the student demonstrations in October 1973, and again in the wake of the popular reactions against the seizure of power by General Suchinda Kraprayoon in May 1992. In both cases, a military junta responded with violence, only to finds its position unsustainable and to be forced to give way to a civilian regime and renewed elections. In both these cases, King Bhumibhol played a critical role.[13] The king was able to play this role because of elements in the traditions that have contributed to the Thai conception of monarchy, some of which go way back. For example, the conception of the king as *dharmaraja*, in the tradition of Ashoka,[14] sees the ruler as charged with establishing dharma in the world.

It was perhaps crucial to the upheavals of 1973 and 1992 that a king with this kind of status played the part he did. The trouble is that the power of the royal office can also be used in the other direction, as happened in 1976 when right-wing groups used the slogan "Nation, King and Religion" as a rallying cry in order to attack democratic and radical leaders. The movement of reaction culminated in the October 1976 coup, which relegated the democratic constitution once again to the wastebasket.[15]

The issue arising from all this is the following: Can the immense power to create trust and consensus that resides in the Thai monarchy be in some way stabilized, regularized, and channeled in support of constitutional rule and the defense of certain human rights, such as those concerned with the security of the person? In Weberian terms, could the charisma here be "routinized" enough to impart a stable direction to it without being lost altogether? If a way could be found to draw on this royal charisma, together with the legitimacy enjoyed by certain individuals of proven "merit" who are invested with moral authority as in the Thai tradition, to enhance support for a democratic order respectful of those immunities and liberties we generally describe as human rights, the fact that it might deviate from the standard Western model of judicial review initiated by individuals should be accorded less importance than the fact that it protects human beings from violence and oppression. We would have in fact achieved convergence on the substance of human rights, in spite of differences in form.

ALTERNATIVE FOUNDATIONS

Suppose we take the "communitarian" arguments against Western rights discourse emanating from other societies at another level, not questioning so much the legal forms but expressing disagreement with the underlying philosophical justification. My example is again drawn from Thailand. This society has seen in the last century a number of attempts to formulate reformed interpretations of the majority religion, Theravada Buddhism. Some of these have sought a basis in this form of Buddhism for democracy and human rights. This raises a somewhat broader issue than the one I'm focusing on because it concerns an alternative foundation for both democracy and human rights. The job of attaining a consensus on human rights in today's world will probably be simplified, however, if we don't try—at least at first—to come to agreement about forms of government, but concentrate solely on human rights standards. I believe that the developments in Thai thinking described here illustrate what is involved in coming to an "overlapping consensus" on the narrower basis as well.

One main stream of reform consists of movements that (as they see it) attempt to purify Buddhism, to turn it away from a focus on ritual, on gaining merit and even worldly success through blessings and acts of piety, and to focus more on (what they see as) the original goal of Enlightenment. The late Phutthathat (Buddhadasa) has been a major figure in this regard. This stream tries to return to what (it sees as) the original core of Buddhist teaching, about the unavoidability of suffering, the illusion of the self, and the goal of Nibbana. It attacks the "superstition" of those who seek potent amulets, the blessings of monks, and the like; it wants to separate the search for enlightenment from the seeking of merit through ritual; and it is very critical of the whole metaphysical structure of belief that has developed in mainstream Buddhism about heavens, hells, gods, and demons, which plays a large part in popular belief. It has been described by the Sri Lankan anthropologist, Gananath Obeyesekere, as a "protestant Buddhism."[16]

This stream seems to be producing new reflections on Buddhism as a basis for democratic society and human rights. Sulak Sivaraksa and Saneh Chamarik are among the leading figures whose writings reflect this. They and others in their milieu are highly active in social justice advocacy. They are concerned with alternative models of development, which would be more ecologically sound, concerned to put limits to growth, critical of "consumerism," and conducive to social equality. The Buddhist commitment lies behind all these goals. As Sulak explains it, the Buddhist commitment to nonviolence entails a nonpredatory stance toward the environment and calls also for the limitation of greed, one of the sources of anger and conflict.[17]

We can see here an agenda of universal well-being, but what specifically pushes to democracy, to ensuring that people take charge of their own lives rather than simply being the beneficiaries of benevolent rule? Two things seem to come together in this outlook to underpin a strong democratic commitment. The first is the notion, central to Buddhism, that ultimately each individual must take responsibility for his or her own Enlightenment. The second is a new application of the doctrine of nonviolence, which is now seen to call for a respect for the autonomy of each person, demanding in effect a minimal use of coercion in human affairs. This carries us far from the politics of imposed order, decreed by the wise minority, which has long been the traditional background to various forms and phases of nondemocratic rule. It is also evident that this underpinning for democracy offers a strong support for human rights legislation, and that, indeed, is how it is understood by thinkers like Sulak.[18]

There is an outlook here that converges on a policy of defense of human rights and democratic development but that is rather different from the standard Western justifications of these. It isn't grounded on a doctrine of the dignity of human beings as something commanding respect. The injunction to respect comes rather as a consequence of the fundamental value of nonviolence, which also generates a whole host of other consequences (including the requirement for an ecologically

responsible development and the need to set limits to growth). Human rights don't stand out, as they often do in the West, as a claim on their own, independent from the rest of our moral commitments, even sometimes in potential conflict with them.

This Buddhist conception provides an alternative way of linking together the agenda of human rights and that of democratic development. Whereas in the Western framework, these go together because they are both seen as co-requirements of human dignity, and indeed, as two facets of liberty, a connection of a somewhat different kind is visible among Thai Buddhists of this reform persuasion. Their commitment to people-centered and ecologically sensitive development makes them strong allies of those communities of villagers who are resisting encroachment by the state and big business, fighting to defend their lands and forests. This means that they are heavily into what has been recognized as a crucial part of the agenda of democratization in Thailand—decentralization, and in particular the recovery of local community control over natural resources.[19] They form a significant part of the NGO community committed to this agenda. A rather different route has been traveled to a similar goal.

Other differences stand out. Because of its roots in a certain justice agenda, the politics of establishing rights in the West has often been surrounded with anger, indignation, the imperative to punish historic wrongdoing. From this Buddhist perspective comes a caution against the politics of anger, itself the potential source of new forms of violence. My aim here is not to judge between these approaches, but to point to these differences as the source of a potentially fruitful exchange within a (hopefully) emerging world consensus on the practice of human rights and democracy.

We can in fact see a convergence here on certain norms of action; however, they may be entrenched in law. What is unfamiliar to the Western observer is the entire philosophical basis and its appropriate reference points, as well as the rhetorical source of its appeal. In the West, both democracy and human rights have been furthered by the steady advance of a kind of humanism that stressed that humans stood out from the rest of the cosmos, had a higher status and dignity than anything else. This has its origins in Christianity and certain strands of ancient thought, but the distance is greatly exacerbated by what Weber describes as the disenchantment of the world, the rejection of a view of the cosmos as a meaningful order. The human agent stands out even more starkly from a mechanistic universe. For Pascal, the human being is a mere reed, but of incomparably greater significance than what threatens to crush it, because it is a thinking reed. Kant echoes some of the same reflections in his discussion of the sublime in the third critique[20] and also defines human dignity in terms of the incomparably greater worth of human beings compared to the rest of the contents of the universe.[21]

The human rights doctrine based on this humanism stresses the incomparable importance of the human agent. It centers everything on him or her, makes his or her freedom and self-control a major value, something to be maximized. Consequently, in the Western mind, the defense of human rights seems indissolubly linked with this exaltation of human agency. It is because humans justifiably command all this respect and attention, at least in comparison to anything else, that their rights must be defended.

The Buddhist philosophy that I have been describing starts from a quite different place, the demand of *ahimsa* (nonviolence), and yet seems to ground many of the same norms. (Of course, there will also be differences in the norms grounded, which raises its own problems, but for the moment I just want to note the substantial overlap.) The gamut of Western philosophical emotions, the exaltation at human dignity, the emphasis on freedom as the highest value, the drama of age-old wrongs righted in valor, all the things that move us in seeing *Fidelio* well performed, seem out of place in this alternative setting. So do the models of heroism. The heroes of *ahimsa* are not forceful revolutionaries, not Cola di Rienzi or Garibaldi, and with the philosophy and the models, a whole rhetoric loses its basis.

This perhaps gives us an idea of what an unforced world consensus on human rights might look like. Agreement on norms, yes, but a profound sense of difference, of unfamiliarity, in the ideals, the notions of human excellence, the rhetorical tropes and reference points by which these norms become objects of deep commitment for us. To the extent that we can only acknowledge agreement with people who share the whole package and are moved by the same heroes, the consensus will either never come or must be forced.

This is the situation at the outset, in any case, when consensus on some aspect of human rights has just been attained. Later a process can follow of mutual learning, moving toward a "fusion of horizons" in Gadamer's term, in which the moral universe of the other becomes less strange. Out of this will come further borrowings and the creation of new hybrid forms.

After all, something of this has already occurred with another stream of the philosophy of *ahimsa*, that of Gandhi. Gandhi's practices of nonviolent resistance have been borrowed and adapted in the West, for example, in the American Civil Rights Movement under Martin Luther King. Beyond that, they have become part of a world repertory of political practices, invoked in Manila in 1988 and in Prague in 1989, to name just two examples.

Also worthy of remark is one other facet of this case that may be generalizable as well. An important part of the Western consciousness of human rights lies in the awareness of an historic achievement. Human rights define norms of respect for human beings, more radical and more exigent than have ever existed in the past. They offer in principle greater freedom, greater security from violence, from arbitrary treatment, from discrimination and oppression than humans have enjoyed at least in most major civilizations in history. In a sense they involve taking the exceptional treatment accorded to privileged people in the past, and extending it to everyone. That is why so many of the landmarks of the historical development of rights were in their day instruments of elite privilege, starting with Magna Carta.

There is a curious convergence in this respect with the strand of Reform Buddhism I have been describing. Here too, there is the awareness that very exigent demands are being made that go way beyond what the majority of ordinary believers recognize as required practice. Reform Buddhism is practiced by an elite, as has been the case with most of its analogues in history. But here too, in developing a doctrine of democracy and human rights, Reform Buddhists are proposing to extend what has hitherto been a minority practice and entrench it in society as a whole. Here again, there is a consciousness of the universalization of the highest of traditional minority practice.

It is as though in spite of the difference in philosophy this universalization of an exigent standard, which human rights practice at its best involves, was recognized as a valid move and recreated within a different cultural, philosophical, and religious world. The hope for a world consensus is that this kind of move will be made repeatedly.

HIERARCHY AND IDENTITY

This example drawn from Thailand provides one model for what the path to world consensus might look like—a convergence on certain norms from out of very different philosophical and spiritual backgrounds. The consensus at first doesn't need to be based on any deep mutual understanding of these respective backgrounds. Each may seem strange to the other, even though both recognize and value the practical agreement attained. Of course, this is not to say that there is no borrowing involved at all. Plainly, democracy and human rights practices originated somewhere and are now being creatively recaptured (perhaps in a significantly different variant) elsewhere, but a mutual understanding and appreciation of each other's spiritual basis for signing on to the common norms may be close to nonexistent.

This, however, is not a satisfactory end point. Some attempt at deeper understanding must follow or the gains in agreement will remain fragile, for at least two closely connected reasons. The first is that the agreement is never complete. We already saw that what we can call the *ahimsa* basis for rights connects to ecological concerns differently from the Western humanist basis, in that the place of anger, indignation, righteous condemnation, and punishment is different in the two outlooks. All this must lead to differences of practice, of the detailed schedule of rights, or at least of the priority ordering among them. In practice, these differences may not emerge in variant schedules of rights. They may be reflected in the way a given schedule is interpreted and applied in different societies. After all, entrenched charters have to be applied by courts, and the courts make their interpretations within the framework of the moral views prevalent in their society. Some, like the Canadian charter, specifically provide for this adaptive interpretation by calling on the courts to interpret the charter in the light of social requirements, including those of a democratic society.[22] The demands of a world consensus will often include our squaring these differences in practical contexts, our accommodating or coming to some compromise version that both sides can live with. These negotiations will be inordinately difficult unless each side can come to some more fine-grained understanding of what moves the other.

The second reason follows on from the first and is in a sense just another facet of it. The continued coexistence in a broad consensus that continually generates particular disagreements, which have in turn to be negotiated to renewed consensus, is impossible without mutual respect. If the sense is strong on each side that the spiritual basis of the other is ridiculous, false, inferior, unworthy, these attitudes cannot but sap the will to agree of those who hold these views while engendering anger and resentment among those who are thus depreciated. The only cure for contempt here is understanding. This alone can replace the too-facile depreciatory stories about others with which groups often tend to shore up their own sense of rightness and superiority. Consequently, the bare consensus must strive to go on towards a fusion of horizons.

In this discussion, I have analytically distinguished consensus from mutual understanding and have imagined that they occur sequentially as successive phases. This is certainly a schematic oversimplification, but perhaps not totally wrong in the Thai case I was examining. However, in other situations some degree of mutual understanding is an essential condition of getting to consensus. The two cannot simply occur successively, because the path to agreement lies through some degree of sympathetic mutual comprehension.

I want to look now at another difference that seems to be of this latter type. To lay it out here, I will have to describe more fully another facet of the Western philosophical background of rights, which can hit a wall of incomprehension once one crosses the boundary to other cultures. This is the Western concern for equality, in the form of nondiscrimination. Existing charters of rights in the Western world are no longer concerned only with ensuring certain liberties and immunities to individuals. To an important degree, they also serve to counter various forms of discrimination. This represents a shift in the center of gravity of rights talk over the last centuries. One could argue that the central importance of nondiscrimination enters American judicial review with the Fourteenth Amendment, in the aftermath of the Civil War. Since then nondiscrimination provisions have been an important and growing part of schedules of rights both in the United States and elsewhere.

This connection is perhaps not surprising, although it took a long time to come to fruition. In a sense, the notion of equality was closely linked from the beginning to that of Natural Right, in contradistinction to the place of subjective rights in medieval systems of law, which were also those of certain estates or privileged individuals. Once right inheres in nature, then it is hard in the long run to deny it to anyone. The connection to equality is the stronger because of the thrust of modern humanism mentioned earlier, which defines itself against the view that we are embedded in a meaningful cosmic order. This latter has been a background against which various forms of human differentiation could appear natural, unchallengeable—be they social, racial, or sexual. The differences in human society, or gender roles, could be understood to reflect differentiations in the order of things and to correspond to differences in the cosmos, as with Plato's myth of the metals. This has been a very common form of thinking in almost all human societies.[23]

The destruction of this order has allowed for a process of unmasking existing social and gender differences as merely socially constructed, as without basis in the nature of things, as revocable and hence ultimately without justification. The process of working this out has been long, and we are not yet at the end, but it has been hard to resist in Western civilization in the last two centuries.

This aspect of Western rights talk is often very hard to export because it encounters societies in which certain social differences are still considered very meaningful, and they are seen in turn as intrinsically linked to certain practices that in Western societies are now regarded as discriminatory. However hard these sticking points may be for a Westerner to grasp in detail, it is not difficult to understand the general shape of the conflict, particularly because we in the West are far from having worked out how to combine gender equality with our conflicted ideas of gender difference.

To take this issue of gender equality as our example, we can readily understand that a certain way of framing the difference, however oppressive it may be in practice, also serves as the reference point for deeply felt human identities. The rejection of the framework can be felt as the utter denial of the basis of identity, and this not just for the favored gender, but also for the oppressed one. The gender definitions of a culture are interwoven with, among other things, its love stories, both those people tell and those they live.[24] Throwing off a traditional identity can be an act of liberation, but more than just liberation is involved here; without an alternative sense of identity, the loss of the traditional one is disorienting and potentially unbearable.

The whole shape of the change that could allow for an unforced consensus on human rights here includes a redefinition of identity, perhaps building on transformed traditional reference points in such a way as to allow for a recognition of an operative equality between the sexes. This can be a tall order, something we should have no trouble appreciating in the West because we have yet to complete our own redefinitions in this regard. This identity redefinition will be the easier to effect the more it can be presented as being in continuity with the most important traditions and reference points, properly understood. Correspondingly, it gets maximally difficult when it comes across as a brutal break with the past involving a condemnation and rejection of it. To some extent, which of these two scenarios gets enacted depends on developments internal to the society, but the relation with the outside world, and particularly the West, can also be determining.

The more the outside portrayal, or attempt at influence, comes across as a blanket condemnation of or contempt for the tradition, the more the dynamic of a "fundamentalist" resistance to all redefinition tends to get in train, and the harder it will be to find unforced consensus. This is a self-reinforcing dynamic, in which perceived external condemnation helps to feed extreme reaction, which calls down further condemnation, and hence further reaction, in a vicious spiral. The world is already drearily familiar with this dynamic in the unhealthy relation between the West and great parts of the Islamic world in our time.

In a sense, therefore, the road to consensus in relation to this difference is the opposite from the one mentioned earlier. There, the convergence on norms between Western humanism and reform Buddhism might be seen as preceding a phase in which they come better to understand and appreciate and learn from each other. In the field of gender discrimination, it may well be that the order would be better reversed, that is, that the path to consensus passes through greater sympathetic understanding of the situation of each party by the other. In this respect, the West with its own hugely unresolved issues about equality and difference is often more of a menace than a help.

THE POLYVALENCE OF TRADITION

Before concluding, I want to look at another difference, which resembles in different respects both of the preceding. That is, it is certainly one in which the dynamic of mutual miscomprehension and condemnation is driving us away from consensus, but it also has potentialities like the Thai case, in that we can see how a quite different

spiritual or theological basis might be found for a convergence on norms. I am thinking of the difference between international human rights standards and certain facets of the *Shari'a*, recently discussed in so illuminating a fashion by Abdullahi Ahmed An-Na'im.[25] Certain punishments prescribed by the *Shari'a*, such as amputation of the hand for theft or stoning for adultery, appear excessive and cruel in the light of standards prevalent in other countries.

It is worthwhile developing here, as I have in the other cases, the facet of Western philosophical thought and sensibility which has given particular force to this condemnation. This can best be shown through an example. When we read the opening pages of Michel Foucault's *Surveiller et Punir* we are struck by its riveting description of the torture, execution, and dismemberment of Damien, the attempted assassin of Louis XV in the mid-eighteenth century.[26] We cannot but be aware of the cultural change that we have gone through since the Enlightenment.[27] We are much more concerned about pain and suffering than our forebears; we shrink more from infliction of gratuitous suffering. It would be hard to imagine people today taking their children to such a spectacle, at least openly and without some sense of unease and shame.

What has changed? We can distinguish two factors, one positive and one negative. On the positive side, we see pain and suffering and gratuitously inflicted death in a new light because of the immense cultural revolution that has been taking place in modernity, which I called elsewhere "the affirmation of ordinary life."[28] What I was trying to gesture at with this term is the momentous cultural and spiritual change of the early modern period, which dethroned the supposedly higher activities of contemplation and the citizen life, and put the center of gravity of goodness in ordinary living, production, and the family. It belongs to this spiritual outlook that our first concern ought to be to increase life, relieve suffering, foster prosperity. Concern above all for the "good life" smacked of pride, of self-absorption. Beyond that, it was inherently inegalitarian, because the alleged "higher" activities could only be carried out by an elite minority, whereas leading rightly one's ordinary life was open to everyone. This is a moral temper to which it seems obvious that our major concern must be our dealings with others, in justice and benevolence, and these dealings must be on a level of equality. This affirmation, which constitutes a major component of our modern ethical outlook, was originally inspired by a mode of Christian piety. It exalted practical agape, and was polemically directed against the pride, elitism, and one might say self-absorption of those who believed in "higher" activities or spiritualities.

We can easily see how much this development is interwoven with the rise of the humanism that stands behind the Western discourse of human rights. They converge on the concern for equality, and also for the security of the person against burdens, dangers, and suffering imposed from outside.

But this is not the whole story. There is also a negative change; something has been cast off. It is not as though our ancestors would have simply thought the level of pain irrelevant, providing no reason at all to desist from some course of action involving torture and wounds. For us, the relief of suffering has become a supreme value, but it was always an important consideration. It is rather that, in cases like that of Damien, the negative significance of pain was subordinated to other, weightier considerations. If it is necessary that punishment in a sense undo the evil of the crime, restore the balance—what is implicit in the whole notion of the criminal making *amende honorable*—then the very horror of regicide calls for a kind of theatre of the horrible as the medium in which this undoing can take place. In this context, pain takes on a different significance; there has to be lots of it to do the trick. A principle of minimizing pain is trumped.

Thus, we relate doubly to our forebears of two centuries ago. We have new reasons to minimize suffering, but we also lack a reason to override the minimizing of suffering. We no longer have the whole outlook—linked as it was to the cosmos as meaningful order—that made sense of the necessity of undoing the crime, restoring the breached order of things, in and through the punishment of the criminal.

In general, contemporaries in the West are so little aware of the positive change they have gone through—they tend anachronistically to think that people must always have felt this way—that they generally believe that the negative change is the crucial one that explains our difference from our predecessors. With this in mind, they look at the *Shari'a* punishments as the simple result of premodern illusions, in the same category in which they now place the *ancien régime* execution scenarios. With this dismissive condemnation, the stage is set for the dynamic I described earlier, in which contemptuous denunciation leads to "fundamentalist" reaffirmations, which in turn provoke even more strident denunciations, and so on.

What gets lost in this struggle is what An-Na'im shows so clearly: the possibilities of reinterpretation and reappropriation that the tradition itself contains. What also becomes invisible is what could be the motor of this change, analogous to the role played by the cultural revolution affirming ordinary life in the West. What this or these could be is not easy for an outsider to determine, but the striking Islamic theme of the mercy and compassion of God, reinvoked at the beginning of almost every sura of the *Qur'an*, might be the locus of a creative theological development. This might help toward a convergence in this domain, in which case we might see a consensus among those of very different spiritual backgrounds, analogous to the Thai Buddhist views I discussed earlier.

CONCLUSION

I started this chapter with the basic notion that an unforced world consensus on human rights would be something like a Rawlsian "overlapping consensus," in which convergent norms would be justified in very different underlying spiritual and philosophical outlooks. I then argued that these norms have to be distinguished and analytically separated not just from the background justifications, but also from the legal forms that give them force. These two could vary with good reason from society to society, even though the norms we crucially want to preserve remain constant. We need, in other words, a threefold distinction: norms, legal forms, and background justifications, which each have to be distinguished from the others.

I then looked at four examples of differences. These by no means exhaust the field, though each is important in the present international exchange on human rights. One of these dealt with the issue of variations in legal forms. In the other three, I tried to discuss issues around the convergence on norms out of different philosophical and spiritual backgrounds.

Two important facets of these convergences emerged. In one way, they involve the meeting of very different minds, worlds apart in their premises, uniting only in the immediate practical conclusions. From another side, it is clear that consensus requires that this extreme distance be closed, that we come better to understand each other in our differences, that we learn to recognize what is great and admirable in our different spiritual traditions. In some cases, this kind of mutual understanding can come after convergence, but in others it seems almost to be condition of it.

An obstacle in the path to this mutual understanding comes from the inability of many Westerners to see their culture as one among many. An example of this difficulty was visible in the last difference discussed. To an extent, Westerners see their human rights doctrine as arising simply out of the falling away of previous countervailing ideas—such as the punishment scenarios of the *ancien régime*—that have now been discredited to leave the field free for the preoccupations with human life, freedom, the avoidance of suffering. To this extent they will tend to think that the path to convergence requires that others too cast off their traditional ideas, that they even reject their religious heritage, and become "unmarked" moderns like us. Only if we in the West can recapture a more adequate view of our own history, can we learn to understand better the spiritual ideas that have been interwoven in our development and hence be prepared to understand sympathetically the spiritual paths of others toward the converging goal.[29] Contrary to

what many people think, world convergence will not come through a loss or denial of traditions all around, but rather by creative reimmersions of different groups, each in their own spiritual heritage, traveling different routes to the same goal.

NOTES

1. John Rawls, *Political Liberalism* (New York: Columbia University Press, 1993), lecture IV.
2. From the Introduction to UNESCO, *Human Rights: Comments and Interpretations* (London: Allan Wingate, 1949), pp. 10–11; cited in Abdullahi An-Na'im, "Towards a Cross-Cultural Approach to Defining International Standards of Human Rights: The Meaning of Cruel, Inhuman, or Degrading Treatment or Punishment," in Abdullahi Ahmed An-Na'im, ed. *Human Rights in Cross Cultural Perspectives* (Philadelphia: University of Pennsylvania Press, 1992), pp. 28–29.
3. Jack Donnelly, *Universal Human Rights in Theory and Practice* (Ithaca: Cornell University Press, 1989), pp. 28–37.
4. See chapter 4.
5. See Sidney Jones, "The Impact of Asian Economic Growth on Human Rights," *Asia Project Working Paper Series* (New York: Council on Foreign Relations, January 1995), p. 9.
6. "I find parts of [the American system] totally unacceptable: guns, drugs, violent crime, vagrancy, unbecoming behaviour in public—in sum, the breakdown of civil society. The expansion of the right of the individual to behave or misbehave as he pleases has come at the expense of orderly society. In the East the main object is to have a well-ordered society so that everybody can have maximum enjoyment of his freedoms. This freedom can only exist in an ordered state and not in a natural state of contention." Fareed Zakaria, "Culture Is Destiny: A Conversation with Lee Kuan Yew," *Foreign Affairs* (March/April 1994), p. 111.
7. Which is why Locke had to introduce a restrictive adjective to block this option of waiver, when he spoke of "inalienable rights." The notion of inalienability had no place in earlier natural right discourse, because this had no option of waiver.
8. According to Louis Henkin, "The Human Rights Idea in Contemporary China: A Comparative Perspective," in R. Randle Edwards, Louis Henkin, and Andrew J. Nathan, *Human Rights in Contemporary China* (New York: Columbia University Press, 1986), p. 21:

    In the Chinese tradition the individual was not central, and no conception of individual rights existed in the sense known to the United States. The individual's participation in society was not voluntary, and the legitimacy of government did not depend on his consent or the consent of the whole people of individuals. . . .

    In traditional China, the idea was not individual liberty or equality but order and harmony, not individual independence but selflessness and cooperation, not freedom of individual conscience but conformity to orthodox truth. . . . The purpose of society was not to preserve and promote individual liberty but to maintain the harmony of the hierarchical order and to see to it that truth prevailed.

9. See Sulka Sivaraksa, "Buddhism and Human Rights in Siam" (unpublished paper presented at Bangkok Workshop of the Human Rights Initiative, Carnegie Council on Ethics and International Affairs, March 1996), pp. 4–5. Sulak wonders whether the Western concept of freedom, closely allied with that of right, "has reached an end point in environmental degradation."

10. "L'égalité place les hommes à côté les uns des autres, sans rien commun qui les retienne. Le despotisme élève des barrières entre eux et les sépare. Elle les dispose ne point songer à leurs semblables et il leur fait une sorte de verru publique de l'indifférance." [Equality places people next to each other, without a common link that really keeps them together. Despotism elevates barriers between people and keeps them apart. It predisposes individuals not to think of their compatriots and makes a kind of public virtue out of their indifference.] *La Démocratie en Amérique* vol. 2, IIe partie, chapitre IV (Paris: Édition Garnier-Flammarion, 1981), vol. 2, p. 131.

11. I have talked about substantially similar issues in somewhat different terms in the last chapter of *The Malaise of Modernity* (Toronto: Anansi Press, 1991), and in "Liberalism and the Public Sphere," *Philosophical Arguments* (Cambridge, MA: Harvard University Press, 1995), chapter 13.

12. This is what is so dangerous to public order in cases like the 1995 O. J. Simpson trial, which both show up and further entrench a deep lack of respect for and trust in the judicial process.

13. There is a Western analogue in the positive part played by Juan Carlos during the coup in Madrid in 1974.

14. See Stanley Tambiah, *World Conqueror and World Renouncer* (New York: Cambridge University Press, 1976).

15. See the discussion in John Girling, *Thailand: Society and Politics* (Ithaca: Cornell University Press, 1981), pp. 154–7. Frank Reynolds in his "Legitimation and Rebellion: Thailand's Civic Religion and the Student Uprising of October, 1973," in Bardwell L. Smith, ed., *Religion and Legitimation of Power in Thailand, Laos, and Burma* (Chambersburg, PA: Anima Books, 1978), discusses the use by the student demonstrators of the symbols of "Nation, Religion, Monarchy."

16. Richard Gombrich and Gananath Obeyesekere, *Buddhism Transformed: Religious Change in Sri Lanka* (Princeton, NJ: Princeton University Press, 1988), chapters 6 and 7.

17. See Sulak Sivaraksa, *Seeds of Peace: A Buddhist Vision for Renewing Society* (Berkeley and Bangkok: Parallax Press, 1992), chapter 9.

18. See Sulak Sivaraksa, *Seeds of Peace*, especially Part Two.

19. See the discussion in Vitit Muntarbhorn and Charles Taylor, *Roads to Democracy: Human Rights and Democratic Development in Thailand, Bangkok and Montréal* (International Centre for Human Rights and Democratic Development, July 1994), part 3.

20. *Kants Werke*, vol. 6: *Kritik der Urteilskraft* (Berlin: Walter de Gruyter, 1964), first part, second book, sections 28–9.

21. *Grundlegung zur Metaphysik der Sitten*. Berlin Academy edition (Berlin: Walter de Gruyter, 1968), vol. 4, p. 434.

22. See the discussion in Joseph Chan, "The Asian Challenge to Universal Human Rights: A Philosophical Appraisal," in James T. H. Tang, ed., *Human Rights and International Relations in the Asia-Pacific Region* (London: Pinter, 1995).

23. A good example is Pierre Bourdieu's description of the "correspondences" between the male–female difference and different colors, cardinal points, and oppositions like wet–dry, up–down, etc. See his *Outline of a Theory of Practice* (Cambridge: Cambridge University Press, 1977), chapter 3.

24. See, for example, Sudhir Kakar, *The Inner World* (Delhi: Oxford University Press, 1978), who claims that Hindu culture foregrounds a love story of the young married couple, already with children, as against the prevalent Western tale of the love intrigue that leads to marriage.

25. See his "Towards a Cross-Cultural Approach to Defining International Standards of Human Rights," chapter 1; also see chapter 6 in this volume.

26. Foucault, *Surveiller et Punir* (Paris: Gallimard, 1976).

27. Tocqueville was already aware of the change when he commented on a passage from Mme. de Sévigny in *La Démocratie en Amérique*.

28. See Charles Taylor, *Sources of the Self* (Cambridge, MA: Harvard University Press, 1989), chapter 13.

29. I have discussed at greater length the two opposed understandings of the rise of modernity that are invoked here in "Modernity and the Rise of the Public Sphere," Grethe B. Peterson, ed., *The Tanner Lectures on Human Values* (Salt Lake City: University of Utah Press, 1993).

Democracy as a Universal Value

Amartya Sen

Amartya Sen was born in India. He has taught at Cambridge and Oxford and is now a professor of economics and philosophy at Harvard University. He is the author of many books including *Identity and Violence: The Illusion of Destiny* (2006), *Rationality and Freedom* (2002), *Development as Freedom* (1999), and *Inequality Reexamined* (1992). Sen won the Nobel Prize in economics in 1998.

Sen maintains that democracy is a universal value in the sense that "people anywhere may have reason to see it as valuable" regardless of cultural difference. In particular, Sen argues that democracy is valuable in three respects: intrinsically, it enhances people's well-being through political participation; instrumentally, it serves as a means for promoting open and informed discussion that could restrain the excesses of government; and constructively, it allows individuals to understand and shape each other's needs and values.

In the summer of 1997, I was asked by a leading Japanese newspaper what I thought was the most important thing that had happened in the twentieth century. I found this to be an unusually thought-provoking question, since so many things of gravity have happened over the last hundred years. The European empires, especially the British and French ones that had so dominated the nineteenth century, came to an end. We witnessed two world wars. We saw the rise and fall of fascism and Nazism. The century witnessed the rise of communism, and its fall (as in the former Soviet bloc) or radical transformation (as in China). We also saw a shift from the economic dominance of the West to a new economic balance much more dominated by Japan and East and Southeast Asia. Even though that region is going through some financial and economic problems right now, this is not going to nullify the shift in the balance of the world economy that has occurred over many decades (in the case of Japan, through nearly the entire century). The past hundred years are not lacking in important events.

Nevertheless, among the great variety of developments that have occurred in the twentieth century, I did not, ultimately, have any difficulty in choosing one as the preeminent development of the period: the rise of democracy. This is not to deny that other occurrences have also been important, but I would argue that in the distant future, when people look back at what happened in this century, they will find it difficult not to accord primacy to the emergence of democracy as the preeminently acceptable form of governance.

The idea of democracy originated, of course, in ancient Greece, more than two millennia ago. Piecemeal efforts at democratization were attempted elsewhere as well, including in India.[1] But it is really in ancient Greece that the idea of democracy took shape and was seriously put into practice (albeit on a limited scale), before it collapsed and was replaced by more authoritarian and asymmetric forms of government. There were no other kinds anywhere else.

Thereafter, democracy as we know it took a long time to emerge. Its gradual—and ultimately triumphant—emergence as a working system of governance was bolstered by many developments, from the signing of the Magna Carta in 1215, to the French and the American Revolutions in the eighteenth century, to the widening of the franchise in Europe and North America in the nineteenth century. It was in the twentieth century, however, that the idea of democracy became established as the "normal" form of government to which any nation is entitled—whether in Europe, America, Asia, or Africa.

The idea of democracy as a universal commitment is quite new, and it is quintessentially a product of the twentieth century. The rebels who forced restraint on the king of England through the Magna Carta saw the need as an entirely local one. In contrast, the American fighters for independence and the revolutionaries in France contributed greatly to an understanding of the need for democracy as a general system. Yet the focus of their practical demands remained quite local—confined, in effect, to the two sides of the North Atlantic, and founded on the special economic, social, and political history of the region.

Throughout the nineteenth century, theorists of democracy found it quite natural to discuss whether one country or another was "fit for democracy." This thinking changed only in the twentieth century, with the recognition that the question itself was wrong: A country does not have to be deemed fit *for* democracy; rather, it has to become fit *through* democracy. This is indeed a momentous change, extending the potential reach of democracy to cover billions of people, with their varying histories and cultures and disparate levels of affluence.

It was also in this century that people finally accepted that "franchise for all adults" must mean *all*—not just men but also women. When in January of this year I had the opportunity to meet Ruth Dreyfuss, the president of Switzerland and a woman of remarkable distinction, it gave me occasion to recollect that only a quarter century ago Swiss women could not even vote. We have

at last reached the point of recognizing that the coverage of universality, like the quality of mercy, is not strained.

I do not deny that there are challenges to democracy's claim to universality. These challenges come in many shapes and forms—and from different directions. Indeed, that is part of the subject of this essay. I have to examine the claim of democracy as a universal value and the disputes that surround that claim. Before I begin that exercise, however, it is necessary to grasp clearly the sense in which democracy has become a dominant belief in the contemporary world.

In any age and social climate, there are some sweeping beliefs that seem to command respect as a kind of general rule—like a "default" setting in a computer program; they are considered right *unless* their claim is somehow precisely negated. While democracy is not yet universally practiced, nor indeed uniformly accepted, in the general climate of world opinion, democratic governance has now achieved the status of being taken to be generally right. The ball is very much in the court of those who want to rubbish democracy to provide justification for that rejection.

This is a historic change from not very long ago, when the advocates of democracy for Asia or Africa had to argue for democracy with their backs to the wall. While we still have reason enough to dispute those who, implicitly or explicitly, reject the need for democracy, we must also note clearly how the general climate of opinion has sh`ifted from what it was in previous centuries. We do not have to establish afresh, each time, whether such and such a country (South Africa, or Cambodia, or Chile) is "fit for democracy" (a question that was prominent in the discourse of the nineteenth century); we now take that for granted. This recognition of democracy as a universally relevant system, which moves in the direction of its acceptance as a universal value, is a major revolution in thinking, and one of the main contributions of the twentieth century. It is in this context that we have to examine the question of democracy as a universal value.

THE INDIAN EXPERIENCE

How well has democracy worked? While no one really questions the role of democracy in, say, the United States or Britain or France, it is still a matter of dispute for many of the poorer countries in the world. This is not the occasion for a detailed examination of the historical record, but I would argue that democracy has worked well enough.

India, of course, was one of the major battlegrounds of this debate. In denying Indians independence, the British expressed anxiety over the Indians' ability to govern themselves. India was indeed in some disarray in 1947, the year it became independent. It had an untried government, an undigested partition, and unclear political alignments, combined with widespread communal violence and social disorder. It was hard to have faith in the future of a united and democratic India. And yet, half a century later, we find a democracy that has, taking the rough with the smooth, worked remarkably well. Political differences have been largely tackled within the constitutional guidelines, and governments have risen and fallen according to electoral and parliamentary rules. An ungainly, unlikely, inelegant combination of differences, India nonetheless survives and functions remarkably well as a political unit with a democratic system. Indeed, it is held together by its working democracy.

India has also survived the tremendous challenge of dealing with a variety of major languages and a spectrum of religions. Religious and communal differences are, of course, vulnerable to exploitation by sectarian politicians, and have indeed been so used on several occasions (including in recent months), causing massive consternation in the country. Yet the fact that consternation greets sectarian violence and that condemnation of such violence comes from all sections of the country ultimately provides the main democratic guarantee against the narrowly factional exploitation of sectarianism. This is, of course, essential for the survival and prosperity of a country as remarkably varied as India, which is home not only to a Hindu majority but also to the world's third largest Muslim population, to millions of Christians and Buddhists, and to most of the world's Sikhs, Parsees, and Jains.

DEMOCRACY AND ECONOMIC DEVELOPMENT

It is often claimed that nondemocratic systems are better at bringing about economic development. This belief sometimes goes by the name of "the Lee hypothesis," due to its advocacy by Lee Kuan Yew, the leader and former president of Singapore. He is certainly right that some disciplinarian states (such as South Korea, his own Singapore, and postreform China) have had faster rates of economic growth than many less authoritarian ones (including India, Jamaica, and Costa Rica). The "Lee hypothesis," however, is based on sporadic empiricism, drawing on very selective and limited information, rather than on any general statistical testing over the wide-ranging data that are available. A general relation of this kind cannot be established on the basis of very selective evidence. For example, we cannot really take the high economic growth of Singapore or China as "definitive proof" that authoritarianism does better in promoting economic growth, any more than we can draw the opposite conclusion from the fact that Botswana, the country with the best record of economic growth in Africa, indeed with one of the finest records of economic growth in the whole world, has been an oasis of democracy on that continent over the decades. We need more systematic empirical studies to sort out the claims and counterclaims.

There is, in fact, no convincing general evidence that authoritarian governance and the suppression of political and civil rights are really beneficial to economic development. Indeed, the general statistical picture does not permit any such induction. Systematic empirical studies (for example, by Robert Barro or by Adam Przeworski) give no real support to the claim that there is a general conflict between political rights and economic performance.[2] The directional linkage seems to depend on many other circumstances, and while some statistical investigations note a weakly negative relation, others find a strongly positive one. If all the comparative studies are viewed together, the hypothesis that there is no clear relation between economic growth and democracy in *either* direction remains extremely plausible. Since democracy and political liberty have importance in themselves, the case for them therefore remains untarnished.[3]

The question also involves a fundamental issue of methods of economic research. We must not only look at statistical connections but also examine and scrutinize the *causal* processes that are involved in economic growth and development. The economic policies and circumstances that led to the economic success of countries in East Asia are by now reasonably well understood. While different empirical studies have varied in emphasis, there is by now broad consensus on a list of "helpful policies" that includes openness to competition, the use of international markets, public provision of incentives for investment and export, a high level of literacy and schooling, successful land reforms, and other social opportunities that widen participation in the process of economic expansion. There is no reason at all to assume that any of these policies is inconsistent with greater democracy and had to be forcibly sustained by the elements of authoritarianism that happened to be present in South Korea or Singapore or China. Indeed, there is overwhelming evidence to show that what is needed for generating faster economic growth is a friendlier economic climate rather than a harsher political system.

To complete this examination, we must go beyond the narrow confines of economic growth and scrutinize the broader demands of economic development, including the need for economic and social security. In that context, we have to look at the connection between political and civil rights, on the one hand, and the prevention of major economic disasters, on the other. Political and civil rights give people the opportunity to draw attention forcefully to general needs and to demand appropriate public action. The response of a government to the acute suffering of its people often depends on the pressure that is put on it. The exercise of political rights (such as voting, criticizing, protesting, and the like) can make a real difference to the political incentives that operate on a government.

I have discussed elsewhere the remarkable fact that, in the terrible history of famines in the world, no substantial famine has ever occurred in any independent and democratic country with a relatively free press.[4] We cannot find exceptions to this rule, no matter where we look: the recent famines of Ethiopia, Somalia, or other dictatorial regimes: famines in the Soviet Union in the 1930s; China's 1958–61 famine with the failure of the Great Leap Forward; or earlier still, the famines in Ireland or India under alien rule. China, although it was in many ways doing much better economically than India, still managed (unlike India) to have a famine, indeed the largest recorded famine in world history: Nearly 30 million people died in the famine of 1958–61, while faulty governmental policies remained uncorrected for three full years. The policies went uncriticized because there were no opposition parties in parliament, no free press, and no multiparty elections. Indeed, it is precisely this lack of challenge that allowed the deeply defective policies to continue even though they were killing millions each year. The same can be said about the world's two contemporary famines, occurring right now in North Korea and Sudan.

Famines are often associated with what look like natural disasters, and commentators often settle for the simplicity of explaining famines by pointing to these events: the floods in China during the failed Great Leap Forward, the droughts in Ethiopia, or crop failures in North Korea. Nevertheless, many countries with similar natural problems, or even worse ones, manage perfectly well, because a responsive government intervenes to help alleviate hunger. Since the primary victims of a famine are the indigent, deaths can be prevented by recreating incomes (for example, through employment programs), which makes food accessible to potential famine victims. Even the poorest democratic countries that have faced terrible droughts or floods or other natural disasters (such as India in 1973, or Zimbabwe and Botswana in the early 1980s) have been able to feed their people without experiencing a famine.

Famines are easy to prevent if there is a serious effort to do so, and a democratic government, facing elections and criticisms from opposition parties and independent newspapers, cannot help but make such an effort. Not surprisingly, while India continued to have famines under British rule right up to independence (the last famine, which I witnessed as a child, was in 1943, four years before independence), they disappeared suddenly with the establishment of a multiparty democracy and a free press.

I have discussed these issues elsewhere, particularly in my joint work with Jean Dr'eze, so I will not dwell further on them here.[5] Indeed, the issue of famine is only one example of the reach of democracy, though it is, in many ways, the easiest case to analyze. The positive role of political and civil rights applies to the prevention of economic and social disasters in general. When things go fine and everything is routinely good, this instrumental role of democracy may not be particularly missed, it is when things get fouled up, for one reason or another, that the political incentives provided by democratic governance acquire great practical value.

There is, I believe, an important lesson here. Many economic technocrats recommend the use of economic incentives (which the market system provides) while ignoring political incentives (which democratic systems could guarantee). This is to opt for a deeply unbalanced set of ground rules. The protective power of democracy may not be missed much when a country is lucky enough to be facing no serious calamity, when everything is going quite smoothly. Yet the danger of insecurity, arising from changed economic or other circumstances, or from uncorrected mistakes of policy, can lurk behind what looks like a healthy state.

The recent problems of East and Southeast Asia bring out, among other things, the penalties of undemocratic governance. This is so in two striking respects. First, the development of the financial crisis in some of these economies (including South Korea, Thailand, Indonesia) has been closely linked to the lack of transparency in business, in particular the lack of public participation in reviewing financial arrangements. The absence of an effective democratic forum has been central to this failing. Second, once the financial crisis led to a general economic recession, the protective power of democracy—not unlike that which prevents famines in democratic countries—was badly missed in a country like Indonesia. The newly dispossessed did not have the hearing they needed.

A fall in total gross national product of, say, 10 percent may not look like much if it follows in the wake of a growth rate of 5 or 10 percent every year over the past few decades, and yet that decline can decimate lives and create misery for millions if the burden of contraction is not widely shared but allowed to be heaped on those—the unemployed or the economically redundant—who can least bear it. The vulnerable in Indonesia may not have missed democracy when things went up and up, but that lacuna kept their voice low and muffled as the unequally shared crisis developed. The protective role of democracy is strongly missed when it is most needed.

THE FUNCTIONS OF DEMOCRACY

I have so far allowed the agenda of this essay to be determined by the critics of democracy, especially the economic critics. I shall return to criticisms again, taking up the arguments of the cultural critics in particular, but the time has come for me to pursue further the positive analysis of what democracy does and what may lie at the base of its claim to be a universal value.

What exactly is democracy? We must net identify democracy with majority rule. Democracy has complex demands, which certainly include voting and respect for election results, but it also requires the protection of liberties and freedoms, respect for legal entitlements, and the guaranteeing of free discussion and uncensored distribution of news and fair comment. Even elections can be deeply defective if they occur without the different sides getting an adequate opportunity to present their respective cases, or without the electorate enjoying the freedom to obtain news and to consider the views of the competing protagonists. Democracy is a demanding system, and not just a mechanical condition (like majority ruse) taken in isolation.

Viewed in this light, the merits of democracy and its claim as a universal value can be related to certain distinct virtues that go with its unfettered practice. Indeed, we can distinguish three different ways in which democracy enriches the lives of the citizens. First, political freedom is a part of human freedom in general, and exercising civil and political rights is a crucial part of good lives of individuals as social beings Political and social participation has *intrinsic value* for human life and well-being. To be prevented from participation in the political life of the community is a major deprivation.

Second, as I have just discussed (in disputing the claim that democracy is in tension with economic development), democracy has an important *instrumental value* in enhancing the hearing that people get in expressing and supporting their claims to political attention (including claims of economic needs). Third—and this is a point to be explored further—the practice of democracy gives citizens an opportunity to learn from one another, and helps society to form its values and priorities. Even the idea of "needs," including the understanding of "economic needs," requires public discussion and exchange of information, views, and analyses. In this sense, democracy has *constructive* importance, in addition to its intrinsic value for the lives of the citizens and its instrumental importance in political decisions. The claims of democracy as a universal value have to take note of this diversity of considerations.

The conceptualization–even comprehension— of what are to count as "needs," including "economic needs," may itself require the exercise of political and civil rights. A proper understanding of what economic needs are—their content and their force—may require discussion and exchange. Political and civil rights, especially those related to the guaranteeing of open discussion, debate, criticism, and dissent, are central to the process of generating informed and considered choices. These processes are crucial to the formation of values and priorities, and we cannot, in general, take preferences as given independently of public discussion, that is, irrespective of whether open interchange and debate are permitted or not.

In fact, the reach and effectiveness of open dialogue are often underestimated in assessing social and political problems. For example, public discussion has an important role to play in reducing the high rates of fertility that characterize many developing countries. There is substantial evidence that the sharp decline in fertility rates in

India's more literate states has been much influenced by public discussion of the bad effects of high fertility rates on the community at large, and especially on the lives of young women. If the view has emerged in, say, the Indian state of Kerala or of Tamil Nadu that a happy family in the modern age is a small family, much discussion and debate have gone into the formation of these perspectives. Kerala now has a fertility rate of 1.7 (similar to that of Britain and France, and well below China's 1.9), and this has been achieved with no coercion, but mainly through the emergence of new values—a process in which political and social dialogue has played a major part. Kerala's high literacy rate (it ranks higher in literacy than any province in China), especially among women, has greatly contributed to making such social and political dialogue possible.

Miseries and deprivations can be of various kinds, some more amenable to social remedies than others. The totality of the human predicament would be a gross basis for identifying our "needs." For example, there are many things that we might have good reason to value and thus could be taken as "needs" if they were feasible. We could even want immortality, as Maitreyee, that remarkable inquiring mind in the *Upanishads,* famously did in her 3000-year old conversation with Yajnvalkya. But we do not see immortality as a "need" because it is clearly unfeasible. Our conception of needs relates to our ideas of the preventable nature of some deprivations and to our understanding of what can be done about them. In the formation of understandings and beliefs about feasibility (particularly, *social* feasibility), public discussions play a crucial role. Political rights, including freedom of expression and discussion, are not only pivotal in inducing social responses to economic needs, they are also central to the conceptualization of economic needs themselves.

UNIVERSALITY OF VALUES

If the above analysis is correct, then democracy's claim to be valuable does not rest on just one particular merit. There is a plurality of virtues here, including, first, the *intrinsic* importance of political participation and freedom in human life; second, the *instrumental* importance of political incentives in keeping governments responsible and accountable; and third, the *constructive* role of democracy in the formation of values and in the understanding of needs, rights, and duties. In the light of this diagnosis, we may now address the motivating question of this essay, namely the case for seeing democracy as a universal value.

In disputing this claim, it is sometimes argued that not everyone agrees on the decisive importance of democracy, particularly when it competes with other desirable things for our attention and loyalty. This is indeed so, and there is no unanimity here. This lack of unanimity is seen by some as sufficient evidence that democracy is not a universal value.

Clearly, we must begin by dealing with a methodological question: What is a universal value? For a value to be considered universal, must it have the consent of everyone? If that were indeed necessary, then the category of universal values might well be empty. I know of no value—not even motherhood (I think of *Mommie Dearest*)—to which no one has ever objected. I would argue that universal consent is not required for something to be a universal value. Rather, the claim of a universal value is that people anywhere may have reason to see it as valuable.

When Mahatma Gandhi argued for the universal value of non-violence, he was not arguing that people everywhere already acted according to this value, but rather that they had good reason to see it as valuable. Similarly, when Rabindranath Tagore argued for "the freedom of the mind" as a universal value, he was not saying that this claim is accepted by all, but that all do have reason enough to accept it—a reason that he did much to explore, present, and propagate.[6] Understood in this way, any claim that something is a universal value involves some counterfactual analysis—in particular, whether people might see some value in a claim that they have not yet considered adequately. All claims to universal value—not just that of democracy—have this implicit presumption.

I would argue that it is with regard to this often *implicit* presumption that the biggest attitudinal shift toward democracy has occurred in the twentieth century. In considering democracy for a country that does not have it and where many people may not yet have had the opportunity to consider it for actual practice, it is now presumed that the people involved would approve of it once it becomes a reality in their lives. In the nineteenth century this assumption typically would have not been made, but the presumption that is taken to be natural (what I earlier called the "default" position) has changed radically during the twentieth century.

It must also be noted that this change is, to a great extent, based on observing the history of the twentieth century. As democracy has spread, its adherents have grown, not shrunk. Starting off from Europe and America, democracy as a system has reached very many distant shores, where it has been met with willing participation and acceptance. Moreover, when an existing democracy has been overthrown, there have been widespread protests, even though these protests have often been brutally suppressed. Many people have been willing to risk their lives in the fight to bring back democracy.

Some who dispute the status of democracy as a universal value base their argument not on the absence of unanimity, but on the presence of regional contrasts. These alleged contrasts are sometimes related to the poverty of some nations. According to this argument, poor people are interested, and have reason to be interested, in bread, not in democracy. This oft-repeated argument is fallacious at two different levels.

First, as discussed above, the protective role of democracy may be particularly important for the poor. This obviously applies to potential famine victims who face starvation. It also applies to the destitute thrown off the economic ladder in a financial crisis. People in economic need also need a political voice. Democracy is not a luxury that can await the arrival of general prosperity.

Second, there is very little evidence that poor people, given the choice, prefer to reject democracy. It is thus of some interest to note that when an erstwhile Indian government in the mid-1970s tried out a similar argument to justify the alleged "emergency" (and the suppression of various political and civil rights) that it had declared, an election was called that divided the voters precisely on this issue. In that fateful election, fought largely on this one overriding theme, the suppression of basic political and civil rights was firmly rejected, and the Indian electorate–one of the poorest in the world—showed itself to be no less keen on protesting against the denial of basic liberties and rights than on complaining about economic deprivation.

To the extent that there has been any testing of the proposition that the poor do not care about civil and political rights, the evidence is entirely against that claim. Similar points can be made by observing the struggle for democratic freedoms in South Korea, Thailand, Bangladesh, Pakistan, Burma, Indonesia, and elsewhere in Asia. Similarly, while political freedom is widely denied in Africa, there have been movements and protests against such repression whenever circumstances have permitted them.

THE ARGUMENT FROM CULTURAL DIFFERENCES

There is also another argument in defense of an allegedly fundamental regional contrast, one related not to economic circumstances but to cultural differences. Perhaps the most famous of these claims relates to what have been called "Asian values." It has been claimed that Asians traditionally value discipline, not political freedom, and thus the attitude to democracy must inevitably be much more skeptical in these countries. I have discussed this thesis in some detail in my Morganthau Memorial Lecture at the Carnegie Council on Ethics and International Affairs.[7]

It is very hard to find any real basis for this intellectual claim in the history of Asian cultures, especially if we look at the classical traditions of India, the Middle East, Iran, and other parts of Asia. For example, one of the earliest and most emphatic statements advocating the

tolerance of pluralism and the duty of the state to protect minorities can be found in the inscriptions of the Indian emperor Ashoka in the third century B.C.

Asia is, of course, a very large area, containing 60 percent of the world's population, and generalizations about such a vast set of peoples is not easy. Sometimes the advocates of "Asian values" have tended to look primarily at East Asia as the region of particular applicability. The general thesis of a contrast between the West and Asia often concentrates on the lands to the east of Thailand, even though there is also a more ambitious claim that the rest of Asia is rather "similar." Lee Kuan Yew, to whom we must be grateful for being such a clear expositor (and for articulating fully what is often stated vaguely in this tangled literature), outlines "the fundamental difference between Western concepts of society and government and East Asian concepts" by explaining, "when I say East Asians, I mean Korea, Japan, China, Vietnam, as distinct from Southeast Asia, which is a mix between the Sinic and the Indian, though Indian culture itself emphasizes similar values."[8]

Even East Asia itself, however, is remarkably diverse, with many variations to be found not only among Japan, China, Korea, and other countries of the region but also *within* each country. Confucius is the standard author quoted in interpreting Asian values, but he is not the only intellectual influence in these countries (in Japan, China, and Korea for example, there are very old and very widespread Buddhist traditions, powerful for over a millennium and a half, and there are also other influences, including a considerable Christian presence). There is no homogeneous worship of order over freedom in any of these cultures.

Furthermore, Confucius himself did not recommend blind allegiance to the state. When Zilu asks him "how to serve a prince," Confucius replies (in a statement that the censors of authoritarian regimes may want to ponder), "Tell him the truth even if it offends him."[9] Confucius is not averse to practical caution and tact, but does not forgo the recommendation to oppose a bad government (tactfully, if necessary): "When the [good] way prevails in the state, speak boldly and act boldly. When the state has lost the way, act boldly and speak softly."[10]

Indeed, Confucius provides a clear pointer to the fact that the two pillars of the imagined edifice of Asian values, loyalty to family and obedience to the state, can be in severe conflict with each other. Many advocates of the power of "Asian values" see the role of the state as an extension of the role of the family, but as Confucius noted, there can be tension between the two. The Governor of She told Confucius, "Among my people, there is a man of unbending integrity: when his father stole a sheep, he denounced him." To this Confucius replied, "Among my people, men of integrity do things differently: a father covers up for his son, a son covers up for his father—and there is integrity in what they do."[11]

The monolithic interpretation of Asian values as hostile to democracy and political rights does not bear critical scrutiny. I should not, I suppose, be too critical of the lack of scholarship supporting these beliefs, since those who have made these claims are not scholars but political leaders, often official or unofficial spokesmen for authoritarian governments. It is, however, interesting to see that while we academics can be impractical about practical politics, practical politicians can, in turn, be rather impractical about scholarship.

It is not hard, of course, to find authoritarian writings within the Asian traditions. But neither is it hard to find them in Western classics: One has only to reflect on the writings of Plato or Aquinas to see that devotion to discipline is not a special Asian taste. To dismiss the plausibility of democracy as a universal value because of the presence of some Asian writings on discipline and order would be similar to rejecting the plausibility of democracy as a natural form of government in Europe or America today on the basis of the writings of Plato or Aquinas (not to mention the substantial medieval literature in support of the Inquisitions).

Due to the experience of contemporary political battles, especially in the Middle East, Islam is often portrayed as fundamentally intolerant of and hostile to individual freedom. But the presence of diversity and variety *within* a tradition applies very much to

Islam as well. In India, Akbar and most of the other Moghul emperors (with the notable exception of Aurangzeb) provide good examples of both the theory and practice of political and religious tolerance. The Turkish emperors were often more tolerant than their European contemporaries. Abundant examples can also be found among rulers in Cairo and Baghdad. Indeed, in the twelfth century, the great Jewish scholar Maimonides had to run away from an intolerant Europe (where he was born), and from its persecution of Jews, to the security of a tolerant and urbane Cairo and the patronage of Sultan Saladin.

Diversity is a feature of most cultures in the world. Western civilization is no exception. The practice of democracy that has won out in the *modern* West is largely a result of a consensus that has emerged since the Enlightenment and the Industrial Revolution, and particularly in the last century or so. To read in this a historical commitment of the West—over the millennia—to democracy, and then to contrast it with non-Western traditions (treating each as monolithic) would be a great mistake. This tendency toward oversimplification can be seen not only in the writings of some governmental spokesmen in Asia but also in the theories of some of the finest Western scholars themselves.

As an example from the writings of a major scholar whose works, in many other ways, have been totally impressive, let me cite Samuel Huntington's thesis on the clash of civilizations, where the heterogeneities *within* each culture get quite inadequate recognition. His study comes to the clear conclusion that "a sense of individualism and a tradition of rights and liberties" can be found in the West that are "unique among civilized societies."[12] Huntington also argues that "the central characteristics of the West, those which distinguish it from other civilizations, antedate the modernization of the West." In his view, "The West was West long before it was modern."[13] It is this thesis that—I have argued—does not survive historical scrutiny.

For every attempt by an Asian government spokesman to contrast alleged "Asian values" with alleged Western ones, there is, it seems, an attempt by a Western intellectual to make a similar contrast from the other side. But even though every Asian pull may be matched by a Western push, the two together do not really manage to dent democracy's claim to be a universal value.

WHERE THE DEBATE BELONGS

I have tried to cover a number of issues related to the claim that democracy is a universal value. The value of democracy includes its *intrinsic importance* in human life, its *instrumental role* in generating political incentives, and its *constructive function* in the formation of values (and in understanding the force and feasibility of claims of needs, rights, and duties). These merits are not regional in character. Nor is the advocacy of discipline or order. Heterogeneity of values seems to characterize most, perhaps all, major cultures. The cultural argument does not foreclose, nor indeed deeply constrain, the choices we can make today.

Those choices have to be made here and now, taking note of the functional roles of democracy, on which the case for democracy in the contemporary world depends. I have argued that this case is indeed strong and not regionally contingent. The force of the claim that democracy is a universal value lies, ultimately, in that strength. That is where the debate belongs. It cannot be disposed of by imagined cultural taboos or assumed civilizational predispositions imposed by our various pasts.

NOTES

1. In Aldous Huxley's novel *Point Counter Point,* this was enough to give an adequate excuse to a cheating husband, who tells his wife that he must go to London to study democracy in ancient India in the library of the British Museum, while in reality he goes to see his mistress.
2. Adam Przeworski et al., *Sustainable Democracy* (Cambridge: Cambridge University Press, 1995); Robert J. Barro, *Getting It Right: Markets and Choices in a Free Society* (Cambridge, Mass.: MIT Press, 1996).
3. I have examined the empirical evidence and causal connections in some detail in my book *Development as Freedom,* forthcoming from Knopf in 1999.
4. See my "Development: Which Way Now?" *Economic Journal* 93 (December 1983); *Resources, Values, and Development* (Cambridge, Mass.; Harvard University Press. 1984); and my "Rationality and Social Choice,"

presidential address to the American Economic Association, published in *American Economic Review* in March 1995. See also Jean Dr'eze and Amartya Sen, *Hunger and Public Action* (Oxford: Clarendon Press, 1987); Frances D'Souza, ed., *Starving in Silence: A Report on Famine and Censorship* (London: Article 19 International Centre on Censorship, 1990); Human Rights Watch, *Indivisible Human Rights: The Relationship between Political and Civil Rights to Survival, Subsistence and Poverty* (New York: Human Rights Watch, 1992); and International Federation of Red Cross and Red Crescent Societies, *World Disaster Report 1994* (Geneva: Red Cross, 1994).
5. Dr'eze and Sen, *Hunger and Public Action.*
6. See my "Tagore and His India," New *York Review of Books,* 26 June 1997.
7. Amartya Sen, "Human Rights and Asian Values," Morgenthau Memorial Lecture (New York: Carnegie Council on Ethics and International Affairs. 1997), published in a shortened form in *The New Republic,* 14–21 July 1997.
8. Fareed Zakaria, "Culture is Destiny: A Conversation with Lee Kuan Yew," *Foreign Affairs* 73 (March–April 1994): 113.
9. *The Analects of Confucius,* Simon Leys, trans. (New York: Norton, 1997), 14.22, 70.
10. *The Analects of Confucius,* 14.3, 66.
11. *The Analects of Confucius,* 13.18, 63.
12. Samuel P. Huntington, *The Clash of Civilizations and the Remaking of World Order* (New York: Simon and Schuster, 1996). 71.
13. Huntington, *The Clash of Civilizations,* 69.

STUDY QUESTIONS: HUMAN RIGHTS

1. The United Nations Declaration of Human Rights claims to protect the rights of individuals. Do you see any problem with such a conception of human rights when the interests of ethnic or cultural minorities are taken into account, for example, when the rights of members of the majority to freedom of movement or to vote are restricted as a result of protecting the rights of minorities?
2. How does Bunch relate violence against women to issues of human rights? What objections might be made against the identification of women's rights with human rights? Are these good objections? Why or why not?
3. Abdullahi Ahmed An-Na'im presents one cultural example of the rejection of universal human rights that is mandated and sanctified by religion. Do you think that we should reject certain aspects of Shari'a while remaining respectful of others? Is such a piecemeal approach justified?
4. It is sometimes argued that the use of child labor (children as young as fourteen years of age) in underdeveloped countries is morally justified on grounds that the alternative for these children would be worse off because of the absence of independent means of support and the opportunity for education. In what ways does Claude Ake's perspective shed light on how we in the West should consider the human rights situations in Third World countries?
5. According to Bell, how can human rights be justified from an East Asian perspective? And how does this approach differ from the Western liberal approach to human rights?

Do you think that there is a right of elderly parents to demand financial support from grown children? If so, can it be considered a human right?

6. Outline Inada's distinction between "hard relationships" and "soft relationships." How might taking this distinction seriously affect the way we talk about human rights, and would such a change be a good thing? Justify your response.

7. Charles Taylor argues that an unforced consensus on human rights norms is possible with different groups, countries, and cultures justifying these norms on the basis of their own conceptions. How broadly inclusive do you think this list of norms would be? Do you think it would be very limited? Or do you think it could be extensive? Explain.

8. Although the Universal Declaration of Human Rights does not explicitly claim that democracy is a human right, Article 21 seems to suggest that this is the case. Taking into account what Sen says in his piece, "Democracy as a Universal Value," do you think that democracy is a human right? That is to say, do you think that if you are a human being, then you have a right to a democratic form of government? Why or why not?

SUPPLEMENTARY READINGS: HUMAN RIGHTS

ABE, MASEO. "A Buddhist View of Human Rights." In *Human Rights and Religious Values: An Uneasy Relationship?* An-Na'im, Jansen, and Vroom, ed. (Grand Rapids, MI: William B. Eerdmans Publishing Company, 1995).

ANAYA, S. JAMES, and CRIDER, S. TODD. "Indigenous People, the Environment, and Commercial Forestry in Developing Countries: The Case of Awas Tingni, Nicaragua." *Human Rights Quarterly* vol. 18 (1996).

ANIKPO, MARK. "Human Rights and Self-Reliance in Africa." In *Emerging Human Rights*, Shepherd and Anikpo, ed. (New York: Greenwood Press, 1990).

BADRAN, MARGOT. *Feminists, Islam, and Nation: Gender and the Making of Modern Egypt.* (Princeton, NJ: Princeton University Press, 1995).

BAUER, JOANNE R., and DANIEL A. BELL (eds). *The East Asian Challenge for Human Rights.* (Cambridge, MA: Cambridge University Press, 1999).

BELL, DANIEL A. "The East Asian Challenge to Human Rights: Reflections on an East West Dialogue." *Human Rights Quarterly* vol. 18 (1996).

———. *East Meets West: Human Rights and Democracy in East Asia.* (Princeton, NJ: Princeton University Press, 2000).

BELL, DIANE. "Considering Gender: Are Human Rights for Women Too? An Australian Case." In *Human Rights in Cross Cultural Perspective*, An-Na'im, ed. (Philadelphia: University of Pennsylvania Press, 1991).

BERTING, JAN, et al. (ed). *Human Rights in a Pluralist World: Individuals and Collectivities.* (Westport, CT: Meckler, Inc., 1990).

COBBAH, JOSIAH. "African Values and the Human Rights Debate." *Human Rights Quarterly* vol. 9(3), August 1987.

DE BARY, THEODORE, and TU, WEI-MING (eds). *Confucianism and Human Rights.* (New York: Columbia University Press, 1998).

DONNELLEY, JACK. "Human Rights and Development: Complementary or Competing Concerns." In *Human Rights and Third World Development*, Shepherd and Nanda, ed. (New York: Greenwood Press, 1985).

DROOGERS, ANDRE F. "Cultural Relativism and Universal Human Rights?" In *Human Rights and Religious Values: An Uneasy Relationship?* An-Na'im, Jansen, and Vroom, ed. (Grand Rapids, MI: William B. Eerdmans Publishing Company, 1995).

HARE, R. M. "Rights and Justice." In *Moral Thinking.* (Oxford: Oxford University Press, 1981).

LANE, SANDRA D., and RUBINSTEIN, ROBERT A. "Judging the Other: Responding to Traditional Female Genital Surgeries." *Hastings Center Report* vol. 26(3) (1996).

LIXIAN, CHENG. "A Tentative Discussion of Human Rights." *Chinese Studies in Philosophy* vol. 17(1), Fall 1985.

NIARCHOS, N. CATHERINE. "Women, War, and Rape: Challenges Facing the International Tribunal for the Former Yugoslavia." *Human Rights Quarterly* vol. 17 (1995).

PENNOCK, J. ROLAND. "Rights, Natural Rights, and Human Rights—A General View." *NOMOS 23: Human Rights.* (New York: New York University Press, 1981).

SCANLON, THOMAS. "Rights, Goals and Fairness." In *Public and Private Morality*, Hampshire, ed. (Cambridge, England: Cambridge University Press, 1978).

TIBI, BASSAM. "The European Tradition of Human Rights and the Culture of Islam." In *Human Rights in Africa*, An-Na'im and Deng, ed. (Washington, DC: The Brookings Institution, 1990).

VAN DER BERG, CHRISTIAN J. G. "Fundamentalist Hindu Values and Human Rights: Two Worlds Apart?" In *Human Rights and Religious Values: An Uneasy Relationship?* An-Na'im, Jansen, and Vroom, ed. (Grand Rapids, MI: William B. Eerdmans Publishing Company, 1995).

WIREDU, KWASI. "An Akan Perspective on Human Rights." In *Human Rights in Africa*, An-Na'im and Deng, ed. (Washington, DC: The Brookings Institution, 1990).

ZEIDAIN, SHAWKY. "A Human Rights Settlement: The West Bank and Gaza." In *Human Rights and Third World Development*, Shepherd and Nanda, ed. (New York: Greenwood Press, 1985).

ZION, JAMES. "North American Indian Perspectives on Human Rights." In *Human Rights in Cross Cultural Perspectives*, An-Na'im, ed. (Philadelphia: University of Pennsylvania Press, 1991).

Part III

ENVIRONMENTAL ETHICS

When we try to pick out anything by itself, we find it hitched to everything else in the Universe.
—JOHN MUIR

A thing is right when it tends to preserve the integrity, stability, and beauty of the biotic community. It is wrong when it tends otherwise.
—ALDO LEOPOLD

When we consider that philosophy has been around for thousands of years, it becomes clear that environmental ethics, which only became a fully fledged academic field forty or so years ago, is extremely new. However, there are many ways in which environmental ethics is the logical extension of the more established fields of ethics, as we shall soon see. There are at least two separate orientations to environmental ethics, both of which are covered in this book. The first divides anthropocentric, or human-centered approaches to environmental ethics from ones that assert that there is intrinsic value in at least some non-human entities. The second divides those that concentrate on the value of individuals from those that concentrate on the value of groups or systems.

Some environmental ethicists argue that we should be anthropocentric in our attitudes toward nature: all reasons to care about nature relate to human needs and desires. According to this view, nature is instrumentally valuable because it is the source of things that human beings need. Anthropocentric views also deny any other value in nature besides this instrumental value, arguing that our attitudes to the environment should be shaped by what is best for present and future human beings.

Anthropocentric views of environmental ethics can be very powerful because they rely on premises that most of us already hold. If there are self-interested or human-centered reasons for protecting the environment, then it should not be difficult to convince the majority of people that we should take the requisite action to protect the environment. The rhetorical power of such arguments makes anthropocentric environmental ethics important even for those who think that there is intrinsic value in nature.

And, indeed, there are many anthropocentric reasons to take care of the environment. Global warming promises to have a massive impact on the human population. By 2025, half the world's population is expected to be at risk from weather extremes as a result of global warming.[1] Natural disasters have quadrupled since the 1980s, and the number of people affected by natural disasters has increased by 250 percent.[2] In addition to increasing in frequency, natural disasters have also increased in severity. Category 4 and 5 hurricanes have doubled in the past thirty years.[3] Droughts, flooding, and heat waves are also becoming more prevalent. Land affected by droughts has tripled over the past ten years, and up to 250 million people are thought to be at risk from droughts by 2020, which are particularly acute in sub-Saharan Africa.[4] Meanwhile, 2007 saw the worst flooding in recorded history in Asia, affecting some 248 million people.[5] Heat waves are also increasing in severity and number. There are five times more heat waves today than there were twenty years ago. In addition to directly killing and harming individuals, these weather

I thank Clare Palmer for her comments and input.

changes have indirect effects. Natural disasters, heat waves, droughts, and flooding harm agriculture and decrease the food supply and the ability to access food. Furthermore, global warming is to blame for an increase in tropical diseases as well as an increase in the range of land that tropical diseases affect in recent years. According to the World Bank, a child dies from malaria every thirty seconds.

Climate change seems to be disproportionately affecting already vulnerable populations such as the poor, women, and children. Developing countries bear the brunt of problems arising from global climate change[6] in part due to inability to respond to natural disasters and in part due to geographical location. In addition, much more than half those affected by natural disasters are women and children.[7] Women are more adversely affected by global climate change because in many societies it is the woman's responsibility to provide drinking water, because they tend not to have property rights or access to lending, and because most female farmers rely on rain-fed agriculture as opposed to irrigated agriculture.

Global climate change is not our only concern. Every year, forests the size of Panama are destroyed, with deforestation concentrated in Latin America and sub-Saharan Africa.[8] In short, there are overwhelming anthropocentric reasons to take drastic action in addressing global climate change,[9] pollution, deforestation, and other negative human impacts on the environment. However, there are also problems with anthropocentric views. Do they go far enough in giving us reason to protect the environment? When weighing human values with the environment, will we sacrifice too much of the environment? And is it really true that humans are the only intrinsically valuable entities on earth?

Some environmental ethicists, then, propose that nonhuman things have intrinsic value—not solely instrumental value. Intrinsic value is a complex concept, one that will be addressed in the chapters in this section and throughout the book. However, one way of understanding intrinsic value is value something has *for its own sake* or *in itself.* Like anthropocentric views, this type of environmental ethic can also be seen as a logical extension of existing approaches to ethics. Aldo Leopold,

who was one of the first environmental ethicists, views environmental ethics as the next step in a set of expanding spheres of value. On this view, our attribution of intrinsic value has been, historically, narrow but ever increasing. For example, thousands of years ago we thought human beings had intrinsic value, but not all human beings. Slavery, tribalism, and xenophobia were evidence that only narrow groups of people were considered as having value. Over time, those groups whose members were thought to have intrinsic value were extended further and further until it was thought that all human beings have equal intrinsic value (although questions remain, for instance, about very early fetuses). Similarly, that trend of inclusivity extended to include animals. With the recognition that animals could feel pain and suffer came the attribution of intrinsic value to them.[10] However, the thought that non-human entities have intrinsic value does not necessarily mean they have equal intrinsic value to human persons. Environmental ethicists will still have to cash out just what it means to attribute intrinsic value to some aspects of nature.

Similarly, there are both individualistic strands in environmental ethics and holistic strands. For example, is there any value in an ecosystem, or a species? Some argue that there is. These approaches to environmental ethics de-emphasizes the importance of individuals. Concerns over species extinction and biodiversity suggest that species may be valuable over and above the value of their component parts. No one knows exactly how many species exist, making our knowledge of species extinction limited. Estimates of the total number of species range from 5 million to 30 million, with only a small fraction of these species identified. However, we do have some knowledge of species extinction. Species extinction today occurs at as much as 1,000 times the background rate of extinction, when compared to fossil records.[11] Of 47,677 assessed species, 17,291 are threatened with extinction.[12] Furthermore, the rate of extinction seems to be accelerating. Between 1970 and 2005 there was a 27 percent decrease in populations of vertebrates.[13] About one third of known amphibian extinctions have occurred since 1980.[14] These figures would be troubling if species were morally relevant entities or had moral worth. Do species have intrinsic value? Species extinction also adversely affects agriculture and food supply, which rely on species diversity and land viability. In other words, there may be anthropocentric reasons for wanting to prevent species extinction.

Some argue that species, groups, or ecosystems have no moral relevance beyond the sum of their parts. These views focus on the value of individual organisms, either sentient or not. They place the focus on individuals over and above issues of species, ecosystems, population control, and biodiversity. It would be wrong, for example, to kill or harm individual organisms to save a species, protect an ecosystem, or control a population. This division in individualistic and holistic approaches to environmental ethics suggests a need not only to determine what type of value exists in nature, but also to determine what in nature has value.

The first selection in the book proposes a complete overhaul in our attitudes toward the environment. In "The Historical Roots of Our Ecologic Crisis," Lynn White, Jr., argues that Christianity is to blame for our problematic relationship with nature but in Christianity we can also find our redemption. According to White, modern science and technology, although influenced by all parts of the world, are distinctly Western. Because modern science and technology can be traced to Western roots, they can also be traced to individuals shaped by the Christian worldview. The combination of these features proved deadly. Christianity, especially in its earliest forms, asserted the dominance of human beings over nature; they transcend nature and they are given dominion over nature by God. As a result, human beings combined a justification to destroy nature from Christianity with the ability to destroy nature from technology and science, and therefore over thousands of years have pieced together the necessary parts for the ecological crisis that we face today. Being so shaped by Christianity, we cannot turn to Eastern worldviews to reinvent our attitudes of nature. Instead, White points us to an alternative Christian theology, that of St. Francis of Assisi, to help us reshape our attitudes from the inside out.

If White's article serves as warning on how anthropocentric views can be compatible with an indefensible destruction of nature, then Dale Jamieson continues on that theme in the next article, "Animal Liberation is an Environmental Ethic." Jamieson addresses the instrumental versus intrinsic value divide most explicitly. He, too, argues against an anthropocentric view that takes the value in nature to be instrumental with a detailed account of what intrinsic value means. However, he addresses this issue in the context of bridging the gap that has historically divided environmentalists and animal liberation activists. According to Jamieson, animal liberationists and environmentalists hold many of the same beliefs, pursue many of the same goals, and have many overlapping concerns. Although he acknowledges important differences between the two groups, such as their differing opinions on the matter of killing individual animals for the sake of saving a species, he argues that the theoretical grounding between the two movements unites them.

In the next article, "Faking Nature," Robert Elliot continues in the theme of defending intrinsic value in nature. He addresses a commonly suggested solution to environmental degradation: restoration. Often our response to the destruction of nature for the purposes of construction, mining, agriculture, or as a result of pollution is simply to recreate the lost environment with a human-made restoration. It might be assumed that such reconstructions are equal in value to what was destroyed. If they completely restore the damage that was done, then restoration could legitimize further destruction. But Elliot questions whether such restoration projects really restore what is lost. He argues that there is intrinsic value in nature that cannot be recreated. When we destroy a priceless Monet, for example, we cannot make up for what was lost when we order a computer-generated painting to replace it, even if the replica looks identical to the brushstrokes Monet himself painted. Similarly, a rainforest planted by construction workers to make up for the rainforest that has been around for a millennia misses out on an important source of value. That is because something's genesis or origin contributes to its value.

William Baxter breaks with this conception of nature having intrinsic value and defends an anthropocentric approach to nature. His view perhaps represents the dominant view of nature in U.S. society. According to Baxter, the reasoning employed by those who defend intrinsic value in nature is flawed. First, he argues against the premise that nature has intrinsic value. There is nothing good or bad about nature and nothing valuable about that which is untouched by human hands. Instead, the only reasons we have to preserve nature refer back to our own values and goals. As such, we need to weigh our protection of the environment against other human values and goals. If the cost of saving a species is too great, it is rational to abandon the cause and use our resources elsewhere. According to Baxter, we must do cost-benefit analyses against other human concerns to determine what resources we should spend on the environment.

In contrast to Lynn White's account of the Christian relationship with the environment, Gregory Cajete offers an account of an indigenous people's environmental ethics. According to the view Cajete describes, nature and the environment are an integral part of daily human life, including survival, art, culture, and self-understanding. Cajete describes this view as a "theology of place," in which people not only have a physical connection to their surroundings but also a spiritual one. Rather than transcend nature or dominate it, indigenous cultures feel at one with nature and humbled by nature. Cajete's account is far-reaching in that it offers a unifying theory of multiple indigenous cultures as well as a theory that encompasses both history and modern times.

In the last piece of this chapter, Shari Collins-Chobanian addresses "environmental racism," the idea that environmental burdens fall disproportionately on minority groups. Environmental racism falls under the larger issue of environmental justice, proponents of which argue that all people should be treated fairly with respect to burdening environmental hazards and receiving the benefits of natural resources, regardless of race, ethnicity, religion, socio-economic status, national origin, or gender. Both environmental justice and environmental racism have become increasingly important areas of environmental ethics. Collins-Chobanian focuses on the disposal radioactive waste, which

has largely been concentrated in American Indian territory. She argues that the practice of dumping radioactive waste in American Indian territory is unjustified in part because it targets a vulnerable population. The issue is made more complicated by the fact that American Indians have ostensibly consented to and been paid compensation for hosting radioactive storage sites. However, Collins-Chobanian questions the validity of this consent by looking at the component parts of the theoretical concept and challenging that the proper standards for consent historically have been met.

Environmental ethics forces us to consider what sort of value exists in nature. Our views on environmental ethics shape not only the choices we make with respect to the environment and natural resources, and not only our reaction to environmental degradation, but also our very understanding of the world around us.

—JILL DELSTON

NOTES

1. According to World Water Council statistics.
2. OXFAM, "Climate Alarm: Disasters Increase as Climate Change Bites," November 2007.
3. K. Emanuel, "Increasing Destructiveness of Tropical Cyclones over the Past 30 Years," *Nature* 436 (2005): 686–688.
4. Save the Children, "In the Face of Disaster: Children and Climate Change," 2008.
5. OXFAM, "Climate Alarm: Disasters Increase as Climate Change Bites," November 2007.
6. The World Bank, "Developing Countries Are Hardest Hit from Climate Change: New World Bank Report Says that Poorest Countries and People Will Suffer Earliest and Most," February 2008.
7. UNICEF, "2009 Humanitarian Action Report."
8. According to the World Bank.
9. Economists also agree that inaction would be much more expensive than action.
10. Although utilitarians would not say that animals have intrinsic value, they might say that pleasure has intrinsic value and by extension that anything capable of pleasure is morally relevant.
11. Millenium Ecosystem Assessment, 2005. *Ecosystems and Human Well-Being: Biodiversity Synthesis.* World Resources Institute, Washington, D.C. More conservative estimates place current extinction rates at 100 times the background rate of extinction. Extinction rates are expected to increase ten-fold the current rates by 2050.
12. According to 2009 statistics from the International Union for the Conservation of Nature (IUCN).
13. According to the Living Planet Index.
14. According to the IUCN 2008 Red List.

The Historical Roots of Our Ecological Crisis

Lynn White, Jr.

Lynn White (1907–1987) was a professor at Princeton University, served as president of Mills College, and was a founder of the Center for Medieval and Renaissance Studies at UCLA. This paper originated as a talk to the American Association for the Advancement of Science about an environmental crisis. The talk was so influential, it was soon published in one of the most prestigious scientific journals, *Science*.

White was one of the first to point out a mounting environmental crisis. According to his analysis, the crisis comes about as a result of our attitudes toward nature, which are shaped by Western Christian thought. If Christianity is indeed responsible for our poor treatment of nature through science and technology, then a revised Christian perspective may be able to help us out of the crisis. White argues that a new Christian philosophy, one that respects nature, should replace our current one.

A conversation with Aldous Huxley not infrequently put one at the receiving end of an unforgettable monologue. About a year before his lamented death he was discoursing on a favorite topic: Man's unnatural treatment of nature and its sad results. To illustrate his point he told how, during the previous summer, he had returned to a little valley in England where he had spent many happy months as a child. Once it had been composed of delightful grassy glades: now it was becoming overgrown with unsightly brush because the rabbits that formerly kept such growth under control had largely succumbed to a disease, myxomatosis, that was deliberately introduced by the local farmers to reduce the rabbits' destruction of crops. Being something of a Philistine, I could be silent no longer, even in the interests of great rhetoric. I interrupted to point out

Lynn White, Jr., "The Historical Roots of our Ecological Crisis" from paper originally presented to the American Association for the Advancement of Science.

that the rabbit itself had been brought as a domestic animal to England in 1176, presumably to improve the protein diet of the peasantry.

All forms of life modify their contexts. The most spectacular and benign instance is doubtless the coral polyp. By serving its own ends, it has created a vast undersea world favorable to thousands of other kinds of animals and plants. Ever since man became a numerous species he has affected his environment notably. The hypothesis that his fire-drive method of hunting created the world's great grasslands and helped to exterminate the monster mammals of the Pleistocene from much of the globe is plausible, if not proved. For 6 millennia at least, the banks of the lower Nile have been a human artifact rather than the swampy African jungle which nature, apart from man, would have made it. The Aswan Dam, flooding 5000 square miles, is only the latest stage in a long process. In many regions terracing or irrigation, overgrazing, the cutting of forests by Romans to build ships to fight Carthaginians or by Crusaders to solve the logistics problems of their expeditions, have profoundly changed some ecologies. Observation that the French landscape falls into two basic types, the open fields of the north and the bocage of the south and west, inspired Marc Bloch to undertake his classic study of medieval agricultural methods. Quite unintentionally, changes in human ways often affect nonhuman nature. It has been noted, for example, that the advent of the automobile eliminated huge flocks of sparrows that once fed on the horse manure littering every street.

The history of ecologic change is still so rudimentary that we know little about what really happened, or what the results were. The extinction of the European aurochs as late as 1627 would seem to have been a simple case of overenthusiastic hunting. On more intricate matters it often is impossible to find solid information. For a thousand years or more the Frisians and Hollanders have been pushing back the North Sea, and the process is culminating in our own time in the reclamation of the Zuider Zee. What, if any, species of animals, birds, fish, shore life, or plants have died out in the process? In their epic combat with Neptune have the Netherlanders overlooked ecological values in such a way that the quality of human life in the Netherlands has suffered? I cannot discover that the questions have ever been asked, much less answered.

People, then, have often been a dynamic element in their own environment, but in the present state of historical scholarship we usually do not know exactly when, where, or with what effects man-induced changes came. As we enter the last third of the 20th century, however, concern for the problem of ecologic backlash is mounting feverishly. Natural science, conceived as the effort to understand the nature of things, had flourished in several eras and among several peoples. Similarly there had been an age-old accumulation of technological skills, sometimes growing rapidly, sometimes slowly. But it was not until about four generations ago that Western Europe and North America arranged a marriage between science and technology, a union of the theoretical and the empirical approaches to our natural environment.

The emergence in widespread practice of the Baconian creed that scientific knowledge means technological power over nature can scarcely be dated before about 1850, save in the chemical industries, where it is anticipated in the 18th century. Its acceptance as a normal pattern of action may mark the greatest event in human history since the invention of agriculture, and perhaps in nonhuman terrestrial history as well.

Almost at once the new situation forced the crystallization of the novel concept of ecology; indeed, the word ecology first appeared in the English language in 1873. Today, less than a century later, the impact of our race upon the environment has so increased in force that it has changed in essence. When the first cannons were fired, in the early 14th century, they affected ecology by sending workers scrambling to the forests and mountains for more potash, sulphur, iron ore, and charcoal, with some resulting erosion and deforestation. Hydrogen bombs are of a different order: a war fought with them might alter the genetics of all life on this planet. By 1285 London had a smog problem arising from the burning of soft coal, but our present combustion of fossil fuels threatens to change the chemistry of the globe's atmosphere as a whole, with consequences which we are only beginning to guess. With the population explosion, the carcinoma of planless urbanism, the now geological deposits of sewage and garbage, surely no creature other than man has ever managed to foul its nest in such short order.

There are many calls to action, but specific proposals, however worthy as individual items, seem too partial, palliative, negative: ban the bomb, tear down the billboards, give the Hindus contraceptives and tell them to eat their sacred cows. The simplest solution to any suspect change is, of course, to stop it, or better yet, to revert to a romanticized past: make those ugly gasoline stations look like Anne Hathaway's cottage or (in the Far West) like ghost-town saloons. The "wilderness area" mentality invariably advocates deep-freezing an ecology, whether San Gimignano or the High Sierra, as it was before the first Kleenex was dropped. But neither atavism nor prettification will cope with the ecologic crisis of our time.

What shall we do? No one yet knows. Unless we think about fundamentals, our specific measures may produce new backlashes more serious than those they are designed to remedy.

As a beginning we should try to clarify our thinking by looking, in some historical depth, at the presuppositions that underlie modem technology and science. Science was traditionally aristocratic, speculative, intellectual in intent; technology was lower-class, empirical, action-oriented. The quite sudden fusion of these two, towards the middle of the 19th century, is surely related to the slightly prior and contemporary democratic revolutions which, by reducing social barriers, tended to assert a functional unity of brain and hand. Our ecologic crisis is the product of an emerging, entirely novel, democratic culture. The issue is whether a democratized world can survive its own implications. Presumably we cannot unless we rethink our axioms.

THE WESTERN TRADITIONS OF TECHNOLOGY AND SCIENCE

One thing is so certain that it seems stupid to verbalize it: both modern technology and modern science are distinctively Occidental. Our technology has absorbed elements from all over the world, notably from China; yet everywhere today, whether in Japan or in Nigeria, successful technology is Western. Our science is the heir to all the sciences of the past, especially perhaps to the work of the great Islamic scientists of the Middle Ages, who so often outdid the ancient Greeks in skill and perspicacity; al-Razi in medicine, for example: or ibn-al-Haytham in optics; or Omar Khayyam in mathematics. Indeed, not a few works of such geniuses seem to have vanished in the original Arabic and to survive only in medieval Latin translations that helped to lay the foundations for later Western developments. Today, around the globe, all significant science is Western in style and method, whatever the pigmentation or language of the scientists.

A second pair of facts is less well recognized because they result from quite recent historical scholarship. The leadership of the West, both in technology and in science, is far older than the so-called Scientific Revolution of the 17th century or the so-called Industrial Revolution of the 18th century. These terms are in fact outmoded and obscure the true nature of what they try to describe— significant stages in two long and separate developments. By A.D. 1000 at the latest—and perhaps, feebly, as much as 200 years earlier—the West began to apply water power to industrial processes other than milling grain. This was followed in the late 12th century by the harnessing of wind power. From simple beginnings, but with remarkable consistency of style, the West rapidly expanded its skills in the development of power machinery, labor-saving devices, and automation. Those who doubt should contemplate that most monumental achievement in the history of automation: the weight-driven mechanical clock, which appeared in two forms in the early 14th century. Not in craftsmanship but in basic technological capacity, the Latin West of the later Middle Ages far outstripped its elaborate, sophisticated, and esthetically magnificent sister cultures, Byzantium and Islam. In 1444 a great Greek ecclesiastic, Bessarion, who had gone to Italy, wrote a letter to a prince in Greece. He is amazed by the superiority of Western ships, arms, textiles, glass. But above all he is astonished by the spectacle of waterwheels sawing timbers and pumping the bellows of blast furnaces. Clearly, he had seen nothing of the sort in the Near East.

By the end of the 15th century the technological superiority of Europe was such that its small, mutually hostile nations could spill out over all the rest of the world, conquering, looting, and colonizing. The symbol of this technological superiority is the fact that Portugal, one of the weakest states of the Occident, was able to become, and to remain for a century, mistress of the East Indies. And we must remember that the technology of Vasco da Gama and Albuquerque was built by pure empiricism, drawing remarkably little support or inspiration from science.

In the present-day vernacular understanding, modern science is supposed to have begun in 1543, when both Copernicus and Vesalius published their great works. It is no derogation of their accomplishments, however, to point out that such structures as the Fabrica and the De revolutionibus do not appear overnight. The distinctive Western tradition of science, in fact, began in the late 11th century with a massive movement of translation of Arabic and Greek scientific works into Latin. A few notable books—Theophrastus, for example— escaped the West's avid new appetite for science, but within less than 200 years effectively the entire corpus of Greek and Muslim science was available in Latin, and was being eagerly read and criticized in the new European universities. Out of criticism arose new observation, speculation, and increasing distrust of ancient authorities. By the late 13th century Europe had seized global scientific leadership from the faltering hands of Islam. It would be as absurd to deny the profound originality of Newton, Galileo, or Copernicus as to deny that of the 14th century scholastic scientists like Buridan or Oresme on whose work they built. Before the 11th century, science scarcely existed in the Latin West, even in Roman times. From the 11th century onward, the scientific sector of Occidental culture has increased in a steady crescendo.

Since both our technological and our scientific movements got their start, acquired their character, and achieved world dominance in the Middle Ages, it would seem that we cannot understand their nature or their present impact upon ecology without examining fundamental medieval assumptions and developments.

MEDIEVAL VIEW OF MAN AND NATURE

Until recently, agriculture has been the chief occupation even in "advanced" societies; hence, any change in methods of tillage has much importance. Early plows, drawn by two oxen, did not normally turn the sod but merely scratched it. Thus, cross-plowing was needed and fields tended to be squarish. In the fairly light soils and semi-arid climates of the Near East and Mediterranean, this worked well. But such a plow was inappropriate to the wet climate and often sticky soils of northern Europe. By the latter part of the 7th century after Christ, however, following obscure beginnings, certain northern peasants were using an entirely new kind of plow, equipped with a vertical knife to cut the line of the furrow, a horizontal share to slice under the sod, and a moldboard to turn it over. The friction of this plow with the soil was so great that it normally required not two but eight oxen. It attacked the land with such violence that cross-plowing was not needed, and fields tended to be shaped in long strips.

In the days of the scratch-plow, fields were distributed generally in units capable of supporting a single family. Subsistence farming was the presupposition, But no peasant owned eight oxen: to use the new and more efficient plow, peasants pooled their oxen to form large plow-teams, originally receiving (it would appear) plowed strips in proportion to their contribution. Thus, distribution of land was based no longer on the needs of a family but, rather, on the capacity of a power machine to till the earth. Man's relation to the soil was profoundly changed. Formerly man had been pan of nature; now he was the exploiter of nature. Nowhere else in the world did farmers develop any analogous agricultural implement. Is it coincidence that modern technology, with its ruthlessness toward nature, has so largely been produced by descendants of these peasants of northern Europe?

This same exploitive attitude appears slightly before A.D. 830 in Western illustrated calendars. In older calendars the months were shown as passive personifications. The new Frankish calendars, which set the style for the Middle Ages, are very different: they show men coercing the world around them—plowing, harvesting, chopping trees, butchering pigs. Man and nature are two things, and man is master.

These novelties seem to be in harmony with larger intellectual patterns. What people do about their ecology depends on what they think about themselves in relation to things around them. Human ecology is deeply conditioned by beliefs about our nature and destiny—that is, by religion. To Western eyes this is very evident in, say, India or Ceylon. It is equally true of ourselves and of our medieval ancestors.

The victory of Christianity over paganism was the greatest psychic revolution in the history of our culture. It has become fashionable today to say that, for better or worse, we live in the "post-Christian age." Certainly the forms of our thinking and language have largely ceased to be Christian, but to my eye the substance often remains amazingly akin to that of the past. Our daily habits of action, for example, are dominated by an implicit faith in perpetual progress which was unknown either to Greco-Roman antiquity or to the Orient. It is rooted in, and is indefensible apart from, Judeo-Christian theology. The fact that Communists share it merely helps to show what can be demonstrated on many other grounds: that Marxism, like Islam, is a Judeo-Christian heresy. We continue today to live, as we have lived for about 1700 years, very largely in a context of Christian axioms.

What did Christianity tell people about their relations with the environment? While many of the world's mythologies provide stories of creation, Greco-Roman mythology was singularly incoherent in this respect. Like Aristotle, the intellectuals of the ancient West denied that the visible world had a beginning. Indeed, the idea of a beginning was impossible in the framework of their cyclical notion of time. In sharp contrast, Christianity inherited from Judaism not only a concept of time as nonrepetitive and linear but also a striking story of creation. By gradual stages a loving and all-powerful God had created light and darkness, the heavenly bodies, the earth and all its plants, animals, birds, and fishes. Finally, God had created Adam and, as an afterthought, Eve to keep man from being lonely. Man named all the animals, thus establishing his dominance over them. God planned all of this explicitly for man's benefit and rule: no item in the physical creation had any purpose save to serve man's purposes. And, although man's body is made of clay, he is not simply part of nature: he is made in God's image.

Especially in its Western form, Christianity is the most anthropocentric religion the world has seen. As early as the 2nd century both Tertullian and Saint Irenaeus of Lyons were insisting that when God shaped Adam he was foreshadowing the image of the incarnate Christ, the Second Adam. Man shares, in great measure, God's transcendence of nature. Christianity, in absolute contrast to ancient paganism and Asia's religions (except, perhaps, Zorastrianism [sic]), not only established a dualism of man and nature but also insisted that it is God's will that man exploit nature for his proper ends.

At the level of the common people this worked out in an interesting way. In Antiquity every tree, every spring, every stream, every hill had its own genius loci, its guardian spirit. These Spirits were accessible to men, but were very unlike men; centaurs, fauns, and mermaids show their ambivalence. Before one cut a tree, mined a mountain, or dammed a brook, it was important to placate the spirit in charge of that particular situation, and to keep it placated. By destroying pagan animism, Christianity made it possible to exploit nature in a mood of indifference to the feelings of natural objects.

It is often said that for animism the Church substituted the cult of saints. True; but the cult of saints is functionally quite different from animism. The saint is not in natural objects: he may have special shrines, but his citizenship is in heaven. Moreover, a saint is entirely a man; he can be approached in human terms. In addition to saints, Christianity of course also had angels and demons inherited from Judaism and perhaps, at one remove, from Zorastrianism. But these were all as mobile as the saints themselves. The spirits in natural objects, which formerly had protected nature from man, evaporated. Man's effective monopoly on spirit in this world was confirmed, and the old inhibitions to the exploitation of nature crumbled.

When one speaks in such sweeping terms, a note of caution is in order. Christianity is a complex faith, and its consequences differ in differing contexts. What I have said may well apply to the medieval West, where in fact technology made spectacular advances. But the Greek East, a highly civilized realm of equal Christian devotion, seems to have produced no marked technological innovation after the late 7th century, when Greek fire was invented. The key to the contrast may perhaps be found in a difference in the tonality of piety and thought which students of comparative theology find between the Greek and the Latin Churches. The Greeks believed that sin was intellectual blindness, and that salvation was found in illumination, orthodoxy—that is, clear thinking. The Latins, on the other hand, felt that sin was moral evil, and that salvation was to be found in right conduct. Eastern theology has been intellectualist. Western theology has been voluntarist. The Greek saint contemplates; the Western saint acts. The implications of Christianity for the conquest of nature would emerge more easily in the Western atmosphere.

The Christian dogma of creation, which is found in the first clause of all the Creeds, has another meaning for our comprehension of today's ecologic crisis. By revelation, God had given man the Bible, the Book of Scripture. But since God had made nature, nature also must reveal the divine mentality. The religious study of nature for the better understanding of God was known as natural theology. In the early Church, and always in the Greek East, nature was conceived primarily as a symbolic system through which God speaks to men: the ant is a sermon to sluggards; rising flames are the symbol of the soul's aspiration. The view of nature was essentially artistic rather than scientific. While Byzantium preserved and copied great numbers of ancient Greek scientific texts, science as we conceive it could scarcely flourish in such an ambience.

However, in the Latin West by the early 13th century natural theology was following a very different bent. It was ceasing to be the decoding of the physical symbols of God's communication with man and was becoming the effort to understand God's mind by discovering how his creation operates. The rainbow was no longer simply a symbol of hope first sent to Noah after the Deluge: Robert Grosseteste, Friar Roger Bacon, and Theodoric of Freiberg produced startlingly sophisticated work on the optics of the rainbow, but they did it as a venture in religious understanding. From the 13th century onward, up to and including Leitnitz and Newton, every major scientist, in effect, explained his motivations in religious terms. Indeed, if Galileo had not been so expert an

amateur theologian he would have got into far less trouble: the professionals resented his intrusion. And Newton seems to have regarded himself more as a theologian than as a scientist. It was not until the late 18th century that the hypothesis of God became unnecessary to many scientists.

It is often hard for the historian to judge, when men explain why they are doing what they want to do, whether they are offering real reasons or merely culturally acceptable reasons. The consistency with which scientists during the long formative centuries of Western science said that the task and the reward of the scientist was "to think God's thoughts after him" leads one to believe that this was their real motivation. If so, then modern Western science was cast in a matrix of Christian theology. The dynamism of religious devotion shaped by the Judeo-Christian dogma of creation, gave it impetus.

AN ALTERNATIVE CHRISTIAN VIEW

We would seem to be headed toward conclusions unpalatable to many Christians. Since both science and technology are blessed words in our contemporary vocabulary, some may be happy at the notions, first, that viewed historically, modern science is an extrapolation of natural theology and, second, that modern technology is at least partly to be explained as an Occidental, voluntarist realization of the Christian dogma of man's transcendence of, and rightful master over, nature. But, as we now recognize, somewhat over a century ago science and technology—hitherto quite separate activities—joined to give mankind powers which, to judge by many of the ecologic effects, are out of control. If so, Christianity bears a huge burden of guilt.

I personally doubt that disastrous ecologic backlash can be avoided simply by applying to our problems more science and more technology. Our science and technology have grown out of Christian attitudes toward man's relation to nature which are almost universally held not only by Christians and neo-Christians but also by those who fondly regard themselves as post-Christians.

Despite Copernicus, all the cosmos rotates around our little globe. Despite Darwin, we are not, in our hearts, part of the natural process. We are superior to nature, contemptuous of it, willing to use it for our slightest whim. The newly elected Governor of California, like myself a churchman but less troubled than I, spoke for the Christian tradition when he said (as is alleged), "when you've seen one redwood tree, you've seen them all." To a Christian a tree can be no more than a physical fact. The whole concept of the sacred grove is alien to Christianity and to the ethos of the West. For nearly 2 millennia Christian missionaries have been chopping down sacred groves, which are idolatrous because they assume spirit in nature.

What we do about ecology depends on our ideas of the man-nature relationship. More science and more technology are not going to get us out of the present ecologic crisis until we find a new religion, or rethink our old one. The beatniks, who are the basic revolutionaries of our time, show a sound instinct in their affinity for Zen Buddhism, which conceives of the man-nature relationship as very nearly the mirror image of the Christian view. Zen, however, is as deeply conditioned by Asian history as Christianity is by the experience of the West, and I am dubious of its viability among us.

Possibly we should ponder the greatest radical in Christian history since Christ: Saint Francis of Assisi. The prime miracle of Saint Francis is the fact that he did not end at the stake, as many of his left-wing followers did. He was so clearly heretical that a General of the Franciscan Order, Saint Bonavlentura, a great and perceptive Christian, tried to suppress the early accounts of Franciscanism. The key to an understanding of Francis is his belief in the virtue of humility—not merely for the individual but for man as a species. Francis tried to depose man from his monarchy over creation and set up a democracy of all God's creatures. With him the ant is no longer simply a homily for the lazy, flames a sign of the thrust of the soul toward union with God; now they are Brother Ant and Sister Fire, praising the Creator in their own ways as Brother Man does in his.

Later commentators have said that Francis preached to the birds as a rebuke to men who would not listen. The records do not read so: he urged the little birds to praise God, and in spiritual ecstasy they flapped their wings and chirped rejoicing. Legends of saints, especially the Irish saints, had long told of their dealings with animals but always, I believe to show their human dominance over creatures. With Francis it is different. The land around Gubbio in the Apennines was ravaged by a fierce wolf. Saint Francis, says the legend, talked to the wolf and persuaded him of the error of his ways. The wolf repented, died in the odor of sanctity, and was buried in consecrated ground.

What Sir Steven Ruciman calls "the Franciscan doctrine of the animal soul" was quickly stamped out. Quite possibly it was in part inspired, consciously or unconsciously, by the belief in reincarnation held by the Cathar heretics who at that time teemed in Italy and southern France, and who presumably had got it originally from India. It is significant that at just the same moment, about 1200, traces of metempsychosis are found also in western Judaism, in the Provencal Cabbala. But Francis held neither to transmigration of souls nor to pantheism. His view of nature and of man rested on a unique sort of pan-psychism of all things animate and inanimate, designed for the glorification of their transcendent Creator, who, in the ultimate gesture of cosmic humility, assumed flesh, lay helpless in a manger, and hung dying on a scaffold.

I am not suggesting that many contemporary Americans who are concerned about our ecologic crisis will be either able or willing to counsel with wolves or exhort birds. However, the present increasing disruption of the global environment is the product of a dynamic technology and science which were originating in the Western medieval world against which Saint Francis was rebelling in so original a way. Their growth cannot be understood historically apart from distinctive attitudes toward nature which are deeply grounded in Christian dogma. The fact that most people do not think of these attitudes as Christian is irrelevant. No new set of basic values has been accepted in our society to displace those of Christianity. Hence we shall continue to have a worsening ecologic crisis until we reject the Christian axiom that nature has no reason for existence save to serve man.

The greatest spiritual revolutionary in Western history, Saint Francis, proposed what he thought was an alternative Christian view of nature and man's relation to it; he tried to substitute the idea of the equality of all creatures, including man, for the idea of man's limitless rule of creation. He failed. Both our present science and our present technology are so tinctured with orthodox Christian arrogance toward nature that no solution for our ecologic crisis can be expected from them alone. Since the roots of our trouble are so largely religious, the remedy must also be essentially religious, whether we call it that or not. We must rethink and refeel our nature and destiny. The profoundly religious, but heretical, sense of the primitive Franciscans for the spiritual autonomy of all parts of nature may point a direction. I propose Francis as a patron saint for ecologists.

Animal Liberation
is an Environmental Ethic

Dale Jamieson

Dale Jamieson is professor of environmental studies and philosophy at New York University. He is the author of *Morality's Progress: Essays on Humans, Other Animals, and the Rest of Nature* (2003), and coeditor of *A Companion to Environmental Philosophy* (2001).

Jamieson argues for a recognition of the convergence that exists between environmental ethics and animal liberation. He uses the example of eating meat to illustrate the existing overlap between the two fields. Eating meat, especially factory farmed meat, results in environmental pollution, is high in energy consumption, and causes immeasurable suffering. He asserts that the recognition that animal liberation is an environmental ethic would strengthen the environmental movement.

. . . The idea that environmental ethics and animal liberation are conceptually distinct, and that animal liberation has more in common with conventional morality than with environmental ethics, would come as a surprise to many people concerned about the human domination of nature. For one thing, environmentalists and animal liberationists have many of the same enemies: those who dump poisons into the air and water, drive whales to extinction, or clear rainforests to create pastures for cattle, to name just a few. Moreover, however one traces the history of the environmental movement, it is clear that it comes out of a tradition that expresses strong concern for animal suffering and autonomy. Certainly both the modern environmental and animal liberation movements spring from the same sources in the post-World War II period: a disgust with the sacrifice of everything else to the construction of military machines,

the creation of a culture which views humans and other animals as replaceable commodities, and the prevailing faith in the ability of science to solve all of our problems. It is no coincidence that, in the United States at least, both of these movements developed during the same period. Peter Singer's first article on animal liberation appeared less than three years after the first Earth Day.[1] Even today people who identify themselves as environmentalists are likely to be as concerned about spotted owls as old growth forests and to think that vegetarianism is a good idea. Many people are members of both environmental and animal liberation organisations and feel no tension between these commitments.

This is not to say that there are no differences between environmentalists and animal liberationists.[2] Such differences exist, but so do deep divisions among environmentalists and among animal liberationists. My thesis is that the divisions within each of these groups are just as deep and profound as the differences between them. Leopold's land ethic is one environmental ethic on offer, but so is animal liberation. The superiority of one to the other must be demonstrated by

Edited Excerpt from Dale Jamieson, "Animal Liberation is an Environmental Ethics" from Environmental Values, No. 7, pp. 41–57, 1998. Reprinted by permission of The White Horse Press.

argument, not by appeal to paradigm cases or established by definitional fiat.

I begin by briefly tracing the history of the split between environmental ethics and animal liberation, go on to sketch a theory of value that I think is implicit in animal liberation, and explain how this theory is consistent with strong environmental commitments. I conclude with some observations about problems that remain.

1. ORIGINS

• • •

The origins of the contemporary environmental movement were deeply entangled in the counterculture of the 1960s. Generally in the counterculture there was a feeling that sex was good, drugs were liberating, opposing the government was a moral obligation, and that new values were needed to vindicate, sustain, and encourage this shift in outlook and behaviour. In 1967 (during the "Summer of Love" in San Francisco's Haight-Ashbury), the UCLA historian Lynn White Jr. published an essay in which he argued that the dominant tendencies in the Judaeo-Christian tradition were the real source of our environmental problems. Only by overthrowing these traditions and embracing the suppressed insights of other traditions could we come to live peaceably with nature.[3]

This view gained philosophical expression in a 1973 paper by Richard Routley.[4] Routley produced a series of cases about which he thought we have moral intuitions that cannot be accounted for by traditional ethics. Routley asked us to consider a "last man" whose final act is to destroy such natural objects as mountains and salt marshes. Although these natural objects would not be appreciated by conscious beings even if they were not destroyed, Routley thought that it would still be wrong for the "last man" to destroy them. These intuitions were widely shared, and many environmental philosophers thought that they could only be explained by supposing that nonsentient nature has mind-independent value.[5]

Throughout the 1970s there was a great deal of discussion about whether a new environmental ethic was needed, possible, or defensible. In a widely discussed 1981 paper Tom Regan clearly distinguished what he called an "environmental ethic" from a "management ethic."[6] In order to be an environmental ethic, according to Regan, a theory must hold that there are nonconscious beings that have "moral standing." Passmore had argued in his 1974 book that such an ethic was not required to explain our duties concerning nature, but in a 1973 paper Naess had already begun the attempt to develop a new ethic that he called Deep Ecology.[7]

• • •

By the early 1980s it seemed clear that environmental ethics and animal liberation were conceptually distinct. To be an environmental ethicist one had to embrace new values. One had to believe that some nonsentient entities have inherent value; that these entities include such collectives as species, ecosystems, and the community of the land; and that value is mind-independent in the following respect: even if there were no conscious beings, aspects of nature would still be inherently valuable. What remained to be seen was whether any plausible ethic satisfied these conditions.

• • •

2. ANIMAL LIBERATION AND THE VALUE OF NATURE

In my view any plausible ethic must address concerns about both animals and the environment. (Indeed, I think that it is an embarrassment to philosophy that those who are most influential within the discipline typically ignore these issues or treat them as marginal.) Some issues that directly concern animals are obviously of great environmental import as well. The production and consumption of beef may well be the most important of them.[8] The addiction to beef that is characteristic of people in the industrialised countries is not only a moral atrocity for animals but also causes health problems for consumers, reduces grain supplies for the poor, precipitates social divisions in developing countries, contributes to climate change, leads to the conversion of forests to pasture lands, is a causal factor in overgrazing, and is implicated in the destruction of native plants and animals. If there is one issue on which animal liberationists and environmentalists should speak with a single voice it is on this issue.

• • •

In addition to there being clear issues on which animal liberationists and environmentalists should agree, it is also important to remember that nonhuman animals, like humans, live in environments. One reason to oppose the destruction of wilderness and the poisoning of nature is that these actions harm both human and nonhuman animals. I believe that one can go quite far towards protecting the environment solely on the basis of concern for animals.

Finally, and most importantly, environmental ethicists have no monopoly on valuing such collectives as species, ecosystems, and the community of the land. It has only seemed that they do because parties to the dispute have not attended to the proper distinctions.

One relevant distinction . . . is between the source and content of values.[9] We can be sentientist with respect to the source of values, yet nonsentientist with respect to their content. Were there no sentient beings there would be no values, but it doesn't follow from this that only sentient beings are valuable.[10]

The second important distinction is between primary and derivative value. Creatures who can suffer, take pleasure in their experiences, and whose lives go better or worse from their own point of view are of primary value. Failure to value them involves failures of objectivity or impartiality in our reasoning or sentiments.

Suppose that I recognise that I matter morally in virtue of instantiating some particular property, but I withhold the judgement that some other creature matters morally, although I recognise that this other creature also instantiates this property. On the face of it, I hold inconsistent beliefs, though they can be made consistent by conceptual gerrymandering.

Just as I can appear to assert P & -P, but limit the interpretation of P to "then or there" and -P to "now or here," so I can say that a particular property is morally relevant only if it is instantiated in me or my close relatives. However, such consistency is not worth having since it rests on an absurd view of how morally relevant properties function. Indeed, it seems to strip them of their significance. Contrary to what has been granted, what makes me morally significant in this case is not instantiating the property under consideration, but rather instantiating the property of being me or my kin. Similar points apply with respect to the sentiments. If I fail to value a creature who instantiates a property in virtue of which I matter morally, then the reach and power of my sentiments are in some way defective. Whether it is reason or sentiment that is involved, in both cases I look out into the world and see creatures who instantiate properties that bestow moral value, yet I deny moral value to those who are not me or biologically close to me. It is natural to say about these cases that I lack objectivity or impartiality. Sidgwick would have chided me for failing to take the point of view of the universe.

Nonsentient entities are not of primary value because they do not have a perspective from which their lives go better or worse. Ultimately the value of nonsentient entities rests on how they fit into the lives of sentient beings. But although nonsentient entities are not of primary value, their value can be very great and urgent. In some cases their value may even trump the value of sentient entities. The distinction between primary and derivative value is not a distinction in degree of value, but rather in the ways different entities can be valuable.

A third distinction is that between intrinsic and nonintrinsic value. Before explaining how I use this distinction, I want to be clear about how I do not use it. G. E. Moore inaugurated a tradition in which some entities were supposed to be of value because of properties intrinsic to themselves, while other entities were of value because of properties that were extrinsic to them (i.e., relational properties).[11] At first glance it might be thought that this is the same distinction as that between primary and derivative value. What underwrites the value of a sentient creature is that its life can go better or worse, and these properties may be thought to be intrinsic to the creature. But whether a creature's life goes well or ill depends on its relation to the world. These value-relevant, world-relating properties are not intrinsic in Moore's sense. A further reason for avoiding Moore's distinction is that it invites conflating the source and content of values. One and the same property may appear intrinsic under one description and extrinsic under another. For example, the properties that make a creature internally goal-directed may appear intrinsic, but when these properties are described as value-conferring they may appear extrinsic because they require the existence of sentient beings in order to be of value. Various responses can be made to these concerns, but I think that enough has been said to show at least that Moore's distinction is troublingly difficult to make out.

The distinction that I think is useful is that between intrinsically and nonintrinsically valuing something. I speak of "intrinsically valuing" rather than "intrinsic value" because it makes clear that the intended distinction is in the structure of valuing rather than in the sorts of things that are valued.[12] We intrinsically value something when we value it for its own sake. Making the distinction in this way also makes clear that one and the same entity can be valued both intrinsically and nonintrinsically at different times, in different contexts, by different valuers, or even by the same valuer at the same time. For example, I can intrinsically value Sean (i.e. value her for her own sake) yet nonintrinsically value her as an efficient mail-delivering device (i.e. for how she conduces to my ends).

Collecting these distinctions we can entertain the possibility that the content of our values may include our intrinsically valuing an entity that is of derivative value, and that this valuing may be urgent and intense, even trumping something of primary value. The obvious candidates for satisfying this description are works of art. Many of us would say that the greatest works of art are very valuable indeed. We value them intrinsically, yet ultimately an account of their value devolves into

understandings about their relations to people (e.g., artists, audiences, potential audiences, those who know of their existence, etc.).

During the Second World War, Churchill evacuated art from London to the countryside in order to protect it from the blitz. Resources devoted to this evacuation could have been allocated to life-saving. Although he may not have represented the decision in this way, Churchill made the judgement that evacuating the art was more important than saving some number of human lives. I don't know whether he was correct in his specific calculation, but he might well have been. Quantity of life is not the only thing that matters; quality of life matters too, and it is to this concern that Churchill's judgement was responsive.

A similar point could be made concerning the destruction of parts of the old city of Dubrovnik by Serbian gunners. I believe that over the course of human history the destruction of the old city would be a greater crime than some measure of death and destruction wrought upon the people of Dubrovnik. Indeed, I believe that some of the people of Dubrovnik share this view. This particular judgement need not be shared, however, in order to accept the basic point that I am making.

Nonsentient features of the environment are of derivative value, but they can be of extreme value and can be valued intrinsically. There are geological features of the Dolomites that are profoundly important to preserve. Rivers and forests can have the same degree of importance. Indeed, there may be features of the Italian natural environment that are as important to preserve as the city of Venice.

The main point I am making here is that many people have traditional evaluational outlooks yet value works of art intrinsically and intensely. There is no great puzzle about how they can both intrinsically value persons and works of art. Similarly, animal liberationists can value nature intrinsically and intensely, even though they believe that nonsentient nature is of derivative value. Because what is of derivative value can be valued intensely and intrinsically, animal liberationists can join environmental ethicists in fighting for the preservation of wild rivers and wilderness areas. Indeed, rightly understood, they can even agree with environmental ethicists that these natural features are valuable for their own sakes.

But at this point an objection may arise. The most that I have shown is that nonsentient entities can be intrinsically valued. I have not shown that they ought to be intrinsically valued.

• • •

But as a first approximation, we might say that in order to see how environmentalist claims are justified, we should look at the practices of persuasion that environmentalists employ. Consider an example.

Many people think of deserts as horrible places that are not worth protecting. I disagree. I value deserts intrinsically and think you should too. How do I proceed? One thing I might do is take you camping with me. We might see the desert's nocturnal inhabitants, the plants that have adapted to these conditions, the shifting colours of the landscape as the day wears on, and the rising of the moon on stark features of the desert. Together we might experience the feel of the desert wind, hear the silence of the desert, and sense its solitude. You may become interested in how it is that this place was formed, what sustains it, how its plants and animals make a living. As you learn more about the desert, you may come to see it differently and to value it more. This may lead you to spend more time in the desert, seeing it in different seasons, watching the spring with its incredible array of flowers turn to the haunting stillness of summer. You might start reading some desert literature, from the monastic fathers of the church to Edward Abbey. Your appreciation would continue to grow.

But there is no guarantee that things will go this way. You may return from your time in the desert hot, dirty, hungry for a burger, thirsty for a beer, and ready to volunteer your services to the U.S. Army Corps of Engineers (whose *raison d'etre* seems to be to flood as much of the earth's surface as possible). Similarly, some people see Venice as a dysfunctional collection of dirty old buildings, find Kant boring and wrong, and hear Mahler as both excessively romantic

and annoyingly dissonant. More experience only makes matters worse.

If someone fails to appreciate the desert, Venice, or Mahler, they need not have made any logical error. Our evaluative responses are not uniquely determined by our constitution or the world. This fact provokes anxiety in some philosophers. They fear that unless value is mind-independent, anything goes. Experience machines are as good as experience, Disney-desert is the same as the real thing, and the Spice Girls and Mahler are colleagues in the same business (one strikingly more successful than the other). Those who suffer this anxiety confuse a requirement for value with how value is constituted. Value is mind-dependent, but it is things in the world that are valuable or not. The fact that we draw attention to features of objects in our evaluative discourse is the common property of all theories of value.

These anxious philosophers also fail to appreciate how powerful psychological and cultural mechanisms can be in constituting objectivity. Culture, history, tradition, knowledge, and convention mediate our constitutions and the world. Culture, together with our constitutions and the world, determines our evaluative practices. Since the world and our constitutions alone are not sufficient for determining them, common values should be seen in part as cultural achievements rather than simply as true reports about the nature of things or expressions of what we are essentially. Evaluative practices are in the domain of negotiation and collective construction, as well as reflection and recognition. But the fact that these practices are in part constructed does not mean that they cannot be rigid and compelling. We can be brought to appreciate Venice, Mahler, or the desert by collectively and interactively educating our sensibilities, tastes, and judgements, but such change often involves a deep reorientation of how we see the world. When I try to get you to appreciate the desert, I direct your attention to objects in your visual field, but I am trying to change your way of seeing and thinking and your whole outlook towards nature. I am also trying to change our relationship from one of difference to one of solidarity. Similarly, when advocates of the enterprise society point to missed opportunities for profit and competitiveness, they are trying to educate our sensibilities as well as referring us to economic facts. Their descriptions of how economies work are to a great extent stories about the social world they want to construct.

What I have argued in this section is that animal liberationists can hold many of the same normative views as environmental ethicists. This is because many of our most important issues involve serious threats to both humans and animals as well as to the nonsentient environment; because animal liberationists can value nature as a home for sentient beings; and because animal liberationists can embrace environmental values as intensely as environmental ethicists, though they see them as derivative rather than primary values. What animal liberationists cannot do is claim the moral high ground of the mind-independent value of nature which, since the early days of the movement, environmental ethicists have attempted to secure. But, as I have argued, this moral high ground is not there to be claimed anyway. Those who are deep green should not despair because some of our environmental values are to a great extent socially constructed. Constructivism is a story about how our practices come to be, not about how real, rigid, or compelling they are.

Still, many will think that this is a flabby ethic that leans too far in the direction of subjectivism, relativism, constructivism, or some other postmodern heresy. One way of making their point is to return to the distinction between primary and derivative value. Imagine two people: Robin, who thinks that trees are of primary value, and Ted, who denies that humans or gorillas are included in this class. What kind of a mistake are Robin and Ted making? If I say they are making a conceptual mistake then I will be dismissing some very influential views as nonstarters; if I say they are making a normative mistake then my view of what has primary and derivative value will turn out to be just as subjective as my view that deserts are valuable, and therefore just as vulnerable to other people's lack of responsiveness to my concerns.

I want to reiterate that first-order value judgements can be both rigid and compelling, even though to some extent they are relative and

socially constructed. But having said this, I want to reject the idea that Robin and Ted are making a logical or grammatical error. Robin, Ted, and I have a real normative dispute about how to determine what is of primary value. At the same time this dispute has a different feel to it than first-order normative disputes (e.g., the dispute about whether or not to value the desert). We can bring out this difference by saying as a first approximation that someone who fails to value deserts lacks sensitivity while someone who fails to value people or gorillas lacks objectivity. Although in both cases the dispute involves how we can see ourselves in relation to the world, to a great extent, different considerations are relevant in each case. Because questions about primary values are at the centre of how we take the world, abstract principles (e.g., those that concern objectivity and impartiality) are most relevant to settling these disputes. Differences about whether or not to value deserts, on the other hand, turn on a panoply of considerations, some of which I have already discussed.[13]

In this section I have argued that there is a great deal of theoretical convergence between animal liberationists and environmental ethicists. There is also a strong case for convergence at the practical and political level. The environmental movement has numbers and wealth while the animal liberation movement has personal commitment. Both environmental and animal issues figure in the choices people make in their daily lives, but they are so glaringly obvious in the case of animals that they cannot be evaded. Anyone who eats or dresses makes ethical choices that affect animals. Refraining from eating meat makes one part of a social movement: rather than being an abstainer, one is characterised positively as "a vegetarian." While other consumer choices also have profound environmental consequences, somehow they are less visible than the choice of whether to eat meat. This is part of the reason why self-identified environmentalists are often less motivated to save energy, reduce consumption, or refrain from purchasing toxic substances than animal liberationists are to seek out vegetarian alternatives.[14] Not only is animal liberation an environmental ethic, but animal liberation can also help to empower the environmental movement.

3. REMAINING CONUNDRUMS AND COMPLEXITIES

. . . It might be objected that my rosy view only survives because I have not dealt in detail with specific issues that divide animal liberationists and environmental ethicists. For example, there are many cases in which environmentalists may favour "culling" (a polite term for "killing") some animals for the good of a population. In other cases environmentalists may favour eliminating a population of common animals in order to preserve a rare plant. Hovering in the background is the image of "hunt saboteurs," trying to stop not only fox hunting but also the fox's hunting.

These difficult issues cannot be resolved here.[15] For present purposes, what is important to see is that while animal liberationists and environmentalists may have different tendencies, the turf doesn't divide quite so neatly as some may think. Consider one example.

Gary Varner, who writes as an animal liberationist, has defended what he calls "therapeutic hunting" in some circumstances.[16] He defines "therapeutic hunting" as "hunting motivated by and designed to secure the aggregate welfare of the target species and/or the integrity of its ecosystem."[17] Varner goes on to argue that animal liberationists can support this kind of hunting and that this is the only kind of hunting that environmentalists are compelled to support. What might have appeared as a clear difference between the two groups turns out to be more complex.

In addition to such "convergence" arguments, it is important to recognise the diversity of views that exists within both the environmental and animal liberation movements. Differences between animal liberationists are obvious and on the table. At a practical level, animal liberation groups are notorious for their sectarianism. At a philosophical level, Tom Regan has spent much of the last fifteen years distinguishing his view from that of Peter Singer's, and I have already mentioned other

diverse animal liberationist voices. In recent years the same kind of divisions have broken out among environmental philosophers, with the rhetoric between Callicott and Rolston (and more recently Callicott and Norton) increasingly resembling that between Singer and Regan. Generally within the community of environmental philosophers there are disagreements about the nature and value of wilderness, the importance of biodiversity, and approaches to controlling population. At a practical level there are disagreements about the very goals of the movement. Some would say that preservation of nature's diversity is the ultimate goal; others would counter that it is the preservation of evolutionary processes that matters. Sometimes people assert both without appreciating that they can come into conflict.[18]

There are many practical issues on which neither animal liberationists nor environmentalists are of one mind. For example, South African, American, and German scientists working for the South African National Parks Board, with support from the Humane Society of the United States, are currently testing contraceptives on elephants in Kruger National Park as an alternative to "culling." The World Wide Fund for Nature is divided about the project, with its local branch opposing it.[19]

Part of the reason for the divisions within both the environmental and animal liberation movements is that contemporary Western cultures have little by way of positive images of how to relate to animals and nature. Most of us know what is bad—wiping out songbird populations, polluting water ways, causing cats to suffer, contributing to smog, and so on. But when asked to provide a positive vision many people turn to the past, to their conception of what life is like for indigenous peoples, or what it is to be "natural." None of this will do. So long as we have a paucity of positive visions, different views, theories, and philosophies will compete for attention, with no obvious way of resolving some of the most profound disagreements.

These are early days for those who are sensitive to the interests of nature and animals. We are in the midst of a transition from a culture which sees nature as material for exploitation, to one which asserts the importance of living in harmony with nature. It will take a long time to understand exactly what are the terms of the debate. What is important to recognise now is that animal liberationists and environmental ethicists are on the same side in this transition. Animal liberation is not the only environmental ethic, but neither is it some alien ideology. Rather, as I have argued, animal liberation is an environmental ethic and should be welcomed back into the family.[20]

NOTES

1. Singer, 1973.
2. The Norwegian government has appealed to theoretical differences between environmental ethics and animal liberation in its attempt to reconcile its reputation as an environmental leader with its flouting of the international consensus against whaling.
3. White, 1967.
4. Routley, 1973.
5. The intuition that it would be wrong for the last man to destroy nonsentient natural features can also be explained by concerns about character or by appeal to transworld evaluations. For the first strategy, see Hill, 1983; for the second strategy, see Elliot, 1985. Routley himself adopted a version of the second strategy.
6. Regan, 1981.
7. Passmore, 1974; Naess, 1973. Other important early publications directed towards developing a new environmental ethic include Stone, 1972, and Rolston, 1975.
8. The case for this has been very convincingly argued by Jeremy Rifkin (1992).
9. Callicott, 1980. John O'Neill (1993, ch. 2) also makes a similar distinction.
10. Here we border on some important issues in philosophy of mind that cannot be discussed here. For present purposes, I assume that sentience and consciousness determine the same class, and that there is something that it is like to be a "merely conscious" (as well as self-conscious) entity, although a "merely conscious" entity cannot reflect on what it is like to be itself. I say a little more about these matters in Jamieson, 1983. See also various papers collected in Bekoff and Jamieson, 1996.
11. See Moore, 1922.
12. This of course is not to deny that some things are better candidates for intrinsically valuing than others. For further discussion, see Jamieson, 1994.
13. There is much more to say about these questions than I can say here. However, it may help to locate my views if I invoke the Quinean image of the web of belief in which what is at the centre of the web is defended in different ways than what is at the periphery, not because such beliefs enjoy some special epistemological status, but because of the density of their connections to other beliefs.

14. These and related issues are discussed in two reports to the United States Environmental Protection Agency (Jamieson and VanderWerf, 1993, 1995). Both documents are available from the National Pollution Prevention Center at the University of Michigan, or the Center for Values and Social Policy at the University of Colorado.
15. For my approach to some of these conflicts see my contributions to Norton et al., 1995.
16. Varner, 1995.
17. Ibid., p. 257.
18. To some degree differences among environmentalists have been obscured by the rise of "managerialist" forms of environmentalism which are favoured by many scientists and are highly visible in the media. For a critique, see Jamieson, 1990. For alternative forms of environmentalism, see Sachs, 1993.
19. *New Scientist*, 1996.
20. This paper began life as a lecture to the Gruppo di Studio "Scienza & Etica" at the Politecnico di Milano in Italy. Subsequent versions were presented in the Faculty of Philosophy at Monash University in Australia, to an environmental ethics seminar in Oxford, and to an environmental ethics conference in London. I have benefited from the probing questions and comments of many people, especially Paola Cavalieri, Roger Crisp, Lori Gruen, Alan Holland, Steve Kramer, Rae Langston, and several anonymous referees for this journal.

REFERENCES

Bekoff, Marc and Dale Jamieson (eds.), *Readings in Animal Cognition*. (Cambridge, MA: The MIT Press), 1996.

Callicott, J. Baird, "Animal Liberation: A Triangular Affair," *Environmental Ethics* 2: 311–328, 1980.

Callicott, J. Baird, "Rolston on Intrinsic Value: A Deconstruction," *Environmental Ethics* 14(2): 131–132, 1992.

Callicott, J. Baird, "On Norton and the Failure of Monistic Inherentism," *Environmental Ethics* 18(2): 219–221, 1996.

Elliot, Robert, "Metaethics and Environmental Ethics," *Metaphilosophy* 16: 103–117, 1985.

Elliot, Robert (ed.), *Environmental Ethics*. (Oxford: Oxford University Press), 1995.

Hill, Thomas, Jr., "Ideals of Human Excellence and Preserving Natural Environments," *Environmental Ethics* 5: 211–224, 1983.

Jamieson, Dale, "Killing Persons and Other Beings," in H. Miller and W. Williams (eds.), *Ethics and Animals*. (Clifton, NJ: Humana Publishing Company), 1983.

Jamieson, Dale, "Managing the Future: Public Policy, Scientific Uncertainty, and Global Warming," in D. Scherer (ed.), *Upstream/Downstream: Essays in Environmental Ethics*, pp. 67–89. (Philadelphia: Temple University Press), 1990.

Jamieson, Dale, "Method and Moral Theory," in Peter Singer (ed.), *A Companion to Ethics*, pp. 476–487. (Oxford: Basil Blackwell), 1991.

Jamieson, Dale, "Ziff on Shooting an Elephant," in Dale Jamieson (ed.), *Language, Mind, and Art: Essays in Appreciation and Analysis, in Honor of Paul Ziff*, pp. 121–129. (Dordrecht: Kluwer), 1994.

Jamieson, Dale and VanderWerf, Klasina, *Cultural Barriers to Behavioral Change: General Recommendations and Resources for State Pollution Prevention Programs*. Report to US EPA, 1993.

Jamieson, Dale and VanderWerf, Klasina (eds., with the assistance of Sarah Goering), *Preventing Pollution: Perspectives on Cultural Barriers and Facilitators*. Report to US EPA, 1995.

Johnson, Edward, "Animal Liberation versus the Land Ethic," *Environmental Ethics* **3**(3): 265–273, 1981.

Lee, Keekok, "The Source and Locus of Intrinsic Value," *Environmental Ethics* **18**(3): 297–309, 1996.

Leopold, Aldo, *A Sand County Almanac*. (Oxford: Oxford University Press), 1949.

Moore, G. E., "The Conception of Intrinsic Value," in *Philosophical Studies*. (London: Routledge and Kegan Paul), 1922.

Naess, Arne, "The Shallow and the Deep, Long-Range Ecology Movements," *Inquiry* **16**(1): 95–100, 1973.

New Scientist, "Villagers Slam 'Pill for Elephants,'" 30 November, p. 9, 1996.

Norton, Bryan G., "Why I Am Not a Nonanthropocentrist: Callicott and the Failure of Monistic Inherentism," *Environmental Ethics* **17**(4): 341–358, 1995.

Norton, Bryan G.; Hutchins, Michael; Stevens, Elizabeth F.; and Maple, Terry L. (eds.) *Ethics on the Ark: Zoos, Animal Welfare, and Wildlife Conservation*. (Washington: Smithsonian Institution Press), 1995.

O'Neill, John, *Ecology, Policy and Politics: Human Well-Being and the Natural World*. (London: Routledge), 1993.

Passmore, John, *Man's Responsibility For Nature*. (New York: Scribner's), 1974.

Regan, Tom, "The Nature and Possibility of an Environmental Ethic," *Environmental Ethics* **3**: 19–34, 1981.

Regan, Tom, *The Case for Animal Rights*. (Berkeley: University of California Press), 1983.

Rifkin, Jeremy, *Beyond Beef*. (New York: Penguin, Books, USA), 1992.

Rolston, Holmes, III, "Is There an Ecological Ethic?" *Ethics* **85**(1): 93–109, 1975.

Rolston, Holmes, III, *Environmental Ethics*. (Philadelphia: Temple University Press), 1988.

Rolston, Holmes, III, "The Wilderness Idea Affirmed," *The Environmental Professional* **13**(4): 370–377, 1992.

Routley, Richard, "Is There a Need for a New, an Environmental, Ethics?" *Proceedings of the XV World Congress of Philosophy*, (Varna, Bulgaria), No. 1, pp. 205–210, 1973.

Sachs, Wolfgang (ed.), *Global Ecology: A New Arena of Political Conflict*. (London: Zed Books), 1993.

Sagoff, Mark, "Animal Liberation and Environmental Ethics: Bad Marriage, Quick Divorce," *Osgoode Hall Law Journal* **22**(2): 297–307, 1984.

Singer, Peter, "Animal Liberation," *New York Review of Books*, April 5, 1973.

Stone, Christopher, *Should Trees Have Standing?* (Los Altos, CA: William Kaufman), 1972.

Varner, Gary, "Can Animal Rights Activists Be Environmentalists," in Christine Pierce and Donald VanDeVeer (eds.), *People, Penguins, and Plastic Trees*, second edition, pp. 254–273. (Belmont CA: Wadsworth), 1995.

Weston, Anthony, "Beyond Intrinsic Value: Pragmatism in Environmental Ethics," *Environmental Ethics* **7**: 321–339, 1985.

White, Lynn, Jr., "The Historical Roots of Our Ecologic Crisis," *Science* **155**: 1203–1207, 1967.

Faking Nature

Robert Elliot

Robert Elliot is a professor of philosophy at the University of the Sunshine Coast in Queensland, Australia. He later turned this paper into a book-length work of the same title.

In a time when many argue that we are justified in cutting down trees, clearing forests, and destroying habitats as long as we replace or replant them later, Elliot's work is particularly pertinent. Elliot calls this view that the destruction of something valuable is compensated by the recreation of something of equal value, "the restoration thesis." However, Elliot questions this thesis by considering what, if anything, makes nature valuable. For example, he argues that the origin of something contributes to its value, and that this source of value is destroyed when we try to replicate nature after destroying it. In fact, through a series of thought experiments, Elliot argues that value is lost even when we do not know or cannot tell that a restoration is fake.

I

Consider the following case. There is a proposal to mine beach sands for rutile. Large areas of dune are to be cleared of vegetation and the dunes themselves destroyed. It is agreed, by all parties concerned, that the dune area has value quite apart from a utilitarian one. It is agreed, in other words, that it would be a bad thing considered in itself for the dune area to be dramatically altered. Acknowledging this the mining company expresses its willingness, indeed its desire, to restore the dune area to its original condition after the minerals have been extracted.[1] The company goes on to argue that any loss of value is merely temporary and that full value will in fact be restored. In other words they are claiming that the destruction of what has value is compensated for by the later creation (recreation) of something of equal value. I shall call this "the restoration thesis."

In the actual world many such proposals are made, not because of shared conservationist principles, but as a way of undermining the arguments of conservationists. Such proposals are in fact effective in defeating environmentalist protest. They are also notoriously ineffective in putting right, or indeed even seeming to put right, the particular wrong that has been done to the environment. The sandmining case is just one of a number of similar cases involving such things as open-cut mining, clear-felling of forests, river diversion, and highway construction. Across a range of such cases some concession is made by way of acknowledging the value of pieces of landscape, rivers, forests and so forth, and a suggestion is made that this value can be restored once the environmentally disruptive process has been completed.

Imagine, contrary to fact, that restoration projects are largely successful, that the environment is brought back to its original condition, and that even a close inspection will fail to reveal that the area has been mined, clear-felled, or whatever. If this is so then there it temptation to think that one particular environmentalist objection is defeated. The issue is by no means merely academic. I have

With kind permission from Springer Science + Business Media. Excerpt from Robert Elliot, Faking Nature: The Ethics of Environmental Restoration. Routledge. 1997.

already claimed that restoration promises do in fact carry weight against environmental arguments. Thus Mr. Doug Anthony, the Australian deputy prime minister, saw fit to suggest that sand-mining on Fraser Island could be resumed once "the community becomes more informed and more enlightened as to what reclamation work is being carried out by mining companies. . . ."[2] Or consider how the protests of environmentalists might be deflected in the light of the following report of environmental engineering in the United States.

> about 2 km of creek 25 feet wide has been moved to accommodate a highway and in doing so engineers with the aid of landscape architects and biologists have rebuilt the creek to the same standard as before. Boulders, bends, irregularities and natural vegetation have all been designed into the new section. In addition, special log structures have been built to improve the habitat as part of a fish development program.[3]

Not surprisingly the claim that revegetation, rehabilitation, and the like restore value has been strongly contested. J. G. Mosley reports that:

> The Fraser Island Environmental Inquiry Commissioners did in fact face up to the question of the relevance of successful rehabilitation to the decision on whether to ban exports (of beach sand minerals) and were quite unequivocal in saying that if the aim was to protect a natural area such success was irrelevant. . . . The Inquiry said: ". . . even if, contrary to the overwhelming weight of evidence before the Commission, successful rehabilitation of the flora after mining is found to be ecologically possible on all mined sites on the Island . . . the overall impression of a wild, uncultivated island refuge will be destroyed forever by mining."[4]

I want to show both that there is a rational, coherent ethical system which supports decisive objections to the restoration thesis, and that that system is not lacking in normative appeal. The system I have in mind will make valuation depend, in part, on the presence of properties which cannot survive the disruption-restoration process. There is, however, one point that needs clarifying before discussion proceeds. Establishing that restoration projects, even if empirically successful, do not fully restore value does not by any means constitute a knock-down argument against some environmentally disruptive policy. The value that would be lost if such a policy were implemented may be just one value among many which conflict in this situation. Countervailing considerations may be decisive and the policy thereby shown to be the right one. If my argument turns out to be correct it will provide an extra, though by no means decisive, reason for adopting certain environmentalist policies. It will show that the resistance which environmentalists display in the face of restoration promises is not merely silly, or emotional, or irrational. This is important because so much of the debate assumes that settling the dispute about what is ecologically possible automatically settles the value question. The thrust of much of the discussion is that if restoration is shown to be possible, and economically feasible, then recalcitrant environmentalists are behaving irrationally, being merely obstinate, or being selfish.

There are indeed familiar ethical systems which will serve to explain what is wrong with the restoration thesis in a certain range of cases. Thus preference utilitarianism will support objections to some restoration proposal if that proposal fails to maximally satisfy preferences. Likewise classical utilitarianism will lend support to a conservationist stance provided that the restoration proposal fails to maximize happiness and pleasure. However, in both cases the support offered is contingent upon the way in which the preferences and utilities line up. And it is simply not clear that they line up in such a way that the conservationist position is even usually vindicated. While appeal to utilitarian considerations might be strategically useful in certain cases they do not reflect the underlying motivation of the conservationists. The conservationists seem committed to an account of what has value which allows that restoration proposals fail to compensate for environmental destruction despite the fact that such proposals would maximize utility. What, then, is this distinct source of value which motivates and underpins the stance taken by, among others, the Commissioners of the Fraser Island Environmental Inquiry?

II

It is instructive to list some reasons that might be given in support of the claim that something of value would be lost if a certain bit of the environment were destroyed. It may be that the area supports a diversity of plant and animal life, it may be that it is the habitat of some endangered species, it may be that it contains striking rock formations or particularly fine specimens of mountain ash. If it is only considerations such as these that contribute to the area's value then perhaps opposition to the environmentally disruptive project would be irrational provided certain firm guarantees were available; for instance that the mining company or timber company would carry out the restoration and that it would be successful. Presumably there are steps that could be taken to ensure the continuance of species diversity and the continued existence of the endangered species. Some of the other requirements might prove harder to meet, but in some sense or other it is possible to recreate the rock formations and to plant mountain ash that will turn out to be particularly fine specimens. If value consists of the presence of objects of these various kinds, independently of what explains their presence, then the restoration thesis would seem to hold. The environmentalist needs to appeal to some feature which cannot be replicated as a source of some part of a natural area's value.

Putting the point thus indicates the direction the environmentalist could take. He might suggest that an area is valuable, partly, because it is a natural area, one that has not been modified by human hand, one that is undeveloped, unspoiled, or even unsullied. This suggestion is in accordance with much environmentalist rhetoric, and something like it at least must be at the basis of resistance to restoration proposals. One way of teasing out the suggestion and giving it a normative basis is to take over a notion from aesthetics. Thus we might claim that what the environmental engineers are proposing is that we accept a fake or a forgery instead of the real thing. If the claim can be made good then perhaps an adequate response to restoration proposals is to point out that they merely fake nature: that they offer us something

less than was taken away.[5] Certainly there is a weight of opinion to the effect that, in art at least, fakes lack a value possessed by the real thing.[6]

One way in which this argument might be nipped in the bud is by claiming that it is bound to exploit an ultimately unworkable distinction between what is natural and what is not. Admittedly the distinction between the natural and the nonnatural requires detailed working out. This is something I do not propose doing. However, I do think the distinction can be made good in a way sufficient to the present need. For present purposes I shall take it that "natural" means something like "unmodified by human activity." Obviously some areas will be more natural than others according to the degree to which they have been shaped by human hands. Indeed most rural landscapes will, on this view, count as nonnatural to a very high degree. Nor do I intend the natural/non-natural distinction to exactly parallel some dependent moral evaluation, that is, I do not want to be taken as claiming that what is natural is good and what is nonnatural is not. The distinction between natural and nonnatural connects with valuation in a much more subtle way than that. This is something to which I shall presently return. My claim, then, is that restoration policies do not always fully restore value because part of the reason that we value bits of the environment is because they are natural to a high degree. It is time to consider some counterarguments.

An environmental engineer might urge that the exact similarity which holds between the original and the perfectly restored environment leaves no room for a value discrimination between them. He may urge that if they are *exactly* alike, down to the minutest detail (and let us imagine for the sake of argument that this is a technological possibility), then they must be *equally* valuable. The suggestion is that value-discriminations depend on there being intrinsic differences between the states of affairs evaluated. This begs the question against the environmentalist, since it simply discounts the possibility that events temporally and spatially outside the immediate landscape in question can serve as the basis of some valuation of it. It discounts the possibility that the manner of the landscape's genesis, for example, has a legitimate role in determining its value. Here are some examples which suggest that an object's origins do affect its value and our valuations of it.

Imagine that I have a piece of sculpture in my garden which is too fragile to be moved at all. For some reason it would suit the local council to lay sewage pipes just where the sculpture happens to be. The council engineer informs me of this and explains that my sculpture will have to go. However, I need not despair because he promises to replace it with an exactly similar artifact, one which, he assures me, not even the very best experts could tell was not the original. The example may be unlikely, but it does have some point. While I may concede that the replica would be better than nothing at all (and I may not even concede that), it is utterly improbable that I would accept it as full compensation for the original. Nor is my reluctance entirely explained by the monetary value of the original work. My reluctance springs from the fact that I value the original as an aesthetic object, as an object with a specific genesis and history.

Alternatively, imagine I have been promised a Vermeer for my birthday. The day arrives and I am given a painting which looks just like a Vermeer. I am understandably pleased. However, my pleasure does not last for long. I am told that the painting I am holding is not a Vermeer but instead an exact replica of one previously destroyed. Any attempt to allay my disappointment by insisting that there just is no difference between the replica and the original misses the mark completely. There is a difference and it is one which affects my perception, and consequent valuation, of the painting. The difference, of course, lies in the painting's genesis.

I shall offer one last example which perhaps bears even more closely on the environmental issue. I am given a rather beautiful, delicately constructed object. It is something I treasure and admire, something in which I find considerable aesthetic value. Everything is fine until I discover certain facts about its origin. I discover that it is carved out of the bone of someone killed especially for that purpose. This discovery affects me deeply and I cease to value the object in the way that I

once did. I regard it as in some sense sullied, spoiled by the facts of its origin. The object itself has not changed but my perceptions of it have. I now know that it is not quite the kind of thing I thought it was, and that my prior valuation of it was mistaken. The discovery is like the discovery that a painting one believed to be an original is in fact a forgery. The discovery about the object's origin changes the valuation made of it, since it reveals that the object is not of the kind that I value.

What these examples suggest is that there is at least a prima facie case for partially explaining the value of objects in terms of their origins, in terms of the kinds of processes that brought them into being. It is easy to find evidence in the writings of people who have valued nature that things extrinsic to the present, immediate environment determine valuations of it. John Muir's remarks about Hetch Hetchy Valley are a case in point.[7] Muir regarded the valley as a place where he could have direct contact with primeval nature; he valued it not just because it was a place of great beauty, but because it was also a part of the world that had not been shaped by human hand. Muir's valuation was conditional upon certain facts about the valley's genesis; his valuation was of a literally natural object, of an object with a special kind of continuity with the past. The news that it was a carefully contrived elaborate *ecological* artifact would have transformed that valuation immediately and radically.

The appeal that many find in areas of wilderness, in natural forests and wild rivers, depends very much on the naturalness of such places. There may be similarities between the experience one has when confronted with the multifaceted complexity, the magnitude, the awesomeness of a very large city, and the experience one has walking through a rain forest. There may be similarities between the feeling one has listening to the roar of water over the spillway of a dam and the feeling one has listening to a similar roar as a wild river tumbles down rapids. Despite the similarities there are also differences. We value the forest and river in part because they are representative of the world outside our dominion, because their existence is independent of us. We may value the city and the dam because of what they represent of human achievement. Pointing out the differences is not necessarily to denigrate either. However, there will be cases where we rightly judge that it is better to have the natural object than it is to have the artifact.

It is appropriate to return to a point mentioned earlier concerning the relationship between the natural and the valuable. It will not do to argue that what is natural is necessarily of value. The environmentalist can comfortably concede this point. He is not claiming that all natural phenomena have value in virtue of being natural. Sickness and disease are natural in a straightforward sense and are certainly not good. Natural phenomena such as fires, hurricanes, and volcanic eruptions can totally alter landscapes, and alter them for the worse. All of this can be conceded. What the environmentalist wants to claim is that within certain constraints, the naturalness of a landscape is a reason for preserving it, a determinant of its value. Artificially transforming an utterly barren, ecologically bankrupt landscape into something richer and more subtle may be a good thing. That is a view quite compatible with the belief that replacing a rich natural environment with a rich artificial one is a bad thing. What the environmentalist insists on is that naturalness is one factor in determining the value of pieces of the environment. But that, as I have tried to suggest, is no news. The castle by the Scottish loch is a very different kind of object, value-wise, from the exact replica in the appropriately shaped environment of some Disneyland of the future. The barrenness of some Cycladic island would stand in a different, better perspective if it were not brought about by human intervention.

As I have glossed it, the environmentalist's complaint concerning restoration proposals is that nature is not replaceable without depreciation in one aspect of its value which has to do with its genesis, its history. Given this, an opponent might be tempted to argue that there is no longer any such thing as "natural" wilderness, since the preservation of those bits of it which remain is achievable only by deliberate policy. The idea is that by placing boundaries around national parks; by actively discouraging grazing,

trail-biking, and the like; by prohibiting sand-mining, we are turning the wilderness into an artifact, that in some negative or indirect way we are creating an environment. There is some truth in this suggestion. In fact we need to take notice of it if we do value wilderness, since positive policies are required to preserve it. But as an argument against my overall claim, it fails. What is significant about wilderness is its causal continuity with the past. This is something that is not destroyed by demarcating an area and declaring it a national park. There is a distinction between the "naturalness" of the wilderness itself and the means used to maintain and protect it. What remains within the park boundaries is, as it were, the real thing. The environmentalist may regret that such positive policy is required to preserve the wilderness against human, or even natural, assault.[8] However, the regret does not follow from the belief that what remains is of depreciated value. There is a significant difference between preventing damage and repairing damage once it is done. That is the difference that leaves room for an argument in favor of a preservation policy over and above a restoration policy.

There is another important issue which needs highlighting. It might be thought that naturalness only matters insofar as it is perceived, in other words, it might be thought that if the environmental engineer could perform the restoration quickly and secretly, then there would be no room for complaint. Of course, in one sense there would not be, since the knowledge which would motivate complaint would be missing. What this shows is that there can be loss of value without the loss being perceived. It allows room for valuations to be mistaken because of ignorance concerning relevant facts. Thus my Vermeer can be removed and secretly replaced with the perfect replica. I have lost something of value without knowing that I have. This is possible because it is not simply the states of mind engendered by looking at the painting, by gloatingly contemplating my possession of it, by giving myself over to aesthetic pleasure, and so on, which explain why it has value. It has value because of the kind of thing that it is, and one thing that it is is a painting executed by a man with certain intentions, at a certain stage of his artistic development, living in a certain aesthetic milieu. Similarly, it is not just those things which make me feel the joy that wilderness makes me feel that I value. That would be a reason for desiring such things, but that is a distinct consideration. I value the forest because it is of a specific kind, because there is a certain kind of causal history which explains its existence. Of course I can be deceived into thinking that a piece of landscape has that kind of history, has developed in the appropriate way. The success of the deception does not elevate the restored landscape to the level of the original, no more than the success of the deception in the previous example confers on the fake the value of a real Vermeer. What has value in both cases are objects which are of the kind that I value, not merely objects which I think are of that kind. This point, it should be noted, is appropriate independently of views concerning the subjectivity or objectivity of value.

An example might bring the point home. Imagine that John is someone who values wilderness. John may find himself in one of the following situations:

1. He falls into the clutches of a utilitarian-minded supertechnologist. John's captor has erected a rather incredible device which he calls an experience machine. Once the electrodes are attached and the right buttons pressed one can be brought to experience anything whatsoever. John is plugged into the machine, and, since his captor knows full well John's love of wilderness, given an extended experience as of hiking through a spectacular wilderness. This is environmental engineering at its most extreme. Quite assuredly John is being shortchanged. John wants there to be wilderness and he wants to experience it. He wants the world to be a certain way and he wants to have experiences of a certain kind; veridical.
2. John is abducted, blindfolded, and taken to a simulated, plastic wilderness area. When the blindfold is removed John is thrilled by what he sees around him: the tall gums, the wattles, the lichen on the rocks. At least that is what he thinks is there. We know better: We know that John is deceived, that he is once again being shortchanged. He has been presented with an environment which he thinks is of value but isn't. If he knew that the leaves through which the artificially generated breeze now stirred were synthetic he would be profoundly disappointed, perhaps even disgusted at what at best is a cruel joke.
3. John is taken to a place which was once devastated by strip-mining. The forest which had stood there for some thousands of years had been felled and the earth torn up, and the animals either killed or driven from their habitat. Times have changed, however, and the area has been restored. Trees of the species which grew there before the devastation grow there again, and the animal species have returned. John knows nothing of this and thinks he is in pristine forest. Once again, he has been shortchanged, presented with less than what he values most.

In the same way that the plastic trees may be thought a (minimal) improvement on the experience machine, so too the real trees are an improvement on the plastic ones. In fact, in the third situation there is incomparably more of value than in the second, but there could be more. The forest, though real, is not genuinely what John wants it to be. If it were not the product of contrivance he would value it more. It is a product of contrivance. Even in the situation where the devastated area regenerates rather than is restored, it is possible to understand and sympathize with John's claim that the environment does not have the fullest possible value. Admittedly in this case there is not so much room for that claim, since the environment has regenerated of its own accord. Still, the regenerated environment does not have the right kind of continuity with the forest that stood there initially, that continuity has been interfered with by the earlier devastation. (In actual fact the regenerated forest is likely to be perceivably quite different to the kind of thing originally there.)

III

I have argued that the causal genesis of forests, rivers, lakes, and so on is important in establishing their value. I have also tried to give an indication of why this is. In the course of my argument I drew various analogies, implicit rather than explicit, between faking art and faking nature. This should not be taken to suggest, however, that the concepts of aesthetic evaluation and judgment are to be carried straight over to evaluations of, and judgments about, the natural environment. Indeed there is good reason to believe that this cannot be done. For one thing, an apparently integral part of aesthetic evaluation depends on viewing the aesthetic object as an intentional object, as an artifact, as something that is shaped by the purposes and designs of its author. Evaluating works of art involves explaining them, and judging them, in terms of their author's intentions; it involves placing them within the author's corpus of work; it involves locating them in some tradition and in some special milieu. Nature is not a work of art, though works of art (in some suitably broad sense) may look very much like natural objects.

None of this is to deny that certain concepts which are frequently deployed in aesthetic evaluation cannot usefully and legitimately be deployed in evaluations of the environment. We admire the intricacy and delicacy of coloring in paintings as we might admire the intricate and delicate shadings in a eucalyptus forest. We admire the solid grandeur of a building as we might admire the solidity and grandeur of a massive rock outcrop. And of course the ubiquitous notion of the beautiful has a purchase in environmental evaluations as it does in aesthetic evaluations. Even granted all this, there are various arguments which might be developed to drive a wedge between the two kinds of evaluation which would weaken the analogies between faking art and faking nature. One such argument turns on the claim that aesthetic evaluation has, as a central component, a judgmental factor concerning the author's intentions and the like, in the way that was sketched above.[9] The idea is that nature, like works of art, may elicit any of a range of emotional responses in viewers. We may be awed by a mountain, soothed by the sound of water over rocks, excited by the power of a waterfall, and so on. However, the judgmental element in aesthetic evaluation serves to differentiate it from environmental evaluation and serves to explain, or so the argument would go, exactly what it is about fakes and forgeries in art which discount their value with respect to the original. The claim is that if there is no judgmental element in environmental evaluation, then there is rational basis for preferring real to faked nature when the latter is a good replica. The argument can, I think, be met.

Meeting the argument does not require arguing that responses to nature count as aesthetic responses. I agree that they are not. Nevertheless there are analogies which go beyond emotional content, and which may persuade us to take more seriously the claim that faked nature is inferior. It is important to make the point that only in fanciful situations dreamt up by philosophers are there no detectable differences between fakes and originals, both in the case of artifacts and in the case of natural objects. By taking a realistic example where there are discernible, and possibly discernible, differences between the fake and the real thing, it is possible to bring out the judgmental element in responses to, and evaluations of, the environment. Right now I may not be able to tell a real Vermeer from a Van Meegeren, though I might learn to do so. By the same token I might not be able to tell apart a naturally evolved stand of mountain ash from one which has been planted, but might later acquire the ability to make the requisite judgment. Perhaps an anecdote is appropriate here. There is a particular stand of mountain ash that I had long admired. The trees were straight and tall, of uniform stature, neither densely packed nor too openspaced. I then discovered what would have been obvious to a more expert eye, namely that the stand of mountain ash had been planted to replace original forest which had been burnt out. This explained the uniformity in size, the density and so on: It also changed my attitude to that piece of landscape. The evaluation that I make now of that landscape is to a certain extent informed, the response is not merely emotive but cognitive as well. The evaluation is informed and directed by my beliefs about the forest, the type of forest it is, its condition as a member of that kind, its causal genesis, and so on. What is more, the judgmental element affects the emotive one. Knowing that the forest is not a naturally evolved forest causes me to feel differently about it: It causes me to perceive the forest differently and to assign it less value than naturally evolved forests.

Val Routley has eloquently reminded us that people who value wilderness do not do so merely because they like to soak up pretty scenery.[10] They see much more and value much more than this. What they do see, and what they value, is very much a function of the degree to which they understand the ecological mechanisms which maintain the landscape and which determine that it appears the way it does. Similarly, knowledge of art history, of painting techniques and the like, will inform aesthetic evaluations and alter aesthetic perceptions. Knowledge of this kind is capable of transforming a hitherto uninteresting landscape into one that is compelling. Holmes Rolston has discussed at length the way in which an understanding and appreciation of ecology generates new values.[11] He does not claim that ecology reveals values previously unnoticed, but rather that the understanding of the complexity, diversity, and integration of the natural world which ecology affords us opens up a new area of valuation. As the facts are uncovered, the values are generated. What the remarks of Routley and Rolston highlight is the judgmental factor which is present in environmental appraisal. Understanding and evaluation do go hand in hand; and the responses individuals have to forests, wild rivers, and the like are not merely raw, emotional responses.

IV

Not all forests are alike, not all rain forests are alike. There are countless possible discriminations that the informed observer may make. Comparative judgments between areas of the natural environment are possible with regard to ecological richness, stage of development, stability, peculiar local circumstance, and the like. Judgments of this kind will very often underlie hierarchical orderings of environments in terms of their intrinsic worth. Appeal to judgments of this kind will frequently strengthen the case for preserving some bit of the environment. Thus one strong argument against the Tasmanian Hydroelectricity Commission's proposal to dam the Lower Gordon River turns on the fact that it threatens the inundation of an exceedingly fine stand of Huon pine. If the stand of Huon pines could not justifiably he ranked so high on the appropriate ecological scale then the argument against the dam would be to that extent weakened.

One reason that a faked forest is not just as good as a naturally evolved forest is that there is always the possibility that the trained eye will tell the difference.[12] It takes some time to discriminate areas of Alpine plain which are naturally clear of snow gums from those that have been cleared. It takes some time to discriminate regrowth forest which has been logged from forest which has not been touched. These are discriminations which it is possible to make and which are made. Moreover, they are discriminations which affect valuations. The reasons why the "faked" forest counts for less, more often than not, than the real thing are similar to the reasons why faked works of art count for less than the real thing.

Origin is important as an integral part of the evaluation process. It is important because our beliefs about it determine the valuations we make. It is also important in that the discovery that something has an origin quite different to the origin we initially believe that it has can literally alter the way we perceive that thing.[13] The point concerning the possibility of detecting fakes is important in that it stresses just how much detail must be written into the claim that environmental engineers can replicate nature. Even if environmental engineering could achieve such exactitude, there is, I suggest, no compelling reason for accepting the restoration thesis. It is worth stressing, though, that as a matter of strategy, environmentalists must argue the empirical inadequacy of restoration proposals. This is the strongest argument against restoration ploys, because it appeals to diverse value frameworks, and because such proposals are promises to deliver a specific good. Showing that the good won't be delivered is thus a useful move to make.

NOTES

1. In this case *full* restoration will be literally impossible because the minerals are not going to be replaced.
2. J. G. Mosley, "The Revegetation 'Debate': A Trap For Conservationists," *Australian Conservation Foundation Newsletter* 12, no. 8(1980): 1.

3. Peter Dunk, "How New Engineering Can Work with the Environment," *Habitat Australia* 7, no. 5(1979): 12.

4. See Mosley, "The Revegetation 'Debate,'" p. 1.

5. Offering something less is not, of course, always the same as offering nothing. If diversity of animal and plant life, stability of complex ecosystems, tall trees, and so on are things that we value in themselves, then certainly we are offered something. I am not denying this, and I doubt that many would qualify their valuations of the above-mentioned items in a way that leaves the restored environment devoid of value. Environmentalists would count as of worth programs designed to render polluted rivers reinhabitable by fish species. The point is rather that they may, as I hope to show, rationally deem it less valuable than what was originally there.

6. See, e.g., Colin Radford, "Fakes," *Mind* 87, no, 345 (1978): 66–76; and Nelson Goodman, *Languages of Art* (New York: Bobbs-Merrill, 1968) pp. 99–122, though Radford and Goodman have different accounts of why genesis matters.

7. Sec chap. 10 of Roderick Nash, *Wilderness and the American Mind* (New Haven: Yale University Press, 1973).

8. For example, protecting the Great Barrier Reef from damage by the crown-of-thorns starfish.

9. See, e.g., Don Mannison, "A Prolegomenon to a Human Chauvinist Aesthetic," in *Environmental Philosophy,* ed. D. S. Mannison, M. A. McRobbie, and R. Routley, (Canberra: Research and School of Social Sciences, Australian National University, 1980), pp. 212–16.

10. Val Routley, "Critical Notice of Passmore's *Man's Responsibility for Nature.*" *Australasian Journal of Philosophy* 53, no. 2 (1975): 171–85.

11. Holmes Rolston III, "Is There an Ecological Ethic?" *Ethics* 85, no. 2 (1975): 93–109.

12. For a discussion of this point with respect to art forgeries, see Goodman, *Languages of Art,* esp. pp. 103–12.

13. For an excellent discussion of this same point with respect to artifacts, see Radford, "Fakes," esp. pp. 73–6.

REFERENCES

Dunk, Peter. "How Engineering Can Work with the Environment." *Habitat Australia* 7, no. 5 (1979).

Goodman, Nelson. *Languages of Art.* New York: Bobbs-Merrill, 1968.

Mannison, Don. "A Prolegomenon to a Human Chauvinist Aesthetic." In *Environmental Philosophy*, edited by D. S. Mannison, M. A. McRobbie, and R. Routley. Canberra: Research School of Social Sciences, Australian National University, 1980.

Mosley, J. G. "The Revegetation 'Debate': A Trap for Conservationists." *Australian Conservation Foundation Newsletter* 12, no. 8 (1980).

Nash, Roderick. *Wilderness and the American Mind.* New Haven: Yale University Press, 1973.

Radford, Colin. "Fakes." *Mind* 87, no. 345 (1978).

Rolston, Holmes III. "Is There an Ecological Ethic?" *Ethics* 85, no. 2 (1975): 93–109.

Routley, Val. "Critical Notice of Passmore's *Man's Responsibility for Nature.*" *Australasian Journal of Philosophy* 53, no. 2 (1975).

A "Good" Environment: Just One of the Set of Human Objectives

William Baxter

William Baxter (1929–1998) was professor of law at Stanford University. He was also Assistant Attorney General for the Antitrust Division of the Department of Justice under the Reagan administration, where he oversaw the breakup of Bell (AT&T). He was the author of *People or Penguins: The Case for Optimal Pollution* (1974).

Baxter addresses the issue of environmental pollution and argues from a thoroughly anthropocentric point of view. Pollution is the price we pay for the use of resources while in pursuit of benefits to human beings. Baxter does not advocate a "clean environment," but rather an "optimal level of pollution" to be determined by trade-offs between goods produced and methods of controlling pollution. These determinations are not made with any moral concern given to the environment and animals. Rather, these determinations are made in order to promote human good.

I start with the modest proposition that, in dealing with pollution, or indeed with any problem, it is helpful to know what one is attempting to accomplish. Agreement on how and whether to pursue a particular objective, such as pollution control, is not possible unless some more general objective has been identified and stated with reasonable precision. We talk loosely of having clean air and clean water, of preserving our wilderness areas, and so forth. But none of these is a sufficiently general objective: Each is more accurately viewed as a means rather than as an end.

With regard to clean air, for example, one may ask, "how clean?" and "what does clean mean?" It is even reasonable to ask, "why have clean air?" Each of these questions is an implicit demand that a more general community goal be stated—a goal sufficiently general in its scope and enjoying sufficiently general assent among the community of actors that such "why" questions no longer seem admissible with respect to that goal.

If, for example, one states as a goal the proposition that "every person should be free to do whatever he wishes in contexts where his actions do not interfere with the interests of other human beings," the speaker is unlikely to be met with a response of "Why?" The goal may be criticized as uncertain in its implications or difficult to implement, but it is so basic a tenet of our civilization—it reflects a cultural value so broadly shared, at least in the abstract—that the question "why" is seen as impertinent or imponderable or both.

I do not mean to suggest that everyone would agree with the "spheres of freedom" objective just stated. Still less do I mean to suggest that a society could subscribe to four or five such general objectives that would be adequate in their coverage to serve as testing criteria by which all

Excerpt from William Baxter, "A good" environment: Just one of the set of human objectives," from PEOPLE OR PENGUINS. Copyright © 1974 Columbia University Press. Reprinted by permission.

other disagreements might be measured. One difficulty in the attempt to construct such a list is that each new goal added will conflict, in certain applications, with each prior goal listed; and thus each goal serves as a limited qualification on prior goals.

Without any expectation of obtaining unanimous consent to them, let me set forth four goals that I generally use as ultimate testing criteria in attempting to frame solutions to problems of human organization. My position regarding pollution stems from these four criteria. If the criteria appeal to you and any part of what appears hereafter does not, our disagreement will have a helpful focus: which of us is correct, analytically, in supposing that his position on pollution would better serve these general goals. If the criteria do not seem acceptable to you, then it is to be expected that our more particular judgments will differ, and the task will then be yours to identify the basic set of criteria upon which your particular judgments rest.

My criteria are as follows:

1. The spheres of freedom criterion stated above.
2. Waste is a bad thing. The dominant feature of human existence is scarcity—our available resources, our aggregate labors, and our skill in employing both have always been, and will continue for some time to be, inadequate to yield to every man all the tangible and intangible satisfactions he would like to have. Hence, none of those resources, or labors, or skills, should be wasted—that is, employed so as to yield less than they might yield in human satisfactions.
3. Every human being should be regarded as an end rather than as a means to be used for the betterment of another. Each should be afforded dignity and regarded as having an absolute claim to an even-handed application of such rules as the community may adopt for its governance.
4. Both the incentive and the opportunity to improve his share of satisfactions should be preserved to every individual. Preservation of incentive is dictated by the "no-waste" criterion and enjoins against the continuous, totally egalitarian redistribution of satisfactions, or wealth; but subject to that constraint, everyone should receive, by continuous redistribution if necessary, some minimal share of aggregate wealth so as to avoid a level of privation from which the opportunity to improve his situation becomes illusory.

The relationship of these highly general goals to the more specific environmental issues at hand may not be readily apparent, and I am not yet ready to demonstrate their pervasive implications. But let me give one indication of their implications. Recently scientists have informed us that use of DDT in food production is causing damage to the penguin population. For the present purposes let us accept that assertion as an indisputable scientific fact. The scientific fact is often asserted as if the correct implication—that we must stop agricultural use of DDT—followed from the mere statement of the fact of penguin damage. But plainly it does not follow if my criteria are employed.

My criteria are oriented to people, not penguins. Damage to penguins, or sugar pines, or geological marvels is, without more, simply irrelevant. One must go further, by my criteria, and say: Penguins are important because people enjoy seeing them walk about rocks; and furthermore, the well-being of people would be less impaired by halting use of DDT than by giving up penguins. In short, my observations about environmental problems will be people-oriented, as are my criteria. I have no interest in preserving penguins for their own sake.

It may be said by way of objection to this position, that it is very selfish of people to act as if each person represented one unit of importance and nothing else was of any importance. It is undeniably selfish. Nevertheless, I think it is the only tenable starting place for analysis for several reasons. First, no other position corresponds to the way most people really think and act—i.e., corresponds to reality.

Second, this attitude does not portend any massive destruction of nonhuman flora and fauna, and they will be preserved because and to the degree that humans do depend on them.

Third, what is good for humans is, in many respects, good for penguins and pine trees—clean air for example. So that humans are, in these respects, surrogates for plant and animal life.

Fourth, I do not know how we could administer any other system. Our decisions are either private or collective. Insofar as Mr. Jones is free to act privately, he may give such preferences as he wishes to other forms of life: He may feed birds in winter and do with less himself, and he may even decline to resist an advancing polar bear on the ground that the bear's appetite is more important than those portions of himself that the bear may choose to eat. In short my basic premise does not rule out private altruism to competing life-forms. It does rule out, however, Mr. Jones' inclination to feed Mr. Smith to the bear, however hungry the bear, however despicable Mr. Smith.

Insofar as we act collectively on the other hand, only humans can be afforded an opportunity to participate in the collective decisions. Penguins cannot vote now and are unlikely subjects for the franchise—pine trees more unlikely still. Again, each individual is free to cast his vote so as to benefit sugar pines if that is his inclination. But many of the more extreme assertions that one hears from some conservationists amount to tacit assertions that they are specially appointed representatives of sugar pines, and hence, that their preferences should be weighted more heavily than the preferences of other humans who do not enjoy equal rapport with "nature." The simplistic assertion that agricultural use of DDT must stop at once because it is harmful to penguins is of that type.

Fifth, if polar bears or pine trees or penguins, like men, are to be regarded as ends rather than means, if they are to count in our calculus of social organization, someone must tell me how much each one counts, and someone must tell me how these life-forms are to be permitted to express their preferences, for I do not know either answer. If the answer is that certain people are to hold their proxies, then I want to know how those proxy-holders are to be selected: self-appointment does not seem workable to me.

Sixth, and by way of summary of all the foregoing, let me point out that the set of environmental issues under discussion—although they raise very complex technical questions of how to achieve any objective—ultimately raise a normative question: What *ought* we to do? Questions of *ought* are unique to the human mind and world—they are meaningless as applied to a nonhuman situation.

I reject the proposition that we *ought* to respect the "balance of nature" or to "preserve the environment" unless the reason for doing so, express or implied, is the benefit of man.

I reject the idea that there is a "right" or "morally correct" state of nature to which we should return. The word "nature" has no normative connotation. Was it "right" or "wrong" for the earth's crust to heave in contortion and create mountains and seas? Was it "right" for the first amphibian to crawl up out of the primordial ooze? Was it "wrong" for plants to reproduce themselves and alter the atmospheric composition in favor of oxygen? For animals to alter the atmosphere in favor of carbon dioxide both by breathing oxygen and eating plants? No answers can be given to these questions because they are meaningless questions.

All this may seem obvious to the point of being tedious, but much of the present controversy over environment and pollution rests on tacit normative assumptions about just such nonnormative phenomena: that it is "wrong" to impair penguins with DDT, but not to slaughter cattle for prime rib roasts; that it is wrong to kill stands of sugar pines with industrial fumes, but not to cut sugar pines and build housing for the poor. Every man is entitled to his own preferred definition of Walden Pond, but there is no definition that has any moral superiority over another, except by reference to the selfish needs of the human race.

From the fact that there is no normative definition of the natural state, it follows that there is no normative definition of clean air or pure water—hence, no definition of polluted air—or of pollution—except by reference to the needs of man. The "right" composition of the atmosphere is one which has some dust in it and some lead in it and some hydrogen sulfide in it—just those amounts that attend a sensibly organized society thoughtfully and knowledgeably pursuing the greatest possible satisfaction for its human members.

The first and most fundamental step toward solution of our environmental problems is a clear recognition that our objective is not pure air or water but rather some optimal state of pollution. That step immediately suggests the question: How do we define and attain the level of pollution that will yield the maximum possible amount of human satisfaction?

Low levels of pollution contribute to human satisfaction, but so do food and shelter and education and music. To attain ever-lower levels of pollution, we must pay the cost of having less of these other things. I contrast that view of the cost of pollution control with the more popular statement that pollution control will "cost" very large numbers of dollars. The popular statement is true in some senses, false in others; sorting out the true and false senses is of some importance. The first step in that sorting process is to achieve a clear understanding of the difference between dollars and resources. Resources are the wealth of our nation; dollars are merely claim checks upon those resources. Resources are of vital importance; dollars are comparatively trivial.

Four categories of resources are sufficient for our purposes: At any given time a nation, or a planet if you prefer, has a stock of labor, of technological skill, of capital goods, and of natural resources (such as mineral deposits, timber, water, land, etc.). These resources can be used in various combinations to yield goods and services of all kinds—in some limited quantity. The quantity will be larger if they are combined efficiently, smaller if combined inefficiently. But in either event the resource stock is limited, the goods and services that they can be made to yield are limited; even the most efficient use of them will yield less than our population, in the aggregate, would like to have.

If one considers building a new dam, it is appropriate to say that it will be costly in the sense that it will require x hours of labor, y tons of steel and concrete, and z amount of capital goods. If these resources are devoted to the dam, then they cannot be used to build hospitals, fishing rods, schools, or electric can openers. That is the meaningful sense in which the dam is costly.

Quite apart from the very important question of how wisely we can combine our resources to produce goods and services, is the very different question of how they get distributed—who gets how many goods? Dollars constitute the claim checks which are distributed among people and which control their share of national output. Dollars are nearly valueless pieces of paper except to the extent that they do represent claim checks to

some fraction of the output of goods and services. Viewed as claim checks, all the dollars outstanding during any period of time are worth, in the aggregate, the goods and services that are available to be claimed with them during that period—neither more nor less.

It is far easier to increase the supply of dollars than to increase the production of goods and services—printing dollars is easy. But printing more dollars doesn't help because each dollar then simply becomes a claim to fewer goods, i.e., becomes worth less.

The point is this: many people fall into error upon hearing the statement that the decision to build a dam, or to clean up a river, will cost $X million. It is regrettably easy to say, "It's only money. This is a wealthy country, and we have lots of money." But you cannot build a dam or clean a river with $X million—unless you also have a match, you can't even make a fire. One builds a dam or cleans a river by diverting labor and steel and trucks and factories from making one kind of goods to making another. The cost in dollars is merely a shorthand way of describing the extent of the diversion necessary. If we build a dam for $X million, then we must recognize that we will have $X million less housing and food and medical care and electric can openers as a result.

Similarly, the costs of controlling pollution are best expressed in terms of the other goods we will have to give up to do the job. This is not to say the job should not be done. Badly as we need more housing, more medical care, and more can openers, and more symphony orchestras, we could do with somewhat less of them, in my judgment at least, in exchange for somewhat cleaner air and rivers. But that is the nature of the trade-off, and analysis of the problem is advanced if that unpleasant reality is kept in mind. Once the trade-off relationship is clearly perceived, it is possible to state in a very general way what the optimal level of pollution is. I would state it as follows:

People enjoy watching penguins. They enjoy relatively clean air and smog-free vistas. Their health is improved by relatively clean water and air. Each of these benefits is a type of good or service. As a society we would be well advised to give up one washing machine if the resources that would have gone into that washing machine can yield greater human satisfaction when diverted into pollution control. We should give up one hospital if the resources thereby freed would yield more human satisfaction when devoted to elimination of noise in our cities. And so on, trade-off by trade-off, we should divert our productive capacities from the production of existing goods and services to the production of a cleaner, quieter, more pastoral nation up to—and no further than—the point at which we value more highly the next washing machine or hospital that we would have to do without than we value the next unit of environmental improvement that the diverted resources would create.

Now this proposition seems to me unassailable but so general and abstract as to be unhelpful—at least unadministerable in the form stated. It assumes we can measure in some way the incremental units of human satisfaction yielded by very different types of goods. The proposition must remain a pious abstraction until I can explain how this measurement process can occur. But I insist that the proposition stated describes the result for which we should be striving—and again, that it is always useful to know what your target is even if your weapons are too crude to score a bull's-eye.

Look to the Mountain: Reflections on Indigenous Ecology

Gregory Cajete

Gregory Cajete, a Tewa Indian from Santa Clara Pueblo, New Mexico, is a professor in the College of Education at the University of New Mexico. He is the author of *A People's Ecology* (1999), *Ignite the Sparkle: An Indigenous Science Education Model* (1999), and *Native Science: Natural Laws of Interdependence* (1999).

Cajete writes of the "theology of place," an ecological relationship that is manifested in all aspects of traditional American Indian life. Both identity and survival flow from American Indians' relationships to place, landscape, and animals. These relationships, as all relationships, carry ethical obligations including the duty to respect the sanctity of both place and all living things therein, the duty to carry out actions with humility, and the duty to remember and teach the ecological relationships. Cajete notes that American Indians find themselves in a larger society that does not comprehend or respect these relationships and that many American Indians themselves have experienced effects of deteriorated ecological relationships. He calls for a return to indigenous ways of living that are restorative and sustainable.

The Americas are an ensouled and enchanted geography, and the relationship of Indian people to this geography embodies a "theology of place," reflecting the very essence of what may be called spiritual ecology. American Indians' traditional relationship to and participation with the landscape includes not only the land itself, but the way in which they have perceived themselves and all else. Through generations of living in America, Indian people have formed and been formed by the land. Indian kinship with the land, its climate, soil, water, mountains, lakes, forests, streams, plants, and animals has literally determined the expressions of an American Indian theology. The land has become an extension of Indian thought and being because, in the words of a Pueblo elder, "It is this place that holds our memories and the bones of our people . . . This is the place that made us."

There is a metaphor that Pueblo people use, which, when translated into English, means "that place that the People talk about." This metaphor refers not only to a physical place but also a place of consciousness and an orientation to sacred ecology. Sacred orientation to place and space is a key element of the ecological awareness and intimate relationship that Indians have established with the North American landscape for 30,000 years or more. Indian people have names for all places that comprise important environmental features of the landscape. In fact, Indian languages are replete with environmentally derived references based on the kind of natural characteristics and experiences they have had living in relationship with their respective landscapes.

Another metaphor used by Tewa elders is *pin peye obe* (look to the mountain), which is used to remind people of the long view, or the need to think about what we are doing in terms of its impact on future generations. "Look to the mountain" reminds us that when dealing with the landscape we must think in terms of many thousands of years.

THEOLOGY OF PLACE

In the words of an Acoma Pueblo poet, the place "that Indian people talk about" is not only a physical place with sun, wind, rain, water, lakes, rivers, and streams, but a spiritual place, a place of being and understanding. Sense of place is constantly evolving and transforming through the lives and relationships of all participants. Humans naturally have a geographic sensibility and geographic imagination borne of millions of years of interaction with places. Humans have always oriented themselves by establishing direct and personal relationships to places in the landscapes with which they have interacted.

An ecological sense of relationship encompassed every aspect of traditional American Indian life. American Indians understood that an intimate relationship between themselves and their environment was the essence of their survival and identity as people. Native peoples lived in every place in what Europeans called the New World, and in every place they established a direct and enduring relationship with the natural environment. They transmitted this understanding of relationship in every aspect of their lives—language, art, music, dance, social organization, ceremony, and identity as human beings.

Adaptations to place among indigenous groups in America took many forms. Living in the forests of the Northeast, Indians venerated the trees and integrated that reality of their environment into every aspect of their lives and expression as a people. Living on the Plains, Indians followed the buffalo and made themselves portable in the way of all nomadic hunters around the world. They understood and expressed themselves in relationship to the land and the animals upon which they depended for their survival. In the desert Southwest, Pueblo Indians

became dryland farmers and likewise venerated the cycles of water, earth, wind, and fire—all environmental elements essential to life and to the continuance of the Pueblo people in their place. The fisher and forest people in the Pacific Northwest established intimate relationships with the salmon upon which they depended for life, with the sea mammals they encountered, and the great rain forests that characterized the environment of their place. And in similar fashion, relationships to place were established by all other peoples such as the Paiute in the Great Basin, the Seminole in the Everglades, and the various Eskimo groups throughout the far North.

Tribes adapted to specific environments in unique and different ways, which in turn gave rise to a diversity of expressive cultures. However, although native peoples' cultures were quite diverse, there was also adherence to a common set of life principles. They understood that the natural universe was imbued with life and sacredness. They understood that their effects on their place had to be carried out with humility, understanding, and respect for the sacredness of the place and all living things of those places. They expressed a "theology of place," which, while focused specifically on their place, extended to include all of nature. The environments of diverse Indian peoples may have been different, but the basis of their theology was the same. The very word "indigenous" is derived from the Latin root *indu* or *endo*, which in turn is related to the Greek word *endina*, which means "entrails." "Indigenous" means being so completely identified with a place that you reflect its very entrails, its insides, its soul.

For Native people throughout the Americas, the paradigm of thinking, acting, and working evolved because of and through their established relationships to nature. As such, the foundation, expression, and context of indigenous education was environmental. The theology of nature reverberated throughout art, community, myth, and any other aspect of human social or tribal expression. All were inspired and formed through an integrated and direct relationship of making a living in and through the reality of their physical environments.

The environment was not separate or divorced from Native peoples' lives, but rather was the context or set of relationships that tied everything together. They understood ecology not as something apart from themselves or outside their intellectual reality, but rather as the very center and generator of self-understanding. As a center, that environmental understanding became the guiding mechanism for the ways in which they expressed themselves and their sense of sacredness.

WINDOWS INTO NATURAL AFFILIATION

Sacred orientation to place is a key concept in Indigenous education. Indigenous peoples honored their place, and often considered themselves to be situated in the center of a sacred space that had very distinct orientations. They recognized and named their directional relationships in terms of the natural and relational qualities associated with them. For instance, many American Indian tribes named the cardinal directions in a way that included a description of the way people oriented themselves upon facing the sun. Thus, north may be referred to as "to the left side of the sun rising"; south, "to the right side of the sun rising"; east, "to the sun rising"; and west, "to the sun setting."

This is the way Indigenous people metaphorically represent the physical qualities of directionality in their language. Such qualities would be included with others, including colors, plants, animals, winds, kinds of thought, and features of the landscape of place that they associated with each direction. Orientation is essential for Indigenous people because each person belongs to a place. Understanding orientation to place is essential in order to grasp what it means to be related. Many Indigenous peoples recognize seven directions: the four cardinal directions, above, center, and below. This way of viewing orientation creates a (literal) sphere of relationship founded on place that evolves through time and space.

Art is another reflection of Indigenous relational sensibility and education. For example, the design motifs of such ancient Southwestern Mimbres pottery reflect the integration of humans with animals, and the relationship the Mimbres felt with animals, plants, and nature in general. Primal symbols of nature also abound in contemporary Pueblo art forms that represent key features, elements, or foundations of their ecological relationships. One is the Pueblo cloud motif. This important symbol reflects the importance of water, the nature of water to flow in various states and cycles, and the ecological understanding of how water circulates in a semi-arid environment. Pueblo elders recognized many different kinds of rain. They understood that in their arid environment, rain was essential to the life cycle, and therefore their own survival. The elders watched clouds day in and day out. Centuries of such observations permitted them to discern the relationships and characteristics of clouds. They reflected on how water is intimately involved with the nature of clouds. They recognized all types of rain that would be possible from particular kinds of clouds. And they prayed for the kinds of clouds that brought the qualities of water they needed. Whether snow, sleet, wind with rain, baby rain, grandfather rain, or mother rain, they honored the kinds of rain that brought them life.

RELATIONSHIP WITH ANIMALS

Hunting and planting are two strains of mythic tribal expression. In many cultures, such as the Pueblo, both orientations are represented in the evolution of traditional art designs, mythic themes, dance, and ritual. The understanding gained from animals about ecological transformation was portrayed in many forms, and wherever Indian people hunted, these traditions abounded. Once again, while each tribe reflected these understandings in unique ways, core understandings were similar from tribe to tribe. The essential focus was relationship, and the guiding sentiment was respect. The central intent revolved around honoring the entities that gave life to a people. Whether it was hunting in the Southwest or in the Far North, an intimate relationship between the hunter and the hunted was established. There was an ecological understanding that animals transformed themselves, and that while this may not be a literal transformation, indeed it is an ecological reality. Animals eat other animals, and the animals that are eaten become a part of the substance of other life. This is the primary process of transformation of energy in the animal kingdom. Through observation and interaction with animals over generations, Indigenous people understood that animals could teach people something about the essence of transformation.

Indigenous peoples have created many kinds of symbolic ideals in reflections about themselves and their relationship to animals. The essence of one such ideal is captured in the metaphoric construct of the "hunter of good heart." Hunting in and of itself is both a spiritual and educational act. Hunting is one of those 40,000-year courses of study that human beings have been involved with. The hunter of good heart was a bringer of life to his people: he had to have not only a very intimate knowledge of the animals he hunted, but also a deep and abiding respect for their nature, procreation, and continuance as species. While he tracked the animal physically to feed himself and his family, he also tracked the animal ritually, thereby understanding at a deeper level the relationship with the animals he hunted. The hunted animal became one of the guides of relationship and community in Indigenous education.

In the entire process of Indigenous hunting, there was always a time for teaching. That time was often directly expressed when the hunter brought back his catch. A scene in many traditional American Indian and Native Alaska communities is when a hunter returns from the hunt, says prayers of thanksgiving to the animals he has killed, and then gathers his extended family around him. He then tells the story of the animal that has been slain. He talks about the importance of maintaining the proper relationship to the animal that has given its life to perpetuate the life of his family and community. He expresses to his family why it is so important to continue to understand that life is sacred, and that animal life also begets human life through the sacrifice of its flesh to feed and clothe humans. He

reminds all that human beings will provide the repayment of life through their own flesh for the purpose of perpetuating animal life. The necessity of sharing is also symbolically emphasized through the hunter sharing his catch with his extended family. These symbolic acts of respect and remembrance reinforce communal relationship to the animals that gave their lives for a community's benefit. Teaching by the hunter of good heart is a way of remembering to remember relationship.

The myths of Indigenous people in North America are replete with animal characters that embody the people's understanding of what it means to live in reverent relationship with animals and the natural world. Each story is a complex of metaphors that teach the essential importance of proper relationship and respect for the natural world. Each illustrates the fact that all living things and natural entities have a role to play in maintaining the web of life.

The Iroquois relate a myth in which Opossum, who was very conceited about his elegant and bushy tail, was tricked by Cricket and Hare into shaving his tail. Opossum believed his tail would become even more glorious upon shaving it, but of course, he failed. This tale is a reflection on how people can get carried away by egotistical desires.

The Paiutes relate a tale that describes the stealing of fire by Coyote after he challenged powerful shamans who lived on an obsidian mountain. The shamans had captured the fire, and refused to share it with the animals or the rest of the world. So the world remained in cold and darkness. Coyote and other animals challenged the shamans to a dance contest. Coyote and the shamans dance until all except Coyote fall asleep from exhaustion. Coyote then steals the last embers of the dance fire and runs away with the shamans in hot pursuit. As Coyote and the other animals and birds take turns running with the fire throughout the land, they shed light and warmth upon the dark frozen landscape.

There are other myths about human relationships to animals, such as the well-known Northwest Indian myth about the woman who married a bear.

The relationships of bears and the similarities of bears to human beings underlie the importance American Indian people place on treating bears respectfully. The role of birds such as Raven in the creation of the first man and first woman is related in a myth from the Eskimo, which tells of the creation of the first human from a pea pod.

Another way of remembering to remember relationship is the complex of animal dances found among Indigenous people around the world. Animal dances are a commemoration of humans' continued relationship with the animal world. The purpose of Indigenous dances is not only the renewal of opportunities for remembering to remember. They also help to maintain the balance of all essential relationships of the world. Such is the case with the Yurok White Deerskin Dance, which was performed to ensure the balance of the world from one year to the next. Indigenous people felt responsibility not only for themselves, but also for the entire world around them. The world renewal ceremonies conducted by all Indigenous people are reflections of this deep ecological sensibility and responsibility.

Indigenous people created annual ceremonial cycles based on the belief that acknowledgment of the sources of a community's life must be made year in and out. Ceremonial cycles are based on the understanding that people have to continue to remember and perpetuate essential ecological relationships through the lives of individual tribal members and succeeding generations. Once people break the cycles of remembering, they forget essential life-sustaining relationships and behave in ways that have led to the ecological crisis we see today. And so Indigenous people dance the relationship of people to animals as represented in their guiding or creation stories. They represent those symbols of life in their art forms and in the things they create in daily life. These are also symbols that help them to maintain tribal identity by assisting in learning to be responsible for their essential life-affirming relationships. Such honoring and exploration of key relationships are equally reflected in the mythological complex of Indigenous story making and telling.

RELATIONSHIP WITH PLANTS

In the Southwest, plants and agricultural ways of being became part of the way that Pueblo people expressed their essential relationships. Pueblo ancestors learned how to cultivate corn in many different kinds of environments and developed numerous strains of corn that were drought resistant and grew under a variety of conditions. For the Pueblo people corn became a sacrament of life, that is, a representation of life itself and the connection that Pueblo people feel toward the plant world. Corn is reflected in Pueblo art forms and in their ways of understanding themselves as a people.

Contemporary Hopi artists at times depict First Man and First Woman as perfect ears of corn being shrouded and guided by a Corn Mother who is a representation of Earth Mother. Pueblo people express this intimate understanding and relationship by dancing for the perpetuation of corn—in June, July, and August, grand Corn Dances occur in many Pueblos in the Southwest. Indeed, until very recently, corn, beans, squash—all of the things which Pueblo people grew—were the physical foundation of Pueblo life and livelihood. These are the dances that Pueblo people maintain to the present, and they represent themselves and their reflections of each other as a community of relationship. According to one Pueblo proverb, "We are all kernels on the same corn cob."

PUEBLO JOURNEYS

Pueblo ancestors lived and hunted in New Mexico for 10,000 years or more following herds of mastodon and bison retreating from the great glaciers of the north. Those early communities of Pueblo hunter-gatherers evolved and developed as groups comprised of no more than two or three extended families living together. Through the process of utilizing everything in their environment they began to understand the nature of sustaining themselves within the environments in which they lived. They developed understandings of how to use the things around them to clothe themselves, to create baskets and pottery, and to sustain themselves in terms of food and shelter. Gradually, those communities became larger and more complex. In those larger, more complex communities, an understanding evolved that people had to honor relationship and reciprocity, not only in terms of each other, but more important, in the context of the environments they depended on for life.

In the stories Pueblo elders tell, the ancestors journeyed many times and settled in many places, including Chaco Canyon, Mesa Verde, and Canyon de Chelly. And each time they stopped they established a relationship to the place in which they settled, and they learned from each of these places. They came to understand something about the essence of these natural places and something about the delicate environmental balance of nature in such places. They settled by lakes and came to understand the nature of water and its importance and sanctity in an arid environment. They came to understand that water was one of the foundations for maintenance of life on earth. They settled near mountains and came to understand the nature of mountains in terms of the way they provided a context, an environment in which Pueblo people and other living things could live.

The Pueblo people have depicted this sort of ecological understanding in many forms, one of which is the symbolic mythic figure called Kokopelli. Kokopelli is the seed carrier and the creative spirit of nature's fertility, good fortune, culture, art, music, and dance. Kokopelli is a reflection of the procreative powers of nature and the creative powers of the human mind. Pueblos saw themselves as reflections of Kokopelli, as creative spirits in sacred interaction with natural places of the landscape, as bearers of natural gifts, and as planters of seeds. This spiritual ecology is linked to the Pueblo's guiding story in which the People emerged from the earth's navel at the time of creation and began to journey through a sacred landscape. At this time in the remote past, the first people came to understand the meaning of their sacred relationship to the earth and to "that place that the People talk about."

Pueblo peoples, like all Indigenous peoples, have a guiding story. According to some versions of this guiding story, humans now live in the fifth world. There were four worlds before this one, and in each of those worlds human beings had to learn something. They had to come to terms with an evolutionary task to, in a sense, become more complete as human beings. Each world metaphorically represents a stage of natural evolution through which human beings learn how to become more human. Pueblo people believe that they emerged from an earth navel, a place of mountains looked upon lovingly by the sun and the moon. It is believed that those first people were taught by certain animals, and that their thoughts were also guided by the evergreen tree of life. This was "that place that the People talk about."

Through guiding stories of creation many American Indian tribes symbolize the earth as a feminine being to whom all living things relate, and whose body follows the contours of the landscape. Indian people also represent these perceptions of life in relationship with the land in their oral traditions and through the symbols of art, ritual, and the attitudes and activities that all Indians have traditionally practiced. It is through these symbols and participating with the land in a kind of symbolic dance that Pueblo people have traditionally maintained the memory of their relationship to their places. Through traditional art forms such as pottery, which are replete with designs based on their relationship to the land, its plants, animals, Pueblo people have symbolized their sense of identity as a people of place. This continual establishing of relationship is not only for renewal and for remembering to remember who they are as a people, but is also an attempt to perpetuate the spiritual ecology of the world as a whole. This is the complex of relationship, symbolism, attitude, and way of interacting with the land that comprises the Pueblo theology of place.

Today there are still numerous communal reflections of natural affiliation among the Pueblo people of New Mexico. The place currently called "New Mexico" is also sometimes called "the land of enchantment." For some, one reason for the evocation of a feeling of enchantment is that New Mexico has been consecrated by the lives and communities of so many Pueblo people for many centuries. New Mexico is not only a place where geological and ecological regions intersect, it is also a meeting place of ideas, cultures, and ways of community.

INDIGENOUS ECOLOGY IN A POST-MODERN WORLD

Native people throughout the Americas developed environmentally sound ways of living with the land. Traditionally, they deeply understood and venerably practiced the concept of sustainability within a particular environment. This way of sustainable living evolved into numerous ways of maintaining harmony, both at the individual and communal level, in dynamic balance with the places in which Indian people have lived in North America. Ceremonial traditions combined with practical ecological knowledge expressed their orientation to sacred ecology and formed the basis for a theology of place.

However, American Indian people today live a dual existence. At times, it resembles a kind of schizophrenia in which people constantly try to adapt themselves to a mainstream social, political, and cultural system that is not their own. They are constantly faced with living in a larger society that does not really understand or respect their traditional life symbols, ecological perspectives, understanding of relationship to the land, and traditional ways of remembering to remember who they are. Moreover, because of modern education and Native peoples' long-term relationships with the U.S. government, many have moved away from a practiced and conscious relationship with place, or direct connection with their spiritual ecology. The results for many Indian communities are "existential" problems, such as high rates of alcoholism, suicide, abuse of self and others, depression, and other social and spiritual ills.

Tewa people call this state of schizophrenic-like existence *pingeh heh* (split thought or thinking, or doing things with only half of one's mind). As an Indian educator, I believe that modern Indian education ultimately has to be about healing this split. Healing the split is not a task for

Indian people only. It is also the task of others who consider themselves people of place, and thereby experience alienation from mainstream society as do many Indian people. Today everyone must "look to the mountain."

Much of what has been presented in this essay about Native American traditions and an Indigenous ecology is an ideal image. As mentioned above, in many Native communities these traditions have undergone significant deterioration. I am reminded of a sculpture by a former Pueblo student at the Institute of American Indian Arts (Santa Fe, New Mexico). She created a clay piece that symbolized her feelings as a young Native woman attempting to be an artist and live in two worlds (trying to be traditional and also modern). The clay sculpture was an androgynous figure sitting with its arms folded; its hands wrung around each other in such a way that the entire form expressed extreme anxiety. To extend this sculptural metaphor of anxiety, the head of the figure had been split in half. Half of the face was drawn up in a smile, and the other half drawn down in a frown. The artist's deeply felt sense of being split, torn as she was between diametrically opposed world views, captures the sense of fragmentation and the dilemma that we all face as modern people living in an ecologically schizophrenic world. The young artist felt a sense of "splitedness" and incompleteness.

My sense as an educator is that Indigenous education must now focus on the recovery of Native peoples' sensibility for natural affiliation and nurturance of this sensibility in their children. The education of the twenty-first century must be about healing this cultural and ecological split. Once again, healing this schizophrenia is not the task of Indigenous education, but the task of all education. Our quintessential educational task is that of reconnecting with our innate sense and need for natural affiliation.

Human interactive relationships with places give rise to and define human cultures and communities. As we change our landscape and allow the self-serving will of materialist economic systems to have sway over our view of the land, we also allow the natural landscape of mind and soul to be altered in the same measure. When we allow school curricula to serve the will of the "marketplace," we also allow the landscape of students' minds to be altered. The price we pay for such lack of consciousness in school curricula is incalculable. Indeed, with each generation since the turn of the century, Americans have collectively become more materially affluent. Yet, at the same time, each generation of Americans has become significantly more impoverished in terms of collective and individual connection to places that form the biological and geographic tapestry of America.

We must once again ask the perennial question, "What is education for?" Our collective answer to this ancient question carries with it consequences that are more profound now than ever before in the history of humankind. It is important to move beyond the idealization and patronization of Indigenous knowledge, which often leads to marginalization of the most profound Indigenous ways of knowing how human beings and nature interact. Indigenous people must be supported in their collective attempts to restore their traditions while also recreating and revitalizing themselves in ways they feel are appropriate in contemporary society.

Indigenous people have been touted as the spiritual leaders of the environmental movement. Such a designation is more symbolic than tangible since most environmental education is still primarily a reaction to the shortcomings of mainstream Western education. Still, many environmental educators, writers, and philosophers advocate getting back to the basics of relationship to environment and also to each other within communities, thereby paralleling the traditional practices of Indigenous societies. This is appropriate since Indigenous people around the world have much to share and much to give. The same peoples also continue to be among the most exploited and oppressed, and are usually the people who suffer the greatest loss of self and culture when dealing with various economic development and educational schemes. In spite of this, Indigenous groups around the world have a very important message, a message that is related in a number of ways to the evolving disciplines of eco-psychology and eco-philosophy.

As we begin our journeys to find the Indigenous mind-set that will allow for sustainable (and even restorative) ways of living at all levels, we must think about who we are and who we represent. Understand that each of us in our own small way is a vital link within the context of creating and remembering the reciprocal relationships that sustain and enliven the earth, flora and fauna, and human beings—in brief, local to global ecology. Whether the role you play is large or small, know that it has an effect. As you look to and imagine climbing the primordial mountain, reflect on your own life and understanding of what it means to be educated and intelligent. As you move from the mountain down a pathway to resume your journey guided by ecological thought and action, think about the journey of your life in relationship to a "place." It is the task of each of us to "look to the mountain" and build a vision of a sustainable future for the people inhabiting Mother Earth in the year 2000, 3000, and beyond.

Environmental Racism, American Indians, and Monitored Retrievable Storage Sites for Radioactive Waste

Shari Collins-Chobanian

Shari Collins-Chobanian is a professor of philosophy at Arizona State University West in Phoenix. She is coeditor of the first, second, and third editions of this anthology, has published on environmental rights, risk analysis, and harms imposed by technology, and is the editor of *Ethical Challenges to Business as Usual* (2004).

Collins-Chobanian addresses the controversial topic of environmental racism. She provides a brief history of how American Indians have been victims of environmental racism. American Indians have been affected by the generation and handling of radioactive waste and are now targeted for the storage of radioactive waste. She argues that this targeting is ethically unjustified.

I see no reason why those who use lethal methods of going about their business, who knowingly impose on others significant risk of death by radiation-related cancers—by poisoning from slow-seeping chemical wastes, from poisons emitted into air and water—should not be dealt with in the same way and in the same place as we deal with those who, for gain, send poisoned chocolates to their elderly relatives.

—Annette Baier[1]

Many people have claimed that the poor in general, and minorities in particular are not concerned with the quality of their environment, and will not be until they have achieved a certain economic status after their more basic and pressing needs are met.[2] Recently, many people have challenged this claim, arguing that the polluted environment that many live in is an extension of oppression, and bringing empirical evidence to bear regarding what is known as environmental racism. There is a growing body of evidence that confirms the charge that minority communities are targeted for the location of hazardous waste storage, incinerators, and chemical corporations. There is further evidence that where environmental harm has been established, the federal government does not provide the same protection to minority communities as it does to predominantly white communities.

According to Benjamin F. Chavis, Jr., the term "environmental racism" was coined in 1982 in Warren County, NC, a mostly African American community where residents were struggling to prevent a PCB landfill.[3] Environmental racism is defined as

> racial discrimination in environmental policymaking . . . in the enforcement of regulation and laws . . . in the deliberate targeting of communities of color for toxic waste disposal and the siting of polluting industries . . . [and] in the official sanctioning of the life-threatening presence of poisons and pollutants in communities of color.[4]

Awareness of environmental racism has sparked the environmental justice movement. People in this movement are trying to protect areas, especially communities of color, that have become environmental "sacrifice zones." American Indian lands are thought to be one such sacrifice zone. While the phenomenon of environmental racism has recently received much attention within minority, environmental, legal, and academic circles, much of the attention is focused on groups other than American Indians.

The purpose of this paper is to extend the philosophical discussion on environmental racism to include American Indians. American Indians have been harmed by radioactive waste from the generation (mining and milling) and handling of radioactive waste, and have been specifically targeted for the storage of our country's waste via monitored retrievable storage (MRS) site applications. I conclude, especially in light of the past harms in generation and handling of radioactive waste, that the targeting of American Indians for MRS sites is ethically unjustified, even if there is the appearance of consent to the MRS site. Without authentic voluntariness and informedness, this consent to these sites on American Indian land is unjustified.

AMERICAN INDIANS, RADIOACTIVE WASTE, AND THE ENVIRONMENT

The Four Corners region has the largest concentration of American Indians in the United States and includes the Diné (Navajo) and Zuni tribes. Shiprock, New Mexico is in the Four Corners area. In Shiprock, uranium tailings[5] were left from Kerr-McGee's uranium mining. By 1980, 133 of the 150 Navajo uranium miners that worked at the site (beginning in 1952) were either dead or sick from radiation. During operation, Kerr-McGee did not enforce standard safety measures, and this resulted in radiation levels in the mining shafts reaching 90 times the level considered "safe."[6] At the Shiprock site, and in the communities downstream along the San Juan watershed, these radiation levels have resulted in an increase in birth defects and disease which result from radiation

exposure.[7] Further, seventy-one acres of "raw" tailings were abandoned at the Shiprock site when Kerr-McGee left in 1980, and this waste is sixty feet from the San Juan River, the major water source for people in the area. As has subsequently been established in the Shiprock area, Navajo birth defects were "two to eight times as high as the national average," and "Microcephaly occurred at fifteen times the normal rate."[8] The Shiprock area is now thoroughly contaminated by radiation and sections have been targeted for a national nuclear waste dump.[9]

There is, as yet, no permanent storage facility for the disposal of radioactive waste. There is currently a permanent repository being built in Nevada, on seized Western Shoshone land. However, this site is of questionable geologic safety, the facility is over budget, past the projected deadline, and is opposed by the majority of Nevadans. Meanwhile, the federal government has, for more than a decade, been seeking MRS sites to store high-level radioactive waste until a permanent repository is available. At first this search was not focused on any particular group. Then the search narrowed and the DOE (Department of Energy) targeted American Indian tribes by offering them 100,000 dollars to apply for an MRS site, and claimed among other things that American Indian ties to the land and cultural longevity suited them for the stewardship of this waste. One such claim was made by David H. Leroy, a United States "Nuclear Waste Negotiator," who said, "With atomic facilities designed to safely hold radioactive materials with half-lives of thousands of years, *it is the Native American culture and perspective that is best designed to correctly consider and balance the benefits and burdens of these proposals.*"[10] The Council of Energy Resource Tribes has also held joint government, industry, and tribal conferences that were designed to identify tribal practices that could be utilized to build consent to MRS sites.[11]

The above cases concerning the nuclear industry and radioactive waste appear to be examples of environmental racism. I see Kerr-McGee's disregard of safety standards for the Navajo miners (the standards were enforced at other facilities) as an illustration of racial discrimination in the enforcement of environmental regulation, and thus as environmental racism. While I also see the federal government's targeting American Indians for waste storage as the "targeting communities of color for toxic waste disposal" as well as "the official sanctioning of the life-threatening presence of poisons and pollutants in communities of color," and thus, as environmental racism, this is still being debated.

Regarding this debate, I will consider two possible arguments for defending the tribal MRS site application process. In the first, sovereignty and the tribes' right to consent to MRS sites is the focus. Tribes, as sovereign entities, have the legal and ethical right to make decisions without outside interference, and can therefore consent to MRS facilities, even if these facilities place the tribes and their cultural base, land, at risk. In the second, the MRS applications are seen as offers of economic development extended to groups that are in need of such development, and these groups, in weighing the options, can thus consent to the risks involved in MRS sites. However, before turning to these arguments, I need to address a challenge that is often raised against the general claim of environmental racism. This challenge asserts that what is called environmental racism is, at the most, environmental classism.

WHY ENVIRONMENTAL RACISM IS NOT REDUCIBLE TO CLASSISM

One challenge to the claim of environmental racism is that it is not racism, but classism. The argument proceeds by asserting that polluted communities of color that are provided as examples of environmental racism are, more importantly, poor and politically powerless communities. The reason that these areas are targeted is because the land there is inexpensive and not because the areas are populated by people of color.[12] That is, economic reasons provide the overriding explanation for the dumps and location of manufacturing facilities, not race.

While there is an element of classism in the cases of environmental racism, these cases cannot be reduced to classism. Racism often persists even when people of color are wealthy. Examples are myriad, from the manner in which African Americans are treated when buying cars, homes, and insurance (there is a well-known "black tax" that is levied, i.e., a higher price than whites would pay) to the manner in which African American celebrities are discriminated against even though they have money. That is, racism is not reducible to classism.

Further evidence is provided by the statistical significance of race that has been illuminated in many national reports. The United States General Accounting Office issued a report in 1983 that covered eight Southeastern states. The report found that 75 percent of offsite commercial hazardous and toxic waste landfills were in African American and other minority communities, while these minorities make up only 20 percent of the population there. The report further showed that 60 percent of Hispanic and African Americans live in areas with uncontrolled toxic waste sites. Ten years later, in September, 1992, *The National Law Journal* published the results of a special investigation of "the racial divide in environmental law." Their investigation found that:

> Penalties under hazardous waste laws at sites having the greatest white population were about 500 percent higher than penalties at sites with the greatest minority population. . . . The disparity under the toxic waste law occurs by race alone, not income.[13]

Additionally, Superfund cleanup of abandoned sites in minority areas takes 20 percent longer to be placed on the priority list than those in white neighborhoods, and action at the Superfund sites begins 12 percent–42 percent later at minority sites. Given the preceding, the challenge that environmental racism is really a matter of environmental classism will not prevail. Racial bias in environmental policy is not reducible to classism. I now turn to the arguments of sovereignty and economic development that can be advanced against the charge of environmental racism in the MRS sitings.

SOVEREIGNTY AND CONSENT

As established under the Indian Reorganization Act of 1934, American Indian Nations are sovereign. Sovereign status acknowledges a tribe's autonomy, and entails the legal and ethical right to self-determination and to be free from external control. As discussed above, the government has an interest in acquiring MRS sites until a permanent repository is secured. Although MRS sites are "temporary" in that the waste is to be transferred to a permanent site eventually, once the utilities operating the nuclear power plants transfer the waste, they will be relieved of title and liability for the waste they generated. It will then become the tribes' legal and environmental responsibility. Twenty-nine tribes and counties applied for the grants but most dropped out. Two tribes that did not withdraw are the Mescalero Apache tribe and Ft. McDermitt tribe.[14]

The first argument defends the MRS application process by asserting that while American Indians have been encouraged to apply for MRS sites, it is not because of race. Rather the initial 100,000 dollars, and subsequent increased amounts, constitute offers to apply that were open to any community. Unlike cases of imposed dump sites, the MRS sites will not actualize on tribal land without consent of the tribes. Sovereignty, expressed in voluntary, informed consent, provides a prima facie justification for the tribes assuming the liability of radioactive waste.

Because consent is crucial to the above argument, an analysis of the justification for assuming risk(s) provided by voluntary, informed consent is necessary. The standard justification for a person risking harm to himself or herself is that he or she gives explicit, voluntary, and informed consent to that risk. Informed consent, while derived from medical malpractice caselaw, is a general legal and ethical principle that maintains a person's autonomy in ensuring that he or she is able to decide what risks he or she will take, because in deciding, he or she is able to weigh the risks against the benefits.

The following conditions are necessary for informed consent: all known existing relevant information regarding the risk(s) must be disclosed; the information disclosed must be understood; the risk must be undertaken voluntarily; the risk-taker(s) must be competent to decide; and the risk-taker(s) must consent to the risk.[15] If the above conditions are met, the necessary, although not sufficient, criteria for justifying the explicit assumption of a risk are met. I will briefly address the necessity of each of these criteria, and why they are not sufficient to justify assumption of a risk.

The first criterion, disclosure, places a duty on those seeking consent to provide available information. Without all known existing relevant information, an agent will not have the data necessary to make an authentic choice between accepting or rejecting the action and its risk(s). The second criterion, that the information be understood, also places a duty on those providing the information to ensure that what is provided is understood. This prevents a perfunctory disclosure that meets the first criterion in a legalistic sense, and places a duty on those providing the information to impart it in a language and in terms that are understood by the audience. The third criterion of voluntariness is also necessary. For an agent's act to be his own, he must be able to act on his choice, and not be forced to act or restrained from acting by another person, group, or situation. Competence, the fourth criterion, is necessary for it involves the general state of mind of the agent, the ability of that agent to be held responsible for her decisions, and to be able to foresee that responsibility and the risks involved. Competence ensures that a person is not under the influence of a mind-altering substance, under an age competent to make the decision at hand, or unable to understand the issue(s). Competence is necessary for it involves the general state of mind of the agent, the ability of that agent to be held responsible for her decisions, and to be able to forsee that responsibility and risks involved. Consent is the final condition. Without the actual act of consent, the agent has done nothing more than be informed about risks and freely deliberated on them.

Each of the criteria for informed consent will vary along a continuum and need to be considered on a case by case basis. That is, there is not an a priori point at which each criterion can be said to have been fulfilled. However, this variability does not diminish the necessity of each condition being met.

While the above discussion focuses on a single agent giving informed consent, groups can also meet these criteria and give informed consent to an action that risks harm to their group and community. The decision-making procedure will most likely involve group dialogue and an agreed-upon mechanism for making decisions. Issues concerning who will be competent to take part in the dialogue, and issues concerning varying degrees of comprehension within the group will need to be considered on a case by case basis. What will count as consent, whether it is unanimity, majority consent, or some other measure, will also have to be decided in context. What will not vary is that the criteria will need to be met in both individual and group situations. The five conditions remain necessary in order to ensure the autonomy that informed consent is required to secure.

However, authentic informed consent is not sufficient for an agent or a group to undertake a risk, for the conditions of informed consent can be met while violating a more important moral issue. Such issues include harm to others, the degree of harmful effects risked, and whether the risks undertaken are reasonable. While autonomy is an important moral value and is maximized by ensuring informed consent, when there are competing claims of autonomy they cannot be decided by appeal to informed consent, but must be adjudicated in the broader social arena.

In addition, inherent in risk-taking is the notion that there is a benefit from taking the risk.[16] Based on the above discussion, to justify exposure to radioactive waste, those exposed would need to consent freely to the risks after being adequately informed, fully comprehend the risks being taken, be competent to make the decision, and benefit from this risk-taking in a manner that was proportionate to the risk.[17]

The Mescalero Apache tribe, located in Mescalero, New Mexico, has applied for, and received, a final grant of about $3 million to study their land for an MRS site.[18] Wendell Chino, the tribal council president, has tribal constitutional power to negotiate with the federal government on behalf of the tribe without being required to obtain explicit tribal consent. Thus, there is apparent consent via Chino's pursuit on behalf of the Mescalero Apache tribe to an MRS site. However, there is also opposition in the tribe, although it is subdued. Harlyn Geronimo, a tribal member, claims that 70 percent of the tribe is opposed and that more would be if they understood the issues.[19] Francie Magoosh, also a tribal member, claims that 95 percent of the tribe is opposed.[20] Another tribe, the Ft. McDermitt tribe, on the Nevada and Oregon border, has also advanced in the site application process and is in the second stage. Their constitution requires more democratic participation, but it has been disregarded by the tribe's chairperson.[21] It is important to remember that as sovereign entities, tribes can adopt their own constitutions, including bestowing power that does not require the tribal leader to obtain informed consent on every issue.

I heartily agree that, given sovereign status, tribes have the legal and ethical right to negotiate with the federal government, to make decisions free from outside interference, and to consent to risks. However, especially in light of harm from the radioactive waste left from mining and milling, it is necessary to ensure that sovereignty does not bypass the process of informed consent. Given the magnitude of risks associated with waste, the justification of informed consent is necessary for the argument advanced in favor of MRS application. Thus, while sovereignty provides a prima facie justification, informed consent may be absent in a sovereign's decision, and if informed consent is absent, the justification is called into question.

Thus, one criterion for informed consent, informedness is called into question by the apparent lack of authentic participation by most of the tribe in the decision-making process. Informedness is further called into question by a lack of tribal education about nuclear waste. A lack of education is relevant to comprehension of the risks at issue, the options available, and the transfer of the responsibility for the waste. There are many points that illustrate the magnitude of the risks from radioactive waste. For example, if the waste is stored at the generation point, it is, compared to alternatives, cost-efficient, has an established record, and does not require the creation of further risks by transporting the waste. Moreover, an MRS facility on American Indian lands exempts waste manufacturers from liability of harm and transfers the burden from those who in some sense benefited from generation of the waste, to those who did not. It is important to keep in mind that much of this waste has a hazardous life of 240,000 plus years.

The tribes targeted are mostly nontechnical communities and lack knowledge of the full range of harms that nuclear technology and its waste impose. On most levels we all do. This lack of technical knowledge is intensified by the fact that many American Indians may be suspicious of what information is presented to them, especially in light of hundreds of years of lies and broken treaties and promises. Although the tribes are sovereign and can justifiably enter into negotiations, consent of tribal members remains crucial to the justification for MRS siting, and consent was compromised by the lack of informedness. In addition, their criterion of voluntariness is also problematic, as I argue below.

ECONOMIC DEVELOPMENT

According to the 1990 United States Census, American Indians constitute less than 1 percent of the population, yet make up 30.9 percent of those who live in poverty. In contrast, whites constitute more than 80 percent of the population, and only have 9.8 percent living at the poverty level. Unemployment is also a serious problem on the reservations. For example, the Ft. McDermitt Tribe had an 80 percent unemployment rate in 1993, and this is not atypical of reservation statistics.[22] MRS site applications can therefore be defended as offers of economic development extended to groups that are in need of economic benefits that could alleviate poverty. It can be argued that as long as these tribes provide voluntary, informed consent to the risks associated with MRS sites, in exchange for

economic benefit, that this is justifiable economic development and not environmental racism. I will first turn to the issue of economic development.

Far from being a self-evident justification for assuming risks, economic duress compromises voluntary consent. Voluntariness is called into question when the lack of money and jobs provides few to no alternatives to the dangerous proposal of storing unwanted waste. The lack of authentic choices is evident in the following quote:

> Garbage and hazardous waste firms are all too aware of the fact that the majority of reservations, which are governed by sovereign tribal leaders, are void of strict environmental regulations and the technical personnel to properly oversee such facilities. They are also keenly aware that many tribes, often faced with unemployment rates of 80 percent or higher, are desperate for both jobs and capital.[23]

The dilemma is that the closer one is to necessity to consent out of duress, the further one is from the voluntary consent being sought to justify the action. The more one does not appear to have a choice and is in a situation where one must "accept the risks associated with this radioactive waste or remain well below the poverty level," the more difficult it will be to arrive at voluntary consent.

As discussed above, the federal government has targeted American Indian communities through national conferences concerning MRS sites held for American Indians, through attempts to foster consent to the sites on tribal land, through the 100,000 dollar application bonuses, and through claims that American Indians are particularly suited for stewardship of the waste. If the sites were to provide economic development, why were other similar groups not courted? For example, Hispanics account for almost one-third of those living at the poverty level in the United States, yet Hispanic communities have not been the target of these applications. Thus, economic need does not appear to be the overarching factor for site applications. In addition, poor, white communities were not encouraged to negotiate for MRS sites. The defense of economic development devoid of environmental racism, like the above claim of sovereignty and consent, therefore will not prevail.

One final note regarding these sites. Even if MRS sites did provide relief from economic duress, they may be a myopic solution since the health risks could preclude all benefits hoped for. Minorities in general, and American Indians in particular (American Indians as a group have the lowest per capita income in the United States) suffer from a lack of iron, calcium, and zinc, among other nutritional deficiencies, and are therefore at a higher risk from exposure to toxic waste, and have less access to healthcare.[24] Therefore, the risk to these populations is even higher than it is to the majority population. This should, at least, lead to a discussion in the broader social arena concerning the degree of harm that is risked, as well as the reasonableness of the risks themselves. It may be that there are many options that could be taken to improve the economic situation that do not carry the serious risks that accepting an MRS site entail.

CONCLUSION

The above concerns over voluntariness and informedness call the issue of American Indian consent to MRS sites into question. The racist history of this country, from European contact forward, has firmly established groups that suffer disproportionately from poverty and all of its accompanying ills. The imposition of environmental racism further extends this disproportionate suffering. To further burden American Indians with the "offer" to "benefit" from an MRS site is unjustified.

Perhaps American Indians accepting MRS sites could be justified if there were truly no other options. However, the lack of options is an empirical question that entails a very broad picture where all possible measures have been taken to ensure the exhaustion of such possibilities. With the inequalities in wealth, nutrition, healthcare, education, political power, and economic resources that exist between corporate and governmental interests and minorities, advocating a deadly economic

"solution" of storing toxic waste to meet needs that have been created through a racist history is unjustifiable.

Rather, the preferred solution is to end the production and resultant dumping of these hazardous wastes. In cases where this is not possible, then those who benefit from the production of this waste should bear the burden of storage and the resultant risks in a nontransferable manner. Furthermore, those who benefited from past generation of hazardous waste, and transferred those burdens, should be required to take responsibility for the harms that have occurred, and those that continue to occur in the communities such as those in the Shiprock area.

NOTES

1. Annette Baier, "Poisoning the Wells," in *Values at Risk*, Douglas MacLean, editor. (Totowa: Rowan & Allanheld, 1986), p. 64.
2. See William K. Reilly, "The Green Thumb of Capitalism: The Environmental Benefits of Sustainable Growth," *Policy Review*, Fall 1990.
3. Five hundred protesters were arrested, and the protesters saw the authorities' behavior as another instance of institutionalized racism many had encountered in the past. The institutional racism many had experienced in the past included discrimination by law enforcement, in housing, in education, and in employment. Benjamin Chavis, Jr., in the foreword to *Confronting Environmental Racism: Voices from the Grassroots*, Robert D. Bullard, editor. (Boston: South End Press, 1993), p. 3.
4. Chavis, from Bullard, 1993, p. 3.
5. "Uranium tailings—contain dangerously radioactive radium, radon gases, and 'radon daughters'—short-lived radionuclides produced as the radon in the ore decays into lead. 'Radon daughters' are dangerous because they attach themselves to dust particles which can be inhaled. Once lodged in the lung tissue, these particles emit intense alpha radiation, which can damage the surrounding cells and eventually cause lung cancer and other respiratory disease." Leslie J. Freeman, *Nuclear Witnesses: Insiders Speak Out*, (New York: W. W. Norton & Company, 1981), pp. 140–141. There are over 70,000,000 tons of radioactive tailings in New Mexico alone.
6. In addition, Kerr-McGee paid the Navajo miners 2/3 the standard rate for uranium miners.
7. Ward Churchill and Winona LaDuke, "The Political Economy of Radioactive Colonialism," in *The State of Native America*, M. Annette Jaimes, editor, (Boston: South End Press, 1992), p. 248. See also J. M. Samet, et al., "Uranium Mining and Lung Cancer in Navajo Men," *New England Journal of Medicine*, No. 310, 1984,

pp. 1481–1484; and Ward Churchill, *Struggle for the Land: Indigenous Resistance to Genocide, Ecocide, and Expropriation in Contemporary North America,* (Monroe, ME: Common Courage Press, 1993).

8. Quoted in Churchill and LaDuke, Op. Cit., p. 264. From an unpublished paper presented at the May 25, 1984 American Association of Atomic Scientists symposium in New York, "Outcome of 13,300 Navajo Births from 1964–1981 in the Shiprock Uranium Mining Area," by Laura Mangum Shields and Alan B. Goodman.

9. There are many other examples of environmental racism on American Indian land. The Kerr-McGee Sequoyah Fuels Facility lies within the Cherokee nation in Oklahoma. From accidental leaks, as well as intentional use of radioactive waste for "fertilizer," radioactive contamination has spread into water supplies. See Hans Baer, "Kerr-McGee and the NRC: From Indian Country to Silkwood to Gore," *Soc. Sci. Med.,* Vol. 30, No. 2, 1990, pp. 237–248. In 1991, the *St. Louis Post-Dispatch* reported that in the two previous years, more than 50 tribes had been approached by toxic waste companies. See Bill Lambrecht, "Broken Trust" series, *St. Louis Post-Dispatch,* November, 1991. The fact that these companies approach American Indians for waste sites, and not white communities, (poor or affluent), lends further weight to the intentional racism claimed in cases of environmental racism.

10. David H. Leroy, "Federalism on Your Terms: An Invitation for Dialogue, Government to Government," in a speech given to the National Congress of American Indians, San Francisco, December 4, 1991, quoted in Erickson and Chapman, Op. Cit., 1994, p. 3. (emphasis mine)

11. J. A. A. Hernandez, "How the Feds Push Nuclear Waste onto Indian Lands," *SF Weekly,* September 23, Vol XI, No. 30, 1992, cited in Jon D. Erickson and Duane Chapman, "Sovereignty for Sale: Nuclear Waste in Indian Country," *Akwe:kon Journal: A Journal of Indigenous Issues,* Fall, 1993, pp. 8, 10.

12. Some people further argue that minorities move into these neighborhoods because of lower prices, thus the areas were already polluted, and not targeted because of race. For an excellent analysis of this issue and evidence of targeted expansion, see James T. Hamilton, "Testing for Environmental Racism: Prejudice, Profits, Political Power?" in *Journal of Policy Analysis and Management,* Vol. 14, No. 1, 1995, pp. 107–132. Hamilton argues that the targeting is due to the perception of political powerlessness. However, this is intricately tied to race.

13. "Unequal Protection: The Racial Divide in Environmental Law," *The National Law Journal,* Vol. 15, No. 3, September 21, 1992, p. S2.

14. See Jon D. Erickson and Duane Chapman, "Sovereignty for Sale: Nuclear Waste in Indian Country," *Akwe:kon Journal: A Journal of Indigenous Issues,* Fall 1993, pp. 3–10; and Ronald Eagleye Johnny, "Showing Respect for Tribal Law: Siting a Nuclear Waste MRS Facility," *Akwe:kon Journal,* Spring 1994, pp. 16–27.

15. This is drawn from Ruth R. Faden and Tom L. Beauchamp, *A History and Theory of Informed Consent,* (New York: Oxford University Press, 1986).

16. For a discussion of the principle of commensurate burdens and benefit, see Peter Wenz, "Just Garbage," in *Faces of Environmental Racism: Confronting Issues of Global Justice,* Laura Westra and Peter S. Wenz, editors. (Lanham, MD: Rowman & Littlefield Publishers, Inc., 1995), pp. 59–60.

17. Informed consent would provide a justification further assuming that the issue of MRS sites could be justified in broader social arena, as mentioned above.

18. See Matthew L. Wald, "Nuclear Storage Divides Apaches and Neighbors," *The New York Times,* November, 1993, p. 1.

19. Priscilla Feral and Betsy Smart, "Laying Waste: The Future of the Mescalero Apaches," in *Trial Lawyer,* September 1992, pp. 78–82.

20. Jon D. Erickson and Duane Chapman, "Sovereignty for Sale: Nuclear Waste in Indian Country," *Akwe:kon Journal: A Journal of Indigenous Issues,* Fall 1993, p. 8.

21. Ibid.

22. Ibid.

23. Senator Thomas Daschle, "Send Your Poisonous Garbage to the Sioux," *Christian Science Monitor,* February 1991.

24. From discussions with Karen Medville, an American Indian environmental toxicologist who studies environmental toxicology on American Indian lands.

STUDY QUESTIONS: ENVIRONMENTAL ETHICS

1. White contends that Christianity can explain our attitudes to nature even if we ourselves are not Christian. What is his argument? Why do we need to adopt a revised approach to Christianity in order to change our relationship with nature?

2. Jamieson argues that there is convergence between animal rights issues and environmental ethics, and provides an example of consuming beef as an area wherein the goals of both areas converge. Why does he argue that they converge, how do they converge, and how might Leopold's land ethic be used to analyze the consumption of beef?

3. Why does Elliot think that a reconstructed forest has less value than a pristine one, even if no one knows that it is artificial? Do you think a real reconstruction can ever be so successful?

4. Baxter argues that the only normative definition of pollution is in relation to man's needs. Why does he argue that an "optimal state of pollution" and not a clean environment should be our objective? In light of Leopold's essay, can such firm lines be drawn between humans and non-humans?

5. What is the American Indian "theology of place" Cajete writes about? How are relationships—with the entire ecosystem—central to American Indian views as presented by Cajete? What ethical duties result from these relationships?

6. Collins-Chobanian argues that the targeting of American Indian lands for MRS sites, even if there is apparent consent, is unjustified. Briefly explain her argument. If consent to these sites were not compromised, would the siting be justified?

SUPPLEMENTARY READINGS: ENVIRONMENTAL ETHICS

AMES, ROGER T. "Taoism and the Nature of Nature." *Environmental Ethics*, vol. 8, Winter 1986.

BOOTH, ANNIE, and WAYNE JACOBS. "Ties That Bind: Native American Beliefs as a Foundation for Environmental Consciousness." *Environmental Ethics*, vol. 12. Spring 1990.

BROWN, PHIL, and EDWIN J. MIKKELSEN. *No Safe Place: Toxic Waste, Leukemia, and Community Action.* Berkeley: University of California Press, 1990.

BULLARD, ROBERT D., editor. *Confronting Environmental Racism.* Boston: South End Press, 1993.

CALLICOTT, J. BAIRD. "Conceptual Resources for Environmental Ethics in Asian Traditions of Thought: A Propaedeutic." *Philosophy East and West*, vol. 37(2), April 1987.

CHENG, CHUNG-YING. "On the Environmental Ethics of the *Tao* and the *Ch'i*" in *Environmental Ethics,* vol. 8(4), 1986.

GUHA, RAMACHANDRA. "Radical American Environmentalism and Wilderness Preservation: A Third World Critique." *Environmental Ethics*, vol. 11(1), 1989.

HALL, DAVID L. "On Seeking a Change of Environment. A Quasi-Taoist Proposal." *Philosophy East and West.* vol. 37(2), April 1987.

HARGROVE, EUGENE C. "Anglo-American Land Use Attitudes." *Environmental Ethics*, vol. 2, Summer 1980.

INADA, KENNETH K. "Environmental Problematics in the Buddhist Context." *Philosophy East and West*, vol. 37(2), April 1987.

LEOPOLD, ALDO. "The Land Ethic" from *A Sand County Almanac: With Other Essays on Conservation from Round River* by Aldo Leopold. Oxford University Press, 1968.

MAGRAW, DANIEL, and JAMES NICKEL. "Can Today's International System Handle Transboundary Environmental Problems?" In *Upstream/Downstream*, Donald Scherer, editor. Philadelphia: Temple University Press, 1990.

MERCHANT, CAROLYN. "Women of the Progressive Conservation Movement." *Environmental Review*, vol. 8, Spring 1984.

OPHULS, WILLIAM. *Ecology and the Politics of Scarcity.* San Francisco: W. H. Freeman and Company, 1977.

REILLY, WILLIAM K. "The Green Thumb of Capitalism: The Environmental Benefits of Sustainable Growth." *Policy Review*, Fall 1990.

ROLLIN, BERNARD E. "Environmental Ethics and International Justice," in *Problems of International Justice*, Luper-Foy, editor. Boulder, CO: Westview Press, 1988.

SAGOFF, MARK. "Zuckerman's Dilemma: A Plea For Environmental Ethics." *Hastings Center Report*, September–October 1991.

SHIVA, VANDANA. "Deveolpment, Ecology, and Women," from *Staying Alive: Women, Ecology, and Development*, by Vandana Shiva. Zed Books, 1988.

SHRADER-FRECHETTE, KRISTIN. *Nuclear Power and Public Policy.* Dordrecht: D. Reidel Publishing Co., 1980.

WARREN, KAREN J. "The Power and the Promise of Ecological Feminism." *Environmental Ethics*, vol. 12(2), 1990.

ZAIDI, IQTIDAR H. "On the Ethics of Man's Interaction with the Environment: An Islamic Approach." *Environmental Ethics*, vol. 3, Spring 1980.

Part IV

HUNGER AND POVERTY

For ye have the poor with you always, and whensoever ye will ye may do them good. . .
—MARK 14:7

Poverty is the worst form of violence.
—MAHATMA GANDHI

The statistics on poverty and hunger in the world today are staggering. According to the U.N., there were 963 million hungry people in 2008, up 40 million from the year before.[1] One third of children in developing countries suffer from malnutrition.[2] Eighteen million people die each year from hunger and poverty related causes. Since the year 2000, this number totals almost 162 million people. The number of people who live on less than $1 a day is 1.1 billion, and 40 percent of the world's population—more than 2.4 billion people—live on less than $2 a day.[3] Further, 1.1 billion people lack access to clean drinking water, and more than twice that number live without adequate sanitation.[4] In Asia, Sub-Saharan Africa, and the Middle East, half of all women and one third of all men are illiterate.[5]

Recent food shortages such as the food crisis of 2008 and increasing energy prices mean these numbers have gotten worse.[6] The World Bank estimates that 100 million more people may fall below the extreme poverty line as a result of the food shortages in 2008.[7] Between 2007 and 2008, there was an increase of 100 million hungry people.[8] In addition, 2008 saw the price of food increase by 50 percent.[9]

On the other hand, the richest 5 percent of the world's population control one third of the world's income, the richest 10 percent enjoy one half of the world's income,[10] and the richest 20 percent have 80 percent of the world's income.[11] Recent trends suggest global inequality is on the rise.[12] This suggests that the problems we face will only grow worse unless we take swift action.

In addition to the easily preventable suffering that millions of people face, there are also indirect consequences of worldwide poverty. First, poverty can lead to overpopulation. Poor, uneducated women tend to have more children and birth rates tend to drop when poverty is alleviated.[13] Thus poverty and overpopulation become a vicious cycle. Women also tend to have more children when birth mortality rates and child mortality rates are high. In other words, individuals have fewer children when they can be reasonably sure that their children will survive to adulthood.

Furthermore, poverty often leads to war and violence. For example, according to Oxfam, lack of resources, in particular lack of access to clean drinking water, is the cause for many national conflicts. The case of the conflict in Darfur is a particularly well-known, though controversial, example of this phenomenon. According to U.N. reports and U.N. secretary general Ban Ki-moon, the genocide in Darfur can be traced in part to droughts and insufficient water in the region. But Darfur is not the only example. According to research by Oxford economist Paul Collier, "If a country's per capita income doubles, its risk of conflict drops by roughly half."[14] His research suggests that poverty is the most important contributing factor to civil war, above ethnic, racial, and political tensions.

What, then, are we to do? What is the proper response to world poverty? Does the suffering of others impose any duties on us? How stringent are these duties? The articles in this chapter will address these important questions. Each article proceeds from the notion that world poverty exists and that it is a wrong. However, the authors differ on what action these facts warrant. The range of positions the authors take is broad, from Singer, who advocates a drastic change in our lifestyles to immediately eradicate all poverty, to Narveson, who argues that no action is necessary.

In the first article in this section, Garrett Hardin argues against helping the world's poor. Not only are such efforts bound to fail, he claims, but they are also likely to cause more harm than good. First, he argues that past efforts to send food aid abroad have been unsuccessful in reducing the number of hunger-stricken people in the world. Instead, these efforts have merely made a few farmers, lobbyists, and food transport workers very wealthy. Next, he claims that famine relief tends to cause energy crises in the population it targets, arguing that any food aid must be accompanied by supplementary fuel aid. However, sending the amount of food and fuel necessary to combat the problem is unrealistic. Finally, he argues that poverty and hunger reduction will wreak havoc on the victims of poverty and hunger by causing overpopulation and environmental degradation, and by setting the stage for civil unrest and warfare.

While Hardin argues that it is impossible to help the hungry, Jan Narveson argues that we have no responsibility to do so. Our responsibility to provide aid, he argues, is dependent on whether or not we have caused the starvation or poverty in the first place. However, he argues that we have not caused these tragedies, and thus it is our prerogative to decide whether or not to help. In other words, we may choose to be charitable if we wish, but we have no duty to alleviate hunger that we did not cause and the hungry have no positive right to be fed.

The next two articles offer positions on the opposite side of the debate. They both argue that we do have duties to help the poor, and those moral requirements are much stronger than we may have thought. In "Famine, Affluence, and Morality," Singer gives a utilitarian argument for why there are strong moral reasons to help the poor. Unlike Hardin, Singer thinks it is not only within our power to help those worse off than ourselves but also that it is very easy. We can alleviate the world's hunger and poverty without undergoing noticeable sacrifices. However, there is a general moral duty to prevent any easily avoidable harm. Therefore, there is a moral duty to help those who are suffering. According to Singer, it is morally wrong to buy a new pair of shoes when people are starving; every dollar spent on luxuries is an unjustified use of our money.

Thomas Pogge continues this line of thought in his article, "A Cosmopolitan Perspective on the Global Economic Order." In contrast to Narveson, Pogge argues that we are in fact responsible for the poverty and hunger that exist in the world. He argues that we are currently enforcing radical inequalities caused by colonialism. Next, he gives a Lockean account for why our property rights do not hold up against the kind of poverty faced by millions. Third, he argues that the global economic order fails to meet the requirements of justice using consequentialist grounds. By arguing for his thesis on the basis of a range of different ethical and political standpoints, Pogge hopes to give his argument more rhetorical power. Finally, Pogge suggests changes to the status quo to make the world more just.

In the next article, Margaret Battin tackles the problem of poverty from the perspective of overpopulation. Overpopulation, she argues, is a grave problem and is to blame for much of the poverty and hunger that exist in the world. However, she continues, overpopulation does not exist because people want too many children, but rather because too many children are conceived accidentally. For example, according to Battin, 50 percent of pregnancies in the United States are unplanned. Battin argues that the best way to curb population growth is to prevent unwanted pregnancies in the first place with automatic, reversible contraception like intrauterine devices or subdermal implants. These contraceptives prevent pregnancy up to 8 years and are 200 times more effective than the condom, but their effects are completely reversible. If everyone were required to use these "background" contraceptives, then sexual relations would result in pregnancy only when women want them to. This solution to overpopulation, she argues, is ethical as long as every woman worldwide is forced to use such contraceptives and they are reversible without restriction.

Many argue that traditional agriculture cannot sustain current populations and the solution to world hunger is genetically modified organisms (GMOs).[15] In the last article, Mae-Wan Ho challenges this position by attacking the proposed benefits of GMOs. Far from being a solution to our hunger problems, Ho argues that GMOs cause irreparable damage to human populations and the environment. According to Ho, GMOs attack biodiversity by jumping to wild strains of plants, promote unsustainable mono-culture farming that requires harsher pesticides not necessary in farms containing more than one crop, deplete the nutritional value of food, and even cause susceptibility to cancer and E. coli in human beings.

In this chapter, the authors address both normative and practical problems associated with world poverty. Many practical solutions are proposed or attacked, from universal birth control to genetically modified crops. But we also will have to face important theoretical concerns to address this practical problem. In the chapter on human rights, we included the Universal Declaration of Human Rights. It states in Article 25, "Everyone has the right to a standard of living adequate for the health and well-being of himself and of his family, including food, clothing, housing and medical care and necessary social services, and the right to security in the event of unemployment, sickness, disability, widowhood, old age or other lack of livelihood in circumstances beyond his control." In order to address world poverty, we will need to consider the existence and content of human rights, to challenge our preconceived notions about property rights, and to understand the moral force of human suffering according to the utilitarian.

—JILL DELSTON

NOTES

1. Food and Agriculture Organization of the United Nations, "The State of Food Insecurity in the World 2008: High Food Prices and Food Security—Threats and Opportunities."
2. http://www.unicef.org/nutriiton/index_bigpicture.html.
3. Food and Agriculture Organization of the United Nations, "State of Food Insecurity in 2006."
4. World Water Council, "Water Supply and Sanitation."
5. According to the CIA World Fact Book, https://www.cia.gov/library/publications/the-world-factbook/geos/xx.html.
6. Ironically, this food crisis was caused in part by the desire to find environmentally sound alternatives to gasoline and oil. Ethanol, which is made from corn, was purported to be a green solution to the problem. However, by diverting food sources to fuel and spending big government subsidies on corn crops, a shortage in food was created.
7. Although it is not clear, this trend will continue. Since 2008, prices have leveled out. However, they remain high relative to recent years. See OXFAM, "A Billion Hungry People: Governments and Aid Agencies Must Rise to the Challenge."
8. UNICEF, "2009 Humanitarian Action Report," http://www.unicef.org/har09.
9. UNICEF, "2009 Humanitarian Action Report," http://www.unicef.org/har09.
10. United Nations Development Program, "2007 Human Development Report (HDR)," November 27, 2007.
11. Branko Milanovic, "Global Income and Inequality: What It Is and Why It Matters?" DESA Working Paper No. 26, United Nations Department of Economic and Social Affairs.
12. Thomas Pogge, World Poverty and Human Rights. Polity Press, 2002, p. 2.
13. Thomas Pogge, World Poverty and Human Rights. Polity Press, 2002, p. 8.
14. Paul Collier, "The Market for Civil War" in Foreign Policy, No. 136.
15. For example, "golden rice," a genetically modified form of rice that includes vitamin A, is heralded as a solution to Third World nutritional deficiencies.

Carrying Capacity as an Ethical Concept

Garrett Hardin

Garrett Hardin is a professor of biology at the University of California, Santa Barbara. His books include *Population, Evolution, and Birth Control* (1969), *The Limits of Altruism: An Ecologist's View of Survival* (1977), and *Promethean Ethics: Living with Death, Competition, and Triage* (1980).

Hardin supports a "lifeboat ethics" that is adapted from the notion of the tragedy of the commons. He argues that the developed countries should not help countries with starving people, such as those in India, by sending only food. He explains that the notion that those who are starving can be helped by food-only shipments is ill-founded because it assumes a fixed amount of people and progress in conquering starvation. Hardin asserts that in sending food we are seriously harming countries like India. He emphasizes that we can "never merely do one thing," and that supplying only food worsens political and economic strife, agricultural dependency, overpopulation, and environmental degradation.

Lifeboat Ethics is merely a special application of the logic of the commons.[1] The classic paradigm is that of a pasture held as common property by a community and governed by the following rules: first, each herdsman may pasture as many cattle as he wishes on the commons; and second, the gain from the growth of cattle accrues to the individual owners of the cattle. In an underpopulated world the system of the commons may do no harm and may even be the most economic way to manage things, since management costs are kept to a minimum. In an overpopulated (or overexploited) world a system of the commons leads to ruin, because each herdsman has more to gain individually by increasing the size of his herd than he has to lose as a single member of the community guilty of lowering the carrying capacity of the environment. Consequently he (with others) overloads the commons.

Edited Excerpt from Garrett Hardin, "Carrying capacity as an ethical concept" in Soundings: An Interdisciplinary Journal, Vol. 59, No. 1, 1976. Reprinted by permission.

Even if an individual fully perceives the ultimate consequences of his actions he is most unlikely to act in any other way, for he cannot count on the restraint *his* conscience might dictate being matched by a similar restraint on the part of *all* the others. (Anything less than all is not enough.) Since mutual ruin is inevitable, it is quite proper to speak of the *tragedy* of the commons.

Tragedy is the price of freedom in the commons. Only by changing to some other system (socialism or private enterprise, for example) can ruin be averted. In other words, in a crowded world survival requires that some freedom be given up. (We have, however, a choice in the freedom to be sacrificed.) Survival is possible under several different politico-economic systems—but not under the system of the commons. When we understand this point, we reject the ideal of distributive justice stated by Karl Marx a century ago. "From each according to his ability, to each according to his needs."[2] This ideal might be defensible if "needs" were defined by the larger community rather than by the individual (or individual political unit) *and if "needs" were static.*[3] But in the past quarter-century, with the best will in the world, some humanitarians have been asserting that rich populations must supply the needs of poor populations even though the recipient populations increase without restraint. At the United Nations conference on population in Bucharest in 1973, spokesmen for the poor nations repeatedly said in effect: "We poor people have the right to reproduce as much as we want to: you in the rich world have the responsibility of keeping us alive."

Such a Marxian disjunction of rights and responsibilities inevitably tends toward tragic ruin for all. It is almost incredible that this position is supported by thoughtful persons, but it is. How does this come about? In part, I think, because language deceives us. When a disastrous loss of life threatens, people speak of a "crisis," implying that the threat is temporary. More subtle is the implication of quantitative stability built into the pronoun "they" and its relatives. Let me illustrate this point with quantified prototype statements based on two different points of view.

Crisis analysis: "*These* poor people (1,000,000) are starving, because of a crisis (flood, drought, or the like). How can we refuse *them* (1,000,000)? Let us feed *them* (1,000,000). Once the crisis is past, those who are still hungry are few (say 1,000) and there is no further need for our intervention."

Crunch analysis: "*Those* (1,000,000) who are hungry are reproducing. We send food to *them* (1,010,000). *Their* lives (1,020,000) are saved. But since the environment is still essentially the same, the next year *they* (1,030,000) ask for more food. We send it to *them* (1,045,000); and the next year *they* (1,068,000) ask for still more. Since the need has not gone away, it is a mistake to speak of a passing crisis: it is evidently a permanent crunch that this growing 'they' face—a growing disaster, not a passing state of affairs."

"They" increases in size. Rhetoric makes no allowance for a ballooning pronoun. Thus, we can easily be deceived by language. We cannot deal adequately with ethical questions if we ignore quantitative matters. This attitude has been rejected by James Sellers, who dismisses prophets of doom from Malthus[4] to Meadows[5] as "chiliasts."

Chiliasts (or millenialists, to use the Latin-derived equivalent of the Greek term) predict a catastrophic end of things a thousand years from some reference point. The classic example is the prediction of Judgment Day in the year 1000 anno Domini. Those who predicted it were wrong, of course; but the fact that this specific prediction was wrong is no valid criticism of the use of numbers in thinking. Millenialism is numerology, not science.

In science, most of the time, it is not so much exact numbers that are important as it is the relative size of numbers and the direction of change in the magnitude of them. Much productive analysis is accomplished with only the crude quantification of "order of magnitude" thinking. First and second derivatives are often calculated with no finer aim than to find out if they are positive or negative. Survival can hinge on the crude issue of the sign of change, regardless of number. This is a far cry from the spurious precision of numerology. Unfortunately the chasm between the "two cultures," as C.P. Snow called them,[6] keeps many in the nonscientific culture from understanding the significance of the quantitative approach. One is tempted to wonder also whether an additional impediment to understanding may not be the mortal sin called Pride, which some theologians regard as the mother of all sins.

Returning to Marx, it is obvious that the *each* in "to each according to his needs" is not—despite the grammar—a unitary, stable entity: "each" is a place holder for a ballooning variable. Before we commit ourselves to saving the life of *each* and every person in need we had better ask this question: "*And then what?*" That is, what about tomorrow, what about posterity? As Hans Jonas has pointed out,[7] traditional ethics has almost entirely ignored the claims of posterity. In an overpopulated world, humanity cannot long endure under a regime governed by posterity-blind ethics. It is the essence of ecological ethics that it pays attention to posterity.

Since "helping" starving people requires that we who are rich give up some of our wealth, any refusal to do so is almost sure to be attributed to selfishness. Selfishness there may be, but focusing on selfishness is likely to be nonproductive. In truth, a selfish motive can be found in all policy proposals. The selfishness of *not* giving is obvious and need not be elaborated. But the selfishness of giving is no less real, though more subtle.[8] Consider the sources of support for Public Law 480, the act of Congress under which surplus foods were given to poor countries, or sold to them at bargain prices ("concessionary terms" is the euphemism). Why did we give food away? Conventional wisdom says it was because we momentarily transcended our normal selfishness. Is that the whole story?

It is not. The "we" of the above sentence needs to be subdivided. The farmers who grew the grain did not give it away. They sold it to the government (which then gave it away). Farmers received selfish benefits in two ways: the direct sale of grain, and the economic support to farm prices given by this governmental purchase in an otherwise free market. The operation of P.L. 480 during the past quarter-century brought American farmers to a level of prosperity never known before.

Who else benefited—in a selfish way? The stockholders and employees of the railroads that moved grain to seaports benefited. So also did freight-boat operators (U.S. "bottoms" were specified by law). So also did grain elevator operators. So also did agricultural research scientists who were financially supported in a burgeoning but futile effort "to feed a hungry world."[9] And so also did the large bureaucracy required to keep the P.L. 480 system working. In toto, probably several million people personally benefited from the P.L. 480 program. Their labors cannot be called wholly selfless.

Who *did* make a sacrifice for P.L. 480? The citizens generally, nearly two hundred million of them, paying directly or indirectly through taxes. But each of these many millions lost only a little; whereas each of the million or so gainers gained a great deal. The blunt truth is that *philanthropy pays*—if you are hired as a philanthropist. Those on the gaining side of P.L. 480 made a great deal of money and could afford to spend lavishly to persuade Congress to continue the program. Those on the sacrificing side sacrificed only a little bit per capita and could not afford to spend much protecting their pocketbooks against philanthropic inroads. And so P.L. 480 continued, year after year.

Should we condemn philanthropy when we discover that some of its roots are selfish? I think not, otherwise probably no philanthropy would be possible. The secret of practical success in large-scale public philanthropy is this: see to it that the losses are widely distributed so that the per capita loss is small, but concentrate the gains in a relatively few people so that these few will have the economic power needed to pressure the legislature into supporting the program.

I have spent some time on this issue because I would like to dispose once and for all of condemnatory arguments based on "selfishness." As a matter of principle we should always assume that selfishness is *part* of the motivation of every action. But what of it? If Smith proposes a certain public policy, it is far more important to know whether the policy will do public harm or public good than it is to know whether Smith's motives are selfish or selfless. Consequences ("ends") can be more objectively determined than motivations ("means"). Situational ethics wisely uses consequences as the measure of morality. "If the end does not justify the means, what does?" asked Joseph Fletcher.[10] The obsession of older ethical systems with means and motives is no doubt in part a consequence of envy, which has a thousand disguises.[11] (Though I am sure this is true, the situationist should not dwell on envy very long, for it is after all only a motive, and as such not directly verifiable. In any case public policy must be primarily concerned with consequences.)

Even judging an act by its consequences is not easy. We are limited by the basic theorem of ecology, "We can never do merely one thing."[12] The fact that an act has many consequences is all the more reason for deemphasizing motives as we carry out our ethical analyses. Motives by definition apply only to intended consequences. The multitudinous unintended ones are commonly denigrated by the term "side effects." But, "The road to hell is paved with good intentions," so let's have done with motivational evaluations of public policy.

Even after we have agreed to eschew motivational analysis, foreign aid is a tough nut to crack. The literature is large and contradictory, but it all points to the inescapable conclusion that a quarter of a century of earnest effort has not conquered world poverty. To many observers the threat of future disasters is more convincing now than it was a quarter of a century ago—and the disasters are not all in the future either.[13] Where have we gone wrong in foreign aid?

We wanted to do good, of course. The question, "How can we help a poor country?" seems like a simple question, one that should have a simple answer. Our failure to answer it suggests that the question is not as simple as we thought. The variety of contradictory answers offered is disheartening.

How can we find our way through this thicket? I suggest we take a cue from a mathematician. The great algebraist Karl Jacobi (1804–1851) had a simple stratagem that he recommended to students who found themselves butting their heads against a stone wall. *Umkehren, immer umkehren*—"Invert, always invert." Don't just keep asking the same old question over and over: turn it upside down and ask the opposite question. The answer you get then may not be the one you want, but it may throw useful light on the question you started with.

Let's try a Jacobian inversion of the food/population problem. To sharpen the issue, let us take a particular example, say India. The question we want to answer is, "How can we help India?" But, since that approach has repeatedly thrust us against a stone wall, let's pose the Jacobian invert, "How can we *harm* India?" After we've answered this perverse question we will return to the original (and proper) one.

As a matter of method, let us grant ourselves the most malevolent of motives: let us ask, "How can we harm India—*really* harm her?" Of course we might plaster the country with thermonuclear bombs, speedily wiping out most of the 600 million people. But, to the truly malevolent mind, that's not much fun: a dead man is beyond harming. Bacterial warfare could be a bit "better," but not much. No: we want something that will really make India suffer, not merely for a day or a week, but on and on and on. How can we achieve this inhumane goal?

Quite simply: by sending India a bounty of food, year after year. The United States exports about 80 million tons of grain a year. Most of it we

sell: the foreign exchange it yields we use for such needed imports as petroleum (38 percent of our oil consumption in 1974), iron ore, bauxite, chromium, tin, etc. But in the pursuit of our malevolent goal let us "unselfishly" tighten our belts, make sacrifices, and do without that foreign exchange. Let us *give* all 80 million tons of grain to the Indians each year.

On a purely vegetable diet it takes about 400 pounds of grain to keep one person alive and healthy for a year. The 600 million Indians need 120 million tons per year; since their nutrition is less than adequate, presumably they are getting a bit less than that now. So the 80 million tons we give them will almost double India's per capita supply of food. With a surplus, Indians can afford to vary their diet by growing some less efficient crops; they can also convert some of the grain into meat (pork and chickens for the Hindus, beef and chickens for the Moslems). The entire nation can then be supplied not only with plenty of calories, but also with an adequate supply of high-quality protein. The people's eyes will sparkle, their steps will become more elastic, and they will be capable of more work. "Fatalism" will no doubt diminish. (Much so-called fatalism is merely a consequence of malnutrition.) Indians may even become a bit overweight, though they will still be getting only two-thirds as much food as the average inhabitant of a rich country. Surely—we think—surely a well-fed India would be better off?

Not so: *ceteris paribus*, they will ultimately be worse off. Remember, "We can never do merely one thing." A generous gift of food would have not only nutritional consequences, it would also have political and economic consequences. The difficulty of distributing free food to a poor people is well known. Harbor, storage, and transport inadequacies result in great losses of grain to rats and fungi. Political corruption diverts food from those who need it most to those who are more powerful. More abundant supplies depress free market prices and discourage native farmers from growing food in subsequent years. Research into better ways of agriculture is also discouraged. Why look for better ways to grow food when there is food enough already?

There are replies, of sorts, to all the above points. It may be maintained that all these evils are only temporary ones; in time, organizational sense will be brought into the distributional system and the government will crack down on corruption. Realizing the desirability of producing more food, for export if nothing else, a wise government will subsidize agricultural research in spite of an apparent surplus. Experience does not give much support to this optimistic view, but let us grant the conclusions for the sake of getting on to more important matters. Worse is to come.

The Indian unemployment rate is commonly reckoned at 30 percent, but it is acknowledged that this is a minimum figure. *Under*employment is rife. Check into a hotel in Calcutta with four small bags and four bearers will carry your luggage to the room—with another man to carry the key. Custom, and a knowledge of what the traffic will bear, decree this practice. In addition malnutrition justifies it in part. Adequately fed, half as many men would suffice. So one of the early consequences of achieving a higher level of nutrition in the Indian population would be to increase the number of unemployed.

India needs many things that food will not buy. Food will not diminish the unemployment rate (quite the contrary); nor will it increase the supply of minerals, bicycles, clothes, automobiles, gasoline, schools, books, movies, or television. All these things require energy for their manufacture and maintenance.

Of course, food is a form of energy, but it is convertible to other forms only with great loss; so we are practically justified in considering energy and food as mutually exclusive goods. On this basis the most striking difference between poor and rich countries is not in the food they eat but in the energy they use. On a per capita basis rich countries use about three times as much of the primary foods—grains and the like—as do poor countries. (To a large extent, this is because the rich convert much of the grain to more "wasteful" animal meat.) But when it comes to energy, rich countries use ten times as much per capita. (Near the extremes Americans use 60 times as much per person as Indians.) By reasonable standards much

of this energy may be wasted (e.g., in the manufacture of "exercycles" for sweating the fat off people who have eaten too much), but a large share of this energy supplies the goods we regard as civilized: effortless transportation, some luxury foods, a variety of sports, clean space-heating, more than adequate clothing, and energy-consuming arts—music, visual arts, electronic auxiliaries, etc. Merely giving food to a people does almost nothing to satisfy the appetite for any of these other goods.

But a well-nourished people is better fitted to try to wrest more energy from its environment. The question then is this: Is the native environment able to furnish more energy? And at what cost?

In India energy is already being gotten from the environment at a fearful cost. In the past two centuries millions of acres of India have been deforested in the struggle for fuel, with the usual environmental degradation. The Vale of Kashmir, once one of the garden spots of the world, has been denuded to such an extent that the hills no longer hold water as they once did, and the springs supplying the famous gardens are drying up. So desperate is the need for charcoal for fuel that the Kashmiri now make it out of tree leaves. This wasteful practice denies the soil of needed organic mulch.

Throughout India, as is well known, cow dung is burned to cook food. The minerals of the dung are not thereby lost, but the ability of dung to improve soil tilth is. Some of the nitrogen in the dung goes off into the air and does not return to Indian soil. Here we see a classic example of the "vicious circle": because Indians are poor they burn dung, depriving the soil of nitrogen and make themselves still poorer the following year. If we give them plenty of food, as they cook this food with cow dung they will lower still more the ability of their land to produce food.

Let us look at another example of this counterproductive behavior. Twenty-five years ago Western countries brought food and medicine to Nepal. In the summer of 1974 a disastrous flood struck Bangladesh, killing tens of thousands of people, by government admission. (True losses in that part of the world are always greater than admitted losses.) Was there any connection between feeding

Nepal and flooding Bangladesh? Indeed there was, and is.[14]

Nepal nestles amongst the Himalayas. Much of its land is precipitous, and winters are cold. The Nepalese need fuel, which they get from trees. Because more Nepalese are being kept alive now, the demand for timber is escalating. As trees are cut down, the soil under them is washed down the slopes into the rivers that run through India and Bangladesh. Once the absorption capacity of forest soil is gone, floods rise faster and to higher maxima. The flood of 1974 covered two-thirds of Bangladesh, twice the area of "normal" floods—which themselves are the consequence of deforestation in preceding centuries.

By bringing food and medicine to Nepal we intend only to save lives. But we can never do merely one thing, and the Nepalese lives we saved created a Nepalese energy-famine. The lives we saved from starvation in Nepal a quarter of a century ago were paid for in our time by lives lost to flooding and its attendant evils in Bangladesh. The saying, "Man does not live by bread alone," takes on new meaning.

Still we have not described what may be the worst consequence of a food-only policy: revolution and civil disorder. Many kindhearted people who support food aid programs solicit the cooperation of "hard-nosed" doubters by arguing that good nutrition is needed for world peace. Starving people will attack others, they say. Nothing could be further from the truth. The monumental studies of Ancel Keys and others have shown that starving people are completely selfish.[15] They are incapable of cooperating with others; and they are incapable of laying plans for tomorrow and carrying them out. Moreover, modern war is so expensive that even the richest countries can hardly afford it.

The thought that starving people can forcefully wrest subsistence from their richer brothers may appeal to our sense of justice, *but it just ain't so.* Starving people fight only among themselves, and that inefficiently.

So what would happen if we brought ample supplies of food to a population that was still poor in everything else? They would still be incapable of waging war at a distance, but their ability to

fight among themselves would be vastly increased. With vigorous, well-nourished bodies and a keen sense of their impoverishment in other things, they would no doubt soon create massive disorder in their own land. Of course, they might create a strong and united country, but what is the probability of that? Remember how much trouble the thirteen colonies had in forming themselves into a United States. Then remember that India is divided by two major religions, many castes, fourteen major languages, and a hundred dialects. A partial separation of peoples along religious lines in 1947, at the time of the formation of Pakistan and of independent India, cost untold millions of lives. The budding off of Bangladesh (formerly East Pakistan) from the rest of Pakistan in 1971 cost several million more. All these losses were achieved on a low level of nutrition. The possibilities of blood-letting in a population of 600 million well-nourished people of many languages and religions and no appreciable tradition of cooperation stagger the imagination. Philanthropists with any imagination at all should be stunned by the thought of 600 million well-fed Indians seeking to meet their energy needs from their own resources.

So the answer to our Jacobian questions, "How can we harm India?" is clear: send food *only.* Escaping the Jacobian by reinverting the question we now ask, "How can we *help* India?" Immediately we see that we must *never* send food without a matching gift of nonfood energy; but before we go careening off on an intoxicating new program, we had better look at some more quantities.

On a per capita basis, India uses the energy equivalent of one barrel of oil per year; the U.S. uses sixty. The world average of all countries, rich and poor, is ten. If we want to bring India only up to the present world average, we would have to send India about 9×600 million barrels of oil per year (or its equivalent in coal, timber, gas, or whatever). That would be more than five billion barrels of oil equivalent. What is the chance that we will make such a gift?

Surely it is nearly zero. For scale, note that our total yearly petroleum use is seven billion barrels (of which we import three billion). Of course we use (and have) a great deal of coal, too. But, these figures should suffice to give a feeling of scale.

More important is the undoubted psychological fact that a fall in income tends to dry up the springs of philanthropy. Despite wide disagreements about the future of energy it is obvious that from now on, for at least the next twenty years and possibly for centuries, our per capita supply of energy is going to fall, year after year. The food we gave in the past was "surplus." By no accounting do we have an energy surplus. In fact, the perceived deficit is rising year by year.

India has about one-third as much land as the United States. She has about three times as much population. If her people-to-land ratio were the same as ours she would have only about seventy million people (instead of 600 million). With the forested and relatively unspoiled farmlands of four centuries ago, seventy million people was probably well within the carrying capacity of the land. Even in today's India, seventy million people could probably make it in comfort and dignity—provided they didn't increase!

To send food only to a country already populated beyond the carrying capacity of its land is to collaborate in the further destruction of the land and the further impoverishment of its people.

Food plus energy is a recommendable policy; but for a large population under today's conditions, this policy is defensible only by the logic of the old saying, "If wishes were horses, beggars would ride." The fantastic amount of energy needed for such a program is simply not in view. (We have mentioned nothing of the equally monumental "infrastructure" of political, technological, and educational machinery needed to handle unfamiliar forms and quantities of energy in the poor countries. In a short span of time this infrastructure is as difficult to bring into being as is an abundant supply of energy.)

In summary, then, here are the major foreign-aid possibilities that tender minds are willing to entertain:

(a) Food plus energy—a conceivable, but practically impossible program.
(b) Food alone—a conceivable and possible program, but one which would destroy the recipient.

In the light of this analysis, the question of triage shrinks to negligible importance. If any gift of food to overpopulated countries does more harm than good, it is not necessary to decide which countries get the gift and which do not. For posterity's sake we should never send food to any population that is beyond the realistic carrying capacity of its land. The question of triage does not even arise. . .

NOTES

1. Garrett Hardin, 1968. "The Tragedy of the Commons," *Science*, 162: 1243–48.
2. Karl Marx, 1875. "Critique of the Gotha program." (Reprinted in *The Marx-Engels Reader*, Robert C. Tucker, editor. New York: Norton, 1972).
3. Garrett Hardin and John Baden, 1977. *Managing the Commons*. (San Francisco: W. H. Freeman.)
4. Thomas Robert Malthus, 1798. *An Essay on the Principle of Population, as It Affects the Future Improvement of Society*. (Reprinted, inter alia, by the University of Michigan Press, 1959, and The Modern Library, 1960).
5. Donella H. Meadows, Dennis L. Meadows, Jorgen Randers, and William H. Behrens, 1972. *The Limits to Growth* (New York: Universe Books).
6. C.P. Snow, 1963. *The Two Cultures; and a Second Look*. (New York: Mentor).
7. Hans Jonas, 1973. "Technology and Responsibility: Reflections on the New Task of Ethics," *Social Research*, 40: 31–54.
8. William and Paul Paddock, 1967. *Famine—1975* (Boston: Little, Brown & Co.).
9. Garrett Hardin, 1975. "Gregg's Law," *BioScience*, 25: 415.
10. Joseph Fletcher, 1966. *Situation Ethics* (Philadelphia: Westminster Press).
11. Helmut Schoeck, 1969. *Envy* (New York: Harcourt, Brace & World).
12. Garret Hardin, 1972. *Exploring New Ethics for Survival* (New York: Viking).
13. Nicholas Wade, 1974. "Sahelian Drought: No Victory for Western Aid," *Science*, 185: 234–37.
14. Erik P. Eckholm, 1975. "The Deterioration of Mountain Environments," *Science*, 189: 764–70.
15. Ancel Keys, et al., 1950. *The Biology of Human Starvation*. 2 vols. (Minneapolis: University of Minnesota Press).

Feeding the Hungry

Jan Narveson

Jan Narveson is a professor of philosophy at the University of Waterloo. He is the author of *The Libertarian Idea* (2000), and *Morality and Utility* (1967).

Narveson argues that unless there is a direct connection between one's actions that cause the suffering of another, then one does not have a duty or responsibility to alleviate another's suffering. While we might consider the actions of one who did not cause the suffering of another yet works to alleviate that suffering to be morally virtuous, no such duty to provide charity to another (if one did not cause another's situation) exists. Thus, Narveson argues, we are not obligated to feed the hungry whom we did not make hungry.

Throughout history it has been the lot of most people to know that there are others worse off than they, and often enough of others who face starvation. In the contemporary world, television and other mass media enable all of us in the better-off areas to hear about starvation in even the most remote places. What, if any, are our obligations toward the victims of such a terrible situation?

This can be a rather complex subject, for different cases differ significantly. We must begin, then, by distinguishing the main ones. First, we should note that the word "starve" functions both as a passive verb, indicating something that happens to one, and as an active verb, designating something inflicted by one person on another. In the latter case, starvation is a form of killing and comes under the same strictures that any other method of killing is liable to. But when the problem is plague, crop failure due to drought, or sheer

Excerpt from Jan Narveson, "Feeding the Hungry" in Moral Matters 2/e, pp. 143–156. 1999. © 1999 by Jan Narveson. Reprinted by permission of Broadview Press.

lack of know-how, there is no obviously guilty party. Then the question is whether *we*, the amply fed, are guilty parties if we *fail to come to the rescue* of those unfortunate people.

STARVATION AND MURDER

If I lock you in a room with no food and don't let you out, I have murdered you. If group A burns the crops of group B, it has slaughtered the Bs. There is no genuine issue about such cases. It is wrong to kill innocent people, and one way of killing them is as eligible for condemnation as any other. Such cases are happily unusual, and we need say no more about them here other than to note, as I will, that the most substantial recent cases could readily be regarded as cases of something amounting to murder, rather than the other kind.

Our interest, then, is in the cases where murder is not the relevant category, or at least not obviously so. But some writers, such as James Rachels,[1] hold that letting someone die is *morally equivalent* to killing them or, at least, "basically" equivalent. Is this so? Most people do not think so; it takes a subtle philosophical argument to persuade them of this. The difference between a bad thing that I intentionally or at least foreseeably brought about and one that just happened, through no fault of my own, matters to most of us in practice. Is our view sustainable in principle, too? Suppose the case is one I could do something about, as when you are starving and my granary is burgeoning. Does that make a difference?

DUTIES OF JUSTICE AND DUTIES OF CHARITY

Another important question, which has cropped up in some of our discussions but is nowhere more clearly relevant than here, is the distinction between *justice* and *charity*. By justice I here intend those things that we may, if need be, be forced to do—where our actions can be constrained by others to ensure our performance. Charity, on the other hand, "comes from the heart": *charity* means, roughly, caring, an emotionally tinged desire to benefit other people just because they need it.

We should note a special point about this. It is often said that charity "cannot be compelled." Is this true? In one clear sense, it is, for in this sense charity consists *only* of benefits motivated by love or concern. If instead you regard an act as one that we may forcibly compel people to do, then you are taking that act to be a case of *justice*. Can it at the same time be charity? It can if we detach the motive from the act and define charity simply as doing good for others. But the claim that charity in this second sense cannot be compelled is definitely *not* true by definition—and is in fact false. People are frequently compelled to do good for others, especially by our governments, which tax us in order to benefit the poor, educate the uneducated, and so on. Whether they *should* be thus compelled is a genuine moral question, however, and must not be evaded by recourse to semantics. (Whether those programs produce benefits that outweigh their costs is a very complex question; but that they do often produce *some* benefits, at whatever cost, is scarcely deniable.)

On which side of the moral divide, then, shall we place feeding the hungry? Is it to be regarded as unenforceable charity, to be left to individual consciences, or enforceable justice, perhaps to be handled by governments? Here, we are asking whether feeding the hungry is not only something we ought to do but also something we *must* do, as a matter of justice. It is especially this latter that concerns us in the present chapter. A great deal turns on it.

We should note, also, the logical possibility that someone might differ so strongly with most of us on this matter as to think it positively *wrong* to feed the hungry. That is an extreme view, but it looks rather like the view that some writers, such as Garrett Hardin,[2] defend. However, it is misleading to characterize their view in this way. Hardin, for example, thinks that feeding the hungry is an exercise in *misguided* charity, not real charity. In feeding the hungry today, he argues, we merely create a much greater problem tomorrow, for feeding the relatively few now will create an unmanageably large number next time their crops fail, a number we won't be able to feed and who will consequently starve. Thus we actually cause more starvation by feeding people now than we do by not feeding them, hard though that may sound. Hardin, then, is not favouring cruelty towards the weak. The truly charitable, he believes, should be *against* feeding the hungry, at least in some cases.

Hardin's argument brings up the need for another distinction of urgent importance: between *principles* and *policies*. Being in favour of feeding the hungry *in principle* may or may not imply that we should feed the particular persons involved in this or that particular case, for that may depend on further facts about those cases. For example, perhaps trying to feed *these* hungry people runs into the problem that the government of those hungry people doesn't want *you* feeding them. If the price of feeding them is that you must go to war, then it may not be the best thing to do. If enormous starvation faces a group in the further future if the starving among them are fed now, then a policy of feeding them now may not be recommended by a principle of humanity. And so on. Principles are relatively abstract and may be considered just by considering possibilities; but when it comes to policy pursued in the real world, facts cannot be ignored.

Our general question is what sort of moral concerns we have with the starving. The question breaks down into two. First, is there a *basic duty of justice* to feed the starving? And second, if there isn't, then is there a basic requirement of *charity* that we be disposed to do so, and if so, how strong is that requirement?

JUSTICE AND STARVATION

Let's begin with the first. Is it *unjust* to let others starve to death? We must distinguish two very different ways in which someone might try to argue for this. First, there are those who, like Rachels, argue that there is no fundamental distinction between killing and letting die. If that is right, then the duty not to kill is all we need to support the conclusion that there is a duty of justice not to let people starve, and the duty not to kill (innocent) people is uncontroversial. Second, however, some insist that feeding the hungry is a duty of justice even if we don't accept the equivalence of killing and letting die. They therefore need a different argument, in support of a positive right to be fed. The two different views call for very different discussions.

STARVING AND ALLOWING TO STARVE

Starving and allowing to starve are special cases of killing and letting die. Are they the same, as some insist? . . . [There is a] need for a crucial distinction here: between the view that they are literally indistinguishable and the view that even though they are logically distinguishable, they are nevertheless *morally* equivalent.

As to the first, the argument for nonidentity of the two is straightforward. When you kill someone, you do any act, x, which brings it about that the person is dead *when he would otherwise still be alive*. You induce a *change* (for the worse) in his condition. But when you let someone die, this is not so, for she would have died even if you had, say, been in Australia at the time. How can *you* be

said to be the "cause" of something that would have happened if you didn't exist?

To be sure, we do often attribute causality to human inaction. But the clear cases of such attribution are those where the agent in question had an antecedent *responsibility* to do the thing in question. The geraniums may die because you fail to water them, but to say that you thus *caused* them to die is to imply that you were *supposed* to water them. Of course, we may agree that if we have a duty to feed the poor and we don't feed them, then we are at fault. But the question before us is *whether* we have this duty, and the argument we are examining purports to prove this by showing that even when we do nothing, we still "cause" their deaths. If the argument presupposes that very responsibility, it plainly begs the question rather than giving us a good answer to it.

What about the claim that killing and letting die are morally equivalent? Here again, there is a danger of begging the question. *If* we have a duty to feed the hungry and we don't, then not doing so might be morally equivalent to killing them, perhaps—though I doubt that any proponents would seriously propose life imprisonment for failing to contribute to the cause of feeding the hungry! But again, the consequence clearly doesn't follow if we don't have that duty, which is in question. Those who think we do not have fundamental duties to take care of each other, but only duties to refrain from killing and the like, will deny that they are morally equivalent.

The liberty proponent will thus insist that when Beethoven wrote symphonies instead of using his talents to grow food for the starving, like the peasants he depicted in his Pastorale symphony, he was doing what he had a perfect right to do. A connoisseur of music might go further and hold that he was also doing *the right thing*: that someone with the talents of Beethoven does more for people by composing great music than by trying to save lives, even if he would have been *successful* in saving those lives—which is not very likely anyway.

How do we settle this issue? If we were all connoisseurs, it would be easy: If you know and love great music, you will find it easy to believe that a symphony by Beethoven or Mahler is worth more than prolonging the lives of a few hundred starvelings for another few miserable years. If you are one of those starving persons, your view might well be different. (But it might not. Consider the starving artist in his garret, famed in romantic novels and operas: They lived voluntarily in squalor, believing that what they were doing was worth the sacrifice.)

We are not all connoisseurs, nor are most of us starving. Advocates of welfare duties talk glibly as though there were a single point of view ("welfare") that dominates everything else. But it's not true. There are all kinds of points of view, diverse and to a large extent incommensurable. Uniting them is not as simple as the welfarist or utilitarian may think. It is *not* certain, not obvious, that we "add more to the sum of human happiness" by supporting the opera than by supporting OXFAM.[3] How are we to unite diverse people on these evaluative matters? The most plausible answer, I think, is the point of view that allows different people to live their various lives by forbidding interference with the lives of others. Rather than insisting, with threats to back it up, that I *help* someone for whose projects and purposes I have no sympathy whatever, let us all agree to *respect* each other's pursuits. We'll agree to let each person live as that person sees fit, with only our bumpings into each other being subject to public control. To do this, we need to draw a sort of line around each person and insist that others not cross that line without the permission of the occupant. The rule will be not to intervene forcibly in the lives of others, thus requiring that our relations be mutually agreeable. Enforced feeding of the starving, however, does cross the line, invading the farmer or the merchant, forcing him to part with some of his hard-earned produce and give it without compensation to others. That, says the advocate of liberty, is theft, not charity.

So if someone is starving, we may pity him or we may be indifferent, but the question so far as our *obligations* are concerned is this: How did he *get* that way? If it was not the result of my previous activities, then I have no obligation to him and may help him out or not, as I choose. If it was a result of my own doing, then of course I must do something. If you live and have long lived downstream from me, and I decide to dam up the river and divert the water elsewhere, then I have deprived you of your water and must compensate you, by supplying you with the equivalent, or else desist. But if you live in the middle of a parched desert and it does not rain, so that you are faced with death from thirst, that is not my doing and I have no compensating to do.

This liberty-respecting idea avoids, by and large, the need to make the sort of utility comparisons essential to the utility or welfare view. If we have no general obligation to manufacture as much utility for others as possible, then we don't have to concern ourselves about measuring that utility. Being free to pursue our own projects, we will evaluate our results as best we may, each in our own way. There is no need to keep a constant check on others to see whether we ought to be doing more for them and less for ourselves.

THE ETHICS OF THE HAIR SHIRT

In stark contrast to the liberty-respecting view stands the idea that we are to count the satisfactions of others as equal in value to our own. If I can create a little more pleasure for some stranger by spending my dollar on him than I would create for myself by spending it on an ice cream cone, I then have a putative *obligation* to spend it on him. Thus, I am to defer continually to others in the organization of my activities and shall be assailed by guilt whenever I am not bending my energies to the relief of those allegedly less fortunate than I. "Benefit others, at the expense of yourself—and keep doing it until you are as poor and miserable as those whose poverty and misery you are supposed to be relieving![4] That is the ethics of the hair shirt.

How should we react to this idea? Negatively, I suggest. Doesn't that view really make us the slaves of the (supposedly) less well off? Surely a rule of conduct that permits people to be themselves and to try to live the best and most interesting lives they can is better than one that makes us all, in effect, functionaries in a welfare state? The rule that *neither* the rich *nor* the poor ought to be enslaved by the others is surely the better rule.

Some, of course, think that the poor *are*, inherently, the "slaves" of the rich, and the rich inherently the masters of the poor. Such is the Marxist view, for instance. It's an important argument, and very influential. It is also wrong. In the first place, its account of "masterhood" is not what we usually have in mind by that notion: the wealthy do *not* have the right to hold a gun to the heads of the nonwealthy and tell them what to do. Legally and morally, both are held to the same strict requirement, to refrain from inflicting evils on anyone, rich or poor. And second, the idea that the rich and poor are somewhat at loggerheads with each other is, so far as "capitalist" economies are concerned, precisely the opposite of the truth, for insofar as wealth is made in free economies, there is only one way to make it: by selling things to other people that those others *voluntarily* purchase. This means that the purchaser, in his view, is made better off *as well as* the seller by the transaction. Of course, the employees of the owners of businesses also become better off, via their wages. The results of this activity are that there are *more* goods in the world than there would otherwise be and that all concerned are better off.

This is precisely the opposite of the way the thief makes his money. The thief expends time and energy depriving others, involuntarily, of what they worked to produce, rather than devoting his energies to new productive activities. The thief, therefore, leaves the world poorer than it was before he set out on his exploitative ways. Marxists assimilate the honest accumulator to the thief. Rather than being, as so many seem to think, a profound contribution to social theory, that is a ground-floor conceptual error, a failure to appreciate that wealth comes about precisely because of the prohibition of theft, rather than by its wholesale exercise.

Of course this Marxist view also encourages the "poor" to rise up and revolt and "socialize the means of production," with consequences familiar to the world. In socialist countries, almost everyone is worse off than almost everyone in "capitalist" ones: Russian, Chinese, and Cuban poor are poorer than their North American counterparts, and middle-class Russians *far* poorer. If we are

impressed by that result—as it seems to me we should be—then we will consider the Marxist program an effort at wholesale theft, with the expected results that theft always has: making people poorer, not richer.

POVERTY AND WAR

It is hardly surprising if people who feel they are up against the wall—and who might well be right in assessing their situation in just that way—should be tempted to resort to violence in their efforts to stay alive. If they have been persuaded of a claim that they have a *right* against the more fortunate that the latter share the wealth with them, that will give the violence in question an ideological support that is likely to make the results more intransigent and more disruptive. And one natural reaction on the part of middle-class and, perhaps especially, wealthier people is to adopt the attitude that we do indeed have a fundamental duty to help feed the starving, undercutting the reasons for "class war" or theft. It is difficult to say whether this reaction does more harm than good. In one way, surely, it's the former: for this reasoning really does involve an assumption that might makes right after all, and that is a view that undoes the good we can all hope for from morals.

MUTUAL AID

The anti-welfarist idea, however, can be taken too far. Should people be disposed to assist each other in time of need? Certainly they should. But the appropriate rule for this is not that each person is duty-bound to minister to the poor until he himself is a pauper or near-pauper as well. Rather, the appropriate rule is what the characterization "in time of need" more nearly suggests. There are indeed emergencies in life when a modest effort by someone will do a great deal for someone else. People who aren't ready to help others when it is comparatively easy to do so are people who deserve to be avoided when they themselves turn to others in time of need.

But this all assumes that these occasions are, in the first place, relatively unusual, and in the second, that the help offered is genuinely of modest cost to the provider. If a stranger on the street asks for directions, a trifling expenditure of time and effort saves him great frustration and perhaps also makes for a pleasant encounter with another human (which that other human should try to make so, for example, by being polite and saying "thanks!"). But, if as I walk down the street I am accosted on all sides by similar requests, then I shall never get my day's work done if I can't just say, "Sorry, I've got to be going!" or merely ignore them and walk right on. If instead I must minister to each, then soon there will be nothing to give, since its existence depends entirely on the activities of people who produce it. If the stranger asks me to drive him around town all day looking for a long-lost friend, then that's going too far, though of course, I should be free to help him out even to that extent if I am so inclined.

What about parting with the means for making your sweet little daughter's birthday party a memorable one in order to keep a dozen strangers alive on the other side of the world? Is this something you are morally required to do? It is not. She may well *matter* to you more than they—and well she should. This illustrates again the point that people do *not* "count equally" for most of us. Normal people care more about some people than others, and build their very lives around those carings. It is both absurd and arrogant for theorists, talking airily about the equality of all people, to insist on cramming it down our throats—which is how ordinary people do see it.

It is reasonable, then, to arrive at a general understanding that we shall be ready to help when help is urgent and when giving it is not very onerous to us. But a general understanding that we shall help everyone as if they were our spouses or dearest friends is quite another matter. Only a thinker whose heart has been replaced by a calculating machine could suppose that to be reasonable.

Note, too, that the duty to help is a "moral" one in a closely related but not identical sense of the word *duty* to the one I have mainly been employing . . . This is the sense in which morals have to do with what's in our souls rather than what others may enforce by threats of punishment and the like. To feel sympathy for the unfortunate is, we may well think, to be human—even though we realize that apparently some humans manage not to feel so. We have ideals of humanity, and this sense of commiseration and fellow-feeling is prominent on most of our depictions of this ideal. I share this ideal, while realizing that it is far from the only ideal that people might reasonably espouse. And it is precisely that realization that forces us to the conclusion that the duty to relieve others in distress cannot reasonably be classed as one to be enforced with threats of jail terms and the like, that is, by taxation. It is, instead, enforced by the expressed support of one's fellow sympathizers and by our spiritual mettle.

CHARITY

One of the good things we can do in life is to make an effort to care about people whom we don't ordinarily care or think about. This can benefit not only the intended beneficiaries in distant places, but it can also benefit you, by broadening your perspective. There is a place for the enlargement of human sympathies. But then, these are *sympathies*, matters of the heart; and for such matters, family, friends, colleagues, and coworkers are rightly first on your agenda. Why so? First, just because you are you and not somebody else—not, for example, a godlike "impartial observer." But there is another reason of interest, even if you think there is something right about the utilitarian view. This is what amounts to a consideration of *efficiency*. We know ourselves and our loved ones; we do not, by definition, know strangers. We can choose a gift for people we know and love, but are we wise to try to benefit someone of alien culture and diet? If we do a good thing for someone we know well, we make an investment that will be returned as the years go by; but we have little idea of the payoff from charity for the unknown. Of course, that can be overcome, once in awhile—you might end up pen pals with a peasant in Guatemala. But it would not be wise to count on it.

The tendency and desire to do good for others is a virtue. Moreover, it is a *moral* virtue, for we all have an interest in the general acquisition of this quality. Just as anyone can kill anyone else, so anyone can benefit anyone else; and so long as the cost to oneself of participating in the general scheme of helpfulness is low—namely, decidedly less than the return—then it is likely to be worth it. But it is not reasonable to take the matter beyond that. In particular, it is not reasonable to become a busybody, or a fanatic-like Dickens's character Mrs. Jellyby, who is so busy with her charitable work for the natives in the darkest Africa that her own children run around in rags and become the terror of the neighbourhood. Nor is it reasonable to be so concerned for the welfare of distant persons that you resort to armed robbery in your efforts to help them out ("Stick 'em up! I'm collecting for OXFAM!").

• • •

SUMMING UP

The basic question of this chapter is whether the hungry have a positive right to be fed. Of course, we have a right to feed them if we wish, and they have a negative right to be fed. But may we forcibly impose a duty on others to feed them? We may not. If the fact that others are starving is not our fault, then we do not need to provide for them as a duty of justice. To think otherwise is to suppose that we are, in effect, slaves to the badly off. And so we can in good conscience spend our money on the opera instead of on the poor. Even so, feeding the hungry and taking care of the miserable is a nice thing to do and is morally recommended. Charity is a virtue. Moreover, starvation turns out to be almost entirely a function of bad governments rather than of nature's inability to accommodate the burgeoning masses. Our charitable instincts can handle easily the problems that are due to natural disaster. We can feed the starving *and* go to the opera!

NOTES

1. See James Rachels, "Killing and Starving to Death," in Narveson, ed., *Moral Issues*.
2. See Garrett Hardin, "Living on a Lifeboat," in Narveson, ed., *Moral Issues*.
3. In my late utilitarian days, I addressed this problem in "Aesthetics, Charity, Utility, and Distributive Justice," *The Monist* 36, 4 (Autumn, 1972): 527–51. Compare with Peter Singer's famous article, "Famine, Affluence, and Morality," *Philosophy and Public Affairs* 1, 3 (Spring, 1972): 229–43. Of closely related interest is his "Rich and Poor," in Soifer, *Ethical Issues*, 60–76.
4. Lest this be thought a caricature, it is just about the conclusion that Singer comes to: "it does follow from my argument that we ought to be working full-time to relieve great suffering of the sort that occurs as a result of famine and other disasters." Singer, "Famine, Affluence, and Morality," 238.

Famine, Affluence, and Morality

Peter Singer

Peter Singer is a professor of bioethics at the University Center for Human Values at Princeton University. He is the author of numerous books, including *Animal Liberation* (1975), *Practical Ethics* (1980), *Applied Ethics* (1986), and *How Are We to Live?: Ethics in an Age of Self-Interest* (1995).

Singer considers it morally wrong for affluent people to spend money on nonessential goods while others are starving. Concerning the suffering of others, Singer asserts a principle we are morally obligated to follow. The principle states that if we can prevent suffering without sacrificing anything of comparable moral importance, then we ought to do it. Giving monetary assistance to aid the starving is one way to prevent suffering. Those people who have the means are morally obligated to give money away until they sacrifice something of comparable moral importance, even if it requires them to radically alter and drastically reduce their standard of living.

As I write this, in November 1971, people are dying in East Bengal from lack of food, shelter, and medical care. The suffering and death that are occurring there now are not inevitable, not unavoidable in any fatalistic sense of the term. Constant poverty, a cyclone, and a civil war have turned at least nine million people into destitute refugees; nevertheless, it is not beyond the capacity of the richer nations to give enough assistance to reduce any further suffering to very small proportions. The decisions and actions of human beings can prevent this kind of suffering. Unfortunately, human beings have not made the necessary decisions. At the individual level, people have, with very few exceptions, not responded to the situation in any significant way. Generally speaking, people have not given large sums to relief funds; they have not written to their parliamentary representatives demanding increased government assistance;

they have not demonstrated in the streets, held symbolic fasts, or done anything else directed toward providing the refugees with the means to satisfy their essential needs. At the government level, no government has given the sort of massive aid that would enable the refugees to survive for more than a few days. Britain, for instance, has given rather more than most countries. It has, to date, given £14,750,000. For comparative purposes, Britain's share of the nonrecoverable development costs of the Anglo-French Concorde project is already in excess of £275,000,000, and on present estimates will reach £440,000,000. The implication is that the British government values a supersonic transport more than thirty times as highly as it values the lives of the nine million refugees. Australia is another country which, on a per capita basis, is well up in the "aid to Bengal" table. Australia's aid, however, amounts to less than one-twelfth of the cost of Sydney's new opera house. The total amount given, from all sources, now stands at about £65,000,000. The estimated cost of keeping the refugees alive for one year is £464,000,000. Most of the refugees have now

Peter Singer, "Famine, Affluence, and Morality" from *Philosophy and Public Affairs*, vol. 1, No. 3, Spring 1972. Reprinted by permission of the author.

been in the camps for more than six months. The World Bank has said that India needs a minimum of £300,000,000 in assistance from other countries before the end of the year. It seems obvious that assistance on this scale will not be forthcoming. India will be forced to choose between letting the refugees starve or diverting funds from her own development program, which will mean that more of her own people will starve in the future.[1]

These are the essential facts about the present situation in Bengal. So far as it concerns us here, there is nothing unique about this situation except its magnitude. The Bengal emergency is just the latest and most acute of a series of major emergencies in various parts of the world, arising both from natural and from man made causes. There are also many parts of the world in which people die from malnutrition and lack of food independent of any special emergency. I take Bengal as my example only because it is the present concern, and because the size of the problem has ensured that it has been given adequate publicity. Neither individuals nor governments can claim to be unaware of what is happening there.

What are the moral implications of a situation like this? In what follows, I shall argue that the way people in relatively affluent countries react to a situation like that in Bengal cannot be justified; indeed, the whole way we look at moral issues— our moral conceptual scheme—needs to be altered, and with it, the way of life that has come to be taken for granted in our society.

In arguing for this conclusion I will not, of course, claim to be morally neutral. I shall, however, try to argue for the moral position that I take, so that anyone who accepts certain assumptions, to be made explicit, will, I hope, accept my conclusion.

I begin with the assumption that suffering and death from lack of food, shelter, and medical care are bad. I think most people will agree about this, although one may reach the same view by different routes. I shall not argue for this view. People can hold all sorts of eccentric positions, and perhaps for some of them it would not follow that death by starvation is in itself bad. It is difficult, perhaps impossible, to refute such positions, and so for brevity I will henceforth take this

assumption as accepted. Those who disagree need read no further.

My next point is this: if it is in our power to prevent something bad from happening, without thereby sacrificing anything of comparable moral importance, we ought, morally, to do it. By "without sacrificing anything of comparable moral importance" I mean without causing anything else comparably bad to happen, or doing something that is wrong in itself, or failing to promote some moral good, comparable in significance to the bad thing that we can prevent. This principle seems almost as uncontroversial as the last one. It requires us only to prevent what is bad, and not to promote what is good, and it requires this of us only when we can do it without sacrificing anything that is, from the moral point of view, comparably important. I could even, as far as the application of my argument to the Bengal emergency is concerned, qualify the point so as to make it: if it is in our power to prevent something very bad from happening, without thereby sacrificing anything morally significant, we ought, morally, to do it. An application of this principle would be as follows: if I am walking past a shallow pond and see a child drowning in it, I ought to wade in and pull the child out. This will mean getting my clothes muddy, but this is insignificant, while the death of the child would presumably be a very bad thing.

The uncontroversial appearance of the principle just stated is deceptive. If it were acted upon, even in its qualified form, our lives, our society, and our world would be fundamentally changed. For the principle takes, firstly, no account of proximity or distance. It makes no moral difference whether the person I can help is a neighbor's child ten yards from me or a Bengali whose name I shall never know, ten thousand miles away. Secondly, the principle makes no distinction between cases in which I am the only person who could possibly do anything and cases in which I am just one among millions in the same position.

I do not think I need to say much in defense of the refusal to take proximity and distance into account. The fact that a person is physically near to us, so that we have personal contact with him, may make it more likely that we *shall* assist him, but this does not show that we *ought* to help him rather than another who happens to be further away. If we accept any principle of impartiality, universalizability, equality, or whatever, we cannot discriminate against someone merely because he is far away from us (or we are far away from him). Admittedly, it is possible that we are in a better position to judge what needs to be done to help a person near to us than one far away, and perhaps also to provide the assistance we judge to be necessary. If this were the case, it would be a reason for helping those near to us first. This may once have been a justification for being more concerned with the poor in one's own town than with famine victims in India. Unfortunately for those who like to keep their moral responsibilities limited, instant communication and swift transportation have changed the situation. From the moral point of view, the development of the world into a "global village" has made an important, though still unrecognized, difference to our moral situation. Expert observers and supervisors, sent out by famine relief organizations or permanently stationed in famine-prone areas, can direct our aid to a refugee in Bengal almost as effectively as we could get it to someone in our own block. There would seem, therefore, to be no possible justification for discriminating on geographical grounds.

There may be greater need to defend the second implication of my principle—that the fact that there are millions of other people in the same position, in respect to the Bengali refugees, as I am, does not make the situation significantly different from a situation in which I am the only person who can prevent something very bad from occurring. Again, of course, I admit that there is a psychological difference between the cases: One feels less guilty about doing nothing if one can point to others, similarly placed, who have also done nothing. Yet this can make no real difference to our moral obligations.[2] Should I consider that I am less obliged to pull the drowning child out of the pond if on looking around I see other people, no further away than I am, who have also noticed the child but are doing nothing? One has only to ask this question to see the absurdity of the view that

numbers lessen obligation. It is a view that is an ideal excuse for inactivity; unfortunately most of the major evils—poverty, overpopulation, pollution—are problems in which everyone is almost equally involved.

The view that numbers do make a difference can be made plausible if stated in this way: if everyone in circumstances like mine gave £5 to the Bengal Relief Fund, there would be enough to provide food, shelter, and medical care for the refugees; there is no reason why I should give more than anyone else in the same circumstances as I am; therefore, I have no obligation to give more than £5. Each premise in this argument is true, and the argument looks sound. It may convince us, unless we notice that it is based on a hypothetical premise, although the conclusion is not stated hypothetically. The argument would be sound if the conclusion were: if everyone in circumstances like mine were to give £5, I would have no obligation to give more than £5. If the conclusion were so stated, however, it would be obvious that the argument has no bearing on a situation in which it is not the case that everyone else gives £5. This, of course, is the actual situation. It is more or less certain that not everyone in circumstances like mine will give £5. So there will not be enough to provide the needed food, shelter, and medical care. Therefore by giving more than £5 I will prevent more suffering than I would if I gave just £5.

It might be thought that this argument has an absurd consequence. Since the situation appears to be that very few people are likely to give substantial amounts, it follows that I and everyone else in similar circumstances ought to give as much as possible, that is, at least up to the point at which by giving more one would begin to cause serious suffering for oneself and one's dependents—perhaps even beyond this point to the point of marginal utility, at which by giving more one would cause oneself and one's dependents as much suffering as one would prevent in Bengal. If everyone does this, however, there will be more than can be used for the benefit of the refugees, and some of the sacrifice will have been unnecessary. Thus, if everyone does what he ought to do, the result will not be as good as it would be if everyone did a little less than he ought to do, or if only some do all that they ought to do.

The paradox here arises only if we assume that the actions in question—sending money to the relief funds—are performed more or less simultaneously, and are also unexpected. For if it is to be expected that everyone is going to contribute something, then clearly each is not obliged to give as much as he would have been obliged to had others not been giving too. And if everyone is not acting more or less simultaneously, then those giving later will know how much more is needed, and will have no obligation to give more than is necessary to reach this amount. To say this is not to deny the principle that people in the same circumstances have the same obligations, but to point out that the fact that others have given or may be expected to give is a relevant circumstance: those giving after it has become known that many others are giving and those giving before are not in the same circumstances. So the seemingly absurd consequence of the principle I have put forward can occur only if people are in error about the actual circumstances—that is, if they think they are giving when others are not, but in fact they are giving when others are. The result of everyone doing what he really ought to do cannot be worse than the result of everyone doing less than he ought to do, although the result of everyone doing what he reasonably believes he ought to do could be.

If my argument so far has been sound, neither our distance from a preventable evil nor the number of other people who, in respect to that evil, are in the same situation as we are, lessens our obligation to mitigate or prevent that evil. I shall therefore take as established the principle I asserted earlier. As I have already said, I need to assert it only in its qualified form: if it is in our power to prevent something very bad from happening, without thereby sacrificing anything else morally significant, we ought, morally, to do it.

The outcome of this argument is that our traditional moral categories are upset. The traditional distinction between duty and charity cannot be drawn, or at least, not in the place we normally draw it. Giving money to the Bengal Relief Fund is regarded as an act of charity in our society. The bodies which collect money are known as "charities." These organizations see themselves in this way—if you send them a check, you will be thanked for your "generosity." Because giving money is regarded as an act of charity, it is not thought that there is anything wrong with not giving. The charitable man may be praised, but the man who is not charitable is not condemned. People do not feel in any way ashamed or guilty about spending money on new clothes or a new car instead of giving it to famine relief. (Indeed, the alternative does not occur to them.) This way of looking at the matter cannot be justified. When we buy new clothes not to keep ourselves warm but to look "well-dressed," we are not providing for any important need. We would not be sacrificing anything significant if we were to continue to wear our old clothes, and give the money to famine relief. By doing so, we would be preventing another person from starving. It follows from what I have said earlier that we ought to give money away, rather than spend it on clothes which we do not need to keep us warm. To do so is not charitable, or generous. Nor is it the kind of act which philosophers and theologians have called "supererogatory"—an act which it would be good to do, but not wrong not to do. On the contrary, we ought to give the money away, and it is wrong not to do so.

I am not maintaining that there are no acts which are charitable, or that there are no acts which it would be good to do but not wrong not to do. It may be possible to redraw the distinction between duty and charity in some other place. All I am arguing here is that the present way of drawing the distinction, which makes it an act of charity for a man living at the level of affluence which most people in the "developed nations" enjoy to give money to save someone else from starvation, cannot be supported. It is beyond the scope of my argument to consider whether the distinction should be redrawn or abolished altogether. There would be many other possible ways of drawing the distinction—for instance, one might decide that it is good to make other people as happy as possible, but not wrong not to do so.

Despite the limited nature of the revision in our moral conceptual scheme which I am proposing, the revision would, given the extent of both afflu- ence and famine in the world today, have radical implications. These implications may lead to fur- ther objections, distinct from those I have already considered. I shall discuss two of these.

One objection to the position I have taken might be simply that it is too drastic a revision of our moral scheme. People do not ordinarily judge in the way I have suggested they should. Most people reserve their moral condemnation for those who violate some moral norm, such as the norm against taking another person's property. They do not condemn those who indulge in luxury instead of giving to famine relief. But, given that I did not set out to present a morally neutral description of the way people make moral judgments, the way people do in fact judge has nothing to do with the validity of my conclusion. My conclusion follows from the principle which I advanced earlier, and unless that principle is rejected, or the arguments shown to be unsound, I think the conclusion must stand, however strange it appears.

It might, nevertheless, be interesting to con- sider why our society, and most other societies, do judge differently from the way I have suggested they should. In a well-known article, J.O. Urmson suggests that the imperatives of duty, which tell us what we must do, as distinct from what it would be good to do but not wrong not to do, function so as to prohibit behavior that is intolerable if men are to live together in society.[3] This may explain the origin and continued existence of the present divi- sion between acts of duty and acts of charity. Moral attitudes are shaped by the needs of society, and no doubt society needs people who will ob- serve the rules that make social existence tolera- ble. From the point of view of a particular society, it is essential to prevent violations of norms against killing, stealing, and so on. It is quite inessential, however, to help people outside one's own society.

If this is an explanation of our common dis- tinction between duty and supererogation, how- ever, it is not a justification of it. The moral point of view requires us to look beyond the interests of our own society. Previously, as I have already mentioned, this may hardly have been feasible, but it is quite feasible now. From the moral point of view, the prevention of the starvation of millions of people outside our society must be considered at least as pressing as the upholding of property norms within our society.

It has been argued by some writers, among them Sidgwick and Urmson, that we need to have a basic moral code which is not too far beyond the capacities of the ordinary man, for otherwise there will be a general breakdown of compliance with the moral code. Crudely stated, this argument sug- gests that if we tell people that they ought to re- frain from murder and give everything they do not really need to famine relief, they will do neither, whereas if we tell them that they ought to refrain from murder and that it is good to give to famine relief but not wrong not to do so, they will at least refrain from murder. The issue here is: where should we draw the line between conduct that is required and conduct that is good although not re- quired, so as to get the best possible result? This would seem to be an empirical question, although a very difficult one. One objection to the Sidgwick- Urmson line of argument is that it takes insufficient account of the effect that moral standards can have on the decisions we make. Given a society in which a wealthy man who gives five percent of his income to famine relief is regarded as most gener- ous, it is not surprising that a proposal that we all ought to give away half our incomes will be thought to be absurdly unrealistic. In a society which held that no man should have more than enough while others have less than they need, such a proposal might seem narrow-minded. What it is possible for a man to do and what he is likely to do are both, I think, very greatly influenced by what people around him are doing and expecting him to do. In any case, the possibility that by spreading the idea that we ought to be doing very much more than we are to relieve famine we shall bring about a general breakdown of moral behavior seems remote. If the stakes are an end to wide- spread starvation, it is worth the risk. Finally, it should be emphasized that these considerations are relevant only to the issue of what we should require from others, and not to what we ourselves ought to do.

The second objection to my attack on the present distinction between duty and charity is one which has from time to time been made against utilitarianism. It follows from some forms of utilitarian theory that we all ought, morally, to be working full time to increase the balance of happiness over misery. The position I have taken here would not lead to this conclusion in all circumstances, for if there were no bad occurrences that we could prevent without sacrificing something of comparable moral importance, my argument would have no application. Given the present conditions in many parts of the world, however, it does follow from my argument that we ought, morally, to be working full time to relieve great suffering of the sort that occurs as a result of famine or other disasters. Of course, mitigating circumstances can be adduced—for instance, that if we wear ourselves out through overwork, we shall be less effective than we would otherwise have been. Nevertheless, when all considerations of this sort have been taken into account, the conclusion remains: we ought to be preventing as much suffering as we can without sacrificing something else of comparable moral importance. This conclusion is one which we may be reluctant to face. I cannot see, though, why it should be regarded as a criticism of the position for which I have argued, rather than a criticism of our ordinary standards of behavior. Since most people are self-interested to some degree, very few of us are likely to do everything that we ought to do. It would, however, hardly be honest to take this as evidence that it is not the case that we ought to do it.

It may still be thought that my conclusions are so wildly out of line with what everyone else thinks and has always thought that there must be something wrong with the argument somewhere. In order to show that my conclusions, while certainly contrary to contemporary Western moral standards, would not have seemed so extraordinary at other times and in other places, I would like to quote a passage from a writer not normally thought of as a way-out radical, Thomas Aquinas.

> Now, according to the natural order instituted by divine providence, material goods are provided for the satisfaction of human needs. Therefore the division and appropriation of property, which proceeds from human law, must not hinder the satisfaction of man's necessity from such goods. Equally, whatever a man has in superabundance is owed, of natural right, to the poor for their sustenance. So Ambrosius says, and it is also to be found in the *Decretum Gratiani*: "The bread which you withhold belongs to the hungry; the clothing you shut away, to the naked; and the money you bury in the earth is the redemption and freedom of the penniless."[4]

I now want to consider a number of points, more practical than philosophical, which are relevant to the application of the moral conclusion we have reached. These points challenge not the idea that we ought to be doing all we can to prevent starvation, but the idea that giving away a great deal of money is the best means to this end.

It is sometimes said that overseas aid should be a government responsibility, and that therefore one ought not to give to privately run charities. Giving privately, it is said, allows the government and the noncontributing members of society to escape their responsibilities.

This argument seems to assume that the more people there are who give to privately organized famine relief funds, the less likely it is that the government will take over full responsibility for such aid. This assumption is unsupported, and does not strike me as at all plausible. The opposite view—that if no one gives voluntarily, a government will assume that its citizens are uninterested in famine relief and would not wish to be forced into giving aid—seems more plausible. In any case, unless there were a definite probability that by refusing to give one would be helping to bring about massive government assistance, people who do refuse to make voluntary contributions are refusing to prevent a certain amount of suffering without being able to point to any tangible beneficial consequence of their refusal. So the onus of showing how their refusal will bring about government action is on those who refuse to give.

I do not, of course, want to dispute the contention that governments of affluent nations should be giving many times the amount of genuine, no-strings-attached aid that they are giving now. I agree, too, that giving privately is not enough, and that we ought to be campaigning actively for entirely new standards for both public and private contributions to famine relief. Indeed, I would sympathize with someone who thought that campaigning was more important than giving oneself, although I doubt whether preaching what one does not practice would be very effective. Unfortunately, for many people the idea that "it's the government's responsibility" is a reason for not giving which does not appear to entail any political action either.

Another, more serious reason for not giving to famine relief funds is that until there is effective population control, relieving famine merely postpones starvation. If we save the Bengal refugees now, others, perhaps the children of these refugees, will face starvation in a few years' time. In support of this, one may cite the now well-known facts about the population explosion and the relatively limited scope for expanded production.

This point, like the previous one, is an argument against relieving suffering that is happening now, because of a belief about what might happen in the future; it is unlike the previous point in that very good evidence can be adduced in support of their belief about the future. I will not go into the evidence here. I accept that the earth cannot support indefinitely a population rising at the present rate. This certainly poses a problem for anyone who thinks it important to prevent famine. Again, however, one could accept the argument without drawing the conclusion that it absolves one from any obligation to do anything to prevent famine. The conclusion that should be drawn is that the best means of preventing famine, in the long run, is population control. It would then follow from the position reached earlier that one ought to be doing all one can to promote population control (unless one held that all forms of population control were wrong in themselves, or would have significantly bad consequences). Since there are organizations working specifically for population control, one would then support them rather than more orthodox methods of preventing famine.

A third point raised by the conclusion reached earlier relates to the question of just how much we all ought to be giving away. One possibility, which has already been mentioned, is that we ought to give until we reach the level of marginal utility—that is, the level at which, by giving more, I would cause as much suffering to myself or my dependents as I would relieve by my gift. This would mean, of course, that one would reduce oneself to very near the material circumstances of a Bengali refugee. It will be recalled that earlier I put forward both a strong and a moderate version of the principle of preventing bad occurrences. The strong version, which required us to prevent bad things from happening unless in doing so we would be sacrificing something of comparable moral significance, does seem to require reducing ourselves to the level of marginal utility. I should also say that the strong version seems to me to be the correct one. I proposed the more moderate version—that we should prevent bad occurrences unless to do so, we had to sacrifice something morally significant—only in order to show that even on this surely undeniable principle a great change in our way of life is required. On the more moderate principle, it may not follow that we ought to reduce ourselves to the level of marginal utility, for one might hold that to reduce oneself and one's family to this level is to cause something significantly bad to happen. Whether this is so I shall not discuss, since, as I have said, I can see no good reason for holding the moderate version of the principle rather than the strong version. Even if we accepted the principle only in its moderate form, however, it should be clear that we would have to give away enough to ensure that the consumer society, dependent as it is on people spending on trivia rather than giving famine relief, would slow down and perhaps disappear entirely. There are several reasons why this would be desirable in itself. The value and necessity of economic growth are now being questioned not only by conservationists, but by economists as well.[5] There is no doubt, too, that the consumer society has had a distorting effect on the goals and purposes of its members. Yet looking at the matter purely from the point of view of overseas aid, there must be a limit to the extent to which we should deliberately slow down our economy; for it might be the case that if we gave away, say forty percent of our Gross National Product, we would slow down the economy so much that in absolute terms we would be giving less than if we gave twenty-five percent of the much larger GNP that we would have if we limited our contribution to this smaller percentage.

I mention this only as an indication of the sort of factor that one would have to take into account in working out an ideal. Since Western societies generally consider one percent of the GNP an acceptable level for overseas aid, the matter is entirely academic. Nor does it affect the question of how much an individual should give in a society in which very few are giving substantial amounts.

It is sometimes said, though less often now than it used to be, that philosophers have no special role to play in public affairs, since most public issues depend primarily on an assessment of facts. On questions of fact, it is said, philosophers as such have no special expertise, and so it has been possible to engage in philosophy without committing oneself to any position on major public issues. No doubt there are some issues of social policy and foreign policy about which it can truly be said that a really expert assessment of the facts is required before taking sides or acting, but the issue of famine is surely not one of these. The facts about the existence of suffering are beyond dispute. Nor, I think, is it disputed that we can do something about it, either through orthodox methods of famine relief or through population control or both. This is therefore an issue on which philosophers are competent to take a position. The issue is one which faces everyone who has more money than he needs to support himself and his dependents, or who is in a position to take some sort of political action. These categories must include practically every teacher and student of philosophy in the universities of the Western world. If philosophy is to deal with matters that are relevant to both teachers and students, this is an issue that philosophers should discuss.

Discussion, though, is not enough. What is the point of relating philosophy to public (and personal) affairs if we do not take our conclusions seriously? In this instance, taking our conclusion seriously means acting upon it. The philosopher will not find it any easier than anyone else to alter his attitudes and way of life to the extent that, if I am right, is involved in doing everything that we ought to be doing. At the very least, though, one can make a start. The philosopher who does so will have to sacrifice some of the benefits of the consumer society, but he can find compensation in the satisfaction of a way of life in which theory and practice, if not yet in harmony, are at least coming together.

NOTES

1. There was also a third possibility: that India would go to war to enable the refugees to return to their lands. Since I wrote this paper, India has taken this way out. The situation is no longer that described above, but this does not affect my argument, as the next paragraph indicates.

2. In view of the special sense philosophers often give to the term, I should say that I use "obligation" simply as the abstract noun derived from "ought," so that "I have an obligation to" means no more, and no less, than "I ought to." This usage is in accordance with the definition of "ought" given by the *Shorter Oxford English Dictionary*: "the general verb to express duty or obligation." I do not think any issue of substance hangs on the way the term is used; sentences in which I use "obligation" could all be rewritten, although somewhat clumsily, as sentences in which a clause containing "ought" replaces the term "obligation."

3. J. O. Urmson, "Saints and Heroes," in *Essays in Moral Philosophy*, ed. Abraham I. Melden (Seattle and London, 1958), p. 214. For a related but significantly different view see also Henry Sidgwick *The Methods of Ethics*, 7th ed. (London, 1907) pp. 220–221, 492–493.

4. *Summa Theologica*, II–II, Question 66. Article 7, in *Aquinas, Selected Political Writings*, ed. A. P. d'Entreves, trans J. G. Dawson (Oxford, 1948), p. 171.

5. See, for instance. John Kenneth Galbraith, *The New Industrial State* (Boston, 1967); and E. J. Mishan, *The Cost of Economic Growth* (London, 1967).

A Cosmopolitan Perspective on the Global Economic Order

Thomas Pogge

Thomas Pogge's appointments include professor of philosophy at Yale University and a professorial fellow at the Centre for Applied Philosophy and Public Ethics at the Australian National University. His most recent book is *World Poverty and Human Rights: Cosmopolitan Responsibilities and Reforms* (2008).

Many people think that helping the less fortunate is a matter of charity; although it is a good thing to do, it is not morally required. Pogge turns this traditional paradigm on its head. He argues that alleviating global poverty is not a choice, it is a mandate. In part, Pogge derives this duty from the rather unobjectionable negative duty not to harm others. He argues that given the vast disparity in wealth today, the well off are actively harming the world's poor.

In a recent book (Pogge, 2002), I have claimed that we—the more advantaged citizens of the affluent countries—are actively responsible for most of the life-threatening poverty in the world. The book focuses on the fifteen years since the end of the Cold War. In this period, billions of people have suffered greatly from poverty-related causes: from hunger and malnutrition, from child labor and trafficking, from lack of access to basic health care and safe drinking water, from lack of shelter, basic sanitation, electricity, and elementary education.[1] Some 18 million people have died prematurely each year from poverty-related causes, accounting for fully one third of all human deaths. This fifteen-year death toll of 270 million is considerably larger than the 200-million death toll from all the wars, civil wars, genocides, and other government repression of the entire twentieth century combined.[2] . . .

My main claim is then that, by shaping and enforcing the social conditions that, foreseeably and avoidably, cause the monumental suffering of global poverty, we are *harming* the global poor—or, to put it more descriptively, we are active participants in the largest, though not the gravest, crime against humanity ever committed. Hitler and Stalin were vastly more evil than our political leaders, but in terms of killing and harming people they never came anywhere near causing 18 millions deaths per year. . . .

POSITIVE DUTIES

Before doing this, I should dispose of one misunderstanding. My book seeks to show how existing world poverty manifests a violation of our *negative* duties, our duties not to harm. To show this, I leave positive duties aside. I do not assert that there are no positive duties, or that such duties are feeble. Rather, I avoid claims about positive duties so as to make clear that my case does not depend on such claims. My focus is solely on duties not to harm as

Edited Excerpts from Thomas Pogge—A cosmopolitan Perspective on the Global Economic Order—chapter 7 from The Political Philosophy of Cosmopolitanism. © 2005 Cambridge University Press. Reprinted by permission.

well as on duties to avert harms that one's own past conduct may cause in the future. . . .

AN ECUMENICAL APPROACH TO DEMONSTRATING HARM

Let us now look at the arguments of my book. The case I seek to build is broadly ecumenical. I am trying to convince not merely the adherents of some particular moral conception or theory—Lockeans or Rawlsians or libertarians or communitarians for example. Rather, I am trying to convince the adherents of *all* the main views now alive in Western political thought. This ambition makes the task much harder, because I must defend my conclusion on multiple fronts, fielding parallel arguments that address and appeal to diverse and often mutually incompatible moral conceptions and beliefs.

This ecumenical strategy has been confusing to some who complain that I am unclear and inconsistent about the baseline relative to which the global poor are supposedly harmed by existing institutional arrangements.[3] They are right that I do not provide a single consistent such baseline. But they are wrong to see this as a flaw. If I want to convince readers with diverse ideas about morality and justice, then I must support my conclusions with diverse arguments. And these may have to appeal to diverse baselines. A state-of-nature baseline is relevant to a reader with Lockean or Nozickian views. But a Rawlsian will reject such a baseline, insisting that the existing distributional profile should be compared to the profiles achievable under alternative feasible institutional arrangements. To satisfy readers of both kinds, I need to give different arguments to them, each with a different baseline. This is more work, to be sure. But the pay-off is that my case cannot justifiably be dismissed as dependent on some partisan moral premises or theory which readers may feel free to reject.

The ecumenical strategy is broadest and most explicit in the final chapter, which argues for a global resources dividend. My first step there is to show that out world is pervaded by what, following Tom Nagel (Nagel, 1977), I call radical inequality (Pogge, 2002, p. 198);

1. The worse-off are very badly off in absolute terms.
2. They are also very badly off in relative terms—very much worse off than many others.
3. The inequality is impervious: it is difficult or impossible for the worse-off substantially to improve their lot; and most of the better-off never experience life at the bottom for even a few months and have no vivid idea of what it is like to live in that way.
4. The inequality is pervasive: it concerns not merely some aspects of life, such as the climate or access to natural beauty or high culture, but most aspects or all.
5. The inequality is avoidable: the better-off can improve the circumstances of the worse-off without becoming badly off themselves.

I go on to assume that most of my readers demand more than the fact of radical inequality between us and the global poor as proof that we are *harming* them. I also assume that different readers differ on the question of what is missing. To satisfy more readers, I present *in parallel* three second steps of the argument, each of which shows in a different way that the existing radical inequality involves us in harming the global poor. All three strands of the argument lead to the conclusion that today's massive and severe poverty manifests a violation by the affluent of their negative duties: an immense crime in which we affluent citizens of the rich countries (as well as the political and economic "elites" of most poor countries) are implicated.

ENGAGING HISTORICAL CONCEPTIONS OF SOCIAL JUSTICE

In one strand of the argument I invoke the effects of a common and violent history. The present world is characterized not only by radical inequality as defined, but also by the fact that "the social starting positions of the worse-off and the better-off have emerged from a single historical process that was pervaded by massive grievous wrongs" (Pogge, 2002, p. 203). I invoke these historical facts specifically for readers who believe that it matters morally how radical inequality has evolved. Most of the existing international inequality in standards of living was built up in the colonial period when today's affluent countries ruled today's poor regions of the world: trading their people like cattle, destroying their political institutions and cultures, and taking their natural resources. Around 1960, when the colonizers finally left, taking what they could and destroying much else, the inequality in *per capita* income between Europe and Africa had grown to 30:1, and vast inequalities existed also in education, health care, infrastructure, and legal and political organization. These inequalities greatly disadvantaged Africans in their dealings with governments and corporations of the affluent countries. This disadvantage helps explain why the Europe/Africa inequality in *per capita* income has since risen to 40:1. But even if *per capita* income had, since 1960, increased a full percentage point more each year in Africa than in Europe, this inequality would still be 20:1 today and would be fully erased only early in the twenty-fourth century.

Readers attracted to historical-entitlement conceptions of justice disagree about the conditions an historical process must meet in order for it to justify gross inequalities in life chances. On this point, I can once more afford to be ecumenical. The relevant historical crimes were so horrendous, so diverse, and so consequential that no historical-entitlement conception could credibly support the conclusion that our common history was sufficiently benign to justify even the radical inequalities in starting positions we are witnessing today.

In short, then, upholding a radical inequality counts as harming the worse-off when the historical path on which this inequality arose is pervaded by grievous wrongs. "A morally deeply tarnished history must not be allowed to result in *radical* inequality" (Pogge, 2002, p. 203). This is the moral rationale behind Abraham Lincoln's forty-acres-and-a-mule promise of 1863, which of course was quickly rescinded. And it is the rationale for saying that we are not entitled to the huge advantages we enjoy from birth over the global poor, given how these inequalities have been built up.

Some critics may seem to address this strand of the argument when the point out that the radical inequality between Europe and Africa might have

come about even without colonialism.[4] Perhaps Europe could have "taken off" even without slavery and stolen raw materials, and perhaps the resulting inequality would then have been equally great. In the absence of conclusive proof that, without the horrors of European conquest, severe poverty worldwide would he substantially less today, Risse suggests, we are entitled to keep and defend what we possess, even at the cost of millions of deaths each year. (I wonder if he would make the same argument against the forty-acres-and-a-mule proposal.)

As a response to the first strand of the argument, this complaint is irrelevant. The first strand addresses readers who believe that the *actual* history *is* relevant. These readers will say: "Yes, if things had transpired as in Risse's hypothetical, then the citizens of the affluent countries might not, by upholding the radical inequality, be harming the global poor. But this has no bearing on whether such upholding of radical inequality constitutes harm in the *actual* world with its *actual* history."

Still, Risse's complaint resonates with other readers who believe that it is permissible to uphold an economic distribution if merely it *could* have come about on a morally acceptable path. It is such readers that the second strand of my argument addresses. To be sure, *any* distribution, however skewed, *could* have been the outcome of a sequence of voluntary bets or gambles. Appeal to *such* a fictional history would "justify" *anything* and would thus be wholly implausible. Locke does much better, holding that a fictional history can justify the status quo only if the changes in holdings and social rules it involves are ones that all participants could have rationally agreed to. He also holds that in a state of nature persons would be entitled to a proportional share of the world's natural resources. He thus makes the justice of any institutional order depend on whether the worst-off under it are at least as well off as people would be in a Lockean stale of nature with a proportional resource share (see Pogge, 2002, pp. 16, 137–39, and 202–03 for a fuller reading of Locke's argument). Locke held, implausibly, that this condition was fulfilled in his time, claiming that "a King of a large fruitful territory [in the Americas] feeds, lodges, and is clad worse than a day Laborer in England" (Locke, 1960, §41, see §37). I argue that this condition is *not* fulfilled for the global poor today who, living below even the day laborers in Locke's England, are coercively denied "enough and as good" (Locke, 1960, §27, §33) of the world's natural resources without having access to an equivalent substitute.

Readers inclined to a Lockean conception disagree about the relevant state-of-nature baseline that determines how bad the worst social starting positions imposed by a just social order may be. On this question I can once more be ecumenical. However one may want to imagine a state of nature among human beings on this planet, one could not realistically conceive it as producing an enduring poverty death toll or 18 million annually. Only a thoroughly organized state of civilization can sustain horrendous suffering on such a massive scale.

Catering to Lockeans, the second strand of my argument invokes the uncompensated exclusion of the worse-off from a proportional share of global resources: the present world is characterized not merely by radical inequality as defined, but also by the fact that "the better-off enjoy significant advantages in the use of a single natural resource base from whose benefits the worse-off are largely, and without compensation, excluded" (Pogge, 2002, p. 202). The better off—we—are *harming* the worse-off insofar as the radical inequality we uphold excludes the global poor from a proportional share of the world's natural resources and any equivalent substitute.

The point I was making about Locke is quite similar to one Satz puts forth in a tone of criticism. For Locke, she says, "property rights, however acquired, do not prevail In the face of desperate need" because "everyone has an original pre-appropriation claim-right to an adequate subsistence from the resources of the world."[5] This is correct, although the poor can really have a claim only to a proportional resources share, not to adequate subsistence, because there may simply not be enough to go around. But why does Satz speak in this context of a "*positive* 'property right' of the needy in the means of subsistence?"[6] What *are* positive as opposed to negative property rights?

Does Satz want to say that we affluent have merely a positive duty toward the needy? This would suggest that our property rights do prevail after all—that our assets are ours though we ought to give away some. But Satz correctly presents Locke as rejecting this picture: we affluent have *no* rights to property, however acquired, in the face of the excluded. Rather, *they* have a right to what we hold. When we prevent them from exercising this right—when we deprive them of what is justly theirs—then we violate this original right of the poor and we harm them. In this way it is a violation of a *negative* duty to deprive others of "enough and as good"—either through unilateral appropriations or through institutional arrangements such as a radically inegalitarian property regime (this is argued at length in Pogge, 2002, ch. 5).

Let me sum up the first two strands of the argument. These strands address readers for whom the justice of the present economic distribution or of present economic arrangement turns on their actual or imaginable history. I conclude that such conceptions of justice cannot justify the status quo. One may try to justify the coercively upheld radical inequality today by appeal to the historical process that *actually* led up to it. But this appeal fails because the actual historical process is massively pervaded by the most grievous wrongs. Alternatively, one may try to justify this coercively upheld radical inequality by appeal to some morally acceptable *fictional* historical process that *might* have led to it. On Locke's permissive version of this account, some small elite may appropriate all, or almost all, of the huge cooperative surplus produced by modern social organization. But such an elite must not enlarge its share even further by reducing the poor below the state-of-nature baseline so that this elite's share of the cooperative surplus is actually more than IOO percent and the share of the poor correspondingly less than zero. As it is, the citizens and governments of the affluent states are violating this negative duty when we, in collaboration with the ruling cliques of many poor countries, coercively exclude the global poor from a proportional resource share and any equivalent substitute.

ENGAGING BROADLY CONSEQUENTIALIST CONCEPTIONS OF SOCIAL JUSTICE

Most contemporary theorists of justice endorse neither of these historical views. Instead, they hold that an economic order and the economic distribution it shapes should be assessed by its foreseeable effects against the background of its feasible alternatives. Thus Rawls considers a domestic economic order to be just if it produces fair equality of opportunity across social classes and no feasible alternative to it would afford better prospects to the least advantaged.

The third strand of my argument addresses such broadly consequentialist conceptions which invoke the effects of shared social institutions. The present world is characterized not only by radical inequality as defined, but also by the facts that: "There is a shared institutional order that is shaped by the better-off and imposed on the worse-off. This institutional order is implicated in the reproduction of radical inequality in that there is a feasible institutional alternative under which so severe and extensive poverty would not persist. The radical inequality cannot be traced to extra-social factors (such as genetic handicaps or natural disasters) which as such, affect different human beings differentially."[7] When these further facts obtain, so I claim, then the better-off—we—are *harming* the worse-off insofar as we are upholding a shared institutional order that is *unjust* by foreseeably and avoidably (re)producing radical inequality.

Now there are many different such broadly consequentialist conceptions of justice which judge an institutional order by comparing its distributional effects to those its feasible alternatives would have. These conceptions differ along three dimensions. They differ in how they characterize the relevant affected parties (groups, persons, time-slices of persons, etc.). They differ about the metric for assessing relevant effects (social primary goods, capabilities, welfare, etc.). And they differ about how to aggregate relevant effects across affected parties. Once again, my response to such diversity is ecumenical. I am trying to specify very minimal conditions of justice that are

widely accepted. Most broadly consequentialist theorists agree that a national economic order is unjust when it leaves social and economic human rights unfulfilled on a massive scale even while there is a feasible alternative order under which these human rights would be much better realized. Most theorists would demand more, of course. But I need no more for my purpose, because our global economic order does not even meet the very weak requirements that form the common core of the various broadly consequentialist theories of economic justice defended today.

As we have seen, the second strand of my argument, operating on Lockean terrain, conceives justice in terms of harm: prevailing economic arrangements and the present economic distribution are shown to be unjust in virtue of the fact that they harm many by forcing them below any credible state-of-nature baseline. It is worth stressing, then, that the third strand of my argument, catering to broadly consequentialist conceptions of social justice, does not, *pace* Satz,[8] conceive justice and injustice in terms of an independently specified notion of harm. Rather this third strand relates the concepts of *harm* and *justice* in the opposite way, conceiving harm in terms of an independently specified conception of social justice. On my ecumenical response to broadly consequentialist conceptions of social justice, we are *harming* the global poor if and insofar as we collaborate in imposing *unjust* social institutions upon them.

Moreover, *pace* Patten,[9] this third strand of my argument is not addressed to libertarians, who indeed reject any non-historical, broadly consequentialist assessment of social institutions. Libertarians are addressed by the first and, to some extent, by the second strand. To be sure, the third strand, like the two others, is meant to support the conclusion that the immense catastrophe of world poverty manifest not merely the affluents' failure to fulfill their positive duties, but also, and more importantly, their massive violation of their negative duties. But the moral significance of this conclusion can be appreciated far beyond the confines of the libertarian school. Nearly everyone in the affluent countries would agree that our moral duty not to contribute to the imposition of conditions of extreme poverty on people and our moral duty to help protect people from harm in whose production we are implicated in this way are each more stringent than our moral duty to help protect people from harm in whose production we are not materially involved.[10]

As I try to implement the third strand of my argument, specifically for a human right to basic necessities, it involves three main tasks. I seek to show that it is, among broadly consequentialist conceptions, a minimal and widely acceptable demand of justice on all national institutional schemes that these must be designed to avoid life-threatening poverty insofar as this is reasonably possible. I then seek to show that this demand of justice applies not merely to any domestic institutional arrangements, but to the global order as well. And I must then show, thirdly, that there are feasible alternatives to the existing global institutional order under which life-threatening poverty would be wholly or largely avoided.

Task One is easy. There simply is no broadly consequentialist conception of social justice in the field that purports to justify, within one national society, radical inequality of the kind the world at large displays today. To be sure, Paton is right to point out that some libertarians (Nozick) do purport to justify such extreme inequalities. But they do this by appeal to historical conceptions of social justice; and I have sketched my response to such justifications in the preceding section.

Task Two involves a highly complex argument to which I cannot possibly do justice here.[11] So let me here concentrate on Task Three, on which my critics have focused most of their attention.

THE CAUSAL ROLE OF THE GLOBAL INSTITUTIONAL ORDER IN THE REPRODUCTION OF SEVERE POVERTY

Many critics believe that I see the global institutional order as *the main* cause of world poverty. And they respond that, in light of the incompetence, corruption, and oppression prevalent in so many poor countries, this claim is simply not credible or, at the very least, unsupported by empirical evidence. They are wrong on both counts.

Let us begin with a quick general reflection on causes. In the simplest cases, multiple causes *add up* to produce an effect. Thus the smoke in a bar is the sum of the smoke released by all the smokers. In the case of world poverty, however, the relation among causes is more complex in at least two ways. One complexity is that the different causes of poverty, such as global institutional factors and national policies, influence one another's effects.[12] How harmful corrupt leaders in poor countries are, for example, is strongly influenced by whether the global order recognizes such leaders, on the basis of effective power alone, as entitled to sell us their country's resources, to borrow in its name, and to use the proceeds to buy the means of internal repression.

Given this special complexity, it is not correct to identify my assertion that *most* severe poverty worldwide was and is avoidable through global institutional reform with the claim that the existing global institutional order is *the main* cause of world poverty. My assertion is perfectly compatible with the assertion that most severe poverty worldwide was and is avoidable through better national policies and better social institutions in the poor countries. To put it simplistically, the interaction between the two sets of causal factors is not so much additive as multiplicative. The worse each set of factors is, the more it also aggravates the marginal harmful impact of the other.

But if, as development economists like to stress, most severe poverty worldwide was and is avoidable through better national policies and better social institutions in the poor countries, does this not show that our global institutional order is morally acceptable as it is? Am I not, as Patten put it,[13] demanding too much from ourselves, given that the ruling elites in the poor countries could also eradicate much poverty?

Now it is true that many of these elites are incompetent, corrupt, and oppressive. Failing, as badly as we are and often worse, to honor their negative duties not to harm, they are indeed responsible for most severe poverty worldwide. But this is quite compatible with the advantaged citizens in the rich countries also being responsible for most severe poverty worldwide. For it is equally true that most such poverty was and is avoidable through a better global institutional order. Given this basic symmetry, we cannot accept Paton's judgement that *we* should not be required to stop *our* contribution until *they* are ready to stop *theirs*. If this were right, then it would be permissible for two parties together to bring about as much harm as they like, each of them pointing out that it has no obligation to stop so long as the other continues.

The situation is roughly analogous to that of two upstream factories releasing chemicals into a river. The chemicals of each factory would cause little harm by themselves. But the mixture of chemicals from both plants causes huge harm downstream. In this sort of case, we must not hold each factory owner responsible for only the small harm he would be causing if the other did not pollute. This would leave unaccounted-for most of the harm they produce together and would thus be quite implausible. In a case of this kind, provided each factory owner knows about the effluent released by the other and can foresee the harmful effects they together produce, each owner bears responsibility for his marginal contribution, that is, for as much of the harm as would be avoided if he alone were not discharging his chemicals. Each factory owner is then responsible for most of the harm they jointly produce.

Despite this symmetry in my causal account, my critics nonetheless have a point when they accuse me of explanatory globalism[14] (in analogy to the explanatory nationalism of which I am accusing the majority of development economists [see Pogge, 2002, §5.3]). This accusation is accurate in that I *focus* much more on global than on national factors. I do this, because these are the factors that my readers and I are morally responsible for and because, not unrelatedly, these factors are grossly neglected by development economists of all stripes, by the media, and by the citizens of the affluent countries for whom I am writing.

And I have another reason for paying more attention to the causal role of global factors in the reproduction of massive severe poverty. This further reason depends on the second special complexity I mentioned earlier, which is that the causes of world poverty also influence one another. As the global institutional order is *shaped* by the political leaders of the most powerful countries, who in turn are selected and shaped by their domestic institutional arrangements, so the global institutional order powerfully *shapes* the national regimes especially of the weaker countries as well as the composition, incentives, and opportunities of their ruling elites. For example, corrupt rule in poor countries is made much more likely by the fact that our global order accords such rulers, on the basis of effective power alone, the international resource and borrowing privileges just described (see Pogge, 2002, §4.9, 6.3, 6.4). These privileges provide strong incentives to potential predators (military officers, most frequently) to take power by force and compel even the most well-intentioned rulers, if they want to maintain their hold on power, to allow such potential putschists corruptly to divert state revenues. The global order thus exerts a strong influence upon the weaker and poorer countries, which makes them considerably more likely to have corrupt and oppressive national regimes. Not all of them will have such regimes, of course, but many of them will, as is well-illustrated by Nigeria and many other developing countries in which the resource sector accounts for a large fraction of GDP (see Lam and Wantchekon, 1999 and Wantchekon, 1999). This is *another* reason to focus on global factors—especially on those that affect the quality of national regimes in the poorer countries.

Let us now look at the evidence I have for believing that severe poverty is largely avoidable through global institutional reforms. Because the effects of sweeping reforms are harder to assess, I discuss in some detail several small reforms and their likely effects. In the WTO negotiations, the affluent countries insisted on continued and asymmetrical protections of their markets through tariffs, quotas, anti-dumping duties, export credits, and subsidies to domestic producers, greatly impairing the export opportunities of even the very poorest countries. These protections cost developing countries hundreds of billions of dollars in lost export revenues (see Pogge, 2002, §4). Risse believes these protections will be phased out. Let us hope so. Still, these protections certainly account for a sizable fraction of the 270 million poverty deaths since 1989.

MODERATE AND FEASIBLE REFORMS OF THE GLOBAL INSTITUTIONAL ORDER

Are there other feasible reforms of the existing global order through which severe poverty could be largely or wholly avoided? The reform I discuss in most detail involves a small change in international property rights (see Pogge, 2002, ch. 8). In accordance with Locke's inalienable right to a proportional share of the world's resources or some adequate equivalent, this change would set aside a small part of the value of any natural resources used for those who would otherwise be excluded from a proportional share. I show how this *global resources dividend* (GRD) could comfortably raise one percent of the global social product specifically for poverty eradication. And I outline how these funds could be spent so as to provide strong incentives toward better government in the developing countries.

The proposed GRD in the amount of one percent of the global product would currently raise about $320 billion annually, or fifty-six times what all affluent countries combined are now spending on basic social services in the developing world. What sort of impact would this money have? Consider health care. The WHO Commission on Macroeconomics and Health, chaired by Jeffrey Sachs, has put the cost of providing basic medical care in the developing world at $62 billion annually and has estimated that this initiative alone would prevent about 8 million deaths from poverty-related causes each year.[15] Another $20 billion could go to incentivize research into the so-called neglected diseases which, because they affect mostly the poor, are grossly under-researched thus far: hepatitis, meningitis, dengue fever, leprosy, sleeping sickness, Chagas disease, river blindness, leishmaniasis, Buruli ulcer, lymphatic filariasis, bilharzia, malaria, tuberculosis, and pneumonia.

There would be money to give every human being access to clean water and electricity. There would be money for free nutritious meals in schools that children could attend free of charge (thanks to the IMF, many schools in developing countries are now charging attendance fees). There would be money to subsidize micro-lending which has been highly effective in recent decades even while charging interest rates of around 20 percent. And there would be money to relieve the crushing debt burden often accumulated under wholly undemocratic regimes[16] that is weighing down many of the poorest countries.

Critics have worried about domestic cooperation. But how many governments would refuse the offer to spend large amounts of money in their country? Consider India, which has about 30 percent of the world's poor and currently receives about $1.7 billion annually in all kinds of official development assistance from all rich countries combined. Under the reform, some $96 billion of GRD funds could be spent there, greatly benefiting also India's pharmaceutical industry, its agricultural sector, its construction firms, its minimum wage level, its unemployment rate, and its tax intake. India's politicians would be extremely eager to cooperate in securing India's share of the GRD funds.

The GRD, though it re channels money from the consumers of resources to the global poor, is not, *pace* Satz,[17] a form of aid. It does not take away some of what belongs to the affluent. Rather, it modifies conventional property rights so as to give legal effect to an inalienable moral right of the poor. For libertarians, this is the right not to be deprived of a decent start in life through a grievously unjust historical process. For Locke, this is the pre-institutional right not to be excluded, without equivalent substitute, from a proportional share of the world's resources. For broadly consequentialist theorists of justice, this is the right not to have imposed upon one an institutional order that is unjust by virtue of the fact that under this order, foreseeably and avoidably, many human being cannot meet their most basic needs.

Patten claims that mine is just an exercise in re-labeling. But by assuming that I must really be calling for aid and assistance, he is begging the question I raise. Our moral failure in the face of world poverty is a mere failure to aid only if we really are morally entitled to the huge advantages we enjoy, from birth, under present institutional arrangements. And this is exactly what I am denying—by appeal to how our advantages arose historically, by appeal to Locke's resource-share criterion, and by appeal to the massive life-threatening poverty to which the existing global institutional order foreseeably and avoidably exposes the majority of humankind.

Patten worries that if the rich countries were to implement my proposals, they and their citizens would be unfairly disadvantaged vis-à-vis the elites of many poor countries who would continue to refuse to shoulder their fair share of the cost of eradicating global poverty.[18] The details of the GRD proposal show that no country could avoid the levy on resource uses without incurring even greater surcharges on their exports (and possibly imports as well). Still, Patten is right that some politically privileged people in poor countries (and some economically privileged people in rich countries!) will manage to contribute less than their fair share to the eradication of world poverty. What is baffling is how Patten can deem this unfairness a sufficient reason to release us from our duty to contribute.

I suspect he is once more tacitly assuming here that our relevant duty is a duty to aid and that the literature on fair sharing of the burdens of positive duties is therefore relevant. Perhaps one may indeed refuse to contribute one's fair share to a morally urgent aid project on the ground that others similarly placed successfully avoid contributing theirs. But appealing to this thought again assumes what I dispute: that the status quo involves us in violating only *positive* duties toward the global poor. Once it is accepted that we are violating our negative and intermediate duties toward the poor, Patten's postulated permission seems absurd. One may not refuse to bear the opportunity cost of ceasing to harm others on the ground that others similarly placed continue their harming. Thus, in particular, we are not entitled to go on inflicting harm upon the global poor on the ground that

others (predatorial elites in the pool countries) are also continuing. Likewise, we may stop some from harming third parties, and compel some to mitigate harms they have caused, even when we are unable so to stop and to compel all who do harm in a similar way. Thus, in particular, we are no more barred from setting up a GRD by the fact that some of the affluent would unfairly escape its effects than we are barred from setting up a criminal-justice system by the fact that some crimes and criminals are unfairly neither presented, nor deterred, nor punished. Yes, some will get away with murder or with enriching themselves by starving the poor. But this sad fact neither permits us to join their ranks, nor forbids us to reduce such crimes as far as we can.

NOTES

1. Among 6227 million human beings (in 2002), about 831 million were undernourished. 1197 million lacked access to safe drinking water, and 2747 million lacked access to basic sanitation (UNDP, 2004, pp. 129–30). Some 2000 million lacked access to essential drugs (www.fic.nih.gov/about/summary.html). Some 1000 million had no adequate shelter and 2000 million lacked electricity (UNDP, 1998, p. 49). Some 876 million adults were illiterate (www.uis.unesco.org) and 211 million children (aged 5 to 14) did wage work outside their family, 8.4 million of them in the "unconditionally worst" forms of child labor, "defined as slavery, trafficking, debt bondage and other forms of forced labor, forced recruitment of children for use in armed conflict, prostitution and pornography, and illicit activities" (ILO, 2002, pp. 17–18). Females and people of color are heavily overrepresented in all these horrifying statistics (UNDP, 2003, pp. 310–30).
2. See http://users.erols.com/mwhite28/war/1900.htm for the figures and the relevant literature supporting them.
3. Notably Satz: "Comments on Pogge's *World Poverty and Human Rights*," and Patten: "Remarks on Pogge's *World Poverty and Human Rights*."
4. Notably Risse (2003).
5. Satz: "Comments on Pogge's *World Poverty and Human Rights*," p. 16.
6. *Ibid.*
7. *Ibid,* p. 199.
8. Satz: "Comments on Pogge's *World Poverty and Human Rights*."
9. Patten: "Remarks on Pogge's *World Poverty and Human Rights*."
10. These comparisons, once again, hold constant the cost or opportunity cost of the required conduct in the duty bearers as well as the reduction in harm it brings to the beneficiaries.

11. See Pogge (2002), ch. 4, and Pogge (2004).

12. Discussion of the other complexity begins six paragraphs down.

13. Patten: "Remarks on Pogge's *World Poverty and Human Rights*."

14. This accusation is due to Patten: "Remarks on Pogge's *World Poverty and Human Rights*," though he uses the less fitting term "explanatory cosmopolitanism."

15. *The Economist*, 22 December 2001, pp. 82–83.

16. An especially dramatic example of this perverse consequence of the international borrowing privilege is played out in Rwanda: "Perhaps there was no better reflection of the world's shabby treatment of post-genocide Rwanda than the matter of the debt burden incurred by the Habyarimana government. The major source of the unpaid debt was the weapons the regime had purchased for the war against the RPF, which had then been turned against innocent Tutsi during the genocide . . . incredibly enough, the new government was deemed responsible for repaying to those multilateral and national lenders the debt accrued by its predecessors" (International Panel of Eminent Personalities, 2000, §§17.30, 17.33).

17. Satz: "Comments on Pogge's *World Poverty and Human Rights*."

18. Patten: "Remarks on Pogge's *World Poverty and Human Rights*."

Sex & Consequences: World Population Growth vs. Reproductive Rights

Margaret P. Battin

Margaret P. Battin is a professor of philosophy at the University of Utah. Battin is the author of *Ending Life: Ethics and the Way We Die* (2005), and *Ethical Issues in Suicide* (1982, 1995), and is co-author of *Praying for a Cure: When Medical and Religious Practices Conflict* (1999). She has co-edited *Physician-Assisted Dying: The Case for Palliative Care and Patient Choice* (2004) and *Medicine and Social Justice: Essays on the Distribution of Health Care* (2002).

Technology now provides us, via the IUD and subdermal implant, with "automatic" birth control. Due to its nature as "automatic," Battin proposes that contraception, rather than pregnancy, could be the "default mode" for sexual relations. Battin suggests that this technology could be provided as part of routine medical care, such as immunizations, and argues for two criteria, universality and reversibility, in order to justify automatic contraception as a response to overpopulation.

In this short paper, I shall address *two* grave problems: global population growth *and* reproductive rights. It might seem impossible to address these two problems at once, so much at odds the solutions may seem. After all, those worried about population growth insist that individual freedom to have children *must* be limited if the world is to survive, while those concerned with reproductive rights are adamant about protecting women's reproductive liberty—the right to have the children one wants. I plan to step between these two opposing camps to show that, thanks to what may seem to be only a tiny, incremental development in reproductive technology, there is a way of accommodating both

concerns—both limiting children and having the children one wants.

I. THE CONFLICT

World Population Growth

In 1798, Thomas Malthus argued in his famous *Essay on the Principle of Population* that human beings, like other species, may reproduce at a rate that outstrips the "carrying capacity" of the environment they inhabit and so doom themselves to devastation. Malthus' central idea is an extraordinarily simple one: because one reproductive pair can have more children than would simply replace themselves, and because each of these children, together with a reproductive mate, can also have more children than would replace themselves, population growth tends to be exponential. But humans, even if they eat other animal species that can also reproduce exponentially, are ultimately limited by the

Excerpts from paper "Sex & Consequences: World population growth vs. reproductive rights" by Margaret P. Battin, The Center for Philosophic Change, 1977. Reprinted by permission of The Center for Philosophic Exchange and the author.

productive capacity of the land. Since arable land is finite and since (to add modern concerns to the Malthusian argument) enhancement methods like fertilizers and hybridization of plants cannot provide indefinite expansion, cannot renew exhausted natural resources, and cannot guarantee complete disposal of pollutants and waste, if humans reproduce at a rate that exceeds the carrying capacity of their habitat—the earth—they will, literally, eat, litter, and excrete themselves out of house and home. When a species does exceed the carrying capacity of its environment, according to Malthusian theory, it dies off, either partially or completely, and either recovers slowly, adapts sufficiently to change its environmental needs, or becomes extinct. For most species that undergo rapid expansion, population growth is limited by periodic episodes of starvation, epidemics of disease exacerbated by the poor nutritional status of the population, or other similar phenomena. The rule is ironclad: excessive growth brings about dramatic, involuntary population loss.

The human population now stands at 5.8 billion; at its current rate of growth, at which it doubles every 40 years or so, it would rise to 12.5 billion by 2050. Unchecked and proceeding at the same rate of growth, it would then reach 25 billion at the end of the coming century—when our grandchildren or children are still alive—and then 50, 100, 200 billion every additional 40 years. But, of course, this would be impossible, since the food production, natural resources, and waste-disposal capacities of the earth cannot possibly support such an increase. If 200 billion seems barely possible, wait just another 40 years; the number would be 400 billion.

Malthus himself did not advocate "population control" programs; he thought moral restraint might serve as some check, but, a pessimist, he also assumed that the human population, like any overproducing animal species, would go through cycles of expansion and starvation. However, his name has been lent to a wide range of population theorists who hold that if voluntary individual restraint in reproduction cannot be counted on—as Malthus himself believed it could not—population growth controls must be imposed from the outside. These theorists are now often called the neoMalthusians.

Reproductive Rights

Meanwhile, critics—especially the more radical feminist critics—have begun to examine the nature of the programs designed to control population growth. Controlling population growth has meant controlling people, they point out, and has in particular meant controlling women. Population control programs, they insist, are designed largely by men in the First-World, industrialized nations and have been imposed largely without input from the women who are most directly affected: the poor women of the Third World. Contraceptive research has involved technologies designed by scientists, mostly male, in the well-protected northern nations, but they are almost exclusively technologies to be used by the female and are tested, often with grossly inadequate consent, on the "needy" women of the poorer southern nations. They have been imposed by using lies, bribes, pressures, and sometimes outright coercion to achieve population-reduction goals. Furthermore, these feminist critics point out, population-control programs have paid little or no attention to women's subordinate situations in patriarchal societies, their precarious economic circumstances, their lack of education and familiarity with modern medicine, their compromised nutritional status, and their desperate need of other healthcare. Individual "acceptors" are identified as "targets." To be sure, they recognize, some population-control programs have also treated men in problematic ways (the most notorious example has been India's offer of a free transistor radio to men who would have vasectomies), but it has been women who have been the primary targets. As one feminist manifesto succinctly put it, population policy is "racist, sexist, and classist,"[1] imposing the values of those who are privileged on those who are not. And, this critique continues, these programs have committed a conceptual injustice as well: they have *blamed* these women for unrestrained, "excess" fertility, as if problems of global population growth (as well as resulting problems of environmental degradation and immigration pressures on wealthy nations) were exclusively their fault.

• • •

II. THE SOLUTION

I think there is a solution—at least a partial solution—to the conflict between the neo-Malthusians and the feminist and religious defenders of reproductive rights or freedoms. This solution depends on noticing what appears to be minor increment in modern reproductive technology, but it is actually one with major implications. It is easy to notice; but it is difficult to decide what to make of it. I don't know whether you will perceive what I want to discuss as a recommendation, a prediction, a utopian fantasy, a totalitarian plot, a hypothetical conjecture, or a realistic solution; I do know that the topic of contraception often produces discomfort. But it is important to examine the facts. This will mean observing something about the way in which we use contraception, and then noticing that we have already at hand the mechanism of substantial change.

Contraception: How We've Done It in the Past, How We Can Do It Now

What I want to explore is the prospect of what I shall call "changing the default mode" in human reproduction. This is a big—but very simple—idea. As things now work—to get right down to the facts of life as directly as possible—unless something is done to prevent it, in about one occasion in five of sexual intercourse between a male and a female during the female's fertile period, pregnancy results. In this sense, we can say, pregnancy is the normal "default" outcome of sexual intercourse.

To be sure, we have many ways of preventing this outcome. Methods of female contraception, which have in the past included an enormous variety of potions, plugs, timing devices, and barriers made from roots, barks, herbs, and even arsenic and spider eggs, now include a number of sophisticated technologies, including douches, sponges, diaphragms, spermicides, pills, implants, intrauterine devices, injectibles, morning-after drugs, vaccines, timing schedules (including natural family planning), surgical sterilization, and many others. Males, in contrast, are limited to just three basic types of contraception: coitus interruptus, the condom, and vasectomy or other surgical sterilization. But it is possible to divide the full range of contraceptive technologies, both male and female, into two broad groups, and it is this distinction that is crucial to the solution I want to explore.

Most of these technologies share a common cluster of characteristics; they are short-acting, user-controlled, and exposure-sensitive or, more plainly, sex-related. They are addressed to preventing the current episode of possible conception, and must be employed at or near the time of sexual contact in order to prevent it. We can call them "time-of-need" contraceptives. In contrast, a few of the contemporary technologies, plus just one historical example,[2] are long-acting, user-independent, and exposure-insensitive (or "coitus-independent")—they work over an extended period of time, require no effort or attention of the part of the user to be effective, and, most important, require no activation, application, ingestion, or insertion at the time of sex. They do not interfere with sexual activity, and sexual activity does not alter or interfere with them. They are, in a word, "automatic." There are two principal contemporary technologies, which not only have all these characteristics, but are immediately reversible—the intrauterine device, such as the Copper T380A, which is safe and effective in multiparous monogamous women for 8 or more years, and the subdermal implant Norplant, which is placed under the skin of a woman's forearm and, in its current 6-rod formulation, provides contraception for 5 years. There are many other contemporary long-acting contraceptive technologies as well, including oral contraceptives, Depo-Provera, hCG vaccines, and laparoscopic sterilization; but because the former require daily self-dosing and the latter are not immediately reversible or not reversible at all, they do not exhibit all the features of the true "automatic" contraceptive.

These two true automatic technologies, the intrauterine device and the subdermal implant, are both associated with side effects, spotting and bleeding. But both exhibit high efficacy and safety—up to 200 times the contraceptive efficacy of the condom. Indeed, of the modern contraceptive technologies now on the market, all are safer than pregnancy—that is, fewer women will die from using them than would die of pregnancy related causes, a risk which is quite low in this country but in some developing countries is as high as 1:20. There have been no fatalities at all caused by subdermal implants. In terms of risk to life, a woman is almost always safer contracepting than not doing so.

Now notice the difference between the traditional short-acting, "time-of-need" methods and the two truly automatic ones. With the traditional methods pregnancy remains the normal outcome of sexual intercourse, and one must employ the device at or near the time of sexual exposure to prevent it. With the automatic methods, however, the user need do nothing to prevent pregnancy but must do something to make it possible to become pregnant—namely, have the device removed or neutralized. This is what informs the metaphor of "reversing the default mode": it changes what happens if one does nothing to interfere. Just as the word processing program I use in my computer has a default setting for single space, and thus will single space unless I direct it to do something else, so human biology's default is set so that—given fertility and an active sex drive—pregnancy is likely to occur unless one takes steps to have it do something else. But just as I can reset my word processing program to double rather than single space, so these "automatic" forms of contraception in effect reset human biology *not* to result in pregnancy *unless* steps are taken to change it. And it does so in a specific way: it inserts an extra level of choice-making, to be followed by the action of having the device removed, into the reproductive process. With these technologies, it becomes the normal state of affairs that sexual intercourse does *not* result in pregnancy. For it to do so requires an additional, positive act.

We now think of the long-acting methods, including the IUD and Norplant, as just two among the various types of contraceptives from which a woman can choose. (Men currently have no such choice; the only nonpermanent contraceptive methods available for men, withdrawal and

the condom, are both quintessentially exposure-sensitive, "time-of-need" methods that one has to attend to while engaged in sex.) Some women will choose the diaphragm, others rely on their partner's use of a condom, others take the Pill or get an IUD. But this cafeteria array of options, as it is sometimes called, disguises the watershed difference between "time-of-need" and "automatic" methods and their potential for addressing the conflict with which we began, that between global population growth and reproductive rights.

True automatic contraceptives are not yet available for men. But there are several technologies under development which would also be long-acting, user-independent, exposure-insensitive, noninterfering with sexual activity, and immediately reversible: these include the so-called Chinese "cork" device, a small silicon plug inserted in the vas deferens, and its double version, the Shug; a male pill utilizing a testosterone ester; a pizoelectrical cell implanted in the vas which fires at the time of ejaculation, killing sperm; and, perhaps, most promising, SMA, a polymer, styrene maleic anhydride, injected into the vas which lowers the pH of the environment just enough to kill sperm passing through. This latter has been tested for 10 years in rats and monkeys and is now in human trials in India; it has been said to show excellent effectiveness and reversibility, with no toxicity or teratogenicity.[3] None of these male methods really works yet, and you can't buy them yet. But they are under development and, I believe, of incalculable significance in addressing the problems which confront us.

Since we are thinking ahead about the prospects for the world, let us look just ahead to the point where these true automatic contraceptive technologies are fully developed, tested, available and free from side effects, both for women and for men. Let me ask the artless question that so directly addresses the conflict between concerns over world population growth and respect for reproductive rights. It is a remarkably simple question: *What if everybody did it?*—that is, what if everybody used "automatic," background contraception?

The Effects of Universal Automatic Contraceptive Use

What if everybody did it? Remember, after all, the state of the world as we ask this question: Population growth, while declining in rate, is still relentlessly increasing; we can expect world population to double within the next 40 years; and the solutions proposed—development, redistribution, the enhancement of the status of women—are comparatively slow processes, especially in cultures in which traditional values are most firmly entrenched. The population bomb keeps ticking. But suppose everybody were to use "automatic," background contraception. Even in the United States, where about 78% of women use some form of contraception, nonuse, erratic use, and contraceptive failures mean that about 50% of all pregnancies are unplanned. And of these, approximately 50% are terminated in abortion. To be sure, many of the pregnancies which were unplanned would have been planned at a later date, and certainly many of the children born of unplanned pregnancies become welcome and loved, but it is reasonable to estimate that somewhere between 1/2 and 1/4 of the pregnancies now occurring (that is, somewhere between the rate of unplanned and aborted pregnancies) would not occur were the "default mode" reversed and the making of a positive choice were required for pregnancy to occur.

The central assumption here is that women—and parents generally—would *choose to have* fewer children than they would *accept having* if pregnancy occurred. As things now stand, half of all unplanned pregnancies are carried to term—about a third of the total births in the United States. If the default mode were reversed, so that an extra level of choice were inserted into the natural biological process, many of these pregnancies would not be initiated in the first place. If this is so, the result of reversing the default mode on population growth could be dramatic—even in a country, like the U.S., in which the birthrate is already comparatively low and the use of contraception widespread. Presumably, the effect of "reversing the default" would be still greater in the many countries with very high birthrates, where access to contraception is erratic or nonexistent.

It is also important to see that the effect on the birthrate of the universal use of automatic contraception would be greater than if, for instance, RU-486—the so-called French abortion pill—were universally available. Even aside from scruples many women have about abortion, reliance on such technologies to control fertility still requires women to do something to stop pregnancy, rather than do something to start it; and if I am right that they will choose to have fewer children than they would accept having if pregnancy occurs, universal availability of RU-486 would not have nearly the impact on the birthrate that universal use of "automatic" contraception would, even though it would seem to give a woman equally great control over her own reproductive life.

The universal use of automatic contraception would have an equally dramatic effect, I think, on reproductive self-determination. If a woman can become pregnant only when she has made a choice to do so, a choice followed by removal or neutralization of her "automatic" contraceptive device, she is far less vulnerable to being pressured, coerced, or overcome by passion in compromising sexual situations, and hence, risk pregnancy when that has not been her previously considered choice. She cannot become pregnant because she forgot or misused her birth control methods. She cannot become pregnant as the result of rape or involuntary incest, at least unless she is also coerced into requesting removal of her device. Once she has an automatic contraceptive, she cannot be denied access to birth control methods by lack of funds, by pressure from her husband or partner, or by the disapproval of the church or village elders. What reversing the default with "automatic" background contraception does is to alter her decision-making options from a range of negative choices—not to get pregnant now, not to get pregnant tomorrow, not to get pregnant the next day—to a positive one: choosing when to invite pregnancy. She can still reach the same outcome—as many children as she wants, for whatever personal or religious reasons—but she gets there by a different decisional course. Because she cannot become pregnant for a variety of reasons she did not predict or elect, the gain in reproductive freedom is enormous—even if she were always free to abort a pregnancy already in progress.

Furthermore, the universal use of automatic contraceptives by women would also produce a gain in reproductive freedom for men. To be sure, this gain will still be greater where there are automatic contraceptive technologies available for men as well, but even without these future developments there is still a gain in reproductive freedom for men if women routinely, universally, use background methods. Although a man would still be hostage to some degree to the reproductive choices of his female partner, and although he could for instance still be tricked into siring a child by a woman who has her device removed without his knowledge, he is no longer likely to contribute to conception in a nonvoluntary way for a large range of currently fairly frequent reasons, e.g., because his partner made technical errors in contraception—forgot a pill, misused a diaphragm, etc.,—or because in the heat of passion or to avoid interfering with spontaneity and sexual pleasure she or he decided on the spur of the moment to ignore precautions against pregnancy, or because erotic activity which was not intended to be consummatory ended up being that way. Because his female partner can only expose herself to pregnancy as the result of a considered choice followed by a deliberate act, namely having the device removed, a man is protected from the effects of any impulsive or careless decisions or actions on her part that might affect his own reproductive freedom. (Needless to say, reversing the default mode in this way could have substantial impact on paternity issues.) After all, in matters of initiating pregnancy within a sexual relationship, males currently have far less reproductive freedom than females, since the only contraceptive device under male control—the condom—is some 200 times less effective in preventing pregnancy than the most effective technologies under female control. Of course, both parties can say no; but once they've said yes, it is the female who retains the greater degree of control over the reproductive outcome of their intercourse.

For the greatest degree of reproductive freedom, of course, both men and women would be users of similarly long-term, user-independent contraceptive technologies, and the achievement of pregnancy would require considered choices and deliberate acts on the part of both parties. It would take two to tango, so to speak, and conception could not occur without the voluntary, deliberate participation of *both* male and female. We have the female part of the technology for such a world now; we can see the male part on the horizon. And we can see how the universal use of these technologies would produce both a dramatic drop in the birth rate and a concomitant gain in reproductive freedom. Neither effect might be complete—the drop in the birthrate might not reduce population growth rates to zero, and reproductive freedom could still be violated when one partner coerced the other into requesting the removal of the device. But compared to present circumstances, gains both in limiting population growth and in enhancing reproductive freedom would be enormous. This is the central idea I have wanted to bring to you.

III. PROBLEMS WITH THE SOLUTION?

What if everybody did it? But in asking this question, we have skipped over what may seem to be a crucial element, especially if reproductive liberty is an issue: How might it come to be the case that *everybody* did it? Doesn't this have a coercive, almost fascist ring to it, suggesting state control, involuntary imposition, the insertion of contraceptive devices into people with or without their consent? Wouldn't this be just another legacy of colonialism in the Third World, just another manifestation of racist policies in American urban ghettoes, just another expression of "controlista" attitudes on the part of the population-controllers? Wouldn't this be the end of religious freedom? Isn't it important to know just how it might come to be the case that "everybody" did it?

When I said at the outset that I was uncertain whether you would perceive what I am discussing here as a recommendation, a prediction, a utopian fantasy, a totalitarian plot, a hypothetical conjecture, or a realistic solution, it was this point that I had in mind: what reaction there would be to the prospect I've been exploring about "everybody" doing it. After all, at least if current experience is much indication, a simple open market is not likely to result in universal use; not only is there a widespread perception that, if contraception is to be used, any reasonable item from the cafeteria of contraceptive options will do, but the automatic technologies tend to seem quite expensive, with purchase and installation costs all up front, and there is widespread misinformation about their effects. Then there is the ubiquitous assumption "that can't happen to me" among people who perceive themselves as at low risk of unwanted pregnancy, coupled with the assumption that contraceptive use is appropriate only when sexual exposure is actually likely, not as a broad, background precaution. For these reasons, I think an open market would be unlikely to result in sufficiently widespread use of automatic contraception to allow us to speak of the default mechanism as having been reversed, or to produce the predicted effects on either population growth or reproductive freedom.

To engender universal use, then, something more would be required—but this is the point that gives us pause. One can imagine various mechanisms: state control and enforced use is one (not altogether impossible, I imagine, under the doomsday population-control scenarios I described at the outset, either in other countries or eventually even in this one), widespread encouragement by public-advertising and media campaign is another; public bribe (like the transistor-radio program for vasectomies in India) is another; employer or insurer requirement is yet another; and still another—the one I think most probable—is that use of these technologies might become a medical norm, the standard course of gynecological treatment for all adolescent and adult women, and eventually the medical norm for men as well—a health measure much like immunization, to which consent is perhaps superficially solicited but in practice assumed. One can even imagine such technologies—much like routine immunization—required for school entrance, at the junior high or high school level, for both boys and girls. "This is just what I do for all my patients,"

we can imagine the adolescent medicine or ob/gyn physician of the future saying, "I'm just helping them—especially the teenagers—protect themselves from pregnancy or siring pregnancy if they don't want it yet. I vaccinate them against typhoid and diptheria and polio, and I immunize them against pregnancy—until they want it—too."

These ways in which it might come to be the case that "everybody does it" clearly differ in the degree of pressure applied to the user. Some involve persuasion; some involve manipulation or pressure; and some might involve outright coercion. It is these fears that are central to the feminist critique of "controlista" population-limitation programs, and the prospect of eurocentric, racist interference both in other cultures and in minority groups within the United States. After all, it is a frequent observation of population-control enthusiasts that, at current rates of growth, some 80% of the world's population in 2050 will be in the developing nations, and that minority growth rates in the U.S.—especially among Latinos and blacks— are higher than those of whites; these projections fuel concerns about the forcible imposition of biased, targeted, antiminority population-control programs both at home and abroad. There have indeed been aggressive population-control programs, usually involving involuntary sterilization or sterilization with inadequate consent, disproportionately imposed on minority women in the U.S. and Puerto Rico in the past,[4] and we cannot ignore such abuses and the fears they fuel in considering the "solution" examined here.

Thus, we want to ask again, just exactly how would it come to be the case that *everybody* used automatic, background contraception? But it is at this very point in assessing the prospect of universal automatic contraceptive use that we make, I think, a substantial conceptual error. For we focus, I think, on the wrong issue. Assuming, as we have been, that we are speaking of future technologies which are safe, effective, and have no substantial side effects, what is central is not so much how it comes to be the case that they are in universal use, but what would be the conditions under which such use would operate when it is universal.

The Moral Conditions of Universal Automatic Contraceptive Use

I've already argued that reversing the default mode would not only result in potentially dramatic decreases in population growth, but that it would substantially enhance both male and female reproductive freedom. We cannot, I believe, welcome one of these consequences without the other. But the latter—enhanced reproductive freedom— would be the case, I believe, only if two conditions were rigorously met, for instance by being incorporated in law (say, as civil rights or as constitutional guarantees) or in whatever social policies are in effect. Provided these two guarantees are rigorously met, the universal use of background contraceptives can, I think, remain ethically defensible independently of the means it is actually brought about:

(a) *universality.*

If any pressures are to be permitted to secure more widespread use beyond what would be the product of individual, voluntary choice, it must be the case that they are expected or required of everyone—not just those groups perceived to be at the highest risk of unwanted pregnancy. This is true for two principal reasons. For one thing, the requirements of universality are essential to prevent the kind of inequitable treatment and potential genocide that develops as specific racial, ethnic, or behavioral groups are targeted for birth control while others are not. In particular, this precludes the kind of computation of risk, often highly infected with prejudice, that perpetuates stereotypes of group behavior often inapplicable to individuals— for example, the claim that black inner-city teenagers "need" Norplant because their rates of illegitimacy are higher, while white suburban teenagers do not, or that Third World populations "ought" to have the IUD because they are incapable of disciplined economic growth. To be sure, *everyone* means *everyone*—or rather, every fertile woman and, as the technology becomes available, every fertile man, without reference to past, current, or anticipated sexual activity. Universality is

crucial, especially in any program involving pressure of any sort, because it is what guarantees the right not to have oneself, either as an individual or as a member of a group, singled out for the imposition of any contraceptive technology which is not similarly imposed on all other fertile women— and eventually, men—across the board. It is a guarantee of fairness. Thus, the quite legitimate specific fears of minority groups that they will be the special targets of population-control projects— as they often have been in the past—are put to rest by this first condition.

(b) *guaranteed reversibility.*

As a second criterion of morally permissible universal use, it must also be a matter of political, legal, and social guarantee that any woman (and, eventually, any man) can have the device removed or neutralized upon request, without restrictive conditions, though it is to be replaced at the completion of the pregnancy. To do otherwise is to undermine the gain in reproductive freedom that the technology introduces in the first place. This means that there must be no stipulation concerning the maximum number of children a woman or couple may have, the type of child care, the physical or mental health of the mother or father, their income or marital status, their criminal status, or any expected genetic defect in the child. To be sure, guaranteed reversibility will result in some pregnancies which conscientious observers believe ought not occur, but this is not to introduce a new problem; such pregnancies can and do now already occur. Guaranteed removal imposes an obligation upon providers of medical services to make removal upon demand, without financial disincentives, undue waiting periods, or requirements like a minimum-use period before removal. Guaranteed removal would answer some of the objections from population-control programs in the Third World—for example, women's frequent experience of finding physicians trained and available to implant devices, but unavailable, untrained, or unwilling to remove them. It would preclude insurance companies or other cost managers from insisting that in order to obtain "full value" from an expensive device, it must remain in place for the full term of its effective period, or something close to it.

Like the first requirement, universality, there are two principle reasons for this second one, reversibility, as well. First, and obviously, the requirement of reversibility is intended to protect reproductive liberty and to thwart external control: even if a woman can be pressured, manipulated, or coerced into accepting "automatic" contraception in the first place, the brunt of this invasion is mitigated if she is guaranteed removal for any reason, at any time, until after the delivery of a child. Thus, she is still guaranteed the basic choice about whether to have a child—the quintessence of reproductive freedom. This answers the complaint of many critics that the background methods of contraception are "provider-controlled": true, they must be emplaced and removed by a provider, but the provider does not retain control over whether or when it shall be removed; the user does. Of course, if reversibility cannot be guaranteed in a chaotic or unjust society, the only defensible expected use of automatic contraceptives would be if technologies were developed that were self-removable or self-neutralizable, but this would guarantee users far less protection against their own impulses and against abuse by their partners. In any case, such technologies are not yet available.

There is a second, conceptual reason as well here for the criterion of guaranteed reversibility: what is crucial, in changing the default mode in reproduction, is that *reproduction remain a normal, natural process of human biology*—one which one can always have happen.[5] It does not make childbearing a privilege for some; it merely makes childbearing a matter of *deliberate choice* for all. This means that not only women who wish to have one or two children can do so, but those who wish to have a dozen or so can do so as well. The *only* change is to introduce one additional step—the making of a considered choice, followed by a minor medical procedure—into the traditional biological process.

Thus, as we survey our future and our concerns, both about exploding population growth and

authoritarian threats to reproductive and religious rights, I think there is some cause for hope. If we can see that the difference between time-of-need and automatic contraception is not just a little increment in technological progress, but represents a watershed difference, we will be well on our way to resolving *both* problems at once. The solution may not be perfect. And there will be some losses: no "surprise" babies, no leaving reproductive choice to fate, no heady atmosphere of "taking a chance." It will also mean the duplication of protection, where barrier methods are used to prevent the transmission of AIDS and other sexually-transmitted diseases, while the background technologies provide contraception. But there will be gains as well, affecting some of our currently most intractable social issues: except in cases of fetal defect or threat to maternal health, there would be no longer any issue about abortion; there would be no pregnancy resulting from rape or nonvoluntary incest; there would be no nonvoluntary teen pregnancy, no accidental perimenopausal pregnancy, no need for permanent surgical sterilization, and fewer paternity issues. It would even permit much better timing of pregnancy for women with chronic health problems, since pregnancy could be elected at easier points in an ongoing illness rather than coped with when it occurs unexpectedly. Indeed, our ways of thinking about pregnancy and childbearing would undergo radical change—from something one accepts or rejects when it happens to something one chooses to begin.

Now it may seem that this is not such a radical proposal after all. If it does not sound so strange, it is worth remembering that in the developed countries, life is already somewhat like this. Women already have access to contraception, and in many regions, especially Scandinavia and the Netherlands, the use of "automatic" forms and related methods like the Pill is quite widespread. The duplication of protection is also increasingly common, as condoms are used for disease prevention, while the far more reliable background modalities are used for contraception. The timing of pregnancies is routine, as couples try to pick patterns of child-bearing that will enhance their careers, their family lives, and their duties to other family members, and will not unduly strain their physical well-being or their financial resources. And all these things are encouraged by many of their social, governmental, and religious institutions. Furthermore, access to contraception has been increasing in the developing world and, among educated women, childbearing choices tend to follow the same patterns: fewer children, later in life, spaced at greater intervals. So if the picture I've been painting seems in the end oddly familiar, this is just a way of saying that—at least in the privileged parts of the privileged parts of the world, we are almost there, and we can already begin to see the extraordinary significance of the technological developments now occurring. But it is far from completely the case here—after all, half of all pregnancies in the U.S. are unplanned—and it is certainly not that way at all yet in much of the rest of the world.

NOTES

An earlier version of this paper was delivered as the 54th Annual Reynolds Lecture, University of Utah, May 1994. Copyright 1996 by Margaret P. Battin.

1. A. Gabriela, National Women's Coalition of Organizations (Philippines), Resolution, October 1993. *Women's Global Network for Reproductive Rights Newsletter* 43: 8–9 (April–June, 1993), p. 9.
2. The one long-acting, user-independent, exposure-insensitive contraceptive technology recorded from historical times is the fruit pits Arab traders are said to have placed in the uteruses of their camels on long desert trips; this is an early form of the modern intrauterine device.
3. Sujoy K. Guha, "Phase One Clinical Trial of an Injectable Contraceptive for the Male," *Contraception* (October, 1993), 48; pp. 367–375.
4. Loretta Ross, "Why Women of Color Can't Talk About Population," and "Sterilization and 'de facto' Sterilization," *The Amicus Journal* (Winter 1994), pp. 27–29.
5. Of course, some women are infertile for various medical or other reasons. My own view is that the same society that expects or imposes automatic contraception for fertile women ought to provide medical help, including in vitro fertilization and other high-tech modalities, for infertile women who wish it to enable them to increase their own range of reproductive choices; but that is a separate issue.

Perils Amid Promises of Genetically Modified Foods

Mae-Wan Ho

Mae-Wan Ho is a biochemical geneticist and a Reader in Biology at the Open University, United Kingdom, on the Roster of Experts for the Cartagena Protocol on Biosafety, and a Fellow of the National Genetics Foundation. Her many publications include the following books: *The Rainbow and the Worm: The Physics of Organisms* (1993, 1998); *Bioenergetics* (1995); and *Bioelectrodynamics and Biocommunication* (1994).

Ho argues that transgenic agricultural biotechnology will not solve the existing food crises. Rather, agricultural biotechnology is inherently unsustainable, and causes irreparable harm to biodiversity, human, and animal health. Documenting the many risks and harms associated with agricultural biotechnology, Ho argues instead for a return to sustainable traditional agriculture.

THE FOOD "CRISIS"

By the year 2000, the world will need to consume over 2 billion tonnes a year of wheat, rice, maize, barley, and other crops—an increase of 25% compared with 1995 figures.[1] This view was echoed by the World Bank Report for the 1996 World Food Summit in Rome,[2] which warned that the world would have to double food production over the next 30 years. One major solution on offer to "feed the world" is agricultural biotechnology. This, it has been proposed, could be used to genetically modify crops for herbicide, pest, and disease resistance, to improve nutritional value and shelf-life, and also, for the future, to bring about promises of drought and frost resistance, nitrogen fixation,[3] and increased yield.[4]

Agricultural biotechnology is big business, and the mission to feed the world has the irresistible ring of a noble obligation. The same goes for improving the nutritional value of foods. Despite prices having dropped to the lowest on record, more than 800 million people still go hungry, and 82 countries—half of them in Africa—neither grow enough food, nor can afford to import it. Infant mortality rates—a sensitive indicator of nutritional stress—have been experiencing an upturn in recent years, reversing a long-term historical trend. Large numbers of children suffer from malnutrition in developing countries. In India alone, 85% of children under five are below the normal, acceptable state of nutrition.[5]

In view of the current crisis in food production, and the support for agricultural biotechnology as a solution to the crisis—as expressed by the World Bank Report and by Chapter 16 of Agenda 21 of the United Nations Convention on Biological Diversity—it is all the more important to examine the major claims and promises of the technology, as well as the uncertainties and hazards which are not adequately taken into account in existing practices and regulations.

Excerpt from Mae-Wan Ho, "Perils amid promises of genetically modified foods" from Genetic Engineering: Dream or Nightmare?, 1999. Reprinted by permission of the author.

CAN GENETICALLY MODIFIED FOODS FEED THE WORLD OR IMPROVE NUTRITION?

The Poverty Trap of Unequal Power Relationships

Undernutrition and malnutrition, found everywhere in the developing as well as the developed world, stem from poverty, as was admitted in the World Bank Report.

In the Third World, poverty was created, in large measure, by centuries of colonial and postcolonial economic exploitation under the free-trade imperative, and has been exacerbated since the 1970s by the introduction of the intensive, high-input industrial agriculture of the Green revolution.[6] The concentration on growing crops for export has benefited the corporate plant breeders and the elite of the Third World at the expense of ordinary people. In 1973, thirty-six of the nations most seriously affected by hunger and malnutrition exported food to the U.S.—a pattern that continues to the present day.[7] The "liberalisation of trade" under the current World Trade Organisation agreement will make things much worse.[8] While Southern countries are obliged to remove subsidies to their farmers, subsidies to Northern producers have remained untouched. This unequal competition will deprive millions of peasants of their livelihood. In addition, as part of the same WTO agreement, the intellectual property rights of corporate gene manipulators in the North will be protected, and that will restrict the use of indigenous varieties that were previously freely cultivated and sold. Thus, seeds protected by patents will no longer be able to be saved by farmers for replanting without annual royalties being paid to the company which owns them.

Another factor already adversely affecting agricultural biodiversity in Europe is the Seed Trade Act which makes it illegal to grow and sell noncertified seeds, produced by organic farmers from indigenous varieties, certification being biased towards the commercial varieties currently being used in agricultural biotechnology.[9] Far from providing cheaper food for all, agricultural biotechnology will further undermine the livelihoods of small organic farmers all over the world, resulting in increased loss of indigenous agricultural biodiversity.

Discussions on food supply are invariably linked to population growth in the Third World. But these discussions leave out the unequal power relations which exist between different countries and different groups of people. "Food scarcity," like "overpopulation" are both socially generated. While populations in the North are suffering from obesity, cardiovascular diseases, and diabetes from overconsumption, populations in the South are dying of starvation. Simplistic "solutions" which leave out the unequal power relations are oppressive, and ultimately "reinforce the very structures creating ecological damage and hunger."[10]

Biological Diversity, Food Security, and Nutrition

Biological diversity and food security are intimately linked. Communities everywhere have derived livelihoods from natural diversity in wild and domesticated forms. Diversity is the basis of ecological stability.[11] Recent studies show that diverse ecological communities are more resilient to drought and other environmental disturbances which cause the population of individual species to fluctuate widely from year to year.[12] Species within an ecological community are interconnected in an intricate web of mutualistic as well as competitive interactions, of checks and balances that contribute to the survival of the whole. This has important implications for *in situ* conservation, particularly at a time when it is being estimated that 50,000 species will go extinct every year over the next decade.[13]

The same principles of diversity and stability operate in traditional agriculture.[14] Throughout the tropics, traditional agroforestry systems commonly contain well over 100 annual and perennial plant species per field. A profusion of varieties and land races are cultivated which are adapted to different local environmental conditions and possess a range of natural resistances to diseases and pests. Spatial diversity through mixed cropping is augmented by temporal diversity in crop rotation, ensuring the recycling of nutrients that maintain soil fertility. These practices have effectively prevented major outbreaks of diseases and pests and buffered food production from environmental exigencies.

The diversity of agricultural produce is also the basis of a balanced nutrition. Nutrition not only depends on the right balance of protein, carbohydrates, and fats, but also on a combination of vitamins, essential metabolites, cofactors, inorganic ions, and trace metals, which only a varied diet can provide. A major cause of malnutrition worldwide is the substitution of the traditionally varied diet for one based on monoculture crops. The transfer of an exotic gene into a monoculture crop can do little to make up for the dietary deficiencies of those suffering from monoculture malnutrition. The nutritional value of beans, or a combination of rice and beans, will always be greater than that of the transgenic rice with a bean gene.

Monoculture and Transgenic Threats

It is now indisputable that monoculture crops introduced since the Green revolution have adversely affected biodiversity and food security all over the world. According to a FAO report, by the year 2000 the world will have lost 95% of the genetic diversity utilised in agriculture at the beginning of this century.[15] Monoculture crops are genetically uniform and, therefore, notoriously prone to disease and pest outbreaks. The corn belt of the United States was last devastated by corn blight in 1970–1971, while, in 1975, Indonesian farmers lost half a million acres of rice to leaf hoppers. Genetic modification for disease or pest resistance will not solve the problems, as intensive agriculture itself creates the conditions for new pathogens to arise.[16] In 1977, a variety of rice, IR-36, created to be resistant to 8 major diseases and pests, including bacterial blight and tungro, was nevertheless attacked by two new viruses called "ragged stunt" and "wilted stunt." Thus, not only do new varieties have to be substituted every three years, they require heavy input of pesticides to keep pests at bay.

The high inputs of fertilisers, water, pesticides, and heavy mechanisation required by monoculture crops have had devastating environmental effects.[17] Teddy Goldsmith, who started the ecology movement in Britain in 1970, has been a long-time critic of global financial institutions such as the World Bank and the International Monetary Fund for the antiecological projects they finance in the Third World, such as the construction of big dams for irrigation and roads which hasten the clearing of forests. Between 1981 and 1991, the world's agricultural base fell by some 7 percent, primarily due to environmental degradation and water shortages. One-third of the world's croplands suffers from soil erosion, which could reduce agricultural production by a quarter between 1975 and the year 2000. In India, 800,000 square kilometres are affected, with many areas turning into scrub or desert. Deforestation has resulted in 8.6 million hectares of degraded land in Indonesia, which is unable to sustain even subsistence agriculture. Throughout the tropics, vast areas are vulnerable to flooding. Of the world's irrigated land, one-fifth—40 million hectares—suffers from waterlogging or salination. The resultant pressures on agricultural land led to the further marginalisation of small farmers, swelling the ranks of the dispossessed and hungry, while indigenous natural and agricultural biodiversity are eliminated at accelerated rates.

Transgenic crops are created from the same high-input monoculture varieties of the Green revolution, and are likely to make things worse. The greatest proportion of transgenic crop plants is now engineered to be resistant to herbicide, with companies engineering resistance to their own herbicide to increase sales of herbicides with seeds.[18] The immediate hazard from herbicide resistant crops is the spread of transgenes to wild relatives by cross-hybridisation, creating superweeds. Herbicide-resistant transgenic oilseed rape, released in Europe, has now hybridised with several wild relatives.[19]

There are yet other problems. Herbicide-resistant transgenic crops make it possible to apply powerful herbicides, killing many species, directly onto crops. This is so for Monsanto's Roundup®, which is lethal to most herbaceous plants. The U.S. Fish and Wildlife Service has identified 74 endangered plant species threatened by the use of herbicides like glyphosate.[20] This product reduces the nitrogen-fixing activity of soils and is toxic to many species of mycorrhizal fungi which are vital for nutrient recycling in the soil. Glyphosate-type compounds are the third most commonly-reported cause of pesticide illness among agricultural workers. The use of this highly-toxic nondiscriminating herbicide will lead to the large-scale elimination of indigenous species and cultivated varieties, damaging soil fertility and human health besides. Herbicide-resistant transgenic crops also become weeds in the form of "volunteer plants" germinated from seeds after the harvest, so that other herbicides then have to be applied in order to eliminate them, with yet further impact on indigenous biodiversity.

Food Security Depends on Agricultural Biodiversity

In order to counteract the crisis of environmental destruction, loss of agricultural land and indigenous biodiversity created by decades of intensive farming, there has been a global move towards holistic, organic farming methods that revive traditional practices. Previous promoters of the Green revolution are now calling for a shift to sustainable agriculture. Sustainable agriculture is promoted in Chapter 14 of Agenda 21 of the United Nations Convention in Biodiversity, signed by more than 140 countries. Large-scale implementation of biodynamic farming and sustainable agriculture is succeeding in the Philippines.[21] In Latin America, a number of nongovernment organisations have joined forces to form the Latin American Consortium on Agroecology and Development, to promote agroecological techniques which are sensitive to the complexities of local farming methods. Programmes introducing soil conservation practices and organic fertilisation methods tripled or quadrupled yields within a year.[22] Successive studies have highlighted the productivity and sustainability of traditional peasant farming in the Third World[23] as well as in

the North, according to a report published by the U.S. National Academy of Sciences.[24]

Many, if not all, southern countries still possess the indigenous genetic resources—requiring no further genetic modification—that can guarantee a sustainable food supply.

"Over centuries of agricultural practice, traditional societies have developed an incredible variety of crops and livestock. Some 200–250 flowering plants species have been domesticated, and genetic diversity amongst each of these is astonishing: in India alone, for instance, farmers have grown over 50,000 varieties of rice *Oryza sativa*. In a single village in northeast India, 70 varieties are being grown . . . farmers (especially women) repeatedly used and enhanced some varieties which were resistant to disease and drought and flood, some which tasted nice, some which were coloured and useful for ritual purposes, and some which were highly productive."[25]

In Brazil, hundreds of rural communities in the northeast are responding to the current crisis in food production by organising communal seed banks to recover traditional indigenous varieties and to promote sustainable agricultural development, with little or no government support.[26]

It is significant that the World Bank is reported to be planning sharp changes in policy to concentrate its efforts on small farmers in developing countries.[27] It seems obvious that, in order to guarantee long-term food security and feed the world, we can do no better than take the aim of the Convention on Biological Diversity to heart, i.e., help to conserve and sustain existing indigenous agricultural diversity worldwide, and to develop this diversity as the basis of a secure and nutritious food base for all.

Thus, there is no need for genetically modified crops. On the contrary, they will undermine food security and biodiversity. Under the combined efforts of monopoly of transnational genetic manipulators' intellectual property rights and "free trade" agreements of the World Trade Organisation, the livelihoods of small farmers will be further compromised, both by seed royalties and the restrictive practices of seed certification, and unfair competition from subsidised Northern produce. At the same time, the use of toxic, wide-spectrum herbicides with herbicide-resistant transgenic crops will result in irretrievable losses of indigenous agricultural and natural biologic diversity.

There are, in addition, problems and hazards inherent to the practice of the technology itself, which make the regulation of the technology, by a legally binding international Biosafety Protocol under the Convention of Biodiversity, a matter of urgency.

Agricultural Biotechnology Is Misguided by Wilful Ignorance of Genetics

In a publication which aims to "provide consumers with clear and comprehensible information about products of the new [bio]technology," we are told that: "Research scientists can now precisely identify the individual gene that governs a desired trait, extract it, copy it, and insert the copy into another organism. That organism (and its offspring) will then have the desired trait."[28]

This reaffirms the genetic determinist idea that one gene controls one character trait, and that transferring the gene results in the transfer of the corresponding trait to the genetically modified organism, which can then pass it on indefinitely to future generations. It presents the process of genetic modification as a precise and simple operation.

The above account—so typical of that found in publications promoting "public understanding"—is based on a simplistic assumption of genetics that both classical geneticists and plant breeders have rejected for many years, and which has been thoroughly invalidated by all the research findings in the new genetics. Unfortunately, most molecular geneticists, apart from being absorbed into industry, also lack training in classical genetics, and suffer from a severe molecular myopia that prevents them from appreciating the implications and broader perspective of the findings in their own discipline. Damages from intensive agricultural practices have indeed come about because they are based on the old reductionist paradigm, as Vandana Shiva has argued so convincingly.[29] For the same reason,

agricultural biotechnology will bring new problems and hazards. . . .

DANGERS OF IGNORING THE INTERCONNECTED GENETIC NETWORK

Because no gene ever functions in isolation, there will almost always be unexpected and unintended side-effects from the gene or genes transferred into an organism.

One major concern over transgenic foods is their potential to be toxic or allergenic, which has become a concrete issue since a transgenic soybean containing a brazil-nut gene was found to be allergenic.[30] Recent studies suggest that allergenicity in plants is connected to proteins involved in defence against pests and diseases. Thus, transgenic plants engineered for resistance to diseases and pests may have a higher allergenic potential than unmodified plants.[31]

New proteins from bacteria, such as the Bt toxin currently engineered into many transgenic crops, cannot be tested for allergenicity because allergic reactions depend on prior exposures. *This means that post-market monitoring and clear segregation and labelling of transgenic products are essential for proper consumer protection.* Most identified allergens are water-soluble and acid-resistant. Some, such as those derived from soya, peanut, and milk, are very heat-stable, and are not degraded during cooking, whereas fruit-derived allergenic proteins are heat-labile.[32]

A transgenic yeast was engineered for increased rate of fermentation with multiple copies of one of its own genes, which resulted in the accumulation of the metabolite methylglyoxal at toxic, multigenic levels.[33] This case should serve as a warning against applying the "familiarity principle" or "substantial equivalence" in risk assessment. We simply do not have sufficient understanding of the principles of physiological regulation to enable us to categorise, *a priori*, those genetic modifications that pose a risk and those that do not.

• • •

DANGER OF IGNORING THE ECOLOGY OF GENES AND ORGANISMS

Single Genes Impact on the Ecosystem

The most immediate and easily observable impacts of transgenic plants on the ecological environment are due to cross-pollination between transgenic crop-plants and their wild relatives to generate super-weeds. Field trials have shown that cross-hybridisation has occurred between herbicide-resistant transgenic *Brassica napa* and its wild relatives: *B. campestris*,[34] *Hirschfeldia incana*,[35] and *Raphanus raphanistrum*.[36] These impacts have been predicted by ecologists such as Rissler and Mellon,[37] and arise from the introduction of any exotic species, whether genetically engineered or not.

Impacts which are generally underestimated are those due to transgenic soil bacteria. As very few molecular geneticists have any training in soil ecology, they will be ignorant of the important role played by the soil microbes in recycling nutrients for the growth of crop plants. Soil microbiologists Elaine Ingham and her student tested a common soil bacterium, *Klebsiella planticola*, engineered to produce ethanol from crop waste, in jars containing different kinds of soil in which a wheat seedling had been planted.[38] The experiments showed that, in all soil types, the growth of the wheat seedling was drastically inhibited. This was due to the ethanol produced, which had adverse effects on different microbes that were involved in recycling nutrients for the wheat seedling. Elaine has talked about this in several TWN-sponsored seminars, to great effect. She and her colleagues now run a consultancy and research firm for organic farming in the U.S., which is a marvellous way to resist the agrochemical biotechnological encroachment.

The Instability of Transgenic Lines

Traditional breeding methods involve crossing closely-related varieties or species containing different forms of the same genes. Selection is then practised over many generations under field conditions, so that the desired characteristics and the genes influencing those characteristics, *in the appropriate environment*, are tested and harmonised for stable expression over a range of genetic backgrounds. Different genetic combinations, moreover, will perform differently in different environments. This genotype-environment interaction is well-known in traditional breeding, so it is not possible to predict how a new variety will perform in untested environments. In many cases, new varieties will lose their characters in later generations as genes become shuffled and recombined, or as they respond to environmental changes.

In the new genetic modification, completely exotic genes are often introduced into organisms. In the case of plants, the genes are often introduced into plant cells in tissue culture, and transgenic plants are regenerated from the cells after selection in culture. The procedures inherently generate increased genetic instability in the resulting transgenic line.

First, the tissue culture technique itself introduces new genetic variations at high frequencies. These are known as *somaclonal variations*.[39] That is because the cells are removed from the internal, physiological environment of the plant which stabilise their gene expression and genetic complement *in vivo*. It is part of the spectrum of ecological interactions between organism and environment that keep gene expression, genes, and genome structure stable in the organism as a whole. Unilever used tissue culture techniques to regenerate oil palms for planting in Malaysia several years ago. This practice has now been abandoned as many plants have aborted in the field or failed to flower.[40] The second reason for increased instability of transgenic lines is that the process of gene insertion is random and a lot of secondary genetic effects can result, as mentioned earlier. Third, the extra DNA integrated into the transgenic organism's genome disrupts the structure of its chromosome, and can itself cause chromosomal rearrangement,[41] further affecting gene function. Finally, all species have cellular mechanisms which tend to eliminate or inactivate foreign DNA.[42] Transgene instability, particularly "gene-silencing"[43]—the inability of the introduced gene to become expressed in subsequent generations—has been discovered only within the past few years, and is now a recognized problem in both farm animals and plants.[44] In transgenic tobacco, 64% to 92% of the first generation of transgenic plants become unstable. Similarly, the frequency of transgene loss in *Arabidopsis* ranges between 50% and 90%. Instability arises both during the production of germ cells and in cell division during plant growth. The commonest cause is gene silencing due to the chemical modification of the introduced DNA by methylation—a reaction adding a methyl group, $2CH_3$, to the base cytosine or adenosine. Other causes are due to DNA rearrangements and excision of the transgene. The long-term agronomic viability of transgenic crops has yet to be proven. Calgene's Flavr Savr tomato, engineered for improved shelflife, was a financial disaster (as was the transgenic strawberry).[45] Apart from side-effects, such as a skin too soft for the tomato to be successfully shipped, it also failed to grow in Florida, as it was created in California. At least in that regard, commercialisation had been premature. In 1996/7, Monsanto's transgenic Bt-cotton crop, engineered to be resistant to the cotton boll-worm, failed to live up to its promise in the field in both the USA and Australia, partly on account of transgene inactivation.[46] Farmers should beware.

By contrast, the long-established indigenous local varieties and land races are the most stable, as genes and environment have mutually adapted to reinforce the stable expression of desirable characteristics for hundreds, if not thousands, of years. There is no quick fix to establishing ecological balance, which must be restored in order to guarantee our long-term food security.

• • •

HAZARDS FROM HORIZONTAL GENE TRANSFER AND RECOMBINATION

The most underestimated hazards of agricultural biotechnology are from horizontal gene transfers. There is now abundant evidence that gene transfer vectors mediate horizontal gene transfer and recombination, spreading antibiotic resistance and generating new pathogens. Antibiotic resistance arose as the result of the profligate use of antibiotics in intensive farming, which predates genetic engineering. However, current transgenic plants often contain antibiotic-resistant marker genes. When released into the environment, these genes will exacerbate the spread of antibiotic resistance.

• • •

Viral Resistance Transgenes Generate Live Viruses

A major class of transgenic plants are now engineered for resistance to viral diseases by incorporating the gene for the virus's coat protein. Some molecular geneticists have expressed concerns that transgenic crops engineered to be resistant to viral diseases with genes for viral coat proteins might generate new diseases by several known processes. The first, *transcapsidation*, has already been detected, and involves the DNA/RNA of one virus being wrapped up in the coat protein of another so that viral genes can get into cells which otherwise exclude them. The second possibility is that the transgenic coat protein can help defective viruses multiply by *complementation*. The third possibility, *recombination*, has been demonstrated in an experiment in which *Nicotiana benthamiana* plants, expressing a segment of a cowpea chlorotic mottle virus (CCMV) gene, were inoculated with a mutant CCMV, missing that gene. The infectious virus was indeed regenerated by recombination.[47] There is now also evidence that transgenic plants increase the frequency of viral recombination, owing to the continual expression of the viral coat protein gene.[48] As plant cells are frequently infected with several viruses, recombination events will occur and new and virulent strains will be generated. Viral recombination is well documented in animals and the resulting recombinant viruses are strongly implicated in causing diseases. As in animals, plant genomes also contain many endogenous proviruses and related elements which can potentially recombine with the introduced transgene.

Another strategy for viral resistance made use of benign viral "satellite RNAs" as transgenes, thereby attenuating the symptoms of viral infection. However, these were found to mutate to pathogenic forms at high frequencies.[49] These already documented pathogenic recombinants and mutants, regenerated from viral resistant transgenic plants, are particularly significant, as viruses are readily transmitted from one plant to another by many species of aphids and other insects that attack the plants. There is a distinct possibility of new broad-range recombinant viruses arising, which could cause major epidemics.

A potentially major source of new viruses arising from recombination has been pointed out by molecular geneticist Joe Cummins.[50] This is the powerful promoter gene from cauliflower mosaic virus (CaMV), which is routinely used to drive gene expression in transgenic cropplants for herbicide or disease resistance. Like the viral coat protein gene, this viral gene can also recombine with other viruses to generate new broad-range viruses. The CaMV has sequence homologies to human retroviruses such as the AIDS virus, human leukaemic virus, and human hepatitis B virus, and the promoter gene can drive the synthesis of these viruses as well. There is thus a possibility for the CaMV promoter to recombine with human viruses when ingested in food (see below).

Vectors Can Infect Mammalian Cells and Resist Breakdown in the Gut

Among the important factors to consider in the safety of transgenic organisms used as food are the extent to which DNA, particularly vector DNA, can resist breakdown in the gut, and the extent to which it can infect the cells of higher organisms.

Studies made since the 1970s have documented the ability of bacterial plasmids carrying a mammalian virus to infect cultured mammalian cells, which then proceed to synthesise the virus, even though no eukaryotic signals for reading the genes are contained in the plasmid. This is because endogenous provirus and other elements can provide helper-functions which are missing. Similarly, bacterial viruses or baculovirus can also be taken up by mammalian cells.[51] Baculovirus is so effectively taken up by mammalian cells that it

is now being developed as a gene transfer vector in human gene replacement therapy. At the same time, baculovirus is genetically engineered to kill insects more effectively, with genes encoding diuretic hormone, juvenile hormone, Bt endotoxin, mite toxins, and scorpion toxin. The recombinant virus is sprayed directly onto crop plants.[52] Recently, a recombinant baculovirus has even been made containing an anti-sense gene from a human cancer gene, *c-myc*. So, what happens when humans eat foods containing vectors and viral sequences?

It has long been assumed that our gut is full of enzymes which rapidly digest DNA. In a study designed to test the survival of viral DNA in the gut, mice were fed DNA from a bacterial virus, and large fragments were found to survive passage through the gut and to enter the bloodstream.[53] This research group has now shown that ingested DNA end up, not only in the gut cells of the mice, but also in spleen and liver cells as well as white blood cells. "In some cases, as much as one cell in a thousand had viral DNA."[54]

A group of French geneticists found that certain pathogenic bacteria have acquired the ability to enter mammalian cells directly by inducing their own internalisation. They found invasive strains of *Shigella felxneri* and *E. coli* that had undergone lysis upon entering the mammalian cells because of an impairment in cell wall synthesis. The researchers developed these strains as DNA transfer systems into mammalian cells. This transfer was described as "efficient, of broad host cell range, and the replicative or integrative vectors so delivered are stably inherited and expressed by the cell progeny."[55] The researchers are totally unable to recognise the tremendous risks to health involved in developing such a vector. These cross-kingdom transfer vectors are extremely hazardous, as are transgenic vaccines constructed in plants and plants viruses, which are chimeras of animal viral genes inserted into plant viruses. These will have an increased propensity to invade cells, recombine with endogenous viruses and proviruses or insert themselves into the cell's genome.

Within the gut, vectors carrying antibiotic resistance markers may also be taken up by the gut bacteria, which would then serve as a mobile reservoir of antibiotic resistance genes for patho-genic bacteria. Horizontal gene transfer between gut bacteria has already been demonstrated in mice and chickens and in human beings.

In view of all this evidence, it would seem un-wise to ingest transgenic foods, as foreign DNA can resist digestion. It can be taken up by gut bac-teria, as well as by gut cells, and, through the gut, into the blood stream and other cells. DNA uptake into cells can lead to the regeneration of viruses. If the DNA integrates into the cell's genome, a range of harmful effects can result including cancer. Moreover, one cannot assume, without adequate data, that DNA is automatically degraded in *processed* transgenic foods, such as the Zeneca's tomato paste currently on sale in UK supermar-kets, as well as the many foods containing processed transgenic soybean or maize. The public is already being experimented on, *without informed consent*. This is surely against the European BioEthics Convention. Yet, almost noth-ing can be learned, since it is, at present, impossi-ble to collect relevant data when neither labelling nor post-market monitoring is required.

CHECKLIST OF HAZARDS FROM AGRICULTURAL BIOTECHNOLOGY

As a summary, I shall reiterate the arguments on why agricultural biotechnology is unsustainable and poses unique hazards to health and biodiversity.

a. Socio-economic Impacts
1. Increased drain of genetic resources from South to North.
2. Increased marginalisation of small farmers due to intellectual property rights, and other restric-tive practices associated with seed certification.
3. Substitution of traditional technologies and produce.
4. Inherent genetic instability of transgenic lines resulting in crop failures.

b. Hazards to Human and Animal Health
1. Toxic or allergenic effects due to transgene products or products from interactions with host genes.

2. Increased use of toxic pesticides with pesticide-resistant transgenic crops, leading to pesti-cide-related illnesses in farm workers, and the contamination of food and drinking water.
3. Vector-mediated spread of antibiotic resist-ance marker genes to gut bacteria and to pathogens.
4. Vector-mediated spread of virulence among pathogens across species by horizontal gene transfer and recombination.
5. Potential for vector-mediated horizontal gene transfer and recombination to create new pathogenic bacteria and viruses.
6. Potential of vector-mediated infection of cells after ingestion of transgenic foods, to regener-ate disease viruses, or for the vector to insert itself into the cell's genome causing harmful or lethal effects including cancer.

c. Hazards to Agricultural and Natural Biodiversity
1. Spread of transgenes to related weed species, creating super-weeds (e.g. herbicide resist-ance).
2. Increased use of toxic, nondiscriminating her-bicides with herbicide-resistant transgenic plants leading to large-scale elimination of in-digenous agricultural and natural species.
3. Increased use of other herbicides to control herbicide-resistant "volunteers," thus further impacting on indigenous biodiversity.
4. Increased use of toxic herbicides destroying soil fertility and yield.
5. Bioinsecticidal transgenic plants accelerating the evolution of biopesticide resistance in major insect pests, resulting in the loss of a bio-pesticide used by organic farmers for years.
6. Increased exploitation of natural biopesticides in transgenic plants, leading to a correspon-ding range of resistant insects, depriving the ecosystem of its natural pest controls and the ability to rebalance itself to recover from perturbation.
7. Vector-mediated horizontal gene transfer to unrelated species via bacteria and viruses, with the potential of creating many other weed species.

8. Vector recombination to generate new virulent strains of viruses, especially in transgenic plants engineered for viral resistance with viral genes.

9. The vectors carrying the transgene, unlike chemical pollution, can be perpetuated and amplified given the right environmental conditions. It has the potential to unleash cross-species epidemics of infectious plant and animal diseases that will be impossible to control or recall.

CONCLUSION

The World Bank Report for the 1996 Food Summit advocated sustained support for research to develop new plants and technologies, but it also called for "whole new ways" of addressing the problem of the current food crisis, one of which was to concentrate on helping small farmers.

I have presented the reasons why agricultural biotechnology *cannot* alleviate the existing food crisis. On the contrary, *it is inherently unsustainable and extremely hazardous to biodiversity, human, and animal health.* A drastic change of direction is indeed required, targeted to supporting conservation and sustainable development of indigenous agricultural biodiversity. This would both satisfy the stated aims of the Biodiversity Convention and guarantee long-term food security for all.

NOTES

1. See *Food for Our Future, Food and Biotechnology*, Food and Drink Federation, London, 1995.
2. "And still the children go hungry," Geoffrey Lean, *Independent on Sunday*, 10 November, p. 12, 1996.
3. Hardy, 1994.
4. See "Food-population: Experts want to break wheat's yield barrier," A. Aslan, *Inter Press Service*, October 18, 1996.
5. Lester Brown of the World Watch Institute, quoted in Goldsmith and Hildyard, 1991.
6. Goldsmith, 1992.
7. Hildyard, N. (1991). An open letter to Edouard Saouma, Director-General of the Food and Agricultural Organization of the United Nations. *The Ecologist*, 21: 43–46.
8. Watkins, 1996.

9. "Seed action in Germany," E. Beringer, *Landmark*, July/August, p. 13.
10. Hildyard, 1996, p. 282.
11. See DeAngelis, 1992; Pimm, 1991.
12. Moffat, 1996.
13. Raven, 1994.
14. Altieri, 1991.
15. "Throwing out the baby with the bathwater," C. Emerson, *On the Ground*, September, p. 2.
16. Shiva, 1993.
17. See Goldsmith, 1992; Shiva, 1993.
18. Meister and Mayer, 1994.
19. Mikkelsen, *et al*, 1996; see also Ho and Tappeser, 1997.
20. Cox, 1995.
21. Perlas, 1994.
22. See note 14.
23. Shiva, 1993, Introduction; see also note 2.
24. *Alternative Agriculture, Report of the National Academy of Sciences*, Washington. DC, 1989.
25. Kothari, 1994.
26. "Seed action in Brazil," *Landmark*, July/August 1996, p. 10.
27. See note 2.
28. See *Food for Our Future; Food and Biotechnology*, Food and Drink Federation, London, 1995, p. 5.
29. Shiva, 1993.
30. Nordlee, *et al*, 1996.
31. Frank and Keller, 1995.
32. Lemke and Taylor, 1994.
33. Inose and Murata, 1995.
34. See Jorgensen and Anderson, 1994; Mikkelsen *et al*, 1996.
35. See Eber, *et al*, 1994; Darmency, 1994.
36. Eber, *et al*, 1994.
37. Rissler and Mellon, 1993.
38. See Holmes and Ingham, 1995.
39. See Cooking, 1989.
40. Reported by Perlas, 1995.
41. Wahl, *et al*, 1984.
42. See Doerfler, 1992.
43. Finnegan and McEloy, 1994.
44. See Colman, 1996; Lee *et al*, 1995, and references therein.
45. "Monsanto swallows Calgene whole," Vicki Brower, *Nature Biotechnology*, 15, 213, 1997.
46. See "Pests eat Monsanto's profits," *GenEthics News*, 13, p. 1, 1996, also "Bt cotton fiascos in the US and Australia," *Biotechnology Working Group: Briefing Paper Number 2*, BSWG, Montreal, Canada, May 1997.
47. Green and Allison, 1994.
48. Allison, 1995.
49. Paulkaitis and Rossinck, 1996.
50. Cummins, 1994.
51. Heitman and Lopes-Pila, 1993.
52. Cummins, 1997. I thank the author for sending this article to me.
53. Schubert, *et al*, 1994.
54. Cited in "Can DNA in food find its way into cells?" Phillip Cohen, *New Scientist*, 4 January, 1997, p. 14.
55. Courvain *et al*, 1995, p. 1207.

STUDY QUESTIONS: HUNGER AND POVERTY

1. Do you consider it ethically problematic that Hardin bases his conclusion concerning providing aid to countries like India on an assumption of what will happen in the future, rather than being concerned with ending immediate suffering? Provide a utilitarian, Kantian, or rights-based justification for the position you take.
2. Narveson states that "it is both absurd and arrogant for theorists, talking airly about the equality of all people, to insist on cramming it down our throats" when he is arguing against the notion that people should "'count equally' for most of us" regarding our duties to each other, especially the duties of the wealthy to the poor. Evaluate his position, drawing from Singer, the *Declaration of Human Rights*, and other ethical arguments in this book. Are Singer and the *Declaration of Human Rights* "cramming it down our throats" or "tweaking our consciences?"
3. In his essay, Singer quotes Thomas Aquinas from *Summa Theologica:* "whatever a man has in superabundance is owed, of natural right, to the poor for their sustenance." Explain this quote and which of Singer's principles this best illustrates (the strong or the weak version). Why do you think that most people do not live according to this principle?
4. Are we responsible for the poverty and hunger millions face due to the global institutions we endorse or take part in? Are we, as Pogge contends, responsible for the suffering of others due to our inaction? What reasons do you have for your answer, and what changes might these responsibilities warrant in our lifestyles?
5. Battin argues that contraception should be the "default mode" rather than pregnancy, and that contraception should be provided much like routine vaccinations. Why does she argue for automatic contraception, and why does she require universality, and guaranteed reversibility? Given the empirical harms from overpopulation, provide a utilitarian justification for her proposal.
6. What are the major risks of transgenic agricultural biotechnology that Ho documents? What is "sustainable indigenous agriculture" and how does it better address hunger and malnutrition? Ho points out that transgenic products are already in our food supply, and thus the public "is already being experimented on, *without informed consent.*" Drawing from Collins-Chobanian's section on informed consent (in the Environmental Ethics section of this anthology), provide an argument against this experimentation.

SUPPLEMENTARY READINGS: HUNGER AND POVERTY

AIKEN, WILLIAM. "The 'Carrying Capacity' Equivocation." *Social Theory and Practice*, vol. 6(1), Spring 1980.

CHEN, MARTHA. "A Matter of Survival: Women's Right to Employment in India and Bangladesh." In *Women, Culture, and Development*, Nussbaum and Glover, editors. Clarendon Press, 1995.

DONNELLY, JACK. "Satisfying Basic Needs in Africa: Human Rights, Markets and the State." *Africa Today*, vol. 32(1 & 2), 1985.

EMMANUEL, ARGHIRI. "The Multinational Corporations and Inequality of Development." In *Multi-National Corporations and Third World Development*, Ghosh, editor. New York: Greenwood Press, 1984.

FILICE, CARLO. "On the Obligation to Keep Informed about Distant Atrocities" in *Human Rights Quarterly,* vol. 12(3), August 1990, revised 2000.

GENDEL, STEVEN M., et al. *Agricultural Bioethics: Implications of Agricultural Biotechnology.* Ames: Iowa State University Press, 1990.

HARDIN, GARRETT. "Living on a Lifeboat." *BioScience* 24, October 1974.

HARL, NEIL E. *The Farm Debt Crisis of the 1980s.* Ames: Iowa State University Press, 1990.

HERNANDEZ, DONALD. "Fertility Reduction Policies and Poverty in Third World Countries: Ethical Issues." *Journal of Applied Behavioral Science*, vol. 20(4), 1984.

HO, MAE-WAN, Joe Cummins, and Peter Saunders. "GM Food Nightmare Unfolding in Regulatory Sham," *Microbial Ecology in Health and Disease*, 19, 2007.

KAHN, HERMAN. "The Confucian Ethic and Economic Growth." In *The Gap Between Rich and Poor*, Seligson, editor. Boulder, CO: Westview Press, 1984.

KRIMSKY, SHELDON, AND ROGER P. WRUBEL. *Agricultural Biotechnology and the Environment.* Chicago: University of Chicago Press, 1996.

LAFOLLETE, HUGH AND LARRY MAY. "Suffer the Little Children." In *World Hunger and Morality*, second edition, LaFollette and Aiken, editors. Upper Saddle River, NJ: Prentice Hall, 1996.

LAPPE, MARC AND BRITT BAILEY. *Against the Grain: Biotechnology and the Corporate Takeover of Your Food.* Monroe, ME: Common Courage Press, 1998.

LI, LILLIAN M. "Famine and Famine Relief: Viewing Africa in the 1980s from China in the 1920s." In *Drought and Hunger in Africa*, Glantz, editor. New York, NY: Cambridge University Press, 1987.

MAY, LARRY. "Minimal Justice and the World Hunger Problem." In *Agriculture, Change and Human Values.* Gainesville, FL: University of Florida, 1982.

NAGEL, THOMAS. "Poverty and Food: Why Charity Is Not Enough." In *Food Policy*. New York: The Free Press, 1977.

O'NEILL, ONORA. "Rights, Obligations and Needs." *Logos*, 1985.

PARPART, JANE L. "Women's Rights and the Lagos Plan of Action." *Human Rights Quarterly*, vol. 8(2), May 1986.

RIFKIN, JEREMY. *Algeny.* New York: Viking Press, 1983.

SEN, AMARTYA. "The Great Bengal Famine." In *Poverty and Famine*. London, England: Oxford University Press, 1981.

SETHI, J. D. "Human Rights and Development." *Human Rights Quarterly*, vol. 3(3), 1981.

SHIVA, VANDANA. *Biopiracy: The Plunder of Nature and Knowledge.* Boston: South End Press, 1997.

———. *Ecology and the Politics of Survival.* London: Sage Publications, 1991.

———. *Monocultures of the Mind.* London: Zed Books, 1993.

SIMON, LAURENCE. "Social Ethics and Land Reform: The Case of El Salvador." *Agriculture and Human Values*, Summer 1984.

VANDERMEER, JOHN, AND IVETTE PERFECTO. *Breakfast of Biodiversity.* Oakland, CA: The Institute for Food and Development Policy, 1995.

Part V

WAR AND VIOLENCE

I observed that men rushed to arms for slight causes, or no cause at all, and that when arms have once been taken up there is no longer any respect for law, divine or human: It is as if in accordance with a general decree, frenzy had openly been let loose for the committing of all crimes. Confronted with such utter ruthlessness, many men who are the very furthest from being bad men, have come to the point of forbidding all use of arms. . . .

—HUGO GROTIUS[1]

Most justifications for war begin with some reference to the principle of self-defense. Just as it is nearly uncontroversial that a person is morally justified in defending himself or herself from attack, so it is thought that nations are justified in defending themselves from attack by the use of violent force. Recourse is often made to another principle as well, namely, that we are all required to go to the aid of suffering innocent persons. As in the case of self-defense, it is often necessary to use violence to thwart an attack on an innocent person. Finally, many people believe that it is justified to use force to prevent a greater evil than is had by the use of violence. This final view, much more controversial than the first two, is an important element in what has come to be known as the "just war" doctrine.

In sharp contrast to the just war doctrine is the doctrine called pacifism. Pacifists believe that all, or almost all, uses of violence are morally unjustified, especially in relations between nations. This doctrine often starts, as in our quotation from

Grotius (who was not a pacifist), with the claim that individuals are corrupted by engaging in war and violence. In addition, violence is considered a direct affront to the humanity of the person against whom violence is used. The use of violence, even to thwart violence, is always a form of disrespect that fails to treat the other as possessing intrinsic value and as having a life worthy of respect. Most pacifists believe that one need not be passive to be nonviolent; indeed the most famous pacifists of recent times have also developed strategies of collective action and resistance, as we will see in several of the readings in this section.

Those who believe that war can be morally justified usually point to a paradigmatic case of a war waged for a just cause. Typically the Second World War is cited as an example of a war that no reasonable person could have opposed since it had the highest of moral aims, namely, ending the Nazi attempt to exterminate all Jews and subjugate all of Europe. Indeed, some suggest that not only was it morally justified but also there was a strong moral obligation to fight in the Second World War. But even in such wars, pacifists will ask whether there were no other alternative nonviolent courses of action that could have been pursued.

Just as the case for the moral justifiability of some wars is buttressed by the facts of the Second World War, so the case for pacifism is tremendously buttressed by the facts concerning the struggle for India's liberation from British colonial rule. Mohandas K. Gandhi led a successful mass revolution without the use of military arms or violence. And in more recent times, Martin Luther King Jr. led very successful nonviolent confrontations with state governments that engaged in unjust discriminatory practices against Blacks. In both cases, the leaders of these movements were philosophically committed to nonviolence and through their own successful efforts showed the effectiveness of collective political efforts that stop short of war.

There also are moral issues raised by the manner in which war is conducted. A controversy has raged about whether the United States used more bombing runs than necessary in order to achieve their military objectives in the Gulf War. And even more people have claimed that the Iraqis engaged in immoral tactics in using Kuwaiti and American civilian hostages as shields to protect military targets during the same Gulf War. Indeed, many argue that the taking of hostages is always immoral, although it has been a tactic employed by both sides in most of the major wars of the last few hundred years. Even more persuasive arguments are made against the use of nuclear or chemical weapons.

One strand of revolutionary literature argues that most tactics, no matter how violent, are justifiable as long as the cause for which one fights is sufficiently honorable. Indeed, there is a long tradition of important political theorists, from Machiavelli through Lenin, who have argued that the goodness of the cause for which one fights justifies nearly any means one may employ to achieve that end. Such a position, sometimes referred to as "the ends justify the means," has also been roundly criticized for a similarly long period of time.

Our readings begin with an essay by Douglas Lackey, who provides a very careful summary of the main elements and problems of the traditional just war theory. The first part of his essay is devoted to the doctrine of *jus ad bellum*, the principles that justify engaging in war. The two most important considerations are whether the war is planned in defense of a just cause, and whether the war is planned for good intentions. The second half of the essay concerns the doctrine of *jus in bello*, the principles governing justified practices in wars. Here, the two most important considerations are

whether the violence inflicted is proportional to the just objective of the war, and whether the violent instruments of war are directed only at enemy soldiers, rather than at noncombatant civilians.

Gregory Kavka discusses the justifiability of the first Gulf War from 1991. In order to assess this issue, Kavka employs the just war theory's central categories. Kavka raises important questions about how we are to understand right intention, especially in situations where multiple motivations were clearly at work in leading a state to go to war. If the Bush administration was motivated by a desire for cheap oil, things would be very different than if they were motivated by a concern for the people of Kuwait, and for regional stability. Kavka also asks about the predictable collateral damages caused to civilians by the use of long-range missiles. By bombing so as to reduce military casualties, and thereby risking greater civilian casualties, the way the war was waged could have been immoral.

Steven Lee discusses the justifiability of the second Gulf War, the war the United States waged against Iraq beginning in 2003. Like Kavka, Lee approaches this topic from within the just war tradition, asking whether the war satisfied the just cause, proportionality, and last resort conditions. Unlike the first Iraq war, the second Iraq war does not satisfy any of these conditions. Lee then asks whether there were special circumstances about the second Iraq war that made it justifiable nonetheless. Lee also rejects the two most prominent of these arguments, namely that the war was justified because of the nature of the weapons used or the viciousness of the reign of Saddam Hussein. The character of the weapons did not change the justifiability of the war, and the viciousness of the tyrant in question also did not change things enough to overcome the fact that the war failed to meet the minimal conditions for being a just war.

Larry May discusses an aspect of the just war tradition that is underexplored. In addition to *jus ad bellum* considerations about the justifiability of initiating war, and *jus in bello* considerations about the justifiability of fighting war, there are the *jus post bellum* considerations of how to behave after war has ended. May focuses on the question of whether and when to prosecute a state's leaders in the aftermath of war and atrocity. In particular, he focuses on the case of the atrocities in the Darfur region of the Sudan in the first years of the new millennium. Should Al Bashir, the president of the Sudan, be brought to trial for these atrocities? The problem is difficult because it appears that human rights abuses may intensify if the International Criminal Court decided to extradite Bashir to The Hague to stand trial, even though it seems obvious that Bashir had orchestrated these atrocities. May develops a nuanced approach to such questions that follows a fairly straightforward normative principle.

Some feminists have pointed out that they share in common with pacifists a condemnation of a predominantly male-aggressive manner of confronting instances of social injustice. Sara Ruddick sketches several cases of mass movements of resistance inspired by the values which have been traditionally cherished in women's lives. The traditional role of mother as maintainer of love and protector of the innocent has been used, she argues, to combat potentially harmful situations concerning war, state terrorism, and environmental destruction. The efforts of women's groups have resulted, she concludes, in new ways to invent peace.

Martin Luther King Jr. defends a version of nonviolent civil disobedience by reference to several of the main principles of Judeo-Christian morality. Like Gandhi, King sees nonviolence as the expression of love, especially the biblical doctrine of "love thy neighbor as thyself." King outlines a strategy for confronting injustice, which has proven to be the blueprint for many social movements of the last twenty-five years in the United States and Europe. He takes great pains to argue that there is nothing unpatriotic about civil disobedience. Indeed he argues that civil disobedience can be one of the greatest expressions of concern for the laws of a nation.

—LARRY MAY

NOTE

1. Hugo Grotius, *Prolegomena to the Law of War and Peace*, 1625, translated by Francis Kelsey (Indianapolis, IN: Library of Liberal Arts, 1957), p. 21.

Just War Theory

Douglas P. Lackey

Douglas P. Lackey is a professor of philosophy at Baruch College and the Graduate Center of the City University of New York. He is the author of *Moral Principles and Nuclear Weapons* (1984) and *The Ethics of War and Peace* (1989). He is the editor of *Ethics and Strategic Defense* (1989).

Lackey surveys most of the important moral issues involved in the just war tradition. In addition to setting out the traditional justifications for engaging in war and the justifications for various forms of conduct during war, he focuses on several issues that have been quite problematic. For example, he points out that certain practices in the Vietnam War involved terrorist tactics but, according to the traditional doctrine of just war, these practices are justifiable. He also argues that attacks on a nation's citizens living abroad, or the seizure of their property, would not normally count as a just cause that would justify going to war.

WHEN TO FIGHT

Introduction

Rightly or wrongly, pacifism has always been a minority view. Most people believe that *some* wars are morally justifiable; the majority of Americans believe that World War II was a moral war. But though most people have clear-cut intuitions about the moral acceptability of World War II, the Vietnam War, and so forth, few people have a theory that justifies and organizes their intuitive judgments. If morally concerned nonpacifists are to defeat the pacifists to their moral left and the cynics to their moral right, they must develop a theory that will distinguish justifiable wars from unjustifiable wars, using a set of consistent and consistently applied rules.

The work of specifying these rules, which dates at least from Aristotle's *Politics*, traditionally

goes under the heading of "just war theory." The name is slightly misleading, since justice is only one of several primary moral concepts, all of which must be consulted in a complete moral evaluation of war. A just war—a morally good war—is not merely a war dictated by principles of justice. A just war is a morally justifiable war after justice, human rights, the common good, and all other relevant moral concepts have been consulted and weighed against the facts and against each other.

Just war theorists sometimes fail to notice that just war theory describes two sorts of just wars: wars that are morally permissible and wars that are morally obligatory. The distinction between the permissible and the obligatory is persuasively demonstrable at the personal level. If I am unjustly attacked, I have a right to use force in my own defense—assuming that I have no other recourse. But since it is always open for the holder of a right to waive that right, I am not *obliged* to use force in my own defense. But suppose that I have promised to defend Jones, that Jones is now exposed to unjust attack, and that Jones calls for my help. In such a case I am obliged to defend Jones. At the level of nations, the distinction between permissible war and obligatory war has important consequences for policy. Frequently policy analysts demonstrate that a certain use of force passes the tests of just war, and then infer that the war is obligatory, that "justice demands it." But it may well be that the use of force is merely permissible, in which case it is also permissible to forgo the use of force. Indeed, there may be powerful prudential considerations why such a merely permissible just war should not be fought.

Another little point in the logic of just war theory deserves attention. In just war theory, the terms "just" and "unjust" are logical contraries. It follows that in war one side at most can be the just side. But it is possible that both sides may be unjust, and it is fallacious to think that if one side is provably unjust, the other side must be provably just. If your enemy is evil, it does not follow that you are good.

In undertaking the moral evaluation of war, it is natural to distinguish rules that determine *when* it is permissible or obligatory to begin a war (*jus ad bellum*) from rules that determine *how* a war should be fought once it has begun (*jus in bello*). *Jus ad bellum* rules apply principally to political leaders; *jus in bello* rules apply principally to soldiers and their officers. The distinction is not ironclad, since there may be situations in which there is no morally permissible way to wage war, in which case it follows that the war should not be waged in the first place. (Some believe that American intervention in Vietnam was such a case.) In this section we take up *jus ad bellum*; the next section is devoted to *jus in bello*.

Competent Authority

From the time of Augustine, theorists have maintained that a just war can be prosecuted only by a "competent authority." Augustine . . . considered the use of force by private persons to be immoral; consequently the only permissible uses of force were those sanctioned by public authorities. Medieval authors, with a watchful eye for peasant revolts, followed Augustine in confining the just use of force to princes, whose authority and patronage were divinely sanctioned. Given these

scholastic roots, considerations of competent authority might appear archaic, but it is still helpful for purposes of moral judgment to distinguish wars from spontaneous uprisings, and soldiers and officers from pirates and brigands. Just war must, first of all, be war.

To begin, most scholars agree that war is a controlled use of force, undertaken by persons organized in a functioning chain of command. An isolated assassin cannot wage war; New York City's Mad Bomber in the 1950s only metaphorically waged war against Con Edison. In some sense, then, war is the contrary of violence. Second, the use of force in war must be directed to an identifiable political result, a requirement forever associated with the Prussian theorist Karl von Clausewitz. An "identifiable political result" is some change in a government's policy, some alteration in a form of government, or some extension or limitation of the scope of its authority. Since the extermination of a people is not an identifiable political result, most acts of genocide are not acts of war: The Turks did not wage war against the Armenians, nor did Hitler wage war on the Jews. (The American frontier cliché, "the only good Indian is a dead Indian," expresses the hopes of murderers, not soldiers.) And since the religious conversion of people is, in most cases, not a political result, many holy wars, by this definition, have not been wars.

Our definition of war as the controlled use of force for political purposes does not imply that wars can be waged only by the governments of nation-states. Many rebels and revolutionaries have used controlled force through a chain of command for political purposes, and there have been at least as many wars within states as there have been wars between states. If civil wars are genuine wars, the scope of "competent authority" must be extended from princes and political leaders to rebels and revolutionaries as well. But, as the case of Pancho Villa perhaps indicates, it is sometimes difficult to distinguish revolutionaries from bandits. In international law, this difficulty is described as the problem of determining when a rebel movement has obtained "belligerent status."

In the most recent international discussion of this issue, at the Geneva Conference of 1974–1977, delegates agreed that in the case of conflicts arising within a single nation-state between the government and "dissident armed forces or other organized groups," a state of war shall exist, provided the dissident forces are

> . . .under responsible command, exercise such control over part of its territory as to enable them to carry out sustained and concerted military operations and [to implement the laws of war]. (Protocol II, Article 1.1)

This recognition of belligerent status, however,

> shall not apply to situations of internal disturbances and tensions, such as riots, isolated and sporadic acts of violence, and other acts of similar nature, as not being armed conflicts. (Protocol I, Article 1.2)

According to these rules, the American Confederacy in 1860, by virtue of its military organization and control of territory, qualifies for belligerent status, whereas the Symbionese Liberation Army, which controlled no territory, and the Newark rioters of 1967, who obeyed no commands, fail to qualify. By this standard, the American Civil War was war but the Patty Hearst kidnapping was crime, verdicts with which most people would agree.

But the new Geneva standard does not always yield satisfactory results. The partisan movements in World War II—the resistance movements in France, Italy, and the Ukraine, and Tito's great movement in Yugoslavia—rarely could claim specific territory as their own, yet their struggles can hardly be dismissed as unjust on grounds of absence of competent authority. Different perplexities arise in the case of peasant movements, where frequently territory is controlled from the capital by day and by the revolutionaries at night. Perhaps the requirement of "territorial control" is too strong.

The new Geneva standard also requires that genuine belligerents must be capable of carrying out "sustained and concerted military operations." This proviso would deny belligerent status to revolutionary groups that engage primarily in terrorist attacks against civilians, and most people would happily classify such terrorists as international outlaws. But what of revolutionary groups that do not engage in "sustained and concerted

military operations"—which, in many cases, would be suicidal for the revolutionaries—but engage in sustained acts of terror against government buildings and officials of the incumbent regime? The campaign of assassination directed by the National Liberation Front (NLF) in Vietnam against village chiefs and other officials siding with the Saigon government was, at one point, the main form of its revolutionary struggle, and it seems pointless to deny the NLF belligerent status on the ground that its members were not engaging in sustained and concerted military operations. Though it might be criticized on other grounds, the NLF assassination campaign was controlled use of force directed to political ends, not a riot and not sporadic violence. It was dirty, but it was war.

Right Intention

One can imagine cases in which a use of military force might satisfy all the external standards of just war while those who order this use of force have no concern for justice. Unpopular political leaders, for example, might choose to make war in order to stifle domestic dissent and win the next election. The traditional theory of just war insists that a just war be a war for the right, fought for the sake of the right.

In the modern climate of political realism, many authors are inclined to treat the standard of right intention as a quaint relic of a more idealistic age, either on the grounds that moral motives produce disastrous results in international politics or on the grounds that motives are subjective and unobservable. ("I will not speculate on the motives of the North Vietnamese," Henry Kissinger once remarked, "I have too much difficulty understanding our own.") But it is unfair to dismiss idealistic motives on the grounds that they produce disaster in international politics, since realistic motives have produced their own fair share of disasters. It is a mistake to dismiss motives as unobservable, when they are so often clearly exhibited in behavior. The real difficulty with the demand for idealistic motives is that people usually have more than one motive for each of their actions, which makes it difficult or impossible to specify *the* motive for the act.

Despite the difficulty of multiple motives, it is important to retain some version of the rule of right intention as part of the theory of just war. No thoughtful person can fail to be disturbed by current international practice, in which leaders make policy decisions without regard for moral considerations and then have their staffs cook up moral rationalizations after the fact. If it is too much to insist that political leaders make decisions solely on moral grounds or even primarily on moral grounds, we can insist that desire for what is morally right be at least *one* of their motives.

It follows from this qualified insistence on moral motivation in the political leadership that political leaders must be able to justify their decisions on moral grounds. They may not act primarily or solely for the right, but they must have some reason, producible on request, for thinking that they are acting for the right, among other things. For those who let slip the dogs of war, it is not sufficient that things turn out for the best. The evils of even a just war are sufficiently great that we can demand of leaders who initiate war that they understand the moral character of the results they seek.

If desire for the right must be included as one of the motives for just war, are there any motives that must be *excluded*? Various authors have insisted that a just war cannot be motivated by love of violence or hatred of the enemy. Even in the fifth century Augustine wrote, "The real evils in war are love of violence, vengeful cruelty, fierce and implacable enmity, wild resistance, lust for power, and the like" (*Contra Faustum*, XXII.75). Most people will agree that a leader who has love of violence or hatred of the enemy as his sole or chief motivation for war has a bad intention. But Augustine and other authors go further and argue that it is immoral to make war if hatred is just one of the many motivations one has for fighting. The rule is severe, but worth considering.

Consider the American campaign against Japan in World War II. By the usual standards, the American decision to fight against Japan satisfied the rules of just war. But as the war proceeded, many Americans, stirred up by wartime propaganda, were seized with racial animosity and came to hate all Japanese as such. The 4-year internment

of 180,000 innocent Japanese Americans, the campaign of extermination against Japanese cities, and the attack on Hiroshima were all caused or rendered tolerable by this atmosphere of hate. Observing this, Augustine would condemn this hatred of the Japanese as sin and the war against Japan as unjust. Nevertheless, it would be unreasonable to tell the relatives of those who died at Pearl Harbor or on Bataan that they should not feel hatred toward those whose acts and decisions took the lives of those they loved.

The difficulties concerning hatred can perhaps be resolved by distinguishing justifiable from unjustifiable hatred. Hatred of leaders who choose to wage unjust war is justifiable; hatred of their compatriots and coracialists is not, since hatred of human beings as such—apart from their voluntary acts—is not a morally acceptable emotion. By this standard, American leaders who chose wartime policies as a result of race hatred toward the Japanese were not engaged in just war, even if their policies were acceptable by all other moral tests.

Just Cause

The most important of the *jus ad bellum* rules is the rule that the moral use of military force requires a just cause. From the earliest writings, just war theorists rejected love of war and love of conquest as morally acceptable causes for war: "We [should] wage war," Aristotle wrote, "for the sake of peace" (*Politics*, 1333A). Likewise, the seizure of plunder was always rejected as an acceptable cause for war. Beyond these elementary restrictions, however, a wide variety of "just causes" were recognized. The history of the subject is the history of how this repertoire of just causes was progressively cut down to the modern standard, which accepts only the single cause of self-defense.

As early as Cicero in the first century B.C., analysts of just war recognized that the only proper occasion for the use of force was a "wrong received." It follows from this that the condition or characteristics of potential enemies, apart from their actions, cannot supply a just cause for war. Aristotle's suggestion that a war is justified to enslave those who naturally deserve to be slaves,

John Stuart Mill's claim that military intervention is justified in order to bestow the benefits of Western civilization on less advanced peoples, and the historically common view that forcible conversion to some true faith is justified as obedience to divine command are all invalidated by the absence of a "wrong received."

Obviously, the concept of a "wrong received" stands in need of considerable analysis. In the eighteenth century, the notion of wrong included the notion of insult, and sovereigns considered it legitimate to initiate war in response to verbal disrespect, desecrations of national symbols, and so forth. The nineteenth century, which saw the abolition of private duels, likewise saw national honor reduced to a secondary role in the moral justification of war. For most nineteenth century theorists, the primary wrongs were not insults, but acts or policies of a government resulting in violations of the rights of the nation waging just war.

By twentieth-century standards, this definition of international wrongs providing conditions of just war was both too restrictive and too loose. It was too restrictive in that it failed to recognize any rights of *peoples*, as opposed to *states*: rights to cultural integrity, national self-determination, and so forth. It was too loose in that it sanctioned the use of military force in response to wrongs, the commission of which may not have involved military force, thus condoning, on occasion, the first use of arms.

These two excesses were abolished in twentieth-century international law. The right to national self-determination was a prevailing theme at the Versailles conference in 1919 and was repeatedly invoked in the period of decolonization following World War II. Prohibition of first use of force was attempted in drafting of the UN Charter in 1945:

Article 2(4): All Members shall refrain in their international relations from the threat or use of force against the territorial integrity or political independence of any state or in any other manner inconsistent with the Purposes of the United Nations.

Article 51: Nothing in the present Charter shall impair the inherent right of individual or collective self-defense if an armed attack occurs against a member of the United Nations, until the Security Council has taken the measures necessary to maintain international peace and security.

Strictly speaking, Article 51 does not prohibit first use of military force: to say that explicitly, the phrase "if an armed attack occurs" would have to be replaced by "if and only if an armed attack occurs." Nevertheless, Article 51, coupled with Article 2(4), rules out anticipatory self-defense. Legitimate self-defense must be self-defense against an actual attack.

The UN Charter represents the most restrictive analysis of just cause in the history of the subject. In discussions since, members of the United Nations have continued to assume that just cause consists only in self-defense, but "self-defense" has come to be understood as a response to aggression. The definition of "aggression" thus becomes central to the analysis of just cause. In the United Nations, a special committee established to analyze the concept of aggression produced a definition adopted by the General Assembly on 14 December 1974:

Article 1. Aggression is the use of armed force by a State against the sovereignty, territorial integrity, or political independence of another State, or in any other manner inconsistent with the Charter of the United Nations. . . .

Article 2. The first use of armed force by a State in contravention of the Charter shall constitute *prima facie* evidence of an act of aggression [although the Security Council may come to determine that an act of aggression has not in fact been committed] . . .

Article 3. Any of the following acts regardless of a declaration of war shall . . . qualify as an act of aggression:

(a) The invasion or attack by the armed force of a State on the territory of another State, or any military occupation, however temporary;
(b) Bombardment by the armed forces of a State against the territory of another State;
(c) The blockade of the ports or coasts of a State by the armed forces of another State;
(d) An attack by the armed forces of a State on the land, sea, air, or marine and air fleets of another State; . . .
(e) The sending by or on behalf of a State of armed bands, groups, irregulars, or mercenaries, which carry out acts of armed force against another State of such gravity as to amount to the acts listed above. . . .

Article 4. The acts enumerated are not exhaustive.
Article 5. No consideration of whatever nature, whether political, economic, military, or otherwise, may serve as a justification for aggression. . . .
Article 7. Nothing in this definition . . . could in any way prejudice the right to self-determination,

freedom, and independence, as derived from the Charter, of peoples forcibly deprived of that right . . . particularly peoples under colonial and racist regimes or other forms of alien domination; nor the right of these peoples to struggle to that end and to seek and receive support. . . .

By reading between the lines, the intent of the special committee can be easily discerned. In failing to enumerate under "acts of aggression" such traditional causes of war as attacks on citizens abroad, assaults on nonmilitary ships and aircraft on the high seas, and the seizure of property of aliens, the committee counted as aggression only military acts that might substantially affect the physical security of the nation suffering aggression. The only violation of rights that merits the unilateral use of force by nations is the physically threatening use of force by another state. . . .

The Rule of Proportionality

It is a superficially paradoxical feature of just war theory that a just cause need not make for a just war. If the just cause can be achieved by some means other than war, then war for that just cause is not morally justified. If the just cause *might* be achieved by other means that have not been attempted, then war for that just cause is not just war. If the cause is just but cannot be achieved by war, then war for that cause is not just war. These rules, sometimes called the rule of necessity, the rule of last resort, or the "chance of victory" requirement, are part of that section of just war theory which acknowledges that some just causes are not sufficiently weighty, on the moral scales, to justify the evils that war for those just causes might produce. The rule of proportionality states that a war cannot be just unless the evil that can reasonably be expected to ensue from the war is less than the evil that can reasonably be expected to ensue if the war is not fought.

The rule of proportionality is easy to state but hard to interpret, since there are no guidelines as to what counts as an "evil" when the rule is applied. Suppose that we interpret an "evil" as a loss of value, that is, as death, injury, physical and psychological suffering, misery, and so forth. On this view of evil, the rule of proportionality implies that a war is just only if there will be more death,

suffering, and so forth if the war is not fought than if the war is fought: a just and proportionate war does more good than harm. Given the destructiveness of war, the rule of proportionality, on this interpretation would declare that almost all wars, even wars with just causes, have been unjust wars.

Suppose that we count as "evils" not merely losses of welfare but also losses that are violations of someone's rights. Then the rule of proportionality implies that a war is just if more rights would be violated if the war is not fought than if the war is fought. Since we have defined a just cause as a cause that seeks to prevent violations of rights, on this interpretation of the rule of proportionality, almost all wars with just causes have been proportionate wars.

Which interpretation of "evil" is the most appropriate for the moral analysis of war? If we interpret "evil" as "violation of rights," then the rule of proportionality, which was supposed to provide an additional and independent check on the moral permissibility of war, is subsumed into the requirement of just cause. If the rule of proportionality is to do any work, we must consider an "evil" to be the destruction of a value. But then the problem arises that the rule condemns almost all wars and reduces just war theory to antiwar pacifism. Some revision of the rule is in order.

From the standpoint of theories of moral rights, a rule which says that war is unjust unless it does more good than harm is far too restrictive. If a war has a just cause, then it is a war in defense of rights and, according to most theories of rights, the maintenance and protection of rights is morally permissible unless the defense of rights causes a *great deal* more harm than good. Accordingly, in just war theory, we can replace the traditional principle—a just war must cause more good than harm—with the less restrictive rule that a war for a just cause passes the test of proportionality unless it produces a *great deal* more harm than good. Even this greatly liberalized rule of proportionality will declare that many wars fought for just causes have been unjust wars, since many wars for just causes have in fact produced a great deal more harm than good. On the other hand, if a war is fought for a just cause and produces only slightly more harm than good, the liberalized rule of proportionality will not judge that war to be unjust. . . .

HOW TO FIGHT

Introduction

People who believe that there are moral limits defining *when* wars should be fought naturally believe that there are moral limits defining *how* they should be fought. The idea that there are right and wrong ways to conduct war is an ancient one. In the Hebrew Bible, God states that though it may be necessary to kill one's enemy, it is never permissible to cut down his fruit trees (Deut. 20:19). In the sixth century B.C. the Hindu Laws of Manu specified, "When the King fights with his foes in battle, let him not strike with weapons concealed in wood, nor with barbed, poisoned, or flaming arrows."

Over the centuries, a vast array of rules and customs constituting *jus in bello* have been elaborated. There are rules that specify proper behavior toward neutral countries, toward the citizens of neutral countries, and toward neutral ships. There are rules governing what can and cannot be done to enemy civilians, to enemy soldiers on the battlefield, and to enemy soldiers when they are wounded and when they have surrendered. There are rules concerning proper and improper weapons of war, and proper and improper tactics on the battlefield.

In the late nineteenth and twentieth centuries, many of these "laws of war" were codified in a series of treaties, conventions, and protocols, signed and ratified by most of the principal nations of the world. Nations ratifying these sets of rules undertook to impose them on their own military establishments, pledging to prosecute violations and punish wrongdoers. When domestic enforcements have fallen short, nations victorious in war have undertaken the prosecution of violations perpetrated by defeated enemies. (Victorious nations are rarely prosecuted.)

With the exceptions of the Geneva Convention banning chemical warfare (1925) and the Second Protocol to the Fourth Geneva Convention (1977),

the United States has ratified most of the principal international conventions regarding the laws of war. In their field manuals, the various military services of the United States consider themselves bound by the Hague Conventions of 1899 and 1907, by the Geneva Conventions of 1929, and by the four Geneva Conventions of 1949, which govern the sick and wounded on the battlefield (I), the sick and wounded at sea (II), prisoners of war (III), and the protection of civilian persons in time of war (IV).

Necessity, Proportionality, and Discrimination

For the student approaching the laws of war for the first time, the profusion of covenants, treaties, customs, and precedents can be bewildering. But fortunately there are a few leading ideas that have governed the development of the laws of war. The first is that the destruction of life and property, even enemy life and property, is inherently bad. It follows that military forces should cause no more destruction than is strictly necessary to achieve their objectives. (Notice that the principle does not say that whatever is necessary is permissible, but that everything permissible must be necessary.) This is the principle of necessity: that *wanton* destruction is forbidden. More precisely, the principle of necessity specifies that a military operation is forbidden if there is some alternative operation that causes less destruction but has the same probability of producing a successful military result.

The second leading idea is that the amount of destruction permitted in pursuit of a military objective must be proportionate to the importance of the objective. This is the *military* principle of proportionality (which must be distinguished from the *political* principle of proportionality in the *jus ad bellum*). It follows from the military principle of proportionality that certain objectives should be ruled out of consideration on the grounds that too much destruction would be caused in obtaining them.

The third leading idea, the principle of noncombatant immunity, is that civilian life and property should not be subjected to military force: Military force must be directed only at military objectives. Obviously, the principle of noncombatant immunity is useful only if there is a consensus about what counts as "civilian" and what counts as "military." In the older Hague Conventions, a list of explicit nonmilitary targets is developed: "buildings dedicated to religion, art, science, or charitable purposes, historic monuments, hospitals . . . undefended towns, buildings, or dwellings." Anything that is not explicitly mentioned qualifies as a military target. But this list is overly restrictive, and the consensus of modern thought takes "military" targets to include servicemen, weapons, and supplies; the ships and vehicles that transport them; and the factories and workers that produce them. Anything that is not "military" is "civilian." Since, on either definition, the principle of noncombatant immunity distinguishes acceptable military objectives from unacceptable civilian objectives, it is often referred to as the principle of discrimination. (In the morality of war, discrimination is good, not evil.)

There is an objective and subjective version of the principle of noncombatant immunity. The objective version holds that if civilians are killed as a result of military operations, the principle is violated. The subjective version holds that if civilians are *intentionally* killed as a result of military operations, the principle is violated. The interpretation of "intentional" in the subjective version is disputed, but the general idea is that the killing of civilians is intentional if, and only if, they are the chosen *targets* of military force. It follows, on the subjective version, that if civilians are killed in the course of a military operation directed at a military target, the principle of discrimination has *not* been violated. Obviously, the objective version of

the principle of discrimination is far more restrictive than the subjective.

The earlier Hague Conventions leaned toward the objective version of the principle of discrimination. The later Geneva Convention (IV), as interpreted in the Second Protocol of 1977, leans toward the subjective version:

> The civilian population as such, as well as individual civilians, shall not be the object of attack. . . . Indiscriminate attacks are prohibited, [including] those which are not directed at a specific military objective, those which employ a method or means which cannot be directed at a specific objective, or those which employ a method or means the effects of which cannot be limited or which are of a nature to strike military objectives and civilians or civilian objects without distinction.

If we adopt the subjective version of the principle of discrimination, it does not follow that any number of civilians may be permissibly killed so long as they are killed in pursuit of military objectives. The number of civilian deaths resulting from a military operation remains limited by the principle of proportionality. In sum,

> In all military operations, civilians should not be the target of attack. The deaths of civilians or damage to their property which are side-effects of military operations must be necessary for the achievement of the objective and proportionate to its importance.

The principles of necessity, proportionality, and discrimination apply with equal force to all sides in war. Violation of the rules cannot be justified or excused on the grounds that one is fighting on the side of justice. Those who developed the laws of war learned through experience that just causes must have moral limits.

Was the [First] Gulf War a Just War?

Gregory S. Kavka

Gregory S. Kavka was professor of philosophy at the University of California, Irvine. He is the author of *Hobbesian Moral and Political Theory* (1986) and *Moral Paradoxes of Nuclear Deterrence* (1987).

Kavka argues that the first Gulf War might have been justified if it turned out that the reason the Bush administration launched the war was to liberate the people of Kuwait and to stabilize the region rather than to obtain cheap oil. Employing the categories of the just war tradition, Kavka also asks whether the severe risk of collateral damages to civilians might not have rendered the way the war was fought to be unjustified.

In the early months of 1991, the United States—in alliance with a number of other nations—fought a large scale air and ground war to evict Iraq's occupying army from the emirate of Kuwait. In this paper, I will consider the question of whether this U.S. military campaign was a just war according to the criteria of traditional just war theory[1]—the only developed moral theory of warfare that we have.[2] My aim, however, is not so much to reach a verdict about the morality of the Gulf War, as it is to identify relevant moral issues, and to reveal certain serious problems of application that are inherent in just war theory itself.

Just war theory divides into two-parts concerning, respectively, the question of whether or not to fight a particular war (justice of war) and the question of how the war is conducted (justice in war). I begin by considering whether it was just, according to the justice of war criteria, for the U.S. to fight the Gulf War at all. I then turn to the

Gregory S. Kavka, "Was the [first] gulf War a just war?" *Journal of Social Philosophy*, Vol. 22, No. 1, pp. 20–29, 1992. © Blackwell Science. Reprinted by permission.

question of whether the way the war was conducted satisfied the criteria of justice in war.

I. SHOULD THE WAR HAVE BEEN FOUGHT?

To be a just war, a military campaign must satisfy each of four criteria: it must be authorized by *competent authority*, fought for a *just cause*, motivated by the *right intentions*, and must not cause harms that are out of *proportion* with the goods achieved. I think it is fairly clear that the first two criteria were satisfied in the case of the Gulf War. Although there was never a declaration of war by the U.S. Congress, the passage of resolutions by both houses of Congress—and the United Nations security council—which authorized the use of force to expel the Iraqi army from Kuwait, meant that U.S. President George Bush was acting as a competent authority in ordering U.S. troops into battle.[3] And the vindication of the rights of self-protection and self-determination of the Kuwaitis against the occupying Iraqi forces is a paradigm of a just cause. When we turn to the criteria of Right

Intention and Proportionality, however, things get considerably more complicated.

Right Intention

The criterion of Right Intention concerns the subjective motivations of the war-making entities. One general difficulty with just war theory is that it is usually collective entities, like nations, that fight wars and there are two competing philosophical accounts of the nature of the motives and intentions of such collective entities. According to the *individualist account*, statements about the motives and intentions of collective entities are merely convenient abbreviations for more complex statements about the motives and intentions of the particular individual members of those entities. But the competing *collectivist account* says that motives and intentions can be attributed to corporate entities themselves if the actions of the entities' members express corporate policy and flow from corporate decision procedures. As Peter French, a prominent collectivist, puts it: "[A] Corporation's Internal Decision Structure . . . licenses the predication of corporate intentionality. . . . [W]hen the corporate act is consistent with, an instantiation or an implementation of established corporate policy, then it is proper to describe it as having been done for corporate reasons, . . . as corporate intentional."[4] As we shall see, both the collectivist and individualistic accounts pose serious problems of application when applied to a concrete situation such as U.S. actions in the Gulf War.

Consider first the collectivist account. Assuming that proper U.S. procedures were used in authorizing the war, the key question is what U.S. policy or policies the Gulf War implemented or instantiated. Doubtless there were many U.S. policies this war may be said to have implemented, and this fact points immediately to two sorts of problems. First, of the various policies implemented, must they *all* be morally good (or at least morally neutral) policies if the Right Intention criterion is to be satisfied? Or must this be true of only the majority of them, or of the most important ones? Second, at what level of

specificity are the policies to be described and evaluated? U.S. policies, described at the most general levels (e.g., "do the right thing," "help friendly nations in trouble," "protect the national interest,") are likely to be morally good or morally neutral. More specific descriptions of these policies that imply their immorality are likely to be controversial. Thus, while all might agree that "protect Middle East oil supplies to the West" was one policy implemented by the Gulf War, critics and friends of U.S. foreign policy are likely to disagree whether the implicit clause in the policy says "by any means necessary" or "by any proper means." The answer to this question is vital in determining the morality of the policy, and hence of the collective intention which implements it according to the collectivist account.

How, in principle, are such questions (about what the *real* collective policy is) to be answered? Presumably by looking at three sorts of evidence: past behavior of the collective, the nature of the collective's decision procedures and the sorts of considerations that carry weight in that procedure, and the particular descriptions of policy that influenced decision makers in the case at hand. The inclusion of the first two elements suggests that, according to the collectivist account, we cannot give a proper account of U.S. motives in the Gulf War without a more general determination of the morality of U.S. behavior in international relations, and the influence various considerations (including moral ones) have within the foreign-policy decision-making apparatus of the U.S. Since these matters are far beyond the scope of this paper, I turn instead to the individualist account which focuses exclusively on the third element: how the decision makers involved thought of what they were doing and why they did it.

According to the individualist account, "collective motives and intentions" are simply agglomerations of individual motives and intentions among the collectives' members. Unfortunately, we have no good account that tells us how to determine (or accurately describe) the motives of a collective when the motives of its various members are diverse and various, as they typically are. Even among a small leadership group—say a head of state and her small circle of advisors—there are likely to be a variety of motives for embarking on a military campaign. Indeed, even if we focus on a single decision maker like President Bush, there may be a number of motives present, and even the individual in question may not know what they all are and which are the most important ones. And even if we put aside epistemological questions about knowing people's motives, just war theory gives us no guidance as to how to deal with the multiplicity of motives. Whose motives count? Must they all be morally legitimate ones, or only the majority of them, or most of the important ones, or most of the important ones of the most influential decision makers? In the absence of answers to these questions, we cannot—on the individualist account—really apply the criterion of Right Intention with great confidence.

Let us sidestep these problems in applying the individualist account to the Gulf War, together with epistemological problems about determining people's real motivations, by making two assumptions. First, it is the motives of President Bush and his top advisors that matter, and second, their publicly stated intention of promoting a new world order is really what motivated their actions in the Gulf crisis. I am far from convinced that the second assumption is correct. But it would be wrong to dismiss it out of hand, on the grounds that some have, namely that previous U.S. failures to intervene militarily in situations as bad as the Kuwaiti one show that our leaders' motives in the Gulf War were imperialistic (control of the Gulf), economic (cheap oil), or privately political (reelection). Just war theory, or any other plausible account of international morality (e.g., a rule-utilitarian one), does not require nations to intervene militarily in all situations of international injustice or aggression. It is perfectly permissible, indeed wise and desirable, for nations to limit their interventions to situations in which grave aggressions need to be prevented or reversed, the nation possesses the means to reliably bring this about, and the nation's interests would be significantly adversely affected

if it did not do so. The mere fact that a nation picks and chooses its interventions to coincide with feasibility and national interest does not mean its motives are bad, nor that is has no concern for halting aggression. This is not to say that patterns of intervention may not constitute *evidence* about the motivations of a nation's leadership. It just says that a history of selective intervention, in itself, is no evidence of impure motives when there is an intervention, and we may not dismiss the second assumption solely on the grounds that the U.S. has failed to intervene when less oil-laden states have been the victims of aggression.

Similar points apply to two other common objections against U.S. intentions being proper in the Gulf situation: that the U.S. has fought clearly unjust wars in the past (from the conquest of the American Indians to the recent invasion of Panama), and that previously it armed and encouraged the aggressors in this very war—the Saddam Hussein regime in Iraq. At most, on the individualist account, these facts form part of a complex pattern of evidence about U.S. motives and intentions in the current situation. They do not in themselves show that these motives and intentions are bad ones. As regards the first argument, in particular, it must be remembered that just war theory is designed to evaluate particular wars and the way they are conducted, it does not attempt to characterize a nation's history of involvement in wars in general. (Thus, the theory allows that just as a person of bad character may, on occasion, perform a right action, so a nation whose foreign policy is normally immoral may sometimes engage in just wars.) And while the second argument about our prior support for Iraq does have moral implications, they point toward—rather than away from—U.S. involvement in the Gulf War. For if the U.S. negligently created a danger by its prior coddling of the Iraqi regime, and the Kuwaitis suffered grievously as a result, the U.S. might bear a special responsibility to repair the effects of its negligence. On this line of reasoning, what would otherwise be a moral option for the United States—evicting the Iraqi army from Kuwait militarily—would become a moral responsibility or duty.[5]

The New World Order and the Nonaggression Principle

Some of the considerations cited above suggest that promoting U.S. economic and political interests in cheap oil and international influence may have been important motivating factors in determining U.S. actions in the Gulf. But they do not definitely rule out the possibility that the administrations' stated motive—promotion of a new world order—was in fact the predominant one. It is therefore worth inquiring whether the Right Intention criterion would be satisfied if promoting the new world order was indeed the guiding U.S. motive in fighting the Gulf War.

We may begin this inquiry by asking a question to which the Bush administration has not offered a clear answer: What is this new world order supposed to be? A cynical view would be that the new world order consists in the U.S. having its way in the world by force or threats of force, now that the Soviets have been weakened by internal problems.[6] But there is another interpretation of the new world order, one whose promotion—in my view—would count as a motive satisfying the criterion of Right Intention. If I am right, and if it is possible that promoting a new world order in this sense was in fact the main motive of U.S. leaders for going to war, then—on the individualist account of collective intentions—the Right Intention criterion would not necessarily disqualify the Gulf War from being a just one.

The alternative interpretation of the new world order equates it with an old idea. A recent brief statement of it is given by political columnist George Will: "Thou shalt not cross borders with armies."[7] This is a principle of nonaggression by sovereign states against one another, a prohibition against external groups altering status quo international boundaries by the use of military force. This principle is justified because it is a useful convention, not because there is anything inherently desirable about status quo political boundaries. It is just that the status quo represents a unique salient point of compromise between nations and groups who would draw and redraw political boundaries in conflicting ways.[8] On this view of the conventional

status of the international status quo, the principle of nonaggression receives a justification along the lines Churchill is supposed to have offered for democracy: Its only virtue is that it's better than the alternatives. The nature of the alternatives is illustrated by Bernard Lewis' comment about the Gulf crisis. "If Saddam's case against Kuwait is accepted, no frontier in the continent of Africa and few in Asia would be safe, since almost every state could have equally legitimate claims on its neighbors."[9]

The importance of the status quo convention can be illuminated by comparison with David Hume's conventional analysis of property.[10] Everyone benefits, according to Hume, from there being principles of ownership and transfer of property, rather than no such rules. The advantages of having such rules, in terms of rational planning, a sense of security, and incentives for trade and investment, are clear. But different people would fare best (or better) under different sets of rules, and there is no unique set of such rules that is derivable as "best" or "most fair" on a purely rational basis. Nonetheless, since all greatly benefit from their being some such rules, the ones laid down by custom and tradition constitute a uniquely salient—and hence potentially stable—compromise among the various possible sets of property rules that various people would most prefer.

A similar argument can be made, I think, about status quo national boundaries. It seems to be a fact that most people prefer to be governed by others who are like them in race, ethnicity, language, or religion. Whether this is an intrinsic preference, or an instrumental one derived from the belief that they will fare better under the governance of their own kind, does not matter for our purposes. Thus, while all benefit from there being some clearly defined international borders,[11] they have quite diverse preferences regarding where the borders are drawn. In particular, most would prefer to have the boundaries drawn so that their group is in a clear majority position in their nation. Thus, Northern Irish Protestants want borders drawn so that they have a state in which they are the majority, while their Catholic brethren would prefer to merge with the South so that they would be in the majority. Conversely, minority groups concentrated in specific regions may wish to secede so that they can be governed by members of their own groups.

But since there is no way to divide populations into nations so that everyone is in the majority, some compromise solution is called for. The natural one—because it is most salient and because people are likely to have made their plans based on it—is the status quo. Any status quo arrangement is bound to be unsatisfactory to many, and may grow more so as conditions change. Internal political forces and external political and economic pressures will not suffice to overturn all of the unsatisfactory regimes.[12] So the status quo oriented nonaggression principle has its costs. But the disadvantages to all of allowing international boundaries to be legitimately contestable by outside force would be much greater. With everything up for grabs, there is likely to be much more international violence: bloody invasions and escalating warfare. The nonaggression principle, enforced by the use of force if necessary and feasible, is—like the property convention—a highly useful one. If the new world order consists of its implementation, promoting that order is one legitimate motive for engaging in war. And there is some evidence, from journalists' reports, that this was at least one of the primary motives of the U.S. leadership in deciding to fight, if necessary, to expel the Iraqis from Kuwait.[13]

Proportionality

The criterion of Proportionality says that the good aimed at in fighting a war must outweigh the bad involved in, and caused by, the war itself.[14] There are three general difficulties with applying this criterion that make it difficult to determine whether the criterion was satisfied in the case of the Gulf War.

First, and most familiarly, there are enormous empirical difficulties in determining the effects of a war, even when it is over, together with possible disagreements about the scheme of value to be used in assessing the war and its consequences. Even if we waive the latter issue, the question about effects will remain largely unanswered for a very long time, since almost everyone agrees that it is the long-term effects on peace and stability in the Middle East that are most important, and they are not yet evident (if they ever will be).

Second, it is unclear whether we should apply the Proportionality criterion with respect to actual outcomes or what the agents involved reasonably believed at the time they made their decisions.[15] The latter alternative has the advantage of taking the just war theory as a practical, action-guiding theory that is designed to help statesmen and citizens guide their deliberations about going to war, rather than a set of abstract formulas usable only by outsiders to praise or condemn after the fact. We would normally think of the subjective "reasonable belief" version of the criterion of Proportionality as being easier on decision makers: it does not expect them to be prescient and does not subject them to Monday morning quarterbacking. But, in this case, using the "reasonable belief" version of the criterion may make it *harder* for the war in question to satisfy that criterion. For at least as regards the immediate effects, the Gulf War was shorter and involved fewer casualties (on both sides) than was reasonably expected ahead of time by top U.S. officials.

Third, evaluating a war in terms of its good and bad upshots is more complicated than simply observing its actual effects in the world. We must also compare the war and its effects to what the world would have been like had the war not occurred, i.e., to a *counterfactual* situation. But we cannot observe what would have happened, but did not; we can only hypothesize it based on what the world was like and our limited ability to identify and extrapolate trends.

Further, it is not obvious *which* counterfactual situation we are to consider in making our comparison: the one resulting from the nation in question doing nothing,[16] from its doing what it would most likely have done if it did not fight, or from its doing what (besides, possibly, fighting) would have maximized utility. This last way of identifying the relevant alternative may be too strong: it turns the Proportionality criterion into a requirement to maximize utility. But the first way seems too weak: it allows fighting when negotiations (or threats) would achieve the same ends more cheaply.[17] And the middle way can set the baseline of comparison too low. Suppose, for example, a nation would most likely turn its army to slaughtering a domestic minority if it did not fight the war in question. Then even a costly and unnecessary war might satisfy the Proportionality criterion.

Unable to solve this problem of picking out the relevant alternative in a satisfactory way, I will henceforth simply *assume* that the relevant alternative in the Gulf situation was to continue the policy actually pursued prior to the outbreak of fighting: military defense of Saudi Arabia combined with economic sanctions against Iraq. Even given this assumption, however, and even if all the data were in about future actual developments in the region, we would not know for sure whether the war produced a favorable balance of good over evil. For we would not know what *would have happened* had the alliance not fought the war. Perhaps continuation of the economic sanctions would have worked to force Iraq from Kuwait or Saddam Hussein from power. Though I doubt this is likely to have occurred, if it had, it would have set a marvelous precedent for a new world order: cancellation of aggressive gains by united diplomatic and economic action rather than war. A more likely possibility is that a purely defensive force in Saudi Arabia would have sufficed to control Iraq's military ambitions, while Kuwaiti oil riches paid off Iraqi debts and provided the Iraqis with a new interest in regional stability. This outcome, sad as it would have been for Kuwait, would not necessarily have been intolerable for the world as a whole, nor worse than the actual consequences of the Gulf conflict.

The fair conclusion to draw, I think, is that we do not know whether the Gulf War satisfied the criterion of Proportionality and may never know. This is due less to the peculiarities of the Gulf War than to general problems concerning applicability of the Proportionality criterion: potential disagreement about values, factual uncertainty and complexity, necessity of comparison with indeterminate counterfactual situations, and ambiguity between "actual outcomes" and

"reasonable belief" interpretations of the criterion.[18] But even this agnostic conclusion suggests that the Gulf War fares better than most wars as regard proportionality. Most wars have clearly cost much and achieved little in terms of human well being. Supporters of the Gulf War can claim, without absurdity, that something humanly significant (the liberation of Kuwait and the removal of the Iraqi military threat) has been achieved at a reasonable cost.

Last Resort

Some interpretations of just war theory require, as a separate criterion, that all available peaceful alternatives be exhausted before a war can be justified.[19] I prefer to view this principle as a powerful rule of thumb to be used in applying the Proportionality criterion. Given the enormous costs of war, it is highly unlikely that it is proportionate to go to war before pursuing all peaceful alternatives for settling a dispute. But in the odd case where it is proportionate to fight before trying all alternatives that might conceivably work—for example, when an aggressor will use any extra time to make his military position unassailable—a nation is justified in doing so.

Though I do not endorse the last resort idea as a separate criterion that must be satisfied for a war to be just, I think it is instructive to look briefly at whether the U.S. went to war in the Gulf as a last resort. Many members of the U.S. Congress apparently thought not; they voted in favor of continuing economic sanctions rather than going to war. But suppose the administration was right and the economic sanctions would not have been sufficient to force Iraq from Kuwait. (This view is credible in view of the fact that a tremendous air war did not suffice to make the Iraqis withdraw.[20]) Did the Bush Administration go the last mile for peace, as it claimed, by offering—and having—direct talks with Iraq at the highest level in order to prevent war?[21] Their apparent aim was to get Iraq to withdraw by credibly threatening to fight without actually fighting.[22] In this they failed.

But there was an alternative, potentially more effective, way of carrying out this strategy for avoiding this war that was not attempted. The war occurred because the two Presidents—Bush and Hussein—looked at different precedents and drew different lessons. Bush looked at World War II, and saw Hussein as a Hitler-like tyrant who had to be stopped by superior military force.[23] Hussein looked at Vietnam and the barracks-bombing in Lebanon and concluded that the U.S. would not sustain a military operation in which it suffered heavy casualties.[24] To get Iraq out of Kuwait without fighting, it was necessary to erase that conclusion from Hussein's mind, other than by verbal threats that he simply would not believe.

Suppose, however, that President Bush had publicly declared that he would not run for reelection in 1992 unless the Iraqi army was out of Kuwait and the original Kuwaiti government restored to power. This announcement would constitute the kind of precommitment to fight to the end in Kuwait that Hussein—a high political leader who is assumed to value political power above all else—would both believe and understand. If he had any doubts about the determination of top American leadership to drive him from Kuwait by force if necessary, this simple public act would have erased them. It would also erase any illusions that once the war began and there were casualties, American leaders would be inclined to pull back or compromise.

This course of action would have had its moral downside. If this last resort were tried but failed, the administration would have incentives to continue a stalemated war past the point of diminishing returns. Nonetheless, if President Bush had wished to walk the last mile for peace by maximizing his chances of expelling Iraq from Kuwait by threats rather than war, this is a policy he might have been well-advised to pursue. Whether his failure to do so renders the subsequent war "disproportionate" depends upon whether this maneuver would have significantly increased the chances of a peaceful settlement. One may reasonably doubt this if one believes that Iraq's behavior during the war indicates that nothing short of decisive military defeat would have driven them from Kuwait.

There is a further issue concerning satisfaction of the Last Resort criterion in the Gulf War. Just prior to the start of the coalition's brief and decisive ground campaign, the Soviet Union was apparently making some headway toward brokering a diplomatic solution that would involve Iraqi withdrawal from Kuwait. If the Last Resort criterion is regarded as a separate criterion that must be satisfied for a war to be just, the Gulf *ground* war would turn out to be unjust simply because the U.S. and its coalition partners passed up this opportunity to settle the dispute with Iraq without fighting a ground war.

On the other hand, if—as suggested above—we interpret the Last Resort criterion as a rule-of-thumb falling under the Proportionality criterion, the status of the ground war is harder to determine. Beneficial and legitimate objectives were achieved by the ground campaign: weakening of the dangerous Iraqi military, Iraq's commitment to paying reparations and its renunciation of its annexation of Kuwait, and strengthening of the "new world order" principle of nonaggression against one's neighbors. And casualties (especially civilian and coalition casualties) were light, because of the swiftness and one-sidedness of the campaign. Thus, unless we assume a "reasonable belief" interpretation of the proportionality criterion, and suppose that U.S. decision makers expected much heavier casualties from the ground war even just before it commenced, the ground war might well satisfy the Proportionality criterion, despite the fact that the U.S. failed to pursue the Soviet peace initiative.

II. WAS THE WAR CONDUCTED IN A JUST MANNER?

The analysis of the previous section does not rule out the possibility that the Gulf War was a just one. Do the principles of Discrimination and Proportionality, which limit how a nation may fight a war (even one it is just to undertake) rule out that possibility? The principle of Discrimination requires not making civilian populations the object of attack. It allows the killing of civilians only as unintended (though possibly foreseen) consequences of attacking legitimate military targets.[25] Coalition policies of targeting only military assets, and ordering their pilots to withhold dropping their bombs when they could not hone in on assigned targets, taken together with the "relatively light" (given the amount of bombing) casualties suffered by Iraqi citizens, indicate general compliance with the principle of Discrimination by the coalition during the Gulf War.

Nonetheless, given the enormous number of powerful bombs dropped, and the targeting of military assets located in and near cities, there were still large numbers of civilian casualties—"collateral damage" in the euphemism used by the military briefers. These foreseeable Iraqi civilian casualties may not have been enough to render the entire war disproportionate. But the principle of Proportionality *within war* says that each operation or tactic must be proportionate, in terms of its costs and benefits (including, of course, the benefits of making overall victory more likely for the side fighting for justice).

This raises problems concerning the coalition's successful military strategy of postponing the ground war until the air war had reduced the effective capacity of resistance by the Iraqi military. This strategy was explicitly motivated by a legitimate desire to minimize coalition casualties. But even if Iraqi soldiers are eliminated from the calculations of proportionality due to being considered "guilty aggressors,"[26] Iraqi civilians cannot be eliminated from those same calculations. Their deaths may have only been unintended side-effects of the bombing of military targets, but to the extent that they were foreseeable, they must be included—at least on a par with coalition military deaths—in applications of the principle of Proportionality.

Now it is possible that both civilian and military casualties were minimized by the coalition policy of continuing the air war for over a month before commencing the ground campaign. Perhaps a shorter air war would have led to a longer and fiercer ground war, with more casualties—civilian and military—on both

sides. (At least their quick defeat on the ground allowed many Iraqi soldiers to surrender or flee. Even fewer might have survived a longer ground war.[27]) But if this is so, it is probably a lucky accident—there is no guarantee that it had to be so. The just war criterion of Proportionality in war implies that coalition war planners should have aimed at minimizing something different than they apparently did: innocent casualties (where this includes at least Iraqi civilians and neutrals caught on the field of battle) rather than simply coalition casualties.

III. CONCLUSION

Was the Gulf War a just war? The answer provided by the analysis of this paper is a resounding "maybe." It pretty clearly satisfied the criteria of Competent Authority, Just Cause, and Discrimination. It may or may not have satisfied the two Proportionality criteria and the Right Intention criterion. The difficulties with determining whether it did are not so much specific to this particular war, but are generic ones associated with applying just war theory in any real world situation. These include characterizing the nature of collective intentions, determining what the relevant motives and intentions of relevant decision makers were, designating a scheme of value to evaluate outcomes, and making complex factual—and counterfactual—determinations about the effects of large-scale actions (like fighting a war) and their alternatives.

The fact that, after careful scrutiny, it remains at least possible that the Gulf War was a just war (according to the just war theory criteria), leaves that conflict in pretty select company. Even the Allies' effort in World War II, often taken as a paradigm of a moral war, clearly failed to satisfy at least one of the just war theory criteria: the principle of Discrimination. And it is not clear that World War II fares better than the Gulf War on the overall Proportionality criterion.

This is not (despite the analogy drawn in one of President Bush's speeches) because Saddam

Hussein is another Hitler. He has not carried out a large-scale program of genocide justified by a racist ideology, nor—as the leader of Iraq—did he ever pose the threat to the world that was posed by Hitler astride the powerful German state. Nonetheless, in a space of a decade, he invaded—with aggressive intent—two neighboring states in a volatile and vital area of the world. Stopping him in a war with a few hundred thousand casualties may not have been disproportionate compared to stopping Hitler in a world conflict with tens of millions of casualties. Indeed, if over the next decade, the Middle East is more peaceful and stable than before the Gulf War, so that it seems likely that the war was after all a proportionate one, we may expect to see the Gulf War join (or even replace) World War II in common lore as the paradigm of a just war. If the analysis of this paper—based on traditional just war theory—is correct, this would not necessarily constitute a mistake.[28]

NOTES

1. There is no single canonical version of just war theory. The criteria used here to define that theory represent an attempt to distill the main elements of just war theory as portrayed in the recent philosophical literature.

2. The main alternative theories that are frequently applied to these issues are pacifism, which regards all wars as immoral, realism, which is a theory that denies the applicability of moral criteria to war, and utilitarianism, which is a general moral theory not specifically designed to deal with moral issues surrounding warfare.

3. Even the leaders of nondemocratic allied nations were "competent authorities" in the relevant sense for just war theory, which is intended to rule out uses of force by private groups and individuals.

4. Peter A. French, "The Corporation as a Moral Person," in Peter A. French, ed., *The Spectrum of Responsibility* (New York: St. Martin's Press, 1991), pp. 298, 302.

5. This conclusion might not hold if, as some people suspect, the U.S. deliberately enticed Iraq into invading Kuwait in order to have an excuse to destroy its military power. But I do not find that suspicion very credible, despite the conflicting reports about what the U.S. Ambassador told Saddam Hussein in their July 25, 1991 meeting. (For one account, see Tom Mathews, "The Road to War," *Newsweek*, January 28, 1991, pp. 54, 56.) U.S. diplomacy just prior to the invasion is better explained as bureaucratic fumbling and listening to the advice of the other Gulf states to appease Saddam, than it is by conspiracy theories. Nor does the fact that the U.S. government saw Saddam and his military as extremely dangerous

after the invasion of Kuwait imply they saw them in the same light prior to that action.

6. This view gains support from a report that President Bush, and his National Security advisor Brent Scowcroft, "saw in the invasion a challenge to the post-cold-war leadership of the United States" and "a threat to the credibility of American leadership now that only one superpower was left on its feet." (Mathews, "The Road to War," p. 58.)

7. George F. Will, "After the Dust Settles," *Newsweek*, February 25, 1991, p. 70.

8. On the role of salience in settling conflicts, see Thomas Schelling, *The Strategy of Conflict* (Cambridge, MA: Harvard University Press, 1960), ch. 3.

9. Bernard Lewis, "At Stake in the Gulf," *New York Review of Books*, December 20, 1990, p. 44.

10. See, e.g., David Hume, *A Treatise of Human Nature*, ed., L. A. Selby-Bigge (Oxford: Clarendon Press, 1888), Book III, Part II, Section II. For an interpretation of Hume along these general lines, see David Gauthier, "David Hume: Contractarian," *Philosophical Review* 88 (1979), pp. 3–38.

11. I assume that the alternative is to have unclear and disputed borders. I am not addressing the question as to whether it would be better to have a single world government and no borders.

12. For a recent theory of secession, see Allen Buchanan, "Toward A Theory of Secession," *Ethics* 101 (January 1991), pp. 322–42.

13. Mathews, "The Road to War," p. 58, reports the following exchange between President Bush and his top advisors at a key meeting: "[T]he president looked at his top political and military advisors and said, 'What if we do nothing?' The result would be catastrophic. Saddam had hijacked an entire nation. 'This must be reversed,' Bush said as they adjourned."

14. The Proportionality criterion takes account of probabilities: in the presence of uncertainty, good and bad effects are to be weighted by their probabilities. So, in principle, a particular good outcome (e.g., restoration of a legitimate government) may justify a small risk of causing a certain number of casualties, but not a large risk of causing the same number of casualties.

15. The notion of "reasonable belief" used here is intended to mean more than "beliefs that are reasonable given the agent's evidence." There are ways of being unreasonable in gathering evidence, such as deliberately avoiding evidence that might shift one's beliefs in an inconvenient way. Satisfying the "reasonable belief" version of the Proportionality criterion requires having beliefs about outcomes that are "reasonable" in this strict sense.

16. Early in the crisis, President Bush apparently discussed the alternative of "doing nothing" with his top advisors. See Mathews, "The Road to War," p. 58.

17. This problem might be solved if, in contrast to what I propose below, we treat the Last Resort criterion as a separate criterion rather than a useful rule-of-thumb falling under the Proportionality criterion.

18. Of course, many of the same problems apply to competing theories that are consequentialist or have significant consequentialist elements, e.g., utilitarianism,

patriotism (utilitarianism with one's scope of concern restricted to fellow citizens of one's country), and normative realism ("nations should act to best promote their own interests").

19. "Last Resort" is listed as a separate criterion, for example, in the American Catholic Bishops' famous pastoral letter on nuclear war. See U.S. Bishops, "The Challenge of Peace: God's Promise and Our Response," *Origins* 13 (May 19, 1983), pp. 10–11.

20. The fact that the air war was not sufficient to drive the Iraqis from Kuwait is strong, but not conclusive, evidence that sanctions alone would not have worked. It is not conclusive evidence because the air war may have stiffened resistance (or affected internal politics) so as to eliminate the withdrawal option for the Iraqis in ways sanctions would not have.

21. Here I assume, at least for the sake of argument, that the offer of direct talks was more than a play for domestic political support. Cf. Mathews, "The Road to War," p. 64.

22. Mathews, "The Road to War," pp. 63–65.

23. Mathews, "The Road to War," p. 64.

24. In the notorious July 25th meeting with U.S. Ambassador to Iraq, April Glaspie, Hussein is reported to have said, "Yours is a society which cannot accept 10,000 dead in one battle." (Mathews, "The Road to War," p. 56).

25. It thus presupposes the problematic doctrine of double-effect, which ascribes enormous moral significance to the distinction between causing the deaths of innocent people intentionally and doing so nonintentionally. Whatever we may think of that doctrine, it is a central aspect of just war theory, and I will apply it here without questioning its validity.

26. It is unclear whether just war theory ascribes equal status to enemy soldiers under the Proportionality criterion. For the notion of proportioning "good" to "evil" could include within it the idea that harm to the "innocent" counts more, where "innocence" is not moral innocence (which many Iraqi conscripts may have shared with their coalition counterparts), but innocence of participating in an unjust and threatening aggression. On the two notions of innocence, see e.g., G.E.M. Anscombe, "War and Murder," in Richard Wasserstrom, ed., *War and Morality* (Belmont, CA: Wadsworth, 1970). pp. 42–53.

27. An alternative view is that the mass surrenders show the Iraqis would have surrendered as soon as attacked in any case. If this is so, the air war was an unnecessary, and therefore disproportionate, tactic.

28. An earlier version of this paper was presented on March 28, 1991 to a meeting of the Concerned Philosophers for Peace at the American Philosophical Association Pacific Division Meetings in San Francisco. I am grateful to the audience on that occasion, and to Edwin Curley, Peter French, Paul Graves, Ron Hirschbein, and Jeff McMahan for helpful discussion and suggestions.

Was the [Second] Iraq War a Just War?

Steven Lee

Steven Lee is professor of philosophy at Hobart and William Smith Colleges. He has recently edited *Intervention, Terrorism, and Torture: Contemporary Challenges to Just War Theory* (2007). He is the author of *Morality, Prudence, and Nuclear Weapons* (1993).

In this essay written shortly after the war started, Lee examines the arguments that were given by the administration of George W. Bush for the Iraq war that began in 2003. He finds the self-defense arguments to be flawed since Iraq was not involved in aggression against the United States. In addition, the various attempts to show that there were special circumstances that supported the war also do not succeed.

On March 19, 2003, the United States went to war against Iraq with a large air attack on Baghdad in an attempt to eliminate Iraq's ruler, Saddam Hussein. This was followed by further heavy bombings of Baghdad and other areas and the invasion of Iraq by American and British troops from Kuwait. Baghdad fell to American troops on April 9, and organized, large-scale Iraqi military resistance ceased soon thereafter.

Was the United States invasion and conquest of Iraq a just war? What does morality have to say about the U.S. war against Iraq? This is an important question to consider, even if the war, from a military perspective, is over. Our moral judgments are retrospective as well as prospective: some serve to assign responsibility for past action, and some serve to guide future action. The vigorous debates on the morality of the war that preceded the war should not end with the war. One reason it is important to make retrospective moral judgments is the indirect role such judgments often have in later prospective moral judgments. The Iraq war is seen by many as the first application of the new military doctrine of "preemptive" war, announced by the Bush administration in September of 2002. Judging the morality of the Iraq war could help us judge later wars that might be proposed under the doctrine.

To begin, it is important to understand the difference between moral judgments and judgments of self-interest (or prudence), and the role such judgments play in debates about war. Much of a debate about whether a nation should go (or have gone) to war focuses on considerations of the interests of the nation, its self-interest, often under the label of national security.[1] Will (or did) the war serve the nation's interest, whatever its effects on the interests of other nations? In contrast, a moral debate about a war considers not only the impact of the war on the nation, but its impact on all affected parties, including, of course, the nation being warred upon. Judgments about war from the point of view of national sell-interest look at the interests of only one nation, while moral judgments about war look at the interests of all nations and their peoples. Speaking generally, moral judgments of a nation's actions place restrictions on what the nation is permitted to do in pursuit of its self-interest. To take an example from the realm of individual action, the moral rule against theft is a restriction on individuals' pursuit of their

Steven Lee, "Was the [second] Iraq War a just war?" 2003. Reprinted by permission.

self-interest. Likewise, the moral rules applying to war are restrictions on nations' pursuit of their self-interest. It may benefit a nation to go to war without its going to war being morally justified. The Iraq war may or may not have been in the self-interest of the United States, but whether it was morally justified is a different matter.

What is the basis of moral judgments of a nation's military actions? What moral rules apply to a nation's going to war? Just war theory is the tradition in Western thought that examines the morality of the use of military force, and I will address the moral justifiability of the Iraq War in terms of this theory.[2] To begin this discussion, three points should be made about the moral rules of just war theory. First, they are not an external imposition on the military activities of nations. The application of the rules is not a matter of ethicists coming in from the outside and trying to tell military professionals how to run their business. The rules are part of how the military conceives of itself, as much as the rules of chivalry were part of how the medieval knighthood conceived of itself. Just-war rules are part of the military manuals and the substance of the international laws of war.

The second point is that the moral rules of just war theory have the same basic rationale as moral rules concerning the use of violence or force in individual relations. Moral rules concerning the use of violence by individuals serve the purpose of preserving social order. If there were no restraints on the free use of individual violence, social order would not be possible. At the individual level, moral rules generally prohibit the use of individual violence, except when such is necessary to protect oneself or another from attack. In other words, only defensive violence is morally justified. Just war theory extends this idea to the international realm. Generally speaking, nations are prohibited from going to war unless the war is defensive, that is, unless the war is necessary to protect a nation that is under attack by another. Aggression is prohibited, and defense is sometimes permitted. This places just war theory between two extremes, on the one hand pacifism, which would prohibit all war, and, on the other hand, "realism," which holds that there are no applicable moral prohibitions

against the international use of force. For just war theory, some wars are just and some are not.

The third point is that there are two kinds of moral judgments made about war, and consequently, two sets of rules in just war theory. The first kind of moral judgment, which has been the focus our discussion so far, is judgment about whether a nation is justified in going to war. The rules in just war theory that refer to this kind of judgment are known as rules *of jus ad bellum,* justice *of* war. But when a nation is at war, there is another kind of moral judgment made about its actions. Is the nation fighting the war in a just way? The rules relevant to this kind of judgment are rules of *jus in bello,* justice *in* war. For example, one of the most important rules of justice in war is that is wrong to attack civilians. Because war is morally judged in these two different ways, even if a nation is fighting a just war, this does not imply that its military actions in the war will be just. A just war may be fought in an unjust way. Nations should be just both in the wars they fight and in how they fight them.

In the following argument, I will consider primarily how the rules of *jus and bellum* apply to the U.S. war against Iraq. As the title of the paper indicates, the main issue is whether the United States was fighting a just war with Iraq. But, I will address two other matters as well. First, I will discuss briefly how the U.S. military action might be seen in terms the rules of *jus in bello.* This is important to consider because special claims were made for the justice of the war in this respect. Second, I will consider some arguments of supporters of the war that the traditional rules of *jus ad bellum* do not apply to this war. According to these arguments, various special circumstances require that the traditional rules be suspended or overridden in the current case, thus showing the war to be just even if it fails to satisfy the traditional rules.

Now, to the main question: Was the United States justified in going to war against Iraq? Was the war just? Did the war satisfy the traditional rules of *jus ad bellum?* These rules set forth a set of necessary conditions for justifying resort to war. No war can be just unless it satisfies all of the conditions. Three of these conditions are especially relevant to judging the U.S. war against Iraq: (1) just cause, (2) proportionality, and (3) last resort. I will discuss each in turn.

The condition of just cause is that only defensive war may be justified. The defensive character of the war must be clear and demonstrable, such as, in the paradigm case, a direct response to military aggression, and the aggression must be current. The justification for the use of force is to stop and reverse the aggression in progress, not to punish a nation for aggression in the past. The aggression need not be directed against the nation that is responding to it; a nation can come to the defense of a third party that is under attack. But a nation can go to war only against a nation engaged in aggression.

The U.S. war against Iraq did not satisfy this condition. Iraq was not engaged in aggression against the United States or another nation. The U.S. war was not defensive, so was not just. Public discussion on this issue was muddled by an incorrect use of terminology. The Bush administration referred to the war as "preemptive." Preemptive wars are wars in which a nation strikes first in the face of an imminent threat of aggression, and they are sometimes justified, because the defensive nature of the war is clear. For example, if the United States had detected the Japanese fleet approaching Hawaii in 1941, and its intention to attack Pearl Harbor was manifest, then if would have been a defensive action for the United States to strike the first blow by attacking the fleet before it reached Hawaii. The United States war against Japan would have then been preemptive, but just nonetheless, as was the actual war, which was a response to the fact, rather than the imminence, of aggression.

But the United States war against Iraq did not have this character. There was no evidence of imminent Iraqi aggression. The war was not provoked by actual or imminent aggression. Instead of being preemptive, the war was, at best, *preventive*. A preventive war is a war waged against a nation out of concerns about aggressive actions that nation might take in the future.[3] While many supporters of the war speculated about aggressive actions Iraq might take in the future, such speculations cannot justify war against Iraq in the

present. Opposition to preventive war has been a strongly held value in the United States. For example, in the early 1950s, the U.S government rejected proposals for preventive war against the Soviet Union. The Soviet Union was then just beginning to develop is nuclear arsenal, and it was clear that it would soon be able to threaten the United States with nuclear annihilation, a much greater threat than Iraq could ever have posed. Yet, the United States did not undertake this preventive war.

One response to this by supporters of the war is to claim that the war was in fact a reaction to actual Iraqi aggression, namely, the attacks of 9/11. The argument is that the Iraqi regime has close ties to al Qaeda, so that the regime was partly responsible for the attacks of 9/11. But there is little or no information to support this claim. No evidence has been presented to show that there were substantial ties between the Iraqi regime and al Qaeda. Indeed, the existence of such ties is counterintuitive, given that al Qaeda strongly advocates theocracy and the Bathist regime in Iraq is avowedly secular. The Bush administration has alleged that there were ties between the two at a low level, but a low-level connection, even if true, would not show active collaboration between them on the 9/11 attacks. In this regard, it is interesting to note that though a majority of Americans (64%) supported the war against Iraq[4] prior to its initiation, 45% believed that Saddam Hussein was personally involved in the attacks on 9/11.[5] This suggests that a majority of Americans did not support a preventive war against Iraq, that the support of many Americans for the war was contingent on the mistaken belief that the war would be defensive.

The second condition necessary for justifying a war is that the good achieved by the war is reasonably expected to be at least proportional to the harm brought about. In other words, the war, as best we can foresee, should do at least as much good as harm overall. The good and harm in question is the good and harm to everyone affected, not merely, as in the case of national self-interest, the good or harm of the people of one nation. This condition must be couched in terms of reasonable expectations due to the uncertainty of the future. As with calculating the consequence of any action, judgment should be based on an honest and informed appraisal of likely consequences. The moral judgment of proportionality is based on the best estimate of the consequences of the war, the best estimate possible at the time of the war is being considered (not on what consequences actually occur), because only then can a judgment of consequences be prospective. This suggests an important principle in the judging of proportionality. The direct harms of war, the deaths and suffering caused by the military action, must be given strong weight in the proportionality calculations because these harms always accompany war, so are the most certain of the predictable consequences. It is more reasonable to expect that harm than any future good. Predictions of how a war will come out are notoriously uncertain and unreliable, and predictions about the good to come of the war are based on predictions of how it will come out. For example, predictions that the good that will come from a war depend on an assumption about which side will win the war, but this assumption is wrong fifty percent of the time.

So, how does the Iraq war fare in terms of the proportionality condition? What is the most reasonable expectation about the war's outcome? To think through this in a rough way, consider an optimistic scenario and a pessimistic scenario about the war's outcome, and consider which is more reasonable. Here is a rough optimistic scenario: the war ends quickly and social order in Iraq is soon restored; a reasonably liberal and democratic regime is establish in short order; other nations in the region liberalize and become more supportive of the United States; the threat of international terrorism is reduced; other nations come to have greater respect for and willingness to cooperate with the United States. Here is a rough pessimistic scenario: the war is lengthy; social order in Iraq is not quickly restored; a reasonably liberal regime cannot be established in Iraq in the near term; the war strengthens international terrorism; other nations become more suspicious and less supportive of the United States and international cooperation becomes more difficult to achieve.

There is a strong argument that the actual outcome of the war, which has yet to play itself out, will be closer to the pessimistic scenario than the optimistic scenario. While the war did in fact end quickly, and it was probably reasonable to expect that it would, the other outcomes are more likely to fall out as the pessimists expect. Factors lending support to the pessimists' expectations are these: the deep ethnic divisions in the Iraqi population among Sunnis, Shiites, Kurds, and others; the Iraqi state's having come into existence only recently;[6] Iraq's lack of experience with nonautocratic self-government; America's unwillingness historically to commit itself to long-term and costly projects of nation-building; America's going to war in the face of the opposition of most other nations. These factors do not, of course, show that an outcome close to the optimistic scenario is impossible, only that it is not a reasonable expectation. These factors make the pessimistic scenario more reasonable than the optimistic scenario. Given the harm and suffering that has already been inflicted by the war itself, and given a reasonable expectation that the future outcome will be closer to what the pessimists expect, the proportionality condition for a just war fails to be satisfied. There is no case that the war is likely to bring about at least as much good as harm.

It is interesting to note in passing that the factors favoring the pessimistic scenario not only support a negative moral judgment on the war, but a negative judgment regarding national self-interest as well. Despite the fact that, in general, judgments of morality are different from judgments of self-interest, in this case a consideration of the likely consequences shows not only the war was morally wrong, but that it was not in the U.S. self-interest. But, this should not be surprising. The deep interdependence of nations characteristic of the modern international order tends to bring about a confluence of the value of the consequences of actions for each nation and for all nations taken together. Growing interdependence leads to a state of affairs in which harm to one nation corresponds to harm for all nations, and good for one nation corresponds to good for all nations. The deep cooperation among nations, especially economic cooperation, characteristic of the contemporary global order makes international action positive-sum rather than zero-sum. This is a strong argument against the unilateralism characteristic of U.S. policy, especially under the Bush administration. When a nation acts unilaterally, that is, in ways the international community does not support, it is likely to be acting against its self-interest.

The third condition necessary for justifying a war is that the war be a last resort. War is a last resort when there are no alternative means that could be reasonably expected to achieve the justifiable war aims (or a substantial part of them) short of using military force. If there are alternatives short of war that could be reasonably expected to bring about the defensive aims of a war, then going to war is not justified. The war cannot be justified until there are no such alternatives, or until such alternatives are tried and found wanting. To count as an alternative, it must be reasonably expectable, not merely logically possible, that the proposed action can achieve the defensible war aims. Otherwise, the last resort condition would reduce just war theory to pacifism, since there are always alternative actions that have some possibility, however remote, of achieving the defensible war aims.

How does the U.S. war against Iraq stand in regard to the last-resort condition? The chief stated concern of the Bush administration was that Iraq would use its weapons of mass destruction against the United States or its allies or give them to terrorists to use. This is what the war would prevent. Aside from the issue of the justifiability of such a preventive war, it is clear that there was at least one alternative to war that had a reasonable chance of achieving the aim of avoiding such future aggression. This was the United Nations program of weapons inspections in Iraq, ongoing in the months prior to March 19, but cut short by the U.S. decision to go to war. There may have been other alternatives as well. Many argue that Iraq could have been deterred from either using any weapons of mass destruction it had or giving them to terrorists to use by the threat of massive U.S. retaliation were it to do so. If so, this would make the adoption of a policy of deterrent threats against Iraq another alternative showing the war not to have been a last resort.

It is worth noting in passing that some alternatives that would achieve the defensive aims without war might not themselves be morally justifiable. For example, one alternative to war with Iraq, which was meant to achieve some of the same aims, has been applied for over a decade, namely, economic sanctions. It is a contentious issue as to whether economic sanctions could achieve the defensive aims for which a war would be fought, but consider a different issue regarding sanctions. There is strong evidence that the sanctions against Iraq have been responsible for the deaths of thousands of civilians from malnutrition and lack of medical care due to the unavailability of medical supplies. A policy with these consequences is not morally justifiable because most of those who die, as civilians, are not responsible for governmental policies that sanctions are designed to affect. So, economic sanctions should not count as an alternative in applying the condition of last resort, even if the alternative could achieve the defensive aims of the war.

Thus, the U.S. war against Iraq fails all three of the *jus ad bellum* conditions it would have to satisfy in order to be just. It is important to appreciate that each of the three is a necessary condition. Even if it were shown that some of the arguments presented above are not sound, it would remain true that the war was not justified. To show that the war was justified, supporters of the war must show not simply that the arguments fail for one or two of the conditions, but that they fail for all three of the conditions.

The second main task of this essay is to see if this conclusion stands in the light of arguments made by supporters of the war that special circumstances require that, in cases like the war against Iraq, the rules of just war theory be set aside or overridden, so that the war may be seen as justified even if it fails to satisfy the requirements *of jus ad bellum*. Before turning to this task, however, I would like to make some brief remarks about the war and the rules of *jus in bello,* justice in war.

The two most important rules of justice in war are the principles of proportionality and discrimination. The principle of proportionality applies to military actions in war the same requirement represented by the condition of proportionality at the level of *jus ad bellum*. Roughly, a particular military action in a war is justified only if it brings about at least as much good as harm. More precisely, a particular military action is justified only if it makes a contribution to the overall war effort sufficient to outweigh the harm that it does. Part of the point of the principle of proportionality is to rule out the gratuitous violence characteristic of war. The principle of discrimination prohibits attacks on civilians. More precisely, it is wrong to engage in military action that is intended to harm civilians.[7] This principle is complicated to apply because there are few large-sunk military actions that do not result in harm to civilians. Thus, those who undertake such actions know that civilians are likely or certainly to die as a result. In order that the principle of discrimination not be construed as prohibiting all such actions (and thereby effectively prohibiting war), the moral analysis of such actions focuses on the intention with which the action is taken. If the action is intended to destroy a military target and the likely civilian deaths are merely foreseen and not intended, and if efforts are made to minimize the magnitude of the civilian damage, then the military action may be permissible.[8]

In the light of the principle of discrimination, an important and novel feature of the Iraq war was the extensive use by the United States of precision-guided munitions. The technology behind these weapons has been improving at a rapid rate, and a far larger portion of the munitions used in the war were precision-guided than in the last U.S. war against Iraq, the Gulf War of 1991. The development and deployment of these munitions has been heralded as a significant moral advance in the means of war because they allow military action to more closely follow the principle of discrimination. If weapons can be more precisely directed on military targets, then fewer civilians will be harmed because civilian areas are less likely to be hit, but also because the yield of the explosives can be lower due to the greater accuracy of their delivery.

But some caveats are in order. First, precision-guided munitions are a means to better adherence to the principle of discrimination, but they do not guarantee it. The targets against which the munitions are directed must be chosen based on intelligence. Only strong efforts to obtain reliable intelligence regarding the targets and restraint in acting on intelligence that is doubtful or uncorroborated will insure adherence to the principle. Second, there is a danger that these weapons will, in the eyes of those who use them, come to carry the whole moral load, that the technology will be seen as imparting moral acceptability to any military action. The whiz-bang character of the weapons may give them a morally seductive quality. Military leaders may mistakenly come to view the weapons themselves as imparting moral acceptability to military action. But their use does not even guarantee adherence to the principle of discrimination, let alone adherence to the other moral requirements to which military action and policy must conform.

Now, what about the arguments of those who claim that the circumstances of our era require revisions in the traditional rules of just war theory, that in cases like the U.S. war against Iraq the traditional rules must be set aside or overridden? Some supporters of the war would concede that the war was not just in terms of the traditional *jus ad bellum* rules, but contend that such a judgment is irrelevant because the special circumstances in which the war was fought show the need to revise or abandon some of the traditional rules. The special circumstances are both social and technological, specifically, recent changes in the nature of the international order and in military technology. The idea is that the rules of just war theory, given their historical origins, implicitly assume that the international order and technology have certain characteristics, so that if these characteristics have changed in relevant ways, the rules themselves may need to be changed.

Just war theory has faced many such arguments over its long history. Since the Middle Ages, change in social order and technology has been a constant. But despite this, just war theory has remained remarkably constant, showing an ability to sustain the substance of its basic rules, supporting interpretations of those rules that incorporate the ongoing social and technological changes. So, it remains to be seen whether recent social and technological changes require changes in the rules, as these supporters of the war contend.

I will consider three arguments that recent social and technological changes should lead to modifications of the traditional just-war rules, specifically, modifications that imply that the U.S. war against Iraq was justified. (1) The first argument is that changes in the case with which weapons of mass destruction can be produced, coupled with the rise of international terrorism an so-called rogue states, imply the need for a change in the just-cause condition of *jus ad bellum*, namely, that preventive war is sometimes justified. (2) Second, the growth of the global human-rights movement shows the need to recognize an exception to the just-cause condition that only defensive wars are permitted in cases where a regime is grossly violating the human rights of its citizens. In other words, humanitarian intervention is sometimes permitted. (3) The third argument is the most far reaching in its implications. The postcold war status of the United States as a hyperpower, as being far and away the most powerful nation, suggests that the sovereign-state model on which just war theory is based may no longer apply, and that we may need to replace or augment just war theory with a moral theory suited to the fact of U.S. hegemony, an ethics of hegemony. Such an ethics would justify U.S. unilateral action to maintain order in the world. I will consider each of these arguments in turn.

The gist of the first argument is that three circumstances new to our era imply that in some cases waging preventive war is as necessary for a nation's defense as waging preemptive war was in the past, and hence that preventive war should sometimes be permitted by just war theory. Whereas just war theory traditionally prohibits all preventive wars, it must now permit at least some. The three circumstances are: (a) the case with which weapons of mass destruction can now be manufactured; (b) the existence and reach of international terrorism of the sort represented by al Qaeda; and (c) the existence of rogue states, states that are willing either to use weapons of mass destruction or to supply these weapons to

international terrorists for their use. The first of these is a result largely of technological change; the second, a result partly of a technological change and partly of a change in international order (for example, cultural globalization); and the third, a result largely of a change in international order.

This is an interesting argument, but it is not a sound one. The confluence of these three factors do not provide anything like a strong enough case for revising the basic rules of *jus ad bellum,* as the argument claims. Speaking generally, there is no reason to think that rogue states cannot be deterred from using weapons of mass destruction as other states can be, that is, by threats of massive retaliation. Rulers of rogue states may be brutal and violent, but their ability to achieve and maintain domestic power shows that they are quite rational about preserving that power, which is precisely what deterrence threatens to deprive them of. Deterrence also makes unlikely the rulers' giving their weapons of mass destruction to international terrorists, given the prospect that the weapons could be traced back to them. In addition, international anti-proliferation efforts (one example being the U.N. inspections in Iraq) can go far to reduce the likelihood that states without weapons of mass destruction, rogue or other, will develop the weapons. Finally, international terrorism can be treated with some success through international cooperation as largely a criminal rather than a military problem. All in all, there is not a strong case that the rules of just war theory must be revised so that preventive war is permitted as a form of defensive war.

But note that even if the case could be make that the three factors support the argument that in our era preventive war should sometimes be permitted by just war theory, and that this would apply in the case of the U.S. war against Iraq, this would not show that the war was justified. For this would be a revision to only one of the rules of *jus ad bellum.* It would remain to be shown that the war also satisfied the other two *jus ad bellum* conditions, proportionality and last resort, and, as argued above, it does not.

The second argument is the strongest and most appealing of the three. The popular form of the argument is this: Saddam Hussein was a savage ruler, responsible for the imprisonment, torture, and death of many of his own people, so that ridding Iraq of him justified the U.S. war against Iraq, In terms of the idea of the need to revise they *jus ad bellum* rules, the argument could be put in this way. The changing circumstance is the growth of the international human rights movement, which has brought about the recognition that all individuals have basic rights their states are obligated to respect. As a result, the sovereignty of the state is no longer a barrier to international demands that states respect those rights. When a state is violating the basic rights of its citizens in a massive way, it may be permissible for other states to use force to put an end to the violations. This is the idea of humanitarian intervention, and it occurs when military force is used against a state for the good of its citizens. This argument is a call for a *humanitarian exception* to *the jus ad bellum* rule of just cause, that a war may be undertaken only in response to a state's external aggression. The humanitarian exception, the argument goes, justifies the U.S. war against Iraq.

There is little question that there exists a recognized humanitarian exception to the just-cause rule of *jus ad bellum*, and that there should be such an exception. This is recognized by most supporters of just war theory,[9] and it is the basis for the justification offered of some recent military actions, such as those in Bosnia and Kosovo. The question here is whether the exception applies to the U.S. war against Iraq. Is the humanitarian exception of sufficient scope to cover this war?

One issue sometimes raised regarding the applicability of the humanitarian exception is that of motivation. Must humanitarianism be the motive for a war in order to justify that war? What if a war has a humanitarian result, but the nation going to war had other reasons for fighting? The claim that a humanitarian justification requires a pure or at least predominant humanitarian motivation might be used to deny that the U.S. war against Iraq could have such a justification. But this is not a line of criticism I will pursue. Motives are always mixed, and are hard to fathom in any case, especially when they apply to a group action. I wish to consider a different approach to the question.

It is important to recognize that the humanitarian exception must have a limited scope. If any series of human rights violations by a state against its own citizens would justify armed intervention by another state, the results could be a massive disproportion between the harm caused by the intervention and the harm avoided through ending the rights violations. To attempt to remedy this problem, one might propose that a proportionality condition by itself be used to set the proper scope for the humanitarian exception: intervention would be justified on humanitarian grounds whenever the amount the good to be achieved by ending the human-rights violations is likely to be sufficient to outweigh the amount of harm the war would cause. But it would be a mistake to construe the humanitarian exception as a proportionality condition, because a proportionality condition is already included as a separate condition under the rules of *jus ad bellum.* The humanitarian exception is an exception to the just-cause condition of *jus ad bellum,* and the exception should be understood as a rule that substitutes for the condition that a war must be defensive. As was pointed out in the case of the first argument, even were the U.S. war against Iraq to satisfy the humanitarian exception, it would also have to satisfy the conditions of proportionality and last resort to be justified.

So, what should be the scope of the humanitarian exception be? The examples usually given of the sort of massive human rights violations that would bring into play the humanitarian exception are policies like genocide and ethnic cleansing. These policies involve severe rights violations directed at people not because of what they have done, but because of who they are, of what kind they are, of what non-voluntary group they belong to. This represents an appropriate basis for setting the scope of the humanitarian exception. On this view, the humanitarian exception comes into play, replacing the defense requirement of the just-cause condition, when the nation against whom the war is contemplated is imposing severe human rights violations on its own people, the victims being selected on the basis of the non-voluntary group to which they belong rather than on the basis of what they have done, the choices they have made.

This is an appropriate demarcation line for the scope of the humanitarian exception because it distinguishes between two fundamentally different kinds of immoral regimes. The first kind of regime is one that commits crimes with the "gen" prefix, genocide, ethnic cleansing, and so forth. The second kind of regime is one that commits crimes that, while often morally horrendous, are recognizably political, in the sense that the rights violations involve the regime's oppressing its population for the sake of maintaining political power by, for example, using violence, torture, and assassination against its political opponents. Regimes of this kind and not concerned with destroying people because of who they are, as regimes of the first kind are, but with intimidating people who threaten their power, that is, those who have chosen, often heroically, to oppose them. Regimes of the second kind may be morally horrendous, but their moral crimes are of a lesser order of magnitude than those of the first kind. In regimes of the first kind, a person's choices cannot determine whether that person lives or dies at the hands of the leaders. In regimes of the second kind, a person's choices can generally determine this. If a person chooses not to be a problem to the regime, the regime will generally leave that person alone. Because of this basic moral difference between these two kinds of regimes, and because the humanitarian exception must be of limited scope, it is appropriate to reserve the humanitarian exception for cases of wars against regimes of the first kind.

It seems clear that the Iraqi regime was of the second kind rather than the first. The people it punished were its political opponents, not those who were merely of a certain kind. The Kurds and the Shiites that the Sunni regime killed were largely those who had taken up military or political opposition to the regime. There was governmental policy to kill Kurds and Shiites because they were Kurds or Shiites. Even if the regime has engaged in "gen" crimes in the past, such crimes can justify the humanitarian exception only when they are occurring in the present, so that the war could put a halt to them.

To many, this argument, whose implication is that the Iraqis should have been left to the torment of Saddam Hussein will sound callous. Indeed, the Iraq war has caused a split within the camp of those who are usually opposed to the United States going to war. Nearly everyone in this camp is delighted to see the Hussein regime gone, but some in this camp see his being gone as sufficient to justify the war, while many do not. Those who would see the war as justified on humanitarian grounds give a wider scope to the humanitarian exception than those who do not. But the cost of that wider scope is justifying a wider range of wars, in the face of the certainty of the great harm war does and the uncertainty of its achieving the desired results.

The third argument is the most radical and intriguing of the three. The first two arguments were based on the claim that special circumstances require changing the rules of *jus ad bellum* in certain ways. The third argument suggests that the new circumstances may be so significant, that they may cut so deep into the assumptions behind just war theory, that just war theory should be replaced or significantly augmented with another.

The basic assumption behind just war theory is that the world is divided into sovereign states. Just war theory governs the military interaction of sovereign states. If state sovereignty is no longer the basic principle of international organization, just war theory may no longer be relevant. State sovereignty has been proclaimed by many to be dead or dying as a principle of global organization due to a variety of factors, such as the growth of economic integration, the technological "shrinking" of the planet, the global effects of many actions of individual states, and so forth. So, one question is whether state sovereignty has declined to the extent that just war theory may need to be replaced. But a further question is what sort of moral perspective would replace or augment just war theory, if it needs to be replaced or augmented, and this would depend on what form of international organization has replaced state sovereignty.

The U.S. war against Iraq and debates leading up to it have suggested two different ideas about a moral perspective that could replace or augment the just-war perspective, given that state sovereignty has declined. The first was embodied in the argument that the war against Iraq would be justified only if it were endorsed by the United Nations. The claim that the United Nations and only the United Nations has the authority to legitimate a war that would not be justified on just-war grounds represents one of the two ideas about a moral perspective that might replace or augment just war theory. This is the idea that there is a genuine global community which has some authority over its member states the way that a federal government has authority over its political units. The global community can authorize the use of force against one of its members even if that member is not engaged in aggression against another of the members. This is what the United States argued that the United Nations Security Council should do in the case of Iraq.

But the Council refused this authorization, and the United States went to war anyway, suggesting that its appeal for U.N. support was not a genuine commitment to the idea that rests moral (and legal) authority in a world body. Instead, the fact that the United States went to war in the face of the United Nations refusal, as well as in contravention to traditional just war rules, suggests that it was committing itself it to a different idea about the decline of state sovereignty and, by implication, about a moral perspective to replace or augment just war theory. This idea is the notion of U.S. hegemony. The United States is by far the most powerful single state in the international system, which suggests that it has, or could achieve, a degree of hegemony over all other states. If this hegemony were strong enough, then perhaps the power lost by individual states through their declining sovereignty would coalesce not in an international body, as the first idea would have it, but in a single most powerful state. Sovereignty would have been lost because the United States can, within limits, do what it wants in the world.

The moral perspective corresponding to this view is an ethics of hegemony. The point is that hegemony has an ethics of its own, and a hegemon may be judged in its terms. What would constitute an ethics of the imperium? An ethics of hegemony would presumably specify a set of responsibilities belonging to the hegemon, a demand that it use its unrivaled power in a responsible way, that it assist lesser states and avoid taking advantage of them. Whereas just way theory is an ethics of individualism, with all states having equal rights, an ethics of hegemony would be paternalistic, a call for the hegemon to use its power for the benefit of other states, and for the others to acknowledge the hegemon's benevolent governance.

There are three questions to consider. First, is the international order such that a hegemon could exist? Second, if so, is the United States in fact that hegemon? Third, if so, would the U.S. war against Iraq be in accord with an ethics of hegemony? The answer to the first question is probably no. Power is too disbursed in the international system for there to be a hegemon. It is easy to lose sight of this when focusing on military power and the preponderance the United States has in this area. But the real power in the world today is economic, and however powerful the U.S. economy is, the economic power of the United States is nothing like as preponderant as its military power. Indeed, the fact that the economy is the surest indicator of power, and that economic power is well disbursed, makes it more plausible to see the power lost through the decline in state sovereignty as being collected in an international authority, not in a hegemon.

Turning to the second question, if the international order were such that a hegemon could exist, would the United States be playing that role? The United States has in many respects certainly acted like a hegemonic power in recent years. The National Security Strategy of the United States of America, published in September of 2002, has been seen by some as a proclamation of U.S. hegemony.[10] But in most respects the U.S. has not acted as a hegemon. Its unilateral instincts seem more to come out of isolationism, not out of a desire to dominate the world. The first requirement of a hegemon is that it use its power to create international order, and the United States has been reluctant to do this. It is not, in image or reality, the policeman of the world, which a hegemon needs to be willing to be. In other words, there is little indication that the United States recognizes, in its rhetoric or its actions, that it has the duties of a hegemon. It likes to throw its weight around from time to time, but it does not understand itself to be a hegemon. The third question is, even if it were assumed, contrary to what has just been argued, that the conditions are right for a world hegemon and the United States is it, would the war against Iraq be sanctioned by an ethics of hegemony. The answer apparently is no. Many of the features of the Iraq war cited in the earlier discussion would support the claim that the United States was abusing its power in attacking Iraq, not acting as a responsible agent in power ought to act. In the end, the war is justified neither on the individualistic assumptions of just war theory that a state has a right not to be attacked unless it is itself attacking another, or on the paternalistic assumptions of an ethics of hegemony, that the power a hegemonic agent has over others must be exercised responsibility.

NOTES

1. National security, as the term is usually understood, is a narrower concept than national self-interest. National security tends to focus inordinately on matters of military security, which is only part of what constitutes a nation's true self-interest.

2. Just war theory speaks in terms of whether a war is just or unjust. I will understand the claim that a war is just, the claim that a war is justified, and the claim that a war is moral, or morally acceptable, or morally permissible as meaning the same thing.

3. For a discussion of the distinction between preemptive and preventive war, see Michael Walzer, *Just and Unjust Wars* (New York: Basic Books, 1977), pp. 74–85.

4. During the week prior to the war, support among Americans for the United States going to war even without United Nations backing, according to the Gallup organization, was 64%. At <http://www.gallup.com/subscription/?m=f&c_id=13228>, accessed on June 8, 2003.

5. A New York Times/CBS poll published on March 14, 2003, showed that 45 percent of Americans believe Mr. Hussein was "personally involved" in the Sept. 11 attacks. At <http://www.csmonitor.com/2003/0314/p02s01-woiq.html> accessed on June 8, 2003.

6. In 1916, the British and the French, in Sykes-Picot Agreement, drew arbitrary national borders in Middle East, creating Iraq and assigning it to British administration.

7. We saw a non-military version of this principle operative in the discussion of economic sanctions above.

8. The idea of distinguishing intended from merely foreseen effects in this way is often referred to as the doctrine of double effect. But the additional element in this interpretation of the principle of discrimination, that likely civilian damage should be minimized, is best expressed by Michael Walzer. He argues for a doctrine of "double intention," namely, that a military action is morally justifiable only if there is both an intention to attack only a military target and an intention to reduce risks to civilians, often through an assumption of greater risk on the part of military personal undertaking the action. See *Just and Unjust Wars,* pp. 155–56.

9. For an excellent discussion of the humanitarian exception, see Walzer, *Just and Unjust Wars,* pp. 101–08.

10. The document is available at http://www.whitehouse.gov/nsc/nss.pdf, accessed on June 13, 2003.

Jus Post Bellum and the Prosecution of Al Bashir for Darfur

Larry May

Larry May is W. Alton Jones professor of philosophy, and professor of law, at Vanderbilt University, and also professorial fellow, Centre for Applied Philosophy and Public Ethics, Charles Sturt and Australian National Universities, in Canberra. He has published several recent books on war including *Crimes Against Humanity: A Normative Account* (2005), *War Crimes and Just War* (2007), *Aggression and Crimes Against Peace* (2008), and Genocide: A Normative Account (2010) and Global Justice and Due Process (forthcoming).

May discusses a branch of the just war tradition that concerns what to do in the aftermath of war. He focuses on the situation in the Darfur region of the Sudan where hundreds of thousands of people have lost their lives and many more rendered homeless. The question is whether the president of the Sudan should be prosecuted by the International Criminal Court for the Darfur atrocities. May argues that prosecution of Bashir should only take place if the risk of greater human rights abuses is diminished rather than increased by such action.

As H.L.A. Hart observed over 25 years ago, international law is infirm because it lacks an "international legislature, courts with compulsory jurisdiction, and centrally organized sanctions."[1] The primary rules, such as against murder, of the international legal regime are often virtually the same in content as those of domestic legal systems. But the form of these rules, or at least the form of the underlying secondary rules, especially concerning sanctions, are infirm calling into question whether international law is indeed a system of law or merely a loose set of laws. In the last decade, we have been moving toward an international rule of law but we are definitely not there yet.

We will not soon have a full-scale solution to the problem of compulsory jurisdiction and centrally organized sanctions. But in the mean time, gap-filling can increase the claim to an international

rule of law. Chief among the measures of gap-filling is a system of international procedures including indictments and arrests for violations of international law, especially international criminal law, along with gap-fillers for protecting the of those indicted and arrested such as are found in the call for the institutional protection of the right of habeas corpus and like measures at the global level. The question posed in this essay, whether Bashir should be indicted and arrested for his role in the Darfur genocide and other atrocities, goes directly to the issues of how best to move toward the international rule of law.

I. THEMES FROM THE JUST WAR TRADITION

I will begin with a bit of background from the Just War tradition. The most significant figure concerning the ethics and law of war was Hugo Grotius. Writing in 1625, he proposed that there is an

Footnote:

Larry May, "Just Post Bellum and the Prosecution of Al Bashir for Darfur."

"association which binds together the human race, or binds many nations together'" and that such an association "has need of law."[2] Grotius then famously defended the idea "that there is a common law among nations, which is valid alike for war and in war."[3] As one commentator has recently noted:

> Grotius, too, is of course fully aware of the importance or independent nations. . . . However his ultimate frame of reference remains the Ciceronian *humani generis societas* inherited from Stoicism, a society of mankind rather than States.[4]

Grotius spoke explicitly of such a society bound together "by good faith" and "tempered with humanity."[5]

Grotius recognised that "law fails of its outward effect unless it has a sanction behind it." Even when there is no sanction, law "is not entirely void of effect," as long as "justice is approved, and injustice condemned, by the common agreement of good men."[6] The conscience of humanity can be affected even without sanctions, but the international society is better served yet if the condemnations of injustice can be backed sanctions against those States that act unjustly. Whatever the sanctions of law, even the sanctions of war, these should be governed by the singular task of "the enforcement of rights."[7]

A century and a half later, Vattel expanded on the ideas of the Just War tradition by arguing that:

> Since Nations are bound by the Law of Nature mutually to promote the society of the human race, they owe one another all the duties which the safety and welfare of that society require. The *offices of humanity* consist in the fulfillment of mutual assistance which men owe to one another because they are men.[8]

These duties of humanity are matters of charity tor Vattel, and hence not as strongly binding, as are duties of justice, but the duties of justice, but the duties of humanity are duties nonetheless. So Vattel argued that it may be our duty to go to war to prevent others from being harmed even though "to neglect or to refuse to further the advancement of a Nation does not constitute an act of aggression."[9]

Contrary to many others to write on these topics at his time or before, Vattel argues that the duties of humanity are binding and may even override a State's sovereignty.

> To give help to a brave people who are defending their liberties against an oppressor by force of arms is only the part of justice and generosity. Hence whenever such dissention reaches the state of civil war, foreign Nations may assist that one of the two parties which seems in have justice on its side.[10]

Sometimes it will be difficult to determine which State is in the right. But in clear-cut cases States are bound to intervene in civil wars on the side of the victims.

These days, talk of a global community, especially globalization, is omnipresent. But while such talk seems to be everywhere, there is little discussion of what exactly it means for there to be an international legal community. A good place to start is with Hersch Lauterpacht, who says: "The First function of the legal organization of the Community is the preservation of peace. Its fundamental precept is, 'there shall be no violence.' But this primordial duty of the law is abandoned and the reign of force is sanctioned as soon as it is admitted that the law may" require violence for the purpose of enforcing the law's proscriptions.[11]

Peace is the goal of law, but violence must sometimes be used to maintain the peace. For there to be an international legal community, according to Lauterpacht, there must be two conditions met: first, there must be rules which prohibit the use of violence; and second, the enforcement of the "no violence" principle should not have gaps, that is, there should be no sections of the community that fail to recognize the principle or where the principle is not enforced. These are the guiding ideas behind the founding of the Untied Nations and fifty years later the International Criminal Court.

Because of the shared interests in peace and basic human rights protection, of all humans in all political communities, we can speak non-metaphorically about the human or international community. It seems to me that the solidarity that many people feel with fellow humans is based on common vulnerability to violence and harm; and the shared interests are based on just these characteristic features of being human as well. In this sense there is an international community of humans, *a* humanity, in which individual human identify. And all states have a natural obligation to promote just international institutions that will advance the interests of the international community.

II. MORALITY AND *JUS POST BELLUM* PRINCIPLE

Recent international criminal trials for genocide seem to be a significant advance in the movement toward a global recognition of human rights and the international rule of law. Yet, such trials are necessarily an advance in reconciling parties of ethnic wars. It has seemed to certain theorists that criminal trials are able to do only one of two tasks: either to provide retribution or deterrence for the perpetrators or to teach about the truth of the atrocity as a way toward healing.[12] In the Sudan, the estimates are that 500,000 people have perished in the Darfur genocide, and over two million have become refugees. The newly constituted international criminal Court (ICC) was given the Darfur case in March of 2005 by the security council of the UN. No trials have yet been held, but some critics of the ICC have argued that the impending trials have complicated an already difficult political situation in the Sudan. Even if it is possible to pick out a few of the worst participants in the atrocity, holding trials in which such individuals are convicted and sentenced may not advance other important goals in the aftermath of war.

As one reads widely about reconciliation, there is very little consensus about the elements of reconciliation. William Long and Peter Brecke stipulate that reconciliation requires: "public truth telling; justice short of revenge; redefinition of the identities of former belligerents; and calls for a new relationship."[13] Ronald Slye, whose view comes close to my own, argues that for reconciliation there are two necessary conditions: more is needed than accountability. "A society is not reconciled with its violent past unless it also works toward the creation of respect for fundamental human rights."[14]

There have been two great branches of the just war tradition: the morality of whether to go to war *(jus ad bellum),* and the morality of how to wage war *(jus in bello).* But there is another branch that is equally important even if not as well recognized, namely the morality of how to behave in the aftermath of war *(jus post bellum).* We need a *jus post bellum* principle to guide decisions about whether to indict, arrest, and try political leaders who are responsible for atrocities. Grotius gives us a good beginning when he argues that "after war" we should be guided by a concern for "the preservation of good faith and of peace." Good faith is what holds States together, and this is also true for Grotius for "the greater society of States."[15] Good faith involves eschewal of deception and also the "removal of all obscurity" from transactions. Peace is rendered more likely after war insofar as war and its immediate aftermath are "tempered with humanity." where that includes avoiding "everything else that may arouse anger."[16]

This prohibition on arousing anger has indeed been one of the main problems with the use of criminal trials in the aftermath of war or other forms of armed conflict. Trials, especially of leaders, often arouse significant anger among the populace. Grotius generally argued for amnesty for rulers in the aftermath of war. Yet, there seems to be one class of exceptions for Grotius, namely, when a ruler has done harm to his own subjects, or allowed others in the society to cause such harm on the innocent.[17] Grotius says very little about such things, but it is not too far removed from Grotius' general position on the ethics of war to suggest that the prohibition on making sure that one does not arouse anger may also find an exception if a ruler has caused or allowed massive human rights abuses to occur during war, even if the war is a civil war.

In light of the above discussion, I propose the following *jus post bellum* normative principle:

> There is an obligation of natural justice to
>   engage in actions to support institutions
>   that promote the international rule of law,
> As long as such actions do not jeopardize
>   human rights.

A similar just war principle, what I have called the principle of humaneness, applies to how soldiers should treat civilians as well as other soldiers. According to this principle one should exercise restraint when it is likely to produce positive good for other humans as long as one's own preservation or comparable interests are not jeopardized.[18] In support of such principles, Grotius argued that force may be used as long as it does not "take away the rights of others."[19]

The general idea behind my *jus post bellum* normative principle is that an international system of justice has at least components: the promotion of human rights, that is, the rights of those who are members of the world community, and the fairness and non-arbitrariness that comes from the rule by law rather than by the whim of "men." In moving toward an international system of justice, one of these components should not be sacrificed for the other. We may countenance some loss in one for some gain in the other, but we should prefer solutions that do not diminish either. In *jus post bellum* situations, care must be taken so that criminal trials in the aftermath of war preserve rather than retard the general protection of human rights in the global society. Force may be used to bring leaders to justice for crimes committed during war when human rights are not risked and when such trials promote the rule of law.

III. BASHIR AND THE INTERNATIONAL LEGAL SYSTEM

The situation in the Darfur region of the Sudan is one of the greatest humanitarian crises of our lifetimes. And, at least on the face of it, Bashir has played a large role in the perpetuation of that crisis. The Prosecutor's application for a warrant against Bashir does not accuse him of personally carrying out any of the crimes but of committing genocide, war crimes, and crimes against humanity "through members of the apparatus, the army and the Militia/Janjaweed." The Prosecutor of the ICC alleged that he has evidence that "establishes reasonable grounds to believe that Al Bashir intends to destroy a substantial part of the Fur, Masalit, and Zaghawa ethnic groups as such." The Prosecutor alleges that "forces and agents controlled by Al Bashir attacked civilians in towns and villages inhabited by the target group, committing killings, rapes, torture, and destroying means of livelihood."[20]

The case of Bashir is especially problematic given the principle I have enunciated above. The human rights situation is so perilous at the moment in Darfur that any new instability could result in many more beatings, rapes, and deaths among those who are in refugee camps or otherwise displaced by the civil war that has raged for more than a decade in the Sudan. But if it is Bashir himself who will be the one orchestrating more human rights abuses than the abuses he already has on his hands, other considerations enter in as well. Bashir's continuing war against his own people is highly significant and may offset some of the worries about how trying him would exacerbate human rights problems. For capturing and sending Bashir to The Hague will anger the population but may nonetheless deter some of the worst violence in the Sudan.

In a speech at Nuremberg Germany last year, the Chief Prosecutor of the International Criminal Court, Luis Moreno-Ocampo said:

> The issue is no longer whether we agree or disagree with, the pursuit of justice in moral or practical terms. It is the law. . . . It is the lack of enforcement of the court's decisions which is the real threat to enduring peace.[21]

Ocampo and others who are working at the ICC see their task as to establish a global community based in law. And the main impediment to such a community, as Hart also indicated, is the lack of enforcement mechanisms. Without a world executive branch, the enforcement will have to be by means of gap-fillers and that is indeed how the ICTY, ICTR, and ICC have been proceeding. Indicting, arresting and prosecuting Bashir could be a significant gap-filler in the international rule of law.

I am inclined to agree with Ocampo, but he needs to realize that legal justice is not the only form of justice. It is possible that when legal justice is served, the moral and social justice that undergirds human rights can be hampered. In my view, this only happens in the most extreme of situations, but it can happen. So, Ocampo needs a somewhat more nuanced approach, but he does not need to heed all of his critics, many of whom are opposed to international criminal trials. Indeed, Ocampo needs to proceed ahead to indict and arrest in the vast majority of cases where there is prima facie evidence that a political or military leader has violated the substantive primary rules of international criminal law, especially in those cases of massive human rights abuse. And given the principle of *aut dedere aut judicare,* Ocampo can and should avail himself of the legal resources of other states to arrest and possibly even to try Bashir.

Let us return to H.L.A. Hart's claim that international law lacked "compulsory jurisdiction and centrally organized sanctions." Both of these problems can be partially addressed with gap-filling. One way to go is through *aut dedere aut judicare*—the principle that a State must either extradite or prosecute individuals who are accused of violating international law. Another way to go is by using diplomacy and other means to bring the leaders of the world who commit atrocities to trial in The Hague for what they have done. Most importantly, international courts should not be deterred from issuing indictments and arrest warrants for fear of political repercussions unless those repercussions are so serious as to risk undermining human rights protections. What should bother prosecutors and judges is whether indicting or arresting political leaders will worsen human rights situations.

International criminal law is infirm, both in terms of compulsory jurisdiction and centrally organized sanctions. Ocampo cannot by himself cure this infirmity. He can provide some gap-filling, by working with various States to help him arrest notorious human rights abusers who have violated international law. But he also needs to be careful that in pursuing an indictment and arrest he does not undermine the political capital he has been granted by the United Nations and the ICC's States parties. For he will need to rely on both entities for gap-filling in the future to cure the infirmity of a lack of organized sanctions as well as lack of compulsory jurisdiction. And Ocampo needs to be especially concerned about furthering rather than retarding the protection of human rights in the global community.

NOTES

1. H.L.A. Hart *The Concept of Law*. Oxford: Oxford University Press, 1960, 1984, p. 214.
2. Hugo Grotius, *De Jure Belli Ac Pacis* (On the Law of War and Peace) (1625), translated by Francis W. Kelsey, Oxford: Clarendon Press, 1925, p 17.
3. Ibid., p. 20.
4. Peter Haggenmacher, "Grotius and Gentili," in *Hugo Grotius and International Relations*, edited by Hedley Bull, Benedict Kingsbury, and Adam Roberts, Oxford: Oxford University Press, 1990, p. 172.
5. *De Jure Belli ac Pacis*, pp. 860–861.
6. Ibid., pp. 16–17.
7. Ibid., p. 18.
8. Emir de Vattel, *Le droit des Gens, ou Principes de la Loi Naturelle* (The Law of Nations or the Principles of Natural Law) (1758), translated by Charles G. Fenwick, Washington: Carnegie Institution, 1916, p. 113; reprinted in *The Morality of War*, edited by May, Rovie, and Viner, Englewood Cliffs. NJ: Prentice-Hall, Inc., 2006, p. 100.
9. Ibid., p. 119; and reprinted in *The Morality of War*, p. 106.
10. Ibid., p. 131; and reprinted in *The Morality of War*, 108.
11. Hersch Lauterpacht, *The Function of Law in the International Community*, Oxford UP. 1933, p. 64.
12. See *Truth v. Justice*, edited by Robert I Rotberg and Dennis Thompson, Princeton U, Press, 2000.
13. William J. Long and Peter Brecke, *War and Reconciliation*, MIT Press, 2003.
14. Ronald Slye, "Amnesty Truth, and Reconciliation: Reflections on the South African Amnesty Process," in *Truth v. Justice*, pp. 170–1.
15. *De Jure Belli ac Pacis*, p. 860.
16. Ibid., pp. 861–2.
17. Ibid., p. 816.
18. See my book *War Crimes and Just War*, NY; Cambridge University Press, 2007, p. 60.
19. *De Jure Belli Ac Pacis*, p 53.
20. Situation in Darfur, The Sudan, Summary of the Case, Prosecutor's Application for Warrant of Arrest under Article 58 Against Omar Hassan Ahmad Al Bashir, 14 July 2008.
21. Speech by Luis Moreno-Ocampo, 25 June 2007, Nuremberg.

A Women's Politics of Resistance

Sara Ruddick

Sara Ruddick teaches philosophy and women's studies at the New School for Social Research. She is the author of *Maternal Thinking: Towards a Politics of Peace* (1989). She has also written a monograph entitled "Drafting Women" (1982).

Ruddick discusses what she calls "a feminist material peace politics." The key dimension of her pacifist perspective is the use of feminine symbols as a model for organizing politically to resist various state practices and policies. She is especially interested in the symbolic role of the "mother" in providing for sustenance of children and family. Ruddick directly confronts one of the most common criticisms of pacifism, namely that it is unlikely to be effective over the long run. In drawing on examples from Argentina and Chile, Ruddick shows the power of largely nonviolent collective action taken by groups of women to oppose tyranny and military might.

A women's politics of resistance is identified by three characteristics: its participants are women, they explicitly invoke their culture's symbols of femininity, and their purpose is to resist certain practices or policies of their governors.

Women, like men, typically act out of social locations and political allegiances unconnected to their sex; women are socialists or capitalists, patriots or dissidents, colonialists or nationalists. Unlike other politics, a women's politics is organized and acted out by women. Women "riot" for bread, picket against alcohol, form peace camps outside missile bases, protect their schools from government interference, or sit in against nuclear testing. A women's politics often includes men: Women call on men's physical strength or welcome the protection that powerful male allies offer. Nonetheless it is women who organize themselves self-consciously as women. The reasons women give for organizing range from an appreciation of the protection afforded by "womanliness" to men's unwillingness to participate in "sentimental" politics to the difficulty in speaking, much less being taken seriously, with men around. Typically, the point of women's politics is not to claim independence from men but, positively, to organize as women. Whatever the reasons for their separatism, the fact that women organize, direct, and enact a politics enables them to exploit their culture's symbols of femininity.

Women can also organize together without evoking common understandings of femininity. Feminist actions, for example, are often organized by women who explicitly repudiate the roles, behavior, and attitudes expected of "women." What I am calling a women's politics of resistance affirms obligations traditionally assigned to women and calls on the community to respect them. Women are responsible for their children's health; in the name of their maternal duty they call on the government to halt nuclear testing, which, epitomizing a general unhealthiness, leaves strontium-90 in nursing mothers' milk. If women are to be able to feed their families, then the community must produce sufficient food and sell it at prices homemakers can afford. If women are responsible for educating young children, then they resist government efforts to interfere with local schools.

Not all women's politics are politics of resistance. There are politics organized by women that celebrate women's roles and attitudes but that serve rather than resist the state. In almost every war, mothers of heroes and martyrs join together in support of military sons, knitting, writing, and then mourning, in the service of the military state. The best-known instance of women's politics is the organization of Nazi women in praise of *Kinder, Küche, Kirche*.[1] Today in Chile, a women's organization under the direction of the dictator Pinochet's wife celebrates "feminine power" (*el poder femenino*), which expresses itself through loyalty to family and fatherland.

A women's politics of *resistance* is composed of women who take responsibility for the tasks of caring labor and then find themselves confronted with policies or actions that interfere with their right or capacity to do their work. In the name of womanly duties that they have assumed and that their communities expect of them, they resist. This feminine resistance has made some philosophers and feminists uneasy. Much like organized violence, women's resistance is difficult to predict or control. Women in South Boston resist racial integration; mothers resist the conscription of their children in just wars.

Even where women aim to resist tyranny, their "feminine" protest seems too acceptable to be effective. As Dorothy Dinnerstein eloquently laments, women are *meant* to weep while men rule and fight:

> Women's resigned, implicitly collusive, ventilation of everybody's intuition that the world men rule is murderously crazy is a central theme in folklore, literature, drama [and women's politics of resistance].
> Think, for instance, of the proverb that groups woman with wine and song as a necessary counterpoint to battle, a counterpoint that makes it possible for men to draw back from their will to kill just long and far enough so that they can then take it up again with new vigor. Or think of the saying "Men must work and women must weep." Woman's tears over what is lethal in man's work, this saying implies, are part of the world's eternal, unalterable way. . . . [Her] tears serve not to deter man but to

help him go on, for she is doing his weeping for him and he is doing what she weeps about for her.[2]

Christa Wolf expresses a related fear that women's resistance is as fragile as their dependence on individual men, loyalty to kin, and privileges of class:

> I was slow on the uptake. My privileges intruded between me and the most necessary insights; so did my attachment to my own family, which did not depend upon the privileges I enjoyed.[3]

For whatever reasons, feminists are apt to be disappointed in the sturdiness and extent of women's resistance. Dorothy Dinnerstein expresses this feminist disappointment:

> The absurd self-importance of his striving has been matched by the abject servility of her derision, which has on the whole been expressed only with his consent and within boundaries set by him, and which has on the whole worked to support the stability of the realm he rules.[4]

While some people fear that "feminine" resistance is inevitably limited—and their fears seem to me not groundless—I place my hope in its unique potential effectiveness, namely, women's social position makes them inherently "disloyal to the civilization"[5] that depends on them. Thus Hegel worries, and I hope, that ostensibly compliant women are on the edge of dissidence. The state, whose most powerful governors depend on women's work and whose stability rests on the authority of the Fathers, "creates for itself in what it suppresses and what it depends upon an internal enemy—womankind in general."[6] Underlining as Hegel does women's exclusion from power, Julia Kristeva celebrates a woman who is "an eternal dissident in relation to social and political consensus, in exile from power, and therefore always singular, fragmentary, demonic, a witch."[7] Yet like Kristeva, I find that the dissident mother, perhaps unlike other witches, is not only a potential critic of the order that excludes her but also and equally a conserver and legitimator of the order it is her duty to instill in her children. Kristeva expects from this dissident mother an "attentiveness to ethics" rooted in a collective experience and tradition of mothering. And I would expect from her the ambivalence that Jane Lazarre believes keeps the head alive, even as it slows the trigger finger. This attentiveness to ethics can become effectively militant in a women's politics of resistance. Its ambivalence, while a spur to compassion, does not slow action if women are governed by principles of nonviolence that allow them to hate and frustrate oppressors they neither mutilate nor murder.

Women's politics of resistance are as various as the cultures from which they arise. Of the many examples I could choose, I select one, the resistance of Argentinian and Chilean women to military dictatorship, specifically to the policy of kidnapping, imprisonment, torture, and murder of the "disappeared." The resistance of the Madres (mothers) of Argentina to its military regime and the similar, ongoing resistance of Chilean women to the Pinochet dictatorship politically exemplify central maternal concepts such as the primacy of bodily life and the connectedness of self and other. At the same time, these movements politically transform certain tendencies of maternal militarism such as cheery denial and parochialism.

Although women's work is always threatened by violence and although women in war always suffer the hunger, illness, mutilation, and loss of their loved ones, the crime of "disappearance" is especially haunting. Kidnapping and rumors of torture and murder destroy lives and families. Yet because the fate of the disappeared person is unclear, because no one in power acknowledges her or his existence, let alone disappearance, even mourning is impossible:

> To disappear means to be snatched off a street corner, or dragged from one's bed, or taken from a movie theater or cafe, either by police, or soldiers, or men in civilian clothes, and from that moment on to disappear from the face of the earth leaving not a single trace. It means that all knowledge of the disappeared is totally lost. Absolutely nothing is known about them. What was their fate? If they are alive, where are they? What are they enduring? If they are dead, where are their bones?[8]

Nathan Laks describes the Argentinian protest that began in Buenos Aires in 1976:

> Once in power [in Argentina in 1976], the military systematized and accelerated the campaign of terror, quickly annihilating the armed organizations of the Left and the unarmed ones, as well as many individuals with little or no connection to either. The indiscriminate nature of the kidnapping campaign and the impunity with which it was carried out spread terror—as intended. Relationships among friends and relatives were shattered by unprecedented fear. Perfectly decent individuals suddenly became afraid even to visit the parents of a kidnap victim, for any such gesture of compassion might condemn the visitor to a terrible fate. In this terrorized society, a small organization of women, mothers and other relatives of kidnapped Argentines staged a stunning act of defiance. One Thursday afternoon they gathered in the Plaza de Mayo, the main square in Buenos Aires and the site of countless historic incidents beginning in 1810 with the events that led to Argentina's separation from the Spanish Empire. In the center of the Plaza de Mayo, within clear sight of the presidential palace, the national cathedral, and several headquarters of ministries and corporations, the Mothers paraded in a closed circle.[9]

The Madres met each other outside hospitals or prisons, where they took food and other provisions and looked for traces of the disappeared, or outside government offices, where they tried, almost invariably without success, to get some accounting of their loved ones' whereabouts. When they marched, the Madres wore white kerchiefs with the names of the disappeared embroidered on them. Often they carried lighted candles and almost always they wore or carried photographs of the disappeared. In Chile, women chained themselves to the steps of the capitol, formed a human chain to a mine, Lonquen, where a mass grave was discovered, and took over a stadium where disappeared people had been rounded up, later to be tortured and killed.

The Latin American women's movements are clearly politics of resistance. The women who engage in them court imprisonment and torture and in some cases have become "disappeared" themselves. Knowing what fearful things could happen to them, women in Chile trained themselves to name and deal with what they feared:

> If they were afraid of facing police, they were told simply to find a policeman and stare at him until they could see him as a man and not as a representative of the state. [They] circled police vans on

foot, until these symbols of the regime appeared as just another kind of motor vehicle. . . . The women also instructed one another how to deal with the tear gas . . . to stop eating two hours before demonstrations, to dress in casual clothing, to take off makeup but to put salt on their cheekbones to keep teargas powder from entering their eyes, . . . to carry lemon to avoid teargas sting and to get a jar with home-made smelling salts made up of salt and ammonia.[10]

The women talked among themselves about their terrors, found others who shared their fears, and marched with them in affinity groups. And thus they brought their bodies to bear against the state.

As in many women's politics of resistance, the Argentinian and Chilean women emphasize mothering among women's many relations. They are Madres, whether or not they are biological or adoptive mothers of individual disappeared; a later group is made up of Abuelas (grandmothers). Their presence and the character of their action, as well as the interviews they have given, invariably evoke an experience of mothering that is central to their lives, whatever other home work or wage labor they engage in. Repeatedly they remember and allude to ordinary tasks—clothing, feeding, sheltering, and most of all tending to extensive kin work. All these works, ordinarily taken for granted, are dramatically present just because they are interrupted; they are made starkly visible through the eerie "disappearance," the shattering mockery of a maternal and childlike "unchanging expectation of good in the head."[11]

As these women honor mothering, they honor themselves. The destruction of the lives of their children, often just on the verge of adulthood, destroys years of their work; their loss and the impossibility of mourning it constitutes a violent outrage against them. Yet there is something misleading about this way of talking. The women do not speak of their work but of their children; they carry children's photographs, not their own. The distinctive structuring of the relation between self and other, symbolized in birth and enacted in mothering, is now politicized. The children, the absent ones, are *not* their mothers, who have decidedly *not* disappeared but are bodily present. The singular, irreplaceable children are lost. Yet as the pictures the Madres carry suggest, the children

are not, even in disappearance, apart from their mothers but, in their absence, are still inseparable from them.

For these Argentinian and Chilean women, as for women in most cultures, mothering is intuitively or "naturally" connected to giving birth. The Abuelas, especially, have made a political point of the emotional significance of genetic continuity. Since the fall of the military regime, one of their projects has been to form a genetic bank to trace the biological parentage of children adopted by people close to the ruling class at the time the military was in power. The insistence on genetic connection is one aspect of a general affirmation of the body. Indeed, the vulnerability, promise, and power of human bodies is central to this women's politics of resistance, as it is to maternal practice:

> Together with the affirmation of life, the human body is a very important reference for these women. They often speak of physical pain, the wounds caused by the disappearances. It seems that wearing a photograph of the missing one attached to the clothing or in a locket around the neck is a way of feeling closer to them.[12]

Because they have suffered military violence—have been stripped naked, sexually humiliated, and tortured—children's bodies have become a locus of pain. Because the violation of bodies is meant to terrify, the body itself becomes a place where terror is wrought. In resistance to this violation mothers' bodies become instruments of nonviolent power. Adorned with representations of bodies loved and violated, they express the necessity of love even amid terror, "in the teeth of all experience of crimes committed, suffered and witnessed."[13]

In their protests, these women fulfill traditional expectations of femininity and at the same time violate them. These are women who may well have expected to live out an ideology of "separate spheres" in which men and women had distinct but complementary tasks. Whatever ideology of the sexual division of labor they may have espoused, their political circumstances, as well as the apparently greater vulnerability and the apparently greater timidity and conventionality of the men they lived among, required that they act publicly as women. Women who bring to the public plazas of a police state pictures of their loved ones, like women who put pillowcases, toys, and other artifacts of attachment against the barbed wire fences of missile bases, translate the symbols of mothering into political speech. Preservative love, singularity in connection, the promise of birth and the resilience of hope, the irreplaceable treasure of vulnerable bodily being—these clichés of maternal work are enacted in public, by women insisting that their governors name and take responsibility for their crimes. They speak a "women's language" of loyalty, love, and outrage; but they speak with a public anger in a public place in ways they were never meant to do.

Although not a "peace politics" in a conventional sense, the Latin American protest undermines tendencies of maternal practice and thinking that are identifiably militarist. To some extent, this is a matter of shifting a balance between tendencies in mothering that support militarism toward tendencies that subvert it. In this case, the balance shifts from denial to truthfulness, from parochialism to solidarity, and from inauthenticity to active responsibility. Writing about André Trocme and his parishioners in the French village of Le Chambon during World War II, Phillip Hallie identified three characteristics that enabled them to penetrate the confusion and misinformation with which Nazis covered their policy and then to act on their knowledge. "*Lucid knowledge, awareness of the pain of others*, and *stubborn decision* dissipated for the Chambonnais the Night and Fog that inhabited the minds of so many people in Europe, and the world at large, in 1942."[14] In the transformed maternal practice of the Argentinian and Chilean women, these same virtues of nonviolent resistance are at work.

Cheery denial is an endemic maternal temptation. A similar "willingness to be self-deceived," as the resistance leader André Trocme called it, also sustains many decent citizens' support of war policy. It is notorious that few people can bear, except very briefly, to acknowledge the dangers of nuclear weapons and the damage they have done and could still do. Similarly, few citizens really look at the political aims and material-emotional lives of people affected by their own country's interventionist war policies. By contrast, the Argentinian and Chilean women insist on, and then disseminate, "lucid knowledge" of military crimes. "What is so profoundly moving about them is their determination to find out the truth."[15] They insist that others, too, hear the truth. They are "ready to talk immediately; they need to talk, to make sure their story, so tragic and so common, . . . be told, be known."[16] In addition to talking, they make tapestries, arpilleras, that tell stories of daily life including workers' organizing, police brutality, kidnapping, and resistance. The protests, tales, and arpilleras extend the maternal task of storytelling, maintaining ordinary maternal values of realism in the face of temptation to deny or distort. In this context, their ordinary extraordinary work becomes a politics of remembering.

After fighting in World War II the philosopher J. Glenn Gray wrote:

> The great god Mars tries to blind us when we enter his realm, and when we leave he gives us a generous cup of the waters of Lethe to drink. . . . When I consider how easily we forget the millions who suffered unbearably, either permanently maimed in body or mind, or who gave up their lives before they realized their purpose, I rebel at the whole insane spectacle of human existence.[17]

After the junta fell, Argentinian women insisted that violated bodies be *remembered*, which required that crimes be named, the men who committed them be brought to trial, and the bodies themselves, alive or dead, be accounted for and, where possible, returned.

"Awareness of the pain of others." The Argentinian and Chilean Madres spoke first of their own pain and the pain of relatives and friends of others disappeared. Similarly, maternal nonviolence is rooted, and typically limited by, a commitment to one's "own" children and the people they live among. . . . I spoke of this limitation as a principal source of maternal militarism; the parochialism of maternal practice can become the racialism that fuels organized violence. This tribal parochialism was also broken down in the Argentinian and Chilean protests.

As in mothering generally, women found it easiest to extend their concern for their own children to other mothers "like them"; only in this political context likeness had to do not with race or ethnicity but with common suffering. In Argentina, where protests are marked by the "singularity" of photographs, the women came to wear identical masks to mark their commonality. In Chile one woman said:

> Because of all this suffering we are united. I do not ask for justice for my child alone, or the other women just for their children. We are asking for justice for all. All of us are equal. If we find one disappeared one I will rejoice as much as if they had found mine.[18]

Concern for all victims then sometimes extended to collective concern for all the people of the nation:

> We are the women and mothers of this land, of the workers, of the professionals, of the students, and of future generations.[19]

This is still "nationalism," though of a noble sort. Many of the women went further as they explicitly identified with all victims of military or economic violence:

> In the beginning we only wanted to rescue our children. But as time passed we acquired a different comprehension. We understood better what is going on in the world. We know that when babies do not have enough to eat that, too, is a violation of human rights.[20]

> We should commit ourselves to make Lonquen [the mine where a mass grave was discovered] a blessed spot. May it be a revered spot, so that never again will a hostile hand be raised against any other person that lives on the earth.[21]

It would be foolish to believe that every woman in the Argentinian and Chilean protest movements extended concern from her own children to all the disappeared then to all of the nation, and finally to all victims everywhere. Why should women whose children and loved ones have been singularly persecuted extend sympathetic protection to all victims, an extension that is extraordinary even among women and men who do not suffer singular assault? Yet many of these women did so

extend themselves—intellectually, politically, emotionally. They did not "transcend" their particular loss and love; particularity was the emotional root and source of their protest. It is through acting on that particularity that they extended mothering to include sustaining and protecting any people whose lives are blighted by violence.

"Stubborn decision." As children remind us, stubborn decision is a hallmark of maternity. And mothers reply: What looks like stubborn decision may well be a compound of timidity, vacillation, and desperation. Women in resistance are (almost certainly) not free from ordinary mothers' temptations to inauthenticity, to letting others—teachers, employers, generals, fathers, grandparents—establish standards of acceptability and delegating to them responsibility for children's lives. And like ordinary mothers, women in resistance probably include in their ranks *individuals* who in ordinary times could speak back to the teacher or organize opposition to the local corporate polluter. But "stubborn decision" takes on a new and collective political meaning when women acting together walk out of their homes to appropriate spaces they never were meant to occupy.

Like their counterparts in resistance elsewhere, these stubbornly decisive Argentinian and Chilean women, whatever their personal timidities, publicly announce that they take responsibility for protecting the world in which they and their children must live. These women are the daughters, the heirs, of Kollwitz's *mater dolorosa*. As in Kollwitz's representations, a mother is victimized through the victimization of her children. These women are themselves victims; moreover, they bear witness to victimization first of loved ones, then of strangers; they stand against those in power, in solidarity with those who are hurt. Yet there is also a sense in which, by their active courage, they refuse victimization. More accurately, they mock dichotomies that still riddle political thought. There is no contradiction between "playing the role of victim" and taking responsibility for public policies. It is possible to act powerfully while standing with those who are hurt. It is neither weak nor passive to reveal one's own suffering while refusing to damage or mutilate in return. The Latin American *mater dolorosa* has learned how to fight as a victim for victims, not by joining the strong, but by resisting them.

A women's politics of resistance is not inherently a peace politics. Women can organize to sabotage peace treaties or to celebrate the heroes and martyrs of organized violence. During the Malvinas-Falklands war, Argentinian and English women sought each other out at a women's meeting in New York to denounce together their countries' militarism and imperialism. Yet during that same war, the Argentinian Madres were reported to use patriotic rhetoric to reinforce their own aims: "The Malvinas belong to us and so do our sons."

Nonetheless, in their own contexts, the Argentinian protest had, and the Chilean protest still has, antimilitarist implications. The regimes against which the women protest were and are militarist; the omnipresence of the soldier as oppressor and the general as the torturers' commander was—and in Chile still is—sufficient to symbolize a contrast between women and war. Moreover, the generals' actions have not been accidentally related to militarism. As Plato saw, when he rejected militarist rule in his totalitarian state, torture, kidnapping and other physical terrorism infect the rule of fearful tyrants, just as atrocities infect the best organized war. In their deliberately and increasingly brutal strategies to ensure absolute control, the generals exemplify the excesses inherent in militarized tyranny. Hence in the women's protests, not only a particular government but military rule is brought to trial.

Whatever their militarist sentiments or rhetoric, the Argentinian and Chilean protests express to the world the ideals of nonviolence. Although effective protest inevitably hurts its opponents and those associated with them, the protesters did not set out to injure but to end injuring. None of their actions even risked serious, lasting physical damage. Their aim was steadfastly one of reconnection and restoration of a just community, even though and because those responsible for violence were held accountable and were punished. By providing an example of persistent, stubborn action, the

Argentinian and Chilean women have offered a model of nonviolent resistance to other Latin American countries and to the world. They have therefore contributed to collective efforts to invent peace, whatever their degree of effectiveness within their own countries. Like the maternal practice from which it grows, a women's politics of resistance may remain racial, tribal, or chauvinist; we cannot expect of women in resistance the rare human ability to stand in solidarity with all victims of violence. Yet if these Latin American protests are at all emblematic, they suggest that the peacefulness latent in maternal practice tends to be realized as participants act against, and therefore reflect on, violence itself.

NOTES

1. For a discussion of women's participation in (and occasional resistance to) the Nazi German government, see Claudia Koonz, *Mothers in the Fatherland: Women, the Family, and Nazi Politics* (New York: St. Martin's, 1987). Among the many virtues of this fascinating book is its tracing of the complex interconnections between women's separate spheres, the Nazi and feminist use of women's difference, and women's participation in but also disappointment in the Nazi state.
2. Dorothy Dinnerstein, *The Mermaid and the Minotaur* (New York: Harper & Row, 1976), p. 226.
3. Christa Wolf, *Cassandra* (New York: Farrar Straus & Giroux, 1984), p. 53.
4. Dorothy Dinnerstein, "The Mobilization of Eros," in *Face to Face* (Greenwood Press, 1982). Manuscript courtesy of the author. For an intellectually sophisticated and high-spirited account of an American women's politics of resistance, see Amy Swerdlow's work on Women's Strike for Peace, forthcoming from the University of Chicago Press. For an example of her work, see "Pure Milk, Not Poison: Women's Strike for Peace and the Test Ban Treaty of 1963," in *Rocking the Ship of State: Toward a Feminist Peace Politics*, ed. Adrienne Harris and Ynestra King (Westview Press, 1989).
5. The title of a well-known essay by Adrienne Rich in *Lies, Secrets and Silence* (New York: Norton, 1979), pp. 275–310.
6. Hegel, *The Phenomenology of Mind*, part VI, A, b, "Ethical Action: Knowledge Human and Divine: Guilt and Destiny" (New York: Harper, 1967), p. 496.
7. Julia Kristeva, "Talking about *Polygoue*" (an interview with Francoise van Rossum-Guyon), in *French Feminist Thought*, ed. Toril Moi (Oxford: Basil Blackwell, 1987), p. 113.
8. Marjorie Agosin, "Emerging from the Shadows: Women of Chile," *Barnard Occasional Papers on Women's*

Issues, vol. 2, no. 3, Fall 1987, p. 12. I am very grateful to Temma Kaplan, historian and director of the Barnard College Women's Center, whose interest in "motherist" and grass-roots womens' resistance movements inspired this section. Temma Kaplan provided me with material on the Madres and discussed an earlier draft of the chapter.

9. Nathan Laks, cited in Nora Amalia Femenia, "Argentina's Mothers of Plaza de Mayo: The Mourning Process from Junta to Democracy," *Feminist Studies*, vol. 13, no. 1, p. 10. The Argentinian Madres protested until the fall of the military regime and still exist today, though they are now divided in their political aims.

10. Marjorie Agosin, Temma Kaplan, Teresa Valduz, "The Politics of Spectacle in Chile," *Barnard Occasional Papers on Women's Issues*, vol. 2, no. 3, Fall 1987, p. 6.

11. Simone Weil, "Human Personality," in *Simone Weil Reader*, p. 315.

12. Agosin, "Emerging," p. 18.

13. Simone Weil, "Human Personality," in *Simone Weil Reader* p. 315.

14. Phillip Hallie, *Lest Innocent Blood Be Shed* (New York: Harper & Row, 1979), p. 104. (Italics added.)

15. Agosin, "Emerging," p. 16.

16. Agosin, "Emerging," p. 14.

17. J. Glenn Gray, *The Warriors* (New York: Harper & Row, 1970), pp. 21, 23.

18. Agosin, "Emerging," p. 21.

19. Patricia M. Chuchryk, "Subversive Mothers: The Women's Opposition to the Military Regime in Chile," paper presented at the International Congress of the Latin American Studies Association, Boston, 1986, p. 9.

20. Rene Epelbaum, member of the Argentinian protest, in an interview with Jean Bethke Elshtain, personal communication.

21. Agosin, "Emerging," p. 18.

Letter from the Birmingham City Jail

Martin Luther King, Jr.

Martin Luther King Jr. was a minister and one of the most important leaders of the civil rights movement in the United States. He was awarded the Nobel Peace Prize in 1964. He was the author of *Strive Toward Freedom* (1958), *Why We Can't Wait* (1964), and *The Trumpet of Conscience* (1968).

King provides another extremely influential account of nonviolent civil disobedience. He defines a nonviolent campaign as one that has four stages: (a) a determination that injustice is occurring; (b) negotiation to try to end the injustice; (c) a cleansing process that steels one against hatred and revenge; (d) nonviolent direct action. He offers a defense of this strategy, as opposed to a strategy of violence, by reference to traditional Judeo-Christian moral principles. Of central concern to King is the contention that we all share in responsibility for stopping injustice wherever it occurs. This contention is supported by reference to the principle of "love your neighbor," a principle which King believed to be strongly opposed to violence.

My dear Fellow Clergymen,

While confined here in the Birmingham City Jail, I came across your recent statement calling our present activities "unwise and untimely." Seldom, if ever, do I pause to answer criticisms of my work and ideas. If I sought to answer all of the criticisms that cross my desk, my secretaries would be engaged in little else in the course of the day, and I would have no time for constructive work. But since I feel that you are men of genuine goodwill and your criticisms are sincerely set forth, I would like to answer your statement in what I hope will be patient and reasonable terms.

I think I should give the reason for my being in Birmingham, since you have been influenced by the argument of "outsiders coming in." I have the honor of serving as president of the Southern Christian Leadership Conference, an organization operating in every Southern state, with headquarters in Atlanta, Georgia. We have some eighty-five affiliate organizations all across the South—one being the Alabama Christian Movement for Human Rights. Whenever necessary and possible we share staff, educational and financial resources with our affiliates. Several months ago our local affiliate here in Birmingham invited us to be on call to engage in a nonviolent direct action program if such were deemed necessary. We readily consented and when the hour came we lived up to our promises. So I am here, along with several members of my staff, because we were invited here. I am here because I have basic organizational ties here.

Beyond this, I am in Birmingham because injustice is here. Just as the eighth century prophets left their little villages and carried their "thus saith the Lord" far beyond the boundaries of their home towns; and just as the Apostle Paul left his little village of Tarsus and carried the gospel of Jesus Christ to practically every hamlet and city of the Greco-Roman world, I too am compelled to carry the gospel of freedom beyond my particular home town. Like Paul, I must constantly respond to the Macedonian call for aid.

Moreover, I am cognizant of the interrelatedness of all communities and states. I cannot sit idly by in Atlanta and not be concerned about what happens in Birmingham. Injustice anywhere is a threat to justice everywhere. We are caught in an inescapable network of mutuality, tied in a single garment of destiny. Whatever affects one directly affects all indirectly. Never again can we afford to live with the narrow, provincial "outside agitator" idea. Anyone who lives inside the United States can never be considered an outsider anywhere in this country.

You deplore the demonstrations that are presently taking place in Birmingham. But I am sorry your statement did not express a similar concern for the conditions that brought the demonstrations into being. I am sure that each of you would want to go beyond the superficial social analyst who looks merely at effects, and does not grapple with underlying causes. I would not hesitate to say that it is unfortunate that so-called demonstrations are taking place in Birmingham at this time, but I would say in more emphatic terms that it is even more unfortunate that the white power structure of this city left the Negro community with no other alternative.

In any nonviolent campaign there are four basic steps: (1) Collection of the facts to determine whether injustices are alive, (2) Negotiation, (3) Self-purification, and (4) Direct Action. We have gone through all of these steps in Birmingham. There can be no gainsaying of the fact that racial injustice engulfs this community.

Birmingham is probably the most thoroughly segregated city in the United States. Its ugly record of police brutality is known in every section of this country. Its unjust treatment of Negroes in the courts is a notorious reality. There have been more unsolved bombings of Negro homes and churches in Birmingham than any city in this nation. These are hard, brutal, and unbelievable facts. On the basis of these conditions Negro leaders sought to negotiate with the city fathers. But the political leaders consistently refused to engage in good faith negotiation.

Then came the opportunity last September to talk with some of these leaders of the economic community. In the negotiating sessions certain promises were made by the merchants—such as the promise to remove the humiliating racial signs from the stores. On the basis of these promises Rev. Shuttlesworth and the leaders of the Alabama Christian Movement for Human Rights agreed to call a moratorium on any type of demonstrations. As the weeks and months unfolded we realized that we were the victims of a broken promise. The signs remained. Like so many experiences of the past we were confronted with blasted hopes, and the dark shadow of a deep disappointment settled upon us. So we had no alternative except that of preparing for direct action, whereby we would present our very bodies as a means of laying our case before the conscience of the local and national community. We were not unmindful of the difficulties involved. So we decided to go through a process of self-purification. We started having workshops on nonviolence and repeatedly asked ourselves the questions, "Are you able to accept blows without retaliating?" "Are you able to endure the ordeals of jail?" We decided to set our direct action program around the Easter season, realizing that with the exception of Christmas, this was the largest shopping period of the year. Knowing that a strong economic withdrawal program would be the by-product of direct action, we felt that this was the best time to bring pressure on the merchants for the needed changes. Then it occurred to us that the March election was ahead and so we speedily decided to postpone action until after election day. When we discovered that Mr. Connor was in the run-off, we decided again to postpone action so that the demonstrations could not be used to cloud the issues. At this time we agreed to begin our nonviolent witness the day after the run-off.

This reveals that we did not move irresponsibly into direct action. We too wanted to see Mr. Connor defeated; so we went through postponement after postponement to aid in this community need. After this we felt that direct action could be delayed no longer.

You may well ask, "Why direct action? Why sit-ins, marches, etc.? Isn't negotiation a better path?" You are exactly right in your call for negotiation. Indeed, this is the purpose of direct action. Nonviolent direct action seeks to create such a crisis and establish such creative tension that a community that has constantly refused to negotiate is forced to confront the issue. It seeks so to dramatize the issue that it can no longer be ignored. I just referred to the creation of tension as a part of the work of the nonviolent resister. This may sound rather shocking. But I must confess that I am not afraid of the word tension. I have earnestly worked and preached against violent tension, but there is a type of constructive nonviolent tension that is necessary for growth. Just as Socrates felt that it was necessary to create a tension in the mind so that individuals could rise from the bondage of myths and half-truths to the unfettered realm of creative analysis and objective appraisal, we must see the need of having nonviolent gadflies to create the kind of tension in society that will help men to rise from the dark depths of prejudice and racism to the majestic heights of understanding and brotherhood. So the purpose of the direct action is to create a situation so crisis-packed that it will inevitably open the door to negotiation. We, therefore, concur with you in your call for negotiation. Too long has our beloved Southland been bogged down in the tragic attempt to live in monologue rather than dialogue.

One of the basic points in your statement is that our acts are untimely. Some have asked, "Why didn't you give the new administration time to act?" The only answer I can give to this inquiry is that the new administration must be prodded about as much as the outgoing one before it acts. We will be sadly mistaken if we feel the election of Mr. Boutwell will bring the millenium to Birmingham. While Mr. Boutwell is much more articulate and gentle than Mr. Connor, they are both segregationists, dedicated to the task of maintaining the status quo. The hope I see in Mr. Boutwell is that he will be reasonable enough to see the futility of massive resistance to desegregation. But he will not see this without pressure from the devotees of civil rights. My friends, I must say to you that we have not made a single gain in civil rights without determined legal and nonviolent pressure. History is the long and tragic story of the fact that privileged groups seldom give up their privileges voluntarily. Individuals may see the moral light and voluntarily give up this unjust posture; but as Reinhold Niebuhr has reminded us, groups are more immoral than individuals.

We know through painful experience that freedom is never voluntarily given by the oppressor; it must be demanded by the oppressed. Frankly, I have never yet engaged in a direct action movement that was "well timed," according to the timetable of those who have not suffered unduly from the disease of segregation. For years now I have heard the word "Wait!" It rings in the ear of every Negro with piercing familiarity. This "Wait" has almost always meant "Never." It has been a tranquilizing thalidomide, relieving the emotional stress for a moment, only to give birth to an ill-formed infant of frustration. We must come to see with the distinguished jurist of yesterday that "justice too long delayed is justice denied." We have waited for more than three hundred and forty years for our constitutional and God-given rights. The nations of Asia and Africa are moving with jet-like speed toward the goal of political independence, and we still creep at horse and buggy pace toward the gaining of a cup of coffee at a lunch counter. I guess it is easy for those who have never felt the stinging darts of segregation to say, "Wait." But when you have seen vicious mobs lynch your mothers and fathers at will and drown your sisters and brothers at whim; when you have seen hate-filled policemen curse, kick, brutalize and even kill your black brothers and sisters with impunity; when you see the vast majority of your twenty million Negro brothers smoldering in an air-tight cage of poverty in the midst of an affluent society; when you suddenly find your tongue twisted and your speech stammering as you seek to explain to your six-year-old daughter why she can't go to the public amusement park that has just been advertised on television, and see tears welling up in her little eyes when she is told that Funtown is closed to colored children, and see the depressing clouds of inferiority begin to form in her little mental sky, and see her begin to distort her little personality by unconsciously developing a bitterness toward white people; when you have to concoct an answer for a five-year-old son asking in agonizing pathos: "Daddy, why do white people treat colored people so mean?"; when you take a cross-country drive and find it necessary to sleep night after night in the uncomfortable corners of your automobile because no motel will accept you; when you are humiliated day in and day out by nagging signs reading "white" and "colored"; when your first name becomes "nigger" and your middle name becomes "boy" (however old you are) and your last name becomes "John," and when your wife and mother are never given the respected title "Mrs."; when you are harried by day and haunted at night by the fact that you are a Negro, living constantly at tip-toe stance never quite knowing what to expect next, and plagued with inner fears and outer resentments; when you are forever fighting a degenerating sense of "nobodiness"; then you will understand why we find it difficult to wait. There comes a time when the cup of endurance runs over, and men are no longer willing to be plunged into an abyss of injustice where they experience the blackness of corroding despair. I hope, sirs, you can understand our legitimate and unavoidable impatience.

You express a great deal of anxiety over our willingness to break laws. This is certainly a legitimate concern. Since we so diligently urge people to obey the Supreme Court's decision of 1954 outlawing segregation in the public schools, it is rather strange and paradoxical to find us consciously breaking laws. One may well ask, "How can you advocate breaking some laws and obeying others?" The answer is found in the fact that there are two types of laws: There are *just* and there are *unjust* laws. I would agree with Saint Augustine that "An unjust law is no law at all."

Now what is the difference between the two? How does one determine when a law is just or unjust? A just law is a man-made code that squares with the moral law or the law of God. An unjust law is a code that is out of harmony with the moral law. To put it in the terms of Saint Thomas Aquinas, an unjust law is a human law that is not rooted in eternal and natural law. Any law that uplifts human personality is just. Any law that degrades human

personality is unjust. All segregation statutes are unjust because segregation distorts the soul and damages the personality. It gives the segregator a false sense of superiority, and the segregated a false sense of inferiority. To use the words of Martin Buber, the great Jewish philosopher, segregation substitutes an "I-it" relationship for the "I-thou" relationship, and ends up relegating persons to the status of things. So segregation is not only politically, economically, and sociologically unsound, but it is morally wrong and sinful. Paul Tillich has said that sin is separation. Isn't segregation an existential expression of man's tragic separation, an expression of his awful estrangement, his terrible sinfulness? So I can urge men to disobey segregation ordinances because they are morally wrong.

Let us turn to a more concrete example of just and unjust laws. An unjust law is a code that a majority inflicts on a minority that is not binding on itself. This is difference made legal. On the other hand a just law is a code that a majority compels a minority to follow that it is willing to follow itself. This is sameness made legal.

Let me give you another explanation. An unjust law is a code inflicted upon a minority which that minority had no part in enacting or creating because they did not have the unhampered right to vote. Who can say that the legislature of Alabama which set up the segregation laws was democratically elected? Throughout the state of Alabama all types of conniving methods are used to prevent Negroes from becoming registered voters, and there are some counties without a single Negro registered to vote despite the fact that the Negro constitutes a majority of the population. Can any law set up in such a state be considered democratically structured?

These are just a few examples of unjust and just laws. There are some instances when a law is just on its face and unjust in its application. For instance, I was arrested Friday on a charge of parading without a permit. Now there is nothing wrong with an ordinance which requires a permit for a parade, but when the ordinance is used to preserve segregation and to deny citizens the First Amendment privilege of peaceful assembly and peaceful protest, then it becomes unjust.

I hope you can see the distinction I am trying to point out. In no sense do I advocate evading or defying the law as the rabid segregationist would do. This would lead to anarchy. One who breaks an unjust law must do it *openly, lovingly* (not hatefully as the white mothers did in New Orleans when they were seen on television screaming "nigger, nigger, nigger"), and with a willingness to accept the penalty. I submit that an individual who breaks a law that conscience tells him is unjust, and willingly accepts the penalty by staying in jail to arouse the conscience of the community over its injustice, is in reality expressing the very highest respect for law.

Of course, there is nothing new about this kind of civil disobedience. It was seen sublimely in the refusal of Shadrach, Meshach, and Abednego to obey the laws of Nebuchadnezzar because a higher moral law was involved. It was practiced superbly by the early Christians who were willing to face hungry lions and the excruciating pain of chopping blocks, before submitting to certain unjust laws of the Roman empire. To a degree academic freedom is a reality today because Socrates practiced civil disobedience.

We can never forget that everything Hitler did in Germany was "legal" and everything the Hungarian freedom fighters did in Hungary was "illegal." It was "illegal" to aid and comfort a Jew in Hitler's Germany. But I am sure that if I had lived in Germany during that time I would have aided and comforted my Jewish brothers even though it was illegal. If I lived in a Communist country today where certain principles dear to the Christian faith are suppressed, I believe I would openly advocate disobeying these antireligious laws. I must make two honest confessions to you, my Christian and Jewish brothers. First, I must confess that over the last few years I have been gravely disappointed with the white moderate. I have almost reached the regrettable conclusion that the Negro's great stumbling block in the stride toward freedom is not the White Citizen's Counciler or the Ku Klux Klanner, but the white moderate who is more devoted to "order" than to justice; who prefers a negative peace which is the absence of tension to a positive peace which is the presence of justice; who constantly says, "I agree with you in the goal you seek, but I can't agree with your methods of direct action"; who paternalistically feels that he can set the timetable for another man's freedom; who lives by the myth of time and who constantly advises the Negro to wait until a "more convenient season." Shallow understanding from people of goodwill is more frustrating than absolute misunderstanding from people of ill will. Lukewarm acceptance is much more bewildering than outright rejection.

I had hoped that the white moderate would understand that law and order exist for the purpose of establishing justice, and that when they fail to do this they become dangerously structured dams that block the flow of social progress. I had hoped that the white moderate would understand that the present tension of the South is merely a necessary phase of the transition from an obnoxious negative peace, where the Negro passively accepted his unjust plight, to a substance-filled positive peace, where all men will respect the dignity and worth of human personality. Actually, we who engage in nonviolent direct action are not the creators of tension. We merely bring to the surface the hidden tension that is already alive. We bring it out in the open where it can be seen and dealt with. Like a boil that can never be cured as long as it is covered up but must be opened with all its pus-flowing ugliness to the natural medicines of air and light, injustice must likewise be exposed, with all of the tension its exposing creates, to the light of human conscience and the air of national opinion before it can be cured.

In your statement you asserted that our actions, even though peaceful, must be condemned because they precipitate violence. But can this assertion be logically made? Isn't this like condemning the robbed man because his possession of money precipitated the evil act of robbery? Isn't this like condemning Socrates because his unswerving commitment to truth and his philosophical delvings precipitated the misguided popular mind to make him drink the hemlock? Isn't this like condemning Jesus because His unique God-Consciousness and never-ceasing devotion to His will precipitated the evil act of crucifixion?

We must come to see, as federal courts have consistently affirmed, that it is immoral to urge an individual to withdraw his efforts to gain his basic constitutional rights because the quest precipitates violence. Society must protect the robbed and punish the robber.

I had also hoped that the white moderate would reject the myth of time. I received a letter this morning from a white brother in Texas which said: "All Christians know that the colored people will receive equal rights eventually, but it is possible that you are in too great of a religious hurry. It has taken Christianity almost 2000 years to accomplish what it has. The teachings of Christ take time to come to earth." All that is said here grows out of a tragic misconception of time. It is the strangely irrational notion that there is something in the flow of time that will inevitably cure all ills. Actually time is neutral. It can be used either destructively or constructively. I am coming to feel that the people of ill will have used time much more effectively than the people of goodwill. We will have to repent in this generation not merely for the vitriolic words and actions of the bad people, but for the appalling silence of the good people. We must come to see that human progress never rolls in on wheels of inevitability. It comes through the tireless efforts and persistent work of men willing to be co-workers with God, and without this hard work time itself becomes an ally of the forces of social stagnation. We must use time creatively, and forever realize that the time is always ripe to do right. Now is the time to make real the promise of democracy, and transform our pending national elegy into a creative psalm of brotherhood. Now is the time to lift our national policy from the quicksand of racial injustice to the solid rock of human dignity.

You spoke of our activity in Birmingham as extreme. At first I was rather disappointed that fellow clergymen would see my nonviolent efforts as those of an extremist. I started thinking about the fact that I stand in the middle of two opposing forces in the Negro community. One is a force of complacency made up of Negroes who, as a result of long years of oppression, have been so completely drained of self-respect and a sense of

"somebodiness" that they have adjusted to segregation, and, of a few Negroes in the middle class who, because of a degree of academic and economic security, and because at points they profit by segregation, have unconsciously become insensitive to the problems of the masses. The other force is one of bitterness and hatred, and comes perilously close to advocating violence. It is expressed in the various black nationalist groups that are springing up over the nation, the largest and best known being Elijah Muhammad's Muslim movement. This movement is nourished by the contemporary frustration over the continued existence of racial discrimination. It is made up of people who have lost faith in America, who have absolutely repudiated Christianity, and who have concluded that the white man is an incurable "devil." I have tried to stand between these two forces, saying that we need not follow the "do-nothingism" of the complacent or the hatred and despair of the black nationalist. There is the more excellent way of love and nonviolent protest. I'm grateful to God that, through the Negro church, the dimension of nonviolence entered our struggle. If this philosophy had not emerged, I am convinced that by now many streets in the South would be flowing with floods of blood. And I am further convinced that if our white brothers dismiss as "rabble rousers" and "outside agitators" those of us who are working through the channels of nonviolent direct action and refuse to support our nonviolent efforts, millions of Negroes, out of frustration and despair, will seek solace and security in black nationalist ideologies, a development that will inevitably lead to a frightening racial nightmare.

Oppressed people cannot remain oppressed forever. The urge for freedom will eventually come. This is what happened to the American Negro. Something within has reminded him of his birthright of freedom; something without has reminded him that he can gain it. Consciously and unconsciously, he has been swept in by what the Germans called the *Zeitgeist*, and with his black brothers of Africa, and his brown and yellow brothers of Asia, South America and the Caribbean, he is moving with a sense of cosmic urgency toward the promised land of racial justice. Recognizing this vital urge that has engulfed the Negro community, one should readily understand public demonstrations. The Negro has many pent-up resentments and latent frustrations. He has to get them out. So let him march sometime; let him have his prayer pilgrimages to the city hall; understand why he must have sit-ins and freedom rides. If his repressed emotions do not come out in these nonviolent ways, they will come out in ominous expressions of violence. This is not a threat; it is a fact of history. So I have not said to my people "get rid of your discontent." But I have tried to say that this normal and healthy discontent can be channelized through the creative outlet of nonviolent direct action. Now this approach is being dismissed as extremist. I must admit that I was initially disappointed in being so categorized.

But as I continued to think about the matter I gradually gained a bit of satisfaction from being considered an extremist. Was not Jesus an extremist in love—"Love your enemies, bless them that curse you, pray for them that despitefully use you." Was not Amos an extremist for justice—"Let justice roll down like waters and righteousness like a mighty stream." Was not Paul an extremist for the gospel of Jesus Christ—"I bear in my body the marks of the Lord Jesus." Was not Martin Luther an extremist—"Here I stand; I can do none other so help me God." Was not John Bunyan an extremist—"I will stay in jail to the end of my days before I make a butchery of my conscience." Was not Abraham Lincoln an extremist—"This nation cannot survive half slave and half free." Was not Thomas Jefferson an extremist—"We hold these truths to be self-evident, that all men are created equal." So the question is not whether we will be extremist but what kind of extremist will we be. Will we be extremists for hate or will we be extremists for love? Will we be extremists for the preservation of injustice—or will we be extremists for the cause of justice? In that dramatic scene on Calvary's hill, three men were crucified. We must not forget that all three men were crucified for the same crime—the crime of extremism. Two were extremists for immorality, and thusly fell below their environment. The other, Jesus Christ, was an extremist for love, truth and goodness, and thereby rose above His environment. So, after all, maybe the South, the nation and the world are in dire need of creative extremists.

I had hoped that the white moderate would see this. Maybe I was too optimistic. Maybe I expected too much. I guess I should have realized that few members of a race that has oppressed another race can understand or appreciate the deep groans and passionate yearnings of those that have been oppressed and still fewer have the vision to see that injustice must be rooted out by strong, persistent and determined action. I am thankful, however, that some of our white brothers have grasped the meaning of this social revolution and committed themselves to it. They are still all too small in quantity, but they are big in quality. Some like Ralph McGill, Lillian Smith, Harry Golden, and James Dabbs have written about our struggle in eloquent, prophetic, and understanding terms. Others have marched with us down nameless streets of the South. They have languished in filthy roach-infested jails, suffering the abuse and brutality of angry policemen who see them as "dirty nigger lovers." They, unlike so many of their moderate brothers and sisters, have recognized the urgency of the moment and sensed the need for powerful "action" antidotes to combat the disease of segregation.

Let me rush on to mention my other disappointment. I have been so greatly disappointed with the white church and its leadership. Of course, there are some notable exceptions. I am not unmindful of the fact that each of you has taken some significant stands on this issue. I commend you, Rev. Stallings, for your Christian stand on this past Sunday, in welcoming Negroes to your worship service on a non-segregated basis. I commend the Catholic leaders of this state for integrating Springhill College several years ago.

But despite these notable exceptions I must honestly reiterate that I have been disappointed with the church. I do not say that as one of the negative critics who can always find something wrong with the church. I say it as a minister of the gospel, who loves the church; who was nurtured in its bosom; who has been sustained by its spiritual blessings and who will remain true to it as long as the cord of life shall lengthen.

I had the strange feeling when I was suddenly catapulted into the leadership of the bus protest in Montgomery several years ago that we would have the support of the white church. I felt that the white ministers, priests, and rabbis of the South would be some of our strongest allies. Instead, some have been outright opponents, refusing to understand the freedom movement and misrepresenting its leaders; all too many others have been more cautious than courageous and have remained silent behind the anesthetizing security of the stained-glass windows.

In spite of my shattered dreams of the past, I came to Birmingham with the hope that the white religious leadership of this community would see the justice of our cause, and with deep moral concern, serve as the channel through which our just grievances would get to the power structure. I had hoped that each of you would understand. But again I have been disappointed. I have heard numerous religious leaders of the South call upon their worshippers to comply with a desegregation decision because it is the *law*, but I have longed to hear white ministers say, "Follow this decree because integration is morally *right* and the Negro is your brother." In the midst of blatant injustices inflicted upon the Negro, I have watched white churches stand on the sideline and merely mouth pious irrelevancies and sanctimonious trivialities. In the midst of a mighty struggle to rid our nation of racial and economic injustice, I have heard so many ministers say "Those are social issues with which the gospel has no real concern," and I have watched so many churches commit themselves to a completely other-worldly religion which made a strange distinction between the body and soul, the sacred and the secular.

So here we are moving toward the exit of the twentieth century with a religious community largely adjusted to the status quo, standing as a taillight behind other community agencies rather than a headlight leading men to higher levels of justice.

I have traveled the length and breadth of Alabama, Mississippi, and all the other southern states. On sweltering summer days and crisp autumn mornings I have looked at her beautiful churches with their lofty spires pointing heavenward. I have beheld the impressive outlay of her massive religious education buildings. Over and over again I have found myself asking: "What kind of people worship here? Who is their God? Where were their voices when the lips of Governor Barnett dripped the words of interposition and nullification? Where were they when Governor Wallace gave the clarion call for defiance and hatred? Where were their voices of support when tired, bruised and weary Negro men and women decided to rise from the dark dungeons of complacency to the bright hills of creative protest?"

Yes, these questions are still in my mind. In deep disappointment, I have swept over the laxity of the church. But be assured that my tears have been tears of love. There can be no deep disappointment where there is not deep love. Yes, I love the church; I love her sacred walls. How could I do otherwise? I am in the rather unique position of being the son, the grandson and the great-grandson of preachers. Yes, I see the church as the body of Christ. But, oh! How we have blemished and scarred that body through social neglect and fear of being nonconformists.

There was a time when the church was very powerful. It was during that period when the early Christians rejoiced when they were deemed worthy to suffer for what they believed. In those days the church was not merely a thermometer that recorded the ideas and principles of popular opinion; it was a thermostat that transformed the mores of society. Wherever the early Christians entered a town the power structure got disturbed and immediately sought to convict them for being "disturbers of the peace" and "outside agitators." But they went on with the conviction that they were "a colony of heaven," and had to obey God rather than man. They were small in number but big in commitment. They were too God-intoxicated to be "astronomically intimidated." They brought an end to such ancient evils as infanticide and gladiatorial contest.

Things are different now. The contemporary church is often a weak, ineffectual voice with an uncertain sound. It is so often the arch supporter of the status quo. Far from being disturbed by the presence of the church the power structure of the average community is consoled by the church's silent and often vocal sanction of things as they are.

But the judgment of God is upon the church as never before. If the church of today does not recapture the sacrificial spirit of the early church, it will lose its authentic ring, forfeit the loyalty of millions, and be dismissed as an irrelevant social club with no meaning for the twentieth century. I am meeting young people every day whose disappointment with the church has risen to outright disgust.

Maybe again, I have been too optimistic. Is organized religion too inextricably bound to the status quo to save our nation and the world? Maybe I must turn my faith to the inner spiritual church, the church within the church, as the true *ecclesia* and the hope of the world. But again I am thankful to God that some noble souls from the ranks of organized religion have broken loose from the paralyzing chains of conformity and joined us as active partners in the struggle for freedom. They have left their secure congregations and walked the streets of Albany, Georgia, with us. They have gone through the highways of the South in tortuous rides for freedom. Yes, they have gone to jail with us. Some have been kicked out of their churches, and lost support of their bishops and fellow ministers. But they have gone with the faith that right defeated is stronger than evil triumphant. These men have been the leaven in the lump of the race. Their witness has been the spiritual salt that has preserved the true meaning of the Gospel in these troubled times. They have carved a tunnel of hope through the dark mountain of disappointment.

I hope the church as a whole will meet the challenge of this decisive hour. But even if the church does not come to the aid of justice, I have no despair about the future. I have no fear about the outcome of our struggle in Birmingham, even if our motives are presently misunderstood. We will reach the goal of freedom in Birmingham and all over the nation, because the goal of America is

freedom. Abused and scorned though we may be, our destiny is tied up with the destiny of America. Before the pilgrims landed at Plymouth, we were here. Before the pen of Jefferson etched across the pages of history the majestic words of the Declaration of Independence, we were here. For more than two centuries our foreparents labored in this country without wages; they made cotton king; and they built the homes of their masters in the midst of brutal injustice and shameful humiliation—and yet out of a bottomless vitality they continued to thrive and develop. If the inexpressible cruelties of slavery did not stop us, the opposition we now face will surely fail. We will win our freedom because the sacred heritage of our nation and the eternal will of God are embodied in our echoing demands.

I must close now. But before closing I am impelled to mention one other point in your statement that troubled me profoundly. You warmly commended the Birmingham police for keeping "order" and "preventing violence." I don't believe you would have so warmly commended the police force if you had seen its angry violent dogs literally biting six unarmed, nonviolent Negroes. I don't believe you would so quickly commend the policemen if you would observe their ugly and inhuman treatment of Negroes here in the city jail; if you would watch them push and curse old Negro women and young Negro girls; if you would see them slap and kick old Negro men and young boys; if you will observe them, as they did on two occasions, refuse to give us food because we wanted to sing our grace together. I'm sorry that I can't join you in your praise for the police department.

It is true that they have been rather disciplined in their public handling of the demonstrators. In this sense they have been rather publicly "nonviolent." But for what purpose? To preserve the evil system of segregation. Over the last few years I have consistently preached that nonviolence demands that the means we use must be as pure as the ends we seek. So I have tried to make it clear that it is wrong to use immoral means to attain moral ends. But now I must affirm that it is just as wrong or even more so, to use moral means to provide immoral ends. Maybe Mr. Connor and his policemen have been rather publicly nonviolent, as Chief Pritchett was in Albany, Georgia, but they have used the moral means of nonviolence to maintain the immoral end of flagrant racial injustice. T.S. Eliot has said that there is no greater treason than to do the right deed for the wrong reason.

I wish you had commended the Negro sit-inners and demonstrators of Birmingham for their sublime courage, their willingness to suffer and their amazing discipline in the midst of the most inhuman provocation. One day the South will recognize its real heroes. They will be the James Merediths, courageously and with a majestic sense of purpose facing jeering and hostile mobs and the agonizing loneliness that characterizes the life of the pioneer. They will be old, oppressed, battered Negro women, symbolized in a seventy-two-year-old woman of Montgomery, Alabama, who rose up with a sense of dignity and with her people decided not to ride the segregated buses, and responded to one who inquired about her tiredness with ungrammatical profundity: "My feet is tired, but my soul is rested." They will be the young high school and college students, young ministers of the Gospel and a host of their elders courageously and nonviolently sitting-in at lunch counters and willingly going to jail for conscience's sake. One day the South will know that when these disinherited children of God sat down at lunch counters they were in reality standing up for the best in the American dream and the most sacred values in our Judeo-Christian heritage, and thusly, carrying our whole nation back to those great wells of democracy which were dug deep by the founding fathers in the formulation of the Constitution and the Declaration of Independence.

Never before have I written a letter this long (or should I say a book?). I'm afraid that it is much too long to take your precious time. I can assure you that it would have been much shorter if I had been writing from a comfortable desk, but what else is there to do when you are alone for days in the dull monotony of a narrow jail cell other than to write long letters, think strange thoughts, and pray long prayers?

If I have said anything in this letter that is an overstatement of the truth and is indicative of an unreasonable impatience, I beg you to forgive me. If I have said anything in this letter that is an understatement of the truth and is indicative of my having a patience that makes me patient with anything less than brotherhood, I beg God to forgive me.

I hope this letter finds you strong in the faith. I also hope that circumstances will soon make it possible for me to meet each of you, not as an integrationist or a civil-rights leader, but as a fellow clergyman and a Christian brother. Let us all hope that the dark clouds of racial prejudice will soon pass away and the deep fog of misunderstanding will be lifted from our fear-drenched communities and in some not too distant tomorrow the radiant stars of love and brotherhood will shine over our great nation with all their scintillating beauty.

Yours for the cause of Peace and Brotherhood,

—MARTIN LUTHER KING JR.

STUDY QUESTIONS: WAR AND VIOLENCE

1. Apply the criteria Douglas P. Lackey discusses in his essay to the Gulf War, the action taken by the United States in Somalia, and the inaction taken in Bosnia. Do these criteria justify the actions and inaction, or not?

2. Kavka provides a good basis for evaluating the first Gulf War, but he does not really draw any final conclusions. What conclusions do you draw from his analysis? Where would you disagree with that analysis?

3. What are the differences between the two Gulf (Iraq) wars? Which of these differences should matter for the moral assessment of these wars? Do you think that Lee would reach the same conclusions about the first Iraq war as he does for the second?

4. Does May's principle resolve the question of whether to indict and extradite Bashir to stand trial in The Hague for the Darfur atrocities? Either construct an argument against May's principle or construct an alternative principle that would have relevance for deciding whether to prosecute Bashir in The Hague.

5. Sara Ruddick discusses the Madres of Argentina and the Chilean women and their emphases on the "primacy of bodily life and the connectedness of self and others." Discuss the implications of these emphases for obtaining peace, in environmental ethics, and as an overall approach in ethics.

6. What does King mean by saying that injustice anywhere is a threat to justice everywhere? If the injustice is extreme enough, why would violence not be justified to confront it so that it does not threaten justice everywhere? Construct an argument both pro and con.

SUPPLEMENTARY READINGS: WAR AND VIOLENCE

ANSBORO, J. J. *Martin Luther King Jr.: The Making of a Mind*. (New York: Orbis, 1983.)

BACK, ALLAN, and DAESHIK KIM. "Pacifism and the Eastern Martial Arts." *Philosophy East and West*, April 1982.

BELL, L. *Rethinking Ethics in the Midst of Violence: A Feminist Approach to Freedom*. (Lanham, MD: Rowman & Littlefield, 1993.)

BELLIOTTI, RAYMOND. "Are All Modern Wars Morally Wrong?" *Journal of Social Philosophy*, vol. 26 (2), Fall 1995.

CAUTE, D. *Franz Fanon*. (New York: Viking 1970.)

CHILDRESS, JAMES F. "Just War Theories." *Theological Studies*, 1978.

DOMBROWSKI, DANIEL M. "Gandhi, Sainthood, and Nuclear Weapons." *Philosophy East and West*, vol. 33 (4), October 1983.

DU BOIS, W.E.B. *The Souls of Black Folk*. Intros. By N. Hare and A. Poussaint. (New York: Signet Classics, 1969.)

FANON, F. *Black Skins, White Masks*. Trans. C.L. Markmann. (New York: Grove, 1967.)

FANON, F. *Sociologie d'une Revolution*. (Paris: Francois Maspero, 1968.)

FASHINA, OLADIPO. "Frantz Fanon and the Ethical Justification of Anti-Colonial Violence." *Social Theory and Practice*, Summer 1989.

GILLESPIE, C.K. *Justifiable Homicide: Battered Woman, Self Defense, and the Law*. (Columbus: Ohio State University, 1989.)

GORDON, L.R. *Fanon and the Crisis of European Man: An Essay on Philosophy and the Human Sciences*. (New York and London: Routledge, 1995.)

GRAY, J. GLENN. "The Enduring Appeals of Battle." In *The Warriors*. (New York: Harcourt Brace, 1959.)

GUINIER, L. *The Tyranny of the Majority*. (New York: Free Press, 1994.)

HAJJAR, SAMI G. and R. KIERON SWAINE. "Social Justice: The Philosophical Justifications of Qadhafi's Construction." *Africa Today*, vol. 31 (3), 1984.

HOCHSCHILD, J.L., and M. HERK. "'Yes, But . . .': Caveats in American Racial Attitudes," in *Majorities and Minorities: NOMOS XXXII*, ed. by J.W. Chapman and A. Wertheimer. (New York: New York University, 1990.)

HOLMES, ROBERT L. "Violence and the Perspective of Morality." In *On War and Morality*. (Princeton, NJ: Princeton University Press, 1989.)

IHARA, CRAIG K. "Pacifism as a Moral Ideal." *Journal of Value Inquiry*, vol. 22, 1988.

KAINZ, HOWARD. "Is Just War Theory Justifiable?" *Journal of Social Philosophy*, vol. 27 (2), Fall 1996.

LLOYD, GENEVIEVE. "Selfhood, War and Masculinity." In *Feminist Challenges*, Pateman and Gross, editors. (Boston: Northeastern University Press, 1986.)

MAGNO, JOSEPH A. "Hinduism on the Morality of Violence." *International Philosophical Quarterly*, vol. 28 (1), March 1988.

MAY, LARRY, ERIC ROVIE, and STEVE VINER, editors. *The Morality of War*. (Upper Saddle River, NJ: Pearson/Prentice-Hall, 2006.)

MAY, LARRY., editor. *War: Essays in Political Philosophy*. (NY: Cambridge University Press, 2008.)

MCGARY, H. "Alienation and the African-American Experience," in *The Philosophical Forum* 24, nos. 1–3, 1992–93.

MCGARY, H. "Racial Integration and Racial Separatism: Conceptual Clarification," in *Philosophy Born of Struggle: Afro-American Philosophy Since 1917*, ed. by L. Harris. Dubuque, IA: Kendall/Hunt, 1983.

NICKEL, JAMES W. "Ethnocide and Indigenous Peoples." *Journal of Social Philosophy*, vol. 25, special issue, June 1994.

NIELSEN, KAI. "Violence and Terrorism: Its Uses and Abuses." In *Values in Conflict*, Leiser, editor. (New York: Macmillan, 1981.)

NNOLI, OKWUDIBIA. "Revolutionary Violence, Development, Equality, and Justice in South Africa." In *Emerging Human Rights*, Shephard and Anikpo, editors. (New York: Greenwood Press, 1990.)

O'BRIEN, WILLIAM. "Just-War Theory." *The Conduct of Just and Limited War*. (New York: Praeger, 1981.)

RICHARDS, GLYN. *The Philosophy of Gandhi*. (Atlantic Highlands, NJ: Humanities Press, 1991.)

RUESGA, G. ALBERT. "Selective Conscientious Objection and the Right Not to Kill." *Social Theory and Practice*, vol. 21 (1), Spring 1995.

SONN, TAMARA. "Irregular Warfare and Terrorism in Islam: Asking the Right Questions." In *Cross, Crescent, and Sword: The Justification and Limitation of War in Western and Islamic Tradition*, Johnson and Kelsay, editors. (New York: Greenwood Press, 1990.)

WALZER, MICHAEL. "War Crimes: Soldiers and Their Officers." In *Just and Unjust Wars*. (New York: Harper Torchbooks, 1977.)

Part VI

GENDER ROLES AND MORALITY

Traditionally in many societies, being male or female meant that one had different moral obligations and a different moral status. In the West, women were thought to be more emotional and less rational than men, and so women were assigned the task of primary child-raisers and not given much of a voice in the political affairs of their societies. In most societies, women are considered weak and in need of protection by a man. As women have become increasingly involved in public affairs, they have been subjected to discriminatory treatment of various forms, often explicitly rationalized by reference to the fact that they have different natures from men.

There are indeed biological differences between men and women. Women menstruate, gestate, and lactate, whereas men do not. Men ejaculate, whereas women do not. Beyond these differences, it is true that in general women as a group differ from men as a group. Men have greater upper-body strength than women. Women in the West score more highly on verbal tests than men, and men score more highly on mathematical tests than women. Here, though, the differences are statistical, not natural, for there are some women who have greater upper-body strength than most men. The question to be raised is this: Do these natural and statistical differences between males and females call for differences in moral obligation or moral status? This is the topic of this part.

In many societies, natural and statistical differences between men and women are indeed thought to justify differential treatment of the sexes. In some Islamic societies, it is considered immoral for women to appear in public without being veiled, whereas this is not true for men. In many societies, especially in Asia, there is a strong preference for male children over female children, which has resulted in the commonly accepted practice of neglect of female newborns. Such practices have led to a disproportionate female mortality rate. In the United States, parents continue to voice a similarly strong preference for male over female children, and they spend a disproportionate amount of money educating their sons. Until quite recently the term "lady lawyer" was a commonly accepted term of derision.

Crimes that are gender-linked have also not been given the same status in many societies. Rape and sexual harassment in the United States are often not taken as seriously as are similar assault crimes that are not predominantly directed against women. The public humiliation of Anita Hill who accused Clarence Thomas of sexually harassing her when he was her supervisor at the Equal Employment Opportunity Commission is only the most recent example. Sexual harassment and even sexual slavery are severe problems in many parts of the world and are generally not considered as important as other crimes. In what follows we will survey some of the main viewpoints on the moral justifiability of differential treatment based on gender.

We begin this part with a selection from Sally Haslanger. She discusses how best to characterize "women" and "men" given that these are not natural, but rather social, categories. Haslanger first explains what it means for categories to be socially constructed. Despite appearances, who are called "women" and "men" are not so-called primarily because of immutable natural characteristics. Physical or anatomical features do not determine membership in these groups or categories. Instead, she argues, these gender categories are socially constructed; they are caused by social forces in given societies. She then provides a philosophical definition of "women" and "men." These definitions make reference to the common observations of people as well as the dominant ideology of a given society. In addition, Haslanger argues that "women" refers to those who are systematically subordinated and that "men" refers to those who have a systematic privilege in their society.

Marilyn Friedman addresses one of the most difficult of problems confronting public policy today: What stance should be taken to cases of domestic abuse, especially in those situations where the woman being abused refuses to press charges against her male abuser or refuses to testify against him? In general, domestic violence, and the threat of domestic violence, greatly diminishes the autonomy of women in a given society. After explaining precisely how it is that women's autonomy is curtailed, Friedman argues that even if women choose not to help prosecute their abusers, it may be justified not to follow their wishes.

Joel Anderson counters common arguments by pointing out that "genderless parenting" need not lead to a problematic "decline of the family," since it demands only that we open up access to the social roles of father and mother on an equal basis. Anderson argues that traditional assumptions about gendered roles have violated women's claim to equal treatment. Against neotraditionalists he argues that promoting family stability is compatible with a commitment to gender equality, even when that is seen to require promoting equal power between spouses and expanding job opportunities for women.

Brook Sadler tackles the difficult question of whether same-sex marriage should be recognized as legitimate. Both opponents and proponents of same-sex marriage agree that marriage is a good thing, and they feel that this assumption is significant in their arguments about whether the good of

marriage should be available for same-sex as well as heterosexual couples. Sadler begins by arguing that marriage is not a civil institution worth preserving because it actually is not a significant good for couples. The responsibilities, benefits and rewards of marriage simply do not outweigh its detriments. Sadler argues that the same is not true of civil unions, and so she sees civil unions for both same-sex and heterosexual couples as a progressive alternative to marriage. Sadler also argues that the state does not have a sufficient interest in marriage to regulate it in any event. This argument does not deny that religious marriage might be of value, but sees the state regulation of civil marriage as not justified.

Jeff Jordan argues that in some cases forms of discrimination not acceptable for heterosexuals may be acceptable for homosexuals. This would not be true, he claims, in the private realm but only in the public domain where more people are involved than just those who are willing participants. Specifically, Jordan worries about the various members of certain religious groups who have strongly condemnatory views of homosexual behavior. If the state were to publicly sanction gay marriage, this would be for the state to take sides in a deeply divisive public policy debate where many religious members of a society will be deeply offended. Because of this, it may be justifiable for the state to withhold sanctions for gay marriage even though the state gives its blessing for heterosexual marriage.

Sarah Song discusses the very difficult case of how to respond to Mormon polygamy in a majority society that is monogamous. The problem is that women, and especially girls, are often thought to be at risk in societies that practice polygamy. Within Mormon polygamous societies themselves, women tell deeply conflicted stories about the role of women and the protection of girls in such a society. Nonetheless, Song argues that in a multicultural society, some recognition should be extended to Mormon polygamists so as to show respect for their religious liberty, even as the larger society tries to make sure that basic rights are protected for everyone in the society. Many women and girls are free to leave these polygamous societies, but in some cases, especially where there is strong social pressure, governmental intervention can be justified. In the end, though, Song argues that criminal charges should be ones of misdemeanor rather than felony. And in any event the same kind of governmental scrutiny of polygamous societies should be extended to the rest of the society to prevent sexual abuse.

As will become evident in the next section, many of the issues facing women overlap with those of racial and ethnic minorities, as both groups have been systematically denied economic, social, and political power.

—LARRY MAY

Gender and Social Construction:
Who? What? When? Where? How?

Sally Haslanger

Sally Haslanger is professor of philosophy at the Massachusetts Institute of Technology. She is the co-editor of *Adoption Matters: Philosophical and Feminist Essays* (2005). Among her many articles are: "Ontology and Social Construction," *Philosophical Topics*, vol. 23, no. 2, 1995, and "Gender and Race: (What) Are They? (What) Do We Want Them to Be?" *Nous*, vol. 34, no. 1, 2000.

Haslanger argues that gender is a category that has been socially constructed. She then attempts to provide a philosophical definition of "woman" and "man" that takes this reality into account, and does not treat these categories as natural. But these categories have reality since they are caused by social forces. Haslanger ends with the hope that men and women can construct new and different practices that are less oppressive than current ones.

I. INTRODUCTION[1]

The idea of social construction is a crucial tool of contemporary feminist theory. No longer willing to regard the differences between women and men as "natural", feminists have studied the variety of cultural processes by which one "becomes" a woman (or a man), ultimately with the hope of subverting them. Along with this has come a critique of those patterns of thought by which gender, as well as other hierarchical social relations, has been sustained.

Although there is consensus that we need the notion of social construction to theorize adequately about women, there is a broad diversity in how the term "social construction" is used and where it should be applied. As just indicated, beyond the thesis that *gender* and other social categories such as *race* and *nationality* are socially constructed, one also finds the claims that the "subject", "knowledge" and "truth" are each socially constructed. On occasion it is possible to find the claim that "everything" is socially constructed, or that "reality" is socially constructed. But once we come to the claim that everything is socially constructed, it appears a short step to the conclusion that there is no reality independent of our practices or of our language, and that "truth" and "reality" are only fictions employed by the dominant to mask their power.

Dramatic claims rejecting the legitimacy of such notions as "truth" and "reality" do appear in the work of feminist theorists, yet one also finds there a deep resistance to slipping into any form of idealism or relativism. For example, to quote Catharine MacKinnon's typically vivid words:

> Epistemologically speaking, women know the male world is out there because it hits them in the face. No matter how they think about it, try to think it out of existence or into a different shape, it remains independently real, keeps forcing them into certain molds. No matter what they think or do,

Excerpt from Sally Haslanger, "Gender and Social Construction" in Theorizing Feminisms: A Reader, edited by Elizabeth Hackett and Sally Haslanger, pp. 16–23, 2006. Reprinted by permission of Oxford University Press.

they cannot get out of it. It has all the indeterminacy of a bridge abutment hit at sixty miles per hour. (MacKinnon 1989: 123)

To start, it will be useful to consider carefully different things one might mean in saying that something is socially constructed. Although I won't address the full range of cases mentioned above, I hope that the distinctions. I discuss will be useful in exploring options for interpreting, criticizing or defending such claims. My focus here will be to consider how the different senses of construction might apply in the case of gender.

II. KINDS OF SOCIAL CONSTRUCTION

In the very broadest sense, something is a social construction if it is an intended or unintended product of a social practice. Artifacts such as washing machines and power drills might on some views count as social constructions, but more interesting cases include: the Supreme Court of the US, chess games, languages, literature, and scientific inquiry.[2] Because each of these depend for their existence on a complex social context, they are in the broad sense in question social constructions. Note, however, that there is also a sense in which professors and wives are only possible within a social context: you can't be a *wife* unless you stand in a marriage relationship to a man that is sanctioned by the state. Insofar as the features which notify one as a member of a particular type or kind include *social* (properties and) relations, things of that kind could count as social constructions too. Although these various items, be they objects, events, sets of individuals, etc., are very different sorts of things and are "constructed" in different ways, at this point there is no reason whatsoever to think they are anything less than fully *real*; and their reality is perfectly concrete, i.e., they don't just exist "in our heads".

A. The Construction of Ideas and Concepts

However, things get more complicated quite quickly. It is important to distinguish first the construction of *ideas* and the construction of

objects. (Hacking 1999: 9–16). Let's start with ideas.[3] On one reading, the claim that an idea or a concept is only possible within and due to a social context is utterly obvious. It would seem to be a matter of common sense that concepts are taught to us by our parents through our language; different cultures have different concepts (that go along with their different languages); and concepts evolve over time as a result of historical changes, science, technological advances, etc. Let's (albeit contentiously) call this the "ordinary view" of concepts and ideas. Even someone who believes that our scientific concepts perfectly map "nature's joints" can allow that scientists come to have the ideas and concepts they do through social-historical processes. After all, social and cultural forces (including, possibly, the practices and methods of science) may help us develop concepts that are apt or accurate, and beliefs that are true.

We may sometimes forget that what and how we think is affected by social forces because our experiences seem to be caused simply and directly by world itself. However, it does not take much prompting to recall that our culture is largely responsible for the interpretive tools we bring to the world in order to understand it. Once we've noted that our experience of the world is already an interpretation of it, we can begin to raise questions about the adequacy of our conceptual framework. Concepts help us organize phenomena; different concepts organize it in different ways. It is important, then, to ask: what phenomena are highlighted and what are eclipsed by a particular framework of concepts? What assumptions provide structure for the framework?

For example, our everyday framework for thinking about human beings is structured by the assumptions that there are two (and only two) sexes, and that every human is either a male or a female. But in fact a significant percentage of humans have a mix of male and female anatomical features. Intersexed bodies are eclipsed in our everyday framework (Fausto-Sterling 1993). This should invite us to ask: why? Whose interests are served, if anyone's, by the intersexed being ignored in the dominant conceptual framework? (It can't be plausibly argued that sex isn't important enough to us to make fine-grained distinctions between bodies!) Further, once we recognize the intersexed, how should we revise our conceptual framework? Should we group bodies into more than two sexes, or are there reasons instead to complicate the definitions of male and female to include everyone in just two sex categories? More generally, on what basis should we decide what categories to use? (Fausto-Sterling 1993; Butler 1990, Ch. 1) In asking these questions it is important to remember that an idea or conceptual framework may be inadequate without being false, e.g., a claim might be true and yet incomplete, misleading, unjustified, biased, etc. (Anderson 1995).

The point of saying that a concept or idea is socially constructed will vary depending on context; sometimes it may have little or no point, if everyone is fully aware of the social history of the idea in question or if the social history isn't relevant to the issue at hand. On other occasions, saying that this or that idea is socially constructed is a reminder of the ordinary view of concepts and, more importantly, an invitation to notice the motivations behind and limitations of our current framework. Every framework will have some limits; the issue is whether the limits eclipse something that, given the (legitimate) goals of our inquiry, matters. However, sometimes a social constructionist is making a more controversial claim. The suggestion would be that something or other is "merely" a social construction, in other words, that what we are taking to be real is only a fiction, an idea that fails to capture reality. Feminists have argued, for example, that certain mental "disorders" that have been used to diagnose battered women are *merely* social constructions. Andrea Westlund points out how

> [b]attered women's "abnormalities" have been described and redescribed within the psychiatric literature of the twentieth century, characterized as everything from hysteria to masochistic or self-defeating personality disorders (SDPD) to co-dependency . . . Moreover, such pathologies measure, classify, and define battered women's deviance not just from "normal" female behavior but also from universalized male norms of independence and self-interest. (Westlund 1999)

Such diagnoses invite us to explain domestic violence by reference to the woman's psychological state rather than the batterer's need for power and control; they also "deflect attention from the social and political aspects of domestic violence to the private neuroses to which women as a group are thought to be prone" (Westlund 1999, 1051). Westlund and others have argued that although victims of domestic violence often do suffer from psychological conditions, e.g., major depression, there is a range of gender coded mental disorders included in the *Diagnostic and Statistical Manual of Mental Disorder* (DSM) for which there is little, if any, good evidence. These diagnoses, it could be claimed, are *merely* social constructions in the sense that they are ideas used to interpret and regulate social phenomena, but do not describe anything real. Applying this to the case at hand would entail that "Self-Defeating Personality Disorder" doesn't really exist. The description of SDPD, if it captures anything at all, isn't a mental disorder of the sort alleged.

So in considering the claim that something is socially constructed, we should ask first: Is it an object or an idea? If it is an idea, it is important to determine how that idea functions within a broader framework of ideas and concepts and to consider how the framework structures our experience: does it illegitimately or inappropriately privilege one set of phenomena over another? Of course in some contexts privileging certain phenomena is useful and even necessary: medical sciences are not "neutral" with respect to what phenomena count as significant and how they are categorized; medicine has a legitimate concern with human health and the organisms that affect human health. However, other things being equal, medicine that privileges phenomena related to men's health, or the health of the wealthy, would not be epistemically or politically legitimate. (Anderson 1995). Considering what is left out of a framework of categories and what assumptions structure it can reveal biases of many sorts. In extreme cases we may find that the idea in question does not describe anything real at all, and instead is just a fiction being treated as real. In such cases work must be done to demonstrate that what's at issue is only a fiction. But that's not all, for we should also ask: How are such fictions established and maintained? Whose interests do they serve?

B. The Construction of Objects

Now consider objects (understanding "objects" in the broadest sense as virtually anything that's not an idea). There is a sense in which any artifact is a construction; but claiming that scissors or cars are social constructions would not have much point, given how obvious it is. Social constructionists, on the whole, are arguing for a surprising thesis that they believe challenges our everyday view of things. It is much more surprising to say that women or Asian-Americans, homosexuals, child abusers, or refugees, are social constructions. What could this mean?

In considering the construction of objects the first point to note is that our classificatory schemes, at least in social contexts, may do more than just map pre-existing groups of individuals; rather our attributions have the power to both establish and reinforce groupings which may eventually come to "fit" the classifications. This works in several ways. Forms of description or classification provide for kinds of intention; e.g., given the classification "cool", I can set about to become cool, or avoid being cool, etc. But also, such classifications can function in justifying behavior; e.g., "we didn't invite him because he's not cool", and such justifications, in turn, can reinforce the distinction between those who are cool and those who are uncool. In an earlier essay, drawing on Ian Hacking's work, I referred to this as "discursive" construction:

> *discursive construction:* something is discursively constructed just in case it is (to a significant extent) the way it is because of what is attributed to it or how it is classified. (Haslanger 1995, 99)

Admittedly, the idea here is quite vague (e.g., how much is "a significant extent"?). However, social construction in this sense is ubiquitous. Each of us is socially constructed in this sense because we are (to a significant extent) the individuals we are today as a result of what has been attributed (and self-attributed) to us. For example, being classified as an able-bodied female from birth has profoundly affected the paths available to me in life and the sort of person I have become.

Note, however, that to say that an entity is "discursively constructed", is not to say that language or discourse brings a material object into existence de novo. Rather something in existence comes to have—partly as a result of having been categorized in a certain way—a set of features that qualify it as a member of a certain kind or sort.[4] My having been categorized as a female at birth (and consistently since then) has been a factor in how I've been viewed and treated; these views and treatments have, in turn, played an important causal role in my becoming gendered a woman (See also Haslanger 1993). But discourse didn't bring me into existence.

It would appear that gender (in different senses) is both an idea-construction and an object-construction. Gender is an idea-construction because the *classification* men/women is the contingent result of historical events and forces. As we saw above, the everyday distinction between males and females leaves out the intersexed population that might have been given its own sex/gender category. Arguably, in fact, some cultures have divided bodies into three sexual/reproductive groups (Herdt 1993). At the same time the classifications "woman" and "man" are what Hacking calls "interactive kinds": gender classifications occur within a complex matrix of institutions and practices, and being classified as a woman (or not), or a man (or not), or third, fourth, fifth . . . sex/gender or not, has a profound effect on an individual. Such classification will have a material affect on her social position as well as effect her experience and self-understanding. In this sense, women and men—concrete individuals—are constructed *as gendered kinds of people,* i.e., we are each object constructions.

There is yet a further sense, I'd like to argue, in which something might be a social construction (Haslanger 2003). So far we've been focusing on social *causation*: to say that something is socially constructed is to say that it is caused to be a certain way, and the causal process involves social factors, e.g., social forces were largely responsible for my coming to have the idea of a husband, and social forces were largely responsible for there being husbands. But often when theorists argue that something is a social construction their point is not about causation. Rather, the point is to distinguish social kinds from physical kinds. In the case of gender, the idea would be that gender is not a classification scheme based simply on anatomical or biological differences, but marks social differences between individuals. Gender, as opposed to sex, is not about testicles and ovaries, the penis and the uterus, but about the location of groups within a system of social relations.

Consider, for example, the category of landlords. To be a landlord one must be located within a broad system of social and economic relations, which includes tenants, private property, and the like. It might be that all and only landlords have a mole behind their left ear. But even if this were the case, having this physical mark is not what it is to be a landlord. Similarly, one might want to draw a distinction between sex and gender, *sex* being an anatomical distinction based on locally salient sexual/reproductive differences, and *gender* being a distinction between the social/political positions of those with bodies marked as of different sexes. One could allow that the categories of sex and gender interact (so concerns with distinctions between bodies will influence social divisions and vice versa); but even to be clear how they interact, we should differentiate them. Using the terms "male"/"female" to mark the current familiar sex distinction and "man"/"woman" the gender distinction, one should allow that on this account of gender, it is plausible that some males are women and some females are men. Because one is a female by virtue of some (variable) set of anatomical features, and one is a woman by virtue of one's position within a social and economic system, the sex/gender distinction gives us some (at least preliminary) resources for including transgendered as well as transsexual persons within our conceptual framework.

I shall return to the question of what social positions might constitute gender below. Before that, however, it is important to note that social kinds cannot be equated with things that have social causes. Sociobiologists claim that some social phenomena have biological causes; some feminists claim that some anatomical phenomena have social causes, e.g., that height and strength differences between the sexes are caused by a long history of gender norms concerning food and exercise.[5] It is also significant that not all social kinds are *obviously* social. Sometimes it is assumed that the conditions for membership in a kind concern only or primarily biological or physical facts. Pointing out that this is wrong can have important consequences. For example, the idea that whether or not a person is White is not simply a matter of their physical features but concerns their position in a social matrix, has been politically significant, and to many surprising. How should we construe the constructionist project of arguing that a particular kind is a social kind? What could be interesting or radical about such a project?

I am a White woman. What does this mean? Suppose we pose these questions to someone who is not a philosopher, someone not familiar with the academic social constructionist literature. A likely response will involve mention of my physical features: reproductive organs, skin color, etc. The gender and race constructionists will reject this response and will argue that what makes the claim apt concerns the social relations in which I stand. On this construal, the important social constructionist import in Beauvoir's claim that "one is not born but rather becomes a woman" (de Beauvoir 1989/1949) is not that one is caused to be feminine by social forces (even if this is true); rather, the important insight was that being a woman is not an anatomical matter concerning, e.g., one's reproductive organs, but a social matter.[6]

Because being a woman is a function of one's role in a social framework broadly speaking, if we allow that social phenomena are highly variable across time, cultures, groups, then this also allows us to recognize that the specific details of what it is to be a woman will differ depending on one's race, ethnicity, class, etc. My being a woman occurs in a context in which I am also White and privileged; my actual social position will therefore be affected by multiple factors simultaneously. I learned the norms of WASP womanhood, not Black womanhood. And even if I reject many of those norms, I benefit from the fact that they are broadly accepted.

The social constructionist's goal is often to challenge the appearance of inevitability of the category in question; as things are arranged now, there are men and women, and people of different races. But if social conditions changed substantially, there would be no men and women, and no people of different races. It would be possible, then, to do away with the conceptual frameworks that we currently use. But an important first step is to make the category visible as a *social* as opposed to *physical* category. This sometimes requires a rather radical change in our thinking. For example, elsewhere, following in Beauvoir's now long tradition, I have argued for the following definitions of man and woman (Haslanger 2000)[7]:

S *is a woman* if and only if

> **i.** S is regularly and for the most part observed or imagined to have certain bodily features presumed to be evidence of a female's biological role in reproduction;
> **ii.** that S has these features marks S within the dominant ideology of S's society as someone who ought to occupy certain kinds of social position that are in fact subordinate (and so motivates and justifies S's occupying such a position); and
> **iii.** the fact that S satisfies (i) and (ii) plays a role in S's systematic subordination, i.e., *along some dimension,* S's social position is oppressive, and S's satisfying (i) and (ii) plays a role in that dimension of subordination.

S *is a man* if and only if

> **i.** S is regularly and for the most part observed or imagined to have certain bodily features presumed to be evidence of a male's biological role in reproduction;
> **ii.** that S has these features marks S within the dominant ideology of S's society as someone who ought to occupy certain kinds of social

position that are in fact privileged (and so motivates and justifies S's occupying such a position); and

> **iii.** the fact that S satisfies (i) and (ii) plays a role in S's systematic privilege, i.e., *along some dimension,* S's social position is privileged, and S's satisfying (i) and (ii) plays a role in that dimension of privilege.

Allowing for the possibility of new and non-hierarchical genders, I also suggest:

A group G *is a gender* relative to context C if and only if members of G are (all and only) those:

> **i.** who are regularly observed or imagined to have certain bodily features presumed in C to be evidence of their reproductive capacities;[8]
> **ii.** whose having (or being imagined to have) these features marks them within the context of the ideology in C as motivating and justifying some aspect(s) of their social position; and
> **iii.** whose satisfying (i) and (ii) plays (or would play) a role in C in their social position's having one or another of these designated aspects.

These definitions are proposed, not as reconstructions of our common sense understanding of the terms "man" and "woman", but as providing a better explanation of how gender works.

What is involved in explaining "how gender works"? There are two clusters of questions that should be distinguished:

> **1.** Is the classification C (e.g., a distinction between the two groups as defined above) theoretically or politically useful?
> **2.** Does the proposed theoretical understanding of C capture an ordinary social category? Is it legitimate or warranted to claim that the proposed definitions reveal the commitments of our ordinary discourse?

I offer the definitions above as a "debunking" of our ordinary understanding of the distinction between men and women as primarily anatomical/biological. The best way of understanding the groups of individuals so familiar to us, men and women, is to understand them in social and hierarchical terms. The anatomical understandings we take for granted, in effect, mask the social reality.

So in response to question (1) I claim that the definitions proposed are theoretically and politically useful; but in response to question (2) I allow that I have not captured our ordinary understanding of the terms. But this is intentional.

III. CONCLUSION

On the account of social construction I've sketched, there are several different senses in which gender, race, and the like are socially constructed. First, the conceptual framework of gender that we take as just "common sense" is only one way of dividing up people according to the shape and functioning of their bodies. There are (and have been) other ways; there are (I believe) better ways.

Moreover, there are ideas associated with gender that are "merely" constructions, e.g., fictions about biological essences and genetic determination are used to reinforce belief in the rightness and inevitability of the classifications. This is not to say, however, that gender is not "real". Although some ideas about gender are fictions, these fictional ideas have functioned to create and reinforce gender reality, i.e., hierarchical social groups based on beliefs about reproductive differences, that are all too real. These categories of people are, I would argue, not just ideas, but are social entities. Such entities are socially constructed in the sense that they are caused by social forces, but also because the conditions for membership in a gender group are social (as opposed to, say, merely physical or anatomical) conditions.

Finally, individual members of such groups are, in a rather extended sense socially constructed, insofar as they are affected by the social processes that constitute the groups. Human beings are social beings in the sense that we are deeply responsive to our social context and become the physical and psychological beings we become through interaction with others. One feminist hope is that we can become, through the construction of new and different practices, no longer men and women, but new sorts of beings.

NOTES

1. Note that this essay draws significantly from my previous work, in particular (Haslanger 1995, Haslanger 2000, Haslanger 2003).
2. Some (e.g., Hacking 1999, Ch. 1) have argued that in cases of something obviously social, it is incorrect, or at least inapt, to say that it is socially constructed, suggesting that it is part of the meaning of the claim that the item in question is typically "taken for granted," "inevitable". (Hacking 1999, 12). I prefer to say that the unmasking element of social construction claims are not part of the meaning, though it may be inapt to make such claims in the case of obviously social phenomena. The inaptness of the assertion can be explained by saying that in general, there is a linguistic maxim against stating the obvious. (Grice 1975).
3. Like Hacking, I will use the terms "idea" and "concept" without making precise distinctions between them for the purposes of our discussion. In contrast to concepts, ideas are often prepositional, and plausibly more specific to the individual.
4. Note that the notion of *kind* in philosophy has several different uses. On one use it is meant to capture a classification of things by essence: things fall into kinds based on their essence, and each thing falls only into one kind. On this view, horses constitute a kind because they share an equine essence, but red things don't constitute a kind because apples, t-shirts, and sunsets don't share an essence. However, on a more common use, the term "kind" is used as equivalent to "type" or "sort" or "grouping." So far I've been using the term "kind" in the latter sense, and will continue to do so.
5. More generally, it is an error to treat the conditions by virtue of which a social entity exists as causing the entity. Consider, for example, what must be the case in order for someone to be a husband in the contemporary US: A husband is a man legally married to a woman. Being a man legally married to a woman does not *cause* one to be a husband; it is just what being a husband consists in.
6. For Beauvoir, roughly, women are positioned as "Absolute Other," i.e., as "Other" in relation to a group counting as "Subject" where the relation between these two groups never reverses so the "Other" becomes "Subject". (Beauvoir 1989, xxii; also Beauvoir 1989, xv–xxxiv).
7. Note that in the fuller account I suggest a "focal analysis" of gender that distinguishes gender as a social category from gender norms, gender identity, gender symbolism, and other gendered phenomena. For example, on my account one may be in the social category of woman if one is socially positioned in the way described, but still not have a woman's *gender identity*, understanding gender identity to be a psychological or subjective matter.
8. It is important here that the "observations" or "imaginings" in question not be idiosyncratic but part of a broader pattern of social perception; however, they need not occur, as in the case of *man* and *woman*, "for the most part." They may even be both regular and rare.

REFERENCES

Anderson, Elizabeth. (1995) "Knowledge, Human Interests, and Objectivity in Feminist Epistemology," *Philosophical Topics* 23:2: 27–58.

Butler, Judith. (1990) *Gender Trouble.* New York: Routledge.

de Beauvoir, Simone. (1989/1949) *The Second Sex.* Trans. H. M. Parshley. New York: Vintage.

Fausto-Sterling, Anne. (1993) "The Five Sexes: Why Male and Female Are Not Enough," *The Sciences* 33:2: 20–24.

Grice, H. Paul. (1975) "Logic and Conversation." In *Syntax and Semantics,* vol. 3, ed., P. Cole and J. L. Morgan. New York: Academic Press, pp. 41–58.

Hacking, Ian. (1999) *The Social Construction of What?* Cambridge, MA: Harvard University Press.

Haslanger, Sally. (1993) "On Being Objective and Being Objectified," *A Mind of One's Own,* ed., L. Antony and C. Witt. Boulder: Westview, 85–125.

___. (1995) "Ontology and Social Construction," *Philosophical Topics* 23:2: 95–125.

___. (2000) "Gender and Race: (What) Are They? (What) Do We Want Them To Be?" *Nous* 34(1): 31–55.

___. (2003) "Social Construction: The 'Debunking' Project," in *Socializing Metaphysics,* ed., F. Schmitt. (Lanham, MD: Rowman and Littlefield).

Herdt, Gilbert. (1993) *Third Sex, Third Gender: Beyond Sexual Dimorphism in Culture and History.* New York: Zone Books.

MacKinnon, Catharine. (1989) *Towards a Feminist Theory of the State.* Cambridge, MA: Harvard University Press.

Westlund, Andrea. (1999) "Pre-Modern and Modern Power: Foucault and the Case of Domestic Violence." *Signs* 24(4): 1045–1066.

Domestic Violence Against Women and Autonomy

Marilyn Friedman

Marilyn Friedman is W. Alton Jones professor of philosophy at Vanderbilt University. She is the author of *What are Friends For?* (1993), *Political Correctness: For and Against* (1995); and *Autonomy, Gender, Politics* (2003). She works in the areas of feminist philosophy, political philosophy, and ethics.

Friedman argues that domestic violence by a man against a woman who are in an intimate relationship severely diminishes the autonomy of the woman. This is true to such an extent that the law should not allow women who are the victims of domestic abuse to shield their male partners by withdrawing complaints or failing to testify against them.

Women who are abused by their intimate partners have often sought help from the legal system and from professional caregiving services. In the past, the legal system virtually ignored the problem, leaving women to fend for themselves against violent partners. In recent years, partly as a result of feminist outcry and partly as a result of lawsuits against them, various legal jurisdictions have made efforts to respond more effectively to women's calls for help against abusive partners. While these efforts still need improvement, the legal response is generally better now than it was a few decades ago.

Certain types of cases, however, continue to pose legal challenges. These are cases in which the abused women[1] themselves act in ways that make it harder for the law to seek justice. Women may, for example, refuse to press charges against their abusers, making it difficult for prosecutors to gain

convictions. Or women may return to live with their abusers, making it more difficult for police to protect them against future violence by those same abusers. Thus, *some* abused women act in ways that hinder even the still-inadequate efforts of the state to protect them or punish the offenders.

Suppose, fantastically, that the law had the resources, capacity, and will to provide full protection and justice to every abused woman who leaves her abuser or who cooperates in bringing him to justice. It would still not be clear how the law should respond to women who do not leave their abusers and who do not cooperate with the state in punishing them. Should the law continue to try to protect such women and to punish the offenders against the wishes of the women? Or should the law simply refrain from punishing offenders when that is what the victims want?

A related but different question is this: How should professional caregivers respond to women who seek help from them in coping with abusive relationships, but who nevertheless choose to remain in those relationships? The aim of this chapter is to explore these two related issues. First,

Excerpt from Marilyn Friedman, "Domestic violence against women and autonomy" from Autonomy, Gender, Politics, pp. 368–378, 2003. Reprinted by permission of Oxford University Press.

how should the *law* respond to women who are being abused by intimate partners but who do not leave their abusers? Second, how should *professional caregivers* respond to women in those circumstances?

To anticipate, I shall argue that legal responses should lean toward penalizing abusers even when the abused women in question fail to cooperate with the law. Professional caregivers, however, should lean toward providing support for abused women who remain in abusive relationships, even if this hampers efforts by all concerned to control the abusers—with exceptions in case there is a risk of serious future abuse. That is, the law should tend to try to prevent domestic abuse with or without the cooperation of the victim while professional caregiving services should tend to support the victim even though this might hamper efforts by outsiders to help prevent her future abuse. Respect for the autonomy of abused women, and the different forms such respect can take, will constitute important considerations in exploring these issues.

The following discussion focuses only on women as abuse victims and only on those who are abused by intimate male partners. This is overwhelmingly the most reported sort of domestic violence, and there are good reasons to believe that it is the most commonly occurring sort. In 1994, according to statistics from the Department of Justice, as reported by social theorists Susan L. Miller and Charles F. Wellford, women experienced violence from an intimate partner at a rate almost ten times that experienced by men.[2]

Before answering my two main questions, we should first consider three other issues: How exactly does domestic violence diminish a woman's autonomy? Why do some women stay in abusive relationships they could safely leave? Is there anything *wrong with asking* why some women stay?

HOW INTIMATE PARTNER ABUSE DIMINISHES AUTONOMY

Intimate relationships affect us in our very homes, our "havens in a heartless world" (to recycle a contemporary cliché),[3] the places where we are supposed to be safe, nurtured, and protected. In intimate relationships, we expose our bodies and bare our souls, making ourselves vulnerable at the very core of our beings. When one's haven *is* a heartless world, there is no further place of refuge, no sanctuary in which one can rest secure from the violence that threatens one's exposed and vulnerable core self.

Abuse by an intimate partner can include: (1) physical battering, ranging from shoving and hitting to attacks with lethal weapons; (2) emotional and psychological abuse, such as humiliation, isolation, threats to take the children away, or the killing of beloved pets; (3) financial control, such as withholding support money or stealing the abused person's own money; and (4) sexual abuse, such as rape or other forced sex acts.[4]

Autonomy, to reiterate, involves reflecting on one's deeper values and concerns and acting in accordance with them. It involves some capacity to persist in acting according to one's deeper concerns in the face of a minimum of opposition by others. One's reflections should, furthermore, have been made without undue manipulation or coercion.

Intimate partner abuse undermines autonomy in at least three related ways. First, intimate partner abuse is coercive; it threatens an abused woman's survival and safety. Intimate partner abuse denies to the abused person, in her very home life and her intimate bodily existence, the safety and security she needs to try to live her life as she thinks she ought to do. Instead of being able to live according to her values and commitments, an abused woman is reduced to seeking bare survival and security. Some philosophers have argued that a person cannot live an autonomous life unless she lives under circumstances that afford her a plurality of acceptable options and do not reduce her to the level of being governed by her basic needs, such as those of survival or security.[5] Basic survival and security are not commitments or self-conceptions that define us as particular persons; they are universal needs of all living beings. Merely to survive, even against great odds, is not (yet) to exemplify self-determination in any significant sense. I argued . . . that someone could still exemplify autonomy, when facing dangerous or tragic circumstances, by nevertheless acting, admittedly at great risk to herself, to preserve and protect what she cares about. Autonomy is thus not eliminated by dangers such as domestic abuse. It is certainly, however, much more difficult to achieve under those conditions and is, in that sense, undermined.

Intimate partner abuse undermines autonomy in a second way as a consequence of the threat it poses to an abused person's survival. This threat focuses an abused woman's attention constantly on the desires and demands of her abuser. An abused woman tends to develop a heightened awareness of what her partner wants and needs as she tries to accommodate his wishes and whims, all this as a way to minimize his violent reactions.[6] Such focused attention on what another person wants distracts someone from the task of understanding herself or being guided by her own self-defining concerns.[7] Her goals are survival and security, which are not, as such, autonomy-conferring goals. And her means of pursuing those goals involve mere deferential or heteronomous reactions to the abuser's actual or anticipated desires or moods.

Third, abusers are people who attempt in general to exercise inordinate control over their intimate partners. One significance of autonomy is that of not being consistently or deeply subjected to the will of other persons. Chronic abuse, however, is precisely a form of willful control by another person.[8] According to Angela Browne, the "early warning signs" of an abusive personality include possessiveness, excessive jealousy, quickness to anger, an insistence on knowing a woman's whereabouts and activities at all times, and a tendency to discourage the woman from maintaining relationships with others.[9] It is much harder for a woman to avoid subjection to the will of another if that other is an intimate partner with substantial access to her at private and vulnerable moments who tries continually to exert control over her.

Over the past several decades, professional caregivers and feminist activists have worked hard to reform the legal system and social support services so that these agencies will help abused women more effectively to avoid or end abuse.[10] Many counseling programs, for example, have emerged to rehabilitate batterers. Studies of the effectiveness of these programs suggest some degree of success, but the studies have been criticized for methodological weaknesses.[11] In the absence of programs with confirmably high or widespread success rates at rehabilitating abusers, much effort continues to be directed toward empowering abused women so that they can improve their own lives.[12] Some studies suggest that the only sure way for most women to stop being abused is to end their relationships with their abusers.[13] What professional caregivers and legal personnel often find, however, is that some women keep returning to their abusive relationships even after receiving the support of social services and finding out about opportunities to leave their relationships with relative safety. The question of how best to respond to abused women arises most acutely in such cases. To answer the question carefully, we need to know why some women stay in abusive relationships.

WHY ASK, "WHY DO WOMEN STAY?"?

Some social theorists have argued that we should stop asking why women stay in abusive relationships. This question seems to blame the victim for the abuse she experiences and perhaps even to excuse the abuser. Instead of this question, it is argued, we should ask, "Why do men abuse women?"[14]

We should certainly ask why some men batter and abuse women, and we should continue to support the important research addressing this question. At the same time, there is value in asking the question why women stay—provided it is asked in the right way. The question is ambiguous in its presuppositions. It could be meant as a rhetorical question intended to *blame* an abused woman for the abuse she suffers. On this mistaken view, the abused woman's action of staying in the relationship is what enables the abuser to continue abusing her, and, for that reason, she is somehow morally responsible for the abuse.

The questions "Why do women stay?" or "Why does she stay?" could be meant, on the other hand, as sincere attempts to understand women's motivations. We assume, with good reason, that human beings tend to be self-protective. When someone defends herself against attack, this is understandable on the face of it. It requires no further explanation. Against this background expectation, it is reasonable to be perplexed when a competent adult seems to take no action to protect herself against attack and even knowingly remains in a situation that exposes herself to further danger. Such behavior does not make sense in those terms. Some further explanation is needed: more information, perhaps, about the behavior in question or the conditions under which it occurs.

It seems furthermore that there is indeed *something* wrong with the choice to stay in an abusive relationship. Exactly what kind of wrong is involved, however, must be specified precisely. Staying in an abusive relationship is not a moral wrong—unless it is morally wrong to endure mistreatment. This notion would require a self-regarding morality, a morality of duties to oneself. Even in the context of a self-regarding morality, it is not obvious that enduring mistreatment would be as wrong as inflicting mistreatment or that it would deserve the same degree of reproach. Without the backing of a self-regarding morality, we should say only that staying in an abusive relationship is at most a prudential mistake. It would be, furthermore, only a prima facie prudential mistake; the action in question could be justified if there were good enough reasons for it. The assumption to which we are entitled, then, in the absence of a self-regarding morality, is that a woman who stays in an abusive relationship that she could have safely left is *imprudent* if she thereby knowingly risks future abuse *for no good reason.*

To be sure, one should not belabor even this qualified point to a woman who has just entered the emergency ward with life-threatening wounds. In a more contemplative and detached context, however, we can certainly entertain the abstract, defeasible assumption that physically capable women should act to protect themselves (to the extent that they can do so) against foreseeable and

unnecessary dangers. Many women stay in abusive relationships for understandable reasons, given the constraints under which they live (more on this below). The prima facie presumption that women do something prudentially wrong by remaining with their abusers can thus be rebutted by evidence in most cases. However, the possibility of rebuttal does not make the request for explanation wrongheaded.[15]

Taking responsibility for one's own well-being does not mean never being dependent on others. Indeed, in a world of scarce resources and human limitations, one's well-being requires depending on others for at least some things most of the time. Depending on others, however, should not lead someone who could defend herself to become utterly defenseless in her own right. There is something amiss about a person who could act to protect herself from a harm she is suffering but fails to do so. Such a failure calls for some explanation.

There might, furthermore, be value in a culturewide expectation that women *as women*, so far as they are able, should try to protect themselves against foreseeable and unnecessary dangers. According to traditional gender norms, women are relatively weak and defenseless and need men to protect them. Expecting or encouraging this dependence in women is part of the same gender role framework that celebrates dominant and controlling tendencies in men, the very tendencies that are at the root of most intimate partner abuse. When we assume that women should try to protect themselves to the best of their abilities, and when we go on to raise our daughters to do so, we are helping in part to reverse the very gender traditions that give rise in the first place to the problem of intimate partner abuse.[16]

SO WHY *DO* WOMEN STAY?

Years ago, some psychoanalysts and psychological theorists argued that women stayed in abusive relationships because they were masochists. They enjoyed the abuse. This explanation has, thankfully, lost credibility in recent years due to mounting contradictory evidence.[17] Women rarely submit to abuse as something desired for its own sake. Nor are women typically mere passive victims of abuse. In general, they try to resist in some way. Even Lenore Walker's famous thesis of the early 1980s that abused women suffer from "learned helplessness"[18] has come under recent criticism. Edward W. Gondolf and Ellen R. Fisher, among others, argue that battered women are not passive or helpless and should not even be thought of as victims. Instead, they should be regarded as survivors, as people who try to resist abuse but encounter obstacles when doing so. Studies show, for example, that many abused women contact professional services for help in coping with their abuser but find these services to be either unresponsive or ineffective. Gondolf and Fisher suggest that professional caregivers may be the ones suffering from learned helplessness![19]

Empirical research in the past few decades has revealed that many women stay in abusive relationships because leaving the relationships would impose even greater hardships on them. Many abused women, for example, are financially dependent on their abusers; leaving the relationship would risk the loss of financial support.[20] Some women stay with their abusers in order to protect their children. A woman may feel that her children are simply better off for having a father in the home; perhaps the man is not abusive toward the children. Or an abuser may frighten a woman into staying with him by warning that he will get custody of the children in case she leaves.[21]

Finally, some abusers threaten to retaliate violently against their female partners for leaving. Sociologist Martha Mahoney calls this sort of abuse "separation assault." Separation assault consists of threats and violence that a batterer inflicts on his partner when she tries to leave, precisely in order to intimidate her into staying.[22]

Some women who leave violent men are pursued and harassed for months or even years afterward. Some abusive men murder their ex-partners. The first few months after leaving are especially dangerous. An abusive man may stalk his former partner, telephoning her family and friends repeatedly, showing up at her place of employment,

hanging out at playgrounds and other places that she frequents. Some women who leave such vindictive men go into hiding, but the women's anxieties continue. They may worry constantly, afraid to enter their apartments, afraid to approach their own cars in parking lots, afraid of headlights that pull up behind them at night. These women sometimes report that living or hiding in fear of reprisal or death seems worse than remaining with the abuser.[23] Some women report that their abusers attempted to maintain a coercive tie for years after the actual relationship ended.[24]

Lack of financial means, worries about children's welfare, and fear of separation assault all provide indisputably legitimate, prima facie reasons for someone to stay in an abusive relationship. A woman who stays under such conditions has good reason to do so. She may have no better alternative. A professional caregiver trying to respect a woman's capacity for autonomy in such a case has a clear responsibility: support the woman's (rational) choice uncritically and, perhaps, try to help her to alter the circumstances that so constrict her life as to make staying in a dangerous relationship the optimal thing for her to do.

There are some other cases, however, that are less clear-cut, cases in which, to outsiders at any rate, the women seem somehow to be misguided. Abused women might, for example, misunderstand what is happening to them, a misunderstanding that can be perplexing to outsiders to whom the existence and nature of the abuse seems obvious. According to Kathleen Ferraro and John Johnson, many abused women deny that the abuse they suffered was really injurious. Or they deny that their partner was to blame for the abuse, perhaps by blaming alcohol or by blaming themselves for not being conciliatory enough. Abused women may also underestimate their abilities to survive on their own.[25]

Women may also be motivated to stay in abusive relationships by questionable normative commitments. Women may have what Ferraro and Johnson call "higher loyalties" to religious or moral norms that require, for instance, that a woman keep her marriage together despite high personal costs to herself. Or women may have what Ferraro and Johnson call a "salvation ethic," an outlook according to which a woman holds herself responsible for trying to "save" or "redeem" her abusive husband or partner from the "sickness" of abusiveness that "afflicts" him.[26]

Women who stay for these sorts of reasons are living their lives in accord with norms that are evidently very important to them. The women are, after all, risking their safety and security to adhere to those norms. On content-neutral accounts of autonomy, these women might well qualify as autonomous. Content-neutral accounts take no account of the substance of what someone chooses. On these accounts, someone is autonomous so long as her choice meets certain nonsubstantive criteria, such as being the result of reflection on her deeper values and commitments.[27] An abusive relationship is, of course, coercive. Someone's self-reflections and choices under those conditions are less likely than otherwise to be reliable reflections of what she really cares about. Yet it is not impossible to discern or act according to one's deeper concerns under coercive conditions. This possibility makes it imperative that a woman's "own" choices, even to continue enduring domestic abuse, should carry some weight in her interactions with the array of social agents who can become involved in domestic violence cases. The question is: What weight should her choices carry and which social agents in particular are best suited to take account of what the abused woman herself wants to do?

EARLIER FEMINIST LEGAL RESPONSES

In the 1970s and 1980s, feminists began arguing and litigating to make the criminal justice system abandon its previously shameful neglect of domestic violence against women. These efforts were successful, and, as a result, jurisdictions around the country began to improve their police and court practices to respond more effectively to domestic violence. The improved policies did not seem to help, however, in cases in which an abused woman asks police not to arrest her abuser or refuses to press charges against him once he has

been arrested. When first reflecting on these sorts of cases, feminists assumed that these women really wanted to leave their abusers or press charges against them but refrained from doing so because the women lacked information about their legal rights or were pressured into backing down, perhaps by law enforcement personnel who discouraged them or by their own fears of retaliation from their abusers. Requiring law enforcement personnel to take the initiative in arresting and prosecuting batterers promised to solve these problems.

This view was supported by a landmark Minneapolis study, published in 1984, that suggested that arrest was more effective in deterring subsequent violence by domestic abusers than either of the two alternatives with which it was compared: mediation or removing the abuser from the premises for eight hours. Nationwide legal reform followed the publication of this study, and by 1996 all fifty states permitted a police officer to arrest someone without a warrant whenever the officer has probable cause to believe the person has committed a misdemeanor or violated a restraining order.[28]

In addition to police practices, legal reformers focused on the problem of inadequate prosecution efforts. Prosecutors had often been lax in pursing criminal prosecution in domestic violence cases. Domestic violence advocacy groups argued that woman-battering was a crime and that it should be prosecuted like any other crime.[29] A crime is, in some sense, a harm to *society*, and "the state itself [is supposed to] bring . . . criminal proceedings" against those accused of crime.[30] Victims themselves do not have to press charges.[31] In recent years, in an effort to ensure that domestic violence is treated as a crime, "no-drop" prosecution policies have been implemented in many jurisdictions.[32] Essentially, these policies require prosecutors to make serious efforts to follow through with the prosecution of domestic violence cases that come to their offices.

The most stringent, and also the most controversial, sorts of no-drop policies call for prosecutors to go forward with a case "regardless of the victim's wishes," so long as there is enough evidence to do so. Stringent no-drop policies mandate some degree of participation by the victim, requiring, for example, that she be photographed to document injuries or provide the state with other evidence or information. Under these policies, a victim may also be forced to testify if the case proceeds to trial. Victims who fail to cooperate might be penalized. Cheryl Hanna notes that forced testimony is "unlikely given that 90% to 95% of all criminal cases end in plea bargains," but, in cases that do go to trial, this "extreme measure" may well be employed under a stringent no-drop policy.[33]

What are the success rates of no-drop prosecution policies? A stringent no-drop policy in San Diego is credited with lowering the annual number of homicides connected with domestic violence there from thirty to seven in the decade from 1985 to 1994. A stringent no-drop policy in Duluth, Minnesota, is credited with lowering the recidivism rate there. And programs in Seattle, Indianapolis, and Quincy, Massachusetts, have also been hailed as successes.[34]

For the rest of this discussion, I am going to assume that these findings are reliable and generalizable and that mandated legal procedures do tend to reduce the overall level of woman battering.[35] On that assumption, the original victims might benefit from less future violence from their abusers, and other women would benefit from a generalized deterrent effect. The primary argument for mandated procedures is thus that they tend overall to reduce the level of woman abuse. So what's the problem?

REASONS FOR AND AGAINST MANDATED PROCEEDINGS

One of the major arguments against mandatory arrest and no-drop prosecutions is that they may impose hardships and risks on an abused woman while at the same time undermining her autonomous capacity to choose or control the legal process that does so. The process proceeds without the woman's agency and possibly against her wishes. As an assistant prosecutor in Baltimore, Cheryl Hanna found that abused women want the abuse to stop but usually prefer the batterer to go into counseling than to be punished.[36] Punishment, if it occurs, would typically consist of jail time. Jailing the abuser would impose hardships on a financially dependent abused woman and her children. In addition, a trial itself can be a harrowing experience for a victim. Attorneys defending the accused batterer may cross-examine the woman about such embarrassing matters as her sexual preferences, in order to try to show that she "likes it rough."[37] And mandatory proceedings do not necessarily prevent abusers from retaliating against victims. The assumption that he won't retaliate against her for mandated legal proceedings against him may credit him with more rationality and integrity than he actually possesses.

A woman's loss of control over the legal process mimics in a way the disempowerment that the violence itself inflicted on her, so the loss of autonomy amounts to her "revictimization," this time by the law enforcement system. In addition, since the legal procedures are portrayed as being for her own good, imposing them on her amounts to paternalism. This interlocking set of hardships for the victim—disempowerment, revictimization, and paternalistic treatment—all stem from the way in which mandated procedures, by definition, largely ignore the victim's preferences and thereby seem to undermine her autonomy.[38] This is the major argument against mandated proceedings.

So on the face of it, we confront a dilemma: If the law *respects* the autonomy of abused women who don't want to cooperate and does not mandate their participation, it will be less effective in reducing woman abuse overall. On the other hand, if the law *mandates* the participation of reluctant abuse victims, it will fail to respect the autonomy of those particular women and may impose additional hardships on them. What should the law do?

The harms and risks that may befall an abused woman during criminal proceedings against her abuser are substantial and deserve serious consideration. I think, however, that they do not outweigh the major reason for mandated legal procedures, namely, a reduction in the level of woman abuse. Let us look more closely at the risks of financial hardship and retaliatory violence.

First, financial hardship. It is true that if an abusive man is put into prison, his family will suffer financially from the loss of any income that he contributed to the household. A family *always* suffers financially, however, when one of its adult, wage-earning members goes to prison for the commission of a crime. This problem is not unique to the families of domestic batterers, and it is not sufficient by itself to entail that no one ought ever to be imprisoned for harming others. We need some sort of policy to deter people from beating each other up. If imprisonment is successful as a deterrent (admittedly, a big "if"), then its value in deterring harmful acts may well outweigh the costs it imposes on the families of offenders. At any rate, there is no special argument based on family need for keeping woman batterers in particular out of prison—no more than there would be for any other offender whose family was financially dependent on him or her.

What about the problem of retaliatory violence? This problem is unique to domestic violence cases. The crime in this case is that of beating up an intimate partner, an action that is typically part of a pattern of behavior in which an abuser tends to blame his partner and "punish" her for things that go wrong in his life. It is certainly possible that the threat of being prosecuted might stimulate an abuser to be more abusive. Yet Cheryl Hanna argues plausibly that abusers might actually be more motivated to retaliate against their victims under a system in which the criminal law did *not* mandate victim cooperation. If an abuser knew that the victim's cooperation would not be mandated, then he would have a powerful incentive to try to scare her into dropping the charges against him, and this could increase the risk of retaliatory violence in nonmandated proceedings.[39]

Another argument against mandated legal proceedings is that they show disrespect, in the Kantian sense, to the abused women who are directly affected by those proceedings. An abused woman whose preference not to press charges was disregarded by the law would be used by the law as a mere means to gain criminal convictions for the sake of deterring future woman battering. We could try to argue that no individual woman should ever be used merely as a means to a social welfare end, even that of protecting other women.

It seems to me, however, that such "usage" cannot be avoided in these difficult cases. *Respecting* the preferences of current victims of domestic abuse and failing to prosecute their abusers would increase the risk of future abuse of both those current victims and other women. In that case, future potential victims would, in a sense, be "used" as a means to promoting respect for the preferences of current reluctant abuse victims. Whichever policy is adopted, *some* woman or women would be used as a means to the end of protecting or respecting some *other* woman or women. Trade-offs of this sort are unavoidable.

In any case, does the law even have a particular duty to respect the autonomy of those whom it affects? Even if it did, that requirement would not by itself tell us whether mandated legal proceedings are right or wrong, good or bad. The difference between autonomy in the short run and autonomy in the long run must be considered. Domestic violence, as I noted earlier, itself profoundly undermines a woman's autonomy. Anything that succeeds in deterring an abuser's future abusiveness promotes his victim's long-run autonomy. Thus, the short-run interference with an abused woman's autonomy that comes from a legal process over which she has no control may well be outweighed by her long-run gain in autonomy if the mandatory legal processes are successful in deterring her future abuse.

In addition, the law's treatment of each particular abused woman is a public matter with potential impact on many other women. The impact is at once both material and symbolic. Materially, the legal treatment of each individual domestic violence case has an impact on the level of domestic violence in the future. The best reason for mandated legal proceedings in domestic violence cases is their apparent effectiveness in reducing the level of domestic violence in a community.

Symbolically, the legal response to each case makes a public statement about how society regards the seriousness of domestic violence. Legal policies deal with whole populations. Feminists have long argued that woman abuse is the sort of harmful moral wrong that should be treated as a *crime* by society at large. Domestic violence is a public crime, not simply a private family matter, and this imposes a duty on the state to intervene with the full power of criminal law.[40] By "going public," we bring domestic life, where relevant, into the public sphere and make domestic violence an offense against the state, not simply against the abused woman. We thereby gain the right to legal protection against woman battering.

If feminists have been right that domestic violence is a public, political matter, then these acts should receive the same treatment under the criminal law as other crimes. The framework of the criminal law, however, changes the conception of a violent act. It is no longer merely an injury to a private woman. As legal theorists have argued, the overriding aims of the criminal justice system are to deter crime, to punish or rehabilitate criminals, and to seek justice. As Wayne LaFave and Austin Scott Jr. write in their textbook on criminal law, "The broad aim of the criminal law is . . . to prevent harm to society" and "to protect the public interest."[41] Respecting the autonomy of victims is not a particular aim of criminal law.

The status of citizen is the status of being a full member of the community. Citizenship transforms violence to oneself into an injury to the community of which one is a member. The community, organized as a state with a formal system of criminal law, may act to punish those who are found guilty of committing the violent acts. The advantage of the public criminalization of domestic woman battering is that the full power of the state may not be enlisted in protecting women against domestic tyranny. As Cheryl Hanna puts it, "One of the most important ways to curb domestic violence is to ensure that abusers understand that *society* will not tolerate their behavior."[42] In her view, it would be paternalistic and sexist to dismiss domestic violence cases based on victim reluctance while not doing so in other areas of criminal law.[43]

This incremental move toward full citizenship status for women, however, does carry a cost. One of the things we may have to give up is private control over the response to domestic violence

done to us. Gaining respect for our autonomous—and our nonautonomous—preferences about how our abusers are to be treated ceases to be an overriding concern. It is important that in seeking to deter future crime, the criminal law does aim at promoting some of the conditions, such as personal safety and security, that happen to undergird the possibility of future autonomy for abuse victims. In any case, it was precisely because women alone *couldn't* control domestic violence that we needed legal protection in the first place.

To be sure, some feminists have recently argued in favor of retaining the public-private distinction on the grounds that it sometimes benefits women. In women's reproductive activities, for example, and in those consensual relationships in which consent and freedom are genuine, we should *want* the state to refrain from interfering in our lives.[44] As Laura stein writes, there is more to the realm of privacy than simply individual men being "left alone to oppress women."[45] Surely, however, domestic violence is not an area in which women benefit from privacy. Left to our own devices, as we were for centuries, we were not able to stop woman battering. To combat it, women need supportive networks and institutions, including the criminal law. This protection, however, comes at a price. Part of the price is a loss of control over the legal consequences that follow domestic violence.

Granted, the criminal law may need to adjust its proceedings so as to respond more sensitively to the needs of crime victims in general. Women know this well from the area of rape law. A victims' rights movement in recent decades has called for such responsiveness across the board. This is not an issue that is peculiar to the crime of woman battering. If there were a good *general* argument against mandating the participation of crime victims, this would cover the case of domestic violence as well. I do not rule out that possibility. Cases of woman battering by themselves, however, do not seem to provide distinctive overriding reasons against mandated victim participation.

I therefore conclude that the deterrent and citizenship benefits to women in general of mandated criminal law proceedings in domestic violence cases outweigh the risks, hardships, and loss of autonomy experienced by those abused women who prefer not to cooperate with such proceedings. Criminal law procedures that genuinely reduced the level of woman abuse would incidentally also promote the (merely) content-neutral autonomy of women in the long run. The law should therefore do what it can to prevent men from abusing their intimate female partners, even if it must do so against the wishes of the victims and by mandating the victims' cooperation.

This does not mean that our society should disregard altogether the concerns of reluctant abuse victims. In the following sections of this chapter, I explore how professional caregivers (therapists, social workers, and so on) should respond to women who choose to remain in abusive relationships. We may find that the domain of caregiving, especially that of professional caregiving, is the appropriate institutional domain in which a society can respect the preferences of particular women without having to consider the impact of that respect on anonymous society at large.

NOTES

1. Some social theorists worry that terms such as "abused woman" and "battered woman" suggest the women in question are the problem; they are marred by the identity of being "abused" or "battered." I share this worry, but to avoid unnecessary complexity tangential to this chapter, I retain the common usage.
2. Susan L. Miller and Charles F. Wellford, "Patterns and Correlates of Interpersonal Violence," in *Violence Between Intimate Partners: Patterns, Causes, and Effects,* ed. Albert P. Cardarelli (Boston: Allyn and Bacon, 1997), p. 17. The fraction of this abuse of women that was inflicted by other women was negligible.
3. This contemporary cliché is of course the main title of Christopher Lasch's *Haven in a Heartless World: The Family Besieged* (New York: Basic Books, 1977).
4. See, for example, Susan Schechter and Lisa T. Gray, "A Framework for Understanding and Empowering Battered Women," in *Abuse and Victimization across the Life Span,* ed. Martha B. Straus (Baltimore: Johns Hopkins University Press, 1988), p. 241.

   In one Massachusetts study of women who sought court restraining orders against their intimate male partners, it was found that the majority of incidents alleged by the women constituted clear-cut criminal offenses, in most cases assault and battery; see James Ptacek, "The Tactics and Strategies of Men Who Batter: Testimony from Women Seeking Restraining Orders," in *Violence*

Between Intimate Partners: Patterns, Causes, and Effects, ed. Albert P. Cardarelli (Boston: Allyn and Bacon, 1997), pp. 109–11.
5. See, for example, Joseph Raz, *The Morality of Freedom* (Oxford: Clarendon Press, 1986), pp. 155–56.
6. See, for example, Lenore Walker, *The Battered Woman Syndrome* (New York: Springer, 1984), p. 79; and Kathleen J. Ferraro, "Battered Women: Strategies for Survival," in *Violence between Intimate Partners,* ed. Albert P. Cardarelli (Boston: Allyn and Bacon, 1977), pp. 128–29.
7. Ferraro, "Battered Women," pp. 124–40. See also Dee L. R. Graham, Edna Rawlings, and Nelly Rimini, "Survivors of Terror: Battered Women, Hostages, and the Stockholm Syndrome," in *Feminist Perspectives on Wife Abuse,* ed. Kersti Yllö and Michele Bograd (Newbury Park, Calif.: Sage, 1990), pp. 223–24.
8. This is the theme of Ann Jones and Susan Schechter, *When Love Goes Wrong: What to Do When You Can't Do Anything Right* (New York: HarperCollins, 1992). See also Martha Mahoney, "Legal Images of Battered Women: Redefining the Issue of Separation," *Michigan Law Review* 90, 1 (October 1991), esp. pp. 53–71.
9. Angela Browne, "Violence in Marriage: Until Death Do Us Part?" in *Violence Between Intimate Partners,* ed. Albert P. Cardarelli (Boston: Allyn and Bacon, 1997), pp. 57–58. Unfortunately for women, our culture values controlling tendencies in men, including control exercised in intimate relationships. A man's jealousy and possessiveness, for example, are often regarded as endearing signs that he loves a woman deeply. Browne, by contrast, emphasizes the "potential for violence" latent in such culturally sanctioned behavior.
10. More than twelve hundred battered women's shelters, for example, were created around the country between 1975 and 1995 as places of refuge for women and their children who are endangered by domestic violence (Albert P. Cardarelli, "Violence and Intimacy: An Overview," in *Violence Between Intimate Partners,* ed. Cardarelli [Boston: Allyn and Bacon, 1997], p. 7). I discuss recent legal innovations later in this chapter.
11. See, for example, Nancy A. Crowell and Ann W. Burgess, eds., *Understanding Violence Against Women* (Washington, D.C.: National Academy Press, 1996), 130–33.
12. "Empowerment" is the key word in the treatment of abused women; see, for example, M. A. Dutton, *Empowering and Healing the Battered Woman: A Model for Assessment and Intervention* (New York: Springer, 1992).
13. See, for example, B. Pressman, "Wife-Abused Couples: The Need for Comprehensive Theoretical Perspectives and Integrated Treatment Models," *Journal of Feminist Family Therapy* 1 (1989): 23–43.
14. Cf. Kathleen Ferraro, "Battered Women," p. 124; Elizabeth Schneider, "Particularity and Generality: Challenges of Feminist Theory and Practice in Work on Woman-Abuse," *New York University Law Review* 67 (June 1992): 558; and Ann Jones, *Next Time She'll Be Dead: Battering & How to Stop It* (Boston: Beacon Press, 1994), chap. 5.
15. To be sure, the question does reveal ignorance on the part of the questioner. Recent decades have witnessed an explosion of knowledge about women's lives. Anyone at all

familiar with this literature already has some idea about why some women stay in abusive relationships.

16. This approach certainly does not mean we should give up on rehabilitating abusive men. Unfortunately, however, as I noted earlier, the rehabilitation project is going slowly. Something else has to be done in the meantime in order to diminish the level of intimate partner abuse of women in the immediate future.

17. See, for example, Paula Caplan, *The Myth of Female Masochism* (New York: Dutton, 1985); and Edward W. Gondolf with Ellen R. Fisher, *Battered Women as Survivors: An Alternative to Treating Learned Helplessness* (New York: Macmillan, 1988), chap. 2.

18. Lenore Walker, *The Battered Woman* (New York: Harper Collins, 1979); and Walker, *Battered Woman Syndrome*.

19. Gondolf and Fisher, *Battered Women as Survivors*, chap. 2 and passim. For example, Gondolf and Fisher classify some batterers as "sociopaths." The typical counseling techniques used for abusers, however, are simply ineffective with sociopaths (pp. 65–66). Yet, women often remain in abusive relationships because the abuser has gone into counseling.

20. According to some studies, women in households with incomes under $10,000 have the highest rates of intimate partner abuse. These women often have less than a full high school education and no employment experience. Their abusive partners may be their only means of financial support. See, for example, Angela M. Moore, "Intimate Violence: Does Socioeconomic Status Matter?" in *Violence Between Intimate Partners*, ed. Albert P. Cardarelli (Boston: Allyn and Bacon, 1997), pp. 94, 96.

21. Browne, "Violence in Marriage," p. 68. The man may not be able to carry out such a threat, especially if there is a legal record of his abusiveness, but the woman may not be legally informed enough to know this.

22. Mahoney, "Legal Images of Battered Women," p. 87. Abusive relationships in which the abuser batters a woman who tries to leave are, in Mahoney's view, a kind of captivity. She compares the women who endure such relationships to hostages and prisoners of war.

23. Browne, "Violence in Marriage," pp. 67–68.

24. Ptacek, "Tactics and Strategies," pp. 113–14.

25. Kathleen J. Ferraro and John M. Johnson, "How Women Experience Battering: The Process of Victimization," *Social Problems* 30, 3 (February 1983): 328–29.

26. Ibid.

27. In the view of Gerald Dworkin, it must be the product of reflection that was not coerced or manipulated; Gerald Dworkin, *The Theory and Practice of Autonomy* (Cambridge: Cambridge University Press, 1988), chap. 1. On John Christman's view, the reflection must also include accepting the history by which the underlying desire was formed; see his "Autonomy and Personal History," *Canadian Journal of Philosophy* 21, 1 (March 1991): 1–24.

28. Cheryl Hanna, "No Right to Choose: Mandated Victim Participation in Domestic Violence Prosecutions,"

Harvard Law Review 109, 8 (June 1996): 1859. In general, police were already permitted to arrest someone on probable cause who had committed a felony.

The results of the Minneapolis study have been challenged by subsequent studies that did not fully replicate its findings. The general view now seems to be that arrest has a qualified deterrent effect. Cf. Donald G. Dutton, *The Domestic Assault of Women: Psychological and Criminal Justice Perspectives* (Vancouver: University of British Columbia Press, 1995), chap. 8.

29. Hanna, "No Right to Choose," p. 1861.

30. Wayne R. LaFave and Austin W. Scott Jr., *Criminal Law*, 2nd ed. (St. Paul, Minn.: West Publishing, 1986), p. 13.

31. Ibid., p. 14.

32. Hanna, "No Right to Choose," p. 1862.

33. Ibid., pp. 1867, 1892. Moderate no-drop policies do not force the participation of uncooperative victims. Instead, counseling and support services are made available to uncooperative victims, and they are *encouraged* to continue the legal process. If, after this support, an abused woman still refuses to cooperate, and the evidence apart from her testimony would not be likely to gain a conviction, the prosecutor following a moderate no-drop policy will usually drop the charges (Hanna, "No Right to Choose," pp. 1862–63). The stringent no-drop policies with their mandated victim participation are the ones that have generated the most controversy, so these are what I will focus on in the remainder of the discussion.

34. Hanna, "No Right to Choose," pp. 1864–65; p. 1865 n. 71; p. 1887 nn. 169, 170.

35. This assumption is crucial for the discussion that follows. If the assumption is not empirically warranted, the argument below would need substantial revision. For a brief summary of some of the evidence, see Crowell and Burgess, *Understanding Violence Against Women*, pp. 114–24; and Rosemary Chalk and Patricia A. King, eds., *Violence in Families: Assessing Prevention and Treatment Programs* (Washington, D.C.: National Academy Press, 1998), pp. 174–81.

36. Hanna, "No Right to Choose," p. 1884.

37. Ibid., p. 1876.

38. Ibid., p. 1866.

39. Ibid., pp. 1891–92.

40. See, for example, Elizabeth A. Stanko, "Fear of Crime and the Myth of the Safe Home: A Feminist Critique of Criminology," in *Feminist Perspectives on Wife Abuse*, ed. Kersti Yllö and Michele Bograd (Newbury Park, Calif.: Sage, 1990), pp. 75–88.

41. LaFave and Scott, *Criminal Law*, pp. 10, 13.

42. Hanna, "No Right to Choose," p. 1890; italics mine.

43. Ibid., p. 1891.

44. See Ruth Gavison, "Feminism and the Public/Private Distinction," *Stanford Law Review* 45 (1992): 37.

45. See Laura Stein, "Living with the Risk of Backfire: A Response to the Feminist Critique of Privacy and Equality," *Minnesota Law Review* 77 (1993): 1173.

Is Equality Tearing Families Apart?

Joel Anderson

Joel Anderson is a University Lecturer-Research in the Philosophy Department at Utrecht University (The Netherlands). He works in the areas of ethical theory (especially on issues regarding autonomy and communicative ethics), applied ethics (especially neuro-ethics), and theories of human agency (especially on the centrality of mutual recognition to the development of fundamental human capabilities). He has edited, with John Christman, *Autonomy and the Challenges to Liberalism: New Essays* (2005).

Anderson defends the principle of gender equality against the charge that it leads to a decline of the family. In his criticism of neotraditionalist approaches such as that of Blankenhorn, he argues that stable, rewarding family life is perfectly compatible with egalitarian feminists' demands for genderless parenting, equal power, and freedom of opportunity. He concludes that the perceived conflict between pro-family and pro-equality positions is an illusion.

Let me begin with what I take to be two basic truths. First, social inequality between the sexes should be eliminated. Second, anything that systematically undermines the possibility for healthy, stable, fulfilling family life should be eliminated as well. Put positively, a good society must be *both* pro-equality and pro-family.

On its own, neither position is particularly controversial. Treating women as inferior to men clearly denies them their dignity and moral worth. Insofar as the majority of society's rewards go to men solely because of their sex, women are victims of injustice. Similarly, clear intuitions hold with regard to the importance of stable, caring, mutually rewarding marriages and families. Assuming (as I do here) that "married couple" and "family" are understood broadly, as including both traditional and nontraditional household arrangements,[1] what is at issue is one of the most basic forms of social relationships around which

individuals build their understanding of the good life. A society that denied its members something that is so widely held to be an essential component of a life worth living would be gravely depriving them. Properly understood, then, a "decline of the family" would pose a genuine threat to human well-being.

My concern here is with the perceived conflict between pro-equality and pro family approaches. Those who have fought hardest for gender equality often view "pro-family" rhetoric with suspicion and even hostility. And those who have worried most about the decline of the family often view campaigns for gender equality with a similar degree of suspicion and hostility. In this essay, I examine this second set of worries, put forward by a range of social critics and philosophers whom I will label "neotraditionalists."[2] I shall be focusing on three ways in which promoting equality is thought to contribute to the disintegration of families. In each case, these neotraditionalist critics argue that the egalitarian policies of feminists entail further social developments—specifically, genderless parenting, selfish individualism, and

Joel Anderson, "Is Equality Tearing Families Apart?" Reprinted by permission of the author.

competing agendas—that are tearing families apart. I shall be arguing that this entailment is rarely plausible, and that even when it is, the risks of social fragmentation should not overshadow the importance of gender equality.

Before continuing, a brief clarification is in order with regard to what it means to say that the family is "in decline" or is being "torn apart." I do not mean this as simply a matter of a demographic shift from "intact" families (a couple in their first marriage plus their children) to single-parent families and "step-families." Unless one assumes that particular structures for living together are ordained by God or biology, it is an open question whether the increase in single-parent households or common-law marriages represents a problem. What clearly would represent a problem, however, are developments that threaten to rob family life of its meaning and purpose. If, for example, the very point of families is to provide a context in which family members are nurtured, cared for, socialized, etc., then a lack of contact between family members represents a decline of the family. In this sense, a family can be torn apart even without a divorce. Being torn apart is thus also a matter of degree. Again, however, what would be problematic is not that a particular form of household is on the decline,[3] but that people are having trouble maintaining the interpersonal commitments about which they care deeply. On the broad understanding assumed here, the break-up of an unmarried couple can be an instance of family disintegration.

There is mounting evidence that the family is suffering from social fragmentation: half of all marriages end in divorce; "in disrupted families, only one child in six, on average, saw his or her father as often as once a week in the past year";[4] and "parents had roughly 10 fewer hours per week for their children in 1986 than in 1960."[5] None of this demonstrates that we should return to the past, but if some degree of stability and integration is a necessary condition for the sort of family life that so many people deeply value, then the criticisms raised by neotraditionalists must be taken seriously.

EQUALITY AND GENDERLESS PARENTING

Neotraditionalist critics of egalitarian feminism sometimes claim that promoting equality involves endorsing the idea of a genderless family in which breadwinning, homemaking, and child-rearing are divided evenly between husband and wife.[6] Neotraditionalists then argue that eliminating distinctions between the role of father and mother forces both men and women to deny essential components of their identity as parents, which is not only bad in itself but also denies families the much-needed stability and complementarity provided by the male-breadwinner/female-homemaker model.

Arguments for this position come from a wide range of viewpoints. The most familiar neotraditionalist arguments in this connection focus on women's "natural" role as nurturers and their greater suitability for the role of primary caregiver.[7] But neotraditionalists such as David Blankenhorn also argue that the role of fathers has been unduly neglected and that men have a special contribution to make in the distinctive role of "father."[8] I shall focus on this latter discussion.

Neotraditionalists have taken issue with the ideal of the sensitive, caring, supportive "New Father" who changes half the diapers and whose sense of self-worth depends as much on his homemaking as his breadwinning.[9] Against this ideal, they argue that it is vitally important to recognize the distinctiveness of a father's contribution to the family, especially as a good provider and a strong protector. According to these critics of egalitarian feminism, recognizing this is important for three reasons.

First, if we eliminate the differences between what it means to be a father and what it means to be a mother, we will lose the benefits of diverse role models within the family. For example, Blankenhorn cites studies that have shown that men tend to inspire adventurousness, assertiveness, and risk-taking in their children, whereas women tend to be more risk-averse and protective. If, as seems plausible, children need to learn to balance these two modes of behavior, then it would be a genuine loss if this diversity were eliminated.

Second, as with many social organizations, the family benefits from functional differentiation, that is, from having a diversity of roles and functions that complement one another, rather than having everyone performing the same roles. On these grounds, neotraditionalists hold, for example, that children do best in a situation in which the authority figure of the father contrasts with the sympathetic ear of a mother.

Third, neotraditionalists argue that by telling men that they must think of themselves as homemakers, proponents of gender equality exacerbate family disintegration by leaving men feeling that they have nothing special to contribute.[10] Without the feeling of masculine pride that comes from being a good provider and a role model of strength in the family, it is argued, men's attachment to the responsibilities of fatherhood is diminished. Thus, genderless parenting denies men this feeling of pride.

These neotraditionalist arguments all attempt to link genderless parenting to the depletion of crucial resources for healthy families. Though some critics might go so far as to claim that this means we should reinstate the traditional, male-breadwinner/female-homemaker family as the normative model, the more moderate position is that the differences between men and women should be accepted, thereby "allowing" women to choose full-time homemaking without guilt and men to focus on breadwinning without shame.

There are several difficulties with this line of argument. To begin with, it is not entirely clear that promoting equality between men and women requires eliminating the distinctive roles of mothers and fathers. "Genderless" parenting does not deny that there will be role differences ("father" and "mother"), but only that parents should not be trapped in one role or the other. Thus one can maintain the diversity of roles on which neotraditionalists insist, while keeping open the question of *who* must fill the roles. Neither of the first two arguments has given us reason to think that men should not occupy the socio-cultural role of "mothers" nor women that of "fathers."

The third argument does aim to provide such reasons. At this point, neotraditionalists often appeal to claims about what is "natural." They reject the idea that men can be "mothers" and women can be "fathers." Given how much of what gives humans their dignity is the ability to refrain from doing "what comes naturally," such direct appeals to nature are generally dubious. Even so, many people are impressed with the purported "brute fact" that women are more emotionally attached to their children, so that they have a much harder time leaving them in the care of others, and are much more reluctant to put young children in child care.[11] Assuming, charitably, that there is empirical evidence for a persistent and fairly general trend, would this show what the neotraditionalists want it to show? Not necessarily. For it might turn out that the persistence of this phenomenon may be traceable to inequalities that are the result of socialization rather than chromosomes.

Consider, for example, Rhona Mahony's suggestion that women's "headstart effect" can be overcome through the use of "affirmative action for fathers."[12] Mahony acknowledges that pregnancy often gives mothers an inevitable "headstart" over fathers when it comes to their emotional attachment and sensitive attunement to the infant, but she stresses that what happens after the birth is not biologically predetermined. Typically, of course, mothers' headstart leads to quicker and more successful responses. Even without the greater degree of coaching and encouragement women generally receive from female friends and relatives, the headstart effect can quickly lead to a situation in which mothers are able to quiet a child quickly and generally set a standard of care that fathers have difficulty living up to. Even when a couple is resolved to share the parenting, Mahony argues, there are unintentional mechanisms that tend to snowball, so that after only a few months it becomes much more efficient for mothers to take over the greater share of the childcare. She gets exasperated, and he gets frustrated. This may look like a "natural" outcome, but biology does not determine this outcome beyond the "headstart effect." In fact, if fathers are given significant periods of time in which they have sole responsibility for the young infant, there is every reason to expect that such "affirmative action" will correct the balance. Before large numbers of fathers have had the opportunity to become equally expert with their children, speculation about what men and women "naturally" want is a poor basis for legitimating practices that perpetuate the unequal status of women.

In this connection, we must be very clear about what is at stake for women in the present discussion. Neotraditionalist attempts to restore the idea that women and men have specific roles to play as mothers and fathers threaten to re-entrench the situation in which women who have the primary childcare responsibilities see their chances diminished of later returning to interesting jobs. As recent discussions of "mommy tracks" and "glass ceilings" have made clear, being the primary care-giver for their children often hinders women on the job front, both by restricting the amount of time they can devote to their work and by making them less attractive candidates for being promoted to positions of responsibility.[13] I shall return to this point below.

EQUAL NEGOTIATING POSITIONS

A second set of neotraditionalist suspicions about the egalitarian agenda has to do with the destabilizing effects of a focus on equal power. Here the argument is that, although some equality of power in the family is probably a good thing, a concern with it should not become a dominant principle. The family, it is argued, follows a different logic than that of politics or business. It is a place of unconditional love and fidelity, a "haven in a heartless world."[14] This climate of love and trust can easily be destroyed by a focus on equal power and equal negotiating positions.

Neotraditionalists do not advocate inequality. They agree with egalitarians that wives should be equal before the law, should be able to own and inherit property, and (for the most part) should not be required to submit to the wishes of their husbands. What they object to is the stronger position taken by egalitarians.

According to this egalitarian position, genuine equality demands both a commitment to equalizing power imbalances as much as possible and an adequate awareness of one's relative power in the relationship. If they care about equality, couples must be concerned with how the choices they make are shaped in subtle ways. Unless the negotiating positions are equal, the appearance of fair decision making may be easily misleading. Furthermore, and this is the importance of *awareness*, even if neither spouse perceives a problematic imbalance, that may simply be because some spouses may be in such a vulnerable position that they cannot *afford* to think about their inequalities.[15]

To understand the egalitarian position, it is best to focus on the difficult decisions that families inevitably face, because it is there that subtle differences on a person's negotiating position can have a huge impact. Take the case of young parents making decisions about who will cut back on his or her hours at work (or quit altogether) in order to care for the newborn, when both spouses are in careers that they love but that will be jeopardized if they cut back on work. Equality demands that the interests of each spouse should weigh as much as those of the other (which is not to say that the only fair outcome is a 50/50 split). That requires, in turn, that it is a genuinely open question whether the mother or the father will go part-time to take care of the babies. But if, as is very often the case, the husband's more established career provides a better income, or if he has little idea how to take care of children by himself, then the wife's negotiating position is seriously weakened. Whether the mother wants to or not, the "obvious" thing to do will be for her to cut back on her hours and thereby jeopardize her career. In this way, even among spouses who love each other, an unequal negotiating position can deny women the opportunity to have their career plans adequately considered.

In a similar way, ensuring equal negotiating positions requires guaranteeing that divorce is not available to one spouse on more advantageous terms. This point is important, because when family conflicts arise, they are played out against the background of the possibility that the marriage may break down. The possibility of divorce gives partners not only a way of escaping an unacceptable position—not insignificant in a world of marital rape and spousal abuse—but also a way of increasing the chances of their criticism being taken seriously. As Albert O. Hirschman observes, "The chances for voice to function effectively as a recuperation mechanism are appreciably strengthened if voice is backed up by the *threat of exit*, whether it is made openly or whether the possibility of exit is merely well understood to be an element in the situation by all concerned."[16] Thus, the equal availability of an "exit option" may actually serve to *prevent* divorce by ensuring that both men and women have a threat at their disposal that will ensure that their voice gets heard.

Beyond formal access to divorce, it is crucially important that the consequences of divorce are equally costly. Otherwise, the negotiating position of one spouse will be stronger. Currently, men's exit options are generally better than those of women: "income for mothers and children declines on average about 30 percent, while fathers experience a 10 to 15 percent increase in their incomes in the year following the separation."[17] The causes of this disparity are complex, but they surely include not only lax enforcement of child support payments but also the fact that while fathers were improving their employment position, mothers have often focused on childcare and housekeeping rather than job experience and networking. Whatever the reasons, however, in this situation of unequal negotiating positions, when the disagreements are intense or the decisions of great consequence, women's awareness that they will be the bigger losers in a divorce can make them willing to tolerate treatment that their husbands would not tolerate. Eliminating these forms of inequality is a major task. It calls for significant changes in family law, public policy, and business practices. But it also calls for spouses to be vigilant about their relative negotiating positions.

For neotraditionalists, this vigilant attitude threatens to increase marital instability, for the more a couple focuses on the equality of their negotiating positions, the more they are likely to undermine the climate of trust, commitment, and self-sacrifice that makes families both stable and worthwhile. From this perspective, when spouses start closely monitoring who is taking advantage of whom or thinking about who will lose out in a divorce, they introduce ways of relating to each other that are antithetical to good marriages (as well as being symptomatic of deeper problems). This is often expressed by saying that the culture of the public world of contracts and self-interest has invaded the private domain of the family, where a distinctive culture is to be cherished.

> The goals of women (and of men, too) in the workplace are primarily individualistic: social recognition, wages, opportunities for advancement, and self-fulfillment. But the family is about collective goals that by definition extend beyond individuals: procreation, socializing the young, caring for the old, and building life's most enduring bonds of affection, nurturance, mutual support, and long-term commitment.[18]

Without this commitment to the larger whole, it is argued, families lack the glue that holds them together, and they tend to disintegrate as soon as sacrifices are required. On this view, if family members are focused on making sure that they get their share, they will have trouble weathering the short-term conflicts that inevitably arise.

But does equalizing negotiating positions between spouses really lead to the sort of self-interested culture that tears families apart? Ultimately, this is an empirical question, but given the complexity of the issue and the sort of data needed, some philosophical analysis may help to clarify which hypotheses are most plausible. Where we should come down on this issue will certainly depend, in part, on the sorts of families that one has in mind. Here we can distinguish three different cases.

(1) In some families, the negotiating positions will be roughly equal. When spouses must make choices that jeopardize their chances of career advancement and financial independence in the future, the sacrifices are made equally; various arrangements are in place to ensure that neither spouse will end up benefiting financially from a divorce; furthermore, when applicable, childcare responsibilities are distributed in such a way that parents' emotional investment in the children and

expertise in childcare is likely to be fairly decided on an equal basis. In such cases, an awareness of their equal negotiating positions seems likely to strengthen the stability of the family, for spouses will know that *even when they are not getting along*, they are not in a position to take advantage of the other. Of course, equality of negotiating positions is not sufficient to hold a marriage together. My point is simply that there is no reason to think that if a couple knows that their interests are balanced, this will threaten their mutual love.

(2) In families where inequalities of power are actually exploited, the different issue arises as to whether keeping the family together is really the best option. I said at the outset that family disintegration is *usually* something that no one wants, and it is bad for that reason—but not always. If we care about human dignity and autonomy, we must recognize that only if people are aware of the possibility of inequality arising in a relationship will they have any chance of correcting a situation in which someone is taking advantage of them. In a family with young children, of course, the choice to end a marriage often represents a tragic situation, and neotraditionalists are right to point out that parents may have an obligation to accept some sacrifices for the sake of a maintaining a tense but stable situation at home. But a situation in which it was typically *women* who made the sacrifices would be a situation of (at least) indirect sexism and would deserve moral condemnation.

(3) The neotraditionalist objection is perhaps on its best footing in cases in which there are unequal negotiating positions, but the more powerful spouse does not exploit the other. If the power imbalance is *temporary*—say, if one parent loses a job—then it may well be just a matter of family members needing to take the long view and to trust that advantages will balance out over time. In a situation of lasting and structural inequality, matters may also seem benign, as long as both spouses feel that they have an equal say. An insistence that spouses be aware of the imbalance may then seem unnecessarily risky to the relationship. As long as we are talking about *adequate* and not *maximal* awareness of relative negotiating positions, however, the greater

danger, I would suggest, lies in being blind to the presence of serious inequality. For an awareness of it allows both spouses to be attentive to the ways in which they may inadvertently slide into patterns that they would not have accepted if their negotiating positions had been equal. Furthermore, only with an awareness of such imbalances is it possible for spouses to make a moral appeal to each other based on a special vulnerability, which itself can contribute to marital stability.

This last point can be generalized. If neotraditionalists are concerned with genuine stability in a relationship, they would do well to acknowledge the ways in which genuine equality provides a basis that is at least as stable as the reliance on traditional family models. To ensure that the stability is more than skin-deep conventionalism, some awareness of and concern with spouses relative negotiating positions is vitally important.

EQUALITY OF INDIVIDUAL OPPORTUNITY

The third neotraditionalist criticism that I wish to consider focuses, like the one just discussed, on the threat that increasing individualism poses to the family. The central suspicion is that feminist egalitarianism undermines the stability of families by allowing the centrifugal forces of the labor market to affect the family more brutally than ever before. Neotraditionalists suggest that, in the push for women's equality, traditional assumptions about the family have been dismantled, taking with them one of the best bulwarks against the divisive demands of the labor market.

In order to examine this claim, we need to understand something of the importance of freedom of choice, especially with regard to the choice of occupation. Historically, the process of industrialization has led to fundamental transformations of family life, for example, in nineteenth-century Europe.[19] Whereas the vast majority of people in pre-industrial societies had no choice of occupation (to the point that their role, usually as peasant, was prescribed by the metaphysical world order), in modern industrial societies the possibilities for choice expanded both in scope and significance. The modern view emerged that free choice of occupation is an important basic liberty, one that guaranteed the opportunity for self-realization. Freedom of choice—and particularly freedom to choose one's occupation—thus became a fundamentally important moral claim of modern individuals, for it affects the very possibility of leading one's life as one's own. Only if people could choose their line of work could they truly be free to develop their own sense of individual identity and self-worth.

Women were, of course, long denied this freedom. Men planned their careers, and women planned their weddings. Insofar as that is still the case, promoting equality will indeed demand that the roles available to women be expanded so as to be equal with that of men. As a general proposition, few would deny that women have an equal moral claim to opportunities for self-determination and self-realization. What feminists have shown, however, is that developing the social conditions under which women have *real* opportunities requires significant transformations. In particular, it involves eliminating the automatic assumption that women will be the ones staying home to care for small children. For as long as employers have reason to believe that young women are more likely to leave the work force, request a shift to a part-time position, decline positions that require overtime or travel, and take time off to care for a sick relative, employers have significant economic incentives to invest in training and promoting men rather than women, thus reducing women's opportunities for self-realization.[20] Rectifying this situation is not, it should be noted, a matter of making special accommodations to women but of realizing more consistently the principles of a free and fair labor market.[21]

As neotraditionalists point out, however, the labor market does not operate on the basis of family-friendly principles.[22] Especially in a world in which global competition is intense and labor unions are relatively weak, the labor market often demands, for example, that workers relocate to find work and that they put in extra hours if they are to remain competitive. The German sociologist

Ulrich Beck follows out this line of thought to its logical extreme:

> Ultimately, the market model of modernity presupposes a society without families or marriages. Everyone must be free and independent for the requirements of the market, in order to secure his or her existence. . . . Accordingly, a fully realized market society is also a society without children— unless the children grow up with mobile, single-parent fathers and mothers.[23]

Given this, even some feminists have recently discussed the costs to women (and their families) of their entry into the labor market, even if it is something that equality demands.[24] Neotraditionalists tend to blame these costs on feminists' campaign for equal opportunity. But it seems far more accurate to say, as Beck does, that this transformation was a matter of artificial barriers to womens' participation in the workplace finally being removed.

Whatever the cause, having both men and women in the labor market has added strains on the family as a result of the increasing number of difficult decisions that must be made. The more options people have, the more complicated the task becomes of trying to coordinate cooperative relationships. As a result of the constant demands to communicate needs and arrive at agreements, the potential for conflict rises dramatically. Take the case of being relocated for a job. In a world in which tradition clearly dictates that the family will move wherever the father's job takes him, no decision really needs to be made. There may still be unhappiness and conflict about the move, but the source of the conflict is situated outside the family. As those traditional assumptions crumble, it becomes a contingent matter how families should resolve such situations. Simple appeals to "how we have always done things" must be replaced by the hard work of finding a way to take everyone's needs into consideration. As a result, to quote Beck again, "The family becomes a constant juggling act of disparate multiple ambitions among careers and their requirements for mobility, educational demands, conflicting parental obligations, and bothersome housework."[25] If this is what women's equality of opportunity brings us, neotraditionalists ask, is it really worth it?

With regard to what women's full participation in the labor market has *taken away*, the critics argue that given how promoting equality involves challenging traditional assumptions about how parental responsibilities will be divided, the egalitarian agenda may be undermining the very bulwark that it needs against the centrifugal pressures of the labor market. When women did not insist on working outside the home, they argue, family stability was less threatened by employers' demands for mobility, because the pressures were again construed as lying *outside the private sphere of the family*. On this view, the head of household faced the competitive, interest-based public world, but came home to a world free of competing agendas. Furthermore, the traditional family model also provided clear roles and expectations, such that much less was open to the sort of debates that can tear families apart.

The difficulties with this neotraditionalist line of argument lie both in what it advocates and what it fails to advocate. On the first count, the neotraditionalist proposal that we restore our faith in certain traditional assumptions about the family—such as the model of men as family providers—is not really an option available in modern industrial societies, even if we could afford it. Aside from the fact that returning to more traditional approaches would involve unconscionably disproportionate sacrifices from women, it would not actually eliminate the need to make complex and conflict-ridden decisions. Once "how we do things" has become a contingent matter, every form of traditionalism is a *neo*traditionalism. You have to argue for it, or at least choose it. Today, when a couple picks the traditional male-breadwinner/female-homemaker pattern, the modern understanding of mutual and just respect demands that it be a *choice* made by *equals*—and that it be done in a way that does not jeopardize future possibilities for self-determination.

What neotraditionalists overlook are the posttraditional alternatives. Since industrial societies have been based on the assumption that only half of the potential work force would participate, it is not really all that surprising that fundamental changes are needed as part of the shift to genuinely full employment (that is, of both men and women). There are numerous proposals regarding *structural changes* that can be made in the way in which homemaking and breadwinning are distributed.[26] For example, some have proposed policies that would enable couples to participate effectively in the labor market *as couples*.[27]

Much of the appeal of the call for retraditionalization is based on the assumption that people will necessarily be overwhelmed by the complexities of a world without traditional gender roles. Talk of "disorientation" is common here. Such talk is premature, however. With the appropriate support, there is clearly room to increase people's capacities to handle these complex new decisions, not simply as individuals but also as families, concerned with their well-being as families. This will involve developing, for example, capacities to listen sympathetically and express oneself clearly, commitments to ensuring that no one is inadvertently silenced and that even unconventional solutions are given due consideration, and clearly established (but revisable) procedures for family deliberations. Developing and maintaining these capacities can empower individuals to build and maintain their families amidst growing complexity.

Although providing a full blueprint for change is beyond the scope of the present essay, these brief sketches serve to highlight the possibilities for responding effectively to contemporary challenges to family stability without having to follow the neotraditionalists in compromising a commitment to equality.

There is no denying the difficulties involved in keeping a family together today, and many of these challenges result partly from the increasing equality of men and women. But it would be a narrow-minded mistake to say that the current challenges are generated by demands for gender equality. Rather, they are part of the larger challenge posed by living in a world in which the artificial constraints of tradition and conventions are increasingly dissolving. What I have argued here is that neotraditionalism presents us with a false dichotomy between genuine gender equality and a supportive climate for stable family life. These critics of feminist egalitarianism would have us choose between pro-family and pro-equality positions. Fortunately, even in complex modern societies, that is one decision that no one has to make.[28]

NOTES

1. In "Of Mothers and Families, Men and Sex" (in the present anthology), Marilyn Friedman provides a suitably broad definition of "family" as an "enduring household based on interpersonal commitment," which rightly includes homosexual couples. I shall focus on heterosexual couples, however, since I am concerned with gender equality and thus on relations between men and women.

2. In this essay, "neotraditionalism" represents a composite portrait of positions defended by a wide range of authors, most typically by the members of The Council on Families in America and the Institute for American Values. See the essays collected in *Rebuilding the Nest: A New Commitment to the American Family*, ed. David Blankenhorn, Steven Bayme, and Jean Bethke Elshtain (Milwaukee, WI: Family Service America, 1990); and *Promises to Keep: Decline and Renewal of Marriage in America*, ed. David Popenoe, Jean Bethke Elshtain, and David Blankenhorn (Lanham, MD: Rowman and Littlefield, 1996). Although the positions I outline are typical of this approach, my concern here is with widely held viewpoints rather than the claims of particular authors.

3. After all, social critics in the past decried the breakdown of the extended family and the rise of the nuclear family.

4. Barbara Defoe Whitehead, "Dan Quayle was Right," *The Atlantic Monthly* (April 1993), 65.

5. Janet Z. Giele, "Decline of the Family: Conservative, Liberal, and Feminist Views," in Popenoe (ed.), *Promises to Keep*, 91.

6. E.g., Susan Moller Okin, *Justice, Gender, and the Family* (New York: Basic Books, 1989).

7. Similar views are defended by some feminists, e.g., Nel Noddings, *Caring: A Feminine Approach to Ethics and Moral Education* (Berkeley: University of California Press, 1984) and Virginia Held, "Feminism and Moral Theory," in *Women and Moral Theory*, ed. Eva Feder Kittay and Diana T. Meyers (Totowa, NJ: Rowman and Littlefield, 1987), 111–28.

8. David Blankenhorn, *Fatherless America: Confronting Our Most Urgent Social Problem* (New York: Basic Books, 1995).

9. In addition to Blankenhorn's *Fatherless America*, see Bruno Bettleheim's earlier piece, "Fathers Shouldn't Try to Be Mothers," *Parents Magazine* (October 1956).

10. This is the main theme of Blankenhorn's *Fatherless America*. It is also a prominent message in various recent "men's movements," including the "Promise-Keepers" and the Nation of Islam's "Million Man March."

11. A recent *New York Times* op-ed presents the greater attachment of mothers as a fact of "genetic wiring" (see Danielle Crittenden, "Yes, Motherhood Lowers Pay," *The New York Times*, op. ed. page, August 22, 1995).

12. Rhona Mahony, *Kidding Ourselves: Breadwinning, Babies, and Bargaining Power* (New York: Basic Books, 1995), 102–6. It should be noted that the biological headstart effect may be absent in the case of adoptive mothers.

13. See, e.g., Mahony, *Kidding Ourselves*, 14–17.

14. Christopher Lasch, *Haven in a Heartless World* (New York: Basic Books, 1977).

15. See Okin, *Justice, Gender, and the Family*, ch. 7; and Laura Sanchez and Emily W. Kane, "Women's and Men's Constructions of Perceptions of Housework Fairness," *Journal of Family Issues* 17 (1996): 358–87.

16. *Exit, Voice, and Loyalty: Responses to Decline in Firms, Organization, and States* (Cambridge, MA: Harvard University Press, 1970), p. 82.

17. Whitehead, "Dan Quayle Was Right," 62. See also Lenore J. Weitzman, *The Divorce Revolution: The Unexpected Social and Economic Consequences for Women and Children in America* (New York: The Free Press, 1985). For a discussion of how this affects women's negotiating position, see Mahony, *Kidding Ourselves*, ch. 3. It should be noted that different issues affect the very poor: insofar as welfare assistance is restricted to unmarried mothers, the breakdown of a marriage may leave men with even fewer resources than women (with custody).

18. David Blankenhorn, "American Family Dilemmas," in Blankenhorn (ed.), *Rebuilding the Nest*, 10f.

19. For an excellent analysis of this development, see Elisabeth Beck-Gernsheim, "Auf dem Weg in die postfamiliale Familie: Von der Notgemeinschaft zur Wahlverwandtschaft," in *Riskante Freiheiten: Individualisierung in modernen Gesellschaften*, ed. Ulrich Beck and Elisabeth Beck-Gernsheim (Frankfurt: Suhrkamp, 1994), 115–38.

20. Felice N. Schwartz makes clear what it currently costs companies to ensure that mothers make their way into the executive ranks in "Management Women and the New Facts of Life," *Harvard Business Review* (Jan./Feb. 1989).

21. Ulrich Beck, *Risk Society: Toward a New Modernity* (London: Sage, 1992), 176–81.

22. Robert N. Bellah, "The Invasion of the Money World," in *Rebuilding the Nest*, 227.

23. Beck, *Risk Society*, 191.

24. Judith Stacey, *Brave New Families: Stories of Domestic Upheaval in Late Twentieth Century* (New York: Basic Books, 1990).

25. Beck, *Risk Society*, 184.

26. E.g., Okin, *Justice, Gender, and the Family*, ch. 8; and Mahony, *Kidding Ourselves*, ch. 9–10. Neotraditionalists make some of these proposals themselves but see structural change as far from sufficient to counter the pressures towards social fragmentation: see, esp., The Council on Families in America, "Marriage in America: A Report to the Nation," in Popenoe (ed.), *Promises to Keep*, 310.

27. Beck, *Risk Society*, 194–204.

28. I would like to thank Larry May, Herbert Anderson, and Pauline Kleingeld for comments on earlier drafts.

Re-Thinking Civil Unions and Same-Sex Marriage*

Brook J. Sadler

Brook J. Sadler is associate professor of philosophy at the University of South Florida. Among her articles are: "Shared Intentions and Shared Responsibility," *Midwest Studies in Philosophy*, vol. 30, 2006, "Collective Responsibility, Universalizability, and Social Practices," *Journal of Social Philosophy*, vol. 38, no. 3, Fall 2007.

Sadler argues that civil marriage is actually not worth preserving. She then argues that civil unions are a progressive alternative to marriage and that these institutions should be embraced by both opponents and proponents of same-sex marriage. Along the way she examines the kind of good that marriage is and whether the state has an interest in marriage.

INTRODUCTION

The current debate about same-sex marriage in the United States has largely overlooked two substantial assumptions shared by both proponents and opponents of same-sex marriage.[1] First, both proponents and opponents of same-sex marriage generally agree that marriage is a valuable practice and institution with a status and significance that elevates it above civil unions. For this reason, *proponents* of same-sex marriage regard civil unions as an unsatisfactory, second-class alternative to marriage that debars gays and lesbians from participating in a practice that not only offers legal rights and benefits but also has an important social and cultural value worth preserving. At best, they see civil unions as an interim solution that should

give way to same-sex marriage when the political climate changes. *Opponents* of same-sex marriage, whether or not they support civil unions, are similarly anxious to protect the special status of marriage, which they believe requires preserving its exclusively heterosexual form. Second, both proponents and opponents of same-sex marriage generally agree that the question of same-sex marriage ought to be decided by the state; implicit in this belief is the idea that the state has a legitimate interest in marriage, indeed a legitimate interest in regulating or authorizing personal, sexual relationships. *Proponents* of same-sex marriage seek to rectify a perceived injustice, which consists in unwarranted legal discrimination on the basis of sexual orientation or sex.[2] Accordingly, even if civil unions provide exactly the same legal rights and benefits as marriage, civil unions sidestep the moral problem by tacitly endorsing the state's right to discriminate on the basis of sexual orientation; nothing short of legal intervention to expand access to marriage for same-sex partners will suffice. On the other hand, *opponents* of same-sex marriage also believe legal intervention is necessary, and they seek to make explicit in the law what has until

Edited Excerpt from Brook Sadler, "Re-thinking civil unions and same-sex marriage" from The Monist, Vol. 91, nos. 3 & 4, pp. 578–605, 2008. Copyright © The Monist: An International Quarterly Journal of General Philosophical Inquiry. Open court Publishing Company, Chicago, Ilinois. Reprinted by permission.

recently been taken for granted: that marriage is an exclusively heterosexual institution.[3]

The ethical value and political advisability of some-sex marriage as a means of rectifying injustices toward gays and lesbians, promoting their welfare, and respecting their interests depends upon the ultimate defensibility of the two assumptions shared by both proponents and opponents of same-sex marriage. If the practice and institution of marriage does more harm than good for married people or for society, and if civil unions can offer the legal benefits of marriage without its disadvantages, then gays and lesbians, as well as heterosexuals, have reason to reject (same-sex) marriage in favor of civil unions.

In this essay I argue against both of the assumptions shared by proponents and opponents of same-sex marriage: I argue that civil marriage is not an institution or practice worth preserving and that we have good reasons to oppose state authorization and regulation of personal, sexual relationships.[4] I suggest that civil unions have the potential to provide a radical, progressive alternative to marriage and that, consequently, we have reason to rethink the relative value of same-sex marriage and civil unions. Admittedly, in a short paper, the arguments must be abbreviated; my aim is to outline the general shape of the overall position, in order to bring into view a possibility that has been largely overlooked in both public and academic debate on the subject of same-sex marriage.[5]

THE FIRST ASSUMPTION: THE GOODS OF MARRIAGE

The alleged goods of marriage, from a secular point of view, seem to divide into three categories: 1) the legal rights and responsibilities conferred by marital status; 2) the benefits to society of the institution of marriage; and 3) the personal rewards of a committed, loving relationship recognized in marriage. I will briefly address each in turn.[6]

Jonathan Rauch, a prominent supporter of same-sex marriage, writes, "If 1 had to pare marriage to its essential core, I would say that marriage is two people's lifelong commitment, recognized by law and by society, to care for each other."[7]

What is wrong with this claim—rather, what is false about this claim—is that the law does not "recognize," define, stipulate, or enforce any form of "care" between spouses.[8] The legal view of marriage today is virtually without content. The law determines who is eligible for marriage, licenses marriages, arbitrates divorces, and assigns special rights and responsibilities on the basis of marital status, but it says almost nothing about what marriage itself consists in; it is a contract without content. The law prescribes no behaviors, not even sexual consummation, that must be exhibited in order to marry or to stay married. It dictates no requirements for the living arrangements of married people. For example, cohabitation is not required, nor is sharing a bank account or having shared financial assets, nor is mutual care for dependents.[9] It prohibits no behaviors on the basis of marital status; not even life-threatening abuse automatically invalidates or nullifies a marriage. The law certainly does not specify the appropriate forms of care or the requirements of caregiving that married people are expected to exhibit toward a spouse. The law does not stipulate the specific obligations that a marital commitment entails. My point is not that the law ought to be specified in these ways; it is a good thing that there are no legally enforceable regulations or restrictions on the conduct of relations between married people as such. My point is, rather, that the legal significance of marriage today centers on the rights and benefits that are established by legal marital *status*. The legal significance of marriage is primarily the way that it distinguishes married people from unmarried people so as to assign certain rights and responsibilities.

For better or worse, the legal rights and responsibilities afforded by marriage are significant and non-trivial. They include financial responsibilities—for example, for a spouse's debts—but also financial benefits, such as social security benefits and transference of property without taxation. Other rights and responsibilities that attach to marital status include healthcare benefits; hospital visitation rights; jail or prison visitation rights; access to records; worker's compensation benefits; rights to make decisions about end-of-life care; child custody; rights of inheritance; tax deductions and exemptions; and many others.

Insofar as these rights and responsibilities are automatically incurred by marrying, marriage can be a mixed blessing. Depending on the individuals and their circumstances, some of these rights and responsibilities can be tremendously useful and important—such as the right to visit one's spouse in the hospital. But where a spouse is abusive, deceptive, or simply irresponsible, these same rights and responsibilities can become a tremendous burden, even an obstacle to the exercise of one's autonomy or independence. They can also make it difficult for a married person to assert his or her individual privacy, which is arguably an important personal good, or to extricate oneself from a failed or abusive relationship.[10] Although many of these rights and responsibilities are important ones, they are not necessarily goods. And insofar as they *are* goods, it is not clear why access to them should be limited to married persons. For each legal right conferred by marriage, an independent argument is required to show why *only* married people ought to have that right. If some or all of the legal rights and benefits of marriage are genuine goods, it is difficult to see why such goods should be denied to non-married people who sustain relationships of financial, emotional, and practical support with others (friends, family, lovers, children) to whom they are not married. If indeed the legal rights and benefits of marriage are goods, the presumption ought to be that all citizens ought to have access to them, regardless of marital status. In other words, simple tradition aside, the burden of proof is on those who would argue that marital status justifies a differential distribution of legal rights and benefits, not on those who would defend greater legal equality by eradicating the arbitrary or antiquated idea that marital status alone confers special rights.[11]

The *social* goods most often associated with and believed to be established by the practice and institution of marriage include promoting reproduction, providing for the welfare of children, and domesticating (young) men, suppressing their tendencies toward violence and "mischief" and encouraging them to fulfill paternal responsibilities.[12] I will not offer comprehensive arguments here to

show that these purported goods can be established without marriage or that these are not indubitable goods. With respect to the claims about reproduction and childcare, suffice it to note, in quick succession, (1) that people can and do reproduce outside of marriage; (2) that marriage does not always result in reproduction; (3) that population growth can be managed through immigration[13]; (4) that it is not obvious that population growth is a good; (5) that children can be well cared-for by non-married people; (6) that the state could promote childcare, education, and healthcare for children, rather than marriage, to ensure the welfare of children; (7) that marriage does not guarantee the emotional and educational support of fathers; and (8) that the financial support of fathers can be (and often is) legislated without marriage. In other words, marriage is neither necessary nor sufficient for establishing the social goods of reproduction and child welfare.

As for the claim about marriage domesticating men, I suspect that it is based on insupportable, essentialist views of men and women—about what their natural, essential, not socially constructed propensities are. Andrew Sullivan observes, strictly for the sake of argument, that the conservative claim seems to be that "women are naturally more prone to be stable, nurturing, supportive of stability, fiscally prudent, and family-oriented than men."[14] In marriage, it is argued, men are benefited by their association with women; they are healthier, happier, more productive, and more responsible. But even if it is true that marriage succeeds in taming the wild, restless impulses in men by their association with women, this alleged social good of marriage needs to be counterbalanced with observation of the effects of marriage on women.[15]

Specifically, the claim ignores the way in which marriage domesticates *women,* arguably a more pronounced and seriously detrimental function of marriage. The *domestication* of women may not only tame *their* wild, restless impulses, but also perpetuate women's economic dependence on men and make it difficult for them to fully participate in social and political life beyond the home. In other words, in a time in which women have access to education and to paid employment, marriage may function to reinforce women's domestic responsibilities at the expense of their greater participation in the public sphere. Marriage reinforces an expectation of shared domestic and financial responsibilities, which in itself is not necessarily a bad thing. Yet, women are still relegated to low-paying jobs and are compensated less than their male peers for the same work, and women still shoulder a disproportionate amount of domestic responsibilities (eldercare, childcare, and housework). These economic realities and domestic arrangements perpetuate a grim gender asymmetry at the heart of marriage. In marriage, women either work fulltime to sustain and care for their families, sacrificing their jobs and hence their (relative) financial independence, or pursue employment or a career while working overtime to provide care to family members and attend to the necessities of daily life (cooking, cleaning, tending the sick). Insofar as marriage is socially compulsory or is the only way to gain access to important legal rights and benefits, women may be conscripted into a living arrangement (and legal contract) that purports to secure shared responsibility and find themselves unfairly burdened by the project of "domesticating" their husbands while their own resources dwindle. In other words, the argument that marriage is a social good because in marriage men are domesticated by women overlooks two important considerations about the effects of marriage on women: First, marriage may "domesticate" women in an altogether different sense; it may confine them to domestic or family life at the expense of other pursuits, including participation in the larger political and cultural spheres. Second, it may unfairly demand that women take on the job, surely unappreciated by many husbands, of training men in the ways of stability, prudence, family, and responsibility: The wife becomes the "old ball-and-chain," the symbol of lost liberty, and the target of interpersonal resentment (even as she may come to resent her husband for the bind she's in). I hope to have carried the argument only far enough here to establish that the domestication of men in marriage, even if a social good, must be weighed

against the problems generated for women as they, too, are domesticated by marriage.[16]

I've suggested that two primary social goods—promoting reproduction and providing for the welfare of children—can be attained without marriage and that the third alleged social good of marriage, the domestication of men, tells a one-sided story, and a dubious one at that, based on questionable assumptions about gender essentialism.[17] Such considerations suggest that the alleged social goods of marriage require greater scrutiny. But even if the things marriage functions to promote *are* important social goods, a further argument must be made to show that the best or only means of attaining them is through the institution of marriage.

If the legal and social goods of marriage are dubious or can be established through other means, perhaps the appeal of marriage for both opponents and proponents of same-sex marriage lies with the *personal* goods obtainable in marriage. What are the personal goods of marriage? In addition to sheer romanticism about true love, finding a soul mate, and living happily-ever-after, among the goods that inspire people to seek marriage are the stability, personal assurance, protection from the vulnerabilities of being alone or lonely, and the prospect for mutual care and development that are thought to come with the marital commitment.[18] If, however, this kind of commitment can be exhibited and sustained outside of marriage, then gays and lesbians (and indeed heterosexuals) have access to such goods without participating in the institution of marriage.

And I see no reason to believe that such a commitment cannot be attained and sustained outside of marriage. Indeed, many gay and lesbian couples succeed in establishing just this sort of deep, lasting relationship built on mutual love and shared responsibility without being married (as do some heterosexual couples). Moreover, the high rate of divorce is compelling evidence that marriage does not succeed in guaranteeing this kind of lasting commitment.[19] And, as I've already observed, the law itself does nothing to clarify the nature of the commitment or care that spouses must exhibit, let alone to ensure or enforce it.

If the nature of the lifelong commitment to another person currently marked through marriage is distinct from the legal practice of marriage and is specified through the particular understanding and form of relating adopted by individual couples, rather than stipulated by law, then marriage is not essential to participating in this kind of commitment. The personal goods of marriage can all be achieved outside of marriage.

With respect to achieving the personal goods of a loving, committed relationship, the sole advantage that marriage provides is the force of social recognition and approval. I do not underestimate the power of this reinforcement (although, again, the divorce rate provides some evidence to the contrary). Nonetheless, it would be strange to suggest that the massive web of social expectations that structure marriage provides a normative grounding for it. (In fact, what I find remarkable is that the social reinforcement for marriage persists even though so many marriages fail, so many marriages are unhappy, and even though people can build successful relationships without marriage.) Disestablishing civil marriage could shift the weight of social expectations and reinforcements and could motivate a deeper understanding of the ethical values appropriate to caring for another person or undertaking a lifelong commitment to another person.[20] Disestablishing civil marriage might also serve to remove material incentives to marry—for the sake of shared health insurance benefits or tax breaks, for example—that may muddy the motives partners have for undertaking a serious, lifelong commitment to one another.

In this section, I have sketched the contours of an argument against the first assumption shared by many opponents and proponents of same-sex marriage. I have suggested that the legal goods of marriage ought to be available to all citizens, regardless of marital status, and that the burden of proof rests with those who would argue that marriage ought to confer special rights. I have challenged the idea that there are substantial social goods generated by marriage or only by marriage, and I have argued, by plain observation of the counterexamples, that marriage does not guarantee the personal goods that many people hope to obtain through marriage.

THE SECOND ASSUMPTION: A STATE INTEREST IN MARRIAGE

The presumptive state interest in marriage is usually thought to consist in the social goods that marriage functions to establish: promoting reproduction, providing for the welfare of children, and domesticating men. I suggested in the first section that the first and last are not unquestionably goods, and that the first and second may be secured through other means. I think this is a good *prima facie* case against a strong state interest in marriage. A further argument against a state interest in marriage might be summoned by looking at the intertwining of civil marriage and religious marriage practices in the United States, where separation of church and state is, arguably, intended not only to allow for freedom of religious practice, but also freedom from religion. Insofar as current marriage contracts are devoid of content—the contracting parties take on no specific, legally enforceable obligations with respect to each other—it appears that civil marriage is but a relic of religious practices, that ought properly to be left to religion. Exploring such arguments is not my aim here. In this section, I want to suggest that, absent compelling arguments for a strong state interest in marriage, we have reason to favor civil unions as a superior alternative to civil marriage, contrary to the views of both proponents and opponents of same-sex marriage.

Although many liberals and progressives have decried civil unions as a second-class alternative to marriage that would perpetuate the marginalization of gays and lesbians,[21] civil unions could provide an alternative model for both heterosexual and homosexual couples and an opportunity to reconceive the appropriate role of the state in personal and sexual relationships. The idea that civil unions would represent a departure from the (sexist, patriarchal) history of marriage and its accreted social expectations is a reason to favor them (rather than denounce them as an unacceptable substitute for marriage). It is also reason to think carefully about the potential for civil unions to constitute a substantively different approach to the relation between government sanction or authority and personal relationships.

Because the law gives no substantial content to marriage, the law does little to establish the value of marriage and provides little recourse to married people who believe their spouse has reneged on perceived marital responsibilities, while holding married people accountable for and subject to forms of regulation that may not benefit them. Whatever forms of action may properly be thought to indicate or manifest a morally defensible form of interpersonal commitment, wedding vows and the speech acts that establish a couple as married do nothing to specify them. The inherent indeterminateness and comprehensiveness of personal commitments makes them ill-suited to government regulation.[22] The private and moral nature of personal commitments should be shielded from unwarranted government interference or regulation. To the extent that marriage is designed to promote such commitments, to that extent the government should stay out of marriage. To the extent dial certain, specific legal rights and responsibilities attach to marriage, it should be viewed as an explicit, contractual relationship. But if these rights and responsibilities are made explicit and incurred voluntarily by consenting adults, they should be available to everyone, regardless of sexual orientation and without reference to the sexual or intimate nature of the relationship between the contracting parties. Civil unions have the potential to be shaped toward these ends.

Civil unions could be conceived as contractual relations, giving those who desire the safeguards of governmental regulation or adjudication the opportunity to specify the relevant terms of their relationship and the conditions under which it is dissolved, without giving the government any further say in how the couple is to arrange their lives, exhibit their love, or manifest their commitment—unwanted forms of government intrusion into the most private of our affairs. Moreover, civil unions—as the vagueness of the tide aptly suggests—could be conceived as a means for one to choose the person in one's life who will be the recipient of (some or all of) the social rights and benefits that normally attach to marriage, without the signification that one has an intimate, romantic, or sexual relationship with that person. In other words, one could choose the person most in need of such systems of support, whether that is one's lover, one's parent, or one's friend. One could even enter into multiple civil unions, specifying their contractual obligations distinctly. Although some paperwork would be required, I doubt that a shortage of lawyers will impede our ability to invent a variety of appropriate forms and designations by which one could individualize one's civil union(s) and its contractual obligations.[23]

Disestablishing marriage in favor of civil unions could have other benefits. Civil unions could inspire people to reflect more seriously on the choices they make regarding their legal obligations to others and the appropriate role of government in sanctioning, endorsing, and interfering in personal and sexual relationships. Civil unions could allow us to perceive more cleanly the break between church and state in the governing of our personal and familial lives, thereby opening the door to public policies that are less controlled by the intertwining history of legal and religious interests in marriage, family, and the control of women and children. Moreover, a lively public debate about the potential of a contractual notion of civil unions could call attention to the fact that all citizens, not just those who are married, should have their basic needs met in times of sickness, disability, or unemployment. Given the practical and economic impact of the rights and benefits that currently attach to marriage, it is worth asking why access to them is limited to marriage and not more widely available to all citizens regardless of their chosen forms of personal and sexual relationships.

In time, if civil unions came to replace or outnumber (religious) marriages, their contractual nature could inspire people to reflect more substantively on what the goods of interpersonal relationships are, what comprises a genuine commitment to someone, and what is required to fulfill the substantial moral obligation of a personal commitment. Although these suggestions regarding the potential of civil unions—as opposed to same-sex marriage—may seem far-fetched, they are not too far removed from some current legislation and policy regarding domestic partnerships, civil unions, guardianship, and health-care surrogates. In these various legal arrangements, adults choose to acquire particular legal rights and responsibilities regarding their relations with particular others. Whereas the state of Vermont established civil unions as a way of giving gay and lesbian couples access to the panoply of benefits conferred by marriage (but without attaining the title of participation in the institution of marriage itself), what I am suggesting is somewhat different: Civil marriage ought to be replaced with civil unions, which can be entered into as individualized contracts by consenting adults who choose from among a variety of legal rights and responsibilities those that they wish to exercise. On my conception, civil unions would not merely replicate marriage, constituting a "separate but equal" institution; rather, civil unions would give consenting adults choices about how to organize the financial and material components of their personal relationships and about how much, if any, government involvement in their personal relationships they desire. Moreover, because civil unions have no religious counterpart and no history of sexism, civil unions have the potential to organize personal relations in a manner that is free from gender norms, which still deeply inform and construct current marriage practice. Although same-sex marriage *may* have the power to symbolically disrupt the gender-identifications that underwrite the social roles of wife and husband (as I discussed in the last section), civil unions *already* represent a break with the tradition of sex-based gender identifications and hence with patriarchy.

One outstanding concern is that marriage is recognized from state to state; whereas, it is currently unclear what status civil unions licensed in one state will have in another. Considering that a growing number of states are passing laws foreclosing recognition of same-sex marriages licensed in other states, in accord with the federal Defense of Marriage Act (DOMA) that established this state prerogative, the prospect of interstate recognition of civil unions could prove to be a fortuitous loophole in the systematic effort to deny legal recognition of same-sex marriages. Somewhat curiously, DOMA says that

> No State, territory, or possession of the United States, or Indian tribe, shall be required to give effect to any public act, record, or judicial proceeding of any other State, territory, possession, or tribe respecting a relationship between persons of the same sex *that is treated as a marriage* under the laws of such other State, territory, possession, or tribe, or a right or claim arising from such relationship.[24] [emphasis added]

This language seems to allow that so long as civil unions are conceived as I have suggested—as particular contractual arrangements that are *not* designed to mimic and replicate marriage contracts—States may be required to recognize them; whereas, if civil unions are designed to imitate marriage, as they are in Vermont, other States will not be required to recognize them. I merely observe this here in order to point out that retaining the rights gained *via* civil unions when crossing state borders will depend upon whether the State conferring the civil union takes it to be a substitution for marriage. In addition to providing the same legal goods as marriage, civil unions might offer other legal options and benefits that marriage lacks.[25]

CONCLUSION

One may wonder whether political wisdom does not recommend suspending the larger critique of the general practice of marriage and advancing the cause of same-sex marriage in order to promote shorter-term, more realistic social and political ends. Accordingly, advancing the cause of same-sex marriage would unquestionably delay a full-scale assault on the general practice of marriage and would favor more immediate gains for gays and lesbians. With access to marriage, gay and lesbian relationships could enjoy greater social visibility and acceptance, and the end to legal discrimination would bring gay and lesbian couples the same rights and benefits that married heterosexuals now enjoy, a substantial, concrete improvement in the lives of many same-sex couples. This argument is important. The trade-off is between a full-scale and fundamental critique and disestablishment of civil marriage and a more limited, but more realistic and achievable aim of expanding the current practice of marriage to include same-sex couples. This easily appears to be a choice between an unobtainable ideal or ethical end, on the one hand, and a concrete, not-insignificant political end, on the other. Whatever political strategy is ultimately advisable, it is important to scrutinize our ends in philosophical and ethical terms. Civil unions could provide a more flexible and individualized and less intrusive form of government involvement in interpersonal relations; make key rights and responsibilities open to all citizens without concern for sexual orientation or marital status; inspire a more socially just distribution of goods such as healthcare; challenge the patriarchal organization of family life; undermine the presumptive state interest in sexuality; and inspire deeper public reflection about the value of committed relationships. A critique of marriage suggests that civil unions may provide a socially progressive, politically radical, and ethically defensible alternative to same-sex marriage.

—Brook J. Sadler
University of South Florida Tampa

NOTES

*Work on this paper was supported, in part, by the University of South Florida Internal Awards Program under Grant Number R043929. I am grateful to many people for comments on drafts of this paper and for discussion of the topic, including Steven Geisz, Avram Hiller, Rebecca Kukla, Eva LaFollette, Hugh LaFollette, Eddy Nahmias, Bruce Silver, and participants at the 2006 Eastern Division meeting of the Society for Women in Philosophy.

1. I focus my discussion on the debate in the United States, though some of what I argue is applicable to other liberal democracies. The outcome of debate concerning same-sex marriage has taken different forms in different jurisdictions. For example, the State of Massachusetts has legalized same-sex marriage; the United Kingdom's 2004 Civil Partnership Act adopts civil unions, open only to same-sex partners, that mimic the legal rights of marriage; and the Netherlands has recognized civil partnerships that are open to both same-sex and opposite-sex couples.

2. In *Baehr* v. *Lewin* (1993), the Supreme Court of Hawaii found that barring same-sex marriage was unconstitutional insofar as it violated equal protection by discriminating on the basis of *sex*. Cheshire Calhoun (2000) discusses the link between sex and gender, on the one hand, and same-sex marriage, on the other, in "Defending Marriage" (reprinted in Alan Soble, ed., *The Philosophy of Sex*, Lanham, MD: Rowman and Littlefield, 2002).

3. The United States Congress approved the Defense of Marriage Act (DOMA) in September 1996. DOMA allows states not to recognize same-sex marriages licensed by other states. It also provides a federal definition of marriage: "the word 'marriage' means only a legal union between one man and one woman as husband and wife." The text of DOMA is reprinted in Andrew Sullivan, ed., (2004) *Same-Sex Marriage Pro & Con: A Reader,* 2nd ed'n. (New York: Vintage Books). John Boswell (1994) challenges the presumption that marriage has always been exclusively heterosexual in *Same Sex Unions in Pre-Modern Europe* (New York: Villard Books).

4. I will not address the question of whether the religious practice of marriage is worth preserving. Note that the disestablishment of *civil* marriage is perfectly compatible with maintaining religious practices of marriage in a nation that separates church and state.

5. Critical discussions of marriage in the philosophical literature include Claudia Card, "Against Marriage" (in *Same Sex: Debating the Ethics, Science, and Culture of Homosexuality,* John Corvino, ed. Lanham, MD: Rowman and Littlefield, 1997); Ralph Wedgwood, "Same-Sex Marriage: A Philosophical Defense" and Richard D. Mohr, "The Case for Gay Marriage" (both in *Philosophy and Sex,* 3rd ed'n., Robert Baker, *et al.,* eds. Amherst, NY: Prometheus, 1998); Jeff Jordan, "Contra Same-Sex Marriage" (reprinted in *Taking Sides,* 11th ed'n., Stephen Satris, ed., McGraw Hill, 2008); and Dan Moller's "An Argument Against Marriage" (2003) in *Philosophy,* 78, pp. 79–91. For relevant discussions of the history of marriage, see Denis de Rougemont (1940), *Love in the Western World* (Princeton, NJ: Princeton University Press); John Boswell (1994), *op. cit.*; and Stephanie Coontz (2005), *Marriage, A History: From Obedience to Intimacy or How Love Conquered Marriage* (New York: Viking). A useful compilation of disparate views on same-sex marriage can be found in Andrew Sullivan (2004), *op. cit.*, and in Lynn D. Wardle, et al., eds., *Marriage and Same-Sex Unions: A Debate* (Westport, CT: Praeger, 2003). Jonathan Rauch (2004), *Gay Marriage: Why It Is Good for Gays, Good for Straights, and Good for America* (New York: Henry Holt and Company) provides the most thorough-going argument for same-sex marriage.

6. I restrict my attention to marriage as recognized by the state to avoid the substantial complications involved in invoking the religious history of marriage; however, I think a reasonable argument, grounded in part on the separation of church and state in the U.S., can be offered to show that the state has no legitimate interest in marriage.

7. Jonathan Rauch, *op. cit.,* p. 24.

8. It is not clear that the law enforces "commitment" either, and with the advent of no-fault divorce laws, it certainly does not insist that the commitment be "lifelong."

9. To apply for domestic partnership, typically one must prove the seriousness of one's commitment to the partner by giving evidence of cohabitation, shared finances, mutual care for dependents (children), etc. No such evidence

is required either to marry or to remain married, with the exception of immigrants seeking American citizenship who marry American citizens.

10. Claudia Card addressed this point in a symposium paper at the Eastern Division meeting of the American Philosophical Association in December of 2004. It also arises in her essay "Against Marriage," *op. cit.*

11. Indeed, the history of civil marriage suggests that its *raison d' être* consisted in protecting male interests. The legal content of marriage consisted primarily in sexist laws that gave husbands control and authority over their wives, their wives' property, and their children. As these sexist laws have been overturned and eradicated, civil marriage has been emptied of content. Arguably, the popularity of civil marriage rose as the middle-class grew, expanding the need for protecting and controlling private property. Marriage continues to serve this function. Insofar as the protection and control of private property is important, marital status ought not to be a determinant in gaining access to the relevant civil protections.

12. Jonathan Rauch *(op. cit.,* pp.18–21) argues that domesticating or civilizing young men and "providing reliable caregivers" are the two primary purposes of marriage. Another alleged social function of marriage (or state interest in marriage) concerns safeguarding public health through the control of sexually transmitted diseases. Given the high rates of premarital sex and adultery and the availability of condoms, it is not at all clear that marriage can or need serve this function.

13. U.S. reproduction rates are relatively low, but population growth is considered healthy (by economists) due in part to immigration. Unlike Japan, where the birthrate is very low and anti-immigration policies are in effect, the U.S. does not face the prospect of a depleted workforce. For information regarding the situation in Japan, see Martin Muhliesen and Hamid Faruqee's "Japan: Population Aging and the Fiscal Challenge" *(IMF's Finance and Development,* 38, 1, 2001), and the Japanese Ministry of International Affairs and Communications' Statistics Bureau website at: (www.stat.go.jp/english/data/handbook/c02).

14. Andrew Sullivan, *op cit.,* pp. 151–52. Sullivan is responding to the domestication argument as presented by Hadley Arkes.

15. Marriage clearly does not succeed in stopping male violence, though it is conceivable that it redirects it—toward women. Domestic violence against women often occurs within marriage; those who argue that marriage functions to curb men's violence should not ignore this significant fact.

16. There is good empirical evidence that women are overrepresented in low-paying or dead-end jobs and in domestic-service jobs, are underrepresented in political life, and are responsible for a larger proportion of childcare and domestic labor (regardless of whether they work outside the home) than their husbands, etc. And although some women's expectations regarding married life picture a more equitable domestic arrangement, the social ideal of the stay-at-home mom or housewife is still prominent. But the point about the domestication of women is not merely an empirical one, nor a claim about women's own attitudes in seeking marriage; it is a conceptual point about how the complex interplay between the public and the private (domestic) reinforces (or generates) a gendered division of labor and gender asymmetry in the socio-political world. Data on women in the labor force in the United States can be found at the U.S. Department of Labor Bureau of Labor Statistics website at: http://www.bls.gov/cps/wlf-databook2006.htm.

17. It is also based on questionable statistical measures about the health and happiness of married men. Andrew Sullivan considers this problem, but quickly passes over it (Sullivan, *op. cit.,* p. 151).

18. Rauch *(op. cit.)* argues that such personal goods comprise the intrinsic value of marriage. I agree that these things are *goods*, but not that they are intrinsic to marriage; they can be attained outside of marriage. The desire to have children is often said to be the attraction or even the purpose of marriage. I would argue that having and raising children can be done outside of marriage, and to the extent that people desire having children within marriage, it is largely because of the normative ideal of marriage, which I discuss briefly below.

19. Exactly how to determine the divorce rate is a matter of some dispute. The National Center for Health Statistics, which tracks the number of marriages and divorces, puts the number of divorces at about half the number of marriages in recent years; but, this does not necessarily mean that half of those who marry will divorce. Even so, low estimates put the divorce rate at 41 percent. See Dan Hurley's article, "Divorce Rate: It's Not as High as You Think" *(New York Times,* April 19, 2005) and the NCHS website at: www.cdc.gov/nchs/fastats/divorce.htm.

20. It is worth noting that a lifelong commitment to care for a spouse is a burden that falls disproportionately on women, who are more likely to outlive their husbands, which means that they are more likely to have to provide substantial support for their aging husbands and to be left without such support when they are widowed. Such a lifelong commitment has become increasingly difficult to fulfill as average life expectancy has risen.

21. For a leading example, see Evan Wolfson's contributions to *Marriage and Same-Sex Unions: A Debate* (Lynn D. Wardle, et al., eds. Westport, CT: Praeger, 2003).

22. I have provided an analysis of this point in "Two Kinds of Obligation: Commitments and Promises" (unpublished manuscript).

23. Living wills and testamentary wills already operate in a similar fashion; within a certain range of choices, there are several standard ways of writing a living will to express one's individual desires regarding end-of-life care.

24. DOMA, reprinted in Sullivan (2004), *op. cit.,* pp. 206–07, emphasis added.

25. For a discussion of Vermont's civil unions law, see Greg Johnson's "Vermont Civil Unions: A Success Story" (in *Marriage and Same-Sex Unions: A Debate, op. cit.,* pp. 284–93). Johnson argues that other states have reason to recognize civil unions licensed in Vermont. I differ from Johnson insofar as he embraces the very close parallel between Vermont's civil unions and marriage. In considering the potential of civil unions, I suggest that some differences from current law regarding marriage and benefits that attach to marital status would be a good thing.

Is it Wrong to Discriminate on the Basis of Homosexuality?

Jeff Jordan

Jeff Jordan is professor of philosophy at the University of Delaware. He works in the areas of philosophy of religion, ethics, and social philosophy.

    Jordan argues that in some situations, discrimination against homosexuals can be justified. He focuses on the example of marriage, arguing that public policy ramifications of gay marriage make it justifiable not to allow homosexuals to marry even though we allow heterosexuals to marry.

Much like the issue of abortion in the early 1970s, the issue of homosexuality has exploded to the forefront of social discussion. Is homosexual sex on a moral par with heterosexual sex? Or is homosexuality in some way morally inferior? Is it wrong to discriminate against homosexuals—to treat homosexuals in less favorable ways than one does heterosexuals? Or is some discrimination against homosexuals morally justified? These questions are the focus of this essay.

    In what follows, I argue that there are situations in which it is morally permissible to discriminate against homosexuals because of their homosexuality. That is, there are some morally relevant differences between heterosexuality and homosexuality which, in some instances, permit a difference in treatment. The issue of marriage provides a good example. While it is clear that heterosexual unions merit the state recognition known as marriage, along with all the attendant advantages—spousal insurance coverage, inheritance rights, ready eligibility of adoption—it is far

from clear that homosexual couples ought to be accorded that state recognition.

    The argument of this essay makes no claim about the moral status of homosexuality per se. Briefly put, it is the argument of this essay that the moral impasse generated by conflicting views concerning homosexuality, and the public policy ramifications of those conflicting views justify the claim that it is morally permissible, in certain circumstances, to discriminate against homosexuals.[1]

1. THE ISSUE

The relevant issue is this: Does homosexuality have the same moral status as heterosexuality? Put differently, since there are no occasions in which it is morally permissible to treat heterosexuals unfavorably, whether because they are heterosexual or because of heterosexual acts, are there occasions in which it is morally permissible to treat homosexuals unfavorably, whether because they are homosexuals or because of homosexual acts?

    A negative answer to the above can be termed the "parity thesis." The parity thesis contends that *homosexuality has the same moral status as heterosexuality.* If the parity thesis is correct, then it

Excerpt from Jeff Jordan, "Is it wrong to discriminate on the basis of homosexuality?" *Journal of Social Philosophy*, Vol. 25, No. 1, Spring 1995, pp. 39–52.

would be immoral to discriminate against homosexuals because of their homosexuality. An affirmative answer can be termed the "difference thesis" and contends that there are morally relevant differences between heterosexuality and homosexuality which justify a difference in moral status and treatment between homosexuals and heterosexuals. The difference thesis entails that *there are situations in which it is normally permissible to discriminate against homosexuals.*

It is perhaps needless to point out that the difference thesis follows as long as there is at least one occasion in which it is morally permissible to discriminate against homosexuals. If the parity thesis were true, then on no occasion would a difference in treatment between heterosexuals and homosexuals ever be justified. The difference thesis does not, even if true, justify discriminatory actions on every occasion. Nonetheless, even though the scope of the difference thesis is relatively modest, it is, if true, a significant principle which has not only theoretical import but import practical consequences as well.[2]

A word should be said about the notion of discrimination. To discriminate against X means treating X in an unfavorable way. The word "discrimination" is not a synonym for "morally unjustifiable treatment." Some discrimination is morally unjustifiable; some is not. For example, we discriminate against convicted felons in that they are disenfranchised. This legal discrimination is morally permissible even though it involves treating one person unfavorably different from how other persons are treated. The difference thesis entails that there are circumstances in which it is morally permissible to discriminate against homosexuals.

2. AN ARGUMENT FOR THE PARITY THESIS

One might suppose that an appeal to a moral right, the right to privacy, perhaps, or the right to liberty, would provide the strongest grounds for the parity thesis. Rights talk, though sometimes helpful, is not very helpful here. If there is reason to think that the right to privacy or the right to liberty encompasses sexuality (which seems plausible enough), it would do so only with regard to private

acts and not public acts. Sexual acts performed in public (whether heterosexual or homosexual) are properly suppressible. It does not take too much imagination to see that the right to be free from offense would soon be offered as a counter consideration by those who find homosexuality morally problematic. Furthermore, how one adjudicates between the competing rights claims is far from clear. Hence, the bald appeal to a right will not, in this case anyway, take one very far.

Perhaps the strongest reason to hold that the parity thesis is true is something like the following:

(1) Homosexual acts between consenting adults harm no one. And,

(2) respecting persons' privacy and choices in harmless sexual matters maximizes individual freedom. And,

(3) individual freedom should be maximized. But,

(4) discrimination against homosexuals, because of their homosexuality, diminishes individual freedom since it ignores personal choice and privacy. So,

(5) the toleration of homosexuality rather than discriminating against homosexuals is the preferable option since it would maximize individual freedom. Therefore,

(6) the parity thesis is more plausible than the difference thesis.

Premise (2) is unimpeachable: if an act is harmless and if there are persons who want to do it and who choose to do it, then it seems clear that respecting the choices of those people would tend to maximize their freedom.[3] Step (3) is also beyond reproach: since freedom is arguably a great good and since there does not appear to be any ceiling on the amount of individual freedom—no "too much of a good thing"—(3) appears to be true.

At first glance, premise (1) seems true enough as long as we recognize that if there is any harm involved in the homosexual acts of consenting adults, it would be harm absorbed by the freely consenting participants. This is true, however, only if the acts in question are done in private. Public acts may involve more than just the willing participants. Persons who have no desire to participate, even if only as spectators, may have no choice if the acts are done in public. A real probability of there being unwilling participants is indicative of the public realm and not the private. However, where one draws the line between private acts and public acts is not always easy to discern, it is clear that different moral standards apply to public acts than to private acts.[4]

If premise (1) is understood to apply only to acts done in private, then it would appear to be true. The same goes for (4): discrimination against homosexuals for acts done in private would result in a diminishing of freedom. So (1)–(4) would lend support to (5) only if we understand (1)–(4) to refer to acts done in private. Hence, (5) must be understood as referring to private acts; and, as a consequence, (6) also must be read as referring only to acts done in private.

With regard to acts which involve only willing adult participants, there may be no morally relevant difference between homosexuality and heterosexuality. In other words, acts done in private. However, acts done in public add a new ingredient to the mix; an ingredient which has moral consequence. Consequently, the argument (1)–(6) fails in supporting the parity thesis. The argument (1)–(6) may show that there are some circumstances in which the moral status of homosexuality and heterosexuality are the same, but it gives us no reason for thinking that this result holds for all circumstances.[5]

3. MORAL IMPASSES AND PUBLIC DILEMMAS

Suppose one person believes that X is morally wrong, while another believes that X is morally permissible. The two people, let's stipulate, are not involved in a semantical quibble; they hold genuinely conflicting beliefs regarding the moral status of X. If the first person is correct, then the second person is wrong; and, of course, if the second person is right, then the first must be wrong. This situation of conflicting claims is what we will call an "impasse." Impasses arise out of moral disputes. Since the conflicting parties in an impasse take contrary views, the conflicting views cannot all be true, nor can they all be false.[6] Moral impasses may concern matters only of a personal nature, but moral impasses can involve public policy. An impasse is likely to have public policy ramifications if large numbers of people hold the conflicting views, and the conflict involves matters which are fundamental to a person's moral identity

(and, hence, from a practical point of view, are probably irresolvable) and it involves acts done in public. Since not every impasse has public policy ramifications, one can mark off "public dilemma" as a special case of moral impasses: those moral impasses that have public policy consequences. Public dilemmas, then, are impasses located in the public square. Since they have public policy ramifications and since they arise from impasses, one side or another of the dispute will have its views implemented as public policy. Because of the public policy ramifications, and also because social order is sometimes threatened by the volatile parties involved in the impasse, the state has a role to play in resolving a public dilemma.

A public dilemma can be actively resolved in two ways.[7] The first is when the government allies itself with one side of the impasse and, by state coercion and sanction, declares that side of the impasse the correct side. The American Civil War was an example of this: the federal government forcibly ended slavery by aligning itself with the Abolitionist side of the impasse.[8] Prohibition is another example. The 18th Amendment and the Volstead Act allied the state with the Temperance side of the impasse. State mandated affirmative action programs provide a modern example of this. This kind of resolution of a public dilemma we can call a "resolution by declaration." The first of the examples cited above indicates that declarations can be morally proper, the right thing to do. The second example, however, indicates that declarations are not always morally proper. The state does not always take the side of the morally correct; nor is it always clear which side is the correct one.

The second way of actively resolving a public dilemma is that of accommodation. An accommodation in this context means resolving the public dilemma in a way that gives as much as possible to all sides of the impasse. A resolution by accommodation involves staking out some middle ground in a dispute and placing public policy in that location. The middle ground location of a resolution via accommodation is a virtue since it entails that there are no absolute victors and no absolute losers. The middle ground is reached in order to resolve the public dilemma in a way which respects the relevant views of the conflicting parties and which maintains social order. The Federal Fair Housing Act and, perhaps, the current status of abortion (legal but with restrictions) provide examples of actual resolutions via accommodation.[9]

In general, governments should be, at least as far as possible, neutral with regard to the disputing parties in a public dilemma. Unless there is some overriding reason why the state should take sides in a public dilemma—the protection of innocent life, or abolishing slavery, for instance—the state should be neutral, because no matter which side of the public dilemma the state takes, the other side will be the recipient of unequal treatment by the state. A state which is partial and takes sides in moral disputes via declaration, when there is no overriding reason why it should, is tyrannical. Overriding reasons involve, typically, the protection of generally recognized rights.[10] In the case of slavery, the right to liberty; in the case of protecting innocent life, the right involved is the negative right to life. If a public dilemma must be actively resolved, the state should do so (in the absence of an overriding reason) via accommodation and not declaration since the latter entails that a sizable number of people would be forced to live under a government which "legitimizes" and does not just tolerate activities which they find immoral. Resolution via declaration is appropriate only if there is an overriding reason for the state to throw its weight behind one side in a public dilemma.

Is moral rightness an overriding reason for a resolution via declaration? What better reason might there be for a resolution by declaration than that it is the right thing to do? Unless one is prepared to endorse a view that is called "legal moralism"—that immorality alone is a sufficient reason for the state to curtail individual liberty—then one had best hold that moral rightness alone is not an overriding reason. Since some immoral acts neither harm nor offend nor violate another's rights, it seems clear enough that too much liberty would be lost if legal moralism were adopted as public policy.[11]

Though we do not have a definite rule for determining *a priori* which moral impasses genuinely constitute public dilemmas, we can proceed via a case by case method. For example, many people hold that cigarette smoking is harmful and, on that basis, is properly suppressible. Others

disagree. Is this a public dilemma? Probably not. Whether someone engages in an imprudent action is, as long as it involves no unwilling participants, a private matter and does not, on that account, constitute a public dilemma. What about abortion? Is abortion a public dilemma? Unlike cigarette smoking, abortion is a public dilemma. This is clear from the adamant and even violent contrary positions involved in the impasse. Abortion is an issue which forces itself into the public square. So, it is clear that, even though we lack a rule which filters through moral impasses designating some as public dilemmas, not every impasse constitute a public dilemma.

4. CONFLICTING CLAIMS ON HOMOSEXUALITY

The theistic tradition, Judaism and Christianity and Islam, has a clear and deeply entrenched position on homosexual acts: they are prohibited. Now it seems clear enough that if one is going to take seriously the authoritative texts of the respective religions, then one will have to adopt the views of those texts, unless one wishes to engage in a demythologizing of them with the result that one ends up being only a nominal adherent of that tradition.[12] As a consequence, many contemporary theistic adherents of the theistic tradition, in no small part because they can read, hold that homosexual behavior is sinful. Though God loves the homosexual, these folk say, God hates the sinful behavior. To say that act X is a sin entails that X is morally wrong, not necessarily because it is harmful or offensive, but because X violates God's will. So, the claim that homosexuality is sinful entails the claim that it is also morally wrong. And, it is clear, many people adopt the difference thesis just because of their religious views: because the Bible or the Koran holds that homosexuality is wrong, they too hold that view.

Well, what should we make of these observations? We do not, for one thing, have to base our moral conclusions on those views, if for no other reason than not every one is a theist. If one does not adopt the religion-based moral view, one must still respect those who do; they cannot just be dismissed out of hand.[13] And, significantly, this situation yields a reason for thinking that the difference thesis is probably true. Because many religious people sincerely believe homosexual acts to be morally wrong and many others believe that homosexual acts are not morally wrong, there results a public dilemma.[14]

The existence of this public dilemma gives us reason for thinking that the difference thesis is true. It is only via the difference thesis and not the parity thesis, that an accommodation can be reached. Here again, the private/public distinction will come into play.

To see this, take as an example the issue of homosexual marriages. A same-sex marriage would be a public matter. For the government to sanction same-sex marriages—to grant the recognition and reciprocal benefits which attach to marriage—would ally the government with one side of the public dilemma and against the adherents of religion-based moralities. This is especially true given that, historically, no government has sanctioned same-sex marriages. The status quo has been no same-sex marriages. If the state were to change its practice now, it would be clear that the state has taken sides in the impasse. Given the history, for a state to sanction a same-sex marriage now would not be a neutral act.

Of course, some would respond here that by not sanctioning same sex marriages, the state is, and historically has been, taking sides to the detriment of homosexuals. There is some truth in this claim. But one must be careful here. The respective resolutions of this issue—whether the state should recognize and sanction same-sex marriages—do not have symmetrical implications. The asymmetry of this issue is a function of the private/public distinction and the fact that marriage is a public matter. If the state sanctions same-sex marriages, then there is no accommodation available. In that event, the religion-based morality proponents are faced with a public, state-sanctioned matter which they find seriously immoral. This would be an example of a resolution via declaration. On the other hand, if the state does not sanction same-sex marriages, there is an accommodation available: in the public realm the state sides with the religion-based moral view, but the state can tolerate private homosexual acts. That is,

since homosexual acts are not essentially public acts, they can be, and historically have been, performed in private. The state, by not sanctioning same-sex marriages is acting in the public realm, but it can leave the private realm to personal choice.[15]

5. THE ARGUMENT FROM CONFLICTING CLAIMS

It was suggested in the previous section that the public dilemma concerning homosexuality, and in particular whether states should sanction same-sex marriages, generates an argument in support of the difference thesis. The argument, again using same-sex marriages as the particular case, is as follows:

(7) There are conflicting claims regarding whether the state should sanction same-sex marriages. And,

(8) this controversy constitutes a public dilemma. And,

(9) there is an accommodation possible if the state does not recognize same-sex marriages. And,

(10) there is no accommodation possible if the state does sanction same-sex marriages. And,

(11) there is no overriding reason for a resolution via declaration. Hence,

(12) the state ought not sanction same-sex marriages. And,

(13) the state ought to sanction heterosexual marriages. So,

(14) there is at least one morally relevant case in which discrimination against homosexuals, because of their homosexuality, is morally permissible. Therefore,

(15) the difference thesis is true.

Since proposition (14) is logically equivalent to the difference thesis, then, if (7)–(14) are sound, proposition (15) certainly follows.

Premises (7) and (8) are uncontroversial. Premises (9) and (10) are based on the asymmetry that results from the public nature of marriage. Proposition (11) is based on our earlier analysis of the argument (1)–(6). Since the strongest argument in support of the parity thesis fails, we have reason to think that there is no overriding reason why the state ought to resolve the public dilemma via declaration in favor of same-sex marriages. We have reason, in other words, to think that (11) is true.

Proposition (12) is based on the conjunction of (7)–(11) and the principle that, in the absence of an overriding reason for state intervention via declaration, resolution by accommodation is the preferable route. Proposition (13) is just trivially true. So, given the moral difference mentioned in (12) and (13), proposition (14) logically follows.

6. TWO OBJECTIONS CONSIDERED

The first objection to the argument from conflicting claims would contend that it is unsound because a similar sort of argument would permit discrimination against some practice which, though perhaps controversial at some earlier time, is now widely thought to be morally permissible. Take mixed-race marriages, for example. The opponent of the argument from conflicting claims could argue that a similar argument would warrant prohibition against mixed-race marriages. If it does, we would have good reason to reject (7)–(14) as unsound.

There are three responses to this objection. The first response denies that the issue of mixed-race marriages is in fact a public dilemma. It may have been so at one time, but it does not seem to generate much, if any, controversy today. Hence, the objection is based upon a faulty analogy.

The second response grants for the sake of the argument that the issue of mixed-race marriages generates a public dilemma. But the second response points out that there is a relevant difference between mixed-race marriages and same-sex marriages that allows for a resolution by declaration in the case but not the other. As evident from the earlier analysis of the argument in support of (1)–(6), there is reason to think that there is no overriding reason for a resolution by declaration in support of the parity thesis. On the other hand, it is a settled matter that state protection from racial discrimination is a reason sufficient for a resolution via declaration. Hence, the two cases are only apparently similar, and, in reality, they are crucially different. They are quite different because, clearly enough, if mixed-race marriages do generate a public dilemma, the state should use resolution by declaration in support of such marriages. The same cannot be said for same-sex marriages.

One should note that the second response to the objection does not beg the question against the proponent of the parity thesis. Though the second response denies that race and sexuality are strict analogues, it does so for a defensible and independent reason: it is a settled matter that race is not a sufficient reason for disparate treatment; but, as we have seen from the analysis of (1)–(6), there is no overriding reason to think the same about sexuality.[16]

The third response to the first objection is that the grounds of objection differ in the respective cases: one concerns racial identity; the other concerns behavior thought to be morally problematic. A same-sex marriage would involve behavior which many people find morally objectionable; a mixed-race marriage is objectionable to some, not because of the participants' behavior, but because of the racial identity of the participants. It is the race of the marriage partners which some find of primary complaint concerning mixed-race marriages. With same-sex marriages, however, it is the behavior which is primarily objectionable. To see this latter point, one should note that, though promiscuously Puritan in tone, the kind of sexual acts that are likely involved in a same-sex marriage are objectionable to some, regardless of whether done by homosexuals or heterosexuals.[17] So again, there is reason to reject the analogy between same-sex marriages and mixed-race marriages. Racial identity is an immutable trait and a complaint about mixed-race marriages necessarily involves, then, a complaint about an immutable trait. Sexual behavior is not an immutable trait and it is possible to object to same-sex marriages based on the behavior which would be involved in such marriages. Put succinctly, the third response could be formulated as follows: objections to mixed-race marriages necessarily involve objections over status, while objections to same-sex marriages could involve objections over behavior. Therefore, the two cases are not analogues since there is a significant modal difference in the ground of the objection.

The second objection to the argument from conflicting claims can be stated so: if homosexuality is biologically based—if it is inborn[18]—then how can discrimination ever be justified? If it is not a matter of choice, homosexuality is an immutable trait which is, as a consequence, morally permissible.

Just as it would be absurd to hold someone morally culpable for being of a certain race, likewise it would be absurd to hold someone morally culpable for being a homosexual. Consequently, according to this objection, the argument from conflicting claims "legitimizes" unjustifiable discrimination.

But this second objection is not cogent, primarily because it ignores an important distinction. No one could plausibly hold that homosexuals act by some sort of biological compulsion. If there is a biological component involved in sexual identity, it would incline but it would not compel. Just because one naturally (without any choice) has certain dispositions, is not in itself a morally cogent reason for acting upon that disposition. Most people are naturally selfish, but it clearly does not follow that selfishness is in any way permissible on that account. Even if it is true that one has a predisposition to do X as a matter of biology and not as a matter of choice, it does not follow that doing X is morally permissible. For example, suppose that pyromania is an inborn predisposition. Just because one has an inborn and, in that sense, natural desire to set fires, one still has to decide whether or not to act on that desire.[19] The reason that the appeal to biology is specious is that it ignores the important distinction between being a homosexual and homosexual acts. One is status; the other is behavior. Even if one has the status naturally, it does not follow that the behavior is morally permissible, nor that others have a duty to tolerate the behavior.

But, while moral permissibility does not necessarily follow if homosexuality should turn out to be biologically based, what does follow is this: in the absence of a good reason to discriminate between homosexuals and heterosexuals, then, assuming that homosexuality is inborn, one ought not discriminate between them. If a certain phenomenon X is natural in the sense of being involuntary and nonpathological, and if there is no good reason to hold that X is morally problematic, then that is reason enough to think that X is morally permissible. In the absence of a good reason to repress X, one should tolerate it since, as per supposition, it is largely nonvoluntary. The argument from conflicting claims, however, provides a good reason which overrides this presumption.

7. A SECOND ARGUMENT FOR THE DIFFERENCE THESIS

A second argument for the difference thesis, similar to the argument from conflicting claims, is what might be called the "no-exit argument." This argument is based on the principle that:

(A) no just government can coerce a citizen into violating a deeply held moral belief or religious belief.

Is (A) plausible? It seems to be since the prospect of a citizen being coerced by the state into a practice which she finds profoundly immoral appears to be a clear example of an injustice. Principle (A), conjoined with there being a public dilemma arising over the issue of same-sex marriages, leads to the observation that if the state were to sanction same-sex marriages, then persons who have profound religious or moral objections to such unions would be legally mandated to violate their beliefs since there does not appear to be any feasible "exit right" possible with regard to state sanctioned marriage. An exit right is an exemption from some legally mandated practice, granted to a person or group, the purpose of which is to protect the religious or moral integrity of that person or group. Prominent examples of exit rights include conscientious objection and military service, home-schooling of the young because of some religious concern, and property used for religious purposes being free from taxation.

It is important to note that marriage is a public matter in the sense that, for instance, if one is an employer who provides health care benefits to the spouses of employees, one must provide those benefits to any employee who is married. Since there is no exit right possible in this case, one would be coerced, by force of law, into subsidizing a practice one finds morally or religiously objectionable.[20]

In the absence of an exit right, and if (A) is plausible, then the state cannot morally force persons to violate deeply held beliefs that are moral or religious in nature. In particular, the state morally could not sanction same-sex marriages since this would result in coercing some into violating a deeply held religious conviction.

8. A CONCLUSION

It is important to note that neither the argument from conflicting claims nor the no-exit argument licenses wholesale discrimination against homosexuals. What they do show is that some discrimination against homosexuals, in this case refusal to sanction same-sex marriages, is not only legally permissible but also morally permissible. The discrimination is a way of resolving a public policy dilemma that accommodates, to an extent, each side of the impasse and, further, protects the religious and moral integrity of a good number of people. In short, the arguments show us that there are occasions in which it is morally permissible to discriminate on the basis of homosexuality.[21]

NOTES

1. The terms "homosexuality" and "heterosexuality" are defined as follows: The former is defined as sexual feelings or behavior directed toward individuals of the same sex; the latter, naturally enough, is defined as sexual feelings or behavior directed toward individuals of the opposite sex.

   Sometimes the term "gay" is offered as an alternative to "homosexual." Ordinary use of "gay" has it as a synonym of a male homosexual (hence, the common expression, "gays and lesbians"). Given this ordinary usage, the substitution would lead to a confusing equivocation. Since there are female homosexuals, it is best to use "homosexual" to refer to both male and female homosexuals, and reserve "gay" to signify male homosexuals, and "lesbian" for female homosexuals in order to avoid the equivocation.

2. Perhaps we should distinguish the weak difference thesis (permissible discrimination on *some* occasions) from the strong difference thesis (given the relevant moral differences, discrimination on *any* occasion is permissible).

3. This would be true even if the act in question is immoral.

4. The standard answer is, of course, that the line between public and private is based on the notion of harm. Acts which carry a real probability of harming third parties are public acts.

5. For other arguments supporting the moral parity of homosexuality and heterosexuality, see Richard Mohr, *Gays/Justice: A Study of Ethics, Society and Law* (NY: Columbia, 1988); and see Michael Ruse, "The Morality of Homosexuality" in *Philosophy and Sex*, eds. R. Baker & F. Elliston, (Buffalo, NY: Prometheus Books, 1984), pp. 370–390.

6. Perhaps it would be better to term the disputing positions "contradictory" views rather than "contrary" views.

7. Resolutions can also be passive in the sense of the state doing nothing. If the state does nothing to resolve the public dilemma, it stands pat with the status quo, and the public dilemma is resolved gradually by sociological changes (changes in mores and in beliefs).

8. Assuming, plausibly enough, that the disputes over the sovereignty of the Union and concerning states' rights were at bottom disputes about slavery.

9. The Federal Fair Housing Act prohibits discrimination in housing on the basis of race, religion, and sex. But it does not apply to the rental of rooms in single-family houses, or to a building of five units or less if the owner lives in one of the units. See 42 U.S.C. Section 3603.

10. Note that overriding reasons involve *generally recognized* rights. If a right is not widely recognized and the state nonetheless uses coercion to enforce it, there is a considerable risk that the state will be seen by many or even most people as tyrannical.

11. This claim is, perhaps, controversial. For a contrary view see Richard George, *Making Men Moral* (Oxford: Clarendon Press, 1993).

12. See, for example, Leviticus 18:22, 21:3; and Romans 1: 22–32; and Koran IV:13.

13. For an argument that religiously-based moral views should not be dismissed out of hand, see Stephen Carter, *The Culture of Disbelief: How American Law and Politics Trivialize Religious Devotion* (NY: Basic Books, 1993).

14. Two assumptions are these: that the prohibitions against homosexuality activity are part of the religious doctrine and not just an extraneous addition; second, that if X is part of one's religious belief or religious doctrine, then it is morally permissible to hold X. Though this latter principle is vague, it is, I think, clear enough for our purposes here (I ignore here any points concerning the rationality of religious belief in general, or in particular cases).

15. This point has implications for the moral legitimacy of sodomy laws. One implication would be this: the private acts of consenting adults should not be criminalized.

16. An *ad hominem* point: If this response begs the question against the proponent of the parity thesis, it does not beg the question any more than the original objection does by presupposing that sexuality is analogous with race.

17. Think of the sodomy laws found in some states which criminalize certain sexual acts, whether performed by heterosexuals or homosexuals.

18. There is some interesting recent research which, though still tentative, strongly suggests that homosexuality is, at least in part, biologically based. See Simon LeVay, *The Sexual Brain* (Cambridge, MA: MIT Press, 1993), pp. 120–122; and J.M. Bailey & R.C. Pillard "A Genetic Study of Male Sexual Orientation," *Archives of General Psychiatry* 48 (1991): 1089–1096; and C. Burr, "Homosexuality and Biology," *The Atlantic* 271/3 (March, 1993): 64; and D. Hamer, S. Hu, V. Magnuson, N. Hu, A. Pattatucci, "A Linkage Between DNA Markers on the X Chromosome and Male Sexual Orientation," *Science* 261 (16 July 1993): 321–327; and see the summary of this article by Robert Pool, "Evidence for Homosexuality Gene," *Science* 261 (16 July 1993): 291–292.

19. I do not mean to suggest that homosexuality is morally equivalent or even comparable to pyromania.

20. Is the use of subsidy here inappropriate? It does not seem so since providing health care to spouses, in a society where this is not legally mandatory, seems to be more than part of a salary and is a case of providing supporting funds for a certain end.

21. I thank David Haslett, Kate Rogers, Louis Pojman, and Jim Fieser for helpful and critical comments.

Justice, Gender, and the Politics of Multiculturalism

Sarah Song

Sarah Song is assistant professor of law and political science at the University of California, Berkeley. She is the author of Justice, Gender, and the Politics of Multiculturalism (2007).

Song argues that Mormon polygamy is the kind of religious practice that should be tolerated in a multicultural society. Government intervention should occur to make sure that women and girls are not coerced and harmed by the practice. If so, criminal penalties should not be excessive, and government oversight should be as vigilant concerning sexual abuse in polygamous societies as in non polygamous ones.

"MORMON POLYGAMY TODAY"

Which arguments from the nineteenth-century debate on polygamy, if any, are relevant for the contemporary practice of polygamy among fundamentalist Mormons in America or any minority group engaging in the practice in liberal democratic societies?

With regard to Mormon polygamy today, government officials have largely taken a laissez-faire approach, a departure from their approach in the earlier part of the twentieth century. In 1935, the Utah legislature declared cohabitation with "more than one person of the opposite sex" a criminal felony.[1] Although the code is vaguely worded, this law was invoked in several polygamy cases in the 1930s and 1940s. Using the 1935 legislation on cohabitation, Utah and Arizona authorities took several actions against fundamentalists, including a raid on the Short Creek fundamentalist Mormon community in 1935 and a raid on various locales on charges of kidnapping, cohabitation, criminal conspiracy, and "white slavery" in 1944. The charges of kidnapping and conspiracy were not upheld, but on appeal, the US Supreme Court affirmed convictions based on the Mann or White Slave Traffic Act, which forbids the transportation of women across state lines for immoral purposes. The Court focused on the question of whether Mormon polygamy was a practice of debauchery and immorality within the reach of federal law. Drawing upon arguments from nineteenth-century decisions against Mormon polygamy discussed above, Justice William O. Douglas, writing for the majority, affirmed that it was. In his dissent, Justice Frank Murphy introduced an unprecedented pluralistic perspective into the nation's highest court. He called polygamy "one of the basic forms of marriage" and argued that it did not constitute sexual enslavement, nor was it "in the same genus" as prostitution or debauchery. Citing anthropological findings that monogamy, polygamy, polyandry, and group marriage were four different forms of marriage practiced by different cultures, Justice Murphy argued that Mormon polygamy was "a form of marriage built upon a set of social and moral principles" and ought to be recognized as such.[2]

Excerpts from Sarah Song, Justice, Gender, and the Politics of Multiculturalism, 2007, pp. 156–166. © 2007 Cambridge University Press. Reprinted by permisssion.

State and federal authorities have not followed Murphy's lead and gone as far as recognizing polygamy as a legitimate form of marriage; polygamy is still illegal.[3] In practice, however, government officials have increasingly taken a "don't ask, don't tell" approach toward Mormon polygamy. The last major raid against Mormon polygamy took place in 1953 against the Short Creek community in Arizona. There was much public criticism in reaction to photographs of children being torn from their parents and taken to foster homes.[4] Since then, government officials have taken a more tolerant stance. In 1991, the Utah Supreme Court ruled that polygamous families were eligible to adopt. A leader of the Fundamentalist Church of Jesus Christ of Latter-day Saints hailed the Canadian court decision that overturned the ban on polygamy on grounds of religious freedom as a sign that the United States would soon legalize polygamy.[5] This prediction was supported by then Republican Governor Michael O. Leavitt's public statement that polygamy might enjoy protection as a religious freedom. After protests from women who had left polygamous marriages, the governor quickly amended his stance, saying that "plural marriage is wrong, it should stay against the law, and there is no place for it in modern society."[6]

In such a laissez-faire legal climate, the number of individuals living in polygamous families in various communities in Utah and Arizona has increased steadily, and the total number of individuals living in polygamous families is estimated to be between 20,000 and 40,000.[7] In explaining why these communities are growing and few people exit, anthropologists Irwin Altman and Joseph Ginat suggest that the main reason appears to be religious devotion. Mormon fundamentalists are committed to the founding doctrines regarding plural marriage. In speculating about whether there are sexual motives, Altman and Ginat contend that for men "any sexual motives must surely pall after a while, as the day-to-day pressures of plural family life cumulate—the financial burdens, the needs of large families, family tensions and conflicts."[8] They add that the widespread occurrences in American society of serial marriages and divorces, cohabitation of unmarried couples, and affairs and mistresses appear much simpler and more "romantic."

For Mormon women today, as in the nineteenth century, there are strong economic motivations to enter and remain within polygamous relationships. While many women convert to fundamentalism on the grounds that they've discovered the true and underlying basis of Mormonism, many are also divorcées or widows in need of economic support. These women gain "the security of a community and family, the support and assistance of other women, someone to care for their children, and a highly structured set of roles with respect to their husband and children."[9] Women who enter polygamous marriages tend to be women seeking economic security; for them, conversion to the group is usually followed by striking upward social and economic mobility. Janet Bennion notes that the Mormon fundamentalist group provides "lower-class female recruits" the chance to "ascend to a position of higher marriage (hypergamy)" and a higher level of economic satisfaction than male recruits to Mormon fundamentalism.[10] Compared to women from the mainstream LDS Church, Bennion finds that Mormon fundamentalist women participate more in social and religious work and also pursue paid work outside the home at higher rates. She argues that polygyny "develops independent women who bear much of the financial responsibility for their families." But her study also finds that men in these communities seek to counteract egalitarian values from the wider society with harsher rules and restrictions for women.[11]

If we listen to what Mormon women themselves are saying about polygamy, we find a contested practice. On one side is Tapestry of Polygamy, a group of former polygamous wives, who support the legal ban on polygamy and favor its strong enforcement. They argue that de facto accommodation of polygamy reinforces women's subordination within fundamentalist Mormon communities. On the other side are women living in polygamous relationships, such as members of Women's Religious Liberties Union, who favor decriminalization of polygamy in the name of religious freedom. They also argue that polygamous arrangements are good for women because they allow them to pursue both career and family by sharing childcare and household responsibilities. A website they maintain denounces forced marriage and incest, and echoing the sentiments of Stanton and Anthony, states that "[a]buse is not inherent in polygamy and can exist in any society."[12] Non-Mormons have also made secular arguments in favor of polygamy. In contrasting monogamy and polygamy, one advocate maintains that frequent divorce and remarriage, separation of children from parents, multiplication of step-relationships, and total breakdown of paternal responsibility suggest that the institution of serial monogamy is in serious trouble and may be no better than polygamy per se.[13]

A CASE FOR QUALIFIED RECOGNITION

What then is the appropriate response to the contemporary practice of polygamy? The charge that polygamous relationships are oppressive is contingent, and needs to be investigated by looking at individual relationships and their context, just as monogamous relationships should be. On a rights-respecting accommodationist approach, the importance of polygamy for Mormon fundamentalists must be weighed against protecting the basic rights of Mormon women and children. On the one hand, liberal democracies should respect people's religious liberty and the liberty to pursue the kinds of intimate relationships that accord with their convictions and desires.[14] Mormon fundamentalists maintain that polygamy is of great importance to their beliefs and way of life. If Mormon women maintain that they have freely chosen to remain in polygamous marriage in accordance with their religious convictions, the state should respect their choices but on the condition that they are free to exit. Determining whether women have realistic rights of exit is no easy matter; it requires consideration of the sorts of conditions necessary for genuine consent and exit, as well as contextual inquiry to see whether such conditions obtain in any given case.

Exit has recently received considerable attention as a solution to the problem of internal minorities. Some liberal political theorists defend toleration of illiberal religious and cultural groups, endorsing a principle of state nonintervention, when these groups meet certain minimal conditions necessary for exit.[15] The central claim here is that religious and cultural groups should be let alone so long as membership in these groups is voluntary. Not voluntary in the sense that a religious belief and cultural attachments are experienced as choices, but rather that individual members can, if they wish, exit groups. The appeal of exit as a solution to the problem of internal minorities has not only to do with its providing vulnerable members with a way to escape internal oppression but also with the transformative potential that the *threat* of exit can have. As Albert O. Hirschman famously argued, the threat of exit can enhance one's voice in decision-making.[16] In the context of minority groups, the idea is that if many members can credibly threaten to exit the group on account of their disagreement with particular aspects of group life, the group's leaders would be compelled to reform those aspects. In the Mormon polygamy case, if the threat of exit by women opposed to polygamous marriage was serious enough, it could compel group leaders to reform their marriage practices or to abolish polygamy altogether.

While exit is a real option for members of many religious and cultural minority groups in contemporary America, whether it really is in any particular case depends on the costs of exit and the nature of the group in question. Describing people's convictions and attachments as voluntary seems appropriate against, as Nancy Rosenblum puts it, "a background of fluid pluralism, where other religious homes are open to splitters and the formation of new associations is a real possibility." So long as members are free to exit, religious and cultural associations need not be congruent with public norms and institutions "all the way down."[17] But how far down state intervention will have to go in order to ensure realistic rights of exit for vulnerable internal minorities is an open question. First, there is the issue of how isolated or open the group is to the wider society. Groups that are relatively isolated and which socialize their members into the inevitability of sex hierarchy, as may well be the case with Mormon fundamentalist communities, are especially worrisome. There is also the issue of the costs of exit, not just the material costs of leaving but also intrinsic and social costs. Leaving means losing not just the cultural or religious affiliations themselves and the intrinsic value they hold for members (intrinsic costs) but also the social relationships afforded by membership (associative costs). In addition, there may be extrinsic costs of educational and employment opportunities or other material benefits associated with membership.[18] There is not much the state or the wider society can do about intrinsic or associative costs, but it can assist those trying to leave their communities with the extrinsic costs of exit.

Okin's criticism of the strategy of exit highlights a different kind of obstacle having to do with the *capacity* for exit, conditions of knowledge and psychology, which require a different sort of response than providing material resources. In many minority groups, there may be strong countervailing pressures that undermine the capacity for exit for women and girls in particular. Okin highlights three such pressures: girls are much more likely to be shortchanged than boys in education; they are more likely to be socialized in ways that undermine their self-esteem and that encourage them to defer to existing hierarchies; and they are likely to be forced into early marriages from which they lack the power to exit.[19] Under such conditions, women and girls within religious groups can hardly be said to enjoy a realistic right of exit.

These concerns suggest the need to think carefully about the sorts of conditions under which women can genuinely make free choices to stay or leave and what the state can do to foster those conditions. Minimal standards necessary to ensure the worth of a right of exit include members' freedom from abuse and coercion; access to decent health care, nutrition, and education; and the existence of genuine alternatives among which to make choices, including real access to a mainstream society to exit to.[20] To address the concerns about capacity raised by Okin, education must play a key role. Children should be taught about their basic constitutional and civic rights so they know that liberty of conscience exists in their society and that apostasy is not a legal crime.

Some argue that even these minimal standards are too robust, and that the existence of a surrounding market society is all that is required for exit to be a meaningful option.[21] But such an approach overlooks the serious obstacles to exit that the state can help ameliorate and assumes that any state action to address these obstacles would be worse in terms of violating basic individual freedoms (especially freedom of association) than leaving vulnerable members to cope on their own. This minimalist position is right to stress that states have oppressed minority groups. As I argued in chapter 3, this fact supports some minority group claims for accommodation. But the fact of past oppression of minority groups should not rule out state involvement in contemporary problems. For some individual members of minority groups, group authorities may be experienced as more oppressive than the state. Here the state can play a role in protecting the basic rights of individuals. Giving a role to the state does not mean any form of intervention goes; rather, the state's role should be limited to meeting the minimal conditions necessary for exit.

What do these considerations about exit suggest for the contemporary case of Mormon polygamy? A legal regime of qualified recognition of polygamy can, I think, more effectively ensure Mormon women's rights to exit their communities than outright proscription. The current ban on polygamy leaves polygamous wives and their children even more vulnerable to domination by driving polygamous communities into hiding. In May 2001, Tom Green, a husband of five and father of twenty-nine, was convicted on four counts of bigamy, the first prosecution of polygamy since 1953. Green's conviction has caused anxiety among some members of polygamous communities. They fear that prosecution of polygamy will discourage the group's most vulnerable members from reporting abuse of women and children. As Anne Wilde, who has been in a polygamous marriage for thirty-two years, put it, "This has pushed people a little further underground." She adds that the *Green* case had done a major disservice to the estimated 30,000 polygamists who live in Utah and neighboring states by presenting a false image of their chosen way of life. She contends that Green is an anomaly among polygamists for having wives and children in far greater numbers than average polygamist husbands. A more common family includes two to three wives and eight to ten children. Even worse, she says, the separate charge of child rape against Green for having one wife who was thirteen at the time of their marriage may leave the impression that all polygamist husbands marry under-age girls and abuse children when in fact most do not. Sidney Anderson, director of Women's Religious Liberties Union, also argues that fear of prosecution for polygamy almost assures that when child abuse does happen it is more likely to go unreported: "The state is forcing them into an abusive situation, and some men are using it to convince women that they have to live in isolation for the unit to be safe. So women who need help can't get it out of fear." Ms. Anderson argues that the best way to help vulnerable members within polygamous communities is to decriminalize bigamy altogether, which would make it easier for members of plural families to seek help when they need it.[22]

A strategy of qualified recognition of polygamy was pursued in reforming the customary marriage laws in South Africa, and this case is instructive for the case of Mormon polygamy. Drawing on provisions in the South African constitution, reformers sought simultaneously to respect customary law and protect women's rights.[23] On the one hand, the constitution recognizes the rights of cultural and religious groups, including various systems of customary African law. On the other hand, it specifies equal individual rights and prohibits racial and sexual discrimination, among other forms of discrimination. In the discussions leading up to reform, many different groups were consulted, including the traditional leaders' Congress, women's groups, legal reform groups, and scholars of constitutional and customary law. The actual lived practices of customary marriage were at the center of discussion. The chiefs were persuaded that reforming the customary marriage laws was less likely to erode their authority than retaining traditional customary marriage laws.

What emerged from the deliberations was the Recognition of Customary Marriages Act of 1998. It recognizes all past customary unions as "marriages"

while also reforming customary marriage itself. The law declares women and men formal equals within marriage and grants the state a role in regulating customary marriage. The law requires all marriages to be registered with a government agency, and it requires that divorce and child custody proceedings be conducted by a family court judge, as opposed to a tribal court. Customary groups are permitted to retain *lobolo* (bride price) as a condition of valid marriage, and polygyny was preserved in a modified form. In order to take a second wife, a man must make a written contract with his existing wife fairly dividing the property accrued at that point and persuade a family court that the contract is fair for all involved.[24]

Qualified recognition of polygamy, as in the case of the modified customary marriage law in South Africa, can offer Mormon women the protection of the law while also respecting their religious commitments. If the law were to recognize polygamy, it could secure legal rights for polygamous wives and ex-wives by regulating the conditions of entry into and exit from such relations. As in the South African case, the state might require a man seeking an additional wife to obtain the consent of his existing wife and to draw up a contract that fairly divides the property they had accrued at that point. If she approved, the couple would then have to obtain the approval of a family court judge. A state that recognizes polygamy could also secure rights for ex-wives and the rights of inheritance for children of polygamous relationships by regulating the terms of property division after divorce. Currently, a polygamous husband may abandon any wife beyond his first without providing any assistance to her and her children. Securing Mormon wives' exit rights could help strengthen their voice within polygamous relationships.

Utah authorities have moved toward a *de facto* regime of qualified recognition. They have shifted away from prosecuting polygamy per se toward cracking down on abuses that occur within polygamous marriages. The Utah attorney general publicly advised prosecutors to avoid prosecuting cases of consensual adult bigamy. Instead, Utah authorities have reached a consensus to crack down on child abuse, statutory rape, and incest. In 1998, the Utah Legislature raised the age for statutory rape to seventeen from sixteen. In 1999, the Legislature raised the minimum marriage age from fourteen to sixteen:[25] The attorney general said he planned to ask the state legislature for money to hire additional investigators for matters relating to "closed societies" so that more traditional crimes do not go unpunished. He favors reducing the charge of bigamy from a felony to a misdemeanor in order to encourage people to provide information about serious crimes in polygamous families.[26] These reforms may stem more from the practical difficulties of prosecuting polygamy: as in the nineteenth century polygamous men generally obtain marriage licenses only for their first wives and subsequent marriages are performed secretly. But in addition to these prudential concerns, there are principled arguments in favor of decriminalization. The public morals argument pressed by nineteenth-century antipolygamy activists, that polygamy was offensive to Christian public morals, does not offer a compelling reason, but the other argument, the concern for equal protection, does. We have good reasons to think that qualified recognition of polygamy can better protect the basic rights of Mormon women and children in polygamous households than a ban on polygamy.

CONCLUSION

In this chapter, as in the previous two chapters, we have seen how the gender norms of the dominant culture have shaped its responses to the gender practices of minority cultures. In the case of nineteenth-century Mormon polygamy, the dominant culture's opposition to polygamy appears to have been motivated less by a concern to empower women and more by a desire to uphold the public morals of the dominant culture. Citizens and public officials opposing polygamy sought to protect Christian-model monogamy, and the focus on Mormon polygamy helped shield the dominant culture's own patriarchal practices from criticism.

The diversionary effect can be seen beyond the case of Mormon polygamy. Focusing on cases of domestic violence and forced marriage in immigrant communities can serve to reinforce a false dichotomy between oppressive minority cultures and egalitarian Western majority cultures, deflecting attention from the reality of domestic violence and underage marriage within the latter. Marriage practices within immigrant communities should be evaluated alongside practices that are common to the majority culture: parental pressure over whom to marry and parent-arranged blind dates. Mainstream marriage practices should receive the same kind of scrutiny as the marriage practices of minority communities with the issue of a woman's consent to marriage and a minimum age for all marriages at the forefront of these considerations.

NOTES

1. The Utah penal code states: "If any person cohabits with more than one person of the opposite sex, such a person is guilty of a felony" (Chapter 112, Section 103–51–2).
2. *Cleveland* v. *United States,* 329 US 14 (1946) at 24–29.
3. The Utah Criminal Code states, "A person is guilty of bigamy when, knowing he has a husband or wife or knowing the other person has a husband or wife, the person purports to marry another person or cohabits with another person." Bigamy is a felony of the third degree (Utah Criminal Code, 76–7–101). The Utah Constitution also states, "Perfect toleration of religious sentiment is guaranteed. No inhabitant of this State shall ever be molested in person or property on account of his or her mode of religious worship; but polygamous or plural marriages are forever prohibited" (Article III, § 2).
4. Altman and Ginat 1996: 46.
5. The Canadian case involved a small group in British Columbia affiliated with the fundamentalists of Hildale, Utah, and Colorado City, Arizona (*Sail Lake Tribune,* June 16, 1992).
6. Brooke 1998: 12.
7. Altman and Ginat estimate between 20,000 and 50,000 (1996: 51, 54).
8. Ibid. 439.
9. Ibid. 440.
10. Bennion (1998: 64–65) finds that of the women who converted to the Allred fundamentalist Mormon group, 69 percent (706 women) had graduated from high school, and of that number, 12 percent (143) had earned a college degree. Overall most women who became plural wives and who worked for wages were low-skilled workers.
11. At least 25 percent of women Bennion interviewed expressed desire to leave if they could do so without losing their children (Bennion 1998: 134, 136, 151–52).

12. See Mary Batchelor, Marianne Watson, and Anne Wilde's *Voices in Harmony: Contemporary Women Celebrate Plural Marriage* (2000) and www.principlevoices.org.
13. See Kilbride 1994.
14. Laurence Tribe has long maintained on civil libertarian grounds that polygamy should be constitutionally protected and has predicted for the last two decades that *Reynolds* would be overruled (1988: 521–28).
15. See Rosenblum 1998; Spinner-Halev 2000 and 2005; Shachar 2001; Galston 2002; Kukathas 2003.
16. Hirschman 1970.
17. Rosenblum 1998: 85, 4.
18. For an excellent discussion of different types of exit costs, see Barry 2001: 150–51.
19. Okin 1999: 128; 2002: 216–22.
20. Other specific proposals include an exit fund to which group members must contribute to enable members to meet the economic costs of exit should they decide to leave (Spinner-Halev 2000: 77–79) and state regulation of the economic aspects of divorce in the context of legal pluralistic arrangements (Shachar 2001: 124–25, 134–35).
21. See, e.g., Kukathas 1992, 2003.
22. Janofsky 2001: A14.
23. Here I draw on Chambers 2000 and Deveaux 2003.
24. Chambers 2000: 112–13.
25. Utah Statutes, §76, ch. 5, 401.2; §30, chs. 1, 9.
26. Janofsky 2001. In contrast to the case of Tom Green, in the more recent case of Warren Jeffs, the leader of the Fundamentalist Church of Jesus Christ of Latter-day Saints, state authorities are not charging him with bigamy itself but with being an accessory to rape by arranging marriages between underage girls and older men (Newman 2006).

STUDY QUESTIONS:
GENDER ROLES AND MORALITY

1. What does Haslanger mean by social construction? What role do facts play in the social construction of gender? Do you agree with the limited role that Haslanger thinks facts play here? Why?
2. According to Friedman, there are serious autonomy issues that arise in situations of domestic violence. Pick one of these issues and construct a debate on the issue. Which position do you find most plausible and why?
3. Anderson argues that gender equality in the home does not necessarily lead to the "decline of the family." Set out some of his reasons in support of this claim. Then provide a sustained counterargument to his view.
4. Take one of the arguments advanced by Sadler in favor of civil unions for gays and then try to argue against her view from Jordan's perspective. Which of these positions do you favor and why?
5. In 1991, Antioch College in Ohio instituted a Sexual Offense Policy. In part it required that (a) consent must be obtained verbally before there is any sexual contact or conduct; (b) if the level of sexual intimacy increases during an interaction (e.g., if two people move from kissing while fully clothed—which is one level—to undressing

for direct physical contact, which is another level), the people involved need to express their clear verbal consent before moving to that new level. First, offer arguments defending such a policy. Second mount a counterargument to this policy.

SUPPLEMENTARY READINGS:
GENDER ROLES AND MORALITY

ACCAD, EVELYNE. "Sexuality and Sexual Politics: Conflicts and Contradictions for Contemporary Women in the Middle East." In *Third World Women and the Politics of Feminism,* Mohanty, Russo, and Torres, editors. (Bloomington, IN: Indiana University Press, 1991.)

ALCOFF, LINDA MARTIN, and EVA FEDER KITTAY, editors. *The Blackwell Guide to Feminist Philosophy.* (Oxford: Blackwell Publishing, 2007.)

ALEXANDER, M. JACQUI. "Redrafting Morality: The Post-colonial State and the Sexual Offenses Bill of Trinidad and Tobago." In *Third World Women and the Politics of Feminism,* Mohanty, Russo, and Torres, editors. (Bloomington, IN: Indiana University Press, 1991.)

ANAGOL-MCGINN, PADMA. "Sexual Harassment in India: A Case Study of Eve-teasing in Historical Perspective," In *Rethinking Sexual Harassment,* Brant and Too, editors. (London: Pluto Press, 1994.)

BAIER, ANNETTE. "Whom Can Women Trust?" In *Feminist Ethics,* Card, editor. (Lawrence, KS: University of Kansas Press 1991.)

BARRY, KATHLEEN. "Female Sexual Slavery: Understanding the International Dimensions of Women's Oppression." *Human Rights Quarterly,* vol. 3(2), Spring 1981.

CHEN, MARTHA. "A Matter of Survival: Women's Right to Employment in India and Bangladesh." In *Women, Culture, and Development,* Nussbaum and Glover, editors. (Oxford: Clarendon Press, 1995.)

CHOW, ESTHER NGAN-LING. "The Feminist Movement: Where Are All the Asian American Women?" In *From Different Shores: Perspectives on Race and Ethnicity in America,* second edition, Takaki, editor. (New York: Oxford University Press, 1994.)

CUDD, ANN E. and ROBIN O. ANDREASEN, editors. *Feminist Theory: A Philosophical Anthology. (*Oxford: Blackwell Publishing. 2005.)

DILLON, ROBIN S. "Care and Respect." In *Explorations in Feminist Ethics,* Cole and Coultrap-McQuin, editors. (Bloomington, IN: Indiana University Press, 1992.)

EL MERNISSI, FATIMA. "Democracy as Moral Disintegration: The Contradiction Between Religious Belief and Citizenship as a Manifestation of the Ahistoricity of the Arab Identity." In *Women of the Arab World,* Toubia, editor. (London: Zed Books, 1988.)

HACKETT, ELIZABETH, and SALLY HASLANGER, editors. *Theorizing Feminisms: A Reader.* (Oxford: Oxford University Press, 2006.)

HARDING, SANDRA. "The Curious Coincidence of Feminine and African Moralities." In *Women and Moral Theory,* Kittay and Meyers, editors. (Totowa, NJ: Rowman & Littlefield, 1987.)

HOAGLAND, SARAH LUCIA. "Lesbian Ethics and Female Agency." In *Explorations in Feminist Ethics,* Cole and Coultrap-McQuin, editors. (Bloomington, IN: Indiana University Press, 1992.)

JAGGAR, ALISON. "On Sexual Equality." *Ethics,* 1974.

LEVIN, MICHAEL, "Sex, The Family, and the Liberal Order." In *Feminism and Freedom.* (New Brunswick, NJ: Transaction Books, 1987.)

MACKINNON, CATHERINE. "Racial and Sexual Harassment." In *Only Words.* (Cambridge, MA: Harvard University Press, 1993.)

MAJOR, BRENDA. "Gender, Entitlement, and the Distribution of Family Labor." *Journal of Social Issues,* vol. 49(3), 1993.

MOODY-ADAMS, MICHELLE. "Gender and the Complexity of Moral Voices." In *Feminist Ethics,* Card, editor. (Lawrence, KS: University of Kansas Press, 1991.)

STEVENS, EVELYN P. *"Marianismo:* The Other Face of *Machismo* in Latin America." In *Female and Male in Latin America,* edited by Pascatello. (Pittsburgh, PA: University of Pittsburgh Press, 1973.)

SWANTON, CHRISTINE, VIVIANE ROBINSON, and JAN CROSTHWAITE. "Treating Women as Sex-Objects." *Journal of Social Philosophy,* vol. 20(3), Winter 1989.

TONG, ROSEMARY. "Sexual Harassment." In *Women, Sex and the Law.* (Totowa, NJ: Rowman and Allenheld, 1984.)

Part VII

RACIAL AND ETHNIC DISCRIMINATION

Shallow understanding from people of good will is more frustrating than absolute misunderstanding from people of ill will.

—MARTIN LUTHER KING, JR.

Part of the reason racism is so pernicious is because we often fail to realize its existence. In our desire to become "post-racial", many of us overlook ways in which racism is still prevalent. Although we should not disregard the important strides we have made toward eliminating racism altogether, pride in our progress always should be accompanied by the open admission of the work that still needs to be done.

One way in which racism still persists in the United States today is in the justice system. For example, many people are familiar with the policy differences in sentencing between crack cocaine and powdered cocaine and the racial implications. Although very similar drugs with identical physiological effects, pharmacological makeup, and accompanying dangers, it takes one hundred times more powder cocaine than crack cocaine to bring about the same sentence in the federal court system. Furthermore, crack cocaine, not powder cocaine, requires a mandatory prison sentence, even for first-time offenders. When we couple these facts with the fact that the only difference between the two illicit drugs is that crack cocaine is more commonly used by African Americans while cocaine powder is primarily used by whites, it should

be no surprise that the result of such laws is racially discriminatory.[1]

But the racial problems with drug sentencing do not end with cocaine. According to the Human Rights Watch, "Although whites commit more drug offenses, African Americans are arrested and imprisoned on drug charges at much higher rates. . . . ." African Americans are disproportionately targeted at every stage of the justice system: arrest, conviction, and length of sentencing. In fact, a black man is thirteen times more likely to go to jail on drug charges than a white man in the United States nationwide and in some states he is fifty-seven times more likely to go to jail on drug charges.[2]

These statistics should be alarming, but because they address only one instantiation of racism towards African Americans in the United States justice system, they do not even scratch the surface of racism or ethnic discrimination today. They do not address racism or ethnic discrimination in education, the workforce, immigration policy, international relations, or racism and ethnic discrimination beyond the context of the United States.

Many people like to jump to the problem of how to deal with racism, race relations, and reparations for past harms against races and ethnicities with a discussion of what justice requires. In this section, we take a more measured approach, first asking whether or not we can define the groups relevant in such discussions. Can we define races or ethnicities? Can we define racism itself? If not, how can we proceed in our pursuit of justice? We hope that by facing these difficult definitional problems head on, we can help bring clarity to the debate.

Naomi Zack weighs in on this dilemma of defining race. She argues against the biological existence of race as lacking in any scientific basis, meaning that race can only be a social construction. However, it is not enough simply to disprove the notion of biological race. Zack argues that we must accept this fact as a society. Fully realizing the falsity of biological taxonomies of race will require widespread scientific literacy on this matter. Next, it will require us to purge our discourse, institutions, and practices of all reliance on the biological category of race. Zack acknowledges that racism might continue even in the face of this scientific enlightenment. Nevertheless, she has hope that it will change our society. Says Zack, "Race is like the liar who says he speaks the truth, the social construction that is constructed around the denial that it is a social construction."

In the next article, Kai Wong grapples with the problem of defining racial, ethnic, and cultural categories even after we dispense with the alleged scientific taxonomy. Wong advocates a theory of "overlapping characteristics" for defining communities. In other words, although there is not one single characteristic that all individuals of a given community share, as long as individuals partake in a set of nontrivial characteristics in some way they can be said to belong to the same racial, ethnic, or cultural group. Wong applies this theory to a problem in justice: collective responsibility. He argues that individuals can share responsibility for injustices by being members of the harm-causing community.

Kwame Anthony Appiah contends not with the problem of defining race, but with the problem of defining racism in his article, "Racisms." Defining racism, as Appiah points out, is not as easy as we might think. Through a careful analysis, Appiah draws out subtle distinctions in types of racism. One difference he focuses on is the difference between extrinsic and intrinsic racism. Extrinsic racism is the view that different races warrant different treatment based on proposed morally relevant characteristics. This view purports

to be based on empirical fact. On In contrast, intrinsic racism is the view that each race has its own moral status independent of any morally relevant characteristics. According to Appiah, although both types of racism are morally wrong, and although both types of racism constitute failures in rationality, the two racisms play out very differently in society. For example, extrinsic racism tends to lead to oppression and genocide, as in Nazi racism and South African racism. On the other hand, intrinsic racism does not tend to be used as a justification for violence but rather leads to "racial solidarity" as in the case of Zionism or Black Nationalism.

The final three articles move past the problems with defining the relevant terms to discuss the pursuit of racial justice. In "Affirmative Action: The Price of Preference," Shelby Steele argues against affirmative action in the United States as not only ineffective in eradicating inequality but also harmful to the intended beneficiaries of the policy. According to Steele, affirmative action is a solution for white guilt, not racial inequality. Furthermore, it is pernicious because it upsets healthy conceptions of self in minorities by introducing self-doubt and victimization and it suggests that affirmative action can make up for past wrongs, an impossible task. Instead, Steele proposes a shift to policies that help the disadvantaged regardless of race or ethnicity.

Amy Gutmann addresses just this proposed social policy in her article, "Should Public Policy Be Class Conscious Rather than Color Conscious?" and comes to the opposite conclusion. Through analysis of empirical data, Gutmann argues that while class is a contributing factor to inequality, it does not account for further disparities between whites and minorities of the same income bracket. According to Gutmann, any reasoning that supports class-based affirmative action logically must also apply to race-based affirmative action. In other words, any view that educational obstacles should be taken into account when considering applicants must apply to race and not just class. Instead, fairness seems to require taking both class and race as independent criteria in affirmative action policy. Finally, Gutmann argues against the view that affirmative action causes racism, as Steele seems to suggest. Instead, she suggests that perhaps affirmative action merely triggers the open expression of already existing racism.

The last article in this chapter is "The Color-Blind Principle" by Bernard Boxill. Boxill argues against color-blind policies although he does not argue that color-conscious policies are necessarily just. By addressing a series of arguments in favor of color-blind policies, Boxill comes to the conclusion that none of these reasons to prefer color-blind policies can consistently rule out the possibility of a just color-conscious policy. For example, some think that it is wrong to give preference to individuals based on characteristics they cannot change and have no responsibility over, such as race, sex, or age. However, Boxill contends, if this were the case, it would be wrong to give preference to individuals based on talent, which they cannot change and over which they have no responsibility. This *reductio ad absurdum* argument is meant to show that the common reasons for opposing color-conscious policies are themselves flawed.

In this section, we have focused on two important themes within the race and ethnicity literature: defining race and ethnicity and evaluating affirmative action. In choosing these two important dilemmas, we hope to address not only the practical solutions to racism but also the theoretical grounding necessary to determine those solutions.

—JILL DELSTON

NOTES

1. Carol Chodroff, US Advocacy Director, "Cracked Justice: Addressing the Unfairness in Cocaine Sentencing," February, 2008, Human Rights Watch.
2. Human Rights Watch Report, "Targeting Blacks: Drug Law Enforcement and Race in the United States," May 2008.

Philosophical and Social Implications of Race

Naomi Zack

Naomi Zack is a professor of philosophy at the University of Oregon. Her books include *Inclusive Feminism: A Third Wave Theory of Women's Commonality* (2005), *Philosophy of Science and Race* (2002), *Bachelors of Science: Seventeenth Century Identity, Then and Now* (1996), and *Race and Mixed Race* (1993).

Building upon the clear scientific evidence that there is no biological basis for race, Zack argues that in order to dismantle racism and its foundation, we will need to progress through two phases. The first phase requires those in all significant societal positions, from education to policy-making, to be scientifically literate regarding the absence of biological races. The second phase requires a thorough paradigm-shift in all cultural, economic, and political practices and institutions. Evident throughout Zack's essay is the paradox that while races are not real, racism is and must continue to be treated as a separate issue from race, "even though the facts about race represent its [racism's] ultimate demise, now in theory, later in practice."

SCIENTIFIC LITERACY ABOUT RACE

. . . The public, which is broadly committed to the results of the physical sciences as a source of information about reality, now maintains anachronistic beliefs about race. The present challenge to members of both oppressive and liberatory traditions regarding what they continue to assume about racial taxonomies is, to begin with, an intellectual challenge. In "The Conservation of Races," after Du Bois claimed that the notion of race overflowed the scientific definition of it in 1897, he asserted that the history of the world is the history of races and that "he who ignores or seeks to override the race idea in human history ignores and overrides the central thought of all history."[1] Race lacks the basis in biology assumed by late-nineteenth-century scientists, and as Anthony Appiah showed, by Du Bois himself in his definition of races as families with common histories. Therefore, it cannot be the case that the history of the world is the history of races. Neither is the history of the world the history of the idea of race, because world history extends further back in time than the modern period, when the idea of biological race was first constructed, and the history of the world that lies ahead will have to take the fact that race is biologically unreal into account—somehow. So, we can now say simply that Du Bois is mistaken here. It is time to put to rest his fantasy that African Americans *could* acquit themselves within a false taxonomy, much less that they *should*.

All of the discussion about science is accessible to educated communities. Most of it is no more difficult to understand than information routinely absorbed in senior high school and introductory college courses. The contemporary information from population genetics, the study of phenotypes, transmission genetics, genealogy, and their relevance to anthropology does not require special talents for absorption by liberal arts educators and their students. What is required is a willingness to acquire scientific literacy relevant to a subject that is one of the major preoccupations of present life in the United States (at least). I would submit that this racially relevant scientific literacy is an obligation for all scholars of race, particularly those who teach and especially those who teach future teachers.

The burning questions evoked by this scientific literacy are social and political. I want to finish with suggestions about how those questions can be answered, but, beforehand, some additional philosophical issues need to be addressed: the connection between "race" and "IQ" and race as a social construction.

THE GORDIAN KNOT OF RACE AND IQ

As Stephen Jay Gould lucidly notes, assumptions of nonwhite and particularly black intellectual inferiority in comparison to whites have always accompanied modern racial taxonomies. The recurrent debate about the connection between race and IQ is thus no more than a contemporary version of nineteenth-century debates about different racial cranial capacities and intelligence.[2] Ashley Montagu points out that no one can say exactly what intelligence is, and Gould has explained how the notion of a general IQ factor, referred to as *g* or "general intelligence," is highly dependent on the statistical methods used in designing and scoring IQ tests.[3] Nonetheless, the numerical nature of IQ test scores casts an illusory mantle of scientific authority over popularized presentations of statistical correlations between IQ scores and membership in social racial groups. In the 1970s, Arthur Jensen presented arguments against integration and funding programs intended to improve the opportunities of African American schoolchildren, on the grounds that IQ cannot be changed because it is biologically determined in ways that correspond to race.[4] During the 1990s, Robert Herrnstein and

Charles Murray presented essentially the same arguments, with more statistics.[5] Montagu notes that both Jensen's and Herrnstein's and Murray's publications appeared at times of federal fiscal retrenchment and should therefore be interpreted as politically motivated.[6] But, though this may be true, it does not address the content of the claims.

IQ, as measured by available tests, is broadly considered to be 60 to 80 percent *heritable* within the white population in the United States. This heritability of IQ is "the proportion of a population's IQ variability attributable to genes."[7] However, biologists do not equate heritability with biological determinism that is invariant over changing environmental and developmental factors. Height is highly heritable from parents to children within groups if environmental factors are constant, but if dairy products are freely added to diets previously lacking them, the height of a whole generation may increase. Ned Block, among others who have written forcefully about the limits to the genetic component of heritability, painstakingly explicates the ways in which the heritability of a trait does not mean that its expression is independent of environmental conditions.[8] Many evidentiary claims have been made against the conclusions drawn by Jensen and Herrnstein and Murray, including references to studies in which IQ scores have risen as environmental conditions have changed.[9] Furthermore, the 60 to 80 percent heritability figure does not take maternal effects in the womb into account. When those effects are allowed for in statistical studies of identical twins reared apart, the genetic effect on IQ appears to be only 48 percent when the total effect of genes on IQ is calculated. But the genetic effect is only about 34 percent when the additive effect of genes on IQ is calculated and that figure is more relevant in evolutionary arguments.[10]

If conservatives have been strongly motivated to link IQ and race, the liberatory motivation to disprove alleged connections between race and IQ has been passionate. The 1998 American Anthropological Association Statement on "Race" was partly prompted by a desire to correct the public misinformation cast by Herrnstein and Murray's *The Bell Curve*.[11] The 1998 AAA Statement on

"Race" began with a claim that biological human races did not exist. However, *if races do not exist*, then regardless of whether or not there is some *g* or "general intelligence" factor and regardless of whether, or to what degree, that factor has a genetic component or is heritable, *it is logically impossible that there could be a connection between the genetics of IQ and the genetics of race*. While discussion of the heritability, malleability, and distribution of "intelligence quotients" and of the cultural objectivity of IQ tests is of considerable interest in its own right, such discussion is irrelevant to race in any biological sense.

RACE AND SOCIAL CONSTRUCTION

Publications such as *The Bell Curve* distress many people because they know that there are millions of young African Americans who do not do as well as their white contemporaries on IQ tests. The reasons for that are social, not biological, but in the absence of a biological foundation for racial difference, there seems to be no difficulty in identifying the different groups by race. For this case and other statistically compelling ones, such as race-related differences in public health and imprisonment, it is necessary to give an account of how people are able to sort others into races, and of the coherent persistence of racial identities. Since races are not natural kinds, they must be social constructions, and indeed, mention of the biological emptiness of race is often now followed by the proclamation that race is nothing but a social construction. But that alone is mild news ontologically, because almost all of the important ingredients of contemporary life are social constructions: money, marriage, social class, education, work, gender, beauty, and perhaps even health itself (physical as well as mental). Anything that is the result of human interaction and intention in contexts where past actions, decisions, and agreements have present consequences is, trivially, a social construction. It is therefore necessary to dig a little into the meaning of "social construction" before it can be informative to park race in that category. Ian Hacking observes that the label "social construction" is currently applied to matters of concern to signal that they are not inevitable when it is otherwise assumed that they are inevitable. Imputation of contingency is an important starting point for change, because, usually, the thing asserted to be socially constructed is also believed to be harmful and/or unjust.[12] Hacking also points out that objects, interactions, people in specified social roles or with specific ascribed identities, processes, and results of processes have all been viewed as social constructions in this way.[13] Applying Hacking's insight to race, we could say that each of the following is a social construction: the common sense notion of race, race relations, black, white, Asian, Native American, mixed, and any other racial identity, the histories of the foregoing, and the present results of those histories. So far, we know the point of saying that race is a social construction, and we know what particular aspects of "race" are social constructions, but we do not know what constitutes something like race as a social construction, that is, how saying that race is a social construction, can give an account of the way race works in society. We need an answer to this question: If race is not biologically real as people think it is, how does it come to be real in society, which it surely is?

Here is an answer to how race is real in society, but no more than a social construction. Racial taxonomy, or the conceptual scheme whereby everyone belongs to one of three or four races, is a simple scheme of classification, much simpler than astrology, for instance. This taxonomy is taught to children early on in their socialization. Along with the classification go physical, cultural, and psychological stereotypes for each race, which are less complicated than the (astrological) traits of Aquarius, Pisces, Leo, and so forth. More complicated, however, is the epistemology of racial sorting, and that is the most interesting part of the social construction of race. People are sorted into racial categories based on criteria that differ for different races and different individuals within the same race. To consider the big three: blacks require but one black ancestor to be black, but they can have any number of nonblack ancestors; whites require no nonwhite ancestors and a white appearance; Asians require ancestors from a list of countries believed to be "Asian." All of the failed scientific bases of race, except for genetics, which is assumed because it is not visible in ordinary experience, are used to sort people into relevant races. Appearance or phenotype is always the favored criterion, but it has to be confirmed by geographical location of ancestors and the race of an individual's social family. If the sorting cannot be done by direct observation, because the individual is filling out a form, or the individual's appearance is ambiguous, the individual can be asked, directly or indirectly, crudely or with finesse, "What race are you?" Thus, stated racial membership is another criterion (except for cases of "passing").

We can see from this account that first of all, the taxonomy of race, like all taxonomies, is socially constructed in the trivial way. People invented and embellished the taxonomy as a symbolic system. Once the taxonomy was broadly accepted, specific traits of individuals could be used to construct the races of those individuals. Conveniently, racial sorting did not have to take place on an individual basis, but entire geographical groups have been, and still are, lined up with components of the taxonomy, for example, inhabitants of Africa were, and still are, designated members of the black race. Racial sorting is a complicated, dynamic system, and since it changes over history and has different nuances within the United States and over the world, it is arbitrary.

However, it is not the problems with the epistemology of race, which qualify it as a social construction in the nontrivial sense, but the fact that the taxonomy of race is itself fictitious—it does not have the physical basis that it is assumed to have. If people viewed race as what used to be called a "parlor game" and did not regard the taxonomy itself as real, there would be no problem with it. It might even be a good social construction in a part of social reality, as many games are. The problematic aspect of race, which underlies what qualifies it as a social construction in the harmful sense that Hacking draws attention to, is twofold: people regard the taxonomy as biologically real;

the components of the taxonomy have different connotations of human psychic worth.

• • •

The ingredients of a racial paradigm at any given time would include a taxonomy of race, the criteria for membership in different races and their application to individuals, social customs and laws that pertain to race, moral beliefs about different race relations, expectations for change in social areas pertaining to race, ideologies of race, and beliefs about the connections between physical race and human psychic attributes. Because beliefs, rules, practices, and formal social structures are all parts of it, a racial paradigm is not merely a symbolic system but its accompanying life world, as well. From this theoretical perspective, we can distinguish at least three paradigms of race. The first, from the late eighteenth century to the early twentieth, had hierarchical racial taxonomies favoring whites, which rankings were believed to be unchanging and morally just. Different human psychic capacities and their expressions were held to be determined by racial heredity, as were physical characteristics.

The second paradigm of race took up most of the twentieth century, and except for revisions in the biological sciences, where they were previously racialist, and philosophical inquiries such as this one, it remains culturally dominant. Ideas of human psychic endowments have been disengaged from physical racial taxonomies. The white-supremacist customs and institutional practices that were considered morally right under the first paradigm have been subjected to intense criticism, with considerable progress toward their elimination.

The third paradigm of race would be the last one. Its core positive belief and principle underlying action is that race is biologically unreal. Once social racial taxonomies are eliminated, the correction of racialist white-supremacist customs and institutional practices would continue. But, the theoretical basis on which they are corrected will likely move away from direct or emic conceptualizations of race, in favor of the descriptions of beliefs and empirical descriptions of economic and social inequalities that can be addressed by changes in education and public policy.[14]

SOCIAL JUSTICE IMPLICATIONS

Race is not biologically real as most people still think, but the existence of racism past and present cannot be denied. There is no paradox here. People believe that race is real, and their belief has been enlivened by greed, fear, anger, and cruelty that often have nothing to do with race, as a motivating idea. But the belief in race has also itself been sufficient to occasion distinctive emotions, motives, and moral attitudes. The results have been racist psychic states and dispositions and racist practices. Racism has been the main use for the social construction of race.

Racism consists of individual and social preferences and aversions based on different racial identities. It has both deliberate forms and socially mechanistic ones that perpetuate themselves in the apparent absence of ill will toward victims. For example, some philosophy professors assume that African American students are not likely to want to learn philosophy, so they reserve their intensive pedagogy for white students. Over their careers, these academics tend not to recruit many or any African American philosophy majors or graduate students. Over time, the field of philosophy does not change in its predominantly white membership. Where blacks were once explicitly excluded as a consequence of their more general exclusion from higher education, they now simply—not that anything like this is ever simple—continue to fail to develop enduring interests in philosophy.[15] Furthermore, some philosophers do not believe that the present situation is racist, because many of the white philosophers involved do not have self-acknowledged feelings of hatred, aversion, or contempt for blacks. But if one views the situation in terms of a concept of institutional racism, it is racist.

When victims of racism racially identify themselves in order to resist and combat racism, they positively affirm the very identities that are used by racists in ways that have victimized them.

Even if they have *transvalued* the oppressive identities within communities of resistance, the identities still refer back to their racialist or racist origins. There would be no point to the transvaluation if external racism did not exist as something to be resisted and overcome. If racial identities were biological facts, then those identities would not be part of racial injustice. Racial identities have not been biological facts as those are understood by biologists since the early twentieth century, and persistent racial taxonomies depend on an ontological commitment to the existence of race as something that can be studied by science. Moreover, all racial taxonomies make a division between whites and nonwhites, which was originally posited by European whites for their own advantage. For these reasons, the affirmation of nonwhite identities probably has an intrinsic ceiling concerning the degree of justice that it can achieve. Such affirmation has been the road most traveled ever since Du Bois cautioned American blacks against minimizing racial difference, because he believed that they needed to strive to fulfill the destiny of their race.[16]

The lack of a biological basis for race is not a political issue. Still, interested parties will want to know exactly how that information will affect the politics of race as it has thus far developed in the service of social justice. If politics is a struggle for power and advantage or decreased disadvantage, the scientific facts are irrelevant unless they can be translated into motivating and empowering rhetoric. For such rhetorical purposes, emic racial identities are probably more useful because they require less intellectual effort to evoke. But stating it this way expresses a cynical condescension toward politicians, activists, and their public(s). Politics, political action, and rhetoric should be principled, with the aim of bettering the human condition and not merely obtaining more desirable relations of power. The core of good politics is a commitment to the life and dignity of all human beings. Such universalism would be compatible with common sense racial taxonomy if it were a system of mere variety and not one of value-laden difference. Twentieth-century liberatory racial politics was a series of footnotes to Du Bois played out as an insistence on the compatibility of existing racial taxonomy (containing an ontological commitment to biological race) with universal equality. Many liberatory and radical activists and scholars of race do not trust whites not to discriminate and behave unjustly to nonwhites unless nonwhite racial identities are explicitly mentioned, noticed, and acknowledged. Legal critical race theorists have argued that the race-neutral language of egalitarian law does not address existing racism, because it assumes it is possible to view all citizens as though they had no racial identities. In fact, unquestioned and pervasive discrimination on the basis of race often excludes nonwhites completely, so that contexts in apparent compliance with legal race neutrality are often contexts inhabited exclusively by whites.[17] The resulting political strategy has been to insist on visible and recognized nonwhite racial identities as integral ingredients in a new democratic pluralism.

What would happen if it became common knowledge that race in the emic biological sense did not exist? Possibly, new pseudobiological grounds for discrimination and aversion would be constructed. Certainly, there would continue to be social injustice against the poor, because they are the most vulnerable component of the capitalistic global corporate enterprise. But it is an empirical question exactly whether and how the present victims of racism might benefit from being relieved of false biological identities. It will require great courage to allow such a question to be answered through the actions of others, whom those most concerned with outcomes have no direct influence over and small reason to trust. The individual and small group project of relinquishing false biological notions of race will have two phases. The first is the acquisition and distribution of the required information about human biology. This scientific literacy will proceed at a slow pace through the academy until it is disseminated at the secondary and primary school levels. On the way, the resistance of the mass media to educated opinion that is not sensationalistic about race will have to be worn down, something that will probably happen only as the three-race generation is replaced by the no-race generation in research, business, and policy-making positions. That is the cognitive phase of the project.

The second phase of relinquishing false biological notions of race is the practical one of rethinking, undoing, and redoing those aspects of ordinary life and discourse, both oppressive and liberatory, which rely on assumptions that racial taxonomies and individual racial differences are real in ways that can be studied by biology. This revision will require a reexamination of received texts and the discovery and creation of new ones in many different fields. So far, the racial liberatory focus has been confined to issues of racism and reactions against it. Needed now will be concentration on the ways in which ungrounded taxonomies of race inform discourse. It will be necessary to reach a lucid understanding of what it literally and metaphorically means to use words and phrases such as these: black, Indian, Jewish, or any kind of racial blood, bloodlines, mixed blood, pure blood, racial solidarity, brotherhood, sisterhood, black ancestry, racial heritage, racial identity, or racial authenticity. These are just a few polite examples.

Discourse affects perception. It has become a sign of astuteness for African Americans to claim that when they look into the mirror, they do not see a man or woman before the glass, but a black man or a black woman. It has also become a sign of social awareness for everyone to notice whether or not a group or institution is racially diverse. Both self-perception and the perception of others as racially identified presuppose that racial identity is given in perception, whether one makes a point of noticing it or not. Suppose one looked at oneself and others and merely noted those physical characteristics that are used to socially construct race, without thereby constructing race? What will we see? How will what we see affect the humanity we take for granted or withhold from ourselves and others?

Where general discourse is embedded with a persistent idea, the idea has an effect on actions and institutions that go beyond the medium of discourse. For instance, is it racism that keeps the United States residentially segregated, or might it not also at core be *racialism*? Much more would be at stake in the shift from the second to the last paradigm of race, than cognition, perception, discourse, and social habit. Economics and politics would be involved, and it is money that could speed up a process of cultural change otherwise requiring centuries. It is not a coincidence that the widespread presence of women in the American workplace accompanied the shift from a manufacturing to an informational and service economy during a period of inflation that made it necessary for women to contribute to household income. Slavery was a profitable form of agricultural business for the South, and during the period of intense segregation, blacks in the workforce continued to be exploited by whites who despised them socially and excluded them politically. The hatred and genocide of Native Americans accompanied their dispossession from ancestral lands. In the West, during the late nineteenth and early twentieth centuries, Asian immigrants were a source of cheap labor for railroad construction and agriculture, and they were treated with great cruelty and contempt. Today, disproportionate numbers of African Americans are "in" the criminal justice system, and some critics now call it "the prison industrial complex," because inmates represent jobs for prison personnel and profits for contractors.

I don't want to milk what alert adolescents now know or put too great a burden on neo-Marxian insights. But, it is important to realize that while the racial identities assigned to those exploited have oiled the wheels of exploitation, those identities have often been extrinsic and ad hoc to the brute facts of exploitation. It couldn't have been otherwise, given that there never existed any such thing as biological race. The more brutal the exploitation, the greater the vilification of its victims by those benefiting from their servitude and death. The fulcrum for historical change on behalf of the victims of exploitation is not a matter of how they are identified before, during, or after exploitation, but the material conditions that make them vulnerable to exploitation in the first place. Because American economic exploitation is mostly a matter of profit, and the business of America is still business, material conditions are most of the story. This subject exceeds the scope of this book, but it is the next subject after the disabuse of "race."[18]

As a practice, the revision of biological ideas of race will reach so deeply into lives based on racial affinities and aversions that the world will not merely become a more just place in issues of race, but it will no longer be the same world.[19] Even the most dedicated and idealistically motivated, and especially them, barely have enough minutes in the day to fulfill their present work, family, social, and civic obligations. How will they have time to effect such change, and with little thanks at the outset? As the practical project of revising life worlds imbued with false ideas of race progresses, it will free up the time and effort presently consumed by race. Because race is a construction requiring constant sorting and identification, it is a dynamic, ongoing, performative process. There is nothing about anyone's racial membership that is simply attached once. Racial membership must constantly be tended, remembered, enacted, and reenacted. Some nonracial part of consciousness must always be ready to assess what is required from a racial self. Under Jim Crow, black men had to remember not to look at white women, and today they have to remember not to scare white women if they encounter them alone at night on city streets. Whites have to remember that they can count on certain unearned advantages that increase directly with the degree of racism in the context. Asian Americans have to remember to let white Americans know that they were born in the United States and to forgive them for assuming that they were instead born somewhere "in Asia." As I revise this manuscript, the current war following September 11, 2001, is contributing to many things that Islamic Americans will have to remember about how they are perceived. Children of all races need to be periodically reminded of their racial membership and of what their elders consider to be the obligations or "dues" that accompany it. Given all this, it's probably not a matter of finding the time to undo race, but of appreciating in retrospect how much time was spent doing it, and making good use of the resources thus liberated.

In immediate pragmatic terms, interested parties will want to know how, while this great revision is occurring, they are expected to view contemporary laws against racial discrimination, as well as the remnants of affirmative action. Will the acknowledged demise of biological race render such measures redundant? I think that anyone who is familiar with race relations in the United States, both past and present, anyone who lives in the culture with a modicum of awareness of how advantages and disadvantages get distributed, would sense that the acknowledged biological emptiness of race is no guarantee that old epistemologies of common sense race won't continue to operate, or that biological race will not still be constructed. But the construction will be driven underground. Witches were believed to be real, the majority thought that they could identify them, and when it was convenient, they tormented and persecuted them. After it came to be generally acknowledged that witches did not exist, it was witch hunters and witch tormentors, in a word, "witchists," who were on the defensive. Even private social discrimination against witches in cultures failing to believe that witches existed would be difficult to imagine. We have already seen such a process at work between the first and second paradigms of race. The first paradigm belief that inferior psyches and cultures accompanied nonwhite racial identities has been rejected as an unacceptable form of racism under the second paradigm. However, the pragmatic answer to the above question is that all of the laws protecting nonwhites against racism, and probably more such laws, are necessary until racism no longer exists, *no matter how long that takes*. In short, racism must be treated separately from the facts about race, even though the facts about race represent its ultimate demise, now in theory, later in practice.

THE STAKES

During the mid 1990s, an erudite and well-published African philosopher of my acquaintance, who had been an American citizen for several years, applied to be nominated for a university affirmative action position in a department of philosophy, also of my acquaintance. The candidate gave a talk about his work to the philosophy department and was interviewed on campus. The members of the philosophy department who participated in the interviewing process were all white males. Much to his disappointment, the candidate was not accepted for nomination by the philosophy department, because they did not think he was "really" a philosopher. He was a mature man, much traveled, and educated in England, so he was aware firsthand of the history of colonialism and postcolonialism in Africa and beyond. He said to me, "Oh, I know these white guys from way back. They don't change much. Maybe an inch a century."

There remains much ongoing institutional racism in the United States, as well as recalcitrant pockets of overt and deliberate individual racism against nonwhites. However, given that the public still lives within a racial paradigm, the civil rights, voting rights, and immigration rights secured by nonwhites in the United States over the twentieth century are at least an inch of change. The next inch will have to be gained first within educated liberatory movements that have disabused themselves of empirically ungrounded biological notions of race, races, racial identities, and individual racial projects.

Some will say, "So what if race is a social construction? Ordinary racist life will not be disturbed by this so-called news of the lack of biological foundation." How do they know that this news will have no effect, when the belief that race is biological is embedded in "race" as a social construction? Race is like the liar who says he speaks the truth, the social construction that is constructed around denial that it is a social construction.

The notion of race as biological is not an abstract fact that is independent of other vital beliefs held by people. Race as biological has been a vast network of practical ideas and thought, which to name a few includes: ideals of beauty, sexuality and forms of gender, notions of special skills, ideas about character, virtue, vice, wealth, the family, and superiority and inferiority. And each of those ideas and more has been lived out in emotion, experience, and behavior.

Du Bois's envisioned dawn was an idea of legal equality and economic and educational opportunity for blacks in America. The civil rights legislation of the 1960s was the historical face of Du Bois's dawn. That time has been succeeded by morning and the fatigue of late morning. We are now at a High Noon, when war, terror, new projects of racialization, the complete corporate colonization of the world, and its attendant ecological depletion, demand a degree of vigilance, against which attachment to identities based on outdated science is frivolous. It would also be frivolous for me, here, to attempt further *rhetoric* toward getting those who think "left" to recognize a basic scientific truth about humankind. Those to the "right" are still not off the hook concerning institutional racism. We should all think straight about this matter that runs deeper than politics.

NOTES

1. W. E. B. Du Bois, "The Conservation of Races," in *The Idea of Race*, eds. Robert Bernasconi and Tommy L. Lott (Indianapolis, IN: Hackett, 2000), p. 110.
2. Stephen J. Gould, "Racist Arguments and IQ," in *Race and IQ: Expanded Edition*, ed. Ashley Montagu (New York: Oxford University Press, 1999), pp. 183–89.
3. Ashley Montagu, "Introduction" in *Race and IQ*, p. 1; Stephen Jay Gould, "Critique of the Bell Curve," in Gould, *The Mismeasure of Man* (New York: W. W. Norton, 1996), pp. 367–90.
4. A. R. Jensen, *Educability and Group Differences* (New York: Harper and Row, 1973).
5. R. J. Herrnstein and Charles Murray, *The Bell Curve* (New York: The Free Press, 1994).
6. Gould, "Racist Arguments and IQ," p. 189, n. 1.
7. B. Devlin, Michael Daniels, and Kathryn Roeder, "The Heritability of IQ," *Nature* 388, no. 31 (July 1997): 468–71.
8. Ned Block, "How Heredity Misleads About Race," in Montagu, *Race and IQ*, pp. 444–81.
9. Ibid.
10. Ibid.
11. American Anthropological Association, "Should the AAA Adopt a Position Paper on 'Race?'" *Anthropology Newsletter* 38, no. 7 (1997): 27.
12. See Ian Hacking, *The Social Construction of What?* (Cambridge, MA: Harvard University Press, 1999), pp. 5–8ff.
13. Ibid., pp. 8–62.
14. For a more comprehensive discussion of race and paradigm theory, see Zack, "Philosophy and Racial Paradigms," loc. cit. note 16.
15. See Leonard Harris, "The Status of Blacks in Academic Philosophy," *The Journal of Blacks in Higher Education* (Winter, 1994/5), reprinted in *Race, Class, Gender and Sexuality: The Big Questions*, eds. Naomi Zack, Laurie Schrage, and Crispin Sartwell (Malden, MA: Blackwell, 1998), pp. 48–49.
16. W. E. B. Du Bois, "The Conservation of Races," reprinted in *The Idea of Race*, eds. Robert Bernasconi and Tommy L. Lott (Indianapolis, IN: Hackett, 2000), pp. 108–17.
17. On these issues, see Patricia J. Williams, *The Alchemy of Race and Rights* (Cambridge, MA: Harvard University Press, 1991).
18. On these issues, see Naomi Zack, "Lockean Money, Globalism and Indigenism," *Canadian Journal of Philosophy*, 1999 Supplementary vol. 25; Catherine Wilson, ed., *Civilization and Oppression* (Calgary: University of Calgary Press, 1999), pp. 31–53; Zack, "Goldberg on Segregation and Prisons," *African Philosophy* 13, no. 2 (2000): 164–71.
19. See Hacking, *The Social Construction of What?*, pp. 128–32.

Collective Responsibility and Multiple Racial, Ethnic, and Cultural Identities

Kai C. Wong

Kai Wong teaches philosophy at Maryville University. He is a coeditor of this anthology. He writes in the areas of ethics, political philosophy, and continental philosophy.

In this article, Wong questions our ability to define races, ethnicities, and cultures, since it is not clear that such groups have a unique identifying feature. This complexity in group membership attribution has practical implications. For example, affirmative action and other policies aimed at addressing wrongs against groups might not be coherent if membership in a group is itself questionable. In such a scenario, it would be impossible to identify either the victims or the perpetrators. Ultimately, Wong argues that we can define group membership on the basis of a set of overlapping characteristics such that we can make sense of two individuals' membership in the same group even if they share no common characteristic.

"We cannot help but believe that the old hatreds shall someday pass, that the lines of tribe shall soon dissolve."
—BARACK OBAMA'S INAUGURAL ADDRESS

Contemporary discourse surrounding collective responsibility is largely dominated by the (working) assumption that a community has more or less well-established boundaries, with its members sharing a set of similar characteristics, beliefs, values, interest, and practices that distinguishes them from members of other communities.[1] Joel Feinberg for one maintains that at the heart of collective responsibility (liability) is a sense of solidarity, which unites the members of a group in terms of reciprocal interests and bonds of sentiment, as well as the sharing of benefits and harms in a common destiny.[2] Albeit dissenting from Feinberg's requirement of a high degree of solidarity, Howard McGary believes that even loosely organized groups such as the residents of a particular state, may manifest solidarity, not because of reciprocal interests but because of a strategic need for security and benefits.[3] Virginia Held argues that even a random collection of individuals can be held responsible just because they have failed to organize themselves into a group that is capable of making decisions when the situation so requires them to.[4] On the other hand, in discussing collective responsibility in the context of corporations, Peter French speaks of an "internal decision structure" which synthesizes "the intentions and acts of various biological persons into a corporate decision."[5] Despite the varying focus of these commentators, underlying their arguments is the same assumption of common or shared interests and characteristics in a group or a community.

Admittedly, this presumption of common or shared interests and characteristics works fairly well for the ascription of group blame when communities were less fluid and permeable—or perhaps when it is applied to the analysis of corporations whose members are brought together through some

Kai Wong, "Collective Responsibility and Multiple Racial, Ethnic, and Cultural Identities."

383

specific interest or purpose. When different racial or ethnic groups lived in compulsorily segregated communities, when exclusionary immigration laws were in place, it is arguably not very difficult to assess from a collective standpoint who was responsible for harming whom. This is because there is some set of characteristics that is shared by most, if not all, of the members of the same community. However, the more we see people cross ethnic and cultural boundaries, the more we see individuals like Barack Obama appearing in the public eye, the harder it is for this conception of community to capture the multifaceted nature of contemporary identities with multiple belief systems and value orientations. The fact that the US government began to allow individuals to check off more than one racial/ethnic category on the 2000 census form represented an official admission that racial, ethnic, and even cultural identifications in this country are not as clear-cut and restrictive as they have been in the past. The emergence of multiracial, multiethnic, and multicultural communities poses a daunting challenge as to whether we can properly speak of a "collective" and thereby whether we can speak of any group as collectively responsible for historical misdeeds.

The weight of this challenge could be better appraised if we consider a concrete example—the claim that whites are responsible for past and current injustice endured by minorities. Even setting aside the question of how guilt can be transferred from one generation to another for the moment,[6] what does it mean to say that whites as a group are responsible for harming minorities? Needless to say, there are whites who are diehard supremacists and who we can say are still responsible for injustice committed against racial and ethnic minorities. But one must not forget that there are whites whose ancestors not only did not own slaves but were themselves opposed to slavery and other kinds of racial injustice. Then there are children of poor whites who have themselves been the victims of economic and class oppressions and might not have contributed to harming minorities after all. Adding to this complexity is of course the fact that many whites have embraced multiple ethnic and cultural heritages: they are "a multicultural event"[7]— Jewish, African American, and Native American all

rolled into one, for example.[8] On top of this, there are cases in which a white person of German descent chooses to marry someone with a Jewish descent. Does it mean then that their children somehow end up being both oppressors and victims? What *could* that mean? Therefore, all things considered, except for the mere coincidence of skin color, what do all whites have in common by which we can judge they belong to the same community, much less the community of oppressors?[9]

Conversely, we can examine the challenge from the perspective of those historically victimized. Consider the larger Jewish community, which is as diverse as it is heterogeneous. Without doubt, there are very religious, orthodox Jews, but there are also conservative Jews, assimilated secular Jews, and black Jews. These groups don't seem to share any single (set of) feature(s) by which we can say definitively that one is Jewish while the other is not. Thus, it does not appear that there are any non-arbitrary criteria for defining the meaning of being Jewish, because there are so many different ways in which people *can be* Jewish. And if we cannot define Jewish identity in virtue of some overarching characteristic, as it can be argued, we are at a loss to say precisely who have been harmed and who should be compensated for enduring such harms. Accordingly, the concept of collective historical responsibility, whether approached from the perspective of the victims or that of the perpetrators, arguably makes little sense in our era of multiple community participation. We would have to forget about inter-group wrongdoings and discard such policies as affirmative action aimed at mitigating the effects of collective past injustice, not necessarily because such wrongdoings together with their legacies have been properly dealt with, but because they are somehow "diluted" by a contingent sociohistorical development that confounds the traditional understanding of community.

It would be, however, too hasty to jump to the conclusion that we can just dispense with the idea of community as a collective and thus the idea of collective responsibility altogether as applied to the racial, ethnic, and cultural categories. For one thing, we *do* mean something when we say that Sally is "very Americanized" even though she has been in the United States for only a short while and even if the United States is as diverse as it has ever been as a society. We also intend that our comparative judgments make some sense when we say that one Lebanese restaurant serves more "authentic" Lebanese cuisine than another does. These attributions purport to pick out something or other held to be characteristic of the community in question—in spite of the fact that these attributions may turn out to be mistaken. Second, our considered judgment also tells us that not anybody who casually claims to be Irish, say, is automatically considered Irish. There has to be some characteristic or other that this person must have in order for her to belong to that community. The challenge, then, is to spell out what underlies our considered judgments.[10]

In this essay, I show that a community's identity can be established on the basis of overlapping and crisscrossing characteristics which link members together directly or indirectly via a "family resemblance" of relationships. On this understanding, the idea of collective responsibility remains meaningful despite the fact that contemporary racial, ethnic, and cultural communities are more open-ended and diverse than they were before. In the first section I present this model of community. In the second section, I outline two general norms for assessing a person's share of collective responsibility. I end this essay by considering an objection to this paradigm of community, namely, that the absence of concrete criteria for determining and ranking community identifications would make it difficult to assess the responsibility that an individual may share in virtue of her community memberships.

I. THE "OVERLAPPING CHARACTERISTICS" APPROACH TO DEFINING A COMMUNITY

To begin with, it seems correct to say that there is neither a necessary nor a sufficient condition (nor a set of unchanging and "essential" conditions) by which to delimit memberships in our age of fluid identities and blurred community borders. Neither language, culture, race, nationality, place of origin or adoption, history, nor tradition, nor even a combination of these, can be conclusively said to constitute a defining (set of) characteristic(s) of community identity. But it is also obvious that if one lacks *all* of these relevant conditions, one *cannot* be a member of a given community. If one has never been to Italy, does not speak Italian, knows hardly anything about Italian art or history, has no friends or relatives who are Italian, and so on, it is mistaken to claim that one is Italian in any sense of the word. While no one single characteristic is necessary, the absence of all these conditions would unequivocally rule out as justifiable any claim of membership association in a given community. The task is, then, to figure out how these different conditions come into play in the definition of community memberships.

My central claim is this: Although it is not necessary that members share all the characteristics in order for them to belong to the same community, they must share some characteristic (or some set of characteristics thereof) that overlaps in one way or another.

Otherwise, they do not belong together in the same community. Represented more formally, my idea goes as follows:

> X and Y belong to community *C* if and only if X shares some (nontrivial) characteristic (language, culture, history, place of origin or adoption, values, ends, etc.) or some such set thereof with Y *directly,* or *indirectly* through some (nontrivial) characteristic (or set of characteristics) that Z has.

I call this paradigm of community membership an "overlapping characteristics model," or, in Wittgensteinian terms if you will, a "family resemblance model."[11]

According to Wittgenstein, there is no necessary or sufficient condition for defining a general term. There isn't anything in common to all the leaves or games by which we can judge whether a given instance is a leaf or a game. What they all have instead is a family of resemblances, "a complicated network of similarities overlapping and criss-crossing. . . ."[12] As a first approximation, take the following group of individuals with members X, Y, and Z that have properties as follows: X(*p, q, r*), Y(*q, r, s*), and Z(*s, t, u*). It can be readily seen that X, Y, and Z do not all share any property in common; nonetheless, they are related to each other through some overlapping characteristics, with X in this case more directly related to Y than to Z due to two shared properties q and r. On the other hand, X and Z are not completely unrelated either, because of Y's sharing s with Z.

To further clarify my approach to community definition, let me take up the question of Asian identity. As it stands, the term is popularly read in the North American context to refer to people from East Asia, including parts if not all of Southeast Asia and descendants of immigrants from such regions who now live in this part of the world. On this understanding, a Thai Buddhist and a third-generation Chinese American may share very little in terms of life experiences, but if they are both avid learner of Chinese culture and have studied in China, they can be said to be associated with the Asian community.

On the other hand, two individuals might not share any property directly but could still be considered to belong to the larger Asian community due to their connection to other people who share overlapping characteristics with them. Take a native-born South Korean, and a second-generation American born of mixed Korean and European heritage, who may not have any strong personal feelings about South Korea. These two individuals do not necessarily share anything in terms of language, culture, territorial identification, etc. But suppose the Korean American of mixed heritage has parents who lived in Korea, and because of this connection, both the native Korean and the Korean American can be said to be associated with the Asian community, broadly understood. This is an example of "indirect overlapping."

Accordingly, under this model, a community consists of plural and diverse subgroups with sometimes conflicting value orientations. The Korean American and the native Korean may have very different views concerning America's role in Korea and that part of the region. Despite diverse and even conflicting value conceptions, both parties can still think of themselves as falling under the umbrella of the term 'Asian.' What is critical under this paradigm of community definition is that there are many ways people can be "-ish", "-ese" or "-ian"

insofar as they possess some (nontrivial) characteristic that can be linked directly or indirectly to others in the existing community. Unlike the more traditional community, the contemporary community on this analysis is not bounded by rigid boundaries, "not closed by a frontier."[13]

Note that in proposing that community memberships are to be defined more in terms of overlapping characteristics than of universally shared ones, I do not rule out the possibility of overarching characteristics for a community at any given time. As an example, the Civil Rights Movement represents such a pivotal moment in recent American experience that one claiming to be an American today cannot simply disregard its significance. Similarly, the Holocaust continues to be a constitutive moment in contemporary German identity, so much so that it is difficult to be a Holocaust-denier without a serious disruption in the historical self-understanding of anyone claiming to be German today.[14] These are events or historical experiences that are so crucial that members of the community individually cannot dismiss them by fiat.

In a nutshell, on this model, the community as a whole is built through a matrix of interconnected and overlapping properties that diverse individuals share, as differently situated as they are. While one subgroup in a community might not feel an immediate sense of identification or solidarity with another subgroup, these two subgroups can nonetheless see how they are connected to the larger entity via various links to other subgroups. Although a community is loser in this sense than is conventionally conceived, understanding of the community as a collective is still possible despite the community's diverse values and practices.

II. TWO GENERAL NORMS OF ASSESSING COLLECTIVE RESPONSIBILITY

Thus far, I have shown that it is conceptually viable to define the contemporary community despite its intrinsic diversity. I have yet to establish the relationship of collective responsibility to this "overlapping characteristics model." In this section, I outline two general norms by which collective responsibility can be assessed. A more robust account of deliberating about sharing responsibility historically is developed elsewhere.[15]

Since there are two ways in which a member of a community can be related to another member under this new paradigm of defining community, there are also two ways in which a member can be held responsible for harms done by other members of the community. First, a person can be held responsible for harm done by other members whose beliefs, values, and attitudes she immediately shares. For instance, a person with racist attitudes toward a particular ethnic group can be held responsible for the harm caused by those who go out to harass members of that group, even though she herself has never actually inflicted harm on the victims. This is because her attitudes increase the risk of the occurrence of such crimes.[16] In more formal terms, the following norm of appraisal of responsibility applies when a member comes from the same *subgroup* of the same community:

> Given that X and Y belong to the same subgroup S of the same community C, the more X shares with Y the harm-causing or blameworthy qualities, i. e., morally objectionable intentions, attitudes, decisions, actions, ends, values, and practices, the more X shares responsibility for (responding to or failing to respond to) the harm (already) caused by Y to Z of community D.

It is important to note that there are two ways of reading this norm (and the next one). The first way is to leave out the parenthesis, that is, when we are dealing with the responsibility of contemporaneous offenders. That is to say, X and Y can influence each other in their actions and attitudes. The second way of reading it is to include the parenthesis. That is when we are dealing with intergenerational responsibility: we suppose that later generations cannot go back in time to hurt the victims of departed generations.[17] Responsibility in this sense is not causal, but has to do with a response or a failure to respond to some harm already done.[18]

However, not only can a person be held culpable for directly related to members who have caused harm but also she can be guilty for wrongs done because of the indirect connections to other subgroups of the same community. As an example, consider the parents of a daughter married to someone from another race and culture. Suppose they invited to their dinner party a friend who shares neither their racial and cultural backgrounds nor their son-in-law's. During the course of the conversation, their son-in-law made a racist joke pertaining to the racial background of the guest. Not only did they fail to confront him but they also joined in the chorus of laughter. They were guilty of contributing to racial harm not only because they insulted the guest directly but also arguably because they were indirectly related to the culprit through their daughter. Hence, for members linked to different subgroups within a community, this second norm of evaluating responsibility applies:

> Given that X belongs to subgroup S_1, Y to subgroup S_2, and that both X and Y belong to the same community C, the more X shares, through indirect connections, harm-causing or blameworthy qualities with Y, the more X shares responsibility for (responding to or failing to respond to) the harm (already) caused by Y to Z of community D.

In formulating these two norms I don't mean to rule out a *qualitative* assessment of responsibility: some qualities can be more prominent than others as harm-causing ones. It is certainly possible that, given two individuals X and Y in C, X can be considered more responsible for harming members of D because X has an attribute *f* which is far more harm-causing than *g* and *h* combined, which Y has. I want to leave open the interpretation of "more" in the two norms so as to embrace a qualitative as well as a quantitative dimension in the assessment of degrees of responsibility.

In conclusion, despite the heterogeneous character of contemporary communities, there is a promising way of defining a community and evaluating shared responsibility. Admittedly, these norms of evaluation are merely general criteria, but they demonstrate that the notion of collective moral responsibility can still be preserved despite the fact that identities are more fluid and open in our contemporary setting.[19] But first, I turn to a challenge to my model of defining community.

III. ANSWERING AN OBJECTION TO THE "OVERLAPPING CHARACTERISTICS" MODEL OF COMMUNITY

Even if one can analyze a community in terms of overlapping and crisscrossing properties, one might still insist that the absence of concrete criteria for determining and ranking community memberships and for attributing blame to individuals would render my account arbitrary, for it would still be difficult to draw the line between where a community ends and where another begins. Consider the following objection:

> "Consider two groups of, say, six individuals each which we wish to distinguish from each other: Group 1 is composed of members A, B, C, D, E, and F. And Group 2 is composed of members G, H, I, J, K, and L . . . For the first group the properties would be as follows, (in parentheses): A(*a, b*), B(*b, c*), C(*c, d*), D(*d, e*), E(*e, f*), and F(*f, g*). For the second group the properties would be as follows: G(*g, h*), H(*h, i*), I(*i, j*), J(*j, k*), K(*k, i*), and L(*l, m*). Now, the point to note is that the last member of the first group has one property in common with the first member of the second group. The significance of this fact is that this makes the break between the two groups arbitrary. That is, there is no more reason to end the first group with F and to begin the second group with G than to end the first group with B and begin the second group with C."[20]

If the contemporary open-ended communities were linked together mostly in the way represented in the objection, then it would indeed spell serious trouble for my account here, for there would simply be no non-arbitrary way to make a break anywhere. Defining community membership and responsibility would then be as good as anybody's guess. Fortunately, such representation does not come close to capturing the nature of contemporary community, in my judgment. A more refined characterization is attributed to Jorge Gracia, who proposes the so-called "Common-Bundle View":[21]

> Say that we identify a group [call it group 1'] with six members A, B, C, D, E and F. And let us propose a set of six properties, *a, b, c, d, e* and *f* . . . [E]ach member of the group would have several of these

properties as, for instance, A(*a, b*), B(*a, b, e, f*), C(*c, d, f*), D(*b, c, d, e, f*), E(*a, e*), and F(*b, e, f*).[22]

On this view, there is a tighter connection amongst the group's members than there is amongst non-members. Instead of linking together via only one property, there are now multiple connections shared by all members, with some having stronger connections with each other than others. In this case, D has more properties than E and hence is more paradigmatic as a member of group 1' than E is. D is also more similar to B than to A. To make the point even more clearly, one can go one step further to introduce another group (group 2') with G, H, I, J, K, L as members and also a set of six properties, *g, h, i, j, a,* and *c*. Suppose members of this latter group have the following properties: G(*g, h, i, j, c*), H(*h, i, j, a*), I(*i, j, h, a, c*), J(*g, h, i, j*), K(*a, c*), L(*a, j*). Each member except J in this group is connected to group 1' in one way or another. G and J are more similar to each other than they are to L or K, since they have four properties in common. J has no immediate connection to members of group 1', What is interesting is that K shares two frequently occurring properties from the two groups, whereas L can be considered marginal to group 1', since L carries only one frequently occurring property from that group. The upshot is that we can identify the clear cases of memberships and come up with a set of properties that we believe to be characteristic of that group. And on that basis, judgments about marginal cases can be made.

The Common-Bundle View seems to alleviate the concern that the boundaries between communities would be arbitrary. It also shows that some individuals can be said to be more of a member, or more paradigmatic, of a community than others. Thus someone who speaks Portuguese, has spent substantial periods of his life in Portugal, knows the history and politics of that country well, and has learnt to discern the nuances of various kinds of Port wine is more Portuguese than a person who holds merely a Portuguese passport. Nonetheless, there are situations where it is difficult to compare who is more of member than others in a given community. Is a Puerto Rican more Hispanic than a Columbian? Is a Shintoist Japanese more Asian than a Confucian born in Singapore? It is difficult to give a definite answer in these kinds of cases. In light of such difficulty, how are we going to arrive at the set of properties most distinctive of a given community? Besides, given the open-ended nature of community, the set of properties may simply be too provisional: the list of characteristics regarded as significant in the past and for the present may cease to be important in the future. Consequently, even granting that the Common-Bundle characterization more closely captures the nature of the contemporary community, because of the difficulty in fixing characteristics, this paradigm is arguably not very useful.

This point is well taken, and I do not mean to underestimate the practical difficulties in fixing properties for a given community. What I propose to do in the ensuing discussion is to show by means of an example how evaluative criteria could figure into the assessment of distinctive properties for a community, in the hope of alleviating the concern that determining a set of distinctive properties for a community would become prohibitively complex.

Take the notion of the "Asian" community. The term 'Asian' is popularly used here in the United States to refer primarily to East Asia—which may include parts of Southeast Asia, and the Asian Pacific communities living in this country.[23] It designates a community that encompasses a diversity of peoples speaking a plurality of languages ranging from Malay, to Korean, Japanese, Chinese, English and other European languages. Unlike the Hispanic identity, which has historically been shaped by a particular event, namely, the arrival of Columbus in 1492, no comparable historical moment can be singularly identified that has exercised such a pervasive impact upon all the peoples and nations in the Asian community. Undoubtedly, there were periods of Western colonization and domination in the region, but its penetration has not been as all-encompassing as it was, say, in Africa. This complexity is compounded by the historical rivalry and grievances amongst various countries, especially between Japan and those hurt by the Japanese invasion and occupation in the last world war. In this regard, the Asian community is arguably far too diverse and heterogeneous to be called a community at all.

Nonetheless, amidst the divisions of race, ethnicities, and languages there exists underlying strands of overlapping connections found in such traditions as Buddhism and Confucianism, which happened to have crossed many national and ethnic boundaries. Buddhism originated in India, but its influence has disseminated throughout much of East and Southeast Asia, and its strongholds have since migrated to places like Thailand, Tibet, and Japan. Confucianism, on the other hand, finds its conspicuous appearance in Singapore, Taiwan, Japan, and some places of Southeast Asia, besides its place of origin, China. Even in the most modernized and Westernized metropolitan cities like Hong Kong, Confucianism and Buddhism in both religious and philosophical forms still make their presence felt, albeit arguably to a less visible degree. What is interesting is that when Christianity was first introduced to a region heavily influenced by Confucianism, it was made to rethink issues barely discussed in the Western context, for instance, filial piety.[24]

A salient illustration of an "Asian cultural character" is perhaps found in Asian views of human rights, which differ at least to some extent from the mainstream Western liberal conception. The liberal conception sees individuals as the bearers of rights regardless of their social and cultural characteristics; it also views individuals as making claims against one another in antagonistic terms even at the risk of serious disruptions in human relationships. To be sure, even contemporary commentators of the Confucian tradition disagree concerning the compatibility of Confucianism with human rights, but they seem to agree that the Confucian society favors a less litigious and more harmonious ordering of human relationships.[25] Some Asian countries even legally require grown children to support financially their aging parents, a notion that is quite alien to Western sensibility. On the other hand, some Buddhist thinkers have proposed what is known as the "soft conception" of human rights, namely, a more relational approach based on sympathy and compassion rather than justice.[26] It is not my objective in this essay to debate the respective merits of Asian and Western views. My point is that when confronted with values that could entail wholescale disruptions in the existing way of life or the loss of cultural uniqueness, a community may have some grounds for limiting the adoption of such values. This is what has happened to French-speaking Quebec, whose aim it is to protect their culture from erosion by the Anglophone culture. But one should not jump to the conclusion that a community may not incorporate in the future values that appear to be alien at the present time, given that cultural values and practices are amenable to change. Nevertheless, in the interest of reducing disruptions to their way of life, a community may be justified in limiting the appropriation of such values or at least streamlining them in such a way that they could be more compatible with their existing practices.

What I meant to show with this example is that some properties, whether historical connectedness, cultural traits or ethnic qualities, and so forth, could figure more prominently than others in the determination of the distinctive character of a community. Because communities originate or come to be shaped in different ways, these preexisting scripts provide certain parameters for determining which qualities are most paradigmatic of those communities. Even conceding that community boundaries are more open-ended than before, one does not have to accept that evaluating which qualities are most salient in a community is completely arbitrary. That is why even if it is true that the set of distinctive properties for a community is subject to change, changes take place within certain historical or cultural givens. Once again, I do not mean to downplay the practical difficulty of fixing properties for a community; what I hope to have done is to assuage the worry that deciding on a set of properties for a community is a hopeless undertaking.

If the foregoing reasoning is correct, collective responsibility could be assessed by examining characteristics paradigmatic of a community. For instance, a case could be made that within the larger Asian community one subgroup S_1 can share a measure of responsibility for injustice perpetrated by another subgroup S_2 against women in S_2

in virtue of their common identification with the traditionally patriarchal and hierarchical nature of Confucian society, even though the former subgroup is not directly responsible for such wrongs.[27] Needless to say, this new model of community provides only a conceptual framework to evaluate the burden of responsibilities; it cannot yield definite or precise answers. Moreover, deliberating about one's share of responsibility for wrongdoings in the contemporary setting requires that one clarify and integrate one's various community identifications: one cannot meaningfully participate in an infinite number of racial, ethnic, and cultural communities; one has to draw some boundaries and make some sensible choices regarding which communities one most wants to associate with. Questions about the share of responsibilities cannot be answered without first addressing questions about the extent of one's community identifications or commitments.[28] Nonetheless, it is my hope that the framework I have outlined presents a fruitful approach for thinking about participating in multiple communities and sharing responsibility for collective historical wrongdoings.[29]

NOTES

1. The following commentators seem to have presupposed this conception of a group or a community in the debate: D. E. Cooper, "Collective Responsibility," *Philosophy* 44 (1969): 66–9, and "Responsibility and the 'System,'" in *Individual and Collective Responsibility: The Massacre at My Lai,* 2nd ed., ed. Peter A. French (Cambridge, Mass.: Schenkman Publishing Co., 1998), pp. 133–50; David Copp, "What Collectives are: Agency, Individualism and Legal Theory," *Dialogue* 23 (1984): 249–70, and "Collective Actions and Secondary Actions," *American Philosophical Quarterly* 16 (1979): 177–86; Richard DeGeorge, "Social Reality and Social Relations," *The Review of Metaphysics* 37 (1983): 1–20; Joel Feinberg, "Collective Responsibility," in *Doing and Deserving* (Princeton, N.J.: Princeton University Press, 1970), pp. 222–51; Peter French, "The Corporation as a Moral Person," *American Philosophical Quarterly* 16 (1979): 207–15, and *Collective and Corporate Responsibility* (New York: Columbia University Press, 1984); Virginia Held, "Can a Random Collection of Individuals be Morally Responsible?" *Journal of Philosophy* 23 (1970): 471–81, and "Moral Responsibility and Collective Action," in *Individual and Collective Responsibility,* 2nd ed., ed. Peter French; Larry May, *The Morality of Groups* (Notre Dame, IN: The University of Notre Dame Press,

1987), pp. 151–66, and *Sharing Responsibility* (Chicago: The University of Chicago Press, 1992); Howard McGary, "Morality and Collective Liability," *Journal of Value Inquiry* 20 (1986): 157–65, reprinted in *Collective Responsibility: Five Decades of Debate in Theoretical and Applied Ethics,* ed. Larry May and Stacy Hoffman (Savage, MD: Rowman & Littlefield, 1991), pp. 77–87; and Michael Zimmerman, "Sharing Responsibility," *American Philosophical Quarterly* 22 (1985): 115–22.

It is noteworthy that we are seeing signs of change in some recent works on collective responsibility. See for example, Larry May, *The Socially Responsible Self* (Chicago: University of Chicago Press, 1996), pp. 13–4 and pp. 103–4 and Marion Smiley, *Moral Responsibility and the Boundaries of Community* (Chicago: University of Chicago Press, 1992), esp. chapter 8, where the possibility of multiple community identities is briefly explored.

2. Feinberg, "Collective Responsibility," p. 234.

3. McGary, "Morality and Collective Liability," in *Collective Responsibility,* pp. 77–87. See note 1 above.

4. Held, "Can a Random Collection of Individuals be Morally Responsible?" pp. 471–81. See note 1 above.

5. French, "The Corporation as a Moral Person," p. 212. See the previous note.

6. This issue is dealt with at length in the second chapter of my doctoral dissertation, *Collective Historical Responsibility and Multiple Community Identities: Deliberating about Identity and Responsibility in an Age of Diversity and Ambiguity* (St. Louis, Missouri: Washington University in St. Louis, 2005).

7. From Ronald Takaki, *A Different Mirror: A History of Multicultural America* (Boston: Little, Brown & Company, 1993), p. 427.

8. As in the case of Naomi Zack. See her "On Being and Not-Being Black and Jewish," in *Racially Mixed People in America,* ed. Maria P. P. Root (Newbury Park, CA: Sage, 1992) and *Race and Mixed Race* (Philadelphia: Temple University Press, 1993). See also the collections of essays in *American Mixed Race: The Culture of Microdiversity,* ed. Naomi Zack (Lanham, Md.: Rowman & Littlefield Publishers, 1995).

9. Not to mention that "probably about 1 percent of the genes of the white population [in the United States] are from African ancestors, and there are millions of white Americans who have at least small amounts of black genetic heritage." See F. James Davis, *Who is Black?* (University Park, Pennsylvania: Pennsylvania State University Press, 1991), p. 29.

10. Leon J. Goldstein stops short of doing that in his attempt to conceptualize Jewish identity: "I venture to suggest that the only solution to the problem of Jewish identity—a solution in the sense that we could approach an understanding of why there is such difference and why there seems to be no way to characterize conceptually what Jewish identity is, though, for the most part, we identify the same people as Jewish and have strong intuition that there is something shared by this diversity of individuals—is to come to see why it is that these questions have no answers." See his "Thoughts on Jewish Identity," in *Jewish Identity,* ed. David Theo Goldberg and Michael Krausz (Philadelphia: Temple University Press, 1993), pp. 56–78, esp. pp. 70–1.

11. Asa Kasher has made a similar—though undeveloped—suggestion along this line. See "Jewish Collective Identity," in *Jewish Identity,* ed. David Theo Goldberg and Michael Krausz, pp. 56–78, esp. pp. 70–1.

12. *Philosophical Investigations,* trans. G. E. M. Anscombe (Oxford: Blackwell Publishers Ltd., 1953, 1958, 1997), remark #66.

13. *Philosophical Investigations,* trans. G. E. M. Anscombe (Oxford: Blackwell Publishers Ltd., 1953, 1958, 1997), remark #66.

14. Thus Björn Kronderfer argues that the "ethos" of contemporary German identity is guilt and forgiveness, whereas that of the Jewish identity is remembrance and forgiveness. See his *Remembrance and Reconciliation* (New Haven and London: Yale University Press, 1995), chap. 2.

15. See Chapter 2 of my dissertation, *Collective Historical Responsibility and Multiple Community Identities,* note 6 above.

16. See Larry May, *Sharing Responsibility* (Chicago: University of Chicago Press, 1992), esp. chapter 2.

17. Joel Feinberg attempts to defend the idea that the dead can be harmed by arguing that posthumous harm does not involve physical or backward causation. Drawing on George Pitcher, he contends that "the occurrence of the harmful posthumous event, . . ., *makes it true* that the antemortem [the person before he died] is harmed, ... It does not suddenly "become true" that the antemortem [person] was harmed. Rather it becomes apparent to us for the first time that it was true all along—. . ." (Feinberg, *Harm to Others* [New York: Oxford University Press, 1984], pp. 79–91, p. 91). In other words, the person was in a harmed condition before he died but it only became true to us afterwards. See also George Pitcher, "The Misfortunes of the Dead," *American Philosophical Quarterly* 21(1984): 183–8.

I don't think this kind of response answers adequately Ernest Partridge's challenge that in order for a person to be harmed, she has to be a bearer of interests, and since a dead person can no longer be a subject of interests, it is beyond harm. (See Partridge, "Posthumous Interests," *Ethics* 91 [1981]: 243–64.) Although a person doesn't have to know that a harm has been done in order to be harmed—which is a epistemological issue, the way Feinberg (as well as Pitcher) responds still leaves open the question of *when* the person was put in a harmed state. Even if "it does not suddenly 'become true' that the antemortem [person] was harmed" from the standpoint of prepositional truth, it still makes sense to ask in the natural order of events whether she was harmed before or after she died. And what caused her to be in that harmed condition, to begin with? Thus the same metaphysical issue of "backward causation" comes back in full circle. However much common sense tells us that a person can be harmed after her death, metaphysical attempts to resolve this problem still get us nowhere.

18. To deal with this problem, I have developed a theory of deliberating intergenerational responsibility in the second chapter of my dissertation.

19. To make such norms of assessment more robust as criteria for assessment, I discuss the different ways of how people share responsibility on account of their community memberships in the second chapter of my dissertation.

20. See Jorge Gracia, *Hispanic/Latino Identity* (Malden, Mass.: Blackwell, 2000), p. 57.

21. Ibid, p. 58–9.

22. Ibid, p. 58.

23. The popular usage of the term may depart from official or formal usage that includes people from South Asia such as India and Pakistan.

24. For instance, Matteo Ricci, the sixteenth century Jesuit missionary, was confronted with questions about filial piety and ancestor worship, ideas that are quite alien to the West but deeply ingrained in the traditional Chinese culture.

25. Roger T. Ames for instance emphasizes the role-based conception of the person in Confucianism whereas Joseph Chan believes that Confucian ethics is not synonymous with role-based ethics. For Chan, the qualities of benevolence (*ren*) and justice (*yi*) rise above particular roles. See Roger Ames, "Rites as Rights: The Confucian Alternative" in *Human Rights and the World's Religion,* edited by Leroy R. Rouner (Notre Dame: University of Notre Dame Press, 1988); and Joseph Chan, "A Confucian Perspective on Human Rights for Contemporary China," in *The East Asian Challenge for Human Rights,* edited by Joanne R. Bauer and Daniel A. Bell (New York: Cambridge University Press, 1999).

26. See, for example, Kenneth Inada, "A Buddhist Response to the Nature of Human Rights," in *Asian Perspectives on Human Rights,* ed. Claude Welsh and Virginia Leary (Boulder: Westview Press, 1990), pp. 91–102.

27. This is not to suggest that Confucians today subscribe to the traditional understanding of Confucianism.

28. I have dealt with this subject at length in the first chapter of my dissertation.

29. Earlier versions of this chapter were presented at the 1998 and 1999 meetings of the American Philosophical Association. I thank my commentators, Rebecca Kukla and Jason Hill for their helpful suggestions. I also thank Larry May and Marilyn Friedman for their incisive comments. Credit also goes to Jill Delston for catching a couple of mindless blunders on subsequent drafts.

Racisms

Kwame Anthony Appiah

Kwame Anthony Appiah is a professor of philosophy and African-American studies at Harvard University. He is the author of several books, including *Experiments in Ethics (Mary Flexner Lecture Series of Bryn Mawr College)* (2008), and *Cosmopolitanism: Ethics in a World of Strangers (Issues of Our Time)* (2006).

Appiah distinguishes various aspects of racism, including racialism, as well as intrinsic and extrinsic racism. Racialism is the view that there are inherent traits and tendencies of each race that are not shared with members of other races, and that allow us to divide people into distinct races. Extrinsic racism is the view that the races inherently have different essences that entail different morally relevant traits. Intrinsic racism is the view that moral differentiation between races is justified because each race has a different moral status, irrespective of its racial essence. The disposition he calls "racial prejudice" is the tendency to subscribe to false moral and theoretical propositions about races. Appiah asserts that racialism is false, and that both kinds of racism are theoretically and morally wrong.

If the people I talk to and the newspapers I read are representative and reliable, there is a good deal of racism about. People and policies in the United States, in Eastern and Western Europe, in Asia and Africa and Latin America are regularly described as "racist." Australia had, until recently, a racist immigration policy; Britain still has one; racism is on the rise in France; many Israelis support Meir Kahane, an anti-Arab racist; many Arabs, according to a leading authority, are anti-Semitic racists;[1] and the movement to establish English as the "official language" of the United States is motivated by racism. Or, at least, so many of the people I talk to and many of the journalists with the newspapers I read believe.

Excerpt from Kwame Anthony Appiah, "Racism" in Anatomy of Racism, edited by David Theo Goldberg, 1990, pp. 3–17. © 1990 University of Minnesota Press. Reprinted by permission.

But visitors from Mars—or from Malawi—unfamiliar with the Western concept of racism could be excused if they had some difficulty in identifying what exactly racism was. We see it everywhere, but rarely does anyone stop to say what it is, or to explain what is wrong with it. Our visitors from Mars would soon grasp that it had become at least conventional in recent years to express abhorrence for racism. They might even notice that those most often accused of it—members of the South African Nationalist party, for example—may officially abhor it also. But if they sought in the popular media of our day—in newspapers and magazines, on television or radio, in novels or films—for an explicit definition of this thing "we" all abhor, they would very likely be disappointed.

Now, of course, this would be true of many of our most familiar concepts. *Sister, chair, tomato*—none of these gets defined in the course of our daily business. But the concept of racism is in worse shape than these. For much of what we say about it is, on the face of it, inconsistent.

It is, for example, held by many to be racist to refuse entry to a university to an otherwise qualified "Negro" candidate, but not to be so to refuse entry to an equally qualified "Caucasian" one. But "Negro" and "Caucasian" are both alleged to be names of races, and invidious discrimination on the basis of race is usually held to be a paradigm case of racism. Or, to take another example, it is widely believed to be evidence of an unacceptable racism to exclude people from clubs on the basis of race; yet most people, even those who think of "Jewish" as a racial term, seem to think that there is nothing wrong with Jewish clubs, whose members do not share any particular religious beliefs, or Afro-American societies, whose members share the juridical characteristic of American citizenship and the "racial" characteristic of being black.

I say that these are inconsistencies "on the face of it," because, for example, affirmative action in university admissions is importantly different from the earlier refusal to admit blacks or Jews (or other "Others") that it is meant, in part, to correct. Deep enough analysis may reveal it to be quite consistent with the abhorrence of racism; even a shallow analysis suggests that it is intended to be so. Similarly, justifications can be offered for "racial" associations in a plural society that are not available for the racial exclusivism of the country club. But if we take racism seriously we ought to be concerned about the adequacy of these justifications.

In this essay, then, I propose to take our ordinary ways of thinking about race and racism and point up some of their presuppositions. And since popular concepts are, of course, usually fairly fuzzily and untheoretically conceived, much of what I have to say will seem to be both more theoretically and more precisely committed than the talk of racism and racists in our newspapers and on television. My claim is that these theoretical claims are required to make sense of racism as the practice of reasoning human beings. If anyone were to suggest that much, perhaps most, of what goes under the name "racism" in our world cannot be given such a rationalized foundation, I should not disagree; but to the extent that a practice cannot be rationally

reconstructed it ought, surely, to be given up by reasonable people. The right tactic with racism, if you really want to oppose it, is to object to it rationally in the form in which it stands the best chance of meeting objections. The doctrines I want to discuss can be rationally articulated: and they are worth articulating rationally in order that we can rationally say what we object to in them.

RACIST PROPOSITIONS

There are at least three distinct doctrines that might be held to express the theoretical content of what we call "racism." One is the view—which I shall call *racialism*[2]—that there are heritable characteristics, possessed by members of our species, that allow us to divide them into a small set of races, in such a way that all the members of these races share certain traits and tendencies with each other that they do not share with members of any other race. These traits and tendencies characteristic of a race constitute, on the racialist view, a sort of racial essence; and it is part of the content of racialism that the essential heritable characteristics of what the nineteenth century called the "Races of Man" account for more than the visible morphological characteristics—skin color, hair type, facial features—on the basis of which we make our informal classifications. Racialism is at the heart of nineteenth-century Western attempts to develop a science of racial difference; but it appears to have been believed by others—for example, Hegel, before then, and many in other parts of the non-Western world since—who have had no interest in developing scientific theories.

Racialism is not, in itself, a doctrine that must be dangerous, even if the racial essence is thought to entail moral and intellectual dispositions. Provided positive moral qualities are distributed across the races, each can be respected, can have its "separate but equal" place. Unlike most Western-educated people, I believe—and I have argued elsewhere[3]—that racialism is false; but by itself, it seems to be a cognitive rather than a moral problem. The issue is how the world is, not how we would want it to be.

Racialism is, however, a presupposition of other doctrines that have been called "racism," and these other doctrines have been, in the last few centuries, the basis of a great deal of human suffering and the source of a great deal of moral error.

One such doctrine we might call "extrinsic racism:" extrinsic racists make moral distinctions between members of different races because they believe that the racial essence entails certain morally relevant qualities. The basis for the extrinsic racists' discrimination between people is their belief that members of different races differ in respects that *warrant* the differential treatment, respects—such as honesty or courage or intelligence—that are uncontroversially held (at least in most contemporary cultures) to be acceptable as a basis for treating people differently. Evidence that there are no such differences in morally relevant characteristics—that Negroes do not necessarily lack intellectual capacities, that Jews are not especially avaricious—should thus lead people out of their racism if it is purely extrinsic. As we know, such evidence often fails to change an extrinsic racist's attitudes substantially, for some of the extrinsic racist's best friends have always been Jewish. But at this point—if the racist is sincere—what we have is no longer a false doctrine but a cognitive incapacity, one whose significance I shall discuss later in this essay.

I say that the *sincere* extrinsic racist may suffer from a cognitive incapacity. But some who espouse extrinsic racist doctrines are simply insincere intrinsic racists. For *intrinsic racists*, on my definition, are people who differentiate morally between members of different races because they believe that each race has a different moral status, quite independent of the moral characteristics entailed by its racial essence. Just as, for example, many people assume that the fact that they are biologically related to another person—a brother, an aunt, a cousin—gives them a moral interest in that person,[4] so an intrinsic racist holds that the bare fact of being of the same race is a reason for preferring one person to another. (I shall return to this parallel later as well.)

For an intrinsic racist, no amount of evidence that a member of another race is capable of great moral, intellectual, or cultural achievements, or has characteristics that, in members of one's own

race, would make them admirable or attractive, offers any ground for treating that person as he or she would treat similarly endowed members of his or her own race. Just so, some sexists are "intrinsic sexists," holding that the bare fact that someone is a woman (or man) is a reason for treating her (or him) in certain ways.

There are interesting possibilities for complicating these distinctions: some racists, for example, claim, as the Mormons once did, that they discriminate between people because they believe that God requires them to do so. Is this an extrinsic racism, predicated on the combination of God's being an intrinsic racist and the belief that it is right to do what God wills? Or is it intrinsic racism because it is based on the belief that God requires these discriminations because they are right? (Is an act pious because the gods love it, or do they love it because it is pious?) Nevertheless, the distinctions between racialism and racism and between two potentially overlapping kinds of racism provide us with the skeleton of an anatomy of the propositional contents of racial attitudes.

RACIST DISPOSITIONS

Most people will want to object already that this discussion of the propositional content of racist moral and factual beliefs misses something absolutely crucial to the character of the psychological and sociological reality of racism, something I touched on when I mentioned that extrinsic racist utterances are often made by people who suffer from what I called a "cognitive incapacity." Part of the standard force of accusations of racism is that their objects are in some way *irrational*. The objection to Professor Shockley's claims about the intelligence of blacks is not just that they are false; it is rather that Professor Shockley seems, like many people we call "racist," to be unable to see that the evidence does not support his factual claims and that the connection between his factual claims and his policy prescriptions involves a series of nonsequiturs.

What makes these cognitive incapacities especially troubling—something we should respond to with more than a recommendation that the individual, Professor Shockley, be offered psychotherapy—is that they conform to a certain pattern: namely, that it is especially where beliefs and policies are to the disadvantage of nonwhite people that he shows the sorts of disturbing failure that have made his views both notorious and notoriously unreliable. Indeed, Professor Shockley's reasoning works extremely well in some other areas: that he is a Nobel Laureate in physics is part of what makes him so interesting an example.

This cognitive incapacity is not, of course, a rare one. Many of us are unable to give up beliefs that play a part in justifying the special advantages we gain (or hope to gain) from our positions in the social order—in particular, beliefs about the positive characters of the class of people who share that position. Many people who express extrinsic racist beliefs—many white South Africans, for example—are beneficiaries of social orders that deliver advantages to them by virtue of their "race," so that their disinclination to accept evidence that would deprive them of a justification for those advantages is just an instance of this general phenomenon.

So, too, evidence that access to higher education is as largely determined by the quality of our earlier educations as by our own innate talents, does not, on the whole, undermine the confidence of college entrants from private schools in England or the United States or Ghana. Many of them continue to believe in the face of this evidence that their acceptance at "good" universities shows them to be intellectually better endowed (and not just better prepared) than those who are rejected. It is facts such as these that give sense to the notion of false consciousness, the idea that an ideology can prevent us from acknowledging facts that would threaten our position.

The most interesting cases of this sort of ideological resistance to the truth are not, perhaps, the ones I have just mentioned. On the whole, it is less surprising, once we accept the admittedly problematic notion of self-deception, that people who think that certain attitudes or beliefs advantage them or those they care about should be able, as we say, to "persuade" themselves to ignore evidence that undermines those

beliefs or attitudes. What is more interesting is the existence of people who resist the truth of a proposition while thinking that its wider acceptance would in no way disadvantage them or those individuals about whom they care—this might be thought to describe Professor Shockley; or who resist the truth when they recognize that its acceptance would actually advantage them—this might be the case with some black people who have internalized negative racist stereotypes; or who fail, by virtue of their ideological attachments, to recognize what is in their own best interests at all.

My business here is not with the psychological or social processes by which these forms of ideological resistance operate, but it is important, I think, to see the refusal on the part of some extrinsic racists to accept evidence against the beliefs as an instance of a widespread phenomenon in human affairs. It is a plain fact, to which theories of ideology must address themselves, that our species is prone both morally and intellectually to such distortions of judgment, in particular to distortions of judgment that reflect partiality. An inability to change your mind in the face of appropriate[5] evidence is a cognitive incapacity; but it is one that all of us surely suffer from in some areas of belief; especially in areas where our own interests or self-images are (or seem to be) at stake.

It is not, however, as some have held, a tendency that we are powerless to resist. No one, no doubt, can be impartial about everything—even about everything to which the notion of partiality applies; but there is no subject matter about which most sane people cannot, in the end, be persuaded to avoid partiality in judgment. And it may help to shake the convictions of those whose incapacity derives from this sort of ideological defense if we show them how their reaction fits into this general pattern. It is, indeed, because it generally *does* fit this pattern that we call such views "racism"—the suffix "-ism" indicating that what we have in mind is not simply a theory but an ideology. It would be odd to call someone brought up in a remote corner of the world with false and demeaning views about white people a "racist" if that person gave up these beliefs quite easily in the face of appropriate evidence.

Real live racists, then, exhibit a systematically distorted rationality, the kind of systematically distorted rationality that we are likely to call "ideological." And it is a distortion that is especially striking in the cognitive domain: Extrinsic racists, as I said earlier, however intelligent or otherwise well informed, often fail to treat evidence against the theoretical propositions of extrinsic racism dispassionately. Like extrinsic racism, intrinsic racism can also often be seen as ideological; but since scientific evidence is not going to settle the issue, a failure to see that it is wrong represents a cognitive incapacity only on controversially realist views about morality. What makes intrinsic racism similarly ideological is not so much the failure of inductive or deductive rationality that is so striking in someone like Professor Shockley but rather the connection that it, like extrinsic racism, has with the interests—real or perceived—of the dominant group.[6] Shockley's racism is in a certain sense directed *against* nonwhite people: many believe that his views would, if accepted, operate against their objective interests, and he certainly presents the black "race" in a less than flattering light.

I propose to use the old-fashioned term "racial prejudice" in the rest of this essay to refer to the deformation of rationality in judgment that characterizes those whose racism is more than a theoretical attachment to certain propositions about race.

RACIAL PREJUDICE

It is hardly necessary to raise objections to what I am calling "racial prejudice"; someone who exhibits such deformations of rationality is plainly in trouble. But it is important to remember that propositional racists in a racist culture have false moral beliefs but may not suffer from racial prejudice. Once we show them how society has enforced extrinsic racist stereotypes; once we ask them whether they really believe that race in itself, independently of those extrinsic racist beliefs, justifies differential treatment, many will come to give up racist propositions, although we must remember how powerful a weight of authority our arguments

have to overcome. Reasonable people may insist on substantial evidence if they are to give up beliefs that are central to their cultures.

Still, in the end, many will resist such reasoning; and to the extent that their prejudices are really not subject to any kind of rational control, we may wonder whether it is right to treat such people as morally responsible for the acts their racial prejudice motivates, or morally reprehensible for holding the views to which their prejudice leads them. It is a bad thing that such people exist; they are, in a certain sense, bad people. But it is not clear to me that they are responsible for the fact that they are bad. Racial prejudice, like prejudice generally, may threaten an agent's autonomy, making it appropriate to treat or train rather than to reason with them.

But once someone has been offered evidence both (1) that their reasoning in a certain domain is distorted by prejudice, and (2) that the distortions conform to a pattern that suggests a lack of impartiality, they ought to take special care in articulating views and proposing policies in that domain. They ought to do so because, as I have already said, the phenomenon of partiality in judgment is well attested in human affairs. Even if you are not immediately persuaded that you are yourself a victim of such a distorted rationality in a certain domain, you should keep in mind always that this is the usual position of those who suffer from such prejudices. To the extent that this line of thought is not one that itself falls within the domain in question, one can be held responsible for not subjecting judgments that *are* within that domain to an especially extended scrutiny; and this is a *fortiori* true if the policies one is recommending are plainly of enormous consequence.

If it is clear that racial prejudice is regrettable, it is also clear in the nature of the case that providing even a superabundance of reasons and evidence will often not be a successful way of removing it. Nevertheless, the racist's prejudice will be articulated through the sorts of theoretical propositions I dubbed extrinsic and intrinsic racism. And we should certainly be able to say something reasonable about why these theoretical propositions should be rejected.

Part of the reason that this is worth doing is precisely the fact that many of those who assent to the propositional content of racism do not suffer from racial prejudice. In a country like the United States, where racist propositions were once part of the national ideology, there will be many who assent to racist propositions simply because they were raised to do so. Rational objection to racist propositions has a fair chance of changing such people's beliefs.

EXTRINSIC AND INTRINSIC RACISM

It is not always clear whether someone's theoretical racism is intrinsic or extrinsic, and there is certainly no reason why we should expect to be able to settle the question. Since the issue probably never occurs to most people in these terms, we cannot suppose that they must have an answer. In fact, given the definition of the terms I offered, there is nothing barring someone from being both an intrinsic and an extrinsic racist, holding both that the bare fact of race provides a basis for treating members of his or her own race differently from others and that there are morally relevant characteristics that are differentially distributed among the races. Indeed, for reasons I shall discuss in a moment, *most* intrinsic racists are likely to express extrinsic racist beliefs, so that we should not be surprised that many people seem, in fact, to be committed to both forms of racism.

The Holocaust made unreservedly clear the threat that racism poses to human decency. But it also blurred our thinking because in focusing our attention on the racist character of the Nazi atrocities, it obscured their character as atrocities. What is appalling about Nazi racism is not just that it presupposes, as all racism does, false (racialist) beliefs—not simply that it involves a moral incapacity (the inability to extend our moral sentiments to all our fellow creatures) and a moral failing (the making of moral distinctions without moral differences)—but that it leads, first, to oppression and then to mass slaughter. In recent years, South African racism has had a similar distorting effect. For although South African racism

has not led to killings on the scale of the Holocaust—even if it has both left South Africa judicially executing more (mostly black) people per head of population than most other countries and led to massive differences between the life chances of white and nonwhite South Africans—it *has* led to the systematic oppression and economic exploitation of people who are not classified as "white," and to the infliction of suffering on citizens of all racial classifications, not least by the police state that is required to maintain that exploitation and oppression.

Part of our resistance, therefore, to calling the racial ideas of those, such as the Black Nationalists of the 1960s, who advocate racial solidarity, by the same term that we use to describe the attitudes of Nazis or of members of the South African Nationalist party, surely resides in the fact that they largely did not contemplate using race as a basis for inflicting harm. Indeed, it seems to me that there is a significant pattern in the modern rhetoric of race, such that the discourse of racial solidarity is usually expressed through the language of *intrinsic* racism, while those who have used race as the basis for oppression and hatred have appealed to *extrinsic* racist ideas. This point is important for understanding the character of contemporary racial attitudes.

The two major uses of race as a basis for moral solidarity that are most familiar in the West are varieties of Pan-Africanism and Zionism. In each case it is presupposed that a "people," Negroes or Jews, has the basis for shared political life in the fact of being of the same race. There are varieties of each form of "nationalism" that make the basis lie in shared traditions; but however plausible this may be in the case of Zionism, which has in Judaism, the religion, a realistic candidate for a common and nonracial focus for nationality, the peoples of Africa have a good deal less in common culturally than is usually assumed. I discuss this issue at length in *In My Father's House: Essays in the Philosophy of African Culture*, but let me say here that I believe the central fact is this: what blacks in the West, like secularized Jews, have mostly in common is that they are perceived—both by themselves and by others—as belonging to the same race, and that this common race is used by others as the basis for discriminating against them. "If you ever forget you're a Jew, a goy will remind you." The Black Nationalists, like some Zionists, responded to their experience of racial discrimination by accepting the racialism it presupposed.[7]

Although race is indeed at the heart of Black Nationalism, however, it seems that it is the fact of a shared race, not the fact of a shared racial character, that provides the basis for solidarity. Where racism is implicated in the basis for national solidarity, it is intrinsic, not (or not only) extrinsic. It is this that makes the idea of fraternity one that is naturally applied in nationalist discourse. For, as I have already observed, the moral status of close family members is not normally thought of in most cultures as depending on qualities of character; we are supposed to love our brothers and sisters in spite of their faults and not because of their virtues. Alexander Crummell, one of the founding fathers of Black Nationalism, literalizes the metaphor of family in these startling words:

> Races, like families, are the organisms and ordinances of God; and race feeling, like family feeling, is of divine origin. The extinction of race feeling is just as possible as the extinction of family feeling. Indeed, a race *is* a family.[8]

It is the assimilation of "race feeling" to "family feeling" that makes intrinsic racism seem so much less objectionable than extrinsic racism. For this metaphorical identification reflects the fact that, in the modern world (unlike the nineteenth century), intrinsic racism is acknowledged almost exclusively as the basis of feelings of community. We can surely, then, share a sense of what Crummell's friend and co-worker Edward Blyden called "the poetry of politics," that is, "the feeling of race," the feeling of "people with whom we are connected."[9] The racism here is the basis of acts of supererogation, the treatment of others better than we otherwise might, better than moral duty demands of us.

This is a contingent fact. There is no logical impossibility in the idea of racialists whose moral beliefs lead them to feelings of hatred for other races while leaving no room for love of members of their own. Nevertheless most racial hatred is in fact expressed through extrinsic racism: Most people who have used race as the basis for causing harm to others, have felt the need to see the others as independently morally flawed. It is one thing to espouse fraternity without claiming that your brothers and sisters have any special qualities that deserve recognition, and another to espouse hatred of others who have done nothing to deserve it.[10]

Many Afrikaners—like many in the American South until recently—have a long list of extrinsic racist answers to the question why blacks should not have full civil rights. Extrinsic racism has usually been the basis for treating people worse than we otherwise might, for giving them less than their humanity entitles them to. But this too is a contingent fact. Indeed, Crummell's guarded respect for white people derived from a belief in the superior moral qualities of the Anglo-Saxon race.

Intrinsic racism is, in my view, a moral error. Even if racialism were correct, the bare fact that someone was of another race would be no reason to treat them worse—or better—than someone of my race. In our public lives, people are owed treatment independently of their biological characters: if they are to be differently treated there must be some morally relevant difference between them. In our private lives, we are morally free to have aesthetic preferences between people, but once our treatment of people raises moral issues, we may not make arbitrary distinctions. Using race in itself as a morally relevant distinction strikes most of us as obviously arbitrary. Without associated moral characteristics, why should race provide a better basis than hair color or height or timbre of voice? And if two people share all the properties morally relevant to some action we ought to do, it will be an error—a failure to apply the Kantian injunction to universalize our moral judgments—to use the bare facts of race as the basis for treating them differently. No one should deny that a common ancestry might, in particular cases, account for similarities in moral character. But then it would be the moral similarities that justified the different treatment.

It is presumably because most people—outside the South African Nationalist party and the

Ku Klux Klan—share the sense that intrinsic racism requires arbitrary distinctions that they are largely unwilling to express it in situations that invite moral criticism. But I do not know how I would argue with someone who was willing to announce an intrinsic racism as a basic moral idea; the best one can do, perhaps, is to provide objections to possible lines of defense of it.

DE GUSTIBUS

It might be thought that intrinsic racism should be regarded not so much as an adherence to a (moral) proposition as the expression of a taste, analogous, say, to the food prejudice that makes most English people unwilling to eat horse meat, and most Westerners unwilling to eat the insect grubs that the !Kung people find so appetizing. The analogy does at least this much for us, namely, to provide a model of the way that *extrinsic* racist propositions can be a reflection of an underlying prejudice. For, of course, in most cultures food prejudices are rationalized: we say insects are unhygienic and cats taste horrible. Yet a cooked insect is no more health-threatening than a cooked carrot, and the unpleasant taste of cat meat, far from justifying our prejudice against it, probably derives from that prejudice.

But there the usefulness of the analogy ends. For intrinsic racism, as I have defined it, is not simply a taste for the company of one's "own kind," but a moral doctrine, one that is supposed to underlie differences in the treatment of people in contexts where moral evaluation is appropriate. And for moral distinctions we cannot accept that "de gustibus non est disputandum." We do not need the full apparatus of Kantian ethics to require that public morality be constrained by reason.

A proper analogy would be with someone who thought that we could continue to kill cattle for beef, even if cattle exercised all the complex cultural skills of human beings. I think it is obvious that creatures that shared our capacity for understanding as well as our capacity for pain should not be treated the way we actually treat cattle— that "intrinsic speciesism" would be as wrong as racism. And the fact that most people think it is

worse to be cruel to chimpanzees than to frogs suggests that they may agree with me. The distinction in attitudes surely reflects a belief in the greater richness of the mental life of chimps. Still, I do not know how I would *argue* against someone who could not see this; someone who continued to act on the contrary belief might, in the end, simply have to be locked up.

THE FAMILY MODEL

I have suggested that intrinsic racism is, at least sometimes, a metaphorical extension of the moral priority of one's family; it might, therefore, be suggested that a defense of intrinsic racism could proceed along the same lines as a defense of the family as a center of moral interest. The possibility of a defense of family relations as morally relevant—or, more precisely, of the claim that one may be morally entitled (or even obliged) to make distinctions between two otherwise morally indistinguishable people because one is related to one and not to the other—is theoretically important for the prospects of a philosophical defense of intrinsic racism. This is because such a defense of the family involves—like intrinsic racism—a denial of the basic claim, expressed so clearly by Kant, that from the perspective of morality, it is as rational agents *simpliciter* that we are to assess and be assessed. For anyone who follows Kant in this, what matters, as we might say, is not who you are but how you try to live. Intrinsic racism denies this fundamental claim also. And, in so doing, as I have argued elsewhere, it runs against the mainstream of the history of Western moral theory.[11]

The importance of drawing attention to the similarities between the defense of the family and the defense of the race, then, is not merely that the metaphor of family is often invoked by racism; it is that each of them offers the same general challenge to the Kantian stream of our moral thought. And the parallel with the defense of the family should be especially appealing to an intrinsic racist, since many of us who have little time for racism would hope that the family is susceptible to some such defense.

The problem in generalizing the defense of the family, however, is that such defenses standardly begin at a point that makes the argument for intrinsic racism immediately implausible: namely, with the family as the unit through which we live what is most intimate, as the center of private life. If we distinguish, with Bernard Williams, between ethical thought, which takes seriously "the demands, needs, claims, desires, and generally, the lives of other people,"[12] and morality, which focuses more narrowly on obligation, it may well be that private life matters to us precisely because it is altogether unsuited to the universalizing tendencies of morality.

The functioning family unit has contracted substantially with industrialization, the disappearance of the family as the unit of production, and the increasing mobility of labor, but there remains that irreducible minimum: the parent or parents with the child or children. In this "nuclear" family, there is, of course, a substantial body of shared experience, shared attitudes, shared knowledge and beliefs; and the mutual psychological investment that exists within this group is, for most of us, one of the things that gives meaning to our lives. It is a natural enough confusion—which we find again and again in discussions of adoption in the popular media—that identifies the relevant group with the biological unit of *genitor, genetrix,* and *offspring* rather than with the social unit of those who share a common domestic life.

The relations of parent and their biological children are of moral importance, of course, in part because children are standardly the product of behavior voluntarily undertaken by their biological parents. But the moral relations between biological siblings and half-siblings cannot, as I have already pointed out, be accounted for in such terms. A rational defense of the family ought to appeal to the causal responsibility of the biological parent and the common life of the domestic unit, and not to the brute fact of biological relatedness, even if the former pair of considerations defines groups that are often coextensive with the groups generated by the latter. For brute biological relatedness bears no necessary connection to the sorts of human purposes that seem likely to be relevant at the most basic level of ethical thought.

An argument that such a central group is bound to be crucially important in the lives of most human beings in societies like ours is not, of course, an argument for any specific mode of organization of the "family:" feminism and the gay liberation movement have offered candidate groups that could (and sometimes do) occupy the same sort of role in the lives of those whose sexualities or whose dispositions otherwise make the nuclear family uncongenial; and these candidates have been offered specifically in the course of defenses of a move toward societies that are agreeably beyond patriarchy and homophobia. The central thought of these feminist and gay critiques of the nuclear family is that we cannot continue to view any one organization of private life as "natural," once we have seen even the broadest outlines of the archaeology of the family concept.

If that is right, then the argument for the family must be an argument for a mode of organization of life and feeling that subserves certain positive functions; and however the details of such an argument would proceed it is highly unlikely that the same functions could be served by groups on the scale of races, simply because, as I say, the family is attractive in part exactly for reasons of its personal scale.

I need hardly say that rational defenses of intrinsic racism along the lines I have been considering are not easily found. In the absence of detailed defenses to consider, I can only offer these general reasons for doubting that they can succeed. The generally Kantian tenor of much of our moral thought threatens the project from the start; and the essentially unintimate nature of relations within "races" suggests that there is little prospect that the defense of the family—which seems an attractive and plausible project that extends ethical life beyond the narrow range of a universalizing morality—can be applied to a defense of races.

CONCLUSIONS

I have suggested that what we call "racism" involves both propositions and dispositions.

The propositions were, first, that there are races (this was *racialism*) and, second, that these races are morally significant either (a) because they are contingently correlated with morally relevant properties (this was *extrinsic racism*) or (b) because they are intrinsically morally significant (this was *intrinsic racism*).

The disposition was a tendency to assent to false propositions, both moral and theoretical, about races—propositions that support policies or beliefs that are to the disadvantage of some race (or races) as opposed to others, and to do so even in the face of evidence and argument that should appropriately lead to giving those propositions up. This disposition I called "racial prejudice."

I suggested that intrinsic racism had tended in our own time to be the natural expression of feelings of community, and this is, of course, one of the reasons why we are not inclined to call it racist. For, to the extent that a theoretical position is not associated with irrationally held beliefs that tend to the *dis*advantage of some group, it fails to display the *directedness* of the distortions of rationality characteristic of racial prejudice. Intrinsic racism may be as irrationally held as any other view, but it does not *have* to be directed *against* anyone.

So far as theory is concerned I believe racialism to be false: since theoretical racism of both kinds presupposes racialism, I could not logically support racism of either variety. But even if racialism were true, both forms of theoretical racism would be incorrect. Extrinsic racism is false because the genes that account for the gross morphological differences that underlie our standard racial categories are not linked to those genes that determine, to whatever degree such matters are determined genetically, our moral and intellectual characters. Intrinsic racism is mistaken because it breaches the Kantian imperative to make moral distinctions only on morally relevant grounds—granted that there is no reason to believe that race, *in se*, is morally relevant, and also no reason to suppose that races are like families in providing a sphere of ethical life that legitimately escapes the demands of a universalizing morality.

NOTES

1. Bernard Lewis, *Semites and Anti-Semites* (New York: Norton, 1986).
2. I shall be using the words "racism" and "racialism" with the meanings I stipulate: in some dialects of English they are synonyms, and in most dialects their definition is less than precise. For discussion of recent biological evidence see M. Nei and A. K. Roychoudhury, "Genetic Relationship and Evolution of Human Races," *Evolutionary Biology*, vol. 14 (New York: Plenum, 1983), pp. 1–59; for useful background see also M. Nei and A. K. Roychoudhury, "Gene Differences between Caucasian, Negro, and Japanese Populations," *Science*, 177 (August 1972), pp. 434–35.
3. See my "The Uncompleted Argument: Du Bois and the Illusion of Race," *Critical Inquiry*, 12 (Autumn 1985); reprinted in Henry Louis Gates (ed.), *"Race," Writing, and Difference* (Chicago: University of Chicago Press, 1986), pp. 21–37.
4. This fact shows up most obviously in the assumption that adopted children intelligibly make claims against their natural siblings: natural parents are, of course, causally responsible for their child's existence and that could be the basis of moral claims, without any sense that biological relatedness entailed rights or responsibilities. But no such basis exists for an interest in natural *siblings*; my sisters are not causally responsible for my existence.
5. Obviously what evidence should *appropriately* change your beliefs is not independent of your social or historical situation. In mid-nineteenth-century America, in New England quite as much as in the heart of Dixie, the pervasiveness of the institutional support for the prevailing system of racist belief—the fact that it was reinforced by religion and state, and defended by people in the universities and colleges, who had the greatest cognitive authority—meant that it would have been appropriate to insist on a substantial body of evidence and argument before giving up assent to racist propositions. In California in the 1980s, of course, matters stand rather differently. To acknowledge this is not to admit to a cognitive relativism; rather, it is to hold that, at least in some domains, the fact that a belief is widely held—and especially by people in positions of cognitive authority—may be a good prima facie reason for believing it.
6. Ideologies, as most theorists of ideology have admitted, standardly outlive the period in which they conform to the objective interests of the dominant group in a society, so even someone who thinks that the dominant group in our society no longer needs racism to buttress its position can see racism as the persisting ideology of an earlier phase of society. (I say "group" to keep the claim appropriately general; it seems to me a substantial further claim that the dominant group whose interests an ideology serves is always a class.) I have argued, however, in "The Conservation of 'Race'" that racism continues to serve the interests of the ruling classes in the West; in *Black American Literature Forum*, 23 (Spring 1989), pp. 37–60.

7. As I argued in "The Uncompleted Argument: Du Bois and the Illusion of Race." The reactive (or dialectical) character of this move explains why Sartre calls its manifestations in Négritude an "antiracist racism"; see "Orphée Noir," his preface to Senghor's *Anthologie de la nouvelle poeésie nègre et malagache de langue française* (Paris: PUF, 1948). Sartre believed, of course, that the synthesis of this dialectic would be transcendence of racism; and it was his view of it as a stage—the antithesis—in that process that allowed him to see it as a positive advance over the original "thesis" of European racism. I suspect that the reactive character of antiracist racism accounts for the tolerance that is regularly extended to it in liberal circles; but this tolerance is surely hard to justify unless one shares Sartre's optimistic interpretation of it as a stage in a process that leads to the end of all racisms. (And unless your view of this dialectic is deterministic, you should in any case want to play an argumentative role in moving to this next stage.)

For a similar Zionist response see Horace Kallen's "The Ethics of Zionism," *Maccabean*, August 1906.

8. "The Race Problem in America," in Brotz's *Negro Social and Political Thought* (New York: Basic Books, 1966), p. 184.

9. *Christianity, Islam and the Negro Race* (1887; reprinted Edinburgh: Edinburgh University Press, 1967), p. 197.

10. This is in part a reflection of an important asymmetry: loathing, unlike love, needs justifying; and this, I would argue, is because loathing usually leads to acts that are *in se* undesirable, whereas love leads to acts that are largely *in se* desirable—indeed, supererogatorily so.

11. See my "Racism and Moral Pollution," *Philosophical Forum*, 18 (Winter–Spring 1986–87), pp. 185–202.

12. *Ethics and the Limits of Philosophy* (Cambridge, MA: Harvard University Press, 1985), p. 12. I do not, as is obvious, share Williams's skepticism about morality.

Affirmative Action:
The Price of Preference

Shelby Steele

Shelby Steele is a Research Fellow, author, and columnist at the Hoover Institution at Stanford University. He is the author of *White Guilt: How Blacks and Whites Together Destroyed the Promise of the Civil Rights Era* (2006) and *The Content of Our Character* (1990), and co-author of *The Great Divide: Why Conservatives Fail to Persuade Blacks* (2006).

Steele argues that affirmative action, as it is currently practiced, perpetuates, rather than alleviates, the harm it was meant to address. Steele states that affirmative action policies' emphasis on color has the result of further stereotyping a group that is already perceived as inferior. Steele further argues that affirmative action is a type of shortcut to the goal of equality. Affirmative action is a shortcut because it does not provide educational and economic development and does not provide sanctions for racial, ethnic, and sexual discrimination, which are the real means necessary for overcoming discrimination and inequality.

In a few short years, when my two children will be applying to college, the affirmative action policies by which most universities offer black students some form of preferential treatment will present me with a dilemma. I am a middle-class black, a college professor, far from wealthy, but also well-removed from the kind of deprivation that would qualify my children for the label "disadvantaged." Both of them have endured racial insensitivity from whites. They have been called names, have suffered slights, and have experienced firsthand the peculiar malevolence that racism brings out in people. Yet, they have never experienced racial discrimination, have never been stopped by their race on any path they have chosen to follow. Still, their society now tells them that if they will only designate themselves as black on their college applications, they will likely do better in the college lottery than if they conceal this fact. I think there is something of a Faustian bargain in this.

Of course, many blacks and a considerable number of whites would say that I was sanctimoniously making affirmative action into a test of character. They would say that this small preference is the meagerest recompense for centuries of unrelieved oppression. And to these arguments other very obvious facts must be added. In America, many marginally competent or flatly incompetent whites are hired everyday—some because their white skin suits the conscious or unconscious racial preference of their employer. The white children of alumni are often grandfathered into elite universities in what can only be seen as a residual benefit of historic white privilege. Worse, white incompetence is always an individual matter, while for blacks it is often confirmation of ugly stereotypes. The Peter Principle was not conceived with only blacks in mind. Given that unfairness cuts both ways, doesn't it only balance the scales of history that my children now receive a slight preference over whites? Doesn't this repay, in a small way, the systematic denial under which their grandfather lived out his days?

So, in theory, affirmative action certainly has all the moral symmetry that fairness requires—the injustice of historical and even contemporary white advantage is offset with black advantage; preference replaces prejudice, inclusion answers exclusion. It is reformist and corrective, even repentant and redemptive. And I would never sneer at these good intentions. Born in the late forties in Chicago, I started my education (a charitable term in this case) in a segregated school and suffered all the indignities that come to blacks in a segregated society. My father, born in the South, only made it to the third grade before the white man's fields took permanent priority over his formal education. And though he educated himself into an advanced reader with an almost professional authority, he could only drive a truck for a living and never earned more than ninety dollars a week in his entire life. So, yes, it is crucial to my sense of citizenship, to my ability to identify with the spirit and the interests of America, to know that this country, however imperfectly, recognizes its past sins and wishes to correct them.

Yet good intentions, because of the opportunity for innocence they offer us, are very seductive and can blind us to the effects they generate when implemented. In our society, affirmative action is, among other things, a testament to white goodwill and to black power, and in the midst of these heavy investments, its effects can be hard to see. But after twenty years of implementation, I think affirmative action has shown itself to be more bad than good and that blacks—whom I will focus on in this essay—now stand to lose more from it than they gain.

In talking with affirmative action administrators and with blacks and whites in general, it is clear that supporters of affirmative action focus on its good intentions while detractors emphasize its negative effects. Proponents talk about "diversity" and "pluralism"; opponents speak of "reverse discrimination," the unfairness of quotas and set-asides. It

was virtually impossible to find people outside either camp. The closest I came was a white male manager at a large computer company who said, "I think it amounts to reverse discrimination, but I'll put up with a little of that for a little more diversity." I'll live with a little of the effect to gain a little of the intention, he seemed to be saying. But this only makes him a halfhearted supporter of affirmative action. I think many people who don't really like affirmative action support it to one degree or another anyway.

I believe they do this because of what happened to white and black Americans in the crucible of the sixties when whites were confronted with their racial guilt and blacks tasted their first real power. In this stormy time white absolution and black power coalesced into virtual mandates for society. Affirmative action became a meeting ground for these mandates in the law, and in the late sixties and early seventies it underwent a remarkable escalation of its mission from simple anti-discrimination enforcement to social engineering by means of quotas, goals, timetables, set-asides, and other forms of preferential treatment.

Legally, this was achieved through a series of executive orders and EEOC guidelines that allowed racial imbalances in the workplace to stand as proof of racial discrimination. Once it could be assumed that discrimination explained racial imbalances, it became easy to justify group remedies to presumed discrimination, rather than the normal case-by-case redress for proven discrimination. Preferential treatment through quotas, goals, and so on is designed to correct imbalances based on the assumption that they always indicate discrimination. This expansion of what constitutes discrimination allowed affirmative action to escalate into the business of social engineering in the name of anti-discrimination, to push society toward statistically proportionate racial representation, without any obligation of proving actual discrimination.

What accounted for this shift, I believe, was the white mandate to achieve a new racial innocence and the black mandate to gain power. Even though blacks had made great advances during the sixties without quotas, these mandates, which came to a head in the very late sixties, could no longer be satisfied by anything less than racial preferences. I don't think these mandates in themselves were wrong, since whites clearly needed to do better by blacks and blacks needed more real power in society. But, as they came together in affirmative action, their effect was to distort our understanding of racial discrimination in a way that allowed us to offer the remediation of preference on the basis of mere color rather than actual injury. By making black the color of preference, these mandates have reburdened society with the very marriage of color and preference (in reverse) that we set out to eradicate. The old sin is reaffirmed in a new guise.

But the essential problem with this form of affirmative action is the way it leaps over the hard business of developing a formerly oppressed people to the point where they can achieve proportionate representation on their own (given equal opportunity) and goes straight for the proportionate representation. This may satisfy some whites of their innocence and some blacks of their power, but it does very little to truly uplift blacks.

A white female affirmative action officer at an Ivy League university told me what many supporters of affirmative action now say: "We're after diversity. We ideally want a student body where racial and ethnic groups are represented according to their proportion in society." When affirmative action escalated into social engineering, diversity became a golden word. It grants whites an egalitarian fairness (innocence) and blacks an entitlement to proportionate representation (power). *Diversity* is a term that applies democratic principles to races and cultures rather than to citizens, despite the fact that there is nothing to indicate that real diversity is the same thing as proportionate representation. Too often the result of this on campus (for example) has been a democracy of colors rather than of people, an artificial diversity that gives the appearance of an educational parity between black and white students that has not yet been achieved in reality. Here again, racial preferences allow society to leapfrog over the difficult problem of developing blacks to parity with whites and into a cosmetic diversity that covers the blemish of disparity—a

full six years after admission, only about 26 percent of black students graduate from college.

Racial representation is not the same thing as racial development, yet affirmative action fosters a confusion of these very difficult needs. Representation can be manufactured; development is always hard-earned. However, it is the music of innocence and power that we hear in affirmative action that causes us to cling to it and to its distracting emphasis on representation. The fact is that after twenty years of racial preferences, the gap between white and black median income is greater than it was in the seventies. None of this is to say that blacks don't need policies that ensure our right to equal opportunity, but what we need more is the development that will let us take advantage of society's efforts to include us.

I think that one of the most troubling effects of racial preferences for blacks is a kind of demoralization, or put another way, an enlargement of self-doubt. Under affirmative action the quality that earns us preferential treatment is an implied inferiority. However this inferiority is explained— it is still inferiority. There are explanations, and then there is the fact. And the fact must be borne by the individual as a condition apart from the explanation, apart even from the fact that others like himself also bear this condition. In integrated situations where blacks must compete with whites who may be better prepared these explanations may quickly wear thin and expose the individual to racial as well as personal self-doubt.

All of this is compounded by the cultural myth of black inferiority that blacks have always lived with. What this means in practical terms is that when blacks deliver themselves into integrated situations, they encounter a nasty little reflex in whites, a mindless, atavistic reflex that responds to the color black with alarm. Attributions may follow this alarm if the white cares to indulge them, and if they do, they will most likely be negative—one such attribution is intellectual ineptness. I think this reflex and the attributions that may follow it embarrass most whites today; therefore, it is usually quickly repressed. Nevertheless, on an equally atavistic level, the black will be aware of the reflex his color triggers and will feel a stab of horror at seeing himself reflected in this way. He, too, will do a quick repression, but a lifetime of such stabbings is what constitutes his inner realm of racial doubt.

The effects of this may be a subject for another essay. The point here is that the implication of inferiority that racial preferences engender in both the white and black mind expands rather than contracts this doubt. Even when the black sees no implication of inferiority in racial preferences, he knows that whites do, so that—consciously or unconsciously—the result is virtually the same. The effects of preferential treatment—the lowering of normal standards to increase black representation—puts blacks at war with an expanded realm of debilitating doubt, so that the doubt itself becomes an unrecognized preoccupation that undermines their ability to perform, especially in integrated situations. On largely white campuses, blacks are five times more likely to drop out than whites. Preferential treatment, no matter how it is justified in the light of day, subjects blacks to a midnight of self-doubt, and so often transforms their advantage into a revolving door.

Another liability of affirmative action comes from the fact that it indirectly encourages blacks to exploit their own past victimization as a source of power and privilege. Victimization, like implied inferiority, is what justifies preference, so that to receive the benefits of preferential treatment one must, to some extent, become invested in the view of one's self as a victim. In this way, affirmative action nurtures a victim-focused identity in blacks. The obvious irony here is that we become inadvertently invested in the very condition we are trying to overcome. Racial preferences send us the message that there is more power in our past suffering than our present achievements—none of which could bring us a *preference* over others.

When power itself grows out of suffering, then blacks are encouraged to expand the boundaries of what qualifies as racial oppression, a situation that can lead us to paint our victimization in vivid colors, even as we receive the benefits of preference. The same corporations and institutions that give us preference are also seen as our oppressors. At Stanford University minority students—some of whom enjoy as much as $15,000 a year in financial aid—recently took over the president's office demanding, among other things, more financial aid. The power to be found in victimization, like any power, is intoxicating and can lend itself to the creation of a new class of super-victims who can feel the pea of victimization under twenty mattresses. Preferential treatment rewards us for being underdogs rather than for moving beyond that status—a misplacement of incentives that, along with its deepening of our doubt, is more a yoke than a spur.

But, I think, one of the worst prices that blacks pay for preference has to do with an illusion. I saw this illusion at work recently in the mother of a middle-class black student who was going off to his first semester of college. "They owe us this, so don't think for a minute that you don't belong there." This is the logic by which many blacks, and some whites, justify affirmative action—it is something "owed," a form of reparation. But this logic overlooks a much harder and less digestible reality, that it is impossible to repay blacks living today for the historic suffering of the race. If all blacks were given a million dollars tomorrow morning it would not amount to a dime on the dollar of three centuries of oppression, nor would it obviate the residues of that oppression that we still carry today. The concept of historic reparation grows out of man's need to impose a degree of justice on the world that simply does not exist. Suffering can be endured and overcome; it cannot be repaid. Blacks cannot be repaid for the injustice done to the race, but we can be corrupted by society's guilty gestures of repayment.

Affirmative action is such a gesture. It tells us that racial preferences can do for us what we cannot do for ourselves. The corruption here is in the hidden incentive *not* to do what we believe preferences will do. This is an incentive to be reliant on others just as we are struggling for self-reliance. And it keeps alive the illusion that we can find some deliverance in repayment. The hardest thing for any sufferer to accept is that his suffering excuses him from very little and never has enough currency to restore him. To think otherwise is to prolong the suffering.

Several blacks I spoke with said they were still in favor of affirmative action because of the "subtle" discrimination blacks were subject to once on the job. One photojournalist said, "They have ways of ignoring you." A black female television producer said, "You can't file a lawsuit when your boss doesn't invite you to the insider meetings without ruining your career. So we still need affirmative action." Others mentioned the infamous "glass ceiling" through which blacks can see the top positions of authority but never reach them. But I don't think racial preferences are a protection against this subtle discrimination; I think they contribute to it.

In any workplace, racial preferences will always create two-tiered populations composed of preferreds and unpreferreds. This division makes automatic a perception of enhanced competence for the unpreferreds and of questionable competence for the preferreds—the former earned his way, even though others were given preference, while the latter made it by color as much as by competence. Racial preferences implicitly mark whites with an exaggerated superiority just as they mark blacks with an exaggerated inferiority. They not only reinforce America's oldest racial myth but, for blacks, they have the effect of stigmatizing the already stigmatized.

I think that much of the "subtle" discrimination that blacks talk about is often (not always) discrimination against the stigma of questionable competence that affirmative action delivers to blacks. In this sense, preferences scapegoat the very people they seek to help. And it may be that at a certain level employers impose a glass ceiling, but this may not be against the race so much as against the race's reputation for having advanced by color as much as by competence. Affirmative action makes a glass ceiling virtually necessary as a protection against the corruptions of preferential treatment. This ceiling is the point at which corporations shift the emphasis from color to competency and stop playing the affirmative action game. Here preference backfires for blacks and becomes a taint that holds them back. Of course, one could argue that this taint, which is, after all, in the minds of whites, becomes nothing more than an excuse to discriminate against blacks. And certainly the result is the same in either case— blacks don't get past the glass ceiling. But this argument does not get around the fact that racial preferences now taint this color with a new theme of suspicion that makes it even more vulnerable to the impulse in others to discriminate. In this crucial yet gray area of perceived competence, preferences make whites look better than they are and blacks worse, while doing nothing whatever to stop the very real discrimination that blacks may encounter. I don't wish to justify the glass ceiling here, but only to suggest the very subtle ways that affirmative action revives rather than extinguishes the old rationalizations for racial discrimination.

In education, a revolving door; in employment, a glass ceiling.

I believe affirmative action is problematic in our society because it tries to function like a social program. Rather than ask it to ensure equal opportunity we have demanded that it create parity between the races. But preferential treatment does not teach skills, or educate, or instill motivation. It only passes out entitlement by color, a situation that in my profession has created an unrealistically high demand for black professors. The social engineer's assumption is that this high demand will inspire more blacks to earn Ph.D.s and join the profession. In fact, the number of blacks earning Ph.D.s has declined in recent years. A Ph.D. must be developed from preschool on. He requires family and community support. He must acquire an entire system of values that enables him to work hard while delaying gratification. There are social programs, I believe, that can (and should) help blacks *develop* in all these areas, but entitlement by color is not a social program; it is a dubious reward for being black. . .

I would also like to see affirmative action go back to its original purpose of enforcing equal opportunity—a purpose that in itself disallows racial preferences. We cannot be sure that the discriminatory impulse in America has yet been shamed into extinction, and I believe affirmative action can make its greatest contribution by providing a rigorous vigilance in this area. It can guard constitutional rather than racial rights, and help institutions evolve standards of merit and selecting that are appropriate to the institution's needs yet as free of racial bias as possible (again, with the understanding that racial imbalances are not always an indication of racial bias). One of the most important things affirmative action can do is to define exactly what racial discrimination is and how it might manifest itself within a specific institution. The impulse to discriminate *is* subtle and cannot be ferreted out unless its many guises are made clear to people. Along with this there should be monitoring of institutions and heavy sanctions brought to bear when actual discrimination is found. This is the sort of affirmative action that America owes to blacks and to itself. It goes after the evil of discrimination itself, while preferences only sidestep the evil and grant entitlement to its *presumed* victims.

But if not preferences, then what? I think we need social policies that are committed to two goals: the educational and economic development of disadvantaged people, regardless of race, and the eradication from our society—through close monitoring and severe sanctions—of racial, ethnic, or gender discrimination. Preferences will not deliver us to either of these goals, since they tend to benefit those who are not disadvantaged—middle-class blacks—and attack one form of discrimination with another. Preferences are inexpensive and carry the glamour of good intentions—change the numbers and the good deed is done. To be against them is to be unkind. But I think the unkindest cut is to bestow on children like my own an undeserved advantage while neglecting the development of those disadvantaged children on the East Side of my city who will likely never be in a position to benefit from a preference. Give my children fairness; give disadvantaged children a better shot at development—better elementary and secondary schools, job training, safer neighborhoods, better financial assistance for college, and so on. Fewer blacks go to college today than ten years ago; more black males of college age are in prison or under the control of the criminal justice system than in college. This despite racial preferences.

The mandates of black power and white absolution out of which preferences emerged were not wrong in themselves. What was wrong was that both races focused more on the goals of these mandates than on the means to the goals. Blacks can have no real power without taking responsibility for their own educational and economic development. Whites can have no racial innocence without earning it by eradicating discrimination and helping the disadvantaged to develop. Because we ignored the means, the goals have not been reached, and the real work remains to be done.

Should Public Policy Be Class Conscious Rather Than Color Conscious?

Amy Gutmann

Amy Gutmann is president of the University of Pennsylvania. Her most recent book is *Why Deliberative Democracy?* (2004, with Dennis Thompson).

In this reading, Gutmann answers a question so often posed in contemporary American society rarely addressed in a systematic, philosophical way. Is it really race that serves as the main obstacle to equal opportunity in the United States or is economic class a greater obstacle? By analyzing empirical data and by evaluating arguments from fairness, Gutmann argues that while class is a relevant factor in evaluating disadvantage, race is much more influential.

We have yet carefully to consider a proposal that promises to go a long way toward securing fair opportunity for black Americans while avoiding the pitfalls of color consciousness by shifting the focus of public policy from race to class. One advocate of "class, not race" argues that "it was clear that with the passage of the Civil Rights Act of 1964, class replaced caste as the central impediment to equal opportunity."[1] If class is the central impediment to equal opportunity, then using class as a qualification may be fairer to individuals than using race.[2] Counting poverty as a qualification—on grounds that it is highly correlated with unequal opportunity, with untapped intellectual potential, and with life experience from which more affluent individuals can learn—would help blacks and nonblacks alike, but only those who are poor.[3] In addition to being fairer, its advocates claim, class preferences would be politically more feasible and therefore

potentially more effective in addressing racial as well as class injustice.[4] The apparently rising tide of resentment and distrust between blacks and whites in the United States makes the call to leave race preferences behind all the more appealing.[5]

Advocates most often look to university admissions as the realm in which class should supplant color as a qualification, so it makes sense to focus on the promise of "class, not race" in this extensive and familiar realm. University admissions policies would be fairer if considerations of color were left behind, advocates argue, while considerations of class took their place. Why? Because poverty accompanied by academic accomplishment is, generally speaking, a sign of uncommon effort, untapped intellectual potential, and unusual life experiences from which more affluent students can learn.

One advocate of "class, not race" notes that "we rarely see a breakdown of [SAT] scores by class, which would show enormous gaps between rich and poor, gaps that would help explain differences in scores by race."[6] After breaking down average SAT scores by class and race, we see enormous gaps between rich and poor students. If this were all that we

Excerpt from Amy Gutmann, Part III, "Should public policy be class conscious rather than color conscious?" in Responding to Racial Injustice. Reprinted by permission of the author.

observed, then the shift from class to race could provide fair opportunity for black Americans, since black Americans are disproportionately poor. But when average SAT scores are broken down by class and race, we also see enormous gaps between black and white students *within* the same income groups. Moreover, the very same argument that "class, not race" advocates invoke for counting poverty as a qualification in admissions also supports the idea that being black is a similarly important qualification. The same evidence of a significant gap in SAT scores between groups—whether identified by class or color—lends support to the idea that both poor students and black students face distinctive educational disadvantages. The educational disadvantages faced by black students are not statistically accounted for by the income differentials between white and black students. This is what we should expect if (and only if) color is an independent cause of injustice in this country.

The evidence from SAT scores alone is of course insufficient to provide a full picture of either class or racial injustice, let alone its causes. But the very same kind of evidence that advocates take as sufficient to support class as a consideration for university admissions also supports color as a consideration. There is a significant gap between the average SAT scores of groups, whether those groups are defined by class, color, or both. The average combined SAT scores for black students whose parents earn between $10,000 and $20,000 is 175 points lower than the average combined score for white students whose parents fall in the same income category. The gap between the average SAT scores of black and white students within this income category narrows by only 21 points out of the 196 point gap between all black and white students taking the test.[7]

As long as such gaps persist, a "class, not race" policy in university admissions will do far less to increase the higher educational opportunity of blacks than nonblacks. If selective colleges and universities reject color in order to adopt class as a consideration in admitting disadvantaged students, their student bodies would become almost entirely nonblack.[8] For colleges and universities committed to educating future leaders, this result should be as alarming as the image of an affluent,

multicolored society without well-educated black leaders. It is just as doubtful that nonblack leaders in such a society could be well educated, for their education would have taken place in almost entirely nonblack universities.

Proportional representation by color in selective universities is not an ultimate goal of a just society. Fair equality of opportunity is. The problem in universities' focusing on class considerations to the exclusion of color is not disproportionality of results but unfairness, as indicated by the inconsistency in the reasoning that supports the proposed shift from color to class. The statistical evidence of lower average SAT scores by income categories is taken to indicate that low-income students are disadvantaged in a way that warrants making low income a qualification. But the analogous statistical evidence of lower average SAT scores by the U.S. Census's racial categories is not taken to indicate that black students are disadvantaged in a way that warrants making color a qualification.[9]

The same statistical evidence that is used to establish the case for class as a consideration in admissions is either ignored or discounted when considering color as a consideration, and for no good reason. Some critics say that individual responsibility is undermined when black students who have lower SAT scores than nonblack students are admitted, but precisely the same argument could be made against admitting students from poor families who score lower than their more affluent peers. In both cases, the argument is extremely weak. Holding individuals responsible for their educational achievement is completely consistent with counting class *and* color as qualifications, as long as class and color are not the *only* qualifications, and individuals are not held to be *exclusively* responsible for their educational successes or failures.

The situation is therefore more complex than the "class, not race" perspective admits. In order to be admitted to a selective university, all applicants—whether they be poor, middle-class, rich, black, white, or some other color—must demonstrate unusual educational accomplishment relative to their similarly situated peers. They must also demonstrate the capacity to succeed academically, once admitted. These prerequisites to admission to a selective university ensure that individual applicants are held responsible for educational achievement. But social institutions, including universities, also share responsibility with individuals for overcoming the obstacles associated with color and class in our society. Why? Because to be responsible for accomplishing something entails having the effective power to do so. Individuals often do not have the power to overcome all the obstacles associated with being poor or black. Nor is responsibility a zero-sum quantity. Just because individuals are responsible for working hard does not mean that institutions are not responsible for coming to their aid, when they can thereby help equalize opportunity. It is therefore both unrealistic and unfair to expect individuals alone to overcome all the obstacles that are associated with being black or poor in our society.

The "class, not race" perspective admits half as much by urging universities to consider low income as a qualification for university admission—not the only qualification, to be sure, but a legitimate one that can justify admitting some applicants with lower SAT scores and lower high school grades and passing over other applicants with higher SAT scores and high school grades. Universities fall short of providing fair equality of educational opportunity, according to the "class, not race" perspective, to the extent that their admission policies neglect low income as an obstacle to educational achievement, and therefore refuse to pass over some applicants who score higher on these conventional indices (which do not predict future educational performance past the freshman year, let alone future career success or social leadership). The very same thing can be said about neglecting the extent to which being black is an obstacle to educational achievement in our society. The refusal to count being black as one qualification among many entails falling short of providing fair equality of educational opportunity for black students who demonstrate unusual educational achievement relative to the obstacles that they have faced. The best available evidence suggests that color and class are both obstacles, with interactive effects in the lives of a majority of black Americans.

Why, then, shift from color to class, rather than use both class and color, as independently

important considerations in university admissions? The inconsistency and unfairness in substituting class for color as a qualification becomes vivid when we imagine what universities that adopt the "class, not race" perspective would effectively be saying to their applicants. To the average low-income white student, they would say— "Giving you a boost in admissions is consistent with our expectation that you have worked hard to get where you are and will continue to work hard to earn your future success." To the average low-income black student, they would say—"If we give you an added boost in admissions over the average low-income white student, we will be denying your responsibility for your lower scores and decreasing your incentive to work hard and earn your success." To average middle-income black students, they would say: "We cannot give you any boost in admissions over average middle-income white students because you no more than they have any special obstacles to overcome."

Universities could achieve consistency by refusing to consider any of the educational obstacles faced by applicants, whether they be poor or black or physically handicapped. But the price of this policy would be forsaking fair equality of educational opportunity as well as overlooking the potential for intellectual accomplishment and social leadership of individuals who have faced far greater than average obstacles to academic achievement, as conventionally measured. Yet another price of a policy of "neither class nor color" would be discounting the values—associational as well as educational—of cultural diversity on university campuses. Consistency would also require giving up all the other, nonacademic factors that the most selective universities have traditionally considered relevant in admissions, such as geographical diversity and athletic ability.

Were citizens of this society engaged in designing our system of higher education from scratch, a case might be made for counting only intellectual accomplishment in admissions. But few if any critics of counting color as a consideration in university admissions propose such a radical redesigning of our college and university system. In any case, the fairest way to such radical restructuring would not begin by giving up on color as a consideration in admissions. There are many reasons to doubt whether such a radical re-design would produce a better system of higher education than the one we now have, and there is no reason to believe that this society would demo-cratically support such a restructuring. In this context, we cannot justify rejecting color while accepting class as one among many legitimate considerations for admissions.

What about the critics' claim that when uni-versities give a boost to applicants above and be-yond their actual educational achievements, they foster in that group of applicants a sense of irre-sponsibility for their (relative lack of) educational achievements? This argument from the value of individual responsibility cannot be sustained for two reasons. First, responsibility is not zero-sum. If universities assume some responsibility for helping applicants who have faced unusually great obstacles to educational achievement, they are not denying the responsibility of those applicants to work hard and demonstrate their capacity to suc-ceed once they are admitted. (Perhaps the critics are objecting to universities that admit a high pro-portion of black students who cannot graduate, in which case the critics are pointing to a correctable problem, and not one that besets the strongest case for counting color as a qualification.) Second, the same argument from responsibility is rarely if ever invoked in opposition to giving a boost to low-income or physically handicapped students, even though it applies with the same (weak) force. The force of the argument is weak because responsibil-ity for educational accomplishment is both institu-tional and individual. When universities share responsibility for helping students overcome educational obstacles, they do not therefore relieve them of the responsibility to succeed academi-cally. Students who are given a boost in an admis-sions process still must compete for admissions, work for their grades, and compete for jobs on the basis of their qualifications.

The case for both class *and* color as consid-erations in university admissions is therefore strong: stronger than either consideration taken to the exclusion of the other. The "class, not race"

proposal, by contrast, fails by the color blind test of fairness; it does not treat like cases alike. It dis-criminates against blacks by giving a boost only to students who score low because of disadvan-tages associated with poverty, but not to students who score low because of disadvantages that are as credibly associated with their color.[10]

A more complex way of counting class as a qualification, some critics say, would avoid these inequities and thereby obviate the need to take color into account. A "complex calculus of advan-tage" would take into account not only parental income, education, and occupation but also "net worth, the quality of secondary education, neigh-borhood influences and family structure." The complex calculus of class is fairer than the simple one, which counts only income, because it consid-ers more dimensions of disadvantage. Since blacks "are more likely than whites to live in con-centrated poverty, to go to bad schools and live in single-parent homes," the complex calculus would "disproportionately" benefit blacks.[11] Its advo-cates say that the complex calculus not only is fair but also has a decisive political advantage over any color conscious policy: it would go almost as far toward fair equality of educational opportunity as would explicit considerations of color without calling attention to the enduring racial divisions in our society.

But the political strength of the complex cal-culus of disadvantage is also its weakness. By not calling attention to enduring divisions of color in our society, some suggest, we may be better able to overcome them. But it is at least as likely that we will thereby fail to make much progress in overcoming them. It is impossible to say on the basis of available evidence—and the enduring imperfections of our self-understanding—which is more likely to be the case. What we can say with near certainty is that if blacks who live in concentrated poverty, go to bad schools, or live in single-parent homes are also stigmatized by racial prejudice as whites are not, then even the most complex calculus of *class* is an imperfect substitute for also taking color explicitly into ac-count. Perhaps the disadvantages of color can be adequately addressed by remedies that do not explicitly take color into account, but the adequacy of the complex calculus of disadvantage will then be closely related to the intention of its designers to come as close as possible to achieving the justice demanded by color as well as class consciousness.

Fairness speaks in favor of taking both class and color into account as qualifications. If politics precludes considerations of color, then we are far better off, morally speaking, with a complex calculus of class than with a simple one. But we would be better off still with policies that at least implicitly recognize the independent dimension of color as an obstacle to educational achievement in our society. The color blind principle of fairness has these inclusive implications. It encourages employers and universities to consider both class and color dimensions of disadvantage (along with other dimensions, such as gender) and also to consider a wider range of qualifications for jobs and places in a university.

Even color, class, *and* gender considerations, taken together, however, would not adequately address the problem of racial injustice. None of these considerations, as commonly defended, addresses a more urgent problem: the deprivation experienced by the poorest citizens, over 30 percent of whom are black. The poorest citizens are not in a position to benefit from admissions or hiring policies that count either class or color as added qualifications. This is a weakness shared by all kinds of policies that focus on giving a boost to individuals—whatever their skin color and relative advantage to one another—who are already among the more advantaged of our society. Millions of citizens, a vastly disproportionate number of them black, suffer from economic and educational deprivations so great as to elude the admittedly incomplete and relatively inexpensive remedies of affirmative action.[12] Policies aimed at increasing employment, job training, health care, child care, housing, and education are desperately needed for all these individuals, regardless of their color. These policies, like the admissions policies we have been considering, would not give *preferential* treatment to anyone.[13] They would treat the least advantaged citizens as civic equals

who should not be deprived of a fair chance to live a good life or participate as equals in democratic politics because of the bad luck of the natural lottery of birth or upbringing.

Social welfare and fair workfare policies—which provide jobs that pay and adequate child care for everyone who can work—are a necessary part of any adequate response to racial injustice. They are also far more expensive than admissions and hiring policies that treat class and color as qualifications, and far more expensive than policies of preferential treatment, at least in the short run. Over time, these policies would in all likelihood more than pay for themselves. They would alleviate the increasingly expensive and widespread problems of welfare dependency, unemployment, and crime in this country. Moreover, without fair workfare and welfare policies, we cannot be a society of civic equals. Citizens will be fighting for their fair share of a social pie that cannot provide fairness for everyone; many men and women who are willing and able to work will not be able to find work that pays, and others will work full-time only to earn less, or little more than they would on welfare, while they are also unable to ensure adequate care for their children.

The political fights in such a context will invariably divide us by groups, since effective democratic politics is by its very nature group politics. To build a society in which citizens both help themselves by helping each other and help each other by helping themselves, we must be committed not only to making the economic pie sufficiently large but also to dividing it in such a way that every person who is willing to work can find adequate child care and decent work that pays.

As urgent as social welfare, workfare, and child care policies are, they would not by themselves constitute a sufficient response to racial injustice in the short run. We have seen that color conscious programs are also part of a comprehensive response to injustice, although not the most urgent (or most expensive) part. Suppose that a more comprehensive, color conscious perspective is fair. Is it feasible? An eye-opening study entitled *The Scar of Race* shows that mere mention of the words "affirmative action" elicits negative attitudes about black Americans from white Americans. After affirmative action is mentioned in the course of an interview with white citizens, the proportion of respondents who agree with the claim that "blacks are irresponsible" almost doubles, increasing from 26 percent to 43 percent. (The proportions grow from 20 to 31 percent for the claim that "blacks are lazy" and from 29 to 36 percent for the claim that "blacks are arrogant."[14]) White Americans' "dislike of particular racial policies," the authors conclude, "can provoke dislike of blacks, as well as the other way around."[15]

"Provoking dislike" is importantly ambiguous between *producing* dislike and *triggering* the open expression of it (where the dislike already preceded the mere mention of affirmative action). It is doubtful that the mere mention of affirmative action *creates* racial prejudice. More likely, it *releases greater oral expression* of preexisting racial animosity. Many white Americans seem to take the mention of affirmative action, particularly in a matter-of-fact question that opens up the possibility of their criticizing affirmative action policies, as a signal that it is acceptable to be critical not only of affirmative action but also of blacks. This is cause for concern, but the concern cannot be effectively addressed simply by relabeling affirmative action policies as something else. A good reason to avoid the term "affirmative action" is the massive confusion that surrounds its meaning. An effective and appropriate response to this confusion would be to go beyond simple sound bites, which rarely serve justice well, and distinguish between morally better and worse policies that are color conscious. The negative reaction to the mere mention of the term "affirmative action" surely is not a sufficient reason to abandon affirmative action programs—whatever we call them—that are otherwise fair and beneficial to blacks.

Another finding of this same study suggests why it would be a mistake to oppose affirmative action only on these grounds. The popularity of programs that are perceived to help blacks is highly volatile, shifting with citizens' perception of the state of the law and the moral commitments of political leadership. When white citizens are

asked for their views on a set-aside program for minorities—"a law to ensure that a certain number of federal contracts go to minority contractors," 43 percent say they favor it. But when they are told that the set-aside program for minorities is a law passed by both houses of Congress, the support significantly increases to 57 percent.[16]

Not only does the force of law seem to have the capacity to change people's minds on race matters, so does the force of moral argument. When exposed to counterarguments to their expressed positions on various policy responses to racial problems, many people switch their position in the direction of the counterarguments. This tendency is greatest for social welfare policies, such as government spending for blacks, but the tendency is also significant for affirmative action policies, where an even greater proportion of whites shift to favoring a pro-affirmative action position than switch to an anti-affirmative action position when exposed to counterarguments to their original positions. Twenty-three percent of white respondents shift from a negative to a positive position on affirmative action, compared to 17 percent who shift in the opposite direction.[17]

Moral argument and political leadership, as this study vividly indicates, make a significant difference in public opinion on race matters. This is potentially good news for deliberative democracy. Were we to make our politics more deliberative, we would also—in all likelihood—increase the potential for bringing public policy and color consciousness more in line with the force of moral arguments. There are no guarantees, of course, about where the force of argument will lead citizens and public officials on these complex issues. But as long as the potential exists for changing minds through deliberation, citizens and public officials alike have good reason—moral as well as prudential—not to endorse public policies merely because they conform to public opinion polls. "New majorities can be made—and unmade," Paul Sniderman and Thomas Piazza conclude. "The future is not foreordained. It is the business of politics to decide it.[18]

All the more reason to approach the political morality of race with renewed openness, at least as much openness as ordinary citizens evince in extended discussions of racially charged issues, which include most issues of our public life. Unless we keep the aim of overcoming racial injustice at the front of our minds and at the center of our democratic deliberations, we shall not arrive at an adequate response to racial injustice. I do not pretend to be able to provide that response, or even anything close to it in this essay. But there is value in keeping democratic doors open to exploring new possibilities and to changing minds, including our own, as our deliberations on these issues continue. Only if we keep the aim of overcoming racial injustice at the center of our deliberations about social justice can we realistically hope to develop into a democracy with liberty and justice for all.

NOTES

1. Richard Kahlenberg, "Class, Not Race," *New Republic,* April 3, 1995, p. 21: "As the country's mood swings violently against affirmative action. . . , the whole project of legislating racial equality seems suddenly in doubt. The Democrats, terrified of the issue, are now hoping it will just go away. It won't. But at every political impasse, there is a political opportunity. Bill Clinton now has a chance. . . to turn a glaring liability. . . into an advantage—without betraying basic Democratic principles."

2. Class preferences are sometimes said to be fairer because they are more individualized than race preferences. But the claim that income is an individual characteristic while race is a group characteristic makes little sense. In itself, race is no more nor less a group characteristic than income. Both generalize on the basis of a group characteristic, as do all feasible public policies. As Michael Kinsley puts it: "The generalization 'Black equals disadvantaged' is probably as accurate as many generalizations that go unchallenged, such as 'High test scores equals good doctor' or 'Veteran equals sacrifice for the nation.'" Kinsley, "The Spoils of Victimhood."

3. Disadvantage by race moreover, is not remediable merely by civil criminal penalties for people who are found guilty of racial discrimination. The costs of bringing lawsuits and the difficulty of proving discrimination are so great as to cast doubt on the argument offered by advocates of color blindness that laws against discrimination can serve as an effective deterrent. Compare Swain, "A Cost Too High to Bear," p. 20.

4. There is also a legal case that class preferences are better than race preference, which is based on the claim that class is not a suspect category under the Fourteenth Amendment, while race is. Class preferences therefore have the advantage of not being constitutionally suspect.

The constitutional case against racial preferences, however, is largely dependent on the moral case for color blindness in our social context, which I criticized in the first two parts of this essay. Racial preferences that are used to create fair opportunity for blacks need not be suspect under the Fourteenth Amendment. Only those racial preferences that reflect prejudice against a disadvantaged group and serve to further disadvantage that group should be considered suspect. Racial distinctions that are relevant to carrying out a job well or that are designed to redress disadvantage therefore should not be deemed unconstitutional or even subject to the strictest scrutiny. See esp. Ronald Dworkin, "Reverse Discrimination," *Taking Rights Seriously* (Cambridge: Harvard University Press, 1977), pp. 223–39; and Dworkin, *A Matter of Principle,* pp. 293–334. Compare Kablenberg, "Class, Not Race," p. 24.

5. Advocates of class preferences also argue that class-based preferences are less likely to be stigmatizing because "there is no myth of inferiority in this country about the abilities of poor people comparable to that about African Americans." Kahlenberg, "Class, Not Race," p. 26. This is highly speculative, for once class-based preferences are instituted, they may elicit a similar myth about the inferiority of the poor. For an insightful piece of political fiction on this score, see Michael Young, *The Rise of the Meritocracy* (Baltimore: Penguin Books, 1961).

6. Kohlenberg, "Class, Not Race," p. 24.

7. The gap for parental incomes between $20,000 and $70,000 is 157 points. The gap between white and black students with parental incomes over $70,000 is 144 points. The gap between white and Asian students, by contrast, increases as parental income increases. Asian students on average overtake white students once parental income surpasses about $20,000. The average SAT scores for Hispanic students range from 52 to 89 points greater than the average for black students, controlling for parental income. The source for this information about the 1990 SAT is the College Board. It is reported and discussed in Andrew Hacker, *Two Nations: Black and White, Separate, Hostile, Unequal* (New York: Scribner, 1992), pp. 139–46.

8. Using income as a proxy for both disadvantages discriminates in favor of low-income white students and against low-income and middle-income black students. Need-based preferences in university admissions, as Jeffrey Rosen recently observed, if "honestly applied, would replace middle-class black students with lower-class white students." Rosen, "Affirmative Action: A Solution," p. 22. "This is why," as Andrew Hacker argues in *Two Nations,* "affirmative action that aims at helping blacks must take race into account" (p. 141).

9. After observing that "SAT scores correlate lockstep with income at every increment," Kahlenberg notes that "unless you believe in genetic inferiority, these statistics suggest unfairness is not confined to the underclass." He therefore endorses giving preference to "offspring of the working poor." The same logic applies racial disadvantage. At every income level, SAT scores vary with race. Unless you believe in genetic inferiority (for which no good evidence exists), the statistics suggest that unfairness is not confined to blacks whose parents are poor or working-class. Kahlenberg, "Class, Not Race," p. 26.

10. Giving preferences on the basis of race or class depends on the claim that admissions are not a prize for past merit but a bet on future promise along with a judgment of each student's ability to contribute to the educational institution itself. For discussion of an important distinction between the distribution of social offices, based on qualifications, and the distribution of social prizes, based on merit, see Michael Walzer, *Spheres of Justice,* pp. 135–39.

11. Kahlenberg, "Class, Not Race," p. 25.

12. As William Julius Wilson writes: "Neither programs based on equality of individual opportunity nor those organized in terms of preferential group treatment are sufficient to address the problems of truly disadvantaged minority group members." *The Truly Disadvantaged,* p. 112.

13. For an extended and insightful defense of some of these policies, see Wilson, *The Truly Disadvantaged.* See also Massey and Demon, *American Apartheid,* esp. pp. 229–36.

14. Paul M. Sniderman and Thomas Piazza, *The Scar of Race* (Cambridge: Harvard University Press, 1993), pp. 97–104. Another surprising finding discussed in this study is that larger percentages of black Americans express these negative images of blacks. Larger proportions of blacks also express positive images of blacks.

15. Ibid., p. 104. A few pages later, Sniderman and Piazza claim that "affirmative action is so intensely disliked that it has led some whites to dislike blacks—an ironic example of a policy meant to put the divide of race behind us in fact further widening it" (p. 109). But this claim is without adequate empirical support by their study, since the divide of race must be measured by more than public opinion.

Even if affirmative action does lead some whites to dislike blacks, its beneficial effects in bringing more blacks into skilled jobs and high status positions may far outweigh its negative effects. We have many reasons to doubt that affirmative action suffices to put the divide of race behind us. But we also have many reasons to doubt that affirmative action on balance has widened the divide of race in this country, since that divide must be measured by far more than the expression of white dislike of blacks (or black dislike of whites). The vast increase in the black middle class over the decades that affirmative action has been in effect, and the decrease in the racial stereotyping of jobs, for which affirmative action is at least partly responsible, has helped narrow the divide of race.

16. Ibid., pp. 131–32.

17. Ibid., p. 148.

18. Ibid., p. 165. Sniderman and Piazza are far less certain about this conclusion vis-à-vis what they call the "race conscious agenda," but their findings appear to hold for affirmative action as well as what they call social welfare and fair housing issues. The minority set-aside program certainly counts as preferential treatment, which is part of what Sniderman and Piazza are calling affirmative action. The positive shift in white support of a minority set-aside program upon learning that it has the sanction of law turns out to be among the more striking shifts in opinion that Sniderman and Piazza report.

The Color-Blind Principle

Bernard Boxill

Bernard Boxill is a professor of philosophy at the University of North Carolina at Chapel Hill. He is the author of *Blacks and Social Justice* (1984) and editor of *Race and Racism* (2001).

Boxill attempts to defend affirmative action plans by arguing that there is no reason for selection plans to be strictly colorblind, that is, for race never to be a criterion of selection. He asserts that some theorists misinterpret the reasons why it is unjust to discriminate based on race. Although he acknowledges that color-conscious policies, such as Jim Crow laws, can be heinous, he contends that it may be perfectly justified to discriminate among people according to traits or skills they are not responsible for possessing. He argues that it is just as bad to completely ignore race as it is to completely ignore talent. He concludes that either color or talent may be the foundation of just discrimination.

PLESSY

In 1892, Homer Plessy, an octoroon, was arrested in Louisiana for taking a seat in a train car reserved for whites. He was testing a state law which required the "white and colored races" to ride in "equal but separate" accommodations, and his case eventually reached the Supreme Court.

Part of Plessy's defense, though it must be considered mainly a snare for the opposition, was that he was "seven-eighths Caucasian and one-eighth African blood," and that the "mixture of colored blood was not discernible in him." The bulwark of his argument was, however, that he was "entitled to every right, privilege and immunity secured to citizens of the white race," and that the law violated the Fourteenth Amendment's prohibition against unequal protection of the laws.[1] Cannily, the court refused the snare. Perhaps it feared—and with reason—that the ancestry of too many white

Louisianans held dark secrets. But it attacked boldly enough Plessy's main argument that the Louisiana law was unconstitutional. That argument, Justice Henry Billings Brown wrote for the majority, was unsound. "Its underlying fallacy," he averred, was its "assumption that the enforced separation of the two races stamps the colored race with a badge of inferiority." "If this be so," Brown concluded, "it is not by reason of anything found in the act, but solely because the colored race chooses to put that construction upon it."[2]

Only one judge dissented from the court majority—Justice John Marshall Harlan. It was the occasion on which he pronounced his famous maxim: "Our Constitution is color-blind." In opposition to Justice Brown, Justice Harlan found that the "separation of citizens on the basis of race [was a] badge of servitude . . . wholly inconsistent [with] equality before the law."[3]

Plessy's is the kind of case which makes the color-blind principle seem indubitably right as a basis for action and policy, and its contemporary opponents appear unprincipled, motivated by expediency, and opportunistic. This impression is

Excerpt from Bernard Boxill, "The Color-Blind Principle" in Blacks and Social Justice, 1984, pp. 458–465.

only strengthened by a reading of Justice Brown's tortuously preposterous defense of the "equal but separate" doctrine. It should make every advocate of color-conscious policy wary of the power of arguments of expediency to beguile moral sense and subvert logic. Yet I argue that color-conscious policy can still be justified. The belief that it cannot is the result of a mistaken generalization from *Plessy*. There is no warrant for the idea that the color-blind principle should hold in some general and absolute way.

"I DIDN'T NOTICE" LIBERALS

In his book *Second Wind*, Bill Russell recalls how amazed he used to be by the behavior of what he called "I didn't notice" liberals. These were individuals who claimed not to notice people's color. If they mentioned someone Russell could not place, and Russell asked whether she was black or white, they would answer, "I didn't notice." "Sweet and innocent," Russell recalls, "sometimes a little proud."[4] Now, the kind of color-blindness the "I didn't notice" liberals claim to have may be a worthy ideal—Richard Wasserstrom, for example, argues that society should aim toward it—but it is absolutely different from the color-blind principle which functions as a basis for policy.[5] Thus, while Wasserstrom supports color-conscious policies to secure the ideal of people not noticing each other's color, the principle of color-blindness in the law opposes color-conscious policies and does not necessarily involve any hope that people will not notice each other's color. Its thesis is simple: that no *law* or *public policy* be designed to treat people differently because they are of a different color.

COLOR-BLIND AND COLOR-CONSCIOUS POLICIES

The essential thing about a color-conscious policy is that it is designed to treat people differently because of their race. But there are many different kinds of color-conscious policies. Some, for example the Jim Crow policies now in the main abolished, aim to subordinate blacks, while others, such as busing and preferential treatment, aim at elevating blacks.

Some color-conscious policies explicitly state that persons should be treated differently because of their race, for example the segregation laws at issue in *Plessy*; others make no mention of race, but are still designed so that blacks and whites are treated differently, for example, the "grandfather clauses" in voting laws that many states adopted at the turn of the century. To give one instance, in Louisiana this clause stated that those who had had the right to vote before or on 1 January 1867, or their lineal descendants, did not have to meet the educational, property, or tax requirements for voting. Since no blacks had had the right to vote by that time, this law worked effectively to keep blacks from voting while at the same time allowing many impoverished and illiterate whites to vote—yet it made no mention of race.

My object in this chapter is to demonstrate that the color-blind principle, which considers all color-conscious policies to be invalid, is mistaken. I do not deny that many color-conscious policies are wrong. Jim Crow was certainly wrong, and, for different reasons, proposals for black control of inner cities and inner city schools are probably wrong. But this is not because they are color-conscious, but for reasons which indicate that color conscious policies like busing and affirmative action could be correct.

Advocates of the belief that the law should be color-blind often argue that this would be the best means to an ideal state in which people are color-blind. They appeal to the notion that, only if people notice each other's color can they discriminate on the basis of color and, with considerable plausibility, they argue that color-conscious laws and policies can only heighten people's awareness of each other's color, and exacerbate racial conflict. They maintain that only if the law, with all its weight and influence, sets the example of color-blindness, can there be a realistic hope that people will see through the superficial distinctions of color and become themselves color-blind.

But this argument is not the main thesis of the advocates of legal color-blindness. Generally, they eschew it because of its dependency on the empirical.

Their favorite argument, one that is more direct and intuitively appealing, is simply that it is wicked, unfair, and unreasonable to penalize a person for what he cannot help being. Not only does this seem undeniably true, but it can be immediately applied to the issue of race. No one can help being white or being black, and so it seems to follow that it is wicked, unfair, and unreasonable to disqualify a person from any consideration just because he is white or black. This, the advocates of color-blindness declare, is what made Jim Crow law heinous, and it is what makes affirmative action just as heinous.

The force of this consideration is enhanced because it seems to account for one peculiar harmfulness of racial discrimination—its effect on self-respect and self-esteem. For racial discrimination makes some black people hate their color, and succeeds in doing so because color cannot be changed. Furthermore, a racially conscious society has made color seem an important part of the individual's very essence, and since color is immutable it is easily susceptible to this approach. As a result, the black individual may come, in the end, to hate even himself. Even religion is here a dubious consolation. For if God makes us black or white, to the religious black that by which he is marked may come to seem a curse by the Almighty, and he himself therefore essentially evil.

Of course, there are strategies that attempt to circumvent these effects of racial discrimination, but their weaknesses seem to confirm the need for color-blindness. For example, some black people concede that black is bad and ugly, but attempt to soften the effects of this concession by insisting that black is only "skin deep," we are all brothers beneath the skin, and the body, which is black and ugly, is no part of and does not sully the soul, which is the real self and is good. Thus, black people sometimes protested that although their skins were black, their souls were white, which is to say, good. There is truth to this feeling, in that nothing is more certain than that neither a black nor a white skin can make a person good or bad. Yet it is not a wholly successful approach to the problem of color. It requires that the black person believe that he is in some sense a ghost, which he can believe only if he is a lunatic. Another strategy is

put forth by Black Nationalism. The black nationalist agrees with the racists' view that his color is an important and integral part of his self, but affirms, in opposition to the racists, that it has value. This strategy, which is exemplified by the slogans "black is beautiful" and "black and proud," has the obvious advantage of stimulating pride and self-confidence. Nevertheless, it is no panacea. For one thing, it has to contend with the powerful propaganda stating that black is *not* beautiful. And there is a more subtle problem. Since the black cannot choose *not* to be black, he cannot be altogether confident that he would choose to *be* black, nor, consequently, does he really place a special value in being black. Thus, some people, black and white, have expressed the suspicion that the slogan "black is beautiful" rings hollow, like the words of the man who protests too loudly that he loves the chains he cannot escape. In this respect the black who can pass as white has an advantage over the black who cannot. For, though he cannot choose not to be black, he can choose not to be *known* to be black.

THE RESPONSIBILITY CRITERION

A final argument in favor of legal color-blindness is related to, and further develops, the point that people do not choose to be, and cannot avoid being, black or white. This links the question of color-blindness to the protean idea of individual responsibility. Thus, William Frankena writes, that to use color as a fundamental basis for distributing "opportunities, offices, etc." to persons is "unjust in itself," because it is to distribute goods on the basis of a feature "which the individual has not done, and can do nothing about; we are treating people differently in ways that profoundly affect their lives because of differences for which they have no responsibility."[6] Since this argument requires that people be treated differently in ways which profoundly affect their lives only on the basis of features for which they are responsible, I call it the responsibility criterion.

The responsibility criterion also seems to make the principle of color-blindness follow from principles of equal opportunity. Joel Feinberg takes it to be equivalent to the claim that "properties can be the grounds of just discrimination between persons only if those persons had a fair opportunity to acquire or avoid them."[7] This implies that to discriminate between persons on the basis of a feature for which they can have no responsibility is to violate the principle of fair opportunity. But color (or sex) is a feature of persons for which they can have no responsibility.

The responsibility criterion may seem innocuous because, though, strictly interpreted it supports the case for color-blindness, loosely interpreted it leaves open the possibility that color-conscious policies are justifiable. Thus, Frankena himself allows that color could be an important basis of distribution of goods and offices if it served "as [a] reliable sign[s] of some Q, like ability or merit, which is more justly employed as a touchstone for the treatment of individuals."[8] This sounds like a reasonable compromise and is enough to support some arguments for color-conscious policies. For example, it could support the argument that black and white children should go to the same schools because being white is a reliable sign of being middle-class, and black children, who are often lower-class, learn better when their peers are middle-class. Similarly, it might support the argument that preferential hiring is compensation for the harm of being discriminated against on the basis of color, and that being black is a reliable sign of having been harmed by that discrimination.

But however loosely it is interpreted, the responsibility criterion cannot be adduced in support of all reasons behind color-conscious policies. It cannot, for example, sustain the following argument, sketched by Ronald Dworkin, for preferential admission of blacks to medical school. "If quick hands count as 'merit' in the case of a prospective surgeon this is because quick hands will enable him to serve the public better and for no other reason. If a black skin will, as a matter of regrettable fact, enable another doctor to do a different medical job better, then that black skin is by the same token 'merit' as well."[9] What is proposed here is not that a black skin is a justifiable basis of discrimination because it is a reliable sign of merit

or some other factor Q. A closely related argument does make such a proposal, viz., that blacks should be preferentially admitted to medical school because being black is a reliable sign of a desire to serve the black community. But this is not the argument that Dworkin poses. In the example quoted above what he suggests is that being black is in *itself* merit, or, at least, something very like merit.

According to the responsibility criterion, we ought not to give A a job in surgery rather than B, if A is a better surgeon than B only because he was born with quicker hands. For if we do, we treat A and B "differently in ways that profoundly affect their lives because of differences for which they have no responsibility." This is the kind of result which puts egalitarianism in disrepute. It entails the idea that we might be required to let fumblers do surgery and in general give jobs and offices to incompetents, and this is surely intolerable. But, as I plan to show, true egalitarianism has no such consequences. They are the result of applying the responsibility criterion, not egalitarian principles. Indeed, egalitarianism must scout the responsibility criterion as false and confused.

Egalitarians should notice first, that, while it invalidates the merit-based theories of distribution that they oppose, it also invalidates the need-based theories of distribution they favor. For, if people are born with special talents for which they are not responsible, they are also born with special needs for which they are not responsible. Consequently, if the responsibility criterion forbids choosing A over B to do surgery because A is a better surgeon because he was born with quicker hands, it also forbids choosing C rather than D for remedial education because C needs it more than D only because he was born with a learning disability and D was not.

At this point there may be objections. First, that the responsibility criterion was intended to govern only the distribution of income, not jobs and offices—in Feinberg's discussion, for example, this is made explicit. Second, that it does not mean that people should not be treated differently because of differences, good or bad, which they cannot help, but rather that people should not get less just because they are born without the qualities their society prizes or finds useful. This seems to be implied in Frankena's claim that justice should make the "same proportionate contribution to the best life for everyone" and that this may require spending more on those who are "harder to help"—probably the untalented—than on others. Qualified in these ways, the responsibility criterion becomes more plausible. It no longer implies, for example, that fumblers should be allowed to practice surgery, or that the blind be treated just like the sighted. But with these qualifications it also becomes almost irrelevant to the color-blind issue. For that issue is not only about how income should be distributed. It is also about how jobs and offices should be distributed.

Most jobs and offices are distributed to people in order to produce goods and services to a larger public. To that end, the responsibility criterion is irrelevant. For example, the purpose of admitting people to medical schools and law schools is to provide the community with good medical and legal service. It does not matter whether those who provide them are responsible for having the skills by virtue of which they provide the goods, or whether the positions they occupy are "goods" to them. No just society makes a person a surgeon just because he is responsible for his skills or because making him a surgeon will be good for him. It makes him a surgeon because he will do good surgery.

Accordingly, it may be perfectly just to discriminate between persons on the basis of distinctions they are not responsible for having. It depends on whether or not the discrimination serves a worthy end. It may be permissible for the admissions policies of professional schools to give preference to those with higher scores, even if their scores are higher than others only because they have higher native ability (for which they cannot, of course, be considered responsible), if the object is to provide the community with good professional service. And, given the same object, if for some reason a black skin, whether or not it can be defined as merit, helps a black lawyer or doctor to provide good legal or medical service to black people who would otherwise not have access to it, or avail themselves of it, it is difficult to see how there can be a principled objection to admissions policies which prefer people with black skins—though, again, they are not responsible for the quality by virtue of which they are preferred.

JUSTICE AND THE RESPONSIBILITY CRITERION

A further point needs to be made in order to vindicate color-conscious policies. The principles of justice are distributive: Justice is concerned not only with increasing the total amount of a good a society enjoys, but also with how that good should be distributed among individuals. Generally, judicial principles dictate that people who are similar in ways deemed relevant to the issue of justice, such as in needs or rights, should get equal amounts of a good, and people who are dissimilar in these regards should get unequal amounts of the good. In terms of these principles certain laws and rules must be considered unjust which would not otherwise be thought unjust. Consider, for example, a policy for admitting persons to medical school which resulted in better and better medical service for white people, but worse and worse medical service for black people. This policy would be unjust, however great the medical expertise—certainly a good—it produced, unless color is relevant to the receiving of good medical attention.

In a case like this, where it is not, the theoretical circumstance outlined by Dworkin, in which black skin might be considered a "merit," becomes viable. It is true, of course, that color is not, precisely, merit. But to insist on strict definition in this context is to cavil. The point is that if black clients tend to trust and confide more in black lawyers and doctors, then color—functioning as merit—enables a good to be produced and distributed according to some principle of justice.

If these considerations are sound, then the responsibility criterion thoroughly misconstrues the reasons for which racial discrimination is unjust. Racial discrimination against blacks is unjust because it does not enable goods to be produced and distributed according to principles of justice. It is not unjust because black people do not choose to be black, cannot *not* be black, or are not responsible for being black. This is completely irrelevant. For example, a policy denying university admission to people who parted their hair on the right side would be unjust because the way in which people part their hair is irrelevant to a just policy of school admission. It does not matter in the least, in relation to the nature and object of education, that they choose how they part their hair. Similarly, even if black people could choose to become white, or could all easily pass as white, a law school or medical school that excluded blacks because they were black would still act unjustly. Nothing would have changed.

The arguments in support of color-blindness tend to make the harmfulness of discrimination depend on the difficulty of avoiding it. This is misleading. It diverts attention from the potential harmfulness of discrimination that *can* be avoided and brings the specious responsibility criterion into play. Suppose again, for example, that a person is denied admission to law school because he parts his hair on the right side. Though he, far more easily than the black person, can avoid being unfairly discriminated *against*, he does not thereby more easily avoid being the object, indeed, in a deeper sense, the victim, of unfair discrimination. If he parts his hair on the left side he will presumably be admitted to law school. But then he will have knowingly complied with a foolish and unjust rule and this may well make him expedient and servile. Of course, he will not be harmed to the same extent and in the same way as the victim of racial discrimination. For example, he probably will not hate himself. Unlike color, the cause of his ill-treatment is too easily changed for him to conceive of it as essential to himself. Moreover, if he chooses to keep his hair parted on the right side and thus to forego law school, he *knows* that he is not going to law school because he freely chose to place a greater value on his integrity or on his taste in hairstyles than on a legal education. He knows this because he knows he could have chosen to change his hairstyle. As I noted earlier, this opportunity for self-assertion, and thus for self-knowledge and

self-confidence, is denied the black who is discriminated against on the basis of his color.

Nevertheless, as I stated earlier, the considerations that stem from applying the responsibility criterion to a judgment of racial discrimination are secondary to understanding its peculiar harmfulness. Suppose, for example, that a person is not admitted to medical school to train to be a surgeon because he was born without fingers. If all the things he wants require that he have fingers, he may conceivably come to suffer the same self-hatred and self-doubt as the victim of racial discrimination. Yet his case is different, and if he attends to the difference, he will not suffer as the victim of racial discrimination suffers. The discrimination that excludes him from the practice of surgery is not denigrating his interests because they are his. It is a policy that takes into account a just object—the needs of others in the community for competent surgery. Allowing him to be a surgeon would rate other, equally important, interests below his. But racial discrimination excludes its victims from opportunities on the basis of a belief that their interests are ipso facto less important than the interests of whites. The man without fingers may regret not being born differently, but he cannot resent how he is treated. Though his ambitions may be thwarted, he himself is still treated as a moral equal. There is no attack on his self-respect. Racial discrimination, however, undermines its victims' self-respect through their awareness that they are considered morally inferior. The fact that racial discrimination, or any color-conscious policy, is difficult to avoid through personal choice merely adds to its basic harmfulness if it is in the first place unjust, but is not the *reason* for its being unjust.

It remains to consider Feinberg's claim that if people are discriminated for or against on the basis of factors for which they are not responsible the equal opportunity principle is contravened. This I concede. In particular, I concede that color-conscious policies giving preference to blacks place an insurmountable obstacle in the path of whites, and since such obstacles reduce opportunities, such policies may make opportunities unequal. But this gives no advantage to the advocates of color-blind policies. For giving preference to the competent has exactly the same implications as giving preference to blacks. It, too, places obstacles in the paths of some people, this time the untalented, and just as surely makes opportunities unequal. Consequently, an advocate of color-blindness cannot consistently oppose color-conscious policies on the grounds that they contravene equal opportunity and at the same time support talent-conscious policies. Nor, finally, does my concession raise any further difficulty with the issue of equal opportunity. Equal opportunity is not a fundamental principle of justice, but is derived from its basic principles. Often these basic principles require that opportunities be made more equal. Invariably, however, these same principles require that the process of equalization stop before a condition of perfect equality of opportunity is reached.

To conclude, adopting a color-blind principle entails adopting a talent-blind principle, and since the latter is absurd, so also is the former. Or, in other words, differences in talent, and differences in color, are, from the point of view of justice, on a par. Either, with equal propriety, can be the basis of a just discrimination. Consequently, the color-blind principle is not as simple, straightforward, or self-evident as many of its advocates seem to feel it is. Color-conscious policies can conceivably be just, just as talent-conscious policies can conceivably be—and often are—just. It depends on the circumstances.

NOTES

1. Derrick A. Bell, Jr., ed., *Plessy v. Ferguson* in *Civil Rights: Leading Cases* (Boston: Little, Brown, 1980), 64–77.
2. Ibid., 71.
3. Ibid., 71–77.
4. Bill Russell and Taylor Brand, *Second Wind* (New York: Random House, 1979), 187.
5. Richard A. Wasserstrom, "Racism and Sexism," in Richard A. Wasserstrom, *Philosophy and Social Issues* (Notre Dame, IN: University of Notre Dame Press, 1980), 24, 25.
6. William Frankena, "Some Beliefs About Justice," in *Justice*, ed. Joel Feinberg and Hyman Gross (Encino, CA: Dickenson, 1977), 49.
7. Joel Feinberg, *Social Philosophy* (Upper Saddle River, NJ: Prentice Hall, 1973), 49.
8. Frankena, "Some Beliefs About Justice," 49.
9. Ronald Dworkin, "Why Bakke Has No Case," *New York Review of Books*, 10 Nov. 1977, 14.

STUDY QUESTIONS: RACIAL AND ETHNIC DISCRIMINATION

1. Is it true that society still relies on the definition of race as a biological entity? Zack describes two phases of "relinquishing false biological notions of race." What influence is our progression through these two phases likely to have on racism?
2. What, according to Wong, is collective responsibility? How does it contribute to justice? How does Wong conceive of racial, ethnic, and cultural categories, and why is our ability to define them necessary for this view?
3. Appiah argues that there are no morally relevant differences between the races. What does his view imply for ethical principles that hold that people have a stronger ethical duty to those in their own race? How can Appiah's arguments be further strengthened with Zack's arguments?
4. Provide Steele's argument against affirmative action being used to address the harms of racism (in the present) and the harms from racism's legacy. (Be sure to make clear the various definitions of affirmative action that he is relying on and the harm that he argues will result from these forms of affirmative action.) What is Steele's solution? Do you think that the development he argues for is likely in the absence of affirmative action?
5. Is it, as Gutmann contends, logically inconsistent to hold that class should be a relevant factor in public policy but not race? Why or why not? What role does empirical evidence play in Gutmann's argument?
6. Boxill argues that color, like talent, can be the basis of justified discrimination. Reconstruct his argument, explaining how he justifies this. Part of his justification is that color is a form of merit, in that a black doctor could better serve black patients (often poor) *who would otherwise not have that service*. Does his argument imply that recipients of color-conscious policies *owe* their services to the needy and/or underserved of their race? If so, do white doctors have similar duties in Appalachia?

SUPPLEMENTARY READINGS: RACIAL AND ETHNIC DISCRIMINATION

ANAYA, RUDOLFO A., and FRANCISCO LOMELI. *Aztlán: Essays on the Chicano Homeland.* (Albuquerque: University of New Mexico Press, 1989.)
BANTON, MICHAEL. "The International Defense of Racial Equality." *Ethnic and Racial Studies*, vol. 13(4), October 1990.
BOXILL, BERNARD. "Self-Respect and Protest." In *Philosophy Born of Struggle*, Harris, editor. (Dubuque, IA: Kendall/Hunt, 1983.)
———. *Blacks and Social Justice.* (Boston: Rowman and Littlefield Publishers, 1992.)
CROW, STEPHEN M., and DINAH PAYNE. "Affirmative Action for a Face Only a Mother Could Love." *Journal of Business Ethics*, vol. 11 (11), 1992.
CORNELL, STEPHEN. "Land, Labour and Group Formation: Blacks and Indians in the United States." *Ethnic and Racial Studies*, vol. 13(3), July 1990.

CUÁDRAZ, GOLRIA HOLGUÍN. "Stories of Access and 'Luck': Chicana/os, Higher Education, and the Politics of Incorporation." *Latino Studies Journal,* vol. 10(1), Winter 1999.

ENGLISH, PARKER, and KIBUJJO M. KALUMBA. *African Philosophy: A Classical Approach.* (Upper Saddle River, NJ: Prentice Hall, 1996).

HARRIS, LEONARD. "The Concept of Racism." In *Exploitation and Exclusion*, Zegeye, Harris, and Maxted, editors. (London: Hans Zell, 1991.)

KARENGA, MAULANA. "Society, Culture and the Problem of Self-Consciousness: A Kawaida Analysis." In *Philosophy Born of Struggle*, Harris, editor. (Dubuque, IA: Kendall/Hunt, 1983.)

LAWSON, BILL. "Nobody Knows Our Plight: Moral Discourse, Slavery and Social Progress." *Social Theory and Practice*, vol. 18(1), Spring 1992.

MAPHAI, VINCENT. "Prisoners' Dilemmas: Black Resistance—Government Response." *The Philosophical Forum* (Special Issue on Apartheid), Winter–Spring 1987.

MCGARY, HOWARD. "Race and Class Exploitation." In *Exploitation and Exclusion*, Zegeye, Harris, and Maxted, editors. (London: Hans Zell, 1991.)

MCINTOSH, PEGGY. "White Privilege and Male Privilege: A Personal Account of Coming to See Correspondences Through Work in Women's Studies." Copyright © 1988 by Peggy McIntosh, Center for Research on Women, Wellesley College.

MOSLEY, ALBERT G. *African Philosophy.* (Upper Saddle River, NJ: Prentice Hall, 1995.)

NAILS, DEBRA. "A Human Being Like Any Other: Like No Other." *The Philosophical Forum*, Winter–Spring 1987.

OUTLAW, LUCIUS. "Toward a Critical Theory of Race." In *Anatomy of Racism*, Goldberg, editor. (Minneapolis: University of Minnesota Press, 1990.)

ROMERO, MARY, PIERRETTE HONDAGNEU-SOTELO, and VILMA ORTIZ, eds. *Challenging Fronteras: Structuring Latina and Latino Lives in the U.S.* (New York: Routledge, 1997.)

SAID, EDWARD W. "Zionism from the Standpoint of Its Victims." In *Anatomy of Racism*, Goldberg, editor. (Minneapolis: University of Minnesota Press, 1990.)

WEST, CORNEL. *Race Matters.* (Boston, MA: Beacon Press, 1993.)

Part VIII

ABORTION

Abortion has remained one of the most difficult and controversial ethical issues in the United States for the past forty years. Although many have nothing more than an emotional reaction to this issue, there are important philosophical questions that need to be addressed. In this section, we survey a spectrum of positions in the debate and examine the underlying philosophical justifications of each. In addition, we hope to shed light on what has been a debate conducted exclusively in Western terms, by introducing non-Western perspectives on the problem.

Abortion has become a forefront ethical issue in the United States since 1973 with the Supreme Court's landmark ruling in *Roe* v. *Wade*. In that court case, an overwhelming majority of the Supreme Court judges ruled that abortion constitutes a "fundamental right" of women. Until the fetus is viable (able to live outside the womb), the court ruled that the woman's right to decide what to do with her own body is paramount. After the fetus attains viability (during the third trimester of gestation), then restrictions could be placed on abortion rights, because only at that point is there a competing (human) right. The right to abortion is seen as one of many rights to privacy, along with the right to obtain and use birth control devices. These rights are considered akin to the rights against unreasonable search and seizure and to speech and peaceable assembly. The ruling in *Roe* v. *Wade* could be viewed as representing a triumph in the liberal position in abortion.

The conservative position, on the other hand, generally regards all abortions as morally unjustifiable. The fetus is regarded as a full-fledged human person from the moment of conception: its rights are thought to outweigh the woman's right to control her body. Many who hold the conservative position also believe that any attempt to interfere with the natural process of gestation and birth, even many forms of birth control, is morally unjustifiable. The paramount concern is for the fetus's right to life, a right so important that it overrides all other considerations. Conservatives argue that if a child is unwanted, adoption rather than abortion is the morally acceptable solution.

Various difficulties plague both sides of the abortion dispute in the United States. Many conservatives have long been bothered by cases of pregnancy due to rape or incest, as well as pregnancies that threaten the life of the pregnant woman. Liberals have been bothered by the issue of whether, on their own principles, they are committed to justifying some forms of infanticide, such as the killing of greatly deformed newborn babies. A consideration of such problem cases has caused some people to adopt one of many moderate, compromise positions on abortion, accepting some types of abortion while prohibiting some others.

We begin with John T. Noonan, who defends a conservative position of abortion. Noonan maintains that the fetus has the right to life at the moment of conception. Arguing that none of the popularly invoked criteria—viability, experience, quickening, attitudes of adults, and social viability—is sufficient to establish when a fetus is human, Noonan claims that the only nonarbitrary basis is located at the moment of conception.

As opposed to a mere nonfertilized egg or spermatozoa that have very little chance of developing into full-fledged human beings, the moment of conception is the point at which the fetus acquires the full human genetic code and the potential to develop into a full-fledged human being. Noonan, however, concedes that abortion is permissible on grounds of self-defense.

In contrast to Noonan, Mary Anne Warren assumes a liberal stand on abortion. She believes that a fetus does not have a right to life. This is because only human persons have such a right, and for a human being to have a right to life, he or she must satisfy some of these five criteria: consciousness, reasoning, self-motivated activity, capacity to communicate, and self-awareness. These are the features that enable an individual to participate as members of a moral community. Fetuses do not generally have enough of these features to be considered persons even though they may resemble human persons in other respects. Fetuses are at best potential persons and as such have merely potential rights, not the sort of rights that could override a woman's right to control her own body. In the postscript, Warren takes on the objection that her argument would render not only abortion but also infanticide morally permissible. She replies that this is not the case for two reasons. First, even if the parents do not want the newly born, other people in this country and at this point in time value newborn infants in a way similar to valuing art works, and second, people in this country want the lives of infants preserved.

Don Marquis is not satisfied with either position in the debate, which he believes is preoccupied with a distinction between human life in the genetic sense and moral personhood. He argues that both sides start with different premises, which means that the debate ends in a deadlock. Instead, he attempts to bypass this debate by advancing his own view of abortion—a conservative one. According to Marquis, what is important about a life is its future possibilities of valuable goals and projects, and what makes killing someone like us morally wrong is that it deprives the individual of his or her future of value. And since the future of a fetus is the same as the future of an adult, what

makes it wrong to kill adult human beings is also what makes it wrong to kill fetuses. Marquis thus concludes that most abortions are morally unjustified, and this is true no matter what the current consensus is about abortion.

In response to Marquis, Peter McInerney challenges the assumption that the future of a fetus is identical to the future of a normal adult human. A fetus does not have the same psychological complexity as a normal adult; nor can it control its future the same way as an adult capable of making and executing plans. There is something to be said about humans as a process of development. Questions then linger as to whether one can bypass the debate between human in the genetic sense and human in the moral sense.

It should be noted that the West considers a woman's right to have an abortion as predominantly a matter of an individual's reproductive freedom; it tends to view coercive abortion for the sake of social goals as morally unacceptable. However, as Jing-Bao Nie argues in his discussion of forced abortion in China, coercion is not always morally unjustified: compulsory vaccination is an example. Moreover, given the need to control population growth and for the sake of the well-being of future generations, coercive abortion may be a tragic necessity, even though it violates an individual's right to reproductive freedom and privacy.

William LaFleur points us toward a society that has largely reached a consensus about abortion. In contemporary Japan, a strong emphasis on conservative family values has had an effect opposite to that which has occurred in America. Abortion is regarded as a necessary measure in assuring that families will have only those members who are wanted. Interestingly, the consensus reached in Japan is one that is tempered by the feeling that abortion is a tragic necessity. No matter whether a consensus or compromise is reached on abortion, there will probably always be this tragic dimension to our choices on the abortion issue.

We close this section with a discussion of the Hindu perspective on abortion, which is unfamiliar to most readers in this part of the world. Jilius

Lipner writes that unlike Western debates on the subject, the Hindu tradition does not make a distinction between human in the genetic sense and human in the moral sense. Instead, moral personhood is presumed throughout fetal development, which is one reason why abortion is morally wrong. Another reason why abortion is unacceptable is because terminating the unborn would arrest the unravelling of *karma*, which should normally be allowed to play itself out in the course of one's life.

—KAI WONG

An Almost Absolute Value in History

John T. Noonan, Jr.

John T. Noonan is a professor of law at the University of California, Berkeley. Among his books are *Contraception* (1965) and *A Private Choice: Abortion in America in the Seventies* (1979).

Noonan advances a defense of the conservative position on abortion. He argues that the fetus acquires the right to life at the moment of conception when it receives its human genetic codes. Other criteria such as viability, experience, quickening, sentiments, and visibility all turn out to be arbitrary on his analysis. Moreover, since there is an 80 percent chance that a zygote—as opposed to a spermatozoon or an oocyte—develops into a full-fledged human being, this jump in probabilities provides an important supporting argument for why drawing the line at conception is not arbitrary.

The most fundamental question involved in the long history of thought on abortion is: How do you determine the humanity of a being? To phrase the question that way is to put in comprehensive humanistic terms what the theologians either dealt with as an explicitly theological question under the heading of "ensoulment" or dealt with implicitly in their treatment of abortion. The Christian position as it originated did not depend on a narrow theological or philosophical concept. It had no relation to theories of infant baptism.[1] It appealed to no special theory of instantaneous ensoulment. It took the world's view on ensoulment as that view changed from Aristotle to Zacchia. There was, indeed, theological influence affecting the theory of ensoulment finally adopted, and, of course, ensoulment itself was a theological concept, so that the position was always explained in theological terms. But the theological notion of ensoulment could easily be translated into humanistic language by substituting "human" for "rational soul;" the problem of knowing when a man is common to theology and humanism.

If one steps outside the specific categories used by the theologians, the answer they gave can be analyzed as a refusal to discriminate among human beings on the basis of their varying potentialities. Once conceived, the being was recognized as man because he had man's potential. The criterion for humanity, thus, was simple and all-embracing: If you are conceived by human parents, you are human.

The strength of this position may be tested by a review of some of the other distinctions offered in the contemporary controversy over legalizing abortion. Perhaps the most popular distinction is in terms of viability. Before an age of so many months, the fetus is not viable, that is, it cannot be removed from the mother's womb and live apart from her. To that extent, the life of the fetus is absolutely dependent on the life of the mother. This dependence is made the basis of denying recognition to its humanity.

There are difficulties with this distinction. One is that the perfection of artificial incubation may make the fetus viable at any time: It may be removed and artificially sustained. Experiments with animals already show that such a procedure is possible.[2] This hypothetical extreme case relates to an actual difficulty: There is considerable elasticity to the idea of viability. Mere length of life is not an exact measure. The viability of the fetus depends on the extent of its anatomical and functional development.[3] The weight and length of the fetus are better guides to the state of its development than age, but weight and length vary.[4] Moreover, different racial groups have different ages at which their fetuses are viable. Some evidence, for example, suggests that Negro fetuses mature more quickly than white fetuses.[5] If viability is the norm, the standard would vary with race and with many individual circumstances.

The most important objection to this approach is that dependence is not ended by viability. The fetus is still absolutely dependent on someone's care in order to continue existence; indeed a child of one or three or even five years of age is absolutely dependent on another's care for existence; uncared for, the older fetus or the younger child will die as surely as the early fetus detached from the mother. The unsubstantial lessening in dependence and viability does not seem to signify any special acquisition of humanity.

A second distinction has been attempted in terms of experience. A being who has had experience, has lived and suffered, who possesses memories, is more human than one who has not. Humanity depends on formation by experience. The fetus is thus "unformed" in the most basic human sense.[6]

This distinction is not serviceable for the embryo which is already experiencing and reacting. The embryo is responsive to touch after eight weeks[7] and at least at this point is experiencing. At an earlier stage the zygote is certainly alive and responding to its environment.[8] The distinction may also be challenged by the rare case where aphasia has erased adult memory: Has it erased humanity? More fundamentally, this distinction leaves even the older fetus or the younger child to be treated as an unformed inhuman thing. Finally, it is not clear why experience as such

confers humanity. It could be argued that certain central experiences such as loving or learning are necessary to make a man human. But then human beings who have failed to love or to learn might be excluded from the class called man.

A third distinction is made by appeal to the sentiments of adults. If a fetus dies, the grief of the parents is not the grief they would have for a living child. The fetus is an unnamed "it" till birth, and is not perceived as personality until at least the fourth month of existence when movements in the womb manifest a vigorous presence demanding joyful recognition by the parents.

Yet feeling is notoriously an unsure guide to the humanity of others. Many groups of humans have had difficulty in feeling that persons of another tongue, color, religion, sex, are as human as they. Apart from reactions to alien groups, we mourn the loss of a ten-year-old boy more than the loss of his one-day-old brother or his 90-year-old grandfather. The difference felt and the grief expressed vary with the potentialities extinguished, or the experience wiped out; they do not seem to point to any substantial difference in the humanity of baby, boy, or grandfather.

Distinctions are also made in terms of sensation by the parents. The embryo is felt within the womb only after about the fourth month.[9] The embryo is seen only at birth. What can be neither seen nor felt is different from what is tangible. If the fetus cannot be seen or touched at all, it cannot be perceived as man.

Yet experience shows that sight is even more untrustworthy than feeling in determining humanity. By sight, color became an appropriate index for saying who was a man, and the evil of racial discrimination was given foundation. Nor can touch provide the test; a being confined by sickness, "out of touch" with others, does not thereby seem to lose his humanity. To the extent that touch still has appeal as a criterion, it appears to be a survival of the old English idea of "quickening"—a possible mistranslation of the Latin *animatus* used in the canon law. To that extent touch as a criterion seems to be dependent on the Aristotelian notion of ensoulment, and to fall when this notion is discarded.

Finally, a distinction is sought in social visibility. The fetus is not socially perceived as human. It cannot communicate with others. Thus, both subjectively and objectively, it is not a member of society. As moral rules are rules for the behavior of members of society to each other, they cannot be made for behavior toward what is not yet a member. Excluded from the society of men, the fetus is excluded from the humanity of men.[10]

By force of the argument from the consequences, this distinction is to be rejected. It is more subtle than that founded on an appeal to physical sensation, but it is equally dangerous in its implications. If humanity depends on social recognition, individuals or whole groups may be dehumanized by being denied any status in their society. Such a fate is fictionally portrayed in *1984* and has actually been the lot of many men in many societies. In the Roman empire, for example, condemnation to slavery meant the practical denial of most human rights; in the Chinese Communist world, landlords have been classified as enemies of the people and so treated as nonpersons by the state. Humanity does not depend on social recognition, though often the failure of society to recognize the prisoner, the alien, the heterodox as human has led to the destruction of human beings. Anyone conceived by a man and a woman is human. Recognition of this condition by society follows a real event in the objective order, however imperfect and halting the recognition. Any attempt to limit humanity to exclude some group runs the risk of furnishing authority and precedent for excluding other groups in the name of the consciousness or perception of the controlling group in the society.

A philosopher may reject the appeal to the humanity of the fetus because he views "humanity" as a secular view of the soul and because he doubts the existence of anything real and objective which can be identified as humanity.[11] One answer to such a philosopher is to ask how he reasons about moral questions without supposing that there is a sense in which he and the others of whom he speaks are human. Whatever group is taken as the society which determines who may be killed is thereby taken as human. A second

answer is to ask if he does not believe that there is a right and wrong way of deciding moral questions. If there is such a difference, experience may be appealed to: To decide who is human on the basis of the sentiment of a given society has led to consequences which rational men would characterize as monstrous.[12]

The rejection of the attempted distinctions based on viability and visibility, experience and feeling, may be buttressed by the following considerations: Moral judgments often rest on distinctions, but if the distinctions are not to appear arbitrary fiat, they should relate to some real difference in probabilities. There is a kind of continuity in all Life, but the earlier stages of the elements of human life possess tiny probabilities of development. Consider, for example, the spermatozoa in any normal ejaculate: there are about 200,000,000 in any single ejaculate, of which one has a chance of developing into a zygote.[13] Consider the oocytes which may become ova: there are 100,000 to 1,000,000 oocytes in a female infant, of which a maximum of 390 are ovulated.[14] But once spermatozoon and ovum meet and the conceptus is formed, such studies as have been made show that roughly in only 20 percent of the cases will spontaneous abortion occur.[15] In other words, the chances are about 4 out of 5 that this new being will develop. At this stage in the life of the being there is a sharp shift in probabilities, an immense jump in potentialities. To make a distinction between the rights of spermatozoa and the rights of the fertilized ovum is to respond to an enormous shift in possibilities. For about twenty days after conception the egg may split to form twins or combine with another egg to form a chimera, but the probability of either event happening is very small.

It may be asked, What does a change in biological probabilities have to do with establishing humanity? The argument from probabilities is not aimed at establishing humanity but at establishing an objective discontinuity which may be taken into account in moral discourse. As life itself is a matter of probabilities, as most moral reasoning is an estimate of probabilities, so it seems in accord with the structure of reality and the nature of moral thought to found a moral judgment on the change in probabilities at conception. The appeal to probabilities is the most commonsensical of arguments; to a greater or smaller degree all of us base our actions on probabilities, and in morals, as in law, prudence and negligence are often measured by the account one has taken of the probabilities. If the chance is 200,000,000 to 1 that the movement in the bushes into which you shoot is a man's, I doubt if many persons would hold you careless in shooting; but if the chances are 4 out of 5 that the movement is a human being's, few would acquit you of blame. Would the argument be different if only one out of ten children conceived came to term? Of course this argument would be different. This argument is an appeal to probabilities that actually exist, not to any and all states of affairs which may be imagined.

The probabilities as they do exist do not show the humanity of the embryo in the sense of a demonstration in logic any more than the probabilities of the movement in the bush being a man demonstrate beyond all doubt that the being is a man. The appeal is a "buttressing" consideration, showing the plausibility of the standard adopted. The argument focuses on the decisional factor in any moral judgment and assumes that part of the business of a moralist is drawing lines. One evidence of the nonarbitrary character of the line drawn is the difference of probabilities on either side of it. If a spermatozoon is destroyed, one destroys a being which had a trace of far less than 1 in 200 million of developing into a reasoning being possessed of the genetic code, a heart and other organs, and capable of pain. If a fetus is destroyed, one destroys a being already possessed of the genetic code, organs, and sensitivity to pain, and one which had an 80 percent chance of developing further into a baby outside the womb who, in time, would reason.

The positive argument for conception as the decisive moment of humanization is that at conception the new being receives the genetic code.[16] It is this genetic information which determines his characteristics, which is the biological carrier of the possibility of human wisdom, which makes

him a self-evolving being. A being with a human genetic code is man.

This review of current controversy over the humanity of the fetus emphasizes what a fundamental question the theologians resolved in asserting the inviolability of the fetus. To regard the fetus as possessed of equal rights with other humans was not, however, to decide every case where abortion might be employed. It did decide the case where the argument was that the fetus should be aborted for its own good. To say a being was human was to say it had a destiny to decide for itself which could not be taken from it by another man's decision. But human beings with equal rights often come in conflict with each other, and some decision must be made as [to] whose claims are to prevail. Cases of conflict involving the fetus are different only in two respects: the total inability of the fetus to speak for itself and the fact that the right of the fetus regularly at stake is the right to life itself.

The approach taken by the theologians to these conflicts was articulated in terms of "direct" and "indirect." Again, to look at what they were doing from outside their categories, they may be said to have been drawing lines or "balancing values." "Direct" and "indirect" are spatial metaphors; "line-drawing" is another. "To weigh" or "to balance" values is a metaphor of a more complicated mathematical sort hinting at the process which goes on in moral judgments. All the metaphors suggest that, in the moral judgments made, comparisons were necessary, that no value completely controlled. The principle of double effect was no doctrine fallen from heaven, but a method of analysis appropriate where two relative values were being compared. In Catholic moral theology, as it developed, life even of the innocent was not taken as an absolute. Judgments on acts affecting life issued from a process of weighing. In the weighing, the fetus was always given a value greater than zero, always a value separate and independent from its parents. This valuation was crucial and fundamental in all Christian thought on the subject and marked it off from any approach which considered that only the parents' interests needed to be considered.

Even with the fetus weighed as human, one interest could be weighed as equal or superior: that of the mother in her own life. The casuists between 1450 and 1895 were willing to weigh this interest as superior. Since 1895, that interest was given decisive weight only in the two special cases of the cancerous uterus and the ectopic pregnancy. In both of these cases the fetus itself had little chance of survival even if the abortion were not performed. As the balance was once struck in favor of the mother whenever her life was endangered, it could be so struck again. The balance reached between 1895 and 1930 attempted prudentially and pastorally to forestall a multitude of exceptions for interests less than life.

The perception of the humanity of the fetus and the weighing of fetal rights against other human rights constituted the work of the moral analysts. But what spirit animated their abstract judgments? For the Christian community it was the injunction of Scripture to love your neighbor as yourself. The fetus as human was a neighbor; his life had parity with one's own. The commandment gave life to what otherwise would have been only rational calculation.

The commandment could be put in humanistic as well as theological terms: Do not injure your fellow man without reason. In these terms, once the humanity of the fetus is perceived, abortion is never right except in self-defense. When life must be taken to save life, reason alone cannot say that a mother must prefer a child's life to her own. With this exception, now of great rarity, abortion violates the rational humanist tenet of the equality of human lives.

For Christians the commandment to love had received a special imprint in that the exemplar proposed of love was the love of the Lord for his disciples. In the light given by this example, self-sacrifice carried to the point of death seemed in the extreme situations not without meaning. In the less extreme cases, preference for one's own interests to the life of another seemed to express cruelty or selfishness irreconcilable with the demands of love.

NOTES

1. According to Glanville Williams (*The Sanctity of Human Life and the Criminal Law*, 1957, 193), "The historical reason for the Catholic objection to abortion is the same as for the Christian Church's historical opposition to infanticide: the horror of bringing about the death of an unbaptized child." This statement is made without any citation of evidence. As has been seen, desire to administer baptism could, in the Middle Ages, even be urged as a reason for procuring an abortion. It is highly regrettable that the American Law Institute was apparently misled by Williams' account and repeated after him the same baseless statement. See American Law Institute, *Model Penal Code: Tentative Draft No. 9* (1959), p. 148, n. 12.

2. E.g., R. L. Brinsler and J. L. Thomson, "Development of Eight-Cell Mouse Embryos In Vitro," *Experimental Cell Research*, 42: 308 (1966).

3. J. Edgar Morison, *Fetal and Neonatal Pathology* 99–100 (1963).

4. Peter Gruenwald, "Growth of the Human Fetus," *American Journal of Obstetrics and Gynecology*, 94: 1112 (1966).

5. Morison, *Fetal and Neonatal Pathology, supra* n. 3, at 101.

6. This line of thought was advanced by some participants at the International Conference on Abortion sponsored by the Harvard Divinity School in cooperation with the Joseph P. Kennedy, Jr., Foundation in Washington, D.C., Sept, 8–10, 1967.

7. Frank D. Allan, *Essentials of Human Embryology* 165 (1960).

8. Frederick J. Gottleib, *Developmental Genetics* 28 (1966).

9. Allan, *Essentials of Human Embryology, supra* n. 7, at 165.

10. Another line of thought advanced at the Conference mentioned in n. 6. Thomas Aquinas gave an analogous reason against baptizing a fetus in the womb: "As long as it exists in the womb of the mother, it cannot be subject to the operation of the ministers of the Church as it is not known to men" (*In sententias Petri Lombardi* 4.6 1.1.2).

11. Compare John O'Connor, "Humanity and Abortion," *Natural Law Forum*, 12:128–130 (1968), with John T. Noonan Jr., "Deciding Who Is Human," *Natural Law Forum*, 12:134–138.

12. A famous passage of Montesquieu reads:

    "Ceux dont il s'agit sont noirs depuis les pieds jusqú à la tête; et ils ont le nez si écrasé qu'il est presque impossible de les plaindre.

    "On ne peut se mettre dans l'esprit que Dieu qui est un être très-sage, ait mis une âme, surtout une âme bonne, dans un corps tout noir.

    "Il est si naturel de penser que c'est la couleur qui constitue l'essence de l'humanité, que les peuples d'Asie, qui font des eunuques, privent toujours les noirs du rapport qu'ils ont avec nous d'une façon plus marquée." *Montesquieu, De l'esprit des lois,* in *Oeuvres Complètes* book 15, chap. 5 (Paris, 1843).

13. J. S. Baxter, Frazer's *Manual of Embryology,* 5 (1963).

14. Gregory Pincus, *The Control of Fertility,* 197 (19a).

15. *Idem.* Apparently there is some small variation by region.

16. Gottleib, *Developmental Genetics, supra* n. 8, at 17.

On the Moral and Legal Status of Abortion

Mary Anne Warren

Mary Anne Warren is a professor emeritus of philosophy at San Francisco State University. She is the author of *Moral Status* (1998), *Gendercide: The Implications of Sex Selection* (1985), and *The Nature of Woman* (1980).

Warren provides the classic "liberal" defense of abortion rights. She maintains that once one concedes that the fetus is a person, then one must accept limitations on the right to abortion. However, she argues, the fetus is not a person. She begins by examining the various criteria that have been employed to establish personhood. Then she proceeds to construct what she regards as the most plausible definition of a human person and thereby shows that a fetus does not conform to the definition. Neither the resemblance of the fetus to a person, nor the fact that it may become a human person are sufficient reasons for regarding the fetus as a human person whose rights could override a pregnant woman's right to decide whether or not to have an abortion. In the postscript, Warren attempts to respond to the criticism that infanticide would also be justified on the basis of her argument.

We will be concerned with both the moral status of abortion, which for our purposes we may define as the act which a woman performs in voluntarily terminating, or allowing another person to terminate, her pregnancy, and the legal status which is appropriate for this act. I will argue that, while it is not possible to produce a satisfactory defense of a woman's right to obtain an abortion without showing that a fetus is not a human being, in the morally relevant sense of that term, we ought not to conclude that the difficulties involved in determining whether or not a fetus is human make it impossible to produce any satisfactory solution to the problem of the moral status of abortion. For it is possible to show that, on the basis of intuitions which we may expect even the opponents of abortion to share, a fetus is not a person, and hence not the sort of entity to which it is proper to ascribe full moral rights.

Of course, while some philosophers would deny the possibility of any such proof,[1] others will deny that there is any need for it, since the moral permissibility of abortion appears to them to be too obvious to require proof. But the inadequacy of this attitude should be evident from the fact that both the friends and the foes of abortion consider their position to be morally self-evident. Because proabortionists have never adequately come to grips with the conceptual issues surrounding abortion, most if not all, of the arguments which they advance in opposition to laws restricting access to abortion fail to refute or even weaken the traditional antiabortion argument, i.e., that a fetus is a human being, and therefore abortion is murder.

These arguments are typically of one of two sorts. Either they point to the terrible side effects of the restrictive laws, e.g., the deaths due to illegal abortions, and the fact that it is poor women who suffer the most as a result of these laws, or else they state that to deny a woman access to abortion is to deprive her of her right to control her own body. Unfortunately, however, the fact that restricting access to abortion has tragic side effects does not, in itself, show that the restrictions are unjustified, since murder is wrong regardless of the consequences of prohibiting it; and the appeal to the right to control one's body, which is generally construed as a property right, is at best a rather feeble argument for the permissibility of abortion. Mere ownership does not give me the right to kill innocent people whom I find on my property, and indeed I am apt to be held responsible if such people injure themselves while on my property. It is equally unclear that I have any moral right to expel an innocent person from my property when I know that doing so will result in his death.

Furthermore, it is probably inappropriate to describe a woman's body as her property, since it seems natural to hold that a person is something distinct from her property, but not from her body. Even those who would object to the identification of a person with his body, or with the conjunction of his body and his mind, must admit that it would be very odd to describe, say, breaking a leg, as damaging one's property, and much more appropriate to describe it as injuring *oneself*. Thus, it is probably a mistake to argue that the right to obtain an abortion is in any way derived from the right to own and regulate property.

But, however we wish to construe the right to abortion, we cannot hope to convince those who consider abortion a form of murder of the existence of any such right unless we are able to produce a clear and convincing refutation of the traditional antiabortion argument, and this has not, to my knowledge, been done. With respect to the two most vital issues which that argument involves, i.e., the humanity of the fetus and its implication for the moral status of abortion, confusion has prevailed on both sides of the dispute.

Thus, both proabortionists and antiabortionists have tended to abstract the question of whether abortion is wrong to that of whether it is wrong to destroy a fetus, just as though the rights of another person were not necessarily involved. This mistaken abstraction has led to the almost universal assumption that if a fetus is a human being, with a right to life, then it follows immediately that abortion is wrong (except perhaps when necessary to save the woman's life), and that it ought to be prohibited. It has also been generally assumed that unless the question about the status of the fetus is answered, the moral status of abortion cannot possibly be determined. . . .

The question which we must answer in order to produce a satisfactory solution to the problem of the moral status of abortion is this: How are we to define the moral community, the set of beings with full and equal moral rights, such that we can decide whether a human fetus is a member of this community or not? What sort of entity, exactly, has the inalienable rights to life, liberty, and the pursuit of happiness? Jefferson attributed these right to all *men*, and it may or may not be fair to suggest that he intended to attribute them *only* to men. Perhaps he ought to have attributed them to all human beings. If so, then we arrive, first, at the problem of defining what makes a being human, and, second, at the equally vital question . . . namely, What reason is there for identifying the moral community with the set of all human beings, in whatever way we have chosen to define that term?

ON THE DEFINITION OF "HUMAN"

One reason why this vital second question is so frequently overlooked in the debate over the moral status of abortion is that the term "human" has two distinct, but not often distinguished, senses. This fact results in a slide of meaning, which serves to conceal the fallaciousness of the traditional argument that since (1) it is wrong to kill innocent human beings, and (2) fetuses are innocent human beings, then (3) it is wrong to kill fetuses. For if "human" is used in the same sense in both (1) and (2) then, whichever of the two senses is meant, one of these premises is question-begging. And if it is used in two different senses then of course the conclusion doesn't follow.

Thus, (1) is a self-evident moral truth[2] and avoids begging the question about abortion, only if "human being" is used to mean something like "a full-fledged member of the moral community." (It may or may not also be meant to refer exclusively to members of the species *Homo sapiens*.) We may call this the *moral* sense of "human." It is not to be confused with what we will call the *genetic* sense, i.e., the sense in which *any* member of the species is a human being, and no member of any other species could be. If (1) is acceptable only if the moral sense is intended, (2) is nonquestion-begging only if what is intended is the genetic sense.

In "Deciding Who Is Human," Noonan argues for the classification of fetuses with human beings by pointing to the presence of the full genetic code, and the potential capacity for rational thought.[3] It is clear that what he needs to show, for his version of the traditional argument to be valid, is that fetuses are human in the moral sense, the sense in which it is analytically true that all human beings have full moral rights. But, in the absence of any argument showing that whatever is genetically human is also morally human, and he gives none, nothing more than genetic humanity can be demonstrated by the presence of the human genetic code. And, as we will see, the *potential* capacity for rational thought can at most show that an entity has the potential for *becoming* human in the moral sense.

DEFINING THE MORAL COMMUNITY

Can it be established that genetic humanity is sufficient for moral humanity? I think that there are very good reasons for not defining the moral community in this way. I would like to suggest an alternative way of defining the moral community, which I will argue for only to the extent of explaining why it is, or should be, self-evident. The suggestion is simply that the moral community consists of all and only *people* rather than all and only human beings;[4] and probably the best way of

demonstrating its self-evidence is by considering the concept of personhood, to see what sorts of entity are and are not persons, and what the decision that a being is or is not a person implies about its moral rights.

What characteristics entitle an entity to be considered a person? This is obviously not the place to attempt a complete analysis of the concept of personhood, but we do not need such a fully adequate analysis just to determine whether and why a fetus is or isn't a person. All we need is a rough and approximate list of the most basic criteria of personhood, and some idea of which, or how many, of these an entity must satisfy in order to properly be considered a person.

In searching for such criteria, it is useful to look beyond the set of people with whom we are acquainted, and ask how we would decide whether a totally alien being was a person or not. (For we have no right to assume that genetic humanity is necessary for personhood.) Imagine a space traveler who lands on an unknown planet and encounters a race of beings utterly unlike any he has ever seen or heard of. If he wants to be sure of behaving morally toward these beings, he has to somehow decide whether they are people, and hence have full moral rights, or whether they are the sort of thing which he need not feel guilty about treating as, for example, a source of food.

How should he go about making this decision? If he has some anthropological background, he might look for such things as religion, art, and the manufacturing of tools, weapons, or shelters, since these factors have been used to distinguish our human from our prehuman ancestors, in what seems to be closer to the moral than the genetic sense of "human." And no doubt he would be right to consider the presence of such factors as good evidence that the alien beings were people, and morally human. It would, however, be overly anthropocentric of him to take the absence of these things as adequate evidence that they were not, since we can imagine people who have progressed beyond, or evolved without ever developing, these cultural characteristics.

I suggest that the traits which are most central to the concept of personhood, or humanity in the moral sense, are, very roughly, the following:

1. consciousness (of objects and events external and/or internal to the being), and in particular the capacity to feel pain;
2. reasoning (the *developed* capacity to solve new and relatively complex problems);
3. self-motivated activity (activity which is relatively independent of either genetic or direct external control);
4. the capacity to communicate, by whatever means, messages of an indefinite variety of types, that is, not just with an indefinite number of possible contents, but on indefinitely many possible topics;
5. the presence of self-concepts, and self-awareness, either individual or racial, or both.

Admittedly, there are apt to be a great many problems involved in formulating precise definitions of these criteria, let alone in developing universally valid behavioral criteria for deciding when they apply. But I will assume that both we and our explorer know approximately what (1)–(5) mean, and that he is also able to determine whether or not they apply. How, then, should he use his findings to decide whether or not the alien beings are people? We needn't suppose that an entity must have *all* of these attributes to be properly considered a person; (1) and (2) alone may well be sufficient for personhood, and quite probably (1)–(3) are sufficient. Neither do we need to insist that any one of these criteria is *necessary* for personhood, although once again (1) and (2) look like fairly good candidates for necessary conditions, as does (3), if "activity" is construed so as to include the activity of reasoning.

All we need to claim, to demonstrate that a fetus is not a person, is that any being which satisfies *none* of (1)–(5) is certainly not a person. I consider this claim to be so obvious that I think anyone who denied it, and claimed that a being which satisfied none of (1)–(5) was a person all the same, would thereby demonstrate that he had no notion at all of what a person is—perhaps because he had confused the concept of a person with that of genetic humanity. If the opponents of abortion were to deny the appropriateness of these five criteria, I do not know what further arguments would convince them.

We would probably have to admit that our conceptual schemes were indeed irreconcilably different, and that our dispute could not be settled objectively.

I do not expect this to happen, however, since I think that the concept of a person is one which is very nearly universal (to people), and that it is common to both proabortionists and antiabortionists, even though neither group has fully realized the relevance of this concept to the resolution of their dispute. Furthermore, I think that on reflection even the antiabortionists ought to agree not only that (1)–(5) are central to the concept of personhood, but also that it is a part of this concept that all and only people have full moral rights. The concept of a person is in part a moral concept; once we have admitted that x is a person we have recognized, even if we have not agreed to respect, x's right to be treated as a member of the moral community. It is true that the claim that x is a *human being* is more commonly voiced as part of an appeal to treat x decently than is the claim that x is a person, but this is either because "human being" is here used in the sense which implies personhood, or because the genetic and moral senses of "human" have been confused.

Now if (1)–(5) are indeed the primary criteria of personhood, then it is clear that genetic humanity is neither necessary nor sufficient for establishing that an entity is a person. Some human beings are not people, and there may well be people who are not human beings. A man or woman whose consciousness has been permanently obliterated but who remains alive is a human being which is no longer a person; defective human beings, with no appreciable mental capacity, are not and presumably never will be people; and a fetus is a human being which is not yet a person, and which therefore cannot coherently be said to have full moral rights. Citizens of the next century should be prepared to recognize highly advanced, self-aware robots or computers, should such be developed, and intelligent inhabitants of other worlds, should such be found, as people in the fullest sense, and to respect their moral rights. But to ascribe full moral rights to an entity which is not a person is as absurd as to ascribe moral obligations and responsibilities to such an entity.

FETAL DEVELOPMENT AND THE RIGHT TO LIFE

Two problems arise in the application of these suggestions for the definition of the moral community to the determination of the precise moral status of a human fetus. Given that the paradigm example of a person is a normal adult human being, then (1) How like this paradigm, in particular how far advanced since conception, does a human being need to be before it begins to have a right to life by virtue, not of being fully a person as of yet, but of being *like* a person? and (2) To what extent, if any, does the fact that a fetus has the *potential* for becoming a person endow it with some of the same rights? Each of these questions requires some comment.

In answering the first question, we need not attempt a detailed consideration of the moral rights of organisms which are not developed enough, aware enough, intelligent enough, etc., to be considered people, but which resemble people in some respects. It does seem reasonable to suggest that the more like a person, in the relevant respects, a being is, the stronger is the case for regarding it as having a right to life, and indeed the stronger its right to life is. Thus we ought to take seriously the suggestion that, insofar as "the human individual develops biologically in a continuous fashion . . . the rights of a human person might develop in the same way."[5] But we must keep in mind that the attributes which are relevant in determining whether or not an entity is enough like a person to be regarded as having some of the same moral rights are no different from those which are relevant to determining whether or not it is fully a person—i.e., are no different from (1)–(5)—and that being genetically human, or having recognizably human facial and other physical features, or detectable brain activity, or the capacity to survive outside the uterus, are simply not among these relevant attributes.

Thus it is clear that even though a seven- or eight-month fetus has features which make it apt to arouse in us almost the same powerful protective instinct as is commonly aroused by a small infant, nevertheless it is not significantly more personlike than is a very small embryo. It is *somewhat* more personlike; it can apparently feel and respond to pain, and it may even have a rudimentary form of consciousness, insofar as its brain is quite active. Nevertheless, it seems safe to say that it is not fully conscious, in the way that an infant of a few months is, and that it cannot reason, or communicate messages of indefinitely many sorts, does not engage in self-motivated activity, and has no self-awareness. Thus, in the *relevant* respects, a fetus, even a fully developed one, is considerably less personlike than is the average mature mammal, indeed the average fish. And I think that a rational person must conclude that if the right to life of a fetus is to be based upon its resemblance to a person, then it cannot be said to have any more right to life than, let us say, a newborn guppy (which also seems to be capable of feeling pain), and that a right of that magnitude could never override a woman's right to obtain an abortion, at any stage of her pregnancy.

There may, of course, be other arguments in favor of placing legal limits upon the stage of pregnancy in which an abortion may be performed. Given the relative safety of the new techniques of artificially inducing labor during the third trimester, the danger to the woman's life or health is no longer such an argument. Neither is the fact that people tend to respond to the thought of abortion in the later stages of pregnancy with emotional repulsion, since mere emotional responses cannot take the place of moral reasoning in determining what ought to be permitted. Nor, finally, is the frequently heard argument that legalizing abortion, especially late in the pregnancy, may erode the level of respect for human life, leading, perhaps, to an increase in unjustified euthanasia and other crimes. For this threat, if it is a threat, can be better met by educating people to the kinds of moral distinctions which we are making here than by limiting access to abortion (which limitation may, in its disregard for the rights of women, be just as damaging to the level of respect for human rights).

Thus, since the fact that even a fully developed fetus is not personlike enough to have any significant right to life on the basis of its personlikeness shows that no legal restrictions upon the stage of pregnancy in which an abortion may be performed can be justified on the grounds that we should protect the rights of the older fetus; and since there is no other apparent justification for such restrictions, we may conclude that they are entirely unjustified. Whether or not it would be *indecent* (whatever that means) for a woman in her seventh month to obtain an abortion just to avoid having to postpone a trip to Europe, it would not, in itself, be *immoral* and therefore it ought to be permitted.

POTENTIAL PERSONHOOD AND THE RIGHT TO LIFE

We have seen that a fetus does not resemble a person in any way which can support the claim that it has even some of the same rights. But what about its *potential*, the fact that if nurtured and allowed to develop naturally it will very probably become a person? Doesn't that alone give it at least some right to life? It is hard to deny that the fact that an entity is a potential person is a strong prima facie reason for not destroying it; but we need not conclude from this that a potential person has a right to life, by virtue of that potential. It may be that our feeling that it is better, other things being equal, not to destroy a potential person is better explained by the fact that potential people are still (felt to be) an invaluable resource, not to be lightly squandered. Surely, if every speck of dust were a potential person, we would be much less apt to conclude that every potential person has a right to become actual.

Still, we do not need to insist that a potential person has no right to life whatever. There may be something immoral, and not just imprudent, about wantonly destroying potential people, when doing so isn't necessary to protect anyone's rights. But even if a potential person does have some prima facie right to life, such a right could not possibly outweigh the right of a woman to obtain an abortion, since the rights of any actual person invariably outweigh those of any potential person, whenever the two conflict. Since this may not be

immediately obvious in the case of a human fetus, let us look at another case.

Suppose that our space explorer falls into the hands of an alien culture, whose scientists decide to create a few hundred thousand or more human beings, by breaking his body into its component cells, and using these to create fully developed human beings, with, of course, his genetic code. We may imagine that each of these newly created men will have all of the original man's abilities, skills, knowledge, and so on, and also have an individual self-concept, in short that each of them will be a bona fide (though hardly unique) person. Imagine that the whole project will take only seconds, and that its chances of success are extremely high, and that our explorer knows all of this, and also knows that these people will be treated fairly. I maintain that in such a situation he would have every right to escape if he could, and thus to deprive all of these potential people of their potential lives; for his right to life outweighs all of theirs together, in spite of the fact that they are all genetically human, all innocent, and all have a very high probability of becoming people very soon, if only he refrains from acting.

Indeed, I think he would have a right to escape even if it were not his life which the alien scientists planned to take, but only a year of his freedom, or, indeed, only a day. Nor would he be obligated to stay if he had gotten captured (thus bringing all these people-potentials into existence) because of his own carelessness, or even if he had done so deliberately, knowing the consequences. Regardless of how he got captured, he is not morally obligated to remain in captivity for *any* period of time for the sake of permitting any number of potential people to come into actuality, so great is the margin by which one actual person's right to liberty outweighs whatever right to life even a hundred thousand potential people have. And it seems reasonable to conclude that the rights of a woman will outweigh by a similar margin whatever right to life a fetus may have by virtue of its potential personhood.

Thus, neither a fetus's resemblance to a person, nor its potential for becoming a person provides any basis whatever for the claim that it has any significant right to life. Consequently, a woman's right to protect her health, happiness, freedom, and even her life,[6] by terminating an unwanted pregnancy, will always override whatever right to life it may be appropriate to ascribe to a fetus, even a fully developed one. And thus, in the absence of any overwhelming social need for every possible child, the laws which restrict the right to obtain an abortion, or limit the period of pregnancy during which an abortion may be performed, are a wholly unjustified violation of a woman's most basic moral and constitutional rights.

POSTSCRIPT ON INFANTICIDE*

Since the publication of this article, many people have written to point out that my argument appears to justify not only abortion, but infanticide as well. For a newborn infant is not significantly more personlike than an advanced fetus, and consequently it would seem that if the destruction of the latter is permissible so too must be that of the former. Inasmuch as most people, regardless of how they feel about the morality of abortion, consider infanticide a form of murder, this might appear to represent a serious flaw in my argument.

Now, if I am right in holding that it is only people who have a full-fledged right to life, and who can be murdered, and if the criteria of personhood are as I have described them, then it obviously follows that killing a newborn infant isn't murder. It does *not* follow, however, that infanticide is permissible, for two reasons. In the first place, it would be wrong, at least in this country and in this period of history, and other things being equal, to kill a newborn infant, because even if its parents do not want it and would not suffer from its destruction, there are other people who would like to have it, and would, in all probability, be deprived of a great deal of pleasure by its destruction. Thus, infanticide is wrong for reasons analogous to those

which make it wrong to wantonly destroy natural resources, or great works of art.

Secondly, most people, at least in this country, value infants and would much prefer that they be preserved, even if foster parents are not immediately available. Most of us would rather be taxed to support orphanages than allow unwanted infants to be destroyed. So long as there are people who want an infant preserved, and who are willing and able to provide the means of caring for it, under reasonably humane conditions, it is, *ceteris parabis*, wrong to destroy it.

But, it might be replied, if this argument shows that infanticide is wrong, at least at this time and in this country, doesn't it also show that abortion is wrong? After all, many people value fetuses, are disturbed by their destruction, and would much prefer that they be preserved, even at some cost to themselves. Furthermore, as a potential source of pleasure to some foster family, a fetus is just as valuable as an infant. There is, however, a crucial difference between the two cases: So long as the fetus is unborn, its preservation, contrary to the wishes of the pregnant women, violates her rights to freedom, happiness, and self-determination. Her rights override the rights of those who would like the fetus preserved, just as if someone's life or limb is threatened by a wild animal, his right to protect himself by destroying the animal overrides the rights of those who would prefer that the animal not be harmed.

The minute the infant is born, however, its preservation no longer violates any of its mother's rights, even if she wants it destroyed, because she is free to put it up for adoption. Consequently, while the moment of birth does not mark any sharp discontinuity in the degree to which an infant possesses the right to life, it does mark the end of its mother's right to determine its fate. Indeed, if abortion could be performed without killing the fetus, she would never possess the right to have the fetus destroyed, for the same reasons that she has no right to have an infant destroyed.

On the other hand, it follows from my argument that when an unwanted or defective infant is born into a society which cannot afford and/or is not willing to care for it, then its destruction is permissible. This conclusion will, no doubt, strike

---

*Warren, Mary Anne. "Postscript on Infanticide," in *Today's Moral Problems*, Richard Wasserstrom (ed.). New York: Macmillan, 1975. Reprinted with permission.

many people as heartless and immoral; but remember that the very existence of people who feel this way, and who are willing and able to provide care for unwanted infants, is reason enough to conclude that they should be preserved.

ACKNOWLEDGMENTS

My thanks to the following people, who were kind enough to read and criticize an earlier version of this paper: Herbert Gold, Gene Glass, Anne Lauterbach, Judith Thomson, Mary Mothersill, and Timothy Binkley.

NOTES

1. For example, Roger Wertheimer, who in "Understanding the Abortion Argument" (*Philosophy and Public Affairs*, 1, No. 1 [Fall, 1971], 67–95), argues that the problem of the moral status of abortion is insoluble, in that the dispute over the status of the fetus is not a question of fact at all, but only a question of how one responds to the facts.

2. Of course, the principle that it is (always) wrong to kill innocent human beings is in need of many other modifications, e.g., that it may be permissible to do so to save a greater number of other innocent human beings, but we may safely ignore these complications here.

3. John Noonan Jr., "Deciding Who Is Human," *Natural Law Forum*, vol. 13 (1968), p. 135.

4. From here on, we will use "human" to mean genetically human, since the moral sense seems closely connected to, and perhaps derived from, the assumption that genetic humanity is sufficient for membership in the moral community.

5. Thomas L. Hayes, "A Biological View," *Commonweal*, 85 (March 17, 1967), 677–78; quoted by Daniel Callahan, in *Abortion, Law, Choice, and Morality* (London: Macmillan & Co., 1970).

6. That is, insofar as the death rate, for the woman, is higher for childbirth than for early abortion.

Why Abortion Is Immoral

Don Marquis

Don Marquis is a professor of philosophy at the University of Kansas. He has published many articles in ethics, especially in biomedical ethics.

Marquis provides a sustained defense of one variation of the "conservative" position that abortion is morally unjustified. He begins by explaining why both sides of the conventional debate engage in serious conceptual mistakes in the way they regard the fetus. Then he argues that "it is wrong to kill us" because such killing deprives us of the value of our future. Since fetuses are sufficiently like us with a future of value, it is just as wrong to kill them as it is wrong to kill us. Marquis allows, at the end, that this argument does not make all abortion wrong since there may be overriding considerations in some cases.

The view that abortion is, with rare exceptions, seriously immoral has received little support in the recent philosophical literature. No doubt most philosophers affiliated with secular institutions of higher education believe that the antiabortion position is either a symptom of irrational religious dogma or a conclusion generated by seriously confused philosophical argument. The purpose of this essay is to undermine this general belief. This essay sets out an argument that purports to show, as well as any argument in ethics can show, that abortion is, except possibly in rare cases, seriously immoral, that it is in the same moral category as killing an innocent adult human being.

The argument is based on a major assumption. Many of the most insightful and careful writers on the ethics of abortion—such as Joel Feinberg, Michael Tooley, Mary Anne Warren, H. Tristram Engelhardt Jr., L. W. Sumner, John T. Noonan Jr., and Philip Devine[1]—believe that whether or not abortion is morally permissible stands or falls on whether or not a fetus is the sort of being whose life it is seriously wrong to end. The argument of this essay will assume, but not argue, that they are correct.

Also, this essay will neglect issues of great importance to a complete ethics of abortion. Some antiabortionists will allow that certain abortions, such as abortion before implantation or abortion when the life of a woman is threatened by a pregnancy or abortion after rape, may be morally permissible. This essay will not explore the casuistry of these hard cases. The purpose of this essay is to develop a general argument for the claim that the overwhelming majority of deliberate abortions are seriously immoral.

A sketch of standard antiabortion and prochoice arguments exhibits how those arguments possess certain symmetries that explain why partisans of those positions are so convinced of the correctness of their own positions, why they are not successful in convincing their opponents, and why, to others, this issue seems to be unresolvable. An analysis of the nature of this standoff suggests a strategy for surmounting it.

Excerpts from Don Marquis, "Why abortion is immoral" The Journal of Philosophy, April 1989, pp. 183–202. Reprinted by permission.

Consider the way a typical antiabortionist argues. She will argue or assert that life is present from the moment of conception or that fetuses look like babies or that fetuses possess a characteristic such as a genetic code that is both necessary and sufficient for being human. Antiabortionists seem to believe that (1) the truth of all of these claims is quite obvious, and (2) establishing any of these claims is sufficient to show that abortion is morally akin to murder.

A standard pro-choice strategy exhibits similarities. The pro-choicer will argue or assert that fetuses are not persons or that fetuses are not rational agents or that fetuses are not social beings. Pro-choicers seem to believe that (1) the truth of any of these claims is quite obvious, and (2) establishing any of these claims is sufficient to show that an abortion is not a wrongful killing.

In fact, both the pro-choice and the antiabortion claims do seem to be true, although the "it looks like a baby" claim is more difficult to establish the earlier the pregnancy. We seem to have a standoff. How can it be resolved?

As everyone who has taken a bit of logic knows, if any of these arguments concerning abortion is a good argument, it requires not only some claim characterizing fetuses, but also some general moral principle that ties a characteristic of fetuses to having or not having the right to life or to some other moral characteristic that will generate the obligation or the lack of obligation not to end the life of a fetus. Accordingly, the arguments of the antiabortionist and the pro-choicer need a bit of filling in to be regarded as adequate.

Note what each partisan will say. The antiabortionist will claim that her position is supported by such generally accepted moral principles as "It is always prima facie seriously wrong to take a human life" or "It is always prima facie seriously wrong to end the life of a baby." Since these are generally accepted moral principles, her position is certainly not obviously wrong. The pro-choicer will claim that her position is supported by such plausible moral principles as "Being a person is what gives an individual intrinsic moral worth" or "It is only seriously prima facie wrong to take the life of a member of the human community." Since these are generally accepted moral principles, the pro-choice position is certainly not obviously wrong. Unfortunately, we have again arrived at a standoff.

Now, how might one deal with this standoff? The standard approach is to try to show how the moral principles of one's opponent lose their plausibility under analysis. It is easy to see how this is possible. On the one hand, the antiabortionist will defend a moral principle concerning the wrongness of killing which tends to be broad in scope in order that even fetuses at an early stage of pregnancy will fall under it. The problem with broad principles is that they often embrace too much. In this particular instance, the principle "It is always prima facie wrong to take a human life" seems to entail that it is wrong to end the existence of a living human cancer-cell culture, on the grounds that the culture is both living and human. Therefore, it seems that the antiabortionist's favored principle is too broad.

On the other hand, the pro-choicer wants to find a moral principle concerning the wrongness of killing which tends to be narrow in scope in order that fetuses will *not* fall under it. The problem with narrow principles is that they often do not embrace enough. Hence, the needed principles such as "It is prima facie seriously wrong to kill only persons" or "It is prima facie wrong to kill only rational agents" do not explain why it is wrong to kill infants or young children or the severely retarded or even perhaps the severely mentally ill. Therefore, we seem again to have a standoff. The antiabortionist charges, not unreasonably, that pro-choice principles concerning killing are too narrow to be acceptable; the pro-choicer charges, not unreasonably, that antiabortionist principles concerning killing are too broad to be acceptable.

Attempts by both sides to patch up the difficulties in their positions run into further difficulties. The antiabortionist will try to remove the problem in her position by reformulating her principle concerning killing in terms of human beings. Now we end up with: "It is always prima facie seriously wrong to end the life of a human being." This principle has the advantage of avoiding the problem of the human cancer-cell culture counterexample. But this advantage is purchased at a high price. For although it is clear that a fetus is both human and alive, it is not at all clear that a fetus is a human *being*. There is at least something to be said for the view that something becomes a human being only after a process of development, and that therefore first trimester fetuses and perhaps all fetuses are not yet human beings. Hence, the antiabortionist, by this move, has merely exchanged one problem for another.[2]

The pro-choicer fares no better. She may attempt to find reasons why killing infants, young children, and the severely retarded is wrong which are independent of her major principle that is supposed to explain the wrongness of taking human life, but which will not also make abortion immoral. This is no easy task. Appeals to social utility will seem satisfactory only to those who resolve not to think of the enormous difficulties with a utilitarian account of the wrongness of killing and the significant social costs of preserving the lives of the unproductive.[3] A prochoice strategy that extends the definition of "person" to infants or even to young children seems just as arbitrary as an antiabortion strategy that extends the definition of "human being" to fetuses. Again, we find symmetries in the two positions and we arrive at a standoff.

. . . We can start from the following unproblematic assumption concerning our own case: it is wrong to kill *us*. Why is it wrong? Some answers can be easily eliminated. It might be said that what makes killing us wrong is that a killing brutalizes the one who kills. But the brutalization consists of being inured to the performance of an act that is hideously immoral; hence, the brutalization does not explain the immorality. It might be said that what makes killing us wrong is the great loss others would experience due to our absence. Although such hubris is understandable, such an explanation does not account for the wrongness of killing hermits, or those whose lives are relatively independent and whose friends find it easy to make new friends.

A more obvious answer is better. What primarily makes killing wrong is neither its effect on the murderer nor its effect on the victim's friends and relatives, but its effect on the victim. The loss of one's life is one of the greatest losses one can suffer. The loss of one's life deprives one of all the experiences, activities, projects, and enjoyments that would otherwise have constituted one's future. Therefore, killing someone is wrong, primarily because the killing inflicts (one of) the greatest possible losses on the victim. To describe this as the loss of life can be misleading, however. The change in my biological state does not by itself make killing me wrong. The effect of the loss of my biological life is the loss to me of all those activities, projects, experiences, and enjoyments which would otherwise have constituted my future personal life. These activities, projects, experiences, and enjoyments are either valuable for their own sakes or are means to something else that is valuable for its own sake. Some parts of my future are not valued by me now, but will come to be valued by me as I grow older and as my values and capacities change. When I am killed, I am deprived both of what I now value which would have been part of my future personal life, but also what I would come to value. Therefore, when I die, I am deprived of all of the value of my future. Inflicting this loss on me is ultimately what makes killing me wrong. This being the case, it would seem that what makes killing *any* adult human being prima facie seriously wrong is the loss of his or her future.[4]

How should this rudimentary theory of the wrongness of killing be evaluated? It cannot be faulted for deriving an "ought" from an "is," for it does not. The analysis assumes that killing me (or you, reader) is prima facie seriously wrong. The point of the analysis is to establish which natural property ultimately explains the wrongness of the killing, given that it is wrong. A natural property will ultimately explain the wrongness of killing, only if (1) the explanation fits with our intuitions about the matter and (2) there is no other natural property that provides the basis for a better explanation of the wrongness of killing. This analysis rests on the intuition that what makes killing a particular human or animal wrong is what it does to that particular human or animal. What makes killing wrong is some natural effect or other of the killing. Some would deny this. For instance, a divine-command theorist in ethics would deny it. Surely this denial is, however, one of those features of divine-command theory which renders it so implausible.

The claim that what makes killing wrong is the loss of the victim's future is directly supported by two considerations. In the first place, this theory explains why we regard killing as one of the worst of crimes. Killing is especially wrong, because it deprives the victim of more than perhaps any other crime. In the second place, people with AIDS or cancer who know they are dying believe, of course, that dying is a very bad thing for them. They believe that the loss of a future to them that they would otherwise have experienced is what makes their premature death a very bad thing for them. A better theory of the wrongness of killing would require a different natural property associated with killing which better fits with the attitudes of the dying. What could it be?

The view that what makes killing wrong is the loss to the victim of the value of the victim's future gains additional support when some of its implications are examined. In the first place, it is incompatible with the view that it is wrong to kill only beings who are biologically human. It is possible that there exists a different species from another planet whose members have a future like ours. Since having a future like that is what makes killing someone wrong, this theory entails that it would be wrong to kill members of such a species. Hence, this theory is opposed to the claim that only life that is biologically human has great moral worth, a claim which many antiabortionists have seemed to adopt. This opposition, which this theory has in common with personhood theories, seems to be a merit of the theory.

In the second place, the claim that the loss of one's future is the wrong-making feature of one's being killed entails the possibility that the futures of some actual nonhuman mammals on our own planet are sufficiently like ours that it is seriously wrong to kill them also. Whether some animals do have the same right to life as human beings depends on adding to the account of the wrongness

of killing some additional account of just what it is about my future or the futures of other adult human beings which makes it wrong to kill us. No such additional account will be offered in this essay. Undoubtedly, the provision of such an account would be a very difficult matter. Undoubtedly, any such account would be quite controversial. Hence, it surely should not reflect badly on this sketch of an elementary theory of the wrongness of killing that it is indeterminate with respect to some very difficult issues regarding animal rights.

In the third place, the claim that the loss of one's future is the wrong-making feature of one's being killed does not entail, as sanctity of human life theories do, that active euthanasia is wrong. Persons who are severely and incurably ill, who face a future of pain and despair, and who wish to die will not have suffered a loss if they are killed. It is, strictly speaking, the value of a human's future which makes killing wrong in this theory. This being so, killing does not necessarily wrong some persons who are sick and dying. Of course, there may be other reasons for a prohibition of active euthanasia, but that is another matter. Sanctity-of-human-life theories seem to hold that active euthanasia is seriously wrong even in an individual case where there seems to be good reason for it independently of public policy considerations. This consequence is most implausible, and it is a plus for the claim that the loss of a future of value is what makes killing wrong that it does not share this consequence.

In the fourth place, the account of the wrongness of killing defended in this essay does straightforwardly entail that it is prima facie seriously wrong to kill children and infants, for we do presume that they have futures of value. Since we do believe that it is wrong to kill defenseless little babies, it is important that a theory of the wrongness of killing easily account for this. Personhood theories of the wrongness of killing, on the other hand, cannot straightforwardly account for the wrongness of killing infants and young children.[5] Hence, such theories must add special ad hoc accounts of the wrongness of killing the young. The plausibility of such ad hoc theories seems to be a function of how desperately one wants such theories to work. The claim that the primary wrong-making feature of a killing is the loss to the victim of the value of its future accounts for the wrongness of killing young children and infants directly; it makes the wrongness of such acts as obvious as we actually think it is. This is a further merit of this theory. Accordingly, it seems that this value of a future-like-ours theory of the wrongness of killing shares strengths of both sanctity-of-life and personhood accounts while avoiding weaknesses of both. In addition, it meshes with a central intuition concerning what makes killing wrong.

The claim that the primary wrong-making feature of a killing is the loss to the victim of the value of its future has obvious consequences for the ethics of abortion. The future of a standard fetus includes a set of experiences, projects, activities, and such which are identical with the futures of adult human beings and are identical with the futures of young children. Since the reason that is sufficient to explain why it is wrong to kill human beings after the time of birth is a reason that also applies to fetuses, it follows that abortion is prima facie seriously morally wrong.

This argument does not rely on the invalid inference that, since it is wrong to kill persons, it is wrong to kill potential persons also. The category that is morally central to this analysis is the category of having a valuable future like ours; it is not the category of personhood. The argument to the conclusion that abortion is prima facie seriously morally wrong proceeded independently of the notion of person or potential person or any equivalent. Someone may wish to start with this analysis in terms of the value of a human future, conclude that abortion is, except perhaps in rare circumstances, seriously morally wrong, infer that fetuses have the right to life, and then call fetuses "persons" as a result of their having the right to life. Clearly, in this case, the category of person is being used to state the *conclusion* of the analysis rather than to generate the *argument* of the analysis.

The structure of this antiabortion argument can be both illuminated and defended by comparing it to what appears to be the best argument for the wrongness of the wanton infliction of pain on animals. This latter argument is based on the assumption that it is prima facie wrong to inflict pain on me (or you, reader). What is the natural property associated with the infliction of pain which makes such infliction wrong? The obvious answer seems to be that the infliction of pain causes suffering and that suffering is a misfortune. The suffering caused by the infliction of pain is what makes the wanton infliction of pain on me wrong. The wanton infliction of pain on other adult humans causes suffering. The wanton infliction of pain on animals causes suffering. Since causing suffering is what makes the wanton infliction of pain wrong and since the wanton infliction of pain on animals causes suffering, it follows that the wanton infliction of pain on animals is wrong.

This argument for the wrongness of the wanton infliction of pain on animals shares a number of structural features with the argument for the serious prima facie wrongness of abortion. Both arguments start with an obvious assumption concerning what it is wrong to do to me (or you, reader). Both then look for the characteristic or the consequence of the wrong action which makes the action wrong. Both recognize that the wrong-making feature of these immoral actions is a property of actions sometimes directed at individuals other than postnatal human beings. If the structure of the argument for the wrongness of the wanton infliction of pain on animals is sound, then the structure of the argument for the prima facie serious wrongness of abortion is also sound, for the structure of the two arguments is the same. The structure common to both is the key to the explanation of how the wrongness of abortion can be demonstrated without recourse to the category of person. In neither argument is that category crucial.

This defense of an argument for the wrongness of abortion in terms of a structurally similar argument for the wrongness of the wanton infliction of pain on animals succeeds only if the account regarding animals is the correct account. Is it? In the first place, it seems plausible. In the second place, its major competition is Kant's account. Kant believed that we do not have direct duties to animals at all, because they are not persons. Hence, Kant had to explain and justify the wrongness of inflicting pain on animals on the grounds that "he who is hard in his dealings with animals becomes hard also in his dealing with men."[6] The problem with Kant's account is that there seems to be no reason for accepting this latter claim unless Kant's account is rejected. If the alternative to Kant's account is accepted, then it is easy to understand why someone who is indifferent to inflicting pain on animals is also indifferent to inflicting pain on humans, for one is indifferent to what makes inflicting pain wrong in both cases. But, if Kant's account is accepted, there is no intelligible reason why one who is hard in his dealings with animals (or crabgrass or stones) should also be hard in his dealings with men. After all, men are persons: Animals are no more persons than crabgrass or stones. Persons are Kant's crucial moral category. Why, in short, should a Kantian accept the basic claim in Kant's argument?

Hence, Kant's argument for the wrongness of inflicting pain on animals rests on a claim that, in a world of Kantian moral agents, is demonstrably false. Therefore, the alternative analysis, being more plausible anyway, should be accepted. Since this alternative analysis has the same structure as the antiabortion argument being defended here, we have further support for the argument for the immorality of abortion being defended in this essay.

Of course, this value of a future-like-ours argument, if sound, shows only that abortion is prima facie wrong, not that it is wrong in any and all circumstances. Since the loss of the future to a standard fetus, if killed, is, however, at least as great a loss as the loss of the future to a standard adult human being who is killed, abortion, like ordinary killing, could be justified only by the most compelling reasons. The loss of one's life is almost the greatest misfortune that can happen to one. Presumably abortion could be justified in some circumstances, only if the loss consequent on failing to abort would be at least as great. Accordingly, morally permissible abortions will be rare indeed unless, perhaps, they occur so early in pregnancy that a fetus is not yet definitely an individual. Hence, this argument should be taken as showing that abortion is presumptively very seriously wrong, where the presumption is very

strong—as strong as the presumption that killing another adult human being is wrong. . . .

The purpose of this essay has been to set out an argument for the serious presumptive wrongness of abortion subject to the assumption that the moral permissibility of abortion stands or falls on the moral status of the fetus. Since a fetus possesses a property, the possession of which in adult human beings is sufficient to make killing an adult human being wrong, abortion is wrong. This way of dealing with the problem of abortion seems superior to other approaches to the ethics of abortion, because it rests on an ethics of killing which is close to self-evident, because the crucial morally relevant property clearly applies to fetuses, and because the argument avoids the usual equivocations on "human life," "human being," or "person." The argument rests neither on religious claims nor on Papal dogma. It is not subject to the objection of "speciesism." Its soundness is compatible with the moral permissibility of euthanasia and contraception. It deals with our intuitions concerning young children.

Finally, this analysis can be viewed as resolving a standard problem—indeed, *the* standard problem—concerning the ethics of abortion. Clearly, it is wrong to kill adult human beings. Clearly, it is not wrong to end the life of some arbitrarily chosen single human cell. Fetuses seem to be like arbitrarily chosen human cells in some respects and like adult humans in other respects. The problem of the ethics of abortion is the problem of determining the fetal property that settles this moral controversy. The thesis of this essay is that the problem of the ethics of abortion, so understood, is solvable.

NOTES

1. Feinberg, "Abortion," in *Matters of Life and Death: New Introductory Essays in Moral Philosophy*, Tom Regan, ed. (New York: Random House, 1986), pp. 256–293; Tooley, "Abortion and Infanticide," *Philosophy and Public Affair*, II, 1 (1972): 37–65; Tooley, *Abortion and Infanticide* (New York: Oxford, 1984); Warren, "On the Moral and Legal Status of Abortion," *The Monist*, I. VII, 1 (1993): 43–61; Engelhardt, "The Ontology of Abortion," *Ethics*, I.XXXIV, 3 (1974): 217–234;

Summer, *Abortion and Moral Theory* (Princeton: University Press, 1981); Noonan, "An Almost Absolute Value in History," in *The Morality of Abortion: Legal and Historical Perspectives*, Noonan, ed. (Cambridge: Harvard, 1970); and Devine, *The Ethics of Homicide* (Ithaca: Cornell, 1978).

2. For interesting discussions of this issue, see Warren Quinn, "Abortion: Identity and Loss," *Philosophy and Public Affairs*, XIII, 1 (1984): 24–54; and Lawrence C. Becker, "Human Being: The Boundaries of the Concept," *Philosophy and Public Affairs*, IV, 4 (1975): 334–359.

3. For example, see my "Ethics and The Elderly: Some Problems," in Stuart Spicker, Kathleen Woodward, and David Van Tassel, eds. *Aging and the Elderly: Humanistic Perspectives in Gerontology* (Atlantic Highlands, NJ: Humanities, 1978), pp. 341–355.

4. I have been most influenced on this matter by Jonathan Glover, *Causing Death and Saving Lives* (New York: Penguin, 1977), ch. 3; and Robert Young, "What Is So Wrong with Killing People?" *Philosophy*, 1. IV, 210 (1979): 515–528.

5. Feinberg, Tooley, Warren, and Engelhardt have all dealt with this problem.

6. "Duties to Animals and Spirits," in *Lectures on Ethics*, Louis Infeld, trans. (New York: Harper, 1963), p. 239.

Does a Fetus Already Have a Future-Like-Ours?

Peter McInerney

Peter McInerney is a professor of philosophy at Oberlin College. He has published in philosophy journals and is the author of *Ethics* (1994), *An Introduction to Philosophy* (1992), and *Time and Experience* (1991).

In response to Marquis, McInerney claims that a fetus's future is unlike that of a normal adult human. A fetus is not connected to its future in the same way a normal adult human is; nor does it have the same psychological complexity. A fetus, for instance, cannot plan for the future; nor can it develop skills and capabilities in the way that an adult can to open up new possibilities for his or her future.

Some of the most interesting and underexplored issues in philosophy are those of how human beings are in time. A person's relationship to her future is very complex, particularly if time passes, as we commonsensically believe that it does. In "Why Abortion Is Immoral," Don Marquis[1] argues that what makes killing a person wrong is that it deprives the person of her future. He concludes that abortion is wrong because it deprives the fetus of a "future-like-ours." The line of argument is clear.

> The future of a standard fetus includes a set of experiences, projects, activities, and such which are identical with the futures of adult human beings and are identical with the futures of young children. Since the reason that is sufficient to explain why it is wrong to kill human beings after the time of birth is a reason that also applies to fetuses, it follows that abortion is prima facie seriously morally wrong (192).

The unexamined premise in the argument is that a fetus *already* has a future-like-ours of which it

Excerpt from Peter McInerney, "Does a fetus already have a future like ours?" Journal of Philosophy, Vol. 87, No. 5, May 1990, pp. 264–268. Reprinted by permission.

can be deprived.[2] For the argument to be convincing, it is necessary that a fetus *at its time* "possess" or be related to a future-like-ours in a way that allows the transfer from the wrongness of killing us persons to the wrongness of killing fetuses.

Fetuses are very different from normal adult humans. The connections between a fetus at an earlier time and a person (or person stage) at a significantly later time are very different from the connections between the person stages at different times which compose one person. Philosophical investigations of personal identity through time have revealed the complexity of the biological and psychological connections between the earlier and later stages of one person. These significant differences invalidate the claim that a fetus has a personal future in the same way that a normal adult human has a personal future.

The differences between a person's relationship to her future and a fetus's relationship to its future are striking even when the passage of time is ignored. In B-series time (a time that is composed entirely of earlier and later temporal locations with their occupants), an earlier person stage has many relations with later person stages which make these later person stages be "her future." The most widely considered relations in contemporary discussions of personal identity are those of memory, continuity of character, and intention-to-action.[3] Memory relations are from later person stages to earlier person stages. The later person stages are able to remember the experiences of the earlier person stages or there is an overlapping chain of such memory connections (memory continuity). The relation of continuity of character is that in which later person stages either have a character similar to the earlier person stages or are different in ways that are explicable by the operation of normal causes.[4] The relation of intention-to-action is that between an earlier intention and a later action that carries out that intention. Normal adult humans have all sorts of plans and projects for their short- and long-term futures which take time to implement.

There are other relations that connect earlier and later person stages. Some of the "mental processing" that ordinarily goes on in normal humans, such as forming generalizations from repeated observations or "digesting" an emotionally charged experience, takes a significant amount of time and so can be considered to include relations between person stages. In addition, there are all of the neurophysiological relations that underlie the ordinary continuation of mental life in persons. That a person has pretty much the same beliefs, wants, skills, and habits that she had 30 minutes (or 30 days) earlier depends upon a similarity of neurophysiological conditions between the earlier and later person stages.

Most of these relations to later person stages exist even when the earlier person is asleep or temporarily unconscious. Even intentions to perform later actions might be considered to continue through periods of unconsciousness. Since a temporarily unconscious person is still strongly related to her future, to kill her while she is unconscious is to deprive her of her future.

Young infants do not have all of the psychological complexity that adult persons have. Nevertheless, young infants are commonsensically understood to have perceptions, beliefs, desires, and emotions (whether or not the experimental data confirms this) and to learn from experience. For this reason, the neurophysiological states and processes of young infants can be understood to underlie something like the ordinary continuation of mental life in persons. A good case can be made that young infants are related in some (though not all) ways to a personal future.

The situation of a fetus at an early stage of development is very different.[5] A fetus at an early stage of development has neither a mental life of feelings, beliefs, and desires nor a developed brain and nervous system. There are none of the main relations with a personal future which exist in persons. Although there is some biological continuity between them so that there is a sense in which the later person stages "are the future" or the fetus, the fetus is so little connected to the later personal life that it can not be deprived of that personal life. At its time the fetus does not already "possess" that future personal life in the way that a normal adult human already "possesses" his future personal life.

Our commonsense views about time and entities in time involve a past that is fixed and determinate, a future that includes alternative possibilities whose actualization may be affected by action, and a process of what is future becoming present and past. In a time of this sort, how an entity "has a future" is more complex because when some temporal part (stage) of the entity is present, there is not a fixed and fully determinate future to which that entity can now be related. With respect to persons, a present person stage is not now related to a specific determinate later person stage that will become present. A person's future includes a branching range of possibilities (including his death) from which only one life course can become present. The branching of possibilities is such that most outcomes can become present only if certain earlier possibilities have become present. The actualization of one possibility makes available those later possibilities which presuppose it. This is particularly pronounced for the acquisition of skills, abilities, and capacities, which open up new ranges of possibilities that would otherwise not be available.

Many factors external to the person affect which of the person's possibilities become present. A normal adult human has only limited control over which of his possibilities become present. This control which a person exercises and attempts to exercise over his future is the most important connection that now exists with a specifically personal future. This control also depends upon the person's wants, skills, abilities, and capacities. The person wants various things for his future (including wanting himself to act) and exercises his powers to affect what happens.

A fetus is separated from a personal future by many "layers" of possibility. The possibilities that are available to a person or even to a young infant are not now available to the fetus. Only if the fetus develops in the right ways (favorable possibilities become present) will it acquire the capacities that make available the infant's possibilities. A great deal of favorable development would be necessary before the fetus could control its future in the way that persons do. The fetus does not now have a personal future.

Marquis has succeeded in formulating an important feature of people's opposition to abortion: the notion that abortion "cuts off" the fetus's future. A close examination of what it is "to have a future" reveals that at its time a fetus does not have a personal future of which it can be deprived. A living human cell that might be stimulated to develop into a clone of a person does not now have a personal future. A fetus similarly has only the potentiality to develop a personal future. For this reason, killing a fetus is morally very different from killing a normal adult human.

—PETER K. MCINERNEY
OBERLIN COLLEGE

NOTES

1. This JOURNAL, LXXXVI, 4 (April 1989): 183–202.
2. "Since a fetus possesses a property, the possession of which in adult human beings is sufficient to make killing an adult human being wrong, abortion is wrong" (202).
3. See Derek Parfit, *Reasons and Persons* (New York: Oxford, 1984), pp. 205–7.
4. See *Reasons and Persons*, p. 207, for a brief discussion of "normal causes."
5. As the fetus develops, it becomes more similar to a young infant, and so progressively acquires more of a relationship to a personal future.

The Problem of Coerced Abortion in China and Related Ethical Issues

Jing-Bao Nie

Jing-Bao Nie is a professor of bioethics at the Bioethics Center in the University of Otago, New Zealand. He has written articles in bioethics from cross-cultural perspectives. He is the author of *Behind the Silence: Chinese Voices on Abortion* (2005).

Nie addresses the practice of coercive abortion in China, which has drawn severe criticisms from the West. He believes that while coercion itself is not necessarily morally wrong, coercive abortion violates reproductive rights and women's right to privacy. Nevertheless, he argues that forced abortion should not be viewed as outright evil but as a necessary measure for the social goal of population control in China.

Since the early 1970s, despite popular opposition, to control the rapid growth of population the Chinese government has been carrying out the strictest and most comprehensive family planning policy in the world. In addition to contraceptive methods and sterilization, artificial abortion—both surgical and nonsurgical—has been used as an important measure of birth control under the policy.

Excerpts from Jing-Bao Nie, "The problem of coerced abortion in China and related ethical issues," Cambridge Quarterly of Healthcare Ethics, Vol. 8, No. 4, October 1999. © Cambridge Journals, reproduced with permission.

This article is a part of the research project on contemporary mainland Chinese people's moral views and experiences of abortion. It was written in 1996 at the Institute for the Medical Humanities of the University of Texas Medical Branch at Galveston. I thank Ms. Faith Legay, Prof. Harold Vanderpool, Dr. Kirk Smith, Prof. Mary Winkler, and Dr. John Douard for their valuable suggestions and generous help. I am also grateful to Arthur Kleinman for his valuable comments on the early version of this paper, which was presented at the poster section of the National Meeting of MD/PhD Education and Research in the Humanities and Social Sciences at the University of Chicago in 1996.

Many women have been required, persuaded, and even forced by the authorities to abort fetuses no matter how much they want to give birth.

For centuries artificial abortion has been practiced in China by and large as a private issue. Direct and indirect sources indicate that abortion has been no less frequently induced in traditional China than in other places of the world. Whether or not abortion was regarded as morally acceptable by ancient Chinese medical doctors, philosophers, and common people, the state did not directly interfere and take any official position in prohibiting, permitting, or encouraging the practice until the middle of this century. The founding of the People's Republic of China changed this situation thoroughly and profoundly.

In her social history of birth control in the United States, Linda Gordon points out that "birth control has always been primarily an issue of politics, not of technology."[1] Such is especially the case with respect to fertility control and abortion in China since 1949, as every aspect of the life of the Chinese people has had strong political and ideological coloring. In the years 1949–1976 Mao

Zedong dominated, controlled, and directed Chinese society, from the political operation of the nation to the lifestyle of the common people. In attempting to understand the abortion issue in China one cannot ignore Mao's ideas on population and fertility control.

Until the late 1950s and early 1960s, Mao, born in a rural village in southern China, completely denied that a huge population is a social catastrophe. Rather, he stressed that the more people, the greater the energy for socialist revolution and construction. As a result, importation of contraceptives was banned and abortion was basically prohibited. But after some hesitations and reversals Mao changed his attitude toward birth control. In the 1970s the party and government started to work out policies to reduce the rate of increase of the population. Mao's successor not only continued the birth control policy but enforced it. In 1980 the Central Committee of the Chinese Communist Party and the government announced officially the famous (infamous) "one child per couple" policy with very few exceptions. The ambitious program that would maintain the population at no higher than 1.2 billion by the year 2000 had been formulated and promoted. Thus persuaded or coerced abortion has become an often-used fertility control method.

It seems that most couples in contemporary China, like many couples elsewhere, wish to have two or more children (ideally, one boy and one girl). Therefore, since the beginning, the family planning program, especially the one-child-per-couple policy, has met with strong popular opposition. Women who definitely want more than one child often intentionally try to violate the one-child policy, making every effort to hide their pregnancies in the hope of finally giving birth. When they eventually give up under various kinds of social and political pressure, their pregnancies have often progressed into the second or third trimester. As a result, most persuaded or coerced abortions are also late abortions. So, among others, two closely related moral questions are involved in the thorny issue of coerced abortion: (1) Can late abortion be justified ethically? and (2) Why and how is forced abortion morally acceptable or unacceptable?

Some Chinese scholars have attempted to address the first question.[2] In this paper I will focus on the second—the problem of coerced abortion and related ethical issues.

The political, economic, cultural, historical, and moral factors related to the practice of coerced abortion in China are so complex that even the problem of coercion cannot be properly and fully discussed in a short paper. In the following discussion, I will begin by confirming the existence of forced abortion in China. Then, through the analysis of the concept of coercion, I will point out that coercion itself is not always morally wrong. To demonstrate why coerced abortion is morally objectionable, I will use not only the concepts of individual rights—the right to reproduce and privacy—but also the traditional Confucianist and Taoist moral ideals, i.e., governing by education rather than by extensive employment of compulsion and by letting people govern themselves. Finally, turning to the conflict between the serious problem of overpopulation and the popular will of people to have two or more children, I will try to show that coerced abortion may be a moral tragedy or a genuine ethical dilemma rather than a thorough moral evil as it first appears.

THE PRACTICE OF COERCED ABORTION IN CHINA

The Chinese government never explicitly legitimated coerced abortion. Induced abortion is called a "remedial measure." This term is not only the standard Chinese euphemism for abortion, especially for late-term abortions, but also partly true because, rather than abortion, the preferred means of birth control and family planning are postponing marriage and childbearing until a mature age, use of intrauterine devices (IUD) and other contraceptive methods, and surgical sterilization. Official and semi-official documents always proclaim that the family planning program is carried out "under the principle of voluntaries on the part of the masses with state guidance" and that couples of childbearing age adopt fertility control methods, including abortion, entirely voluntarily or through persuasion but not through coercion. The government insists that the basic means of promoting the family planning program are information, education, and motivation, not "coercion and commandism," which refer to forceful orders and physical force.

However, to many people the statement that the birth control campaign is based on voluntary choice or persuasion is either another lie put out by the communist government, or at least should be assessed with great caution. In his comprehensive study on Chinese family planning policy, *Slaughter of the Innocents*, John Aird has reviewed the historical development of fertility control in the People's Republic of China, especially in the 1980s. He concludes his monograph:

> The Chinese family planning program is being carried out against the popular will by means of a variety of coercive measures. Despite official denials and intermittent efforts to discourage some of the more extreme manifestations, since the early 1970's if not before, coercion has been an integral part of the program.[3]

In *China's Changing Population*, Judith Banister summarizes that the Chinese policy "makes extensive use of compulsory family planning, compulsory limitation of the total number of children to one child, required signing of double contracts and pledges to stop at one child, forced sterilization, compulsory IUD acceptance, forced IUD retention, and forced abortion."[4]

It has been estimated that from 1971 to 1983 the total number of artificial abortions in China was 92 million.[5] According to a 1982 report by Guangdong family planning authorities, 80 percent of the 624,000 abortions in the province were performed "by order," and one-third were in the sixth month of pregnancy or later.[6] These data cannot be taken to be representative before more supportive statistical documents come out. A more recent number is not available, but more recent figures must be no lower because the national population control policy has grown stricter and sexuality freer in the past decade. To know how many abortions are voluntary and how many are compulsory is difficult, if not completely impossible, since the authorities concerned always deny the use of coercion.

Many cases of forced abortion do not necessarily indicate a coercive abortion policy, just as the many cases of "people's policemen" beating people in China do not necessarily mean that the government has a policy legitimating physical abuse by police. Does a central and provincial policy exist that explicitly legitimates coerced abortion in China? The Chinese government and some supporters of the birth control policy contend that mandatory IUD insertions, compulsory sterilizations, and coerced abortion originate not in central policy but in local deviations from central policies. Unfortunately, this argument can hardly hold water.

When "real action," "effective measures," and "practical results" are emphasized by the central policymakers in order to carry out the family planning program "strictly," "firmly," "resolutely," and "effectively" local cadres, in direct confrontation with the strong will of many people to have more than one child, must choose between using coercion and losing their positions. Some articles in the Chinese media have even openly advocated coercion. In 1979 Guangdong province ordered local officials:

> At present, we must shift our work emphasis to women who are pregnant, particularly to women who have more than one child. . . . We must mobilize those who have unplanned pregnancies [i.e., without permission from the authorities concerned] to adopt effective remedial measures to solve the problem. All units and departments must go into immediate action and do well in mobilization, persuasion, and education work.[7]

A municipality in Liaoning was praised as a model for its 1982 performance because "women with unplanned pregnancies were subjected to remedial operation . . . and no time limit was set on the pregnancies." In 1983 the national leadership ordered that "women with unplanned pregnancies must adopt remedial measures as soon as possible."[8] A 1991 official regulation in Shanxi concerning family planning includes the stipulations that "pregnancy must be terminated if it has not been planned" (i.e., permission has not been obtained from the authorities) and "must also be terminated if the woman has not reached the legal age to marry or is pregnant outside marriage."[9]

In sum, as Aird has said, coercion is a "direct, inevitable, and intentional consequence" of policies formulated by the central government.[10] The central and provincial policies have permitted and assured, at least indirectly, that local cadres can and sometimes must use coercion in their work. In Banister's words, "although the problem is seen at the grassroots level, its roots lie with the upper level."[11] The Chinese family planning program remains highly coercive through the whole process; central policies have brought out many forced abortions and other coercive activities in the birth control campaign.

As Aird has documented, many tactics and concrete methods are employed to persuade or compel people to submit to family planning demands against their will, including the following:

- officials go repeatedly to the houses of women with unplanned pregnancies to have "heart-to-heart talks" with the family;
- women pregnant without permission are required to attend "study classes";
- the government initiates the mass "movement" or "mobilizations" for contraception, sterilization, and abortion;
- penalties for resisting policies include measures that threaten family subsistence such as loss of employment for urban residents or removing the houses of rural people;
- collective punishments and rewards are designed to involve the entire membership of a factory, or an institution, or a rural political unit so that peers will participate in persuading and compelling the women with unauthorized pregnancies to follow the central government policies.

Persuasion is involved in some of the above measures (for instance, "heart-to-heart talks" and "study classes"), but local cadres often cross the line between persuasion and coercion.[12] It must be remembered here that the Chinese government exercises almost unlimited power in the lives of citizens.

COERCION ITSELF IS NOT NECESSARILY A MORAL EVIL

A great difficulty in discussing the ethical issues of coerced abortion lies in the definitions of the terms "coercion" or "compulsion" and the related concept "persuasion." To draw a clear line between persuasion and coercion is even more difficult in practice than in theory. The Chinese government and some family planning advocates limit the term "coercion" to the use of physical force. Although physical force is sometimes used by local officials, the Chinese government never openly approves and formally legitimizes such action in any official published directive. Understanding coercion in this narrow sense, Chinese policymakers are able to openly deny the existence of coercion in the family planning program.

For many people, this definition is obviously too narrow. For Aird, a method powerful enough to compel many people to act contrary to their wishes constitutes force or coercion. He states, "Any action in the fertility control to employ force, the threat of force, or extreme penalties and pressure that leave people no choice but to comply should be defined as coercion."[13] Although this definition does grasp the core meaning of the term *coercion* as ordinarily used, it has not distinguished the strategies of persuasion and strong persuasion from the category of coercion or compulsion.

Merriam-Webster's Collegiate Dictionary (10th ed.) defines the word *coerce* as "to restrain or dominate by force," "to compel to an act or choice," "to bring about by force or threat." The word *persuade* is defined as "to move by argument, entreaty, or expostulation to a belief, position, or course of action." Although these dictionary definitions are of little help for moral exploration of coercive activities in Chinese birth control and abortion policies, they are a good starting point.

Following the essay "Coercion" by Robert Nozick and the article "Coercion and Freedom" by Bernard Gert, bioethicists Tom Beauchamp and James Childress claim that coercion "occurs if, and only if, one person intentionally uses a credible and severe threat of harm or force to control another."[14] They point out further, "For a threat to be credible, both parties must believe that the person making the threat can effect it, or the one making the threat must successfully deceive the person threatened into so believing."[15] For them, there is a distinctive line between coercion and persuasion since, as they define persuasion "a person must be convinced to believe in something through the merit of reasons advanced by another person." Thus they do not agree that such measures as "forceful persuasion" exist.[16]

Two points here require attention. First, coercion or compulsion is never absolute, nor essentially value free. Some may think that a decision concerning whether a person is coerced is a fact claim, just an empirical question. But to others, as Alan Wertheimer has argued, "coercion claims are moralized" and "they involve moral judgments at their core."[17] As a matter of fact, different people may respond very differently to the same pressure, threat, or force, not to mention that different cultures have different understandings of and attitudes about coercion.

Second, and more important, coercion in itself is not necessarily morally unacceptable. For Aird, as the title of his book has clearly shown, coercive birth control in China is "slaughter of the innocents." China's use of coercion in family planning violates human rights. He suggests that the Chinese family planning program is morally evil because it is highly coercive. This interpretation seems to be the first response of many Westerners to the practice of coerced abortion in China. Yet coercion itself is not always morally wrong at all. Beauchamp and Childress give two typical examples of coercion: the threat of force or punishment used by policy, courts, and hospitals in acts of involuntary commitment for psychiatric treatment, and society's use of compulsory vaccination laws.[18] However, they do not thereby mean to claim that involuntary civil commitment and compulsory vaccination are morally unacceptable just because coercion is adopted.

Not only is coercion not always morally wrong, it may even be morally required under some circumstances that certain people or institutions control others by coercive or other manipulative means. Red B. Edwards and Edmund L. Erde point out that valid moral justifications exist for using coercion, such as parental coercion of children at times; good laws and penalties for noncompliance; and proper enforcement mechanisms like the police, the courts, and the prisons to coerce lawless persons into behaving themselves.

Edwards and Erde conclude, "Using coercion is often, but not always, the morally right thing to do. Other human values besides freedom must be protected coercively."[19] This fact may be rather sad and unfortunate to acknowledge since modern Western moral and legal traditions are typically based on personal autonomy (self-determination) or, in Wertheimer's term, the voluntariness principle.[20] The crucial question is not whether coercion can be morally justified, but, as Wertheimer poses, "What constitutes the coercion or duress that violates the voluntariness principle?"[21] and, as Edwards and Erde ask, "When is coercion morally unacceptable? And how can we tell when it places morally unjustifiable limits on freedom?"[22]

Thus more and deeper moral exploration is needed to answer the question whether and how coercive birth control programs in general and forced abortion in particular are morally wrong or acceptable. What more fundamental moral principles does the practice of coerced abortion violate? Can compulsory abortion be morally defended for protecting other human values, for instance, the social good? Is compulsory abortion necessarily a moral evil?

COERCED ABORTION AS A MORAL EVIL

For many Westerners, as Geoffrey McNicoll has said, "Browbeating a woman to have an abortion, a practice reported in some studies of China's antinatalist program, would, of course, be found highly objectionable."[23] The conception of individual rights or freedom constitutes one cornerstone of the Western political, legal, and moral system. Promoting the family planning program by coercion then conflicts with and challenges fundamental values and moral principles, such as reproductive rights and women's right to personal privacy. So it is not surprising that the Chinese fertility control programs have raised serious criticisms and strong objections as long as the existence of coercion has been known here in the West.

Coerced abortion undoubtedly violates at least the right of women to personal privacy. The idea of individual rights or the natural rights of human beings plays a dominant role in Western ethical and political life. As a result, the issue of moral and legal rights, the rights of the pregnant woman, is one of the key problems in the contemporary abortion debate. The labels "pro-life" ("right to life") and "pro-choice" ("right to choose") used by opponents in the U.S. abortion debate reveal the fact that the two sides are employing the same language—the language of rights.

The distinction between public and private, which has origins in Greco-Roman political and ethical theory and practice, is crucial to prevent unlimited intervention of the state or community into the life of the individual. The English political philosopher James F. Stephen wrote in 1873 that "Conduct which can be described as indecent is always in one way or another a violation of privacy."[24] The right of personal privacy has been used by the U.S. Supreme Court to favor a woman's decision whether to terminate her pregnancy. Feminists developed this rationale into the popular phrase "a woman's right to control her own body."

Is the right to reproduce a fundamental human right? The Universal Declaration of Human Rights classifies the following rights as the first group: life, liberty, and the security of person; freedom from arbitrary arrest, detention, or exile; right to impartial tribunal; freedom of thought and religion; freedom of opinion and expression; freedom of peaceful assembly and association. The right to decide one's own fertility and reproduction issues is not, at least not explicitly, included as a fundamental right. The U.S. Constitution does not claim the right to reproduce as a constitutional right either. However, the practice of coerced abortion undoubtedly violates at least the personal-privacy of a woman, grounds for a claim of fundamental rights in the West.

Nevertheless, to question whether or not the right to reproduce is fundamental might result in many further questions:

- If the right to reproduce should be seen as a fundamental human right, then why and how?
- If the right to reproduce is fundamental, may individuals have as many children as they wish?
- Like sexual behavior, must reproductive behavior be completely free form state intervention?

- When reproductive rights conflict with some kinds of common good, such as controlling the rapid growth of population, to which should priority be given?

In the moral discussion about abortion and many other medical ethics issues in China, the cultural characteristics of the country and the people must be taken into account, for China has a very different cultural tradition from the West. Among ancient Chinese philosophers, doctors, and lay people, the practice of abortion evoked little explicit discussion (if any concern), not to mention public debate, as is still the case in contemporary China. Even though no ancient Chinese thinker explicitly advocated that both abortion and infanticide are justifiable on utilitarian grounds as did Plato and Aristotle, neither was there a Chinese "Pythagoras" to hold that abortion is killing because of the belief that human life begins at conception. The Chinese did not consider abortion morally objectionable mainly because they, like Jewish law and Platonists in ancient Greece, maintain that human life does not begin until birth. Confucianists and Taoists rarely treated the fetus as a human being. So neither the "Absolute Sincerity of Great Doctor" (the Chinese "Hippocratic Oath") by the "King of Medicine," Sun Simiao, nor any other premodern professional maxims written by medical doctors clearly claimed that the physician should "not give to a woman abortion remedy" as does the well-known Hippocratic Oath.[25] Nevertheless, to conclude that abortion has never evoked moral concern among the people of traditional Chinese society is incorrect. As a matter of fact, the question whether abortion is morally right puzzled Chinese people even in ancient times.[26] Imported Buddhism, the third major philosophical-social-religious doctrine in traditional China, taught that the fetus is a form of life and therefore put limits on artificial abortion.

Paying attention to the importance of cultural difference never means justifying everything in the culture or society. Studies of cultural factors often can provide information on how today's reality came about, but does not always ethically justify the practice itself. That something is so does not mean that it ought to be so. In fact, while traditional

Chinese moral thoughts and culture give priority to the common good of society over individual rights, in Chinese ethical and political philosophy are rich resources to criticize today's various policies that adopt compulsion. For example, Taoist philosophy emphasizes the idea of individual freedom and being free from external coercion. For Lao Zi and Zhuang Zi, no governing is better than letting people govern themselves or letting people alone. Taoism has a strong individualist trend. Although Confucianism gives great importance to the community, the power of the ruler, and the merit of obeying the authorities in human life, it never approves governing by coercion rather than by persuasion. Confucius and his followers defined a good government as one that loves the people and makes them happy and held that the highest technique of governing is teaching or education. Mencius, the Confucian master second only to Confucius, once distinguished two kinds of government; *wang* ("kingly") and *ba* ("forceful"). He exalted the former and rebuked the latter. In contrast to *ba* who govern by means of coercion, *wang*, the leader of kingly government, is a sage. On behalf of the people, the sage-king administers through moral construction and virtues and practices *ren* ("humanity, humaneness"). In fact, the concept of "*ren,*" translated as "benevolence, human-heartedness, goodness," is the heart of Confucianism. In the long history of traditional Chinese thought only the totalitarian thinkers of Legalism advocate the absolute power of strong centralized government, draconian law, and harsh punishment.[27]

COERCED ABORTION AS A NECESSITY FOR THE SOCIAL GOOD

Abortion is practiced in the People's Republic of China mainly as an ultimate mechanism of the family planning program. In the face of the social problem of overpopulation, the one-child family campaign has been proposed and pursued as a significant common good for the whole society. This family planning program is widely regarded as necessary to control and reduce the geometrical rate of increase in population in order to raise common living standards, given China's very limited natural resources.

It is well known that one striking characteristic of Chinese cultural and political life is emphasis on the common good, the state authority, the priority of community. Ren-Zong Qiu, one of the leading Chinese bioethicists and philosophers of science, has well summarized and expressed the common understanding of Chinese culture:

> A quasi-holistic social-political philosophy has been developed from Chinese cultural tradition. It is based on two thousand years of power—centralized, autocratic monarchy—one that has lacked any rights-oriented, individualist, liberal democratic tradition. In recent decades, Marxism—rather, a mixture of Russian and Chinese versions of Marxism—has become the dominant ideology. The historism and social holism of this system, interwoven with traditional ideas, puts the greatest emphasis on nation, society, and country, rather than on individuals.[28]

Even though this summary may be too general because in this widely accepted view the diversity and plurality of Chinese medical morality and cultural traditions have been either totally ignored or minimized,[29] the generalization does suggest a significant reason why coercive abortion can go on in practice and be justified in theory in the name of the common good in China.

Many Chinese medical ethicists agree with the priority of the common good and use the concept to justify the family planning program. On the issue of reproduction, the author of *Essentials of Medical Ethics* proclaims the priority, actually the tyranny, of the society in a very typical way: "when the prenatal care comes into conflict with birth control and eugenics, it must be subordinated to the needs of the latter, because these are in the interest of the whole nation and the whole [of] mankind, as well as in accord with the greatest morality."[30] To morally justify the measure of coerced abortion for the good of society is not difficult starting from this sort of logic and theoretical perspective.

As a matter of fact, the concept of the social good has been used by Chinese officials and scholars as the most powerful approach to justify fertility control in general and "persuaded" abortion in particular. Few deny that overpopulation is one of the most serious social problems in today's China.

To achieve the goal of controlling population growth, government emphasizes that citizens have an obligation to follow family planning policy, i.e., use efficient birth control methods and, if unplanned pregnancy occurs, abort. Actually, the constitution of the People's Republic of China that came into force upon promulgation by the announcement of the 5th National People's Congress, 1982, requires that "Both husband and wife have the duty to put into practice family planning."

To appreciate fully the seriousness of overpopulation in China is not always easy for Westerners, especially people in North America. The concrete numbers—now more than 1.1 billion, more than one-fifth of the world's population, living in the mainland of China—may not make real sense to many people. To put these numbers in North American terms, please imagine that all Canadians live in two cities, Toronto and Quebec. The population of Beijing and Shanghai, the two biggest cities in China, is close to the total population in Canada. Wherever you are in the United States, multiply the number of people you meet five or six times. While the total land areas of the United States and China are almost the same, the population of China is five times that of the United States. Furthermore, China has far fewer natural resources and less habitable area than the United States.

Therefore many Chinese scholars and some Western population experts believe and argue that China must persist in controlling population growth, adjusting population structure, and raising the quality of human resources. The rationale here is very simple: the extant overpopulation and its continuing growth threaten the whole society; thus individuals must make sacrifices for the eventual common good. The argument for the social good is sometimes extended to an obligation to future generations and the world. People living now have a duty to preserve the world so that future societies and individuals will have the resources and health conditions currently available. Fertility control is considered a social good not only for China, but also for the world because overpopulation is a global problem rather than only a local one.

If the present overpopulation is not serious enough, the popular wish of contemporary Chinese people to have two or more children makes the problem of population a real social crisis. Even though the reproductive behavior of individuals in China, as in other places, was never totally free from economic limits and cultural influence, for ages the Chinese were free to have as many children as they wished without the direct intervention of the state. As a matter of fact, under Confucianism, to be without offspring was considered the greatest violation of the principle of filial piety, a fundamental duty and merit of the individual. Chinese people developed this idea into a positive maxim, "More children, more happiness." Some contemporary Chinese, especially some people in rural areas, still hold this belief.

In 1985 a survey of one-child households in the rural suburbs of Tianjing Municipality found that about 80 percent hoped to have two children and that some of them had accepted one-child certificates only because they felt they "have no choice." In 1988 a State Family Planning Commission found that 72 percent of all couples and 90 percent of rural couples wanted more than one child and a demographic journal reported other survey results showing that 88 percent of Chinese couples wanted both a boy and a girl. Even in Beijing a survey found that fewer than 20 percent of a sample of 7,622 married women want only one child; 79.7 percent wanted two or more.[31]

Although being required to pay income tax in the United States and to limit childbearing in China are vastly different, there is an important similarity between them insofar as the conflict between the genuine self-interest of the individual and the general good of society is concerned. In one case, the individual wishes to have as many children as desired while "others" limit fertility. In the other case, the individual wishes to avoid paying taxes while "others" pay theirs. That is to say, both paying tax and limiting reproduction are regarded as necessary for the sake of the social good.

Confronted with overpopulation on the one hand and the strong will of people to have many children on the other, the government seems to have no choice but to adopt both persuasion and compulsion to achieve a decrease in the rate of population growth and thereby raise people's living standard. Coercion is thus considered a necessary evil for the good of society and eventually for the long-term interests of every member.

In the well-known essay *On Liberty*, John Stuart Mill argued that civil or social liberty is mainly concerned with "the nature and limits of the power which can be legitimately exercised by society over the individuals."[32] For him, liberty meant protection not only "against the tyranny of the political rulers" but also "against the tyranny of the prevailing opinion and feeling; against the tendency of society to impose, by other means than civil penalties, its own ideas and practices as rules of conduct on those who dissent from them,"[33] etc. He pointed out that "[t]he only purpose for which power can rightfully be exercised over any member of a civilized community, against his will, is to prevent harm to others. His own good, either physical and moral, is not a sufficient warrant."[34] Adopting coerced abortion to promote the one-child family planning program must first of all answer the question whether having many children really constitutes a harm to others so that state intervention is needed to enforce a number—one child per couple.

Using the social good as a theoretical justification for the one-child policy and coerced abortion must also resolve the following questions:

- Is there really a serious population problem? Or is controlling the population growth rigorously really a social good? In fact, this issue is controversial and some scholars totally deny population size as a real social problem.

- If controlling population increase is a social good, considering the reality of today's China, is the good an equal advantage to every member in the society? If not, who benefits most? Who least? Might some even be harmed?

- Has overpopulation been used by the government as an excuse for other social problems that have resulted from misgoverning? Is promoting family planning policy just an integral part of keeping and enforcing the extant power structure?

- If fertility control is a universal social good, why should and must the interest or right or freedom of individuals be subordinated to the social good of the whole nation and even all humankind? One may argue and the individual may believe that having more children contributes more to society than having just one.

- Even in the one-child policy is a social good to which everyone should be committed, is coerced abortion justified as a measure of birth control? Is there not a better way? In other words, cannot the fertility control program really be built on voluntariness, as the government has openly claimed, rather than on coercion or force?

CONCLUSION

In spite of official denial, coerced abortion has been enforced in China in the name of social good. For Chinese policymakers, officials, and many scholars, the dilemma is seen in terms of either adopting coercive measures or losing the birth control program entirely. Confronted with the reality of overpopulation and the pressure of most people's strong will to have two or more children, coercion is employed as an important measure to limit the rapid growth of population. Even though coercion itself is not necessarily a moral evil, forced abortion and other compulsory fertility control mechanisms do violate the individual right to reproduce, the Chinese women's right to personal privacy. Although traditional Chinese ethical thought gives priority to the common good of society, it cannot be employed to justify the extensive use of coercion.

My conclusion is that coerced abortion is highly morally unacceptable because the practice violates individual rights to reproduction and personal privacy as well as the traditional Chinese—both Confucianist and Taoist—moral and political idea of not governing by coercion. But enforced abortion can be defended for the common good of society. In other words, taking the conflict between the serious problem of overpopulation and the popular will of people to have two or more children into account, forced abortion may be a moral tragedy or a genuine ethical dilemma rather than a thorough moral evil as it first appears.

In my paper I have raised many questions, more than I can resolve. More moral and cultural exploration of the practice is greatly needed, and more important and definitely necessary is an open public discussion or debate among Chinese people on abortion in particular and family planning policy in general. Unfortunately and sadly, this latter necessity seems to be especially difficult to realize. Moreover, if the moral exploration is not so much theoretical meditation in the ivory tower as a social practice of people, then the biggest challenge we now face is how Western ethical theories and traditional Chinese moral wisdom can be applied and transformed to change the present reality in China, if the reality is morally wrong.

NOTES

1. Gordon, L. *Woman's Body, Woman's Right: A Society History of Birth Control in America*. Harmondsworth: Penguin Books, 1977:xli.
2. Qiu, R.Z., Wang, C.Z., Gu, Y. Can late abortion be ethically justified? *Journal of Medicine and Philosophy*, 1989; 14:343–50. Their conclusion is that "the late abortion can be justified ethically in China: 1) if the 'one couple, one child' policy is justifiable; 2) if the couple and the physician take the social good into account; 3) if the mother express[es] her voluntary consent, no matter whether the decision is made on the basis of her own original desire or after persuasion by others that is not coercive; and 4) if the late abortion will entail only a low risk to the mother's health or life" (p. 349). Obviously, more ethical explorations are definitely needed regarding the late abortion problem.
3. Aird, J.S. *Slaughter of the Innocents: Coercive Birth Control in China*. Washington, D.C.: The American Enterprise Institute, 1990:88.
4. Banister, J. *China's Changing Population*. Stanford: Stanford University Press, 1987:216.
5. Qiu, R.Z. Medical ethics and Chinese culture. In: Pellegrino, E.D., Mazzabella, P., Crosi, P., eds. *Transcultural Dimensions in Medical Ethics*. Frederick, Maryland: University Publishing Group, 1992:155–74.
6. See note 4, Banister 1987:208.
7. See note 4, Banister 1987:209–10.
8. See note 4, Banister 1987:209–10.
9. The 20th Meeting of the Standing Committee of the Seventh Provincial People's Congress (3 March 1991), *International Digest of Health Legislation*, 1994:45(3).
10. See note 3, Aird 1990:89.
11. See note 4, Banister 1987:209.
12. See note 3, Aird 1990:16–7.
13. Aird, J.S. Population policies: strategies of fertility control: compulsion. In: Reich W.T., ed. *Encyclopedia of Bioethics*, rev. ed., vol. 4. New York: Simon & Schuster Macmillan, 1995:2023.
14. Beauchamp, T.L., Childress, J.R. *Principles of Biomedical Ethics*, 4th ed. New York: Oxford University Press, 1994:164.
15. See note 14, Beauchamp, Childress 1994.
16. See note 14, Beauchamp, Childress 1994.
17. Wertheimer, A. *Coercion*. Princeton: Princeton University Press, 1990:xi.
18. See note 14, Beauchamp, Childress 1994.
19. Edwards, R.B, Erde, E.L. Freedom and coercion. In: Reich, W.T, ed. *Encyclopedia of Bioethics*, rev. ed., vol. 1. New York: Simon & Schuster Macmillan, 1995:886.
20. See note 17, Wertheimer 1990:4.
21. See note 17, Wertheimer 1990.
22. See note 19, Edwards, Erde 1995:886.
23. McNicoll, G. Strong persuasion. In: Reich, W.T, ed. *Encyclopedia of Bioethics*, rev. ed., vol. 1. New York: Simon & Schuster Macmillan, 1995.
24. Stephen, J.F. *Liberty, Equality and Fraternity*. Cambridge: Cambridge University Press, 1967 [1893]: 160.
25. For ancient Chinese medical ethics, see Unschuld, P.U. *Medical Ethics in Imperial China: A study in Historical Anthropology*. Berkeley: University of California Press, 1979. On the theories and practice of medical ethics in ancient Greece and Rome, see Carrick, P., *Medical Ethics in Antiquity: Philosophical Perspectives on Abortion and Euthanasia*. Dordrecht: D. Reidel Publishing Company, 1985.
26. There does not exist much primary or secondary literature on abortion in premodern China. About ancient Chinese law on abortion, see Luk, B.H. Abortion in Chinese law. *American Journal of Comparative Law* 25(1):372–90. On the traditional Chinese understandings (especially medical professionals' understandings) of abortion and the fetus, see J.B. Nie. Coerced abortion in China: an ethical problem in its historical and cultural context. Paper presented at the 38th National [Medical] Student Research Forum, Galveston, Texas, April 1997.
27. On traditional Chinese moral and political thought in the English language see, for example, Fung, Y.L., ed. Bodde, D. *A Short History of Chinese Philosophy*. New York: Macmillan, 1948; Fung, Y.L, trans. Bodde, D. *A History of Chinese Philosophy*, vols. 1, 2. Princeton: Princeton University Press, 1952, 1953; Greel, H.G. *Chinese Thought from Confucius to Mao Tse-tung*. Chicago: University of Chicago Press, 1954; and Hsiao, K.C. Trans. Mote, F.W. *A History of Chinese Political Thought*. Princeton: Princeton University Press, 1979.
28. See note 5, Qiu 1992:170–1.
29. Nie, J.B. Reexamining the characteristics of American and Chinese medical moralities: toward an interpretive cross-cultural bioethics. Paper presented at the 1996 Joint Meeting of the Society for Health and Human Values and the Society for Bioethics Consultation, Cleveland, Ohio, October 1996. See also Nie, J.B., Inquiring for the foundations of medical morality at the soul of medical ethics. *Zhongguo Yixue Lundixue [Chinese Medical Ethics]* 1996:5.
30. Quoted in Qiu et al. See note 2. Qiu, Wang, Gu 1989.
31. See note 3, Aird 1990:84. The result of an unpublished survey made by the Chinese Society for Sociology in 1979 showed that a considerable percentage of city inhabitants (19.44–30.95%) and the majority of peasants (51.34–79.53%) wanted to have two or more children. The lower percentage of opposition in 1979 hardly means that there were more people then who approved the family planning program of the state. One important factor is that people were more afraid to express what they thought even in the sociological survey, given newly initiated economic and political policies and the fact that the country remained under the shadow of Mao's dictatorship.
32. Mill, J.S. *On Liberty*, ch. 1. In: Burtt, F.A., ed. *The English Philosophers from Bacon to Mill*. New York: Modern Library, 1939:949.
33. See note 32, Mill 1939:952.
34. See note 32, Mill 1939:956.

Contestation and Consensus:
The Morality of Abortion in Japan

William R. LaFleur

William R. LaFleur is a professor of Japanese studies at the University of Pennsylvania. He is the author of *Liquid Life: Abortion and Buddhism in Japan* (1992) and *The Karma of Words: Buddhism and Literary Arts in Medieval Japan* (1983). He is the editor of *Zen and Western Thought: Essays on Masao Abe* (1985) and *Dogen Studies* (1985).

LaFleur examines the traditional Buddhist doctrine that abortion is morally justifiable. Even though abortion is considered justifiable, it is regarded as a necessary evil or sorrow. Abortion is considered to be an important component in the preservation of family values in Japan as well as in keeping the population in check. The Japanese practice of memorializing the aborted fetuses serves a therapeutic purpose of alleviating guilt for parents who have chosen abortions.

. . . The scholarly community, especially in the West, has habitually by-passed or denigrated vast amounts of materials that are important to understand the history of ethical thinking in Japan. It has also led to a systematic pattern of ignoring and down-playing those times and ways in which there was real conflict and contestation in Japanese ethical and religious life. In keeping with the fact that some recent works in Japanese have paid increasing attention to the reality and energy of intellectual contestation in Japanese history,[1] I am here suggesting that we, at least for heuristic purposes, reject as flawed the common assumption that there usually was a neat division of intellectual labor in Japan. To assume that Buddhists merely plugged Confucianism into their teachings as a kind of caretaker for "the world," ethics, and the family is an assumption that tends to flatten the real shape

Excerpts from William R. LaFleur, "Contestation and Consensus; the morality of abortion in Japan," Philosophy East and West, Vol. 40/4, October 1990 edited. © 1990 University of Hawaii Press. Reprinted by permission.

of ethical discourse in Japan. It also reads as complementary and "harmonized" certain points that were, in fact, often fraught with conflict over both principles and practice.

ABORTION IN JAPAN: THE CONTESTATION

I believe this to be eminently true in the case of Japanese thinking about abortion. I have elsewhere narrated what I take to be the history of Japanese Buddhist thinking about abortion as a moral and religious problem.[2] Within that history I have located a phase in the early half of the nineteenth century when what I call a distinct difference between Buddhists on the one hand and Confucians and Shinto-based Kokugaku scholars on the other took shape. I detail why it is clear that the Buddhists for the most part took the position that abortion was what we call a "necessary evil"—although their term was a "necessary sorrow." Their opponents rejected all abortion as morally and religiously wrong. A common Buddhist position, in this sense comparatively "soft" on abortion, is expressed in the tradition of memorial rituals (*kuyō*) provided in cases of abortion; it can also be known from the materials in which Buddhists were attacked on this point by their opponents.

This is not to say that Buddhists had no qualms about abortion or did not recognize a tension between its practice and the precept against taking life. It is merely to note that they were more flexible on this point than were the Confucians and proponents of late Kokugaku. The latter, especially, mixed religion and politics unabashedly; beginning in the nineteenth century a family's reproductivity was read as an index to patriotism. This became intense in the Meiji (1868–1912) period—an eloquent demonstration of Bellah's observation that in Japan "the family does not stand over against the polity but is integrated into it and to an extent penetrated by it."[3]

Therefore, the Buddhist stance at that time was charged with being a threat to national well-being and as a flagrant offense to the gods—gods that protect the nation and are happiest when people's "seeds" germinate into whole persons in great numbers. Of course, the fact that there was a political aspect to the entire discourse also helps explain why the Buddhists dared to express their "soft" stand only indirectly. In fact, the Buddhist "position" on this was articulated not so much through treatises as through ritual, surely a "safer" medium in their situation. I would, however, point out that this indirect, mixed, or muted discourse on specific moral questions had by this point already become "traditional" for Japanese Buddhists. Here was an instance where a traditional mode of expression also happened to be the only politically viable one; that it came in a muted form, however, does not mean it was not a distinct and *discernible* position. Its opponents knew it was at odds with their view and we, too, can reconstruct why that was so—and, therefore, its structure as an ethical stance on abortion.

During the latter half of the nineteenth century much changed within Japan. What the government perceived as a "population stagnation" conflicted with imperial designs. Japan's growing need for human manpower, a need that was to

grow with rapid industrialization and a military buildup for foreign wars, fit hand-in-glove with the antiabortion arguments advanced early in the nineteenth century by Kokugaku advocates and Confucians. This meant that a process was in place that led to the criminalization of abortion soon after the Meiji Restoration in 1868. During the latter half of the nineteenth century and the first half of the twentieth, therefore, the case against abortion, identifiable with this Shinto revival and with Confucian points of view, held sway in Japan. What I call "fecundism" became the order of the day and was associated in the public mind with "family" values.

Given the fact that in 1945 with its total defeat in World War II Japan underwent as thorough and total a crisis as can be imagined, the ban on abortion, too, began to be rethought. Whereas during the decades of rapid industrialization, militarization, colonial expansion, and war, abortion had been proscribed, after the Pacific War things were completely different. To some degree what had been the Kokugaku/Confucian opposition to abortion had been totally discredited by the events of history, most especially Japan's own defeat in 1945. Beginning at that time—especially given the tightness of basic resources—there was a deep concern about an explosion of the population. Thus once again a more "Buddhist" view, traditionally amenable to seeing abortion as a "necessary suffering," was the view that for all practical purposes was adopted when, in 1948, the process was begun to legalize abortion once again. Although what we here call "the Buddhist view" was not articulated in terms of explicit arguments, it was implicit in Buddhism's readiness to provide "rituals of memorial" for aborted fetuses (*mizuko*), a view widely perceived as tolerating abortion. It is probably not an exaggeration to say that, at least since 1948, on this ethical question it has been the Buddhist view which, consciously or not, has been what underlies actual practice.

The point that I want to emphasize here is not the one that ethical positions merely traipse along in the wake of political needs but, in fact, a quite different one—namely, that ethical discourse in Japan has in fact been much more diverse and conflict-ridden than most commentators assume. It also interests me that, once we begin to derive our readings of ethical positions from materials that are "mixed" and do not necessarily come in a genre recognizable as "*the* ethical treatise," we can more readily reconstruct what clearly seems historically to have been a distinctly Buddhist approach to abortion in Japan, a position in actuality quite different from the total opposition—at least from the early nineteenth to the mid-twentieth centuries—to it by persons self-consciously representing Confucianism and the Neo-Shintō phase of Kokugaku. This is not to say that certain schools of Buddhists, especially those in the Pure Land tradition, have not objected both to abortion and to the *mizuko* rites. It is merely to note a trajectory of comparative tolerance of the practice.

ABORTION IN JAPAN: CONSENSUS

What are we to make of the fact that, whereas what I call Japan's conflict over abortion was most aggravated in the middle of the nineteenth century, there is relatively little debate today—when in Europe and America the debate has become strong and often acrimonious?

One might expect that, given the high rate of abortion in Japan as well as the diversity of religious positions represented there, Japan would have been the locus of protracted and spirited debates about the ethics of abortion in recent years. Such, however, has not been the case. What is impressive, at least to the Western scholar looking for such, is the fact that comparatively little has been written on this topic during the past few decades— and that what has appeared has for the most part dealt with the politics of abortion, the legalization of the contraceptive pill, and criticisms of certain entrepreneurial temples for capitalizing on the *mizuko* boom. Voices advocating the repeal of legalized abortion have, by contrast, been almost nonexistent. I think it significant that what a century ago had been strongly expressed Confucian and neo-Shintō objections to legalized abortion have today in Japan largely dissipated and disappeared.

There are groups—such as Seichō no Ie (The House of Life), a "new religion"—that vocally oppose abortion. Such groups during the early 1980s evoked strong opposition from the Women's Movement in Japan, but as far as the general public is concerned these rather small groups opposed to abortion are little more than a blip on the screen of public consciousness. Some Buddhist and Christian groups express alarm at the *number* of abortions performed, yet in Japan today there could hardly be anything that could rightly be called a real or wide public debate on this issue. Books on abortion as a public policy problem can scarcely be found. Many assume that the legalization of the pill will in time cut back the abortion rate. In fact, it is the *absence* of such a debate at the present time which, in my opinion at least, is the salient datum that deserves exploration and interpretation.

I would contend that this absence of public debate also needs to be interpreted as a sign of something *present*—namely, a fairly wide consensus on this matter. There is a consensus that abortion constitutes a painful social necessity and as such must remain legal and available, although religio-psychological mechanisms for relieving bad feelings about abortion—the *mizuko* rites, for instance—in most cases probably play a positive, therapeutic role. And, of course, this is to say that it is now what I have termed a Buddhist position on abortion which has, for all practical purposes, won the day.

A "position" is expressed not only by what is said but also by what goes unsaid. Therefore, in my view, it is significant that within the Japanese Buddhist community the discussion of abortion is now limited largely to criticisms of those temples and temple like organizations which employ the notion of "fetal retribution" to coerce the "parents" of an aborted fetus into performing rituals that memorialize the fetus, remove its "grudges," and facilitate its rebirth or its Buddhahood. Many Buddhists find repugnant such types of manipulation of parental guilt—especially when expressed in the notion that a fetus in limbo will wreak vengeance (*tatari*) on parents who neglect to memorialize it.

But, of course, the focus here is on the morality of using this concept of retribution; the question of the morality of abortion per se is, by comparison, something that goes almost without discussion. In other words, it seems now widely accepted that the Buddhist praxis developed over centuries on this issue is itself basically a moral and viable way of handling this complex and vexing problem.

Although I cannot here recapitulate things discussed in more detail elsewhere, a very rudimentary statement of the matter is that most Japanese Buddhists have accepted abortion as a necessary sorrow but at the same time have contextualized the termination of pregnancy—and also infanticide in an earlier epoch—through Buddhist ritual. One result of my analysis has been to demonstrate that historically the belief in transmigration and rebirth effectively attenuated any sense of "finality" in abortion—thus giving the "parents" of an aborted fetus the expectation that the fetus' entry into the world had been merely postponed.

Thus parental prayers and ritual memorializations were expected to palliate guilt, create what is taken to be a continuing relationship between parents in this world and a fetus in a Buddhist "limbo," and render close to moot many of the West's protracted debates about life's inception, fetal rights, and ownership of the bodies of women. Although those Japanese Buddhists who take this position face various conceptual and ethical problems in its wake, these are rather different—and in terms of upheaval in the larger society certainly less severe—than the problems we have faced in trying to deal with abortion in the West in general and the United States in particular.[4]

This is not to say that women's rights advocates feel no need for vigilance vis-à-vis Buddhist institutions on this matter. It is merely to call attention to the fact that, even though their acknowledged concerns are political and focus on the danger of being, as women, manipulated, those feminists who have written about Buddhism and abortion have tended to focus their criticisms on those who employ the concept of "fetal retribution," and that is something which, as noted above, many

Buddhists themselves are quick to condemn.[5] My sense is that many feminists in Japan find, at least in the present context, a kind of odd, unanticipated ally in the Buddhists. Those feminists who are also ideologically Marxists are troubled by this convergence, but most feminists show reluctance to refuse the Buddhist hand that seems to render indirect help to this part of their cause. Obviously the Marxist critique of religion is itself "softened" in this.

My own personal conversations with representatives of various religious constituencies in Japan leads me to conclude that, especially if the legalization of "the pill" and a wider use of contraceptive devices can effectively reduce the *number* of abortions, there will be no deep objection to the continued legalization of abortion and the tendency to keep in place those Buddhist rituals that ritually memorialize fetuses and may serve as a conscience–solace for parents. The status quo, especially if numbers can be reduced, is acceptable to a surprisingly wide spectrum of persons engaged in discussions of religious and ethical questions. To that degree at least—and in contrast to American society—there is in Japan a fairly wide public consensus on this matter.

MORAL HIGH GROUND

Sometimes on moral questions a consensus forms because the participants in a protracted debate are exhausted or the issue no longer seems so important. On other occasions, however, consensus comes into being because something tagged as a "higher" value is recognized and respected by those who had earlier been partisans of differing positions; in such instances the "higher" can begin to override the former concern to sharpen differences. If a sense of exhaustion happens to coincide with a sense of moving towards a value deemed "higher" by both sides, the potential for consensus becomes eminently realizable.

My view is that in Japan's consensus on abortion today we can observe an instance where these two motives have, in fact, coincided quite remarkably. Interest in opening the old wounds is minimal—especially given the high social cost of the years of abortion-proscription. In addition, there is a widely generalized perception that abortion, however much regarded as a source of suffering, is not only demographically necessary but even a means for protecting what are felt to be "family" values. In most basic terms it is necessary to prevent the hemorrhaging of population in a land where the density is already unusually high. More importantly, however, abortion is perceived as a mechanism whereby families can maximize the opportunities for their children by a "rational" investment of resources in the education and upbringing of a limited number of children, usually two. It would not be too much to say that in Japan the high emphasis placed upon family life is itself a factor in the current consensus in favor of keeping abortion legal and available.

Religious institutions—perhaps Buddhist ones in particular—articulate and reinforce these family values in Japan. This means that in most instances such institutions cannot be expected to move in any significant way to curtail a practice they perceive as a regrettable but necessary component in ensuring the persistence of good family life and national life. The consensus among religious groups to leave abortion legal and available will, I suspect, remain as long as it seems clear to the majority that, however unpleasant and painful abortion may be, family life in the aggregate is far better served by having it available than by criminalizing it once again. In my own conversations with Buddhist clergy in Japan on this problem I detect two concerns, but they are not, it should be noted, of sufficient weight to prompt any strong movement for a change in the rather liberalized law.

The first concern is that people not become inured to abortion and trivialize it. Many Buddhists are worried that, especially if there is no real grief and ritual, a kind of personal degradation becomes the pattern: from repeated abortions to a flippant acceptance of the practice and from there to a deterioration in a person's (read: woman's) capacity for generalized sensitivity. This consists in a "hardening," something serious because in the psychoethical vocabulary of the Japanese this is a matter of the *kokoro* or "heart." If too many people within society become persons who take abortion

as simply a matter of course, then the tenor of society itself will change for the worse.

The legal and social admission of abortion as a practice is different from being psychologically and spiritually inured to it. Japanese Buddhists worry more about the latter than the former and focus their energies accordingly. Japanese Buddhists will often go on to argue that the meaningful performance of remembrance rites can, in fact, offset what is to be most feared. That is, the ritual of *mizuko kuyō*, a kind of "requiem mass" for the fetus, can, it is claimed, do much to prevent this "hardening" of the *kokoro* and dehumanization.

The second concern is for a possible nexus between the accessibility of abortion and an appreciable growth in the numbers of persons who adopt what is now called the "single" (*shingaru*) style of the larger urban centers. Within Buddhist periodicals, for instance, there can be found more and more discussions of the single lifestyle as a threat to family life. A decline is detected and projected: from the extended family to the nuclear family and from there to the single lifestyle and the one-parent "family." It is important to note that virtually every Buddhist institution is committed to the superior values of the traditional family and is itself dependent upon such a family's readiness to support temples for the performance of ancestral rites. Partially no doubt because of this, the single lifestyle is pinpointed as a threat to societal values in general. It is also seen as an index to the growth of a dangerous form of (Western-style) individualism, and fundamentally contrary to traditional values that are at the same time understood to be "national" values.

On the basis of things I have heard and read, it probably can be predicted that, if the single lifestyle were to become really widespread, the ready accessibility of abortion could eventually come under attack. To date, however, this does not seem likely. The anxiety about a nexus between "liberated sex" and a changing structure of the family has for now focused on the danger of making "the pill" readily available. If that anxiety tends to deepen, it will more likely jeopardize the legalization of the contraceptive pill rather than the availability of abortion.

In fact, "conservative" views in Japan can at times take strikingly unexpected turns—at least when judged by what would be expected if they are thought to be the equivalent of "conservative" views in American public life. For instance, one privately will often be told in Japan that the availability of abortion is in fact *protective of family values* to the degree that it makes unnecessary the birthing of unwanted children. Then, because it is assumed, first, that unwanted children are both pitiable and more prone to become problematic for society itself and, second, that family strength and well-being are maximized when it can be assumed that all persons within it are *wanted* and valued, logic seems to compel the conclusion that abortion is needed as a necessary "safety valve" to ensure familial, societal, and national strength. Buddhists go on from this to argue that, especially if the "hearts" of persons who have had abortions can be "softened" via the rituals that keep alive a sensitivity to the departed fetus as still alive in the Buddhist limbo (*sai no kawara*), the cumulative danger to society is reduced.

In Japan, surprisingly then, it seems to be the case that the most politically effective argument for legalized abortion, even though it comes down in muted forms, is based on fairly "conservative" concerns for the quality of family life. To many persons with fairly traditional religious and social views in Japan it is difficult to imagine why "conservative" Americans can be found favoring a public policy—the criminalization of abortion—that will in effect result not only in giving birth to obviously unwanted children but, beyond that, also to the psychic pain, both individual and social, that is bound to follow such a policy. In addition, it is assumed in Japan that there must be some close correlations in any society among the degree to which children are wanted, such children's perceptions of being wanted and loved, the quality of the care they receive, and whether or not their subsequent behavior becomes deviant or criminal.

To criminalize abortion, thus, looks irrational and socially foolhardy. To Japanese ready to express candid views on these things, this scarcely seems to be the direction in which American public life should sensibly be moving today. Given the existing problem of large numbers of unwanted children as well as the

exorbitant crime rate in America, those who push for abortion's recriminalization appear to be courting what to some Japanese looks like a kind of social suicide. To some Japanese it is even somewhat baffling why certain Americans, viewing themselves to be "conservative" in their views of the family, do not recognize that forcing others to have children they do not really want is itself a morally questionable stance.

Clearly that location called the "moral high ground" can be approached from different directions. What is interesting—and potentially instructive—in the Japanese case is that interpretations of the relationship between religion and abortion have not been forced down the either/or chutes of "rights of the unborn" or "rights of the woman." In part that is undoubtedly because the Japanese traditional concern for social order (*chitsujo*) still seems almost automatically to take immediate precedence over any public scenario of "rights" and "liberation."

ABORTION AND THE POLIS

I believe the chief value in the study of Japanese thinking about abortion may be heuristic. That is, in this way we can see a society permitting abortion while avoiding interminable debate over conflicting rights. In a sense we can see a society that, through trial and error, has learned to opt for access to abortion as a way of enhancing the quality of social life itself. Neither the rights of the individual fetus nor those of the individual woman are highlighted; instead these claims—often taken in the West as "opposite"—are both seen as driven by the ideology of individualism. There are other reasons to legitimate abortion, reasons which, it is felt, have to do with the quality of common life of the society itself. The health of the larger society is at issue.

Robert Nisbet grasped this point. As an advocate of the contemporary relevance of the position on these things held by ancient Greeks and Romans rather than by medieval Christians, Nisbet found in the Japanese case a ready instance of exactly what he had in mind. In the entry on "abortion" in his *Prejudices: A Philosophical Dictionary*, he wrote:

> In the contemporary world it would be hard to find a family system more honored and more important in its authority than that of Japan. But abortion there has for long been easily available.[6]

My own analysis has suggested that, although Nisbet did not realize how historically complicated things really had been in Japan and how painful had been the process to legalize abortion there,[7] he was entirely accurate in his grasp of the nexus between tolerance of abortion in Japan and the high valorization of family life there *today*. That is, he grasped that there is an argument for abortion based upon familial and societal values, an argument furthermore that is not bound to prioritize individuals and individual rights.

Alasdair MacIntyre, in his *Whose Justice? Which Rationality?* refers to "the unborn" in a way that suggests how he reads the history of Europe very differently from Nisbet. In depicting what he calls the emergence of the "Augustinian alternative" to Aristotelianism, MacIntyre locates the moral payoff of that alterative as making itself evident in the following way:

> The law of the *civitas Dei* requires a kind of justice to the unborn which Aristotle's proposed measures for controlling the size of the population of a *polis* deny to them.[8]

It would be difficult to find a more pithy statement of what many in the West have often held to be how Christianity gained its own moral high ground, a position assumed to be superior even to that of Aristotle.

The problem, of course, is that the trajectory right into individualism seems to have been prepared at the same time. Augustine, says MacIntyre, had found a way to require "a kind of justice to the unborn" but he neglects to point out that in Augustine the importance of the *polis* was at the same time being drastically reduced. In his *De nuptiis et concupiscentia*, the Bishop of Hippo, having declared that childbearing is "the end and aim of marriage," goes on to judge that, unless they have the intent of being fecund, a man and woman, however legally married, are really only having sinful

sex. Without the aim of propagation a woman is just her "husband's harlot" and the man is his own "wife's adulterer."[9] Ultimately marriage is something for the Church to define, not the state.

Once such views were injected into the consciousness of the West—and later defined in such a way that something uniquely "Western" and morally "higher" was implied in their observance—it became extremely difficult to go back and recapture Aristotle's important and still valid point about eugenics and the quality of life in the polis. That point had been compromised, of course, because Aristotle had viewed it, unnecessarily I think, as something the polis must force upon its citizens. But the Christians went beyond merely objecting to the coercion. With their polemic against paganism, Christians tended toward the obscuring of the view that the *polis* might have eugenic concerns that are legitimate and, in fact, ethically worthy. In this way, what was important in Aristotle was effectively obliterated by the "Augustinian alternative," and with the articulation of that alternative the course of the West was set.

If eugenics became a matter of consensus rather than coercion, however, the picture changes significantly. Then it appears possible to avoid, on one side, the forced compliance that Aristotle mandated and, on the other, the prizing of individual rights—either to "life" in the fetus' case or to "choice" in the pregnant woman's—at the expense of what is good for the larger social entity.[10] While I do not imply that the Japanese have arrived at a perfect solution to these problems, their present practice with respect to abortion and the family avoids, I wish to suggest, some of the most serious pitfalls of our own practices. In addition, an understanding of how their practice has been put together as an instance of moral "reasoning" is—however initially odd by our usual criteria—itself a reason for studying it with care.

NOTES

1. For example, Imai Jun and Ozawa Tomio, eds., *Nihon shisô ronsôshi* (Tokyo: Perikansha, 1979).
2. William R. LaFleur, *Liquid Life: Buddhism, Abortion, and the Family in Japan*, Princeton: Princeton University

Press, 1992. Published studies on *mizuko* in English to date include: Anne Page Brooks, *"Mizuko kuyō* and Japanese Buddhism," *Japanese Journal of Religious Studies*, 8, nos. 3–4 (September–December 1981): 119–147; Emiko Ohnuki-Tierney, *Illness and Culture in Contemporary Japan: An Anthropological View* (Cambridge: Cambridge University Press, 1984), pp: 78–81; Hoshino Eiki and Takeda Dōshō, "Indebtedness and Comfort: The Undercurrents of *Mizuko Kuyō* in Contemporary Japan," *Japanese Journal of Religious Studies*, 14, no. 4 (December 1987): 305–320, and Bardwell Smith, "Buddhism and Abortion in Contemporary Japan: *Mizuko kuyō* and the Confrontation with Death," *Japanese Journal of Religious Studies*, 15, no. 1 (March 1988): 3–24. There is, of course, an extensive bibliography in Japanese.

3. Robert N. Bellah, *Tokugawa Religion: The Values of Pre-Industrial Japan* (Glencoe, Illinois: The Free Press, 1957), p. 19.

4. For the incredulous, somewhat appalled response of a Japanese woman legal expert present at European debates trying to pinpoint the exact time of a soul's entry into the body, see Nakatani Kinko, "Chūzetsu, Dataizai no Toraekata," in Nihon Kazoku Keikaku Renmei, ed., *Onna no jinken to sei* (Tokyo: Komichi Shobō, 1984), p. 29.

5. See, for example, Anzai Atsuko, "Mizuko kuyō" shō bai no ikagawashisa," in Nihon Kazoku Keigaku Renmei, ed., *Kanashimi o sabakemasu ka* (Tokyo: Ningen no Kagakusha, 1983), pp. 137–148. The critique of *tatari* from within Buddhism, however, is also strong. There is widespread censure of it, for instance, in a special issue devoted to this problem in the interdenominational Buddhist Journal *Daihōrin*, vol. 54 (July 1987). For details see my *Liquid Life*, pp. 160–176.

6. Robert Nisbet, *Prejudices: A Philosophical Dictionary* (Cambridge, Massachusetts: Harvard University Press, 1982), p. 1.

7. See my *Liquid Life*, pp. 69–139.

8. Alasdair MacIntyre, *Whose Justice? Which Rationality?* (Notre Dame: University of Notre Dame Press, 1988), p. 163.

9. Augustine, "Of Marriage and Concupiscence" in Marcus Dods, ed., *The works of Aurelius Augustine, Bishop of Hippo*, trans. Peter Holmes (Edinburgh: T & T Clark, 1985), vol. 12, p. 116.

10. For a discussion of how, in fact, history shows there is nothing absolute about "respect for life" in the West's religions, see John A. Miles Jr., "Jain and Judaeo-Christian Respect for Life," *Journal of the American Academy of Religion*, 44, no. 3 (1976): 453–457.

The Classical Hindu View on Abortion and the Moral Status of the Unborn*

Julius J. Lipner

Julius Lipner is a professor of Hinduism at the University of Cambridge. He is the author of *Fruits of Our Desiring: Enquiry into the Ethics of the Bhagawad Gita* (1997) and *The Face of Truth: A Study of Meaning and Metaphysics in the Vedantic Theology of Ramanuja* (1986) and a coauthor of *Hindu Ethics: Purity, Abortion, and Euthanasia* (1989).

Lipner holds that Hindu texts do not seem to make a clear distinction between human being (in the genetic sense) and human personhood (in the moral sense). In fact, moral status is assumed throughout the entire period of fetal development, and hence, abortion is unacceptable except under unusual circumstances. In addition, according to Lipner, abortion blocks the unborn from living out its *karma*, thus depriving it of the opportunity of liberation from rebirth.

It will be helpful to start the discussion by reference to a distinction often made by some contemporary western moralists in the context of the moral status of the embryo/foetus. In this context, these moralists affirm that a distinction is in order between the individual qua HUMAN BEING and the individual qua HUMAN PERSON. The individual qua human being, they say, is a member of the human species but, for various reasons, is not yet a person—in fact, may never be a person. Some of these limiting reasons may be the following: the lack of a recognisable human form (in the embryo/foetus); clear evidence (detected by mechanical devices) of insufficient (rather than abnormal) cerebral activity in some foetuses compared to cerebral activity, in other foetuses, which is accepted and established as pertaining to human person, at that stage of development, and so on. The moralists differ as to whether one or more of such reasons are the sufficient condition to determine human personhood.

It is not to the point here to inquire whether the criteria themselves and the distinction based on them, are valid. The point is that some moralists, having established to their satisfaction criteria for distinguishing between human beings and human persons (or at least, for the validity of this distinction), then go on to affirm that abortion in the case of human BEINGS is morally permissible for reasons which may not be valid when abortion of human PERSONS is in question. In practical terms, they incline to the view that abortion in the early stages of pregnancy cannot be objected to morally with the same force as to abortion in the late stages of pregnancy ("early" and "late" here are given varying interpretations). This is because in early pregnancy, the human being has not yet developed—for one reason or another—into the human person with the

Excerpts from Julius J. Lipner, "The Classical Hindu View on Abortion and Moral Status of the Unborn" in Hindu Ethics: Purity, Abortion and Euthanasia. 1989. © 1989 State University of New York Press. Reprinted by permission. [Edited]

*This essay is dedicated to Fr. George Gispert-Sauch, S.J., of Vidyajyoti, Institute of Religious Studies, Delhi— sound scholar and good friend.

latter's claim to a moral status qualitatively superior to that of the former (however "human person" may then be further defined).

Now, we may ask, is the classical Hindu view on the nature of the prenatal human individual such as to permit us to draw this kind of qualitative distinction between human being and human person, with its repercussions for the (limited) permissibility of abortion? To answer this, we shall have to examine first the traditional Hindu philosophical position on the nature of human personhood.

THE HINDU VIEW OF PERSONHOOD

It is well known that there are many views in Hindu tradition during our period on the nature of the human person. Nevertheless, in this respect, one and only one basic model—with variations on the theme—was accepted from early times in traditional, orthodox Hinduism (viz., in those perspectives or *darśanas* which did not explicitly repudiate the authority of the accredited scriptures). According to this basic model, the human person is a composite of two essentially disparate but intimately conjoined principles—spirit *(ātman, puruṣa)* and matter *(prakrti)*. Spirit is essentially the locus of consciousness and bliss, and is impervious to substantial change; matter is essentially insentient, tending to diversification and change. For reasons we need not go into here, spirit and matter come together to produce the distinctive individual which each of us is. This union, though finally dissoluble, is nevertheless a profound one and engenders the separate centres of self-awareness we experience ourselves to be. This experience is characterised by the congenital illusion which fails to distinguish between the "real" self, that is, the pure spirit, and the "false" or composite self (matter-cum-spirit). Liberation, the human goal, about which the different schools have different views, necessarily consists in at least the internalised awareness of the distinction between the real self and the false self. So long as this enlightened knowledge is not attained, each of

us repeatedly dies and is physically reborn as a continuum of different personalities, each reborn individual being determined as to nature and life situation by the resultant of the continuum's past ego-centred KARMA (i.e., meritorious and unmeritorious action). This process of *karma* and rebirth is beginningless for each individual and may continue indefinitely. It is terminated by enlightenment, and at dead the enlightened soul is liberated from the wheel of rebirth.

This basic model of human personhood is delineated in the *Caraka Saṃhitā*.[1] The quotations that follow are taken from a philosophical section of this treatise called the *Śārīrasthāna*. It was typical of the integral outlook of the Hindu mind that a medical text also contained discussions on the nature of the human subject. The Hindus believed that a physician could not effectively minister to the body unless he viewed it in the perspective of the spirit.

In the section mentioned, the following description of the spirit or *ātman's* essential nature is given as the evidently acceptable one: "Those who know the *ātman* say that it is actionless, self-dependent, sovereign, all-pervading, and omnipresent; that it has conscious control over the body (that is, a *kṣetrajña*) and witnesses its doings."[2] Later the inner self (*antarātman*) of the human person is described as essentially "eternal, free from disease, free from old age, deathless, free from decay; it cannot be pierced, cut or agitated. It takes all forms, performs all actions, is unmanifest, beginningless, endless and immutable."[3] In answer to how it is then that, in the human subject, the *ātman* as described above) seems to manifest the contrary characteristics, viz., being a limited agent, mortal, dependent upon bodily functions, changeable, and so on, we are told that this false appearance of the *ātman* results from the *ātman's* union with matter (in the form or the body). The body, for its part, is described as, "the support of the conscious principle, constitutive of the totality of modifications of the five elementals (which make up matter), and maintaining the harmonious conjunction (of its parts)."[4]

ENSOULMENT, AND CONSCIOUSNESS IN THE WOMB

With this traditional Hindu view of human person-hood in mind, let us consider now, in the context of the distinction between human being and human person and its implications for abortion, what the classical texts have to say about the nature of human conception and the development of the embryo. Here we seem to be confronted with two traditions—what we may call a "major" (because of its apparently weightier authority) and a "minor" (which, in contrast to the major, seems to rely on weaker evidence).

Focusing on the major tradition first, there follows a description of what happens at conception, taken from the section entitled "Descent (of the spirit) into the Womb" of the *Caraka Saṃhitā:* "Conception occurs when intercourse takes place in due season between a man of unimpaired semen and a woman whose generative organ, (menstrual) blood and womb are unvitiated—when, in fact, in the event of intercourse thus described, the individual soul (*jīva*) descends into the union of semen and (menstrual) blood in the womb in keeping with the *(karmically* produced) psychic disposition (of the embryonic matter)."[5] This seems to mean that conception coincides with the "descent" or presence of the spirit in the womb—that from the beginning the embryo is the spirit-matter composite that constitutes the human person. There seems to be no scope according to this seminal authority for drawing the distinction between human being and human person, with the implication that abortion at some early stage of pregnancy may be permissible.

In the minor tradition, however, the soul unites with the embryo some time AFTER conception. Here, it seems that grounds do exist for drawing a distinction between human being (the, embryo before the union with the soul) and human person (the embryo after the union). The minor tradition is (perhaps uniquely) expressed in the *Garbha Upaniṣad* (circa 2d–3d century C.E.?), a minor Upaniṣad and hardly a recognised authority in such matters. The *Garbha Upaniṣad* has it that soul and embryo unite in the seventh month after conception:

> As a result of intercourse in due season, the embryo forms in the space of a night; within seven nights a bubble forms; in the period of a fortnight, there is a lump and by a month this becomes hard. In two months the head develops, in three months the region of the feet, and in the fourth month the ankles, stomach, and loins form. In the fifth month, the back and spine form; in the sixth month, nose, eyes, and ears develop. In the seventh month, (the foetus) is joined to the soul, and in the eighth month it is complete in every (part).[6]

It is important to point out that neither the *Garbha Upaniṣad*, in particular, nor the minor tradition, in general, ever explicitly draws a distinction analogous to that between human being and human person described earlier, either with or without reference to abortion. We cannot derive any conclusions about the permissiblity of abortion, therefore, from any argument which refers specifically to a time lapse between conception and ensoulment, based on the minor tradition.

But, it may be objected, one does not need to appeal to this kind of argument in the attempt to make a case for the permissibility of (early) abortion in our context. For if it can be shown that even according to the major tradition it is only relatively late in pregnancy—if at all—that the mark of ensoulment, viz., conscious experience, occurs, then it can be argued that BEFORE the appearance of this sign only the NECESSARY (not the sufficient) condition obtains for personhood in the embryo. In this instance, abortion may be permissible for reasons and in situations acknowledgedly not valid if and when the SUFFICIENT condition (viz., consciousness) does apply.

This is our cue for examining the evidence, in the classical tradition, as to whether the embryo/foetus has conscious experience or not. In fact, it was commonly believed that, at least in a relatively advanced stage of pregnancy, there is conscious experience in the womb. This awareness is invariably connected with the so-called *garbha-duḥkha* or sufferings of residence in the womb. The *Viṣṇu Purāṇa* says:

> An individual soul (*jantu*), possessing a subtle body (*sukumāratanu*), resides in his mother's womb (*garbha*), which is imbued with various sorts of impurity (*mala*). He stays there being folded in the membrane surrounding the foetus (*ulba*). . . . He experiences severe pains. . . tormented immensely by the foods his mother takes . . . Incapable of extending (*prasāraṇa*) or contracting (*ākuñcana*) his own limbs and reposing amidst a mud of faeces and urine, he is in every way incommoded. He is unable to breathe. Yet, being endowed with consciousness (*sacaitanya*) and thus calling to memory many hundreds (of previous) births, he resides in his mother's womb with great pains, being bound by his previous deeds.[7]

The *Garbha Upaniṣad* elaborates on one aspect of this painful experience:

> Now (when the foetus) is complete in every aspect, it remembers its past births. Action pertains to what is done and not done, and (the foetus) thinks upon its good and bad deeds. Having surveyed (previous births from) thousands of different wombs, (it thinks): "Thus have I enjoyed various foods and suckled various teats. Again and again both the living and the dead are reborn. Alas! I am sunk in this ocean of sorrow and see no remedy. Whatever I've done, good or bad, for those about me—I alone must suffer the consequences, for they've gone on their way, suffering the fruits (of their own deeds). If ever I escape the womb I'll study the *Sāṃkhya-Yoga* which destroys evil and confers the reward of liberation. If ever I escape the womb I'll abandon, myself to Śiva who destroys evil and confers the reward of liberation."[8]

But the trauma of birth—the squeezing in the vaginal passage and the impact of the air outside the mother's body (the so-called Vaiṣṇava Wind)—erases all memories and stupefies (*bālakaraṇa*: makes a child of!) the newborn.[9]

The *Suśruta Saṃhitā* is more specific as to when consciousness develops in the womb:

> In the first month (after conception) the embryo is formed, in the second . . . there results a compact mass. If this is globular (*piṇḍa*), it's a male, if longish (*peśī*) it's a female. . . . In the third month, five protuberances appear for the hands, legs and head, while the division of the other bodily limbs and sections is hardly visible (*sûkṣma*). In the fourth month, the division of these other limbs and

sections appears clearly, while awareness as a distinct category (*cetanādhātu*) manifests itself in relation to the appearance of the foetus' heart. . . . Also in the fourth month, the foetus expresses desires in respect of sense-objects. . . . In the fifth month the coordinating sense (*manas*) becomes more aware, and in the sixth the intellect (*buddhi*) is manifest. In the seventh month, the division of the bodily limbs and sections is more defined; in the eighth month the life-force (*ojas*) concentrates. . . . In one or other of the ninth, tenth, eleventh, or twelfth months, birth takes place, or else (the pregnancy) is void.[10]

Note that nothing is said here to indicate that in its development the embryo undergoes a quantum leap, passing from one kind of human moral status (human being) to another (human person). On the contrary, in characteristic Hindu fashion, the language here is in terms of progressive MANIFESTATION, of a personhood previously only latent rather than origination of personhood *abinitio*.[11] The *Suśruta Saṃhitā* confirms this conclusion when, after describing the development of the foetus, it observes in the face of opposing views that the foetus undergoes an all-round (rather than sporadic) development from the very beginning.[12] For its part, the *Caraka Saṃhitā* implies that the conscious principle is active in the fertilised egg, directing its growth, right from conception.[13] Thus, in respect of the development of the unborn, the language of the manifestation of consciousness in traditional Hinduism cannot be and never has been taken to refer to qualitatively different moral statuses of the embryo/foetus. There is no scope here then for arguing for abortion in a traditional context.

The same stricture applies to the minor tradition, notwithstanding the time lapse it introduces between conception and ensoulment.[14] This hiatus, too, has never been used to distinguish qualitatively, in a moral sense, between one stage of the embryo and another, with or without abortion in mind. So, as noted before, we can deduce nothing positively concerning the permissibility of abortion on the basis of this hiatus. In point of fact, the overriding evidence of the classical texts as a whole speaks in favour of according the status of human personhood to the unborn throughout pregnancy, with consequent implications for (the impermissibility of) abortion, except in extreme circumstances (see earlier).

Other reasons, embracing both traditions, can be adduced for the standard view on abortion.

LINGUISTIC EVIDENCE

There is the argument from the negative evidence of the linguistic terms used to describe different stages in the development of the embryo.[15] At no stage in pregnancy is the embryo/foetus designated by a particular term so as to indicate in any way that it is susceptible of abortion for reasons not obtaining when the embryo/foetus is differently designated. Further, while it is invariably some compound containing *bhrūṇa* (embryo/foetus) which is used to express the reprehensible act of abortion in the literature, *bhrūṇa* is never used, to the best of my knowledge, as a recognised term for designating a particular stage in the development of the embryo. Thus, there is no linguistic evidence to enforce a distinction positing different moral statuses in the unborn, or by implication, favouring abortion.

KARMA AND REBIRTH

Another reason which made abortion unacceptable in traditional Hinduism was the belief in *karma* and rebirth, outlined earlier. This belief, in one or other of its variants, was firmly implanted in the Hindu psyche from very early times and had far-reaching consequences for Hindu practice. It militated against abortion, in that abortion could be regarded as thwarting the unfolding of the *karma* of both the unborn and the perpetrator(s) of the act. The unborn's *karma* matures through its prenatal and postnatal experiences, and abortion unnaturally terminates the possibility of this maturation. Abortion thus gravely affected the outworking of a person's destiny, the more so since it is generally believed that it was as a human being that one could act most effectively to achieve liberation from rebirth.[16]

An objection may be raised here. Why could not abortion be permissible as itself (unwittingly) predetermined by *karma*? The Hindus countered this objection by maintaining that the experience of free choice was not an illusion, that the law of *karma* did not abrogate the laws of *dharma*, of right living in accordance with freedom and responsibility. In other words, deliberate abortion as a free act violates *dharma* and, as such, is reprehensible. In Hindu tradition, the real distinction between "timely" and "untimely" death was recognised. If this distinction did not apply, if everything that happened (abortion included) could indiscriminately be put down to the predetermined unfolding of the *karmic* law, there would be no place for free, responsible action, and the law of *karma*, which is based on such action, would itself be subverted.

Caraka considers the issue raised by the objection and answers:

> If all life-spans were fixed (willy-nilly by the power of *karma*, abortion notwithstanding), then in search of good health none would employ efficacious remedies or verses, herbs . . . oblations . . . fastings . . . There would be no disturbed, ferocious, or ill-mannered cattle, elephants . . . and the like . . . no anxiety about falling from mountains or (into) rough, impassable waters; and none whose minds were negligent. . . . NO VIOLENT ACTS, NO ACTIONS OUT OF PLACE OR UNTIMELY (SUCH AS ABORTION). . . .
>
> For the occurrence of these and the like would not (freely) cause death if the term of all life were fixed and predetermined. Also, the fear of untimely death would not beset those creatures who did not practice the means for fending off fear of untimely death. Undertaking to employ the stories and thoughts of the great seers regarding the prolongation of life would be senseless. Even Indra could not (choose to) slay with his thunderbolt an enemy whose life span was fixed.[17]

Though a number of philosophical questions are begged in this passage, the point is that the decrees of *karma* and the freedoms of *dharma* were not regarded as incompatible in Hindu thought. Thus one could not justify abortion as the instrument of *karma* in the face of the clear condemnations of *dharma*.

THE EMBRYO: A SYMBOL OF LIFE

Again, the embryo in the womb was sacrosanct because it was a potent symbol of a dominant motif regulating the traditional Hindu view of life—that of birth, regeneration, new life, immortality. The theme of the primeval egg of creation from which the world of plurality emerges is a popular one in Hindu folklore. For example, we read in the *Mbh.:* "When all this (universe) was (originally) darkness, unillumined, covered on all sides by obscurity, the Great Egg arose, the sole imperishable seed of creatures. They say that at the beginning of an age this is the great, divine cause, and that on which (it rests) is revealed as the true Light, the eternal Brahman."[18] There are a number of variants of this image of the egg of creation in the scriptural texts.[19] The *Śatapatha Brāhmaṇa* informs us that in certain rituals the initiate was compared or associated with an embryo, no doubt because the latter was suggestive of new birth or life.[20] In the light of this symbolism, we can see why abortion was generally condemned in traditional Hinduism.

SOCIAL AND RELIGIOUS REASONS

A more practical reason for safeguarding the life of the embryo stemmed from the social and religious need to produce, especially male, offspring. Since Hindu society was, in the main, patriarchal, male progeny, in particular, were necessary not only to maintain social and economic stability (by a proper functioning of the caste system) but also for religious purposes (the performance of the priestly and domestic ritual, especially the *śrāddha* rite to ensure that deceased parents entered a satisfactory postmortem existence). Great store was laid by the birth of a son (or sons—there was security in numbers) for this latter purpose.

In fact, the need to produce offspring for these reasons determined to a large extent the attitude of traditional (male-dominated) Hindu society to women. Women fulfilled their role by being wives and mothers, i.e., child-bearers and child-rearers. The following quotations from the *MnS*, a seminal law text of our period, show the interplay of some of the ideas noted above: 1. "The husband, having entered his wife, is born here as an embryo, for that is the wifehood of the wife that he is born again of her"; 2. "As is he to whom a wife cleaves, so is the offspring. Therefore one should protect one's wife with care for the purity of one's progeny"; 3. "Women were made for child-bearing, men for continuing the line, hence public rites are enjoined in the Veda are to include the wife."[21]

A special point to note here is that the production of children was a public duty, rather than a purely individual expression of parental rights and choices. Indeed, one of the traditional debts the householder owed society was maintaining society's numbers by continuing the line in accordance with *dharma*. It would be unHindu, therefore, to regard procreation and concomitant issues (such as abortion) as a private concern of mother (or family) alone. One can understand how in this whole content then—that of the social, economic and religious issues—abortion, in general, was condemned.

AHIṂSĀ

Finally, we may mention the influence of the principle of *ahiṃsā* or non-injury in Hindu tradition as a factor militating against the performance of abortion. While it is true that in Hinduism, in general, this principle never enjoyed the unambivalent status it had in the Jaina and Buddhist traditions (the *Bhagavad-Gītā*, for instance, may be regarded as a defence of just war undertaken out of selfless duty), it still exerted a powerful influence on the Hindu mind with reference to particularly vulnerable forms of life, such as the embryo. Revitalised in contemporary times by the example of M. K. Gandhi, this principle traditionally applied to all living (especially breathing) beings. It had a twofold aspect: negative, that is, avoiding violence in thought and deed; and positive, being well-disposed towards, in thought and deed.

Since abortion entailed the inflicting of (mental and) physical violence to the point of death on the unborn person, it flew in the face of the ingrained

Hindu reverence for (the seed of) life. It ran counter to the Hindu genius to empathise and harmonise with natural forces and processes rather than to exploit and dominate them. This is a main feature of the rationale underlying *ahiṃsā*.

CONCLUSION

. . . We may conclude from our study then, that from earliest times, especially in the formative classical period described, both in canonical and collaborative orthodox Hindu literature, abortion (viz., deliberately caused miscarriage as opposed to involuntary miscarriage) at any stage of pregnancy, has been morally condemned as violating the personal integrity of the unborn, save when it was a question of preserving the mother's life. No other consideration, social or otherwise, seems to have been allowed to override this viewpoint.

After outlining the traditional Hindu model of human personhood, we analysed the reasons for this stance on abortion and the moral status of the unborn. Irrespective of the moment of ensoulment in the womb, no distinction seems to have been made or enforced in the literature analogous to the human being/human person distinction in some western discussions with its bearing on the permissibility of (at least early) abortion. In other words, *de facto,* Hindu tradition has always accorded personal moral status to the embryo/foetus throughout pregnancy. Other reasons converge in shaping the accredited view: advanced conscious experience in the developed foetus; the absence of linguistic evidence endorsing the abortability of the embryo at one point in pregnancy rather than at another; the implications of the law of *karma* and rebirth; the dominant influence of the egg/seed motif as suggestive of new life; the need to preserve caste, line, and race, not to mention family; the importance of ensuring a good postmortem existence for deceased parents by the performance of the *śrāddha* rite; and the reverence for the principle of *ahiṃsā*.

Note that these are not only rational reasons— social, religious, and cultural factors, in general, have played a large part in shaping the traditional Hindu attitude to the unborn. And so it must be in the formation of a genuinely human response. The point is that the classical attitude has grown in a distinctive cultural context and that the modern response to the issue under consideration will also grow out of that context, as well as be determined by the contemporary Indian context. One cannot argue simplistically, as some moralists would have it, that only timeless rational (as opposed to more widely cultural) factors should be brought to bear in this matter. In any case, what counts for the cogency of purely rational reasons/arguments for any people group is often itself culturally determined. The Hindu attitude to abortion and the unborn is the result of a rich cultural matrix. It will continue to be so determined in the present and the future and only as such can contribute distinctively to the discussion on the topic in the world at large. In this respect, the traditional Hindu stress on the wider social and moral obligations attaching to pregnancy (not excluding those to the child-to-be and the father), rather than the making of pregnancy a matter exclusively of individual rights (especially of the mother), must be noted.[22]

Modern India, a secular democracy, permits abortion by law, under certain circumstances. No doubt this is a law availed of by some. Yet it is true to say that the issues relating to the moral status of the unborn and abortion have neither been aired nor even properly identified, in general, in Indian minds and literature. In public, the topic is by and large taboo. Illegal abortionists in the back street or the bush continue to ply their trade, often with dire consequences for their customers. To check exploitation of one kind or another in this matter, the issue must be thrown open.

In this chapter I have not sought to evaluate or to argue for or against any side. Rather, I have provided but a preliminary (and incomplete) historical and analytical study. Others are invited to continue the task.

NOTES

1. The *Caraka Saṃhitā* is said to contain the substance of a comprehensive medical teaching given by the god Indra to a group of seers. One of these, Âtreya Punarvasu,

committed the teaching to six disciples, of whom one again, Agniveśa, composed a treatise of the teaching. Caraka, finally, figures as the àuthoritative redactor of Agniveśa's text. His work, the *Caraka Saṃhitā*, which is said to have been unfinished, was apparently later revised and completed by another savant, Dṛḍhabala. The text itself proceeds, for the most part, by way of a discourse between Ātreya Punarvasu, Agniveśa, and others. Though the received Caraka-Dṛḍhabala version is usually dated between 200–500 C.E., there seems to be no doubt that it represents a medical tradition whose roots dig far deeper into the past. There is much scholarly dispute concerning the roles Caraka-Dṛḍhabala, and perhaps others have played in constructing the received *Saṃhitā*, but for our purposes this debate is irrelevant. Suffice it to say that the *Caraka Saṃhitā* embodies the standard Hindu outlook of the classical period on the conception, nature, and development of the human foetus. For a resume and a bibliography of the origin and composition of the *Caraka Saṃhitā*, see M. C. Weiss's contribution, "Caraka Saṃhitā on the Doctrine of Karma," in *Karma and Rebirth in Classical Indian Traditions*, ed. W. D. O'Flaherty, Berkeley: University of California Press, 1980, pp. 93–4.

2. *niṣkriyaṃ ca svatantraṃ ca vaśinaṃ sarvagaṃ vibhuṃ, vadanty ātmānam āimajñāḥ kṣetrajñaṃ sākṣiṇaṃ tathā.* Pandeya, *Caraka Saṃhitā*, ch. 1, *sū*, 5, p. 690.

3. *garbhātmā hy antarātmā . . . tam . . . ācakṣate śāśvatam arujam ajaram amaram akṣayam abhedyam acchedyam alodyam viśvarūpam viśvakarmānam avyaktam anādim anidhanam akṣaram api.* Pandeya, *Caraka Saṃhitā*, ch. 3, su 8, p. 743.

4. *tatra śarîram nāma cetanādhiṣṭhānabhūtaṃ pañcamihābhūtacikārasamudāyaimakam sámayogavāhi.* Pandeya, *Caraka Saṃhitā* ch. 6, sū. 4, p. 787. "The five elementals" are the fundamental forms of earth, water, fire, air, and ether constitutive of *prakṛti* or the material principle which unfolds from its subtle, unmanifest state into the material world as we experience it.

5. *puruṣasyānupahataretasaḥ striyāś cāpraduṣṭayoniśonitagarbhāśayāyā yadā bhavati saṃsargaḥ rtukāle, yadā cānayos tathāyukte saṃsarge śukraśonitasaṃsargam antargarbhāśayagataṃ jîvo'vakrāmati sattvasaṃprayogāt tadāgarbho'bhiairvartate.* Pandeya, *Caraka Saṃhitā* ch. 3, sū. 3, p. 737. "in due season": in the law texts, intercourse was permitted from the third/fourth day after the appearance of the menses till the sixteenth day. "The union of semen and (menstrual) blood": it was believed that the procreative factor from the woman's side was the menstrual blood. For a discussion of the symbolism/interplay of procreative terms and elements in traditional Hinduism, see W. D. O'Flaherty, "Sexual Fluids," in *Women, Androgynes, and Other Mythical Beasts*, Chicago: Univ. of Chicago Press, 1980, ch. 2.

6. *rtukāle prayogād ekarātroṣitaṃ kaliaṃ (kalalam?) bhavati, saptarātroṣitaṃ budbudaṃ bhavaty, ardhamdsābhyantareṇa piṇḍo bhavati, māsābhyantareṇa kaṭhino bhavati, māsadvayena śiraḥ kurute, māsatrayeṇa pā dapradeśo bhavaty, atha caturthe māse'ṅgulyajatharakaṭipradeśo bhavanti, pañcame māse pṛṣṭhavaṃśo bhavati, ṣaṣṭhe māse nāsākṣiṇiśrotrāṇi bhavanti, saptame māse jîvena saṃyukto bhavaty, aṣṭame māse sarvasaṃpûṭno bhavati.* See, "The Garbha Upaniṣad" in the

Ānandāśrama Sanskrit Series, vol. 29, 1895, p. 161. "(the foetus) is joined to the soul": thus, *jîvena saṃyukto* bhavati. But the commentator, Nārāyaṇa, glosses this as: *Jîvaliṅgena (saṃyukto. . .)*, i.e., is joined TO THE MARK of the soul—which is consciousness. If this interpretation is correct, then the implication is that CONSCIOUSNESS, not ensoulment, occurs in the seventh month. Ensoulment may well have taken place at conception. In this event, the minor tradition collapses into the major.

7. Quoted from Minoru Hara, "A Note on the Buddha's Birth Story," in *Indianisme et Bouddhisme* (Mélanges offerts à Mgr. Étienne Lamotte), Louvain-la-Neuve: Publications de l'institute Orientaliste de Louvain, 23, 1980, pp. 148–9. Hara gives another quotation, to similar effect, from the *Garuḍa Purāṇa*, p. 151.

8. *atha . . . sarvalakṣaṇasaṃpûrṇo bhavati pūrvajātîḥ smarati. kṛtākrtam ca karma bhavati śubhāśubham ca karma vindati. nānāyonisahesrāni dṛṣṭvā caiva tato mayā āhārā vividhā bhuktāḥ pītāś ca vividhāḥ stanāḥ. jātasyaiva mrtasyaioa janme caiva punaḥ punaḥ, aho duhkhodahau mango no paśyāmi pratikriyām. yan mayā parijanasyārthe krtam karma śubhāśubham ekākī tena dahyāmi gatās te phalabhoginsh. yadi yonyāṃ pramuñcāmi sāmkhyam yogam samabhyaset, aśubhakṣayakartāram phalamuktipradāyinom. yadi yonyāṃ pramiñcāmi taṃ prapadye maheśvaram, aśubhak-ṣayakartāraṃ phalamuktipradāyinom.* Garbha Upaniṣad: Ānandāśrama, pp. 162–3. The foetus' rueing of rebirth and of the deeds perpetuating it, as also the resolution to take steps to avoid the process, is a recurrent theme in popular Sanskrit literature. See Hara for more examples.

9. See Hara, "Buddha's Birth Story," esp. pp. 149f.

10. *tatra prathama māst kalaiaṃ jāyate; dvitīye . . . (abhiprapacyamānānāṃ mahābhūtānāṃ) saṃghāto ghanaḥ saṃjāyate. yadi piṇḍaḥ pumān, stri cet peśî . . . trī ye hastapādaśirasāṃ pañcapiṇḍakā nirvartante'ṅgapratyaṅgavibhāgaś ca sūkṣmo bhavati. caturthe sarvā-ṅgapratyangavibhāgaḥ pravyakto bhavati, garbhahrdayapravyaktibhāvāc cetanādhātur abhivyakto bhavati . . . garbhaś caturthe māsy abhiprāyam indriyārtheṣu karoti . . . (sū. 18). pañcame manaṃ pratibuddhataram bhavati, ṣaṣṭhe buddhiḥ. saptame sarvāṅgapratyangaoibhāgaḥ pravyaktctarab, aṣṭame 'sthiri bhavaty ojaḥ . . . navamadasamaikādaśadvādaśānām anyatam asmin jā yate, ato'nyathā vikārîbhavati.* sū. 30; Atrideva: *Suśrutasamhita, Sārîrasthâna*, ch. 3, pp. 299 & 301, "in relation to the appearance of the foetus' heart": it was believed that the heart was the bodily abode of consciousness. The *Caraka Saṃhitā* does not differ substantially in its description of embryonic development. Hara, "Buddha's Birth Story," p. 154, ft. nt. 49, points out that in the *Purā nas* it was generally held that foetal consciousness appeared from the seventh to the ninth month and notes (p. 157, ft nt. 71) that the first reference "in Sanskrit literature to prenatal experience and memory of previous births is found in Rig Veda 4.27.1 (Vāmadeva), and *Aitareya Upaniṣad* 4.6." There is some doubt concerning the interpretation of the *Rg Vedic* reference as bearing on the memory of previous births.

11. Note the frequency in the Sanskrit (see note 10) of terms intimating a transition from an unmanifest to a manifest state: *sūkṣma, pravyakta, abhivyakta.* Also,

there is nothing in this extract of the so-called preformation theory—influential in the West in the 17th century—according to which the fertilised egg was an homunculus, or miniature human, complete with tiny arms, legs, head, and so one who simply grew in size as pregnancy progressed.

12. " 'All the limbs and sections of the body grow simultaneously' says Dhanvantari (Suśruta's reputed teacher)": *sarvāny aṅgapratyaṅgāni yugapat sambhavantīty āha dhanvantarth.* Atrideva: *Suśruta Samhitā, sū.* 32, p. 302. The *Caraka Samhitā* has it that "the senses, limbs and members (of the embryo) develop simultaneously": *evam asyendriyāny aṅgāvayavāś ca yaugapadyenābhinirvartante. Śarīrasthāsa,* ch. 4, sū. 14, p. 762.

13. "There (in the fertilised egg) the conscious principle with the coordinating sense as its instrument, is *already* working towards the realisation of the (various) qualities (of the individual)": *tatra pūrvam cetanādhātuh sattvakarano gunagrahanāya pravartate. . . . Śarīrasthā na,* ch. 4, sū. 8, p. 759.

14. But note our comment on Nārāyana's gloss in note 57.

15. Hara, "Buddha's Birth Story," p. 154, gives a standard list, apparently mainly of Buddhist origin.

16. In theory, the different versions of the rebirth belief allowed for a person's rebirth, on the one hand, in animal and plant form, on the other, as celestials or gods (*devas*). In practice, however, the various texts, including the theological treatises of thinkers like Śaṃkara, Rāmānuja, and Madhva, are preoccupied with the nature, ethics, and destiny of the human person and imply that a qualitative distinction exists between human and (at least) animal and vegetative life. A corollary of this implication, usually taken for granted and not given due philosophical analysis, is that it is in its human form that the soul can most effectively seek liberation.

17. Quotation taken from M. G. Weiss, "Caraka Samhitā on Karma," p. 95, (see note 1). Emphasis and words in brackets have been added.

18. *nisprabhe'smin nirāloke sarvatas tamasāvrte, brhad andam abhūd ekam pra jānām bījam aksayam. yugasyā-dau nimittam tan mahad dīvyam prukṣute, yasminw tac chrūyate satyam jyotir brehma sanātanam. Mbh.* I.1.27–8.

19. See, e.g., *Śatapatha Brāhmana* XI.1.6, 1–2; VI.1.2.,1–2; *Maitri* Up., vi. 8; *MnS* I. 8f.

20. E.g., *Śatapatha Brāhmana* III.1.3.28, where the sacrificial fire becomes the womb (*yoni*) of the sacrifice, and the initiate (*dikṣita*) the embryo (*garbha*); pp. 203–4, Pt. I.

21. 1. *patir bhāryām sampraviśya garbho bhātveha jāyate. jāyāyās tad dhi jāyātvam yad asya jāyate punah. MnS* IX.8, p. 287. Here reference is being made to the "rebirth" of the husband in his progeny. 2. *yādriśam, bhajats hi strī sutam sūle tathāvidham, tasmāt prajā viśuddhyartham striyam rakset prayatnatah. MnS* IX.9, p. 287. 3. *prajanārtham striyah strṣjāh santanārtham ca mānavāh, tastmāt sādhārano dharmah śrutau patnyā sahoditah. MnS* IX.96, p. 298.

22. In this context, Ms. Das writes: ". . . we have been tricked by modern philosophers into thinking that the morality of abortion involves strictly the relation of a WOMAN to the foetus. In fact this dyadic relationship is embedded into a number of relationships involving not only the responsibility of a genitor to the embryo/foetus, but also the relationship of adult men and women. Further, this arrangement of relationships involves the rest of society. Without a discussion of the responsibility of society (either through the State or other agencies) towards the embryo, the foetus, and the infant as also towards those who are charged with caring for them, a discussion on the morality of abortion if incomplete." "Debate on Abortion," p. 34.

STUDY QUESTIONS: ABORTION

1. John T. Noonan argues that a fetus possesses the right to life at the moment of conception because it is when it receives the full human genetic code and the potentiality for developing into a full-fledged human being. What problems do you see in his argument?

2. Mary Anne Warren argues that there are five features central to the concept of human personhood. What are these features, and what do you think are the most important? Do you think that one must achieve personhood as she defines it to have rights? Do you think her example of "the space explorer" is a good one for defending her claim that the rights of an actual person are more important than the right of a potential person?

3. Don Marquis attempts to place himself between two opposing positions with regard to abortion. What are these positions? What problems does he think these positions have? Outline his alternative position. How does Peter McInerney object to Marquis? What other objections can be brought against Marquis?

4. How does Nie argue that coercive abortion can be morally justified? Do you think that the Western debate on abortion fails to take into account larger social and economic contexts?

5. What does William LaFleur think the *mizuko kuyō* ritual accomplishes for the Japanese women who undergo abortions? How is the "necessary sorrow" of abortion connected in the Japanese concern for "family values"? How does this attitude affect the way we view the abortion controversy in the West?

6. What is the Hindu view of the moral standing of the unborn fetus, according to Julius Lipner? Is it any different from the way the West approaches the issue? How does the idea of *karma* influence the morality of abortion from the Hindu point of view?

SUPPLEMENTARY READINGS: ABORTION

ARMSTRONG, ROBERT L. "The Right to Life." *Journal of Social Philosophy*, vol. 8(1), January 1977.

BADGER, W. DOUGLAS. "Abortion: The Judeo-Christian Imperative." In *Whose Values? The Battle for Morality in Pluralistic America*, Horn, editor. Ann Arbor, MI: Servant Books, 1985.

BAYLES, MICHAEL D. "Genetic Choice." In *Ethical Issues in the New Reproductive Technologies*, Hull, editor. Belmont, CA: Wadsworth, 1990.

BOLTON, MARTHA BRANDT. "Responsible Women and Abortion Decisions." In *Having Children*, O'Neill and Ruddick, editors. New York: Oxford University Press, 1979.

HURSTHOUSE, ROSALIND. "Virtue Theory and Abortion." *Philosophy and Public Affairs*, vol. 20(3), Summer, 1991.

KARKAL, MALINI. "Abortion Laws and the Abortion Situation in India." *Issues in Reproductive and Genetic Engineering*, vol. 4(1), 1991.

KELLY, JAMES R. "Learning and Teaching Consistency: Catholics and the Right-to-Life Movement." In *Catholic Church and the Politics of Abortion: A View from the States*, Byrnes and Segers, editors. Boulder, CO: Westview Press, 1992.

KEOWN, DAMIEN, ed. *Buddhism and Abortion*. Honolulu: University of Hawaii Press, 1999.

KOERNER, UWE, and HANNELORE KOERNER. "Ethics in Reproductive Medicine in the German Democratic Republic." *The Journal of Medicine and Philosophy*, vol. 14(3), June 1989.

MACKENZIE, CATRIONA. "Abortion and Embodiment." *Australian Journal of Philosophy*, vol. 70 (2), June 1992.

MARKOWITZ, SALLY. "Abortion and Feminism." *Social Theory and Practice*, Spring 1990.

McCORMICK, RICHARD A., S. J. "Blastomene Separation: Some Concerns." Hastings Center Report, vol. 24(2), 1994.

MENKITI, IFANYI A. "Person and Community in African Traditional Thought." In *African Philosophy: An Introduction*, third edition, Wright, editor. Lanham, MD: University Press of America, 1984.

MURRAY, THOMAS H. "Moral Obligations to the Not-Yet Born: The Fetus as Patient." In *Ethical Issues in the New Reproductive Technologies*, Hull, editor. Belmont, CA: Wadsworth, 1990.

NOONAN, JOHN. "Responding to Persons: Methods of Moral Argument in the Debate over Abortion." *Theology Digest*, 1973.

PAPP, ZOLTAN. "Genetic Counseling and Termination of Pregnancy in Hungary." *Journal of Medicine and Philosophy*, vol. 14(3), June 1989.

ROBERTSON, JOHN A. "The Question of Human Cloning." *Hastings Center Report*, vol. 24(2), 1994.

SISTARE, CHRISTINE. "Reproductive Freedom and Women's Freedom: Surrogacy and Autonomy." *Philosophical Forum*, vol. 19(4), 1987.

STEINBOCK, BONNIE. *Life Before Birth: The Moral and Legal Status of Embryos and Fetuses* (New York: Oxford University Press, 1992).

SUMNER, L. WAYNE. "The Morality of Abortion." *Abortion and Moral Theory*, Princeton, NJ: Princeton University Press, 1981.

SUTHERLAND, GAIL HINICH. "Abortion and Woman's 'Nature': The Idiom of Choice." *Soundings*, vol. 76(4), Winter, 1993.

THOMSON, JUDITH JARVIS. "A Defense of Abortion." *Philosophy and Public Affairs*, vol. 1(1), Fall 1971.

TWORKOV, HELEN. "Anti-abortion/Pro-choice." *Tricycle: The Buddhist Review*, vol. 1(3), Spring 1992.

Part IX

EUTHANASIA, SUSTAINING AND CREATING LIFE

Should his Demand to die be respected? . . . Another question occurred to me as I watched this blind, maimed, and totally helpless man defy and baffle everyone: could his adamant stand be the only way available for him to regain his independence after such a prolonged period of helplessness and total dependence? Consequently I decided to assist him . . .

—ROBERT B. WHITE, M.D.[1]

The American population has been growing older with each passing decade. In fact, that is the demographic trend with many industrialized nations in the world. People do not die of rapidly deteriorating conditions caused by highly infectious diseases such as tuberculosis or malaria as frequently as they did in the past. Instead, increasingly people are dying of degenerative illnesses such as cancer and Alzheimer's. With the advance of medical technology, more and more people who would not otherwise have survived a few decades ago are able to live and even lead a fulfilling life. While such biomedical advances are certainly a blessing for many, the fact that a person can be kept alive for a long time by respirators, heart pumps and pacers, radiation therapy, dialysis machines, and so on could undermine the quality of lives people live, since they have to struggle with progressively debilitating, undignified, and even painful physical conditions. Some may choose to brave such conditions with all their might, but others believe that this is not the kind of life they would envision themselves enduring until their inevitable destiny. Do people have a right to terminate their own lives or request the medical professionals to help end their lives before the illness runs its course? Is withholding life-sustaining treatment from a terminally ill patient the same as giving a lethal injection? What are the potential risks involved in legalizing the right to die in general or the right to physician-assisted suicide in particular? These are some of the key questions we explore in the large portion of this section.

Euthanasia literally means "good death." The term is often equated with mercy killing. There are two types of euthanasia: active and passive. Active euthanasia refers to the practice of directly bringing about a person's death, according to or against that person's wishes. A person who wishes to die may request that a lethal injection be administered, and such an injection would constitute active euthanasia. Passive euthanasia is the practice of doing nothing to prevent death from occurring. If someone is suffering greatly and wants to die, a decision may be made not to treat the person's current pneumonia, for example, thereby allowing the person to die naturally, or to remove someone from life support systems. Some argue that this is a way of directly causing a person's death, while others argue that it is a way of merely allowing a person to die naturally.

In many, but not all societies, active euthanasia is condemned. We will examine the practices and their justification in a number of societies in hopes of understanding the complexities of the morality of euthanasia. We will also examine how decisions are made about whom to save when not all can be saved. In both of these topics we will be forced to confront the possible limits of the right to life, as well as the justification of certain medical practices, such as physician-assisted suicide, that are currently some of the most controversial in Western society and in many other societies.

We begin with a very influential essay written by James Rachels, who argues that the distinction between active and passive euthanasia is not a morally relevant one. He points out that one can directly bring about a person's death with the best of intentions, and one can let someone die with the worst of intentions. Intentions make a moral difference, but whether the death is actively or passively brought about does not. Using two hypothetical cases, Rachels contends that those who argue that there is a difference between killing someone and letting her die are making a conceptual mistake.

In response to Rachels, Bonnie Steinbock contends that there are at least two kinds of circumstances in which the termination of life-sustaining treatment cannot be equated with intentionally letting die. The first has to do with a physician's respecting a patient's rights to decline treatment and to be free from unjustified intervention. The second has to do with the ending of extraordinary means of care deemed to be of little benefit to the patient. In neither of these situations, Steinbock further points out, can the doctor's act of ceasing life-prolonging treatment be construed as one involving intentionally bringing about the death of the patient, for the reason that one can do something knowing what its results will be while having no intention of producing those results.

In an *amici curiae* filed to the U.S. Supreme Court, six moral and political philosophers argue under the Due Process Clause and previous Court decisions for a constitutionally protected right to choose the time and the manner of one's own death in a way consistent with one's moral, philosophical or religious conviction. The philosophers believe that death, like marriage and procreation,

is something most personal and intimate and that this liberty to choose to die and, in particular, the liberty-right to physician-assisted suicide should be protected. Moreover, insofar as proper precautions are implemented, states should not prohibit the right of a terminally ill patient to a willing physician to assist him or her in ending his or her life.

Instead of debating whether individual acts of euthanasia are morally acceptable, Stephen Potts looks at the probable consequences of legalizing euthanasia as a general practice. Potts argues that proponents of voluntary active euthanasia have underestimated the enormous risks involved in the institutionalization of such a practice. He points out, among other things, that social acceptance of voluntary active euthanasia could bring about a slippery slope that goes from curing the patient to eliminating individuals deemed weak or undesirable. He ends by warning that a patient might believe that he or she has a duty to die and that the doctor has a duty to kill once the right to die is extended from a right to refuse life-prolonging treatment to a right to be killed.

Margaret Battin provides a comparative analysis of end-of-life practices in three countries: the Netherlands, Germany, and the United States. Physician-performed euthanasia and physician-assisted suicide are legally permissible in the Netherlands while (self-directed) suicide is the only form of euthanasia legally available in Germany. The only form of dying practice allowed in the United States is withdrawal of life-sustaining treatment, with the exception of Oregon (and more recently, Washington), where physician-assisted suicide is allowed. Battin points out that there is not one single form of dying practice that is best for all societies. Given different cultural climates, economic conditions, and physician-patient relationships, what we need to ask is which form of practice is best for which society.

Approaching from a feminist standpoint, Susan Wolf writes that the debate on physician-assisted suicide and euthanasia has overlooked the effects of gender differences. She argues that neither the rights-based perspective nor the ethics-of-care approach that has been used as a moral argument for the legalization of physician-assisted suicide and euthanasia is adequate. The rights-based approach is wrongheaded because with its exclusive focus on the individual's autonomy or self-determination it ignores the social and economic contexts and the personal history of the patient. The ethics-of-care perspective is problematic in that by emphasizing the physician's obligation to relieve suffering it destroys the very patient who is suffering in the process. Instead she argues that the correct approach must be sensitive to both moral domains.

In contrast with the Western understanding of dying with dignity as ending a life ravaged by biological degradation, Ping-Cheung Lo introduces a Confucian perspective that judges indignity not simply on the basis of biological degradation but more importantly on moral disgrace and dishonor. On that understanding, most self-regarding suicides would be morally objectionable. Instead, according to Lo, teminating one's own life should be done mostly for the sake of others and in conformity with the Confucian ideals of benevolence and justice. Lo's article casts a different light on the meaning of "dying with dignity" from what is currently understood.

Carl Becker enters the debate from a Buddhist perspective. Unlike contemporary Westerners, Buddhists do not regard death as an evil or even as something to be avoided. Indeed, the Buddha is said to have praised certain persons who committed suicide. For Buddhists, what is most important is that a person be mentally and physically prepared to die. Once this has occurred, then the only morally relevant question concerns how this person can best die with dignity. To keep someone alive who is prepared to die and wants to die is generally considered inhumane in Japan, where Buddhism is very strong.

We conclude this section—and this anthology—by examining an ethical issue relating to the beginning of life—human cloning. Speaking of human cloning, one may have a gut revulsion against it. Leon Kass begins his essay with this common response. He believes that as with incest or necrophilia, human cloning falls into the ambit of practices that we find repulsive without being able to give a full rational justification. In addition, on Kass's view, those who argue for the cloning of human beings on the basis of an extension of our existing assisted reproduction, reproductive freedom, or enhancement of human traits overlook the importance of ourselves as essentially embodied and gendered, and the social relationships that depend on our natural kinship. He concludes that not only reproductive cloning but also the cloning of human embryos even for research purposes should be banned.

—KAI WONG

NOTE

1. Robert B. White, M.D., "A Demand To Die," *Hastings Center Report*, June 1975.

Active and Passive Euthanasia

James Rachels

James Rachels was a professor of philosophy at the University of Alabama at Birmingham. He was the author of *Created from Animals: The Moral Implications of Darwinism* (1990), *The Elements of Moral Philosophy* (1986), *The End of Life: Euthanasia and Morality* (1986), and the editor of *The Right Thing To Do* (1989).

In this essay, Rachels considers the distinction between active and passive euthanasia as an example of the distinction between killing and letting die. Rachels argues that there is no morally relevant difference between actively killing someone and passively letting a person die. He argues that if this is true, then policies of the American Medical Association and other institutions that rely on the distinction need to be changed. What is important morally are the motivations or consequences of actively or passively killing, and only after these factors have been evaluated in each case can it be said that euthanasia is morally justifiable.

The distinction between active and passive euthanasia is thought to be crucial for medical ethics. The idea is that it is permissible, at least in some cases, to withhold treatment and allow a patient to die, but it is never permissible to take any direct action designed to kill the patient. This doctrine seems to be accepted by most doctors, and it is endorsed in a statement adopted by the House of Delegates of the American Medical Association on 4 December 1973:

> The intentional termination of the life of one human being by another—mercy killing—is contrary to that for which the medical profession stands and is contrary to the policy of the American Medical Association.
>
> The cessation of the employment of extraordinary means to prolong the life of the body when there is irrefutable evidence that biological death is

imminent is the decision of the patient and/or his immediate family. The advice and judgment of the physician should be freely available to the patient and/or his immediate family.

However, a strong case can be made against this doctrine. In what follows, I will set out some of the relevant arguments, and urge doctors to reconsider their views on this matter.

To begin with a familiar type of situation, a patient who is dying of incurable cancer of the throat is in terrible pain, which can no longer be satisfactorily alleviated. He is certain to die within a few days, even if present treatment is continued, but he does not want to go on living for those days since the pain is unbearable. So he asks the doctor for an end to it, and his family joins in the request.

Suppose the doctor agrees to withhold treatment, as the conventional doctrine says he may. The justification for his doing so is that the patient is in terrible agony, and since he is going to die anyway, it would be wrong to prolong his suffering needlessly. But now notice this—If one simply withholds treatment, it may take the patient longer to die, and so he may suffer more than he would if more direct action were taken and a lethal injection given. This fact provides strong reason for thinking that, once the initial decision not to prolong his agony has been made, active euthanasia is actually preferable to passive euthanasia, rather than the reverse. To say otherwise is to endorse the option that leads to more suffering rather than less, and is contrary to the humanitarian impulse that prompts the decision not to prolong his life in the first place.

Part of my point is that the process of being "allowed to die" can be relatively slow and painful, whereas being given a lethal injection is relatively quick and painless. Let me give a different sort of example. In the United States about one in 600 babies is born with Down's syndrome. Most of these babies are otherwise healthy—that is, with only the usual pediatric care, they will proceed to an otherwise normal infancy. Some, however, are born with congenital defects such as intestinal obstructions that require operations if they are to live. Sometimes, the parents and the doctor will decide not to operate, and let the infant die. Anthony Shaw describes what happens then:

> When surgery is denied [the doctor] must try to keep the infant from suffering while natural forces sap the baby's life away. As a surgeon whose natural inclination is to use the scalpel to fight off death, standing by and watching a salvageable baby die is the most emotionally exhausting experience I know. It is easy at a conference, in a theoretical discussion, to decide that such infants should be allowed to die. It is altogether different to stand by in the nursery and watch as dehydration and infection wither a tiny being over hours and days. This is a terrible ordeal for me and the hospital staff—much more so than for the parents who never set foot in the nursery.[1]

I can understand why some people are opposed to all euthanasia, and insist that such infants must be allowed to live. I think I can also understand why other people favor destroying these babies quickly and painlessly. But why should anyone favor letting "dehydration and infection wither a tiny being over hours and days"? The doctrine that says a baby may be allowed to dehydrate and wither, but may not be

given an injection that would end its life without suffering, seems so patently cruel as to require no further refutation. The strong language is not intended to offend, but only to put the point in the clearest possible way.

My second argument is that the conventional doctrine leads to decisions concerning life and death made on irrelevant grounds.

Consider again the case of the infants with Down's syndrome who need operations for congenital defects unrelated to the syndrome to live. Sometimes, there is no operation, and the baby dies, but when there is no such defect, the baby lives on. Now an operation such as that to remove an intestinal obstruction is not prohibitively difficult. The reason why such operations are not performed in these cases is, clearly, that the child has Down's syndrome and the parents and the doctor judge that because of that fact it is better for the child to die.

But notice that this situation is absurd, no matter what view one takes of the lives and potentials of such babies. If the life of such an infant is worth preserving what does it matter if it needs a simple operation? Or, if one thinks it better that such a baby should not live on, what difference does it make that it happens to have an unobstructed intestinal tract? In either case, the matter of life and death is being decided on irrelevant grounds. It is the Down's syndrome, and not the intestines, that is the issue. The matter should be decided, if at all, on that basis, and not be allowed to depend on the essentially irrelevant question of whether the intestinal tract is blocked.

What makes this situation possible, of course, is the idea that when there is an intestinal blockage, one can "let the baby die," but when there is no such defect there is nothing that can be done, for one must not "kill" it. The fact that this idea leads to such results as deciding life or death on irrelevant grounds is another good reason why the doctrine would be rejected.

One reason why so many people think that there is an important moral difference between active and passive euthanasia is that they think killing someone is morally worse than letting someone die. But is it? Is killing, in itself, worse than letting die? To investigate this issue, two cases may be considered that are exactly alike except that one involves killing whereas the other involves letting someone die. Then, it can be asked whether this difference makes any difference to the moral assessments. It is important that the cases be exactly alike, except for this one difference, since otherwise one cannot be confident that it is this difference and not some other that accounts for any variation in the assessments of the two cases. So, let us consider this pair of cases.

In the first, Smith stands to gain a large inheritance if anything should happen to his six-year-old cousin. One evening while the child is taking his bath, Smith sneaks into the bathroom and drowns the child, and then arranges things so that it will look like an accident.

In the second, Jones also stands to gain if anything should happen to his six-year-old cousin. Like Smith, Jones sneaks in, planning to drown the child in his bath. However, just as he enters the bathroom Jones sees the child slip and hit his head, and fall face down in the water. Jones is delighted; he stands by, ready to push the child's head back under if it is necessary, but it is not necessary. With only a little thrashing about, the child drowns all by himself, "accidentally," as Jones watches and does nothing.

Now Smith killed the child, whereas Jones "merely" let the child die. That is the only difference between them. Did either man behave better, from a moral point of view? If the difference between killing and letting die were in itself a morally important matter, one should say that Jones's behavior was less reprehensible than Smith's. But does one really want to say that? I think not. In the first place, both men acted from the same motive, personal gain, and both had exactly the same end in view when they acted. It may be inferred from Smith's conduct that he is a bad man, although that judgment may be withdrawn or modified if certain further facts are learned about him—for example, that he is mentally deranged. But would not the very same thing be inferred about Jones from his conduct? And would not the same further considerations also be

relevant to any modification of this judgment? Moreover, suppose Jones pleaded, in his own defense, "After all, I didn't do anything except just stand there and watch the child drown. I didn't kill him; I only let him die." Again, if letting die were in itself less bad than killing, this defense should have at least some weight. But it does not. Such a "defense" can only be regarded as a grotesque perversion of moral reasoning. Morally speaking, it is no defense at all.

Now, it may be pointed out, quite properly, that the cases of euthanasia with which doctors are concerned are not like this at all. They do not involve personal gain or the destruction of normal healthy children. Doctors are concerned only with cases in which the patient's life is of no further use to him, or in which the patient's life has become or will soon become a terrible burden. However, the point is the same in these cases: The bare difference between killing and letting die does not, in itself, make a moral difference. If a doctor lets a patient die, for humane reasons, he is in the same moral position as if he had given the patient a lethal injection for humane reasons. If his decision was wrong—if, for example, the patient's illness was in fact curable—the decision would be equally regrettable no matter which method was used to carry it out. And if the doctor's decision was the right one, the method used is not in itself important.

The AMA policy statement isolates the crucial issue very well; the crucial issue is "the intentional termination of the life of one human being by another." But after identifying this issue, and forbidding "mercy killing," the statement goes on to deny that the cessation of treatment is the intentional termination of a life. This is where the mistake comes in, for what is the cessation of treatment, in these circumstances, if it is not "the intentional termination of the life of one human being by another"? Of course it is exactly that, and if it were not, there would be no point to it.

Many people will find this judgment hard to accept. One reason, I think, is that it is very easy to conflate the question of whether killing is, in itself, worse than letting die, with the very different question of whether most actual cases of killing are more reprehensible than most actual cases of letting die. Most actual cases of killing are clearly terrible (think, for example, of all the murders reported in the newspapers), and one hears of such cases every day. On the other hand, one hardly ever hears of a case of letting die, except for the actions of doctors who are motivated by humanitarian reasons. So one learns to think of killing in a much worse light than of letting die. But this does not mean that there is something about killing that makes it in itself worse than letting die, for it is not the bare difference between killing and letting die that makes the difference in these cases. Rather, the other factors—the murderer's motive of personal gain, for example, contrasted with the doctor's humanitarian motivation—account for different reactions to the different cases.

I have argued that killing is not in itself worse than letting die; if my contention is right, it follows that active euthanasia is not any worse than passive euthanasia. What arguments can be given on the other side? The most common, I believe, is the following:

> The important difference between active and passive euthanasia is that, in passive euthanasia, the doctor does not do anything to bring about the patient's death. The doctor does nothing, and the patient dies of whatever ills already afflict him. In active euthanasia, however, the doctor does something to bring about the patient's death: he kills him. The doctor who gives the patient with cancer a lethal injection has himself caused his patient's death; whereas if he merely ceases treatment, the cancer is the cause of death.

A number of points need to be made here. The first is that it is not exactly correct to say that in passive euthanasia the doctor does nothing, for he does do one thing that is very important: He lets the patient die. "Letting someone die" is certainly different, in some respects, from other types of action—mainly in that it is a kind of action that one may perform by way of not performing certain other actions. For example, one may let a patient die by way of not giving medication, just as one may insult someone by way of not shaking his hand. But for any purpose of moral assessment, it is a type of action nonetheless. The decision to let a patient die is subject to moral appraisal in the

same way that a decision to kill him would be subject to moral appraisal: It may be assessed as wise or unwise, compassionate or sadistic, right or wrong. If a doctor deliberately let a patient die who was suffering from a routinely curable illness, the doctor would certainly be to blame for what he had done, just as he would be to blame if he had needlessly killed the patient. Charges against him would then be appropriate. If so, it would be no defense at all for him to insist that he didn't "do anything." He would have done something very serious indeed, for he let his patient die.

Fixing the cause of death may be very important from a legal point of view, for it may determine whether criminal charges are brought against the doctor. But I do not think that this notion can be used to show a moral difference between active and passive euthanasia. The reason why it is considered bad to be the cause of someone's death is that death is regarded as a great evil—and so it is. However, if it has been decided that euthanasia—even passive euthanasia—is desirable in a given case, it has also been decided that in this instance death is no greater an evil than the patient's continued existence. And if this is true, the usual reason for not wanting to be the cause of someone's death simply does not apply.

Finally, doctors may think that all of this is only of academic interest—the sort of thing that philosophers may worry about but that has no practical bearing on their own work. After all, doctors must be concerned about the legal consequences of what they do, and active euthanasia is clearly forbidden by the law. But even so, doctors should also be concerned with the fact that the law is forcing upon them a moral doctrine that may be indefensible, and has a considerable effect on their practices. Of course, most doctors are not now in the position of being coerced in this matter, for they do not regard themselves as merely going along with what the law requires. Rather, in statements such as the AMA policy statement that I have quoted, they are endorsing this doctrine as a central point of medical ethics. In that statement, active euthanasia is condemned not merely as illegal but as "contrary to that for which the medical profession stands," whereas passive euthanasia is approved. However, the preceding considerations suggest that there is really no difference between the two, considered in themselves (there may be important moral differences in some cases in their *consequences*, but as I pointed out, these differences may make active euthanasia, and not passive euthanasia, the morally preferable option). So, whereas doctors may have to discriminate between active and passive euthanasia to satisfy the law, they should not do any more than that.

In particular, they should not give the distinction any added authority and weight by writing it into official statements of medical ethics.

NOTE

1. Shaw, Anthony, "Doctor, Do We Have a Choice?" *The New York Times Magazine*, 30 Jan., 1972, p. 54.

The Intentional Termination of Life

Bonnie Steinbock

Bonnie Steinbock is a professor of philosophy at the State University of New York, Albany. She has published articles on ethical issues relating to life and death. She is the author of *Life Before Birth: The Moral and Legal Status of Embryos and Fetuses* (1992) and the coeditor of *Public Health Ethics: Theory, Policy and Practice* (2006).

Steinbock argues that Rachels misconstrues the American Medical Association policy as endorsing a distinction between active and passive euthanasia by falsely identifying the termination of life-sustaining treatment with passive euthanasia. She claims that this identification cannot hold in situations where the patient chooses to refuse treatment and where the treatment is discontinued when it proves to be of no benefit to the patient. In closing, Steinbock points out that one needs to make a distinction between an act done intentionally and the unintended results brought about by the act.

According to James Rachels and Michael Tooley . . . a common mistake in medical ethics is the belief that there is a moral difference between active and passive euthanasia. This is a mistake, they argue, because the rationale underlying the distinction between active and passive euthanasia is the idea that there is a significant moral difference between intentionally killing and intentionally letting die. "The idea," Tooley says, "is admittedly very common. But I believe that it can be shown to reflect either confused thinking or a moral point of view unrelated to the interests of individuals." Whether or not the belief that there is a significant moral difference is mistaken is not my concern here. For it is far from clear that this distinction *is* the basis of the doctrine of the American Medical Association which Rachels attacks. And if the killing/letting die distinction is not the basis of the AMA doctrine, then arguments showing that the distinction has no moral force do not, in themselves, reveal in the doctrine's adherents either "confused thinking" or "a moral point of view unrelated to the interests of individuals." Indeed, as we examine the AMA doctrine, I think it will become clear that it appeals to and makes use of a number of overlapping distinctions, which may have moral significance in particular cases, such as the distinction between intending and foreseeing, or between ordinary and extraordinary care. Let us then turn to the 1973 statement, from the House of Delegates of the American Medical Association, which Rachels cites:

> The intentional termination of the life of one human being by another—mercy killing—is contrary to that for which the medical profession stands and is contrary to the policy of the American Medical Association.
>
> The cessation of the employment of extraordinary means to prolong the life of the body when there is irrefutable evidence that biological death is imminent is the decision of the patient and/or his immediate family. The advice and judgment of the physician should be freely available to the patient and/or his immediate family.

Excerpts from Bonnie Steinbock, "the intentional termination of life," from Social Science and Medicine, vol. 1, pp. 69–94, 1979. Reprinted by permission.

Rachels attacks this statement because he believes that it contains a moral distinction between active and passive euthanasia. Tooley also believes this to be the position of the AMA, saying:

> Many people hold that there is an important moral distinction between passive euthanasia and active euthanasia. Thus, while the AMA maintains that people have a right "to die with dignity," so that it is morally permissible for a doctor to allow someone to die if that person wants to and is suffering from an incurable illness causing pain that cannot be sufficiently alleviated, the AMA is unwilling to countenance active euthanasia for a person who is in similar straits, but who has the misfortune not to be suffering from an illness that will result in a speedy death.

Both men, then, take the AMA position to prohibit active euthanasia, while allowing, under certain conditions, passive euthanasia.

I intend to show that the AMA statement does not imply support of the active/passive euthanasia distinction. In forbidding the intentional termination of life, the statement rejects both active and passive euthanasia. It does allow for "the cessation of the employment of extraordinary means" to prolong life. The mistake Rachels and Tooley make is in identifying the cessation of life-prolonging treatment with passive euthanasia, or intentionally letting die. If it were right to equate the two, then the AMA statement would be self-contradictory, for it would begin by condemning, and end by allowing, the intentional termination of life. But if the cessation of life-prolonging treatment is not always or necessarily passive euthanasia, then there is no confusion and no contradiction.

Why does Rachels think that the cessation of life-prolonging treatment is the intentional termination of life? He says:

> The AMA policy statement isolates the crucial issue very well: The crucial issue is "the intentional termination of the life of one human being by another." But after identifying this issue, and forbidding "mercy killing," the statement goes on to deny that the cessation of treatment is the intentional termination of a life. This is where the mistake comes in, for what is the cessation of treatment, in these circumstances, if it is not "the intentional termination of the life of one human being by another"? Of course it is exactly that, and if it were not, there would be no point to it.

However, there *can* be a point (to the cessation of life-prolonging treatment) other than an endeavor to bring about the patient's death, and so the blanket identification of cessation of treatment with the intentional termination of a life is inaccurate. There are at least two situations in which the termination of life-prolonging treatment cannot be identified with the intentional termination of the life of one human being by another.

The first situation concerns the patient's right to refuse treatment. Both Tooley and Rachels give the example of a patient dying of an incurable disease, accompanied by unrelievable pain, who wants to end the treatment which cannot cure him but can only prolong his miserable existence. Why, they ask, may a doctor accede to the patient's request to stop treatment, but not provide a patient in a similar situation with a lethal dose? The answer lies in the patient's right to refuse treatment. In general, a competent adult has the right to refuse treatment, even where such treatment is necessary to prolong life. Indeed, the right to refuse treatment has been upheld even when the patient's reason for refusing treatment is generally agreed to be inadequate.[1] This right can be overridden (if, for example, the patient has dependent children) but, in general, no one may legally compel you to undergo treatment to which you have not consented. "Historically, surgical intrusion has always been considered a technical battery upon the person and one to be excused or justified by consent of the patient or justified by necessity created by the circumstances of the moment. . . ."[2]

At this point, an objection might be raised that if one has the right to refuse life-prolonging treatment, then consistency demands that one have the right to decide to end his or her life, and to obtain help in doing so. The idea is that the right to refuse treatment somehow implies a right to voluntary euthanasia, and we need to see why someone might think this. The right to refuse treatment has been considered by legal writers as an example of the right to privacy or, better, the right to bodily self-determination. You have the right to decide what happens to your own body, and the right to refuse treatment is an instance of that right. But if you have the right to determine what happens to your own body, then should you not have the right to choose to end your life, and even a right to get help in doing so?

However, it is important to see that the right to refuse treatment is not the same as, nor does it entail, a right to voluntary euthanasia, even if both can be derived from the right to bodily self-determination. The right to refuse treatment is not itself a "right to die"; that one may choose to exercise this right even at the risk of death, or even *in order to die*, is irrelevant. The purpose of the right to refuse medical treatment is not to give persons a right to decide whether to live or die, but to protect them from the unwanted interferences of others. Perhaps we ought to interpret the right to bodily self-determination more broadly, so as to include a right to die; but this would be a substantial extension of our present understanding of the right to bodily self-determination, and not a consequence of it. If we were to recognize a right to voluntary euthanasia, we would have to agree that people have the right not merely to be left alone but also the right to be killed. I leave to one side that substantive moral issue. My claim is simply that there can be a reason for terminating life-prolonging treatment other than "to bring about the patient's death."

The second case in which termination of treatment cannot be identified with intentional termination of life is where continued treatment has little chance of improving the patient's condition and brings greater discomfort than relief.

The question here is what treatment is appropriate to the particular case. A cancer specialist describes it in this way:

> My general rule is to administer therapy as long as a patient responds well and has the potential for a reasonably good quality of life. But when all feasible therapies have been administered and a patient shows signs of rapid deterioration, the continuation of therapy can cause more discomfort than the cancer. From that time I recommend surgery, radiotherapy, or chemotherapy only as a means of relieving pain. But if a patient's condition should once again stabilize after the withdrawal of active therapy and if it should appear that he could still gain some good time, I would immediately reinstitute active therapy. The decision to cease anticancer treatment is never irrevocable, and often the desire to live will push a patient to try for another remission, or even a few more days of life.[3]

The decision here to cease anticancer treatment cannot be construed as a decision that the patient die, or as the intentional termination of life. It is a decision to provide the most appropriate treatment for that patient at that time. Rachels suggests that the point of the cessation of treatment is the intentional termination of life. But here the point of discontinuing treatment is not to bring about the patient's death but to avoid treatment that will cause more discomfort than the cancer and has little hope of benefiting the patient. Treatment that meets this description is often called "extraordinary."[4] The concept is flexible, and what might be considered "extraordinary" in one situation might be ordinary in another. The use of a respirator to sustain a patient through a severe bout with a respiratory disease would be considered ordinary; its use to sustain the life of a severely brain-damaged person in an irreversible coma would be considered extraordinary.

Contrasted with extraordinary treatment is ordinary treatment, the care a doctor would normally be expected to provide. Failure to provide ordinary care constitutes neglect, and can even be construed as the intentional infliction of harm, where there is a legal obligation to provide care. The importance of the ordinary/extraordinary care distinction lies partly in its connection to the doctor's intention. The withholding of extraordinary care should be seen as a decision not to inflict painful treatment on a patient without reasonable hope of success. The withholding of ordinary care, by contrast, must be seen as neglect. Thus, one doctor says, "We have to draw a distinction between ordinary and extraordinary means. We never withdraw what's needed to make a baby comfortable, we would never withdraw the care a parent would provide. We never kill a baby. . . . But we may decide certain heroic interventions are not worthwhile."[5]

We should keep in mind the ordinary/extraordinary care distinction when considering an example given by both Tooley and Rachels to show the irrationality of the active/passive distinction with regard to infanticide. The example is this: A child is born with Down's syndrome and also has an intestinal obstruction that requires corrective surgery. If the surgery is not performed, the infant will starve to death, since it cannot take food orally. This may take days or even weeks, as dehydration and infection set in. Commenting on this situation in his article in this book Rachels says:

> I can understand why some people are opposed to all euthanasia, and insist that such infants must be allowed to live. I think I can also understand why other people favor destroying these babies quickly and painlessly. But why should anyone favor letting "dehydration and infection wither a tiny being over hours and days"? The doctrine that says that a baby may be allowed to dehydrate and wither, but may not be given an injection that would end its life without suffering, seems so patently cruel as to require no further refutation.

Such a doctrine perhaps does not need further refutation; but this is not the AMA doctrine. The AMA statement criticized by Rachels allows only for the cessation of extraordinary means to prolong life when death is imminent. Neither of these conditions is satisfied in this example. Death is not imminent in this situation, any more than it would be if a normal child had an attack of appendicitis. Neither the corrective surgery to remove the intestinal obstruction nor the intravenous feeding required to keep the infant alive until such surgery is performed can be regarded as extraordinary means, for neither is particularly expensive, nor does either place an overwhelming burden on the patient or others. (The continued existence of the child might be thought to place an overwhelming burden on its parents, but that has nothing to do with the characterization of the means to prolong its life as extraordinary. If it had, then *feeding* a severely defective child who required a great deal of care could be regarded as extraordinary.) The chances of success if the operation is undertaken are quite good, though there is always a risk in operating on infants. Though the Down's syndrome will not be alleviated, the child will proceed to an otherwise normal infancy.

It cannot be argued that the treatment is withheld for the infant's sake, unless one is prepared to argue that all mentally retarded babies are better off dead. This is particularly implausible in the case of Down's syndrome babies, who generally do not suffer and are capable of giving and receiving love, of learning and playing, to varying degrees.

In a film on this subject entitled, "Who Should Survive?" a doctor defended a decision not to operate, saying that since the parents did not consent to the operation, the doctors' hands were tied. As we have seen, surgical intrusion requires consent, and in the case of infants, consent would normally come from the parents. But, as legal guardians, parents are required to provide medical care for their children, and failure to do so can constitute criminal neglect or even homicide. In general, courts have been understandably reluctant to recognize a parental right to terminate life-prolonging treatment.[6] Although prosecution is unlikely, physicians who comply with invalid instructions from the parents and permit the infant's death could be liable for aiding and abetting, failure to report child neglect, or even homicide. So it is not true that, in this situation, doctors are legally bound to do as the parents wish.

To sum up, I think that Rachels is right to regard the decision not to operate in the Down's syndrome example as the intentional termination of life. But there is no reason to believe that either the law or the AMA would regard it otherwise. Certainly the decision to withhold treatment is not justified by the AMA statement. That such infants have been allowed to die cannot be denied; but this, I think, is the result of doctors misunderstanding the law and the AMA position.

Withholding treatment in this case is the intentional termination of life because the infant is deliberately allowed to die; that is the point of not operating. But there are other cases in which that is not the point. If the point is to avoid inflicting painful treatment on a patient with little or no reasonable hope of success, this is not the intentional termination of life. The permissibility of such withholding of treatment, then, would have no implications for the permissibility of euthanasia, active or passive.

The decision whether or not to operate, or to institute vigorous treatment, is particularly agonizing in the case of children born with spina bifida, an opening in the base of the spine usually accompanied by hydrocephalus and mental retardation. If left unoperated, these children usually die of meningitis or kidney failure within the first few years of life. Even if they survive, all affected children face a lifetime of illness, operations, and varying degrees of disability. The policy used to be to save as many as possible, but the trend now is toward selective treatment, based on the physician's estimate of the chances of success. If operating is not likely to improve significantly the child's condition, parents and doctors may agree not to operate. This is not the intentional termination of life, for again the purpose is not the termination of the child's life but the avoidance of painful and pointless treatment. Thus, the fact that withholding treatment is justified does not imply that killing the child would be equally justified.

Throughout the discussion, I have claimed that intentionally ceasing life-prolonging treatment is not the intentional termination of life unless the doctor has, as his or her purpose in stopping treatment, the patient's death.

It may be objected that I have incorrectly characterized the conditions for the intentional termination of life. Perhaps it is enough that the doctor intentionally ceases treatment, foreseeing that the patient will die.

In many cases, if one acts intentionally, foreseeing that a particular result will occur, one can be said to have brought about that result intentionally. Indeed, this is the general legal rule. Why, then, am I not willing to call the cessation of life-prolonging treatment, in compliance with the patient's right to refuse treatment, the intentional termination of life? It is not because such an *identification* is necessarily opprobrious; for we could go on to *discuss* whether such cessation of treatment is a *justifiable* intentional termination of life. Even in the law, some cases of homicide are justifiable; e.g., homicide in self-defense.

However, the cessation of life-prolonging treatment, in the cases which I have discussed, is not regarded in law as being justifiable homicide, because it is not homicide at all. Why is this? Is it because the doctor "doesn't do anything," and so cannot be guilty of homicide? Surely not, since, as I have indicated, the law sometimes treats an omission as the cause of death. A better explanation, I think, has to do with the fact that in the context of the patient's right to refuse treatment, a doctor is not at liberty to continue treatment. It seems a necessary ingredient of intentionally letting die that one could have done something to prevent the death. In this situation, of course, the doctor can physically prevent the patient's death, but since we do not regard the doctor as *free* to continue treatment, we say that there is "nothing he can do." Therefore he does not intentionally let the patient die.

To discuss this suggestion fully, I would need to present a full-scale theory of intentional action. However, at least I have shown, through the discussion of the above examples, that such a theory will be very complex, and that one of the complexities concerns the agent's reason for acting. The reason why an agent acted (or failed to act) may affect the characterization of what he did intentionally. The mere fact that he did *something* intentionally, foreseeing a certain result, does not necessarily mean that he brought about that *result* intentionally.

In order to show that the cessation of life-prolonging treatment, in the cases I've discussed, is the intentional termination of life, one would either have to show that treatment was stopped in order to bring about the patient's death, or provide a theory of intentional action according to which the reason for ceasing treatment is irrelevant to its characterization as the intentional termination of life. I find this suggestion implausible, but am willing to consider arguments for it. Rachels has provided no such arguments: Indeed, he apparently shares my view about the intentional termination of life. For when he claims that the cessation of life-prolonging treatment *is* the intentional termination of life, his reason for making the claim is that "if it were not, there would be no point to it." Rachels believes that the point of ceasing treatment, "in these cases," is to bring about the patient's death. If that were not the point, he suggests, why would the doctor cease treatment? I have shown, however, that there can be a point to ceasing treatment which is not the death of the patient. In showing this, I have refuted Rachels' reason for identifying the cessation of life-prolonging treatment with the intentional termination of life, and thus his argument against the AMA doctrine.

Here someone might say: Even if the withholding of treatment is not the intentional termination of life, does that make a difference, morally speaking? If life-prolonging treatment may be withheld, for the sake of the child, may not an easy death be provided, for the sake of the child, as well? The unoperated child with spina bifida may take months or even years to die. Distressed by the spectacle of children "lying around, waiting to die," one doctor has written, "It is time that society and medicine stopped perpetuating the fiction that withholding treatment is ethically different from terminating a life. It is time that society began to discuss mechanisms by which we can alleviate the pain and suffering for those individuals whom we cannot help."[7]

I do not deny that there may be cases in which death is in the best interests of the patient. In such cases, a quick and painless death may be the best thing. However, I do not think that, once active or vigorous treatment is stopped, a quick death is always preferable to a lingering one. We must be cautious about attributing to defective children *our* distress at seeing them linger. Waiting for them to die may be tough on parents, doctors, and nurses—it isn't necessarily tough on the child. The decision not to operate need not mean a decision to neglect, and it may be possible to make the remaining months of the child's life comfortable, pleasant, and filled with love. If this alternative is possible, surely it is more decent and humane than killing the child. In such a situation, withholding treatment, foreseeing the child's death, is not ethically equivalent to killing the child, and we cannot move from the permissibility of the former to that of the latter. I am worried that there will be a tendency to do precisely that if active euthanasia is regarded as morally equivalent to the withholding of life-prolonging treatment.

CONCLUSION

The AMA statement does not make the distinction Rachels and Tooley wish to attack, that between active and passive euthanasia. Instead, the statement draws a distinction between the intentional termination of life, on the one hand, and the cessation of the employment of extraordinary means to prolong life, on the other. Nothing said by Rachels

and Tooley shows that this distinction is confused. It may be that doctors have misinterpreted the AMA statement, and that this has led, for example, to decisions to allow defective infants to starve slowly to death. I quite agree with Rachels and Tooley that the decisions to which they allude were cruel and made on irrelevant grounds. Certainly it is worth pointing out that allowing someone to die *can* be the intentional termination of life, and that it can be just as bad as, or worse than, killing someone. However, the withholding of life-prolonging treatment is not necessarily the intentional termination of life, so that if it is permissible to withhold life-prolonging treatment it does not follow that, other things being equal, it is permissible to kill. Furthermore, most of the time, other things are not equal. In many of the cases in which it would be right to cease treatment, I do not think that it would also be right to kill.

ACKNOWLEDGMENTS

I would like to express my thanks to Jonathan Bennett, Josiah Gould, Deborah Johnson, David Pratt, Bruce Russell, and David Zimmerman, all of whom provided helpful criticism and suggestions for this article. Reprinted with permission of the publisher and author.

NOTES

1. For example, *In re Yetter*, 62 Pa. D. & C. 2d 619 (C.P., Northampton County Ct. 1974).
2. David W. Meyers, "Legal Aspects of Voluntary Euthanasia," in *Dilemmas of Euthanasia*, ed. John Behnke and Sissela Bok (New York: Anchor Books, 1975), p. 56.
3. Ernest H. Rosenbaum, M.D., *Living with Cancer* (New York: Praeger, 1975), p. 27.
4. See Tristram Engelhardt, Jr., "Ethical Issues in Aiding the Death of Young Children," in *Beneficent Euthanasia*, ed. Marvin Kohl (Buffalo, N.Y.: Prometheus Books, 1975).
5. B. D. Colen, *Karen Ann Quinlan: Living and Dying in the Age of Eternal Life* (Los Angeles: Nash, 1976), p. 115.
6. See Norman L. Cantor, "Law and the Termination of an Incompetent Patient's Life-Preserving Care," in *Dilemmas of Euthanasia*, pp. 69–105.
7. John Freeman, "Is There a Right to Die—Quickly?" *Journal of Pediatrics*, 80, no. 5 (1972), 904–905.

Assisted Suicide:
The Philosophers' Brief

*Ronald Dworkin, Thomas Nagel, Robert Nozick, John Rawls,
Thomas Scanlon, and Judith Jarvis Thomson*

Ronald Dworkin is a professor of philosophy and a professor of law at New York University. His works include *Law's Empire* (1986) and *Taking Rights Seriously* (1977).

Thomas Nagel is also a professor of philosophy and a professor of law at New York University. Among his works are *Concealment and Exposure* (2002), *Equality and Partiality* (1991), *Mortal Questions* (1979), and *The Possibility of Altruism* (1978).

Robert Nozick was a professor of philosophy at Harvard University. He was the author of *Anarchy, State, and Utopia* (1974).

John Rawls was an influential moral and political philosopher who taught at Harvard. His major works include *A Theory of Justice* (1971, 1999) and *Political Liberalism* (1993, 1996).

Thomas Scanlon is a professor of philosophy at Harvard University. He has published many articles. He is also the author of and *The Difficulty of Tolerance* (2003) and *What We Owe to Each Other* (1998).

Judith Jarvis Thomson is a professor of philosophy at MIT. She has published numerous articles in ethics and metaphysics. She is the author of *Goodness and Advice* (2001) and *The Realm of Rights* (1990).

The philosophers believe that the right to assisted suicide could be grounded in the Due Process Clause of the Fourteenth Amendment and in various case decisions in the U.S. Supreme Court. In particular, they argue that an individual has a right to make highly "personal and intimate" choices critical to his or her dignity and autonomy including "marriage, procreation, and death." They also hold that states should protect this right provided that the risks involved are properly controlled through appropriate regulations.

Amici are six moral and political philosophers who differ on many issues of public morality and policy. They are united, however, in their conviction that respect for fundamental principles of liberty and justice, as well as for the American constitutional tradition, requires that the decisions of the Courts of Appeals be affirmed.

INTRODUCTION AND SUMMARY OF ARGUMENT

These cases do not invite or require the Court to make moral, ethical, or religious judgments about how people should approach or confront their death or about when it is ethically appropriate to hasten

Source: Assisted Suicide: The Philosophers' Brief by Thomas Nagel, Judith Jarvis Thomson, Ronald Dworkin, Robert Nozick, John Rawls. New York Review of Books March 27, 1997, Volume 44, Number 5. Reprinted by permission.

one's own death or to ask others for help in doing so. On the contrary, they ask the Court to recognize that individuals have a constitutionally protected interest in making those grave judgments for themselves, free from the imposition of any religious or philosophical orthodoxy by court or legislature. States have a constitutionally legitimate interest in protecting individuals from irrational, ill-informed, pressured, or unstable decisions to hasten their own death. To that end, states may regulate and limit the assistance that doctors may give individuals who express a wish to die. But states may not deny people in the position of the patient-plaintiffs in these cases the opportunity to demonstrate, through whatever reasonable procedures the state might institute— even procedures that err on the side of caution—that their decision to die is indeed informed, stable, and fully free. Denying that opportunity to terminally ill patients who are in agonizing pain or otherwise doomed to an existence they regard as intolerable could only be justified on the basis of a religious or ethical conviction about the value or meaning of life itself. Our Constitution forbids government to impose such convictions on its citizens.

Petitioners [i.e., the state authorities of Washington and New York] and the amici who support them offer two contradictory arguments. Some deny that the patient-plaintiffs have any constitutionally protected liberty interest in hastening their own deaths. But that liberty interest flows directly from this Court's previous decisions. It flows from the right of people to make their own decisions about matters "involving the most intimate and personal choices a person may make in a lifetime, choices central to personal dignity and autonomy." *Planned Parenthood* v. *Casey*, 505 U.S. 833, 851(1992).

The Solicitor General, urging reversal in support of Petitioners, recognizes that the patient-plaintiffs do have a constitutional liberty interest at stake in these cases. See Brief for the United States as Amicus Curiae Supporting Petitioners at 12, *Washington* v. *Vacco* (hereinafter Brief for the United States) ("The term 'liberty' in the Due Process Clause . . . is broad enough to encompass an interest on the part of terminally ill, mentally competent adults in obtaining relief from the kind

of suffering experienced by the plaintiffs in this case, which includes not only severe physical pain, but also the despair and distress that comes from physical deterioration and the inability to control basic bodily functions."); *see also id.* at 13 (*"Cruzan* . . . supports the conclusion that a liberty interest is at stake in this case.").

The Solicitor General nevertheless argues that Washington and New York properly ignored this profound interest when they required the patient-plaintiffs to live on in circumstances they found intolerable. He argues that a state may simply declare that it is unable to devise a regulatory scheme that would adequately protect patients whose desire to die might be ill informed or unstable or foolish or not fully free, and that a state may therefore fall back on a blanket prohibition. This Court has never accepted that patently dangerous rationale for denying protection altogether to a conceded fundamental constitutional interest. It would be a serious mistake to do so now. If that rationale were accepted, an interest acknowledged to be constitutionally protected would be rendered empty.

ARGUMENT

I. The Liberty Interest Asserted Here is Protected by the Due Process Clause

The Due Process Clause of the Fourteenth Amendment protects the liberty interest asserted by the patient-plaintiffs here.

Certain decisions are momentous in their impact on the character of a person's life decisions about religious faith, political and moral allegiance, marriage, procreation, and death, for example. Such deeply personal decisions pose controversial questions about how and why human life has value. In a free society, individuals must be allowed to make those decisions for themselves, out of their own faith, conscience, and convictions. This Court has insisted, in a variety of contexts and circumstances, that this great freedom is among those protected by the Due Process Clause as essential to a community of "ordered liberty." *Palko* v. *Connecticut,* 302 U.S. 319, 325 (1937). In its recent decision in *Planned Parenthood* v. *Casey,* 505 U.S. 833,851 (1992), the Court offered a paradigmatic statement of that principle:

> matters [ ] involving the most intimate and personal choices a person may make in a lifetime, choices central to a person's dignity and autonomy, are central to the liberty protected by the Fourteenth Amendment.

That declaration reflects an idea underlying many of our basic constitutional protections. As the Court explained in *West Virginia State Board of Education* v. *Barnette,* 319 U.S. 624,642 (1943):

> If there is any fixed star in our constitutional constellation, it is that no official . . . can prescribe what shall be orthodox in politics, nationalism, religion, or other matters of opinion or force citizens to confess by word or act their faith therein.

A person's interest in following his own convictions at the end of life is so central a part of the more general right to make "intimate and personal choices" for himself that a failure to protect that particular interest would undermine the general right altogether. Death is, for each of us, among the most significant events of life. As the Chief Justice said in *Cruzan* v. *Missouri,* 497 U.S. 261, 281 (1990), "[t]he choice between life and death is a deeply personal decision of obvious and overwhelming finality." Most of us see death—whatever we think will follow it—as the final act of life's drama, and we want that last act to reflect our own convictions, those we have tried to live by, not the convictions of others forced on us in our most vulnerable moment.

Different people, of different religious and ethical beliefs, embrace very different convictions about which way of dying confirms and which contradicts the value of their lives. Some fight against death with every weapon their doctors can devise. Others will do nothing to hasten death even if they pray it will come soon. Still others, including the patient-plaintiffs in these cases, want to end their lives when they think that living on, in the only way they can, would disfigure rather than enhance the lives they had created. Some people make the latter choice not just to escape pain. Even if it were possible to eliminate all pain for a dying patient—and frequently that is not possible—that would not end or even much alleviate the anguish some would feel at remaining alive, but intubated, helpless, and often sedated near oblivion.

None of these dramatically different attitudes about the meaning of death can be dismissed as irrational. None should be imposed, either by the pressure of doctors or relatives or by the fiat of government, on people who reject it. Just as it would be intolerable for government to dictate that doctors never be permitted to try to keep someone alive as long as possible, when that is what the patient wishes, so it is intolerable for government to dictate that doctors may never, under any circumstances, help someone to die who believes that further life means only degradation. The Constitution insists that people must be free to make these deeply personal decisions for themselves and must not be forced to end their lives in a way that appalls them, just because that is what some majority thinks proper.

II. This Court's Decisions in *Casey* and *Cruzan* Compel Recognition of a Liberty Interest Here

A. CASEY *SUPPORTS THE LIBERTY INTEREST ASSERTED HERE.* In *Casey*, this Court, in holding that a state cannot constitutionally proscribe abortion in all cases, reiterated that the Constitution protects a sphere of autonomy in which individuals must be permitted to make certain decisions for themselves. The Court began its analysis by pointing out that "[a]t the heart of liberty is the right to define one's own concept of existence, of meaning, of the universe, and of the mystery of human life." 505 U.S. at 851. Choices flowing out of these conceptions, on matters "involving the most intimate and personal choices a person may make in a lifetime, choices central to personal dignity and autonomy, are central to the liberty protected by the Fourteenth Amendment." *Id*. "Beliefs about these matters," the Court continued, "could not define the attributes of personhood were they formed under compulsion of the State." *Id*.

In language pertinent to the liberty interest asserted here, the Court explained why decisions about abortion fall within this category of "personal and intimate" decisions. A decision whether or not to have an abortion, "originat[ing] within the zone of conscience and belief," involves conduct in which "the liberty of the woman is at stake in a sense unique to the human condition and so unique to the law." *Id.* at 852. As such, the decision necessarily involves the very "destiny of the woman" and is inevitably "shaped to a large extent on her own conception of her spiritual imperatives and her place in society." *Id.* Precisely because of these characteristics of the decision, "the State is [not] entitled to proscribe [abortion] in all instances." *Id.* Rather, to allow a total prohibition on abortion would be to permit a state to impose one conception of the meaning and value of human existence on all individuals. This the Constitution forbids.

The Solicitor General nevertheless argues that the right to abortion could be supported on grounds other than this autonomy principle, grounds that would not apply here. He argues, for example, that the abortion right might flow from the great burden an unwanted child imposes on its mother's life. Brief for the United States at 14–15. But whether or not abortion rights could be defended on such grounds, they were not the grounds on which this Court in fact relied. To the contrary, the Court explained at length that the right flows from the constitutional protection accorded all individuals to "define one's own concept of existence, of meaning, of the universe, and of the mystery of human life." *Casey,* 505 U.S. at 851.

The analysis in *Casey* compels the conclusion that the patient-plaintiffs have a liberty interest in this case that a state cannot burden with a blanket prohibition. Like a woman's decision whether to have an abortion, a decision to die involves one's very "destiny" and inevitably will be "shaped to a large extent on [one's] own conception of [one's] spiritual imperatives and [one's] place in society." *Id.* at 832. Just as a blanket prohibition on abortion would involve the improper imposition of one conception of the meaning and value of human existence on all individuals, so too would a

blanket prohibition on assisted suicide. The liberty interest asserted here cannot be rejected without undermining the rationale of *Casey.* Indeed, the lower court opinions in the Washington case expressly recognized the parallel between the liberty interest in *Casey* and the interest asserted here, *See Compassion in Dying* v. *Washington,* 79 F.3d 790, 801(9th Cir. 1996) (en banc) ("In deciding right-to-die cases, we are guided by the Court's approach to the abortion cases. *Casey* in particular provides a powerful precedent, for in that case the Court had the opportunity to evaluate its past decisions and to determine whether to adhere to its original judgment"), *aff'g.* 850 F. Supp. 1454, 1459 (W. D. Wash. 1994) ("[T]he reasoning in *Casey* [is] highly instructive and almost prescriptive . . ."). This Court should do the same.

B. CRUZAN *SUPPORTS THE LIBERTY INTEREST ASSERTED HERE.* We agree with the Solicitor General that this Court's decision in "*Cruzan* . . . supports the conclusion that a liberty interest is at stake in this case." Brief for the United States at 8. Petitioners, however, insist that the present cases can be distinguished because the right at issue in *Cruzan* was limited to a right to reject an unwanted invasion of one's body.[1] But this Court repeatedly has held that in appropriate circumstances a state may require individuals to accept unwanted invasions of the body. *See, e.g., Schmerber* v. *California*, 384 U.S. 757 (1966) (extraction of blood sample from individual suspected of driving while intoxicated, notwithstanding defendant's objection, does not violate privilege against self-incrimination or other constitutional rights); *Jacobson* v. *Massachusetts*, 197 U.S. 11 (1905) (upholding compulsory vaccination for smallpox as reasonable regulation for protection of public health).

The liberty interest at stake in *Cruzan* was a more profound one. If a competent patient has a constitutional right to refuse life-sustaining treatment, then, the Court implied, the state could not override that right. The regulations upheld in *Cruzan* were designed only to ensure that the individual's wishes were ascertained correctly. Thus, if *Cruzan* implies a right of competent patients to refuse life-sustaining treatment, that implication must be understood as resting not simply on a right to refuse bodily invasions but on the more profound right to refuse medical intervention when what is at stake is a momentous personal decision, such as the timing and manner of one's death. In her concurrence, Justice O'Connor expressly recognized that the right at issue involved a "deeply personal decision" that is "inextricably intertwined" with our notion of "self-determination." 497 U.S. at 287–89.

Cruzan also supports the proposition that a state may not burden a terminally ill patient's liberty interest in determining the time and manner of his death by prohibiting doctors from terminating life support. Seeking to distinguish *Cruzan,* Petitioners insist that a state may nevertheless burden that right in a different way by forbidding doctors to assist in the suicide of patients who are not on life-support machinery. They argue that doctors who remove life support are only allowing a natural process to end in death whereas doctors who prescribe lethal drugs are intervening to cause death. So, according to this argument, a state has an independent justification for forbidding doctors to assist in suicide that it does not have for forbidding them to remove life support. In the former case though not the latter, it is said, the state forbids an act of killing that is morally much more problematic than merely letting a patient die.

This argument is based on a misunderstanding of the pertinent moral principles. It is certainly true that when a patient does not wish to die, different acts, each of which foreseeably results in his death, nevertheless have very different moral status. When several patients need organ transplants and organs are scarce, for example, it is morally permissible for a doctor to deny an organ to one patient, even though he will die without it, in order to give it to another. But it is certainly not permissible for a doctor to kill one patient in order to use his organs to save another. The morally significant difference between those two acts is not, however, that killing is a positive act and not providing an organ is a mere omission, or that killing someone is worse than merely allowing a "natural" process to result in death. It would be equally

impermissible for a doctor to let an injured patient bleed to death, or to refuse antibiotics to a patient with pneumonia—in each case the doctor would have allowed death to result from a "natural" process—in order to make his organs available for transplant to others. A doctor violates his patient's rights whether the doctor acts or refrains from acting, against the patient's wishes, in a way that is designed to cause death.

When a competent patient does want to die, the moral situation is obviously different, because then it makes no sense to appeal to the patient's right not to be killed as a reason why an act designed to cause his death is impermissible. From the patient's point of view, there is no morally pertinent difference between a doctor's terminating treatment that keeps him alive, if that is what he wishes, and a doctor's helping him to end his own life by providing lethal pills he may take himself, when ready, if that is what he wishes—except that the latter may be quicker and more humane. Nor is that a pertinent difference from the doctor's point of view. If and when it is permissible for him to act with death in view, it does not matter which of those two means he and his patient choose. If it is permissible for a doctor deliberately to withdraw medical treatment in order to allow death to result from a natural process, then it is equally permissible for him to help his patient hasten his own death more actively, if that is the patient's express wish.

It is true that some doctors asked to terminate life support are reluctant and do so only in deference to a patient's right to compel them to remove unwanted invasions of his body. But other doctors, who believe that their most fundamental professional duty is to act in the patient's interests and that, in certain circumstances, it is in their patient's best interests to die, participate willingly in such decisions: they terminate life support to cause death because they know that is what their patient wants. *Cruzan* implied that a state may not absolutely prohibit a doctor from deliberately causing death, at the patient's request, in that way and for that reason. If so, then a state may not prohibit doctors from deliberately using more direct and often more humane means to the same end when that is what a patient prefers. The fact that failing to provide life-sustaining treatment may be regarded as "only letting nature take its course" is no more morally significant in this context, when the patient wishes to die, than in the other, when he wishes to live. Whether a doctor turns off a respirator in accordance with the patient's request or prescribes pills that a patient may take when he is ready to kill himself, the doctor acts with the same intention: to help the patient die.

The two situations do differ in one important respect. Since patients have a right not to have life-support machinery attached to their bodies, they have, in principle, a right to compel its removal. But that is not true in the case of assisted suicide: patients in certain circumstances have a right that the state not forbid doctors to assist in their deaths, but they have no right to compel a doctor to assist them. The right in question, that is, is only a right to the help of a willing doctor.

III. State Interests Do Not Justify a Categorical Prohibition on All Assisted Suicide

The Solicitor General concedes that "a competent, terminally ill adult has a constitutionally cognizable liberty interest in avoiding the kind of suffering experienced by the plaintiffs in this case." Brief for the United States at 8. He agrees that this interest extends not only to avoiding pain, but to avoiding an existence the patient believes to be one of intolerable indignity or incapacity as well. *Id.* at 12. The Solicitor General argues, however, that states nevertheless have the right to "override" this liberty interest altogether, because a state could reasonably conclude that allowing doctors to assist in suicide, even under the most stringent regulations and procedures that could be devised, would unreasonably endanger the lives of a number of patients who might ask for death in circumstances when it is plainly not in their interests to die or when their consent has been improperly obtained.

This argument is unpersuasive, however, for at least three reasons. *First*, in *Cruzan*, this Court noted that its various decisions supported the recognition of a general liberty interest in refusing medical treatment, even when such refusal could result in death. 497 U.S. at 278–79. The various risks described by the Solicitor General apply equally to those situations. For instance, a patient kept alive only by an elaborate and disabling life-support system might well become depressed, and doctors might be equally uncertain whether the depression is curable: such a patient might decide for death only because he has been advised that he will die soon anyway or that he will never live free of the burdensome apparatus, and either diagnosis might conceivably be mistaken. Relatives or doctors might subtly or crudely influence that decision, and state provision for the decision may (to the same degree in this case as if it allowed assisted suicide) be thought to encourage it.

Yet there has been no suggestion that states are incapable of addressing such dangers through regulation. In fact, quite the opposite is true. In *McKay v. Bergstedt*, 106 Nev. 808, 801 P.2d 617 (1990), for example, the Nevada Supreme Court held that "competent adult patients desiring to refuse or discontinue medical treatment" must be examined by two nonattending physicians to determine whether the patient is mentally competent, understands his prognosis and treatment options, and appears free of coercion or pressure in making his decision, *Id.* at 827–28, 801 P.2d at 630. See also: *id.* (in the case of terminally ill patients with natural life expectancy of less than six months, [a] patient's right of self-determination shall be deemed to prevail over state interests, whereas [a] non-terminal patient's decision to terminate life-support systems must first be weighed against relevant state interests by trial judge); [and] *In re Farrell,* 108 N.J. 335, 354, 529 A.2d 404, 413 (1987) ([which held that a] terminally-ill patient requesting termination of life-support must be determined to be competent and properly informed about [his] prognosis, available treatment options and risks, and to have made decision voluntarily and without coercion). Those protocols served to guard against precisely the dangers that the Solicitor General raises. The case law contains no suggestion that such protocols are inevitably insufficient to prevent deaths that should have been prevented.

Indeed, the risks of mistake are overall greater in the case of terminating life support. *Cruzan* implied that a state must allow individuals to make such decisions through an advance directive stipulating either that life support be terminated (or not initiated) in described circumstances when the individual was no longer competent to make such a decision himself, or that a designated proxy be allowed to make that decision. All the risks just described are present when the decision is made through or pursuant to such an advance directive, and a grave further risk is added: that the directive, though still in force, no longer represents the wishes of the patient. The patient might have changed his mind before he became incompetent, though he did not change the directive, or his proxy may make a decision that the patient would not have made himself if still competent. In *Cruzan*, this Court held that a state may limit these risks through reasonable regulation. It did not hold—or even suggest—that a state may avoid them through a blanket prohibition that, in effect, denies the liberty interest altogether.

Second, nothing in the record supports the [Solicitor General's] conclusion that no system of rules and regulations could adequately reduce the risk of mistake. As discussed above, the experience of states in adjudicating requests to have life-sustaining treatment removed indicates the opposite. The Solicitor General has provided no persuasive reason why the same sort of proce dures could not be applied effectively in the case of a competent individual's request for physician-assisted suicide.

Indeed, several very detailed schemes for regulating physician-assisted suicide have been submitted to the voters of some states and one has been enacted. In addition, concerned groups, including a group of distinguished professors of law and other professionals, have drafted and defended such schemes. *See, e.g.,* Charles H. Baron, *et al., A Model State Act to Authorize and Regulate Physician-Assisted Suicide*, 33 Harv. J. Legis. 1 (1996). Such draft statutes propose a variety of protections and review procedures designed to insure against mistakes, and neither Washington nor New York attempted to show that

such schemes would be porous or ineffective. Nor does the Solicitor General's brief: it relies instead mainly on flat and conclusory statements. It cites a New York Task Force report, written before the proposals just described were drafted, whose findings have been widely disputed and were implicitly rejected in the opinion of the Second Circuit below. *See generally Quill* v. *Vacco*, 80 F.3d 716 (2d Cir. 1996). The weakness of the Solicitor General's argument is signaled by his strong reliance on the experience in the Netherlands which, in effect, allows assisted suicide pursuant to published guidelines. Brief for the United States at 23–24. The Dutch guidelines are more permissive than the proposed and model American statutes, however. The Solicitor General deems the Dutch practice of ending the lives of people like neonates who cannot consent particularly noteworthy, for example, but that practice could easily and effectively be made illegal by any state regulatory scheme without violating the Constitution.

The Solicitor General's argument would perhaps have more force if the question before the Court were simply whether a state has any rational basis for an absolute prohibition; if that were the question, then it might be enough to call attention to risks a state might well deem not worth running. But as the Solicitor General concedes, the question here is a very different one: whether a state has interests sufficiently compelling to allow it to take the extraordinary step of altogether refusing the exercise of a liberty interest of constitutional dimension. In those circumstances, the burden is plainly on the state to demonstrate that the risk of mistakes is very high, and that no alternative to complete prohibition would adequately and effectively reduce those risks. Neither of the Petitioners has made such a showing.

Nor could they. The burden of proof on any state attempting to show this would be very high. Consider, for example, the burden a state would have to meet to show that it was entitled altogether to ban public speeches in favor of unpopular causes because it could not guarantee, either by regulations short of an outright ban or by increased police protection, that such speeches would not provoke a riot that would result in serious injury or death to an innocent party. Or that it was entitled to deny those accused of crime the procedural rights that the Constitution guarantees, such as the right to a jury trial, because the security risk those rights would impose on the community would be too great. One can posit extreme circumstances in which some such argument would succeed. *See, e.g., Korematsu* v. *United States*, 323 *U S.*, 214 (1944) (permitting United States to detain individuals of Japanese ancestry during wartime). But these circumstances would be extreme indeed, and the *Korematsu* ruling has been widely and severely criticized.

Third, it is doubtful whether the risks the Solicitor General cites are even of the right character to serve as justification for an absolute prohibition on the exercise of an important liberty interest. The risks fall into two groups. The first is the risk of medical mistake, including a misdiagnosis of competence or terminal illness. To be sure, no scheme of regulation, no matter how rigorous, can altogether guarantee that medical mistakes will not be made. But the Constitution does not allow a state to deny patients a great variety of important choices, for which informed consent is properly deemed necessary, just because the information on which die consent is given may, in spite of the most strenuous efforts to avoid mistake, be wrong. Again, these identical risks are present in decisions to terminate life support, yet they do not justify an absolute prohibition on the exercise of the right.

The second group consists of risks that a patient will be unduly influenced by considerations that the state might deem it not in his best interests to be swayed by, for example, the feelings and views of close family members. Brief for the United States at 20. But what a patient regards as proper grounds for such a decision normally reflects exactly the judgments of personal ethics—of why his life is important and what affects its value—that patients have a crucial liberty interest in deciding for themselves. Even people who are dying have a right to hear and, if they wish, act on what others might wish to tell or suggest or even hint to them, and it would be dangerous to suppose that a state may prevent this on the ground that it knows better than its citizens when they should be moved by or yield to particular advice or suggestion in the exercise of their right to make fateful personal decisions for themselves. It is not a good reply that some people may not decide as they really wish—as they would decide, for example, if free from the "pressure" of others. That possibility could hardly justify the most serious pressure of all—the criminal law which tells them that they may not decide for death if they need the help of a doctor in dying, no matter how firmly they wish it.

There is a fundamental infirmity in the Solicitor General's argument. He asserts that a state may reasonably judge that the risk of "mistake" to some persons justifies a prohibition that not only risks but insures and even aims at what would undoubtedly be a vastly greater number of "mistakes" of the opposite kind—preventing many thousands of competent people who think that it disfigures their lives to continue living, in the only way left to them, from escaping that—to them—terrible injury. A state grievously and irreversibly harms such people when it prohibits that escape. The Solicitor General's argument may seem plausible to those who do not agree that individuals are harmed by being forced to live on in pain and what they regard as indignity. But many other people plainly do think that such individuals are harmed, and a state may not take one side in that essentially ethical or religious controversy as its justification for denying a crucial liberty.

Of course, a state has important interests that justify regulating physician-assisted suicide. It may be legitimate for a state to deny an opportunity for assisted suicide when it acts in what it reasonably judges to be the best interests of the potential suicide, and when its judgment on that issue does not rest on contested judgments about "matters involving the most intimate and personal choices a person may make in a lifetime, choices central to personal dignity and autonomy." *Casey*, 505 U.S. at 851. A state might assert, for example, that people who are not terminally ill, but who have formed a desire to die, are, as a group, very likely later to be grateful if they are prevented from taking their own lives. It might then claim that it is legitimate, out of concern for such people, to deny any of them a doctor's assistance [in taking their own lives].

This Court need not decide now the extent to which such paternalistic interests might override an individual's liberty interest. No one can plausibly claim, however—and it is noteworthy that neither Petitioners nor the Solicitor General does claim—that any such prohibition could serve the interests of any significant number of terminally ill patients. On the contrary, any paternalistic justification for an absolute prohibition of assistance to such patients would of necessity appeal to a widely contested religious or ethical conviction many of them, including the patient-plaintiffs, reject. Allowing *that* justification to prevail would vitiate the liberty interest.

Even in the case of terminally ill patients, a state has a right to take all reasonable measures to insure that a patient requesting such assistance has made an informed, competent, stable and uncoerced decision. It is plainly legitimate for a state to establish procedures through which professional and administrative judgments can be made about these matters, and to forbid doctors to assist in suicide when its reasonable procedures have not been satisfied. States may be permitted considerable leeway in designing such procedures. They may be permitted, within reason, to err on what they take to be the side of caution. But they may not use the bare possibility of error as justification for refusing to establish any procedures at all and relying instead on a flat prohibition.

CONCLUSION

Each individual has a right to make the "most intimate and personal choices central to personal dignity and autonomy." That right encompasses the right to exercise some control over the time and manner of one's death.

The patient-plaintiffs in these cases were all mentally competent individuals in the final phase of terminal illness and died within months of filing their claims.

Jane Doe described how her advanced cancer made even the most basic bodily functions such as swallowing, coughing, and yawning extremely painful and that it was "not possible for [her] to reduce [her] pain to an acceptable level of comfort and to retain an alert state." Faced with such circumstances, she sought to be able to "discuss freely with [her] treating physician [her] intention of hastening [her] death through the consumption of drugs prescribed for that purpose." *Quill* v. *Vacco*, 80 F.2d 716, 720 (2d Cir. 1996) (quoting declaration of Jane Doe).

George A. Kingsley, in advanced stages of AIDS, which included, among other hardships, the attachment of a tube to an artery in his chest which made even routine functions burdensome and the development of lesions on his brain, sought advice from his doctors regarding prescriptions, which could hasten his impending death. *Id.*

Jane Roe, suffering from cancer since 1988, had been almost completely bedridden since 1993 and experienced constant pain which could not be alleviated by medication. After undergoing counseling for herself and her family, she desired to hasten her death by taking prescription drugs. *Compassion in Dying* v. *Washington*, 850 F. Supp. 1454, 1456 (1994).

John Doe, who had experienced numerous AIDS-related ailments since 1991, was "especially cognizant of the suffering imposed by a lingering terminal illness because he was the primary caregiver for his long-term companion who died of AIDS" and sought prescription drugs from his physician to hasten his own death after entering the terminal phase of AIDS. *Id.* at 1456–57.

James Poe suffered from emphysema which caused him "a constant sensation of suffocating" as well as a cardiac condition which caused severe leg pain. Connected to an oxygen tank at all times but unable to calm the panic reaction associated with his feeling of suffocation even with regular doses of morphine, Mr. Poe sought physician-assisted suicide. *Id.* at 1457.

A state may not deny the liberty claimed by the patient-plaintiffs in these cases without providing them an opportunity to demonstrate, in whatever way the state might reasonably think wise and necessary, that the conviction they expressed for an early death is competent, rational, informed, stable, and uncoerced.

Affirming the decisions by the Courts of Appeals would establish nothing more than that there is such a constitutionally protected right in principle. It would establish only that some individuals, whose decisions for suicide plainly cannot be dismissed as irrational or foolish or premature, must be accorded a reasonable opportunity to show that their decision for death is informed and free. It is not necessary to decide precisely which patients are entitled to that opportunity. If, on the other hand, this Court reverses the decisions below, its decision could only be justified by the momentous proposition—a proposition flatly in conflict with the spirit and letter of the Court's past decisions—that an American citizen does not, after all, have the right, even in principle, to live and die in the light of his own religious and ethical beliefs, his own convictions about why his life is valuable and where its value lies.

NOTE

1. In that case, the parents of Nancy Cruzan, a woman who was in a persistent vegetative state following an automobile accident, asked the Missouri courts to authorize doctors to end life support and therefore her life. The Supreme Court held that Missouri was entitled to demand explicit evidence that Ms. Cruzan had made a decision that she would not wish to be kept alive in those circumstances, and to reject the evidence the family had offered as inadequate. But a majority of justices assumed, for the sake of the argument, that a competent patient has a right to reject life-preserving treatment, and it is now widely assumed that the Court would so rule in an appropriate case.

Objections to the Institutionalisation of Euthanasia

Stephen G. Potts

Stephen Potts is a physician at the Royal Edinburgh Hospital in Scotland. He has written in the area of bioethics.

In this essay, Potts examines the probable consequences of institutionalizing voluntary active euthanasia. While not necessarily objecting to individual acts of euthanasia, he argues that the risks of harm are too great to justify its legalization as a practice. In particular, Potts is deeply concerned that the right to die might lead the patient to conclude he or she has a duty to die and that the doctor may be pressured to end the life of the patient.

. . . I object to the institutionalization of euthanasia . . . because the risks of such institutionalisation are so grave as to outweigh the very real suffering of those who might benefit from it.

A. RISKS OF INSTITUTIONALISATION

Among the potential effects of a legalised practice of euthanasia are the following:

1. *Reduced Pressure to Improve Curative or Symptomatic Treatment.* If euthanasia had been legal forty years ago, it is quite possible that there would be no hospice movement today. The improvement in terminal care is a direct result of attempts made to minimize suffering. If that suffering had been extinguished by extinguishing the patients who bore it, then we may never have known the advances in the control of pain, nausea,

breathlessness, and other terminal symptoms that the last twenty years have seen.

Some diseases that were terminal a few decades ago are now routinely cured by newly developed treatments. Earlier acceptance of euthanasia might well have undercut the urgency of the research efforts which lead to the discovery of those treatments. If we accept euthanasia now, we may well delay by decades the discovery of effective treatments for those diseases that are now terminal.

2. *Abandonment of Hope.* Every doctor can tell stories of patients expected to die within days who surprise everyone with their extraordinary recoveries. Every doctor has experienced the wonderful embarrassment of being proven wrong in their pessimistic prognosis. To make euthanasia a legitimate option as soon as the prognosis is pessimistic enough is to reduce the probability of such extraordinary recoveries from low to zero.

3. *Increased Fear of Hospitals and Doctors.* Despite all the efforts at health education, it seems there will always be a transference of the patient's fear of illness from the illness to the doctors and hospitals who treat it. This fear is still very real

Excerpts from Stephen G. Potts, "Objections to the institutionalisation of euthanasia" from "Looking for the Exit Door: Killing and Caring in Modern Medicine," Houston Law Review, Vol. 25, 1988, pp. 504–511. Copyright © 1988 Houston Law Review. Reprinted by permission.

and leads to large numbers of late presentations of illnesses that might have been cured if only the patients had sought help earlier. To institutionalise euthanasia, however carefully, would undoubtedly magnify all the latent fear of doctors and hospitals harbored by the public. The inevitable result would be a rise in late presentations and, therefore, preventable deaths.

4. *Difficulties of Oversight and Regulation.* Both the Dutch and the Californian proposals list sets of precautions designed to prevent abuses. They acknowledge that such abuses are a possibility. I am far from convinced that the precautions are sufficient to prevent either those abuses that have been foreseen or those that may arise after passage of the law. The history of legal "loopholes" is not a cheering one. Abuses might arise when the patient is wealthy and an inheritance is at stake, when the doctor has made mistakes in diagnosis and treatment and hopes to avoid detection, when insurance coverage for treatment costs is about to expire, and in a host of other circumstances.

5. *Pressure on the Patient.* Both sets of proposals seek to limit the influence of the patient's family on the decision, again acknowledging the risks posed by such influence. Families have all kinds of subtle ways, conscious and unconscious, of putting pressure on a patient to request euthanasia and relieve them of the financial and social burden of care. Many patients already feel guilty for imposing burdens on those who care for them, even when the families are happy to bear that burden. To provide an avenue for the discharge of that guilt in a request for euthanasia is to risk putting to death a great many patients who do not wish to die.

6. *Conflict with Aims of Medicine.* The pro-euthanasia movement cheerfully hands the dirty work of the actual killing to the doctors who, by and large, neither seek nor welcome the responsibility. There is little examination of the psychological stresses imposed on those whose training and professional outlook are geared to the saving of lives by asking them to start taking lives on a regular basis. Euthanasia advocates seem very confident that doctors can be relied on to make the enormous

efforts sometimes necessary to save some lives, while at the same time assenting to requests to take other lives. Such confidence reflects, perhaps, a high opinion of doctors' psychic robustness, but it is a confidence seriously undermined by the shocking rates of depression, suicide, alcoholism, drug addiction, and marital discord consistently recorded among this group.

7. *Dangers of Societal Acceptance.* It must never be forgotten that doctors, nurses, and hospital administrators have personal lives, homes, and families, or that they are something more than just doctors, nurses or hospital administrators. They are citizens and a significant part of the society around them. I am very worried about what the institutionalisation of euthanasia will do to society, in general, and, particularly how much it will further erode our attachment to the sixth commandment.[1] How will we regard murderers? What will we say to the terrorist who justifies killing as a means to his political end when we ourselves justify killing as a means to a humanitarian end? I do not know and I daresay the euthanasia advocates do not either, but I worry about it and they appear not to. They need to justify their complacency.

8. *The Slippery Slope.* How long after acceptance of voluntary euthanasia will we hear the calls for nonvoluntary euthanasia? There are thousands of comatose or demented patients sustained by little more than good nursing care. They are an enormous financial and social burden. How soon will the advocates of euthanasia be arguing that we should "assist them in dying"—for, after all, they won't mind, will they?

How soon after *that* will we hear the calls for involuntary euthanasia, the disposal of the burdensome, the unproductive, the polluters of the gene pool? We must never forget the way the Nazi euthanasia programme made this progression in a few short years. "Oh, but they were barbarians," you say, and so they were, but not at the outset.

If developments in terminal care can be represented by a progression from the CURE mode of medical care to the CARE mode, enacting voluntary euthanasia legislation would permit a further progression to the KILL mode. The slippery slope argument represents the fear that, if this step is taken, then it will be difficult to avoid a further progression to the CULL mode, as illustrated:

CURE The central aim of medicine
CARE The central aim of terminal care once patients are beyond cure
KILL The aim of the proponents of euthanasia for those patients beyond cure and not helped by care
CULL The feared result of weakening the prohibition on euthanasia

I do not know how easy these moves will be to resist once voluntary euthanasia is accepted, but I have seen little evidence that the modern euthanasia advocates care about resisting them or even worry that they might be possible.

9. *Costs and Benefits.* Perhaps the most disturbing risk of all is posed by the growing concern over medical costs. Euthanasia is, after all, a very cheap service. The cost of a dose of barbiturates and curare and the few hours in a hospital bed that it takes them to act is minute compared to the massive bills incurred by many patients in the last weeks and months of their lives. Already in Britain, there is a serious under-provision of expensive therapies like renal dialysis and intensive care, with the result that many otherwise preventable deaths occur.[2] Legalising euthanasia would save substantial resources which could be diverted to more "useful" treatments. These economic concerns already exert pressure to accept euthanasia, and, if accepted, they will inevitably tend to enlarge the category of patients for whom euthanasia is permitted.

Each of these objections could, and should, be expanded and pressed harder. I do not propose to do so now, for it is sufficient for my purposes to list them as *risks*, not inevitabilities. Several elements go into our judgment of the severity of a risk: the *probability* that the harm in question will arise (the odds), the *severity* of the harm in question (the stakes), and the ease with which the harm in question can be corrected (the *reversability*). The institutionalisation of euthanasia is such a radical departure from anything that has gone before in Western society that we simply cannot judge the probability of any or all of the listed consequences. Nor can we rule any of them out. There must, however, be agreement that the severity of each of the harms listed is enough to give serious cause for concern, and the severity of all the harms together is enough to horrify. Furthermore, many of the potential harms seem likely to prove very difficult, if not impossible, to reverse by reinstituting a ban on euthanasia.

B. WEIGHING THE RISKS

For all these reasons, the burden of proof *must* lie with those who would have us gamble by legalising euthanasia. They should demonstrate beyond a reasonable doubt that the dangers listed will not arise, just as chemical companies proposing to introduce a new drug are required to demonstrate that it is safe as well as beneficial. Thus far, the proponents of euthanasia have relied exclusively on the compassion they arouse with tales of torment mercifully cut short by death, and have made little or no attempt to shoulder the burden of proving that legalising euthanasia is safe. Until they make such an attempt and carry it off successfully, their proposed legislation must be rejected outright.

C. THE RIGHT TO DIE AND THE DUTY TO KILL

The nature of my arguments should have made it clear by now that I object, not so much to individual acts of euthanasia, but to institutionalising it as a practice. All the pro-euthanasia arguments turn on the individual case of the patient in pain, suffering at the center of an intolerable existence. They exert powerful calls on our compassion, and appeal to our pity, therefore, we assent too readily when it is claimed that such patients have a "*right to die*" as an escape from torment. So long as the right to die means no more than the right to refuse life-prolonging treatment and the right to rational suicide, I agree. The advocates of euthanasia want to go much further than this though. They want to extend the right to die to encompass the right to receive assistance in suicide and, beyond that, the right to be killed. Here, the focus shifts from the patient to the agent, and from the killed to the killer; but, the argument begins to break down because our compassion does not extend this far.

If it is true that there is a right to be assisted in suicide or a right to be killed, then it follows that someone, somewhere, has a *duty* to provide the assistance or to do the killing. When we look at the proposed legislation, it is very clear upon whom the advocates of euthanasia would place this duty: the doctor. It would be the doctor's job to provide the pills and the doctor's job to give the lethal injection. The regulation of euthanasia is meant to prevent anyone, other than a doctor, from doing it. Such regulation would ensure that the doctor does it with the proper precautions and consultations, and would give the doctor security from legal sanctions for doing it. The emotive appeal of euthanasia is undeniably powerful, but it lasts only so long as we can avoid thinking about who has to do the killing, and where, and when, and how. Proposals to institutionalise euthanasia force us to think hard about these things, and the chill that their contemplation generates is deep enough to freeze any proponent's ardor.

Two questions immediately suggest themselves: (1) Why doctors? and (2) Which doctors? The logic of the euthanasia proponents' arguments suggests the likely replies. Euthanasia is portrayed as a natural extension of patient care, not a radical new departure from it. When care and comfort is not enough to avert serious suffering, and the patient seeks an escape in death, is it not reasonable that it should be the doctor who provides the escape route in furtherance of his mission to eliminate the patient's pain? The patient and his doctor have been partners all along—fighting first the disease and then its symptoms. Why not extend their partnership just one stage further? The intended answer to the first question is clear: The doctor is the one who has primary responsibility for patient care from the outset and who should, therefore, take primary responsibility for euthanasia as the final element of patient care when other elements fail.

The intended answer to the second question follows from the answer to the first: The doctor responsible for euthanasia should be the same as the doctor responsible for the rest of a patient's care. If euthanasia is to be properly integrated with other modes of patient care, then it should be expected from the provider of those other modes— the doctor who has provided care throughout. The euthanasia advocates do not usually press this answer very far. Their proposals allow doctors to deny a patient's request for euthanasia on the grounds of conscience, as long as they refer the patient to a doctor more willing to comply.[3] Nevertheless, the *tone* of the pro-euthanasia literature is revealing: Doctors who deny a patient's request to provide the means of suicide are consistently portrayed in a negative light, however sympathetic they may be, in contrast to those heroes who risk their careers to slip a bottle of barbiturates under the patient's pillow. The advocates of euthanasia expect all doctors to comply with requests for euthanasia, but their legislation will not *require* it, though it will require a referral.

Enacting the legislation could result in a general willingness on the part of most doctors to meet expectations and comply with requests for euthanasia, at the one extreme, or, at the other, a general refusal to comply, coupled with reluctant transfers to a small number of more compliant doctors who will become de facto death specialists ("thanatologists" perhaps).[4] Neither alternative, nor any mix of the two, is attractive. Instituting either of them involves a recognition that ceding someone the right to be killed involves imposing on someone else, not just the permission, but the *duty* to kill. It is the institutionalisation of this duty which gives rise to many of the dangers listed above.

This last objection relates to another set out above (#5. Pressure on the Patient). The objection turns on the concern that many requests for euthanasia will not be truly voluntary because of pressure on the patient or the patient's fear of becoming a burden. There is a significant risk that legalising voluntary euthanasia out of respect for the *right* to die will generate many requests for euthanasia out of a perceived *duty* to die.

The right to die is an emotive slogan, used liberally in the pro-euthanasia campaign, but with little attention to its dangerous correlates—specifically, the institutionalisation of a doctor's duty to kill and a patient's duty to die. Euthanasia's proponents must show that the legislation they advocate separates these correlates, but they cannot, nor have they ever really tried.

NOTES

1. "Thou shalt not kill." *Exodus* 20:13 (King James).
2. I have argued elsewhere that cost-effectiveness criteria increasingly employed in resource allocation decisions in Britain would tend to make euthanasia not just a permitted medical intervention, but a high priority one.
3. This is similar to the way that doctors and nurses may refuse to participate in abortions if their religion or conscience so dictates. Nevertheless, they are expected to refer a woman requesting abortion to someone who will provide it.
4. If the latter, there must be a justification for the requirement that transfer should be to another *doctor* rather than anyone else. It takes little medical expertise to kill humanely. If the sole function of the transfer is to grant a request to be killed, then why not appoint a suitably trained hospital executioner, or call in a nearby veterinarian (whom cats and dogs will doubtless thank for having been put out of *their* misery)?

Euthanasia: The Way We Do It, the Way They Do It

Margaret P. Battin

Margaret Battin is a professor of philosophy at the University of Utah. She is the author of *Ending Life: Ethics and the Way We Die* (2005), *The Least Worst Death* (1994), *Ethics in the Sanctuary* (1990), and *Ethical Issues in Suicide* (1982). She is the coeditor of *Medicine and Social Justice: Essays on the Distribution of Health Care* (2002).

Battin examines euthanasia practices in three societies: the Netherlands, where physician-performed euthanasia and physician-assisted suicide are allowed; Germany where active euthanasia is disallowed but suicide is allowed; and the United States, where active euthanasia is disallowed and physician-assisted suicide is allowed only in the state of Oregon,* but where passive euthanasia in the form of withdrawal or withholding of treatment is common. Battin argues that the United States does not supply an adequate range of options to patients who are near death. After considering arguments from many sides of the issue, Battin concludes that physician-assisted suicide works best for the United States as end-of-life practice.

Because we tend to be rather myopic in our discussions of death and dying, especially about the issues of active euthanasia and assisted suicide, it is valuable to place the question of how we go about dying in an international context. We do not always see that our own cultural norms may be quite different from those of other nations and that our background assumptions and actual practices differ dramatically—even when the countries in question are all developed industrial nations with similar cultural ancestries, religious traditions, and economic circumstances. I want to explore the three rather different approaches to end-of-life dilemmas prevalent in the United States, the

Netherlands, and Germany—developments mirrored in Australia, Belgium, Switzerland, and elsewhere in the developed world—and consider how a society might think about which model of approach to dying is most appropriate for it.

THREE BASIC MODELS OF DYING

The Netherlands, Germany, and the United States are all advanced industrial democracies. They all have sophisticated medical establishments and life expectancies over 75 years; their populations are all characterized by an increasing proportion of older persons. They are all in what has been called the fourth stage of the epidemiologic transition[1]— that stage of societal development in which it is no longer the case that the majority of the population dies of acute parasitic or infectious diseases, often with rapid, unpredictable onsets and sharp fatality

From Margaret P. Battin, Ending Life: Ethics and the Way We Die (New York: Oxford University Press, 2005). Reprinted with permission.

*Editors' note: Washington became the second state to legalize physician-assisted suicide in 2008.

curves (as was true in earlier and less developed societies); rather, in modern industrial societies, the majority of a population—estimated in Europe at about 66–71%—dies of degenerative diseases, especially delayed-degenerative diseases that are characterized by late, slow-onset and extended decline.[2] This is the case throughout the developed world. Accidents and suicide claim some, as do infectious diseases like AIDS, pneumonia, and influenza, but most people in highly industrialized countries die from heart disease (by no means always suddenly fatal); cancer; atherosclerosis; chronic obstructive pulmonary disease; diabetes, liver, kidney, or other organ disease; or degenerative neurological disorders. In the developed world, we die not so much from attack by outside diseases but from gradual disintegration. Thus, all three of these modern industrial countries—the United States, the Netherlands, and Germany—are alike in facing a common problem: how to deal with the characteristic new ways in which we die.

Dealing with Dying in the United States

In the United States, we have come to recognize that the maximal extension of life-prolonging treatment in these late-life degenerative conditions is often inappropriate. Although we could keep the machines and tubes—the respirators, intravenous lines, feeding tubes—hooked up for extended periods, we recognize that this is inhumane, pointless, and financially impossible. Instead, as a society we have developed a number of mechanisms for dealing with these hopeless situations, all of which involve withholding or withdrawing various forms of treatment.

Some mechanisms for withholding or withdrawing treatments are exercised by the patient who is confronted by such a situation or who anticipates it. These include refusal of treatment, the patient-executed do-not-resuscitate (DNR) order, the living will, and the durable power of attorney. Others are mechanisms for decision by second parties about a patient who is no longer competent or never was competent, reflected in a long series of court cases from *Quinlan,*

Saikewicz, Spring, Eichner, Barber, Bartling, Conroy, Brophy, and the trio *Farrell, Peter,* and *Jobes* to *Cruzan.* These cases delineate the precise circumstances under which it is appropriate to withhold or withdraw various forms of therapy, including respiratory support, chemotherapy, dialysis, antibiotics in intercurrent infections, and artificial nutrition and hydration. Thus, during the past quarter-century, roughly since *Quinlan* (1976), the United States has developed an impressive body of case law and state statutes that protects, permits, and facilitates the characteristic American strategy of dealing with end-of-life situations. These cases provide a framework for withholding or withdrawing treatment when physicians and family members believe there is no medical or moral point in going on. This has sometimes been termed *passive euthanasia;* more often it is simply called *allowing to die.*

Indeed, "allowing to die" has become ubiquitous in the United States. For example, a 1988 study found that of the 85% of deaths in the United States that occurred in health-care institutions, including hospitals, nursing homes, and other facilities, about 70% involved electively withholding some form of life-sustaining treatment.[3] A 1989 study found that 85–90% of critical care professionals said they were withholding or withdrawing life-sustaining treatments from patients who were "deemed to have irreversible disease and are terminally ill."[4] A 1997 study of limits to life-sustaining care found that between 1987–88 and 1992–93, recommendations to withhold or withdraw life support prior to death increased from 51% to 90% in the intensive-care units studied.[5] Rates of withholding therapy such as ventilator support, surgery, and dialysis were found in yet another study to be substantial, and to increase with age.[6] A 1994/95 study of 167 intensive-care units—all the ICUs associated with U.S. training programs in critical care medicine or pulmonary and critical care medicine—found that in 75% of deaths, some form of care was withheld or withdrawn.[7] It has been estimated that 1.3 million American deaths a year follow decisions to withhold life support;[8] this is a majority of the just over 2 million American deaths per year.

In recent years, the legitimate use of withholding and withdrawing treatment has increasingly been understood to include practices likely or certain to result in death. The administration of escalating doses of morphine in a dying patient, which, it has been claimed, will depress respiration and so hasten death, is accepted under the (Catholic) principle of double effect, provided the medication is intended to relieve pain and merely foreseen but not intended to result in death; this practice is not considered killing or active hastening of death. The use of "terminal sedation," in which a patient dying in pain is sedated into unconsciousness while artificial nutrition and hydration are withheld, is also recognized as medically and legally acceptable; it too is understood as a form of "allowing to die," not active killing. With the single exception of Oregon, where physician-assisted suicide became legal in 1997,[9] withholding and withdrawing treatment and related forms of allowing to die are the only legally recognized ways we in the United States go about dealing with dying. A number of recent studies have shown that many physicians—in all states studied—do receive requests for assistance in suicide or active euthanasia and that a substantial number of these physicians have complied with one or more such requests; however, this more direct assistance in dying takes place entirely out of sight of the law. Except in Oregon, *allowing to die*, but not *causing to die*, has been the only legally protected alternative to maximal treatment legally recognized in the United States; it remains America's—and American medicine's—official posture in the face of death.

Dealing with Dying in the Netherlands

In the Netherlands, although the practice of withholding and withdrawing treatment is similar to that in the United States, voluntary active euthanasia and physician assistance in suicide are also available responses to end-of-life situations.[10] Active euthanasia, understood as the termination of the life of the patient at the patient's explicit and persistent request, is the more frequent form of directly assisted dying, and most discussion in the Netherlands has concerned it rather than assistance in suicide, though the conceptual difference is not regarded as great: many cases of what the Dutch term *euthanasia* involve initial self-administration of the lethal dose by the patient but procurement of death by the physician, and many cases of what is termed *physician-assisted suicide* involve completion of the lethal process by the physician if a self-administered drug does not prove fully effective. Although until 2002 they were still technically illegal under statutory law—and even with legalization remain an "exception" to those provisions of the Dutch Penal Code that prohibit killing on request and intentional assistance in suicide—active euthanasia and assistance in suicide have long been widely regarded as legal, or rather *gedoogd*, legally "tolerated," and have in fact been deemed justified (not only non-punishable) by the courts when performed by a physician if certain conditions were met. Voluntary active euthanasia (in the law, called "life-ending on request") and physician-assisted suicide are now fully legal by statute under these guidelines. Dutch law protects the physician who performs euthanasia or provides assistance in suicide from prosecution for homicide if these guidelines, known as the conditions of "due care," are met.

Over the years, the guidelines have been stated in various ways. They contain six central provisions:

1. That the patient's request be voluntary and well-considered
2. That the patient be undergoing or about to undergo intolerable suffering, that is, suffering that is lasting and unbearable
3. That all alternatives acceptable to the patient for relieving the suffering have been tried, and that in the patient's view there is no other reasonable solution
4. That the patient have full information about his or her situation and prospects
5. That the physician consult with a second physician who has examined the patient and whose judgment can be expected to be independent
6. That in performing euthanasia or assisting in suicide, the physician act with due care

Of these criteria, it is the first that is held to be central: euthanasia may be performed only at the *voluntary* request of the patient. This criterion is also understood to require that the patient's request be a stable, enduring, reflective one—not the product of a transitory impulse. Every attempt is to be made to rule out depression, psychopathology, pressures from family members, unrealistic fears, and other factors compromising voluntariness, though depression is not in itself understood to necessarily preclude such choice. Euthanasia may be performed *only* by a physician, not by a nurse, family member, or other party.

In 1991, a comprehensive, nationwide study requested by the Dutch government, popularly known as the Remmelink Commission report, provided the first objective data about the incidence of euthanasia and physician-assisted suicide.[11] This study also provided information about other medical decisions at the end of life, particularly withholding or withdrawal of treatment and the use of life-shortening doses of opioids for the control of pain, as well as direct termination. The Remmelink report was supplemented by a study focusing particularly carefully on the characteristics of patients and the nature of their euthanasia requests.[12] Five years later, the researchers from these two studies jointly conducted a major new nationwide study replicating much of the previous Remmelink inquiry, providing empirical data both about current practice in the Netherlands and change over a five year period.[13] A third replication of the nationwide study was published in 2003.[14]

About 140,000 people die in the Netherlands every year, and of these deaths, about 30% are sudden and unexpected, while the majority are predictable and foreseen, usually the result of degenerative illness comparatively late in life. Of the total deaths in the Netherlands, according to the 2001 data, about 20.2% involve decisions to withhold or withdraw treatment in situations where continuing treatment would probably have prolonged life; another 20.1% involve the "double effect" use of opioids to relieve pain but in dosages probably sufficient to shorten life. Only a small fraction of people who die do so by euthanasia— about 2.4%—and an even smaller fraction, 0.2%, do so by physician-assisted suicide. Of patients who do receive euthanasia or physician-assisted suicide, about 80% have cancer, while 3% have cardiovascular disease and 4% neurological disease, primarily ALS.

However, the 1990 Remmelink report had also revealed that another 0.8% of patients who died did so as the result of life-terminating procedures not technically called euthanasia, without explicit, current request. These cases, known as "the 1000 cases," unleashed highly exaggerated claims that patients were being killed against their wills. In fact, in about half of these cases, euthanasia had been previously discussed with the patient or the patient had expressed in a previous phase of the disease a wish for euthanasia if his or her suffering became unbearable ("Doctor, please don't let me suffer too long"); and in the other half, the patient was no longer competent and was near death, clearly suffering grievously although verbal contact had become impossible.[15] In 91% of these cases without explicit, current request, life was shortened by less than a week, and in 33% by less than a day.

Over the next decade, as revealed in the 1995 and 2003 nationwide studies, the proportion of cases of euthanasia rose slightly (associated, the authors conjectured, with the aging of the population and an increase in the proportion of deaths due to cancer, that condition in which euthanasia is most frequent); the proportion of cases of assisted suicide had remained about the same. The proportion of cases of life termination without current explicit request declined slightly to 0.7%, down from the notorious 1,000 to about 900. In 1990, a total of 2.9% of all deaths had involved euthanasia and related practices; by 2001 this total was about 3.7%.[16] In the early days of openly tolerated euthanasia, comparatively few cases were reported as required to the Public Prosecutor; there has been a dramatic gain since reporting procedures have been revised to require reporting to a review committee rather than to the police, and about 54% are now reported. However, there are no major differences between reported and unreported cases in terms of the patient's characteristics, clinical conditions, or reasons for the action.[17] Euthanasia is performed in about 1:25 of deaths that occur at home, about 1:75 of hospital deaths, and about 1:800 of nursing home deaths. The Netherlands has now established regional review committees for such cases and has initiated hospice-style pain management programs complete with 24-hour phone-in consultation services for physicians confronted by euthanasia requests.

Although euthanasia is thus not frequent, a small fraction of the total annual mortality, it is nevertheless a conspicuous option in terminal illness, well known to both physicians and the general public. There has been very widespread public discussion of the issues that arise with respect to euthanasia during the last quarter-century, and surveys of public opinion show that public support for a liberal euthanasia policy has been growing: from 40% in 1966 to 81% in 1988, then to about 90% by 2000. Doctors, too, support the practice, and although there has been a vocal opposition group, it has remained in the clear minority. Some 57% of Dutch physicians say that they have performed euthanasia or provided assistance in suicide, and an additional 30% say that although they have not actually done so, they can conceive of situations in which they would be prepared to do so. Ten percent say they would never perform it but would refer the patient to another physician. The proportion of physicians who say they not only would not do so themselves but would not refer a patient who requested it to a physician who would dropped from 4% in 1990 to 3% in 1995 to 1% in 2001. Thus, although many physicians who have performed euthanasia say that they would be most reluctant to do so again and that "only in the face of unbearable suffering and with no alternatives would they be prepared to take such action,"[18] all three nationwide studies have shown that the majority of Dutch physicians accept the practice. Surveying the changes over the 5-year period between 1990 and 1995, the authors of the nationwide study also commented that the data do not support claims of a slippery slope.[19] Work now in progress shows no such pattern either.[20]

In general, pain alone is not the basis for deciding upon euthanasia, since pain can, in most cases, be effectively treated. Only a third of Dutch physicians think that adequate pain control and terminal care make euthanasia redundant, and that number has been dropping. Rather, the "intolerable suffering" mentioned in the second criterion is understood to mean suffering that is intolerable in the patient's (rather than the physician's) view, and can include a fear of or unwillingness to endure *entluistering*, that gradual effacement and loss of personal identity that characterizes the end-stages of many terminal illnesses. In very exceptional circumstances, the Supreme Court ruled in the *Chabot* case of 1994, physician-assisted suicide may be justified for a patient with nonsomatic, psychiatric illness like intractable depression, but such cases are extremely rare and require heightened scrutiny.

In a year, about 35,000 patients seek reassurance from their physicians that they will be granted euthanasia if their suffering becomes severe; there are about 9,700 explicit requests, and about two-thirds of these are turned down, usually on the grounds that there is some other way of treating the patient's suffering. In 14% of cases in 1990, the denial was based on the presence of depression or psychiatric illness.

In the Netherlands, many hospitals now have protocols for the performance of euthanasia; these serve to ensure that the legal guidelines have been met. However, euthanasia is often practiced in the patient's home, typically by the general practitioner who is the patient's long-term family physician. Euthanasia is usually performed after aggressive hospital treatment has failed to arrest the patient's terminal illness: the patient has come home to die, and the family physician is prepared to ease this passing. Whether practiced at home or in the hospital, it is believed that euthanasia usually takes place in the presence of the family members, perhaps the visiting nurse, and often the patient's pastor or priest. Many doctors say that performing euthanasia is never easy but that it is something they believe a doctor ought to do for his or her patient when the patient genuinely wants it and nothing else can help.

Thus, in the Netherlands a patient who is facing the end of life has an option not openly practiced in the United States, except Oregon: to ask the physician to bring his or her life to an end. Although not everyone in the Netherlands does so—indeed, over 96% of people who die in a given year do not do so in this way—it is a choice legally recognized and widely understood.

Facing Death in Germany

In part because of its very painful history of Nazism, German medical culture has insisted that doctors should have no role in directly causing death. As in the other countries with advanced medical systems, withholding and withdrawing of care is widely used to avoid the unwanted or inappropriate prolongation of life when the patient is already dying, but there has been vigorous and nearly universal opposition in German public discourse to the notion of active euthanasia, at least in the horrific, politically motivated sense associated with Nazism. In the last few years, some Germans have begun to approve of euthanasia in the Dutch sense, based on the Greek root, *eu-thanatos,* or "good death," a voluntary choice by the patient for an easier death, but many Germans still associate euthanasia with the politically motivated exterminations by the Nazis and view the Dutch as stepping out on a dangerously slippery slope.

However, although under German law killing on request (including voluntary euthanasia) is illegal, German law has not prohibited assistance in suicide since the time of Frederick the Great (1742), provided the person is *tatherrschaftsfähig,* capable of exercising control over his or her actions, and also acting out of *freiverantwortliche Wille,* freely responsible choice. Doctors are prohibited from assistance in suicide not by law but by the policies and code of ethics of the Bundesärztekammer, the German medical association.[21] Furthermore, any person, physician or otherwise, has a duty to rescue a person who is unconscious. Thus, medical assistance in suicide is limited, but it is possible for a family member or friend to assist in a person's suicide, for instance by providing a lethal drug, as long as the person is competent and acting freely and the assister does not remain with the person after unconsciousness sets in.

Taking advantage of this situation, a private organization, the Deutsche Gesellschaft füt Humanes Sterben (DGHS), or German Society for Dying in Dignity, has developed; it provides support to its very extensive membership in many end-of-life mailers, including choosing suicide as an alternative to terminal illness. Of course, not all Germans are members of this organization, and many are not sympathetic with its aims, yet the notion of self-directed ending of one's own life in terminal illness is widely understood as an option. Although since 1993 the DGHS has not itself supplied such information for legal reasons, it tells its members how to obtain the booklet "Departing Drugs," published in Scotland, and other information about ending life, if they request it, provided they have been a member for one year and have not received medical or psychotherapeutic treatment for depression or other psychiatric illness during the last three years. The information includes a list of prescription drugs, together with the specific dosages necessary for producing a certain, painless death. The DGHS does not itself sell or supply lethal drugs;[22] rather, it recommends that the member approach a physician for a prescription for the drug desired, asking, for example, for a barbiturate to help with sleep. If necessary, the DGHS has been willing to arrange for someone to obtain drugs from neighboring countries, including France, Italy, Spain, Portugal, and Greece, where they may be available without prescription. It also makes available the so-called Exit Bag, a plastic bag used with specific techniques for death by asphyxiation. The DGHS provides and trains family members in what it calls *Sterbebegleitung* (accompaniment in dying), which may take the form of simple presence with a person who is dying but may also involve direct assistance to a person who is committing suicide, up until unconsciousness sets in. The *Sterbebegleiter* is typically a layperson, not someone medically trained, and physicians play no role in assisting in these cases of suicide. Direct active *Sterbehilfe*—active euthanasia—is illegal under German law. But active indirect *Sterbehilfe,* understood as assistance in suicide, is not illegal, and the DGHS provides counseling in how a "death with dignity" may be achieved in this way.

To preclude suspicion by providing evidence of the person's intentions, the DGHS also provides a form—printed on a single sheet of distinctive purple paper—to be signed once when joining the organization, documenting that the person has reflected thoroughly on the possibility of "free death" (*Freitod*) or suicide in terminal illness as a way of releasing oneself from severe suffering, and expressing the intention to determine the time and character of one's own death. The person then signs this "free death directive" or "suicide decision declaration" (*Freitodverfügung*) again at the time of the suicide, leaving it beside the body as evidence that the act is not impetuous or coerced. The form also requests that, if the person is discovered before the suicide is complete, no rescue measures be undertaken. Because assisting suicide is not illegal in Germany (provided the person is competent and in control of his or her own will, and thus not already unconscious), there has been no legal risk for family members, the *Sterbebegleiter*, or others in reporting information about the methods and effectiveness of suicide attempts, and, at least in the past, the DGHS has encouraged its network of regional bureaus, located in major cities throughout the country, to facilitate feedback. On this basis it has regularly updated and revised the drug information provided. There has been no legal risk in remaining with the patient to assist him or her at the bedside—that is, at least until recent legal threats.

Open, legal assistance in suicide has been supported by a feature of the German language that makes it possible to conceptualize it in a comparatively benign way. While English, French, Spanish, and many other languages have just a single primary word for suicide, German has four: *Selbstmord, Selbsttötung, Suizid*, and *Freitod*, of which the last has comparatively positive, even somewhat heroic connotations.[23] Thus German speakers can think about the deliberate termination of their lives in a linguistic way not easily available to speaker of other languages. The negatively rooted term *Selbstmord* ("Self-murder") can be avoided; the comparatively neutral terms *Selbsttötung* ("'self-killing") and

Suizid ("suicide") can be used and the positively rooted term *Freitod* ("free death") can be reinforced. The DGHS has frequently used *Freitod* rather than German's other, more negative terms to describe the practice with which it provides assistance.

No reliable figures are available about the number of suicides with which the DGHS has assisted, and, as in the Netherlands and Oregon, the actual frequency of directly assisted death is probably small: most Germans who die as a result of medical decision making, like most Dutch and most Americans, die as treatment is withheld or withdrawn or as opiates are administered in doses that foreseeably but not intentionally shorten life—that is, by being "allowed to die." Yet it is fair to say, both because of the legal differences and the different conceptual horizons of German-speakers, that the option of self-produced death outside the medical system is more clearly open in Germany than it has been in the Netherlands or the United States.

In recent years, the DGHS has decreased its emphasis on suicide, now thinking of it as a "last resort" when pain control is inadequate—and turned much of its attention to the development of other measures for protecting the rights of the terminally ill, measures already available in many other countries. It distributes newly legalized advance directives, including living wills and durable powers of attorney, as well as organ-donation documents. It provides information about pain control, palliative care, and Hospice. It offers information about suicide prevention. Yet, despite various legal threats, it remains steadfast in defense of the terminally ill patient's right to self-determination, including the right to suicide, and continues to be supportive of patients who make this choice.

To be sure, assisted suicide is not the only option open to terminally ill patients in Germany, and the choice may be infrequent. Reported suicide rates in Germany are only moderately higher than in the Netherlands or the United States, though there is reason to think that terminal-illness suicides in all countries are often reported as deaths from the underlying disease. Although there is political pressure from right-to-die organizations to change the law to permit voluntary active euthanasia in the way understood in the Netherlands, Germany is also seeing increasing emphasis on help in dying, like that offered by Hospice, that does not involve direct termination. Whatever the pressures, the DGHS is a conspicuous, widely known organization, and many Germans appear to be aware that assisted suicide is available and not illegal even if they do not use its services.

OBJECTIONS TO THE THREE MODELS OF DYING

In response to the dilemmas raised by the new circumstances of death, in which the majority of people in the advanced industrial nations die after an extended period of terminal deterioration, different countries develop different practices. The United States, with the sole exception of Oregon, legally permits only withholding and withdrawal of treatment, "double effect" uses of high doses of opiates, and terminal sedation, all conceived of as "allowing to die." The Netherlands permits these but also permits voluntary active euthanasia and physician-assisted suicide. Germany rejects physician-performed euthanasia but, at least until recent legal threats, permits assisted suicide not assisted by a physician. These three serve as the principal types or models of response in end-of-life dilemmas in the developed world. To be sure, all of these practices are currently undergoing evolution, and in some ways they are becoming more alike: Germany is paying new attention to the rights of patients to execute advance directives and thus to have treatment withheld or withdrawn, and public surveys reveal considerable support for euthanasia in the Dutch sense, voluntary active aid-in-dying under careful controls. In the Netherlands, a 1995 policy statement of the Royal Dutch Medical Association expressed a careful preference for physician-assisted suicide over euthanasia, urging that physicians encourage patients who request euthanasia to administer the lethal dose themselves as a further protection for voluntary choice. And, in the United States, the Supreme Court's 1997 ruling that there is no constitutional right to physician-assisted suicide has been understood to countenance the emergence of a "laboratory of the states" in which individual states, following the example of Oregon, may in the future move to legalize physician-assisted suicide, though as of this writing no such further measures have yet succeeded. An attempt by U.S. Attorney General John Ashcroft to reinterpret the Controlled Substances Act to prohibit the use of scheduled drugs for the purpose of causing death and thus undercut Oregon's statute was rejected at the appellate level in 2004, though his further appeal may take the issue to the U.S. Supreme Court. Nevertheless, among these three countries that serve as the principal models of approaches to dying, there remain substantial differences, and while there are ethical and practical advantages to each approach, each approach also raises serious moral objections.

Objections to the German Practice

German low does not prohibit assisting suicide, but postwar German culture and the German physicians' code of ethics discourages physicians from taking an active role in causing death. This gives rise to distinctive moral problems. For one thing, if the physician is not permitted to assist in his or her patient's suicide, there may be little professional help or review provided for the patient's choice about suicide. If patients make such choices essentially outside the medical establishment, medical professionals may not be a position to detect or treat impaired judgment on the part of the patient, especially judgment impaired by depression. Similarly, if the patient must commit suicide assisted only by persons outside the medical profession, there are risks that the patient's diagnosis and prognosis will be inadequately confirmed, that the means chosen for suicide will be unreliable or inappropriately used, that the means used for suicide will fall into the hands of other persons, and that the patient will fail to recognize or be able to resist intrafamilial pressures and manipulation. While it now makes efforts to counter most of these objections, even the DGHS itself has been accused in the past of promoting rather than simply supporting choices of suicide. Finally, as the DGHS now emphasizes, assistance in suicide can be a freely chosen option only in a legal context that also protects the many other choices a patient may make—declining treatment, executing advance, directives, seeking Hospice care—about how his or her life shall end.

Objections to the Dutch Practice

The Dutch practice of physician-performed active voluntary euthanasia and physician-assisted suicide also raises a number of ethical issues, many of which have been discussed vigorously both in the Dutch press and in commentary on the Dutch practices from abroad. For one thing, it is sometimes said that the availability of physician-assisted dying creates a disincentive for providing good terminal care. There is no evidence that this is the case; on the contrary, Peter Admiral, the anesthesiologist who has been perhaps the Netherlands' most vocal defender of voluntary active euthanasia, insists that pain should rarely or never be the occasion for euthanasia, as pain (in contrast to suffering) is comparatively easily treated.[24] In fact, pain is the primary reason for the request in only about 5% of cases. Instead, it is a refusal to endure the final stages of deterioration, both mental and physical, that primarily motivates the majority of requests.

It is also sometimes said that active euthanasia violates the Hippocratic oath. The original Greek version of the oath does prohibit the physician from giving a deadly drug, even when asked for it; but the original version also prohibits the physician from performing surgery and from taking fees for teaching medicine, neither of which prohibitions has survived into contemporary medical practice. At issue is whether deliberately causing the death of one's patient—killing one's patient, some claim—can ever be part of the physician's role. "Doctors must not kill," opponents insist,[25] but Dutch physicians often say that they see performing euthanasia—where it is genuinely requested by the patient and nothing else can be done to relieve the patient's condition—as part of their duty to the patient, not as a violation of it. As the 1995 nationwide report commented, "a large majority of Dutch physicians consider euthanasia an exceptional but accepted part of medical practice."[26] Some Dutch do worry, however, that too many requests for euthanasia or assistance in suicide are refused—only about ⅓ of explicit requests are actually honored. One well-known Dutch commentator points to another, seemingly contrary concern: that some requests are made too early in a terminal course, even shortly after diagnosis, when with good palliative care the patient could live a substantial amount of time longer.[27] However, these are concerns about how euthanasia and physician-assisted suicide are practiced, not about whether they should be legal at all.

The Dutch are also often said to be a risk of starting down the slippery slope, that is, that the practice of voluntary active euthanasia for patients who meet the criteria will erode into practicing less-than-voluntary euthanasia on patients whose problems are not irremediable and perhaps by gradual degrees will develop into terminating the lives of people who are elderly, chronically ill, handicapped, mentally retarded, or otherwise regarded as undesirable. This risk is often expressed in vivid claims of widespread fear and wholesale slaughter—claims based on misinterpretation of the 1,000 cases of life-ending treatment without explicit, current request, claims that are often repeated in the right-to-life press in both the Netherlands and the United States. Work now in progress on the impact of legalized physician-assisted dying in the Netherlands and Oregon shows that these claims are simply not true: except for patients with AIDS, the rates of assisted dying show no evidence of disparate impact on ten groups of potentially vulnerable patients: the elderly, women, the uninsured (not applicable in the Netherlands, where all are insured), people with low educational status, the poor, racial minorities (except Asians in Oregon: data not available in the Netherlands), people with physical disabilities or chronic illness, mature minors, and people with psychiatric illness.[28] However, it is true that in recent years the Dutch have begun to agonize over the problems of the incompetent patient, the mentally ill patient, the newborn with serious deficits, and other patients who cannot make voluntary choices, though these are largely understood is issues about withholding or withdrawing treatment, not about direct termination.[29]

What is not often understood is that this new and acutely painful area of reflection for the Dutch—withholding and withdrawing treatment from incompetent patients—has already led in the United States to the emergence of a vast, highly developed body of law: namely, the long series of cases beginning with *Quinlan* and culminating in *Cruzan*. Americans have been discussing these issues for a long time and have developed a broad set of practices that are regarded as routine in withholding and withdrawing treatment from persons who are no longer or never were competent. The Dutch see Americans as much further out on the slippery slope than they are because Americans have already become accustomed to second-party choices that result in death for other people. Issues involving second-party choices are painful to the Dutch in a way they are not to Americans precisely because *voluntariness* is so central in the Dutch understanding of choices about dying. Concomitantly, the Dutch see the Americans' squeamishness about first-party choices—voluntary euthanasia, assisted suicide—as evidence that we are not genuinely committed to recognizing voluntary choice after all. For this reason, many Dutch commentators believe that the Americans are at a much greater risk of sliding down the slippery slope into involuntary killing than they are.

Objections to the American Practice

The German, Dutch, and American practices all occur within similar conditions—in industrialized nations with highly developed medical systems where a majority of the population die of illnesses exhibiting characteristically extended downhill courses—but the issues raised by the American response to this situation—relying on withholding and withdrawal of treatment—may be even more disturbing than those of the Dutch or the Germans. We Americans often assume that our approach is "safer" because, except in Oregon, it involves only letting someone die, not killing them; but it, too, raises very troubling questions.

The first of these issues is a function of the fact that withdrawing and especially withholding treatment are typically less conspicuous, less pronounced, less evident kinds of actions than direct killing, even though they can equally well lead to death. Decisions about nontreatment have an invisibility that decisions about directly causing death do not have, even though they may have the same result; hence there is a much wider range of occasions in which such decisions can be made. One can decline to treat a patient in many different ways, at many different times—by not providing oxygen, by not instituting dialysis, by not correcting electrolyte imbalances, and so on—all of which will cause the patient's death. Open medical killing also brings about death but is much more overt and conspicuous. Consequently, letting die offers many fewer protections. In contrast to the standard slippery-slope argument, which sees killing as riskier than letting die, the more realistic slippery-slope argument warns that because our culture relies primarily on decisions about nontreatment and practices like terminal sedation construed as "allowing to die," grave decisions about living or dying are not as open to scrutiny as they are under more direct life-terminating practices, hence are more open to abuse. Indeed, in the view of one influential commentator, the Supreme Court's 1997 decision in effect legalized active euthanasia, voluntary and nonvoluntary, in the form of terminal sedation, even as it rejected physician-assisted suicide.[30]

Second, reliance on withholding and withdrawal of treatment invites rationing in an extremely strong way, in part because of the comparative invisibility of these decisions. When a health-care provider does not offer a specific sort of care, it is not always possible to discern the motivation; the line between believing that it would not provide benefit to the patient and that it would not provide benefit worth the investment of resources in the patient can be very thin. This is a particular problem where health-care financing is decentralized, profit-oriented, and nonuniversal, as in the United States, and where rationing decisions without benefit of principle are not always available for easy review.

Third, relying on withholding and withdrawal of treatment can often be cruel. Even with Hospice or with skilled palliative care, it requires that the patient who is dying from one of the diseases that exhibit a characteristic extended, downhill course (as the majority of patients in the developed world all do) must, in effect, wait to die until the absence of a certain treatment will cause death. For instance, the cancer patient who forgoes chemotherapy or surgery does not simply die from this choice; he or she continues to endure the downhill course of the cancer until the tumor finally destroys some crucial bodily function or organ. The patient with ALS who decides in advance to decline respiratory support does not die at the time this choice is made but continues to endure increasing paralysis until breathing is impaired and suffocation occurs. Of course, attempts are made to try to ameliorate these situations by administering pain medication or symptom control at the time treatment is withheld—for instance, by using opiates and paralytics as a respirator is withdrawn—but these are all ways of disguising the fact that we are letting the disease kill the patient rather than directly bringing about death. But the ways diseases kill people can be far more cruel than the ways physicians kill patients when performing euthanasia or assisting in suicide. . . .

THE PROBLEM: A CHOICE OF CULTURES

In the developed world, we see three sorts of models in the three countries just examined in detail. While much of medical practice in them is similar, they do offer three quite different basic options in approaching death. All three of these options generate moral problems; none of them, nor any others we might devise, is free of moral difficulty. The question, then, is this: for a given society, which practices about dying are, morally and practically speaking, best?

It is not possible to answer this question in a less-than-ideal world without attention to the specific characteristics and deficiencies of the society in question. In asking which of these practices is best, we must ask which is best *for us*. That we currently employ one set of these options rather

than others does not prove that it is best for us; the question is whether practices developed in other cultures or those not yet widespread in any culture would be better for our own culture than that which has so far developed here. Thus, it is necessary to consider the differences between our own society and these other societies in the developed world that have real bearing on which model of approach to dying we ought to adopt. This question can be asked by residents of any country or culture: which model of dying is best *for us?* I have been addressing this question from the point of view of an American, but the question could be asked by any member of any culture, anywhere.

First, notice that different cultures exhibit different degrees of closeness between physicians and patients—different patterns of contact and involvement. The German physician is sometimes said to be more distant and more authoritarian than the American physician; on the other hand, the Dutch physician is often said to be closer to his or her patients than either the American or the German physician. In the Netherlands, basic primary care is provided by the *huisarts*, the general practitioner or family physician, who typically lives in the neighborhood, makes house calls frequently, and maintains an office in his or her own home. This physician usually also provides care for the other members of the patient's family and will remain the family's physician throughout his or her practice. Thus, the patient for whom euthanasia becomes an issue—say, the terminal cancer patient who has been hospitalized in the past but who has returned home to die—will be cared for by the trusted family physician on a regular basis. Indeed, for a patient in severe distress, the physician, supported by the visiting nurse, may make house calls as often as once a day, twice a day, or even more frequently (after all, the physician's office is right in the neighborhood) and is in continuous contact with the family. In contrast, the traditional American institution of the family doctor who makes house calls has largely become a thing of the past, and although some patients who die at home have access to hospice services and receive house calls from their long-term physician, many have no such long-term care and receive most of it from staff at a clinic or from house staff rotating through the services of a hospital. Most Americans die in institutions, including hospitals and nursing homes; in the Netherlands, in contrast, the majority of people die at home. The degree of continuing contact that the patient can have with a familiar, trusted physician and the degree of institutionalization clearly influence the nature of the patient's dying and also play a role in whether physician-performed active euthanasia, assisted suicide, and/or withholding and withdrawing treatment is appropriate.

Second, the United States has a much more volatile legal climate than either the Netherlands or Germany; its medical system is highly litigious, much more so than that of any other country in the world. Fears of malpractice actions or criminal prosecution color much of what physicians do in managing the dying of their patients. Americans also tend to develop public policy through court decisions and to assume that the existence of a policy puts an end to any moral issue. A delicate legal and moral balance over the issue of euthanasia, as has been the case in the Netherlands throughout the time it was understood as *gedoogd*, tolerated but not fully legal, would hardly be possible here.

Third, we in the United States have a very different financial climate in which to do our dying. Both the Netherlands and Germany, as well as virtually every other industrialized nation, have systems of national health insurance or national health care. Thus the patient is not directly responsible for the costs of treatment, and consequently the patient's choices about terminal care and/or euthanasia need not take personal financial considerations into account. Even for the patient who does have health insurance in the United States, many kinds of services are not covered, whereas the national health care or health insurance programs of many other countries provide multiple relevant services, including at-home physician care, home nursing care, home respite care, care in a nursing home or other long-term facility, dietician care, rehabilitation care, physical therapy, psychological counseling, and so on. The patient in the United States needs to attend to the financial aspects of dying in a way that

patients in many other countries do not, and in this country both the patient's choices and the recommendations of the physician are very often shaped by financial considerations.

There are many other differences between the United States on the one hand and the Netherlands and Germany, with their different options for dying, on the other, including differences in degrees of paternalism in the medical establishment, in racism, sexism, and ageism in the general culture, and in awareness of a problematic historical past, especially Nazism. All of these cultural, institutional, social, and legal differences influence the appropriateness or inappropriateness of practices such as active euthanasia and assisted suicide. For instance, the Netherlands' tradition of close physician-patient contact, its comparative absence of malpractice-motivated medicine, and its provision of comprehensive health insurance, together with its comparative lack of racism and ageism and its experience in resistance to Nazism, suggest that this culture is able to permit the practice of voluntary active euthanasia, performed by physicians, as well as physician-assisted suicide, without risking abuse. On the other hand, it is sometimes said that Germany still does not trust its physicians, remembering the example of Nazi experimentation, and, given a comparatively authoritarian medical climate in which the contact between physician and patient is quite distanced, the population could not be comfortable with the practice of physician-performed active euthanasia or physician-assisted suicide. There, only a wholly patient-controlled response to terminal situations, as in non-physician-assisted suicide, is a reasonable and prudent practice.

But what about the United States? This is a country where (1) sustained contact with a personal physician has been decreasing, (2) the risk of malpractice action is perceived as substantial, (3) much medical care is not insured, (4) many medical decisions are financial decisions as well, (5) racism remains high, with racial and ethnic minorities tending to receive lower quality health care,[31] and (6) the public has not experienced direct contact with Nazism or similar totalitarian movements. Thus, the United States is in many respects an untrustworthy candidate for practicing active euthanasia. Given the pressures on individuals in an often atomized society, encouraging solo suicide, assisted if at all only by nonprofessionals, might well be open to considerable abuse too.

However, there are several additional differences between the United States and both the Netherlands and Germany that may seem peculiarly relevant here. First, American culture is more confrontational than many others, including Dutch culture. While the Netherlands prides itself rightly on a long tradition of rational discussion of public issues and on toleration of others' views and practices, the United States (and to some degree also Germany) tends to develop highly partisan, moralizing oppositional groups, especially over social issues like abortion. In general, this is a disadvantage, but in the case of euthanasia it may serve to alert the public to issues and possibilities it might not otherwise consider, especially the risks of abuse. Here the role of religions groups may be particularly strong, since in discouraging or prohibiting suicide and euthanasia (as many, though by no means all, religious groups do), they may invite their members to reinspect the reasons for such choices and encourage families, physicians, and health-care institutions to provide adequate, humane alternatives.

Second, though this may at first seem to be not only a peculiar but a trivial difference, it is Americans who are particularly given to self-analysis. This tendency not only is evident in the United States' high rate of utilization of counseling services, including religious counseling, psychological counseling, and psychiatry, but also is more clearly evident in its popular culture: its diet of soap operas, situation comedies, pop psychology books, and reality shows. It is here that the ordinary American absorbs models for analyzing his or her personal relationships and individual psychological characteristics. While, of course, things are changing rapidly and America's cultural tastes are widely exported, the fact remains that the ordinary American's cultural diet contains more in the way of professional and do-it-yourself amateur psychology and self-analysis than anyone else's. This long tradition of self-analysis may put Americans in a better position for certain kinds of end-of-life

practices than many other cultures. Despite whatever other deficiencies U.S. society has, we live in a culture that encourages us to inspect our own motives, anticipate the impact of our actions on others, and scrutinize our own relationships with others, including our physicians. This disposition is of importance in euthanasia and assisted-suicide contexts because these are the kinds of fundamental choices about which one may have somewhat mixed motives, be subject to various interpersonal and situational pressures, and so on. If the voluntary character of choices about one's own dying is to be protected, it may be a good thing to inhabit a culture in which self-inspection of one's own mental habits and motives, not to mention those of one's family, physician, and others who might affect one's choices, is culturally encouraged. Counseling specifically addressed to end-of-life choices is not yet easily or openly available, especially if physician-assisted suicide is at issue—though some groups like Compassion in Dying and End-of-Life Choices (which merged in 2004 but later experienced some fission) now provide it—but I believe it will become more frequent in the future as people facing terminal illnesses characterized by long downhill, deteriorative courses consider how they want to die.

Finally, the United States population, varied as it is, is characterized by a kind of do-it-yourself ethic, an ethic that devalues reliance on others and encourages individual initiative and responsibility. (To be sure, this ethic is little in evidence in the series of court cases from *Quinlan* to *Cruzan*, but these were all cases about patients who had become or always were incapable of decisionmaking.) This ethic seems to be coupled with a sort of resistance to authority that perhaps also is basic to the American temperament, even in all its diversity. If this is really the case, Americans might be especially well served by end-of-life practices that emphasize self-reliance and resistance to authority.

These, of course, are mere conjectures about features of American culture relevant to the practice of euthanasia or assisted suicide. These are the features that one would want to reinforce should these practices become general, in part to minimize the effects of the negative influences. But, of course, these positive features will differ from one country and culture to another, just as the negative features do. In each country, a different architecture of antecedent assumptions and cultural features develops around end-of-life issues, and in each country the practices of euthanasia and assisted or physician-assisted suicide, if they are to be free from abuse, must be adapted to the culture in which they take place.

What, then, is appropriate for the United States' own cultural situation? Physician-performed euthanasia, even if not in itself morally wrong, is morally jeopardized where legal, time-related, and especially financial pressures on both patients and physicians are severe; thus, it is morally problematic in our culture in a way that it is not in the Netherlands. Solo suicide outside the institution of medicine (as in Germany) may be problematic in a country (like the United States) that has an increasingly alienated population, offers deteriorating and uneven social services, is increasingly racist and classist, and in other ways imposes unusual pressures on individuals, despite opportunities for self-analysis. Reliance only on withholding and withdrawing treatment and allowing to die (as in the United States) can be cruel, and its comparative invisibility invites erosion under cost-containment and other pressures. These are the three principal alternatives we have considered, but none of them seems wholly suited to our actual situation for dealing with the new fact that most of us die of extended-decline, deteriorative diseases.

Perhaps, however, there is one that would best suit the United States, certainly better than its current reliance on allowing to die, and better than the Netherlands' more direct physician involvement or Germany's practices entirely outside medicine. The "arm's-length" model of physician-assisted suicide—permitting physicians to supply their terminally ill patients who request it with the means for ending their own lives (as has become legal in Oregon)—still grants physicians some control over the circumstances in which this can happen (for example, only when the prognosis is genuinely grim and the alternatives for symptom control are poor) but leaves the fundamental decision about whether

to use these means to the patient alone. It is up to the patient then—the independent, confrontational, self-analyzing, do-it-yourself, authority-resisting patient—and his or her advisors, including family members, clergy, the physician, and other health-care providers, to be clear about whether he or she really wants to use these means or not. Thus, the physician is involved but not directly, and it is the patient's decision, although the patient is not making it alone. Thus also it is the patient who performs the action of bringing his or her own life to a close, though where the patient is physically incapable of doing so or where the process goes awry the physician must be allowed to intercede. We live in an imperfect world, but of the alternatives for facing death—which we all eventually must—I think that the practice of permitting this somewhat distanced though still medically supported form of physician-assisted suicide is the one most nearly suited to the current state of our own flawed society. This is a model not yet central in any of the three countries examined here—the Netherlands, Germany, or (except in Oregon) the United States, or any of the other industrialized nations with related practices—but it is the one, I think, that suits us best.

NOTES

From *The Journal of Pain and Symptom Management* 6(5), July 1991, pp. 298–305. © 1991 U. S. Cancer Pain Relief Committee. Revised and updated multiple times by the author, most recently in Match 2004 for Bruce N. Waller, ed., *Consider Ethics: Theory, Readings, and Contemporary Issues*, Pearson Education and Longman Publishing, forthcoming 2004. Updated again in June 2004.

1. S. J. Olshansky and A. B. Ault. "The Fourth Stage of the Epidemiological Transition: The Age of Delayed Degenerative Diseases." *Milbank Memorial Fund Quarterly Health and Society* 64 (1986): 355–91.
2. In a study of end-of-life decision making in six European countries, about one-third of all deaths were found to have happened suddenly and unexpectedly, ranging from 29% in Italy to 34% in Belgium. See Agnes van der Heide, Luc Deliens, Karin Faisst, Tore Nilstun, Michael Norup, Eugenio Paci, Gerrit van der Wal, Paul J. van der Maas, on behalf of the EURELD consortium, "End-of-life decision-making in six European countries: Descriptive study," *Lancet* 361 (August 2, 2003): 345–50, table 2, p. 347.
3. S. Miles and C. Gomez, *Protocols for Elective Use of Life-Sustaining Treatment* (New York: Springer-Verlag, 1988).

4. C. L. Sprung, "Changing Attitudes and Practices in Forego-ing Life-Sustaining Treatments," *JAMA* 262 (1990): 2213.

5. T. J. Prendergast and J. M. Luce, "Increasing Incidence of Withholding and Withdrawal of Life Support from the Critically Ill," *American Journal of Respiratory and Critical Care Medicine* 155, 1 (January 1997): 1–2.

6. M. B. Hamel, J. M. Teno, L. Goldman, J. Lynn, R. B. Davis, A. N. Galanos, N. Desbiens, A. F. Connors Jr., N. Wenger, R. S. Phillips (SUPPORT investigators), "Patient Age and Decisions to Withhold Life-Sustaining Treatments from Seriously Ill, Hospitalized Adults," *Annals of Internal Medicine* 130, 2 (January 19, 1999): 116–25.

7. John M. Luce, "Withholding and Withdrawal of Life Support: Ethical, Legal, and Clinical Aspects," *New Horizons* 5, 1 (February 1997): 30–7.

8. *New York Times*, July 23, 1990, A13.

9. Accounts of the use of Oregon's Death with Dignity Act (Measure 16) begin with A. E Chin, K. Hedberg, G. K. Higginson, and D. W. Fleming, "Legalized Physician-Assisted Suicide in Oregon—The First Year's Experience," *New England Journal of Medicine* 340 (1999): 577–83, and are updated annually in this journal and at the website of the Oregon Department of Human Services. The 171 cases of legal physician-assisted suicide that have taken place in the first six years since it became legal in Oregon represent about one-tenth of 1% of the total deaths in Oregon.

10. For a fuller account, see my remarks in "A Dozen Caveats Concerning the Discussion of Euthanasia in the Netherlands," in my book *The Least Worst Death: Essays in Bioethics on the End of Life* (New York: Oxford University Press, 1994), 130–44; John Griffiths, Alex Bood, and Helen Weyers, *Euthanasia and Law in the Netherlands* (Amsterdam: Amsterdam University Press, 1998), and the three nationwide studies of end-of-life decision making mentioned hereafter.

11. P. J. van der Maas, J. J.M. van Deladen, and L. Pijnenborg, "Euthanasia and Other Medical Decisions Concerning the End of Life," published in full in English at a special issue of *Health Policy*, 22, 1–2 (1992), and, with C.W. N. Looman, in summary in *Lancet* 138(1991): 669–74.

12. G. van der Wal, J. T. M. van Eijk, H. J. J. Leenen, and C. Spreeuwenberg, "Euthanasie en hulp bij zelfdoding door artsen in de thuissituatie," pts. 1 and 2, *Nederlands Tijdschrift voor Geneesekunde* 135 (1991): 1593–8, 1599–1604.

13. P. J. van der Mass, G. van der Wal, "Euthanasia, Physician-Assisted Suicide, and Other Medical Practices Involving the End of Life in the Netherlands, 1990–1995," *New England Journal of Medicine* 335 (1996): 1699–1105.

14. Bregje D. Onwuteaka-Philipsen, Agnes van der Heide, Dirk Koper, Ingeborg Keij-Deerenberg, Judith A. C. Rietjens, Mette Rurup, Astrid M. Vrakking, Jean Jacques Georges, Martien T. Muller, Gerrit van der Wal, and Paul J. van der Maas, "Euthanasia and Other End--of-Life Decisions in the Netherlands in 1990, 1995, and 2001," *Lancet* 362, (2003): 395–9. A full account is available in Gerrit van der Wal, Agnes van der Heide, Bregje D. Onwuteaka-Philipsen, Paul J. van der Mass, *Medische besluitvorming aan het einde van het leven: De praktijk en de toetsingsprocedure euthasie* (Utrecht: De Tijdstroom, 2003).

15. L. Pijnenborg, P. J. van der Mass, J. J. M. van Delden, C.W. N. Looman, "Life Terminating Acts without Explicit Request of Patient," *Lancet* 341 (1993): 1196–9.

16. Onwuteaka Philipsen et al., "Euthanasia and Other End-of Life Decisions," 2003. These figures are an average of the results of the two principal parts of the 1990, 1995, and 2001 nationwide studies, the interview study, and the death-certificate study.

17. G van der Wal, P. J. van der Maas, J. M. Bosma, B. D. Onwuteaka-Philipsen, D. L. Willems, I. Haverkate, P. J. Kostense, "Evaluation of the Notification Procedure for Physician-Assisted Death in the Netherlands," *New England Journal of Medicine* 335 (1996): 1706–11.

18. Van der Maas et al., "Euthanasia and other Medical Decisions Concerning the End of Life," 673.

19. Van der Maas et al., "Euthanasia, Physician-Assisted Suicide, and Other Medical Practices Involving the End of Life in the Netherlands, 1990–1995," p. 1705.

20. Margaret P. Battin, Agnes van der Heide, Linda Ganzini, and Gerrit van der Wal, "Legalized Physician-Assisted Dying in Oregon and the Netherlands: The Impact on Patients in Vulnerable Groups," in preparation.

21. Kurt Schobert, "Physician-Assisted Suicide in Germany and Switzerland, with Focus on Some Developments in Recent Years," manuscript in preparation, citing "Grundsätze der Bundesärztekammer zur ärztlichen Sterbebegleitung." in *Ethik in der Medizin*, ed., Urban Wiesing (Stuttgart: Gustav Fischer, 2002): 203–8.

22. That is, it no longer sells or supplies such drugs. A scandal in 1992-93 engulfed the original founder and president of the DGHS, Hans Hennig Atrott, who had been secretly providing some members with cyanide in exchange for substantial contributions; he was convicted of violating the drug laws and tax evasion, though not charged with or convicted of assisting suicides.

23. See my "Assisted Suicide: Can We Learn from Germany?" in *The Least Worst Death*, pp. 254–70.

24. P. Admiraal. "Euthanasia in a General Hospital," paper read at the Eighth World Congress of the International Federation of Right-to-Die Societies, Maastricht, the Netherlands, June 8, 1990.

25. See the editorial "Doctors Must Not Kill," *JAMA* 259 (1988): 2139–40, signed by Willard Gaylin, Leon R. Kass, Edmund D. Pellegrino, and Mark Siegler.

26. Van der Mass et al., "Euthanasia, Physician-Assisted Suicide, and Other Medical Practices," 1705.

27. Govert den Hartogh, personal communication.

28. Margaret P. Battin, Agnes van der Heide, Linda Ganzini, and Gerrit van der Wal, "Legalized Physician-Assisted Dying," in preparation.

29. H. ten Have, "Coma: Controversy and Consensus," *Newsletter of the European Society for Philosophy of Medicine and Health Care*, May 1990, 19–20.

30. David Orentlicher, "The Supreme Court and Terminal Sedation: Rejecting Assisted Suicide, Embracing Euthanasia," *Hastings Constitutional Law Quarterly* 24 (1997): 947–68; see also *New England Journal of Medicine* 337 (1997): 1236–9.

31. Institute of Medicine, *Unequal Treatment: Confronting Racial and Ethical Disparities in Health Care* (Washington, D.C.: National Academy of Sciences, 2002).

Gender, Feminism, and Death: Physician-Assisted Suicide and Euthanasia

Susan M. Wolf

Susan M. Wolf is a professor of philosophy at University of North Carolina at Chapel Hill. She is the editor of *Feminism and Bioethics: Beyond Reproduction* (1996), and the author of *Freedom Within Reason* (1990) and of numerous articles in ethics.

In this essay, Wolf argues that the lack of attention to gender differences in the current debate on physician-assisted suicide or active voluntary euthanasia could put women in greater risks of harm should such a practice be legalized prematurely. She examines two types of arguments: the rights-based approach that emphasizes the patient's autonomy or self-determination and the ethics of care perspective that focuses on the physician's compassion for the suffering patient. She holds that neither of these types of arguments is adequate. Instead, she proposes a "principled caring" approach that takes into account both of these moral perspectives.

The debate in the United States over whether to legitimate physician-assisted suicide and active euthanasia has reached new levels of intensity. Oregon has become the first state to legalize physician-assisted suicide, and there have been campaigns, ballot measures, bills, and litigation in other states in attempts to legalize one or both practices.[1] Scholars and others increasingly urge either outright legalization or some other form of legitimation, through recognition of an affirmative defense of "mercy killing" to a homicide prosecution or other means.[2]

Yet the debate over whether to legitimate physician-assisted suicide and euthanasia (by which I mean active euthanasia, as opposed to the termination of life-sustaining treatment)[3] is most often about a patient who does not exist—a patient with no gender, race, or insurance status. This is the same generic patient featured in most bioethics debates. Little discussion has focused on how differences between patients might alter the equation.

Even though the debate has largely ignored this question, there is ample reason to suspect that gender, among other factors, deserves analysis. The cases prominent in the American debate mostly feature women patients. This occurs against a backdrop of a long history of cultural images revering women's sacrifice and self-sacrifice. Moreover, dimensions of health status and health care that may affect a patient's vulnerability to considering physician-assisted suicide and euthanasia—including depression, poor pain relief, and difficulty obtaining good health care—differentially plague women. And suicide patterns themselves show a

Excerpts from Susan M. Wolf, "Gender, Feminism, and Death" Feminism and Bioethics. 1996, pp. 608–621. Reprinted by permission of Oxford University Press.

strong gender effect: Women less often complete suicide, but more often attempt it.[4] These and other factors raise the question of whether the dynamics surrounding physician-assisted suicide and euthanasia may vary by gender.

Indeed, it would be surprising if gender had no influence. Women in America still live in a society marrd by sexism, a society that particularly disvalues women with illness, disability, or merely advanced age. It would be hard to explain if health care, suicide, and fundamental dimensions of American society showed marked differences by gender, but gender suddenly dropped out of the equation when people became desperate enough to seek a physician's help in ending their lives.

What sort of gender effects might we expect? There are four different possibilities. First, we might anticipate a higher incidence of women than men dying by physician-assisted suicide and euthanasia in this country. This is an empirical claim that we cannot yet test; we currently lack good data in the face of the illegality of the practices in most states[5] and the condemnation of the organized medical professions.[6] The best data we do have are from the Netherlands and are inconclusive. As I discuss below, the Dutch data show that women predominate among patients dying through euthanasia or administration of drugs for pain relief, but not by much. In the smaller categories of physician-assisted suicide and "life-terminating events without . . . request," however, men predominate. And men predominate too in making requests rejected by physicians. It is hard to say what this means for the United States. The Netherlands differs in a number of relevant respects, with universal health care and a more homogeneous society. But the Dutch data suggest that gender differences in the United States will not necessarily translate into higher numbers of women dying. At least one author speculates that there may in fact be a sexist tendency to discount and refuse women's requests.[7]

There may, however, be a second gender effect. Gender differences may translate into women seeking physician-assisted suicide and euthanasia for somewhat different reasons than men. Problems we know to be correlated with

gender—difficulty getting good medical care generally, poor pain relief, a higher incidence of depression, and a higher rate of poverty—may figure more prominently in women's motivation. Society's persisting sexism may figure as well. And the long history of valorizing women's self-sacrifice may be expressed in women's requesting assisted suicide or euthanasia.

The well-recognized gender differences in suicide statistics also suggest that women's requests for physician-assisted suicide and euthanasia may more often than men's requests be an effort to change an oppressive situation rather than a literal request for death. Thus, some suicidologists interpret men's predominance among suicide "completers" and women's among suicide "attempters" to mean that women more often engage in suicidal behavior with a goal other than "completion."[8] The relationship between suicide and the practices of physician-assisted suicide and euthanasia itself deserves further study; not all suicides are even motivated by terminal disease or other factors relevant to the latter practices. But the marked gender differences in suicidal behavior are suggestive.

Third, gender differences may also come to the fore in physicians' decisions about whether to grant or refuse requests for assisted suicide or euthanasia. The same historical valorization of women's self-sacrifice and the same background sexism that may affect women's readiness to request may also affect physicians' responses. Physicians may be susceptible to affirming women's negative self-judgments. This might or might not result in physicians agreeing to assist; other gender-related judgments (such as that women are too emotionally labile, or that their choices should not be taken seriously) may intervene.[9] But the point is that gender may affect not just patient but physician.

Finally, gender may affect the broad public debate. The prominent U.S. cases so far and related historical imagery suggest that in debating physician-assisted suicide and euthanasia, many in our culture may envision a woman patient. Although the AIDS epidemic has called attention to physician-assisted suicide and euthanasia in men, the cases that have dominated the news accounts and scholarly journals in the recent renewal of debate have featured women patients. Thus, we have reason to be concerned that at least some advocacy for these practices may build on the sense that these stories of women's deaths are somehow "right." If there is a felt correctness to these accounts, that may be playing a hidden and undesirable part in catalyzing support for the practices' legitimation.

Thus we have cause to worry whether the debate about and practice of physician-assisted suicide and euthanasia in this country are gendered in a number of respects. Serious attention to gender, therefore, seems essential. Before we license physicians to kill their patients or to assist patients in killing themselves, we had better understand the dynamic at work in that encounter, why the practice seems so alluring that we should court its dangers, and what dangers are likely to manifest. After all, the consequences of permitting killing or assistance in private encounters are serious, indeed fatal. We had better understand what distinguishes this from other forms of private violence, and other relationships of asymmetrical power that result in the deaths of women. And we had better determine whether tacit assumptions about gender are influencing the enthusiasm for legalization.

Yet even that is not enough. Beyond analyzing the way gender figures in our cases, cultural imagery, and practice, we must analyze the substantive arguments. For attention to gender, in the last two decades particularly, has yielded a wealth of feminist critiques and theoretical tools that can fruitfully be brought to bear. After all, the debate over physician-assisted suicide and euthanasia revolves around precisely the kind of issues on which feminist work has focused: what it means to talk about rights of self-determination and autonomy; the reconciliation of those rights with physicians' duties of beneficence and caring; and how to place all of this in a context including the strengths and failures of families, professionals, and communities, as well as real differentials of power and resources.

The debate over physician-assisted suicide and euthanasia so starkly raises questions of rights, caring, and context that at this point it would take determination *not* to bring to bear a literature that has been devoted to understanding those notions. Indeed, the work of Lawrence Kohlberg bears witness to what an obvious candidate this debate is for such analysis.[10] "It was Kohlberg's work on moral development, of course, that provoked Carol Gilligan's *In A Different Voice*, criticizing Kohlberg's vision of progressive stages in moral maturation as one that was partial and gendered.[11] "Gilligan proposed that there were really two different approaches to moral problems, one that emphasized generalized rights and universal principles, and the other that instead emphasized contextualized caring and the maintenance of particular human relationships. She suggested that although women and men could use both approaches, women tended to use the latter and men the former. Both approaches, however, were important to moral maturity. Though Gilligan's and others' work on the ethics of care has been much debated and criticized, a number of bioethicists and health care professionals have found a particular pertinence to questions of physician caregiving.[12]

Embedded in Kohlberg's work, one finds proof that the euthanasia debate in particular calls for analysis in the very terms that he employs, and that Gilligan then critiques, enlarges, and reformulates. For one of the nine moral dilemmas Kohlberg used to gauge subjects' stage of moral development was a euthanasia problem. "Dilemma IV" features "a woman" with "very bad cancer" and "in terrible pain." Her physician, Dr. Jefferson, knows she has "only about six months to live." Between periods in which she is "delirious and almost crazy with pain," she asks the doctor to kill her with morphine. The question is what he should do.[13]

The euthanasia debate thus demands analysis along the care, rights, and context axes that the Kohlberg–Gilligan debate has identified.[14] Kohlberg himself used this problem to reveal how well respondents were doing in elevating general principles over the idiosyncrasies of relationship and context. It is no stretch, then, to apply the fruits of more than a decade of feminist critique. The problem has a genuine pedigree.

The purpose of this chapter thus is twofold. First, I explore gender's significance for analyzing physician-assisted suicide and euthanasia. Thus, I examine the prominent cases and cultural images, against the background of cautions recommended by what little data we have from the Netherlands. Finding indications that gender may well be significant, I investigate what that implies for the debate over physician-assisted suicide and euthanasia. Clearly more research is required. But in the meantime, patients' vulnerability to requesting these fatal interventions because of failures in health care and other background conditions, or because of a desire not to die but to alter circumstances, introduces reasons why we should be reluctant to endorse these practices. Indeed, we should be worried about the role of the physician in these cases, and consider the lessons we have learned from analyzing other relationships that result in women's deaths. What we glean from looking at gender should lead us to look at other characteristics historically associated with disadvantage, and thus should prompt a general caution applicable to all patients.

My second purpose is to go beyond analysis of gender itself, to analysis of the arguments offered on whether to condone and legitimate these practices. Here is where I bring to bear the feminist literature on caring, rights, and context. I criticize the usual argument that patients' rights of self-determination dictate legitimation of physician-assisted suicide and euthanasia, on the grounds that this misconstrues the utility of rights talk for resolving this debate, and ignores essential features of the context. I then turn to arguments based on beneficence and caring. It is no accident that the word "mercy" has figured so large in our language about these problems; they do involve questions of compassion and caring. However, a shallow understanding of caring will lead us astray, and I go on to elaborate what a deep and contextualized understanding demands. I argue that physicians should be guided by a notion of "principled caring." Finally, I step back to suggest what a proper integration of rights and caring would look like in this context, how it can be coupled with attention to the fate of women and other historically disadvantaged groups, and what practical steps all of this counsels.

This chapter takes a position. As I have before, I oppose the legitimation of physician-assisted suicide and euthanasia.[15] Yet the most important part of what I do here is urge the necessity of feminist analysis of this issue. Physician-assisted suicide and euthanasia are difficult problems on which people may disagree. But I hope to persuade that attending to gender and feminist concerns in analyzing these problems is no longer optional.

GENDER IN CASES, IMAGES, AND PRACTICE

The tremendous upsurge in American debate over whether to legitimate physician-assisted suicide and euthanasia in recent years has been fueled by a series of cases featuring women. The case that seems to have begun this series is that of Debbie, published in 1988 by the *Journal of the American Medical Association* (*JAMA*).[16] *JAMA* published this now infamous, first-person, and anonymous account by a resident in obstetrics and gynecology of performing euthanasia. Some subsequently queried whether the account was fiction. Yet it successfully catalyzed an enormous response.

The narrator of the piece tells us that Debbie is a young woman suffering from ovarian cancer. The resident has no prior relationship with her, but is called to her bedside late one night while on call and exhausted. Entering Debbie's room, the resident finds an older woman with her, but never pauses to find out who that second woman is and what relational context Debbie acts within. Instead, the resident responds to the patient's clear discomfort and to her words. Debbie says only one sentence, "Let's get this over with." It is unclear whether she thinks the resident is there to draw blood and wants that over with, or means something else. But on the strength of that one sentence, the resident retreats to the nursing station, prepares a lethal injection, returns to the room, and administers it. The story relates this as an act of mercy under the title "It's Over, Debbie," as if in caring response to the patient's words.

The lack of relationship to the patient; the failure to attend to her own history, relationships, and resources; the failure to explore beyond the patient's presented words and engage her in conversation; the sense that the cancer diagnosis plus the patient's words demand death; and the construal of that response as an act of mercy are all themes that recur in the later cases. The equally infamous Dr. Jack Kevorkian has provided a slew of them.

They begin with Janet Adkins, a 54-year-old Oregon woman diagnosed with Alzheimer's disease.[17] Again, on the basis of almost no relationship with Ms. Adkins, on the basis of a diagnosis by exclusion that Kevorkian could not verify, prompted by a professed desire to die that is a predictable stage in response to a number of dire diagnoses, Kevorkian rigs her up to his "Mercitron" machine in a parking lot outside Detroit in what he presents as an act of mercy.

Then there is Marjorie Wantz, a 58-year-old woman without even a diagnosis.[18] Instead, she has pelvic pain whose source remains undetermined. By the time Kevorkian reaches Ms. Wantz, he is making little pretense of focusing on her needs in the context of a therapeutic relationship. Instead, he tells the press that he is determined to create a new medical specialty of "obitiatry." Ms. Wantz is among the first six potential patients with whom he is conferring. When Kevorkian presides over her death there is another woman who dies as well, Sherry Miller. Miller, 43, has multiple sclerosis. Thus, neither woman is terminal.

The subsequent cases reiterate the basic themes.[19] And it is not until the ninth "patient" that Kevorkian finally presides over the death of a man.[20] By this time, published criticism of the predominance of women had begun to appear.[21]

Kevorkian's actions might be dismissed as the bizarre behavior of one man. But the public and press response has been enormous, attesting to the power of these accounts. Many people have treated these cases as important to the debate over physician-assisted suicide and euthanasia. Nor are Kevorkian's cases so aberrant—they pick up all the themes that emerge in "Debbie."

But we cannot proceed without analysis of Diane. This is the respectable version of what Kevorkian makes strange. I refer to the story published by Dr. Timothy Quill in the *New England*

Journal of Medicine, recounting his assisting the suicide of his patient Diane.[22] She is a woman in her forties diagnosed with leukemia, who seeks and obtains from Dr. Quill a prescription for drugs to take her life. Dr. Quill cures some of the problems with the prior cases. He does have a real relationship with her, he knows her history, and he obtains a psychiatric consult on her mental state. He is a caring, empathetic person. Yet once again we are left wondering about the broader context of Diane's life—why even the history of other problems that Quill describes has so drastically depleted her resources to deal with this one, and whether there were any alternatives. And we are once again left wondering about the physician's role—why he responded to her as he did, what self-scrutiny he brought to bear on his own urge to comply, and how he reconciled this with the arguments that physicians who are moved to so respond should nonetheless resist.[23]

• • •

FEMINISM AND THE ARGUMENTS

Shifting from the images and stories that animate debate and the dynamics operating in practice to analysis of the arguments over physician-assisted suicide and euthanasia takes us further into the concerns of feminist theory. Arguments in favor of these practices have often depended on rights claims. More recently, some authors have grounded their arguments instead on ethical concepts of caring. Yet both argumentative strategies have been flawed in ways that feminist work can illuminate. What is missing is an analysis that integrates notions of physician caring with principled boundaries to physician action, while also attending to the patient's broader context and the community's wider concerns. Such an analysis would pay careful attention to the dangers posed by these practices to the historically most vulnerable populations, including women.

Advocacy of physician-assisted suicide and euthanasia has hinged to a great extent on rights claims. The argument is that the patient has a right of self-determination or autonomy that entitles her to assistance in suicide or euthanasia. The strategy is to extend the argument that self-determination entitles the patient to refuse unwanted life-sustaining treatment by maintaining that the same rationale supports patient entitlement to more active physician assistance in death. Indeed, it is sometimes argued that there is no principled difference between termination of life-sustaining treatment and the more active practices.

The narrowness and mechanical quality of this rights thinking, however, is shown by its application to the stories recounted above. That application suggests that the physicians in these stories are dealing with a simple equation: Given an eligible rights bearer and her assertion of the right, the correct result is death. What makes a person an eligible rights bearer? Kevorkian seems to require neither a terminal disease nor thorough evaluation of whether the patient has nonfatal alternatives. Indeed, the Wantz case shows he does not even require a diagnosis. Nor does the Oregon physician-assisted suicide statute require evaluation or exhaustion of nonfatal alternatives; a patient could be driven by untreated pain, and still receive physician-assisted suicide. And what counts as an assertion of the right? For Debbie's doctor, merely "Let's get this over with." Disease plus demand requires death.

Such a rights approach raises a number of problems that feminist theory has illuminated. In particular, feminist critiques suggest three different sorts of problems with the rights equation offered to justify physician-assisted suicide and euthanasia. First, it ignores context, both the patient's present context and her history. The prior and surrounding failures in her intimate relationships, in her resources to cope with illness and pain, and even in the adequacy of care being offered by the very same physician fade into invisibility next to the bright light of a rights bearer and her demand. In fact, her choices may be severely constrained. Some of those constraints may even be alterable or removable. Yet attention to those dimensions of decision is discouraged by the absolutism of the equation: Either she is an eligible rights bearer or not; either she has asserted

her right or not. There is no room for conceding her competence and request, yet querying whether under all the circumstances her choices are so constrained and alternatives so unexplored that acceding to the request may not be the proper course. Stark examples are provided by cases in which pain or symptomatic discomfort drives a person to request assisted suicide or euthanasia, yet the pain or discomfort are treatable. A number of Kevorkian's cases raise the problem as well: Did Janet Adkins ever receive psychological support for the predictable despair and desire to die that follow dire diagnoses such as Alzheimer's? Would the cause of Marjorie Wantz's undiagnosed pelvic pain been ascertainable and even ameliorable at a better health center? In circumstances in which women and others who have traditionally lacked resources and experienced oppression are likely to have fewer options and a tougher time getting good care, mechanical application of the rights equation will authorize their deaths even when less drastic alternatives are or should be available. It will wrongly assume that all face serious illness and disability with the resources of the idealized rights bearer—a person of means untroubled by oppression. The realities of women and others whose circumstances are far from that abstraction's will be ignored.

Second, in ignoring context and relationship, the rights equation extols the vision of a rights bearer as an isolated monad and denigrates actual dependencies. Thus, it may be seen as improper to ask what family, social, economic, and medical supports she is or is not getting; this insults her individual self-governance. Nor may it be seen as proper to investigate alternatives to acceding to her request for death; this too dilutes self-rule. Yet feminists have reminded us of the actual embeddedness of persons and the descriptive falseness of a vision of each as an isolated individual.[24] In addition, they have argued normatively that a society comprised of isolated individuals, without the pervasive connections and dependencies that we see, would be undesirable.[25] Indeed, the very meaning of the patient's request for death is socially constructed; that is the point of the prior section's review of the images animating the debate. If we construe the patient's request as a rights bearer's assertion of a right and deem that sufficient grounds on which the physician may proceed, it is because we choose to regard background failures as irrelevant even if they are differentially motivating the requests of the most vulnerable. We thereby avoid real scrutiny of the social arrangements, governmental failures, and health coverage exclusions that may underlie these requests. We also ignore the fact that these patients may be seeking improved circumstances more than death. We elect a myopia that makes the patient's request and death seem proper. We construct a story that clothes the patient's terrible despair in the glorious mantle of "rights."

Formulaic application of the rights equation in this realm thus exalts an Enlightenment vision of autonomy as self-governance and the exclusion of interfering others. Yet as feminists such as Jennifer Nedelsky have argued, this is not the only vision of autonomy available.[26] She argues that a superior vision of autonomy is to be found by rejecting "the pathological conception of autonomy as boundaries against others," a conception that takes the exclusion of others from one's property as its central symbol. Instead, "If we ask ourselves what actually enables people to be autonomous, the answer is not isolation but relationships . . . that provide the support and guidance necessary for the development and experience of autonomy." Nedelsky thus proposes that the best "metaphor for autonomy is not property, but childrearing. There we have encapsulated the emergence of autonomy through relationship with others."[27] Martha Minow, too, presents a vision of autonomy that resists the isolation of the self, and instead tries to support the relational context in which the rights bearer is embedded.[28] Neither author counsels abandonment of autonomy and rights. But they propose fundamental revisions that would rule out the mechanical application of a narrow rights equation that would regard diseases or disability, coupled with demand, as adequate warrant for death.[29]

In fact, there are substantial problems with grounding advocacy for the specific practices of physician-assisted suicide and euthanasia in a rights analysis, even if one accepts the general importance of rights and self-determination. I have elsewhere argued repeatedly for an absolute or near-absolute moral and legal right to be free of unwanted life-sustaining treatment.[30] Yet the negative right to be free of unwanted bodily invasion does not imply an affirmative right to obtain bodily invasion (or assistance with bodily invasion) for the purpose of ending your own life.

Moreover, the former right is clearly grounded in fundamental entitlements to liberty, bodily privacy, and freedom from unconsented touching; in contrast there is no clear "right" to kill yourself or be killed. Suicide has been widely decriminalized, but decriminalizing an act does not mean that you have a positive right to do it and to command the help of others. Indeed, if a friend were to tell me that she wished to kill herself, I would not be lauded for giving her the tools. In fact, that act of assistance has *not* been decriminalized. That continued condemnation shows that whatever my friend's relation to the act of suicide (a "liberty," "right," or neither), it does not create a right in her sufficient to command or even permit my aid.

There are even less grounds for concluding that there is a right to be killed deliberately on request, that is, for euthanasia. There are reasons why a victim's consent has traditionally been no defense to an accusation of homicide. One reason is suggested by analogy to Mill's famous argument that one cannot consent to one's own enslavement: "The reason for not interfering . . . with a person's voluntary acts, is consideration for his liberty . . . But by selling himself for a slave, he abdicates his liberty; he foregoes any future use of it. . . ."[31] Similarly, acceding to a patient's request to be killed wipes out the possibility of her future exercise of her liberty. The capacity to command or permit another to take your life deliberately, then, would seem beyond the bounds of those things to which you have a right grounded in notions of liberty. We lack the capacity to bless another's enslavement of us or direct killing of us. How is this compatible then with a right to refuse life-sustaining treatment? That right is not grounded in any so-called "right to die," however frequently the phrase appears in the general press.[32] Instead, it is grounded in rights to be free of unwanted bodily invasion, rights so fundamental that they prevail even when the foreseeable consequence is likely to be death.

Finally, the rights argument in favor of physician-assisted suicide and euthanasia confuses two separate questions: what the patient may do, and what the physician may do. After all, the real question in these debates is not what patients may request or even do. It is not at all infrequent for patients to talk about suicide and request assurance that the physician will help or actively bring on death when the patient wants;[33] that is an expected part of reaction to serious disease and discomfort. The real question is what the doctor may do in response to this predictable occurrence. That question is not answered by talk of what patients may ask; patients may and should be encouraged to reveal everything on their minds. Nor is it answered by the fact that decriminalization of suicide permits the patient to take her own life. The physician and patient are separate moral agents. Those who assert that what a patient may say or do determines the same for the physician, ignore the physician's separate moral and legal agency. They also ignore the fact that she is a professional, bound to act in keeping with a professional role and obligations. They thereby avoid a necessary argument over whether the historic obligations of the physician to "do harm" and "give no deadly drug even if asked" should be abandoned.[34] Assertion of what the patient may do does not resolve that argument.

The inadequacy of rights arguments to legitimate physician-assisted suicide and euthanasia has led to a different approach, grounded on physicians' duties of beneficence. This might seem to be quite in keeping with feminists' development of an ethics of care.[35] Yet the beneficence argument in the euthanasia context is a strange one, because it asserts that the physician's obligation to relieve suffering permits or even commands her to annihilate the person who is experiencing the suffering. Indeed, at the end of this act of beneficence, no patient is left to experience its supposed benefits. Moreover, this argument ignores widespread agreement that fears of patient addiction in these cases should be discarded, physicians may sedate to unconsciousness, and the principle of double effect permits giving pain relief and palliative care in doses that risk inducing respiratory depression and thereby hastening death. Given all of that, it is far from clear what patients remain in the category of those whose pain or discomfort can only be relieved by killing them.

Thus this argument that a physician should provide so much "care" that she kills the patient is deeply flawed. A more sophisticated version, however, is offered by Howard Brody.[36] He acknowledges that both the usual rights arguments and traditional beneficence arguments have failed. Thus, he claims to find a middle path. He advocates legitimation of physician-assisted suicide and euthanasia "as a compassionate response to one sort of medical failure," namely, medical failure to prolong life, restore function, or provide effective palliation. Even in such cases, he does not advocate the creation of a rule providing outright legalization. Instead, "compassionate and competent medical practice" should serve as a defense in a criminal proceeding.[37] Panels should review the practice case by case; a positive review should discourage prosecution.

There are elements of Brody's proposal that seem quite in keeping with much feminist work: his rejection of a binary either-or analysis, his skepticism that a broad rule will yield a proper resolution, his requirement instead of a case-by-case approach. Moreover, the centrality that he accords to "compassion" again echoes feminist work on an ethics of care. Yet ultimately he offers no real arguments for extending compassion to the point of killing a patient, for altering the traditional boundaries of medical practice, or for ignoring the fears that any legitimation of these practices will start us down a slippery slope leading to bad consequences. Brody's is more the proposal of a procedure—what he calls "not resolution but adjudication," following philosopher Hilary Putnam—than it is a true answer to the moral and legal quandaries.

What Brody's analysis does accomplish, however, is that it suggests that attention to method is a necessary, if not sufficient, part of solving the euthanasia problem. Thus, we find that two of the most important current debates in bioethics are linked—the debate over euthanasia and the debate over the proper structure of bioethical analysis and method.[38] The inadequacies of rights arguments to establish patient entitlement to assisted suicide and euthanasia are linked to the inadequacies of a "top-down" or deductive bioethics driven by principles, abstract theories, or rules. They share certain flaws: Both seem to overly ignore context and the nuances of cases; their simple abstractions overlook real power differentials in society and historic subordination; and they avoid the fact that these principles, rules, abstractions, and rights are themselves a product of historically oppressive social arrangements. Similarly, the inadequacies of beneficence and compassion arguments are linked to some of the problems with a "bottom-up"or inductive bioethics built on cases, ethnography, and detailed description. In both instances it is difficult to see where the normative boundaries lie, and where to get a normative keel for the finely described ship.

What does feminism have to offer these debates? Feminists too have struggled extensively with the question of method, with how to integrate detailed attention to individual cases with rights, justice, and principles. Thus, in criticizing Kohlberg and going beyond his vision of moral development, Carol Gilligan argued that human beings should be able to utilize both an ethics of justice and an ethics of care. "To understand how the tension between responsibilities and rights sustains the dialectic of human development is to see the integrity of two disparate modes of experience that are in the end connected. . . . In the representation of maturity, both perspectives converge. . . ."[39] What was less clear was precisely how the two should fit together. And unfortunately for our purposes, Gilligan never took up Kohlberg's mercy killing case to illuminate a care perspective or even more importantly, how the two perspectives might properly be interwoven in that case.

That finally, I would suggest, is the question. Here we must look to those feminist scholars who have struggled directly with how the two perspectives might fit. Lawrence Blum has distinguished eight different positions that one might

take, and that scholars have taken, on "the relation between impartial morality and a morality of care:"[40] (1) acting on care is just acting on complicated moral principles; (2) care is not moral but personal; (3) care is moral but secondary to principle and generally adds mere refinements or supererogatory opportunities; (4) principle supplies a superior basis for moral action by ensuring consistency; (5) care morality concerns evaluation of persons while principles concern evaluation of acts; (6) principles set outer boundaries within which care can operate; (7) the preferability of a care perspective in some circumstances must be justified by reasoning from principles; and (8) care and justice must be integrated. Many others have struggled with the relationship between the two perspectives as well.

Despite this complexity, the core insight is forthrightly stated by Owen Flanagan and Kathryn Jackson: "[T]he most defensible specification of the moral domain will include issues of both right and good."[41] Martha Minow and Elizabeth Spelman go further. Exploring the axis of abstraction versus context, they argue against dichotomizing the two and in favor of recognizing their "constant interactions."[42] Indeed, they maintain that a dichotomy misdescribes the workings of context. "[C]ontextualists do not merely address each situation as a unique one with no relevance for the next one. . . . The basic norm of fairness—treat like cases alike—is fulfilled, not undermined, by attention to what particular traits make one case like, or unlike, another."[43] Similarly, "[w]hen a rule specifies a context, it does not undermine the commitment to universal application to the context specified; it merely identifies the situations to be covered by the rule."[44] If this kind of integration is available, then why do we hear such urgent pleas for attention to context? "[T]he call to context in the late twentieth century reflects a critical argument that prevailing legal and political norms have used the form of abstract, general, and universal prescriptions while neglecting the experiences and needs of women of all races and classes, people of color, and people without wealth."[45]

Here we find the beginning of an answer to our dilemma. It appears that we must attend to both context and abstraction, peering through the lenses of both care and justice. Yet our approach to each will be affected by its mate. Our apprehension and understanding of context or cases inevitably involves categories, while our categories and principles should be refined over time to apply to some contexts and not others.[46] Similarly, our understanding of what caring requires in a particular case will grow in part from our understanding of what sort of case this is and what limits principles set to our expressions of caring; while our principles should be scrutinized and amended according to their impact on real lives, especially the lives of those historically excluded from the process of generating principles.[47]

This last point is crucial and a distinctive feminist contribution to the debate over abstraction versus context, or in bioethics, principles versus cases. Various voices in the bioethics debate over method—be they advocating casuistry, specified principlism, principlism itself, or some other position—present various solutions to the question of how cases and principles or other higher-order abstractions should interconnect. Feminist writers, too, have substantive solutions to offer, as I have suggested. But feminists also urge something that the mainstream writers on bioethics method have overlooked altogether, namely, the need to use cases and context to reveal the systematic biases such as sexism and racism built into the principles or other abstractions themselves. Those biases will rarely be explicit in a principle. Instead, we will frequently have to look at how the principle operates in actual cases, what it presupposes (such as wealth or life options), and what it ignores (such as preexisting sexism or racism among the very health care professionals meant to apply it).[48]

What, then, does all of this counsel in application to the debate over physician-assisted suicide and euthanasia? This debate cannot demand a choice between abstract rules or principles and physician caring. Although the debate has sometimes been framed that way, it is difficult to imagine a practice of medicine founded on one to the exclusion of the other. Few would deny that physician beneficence and caring for the individual

patient are essential. Indeed, they are constitutive parts of the practice of medicine as it has come to us through the centuries and aims to function today. Yet that caring cannot be unbounded. A physician cannot be free to do whatever caring for or empathy with the patient seems to urge in the moment. Physicians practice a profession with standards and limits, the context of a democratic polity that itself imposes further limits.[49] These considerations have led the few who have begun to explore an ethics of care for physicians to argue that the notion of care in that context must be carefully delimited and distinct from the more general caring of a parent for a child (although there are limits, too, on what a caring parent may do).[50] Physicians must pursue what I will call "principled caring."

This notion of principled caring captures the need for limits and standards, whether technically stated as principles or some other form of generalization. Those principles or generalizations will articulate limits and obligations in a provisional way, subject to reconsideration and possible amendment in light of actual cases. Both individual cases and patterns of cases may specifically reveal that generalizations we have embraced are infected by sexism or other bias, either as those generalizations are formulated or as they function in the world. Indeed, given that both medicine and bioethics are cultural practices in a society riddled by such bias and that we have only begun to look carefully for such bias in our bioethical principles and practices, we should expect to find it.

Against this background, arguments for physician-assisted suicide and euthanasia— whether grounded on rights or beneficence—are automatically suspect when they fail to attend to the vulnerability of women and other groups. If our cases, cultural images, and perhaps practice differentially feature the deaths of women, we cannot ignore that. It is one thing to argue for these practices for the patient who is not so vulnerable, the wealthy white male living on Park Avenue in Manhattan who wants to add yet another means of control to his arsenal. It is quite another to suggest that the woman of color with no health care coverage or continuous physician relationship, who is given a dire diagnosis in the city hospital's emergency room, needs then to be offered direct killing.

To institute physician-assisted suicide and euthanasia at this point in this country—in which many millions are denied the resources to cope with serious illness, in which pain relief and palliative care are by all accounts woefully mishandled, and in which we have a long way to go to make proclaimed rights to refuse life-sustaining treatment and to use advance directives working realities in clinical settings—seems, at the very least, to be premature. Were we actually to fix those other problems, we have no idea what demand would remain for these more drastic practices and in what category of patients. We know, for example, that the remaining category is likely to include very few, if any, patients in pain, once inappropriate fears of addiction, reluctance to sedate to unconsciousness, and confusion over the principle of double effect are overcome.

Yet against those background conditions, legitimating the practices is more than just premature. It is a danger to women. Those background conditions pose special problems for them. Women in this country are differentially poorer, more likely to be either uninsured or on government entitlement programs, more likely to be alone in their old age, and more susceptible to depression. Those facts alone would spell danger. But when you combine them with the long (indeed, ancient) history of legitimating the sacrifice and self-sacrifice of women, the danger intensifies. That history suggests that a woman requesting assisted suicide or euthanasia is likely to be seen as doing the "right" thing. She will fit into unspoken cultural stereotypes.[51] She may even be valorized for appropriate feminine self-sacrificing behavior, such as sparing her family further burden or the sight of an unaesthetic deterioration. Thus, she may be subtly encouraged to seek death. At the least, her physician may have a difficult time seeing past the legitimating stereotypes and valorization to explore what is really going on with this particular patient, why she is so desperate, and what can be done about it. If many more patients in the Netherlands ask about assisted suicide and euthanasia than go through with

it,[52] and if such inquiry is a routine part of any patients responding to a dire diagnosis or improperly managed symptoms and pain, then were the practices to be legitimated in the United States, we would expect to see a large group of patients inquiring. Yet given the differential impact of background conditions in the United States by gender and the legitimating stereotypes of women's deaths, we should also expect to see what has been urged as a neutral practice show marked gender effects. . . .

The required interweaving of principles and caring, combined with attention to the heightened vulnerability of women and others, suggests that the right answer to the debate over legitimating these practices is at least "not yet" in this grossly imperfect society and perhaps a flat "no." Beneficence and caring indeed impose positive duties upon physicians, especially with patients who are suffering, despairing, or in pain. Physicians must work with these patients intensively; provide first-rate pain relief, palliative care, and symptomatic relief; and honor patients' exercise of their rights to refuse life-sustaining treatment and use advance directives. Never should the patient's illness, deterioration, or despair occasion physician abandonment. Whatever concerns the patient has should be heard and explored, including thoughts of suicide, or requests for aid or euthanasia.

Such requests should redouble the physician's efforts, prompt consultation with those more expert in pain relief or supportive care, suggest exploration of the details of the patient's circumstance, and a host of other efforts. What such requests should not do is prompt our collective legitimation of the physician's saying "yes" and actively taking the patient's life. The mandates of caring fail to bless killing the person for whom one cares. Any such practice in the United States will inevitably reflect enormous background inequities and persisting societal biases. And there are special reasons to expect gender bias to play a role.

The principles bounding medical practice are not written in stone. They are subject to reconsideration and societal renegotiation over time. Thus the ancient prohibitions against physicians assisting suicide and performing euthanasia do not magically defeat proposals for change. (Nor do mere assertions that "patients want it" mandate change, as I have argued above.)[53] But we ought to have compelling reasons for changing something as serious as the limits on physician killing, and to be rather confident that change will not mire physicians in a practice that is finally untenable.

By situating assisted suicide and euthanasia in a history of women's deaths, by suggesting the social meanings that over time have attached to and justified women's deaths, by revealing the background conditions that may motivate women's requests, and by stating the obvious—that medicine does not somehow sit outside society, exempt from all of this—I have argued that we cannot have that confidence. Moreover, in the real society in which we live, with its actual and for some groups fearful history, there are compelling reasons not to allow doctors to kill. We cannot ignore that such practice would allow what for now remains an elite and predominantly male profession to take the lives of the "other." We cannot explain how we will train the young physician both to care for the patient through difficult straits and to kill. We cannot protect the most vulnerable.

CONCLUSION

Some will find it puzzling that elsewhere we seek to have women's voices heard and moral agency respected, yet here I am urging that physicians not accede to the request for assisted suicide and euthanasia. Indeed, as noted above, I have elsewhere maintained that physicians must honor patients' requests to be free of unwanted life-sustaining treatment. In fact, attention to gender and feminist argument would urge some caution in both realms. As Jay Katz has suggested, any patient request or decision of consequence merits conversation and exploration.[54] And analysis by Steven Miles and Alison August suggests that gender bias may be operating in the realm of the termination of life-sustaining treatment, too.[55] Yet finally there is a difference between the two domains. As I have argued above, there is a strong right to be free of

unwanted bodily invasion. Indeed, for women, a long history of being harmed specifically through unwanted bodily invasion such as rape presents particularly compelling reasons for honoring a woman's refusal of invasion and effort to maintain bodily intactness. When it comes to the question of whether women's suicides should be aided, however, or whether women should be actively killed, there is no right to command physician assistance, the dangers of permitting assistance are immense, and the history of women's subordination cuts the other way. Women have historically been seen as fit objects for bodily invasion, self-sacrifice, and death at the hands of others. The task before us is to challenge all three.[56]

Certainly some women, including some feminists, will see this problem differently. That may be especially true of women who feel in control of their lives, are less subject to subordination by age or race or wealth, and seek yet another option to add to their many. I am not arguing that women should lose control of their lives and selves. Instead, I am arguing that when women request to be put to death or ask help in taking their own lives, they become part of a broader social dynamic of which we have properly learned to be extremely wary. These are fatal practices. We can no longer ignore questions of gender or the insights of feminist argument.

ACKNOWLEDGMENTS

My thanks to Arthur Applbaum, Larry Blum, Alta Charo, Norman Daniels, Johannes J. M. van Delden, Rebecca Dresser, Jorge Garcia, Henk ten Have, Warren Kearney, Elizabeth Kiss, Steven Miles, Christine Mitchell, Remco Oostendorp, Lynn Peterson, Dennis Thompson, and Alan Wertheimer for help at various stages to the *Texas Journal on Women and the Law* at the University of Texas Law School for the opportunity to elicit comments on an earlier version, and to participants in the University of Minnesota Law School Faculty Workshop for valuable suggestions. Kent Spies and Terrence Dwyer of the University of Minnesota Law School provided important research assistance. Work on this chapter was supported in part by a Fellowship in the Program in Ethics and the Professions at Harvard University.

NOTES

1. See, for example, Pamela Carroll, "Proponents of Physician-Assisted Suicide Continuing Efforts," *ACP Observer*, February 1992, p. 29 (describing state initiatives in Washington, California, Michigan, New Hampshire, and Oregon). Subsequently, Oregon voters made that state the first to legalize physician-assisted suicide. See 1995 Oregon Laws, Ch. 3, I. M. No. 16. But see also *Lee v. Oregon*, 869 F. Supp. 1491 (D. Or. 1994), entering an injunction preventing the statute from going into effect. Further legal proceedings will decide the statute's fate. For attempts to legalize physician-assisted suicide through litigation, see Compassion in *Dying v. Washington*, 850 F. Supp. 1454 (W.D. Wash. 1994), *rev'd*, 49 F.Sd 586 (9th Cir. 1995); Quill v. Koppel, 870 F. Supp. 78 (S.D.N.Y. 1994). See also *Hobbins v. Attorney General*, 527 N.W.2d 714 (Mich. 1994).

2. See, for example, Howard Brody, "Assisted Death—A Compassionate Response to a Medical Failure," *New England Journal of Medicine* 327 (1992): 1384–88; Timothy E. Quill, Christine K. Cassel, and Diane E. Meier, "Care of the Hopelessly Ill: Proposed Clinical Criteria for Physician-Assisted Suicide," *New England Journal of Medicine* 327 (1992): 1380–84; Guy I. Benrubi, "Euthanasia—The Need for Procedural Safeguards," *New England Journal of Medicine* 326 (1992): 197–99; Christine K. Cassel and Diane E. Meier, "Morals and Moralism in the Debate Over Euthanasia and Assisted Suicide," *New England Journal of Medicine* 323 (1990): 750–52; James Rachels, *The End of Life* (Oxford, England: Oxford University Press, 1986).

3. I restrict the term "euthanasia" to active euthanasia, excluding the termination of life-sustaining treatment, which has sometimes been called "passive euthanasia." Both law and ethics now treat the termination of treatment quite differently from the way they treat active euthanasia, so to use "euthanasia" to refer to both invites confusion. See generally "Report of the Council on Ethical and Judicial Affairs of the American Medical Association," *Issues in Law & Medicine* 10 (1994): 91–97, 92.

4. See Howard I. Kushner, "Women and Suicide in Historical Perspective," in Joyce McCarl Nielsen, ed., *Feminist Research Methods: Exemplary Readings in the Social Sciences* (Boulder, CO: Westview Press, 1990), 193–206, 198–200.

5. See Alan Meisel, *The Right to Die* (New York, NY: John Wiley & Sons Inc., 1989), 62, & *1993 Cumulative Supplement No. 2*, 50–54.

6. See Council on Ethical and Judicial Affairs, *Code of Medical Ethics: Current Opinions with Annotations* (Chicago, IL: American Medical Association, 1994), 50–51; "Report of the Board of Trustees of the American Medical Association," *Issues in Law & Medicine* 10 (1994): 81–90; "Report of the Council on Ethical and Judicial Affairs;" *Report of the Council on Ethical and Judicial Affairs of the American Medical Association: Euthanasia* (Chicago, IL: American Medical Association, 1989). There are U.S. data on public opinion and physicians' self-reported practices. See, for example, "Report of the Board of Trustees." But the legal and ethical condemnation of physician-assisted suicide and euthanasia in the United States undoubtedly affect the self-reporting and render this a poor indicator of actual practices.

7. See Nancy S. Jecker, "Physician-Assisted Death in the Netherlands and the United States: Ethical and Cultural Aspects of Health Policy Development," *Journal of the American Geriatrics Society* 42 (1994): 672–78, 676.

8. See generally Howard I. Kushner, "Women and Suicidal Behavior: Epidemiology, Gender, and Lethality in Historical Perspective," in Silvia Sara Canetto and David Lester, eds., *Women and Suicidal Behavior* (New York, NY: Springer, 1995).

9. Compare Jecker, "Physician-Assisted Death," 676, on reasons physicians might differentially refuse women's requests.

10. See Lawrence Kohlberg, *The Philosophy of Moral Development: Moral Stages and the Idea of Justice*, vol. I (San Francisco, CA: Harper & Row, 1981); Lawrence Kohlberg, *The Psychology of Moral Development: The Nature and Validity of Moral Stages*, vol. II (San Francisco, CA: Harper & Row, 1984).

11. See Carol Gilligan, *In A Different Voice: Psychological Theory and Women's Development* (Cambridge, MA: Harvard University Press, 1982).

12. Gilligan's work has prompted a large literature, building upon as well as criticizing her insights and methodology. See, for example, the essays collected in Larrabee, ed., *An Ethic of Care*. On attention to the ethics of care in bioethics and on feminist criticism of the ethics of care, see my Introduction to this volume.

13. See Kohlberg, *The Psychology of Moral Development*, 644–47.

14. On the Kohlberg–Gilligan debate, see generally Lawrence A. Blum, "Gilligan and Kohlberg: Implications for Moral Theory," in Larrabee, ed., *An Ethic of Care*, 49–68; Owen Flanagan and Kathryn Jackson, "Justice, Care, and Gender: The Kohlberg-Gilligan Debate Revisited," in Larrabee, ed., *An Ethic of Care*, 69–84, Seyla Benhabib, "The Generalized and the Concrete Other: The Kohlberg–Gilligan Controversy and Feminist Theory," in Seyla Benhabib and Drucilla Cornell, eds., *Feminism as Critique: On the Politics of Gender* (Minneapolis, MN: University of Minnesota Press, 1987), 77–95.

15. See, for example, Susan M. Wolf, "Holding the Line on Euthanasia," *Hastings Center Report* 19 (Jan./Feb. 1989): special supp. 13–15.

16. See "It's Over, Debbie," *Journal of the American Medical Association* 259 (1988): 272.

17. See Timothy Egan, "As Memory and Music Faded, Oregon Woman Chose Death," *The New York Times*, June 7, 1990, p. A1; Lisa Belkin, "Doctor Tells of First Death Using His Suicide Device," *The New York Times*, June 6, 1990, p. A1.

18. See "Doctor Assists in Two More Suicides in Michigan," *The New York Times*, October 24, 1991, p. A1 (Wantz and Miller).

19. See "Death at Kevorkian's Side Is Ruled Homicide," *The New York Times*, June 6, 1992, p. 10; "Doctor Assists in Another Suicide," *The New York Times*, September 27, 1992, p. 32; "Doctor in Michigan Helps a 6th Person To Commit Suicide," *The New York Times*, November 24, 1992, p. A10; "2 Commit Suicide, Aided by Michigan Doctor," *The New York Times*, December 16, 1992, p. A21.

20. See "Why Dr. Kevorkian Was Called in," *The New York Times*, January 25, 1993, P. A16.

21. See B. D. Colen, "Gender Question in Assisted Suicides," *Newsday*, November 25, 1992, p. 17; Ellen Goodman, "Act Now to Stop Dr. Death," *Atlanta Journal and Constitution*, May 27, 1992, p. A11.

22. See Timothy E. Quill, "Death and Dignity—A Case of Individualized Decision Making," *New England Journal of Medicine* 324 (1991): 691–94.

23. On Quill's motivations, see Timothy E. Quill, "The Ambiguity of Clinical Intentions," *New England Journal of Medicine* 329 (1993): 1039–40.

24. See, for example, Jean Grimshaw, *Philosophy and Feminist Thinking* (Minneapolis, MN: University of Minnesota Press, 1986), 175.

25. See, for example, Naomi Scheman, "Individualism and the Objects of Psychology," in Sandra Harding and Merrill B. Hintikka, eds., *Discovering Reality: Feminist Perspectives in Epistemology, Metaphysics, Methodology, and the Philosophy of Science* (Boston, MA: D. Reidel, 1983), 225–44, 240.

26. See Jennifer Nedelsky, "Reconceiving Autonomy: Sources, Thoughts and Possibilities," *Yale Journal of Law and Feminism* 1 (1989): 7–36.

27. *Ibid.*, 12–13.

28. See Martha Minow, *"Making All the Difference: Inclusion, Exclusion, and American Law* (Ithaca, NY: Cornell University Press, 1990).

29. Another author offering a feminist revision of autonomy and rights is Diana T. Meyers in "The Socialized Individual and Individual Autonomy: An Intersection between Philosophy and Psychology," in Eva Feder Kittay and Diana T. Meyers, eds., *Women and Moral Theory* (Savage, MD: Rowman & Littlefield, 1987), 139–53. See also Elizabeth M. Schneider, "The Dialectic of Rights and Politics: Perspectives from the Women's Movement," *New York University Review* 61 (1986): 589–652. There is a large feminist literature presenting a critique of rights, some of it rejecting the utility of such language. See, for example, Catharine MacKinnon, "Feminism, Marxism, Method and the State: Toward Feminist Jurisprudence," *Signs* 8 (1983): 635–58, 658 ("Abstract rights will authorize the male experience of the world.").

30. See, for example, Susan M. Wolf, "Nancy Beth Cruzan: In No Voice At All," *Hastings Center Report* 20 (Jan.–Feb. 1990): 38–41; *Guidelines on the Termination of Life-Sustaining Treatment and the Care of the Dying* (Bloomington, IN: Indiana University Press & The Hastings Center, 1987).

31. John Stuart Mill, "On Liberty," in Marshall Cohen, ed., *The Philosophy of John Stuart Mill: Ethical, Political and Religious* (New York, NY: Random House, 1961), 185–319, 304.

32. Leon R. Kass also argues against the existence of a "right to die" in "Is There a Right to Die?" *Hastings Center Report* 23 (Jan.–Feb. 1993): 34–43.

33. The Dutch studies show that even when patients know they can get assisted suicide and euthanasia, three times more patients ask for such assurance from their physicians than actually die that way. See van der Maas et al., "Euthanasia," *Lancet*, 673.

34. On these obligations and their derivation, see Leon R. Kass, "Neither for Love nor Money: Why Doctors Must Not Kill," *The Public Interest* 94 (Winter 1989): 25–46; Tom L. Beauchamp and James F. Childress, *Principles of Biomedical Ethics*, 4th ed. (New York, NY: Oxford University Press, 1994), 189, 226–27.

35. See Leslie Bender, "A Feminist Analysis of Physician-Assisted Dying and Voluntary Active Euthanasia," *Tennessee Law Review* 59 (1992): 519–46, making a "caring" argument in favor of "physician-assisted death."

36. Brody, "Assisted Death."

37. James Rachels offers a like proposal. See Rachels, *The End of Life*.

38. For a summary of the debate over the proper structure of bioethics, see David DeGrazia, "Moving Forward in Bioethical Theory, Theories, Cases, and Specified Principlism," *Journal of Medicine and Philosophy* 17 (1992): 511–40. There have been several different attacks on a bioethics driven by principles, which is usually taken to be exemplified by Beauchamp and Childress, *Principles of Biomedical Ethics*. Clouser and Gert argue for a bioethics that would be even more "top-down" or deductive, proceeding from theory instead of principles. See K. Danner Clouser and Bernard Gert, "A Critique of Principlism," *Journal of Medicine and Philosophy* 15 (1990): 219–36. A different attack is presented by Ronald M. Green, "Method in Bioethics: A Troubled Assessment," *Journal of Medicine and Philosophy* 15 (1990): 179–97. Hoffmaster argues for an ethnography driven, "bottom-up" or inductive bioethics. Barry Hoffmaster, "The Theory and Practice of Applied Ethics," *Dialogue* XXX (1991): 213–34. Jonsen and Toulmin have urged a revival of casuistry built on case-by-case analysis. Albert R. Jonsen and Stephen Toulmin, *The Abuse of Casuistry: A History of Moral Reasoning* (Berkeley, CA: University of California Press, 1988). Beauchamp and Childress discuss these challenges at length in the 4th edition of *Principles of Biomedical Ethics*.

39. See Gilligan, *In A Different Voice*, 174. Lawrence Blum points out that Kohlberg himself stated that "the final, most mature stage of moral reasoning involves an 'integration of justice and care that forms a single moral principle,'" but that Kohlberg, too, never spelled out what that integration would be. See Lawrence A. Blum, "Gilligan and Kohlberg: Implications for Moral Theory," *Ethics* 98 (1988): 472–91, 482–83 (footnote with citation omitted).

40. See Blum, "Gilligan and Kohlberg," 477.

41. Owen Flanagan and Kathryn Jackson, "Justice, Care, and Gender: The Kohlberg-Gilligan Debate Revisited," in Larrabee, ed., *An Ethic of Care*, 69–84, 71.

42. Martha Minow and Elizabeth V. Spelman, "In Context," *Southern California Law Review* 63 (1990): 1597–652, 1625.

43. *Ibid.*, 1629.

44. *Ibid.*, 1630–31.

45. *Ibid.*, 1632–33.

46. There are significant similarities here to Henry Richardson's proposal of "specified principlism." See DeGrazia, "Moving Forward in Bioethical Theory."

47. On the importance of paying attention to who is doing the theorizing and to what end "including in feminist theorizing, see Maria C. Lugones and Elizabeth V. Spelman, "Have We Got a Theory for You! Feminist Theory, Cultural Imperialism and the Demand for 'The Woman's Voice,'" *Women's Studies International Forum* 6 (1983): 573–81.

48. I have elsewhere argued that health care institutions should create processes to uncover and combat sexism and racism, among other problems. See Susan M. Wolf, "Toward a Theory of Process," *Law, Medicine & Health Care* 20 (1992): 278–90.

49. On the importance of viewing the medical profession in the context of the democratic polity, see Troyen Brennan, *Just Doctoring: Medical Ethics in the Liberal State* (Berkeley, CA: University of California Press, 1991).

50. See, for example, Howard J. Curzer, "Is Care A Virtue For Health Care Professionals?" *Journal of Medicine and Philosophy* 18 (1993): 51–69; Nancy S. Jecker and Donnie J. Self, "Separating Care And Cure: An Analysis Of Historical And Contemporary Images Of Nursing And Medicine," *Journal of Medicine and Philosophy* 16 (1991): 285–306.

51. Compare Canetto, "Elderly Women and Suicidal Behavior," finding evidence of this with respect to elderly women electing suicide.

52. See van der Maas, van Delden, and Pijnenborg, "Euthanasia," *Health Policy*, 51–55, 145–46; van der Wal et al.,

"Voluntary Active Euthanasia and Physician-Assisted Suicide in Dutch Nursing Homes."

53. In these two sentences, I disagree both with Kass's suggestion that the core commitments of medicine are set for all time by the ancient formulation of the doctor's role and with Brock's assertion that the core commitment of medicine is to do whatever the patient wants. See Kass, "Neither for Love Nor Money"; Dan Brock, "Voluntary Active Euthanasia," *Hastings Center Report* 22 (Mar.–Apr. 1992): 10–22.

54. See Jay Katz, *The Silent World of Doctor and Patient* (New York, NY: Free Press, 1984), 121–22.

55. See Miles and August, "Gender, Courts, and the 'Right to Die.'"

56. While a large literature analyzes the relationship between terminating life-sustaining treatment and the practices of physician-assisted suicide and euthanasia, more recently attention has turned to the relationship between those latter practices and abortion. On the question of whether respect for women's choice of abortion requires legitimation of those practices, see, for example, Seth F. Kreimer, "Does Pro-choice Mean Pro-Kevorkian? An Essay on *Roe, Casey*, and the Right to Die," *American University Law Review* 44 (1995): 803–54. Full analysis of why respect for the choice of abortion does not require legitimation of physician-assisted suicide and euthanasia is beyond the scope of this chapter. However, the courts themselves are beginning to argue the distinction. See Compassion in *Dying v. Washington*, 49 F.3d 586 (9th Cir. 1995). On gender specifically, there are strong arguments that gender equity and concern for the fate of women demand respect for the abortion choice, whereas I am arguing that gender concerns cut the other way when it comes to physician-assisted suicide and euthanasia.

Confucian Ethic of Death with Dignity and Its Contemporary Relevance

Ping-Cheung Lo

Ping-Cheung Lo is a professor of philosophy at the Hong Kong Baptist University. He has written extensively in bioethics and comparative religious ethics. He is also the author of *Treating Persons as Ends: An Essay on Kant's Moral Philosophy* (1987).

In this selection, Lo discusses two theses at work in the Confucian ethic of dying with dignity, one other-regarding, the other self-regarding. The other-regarding thesis holds that the moral values of benevolence (*ren*) and justice (*yi*) must not be sacrificed to preserve one's life. The self-regarding thesis, on the other hand, maintains that one should kill oneself to avoid humiliation and disgrace, although this thesis is not without dissent. In the end, he highlights similarities and differences between contemporary and Confucian understandings of physician-assisted suicide and euthanasia.

ABSTRACT

This paper advances three claims. First, according to contemporary Western advocates of physician-assisted-suicide and voluntary euthanasia, "death with dignity" is understood negatively as bringing about death to avoid or prevent indignity, that is, to avoid a degrading existence. Second, there is a similar morally affirmative view on death with dignity in ancient China, in classical Confucianism in particular. Third, there is consonance as well as dissonance between these two ethics of death with dignity, such that the Confucian perspective would regard the argument for physician-assisted-suicide and voluntary euthanasia as less than compelling because of the latter's impoverished vision of human life.

Ping-Cheung Lo, "Confucian Ethic of Death with Dignity and Its Contemporary Relevance" from *Annual of the Society of Christian Ethics* 19 (1999), pp. 313–333. Reprinted by permission.

INTRODUCTION

I want to make three claims in this paper. To begin with, there are several major arguments in favor of physician-assisted suicide and voluntary euthanasia (abbreviated as PAS and VE below) in the contemporary debate in the West. There is much discussion on the arguments from autonomy and from compassion, but not much on the argument from death with dignity as an independent argument. I submit that according to the advocates of PAS and VE, to be explained in a later section, "death with dignity" is to be understood negatively as bringing about death to avoid or prevent indignity, that is, to avoid extreme humiliation or a degrading existence. This is the first claim. The second is that there is a similar morally affirmative view on death with dignity in ancient China, in classical Confucianism in particular. The third claim is that there is consonance as well as dissonance between these two ethics of death with dignity and that the Confucian perspective would deem the PAS and VE death with dignity argument as less than compelling because of its impoverished vision of human life.

A few qualifications are in order before I proceed. First, in discussing PAS and VE my major concern is not with public policy or law, which involve factors other than the moral status of the acts of PAS and VE. In this paper I will focus on the right-making and wrong-making characteristics of these acts in their proper circumstances. Second, this is not an essay in comparative religious ethics or comparative bioethics. My aim is to explore how a religious or quasi-religious tradition very different from Christianity would assess the morality of PAS and VE. Hence in the first part of this essay I will articulate descriptive analyses, and in the second part I will propose certain normative claims.

CONFUCIAN ETHIC OF "DEATH WITH DIGNITY"[1]

Early Confucian Ethic of Suicide

Early Confucian ethics emphasizes that biological life is not of the highest value. As Confucius (551–479 BCE) says:

> For gentlemen of purpose and men of *ren* [benevolence or supreme virtue] while it is inconceivable that they should seek to stay alive at the expense of *ren*, it may happen that they have to accept death in order to have *ren* accomplished.[2]

Likewise, Mencius (372–289 BCE), the second most famous Confucian after Confucius,[3] explains in a famous passage:

> Fish is what I want; bear's palm is also what I want. If I cannot have both, I would rather take bear's palm than fish. Life is what I want; *yi* [justice or dutifulness] is also what I want. If I cannot have both, I would rather take *yi* than life. On the one hand, though life is what I want, there is something I want more than life. That is why I do not cling to life at all cost. On the other hand, though death is what I loathe, there is something I loathe more than death. That is why there are dangers I do not avoid. . . . Yet there are ways of remaining alive and ways of avoiding death to which a person will not resort. In other words, there are things a person wants more than life and there are also things he or she loathes more than death. This is an attitude not confined to the moral person but common to all persons. The moral person simply never loses it.[4]

These two discourses together became the *locus classicus* of the Confucian view on the value of human life, and have been tremendously influential down the ages. According to this classical view, the preservation of our biological life is a good, but not the supreme good; death is an evil, but not the supreme evil. Since the cardinal moral values of *ren* and *yi* (benevolence and justice) are the supreme good, it is morally wrong for one to preserve one's own life at the expense of ignoring *ren* and *yi*. Rather, one should sacrifice one's life, either passively or actively, in order to uphold *ren* and *yi*.[5] The failure to follow *ren* and *yi* is ethically worse than death. Hence suicide is morally permissible, and even praiseworthy, if it is done for the sake of *ren* and *yi*. In some circumstances, furthermore, committing suicide is more than supererogatory; it is even obligatory. There is a doctrine of the sanctity of moral values, but not a doctrine of the sanctity of human life. Sheer living has no intrinsic moral value; to live as a virtuous person does have such value. There is no unconditional duty to preserve and continue life, but there is an unconditional duty to uphold *ren* and *yi*. For convenience sake, I shall summarize this classical Confucian view as Confucian Thesis I: **One should give up one's life, if necessary, either passively or actively, for the sake of upholding the cardinal moral values of *ren* and *yi*.**

There are numerous expositions of this thesis in the history of interpretation. I will summarize only two such expositions here. The first one is articulated by Wen Tianxiang (1236–1282 CE), who points out that since one has to die one way or another, one should die in such a way that renders one's life meaningful or honorable. In other words, though death is the termination of life, dying is still part of life. "How one dies" is part of "how one lives." Hence dying should serve life. To take charge of one's life implies taking charge of one's dying. To secure a noble and honorable life implies that one should secure a noble and honorable dying. To live meaningfully implies managing the time and circumstances of one's dying in such a way that one can also die meaningfully. What matters is not life's quantity (its length), but its quality, which is defined morally with reference to *ren* and *yi*. In order to secure a high quality of life, in some circumstances one has to be prepared to die, lest what transpires in a prolonged life decreases the quality of life.[6]

Another famous interpreter of Confucian Thesis I is Sima Qian (c.190–145 BCE), who explains that though all people have to die, the value of their dying is not necessarily the same. Some deaths are good while others are of no value or even bad. The degree of value depends on the circumstances of the death. If committing suicide can be of significant value, then one ought to do it. One ought not to commit a suicide, however, that will have little significance. In other words, according to Sima Qian, dying is not a bare biological event as far as human beings are concerned. The time and circumstance of one's death have moral significance. The moral issue is not whether one can commit suicide or not, since there is no strict prohibition against it. Rather, the issue is for what kind of reason (trivial or substantial) suicide is committed, and what kind of impact it will produce.[7]

This Confucian teaching of "dying to achieve *ren (shashen chengren)*" (Confucius) and of "laying down one's life for a cause of *yi (shesheng quyi)*" (Mencius) not only have inspired innumerable Chinese to risk and sacrifice their lives for noble causes, but also have motivated many Chinese to commit suicide for noble causes. When people committed suicide for noble reasons, they were not condemned; rather, they were praised for their aspiration and dedication to *ren* and *yi*.[8] This moral view prevails even as late as the early twentieth century.[9]

Furthermore, in the Chinese language these acts were not called "suicide" in the pejorative sense of "self-destruction" or "self-slaughter." A different set of phrases, usually a combination of another word with *xun* (sacrifice) or *jie* (moral integrity), with the connotation of praiseworthiness, were used instead.[10] Hence such suicides were not deemed acts of self-destruction, but rather, acts of moral "construction" or affirmation. Tang Jungyi, a prominent contemporary neo-Confucian, compares such suicide of *xun* and *jie* to the death of martyrs in early Christianity. Just as these Christian martyrs were prepared to endure anything, even death, for the sake of upholding faith, Confucian men and women of integrity (*qijie*) were also prepared to

endure anything, even death, for the sake of upholding *ren* and *yi*. The distinction between letting oneself be killed and actively killing oneself does not make any moral difference here. Tang Jungyi adds that the religiosity (absolute devotion, unconditional dedication, ultimate commitment) of these men and women cannot not be denied.[11]

There were, of course, many suicides in premodern China that were not deemed suicides for the sake of *ren* and *yi*. Most self-regarding suicides—for example, suicide as a result of being tired of life, suicide as a solution to one's troubles or failures (financial or marital), suicide as a solution to chronic depression, suicide as an expiation of one's wrongdoing, suicide out of fear of punishment or public mockery—were not included. These people were both pitied and deplored. Their suicides were evaluated as "self-destruction" or "self-slaughter," and many of them were deemed wrong primarily because of another important Confucian value, namely, *xiao* or filial piety. Committing suicide was deemed contrary to filial piety not because of the trivial reason that it would cause grief to one's parents.[12] Confucian filial piety required that sons and daughters attend to their parents' daily needs throughout life. Terminating one's life would render one unable to fulfill this important filial duty. Furthermore, Confucian literature on filial piety argued that children were permanently indebted to their parents because children owe their very existence to the parents. If one is not the author of one's biological life, then how can one have the authority to dispose of one's life as one wishes? Suicide was then understood as usurping the authority of parents.[13] In short, unless filial piety was outweighed by another moral value such as *ren* or *yi*, the former was usually a moral reason strong enough to forbid suicide.

The Emergence of the Ethic of Death with Dignity

Most self-regarding suicides were regarded as morally wrong in ancient China, and no one felt the need to discuss them. There was one kind of self-regarding suicide, however, that did evoke some discussion, and it can be conveniently called, in modern idiom, "death with dignity." In the former Han Dynasty (206 BCE–8 CE) Confucianism was elevated to the role of the established ideology of the empire. The Confucian instrumental in bringing this about was Dong Zhongshu (C.179–C.104 BCE). Though modern Chinese philosophers often consider him of minor philosophical significance, historically he was of the utmost importance. The imperial policy, advocated by Dong, of establishing the supremacy of Confucianism to the exclusion of other schools of thought, was adopted in 136 BCE and was continued until 1905.[14] Dong has been widely acknowledged as the most religious thinker in the history of Confucianism because be elevated "Heaven" to a personal God in his political theory.

One should note that it was not the original classical Confucianism that was honored in the Han Dynasty, but rather Dong's creative synthesis of various streams of Confucianism together with other schools of thought. Dong's masterpiece was entitled *Chunqiu fanlou (Exuberant Dew of the Spring and Autumn),* which was an exposition of the thought of the *Spring and Autumn Annals,* the authorship of which was attributed to Confucius. Dong regarded the *Spring and Autumn Annals* as the canon within the Confucian Canon.[15] In one chapter of his work, Dong eloquently elaborated a variation of Confucian Thesis I, which was shared by other Confucian writings around the same time in the early Han Dynasty.

In Chapter 8 ("*Zhulin*") of his *Exuberant Dew of the Spring and Autumn,* Dong discussed a certain king and his adviser who lived several hundred years before his time. King Qing of Qi was in a battle with his enemies, and lost. The enemies surrounded his armies, and it was highly likely that he would be captured and killed. His adviser Choufu happened to look quite like him and therefore offered to exchange clothing with him so that the king could escape unnoticed. The strategy succeeded. King Qing escaped and returned to his kingdom in civilian clothing, while Choufu was mistaken as the king, captured, and killed.

Rather than praising Choufu's ingenuity, dedication, and sacrifice, Dong condemned his action.

To have a king dress as an ordinary citizen and escape surreptitiously, according to Dong, was to subject a dignitary to an undignified treatment. Such humiliation should not be tolerated, even if it could save life. This was because, Dong argued, "to survive through accepting a great humiliation is joyless, thus wise people refrain from doing it. . . . A person who has a sense of shame does not live in dishonor." Citing other Confucian writings of the early Han Dynasty, Dong implied that his ethics of suicide was derived from the Confucian canon. "If a dishonor is avoidable, avoid it; if it is unavoidable, *junzi* [a man of noble character] sees death as his destiny [that is, he embraces death with courage]. . . . A *ru* [Confucian] prefers death to humiliation."[16] Dong therefore argued that the morally right thing for Choufu to have done was to have told King Qing. "To bear humiliation and yet refuse to commit suicide is shameless. I shall therefore commit suicide with you." At that moment, for both of them, death was better than staying alive, as "a *junzi* [man of noble character] should prefer dying in honor to surviving in dishonor."

In short, according to Confucianism in the early Han Dynasty, biological life is valuable, but there are self-regarding states of affairs more valuable than biological life, namely, a life with honor and dignity. Although death is undesirable, there are self-regarding states of affairs more undesirable than death, namely, to suffer disgrace, dishonor, and humiliation in life. One should choose death in order to avoid undergoing undignified treatment; and it is honorable, even obligatory, to make such a choice. Such a suicide is honorable because it is a suicide for the sake of *ren* and *yi.* This view is a variation and elaboration of Confucian Thesis I, with the focus shifted from other-regarding concerns to self-regarding concerns. I shall call it Confucian Thesis II: **One should actively terminate one's life for the sake of preventing indignity.**

I suggest that we can use the phrase "death with dignity" to describe the kind of death recommended by Confucian Thesis II. Though Dong did not use the Chinese term for "dignity" in his discussions, the opposite words, such as "indignity," "humiliation," "disgrace," and "dishonor," were frequently used by him. In other words, this Confucian "death with dignity" is to be understood negatively as "death to prevent indignity."

The idea of "death with dignity" was quite common in ancient China and many examples can be found in the *Records of the Historian (Shiji)* by Sima Qian (c.190–145 BCE),[17] the greatest historian of ancient China, and a younger contemporary of Dong Zhongshu. This work records many suicides, often with approval. Among these suicides two types are particularly noteworthy for our purposes. The first type involves those where death is unavoidable in the near future: one hears or predicts that one will be executed by the government, and so commits suicide; suicide after a military defeat (otherwise the defeated general will be killed by his conqueror); and suicide after a failed *coup d'etat* attempt (which means that execution is waiting for the rebel). What is common in all these three cases is that the agents consider the fate of execution a humiliation, a dishonor, and a disgrace. Hence it is better to kill oneself than to be killed by others. Committing suicide is therefore a means of avoiding undignified treatment.

The second noteworthy type of suicide involves those where there is no known threat to one's life: a literati-official commits suicide in order to avoid the indignity of being tried in court, regardless of whether he is guilty of innocent; a literati-official commits suicide in order to avoid the indignity of imprisonment. In these cases, the literati-officials firmly believe that to be tried in court and/or to be imprisoned, even if one is innocent, is a humiliation, a dishonor, and a disgrace. Hence it is better to kill oneself than to suffer such an undignified treatment. Committing suicide is therefore a means of preventing indignity.

In short, both of these types of suicide are instances of Confucian "death with dignity," and they confirm that the Confucian ethic of death with dignity was widely accepted in Chinese antiquity.[18]

A Dissenting Ethic

Although Confucian Thesis II was the mainstream view during Dong's time, a dissenting view soon emerged. Sima Qian, the Grand Historian, who

approved so many "death with dignity" suicides in his *Records of the Historian*, ironically rejected this option when he himself was put in the predicament of an extremely undignified treatment: he suffered castration in prison. This treatment stemmed from his defense of a general who surrendered to the "barbarians" after a military defeat. Subsequent events convinced the emperor that the general was a traitor, and the emperor punished all those who had pleaded for the general. Sima Qian was therefore imprisoned and further punished with castration. The Grand Historian considered this punishment an utmost humiliation and understood that his peers expected him to commit suicide in order to avoid undignified treatment. After much struggle, however, Sima Qian refused to commit suicide and decided to bear this unbearable indignity in order to complete his half-finished masterpiece, the *Shiji*. He understood very well that he had a duty to commit suicide, but he considered it more important to discharge his weightier duty of writing a grand historical book. His *A letter to Ren An* can be read as the account of a tormented soul urging his contemporaries to excuse him for *not* committing suicide.[19]

In short, in the midst of undignified treatment, death with dignity is not the only option. One can continue to live on with a modicum of dignity by fulfilling one's vocation. There are many historical examples of this nature, as Sima Qian also noted in the *Letter*. Sima Qian's decision of not committing suicide has also been influential in the subsequent development of Chinese thought.

Dialectic Balance of These Two Ethics During the "Cultural Revolution"

It is noteworthy that both the Confucian ethic of "death with dignity" and the dissenting ethic have their respective followers even among the contemporary intellectuals in China. During the "Cultural Revolution" (1966–1976) many university professors, literati, and public intellectuals were publicly tortured, brutalized, and humiliated. Many of them committed suicide (e.g. Fu Lei, Lao She).[20] While some terminated lives because they could not stand the physical and emotional suffering, others chose to die because they refused to accept the humiliation. In the case of Lao She, at least two contemporary mainland Chinese writers have used the maxim "literati prefer death to humiliation" to explain his suicide.[21] Whether or not Lao She in fact drowned himself with this motivation is not indisputable.[22] The fact that these writers employed this maxim to explain the suicide shows, however, that the maxim remains persuasive to contemporary Chinese.[23] In 1993, a famous senior philosophy professor at Peking University told me of a colleague who, during the "Cultural Revolution," calmly accepted the purges levied against him. One morning, however, he discovered *on* his front door an accusation poster written by his students. He was so deeply hurt that he left a note, "literati prefer death to humiliation," and then committed suicide. This further indicates that the Confucian ethic of "death with dignity" is accepted by some contemporary Chinese.[24]

On the other hand, many survivors of the "Cultural Revolution" invoke the dissenting ethic to justify their refusal to commit suicide, appealing to the precedent of Sima Qian. They admit, however, that the tension between the ethic of "death with dignity" and the dissenting view provides a helpful check and balance. If all intellectuals rushed to embrace "death with dignity," there would be nobody left to rebuild the country when the political storm was over. If all intellectuals invoked the dissenting ethic and stayed alive, there would be no witness of blood telling society at that time that the indignity they experienced was totally unacceptable.

In other words, the Confucian "death with dignity" is not a uniform moral consensus among either ancient Chinese or contemporary Chinese. This lack of consensus notwithstanding, my claim is that Confucian "death with dignity" is morally persuasive to a significant number of Chinese. This claim is an adequate basis for the next major question of this paper. Given its sympathy to the idea of "'death with dignity," would Confucianism endorse the "death with dignity" argument in favor of PAS and VE? Before I turn to that question, however, I want to further analyze ethically the Confucian notion of death with dignity and examine its normative significance.

FURTHER ETHICAL ANALYSIS OF CONFUCIAN "DEATH WITH DIGNITY" AND ITS NORMATIVE SIGNIFICANCE

As Leon Kass points out, etymologically central to the notion of "dignity" in English and "*dignitas*" in Latin is the notion of "worthiness, elevation, honor, nobility, height—in short, of excellence or virtue . . . . Dignity is, in principle, aristocratic."[25] The same is true in Chinese culture. The ethic of "death with dignity" articulated by Dong Zhongshu was not meant to be binding on all Chinese. In the beginning, it applied only to the nobility and dignitaries, a class comprised exclusively of royalty. Gradually the literati-officials, who assisted the royalty in running the government, were elevated to the class of nobility and dignitary. For a literati-official to have been tried in court or imprisoned would have meant that he would be treated as a commoner, and that would have been degrading and humiliating. Hence he had to kill himself rather than undergoing such humiliation. This was, however, only a superficial reason for committing suicide.

There was a weightier reason for committing this kind of suicide. When an educated person entered public service, becoming a literati-official, in addition to acquiring a higher social status, he also accepted a noble vocation or office in life. He therefore had to live a life worthy of his new station and duty, a life commensurate with his vocation. There was a stronger sense of accountability correlative with this higher status. Out of respect for one's vocation and calling, one should rather die than let the office/vocation be dishonored, despised, and mocked. Hence choosing death to prevent indignity was not solely expressive of a self-regarding concern, but also done from a concern to maintain the dignity of one's office.

There is an ancient Chinese saying that summarizes well the ethic of "death with dignity" in both ancient and contemporary China: "rather be a shattered vessel of jade than an unbroken piece of pottery," which means, "better to die in glory or dignity than live or survive in dishonor." Its ethic of life and death is clear: mere biological life is not intrinsically valuable; there is no sanctity of biological life. When a life in its fullness is irreversibly reduced to an unacceptably low or degrading state, then that life is no longer worth living. This saying is taken further to mean that there is a purpose or vocation in life higher than preserving one's own life: the fulfillment of *ren* and *yi*, or the aspiration for moral sagehood. When one can no longer serve that vocation and is even forced to go against it (to violate *ren* and *yi*, and to descend to immorality), life becomes degraded and one should rather die. To die in this way is analogous to martyrdom—one dies rather than betraying a worthy cause in life; one dies as a witness to the worthy cause. (For example, during the "Cultural Revolution," many people, especially those who enjoyed social esteem, were forced to live the life of a liar, to be a part of the propaganda machinery of the Communist Party, to be an accomplice of the party to destroy its "enemies." Some intellectuals found this kind of life too degrading to live and therefore committed suicide to resist such an indignity.)

We should note that when it is said that "the humiliation, dishonor, disgrace, or degradation is too much to bear and one would rather die than drag on," a normative ideal is being expressed. In fact the state of affairs could be made bearable if one changed one's vocation ("Forget about aspiring to be a vessel of jade, just be happy to be a piece of pottery!"). It is not a matter of "can," but "should." In other words, the claim is that the degradation involved is so serious that one would be forced to betray one's vocation if one continued to live under these circumstances. One should not do this, because one should not trade *ren* and *yi* or moral sagehood for biological life, which is not intrinsically valuable. Death is not the *summum malum*; the betrayal of one's vocation is. Hence, as a last resort, it is morally permissible and even obligatory to bring about one's death in order to resist the true *summum malum*. What matters is not life's quantity (its length), but its quality, which is defined morally with reference to the cardinal Confucian virtues. In order to secure a high quality of life, in some circumstances one has to be prepared to die, lest what transpires decreases the moral quality of life.

THE NATURE OF "DEATH WITH DIGNITY" IN CONTEMPORARY WESTERN DISCUSSIONS

I will now analyze the "death with dignity" argument in favor of PAS and VE in contemporary Western society. Though this argument is not developed as thoroughly as the arguments from compassion (that PAS and VE are the only effective way of relieving patients' intractable pain near life's end) and from autonomy (that self-determination includes deciding the time and manner of one's death), it has much persuasive power. I submit that the argument that PAS and VE are "death with dignity" is more than mere rhetoric and is an argument independent of the arguments from autonomy and compassion. This interpretation needs some substantiation because it is not that widely recognized. Hence my analysis of this argument below will include a number of salient quotations from the pro-PAS and pro-VE literature.

To begin, when Californians debated California Proposition 161 ("Death with Dignity Act") in 1992, a group called Californians against Human Suffering published a pamphlet entitled *Questions and Answers on the California Death with Dignity Act*. Question 9 in this pamphlet asks, "Shouldn't the law be restricted to those who are [in] intractable pain?" The answer provided is as follows:

> No! The *loss of personal dignity* may be as intolerable to a patient as horrific pain. Many are willing to fight back against their terminal disease as long as they can maintain a minimally acceptable quality of life, but many of us do not wish to *live like a zombie*, which is often the result of adequate pain control. For others whose *bodily functions fail* and are *confined to bed, totally dependent on others for every aspect of existence*, their life has become unbearable even if their pain is being controlled.[26]

This passage makes three significant points: (1) the argument of "death with dignity" is distinct from the argument from compassion (the elimination of pain); (2) the concern is negative (the loss of dignity) rather than positive (the conferral of dignity); and (3) indignity happens because of failing health and of the side-effect of large doses of pain-killing medicine.[27]

This abhorrence of failing health seems to suggest an aversion to and rejection of the natural cycle of life, which starts from the dependence of infancy, moves on to the independence of adulthood, and then concludes with the dependence of failing health in old age. As some judges in the United States Court of Appeals for the Ninth Circuit argued in 1996:

> Like the decision of whether or not to have an abortion, the decision how and when to die is one of "the most intimate and personal choices a person may make in a lifetime," a choice "central to *personal dignity* and autonomy." A competent terminally ill adult, having lived nearly the full measure of his life, has a strong liberty interest in choosing a *dignified and humane death* rather than being reduced at the end of his existence to a *childlike state of helplessness, diapered, sedated, incontinent.*[28]

Some people seem to blame this utter dependence of the dying elderly on the relatively long dying process of modern patients. For example, it is reported by a Canadian Senate committee on euthanasia:

> Some witness told the Committee that a *prolonged dying process* can cause a *loss of dignity.* Furthermore, it can lead to a *loss of independence and control over their lives* which for them, is paramount.[29]

This concern is echoed in the Ninth Circuit decision mentioned above.

> As a result, Americans are living longer, and when they finally succumb to illness, *lingering longer,* either in greater pain or in a stuporous, semicomatose condition that results from the infusion of vast amounts of pain killing medications. Despite the marvels of technology, Americans frequently *die with less dignity than they did in the days when ravaging diseases typically ended their lives quickly.* . . . One result has been a growing movement to restore humanity and dignity to the process by which Americans die.[30]

Perhaps being mindful that the "dignity-talk" can be over-used and sound hollow, some authors choose different terms to describe the utterly unpleasant condition of the dying. For example, the Ontario Medical Association states in a recent publication on euthanasia:

> There are concerns about *loss of dignity* and the occurrence of symptoms of situations which are perceived by the individual as *demeaning or degrading.* These concerns are raised by a number of patients but are particularly common in Alzheimer's disease and AIDS. Patients with Alzheimer's disease may perceive euthanasia as a welcome release from the relentless progressive loss of intellectual faculties and worsening physical status which ultimately result in a *completely dependent and institutionalized state.* Similarly, the final stages of AIDS may be extremely unpleasant and unattractive and it has been argued by a number of AIDS groups that euthanasia is a needed option for patients who wish to forgo this *degradation.*[31]

Finally, I want to quote one more passage that contains almost all the ingredients of the argument of "death with dignity" analyzed above. This passage is from a book entitled *Death and Dignity,* authored by Dr. Timothy Quill, a leading physician-spokesperson and activist of the PAS movement in the U.S.:

> Despite the effectiveness of the hospice program, Diane still feared being *out of control, bedbound, and totally dependent.* She had an extreme aversion to *lying passively in bed,* to being *unable to attend to her basic bodily functions,* or to being *sedated or confused while she waited for death.* . . . For some people, such *prolongation of dying* might have a purpose; for others, it is meaningless and even cruel . . . For those who place extreme value on their physical and intellectual integrity, living out their final time with the progressive dementia associated with HIV can be far worse than death. *"What dignity can be found dying demented, lying in my own feces, unaware of my surrounding?"* they ask. . . . a "natural" death that they would find *humiliating.*[32]

I think that a sympathetic reading of the pro-PAS and pro-VE literature supports the claim that the argument of death with dignity is an independent argument. It is more about the process of dying than about the state of death.[33] According to this argument, our biological condition can deteriorate so badly (e.g., incontinence, being brought back to the state of infancy, total dependence on others, entirely bedbound, progressive dementia, disability, comatose, sedated to a semi-conscious state) that the relatively long dying process can be utterly undignified, humiliating, disgraceful, dishonorable, and degrading.[34] Such an indignity can be more intolerable than physical pain. PAS and VE can therefore save people from such an undignified state of existence. In other words, PAS and VE, as death with dignity, while not positively conferring dignity upon a person when s/he dies, negatively prevent a person from falling into an undignified state of existence.[35]

CONSONANCE AND DISSONANCE

The final task of this paper involves examining whether the Confucian conception of "death with dignity" might lend support to the death with dignity position of contemporary PAS and VE. There is consonance as well as dissonance between these two ethics.

Regarding consonance: First, neither ethic deems suicide intrinsically immoral, and both agree that human beings should take full charge of their lives, of which dying is a part. Second, both ethics accept some kind of quality of life consideration, and make a distinction between an acceptable quality of life and an unacceptably low quality of life. Third, both agree that there are cases in which the quality of life is so low that to continue in such a state would be worse than death. When life is too degrading to go on living, to terminate one's biological life boldly is a morally acceptable option. Bringing about death to prevent indignity is morally permissible.

There is dissonance as well. First, the crucial difference is the criterion for unacceptable degradation—what constitutes an indignity so serious and so grave that it is worse than death? For Confucianism, the criterion is always moral, not physiological-psychological. Confucian quality of life considerations are always quality of moral life consideration. Indignity, humiliation, dishonor, disgrace, and degradation are all conceived with reference to one's moral life rather than one's biological life. The metaphor of jade vessel and pottery, for example, is not to be understood physiologically with reference to one's

health condition, but with reference to one's moral character. This is because Confucianism has a definite theory of good and evil. Biological life is a good, but it is not the highest good; the *summum bonum* is moral sagehood. Biological death is an evil, but it is not the worst evil; the *summum malum* is moral depravity. Hence an authentic human life is an ascent to moral sagehood, and an inauthentic human life a descent into immorality (or in Confucian idiom, a descent from the human to the beastly). Exaltation and degradation in human existence are to be understood as moral ascent and moral depravity. Since the degradation and indignity are seated in a person's moral soul rather than in the human body, the circumstances that constitute "death with dignity" (i.e., death to prevent indignity) in Confucianism are quite different from that in contemporary pro-PAS and pro-VE movement.

Second, accordingly, it is not immediately clear in Confucianism that deteriorating biological conditions (e.g., incontinence, being brought back to the state of infancy, total dependence on others, entirely bedbound, progressive dementia, disability, comatose, sedated to a semi-conscious state) are so degrading that to stay in these conditions is worse than death. It may be disturbing to see one's health deteriorate, but this biological circumstance does not degrade human existence. It is probable that Confucianism accepts the idea that "finitude is no disgrace,"[36] because it proffers only a naturalistic account of death—the genesis, growth, decay, and perishing of biological life are phenomena common to all living organisms, including human beings. One should therefore accept pre-death decay with serenity. That one's biological health is deteriorating does not indicate that one's moral health is in jeopardy too.

Third, Confucian "death with dignity" is deemed morally commendable because it is one manifestation of suicide for the sake of *ren* and *yi*. Though biological life is not the highest good, it is the highest price one can pay for a worthy cause,[37] and *ren* and *yi* are such worthy causes. Hence a suicide for the sake of *ren* and *yi* is a sacrificing witness to a worthy cause. One yields one's biological life for the sake of cultivating one's moral life. Biological destruction is brought about for the sake of moral construction. A Confucian "death to prevent indignity" is a morally constructive act because it prevents moral degradation. An act of PAS and VE on grounds of deteriorating biological condition, however, cannot be interpreted as an act of moral construction.[38]

Fourth, it should also be noted that in all the examples of "death with dignity" in ancient and contemporary China, the unacceptable humiliation and degradation stem from unstoppable hostile forces and circumstances. There is no palliation or relief of any kind. In such a case the disjunction of either committing suicide or submitting to humiliation and degradation is more plausible. Hence unless disease, sickness, and degeneration are interpreted as hostile enemies,[39] or corporal punishments or tortures from fate, or malicious assaults from nature, there is another dissonance between these two ethics of "death with dignity."

Fifth, given these differences of the two ethics of "death with dignity," it will not be surprising to note that in contemporary Chinese arguments in favor of PAS and VE, the argument of "death with dignity" is conspicuously absent. This absence is not the result of a weak movement in favor of the decriminalization of PAS and VE in China; quite the contrary, in the larger cities many intellectuals are in its favor, and the pro-PAS and pro-VE literature far exceeds the opposite side in scholarly and professional journals. I suspect that the argument of "death with dignity" is not present because most Chinese, still under some influence of Confucianism, have a different understanding of dignity and indignity, of the quality of life and its degradation.[40]

To conclude, "death with dignity" in the Confucian sense is recommended by Confucian ethics because of "the priority of the moral over the biological." In common with other major world religions, Confucianism acknowledges that there is much more in human life than biological health, which is only a perishable good. One should strive hard to resist the *summum malum*, even at the expense of terminating one's biological life, and the *summum malum*, in this case is much more than biological. By contrast, "death with dignity" in PAS and VE remains within the realm of the

biological. Deteriorating health is deemed the *summum malum* so that one should prevent it from happening even at the expense of biological life. The goal of such suicide does not go beyond the biological; it seeks only to overcome our actual imperfect and finite biological condition through the annihilation of biological life. From the perspective of Confucianism and other world religions, such an understanding of the *summum malum* suffers from a very narrow vision of life. In virtue of its preoccupation with biological health, such an understanding misplaces the source of indignity and degradation in the physical and the corporeal (body, health), and loses sight of the soul or spirit (moral life in Confucianism). To accept PAS and VE as "death with dignity" will render a Confucian "death with dignity" unintelligible because, in the former, exaltation and degradation in human life are confined to the biological dimension. It reduces the human person to the one-dimensional existence of the biological-physical.

What may be more worrisome is that the arguments for, and the practice of, PAS and VE are no longer restricted to the last phase of a terminal illness.[41] Their argument of "death with dignity" is being offered not only as a solution to a problem concerning the manner of dying, but also as a solution to existential problems in human life, namely, mortality, corruptibility, failing health, frailty of human body and mind, and finitude. The superficiality of this latter solution is obvious; it stems from discussing PAS and VE in the absence of comprehensive visions of life, such as provided by Confucianism and many other religious traditions.[42]

NOTES

1. For a fuller discussion of the analysis in this section, see Ping-cheung Lo, "Confucian Values of Life and Death and Euthanasia," (in Chinese) *Chinese & International Philosophy of Medicine* 1:1 (Feb 1998): 35–73, and Ping-cheung Lo, "Confucian Views On Suicide and Their Implications For Euthanasia," in *Confucian Bioethics*, ed. Ruiping Fan (Dordrecht: Kluwer Academic Publishers, 1999), 69–101.
2. *Analects*, trans. D. C. Lau, second edition, (Hong Kong: Chinese University Press. 1992). XV:9D, translation modified.

3. Mencius to Confucius is comparable with Paul to Jesus in Christianity.

4. *Mencius*, trans. D. C. Lau. (Hong Kong: Chinese University Press, 1984), VI A:10, translation modified.

5. *Both ren* and *yi* have a narrow and a wide sense. In the narrow sense, as the first two of the four cardinal virtues, *ren* means benevolence, and *yi* means justice. In the wide sense, however, both words, especially when they are used together, can mean supreme virtue or morality (cf. David S. Nivison. "Jen and I," in *Encyclopedia of Religion,* ed. Mircea Eliade, volume 7, [New York: Macmillan, 1987], 566–567). In the context of "dying to achieve *ren*" and "laying down one's life for a cause of *yi*," *ren* and *yi* were usually understood in the wide sense. One should note, however, since the Han Dynasty morality or *ren* and *yi* have been conceived of manifesting themselves in particular human relationships, rather than in a universal and general way. In other words, *ren* and *yi* were understood not through universal love or duty to society in general, but through interpersonal commitments such as loyalty (in the emperor-subject relationship), filial piety (in the parent-child relationship), chastity (in the husband-wife relationship), and faithfulness (in friendship). In other words, *ren* and *yi* are virtues of other-regarding morality, mediated through concrete familial, social, and political relationship.

6. See the brief biography of Wen Tianxiang in *Song Shi* (*History of Song Dynasty*), biography number 177.

7. See Sima Qian, "BAO Ren An Shu" (Letter to Ren An). For a free English translation, see *Anthology of Chinese Literature: From Early Times to the Fourteenth Century,* ed. Cyril Birch (New York; Grove Press, 1965), 95–102.

8. For detailed historical illustrations of this thesis see my essay, "Confucian Views On Suicide and Their Implications for Euthanasia." For now, it must suffice to cite an illustration that is not entirely unfamiliar in the Western world. During the Yuan Dynasty (1279–1368 AD) there was a famous opera entitled *The Orphan of Zhao* (for a complete English translation, see Chun-hsiang Chi, "The Orphan of Chao," in *Six Yuan Plays,* trans. Liu Jung-en [New York: Penguin Books. 1972], 41–81), whose plot was based on accounts in historical books The Jesuit missionaries in China later brought this opera to Europe. It was immensely popular and was translated into English, French, and German (cf. Adrian Hsia, 'The Orphan of the House Zhao' in French, English, German, and Hong Kong Literature,' *Comparative Literature Studies,* 25:4 [1988]: 335–351. Voltaire not only rendered it into a drama, with the name changed to *L'Orphelin de la Chine,* but also staged it successfully in Paris. The German philosopher Arthur Schopenhauer also mentioned this play with admiration in his essay "On Suicide" (Arthur Schopenhauer, "On Suicide," *The Essential Schopenhauer* [English selections of *Paralipomena*], [London: Allen & Unwin, 1962], 99). The story is about a family of nobility being persecuted by its political enemies, and everybody in the family is killed except a baby. Some friends of the family try their best to save the life of this orphan. In the process, all the noble characters who take part in the saving effort commit suicide, mostly for the reason of ensuring the success of the rescue effort. These are altruistic suicides. At the end of the story, after the rescued orphan has grown up and avenged his father, the architect of the rescue and vengeance, Cheng Ying, also commits suicide for the reason of going to the underworld to tell all the related suicide committers that their deaths were worthwhile.

9. It seems to me that the Western philosopher who comes closest to this classical Confucian view is Immanuel Kant. In his lecture on suicide, he emphasizes repeatedly that "life is not to be highly regarded for its own sake. I should endeavour to preserve my own life only so far as I am worthy to live. . . . Yet there is much in the world far more important than life. To observe morality is far more important. It is better to sacrifice one's life than one's morality. To live is not a necessity; but to live honourably while life lasts is a necessity" (Immanuel Kant, *Lectures on Ethics,* trans. Louis Infield [London: Methuen & Co., 1930], 150–152). Accordingly, though Kant firmly opposes suicide in the sense of self-destruction, he commends self-sacrifice highly. Risking one's life and willing to be killed for the sake of others' good are praiseworthy. Furthermore, altruistic suicide, i.e., actively to kill oneself for others' sake, is also noble, as in the example of Cato the Younger (95–46 BCE), who "knew that the entire Roman nation relied upon him in their resistance to Caesar, but he found that he could not prevent himself from falling into Caesar's hands. What was he to do? If he, the champion of freedom, submitted, every one would say. 'If Cato himself submits, what else can we do?' If, on the other hand, he killed himself, his death might spur on the Romans to fight to the bitter end in defense of their freedom. So he killed himself. He thought that it was necessary for him to die. He thought that if he could not go on living as Cato, he could not go on living at all. It must certainly be admitted that in a case such as this, where suicide is a virtue, appearances are in its favour" (Kant, *Lectures on Ethics,* 149). This high regard for altruistic suicide notwithstanding, one should not overlook that immediately after the this passage, Kant cautions, "But this is the only example which has given the world the opportunity of defending suicide. It is the only example of its kind and there has been no similar case since" (*Ibid.*).

10. It is noteworthy that even the Protestant theologian Karl Barth, who articulates a vigorous theological argument against suicide, makes the distinction between "self-destruction" and "self-offering." In an intriguing passage he says, "While there can be no doubt about this, we must not forget the exceptional case. Not every act of self-destruction is as such suicide in this sense. Self-destruction does not have to be the taking of one's own life. Its meaning and intention might well be a definite if extreme form of the self-offering required of man. . . . Who can say that it is absolutely impossible for the gracious God Himself to help a man in affliction by telling him to take this way out? In some cases perhaps a man can and must choose and do this in the freedom given him by God and not therefore in false sovereignty, in despair at the futility of his existence, of in final, supreme and masterful self-assertion, but in obedience. . . . Can we, therefore make a simple equation of self-destruction with self-murder? Have we not to take into account the possibility that suicide might not be committed as a crime and therefore as murder, but in faith and therefore in peace with God?"

(Karl Barth, *Church Dogmatics*, volume III, *The Doctrine of Creation*, part 4, trans. A.T. MacKay et al. [Edinburgh: T. & T. Clark 1961], 410). Here we can see the convergence of Christian and Confucian ethics of suicide.

11. Jun-yi Tang, "Zhongguo wenhua yu shijie (A Manifesto for a Re-appraisal of Sinology and Reconstruction of Chinese Culture)," *Shuo zhonghua minzu zhi huaguo piaoling (On the Diaspora of the Chinese)* (Taipei: Sanmin Press, 1974), 144.

12. Cf. Margaret Pabst Battin, *The Death Debate: Ethical Issues in Suicide*, (Upper Saddle River, New Jersey: Prentice-Hall, 1996), 67–68.

13. As a famous line from Chapter One of *Xiaojing (Book of Filial Piety*; a Confucian text that was composed in the first century BCE) puts it, "Our body, limbs, hair, and skin all originated from our parents. We should hold them in respect and guard them against injury. This is the beginning of filial piety."

14. It should be noted that although Daoism and Buddhism were not established religions, they flourished in Chinese society. The persecution of non-established religions and ideologies occurred only infrequently in China.

15. For a sampling of passages from *Chunqiu fanlou* see *A Source Book in Chinese Philosophy*, trans. and compiled by Wing-tsit Chan (Princeton: Princeton University Press, 1963), Chapter 14. For a brief overview of his thought, see "Tung Chung-shu," in *The Encyclopedia of Religion,* vol. 15, ed. Mircea Eliade (New York: Macmillan), 81–83. Dong's ethic of "death with dignity," however, does not receive any attention in the general accounts.

16. These two passages are taken from *Liji* (The Book of Rites).

17. For an abridged English translation, see *Records of the Grand Historian of China*, two volumes, trans. Burton Watson (New York; Columbia University Press, 1961).

18. Again, Kant's idea on self-regarding duty comes very close to Confucian Thesis II. "We are in duty bound to take care of our life; but in this connexion it must be remarked that life, in and for itself, is not the greatest of the gifts entrusted to our keeping and of which we must take care. There are duties which are far greater than life and which can often be fulfilled only by sacrificing life. . . . If a man cannot preserve his life except by dishonouring his humanity, he ought rather to sacrifice it. . . . It is not his life that he loses, but only the prolongation of his years, for nature has already decreed that he must die at some time, what matters is that, so long as he lives, man should live honourably and should not disgrace the dignity of humanity. . . . If, then, I cannot preserve my life except by disgraceful conduct, virtue relieves me of this duty because a higher duty here comes into play and commands me to sacrifice my life" (Kant, *Lectures on Ethics*, 154–151). Accordingly, Kant thinks that in the case of an innocent man wrongly accused of treachery, if he is given the choice of death or penal servitude for life, he should choose the former. Similarly, a woman should prefer to be killed to being violated by a man. Kant, however, stops short of recommending suicide in order to avoid such dishonor. Battin therefore points out, I think correctly, that Kant is inconsistent here. If our self-regarding duty of avoiding moral degradation is of such paramount importance, "and if death—the only possibility for nondegradation—is the only morally acceptable alternative, the only way to achieve this alternative would be to take death upon oneself" (Battin, *The Death Debate*, 109). In other words, as an eminent contemporary Kantian scholar argues, the spirit of Kant's ethics should permit some self-regarding suicides (Thomas E. Hill, "Self-Regarding Suicide: A Modified Kantian View," in *Suicide and Ethics: A Special Issue of Suicide and Life Threatening Behavior*, ed. Margaret P. Battin and Ronald W. Maris [New York: Human Sciences Press, 1983], 254–275.

19. Sima, "Bao Ren An Shu (Letter to Ren An)," 95–102.

20. For stimulating discussions on the suicide of these two intellectuals, see Ziping Huang, "Qiangu jiannan wei yisi: tan jibu xie Lao She, Fu Lei zhi si de xiaoshuo (Death as a Difficult Task since Time Immemorial: On Some Novels on the Death of Lao She and Fu Lei)," *Dushu (Reading)* 4 (April 1989): 53–63; Cengqi Wang, "Bayue jiaoyang (Bright Sunshine in August)," *Renmin wenxue (People's Literature)* 9 (1986): 17–21; Cun Chen, "Si: gei 'wenge' (Death: For the 'Cultural Revolution')," *Shanghai wenxue (Literature in Shanghai)* 9 (1986): 4–11; Shuyang Su, "Lao She zhi si (Death of Lao She)," *Renmin wenxue (People's Literature)* 8 (1986): 22–34.

21. Su, "Lao She zhi xi"; Wang. "Bayue jiaoyang."

22. For example, see Huang, "Qiangu jiannan we yisi."

23. Though Huang doubts that this maxim provides the most plausible explanation of the suicide of Lao She, he nonetheless uses this maxim to reflect on the suicide of Fu Lei. See *ibid.*

24. The Japanese term (which is in Chinese characters) for euthanasia used to be one which means "a peaceful and happy death" (*anraku-shi*); it is now replaced by another term which means "death with dignity" (*songen-shi*). Since Confucianism has been very influential in Japanese culture, this change of terminology probably indicates the pervasive influence of the Confucian ethic of "death with dignity" in Japan. See Shigeru Kato, "Japanese Perspectives on Euthanasia," in *To Die or Not to Die? Cross-Disciplinary, Cultural, and Legal Perspective on the Right to Choose Death*, ed. Arthur S. Berger and Joyce Berger (New York; Praeger, 1990), 67–82?

25. Leon R. Kiss, "Death with Dignity and the Sanctity of Life," in *A Time to be Born and a Time to Die: The Ethics of Choice*, ed. Barry S. Kogan (Hawthorne, New York: Aldine DeGruyter, 1991), 133.

26. Californians against Human Suffering, *Questions and Answers on the California Death with Dignity Act* (1992), emphasis added.

27. Likewise, in Holland, when the Dutch Parliament finally approved a law permitting euthanasia in 1993, the *New York Times* reported that "In Dr. Cohen's experience the main motive for requesting death is not only a question of physical suffering. 'Generally, *personal dignity* plays an important role,' he said. 'People don't want to *live on machines*, someone may be *half paralyzed, incontinent*. This can be harder to bear than pain'."(Marlise Simons, "Dutch Parliament Approves Law Permitting Euthanasia," *The New York Times* [February 10, 1993]: A10; emphasis added.) Besides, when Oregonians debated the Oregon Ballot Measure 16 (Death with Dignity Art, 1994), John A. Pridonhoff, then Executive Director of

The Hemlock Society, USA, explains in an essay, "And for some people, the *loss of dignity* and self-respect amid chronic suffering, where the *loss of mental competence and control of bodily functions* are definite prospects, is enough to make some people choose to take control of the time and manner of their death. (John A. Pridonhoff, "Right to Die and Hospice," in *Physician-Assisted Suicide: Report of the Ethics Task Force*, ed. Oregon Hospice Association [1994], 49; emphasis added.)

28. *Compassion in Dying v. State of Washington*, 1996, Majority Opinion, Section IV ("Is There a Liberty Interest?"), subsection F ("Liberty Interest under Casey"); emphasis added. Ronald Dworkin also argues in a similar manner in his book, "many people, as I said, think it *undignified* or bad in some other way to live under certain conditions, however they might feel if they feel at all. Many people do not want to be remembered living in those circumstances; others think it *degrading to be wholly dependent*, or to be the object of continuing anguish. . . . At least part of what people fear about dependence is its impact not on those responsible for their care, but on their own *dignity*." (Ronald Dworkin, *Life's Dominion* [New York: Vintage Books, 1994], 209–210, emphasis added.)

29. Special [Canada] Senate Committee on Euthanasia and Assisted Suicide, *Of Life and Death—Final Report* (June 1995, http://www.parl.gc.ca/english/senate/com-e/euth-e/rep-e/lad-tc-e.htm), chapter VII, emphasis added.

30. *Compassion in Dying v. State of Washington*, Section IV, subsection D, emphasis added.

31. Ontario Medical Association, *Euthanasia and the Role of Medicine: A Discussion Paper* (Toronto, 1991), 11; emphasis added.

32. Timothy E, Quill, *Death and Dignity: Making Choices and Taking Charge* (New York: W. W. Norton, 1993), 105–107; emphasis added.

33. I fully acknowledge that the advocates of PAS and VE as "death with dignity" are not univocal in their arguments, and that some of them indeed employ the phrase "death with dignity" mainly rhetorically without advancing an additional argument. However, I do want to reconstruct their argument as sympathetically as possible, and there is a large amount of literature to substantiate my claim.

34. Catholic theologian Hans Küng also entitled his book on this subject *Dignified Death (Dying with Dignity* in English translation). His identification of the source of indignity in dying, however, is restricted only to the side effects of sedation. "As a result of the tremendous success of modern medicine and eugenics, people today have been given what is in fact a new period of life, often lasting more than twenty years. In certain cases, however, this can lead to an *undignified decline into vegetation*, frequently over many years. In such cases of intolerable suffering it should be possible to help people to ensure that their deaths are not dragged out endlessly and that they can *die a dignified death*—if that is what they want. . . . Palliative medicine has made most welcome progress. . . . However, it is not the answer to all the questions of life and death. All doctors know this: no therapy to relieve pain is possible without sedation. And the higher the dose (and it must often constantly be increased) and the more it relieves pain, the more sedative its effect is. That means that normally *the vigilance, the wakefulness, the spiritual presence of the patient is all the

weaker. So our question is: is a person obliged to live away the last 'artificial' phase of his or her life, perfectly 'tranquillized,' in some circumstances for weeks, months or even years, *dosing away in a twilight state?*" (Hans Küng and Walter Jens, *Dying with Dignity: A Plea for Personal Responsibility,* trans. John Bowden [New York: Continuum. 1995], 119–120; emphasis added.)

35. Accordingly, some theological argument against death with dignity (such as Paul Ramsey's famous article, "The Indignity of 'Death with Dignity,'" *Hastings Center Studies* 2:2 (May 1974): 47–62) is misdirected, and the charge that the phrase "death with dignity" is an oxymoron (Kass, "Death with Dignity and the Sanctity of Life." p.132) is unjustified.

36. Kass, "Death with Dignity and the Sanctity of Life," 141.

37. Barth, *Church Dogmatics*, III/4, 402.

38. However, as one commentator puts it, "if there is reason to think that physical or mental infirmity will diminish [one's] adherence to the moral law—a risk presumably especially great in diseases which involve progressive mental deterioration" (Battin, *The Death Debate,* 112), a preemptive suicide can be considered "death with dignity" in the Confucian sense. I am not sure that human moral health declines with human biological health as this commentator suggests. But if it happens, the dissonance between these two ethics of "death with dignity" may disappear.

39. As suggested in Carl B. Becker, "Buddhist Views of Suicide and Euthanasia," *Philosophy East and West* 40:4 (October 1990): 551–552.

40. It goes without saying, then, that Confucianism's rejection of "death with dignity" argument for PAS and VE does not imply that Confucianism will necessarily reject other arguments for PAS and VE. Whether Confucianism will reject them are topics for other papers (for a brief treatment, see my paper in Chinese, "Confucian Values of Life and Death and Euthanasia").

41. As early as 1979 Peter Singer defines euthanasia as "the killing of those who are incurably ill and in great pain or distress in order to spare them further suffering" (Peter Singer, *Practical Ethics* [Cambridge: Cambridge University Press, 1979], 127). What is noticeable is the replacement of "the incurably ill" for "the terminally ill." Hence the endorsement of the euthanasia of newborns with severe defects (*ibid.,* 131–138). Furthermore, in the Netherlands, since 1973 the courts have dropped the condition of being in the terminal phase of an illness from the prerequisites of permissible PAS and VE. See John Griffiths, Alex Bood, and Heleen Weyers, *Euthanasia and Law in the Netherlands* (Amsterdam: Amsterdam University Press, 1998), 52.

42. This article is part of a research project funded by the Research Grant Council of Hong Kong 1995–1996 Earmarked Research Grant (RGC/95-96/26) and has been assisted by Miss Lee Wing Yi. I am grateful to them for their respective contributions. Some of the research on "death with dignity" in contemporary bioethics was carried out in the Hastings Center and the Kennedy Institute of Ethics, I want to thank them for allowing me to do research in their excellent libraries. I also want to thank Sumner B. Twiss and two anonymous reviewers of *The Annual of the Society of Christian Ethics* for their helpful comments on an earlier version of this essay.

Buddhist Views of Suicide and Euthanasia

Carl B. Becker

Carl B. Becker is a professor at Kyoto University. His research is focused on biomedical ethics and Japanese worldviews. He is the author of *Asian and Jungian Views of Ethics* (1999) and *Breaking the Circle: Buddhist Views of Death and Afterlife* (1993).

Becker explores Buddhist views of death and suicide and attempts to apply these ideas to recent debates about euthanasia. Traditionally, Buddhism does not view death as a bad thing or even as an ending. Rather, death is a transition from one stage of life to another. Because of this, suicide was not condemned, as long as the person had placed himself or herself in the right state of mind. A key to this is that a person accepts responsibility for his or her own life choices. When suicide or euthanasia is prohibited, it means that a person is deprived of the final act of taking responsibility for his or her own life. Hence, Becker argues, disallowing suicide and euthanasia is inhumane.

BIOETHICS AND BRAIN DEATH: THE RECENT DISCUSSION IN JAPAN

Japanese scholars of ethics and religions have been slow to come to grips with issues of bioethics, suicide, and death with dignity. Although the practical problems are frequently addressed in the popular press, and scattered citizen groups are beginning to draw attention to the issues, few people outside of the medical community have seriously addressed these issues.[1] As one recent representative example of this situation, consider the 39th annual meeting of the Japan Ethics Association (the academic association of ethicists from the entire country) held at Waseda University in October of 1988. The title of the annual meeting, in deference to the late Emperor's ailing condition and growing urgency of bioethical issues, was "Life and Ethics." Ostensibly, this was a chance to further the discussion among medical, religious, and philosophical ethicists on topics such as euthanasia and death with dignity. In fact, more than half of the presentations discussed classical views of life, such as those of Hippocrates, Confucius, Vico, Kant, Nietzsche, and so forth. The periods planned for open discussion were entirely usurped by the panelists' overtime reading of such papers. To their credit, however, there were a few Japanese scholars who boldly attempted to establish some more-Japanese views on the topics in bioethics, particularly euthanasia and death with dignity. While not without their problems, these presentations displayed less a Buddhist than a popular Japanese approach to the issue. The majority agreed with Anzai Kazuhiro's early presentation that brain death should not be equated with human death.[2] Anzai's reasoning

Excerpts from Carl Becker, "Buddhist views of suicide and euthanasia" Philosophy East and West, Vol. 40/4, October 1990. © 1990 University of Hawaii Press. Reprinted by permission.

runs as follows: If brain death implies human death, then, by contraposition, human life must imply conscious (brain) life. Now there are clearly segments of our lives in which we are alive but not always conscious. Therefore it is wrong to conclude that a human is dead because he or she lacks consciousness. Of course, this argument can be faulted for collapsing conscious life and brain life, and for failing to distinguish periods of unconsciousness with the expectation of future revival (like deep sleep) from periods of unconsciousness with no expectation of future revival (like irreversible coma). But it is representative of a widely seen Japanese rejection of brain-death criteria.

This rejection comes partly from the Japanese association of brain-death criteria with organ transplantation. Many Japanese continue to manifest a distaste for organ transplantation, a distaste which dates back to Confucian teachings that the body, a gift from heaven and from one's parents, must be buried whole, and never cut. For this reason, dissections and autopsies were late in coming to Japan, and not widely permitted until the nineteenth century. The modern Japanese practices of universal cremation, of surgical operations, and of flying to other countries to have organ transplants all have superseded the old Confucian prejudice against body-cutting. However, there remains a fear that if brain-death criteria were widely accepted, less conservative elements of society might abuse it for the sake of the "distasteful" practice of organ transplantation.

In his keynote address about Buddhist ethics, Tsukuba Professor Shinjō Kawasaki implied that this rejection of brain-death criteria may also be grounded in a Buddhist view of life and death.[3] He cited the *Visuddhimagga*, which indicates that life energy (*ayus*) is supported by body warmth and conscious faculties (broadly interpretable to include reflexes).[4] If either body heat or reflexes remain, then a person cannot be considered dead. Now Buddhism admits situations (such as meditative trances or hypothermia) in which neither body warmth nor reflexes are externally detectable, but the subject is not yet dead. So lack of warmth and reflexes is a necessary but not sufficient indicator of death; if either persists, it can be said that the body is not yet dead. In other words, Buddhism does not equate life with warmth and reflexes, but holds that body heat and reflexes are the "supports" of life, and therefore life cannot be empirically measurable except through such variables. Kawasaki also reaffirms the widespread Japanese Buddhist view that death is not the end of life, but merely a brief transition to another state, commonly thought to last for forty-nine days, intermediate between life in this body and life in the next. The reluctance to dismiss a body as "dead" prior to its loss of warmth and reflexes is not based on a fear of personal extinction or annihilation, but rather on a Buddhist view of the basic components of the life system.[5]

Chiba's Iida Tsunesuke expands this view by arguing that "persons are not merely the meaningless 'subjects of rights,' but personalities, 'faces,' embodying the possibilities of fulfilling the dreams of their parents or loved ones . . . recipients of love, and therefore worthy of honoring."[6] This argument begs the question of "possibilities," since in the case of brain-dead victims, it is precisely such possibilities which are missing. Logically speaking, the "possibilities" argument has long ago been laid to rest by philosophers like Mary Anne Warren, who have demonstrated that we need not treat potential presidents as presidents, potential criminals as criminals, or potential humans as humans.[7] (Japanese society might differ in this respect; until recently, suspicion of crime or likelihood of committing crime were sufficient grounds for arrest, children of nobles [potential lords] were often honored or killed as real lords.)[8]

However, Iida's argument is important less for its logical persuasion than for its revelation of the Japanese attitude: that persons are not subjects with rights and individual free wills, but rather objects of the attention of others. (Japanese treatment of infants and children reinforces this view that Japanese children are not seen as persons but as possessions of their parents; this was the legal as well as philosophical status of women and servants as well as children prior to the twentieth century.)

This position is further developed by Ohara Nobuo, who argues that "although a body may be treated as a 'thing' or a corpse by physicians, it remains a body of value and meaning, and in that sense, a *person*, to members of its family. . . . In this sense, even vegetative humans and brain-dead corpses can give joy to other people."[9] Of course this point of view is pregnant with problems which Ohara himself seems loath to acknowledge. Only in the most metaphorical of senses can a corpse "give" anything to anyone; rather, it is the family who may *derive* some sense of joy by beholding the face of one dear to them, even though that person is incapable of ever being conscious in that body again.

This attitude is akin to the Japanese reverence for pictures, sculptures, and myths; it provides no useful guidelines whatsoever to the medical faculty as to when to continue or desist from what kinds of treatment for the patient. To the question "When does a body stop being a person?", the Oharan answer, "It never stops being a person to those who love it," may be psychologically correct for some people, but is a dead end in medical ethics, for it fails to answer the question, "When should a body be treated not as a living person but as a dead body?"

Moreover, even if it were thought to have some utility in the case where relatives or "significant others" remain alive and concerned with the fate of the deceased, it values the person (or corpse) entirely in terms of his value *to others*. In cases where old people die alone and uncared for, the absence of concerned others leaves the medical practitioner utterly without guidelines. (This is consistent with the frequently noted proposition that Japanese without social contexts seem morally at a loss.)[10]

This position also presumes a wishful naïveté on the part of the parent or family, a failure to distinguish between a living human with a potential for interaction and a dead body with only the resemblance of a loved one. This may not bother many Japanese parents, for whom children are indeed "objects." In fact, there are "rehabilitation hospitals" in Japan in which anencephalic infants are cared for and raised for as many years as their parents' finances and interest dictate; they are propped up and made to "greet" their parents whenever their parents desire to visit.[11]

Such unwillingness to admit the finality of death or the fundamental suffering of the human condition runs counter to the basic tenets of Buddhism. We are reminded of the famous story of the woman who asked the Buddha to revive her baby. In response, the Buddha instructed her to ask for food from any house in which no one had died. In the process of asking around the entire village, the woman came to realize that all humans must die and deal with death. In this way she gained enlightenment, stopped grieving for her dead child, and became a follower of the Buddha. The relatives who refuse to pronounce dead a relative as long as he has a "face," or the parents who insist on artificially prolonging the appearance of life in an anencephalic infant, cannot claim to understand Buddhism.

A much larger misunderstanding lurks behind the whole discussion between "brain-death advocates" and "brain-dead opposers" in Japan. The real issue is not whether or not every body should immediately be scavenged for spare parts as soon as the brain is isoelectric, as some opponents would purport. Rather, the question is whether it is ever acceptable to desist from treatment after brain death (turning the hospital's valuable and limited resources to other waiting patients). In the absence of brain-death criteria, many otherwise hopeless bodies remain on artificial support systems almost indefinitely. Even if the brain death criteria were accepted, nothing would prevent families from finding hospitals which would preserve the bodies of their beloved on artificial support systems indefinitely, nor would anything require organ donation if the patient and family did not desire it. Thus, the issue, like that of suicide and euthanasia, is not, "Should everyone be forced to follow these criteria?" but rather, "May people who desire it be allowed to follow these criteria?" Groundless fears of widespread organ sales or piracy have made this issue into a much greater hobgoblin than it ever needed to become.

This is not merely to criticize the recently voiced opinions of Japanese ethicists. Rather, I introduce this body of evidence to demonstrate the slow growth of Japanese thought in bioethics, and particularly their concerns with *bodies of value to others* rather than with *subjects of value to them-selves*. This concern finds no support either in Japanese Buddhism nor in samurai teaching, but in the level of popular belief, it may have serious ramifications for Japanese bioethics for many generations to come.

The World Federation of the Right To Die Society held an International Conference in Nice (France) in 1984. Although many Japanese attended this conference, apparently none of them contributed to the West's understanding of Buddhist views of euthanasia. When the President of the Society published a book on world attitudes on euthanasia the following year, only 2 percent (2.5 out of 150 pages) was about Buddhist attitudes, and those ideas were gained from California Buddhists, not from the Japanese Buddhists at Nice.[12]

Buddhists have a big contribution to make to the humanization and naturalization of medicine and bioethics. I may not speak for all of Japanese Buddhism, but I shall be happy if this article inspires further dialogue and contributions from the Japanese Buddhist side.

EARLY BUDDHIST VIEWS OF DEATH, SUICIDE, AND EUTHANASIA

Japan has long been more aware of and sensitive to the dying process than modern Western cultures. Moreover, Japan already has its own good philosophical and experiential background to deal effectively with "new" issues of bioethics, such as euthanasia. Japanese Buddhists have long recognized what Westerners are only recently rediscovering: that the manner of dying at the moment of death is very important. This fundamental premise probably predates Buddhism itself, but is made very explicit in the teachings of the Buddha.[13] In his meditations, the Buddha noticed that even people with good karma were sometimes born into bad situations, and even those with bad karma sometimes found inordinately pleasant rebirths. Buddha declared that the crucial variable governing rebirth was the nature of the consciousness at the moment of death. Thereafter, Buddhists placed high

importance on holding the proper thoughts at the moment of death. Many examples of this idea can be found in two works of the Theravada canon. The *Petavatthu* and the *Vimānavatthu* ("Stories of the Departed"). Indeed, in many sutras, monks visit laymen on their deathbeds to ensure that their dying thoughts are wholesome,[14] and the Buddha recommends that lay followers similarly encourage each other on such occasions.[15]

Buddhism sees death as not the end of life, but simply a transition; suicide is therefore no escape from anything. Thus, in the early *sangha* (community of followers of the Buddha), suicide was in principle condemned as an inappropriate action.[16] But the early Buddhist texts include many cases of suicide which the Buddha himself accepted or condoned. For example, the suicides of Vakkali[17] and of Channa[18] were committed in the face of painful and irreversible sickness. It is significant, however, that the Buddha's praise of the suicides is *not* based on the fact that they were in terminal states, but rather that their minds were selfless, desireless, and enlightened at the moments of their passing.

This theme is more dramatically visible in the example of Godhika. This disciple repeatedly achieved an advanced level of *samādhi*, bordering on *parinirvāna*, and then slipped out of the state of enlightenment into normal consciousness again. After this happened six times, Godhika at last vowed to pass on to the next realm while enlightened, and quietly committed suicide during his next period of enlightenment. While cautioning his other disciples against suicide, the Buddha nonetheless blessed and praised Godhika's steadiness of mind and purpose, and declared that he had passed on to *nirvāna*. In short, the acceptability of suicide, even in the early Buddhist community, depended not on terminal illness alone, but upon the state of selfless equanimity with which one was able to pass away. It is interesting in passing that all these suicides were committed by the subject knifing himself, a technique which came to be standardized in later Japanese ritual suicide.

When asked about the morality of committing suicide to move on to the next world, the Buddha did not criticize it.[19] He emphasized that only the uncraving mind would be able to move on towards *nirvāna*, and that, conversely, minds desiring to get free or flee something by their death might achieve nothing. Similarly, there are stories in the Jatāka tales of the Buddha giving his own body (in former lives) to save other beings, both animals and humans. Thus, death out of compassion for others is also lauded in the scriptures.[20] It is also well known that in the Jain tradition, saints were expected to fast until their deaths,[21] and thereafter there have been those both in China and Japan who have followed this tradition.[22]

In China, it is believed that a disciple of Zendō's jumped out of a tree in order to kill himself and reach the Pure Land. Zendō's response was not that the action of suicide was right or wrong in and of itself, but that the disciple who wanted so strongly to see the Pure Land was doubtless ready to reach it.[23] Other more recent examples may be found in the Buddhist suicides of the Vietnamese monks protesting against the Vietnam government.[24] Whether or not these stories are all historical fact is not at issue here. The point is that they demonstrate the consistent Buddhist position toward suicide: There is nothing intrinsically wrong with taking one's own life, if it is not done in hate, anger, or fear. Equanimity or preparedness of mind is the main issue.

In summary, Buddhism realizes that death is not the end of anything, but a transition. Buddhism has long recognized persons' rights to determine when they should move on from this existence to the next. The important consideration here is not whether the body lives or dies, but whether the mind can remain at peace and in harmony with itself.

The Jōdo (Pure Land) tradition tends to stress the continuity of life, while the Zen tradition tends to stress the importance of the time and manner of dying. Both of these ideas are deeply rooted in the Japanese consciousness.

RELIGIOUS SUICIDE AND DEATH WITH DIGNITY IN JAPAN

Japanese Buddhists demonstrated an unconcern with death even more than their neighbors. Japanese valued peace of mind and honor of life over length of life. While the samurai often committed suicide on the battlefield or in court to preserve their dignity in death, countless commoners chose to commit suicide in order to obtain a better future life in the Pure Land. On some occasions, whole masses of people committed suicide at the same time. In others, as in the situation depicted in Kurosawa's famous film "Red Beard," a poverty-stricken family would commit suicide in order to escape unbearable suffering in this life and find a better life in the world to come. Often parents would kill their children first, and then kill themselves; this kind of *shinjū* can still be seen in Japan today. The issue for us today is: How does Buddhism appraise such suicide in order to gain heavenly rebirth?

On a popular level, the desire to "leave this dirty world and approach the Pure Land" (*Enri edo, gongu jōdo*) was fostered by wandering itinerant monks such as Kūya in the Heian period, and Ippen in the Kamakura period. The tradition of committing suicide by entering a river or west-facing seashore apparently began in the Kumano area, but rapidly spread throughout the nation along with the Pure Land faith upon which it was based. The common tradition was to enter the water with a rope tied around one's waist, held by one's retainers or horse.[25] If one's nerve and single-minded resolution failed, then one would not achieve rebirth in the Pure Land as desired. In such an instance, either the suicide himself, or his retainers (judging from his countenance), might pull him out of the water and save him from dying with inappropriate thoughts. However, if the suicide retained a peaceful and unperturbed mind and countenance throughout the drowning, the retainers were to let him die in peace, and simply retain the body for funeral purposes. Such situations clearly demonstrate that what is at stake here is not the individual's right to die, but rather his ability to die with peace of mind. If a death with a calm mind is possible, then it is not condemned.

A paradigmatic example of this situation can be found in the records of Saint Ippen.[26] Ajisaka Nyūdō, a Pure Land aspirant possibly of noble descent, gave up his home and family to follow the teachings of Saint Ippen. For unclear reasons, Ippen refused admission to his band of itinerant mendicants, but advised him that the only way to enter the Pure Land was to die holding the Nembutsu (name and figure of Amida) in mind. Nyūdō then committed suicide by drowning himself in the Fuji River.

The scene is vividly depicted in the scroll paintings.[27] Here, Ajisaka is seen with a rope around his waist. His attendants on the shore hold one end of the rope. As he bobs above the current, he is seen perfectly preserving the gasshō position, at peace and in prayer. Music is heard from the purple clouds above him, a common sign of Ōjō, or rebirth in the Pure Land.

When Ippen heard of this suicide, he praised Ajisaka's faith, interpreting the purple clouds and Ajisaka's unruffled demeanor as proof of his attainment of rebirth in the Pure Land. At the same time, he warned his other disciples, repeating Ajisaka's last words (nagori o oshimuna), not to grieve over their master's passing.[28]

When Ippen himself died, six of his disciples also committed suicide in sympathy, hoping to accompany their master to the Pure Land. This occasioned some other debate about the propriety of "sympathy suicide." Shinkyō, Ippen's disciple and second patriarch of the Ji School, declared that the disciples had failed to obtain rebirth in the Pure Land, for their action was seen as "self-willed," and Pure Land faith relies entirely on the power and will of Amida Buddha. Assertion of self-will is seen as running counter to the reliance on other power demanded by the Amida faith.[29]

Several important points can be learned from these examples. First, suicide is never condemned per se. Rather it is the state of mind which determines the rightness or wrongness of the suicide situation. The dividing line between choosing one's own time and place of death with perfectly assured peace of mind, and self-willing one's own death at the time of one's master's death is perhaps a thin grey one, but this should not obscure the criteria involved: Death with desire leads not to rebirth in the Pure Land, but death with calm assurance does. Even the method

of water suicide, using a rope as a preventative backup, stresses the importance of the state of mind in this action.

Secondly, Ajisaka's famous phrase, "Nagori o oshimuna," means that Buddhists are not to kill themselves in "sympathy" when others die. A literal translation would be that we are not to cling to what remains of the name or person, but to let the deceased go freely on to the next world. In other words, when someone dies with an assured state of mind, it is not for those who remain either to criticize or to wish that he had not died in this situation. Those who are left behind are to respect and not resent, reject, or grieve for a death which might seem to them untimely.

It is not coincidental that the word for euthanasia in Japanese is anrakushi, a term with Buddhist meanings. In Buddhist terminology, anrakukoku is another name for the Pure Land, the next world of Amida Bodhisattva, to which each Japanese expects to go after death. German-educated doctor and historical novelist Mori Ōgai's famous book Takasebune specifically deals with anrakushi; it is the story of Yoshisuke killing his sickly young brother who wants to die but lacks the strength to kill himself.[30] Many famous twentieth-century Japanese authors wrote of suicide, and some, such as Akutagawa, Dazai, Kawabata, and Mishima, actually committed suicide. Following the deaths of each emperor (Meiji, Taishō, and, last year, Shōwa), faithful retainers have also committed suicide in sympathy with their departed leaders. While some of these suicides are not Buddhistic (they show anger, pessimism, nihilism, and so forth), they are still reminders that the Japanese Buddhist world view does not condemn suicide.

Japanese law does not criminalize suicide, and European law is slowly beginning to follow the Japanese model in this regard. However, Japanese law does hold it to be a crime to assist or encourage a suicide. In normal situations, this is only wise and prudent, for healthy people should be encouraged to live and make the most of their lives. But in the situations where songenshi (death with dignity) is requested, it is precisely because the person is facing imminent death that it is morally acceptable to assist his suicide, particularly if the motive is mercy.

SAMURAI, *SEPPUKU,* AND EUTHANASIA

Among the warrior elite, who usually followed Zen Buddhism, suicide was considered an honorable alternative to being killed by others or continuing a life in shame or misery. Beginning with the famous *seppuku* of Minamoto no Tametomo and Minamoto no Yorimasi in 1170, *seppuku* became known as the way that a vanquished but proud Buddhist warrior would end his life.[31] Soon thereafter, headed by Taira Noritsune and Tomomori, hundreds of Taira warriors and their families committed suicide in the battle of Dannoura of 1185. Famous suicides included that of Kusunoki Masashige in 1336, in the battle between Nitta and Hosokawa, and that of Hideyori Toyotomi, under siege by Tokugawa Ieyasu in 1615. In the Tokugawa period, love suicides were dramatized in a dozen plays by Chikamatsu Monzaemon including *Sonezaki shinjū, Shinjū ten no Amijima, and Shinjū mannensō.*[32] The forty-seven Ako *ronin,* who committed suicide after avenging their master's death, was another famous true story, dramatized in the *Chūshingura* plays and films.[33] The samurai's creed, to be willing to die at any moment, was dramatically spelled out by the *Hagakure.*[34] According to the *Hagakure,* the important concern was not whether one lived or died, but (1) being pure, simple, single-minded; (2) taking full responsibility for doing one's duty; and (3) unconditionally serving one's master, without concern for oneself.

Although *seppuku* may seem like a violent death to the observer, it was designed to enable the samurai to die with the greatest dignity and peace.

It is particularly noteworthy that the samurai's code of suicide included a provision for euthanasia: the *kaishakunin* (attendant). Cutting of the *hara* alone was very painful, and would not lead to a swift death. After cutting their *hara,* few samurai had enough strength to cut their own necks or spines. Yet without cutting their necks, the pain of the opened *hara* would continue for minutes or even hours prior to death. Therefore, the samurai would make arrangements with one or more *kaishakunin* to assist his suicide. While the samurai steadied his mind and prepared to die in peace, the *kaishakunin* would wait by his side. If the samurai spoke to the *kaishakunin* before or during the *seppuku* ceremony, the standard response was *"go anshin"* (set your mind at peace). All of the interactions and conversations surrounding an officially ordered *seppuku* were also fixed by tradition, so that the suicide might die with the least tension and greatest peace of mind. After the samurai had finished cutting to the prearranged point, or gave some other signal, it was the duty of the *kaishakunin* to cut the neck of the samurai to terminate his pain by administering the coup de grâce.[35]

Many samurai suicides were in fact the moral equivalent of euthanasia. The reasons for a samurai's suicide were either (1) to avoid an inevitable death at the hands of others, or (2) to escape a longer period of unbearable pain or psychological misery, without being an active, fruitful member of society. These are exactly the sorts of situations when euthanasia is desired today: (1) to avoid an inevitable death at the hands of others (including disease, cancer, or bacteria), (2) to escape a longer period of pain or misery without being a fruitful, active member of society.

In regard to (1), most Japanese are now cut down in their seventies by the enemies of cancer and other diseases, rather than in their youth on a battlefield. Regardless of whether the person is hopelessly surrounded by enemies on a battlefield, or hopelessly defeated by enemy organisms within his body, the morality of the situation is the same. In regard to (2), it might be argued that there is a difference between the pain or misery of the permanent incapacitation of a samurai, and the pain or misery of the permanent incapacitation of a hospital patient. But if anything, the hospital patient is in even less of a position to contribute to society or feel valued than is the samurai, so he has even more reason to be granted the option of leaving this arena (world) when he chooses. The samurai tradition shows that the important issue is not the level of physical pain, but the prospect for meaningful and productive interaction with other members of society. If there are no prospects for such interactions, the samurai society claimed no right to prevent the person from seeking more meaningful experiences in another world.

Now in both cases, there may be relatives or retainers in the area who do not wish to see their friend die. The issue in these cases is not whether or not the besieged person will die; it is only a question of how soon, and in what manner. From ancient times, Japanese have respected the right of the individual to choose the moment and manner of dying. The Buddhist principle ought to apply equally well to the modern medical battles against the enemies of the body. The argument that if a body still has a face, it is still a person to those around him, is a basically un-Buddhist failure to understand (a) the difference between body and life, (b) the importance of each person's determination of his own mental states, and (c) the importance of placing mercy over desire in Buddhism.

Of course there need to be safeguards in such situations, and those safeguards have already been spelled out by the decision of the Nagoya High Court. In case of euthanasia, the Nagoya High Court (22 December 1962) defined certain conditions under which euthanasia could be considered acceptable:

1. The disease is considered terminal and incurable by present medicine.
2. The pain is unbearable—both for the patient and those around him.
3. The death is for the purpose of his peaceful passing.
4. The person himself has requested the death, while conscious and sane.
5. The killing is done by a doctor.
6. The method of killing is humane.

If these safeguards are followed, it seems there is no moral reason that Buddhists should oppose euthanasia.

CONCLUSIONS

There are Japanese who hold that the Japanese lack the independent decision-making abilities of Western people, and that therefore doctors should make the decisions for their patients. This logic is backwards. The reason patients cannot make good independent judgments is because the doctors refuse them the information and freedom to do so, not because they lack the mental abilities or personal characteristics to make judgments.[36] Buddhism has always recognized the importance of individual choice, despite social pressures; examples range from the Buddha himself, through Kūkai, Hōnen, Shinran, and Nagamatsu Nissen. The ability of Japanese to take personal responsibility for important decisions in times of stress, danger, or anguish has been repeatedly shown in the historical examples of these bold Buddhist reformers.

In order for the patient to make an intelligent decision about when and how he wants to die, he needs to know the facts about the nature of his disease, not only its real name, but the realistic prospects and alternative outcomes of all available forms of treatment. This means renouncing the paternalistic model held by present Japanese medicine, and granting substantial freedom to the patient in deciding his own case. Some Japanese doctors have argued that (1) patients do not really want to know the bad news about themselves, that (2) knowing the truth may harm their conditions, and that (3) the physicians can judge more intelligently than the patient. However, studies in the West show that none of these claims is true. As Bok points out, "The attitude that what [the patient] doesn't know won't hurt him is proving unrealistic—it is rather what patients do not know but vaguely suspect that causes them corrosive (destructive) worry."[37] People recover faster from surgery and tolerate pain with less medication when they understand their own medical problems and what can and cannot be done about them.[38] In any case, doctors' withholding of information from patients is based not on statistical proof or ethical principles, but on the physician's desires to retain control over patients.[39] This is a situation that clear-thinking Buddhists naturally oppose. There is no reason to believe that these findings, long known and supported in Western medicine, should prove any different for the Japanese.

One important question for Buddhists today remains: What, if any, are the differences between suicide and euthanasia? Obviously one important difference is in the case where the person receiving euthanasia is unconscious. In this case, we have no way of knowing whether the patient genuinely desires euthanasia, unless he or she has previously made a declaration of wishes in a living will. On the other hand, once the consciousness has permanently disassociated itself from the body, there is no reason in Buddhism to continue to nourish or stimulate the body, for the body deprived of its *skandhas* is not a person. The Japan Songenshi Kyōkai (Association for Death with Dignity) has done much to improve the ability of the individual Japanese to choose his time and manner of death.

Another issue is the relation of painkilling to prolonging life and hastening death itself. The Japan Songenshi Kyōkai proposes the administering of painkilling drugs even if they hasten the death of the patient. Buddhists would agree that relief of pain is desirable, and whether the death is hastened or not is not the primary issue. However, consider a case where the pain is extreme and only very strong drugs will stop the pain. Here there may be a choice between: (a) no treatment at all, (b) painkilling which only blurs or confuses the mind of the patient, and (c) treatment which hastens the end while keeping the mind clear. In such a situation, the Buddhist would first prefer the most natural way of (a) no treatment at all. But if his mind were unable to focus or be at peace because of the great pain, the Buddhist would choose (c) over (b), because clarity of consciousness at the moment of death is so important in Buddhism.

Doctors who do not like the idea of shortening a person's life would prefer to prolong the material life-processes, regardless of the mental quality of that life. This is where Buddhists disagree with materialistic Western medicine. But there need be no conflict between Buddhism and medicine. There is no reason to assign the doctor the "responsibility" for the death of the patient. Following the guidelines of the Nagoya court, patients potentially eligible for euthanasia are going to die soon anyway, so that is not the fault of the doctor. And the patient has the right to determine his own death. The fact that he is too weak to hold a sword or to cut short his own life is not morally significant. If his mind is clear, calm, and ready for death, then the one who understands and compassionately assists that person is also following Buddhist morality. In summary, the important issue for Buddhists here is whether or not the person will be allowed responsibility for his own life and fate. The entire Buddhist tradition, and particularly that of suicide within Japan, argues that personal choice in time and manner of death is of extreme importance, and anything done by others to dim the mind or deprive the dying person of such choice is a violation of Buddhist principles. Japanese Buddhists may respect this decision more than Western cultures, and lead humanitarian bioethics in a different perspective towards dignified death.

NOTES

1. Morioka Masahiro, "Nōshi to wa nan de atta ka" (What was brain death?), in *Nihon Rinri Gakkai kenkyū happyō yoshi* (Japanese Ethics Association outline of presentations) (Japan Ethics Association 39th Annual Conference, Waseda University, October 14–15, 1988), p. 7.
2. Anzai Kazuhiro, "Nō to sono ishiki" (Brain and its consciousness), in *Nihon Rinri Gakkai*, p. 6.
3. Kawasaki Shinjo, "Tōyō kodai no seimei juyō." (The accepted understanding of life in the ancient Orient), in *Nihon Rinri Gakkai*, p. 26.
4. *Visuddhimagga*, pp. 229ff.
5. Kawasaki, "Tōyō kodai no seimei juyō," p. 27.
6. Iida Tsunesuke, "Bioethics wa nani o nasu no ka" (What does bioethics accomplish?), in *Nihon Rinri Gakkai*, pp. 40ff.
7. Mary Anne Warren, "Do Potential People Have Moral Rights?" *Canadian Journal of Philosophy* 7 no. 2 (1978): 275–289.
8. Carl Becker, "Old and New: Japan's Mechanisms for Crime Control and Social Justice," *Howard Journal of Criminal Justice*, 27, no. 4 (November 1988): 284–285.
9. Ohara Nobuo, "Sei to shi no rinrigaku" (The ethics of life and death), in *Nihon Rinri Gakkai*, pp. 54–55.
10. Carl Becker, "Religion and Politics in Japan," chap. 13 of *Movements and Issues in World Religions*, ed. C. W-H. Fu and G. S. Spiegler (New York: Greenwood Press, 1987), p. 278.
11. Among the author's students are nurses at such hospitals.
12. Gerald A. Larue, *Euthanasia and Religion: A Survey of the Attitudes of World Religions to the Right-To-Die* (Los Angeles: The Hemlock Society, 1985).
13. Cf. *Hastings Encyclopedia of Religion*, vol. 4, p. 448.

14. *Majhima Nikāya* II, 91; III, 258.

15. *Samyutta Nikāya* V, 408.

16. Tamaki Koshirō, "Shino oboegaki" (Memoranda on death), in *Bukkyō shisō*, vol. 10, ed. Bukkyō Shisō Kenkyukai, Tokyo (September 1988), pp. 465–475.

17. *Sūtta Vibhanga, Vinaya* III, 74; cf. *Samyutta Nikāya* III, 119–124.

18. *Majhima Nikāya* III, 263–266 (*Channovadasūtta*); *Samyutta Nikāya* IV, 55–60 (*Channavaga*).

19. *Samyutta Nikāya* I, 121.

20. *Jatakā Suvarna Prabhāsa*, p. 206ff.

21. *Acāranga Sūtra* I, 7, 6.

22. A mummified body of one such monk is preserved at the Myorenji temple, close to Tsukuba University.

23. Ogasawara Senshū, *Chūgoku Jōdokyō no kenkyū* (Researches in Chinese Pure Land Buddhism) (Kyoto: Heirakuji, 1951), pp. 60ff.

24. Thich Nhat Hanh, *The Lotus in the Sea of Fire* (London, 1967).

25. Kurita Isamu, *Ippen Shōnin, tabi no shisakuska* (Saint Ippen, the meditative wayfarer) (Tokyo: Shinchosha, 1977), pp. 165–169.

26. Ōhashi Shunnō, *Ippen* (Tokyo: Yoshikawa Kobunkan, 1983), pp. 105ff.

27. *Ippen goroku*, scroll 6, stage 2 (*maki 6, dan 2*).

28. Kurita, *Ippen Shōnin*.

29. Ōhashi, *Ippen*, pp. 107ff.

30. Mori Ōgai, *Takasebune* (Tokyo: Iwanami Bunko, 1978).

31. Jack Seward, *Hara-Kiri: Japanese Ritual Suicide* (Tokyo: Charles E. Tuttle, 1968), Seward describes these and many other significant suicides in detail.

32. Donald Keene, trans., *Major Plays of Chikamatsu* (New York: Columbia University Press, 1961).

33. Fujino Yoshiō, ed., *Kanatehon Chushingura: Kaishaku to kenkyū* (Chushingura) (Tokyo: Ofūsha, 1975).

34. Watsuji Tetsurō, ed., *Hagakure* (Tokyo: Iwanami Bunko, 1970).

35. All condensed from Seward, *Hara-Kiri*.

36. *Kimura Rihito*, "In Japan, Parents Participate but Doctors Decide," *Hastings Center* Report 16, no. 4 (1986): 22–23.

37. Sisela Bok, "Lies to the Sick and Dying," in *Lying: Moral Choice in Public and Private Life* (New York: Pantheon Books, 1978).

38. Lawrence Egbert, George Batitt, et al., "Reduction of Post-Operative Pain by Encouragement and Instruction of Patients," *New England Journal of Medicine* 270 (1964): 825–827; and Howard Waitzskin and John Stoeckle, "The Communication of Information About Illness," *Advances in Psychosomatic Medicine* 8 (1972): 185–215.

39. Cf. Bernard Gert and Charles Culver, "Paternalistic Behavior," *Philosophy and Public Affairs* 6 (Summer 1976); and Allen Buchanan, "Medical Paternalism," ibid., vol. 7 (Summer 1978).

The Wisdom of Repugnance

Leon R. Kass

Leon Kass is the Addie Clark Harking professor on the committee of social thought at the University of Chicago. He is the author of *Toward a More Natural Science: Biology and Human Affairs* (1985), and the coauthor of *The Ethics of Human Cloning* (1998) and *Reproduction and Responsibility* (2004). He was appointed by President George W. Bush as the chair of the Council on Bioethics. His article on cloning, "The Wisdom of Repugnance," is widely read.

Kass maintains that our gut reaction of revulsion against human cloning reveals our feelings toward moral taboos, the significance of which cannot be fully articulated in terms of rational arguments. He also points out that human cloning meddles with biological kinship, which is indelibly connected to our social identity. Against the idea that genotype has little to do with identity, he contends that cloning violates a person's uniqueness, which is connected to genetic distinctiveness. Moreover, in cloning not only do we seek to "manufacture" babies but also we aspire to control and predetermine a child's future, which goes against the meaning of childbearing and parenthood. In view of these reasons, Kass advocates a comprehensive legal prohibition of reproductive cloning as well as cloning of human embryos for research purposes.

THE WISDOM OF REPUGNANCE

"Offensive." "Grotesque." "Revolting." "Repugnant." "Repulsive." These are the words most commonly heard regarding the prospect of human cloning. Such reactions come both from the man or woman in the street and from the intellectuals, from believers and atheists, from humanists and scientists. Even Dolly's creator has said he "would find it offensive" to clone a human being.

People are repelled by many aspects of human cloning. They recoil from the prospect of mass production of human beings, with large clones of lookalikes, compromised in their individuality; the idea of father-son or mother-daughter twins; the bizarre prospects of a woman giving birth to and

Excerpts from Leon Kass, "The Wisdom of Repugnance" from The New Republic, 216, 1997. Reprinted by permission of the author.

rearing a genetic copy of herself, her spouse or even her deceased father or mother; the grotesqueness of conceiving a child as an exact replacement for another who has died; the utilitarian creation of embryonic genetic duplicates of oneself, to be frozen away or created when necessary, in case of need for homologous tissues or organs for transplantation; the narcissism of those who would clone themselves and the arrogance of others who think they know who deserves to be cloned or which genotype any child-to-be should be thrilled to receive; the Frankensteinian hubris to create human life and increasingly to control its destiny; man playing God. Almost no one finds any of the suggested reasons for human cloning compelling; almost everyone anticipates its possible misuses and abuses. Moreover, many people feel oppressed by the sense that there is probably nothing we can do to prevent it from happening. This makes the prospect all the more revolting.

Revulsion is not an argument; and some of yesterday's repugnances are today calmly accepted—though, one must add, not always for the better. In crucial cases, however, repugnance is the emotional expression of deep wisdom, beyond reason's power fully to articulate it. Can anyone really give an argument fully adequate to the horror which is father-daughter incest (even with consent), or having sex with animals, or mutilating a corpse, or eating human flesh, or even just (just!) raping or murdering another human being? Would anybody's failure to give full rational justification for his or her revulsion at these practices make that revulsion ethically suspect? Not at all. On the contrary, we are suspicious of those who think that they can rationalize away our horror, say, by trying to explain the enormity of incest with arguments only about the genetic risks of inbreeding.

The repugnance at human cloning belongs in this category. We are repelled by the prospect of cloning human beings not because of the strangeness or novelty of the undertaking, but because we intuit and feel, immediately and without argument, the violation of things that we rightfully hold dear. Repugnance, here as elsewhere, revolts against the excesses of human willfulness, warning us not to transgress what is unspeakably profound. Indeed, in this age in which everything is held to be permissible so long as it is freely done, in which our given human nature no longer commands respect, in which our bodies are regarded as mere instruments of our autonomous rational wills, repugnance may be the only voice left that speaks up to defend the central core of our humanity. Shallow are the souls that have forgotten how to shudder.

The goods protected by repugnance are generally overlooked by our customary ways of approaching all new biomedical technologies. The way we evaluate cloning ethically will in fact be shaped by how we characterize it descriptively, by the context into which we place it, and by the perspective from which we view it. The first task for ethics is proper description. And here is where our failure begins.

Typically, cloning is discussed in one or more of three familiar contexts, which one might call the technological, the liberal and the meliorist.

Under the first, cloning will be seen as an extension of existing techniques for assisting reproduction and determining the genetic makeup of children. Like them, cloning is to be regarded as a neutral technique, with no inherent meaning or goodness, but subject to multiple uses, some good, some bad. The morality of cloning thus depends absolutely on the goodness or badness of the motives and intentions of the cloners: as one bioethicist defender of cloning puts it, "the ethics must be judged [only] by the way the parents nurture and rear their resulting child and whether they bestow the same love and affection on a child brought into existence by a technique of assisted reproduction as they would on a child born in the usual way."

The liberal (or libertarian or liberationist) perspective sets cloning in the context of rights, freedoms and personal empowerment. Cloning is just a new option for exercising an individual's right to reproduce or to have the kind of child that he or she wants. Alternatively, cloning enhances our liberation (especially women's liberation) from the confines of nature, the vagaries of chance, or the necessity for sexual mating. Indeed, it liberates women from the need for men altogether, for the process requires only eggs, nuclei and (for the time being) uteri—plus, of course, a healthy dose of our (allegedly "masculine") manipulative science that likes to do all these things to mother nature and nature's mothers. For those who hold this outlook, the only moral restraints on cloning are adequately informed consent and the avoidance of bodily harm. If no one is cloned without her consent, and if the clonant is not physically damaged, then the liberal conditions for licit, hence moral, conduct are met. Worries that go beyond violating the will or maiming the body are dismissed as "symbolic"—which is to say, unreal.

The meliorist perspective embraces valetudinarians and also eugenicists. The latter were formerly more vocal in these discussions, but they are now generally happy to see their goals advanced under the less threatening banners of freedom and technological growth. These people see in cloning a new prospect for improving human beings— minimally, by ensuring the perpetuation of healthy individuals by avoiding the risks of genetic disease inherent in the lottery of sex, and maximally, by producing "optimum babies," preserving outstanding genetic material, and (with the help of soon-to-come techniques for precise genetic engineering) enhancing inborn human capacities on many fronts. Here the morality of cloning as a means is justified solely by the excellence of the end, that is, by the outstanding traits or individuals cloned—beauty, or brawn, or brains.

These three approaches, all quintessentially American and all perfectly fine in their places, are sorely wanting as approaches to human procreation. It is, to say the least, grossly distorting to view the wondrous mysteries of birth, renewal and individuality, and the deep meaning of parent-child relations, largely through the lens of our reductive science and its potent technologies. Similarly, considering reproduction (and the intimate relations of family life!) primarily under the political-legal, adversarial and individualistic notion of rights can only undermine the private yet fundamentally social, cooperative and duty-laden character of child-bearing, child-rearing and their bond to the covenant of marriage. Seeking to escape entirely from nature (in order to satisfy a natural desire or a natural right to reproduce!) is self-contradictory in theory and self-alienating in practice. For we are erotic beings only because we are embodied beings, and not merely intellects and wills unfortunately imprisoned in our bodies. And, though health and fitness are clearly great goods, there is something deeply disquieting in looking on our prospective children as artful products perfectible by genetic engineering, increasingly held to our willfully imposed designs, specifications and margins of tolerable error.

The technical, liberal and meliorist approaches all ignore the deeper anthropological, social and, indeed, ontological meanings of bringing forth new life. To this more fitting and profound point of view, cloning shows itself to be a major alteration, indeed, a major violation, of our given nature as embodied, gendered and engendering beings—and of the social relations built on this natural ground. Once this perspective is recognized, the ethical

judgment on cloning can no longer be reduced to a matter of motives and intentions, rights and freedoms, benefits and harms, or even means and ends. It must be regarded primarily as a matter of meaning: Is cloning a fulfillment of human begetting and belonging? Or is cloning rather, as I contend, their pollution and perversion? To pollution and perversion, the fitting response can only be horror and revulsion; and conversely, generalized horror and revulsion are prima facie evidence of foulness and violation. The burden of moral argument must fall entirely on those who want to declare the widespread repugnances of humankind to be mere timidity or superstition.

Yet repugnance need not stand naked before the bar of reason. The wisdom of our horror at human cloning can be partially articulated, even if this is finally one of those instances about which the heart has its reasons that reason cannot entirely know.

The Profundity of Sex

To see cloning in its proper context, we must begin not, as I did before, with laboratory technique, but with the anthropology—natural and social—of sexual reproduction.

Sexual reproduction—by which I mean the generation of new life from (exactly) two complementary elements, one female, one male, (usually) through coitus—is established (if that is the right term) not by human decision, culture or tradition, but by nature; it is the natural way of all mammalian reproduction. By nature, each child has two complementary biological progenitors. Each child thus stems from and unites exactly two lineages. In natural generation, moreover, the precise genetic constitution of the resulting offspring is determined by a combination of nature and chance, not by human design: each human child shares the common natural human species genotype, each child is genetically (equally) kin to each (both) parent(s), yet each child is also genetically unique.

These biological truths about our origins foretell deep truths about our identity and about our human condition altogether. Every one of us is at once equally human, equally enmeshed in a particular familial nexus of origin, and equally individuated in our trajectory from birth to death—and, if all goes well, equally capable (despite our morality) of participating, with a complementary other, in the very same renewal of such human possibility through procreation. Though less momentous than our common humanity, our genetic individuality is not humanly trivial. It shows itself forth in our distinctive appearance through which we are everywhere recognized; it is revealed in our "signature" marks of fingerprints and our self-recognizing immune system; it symbolizes and foreshadows exactly the unique, never-to-be-repeated character of each human life.

Human societies virtually everywhere have structured child-rearing responsibilities and systems of identity and relationship on the bases of these deep natural facts of begetting. The mysterious yet ubiquitous "love of one's own" is everywhere culturally exploited, to make sure that children are not just produced but well cared for and to create for everyone clear ties of meaning, belonging and obligation. But it is wrong to treat such naturally rooted social practices as mere cultural constructs (like left- or right-driving, or like burying or cremating the dead) that we can alter with little human cost. What would kinship be without its clear natural grounding? And what would identity be without kinship? We must resist those who have begun to refer to sexual reproduction as the "traditional method of reproduction," who would have us regard as merely traditional, and by implication arbitrary, what is in truth not only natural but most certainly profound.

Asexual reproduction, which produces "single-parent" offspring, is a radical departure from the natural human way, confounding all normal understandings of father, mother, sibling, grandparent, etc., and all moral relations tied thereto. It becomes even more of a radical departure when the resulting offspring is a clone derived not from an embryo, but from a mature adult to whom the clone would be an identical twin; and when the process occurs not by natural accident (as in natural twinning), but by deliberate human design and manipulation; and when the child's (or children's) genetic constitution is preselected by the parent(s) (or scientists). Accordingly, as we will see, cloning is vulnerable to three kinds of concerns and objections, related to these three points: cloning threatens confusion of identity and individuality, even in small-scale cloning; cloning represents a giant step (though not the first one) toward transforming procreation into manufacture, that is, toward the increasing depersonalization of the process of generation and, increasingly, toward the "production" of human children as artifacts, products of human will and design (what others have called the problem of "commodification" of new life); and cloning—like other forms of eugenic engineering of the next generation—represents a form of despotism of the cloners over the cloned, and thus (even in benevolent cases) represents a blatant violation of the inner meaning of parent-child relations, of what it means to have a child, of what it means to say "yes" to our own demise and "replacement."

Before turning to these specific ethical objections, let me test my claim of the profundity of the natural way by taking up a challenge recently posed by a friend. What if the given natural human way of reproduction were asexual, and we now had to deal with a new technological innovation—artificially induced sexual dimorphism and the fusing of complementary gametes—whose inventors argued that sexual reproduction promised all sorts of advantages, including hybrid vigor and the creation of greatly increased individuality? Would one then be forced to defend natural asexuality because it was natural? Could one claim that it carried deep human meaning?

The response to this challenge broaches the ontological meaning of sexual reproduction. For it is impossible, I submit, for there to have been human life—or even higher forms of animal life—in the absence of sexuality and sexual reproduction. We find asexual reproduction only in the lowest forms of life: bacteria, algae, fungi, some lower invertebrates. Sexuality brings with it a new and enriched relationship to the world. Only sexual animals can seek and find complementary others with whom to pursue a goal that transcends their own existence. For a sexual being, the world is no longer an indifferent and largely homogenous *otherness*, in part edible, in part dangerous. It also contains some very special and related and complementary beings, of the same kind but of opposite sex, toward whom one reaches out with special interest and intensity. In higher birds and mammals, the outward gaze keeps a lookout not only for food and predators, but also for prospective mates; the beholding of the many splendored world is suffused with desire for union, the animal antecedent of human eros and the germ of sociality. Not by accident is the human animal both the sexiest animal—whose females do not go into heat but are receptive throughout the estrous cycle and whose males must therefore have greater sexual appetite and energy in order to reproduce successfully—and also the most aspiring, the most social, the most open and the most intelligent animal.

The soul-elevating power of sexuality is, at bottom, rooted in its strange connection to mortality, which it simultaneously accepts and tries to overcome. Asexual reproduction may be seen as a continuation of the activity of self-preservation. When one organism buds or divides to become two, the original being is (doubly) preserved, and nothing dies. Sexuality, by contrast, means perishability and serves replacement; the two that come together to generate one soon will die. Sexual desire, in human beings as in animals, thus serves an end that is partly hidden from, and finally at odds with, the self-serving individual. Whether we know it or not, when we are sexually active we are voting with our genitalia for our own demise. The salmon swimming upstream to spawn and die tell the universal story: sex is bound up with death, to which it holds a partial answer in procreation.

The salmon and the other animals evince this truth blindly. Only the human being can understand what it means. As we learn so powerfully from the story of the Garden of Eden, our humanization is coincident with sexual self-consciousness, with the recognition of our sexual nakedness and all that it implies: shame at our needy incompleteness, unruly self-division and finitude; awe

before the eternal; hope in the self-transcending possibilities of children and a relationship to the divine. In the sexually self-conscious animal, sexual desire can become eros, lust can become love. Sexual desire humanly regarded is thus sublimated into erotic longing for wholeness, completion and immortality which drives us knowingly into the embrace and its generative fruit—as well as into all the higher human possibilities of deed, speech and song.

Through children, a good common to both husband and wife, male and female achieve some genuine unification (beyond the mere sexual "union," which fails to do so). The two become one through sharing generous (not needy) love for this third being as good. Flesh of their flesh, the child is the parents' own commingled being externalized, and given a separate and persisting existence. Unification is enhanced also by their commingled work of rearing. Providing an opening to the future beyond the grave, carrying not only our seed but also our names, our ways and our hopes that they will surpass us in goodness and happiness, children are a testament to the possibility of transcendence. Gender duality and sexual desire, which first draws our love upward and outside of ourselves, finally provide for the partial overcoming of the confinement and limitation of perishable embodiment altogether.

Human procreation, in sum, is not simply an activity of our rational wills. It is a more complete activity precisely because it engages us bodily, erotically and spiritually, as well as rationally. There is wisdom in the mystery of nature that has joined the pleasure of sex, the inarticulate longing for union, the communication of the loving embrace and the deep-seated and only partly articulate desire for children in the very activity by which we continue the chain of human existence and participate in the renewal of human possibility. Whether or not we know it, the severing of procreation from sex, love and intimacy is inherently dehumanizing, no matter how good the product.

We are now ready for the more specific objections to cloning.

THE PERVERSITIES OF CLONING

First, an important if formal objection: any attempt to clone a human being would constitute an unethical experiment upon the resulting child-to-be. As the animal experiments (frog and sheep) indicate, there are grave risks of mishaps and deformities. Moreover, because of what cloning means, one cannot presume a future cloned child's consent to be a clone, even a healthy one. Thus, ethically speaking, we cannot even get to know whether or not human cloning is feasible.

I understand, of course, the philosophical difficulty of trying to compare a life with defects against nonexistence. Several bioethicists, proud of their philosophical cleverness, use this conundrum to embarrass claims that one can injure a child in its conception, precisely because it is only thanks to that complained-of conception that the child is alive to complain. But common sense tells us that we have no reason to fear such philosophisms. For we surely know that people can harm and even maim children in the very act of conceiving them, say, by paternal transmission of the AIDS virus, maternal transmission of heroin dependence or, arguably, even by bringing them into being as bastards or with no capacity or willingness to look after them properly. And we believe that to do this intentionally, or even negligently, is inexcusable and clearly unethical.

The objection about the impossibility of presuming consent may even go beyond the obvious and sufficient point that a clonant, were he subsequently to be asked, could rightly resent having been made a clone. At issue are not just benefits and harms, but doubts about the very independence needed to give proper (even retroactive) consent, that is, not just the capacity to choose but the disposition and ability to choose freely and well. It is not at all clear to what extent a clone will truly be a moral agent. For, as we shall see, in the very fact of cloning, and of rearing him as a clone, his makers subvert the cloned child's independence, beginning with that aspect that comes from knowing that one was an unbidden surprise, a gift, to the world, rather than the designed result of someone's artful project.

Cloning creates serious issues of identity and individuality. The cloned person may experience concerns about his distinctive identity not only because he will be in genotype and appearance identical to another human being, but, in this case, because he may also be twin to the person who is his "father" or "mother"—if one can still call them that. What would be the psychic burdens of being the "child" or "parent" of your twin? The cloned individual, moreover, will be saddled with a genotype that has already lived. He will not be fully a surprise to the world. People are likely always to compare his performances in life with that of his alter ego. True, his nurture and his circumstance in life will be different; genotype is not exactly destiny. Still, one must also expect parental and other efforts to shape this new life after the original—or at least to view the child with the original version always firmly in mind. Why else did they clone from the star basketball player, mathematician and beauty queen—or even dear old dad—in the first place?

Since the birth of Dolly, there has been a fair amount of doublespeak on this matter of genetic identity. Experts have rushed in to reassure the public that the clone would in no way be the same person, or have any confusions about his or her identity: as previously noted, they are pleased to point out that the clone of Mel Gibson would not be Mel Gibson. Fair enough. But one is shortchanging the truth by emphasizing the additional importance of the intrauterine environment, rearing and social setting: genotype obviously matters plenty. That, after all, is the only reason to clone, whether human beings or sheep. The odds that clones of Wilt Chamberlain will play in the NBA are, I submit, infinitely greater than they are for clones of Robert Reich.

Curiously, this conclusion is supported, inadvertently, by the one ethical sticking point insisted on by friends of cloning: no cloning without the doctor's consent. Though an orthodox liberal objection, it is in fact quite puzzling when it comes from people (such as Ruth Macklin) who also insist that genotype is not identity or individuality, and who deny that a child could reasonably complain about being made a genetic copy. If the clone of Mel Gibson would not be Mel Gibson, why should Mel Gibson have grounds to object that someone had been made his clone? We already allow researchers to use blood and tissue samples for research purposes of no benefit to their sources: my falling hair, my expectorations, my urine, and even my biopsied tissues are "not me" and not mine. Courts have held that the profit gained from uses to which scientists put my discarded tissues do not legally belong to me. Why, then, no cloning without consent—including, I assume, no cloning from the body of someone who just died? What harm is done the donor, if genotype is "not me"? Truth to tell, the only powerful justification for objecting is that genotype really does have something to do with identity, and everybody knows it. If not, on what basis could Michael Jordan object that someone cloned "him," say, from cells taken from a "lost" scraped-off piece of his skin? The insistence on donor consent unwittingly reveals the problem of identity in all cloning.

Genetic distinctiveness not only symbolizes the uniqueness of each human life and the independence of its parents that each human child rightfully attains. It can also be an important support for living a worthy and dignified life. Such arguments apply with great force to any large-scale replication of human individuals. But they are sufficient, in my view, to rebut even the first attempts to clone a human being. One must never forget that these are human beings upon whom our eugenic or merely playful fantasies are to be enacted.

Troubled psychic identity (distinctiveness), based on all-too-evident genetic identity (sameness), will be made much worse by the utter confusion of social identity and kinship ties. For, as already noted, cloning radically confounds lineage and social relations, for "offspring" as for "parents." As bioethicist James Nelson has pointed out, a female child cloned from her "mother" might develop a desire for a relationship to her "father," and might understandably seek out the father of her "mother," who is after all also her biological twin sister. Would "grandpa," who thought his paternal duties concluded, be pleased to discover that the clonant looked to him for paternal attention and support?

Social identity and social ties of relationship and responsibility are widely connected to, and

supported by, biological kinship. Social taboos on incest (and adultery) everywhere serve to keep clear who is related to whom (and especially which child belongs to which parents), as well as to avoid confounding the social identity of parent-and-child (or brother-and-sister) with the social identity of lovers, spouses, and co-parents. True, social identity is altered by adoption (but as a matter of the best interest of already living children: we do not deliberately produce children for adoption). True, artificial insemination and in vitro fertilization with donor sperm, or whole embryo donation, are in some way forms of "parental adoption"—a not altogether unproblematic practice. Even here, though, there is in each case (as in all sexual reproduction) a known male source of sperm and a known single female source of egg—a genetic father and a genetic mother—should anyone care to know (as adopted children often do) who is genetically related to whom.

In the case of cloning, however, there is but one "parent." The usually sad situation of the "single-parent child" is here deliberately planned, and with a vengeance. In the case of self-cloning, the "offspring" is, in addition, one's twin; and so the dreaded result of incest—to be parent to one's sibling—is here brought about deliberately, albeit without any act of coitus. Moreover, all other relationships will be confounded. What will father, grandfather, aunt, cousin, sister mean? Who will bear what ties and what burdens? What sort of social identity will someone have with one whole side— "father's" or "mother's"—necessarily excluded? It is no answer to say that our society, with its high incidence of divorce, remarriage, adoption, extramarital childbearing and the rest, already confounds lineage and confuses kinship and responsibility for children (and everyone else), unless one also wants to argue that this is, for children, a preferable state of affairs.

Human cloning would also represent a giant step toward turning begetting into making, procreation into manufacture (literally, something "handmade"), a process already begun with in vitro fertilization and genetic testing of embryos. With cloning, not only is the process in hand, but the total genetic blueprint of the cloned individual is selected and determined by the human artisans. To be sure, subsequent development will take place according to natural processes; and the resulting children will still be recognizably human. But we here would be taking a major step into making man himself simply another one of the manmade things. Human nature becomes merely the last part of nature to succumb to the technological project, which turns all of nature into raw material at human disposal, to be homogenized by our rationalized technique according to the subjective prejudices of the days.

How does begetting differ from making? In natural procreation, human beings come together, complementarily male and female, to give existence to another being who is formed, exactly as we were, *by what we are:* living, hence perishable, hence aspiringly erotic, human beings. In clonal reproduction, by contrast, and in the more advanced forms of manufacture to which it leads, we give existence to a being not by what we are but by what we intend and design. As with any product of our making, no matter how excellent, the artificer stands above it, not as an equal but as a superior, transcending it by his will and creative prowess. Scientists who clone animals make it perfectly clear that they are engaged in instrumental making; the animals are, from the start, designed as means to serve rational human purposes. In human cloning, scientists and prospective "parents" would be adopting the same technocratic mentality to human children: human children would be their artifacts.

Such an arrangement is profoundly dehumanizing, no matter how good the product. Mass-scale cloning of the same individual makes the point vividly; but the violation of human equality, freedom and dignity are present even in a singly planned clone. And procreation dehumanized into manufacture is further degraded by commodification, a virtually inescapable result of allowing baby-making to proceed under the banner of commerce. Genetic and reproductive biotechnology companies are already growth industries, but they will go into commercial orbit once the Human Genome Project nears completion. Supply will

create enormous demand. Even before the capacity for human cloning arrives, established companies will have invested in the harvesting of eggs from ovaries obtained at autopsy or through ovarian surgery, practiced embryonic genetic alteration, and initiated the stockpiling of prospective donor tissues. Through the rental of surrogate-womb services, and through the buying and selling of tissues and embryos, priced according to the merit of the donor, the commodification of nascent human life will be unstoppable.

Finally, and perhaps most important, the practice of human cloning by nuclear transfer—like other anticipated forms of genetic engineering of the next generation—would enshrine and aggravate a profound and mischievous misunderstanding of the meaning of having children and of the parent-child relationship. When a couple now chooses to procreate, the partners are saying yes to the emergence of new life in its novelty, saying yes not only to having a child but also, tacitly, to having whatever child this child turns out to be. In accepting our finitude and opening ourselves to our replacement, we are tacitly confessing the limits of our control. In this ubiquitous way of nature, embracing the future by procreating means precisely that we are relinquishing our grip, in the very activity of taking up our own share in what we hope will be the immortality of human life and the human species. This means that out children are not *our* children: they are not our property, not our possessions. Neither are they supposed to live our lives for us, or anyone else's life but their own. To be sure, we seek to guide them on their way, imparting to them not just life but nurturing, love, and a way of life; to be sure, they bear our hopes that they will live fine and flourishing lives, enabling us in small measure to transcend our own limitations. Still, their genetic distinctiveness and independence are the natural foreshadowing of the deep truth that they have their own and never-before-enacted life to live. They are sprung from a past, but they take an uncharted course into the future.

Much harm is already done by parents who try to live vicariously through their children. Children are sometimes compelled to fulfill the broken dreams of unhappy parents; John Doe Jr. or the III is under the burden of having to live up to his forebear's name. Still, if most parents have hopes for their children, cloning parents will have expectations. In cloning, such overbearing parents take at the start a decisive step which contradicts the entire meaning of the open and forward-looking nature of parent-child relations. The child is given a genotype that has already lived, with full expectation that this blueprint of a past life ought to be controlling of the life that is to come. Cloning is inherently despotic, for it seeks to make one's children (or someone else's children) after one's own image (or an image of one's choosing) and their future according to one's will. In some cases, the despotism may be mild and benevolent. In other cases, it will be mischievous and downright tyrannical. But despotism—the control of another through one's will—it inevitable will be.

MEETING SOME OBJECTIONS

The defenders of cloning, of course, are not wittingly friends of despotism. Indeed, they regard themselves mainly as friends of freedom: the freedom of individuals to reproduce, the freedom of scientists and inventors to discover and devise and to foster "progress" in genetic knowledge and technique. They want large-scale cloning only for animals, but they wish to preserve cloning as a human option for exercising our "right to reproduce"—our right to have children, and children with "desirable genes." As law professor John Robertson points out, under our "right to reproduce" we already practice early forms of unnatural, artificial and extramarital reproduction, and we already practice early forms of eugenic choice. For this reason, he argues, cloning is no big deal.

We have here a perfect example of the logic of the slippery slope, and the slippery way in which it already works in this area. Only a few years ago, slippery slope arguments were used to oppose artificial insemination and in vitro fertilization using unrelated sperm donors. Principles used to justify these practices, it was said, will be used to justify more artificial and more eugenic practices,

including cloning. Not so, the defenders retorted, since we can make the necessary distinctions. And now, without even a gesture at making the necessary distinctions, the continuity of practice is held by itself to be justificatory.

The principle of reproductive freedom as currently enunciated by the proponents of cloning logically embraces the ethical acceptability of sliding down the entire rest of the slope—to producing children ectogenetically from sperm to term (should it become feasible) and to producing children whose entire genetic makeup will be the product of parental eugenic planning and choice. If reproductive freedom means the right to have a child of one's own choosing, by whatever means, it knows and accepts no limits.

But, far from being legitimated by a "right to reproduce," the emergence of techniques of assisted reproduction and genetic engineering should compel us to reconsider the meaning and limits of such a putative right. In truth, a "right to reproduce" has always been a peculiar and problematic notion. Rights generally belong to individuals, but this is a right which (before cloning) no one can exercise alone. Does the right then inhere only in couples? Only in married couples? Is it a (woman's) right to carry or deliver or a right (of one or more parents) to nurture and rear? Is it a right to have your own biological child? Is it a right only to attempt reproduction, or a right also to succeed? Is it a right to acquire the baby of one's choice?

The assertion of a negative "right to reproduce" certainly makes sense when it claims protection against state interference with procreative liberty, say, through a program of compulsory sterilization. But surely it cannot be the basis of a tort claim against nature, to be made good by technology, should free efforts at natural procreation fail. Some insist that the right to reproduce embraces also the right against state interference with the free use of all technological means to obtain a child. Yet such a position cannot be sustained: for reasons having to do with the means employed, any community may rightfully prohibit surrogate pregnancy, or polygamy, or the sale of babies to infertile couples, without violating anyone's basic human "right to reproduce." When the exercise of a previously innocuous freedom now involves or impinges on troublesome practices that the original freedom never was intended to reach, the general presumption of liberty needs to be reconsidered.

We do indeed already practice negative eugenic selection, through genetic screening and prenatal diagnosis. Yet our practices are governed by a norm of health. We seek to prevent the birth of children who suffer from known (serious) genetic diseases. When and if gene therapy becomes possible, such disease could then be treated, in utero or even before implantation—I have no ethical objection in principle to such a practice (though I have some practical worries), precisely because it serves the medical goal of healing existing individuals. But therapy, to be therapy, implies not only an existing "patient." It also implies a norm of health. In this respect, even germline gene "therapy," though practiced not on a human being but on egg and sperm, is less radical than cloning, which is in no way therapeutic. But once one blurs the distinction between health promotion and genetic enhancement, between so-called negative and positive eugenics, one opens the door to all future eugenic designs. "To make sure that a child will be healthy and have good chances in life"; this is Robertson's principle, and owing to its latter clause it is an utterly elastic principle, with no boundaries. Being over eight feet tall will likely produce some very good chances in life, and so will having the looks of Marilyn Monroe, and so will a genius-level intelligence.

Proponents want us to believe that there are legitimate uses of cloning that can be distinguished from illegitimate uses, but by their own principles no such limits can be found. (Nor could any such limits be enforced in practice.) Reproductive freedom, as they understand it, is governed solely by the subjective wishes of the parents-to-be (plus the avoidance of bodily harm to the child). The sentimentally appealing case of the childless married couple is, on these grounds, indistinguishable from the case of an individual (married or not) who would like to clone someone famous or talented, living or dead. Further, the principle here endorsed justifies not only cloning but, indeed, all future artificial attempts to create (manufacture) "perfect" babies.

A concrete example will show how, in practice no less than in principle, the so-called innocent case will merge with, or even turn into, the more troubling ones. In practice, the eager parents-to-be will necessarily be subject to the tyranny of expertise. Consider an infertile married couple, she lacking eggs or he lacking sperm, that wants a child of their (genetic) own, and propose to clone either husband or wife. The scientist-physician (who is also coowner of the cloning company) points out the likely difficulties—a cloned child is not really their (genetic) child, but the child of only *one* of them; this imbalance may produce strains on the marriage; the child might suffer identity confusion; there is a risk of perpetuating the cause of sterility; and so on—and he also points out the advantages of choosing a donor nucleus. Far better than a child of their own would be a child of their own choosing. Touting his own expertise in selecting healthy and talented donors, the doctor presents the couple with his latest catalog containing the pictures, the health records, and the accomplishments of his stable of cloning donors, samples of whose tissues are in his deep freeze. Why not, dearly beloved, a more perfect baby?

The "perfect baby," of course, is the project not of the infertility doctors, but of the eugenic scientists and their supporters. For them, the paramount right is not the so-called right to reproduce but what biologist Bentley Glass called, a quarter of a century ago, "the right of every child to be born with a sound physical and mental constitution, based on a sound genotype . . . the inalienable right to a sound heritage." But to secure this right, and to achieve the requisite quality control over new human life, human conception and gestation will need to be brought fully into the bright light of the laboratory, beneath which it can be fertilized, nourished, pruned, weeded, watched, inspected, prodded, pinched, cajoled, injected, tested, rated, graded, approved, stamped, wrapped, sealed, and delivered. There is no other way to produce the perfect baby.

Yet we are urged by proponents of cloning to forget about the science fiction scenarios of laboratory manufacture and multiple-copied clones, and to focus only on the homely cases of infertile couples exercising their reproductive rights. But why, if the single cases are so innocent, should multiplying their performance be so off-putting? (Similarly, why do others object to people making money off this practice, if the practice itself is perfectly acceptable?) When we follow the sound ethical principle of universalizing our choice—"would it be right if everyone cloned a Wilt Chamberlain (with his consent, of course)? Would it be right if everyone decided to practice asexual reproduction?"—we discover what is wrong with these seemingly innocent cases. The so-called science fiction cases make vivid the meaning of what looks to us, mistakenly, to be benign.

Though I recognize certain continuities between cloning and, say, in vitro fertilization, I believe that cloning differs in essential and important ways. Yet those who disagree should be reminded that the "continuity" argument cuts both ways. Sometimes we establish bad precedents, and discover that they were bad only when we follow their inexorable logic to places we never meant to go. Can the defenders of cloning show us today how, on their principles, we will be able to see producing babies ("perfect babies") entirely in the laboratory or exercising full control over their genotypes (including so-called enhancement) as ethically different, in any essential way, from present forms of assisted reproduction? Or are they willing to admit, despite their attachment to be principle of continuity, that the complete obliteration of "mother" or "father," the complete depersonalization of procreation, the complete manufacture of human beings and the complete genetic control of one generation over the next would be ethically problematic and essentially different from current forms of assisted reproduction? If so, where and how will they draw the line, and why? I draw it at cloning, for all the reasons given.

BAN THE CLONING OF HUMANS

What, then, should we do? We should declare that human cloning is unethical in itself and dangerous in its likely consequences. In so doing, we shall

have the backing of the overwhelming majority of our fellow Americans, and of the human race, and (I believe) of most practicing scientists. Next, we should do all that we can to prevent the cloning of human beings. We should do this by means of an international legal ban if possible, and by a unilateral national ban, at a minimum. Scientists may secretly undertake to violate such a law, but they will be deterred by not being able to stand up proudly to claim the credit for their technological bravado and success. Such a ban on clonal baby-making, moreover, will not harm the progress of basic genetic science and technology. On the contrary, it will reassure the public that scientists are happy to proceed without violating the deep ethical norms and intuitions of the human community.

This still leaves the vexed question about laboratory research using early embryonic human clones, specially created only for such research purposes, with no intention to implant them into a uterus. There is no question that such research holds great promise for gaining fundamental knowledge about normal (and abnormal) differentiation, and for developing tissue lines for transplantation that might be used, say, in treating leukemia or in repairing brain or spinal cord injuries—to mention just a few of the conceivable benefits. Still, unrestricted clonal embryo research will surely make the production of living human clones much more likely. Once the genies put the cloned embryos into the bottles, who can strictly control where they go (especially in the absence of legal prohibitions against implanting them to produce a child)?

I appreciate the potentially great gains in scientific knowledge and medical treatment available from embryo research, especially with cloned embryos. At the same time, I have serious reservations about creating human embryos for the sole purpose of experimentation. There is something deeply repugnant and fundamentally transgressive about such a utilitarian treatment of prospective human life. This total, shameless exploitation is worse, in my opinion, than the "mere" destruction of nascent life. But I see no added objections, as a matter of principle, to creating and using *cloned* early embryos for research purposes, beyond the objections that I might raise to doing so with embryos produced sexually.

And yet, as a matter of policy and prudence, any opponent of the manufacture of cloned humans must, I think, in the end oppose also the creating of cloned human embryos. Frozen embryonic clones (belonging to whom?) can be shuttled around without detection. Commercial ventures in human cloning will be developed without adequate oversight. In order to build a fence around the law, prudence dictates that one oppose—for this reason alone—all production of cloned human embryos, even for research purposes. We should allow for all cloning research on animals to go forward, but the only safe trench that we can dig across the slippery slope, I suspect, is to insist on the inviolable distinction between animal and human cloning.

Some readers, and certainly most scientists, will not accept such prudent restraints, since they desire the benefits of research. They will prefer, even in fear and trembling, to allow human embryo cloning research to go forward.

Very well. Let us test them. If the scientists want to be taken seriously on ethical grounds, they must at the very least agree that embryonic research may proceed if and only if it is preceded by an absolute and effective ban on all attempts to implant into a uterus a cloned human embryo (cloned from an adult) to produce a living child. Absolutely no permission for the former without the latter.

The National Bioethics Advisory Commission's recommendations regarding this matter should be watched with the greatest care. Yielding to the wishes of the scientists, the commission will almost surely recommend that cloning human embryos for research be permitted. To allay public concern, it will likely also call for a temporary moratorium—not a legislative ban—on implanting cloned embryos to make a child, at least until such time as cloning techniques will have been perfected and rendered "safe" (precisely through the permitted research with cloned embryos). But the call for a moratorium rather than a legal ban would be a moral and a practical failure. Morally, this ethics commis-

sion would (at best) be waffling on the main ethical question, by refusing to declare the production of human clones unethical (or ethical). Practically, a moratorium on implantation cannot provide even the minimum protection needed to prevent the production of cloned humans.

Opponents of cloning need therefore to be vigilant. Indeed, no one should be willing even to consider a recommendation to allow the embryo research to proceed unless it is accompanied by a call for *prohibiting* implantation and until steps are taken to make such a prohibition effective.

• • •

Technically, the National Bioethics Advisory Commission can advise the president only on federal policy, especially federal funding policy. But given the seriousness of the matter at hand, and the grave public concern that goes beyond federal funding, the commission should take a broader view. (If it doesn't, Congress surely will.) Given that most assisted reproduction occurs in the private sector, it would be cowardly and insufficient for the commission to say, simply, "no federal funding" for such practices. It would be disingenuous to argue that we should allow federal funding so that we would then be able to regulate the practice; the private sector will not be bound by such regulations. Far better, for virtually everyone concerned, would be to distinguish between research on embryos and baby-making, and to call for a complete national and international ban (effected by legislation and treaty) of the latter, while allowing the former to proceed (at least in private laboratories).

The proposal for such a legislative ban is without American precedent, at least in technological matters, though the British and others have banned cloning of human beings, and we ourselves ban incest, polygamy, and other forms of "reproductive freedom." Needless to say, working out the details of such a ban, especially a global one, would be tricky, what with the need to develop appropriate sanction for violators. Perhaps such a ban will prove ineffective; perhaps it will eventually be shown to have been a mistake. But it would at least place the burden of practical proof where it belongs: on the proponents of this horror, requiring them to show very clearly what great social or medical good can be had only by the cloning of human beings.

We Americans have lived by, and prospered under, a rosy optimism about scientific and technological progress. The technological imperative—if it can be done, it must be done—has probably served us well, though we should admit that there is no accurate method for weighing benefits and harms. Even when, as in the cases of environmental pollution, urban decay or the lingering deaths that are the unintended by-products of medical success, we recognize the unwelcome outcomes of technological advance, we remain confident in our ability to fix all the "bad" consequences—usually by means of still newer and better technologies. How successful we can continue to be in such post hoc repairing is at least an open question. But there is very good reason for shifting the paradigm around, at least regarding those technological interventions into the human body and mind that will surely effect fundamental (and likely irreversible) changes in human nature, basic human relationships, and what it means to be a human being. Here we surely should not be willing to risk everything in the naive hope that, should things go wrong, we can later set them right.

The president's call for a moratorium on human cloning has given us an important opportunity. In a truly unprecedented way, we can strike a blow for the human control of the technological project, for wisdom, prudence, and human dignity. The prospect of human cloning, so repulsive to contemplate, is the occasion for deciding whether we shall be slaves of unregulated progress, and ultimately its artifacts, or whether we shall remain free human beings who guide our technique toward the enhancement of human dignity. If we are to seize the occasion, we must, as the late Paul Ramsey wrote,

> raise the ethical questions with a serious and not a frivolous conscience. A man of frivolous conscience announces that there are ethical quandaries ahead that we must urgently consider before the future catches up with us. By this he often means that we need to devise a new ethics that will provide the rationalization for doing in the future what men are bound to do because of new actions and

interventions science will have made possible. In contrast a man of serious conscience means to say in raising urgent ethical questions that there may be some things that men should never do. The good things that men do can be made complete only by the things they refuse to do.

STUDY QUESTIONS: EUTHANASIA, SUSTAINING, AND CREATING LIFE

1. Is there any morally relevant difference between killing and letting die, according to James Rachels? What specific hypothetical cases does he use to advance his argument? Is there a problem with his argument?
2. How does Bonnie Steinbock argue against Rachels's identification of the termination of life-sustaining measures with passive euthanasia? Do you think her arguments are effective? Why or why not?
3. How do the six philosophers argue for a right to physician-assisted suicide? What are the legal and moral bases? What sort of duty does this right impose on the doctor? Does it require that every doctor comply with the request of every patient expressing the wish to die?
4. How does Stephen Potts argue against active voluntary euthanasia? Do you think the institutionalization of euthanasia would lead to the kind of consequences of which he warns us? To what extent do you think institutional constraints would be instrumental in preventing the slippery slope effect?
5. Margaret Battin discusses German, Dutch, and American methods of dealing with euthanasia. How do these different medical practices reflect different views of respect for the patient's autonomy?
6. According to Susan Wolf, what is wrong with the rights-based approach to euthanasia and physician-assisted suicide and why? And what is wrong with the ethics of care approach and why? Exactly how does she argue for an integration of these two approaches? How does her discussion throw light on Dutch, German, and American views on euthanasia and physician-assisted suicide?
7. It seems that the Confucian perspective has a different understanding of "dignity" in face of end-of-life suffering from the contemporary Western understanding. How would that understanding shed light on the current debate regarding euthanasia?
8. Outline Carl Becker's discussion of how the traditional Buddhist (Samurai) notion of dying with dignity can be translated into modern medical practice of euthanasia. Is this notion of respect for individual responsibility or autonomy different from or similar to (or different in some ways but similar in others) that of the Western practice of euthanasia? Explain. Are there problems with this view?
9. Kass believes that our genotype is important to our uniqueness and identity, important enough to confer some kind of moral right. Do you think that there is such an important connection? If so, do you think that it is important enough to confer some kind of moral right to uniqueness and identity?

SUPPLEMENTARY READINGS: EUTHANASIA, SUSTAINING AND CREATING LIFE

BATTIN, MARGARET P. "Assisted Suicide: Can We Learn from Germany?" *Hastings Center Report*, March–April 1992.

BAYLES, MICHAEL D. "Allocation of Scarce Medical Resources." *Public Affairs Quarterly*, vol. 4(1), January 1990.

BELL, NORA A. "What Setting Limits Might Mean: A Feminist Critique." *Hypatia*, Summer 1989.

BROADY, BARUCH A., and AMIR HALEVY. "Is Futility a Futile Concept?" *Journal of Medicine and Philosophy*, vol. 20(2), April, 1995.

BROCK, DAN W. "Voluntary Active Euthanasia." *Hastings Center Report*, March–April 1992.

BUCHANAN, ALLEN. "The Right to a Decent Minimum of Health Care." *Philosophy and Public Affairs*, Winter 1984.

CAPRON, ALEXANDER M. "Legalizing Physician-Aided Death." *Cambridge Quarterly of Healthcare Ethics*, vol. 5, 1996.

FENIGSEN, RICHARD. "A Case Against Dutch Euthanasia." *Hastings Center Report*, January–February 1989.

HARAKAS, STANLEY S. "An Eastern Orthodox Approach to Bioethics." *Journal of Medicine and Philosophy*, vol. 18(6), December 1993.

HEVI, JACOB. "In Ghana, Conflict and Complementarity." *Hastings Center Report*, July–August 1989.

HUMPHREY, DEREK, and MARY CLEMENT. *Freedom to Die: Politics, and the Right-To-Die Movement.* New York: St. Martin's Press, 1998.

KIMURA, RIHITO. "Anencephalic Organ Donation: A Japanese Case." *The Journal of Medicine and Philosophy*, vol. 14(1), February 1989.

KOCH, TOM. "Living Versus Dying 'With Dignity': A New Perspective on the Euthanasia Debate." *Cambridge Quarterly of Healthcare Ethics*, vol. 5, 1996.

KUHSE, HELGA, and PETER SINGER. "Age and the Allocation of Medical Resources." *The Journal of Medicine and Philosophy*, vol. 13(1), February 1988.

KUNTZ, TOM. "Helping a Man Kill Himself, as Shown on Dutch TV." *New York Times*, Nov. 13, 1994.

MALM, M.H. "Killing, Letting Die, and Simple Conflicts." *Philosophy and Public Affairs*, vol. 18(3), Summer 1989.

NEWMAN, LONIS E. "Talking Ethics with Strangers: A View from Jewish Tradition." *Journal of Medicine and Philosophy*, vol. 18(6), December, 1993.

ORTMANN, JOHN. "Cutting Bodies to Harvest Organs." *Cambridge Quarterly of Healthcare Ethics*, vol. 8, 1999.

RESCHER, NICHOLAS. "The Allocation of Exotic Lifesaving Therapy." *Ethics*, April 1969.

SHERWIN, SUSAN. *The Politics of Women's Health: Exploring Agency and Autonomy.* Philadelphia: Temple University Press, 1998.

SIMONS, MARLISE. "Dutch Doctors to Tighten Rules on Mercy Killings." *New York Times*, September 11, 1995.

SIVA SUBRAMANIAN, K.N. "In India, Nepal, and Sri Lanka, Quality of Life Weighs Heavily." *Hastings Center Report*, August 1986.

TULSKY, JAMES A., et al. "A Middle Ground on Physician-Assisted Suicide." *Cambridge Quarterly of Healthcare Ethics*, vol. 5, 1996.

WILKINSON, STEPHEN and EVE GARRARD. "Bodily Integrity and the Sale of Human Organs." *Journal of Medicine and Philosophy*, vol. 22, 1996.